The Moneywise Guide to North America

This uniquely informative guide first appeared in 1964 as the 'Guide to the New World', and contained just 64 pages! Since then, tens of thousands of users and contributors later, it has become the most sought-after guidebook for the serious, economy-minded traveller who wants to see and experience all that the North American continent has to offer.

The *Moneywise Guide* continues to be the only guidebook covering all three countries of North America in one sensible-size volume, although the emphasis is on the USA and Canada. It remains the only guide which treats not only all the usual cities and tourist areas of North America, but also those lesser-known cities, towns and communities which form natural way-points on the major travel routes.

Ideal for the traveller just passing through or staying a while, the *Moneywise Guide* will inform you, entertain you and, above all, save you money.

Where to stay—budget accommodation tested, assessed and updated by the users, checked by the editors. Small downtown hostels, economy motels, YMCAs, youth hostels, bed and breakfasts, tourist homes.

Where not to stay— 'no-go' areas, seedy spots, and places to avoid.

Where to eat—the latest in 'mean cuisine' for those who still buy their meals with cash, not plastic.

What to see—the sights you'll want to see, from Disneyland to national parks, the things you'll want to do, throughout the continent. Updated entrance fees. Hundreds of *free* attractions.

General information—the most comprehensive 'General' section of any guide to North America. How to get there to visit or to work, what to take, what to wear. Visas, insurance and other paperwork. Immigration, people and customs. Driving, hiking and other forms of low-budget travel. And where to get further information and how to find places on the Internet.

About the authors: **Anna Crew** has a background in journalism and has edited this Guide for many years. She is British but lives in Connecticut, from where she directs BUNAC'S camp counsellor programme, BUNACAMP Counsellors. **Nicholas Ludlow** is also British, and based in Washington DC. An inveterate traveller throughout North America and the world at large, Nick is a freelance writer and editor and specialist in the economics of developing countries.

Ginny Bull is from Leicestershire and has a degree in English/Drama and Theatre Studies from Royal Holloway College, London. She is a seasoned budget traveller having done an 18-month round-the-world trip and participated on BUNAC's 'Work America' programme.

Margarita Barritt, who revised the Mexico section of this edition, is a free-lance writer and researcher based in Washington D.C. Born in Costa Rica, she majored in tourism management and promotion at the Universidad de Regiomontana in Monterrey, Mexico.

Sarah Eykyn is a widely-travelled and published ex-BUNAC London staff member. Now resident in Boulder, Colorado, she revised the Mountain States for this issue of the *Moneywise Guide*.

Catriona More comes from Scotland and has a degree in publishing studies from Robert Gordon University in Aberdeen, where she also worked on the university newspaper, *Cogno*.

Kerry Anne Ridge is from Edinburgh and also took her degree in publishing studies at Robert Gordon University. She has previously worked as a summer camp counsellor in Vermont and travelled extensively in the USA.

The Moneywise Guide to

NORTH AMERICA

THE USA
CANADA and selected MEXICO

Editors: Anna Crew and
Nicholas Ludlow

Research and Revision 1998 Edition:
Ginny Bull, Margarita Barritt, Sarah Eykyn,
Catriona More, Kerry Anne Ridge.

1998

THE MONEYWISE GUIDE TO NORTH AMERICA
30th Edition

© Copyright BUNAC 1998

Published by BUNAC Travel Services Ltd,
16 Bowling Green Lane, London EC1R 0BD

British Library Cataloguing in Publication Data
Moneywise Guide to North America: USA,
Canada, Mexico. – 30 Rev. ed
  I. Crew, Anna   II. Ludlow, Nicholas H.
  917.04
  ISBN 0–9526872–2–4

General Editors: Anna L. Crew and Nicholas H. Ludlow.

Research and Revision: Margarita Barritt, Ginny Bull, Sarah Eykyn, Catriona More,
Kerry Anne Ridge.

Additional editorial assistance: Jim Buck, Daniella Finn, Elizabeth Hood,
Philippa Howe Ivain, Sally Vivash, plus the many readers who sent in corrections
and additions.

Cover design: Randak Design Consultants Limited
Cover pictures: Trek America, Trevor Hopkins
Design and maps: Vera Brice; Randak Design Consultants Limited.

Set in Postscript Palatino by Create Publishing Services Ltd, Bath.
Printed and bound in Great Britain by The Bath Press, Lower Bristol Road,
Bath BA2 3BL.

Contents

THE FUTURE OF THIS GUIDE

Quoted comments throughout the *Guide* are genuine remarks made by travellers over the years. Comments from present readers—the more descriptive the better—will add to the colour and usefulness of the next edition.

For brief comments, and most importantly for correcting or adding information about accommodation, fares and so on, please use the **Correction and Addition** slips at the back of the *Guide*. Hotel brochures, local bus schedules, maps and similar tidbits are gratefully received. Also welcome are longer accounts, so feel free to send in letters.

In all cases, please write only on one side of each sheet of paper. Thank you for your help.

The Undiscovered Continent

The most amazing thing about North America is that after a spell of travelling you find it so different from what you expected it to be. Everyone thinks they have a good idea of what it is all about. American technology, politics, media and entertainments daily make their mark the world over. North America is the most publicised continent on earth.

But the projected image hides, both from foreigners and North Americans themselves, a largely undiscovered continent. The polyglot of peoples out of which Canada, the United States and Mexico are each differently formed can make Europe, for example, look comparatively homogeneous. Just a ride on the New York City subway is enough to convince anyone of that.

There are huge tracts of magnificent landscapes, unsettled and hardly explored: forests, glaciers, deserts and jungles; mountains, canyons, prairies, vast lakes and seashores; orchards in Oregon, farming valleys in Vermont, pre-Columbian Indian settlements, many of them unchanged and still inhabited, in Mexico and Arizona, totem poles in British Columbia, fishing villages in Nova Scotia.

Then there are the cities, the hubs of late 20th century North America: Los Angeles, an exploding star, San Francisco riding on a sea of hills, New York, a concrete canyon, Chicago scraping the sky with the longest fingers in the world, Houston, a port and rocket centre, New Orleans blowing jazz across the Mississippi, Québec only geographically in the New World, its soul still back across the Atlantic, Vancouver, Canada's golden gateway to the Pacific, and Mexico City a brilliant mosaic of Spanish and Aztec design. In between is the 'heartland', thousands of small communities each with its own distinctive character and way of life.

The reality, variety and complexity of it all, are more than a lifetime of sitting in front of a television set, or searching the Internet will even remotely convey to you. And there is the discovery too of the instant, of even the future, for North America is always reaching ahead and you have to be there, in the running, to get a glimpse of tomorrow.

About The Moneywise Guide

This is a Guide to most of the usual and many of the unusual places in North America and should prove of service to anyone, but most of all the moneywise traveller. North America can be an expensive continent if you let it. But part of its great variety is the many places to eat and sleep and the many different ways of moving about from which you can choose to suit your pocket, and with the help of this guide it can be a real bargain. Anyone who is happy about spending more money will easily find a $90 hotel bed and a $30 meal, in which case this guide is content with showing you the way to the Statue of Liberty or the Grand Canyon. But for people really on a budget, this is also a guide to thousands of inexpensive places to rest your head, eat cheaply and well *and* to get you to the Grand Canyon on a shoestring.

In separate sections this Guide covers the USA, Canada and parts of Mexico. General introductions precede the coverage of each country. Make a point of first reading these background chapters: here you will find general information on each country, facts about visas, currency, health and other things, money-saving tips on eating, accommodation and travel. *Note that much of the information found in the US Background section will also be of value for travel to Canada and Mexico.*

Each country is then divided into regions, e.g. The Midwest, and in the case of the USA and Canada, states and provinces within each region follow *alphabetically*. There is also an Index at the back of the *Guide*.

Hotel and restaurant listings are the result of the first-hand experience of the *Guide*'s authors and its thousands of readers since the preceding edition. Prices quoted are usually the lowest available. Within the same month at the same hotel, one traveller might spend more on a room than another. This is usually because the rooms were of different standards, but never be afraid to question room rates or even to bargain over them. **You should also allow for inflation when budgeting for the trip. It is therefore probably advisable to allow more for the overall cost of accommodation than the rates printed here would indicate. Similarly it should be remembered that all travel/vacation costs tend to rise each year in North America and so it is quite possible that prices will change after the *Guide* has gone to print. Sorry!**

Please remember that the **maps in this *Guide* are only intended to give you a rough orientation**—an artist's impression—when first arriving in the city. They are not, nor are they intended to be, fully comprehensive. If staying anywhere for any length of time, buy a good street map, though first see if you can get one free from the local Chamber of Commerce or tourist office.

Accommodation Listings Abbreviations:
S = single; D = double; T = triple; Q = quad; XP = extra person in room; Bfast = breakfast; facs = facilities; ess = essential; rec = recommended; nec = necessary.

1. USA

BACKGROUND

BEFORE YOU GO
Unless you plan to enter the USA under the *Visa Waiver Program*, before departing you must obtain an entry visa (main categories listed below). Currently citizens of Australia, France, Germany, Italy, Japan, The Netherlands, Sweden, Switzerland and the U.K. are eligible to participate in the Waiver Program under which visitors to the US for less than 90 days can apply for entry permission on arrival. Check with your airline or travel agent about this. If not applicable to you, you will have to obtain one of the following:

Visitors (B) Visa. This allows you to remain in the US for a maximum of six months, the period to be determined on arrival by immigration officials based on how long they think your money will hold out. When you first obtain your visa abroad it may be stamped 'valid indefinitely'. This means it may be used repeatedly; but each stay is limited to the six-month maximum. You may not work on a Visitors Visa.

In Transit (C) Visa. This allows you to go from A to B via the US and to stay in the US a maximum of 29 days. It can be issued for multiple entries.

Student (F) Visa. You must pursue a fulltime course of study for one year minimum at a school that is identified and approved in advance. Sometimes you have to post a money bond before entering the US. It allows you to work, but only under certain, limited, circumstances.

Temporary Workers (H) Visa. Issued only if you offer specialised skills or qualifications, and requires a written offer from your prospective employer. It's very difficult to obtain.

Exchange (J) Visa. For non-immigrant exchange visitors, J-1 visas are obtainable only through an approved, sponsoring organization. The terms are usually very specific. J-1 participants can work, study, train, research or lecture—depending on individual programme conditions—for a specified period of time.

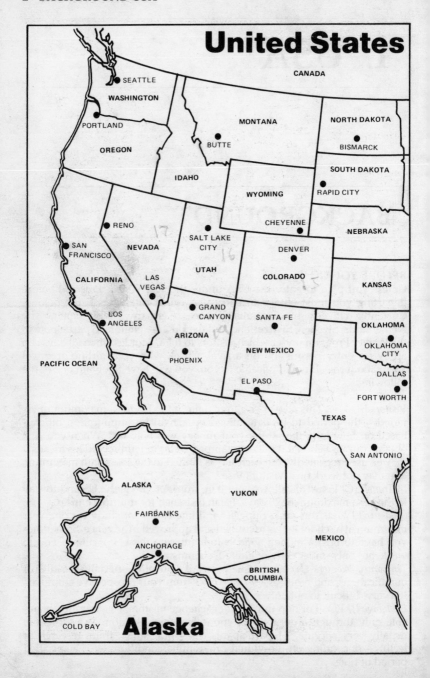

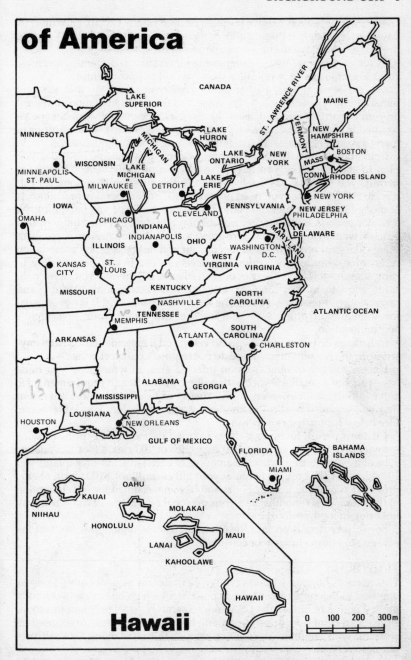

Fiancé (K) Visa. Given for the purpose of marrying a US citizen within 90 days. Unfortunately it doesn't allow you to look for 'Mr/Miss Right' during the first 89; you have to show a petition from the spouse-to-be.

(Q) Cultural Exchange Visa. A programme for certain participants who are on cultural exchanges eg. working at Disneyworld or Epcot Centre.

Permanent Resident Visa. (*Green Card*.) This is the Big One that lets you remain in the US *ad infinitum*. It's subject to the quota limitations imposed on your country of origin. It also subjects you to the possibility of being conscripted into the US military, an eventuality designed to cool the ardour of many a would-be (male) citizen. It takes a long time to obtain.

Immigration officials ask you the purpose of your visit and how long you plan to stay. Probably you have arrived on a pleasure visit. If your visa permits you to work, say so. In answer to the question How long do you plan to stay? note that you need not possess X dollars per day or X amount of money. Rather, immigration officials are looking for proof of planning. As a reader of this Guide, you're probably on a budget anyway. Immigration officials want to know how you're going to manage. You need to show them things like your return ticket home; rail, air and bus passes; accommodation reservations; student or senior identification; etc. If you plan to stay in campsites, hostels, guest houses or with friends, tell them. If you have credit cards, show them. Anything to prove that you've done some planning and can make your resources last for the time you wish to stay. It is not unusual for immigration officials to ask for the address of your first night's accommodation.

Canadians do not require a visa (to visit), and if entering the US from anywhere in the western hemisphere do not require a passport either.

Unless you are coming from an infected area, in which case you must have proof of a smallpox vaccination, there are no **health requirements** for entry into the US. However, on the subject of health, it is most important that you organise medical **insurance** for yourself before you leave home. (See below for further comment.)

Customs permit foreign residents to bring in one litre of spirits or wine (provided you are 21 or over); 200 cigarettes or 100 cigars (not Havana) or 3 lbs of tobacco or proportionate amounts of each (an additional quantity of 100 cigars may be brought in under your gift exemption), $100 worth of gifts provided you stay at least 72 hours and have not claimed the gift exemption in the previous six months, and your personal effects free of duty. You may not bring in food, fruits or meats.

For further details on visa, health and customs regulations, contact the nearest American embassy or consulate.

TEMPORARY WORK

This refers to summer vacation type work under the auspices of a J-1 visa as opposed to the more career-type of position in which one might work for a limited period of time in the USA under, say, an H visa. J programmes cover a great variety of categories: everything from hospital interns to counsellors working with children on summer camps. The regulations for each programme vary.

In Britain, BUNAC (the British Universities North America Club) organises educational work travel exchange programmes to the United States and Canada. The *Work America* programme is for full-time students studying at a British university or college, and provides the student with a work permit for the duration of the summer. Participants can take any job other than that of camp counselling. In Ireland, USIT operate a similar programme for Irish students. BUNAC also runs an 18-month J-1 intern programme, OPT USA (Overseas Practical Training).

In Australia and New Zealand, contact International Exchange Programs, IEP, for their equivalent *Work USA* winter (northern hemisphere) programme.

If you are interested in working with children on an American summer camp, then the *BUNACAMP Counsellors* programme run by BUNAC may be for you. *BUNACAMP Counsellors* will place you as a counsellor on a camp and loan you the round-trip fare across the Atlantic. All you pay to register on the programme is £59. You also have to pay for insurance once you get a definite place. You repay the loan for your airfare etc. out of your salary and are still left with about $420-$480 pocket money at the end of camp. In Australia and New Zealand contact IEP for details on *Summer Camp USA*.

For details on these programmes contact: BUNAC, 16 Bowling Green Lane, London EC1R 0BD. Tel: (0171) 251-3472. IEP, 196 Albert Rd, South Melbourne, Victoria 3205. Tel: (03) 9690-5890. In New Zealand: IEP, PO Box 1786, Shortland St, Auckland. Tel: (09) 366-6255.

Doubtless many people do work in 'underground jobs' such as in casual labour, fruit harvesting, farm work, restaurant work etc., but if you are contemplating this you should be aware of the risks involved. The penalties you would be likely to incur include deportation, with the knowledge that you would have to face an extremely uphill task should you ever want to return to America again. You should also be aware that the terms of the recent Immigration Act mean that an employer hiring an illegal alien faces stiff penalties if caught. This of course acts as a deterrent should an employer be contemplating the possibility and lessens the chances of employment for someone without a work visa.

GETTING THERE

This Guide is used by readers all over the world, and the best and least expensive way of reaching the United States will vary according to where you're starting out. Check advertisements, ask friends and travel agents— including the 'bucket shop' variety. Be alert. Fares are constantly changing.

For the budget traveller, the choice is basically charter, economy, APEX, inclusive package and, possibly, standby. If you are travelling to North America from Britain a group charter fare will probably be cheapest. Watch the press for ads. or ask a travel agent about such fares. Of the scheduled airlines Continental Airlines, flying from Gatwick Airport to Newark, NJ (New York), and Virgin Atlantic flying from Heathrow to JFK and Newark Airports, offer fares from about £390 to £500 return and including tax, depending on when you travel and when you book. Virgin also fly to Boston, Washington DC, Miami and Orlando, FL, and to Los Angeles and San Francisco on the west coast. Continental can connect the traveller on to various US cities (and Mexico) through their domestic network from Newark.

However, don't overlook carriers like British Airways or American Airlines. They will sometimes come in with good deals and are worth investigating. BA also offer regional departures.

Economy fares are pretty expensive; so if you're willing to accept a few restrictions you can save a lot of money on other types of fare.

APEX (Advance Purchase Excursion) tickets are sold by the scheduled airlines themselves and must be purchased at least 21 days before departure. At the time of purchase you must fix your date of departure and return; if you later decide to change either of these dates you'll have to pay a penalty charge.

Advanced Booking Charters (ABCs) have roughly the same restrictions as APEX tickets and you may find yourself either travelling on a plane wholly chartered by the travel operator or else on a scheduled airline from whom the operator will have bought a block of seats at a special charter rate. For the tourist or budget traveller this is probably the most popular method of getting to America. From Britain expect to pay about the same or a little less than the fares quoted above for Virgin and Continental.

Standby fares, if available, are probably the cheapest; you buy the ticket when you like, but space is allocated only on the day of departure. Summer weekends are the most difficult times to get space; midweek departures are usually easier. These tickets are bought directly from the airline, which can advise you of your prospects a day or so before your intended date of departure.

It may be possible to get yourself hired as a *courier* for a one-off flight. Using this method you pay a reduced price on a scheduled flight and in return you carry with you and deliver a package at the other end. Check directly with the many courier operations which make their living shipping business packages back and forth across the Atlantic.

Inclusive packages abound, offering considerable flexibility. Some, however, treat America as a substitute for two weeks on the Costa del Sol— there was never much excuse for fish and chips at Torremolinos when there was all of Spain to see, and there is even less excuse for two weeks of fish and chips in Miami when an entire continent awaits you.

Fly-drive packages including air fare, unlimited mileage car and accommodation vouchers are a good bet, especially if you're travelling as a family or with friends. Prices vary according to size of car, standard of accommodation and the number of people travelling together.

At the same time that you consider how to get to North America, you should be considering how to travel around once there. Certain discounts and travel passes may only be available to non-residents purchasing their tickets abroad. Also, when you buy your tickets outside the US you save the sales tax.

CLIMATE

Remember that you are not travelling over a country but across a vast continent and that the climate varies accordingly. Consider that the distance from New York to Miami is equivalent to that from London to Tangier, and that New York and Los Angeles are as distant from each other as London and

Baghdad, and you get a good idea of what this can mean.

Indoors, these differences are minimised by central heating and air condi-tioning, but outside, winters can be very cold in Washington DC (for instance) and even further south, and summers extremely hot everywhere.

Temperatures approaching 90°F (32°C) day after day, sometimes accom-panied by a suffocating humidity, are not unusual in the summer. New York, Washington DC, New Orleans and the Deep South can be particularly unpleasant. As early as September, however, nights can be cool everywhere, and freezing in mountainous areas.

Some generalisations on climatic regions:

New England, the Northeast, Mid-Atlantic and Midwest. Cold in the winter, often humid in the summer and as hot as anywhere else in America including Florida and southern California.

The Southwest. Warm to hot throughout the year, and nearly always dry.

The Pacific States. Washington, Oregon and northern California have mod-erate climates: not too cold in the winter—though often wet, not too hot in the summer. San Francisco is often bathed in summer afternoon fogs. Southern California is warm to hot the year round, and nearly always dry.

The South. Hot with thunderstorm activity in summer, mild in winter though agreeably warm in Florida. Summer is also the hurricane season in the SouthEast.

The Mountains. In summer, days are warm but nights can be cold. Very cold throughout the winter.

The Deserts. Very hot and dry throughout the year, but can be cold at night.

WHAT TO TAKE AND HOW TO TAKE IT

Take as little as possible, choose clothes for their use in a variety of situa-tions and when you have made your final selection, halve it!

It is always a nuisance to have too much, and anyway if necessary, you can purchase what you need in America. The present exchange rate means that American stores offer many shopping bargains for visitors. In particu-lar items like jeans, shirts, T-shirts and casual clothes are good buys in the US. If you hunt around you can usually find something on sale.

Laundromats are often open 24 hours a day. The cost of a wash is usually $1.50 (in quarters); drying machines usually take 25¢—you just keep feeding in the quarters, total per load is about $1.25.

Whatever luggage you take, make sure it's easy to handle. Getting on and off buses and trains, even just changing planes, can be an ordeal if your bags are too heavy or too many. The best solution is to take one hold-all, be it a suitcase or a backpack, and then a smaller bag which you can sling from your shoulder. When you have to check in your hold-all at the airport or bus station, you must keep all your documents, travellers' cheques and your paperback novel safely and conveniently by your side. It is also a good idea to keep a change of clothing in your shoulder bag in case your suitcase/backpack gets lost by an airline or bus company or your flight is delayed.

For extra security many travellers also wear a neck (or belt) wallet/pouch for passport, cash, travellers cheques and other valuables. It is also a good idea to photocopy your passport and other important documents and keep

City temperatures (in Fahrenheit)		Jan-Feb	Mar-Apr	May-June	Jul-Aug	Sep-Oct	Nov-Dec
CHICAGO	Low	20°	35°	56°	67°	53°	28°
	High	34	51	74	83	69	42
	Average	27	43	65	75	61	35
DENVER	Low	18	29	58	43	43	22
	High	46	57	88	73	73	50
	Average	32	43	73	58	58	36
HONOLULU	Low	68	69	72	74	73	69
	High	74	75	80	84	83	79
	Average	71	72	76	79	78	74
HOUSTON	Low	48	58	71	75	67	50
	High	64	74	89	93	87	68
	Average	56	66	80	84	77	59
LAS VEGAS	Low	35	47	64	76	61	47
	High	57	73	84	102	87	61
	Average	46	60	79	89	74	54
LOS ANGELES	Low	46	50	57	62	59	49
	High	64	66	71	76	75	69
	Average	55	58	64	69	67	59
MIAMI	Low	59	64	72	75	73	61
	High	77	82	88	89	87	79
	Average	68	73	80	82	80	70
NEW ORLEANS	Low	49	59	71	76	68	52
	High	67	75	87	92	84	68
	Average	58	67	79	84	77	60
NEW YORK	Low	26	38	58	68	54	34
	High	40	54	76	84	72	44
	Average	33	46	67	76	63	39
SAN FRANCISCO	Low	43	46	51	54	52	45
	High	57	64	65	72	72	61
	Average	50	55	58	63	62	53
ST LOUIS	Low	24	38	58	67	52	30
	High	42	60	80	89	76	50
	Average	33	49	69	78	64	40
SEATTLE	Low	24	39	47	54	47	37
	High	46	55	69	76	65	49
	Average	35	47	58	65	56	43
WASHINGTON DC	Low	29	41	61	68	56	35
	High	45	61	79	86	74	51
	Average	37	51	70	77	65	43

the copies SEPARATE from the originals. Should you lose your passport you should immediately contact your nearest national consulate (British consulates in Atlanta, Chicago, Houston, Los Angeles, New York and Washington DC).

Some tips: at bus stations in particular, make absolutely certain that your bag is going on your bus and that you get a check-in ticket for it. You would be amazed at the number of times bag and body go off in different directions. And if you're a backpacker just arrived in a big city, you can usually leave your pack at one of the museums for free and then skip off to look for a room, or do a little sightseeing unencumbered.

TIME ZONES

The continental US is divided into four time zones, Eastern Standard Time, Central Standard Time, Mountain Standard Time and Pacific Standard Time. Exact zone boundaries are shown on most road maps.

Noon EST = 11 am CST = 10 am MST = 9 am PST. Standard time in Hawaii is two hours earlier than PST, ie 9 am PST = 7 am HST. Daylight Saving Time occurs widely though not universally throughout the United States; from the end of April to the end of October clocks are put forward one hour. Carefully check air, rail and bus schedules in advance.

THE AMERICAN PEOPLE

Keeping in mind the vastness of the United States and the thought that this is a continent you are visiting rather than a country, it becomes a little easier to appreciate the diversity of the land and its people. America is an incredibly cosmopolitan society. Glance at the names in the telephone book of almost any town anywhere in America for evidence of this. Every nationality on earth, speaking scores of the world's languages, every creed, every race is represented here.

The only true native peoples of the USA, of course are the Indians, who are thought to have arrived in America by way of the Bering Strait from Asia several thousands of years before the Pilgrim Fathers made landfall in Massachusetts. Since the time of the European migration the lot of the 'Native American' has not been a happy one. Harried and hounded by the westward moving white man, Native Americans were eventually pushed into their own 'reservations', inevitably on the poorest and most infertile land around. In more recent times the position of the Native American has improved a little but there is still a long, long way to go. Having Indian blood is a matter for fierce pride and many Indians still harbour great resentment towards the white man. Be aware of this should you visit a reservation and be respectful towards the people and their laws and customs.

Cosmopolitan America may be, but not yet a melting pot. National groups tend to stick together—you will see bumper stickers reading 'Irish-American', 'Proud to be Polish' for instance. At the top of the social heap are still the WASPS (White Anglo Saxon Protestants) represented by the British, Germans and Scandinavians, and followed by the Irish and other European groups. Next come Asians, who predominate in California, then Blacks and the fast-rising Hispanics. It is estimated that Hispanics will soon outnumber the Black-American population and become the largest minority group. As immigration continues and fortunes around the world turn this way or that, so will American society continue to evolve in order to cope with new national groupings and social trends.

It is to this constantly changing society, the moving frontier, that one can perhaps trace the roots of the violence present in American society. Where a nationwide sense of tradition is scarce, where the future is always being built anew, there is often a sense of rootlessness and self-doubt in which violence, crime, drug or alcohol dependency, religious, political or social fads and fancies can easily flourish. There is a great deal of poverty in the land of opportunity, contrasting sharply with the material splendours of those who have in abundance.

That is the down side. On the brighter side, American people in their own land are more hospitable, kind and generous than any other nation. Even the newest immigrants take great pride in their new land. Everywhere there is a flag flying, on private homes as well as on public buildings; allegiance to America is constantly recited and renewed. The USA remains on the whole an optimistic land, still reaching towards the future, trying to stay ahead, and proud of its role in the world. Americans tend to be demanding, enthusiastic; living hard, playing hard; conforming, yet individualistic; still expecting the best of everything.

MEETING PEOPLE

Americans are naturally outgoing and hospitable, more so when they detect a foreign accent. Your novelty value is particularly enhanced outside of the big cities, where curiosity and interest is generated amongst locals as soon as you open your mouth. Don't be surprised if you are invited to dinner, taken places and shown round the local sights. Staying at a private bed and breakfast place is a prime way to mingle with Americans—the services you get and the friendliness you'll receive go far beyond the monetary exchange. State fairs and other such special events—rodeos, clambakes, New England autumn fairs, etc.—are an essential slice of the American pie and another way of meeting people informally.

If you want a more organised approach for meeting Americans, we suggest a number of organisations within our listings and also the following (most of which require making advance arrangements):

1. Contact the **National Council for International Visitors** (NCIV), 1420 K St NW, Suite 800, Washington DC 20005, (202) 842-1414. Ask for their booklet called *Where to Phone*, a complete rundown of local organisations willing to extend hospitality.
2. Enquire at the local **Chambers of Commerce** and Visitors Bureaux about their 'Visit a local family' programmes, if any. Some of them are very active in this area. A number have volunteer language banks also, if you're having difficulty communicating.
3. **Servas**. An organisation of approved hosts and travellers that arranges homestays. Charges membership fee of $55 a year then requires a deposit of $25 for 1-5 host lists. Guests then make their own contacts. US Servas Committee, 11 John St, Rm 407, New York, NY 10038, (212) 267-0252.

HEALTH AND WELFARE

There is no free or subsidised national health service in the United States for anyone under retirement age. For most people, therefore, medical, dental and hospital services have to be paid for and they can be expensive. However, the emergency room of any public hospital provides medical care to anyone who walks in the door (and is prepared for a long wait), and will often only charge those who have insurance or are otherwise able to pay, the government reimbursing them for the rest.

The 'emergency' doesn't have to be a car crash or the like—it can be a high fever or stomach pains, anything of a reasonably acute nature or which you feel needs immediate attention. Teaching hospitals—medical and dental—are other possible sources of free, or cheaper, treatment. Women may find help through the local women's centre.

Nevertheless, it is essential to be insured (ask your travel agent), and a good idea to get a dental checkup before going. If you wear glasses or contact lenses take spares, or at least prescriptions.

MONEY

Dollars and cents are of course the basic units of American money. The back of all denominations of dollar bills are green (hence 'greenbacks'). The commonly used coins are: one cent (penny), five cents (nickel), 10 cents (dime), and 25 cents (quarter). 50¢ pieces (half dollars) and silver dollars (not really silver anymore) are gaining in usage, while there has been talk of phasing out the penny—that's inflation for you. 'Always carry plenty of quarters when travelling. Very useful for phones, soda machines, laundry machines, etc.'

There is generally no problem in using US dollars in Canada, albeit with a loss on the exchange rate; but this is never possible vice versa. It is difficult to change Canadian dollar travellers cheques into American cash.

It's useful always to carry small change for things like exact fare buses, but do not carry large sums of cash. Instead keep the bulk of your money in travellers cheques which can be purchased both in the US and abroad and should be in US dollar denominations. The best known cheques are those of American Express, so you will have the least difficulty cashing these, even in out of the way places. (AMEX card holders may have mail sent to American Express offices—ask for a complete list (800) 528-4800). Thomas Cook travellers cheques are also acceptable, especially as lost ones can be reclaimed at some Hertz Car Rental desks. Dollar denomination cheques can be used like regular money. There's no need to cash them at a bank: use them instead to pay for meals, supermarket purchases or whatever. Ten or 20 dollar cheques are accepted like this almost always and you'll be given change just as though you'd presented the cashier with dollar bills. Be prepared to show I.D when you cash your cheques.

Credit cards can be even more valuable than travellers cheques as they are often used to guarantee room reservations over the phone and are accepted in lieu of a deposit when renting a car—indeed *without* a credit card you may be considered so untrustworthy that not only a deposit but your passport will be held as security too. Or, you may not be able to rent at all without a credit card. The major credit cards are VISA, Master Charge and Access (each with the other's symbol on the reverse), Diners Club and American Express. If you hold a bank card (eg. VISA), it could well be worthwhile to increase your credit limit for travel purposes—you should ask your bank manager.

Banks. Bank hours are usually 9 am—5 pm, Mon-Fri, although some smaller branches, especially in rural areas, have a shorter day. Many banks stay open until 6 pm on Fridays and some open limited hours on Saturdays.

If you ever receive a cheque, it is important to cash it in the same area— i.e. at a branch of the bank on which it is drawn. Without a bank account to pay into, it will be impossible to cash it elsewhere—the American banking system is not as integrated as elsewhere in the world. Some form of photo-identification (eg. passport) is necessary when cashing a personal or company cheque.

Tax. There is usually a three to nine percent sales tax on most items over 20¢ and meals over $1. This is never included in the stated price and varies from place to place according to whether you are being charged state or city sales tax. There is also a 'bed tax' in most cities that ranges from five to ten percent on hotel rooms. 'Bed tax' does not generally apply to bed and break-fast places. *Note that unless stated, accommodation rates in this Guide do not include tax.*

Tipping. It is customary in the US to tip the following: taxi drivers, waiters, chamber maids, hotel bellboys, airport luggage porters. Ten to 15 percent is the accepted amount, although most waiters, especially in cities will expect 15-20 percent. Some restaurants do include service in the menu price so make sure you don't tip them twice.

COMMUNICATIONS

Mail. Post offices are infrequent, but since the alternative is a commercial stamp machine which in the spirit of free enterprise sells stamps but only at a considerable profit, it is advisable to stock up at post offices when you can. As of going to press, first class letters within the US are 32¢; the air mail rate for post cards to Europe is 50¢, aerogrammes 50¢, air mail letters up to 1oz, 60¢.

Mail within the US travels at a snail's pace: allow a week coast to coast or to Canada, and four days for any distance more than around the corner. For two-day (no guarantees!) delivery use Priority Mail, $3. For guaranteed overnight delivery you have to use Express Mail which has a minimum rate of $9.95! You must always include the zip code on a US address. To mail a letter without a zip code is to invite considerable delay if not everlasting loss!

It is possible to have mail sent General Delivery (Poste Restante) for collection (also to American Express offices if you use their travellers cheques). The post office will usually keep it for 10 days before returning it to sender.

American post offices deal *only* with mail.

Telegrams. Internal telegrams are sent by Western Union and not from the post office. Telegrams abroad are cheaper by night rate. You hand or telephone in your message anytime and ask for second class treatment. But it may take 48 hours before the telegram is delivered. Better to fax it if you can!

Telephone. Phones in North America are easy to use. All numbers have an Area Code (3 digits), an Exchange Code (3 digits) and a number (4 digits). You do not dial the Area Code if you are within that dialling area (eg. omit the 202 when calling Washington DC numbers from within Washington). For directory enquiries call 555-1212 wherever you are and that will get you through to information for that state; if you want a number in another state, use that prefix before you dial, eg. To call New York from DC you would dial, (212) 555-1212. For (800) numbers call 1 (800) 555-1212. A reverse charges call is called a collect call.

When calling from pay phones in most areas of North America, you dial the whole number preceded by 1 (if you have enough coins to pay for the call), or by 0 (zero, not the O in MNO) if you are making a collect call. Before dialling, you insert the minimum amount of money as instructed on the pay phone (eg. 25¢). When you have dialled the complete number, the operator will come on the line and tell you how much to put in (if you dialled 1 first). If you dialled 0 first, a recorded message may ask you to 'please dial your card number or zero for an operator now'. Press 0, wait, and the operator will ask how he/she can help you. You then say: 'I'd like to make a collect call, please. My name is...'

Whenever the operator answers, your money is refunded to you. Don't forget to take it out of the machine! You may find that you are being spoken to by a recording which says something like 'Deposit 40 cents, please'. Obey the voice...

If calling at peak time, you may need to have ready up to $3.50 a minute in 25¢, 10¢ and 5¢ coins. The cheapest time to make a long distance call is between 11pm and 8am. Between 5pm and 11pm and at weekends the next cheapest time; 8am-5pm is the most expensive time. Remember to allow for time zone differences when phoning.

If making calls from your hotel, remember that it is cheaper to use the phone in the hotel lobby rather than the one in your bedroom. It's always cheaper to dial direct and not through the operator. In many areas local calls are free from private phones. If you make a pay call from a private phone you can get the operator to tell you how much the call cost.

Look for pay phones in drug stores, gas stations, highway rest areas, in transport terminals and along the street. Phone cards are now more readily available in North America. However, the US-style phone cards work somewhat differently to those available, for example, in the UK. They use a more complicated electronic system and are generally offered initially in $10 or $20 units but with the ability to 'top up' the card once the initial investment runs out. BUNAC members get the special Telekey Card which also offers voice messaging. You will encounter others also, all offering slightly different packages.

ELECTRICITY
Voltage is 110-115V, 60 cycles AC. American plugs have two flat pins. Try to get an adaptor before you go. Even if you have a dual voltage appliance you

will still need an adaptor. You will not be able to use your home hairdryer, shaver or whatever, unless it is dual voltage.

SHOPPING

Major stores in out of town malls often have long opening hours, eg. from 9 am or 10 am to 9 pm or 10 pm—on one, several or even all days of the week. Smaller shops in cities are sometimes open all night: you should have no trouble getting a meal or a drink, or shopping for food and other basics, 24 hours a day—though you'll pay more for the privilege.

Large American supermarkets and department stores can make their foreign equivalents look like they're suffering from war-time rationing. The variety of goods on offer—and at relatively low prices—is amazing. The American consumer is a keen and well practised shopper with an eye for a bargain, seldom in fact, buying anything when it's not on sale. Almost every town has at least one shopping mall (pronounced 'maul') on the outskirts where you can observe the credit card culture in action and brouse to your heart's content from about 10 am to 9 pm.

Good buys in the US include cameras, CDs, electronic goods, sound equipment, denims, winter clothes, and casual clothes, in particular western gear. Just how good a bargain will of course depend upon the exchange rate at the time of your visit. Even if it is not in your favour, if you do as all Americans do and shop only when the item you want is on sale, you will still be able to net some bargains.

THE METRIC SYSTEM

The US still uses feet and miles, pounds and gallons, Fahrenheit instead of Centigrade/Celsius, and it appears as though it will for some time to come. The only things that have gone metric are liquor and wine bottles, some gasoline pumps and the National Park Service. A conversion table is to be found in the Appendix.

DRINKING

Although nationwide Prohibition ended in the US in 1933, you will still find places in which you cannot get a drink at all, or where you cannot stand to drink, or must bring your own bottle—one anomaly after another. This is because each state decides whether it will be 'dry' or 'wet', and sometimes this is left to counties on an optional basis.

American beer (which as a legacy of Prohibition has a relatively low alcohol content) is of the lager variety—Knickerbocker, Miller, Schaeffer, Budweiser, Pabst. Be sure to ask for micro-brewery beers, now standard fare at most bars and restaurants, and tending to eclipse the old standards.There are now scores of interesting micro-brews from honey-brown ale to raspberry wheat.

America is the home of the cocktail. Spirit concoctions are excellent and a major part of American ingenuity is devoted to thinking up new ones—and extraordinary names for them! Bars never close before midnight, stay open sometimes till 4 am, or even 23 hours a day. Try to sample local wines, New York and California turn out the best although Washington State and Michigan also produce a few decent varieties. Visit a winery in these states too.

The minimum drinking age is now 21 in every state in the US. A strong anti-drink climate of opinion exists in the US at present and under-age drinking rules are strictly enforced. Someone under 21 may not be able to drink alcohol at all during their stay in the USA. You will need to carry photo ID when ordering a drink or buying liquor in a store just in case you are asked—even if you think you look much older than 21! Student cards etc. are generally not acceptable as ID and even a passport is sometimes not enough. You can, however, obtain a US ID with your photo on it from any DMV (Department of Motor Vehicles) office (where drivers licences are issued). Check *Yellow Pages* for location.

TOBACCO
Cigarettes are about $2.50 for a pack of 20, five big cigars for about the same price. Pipe tobacco is heavily flavoured—imported brands are better and not much more expensive. Unless you learnt to chew tobacco at the same time as you were breast-fed, forget it. Tobacco addicts should stock up on cartons at supermarkets for substantial savings.

Smoking is increasingly frowned upon and many restaurants (even McDonald's) and other public places now have 'non-smoking' sections. In New York City, the smoking in restaurants ban is total. Smoking is banned in all government buildings; post offices, libraries, subway stations, etc. and on all public transport, including Amtrak and Greyhound. Banks, cinemas and theatres also ban the weed and it is banned on all US internal flights except those of more than 6 hours.

DRUGS
A great deal has been written about the 'drug culture' of the US. Most of it is absolutely true. The best advice is the obvious— stay away from it. Reject all advances made to you on the street, in bus terminals, airports, wherever. It is illegal to possess or sell narcotics. Penalties can be severe.

PUBLIC HOLIDAYS
New Year's Day (1 January)
Martin Luther King Jr's Birthday (15 January)
Washington's Birthday (third Monday in February)
Memorial Day (last Monday in May)
Independence Day (4 July)
Labor Day (first Monday in September)
Columbus Day (second Monday in October)
Veterans' Day (11 November)
Thanksgiving (fourth Thursday in November)
Christmas (25 December)

Though many smaller shops and almost all businesses close on public holidays, many of the biggest stores and multiples will make a point of being open—often offering sales. Outside of cities, supermarkets are often open during at least part of a public holiday. On days of all primary and general elections all bars are closed. There are numerous other public holidays that are not nationwide, eg. Lincoln's Birthday, St Patrick's Day. Jewish New

Year brings New York to a standstill.

The summer tourism and recreational season extends from Memorial Day to Labor Day. After Labor Day you can expect some hours or days of opening to be reduced, or some attractions to be closed altogether. The same may apply to related transport services. Unless otherwise specified, times and days of openings in this guide refer to the summer season. Outside this period, you should phone in advance.

INFORMATION

A multitude of resources exists in the US both to make your stay more informed and enjoyable and to help you out if you encounter problems. Among the most useful:

1. *Libraries*. One in every town, often open late hours and on weekends, libraries and librarians are a traveller's best friend. Besides reference works, atlases, local guidebooks, they offer transit schedules, local and other newspapers, magazines, free community newspapers, phone books, brochures on helping organisations and are unfailingly kind about answering questions and making phone enquiries for you. They also have toilets, comfy chairs and often a social calendar of free evening events.

2. *Travelers Aid*. Their kiosks are found at bus, train and plane terminals across the country—invaluable for cheap lodging and other suggestions, helpful with free maps and brochures, and solid support if your trip runs into a snag (whether it's a medical, financial or practical problem).

3. *Chambers of Commerce and Visitors Bureaux*. Found almost everywhere, with lots of free materials, maps (although you usually have to purchase the really good maps) and advice. Big-city offices have multilingual staff, are open longer hours and sometimes weekends. Smaller places are open 9am-5pm, Monday to Friday; many have recorded events messages for local activities when they are closed. A major drawback is that they are primarily member organisations; few of them will even recognise much less recommend non-member hotels, restaurants, etc. That means that you won't hear much about low-budget places from them and some bureaux will even try to warn you off such places. Don't buy it. If driving, look out for state highway 'welcome stations'. They are a good source of free maps and local information and often provide free juice or coffee.

4. Many communities have a *volunteer clearinghouse phone service* designed to answer a variety of needs, from real emergencies to simple orientation. Usually listed in both the white and yellow pages of the phone book, and variously called Hotline, Helpline, Crisis Center, People's Switchboard, Community Switchboard, We Care, or some such. Their well-trained volunteers can steer you to the resources available in the community— free, cheap and not-so-cheap.

5. *Women's Centers and Senior Centers* provide the same kind of clearing-house info and friendly support on a walk-in basis; you will also find them in nearly every US town and listed in the phone book. The centers also make excellent places to meet people, and often sponsor a range of

free and interesting activities. You might also try the free clinics, which still exist in a number of big cities. Many of them operate hotlines, referral services, crash pad recommendations and other services besides free health care.

6. *Maps*. Besides the free ones from visitor centers, state tourism offices and so forth, you may be interested in specialty maps, such as Greyhound's excellent 'United States of Greyhound', a monster which shows all of the US and Canadian routes clearly marked, plus major parks and monuments. Free.

7. *The Internet*. Imagine a future where you travel with a hand-held computer instead of a guidebook, calling-up information,via satellite, on anything from the weather to which hostels do laundry. Already, from the UK or North America, you can access a wealth of travel info on the internet, including maps, weather reports, timetables and accommodation guides to help you plan your trip. The US is on the fast-track of this information superhighway and coffee/computer hot-spots are springing up in major cities like New York, San Francisco and Washington D.C., where those without their own or a university computer can get onto the net.

Once into the system look for the World Wide Web which has a general travel site full of holiday hints. There are also two excellent internet sites designed specifically for hostellers. *The Internet Guide To Hostelling* is an electronic magazine which offers a mountain of help to travellers. It has a worldwide hostel guide, tips and tales from other budget travelers, info on special events and discounts and the answers to the 'most frequently asked questions about hostelling'. The guide can be accessed on the WorldWide Web at: http://www.hostels.com/hostels/. For information on how to access the guide using other methods contact The Editor, Pacific Tradewinds Hostel, 680 Sacramento St, San Francisco, (415) 433-7970. Email: media@hostels.com.

A second useful site for budget travellers is *Go hostelling on-line magazine*. This features an article on hosteling culture for 'newbies', travel-planning tips and a guide to hostel-hopping the Pacific Northwest. There are even photos of places you might want to stay or visit. All the information can be emailed to a computer and printed out, so you can shove it in your rucksack and take it with you. Find *Go Hostelling* at: http://www.northcoast.com/~ebarnett/go.html or contact the Ave of the Giants/Eel River Redwoods Hostel, 70400 Redwood Highway, Leggett, CA, (707) 925-6469. Email: ebarnett@hostel.com. The *Hostel Handbook for the USA and Canada* is also available on the internet, contact the editor at Sugar Hill Int House, 722 Saint Nicholas Ave, NY, (212) 926-7030. Email: *InfoHostel@aol.com*.

EMERGENCIES/SAFETY

Many towns and cities have '911' as the emergency telephone number—for police, fire, ambulance. Otherwise you would dial '0' for operator. The emergency number is always indicated on public telephones.

Yes, the USA can be a dangerous place, but then so can your own home town if you happen to be in the wrong place at the wrong time. In other words, chance or fate alone may determine what may or may not happen to you. This is not to say that you should not take reasonable, sensible, standard precautions to protect your safety.

Don't wander into parks or dark alleys alone or late at night; carry your valuables in a neck or waist pouch; don't leave your belongings unattended; stay in what you know to be safe areas of towns and cities—if it feels 'wrong', get out; don't hitchhike or drive alone; and stay alert to what is happening around you. Remember, although crime rates are high, most Americans *never* encounter crime in their daily lives.

Listed below are a few helplines and hotlines should you or anyone travelling with you run into difficulties. The first thing to remember is always consult your local telephone directory. Many states have their own 'information lines' or INR numbers (Info 'n' Referral). These lines may help you with anything from suicide prevention to health information, providing you with facts and referrals for counselling and support where needed.

The previously mentioned **Traveler's Aid** can be found at major bus, rail stations and airports and will help in emergency situations. Traveler's Aid can also be found nationwide (locate in directory) and specialise in helping people who are out-of-state get back to where they need to be.

National Aids Hotline, (800) 342-AIDS, 24hrs. Answers questions and gives out information as well as arranging counselling where needed. (See also 'Health Agencies' in Yellow Pages.)

(800) ALCOHOL, (800) 252-6465, 24 hrs. Provides referral in reference to drugs or alcohol.

National Drug Hotline, (800) 662-4357, daytime. Information on drug or alcohol abuse and related issues. Referrals to local drug treatment or counselling centres.

Pregnancy Hotline, (800) 848-5683, 24hrs. Information for pregnant (or suspecting) women, counselling etc. Or (800) 238-4269, free pregnancy testing and counselling.

THE GREAT OUTDOORS

One of the most exciting things about North America is the great tracts of unspoilt land. The most superlative examples have usually been specially preserved as national parks. There are 41 national parks in the United States, all of which offer the visitor beautiful scenery; everything from fantastic seascapes, deep canyons, spectacular volcanoes, to pure lakes and craggy mountains. Many parks are somewhat off the beaten track and although the roadways in all are excellent, the parks are best seen more slowly on foot, by bicycle, horse, or canoe. Most offer camping facilities (see under Accommodation) and some, cabin or hotel accommodation.

Some parks are free but in general the entrance fee will be $10. Should you intend to use the National Park system extensively, purchase a Golden Eagle Passport on sale at all parks, or from the National Park Service, Office of Public Inquiries, room 1013, PO Box 37127, Washington DC 20013, (202) 208-4747. The Pass costs $50 and gives you, and anyone accompanying you in a private vehicle, access to all the parks for a year at no further expense. Also, visitors arriving before 7 am sometimes get in free. Camping, of course, costs extra. Reservations for camping are essential in peak season; apply in advance to be sure of a pitch. 1 (800) 365-2267 is the nationwide no to reserve pitches—persevere, the line is always busy! For further information and much faster reservations, look up *www.destinet.com/*.

There are also numerous national seashores, monuments and forests, and other federally-administered preserves which should not be overlooked. In addition there are thousands of state parks across America, many of which provide facilities for swimming, camping, walking etc. for a modest entry fee.

Almost all the national parks are included in this Guide. For more information write directly to the park, asking for details and brochures. A list of the major national parks in the US follows.

Acadia, Maine.	Kings Canyon, California.
Arches, Utah.	Lassen Volcanic, California.
Badlands, South Dakota.	Mammoth Cave, Kentucky.
Big Bend, Texas.	Mesa Verde, Colorado.
Bryce Canyon, Utah.	Mount Rainier, Washington.
Canyonlands, Utah	National Reef, Utah.
Carlsbad Caverns, New Mexico.	North Cascades, Washington.
Crater Lake, Oregon.	Olympic, Washington.
Denali, Alaska.	Petrified Forest, Arizona.
Everglades, Florida.	Platt, Oklahoma.
Glacier, Montana.	Redwood, California.
Grand Canyon, Arizona.	Rocky Mountain, Colorado.
Grand Teton, Wyoming.	Sequoia, California.
Great Basin, Nevada.	Shenandoah, Virginia.
Great Smoky Mountains.	Theodore Roosevelt, North Dakota.
Tennessee/North Carolina.	Virgin Islands, St John, Virgin Islands.
Guadalupe Mountains, Texas.	Voyageurs, Minnesota.
Haleakala, Island of Maui, Hawaii.	Wind Cave, South Dakota.
Hawaii Volcanoes, Island of Hawaii,	Yellowstone, Wyoming/Montana/
Hawaii.	Idaho.
Hot Springs, Arkansas.	Yosemite, California.
Isle Royale, Michigan.	Zion, Utah.

SPORT AND RECREATION

At times on your travels across America it may seem that every man, woman, child, and dog, jog, run or otherwise 'keep fit' at least four times a week, so many people will you see doing just that. Certainly as a nation Americans tend towards the active, outdoors existence. After all they have the climate and the country to make it all possible.

In summer there's swimming, sailing, 'surfin', waterski-ing, fishing, diving and all the other water-based activities, plus tennis, baseball, athletics, camping, hiking, cycling ... the list is endless. Then just when you begin to get tired of all that, along comes the football (American) season, followed by basketball, and ice hockey. Then it snows and do Americans sit at home and watch it? Silly question. Now it's time for ski-ing (downhill or cross-country), skating, hunting, ice-fishing, more ice hockey and so on. In short if it exists as a sport you will find it somewhere in America—yes, even rugby and croquet.

On the professional scene the biggies are football (American) and baseball. The latter goes from April through until October and football starts at the end of the summer and finishes in January when finally overtaken by the weather. Try and go to a professional game in either sport—it's a real slice of American pie (baseball can be very slow but it is as much about beer, hot-dogs and tailgating as it is about the game). There is a major league team in almost every large city. Soccer is starting to catch on in a big way, although it doesn't cause the same sort of frenzy as it does in Europe. There is a national league but the real strength of the game is at grassroots(!) level. Basketball, athletics, ice hockey, tennis, horse/motor racing and wrestling, are other major spectator sports.

One interesting point about the US sport scene is the attention given nationally to the, often near-professional, college/university teams. This is especially the case with basketball and football where the college teams are often followed with enthusiasm equal to that given to the pros.

MEDIA AND ENTERTAINMENT

In these days of cable and satellite TV it is not unusual to be able to tune into more than 60 channels on your **television** set. Network television can be condescending, boring, total rubbish—an insult to the intelligence but also has excellent and interesting programmes. Best programmes feature old movies (squeezed in between commercials), news coverage, reruns of old sitcoms which always offer an interesting look at bygone America, and the public television channels which show British imports—*Absolutely Fabulous, Mr. Bean, Are You Being Served?, Lovejoy, EastEnders, One Foot In The Grave,* etc., and offer excellent current affairs, science and nature programmes as well as live theatre and music.

At whatever time of night or day there is always something to watch! The proliferation of cable has brought more specialist viewing to the small screen. Sport, religion, local events, movies, Spanish/Japanese/Cuban/whatever, and music videos (MTV) are just a few of the offerings. You will not be able to resist!

And there's even more **radio**, and here the overkill holds promise for in amongst the top-40 musical pop stations there are first-rate classical, jazz, blues, bluegrass, country, gospel, R&B, progressive and regional music stations, as well as some solid all-news stations. Radio is also an excellent way of finding out about an area you're visiting or just driving through.

Every city with any claim to consequence will have its theatres and its own **orchestra** and **opera company**, with performances often to a very high standard. In this respect, Americans arguably enjoy a greater access to culture than Europeans with their brighter but more centralised cultural traditions.

Hollywood still turns out more **movies** than anywhere else in the world except India, and with the decline of the studios there has been more freelancing, more opportunity for outsiders with new ideas to hit the big screen. In writing, directing and acting, America easily holds its own as one of the four or five great film-making nations.

Often movies are cheaper before 6 pm and some are just $2 at weekends. Free papers in every city are essential reading for entertainments/events etc.If you're interested in concerts, plays, etc, one easy solution is to look up **TICKETRON** in the local phone book. They are nationwide agents, but have information on what's on in the particular city you're in—they publish a free monthly list of all events, though take a percentage on any tickets you buy from them. There are half-priced ticket agencies in most major cities.

The *New York Times* is one of the most respected of American **newspapers** and in content comes closest to being the country's national newspaper. The mammoth Sunday edition of *The Times* should keep you going at least until Thursday. There is, of course, an actual, coast-to-coast, national newspaper—*USA Today*. Published weekdays, across America, and using full colour throughout, it manages to a large extent to overcome the problems of time zones, and the diversity of life in the US. In general people still buy their local papers and all towns and cities have at least one. Among the best of the rest are the *Los Angeles Times*, the *Washington Post* and the *Wall Street Journal*. The latter is a good read for the considerable insight it offers into a great variety of topics both inside and well beyond the world of finance. Wherever you are of course, the local paper (perhaps free) is your best resource for local events as well as adding to your picture of American life.

Magazines proliferate, covering every conceivable interest and point of view. Sample the offerings on hot rods, sex, flying saucers, sport, computers, snowmobiles, collectibles and so on if you want to appreciate the American appetite for every sort of information. Also there are growing numbers of magazines for business women and the environmentally aware, plus large circulation African American publications. Some of the best writing is found in *The New Yorker*, *The Atlantic Monthly* —which grew out of the Transcendentalist and anti-slavery movements—and *Esquire*. *Rolling Stone* is still the voice of pop, *MS* is for politically correct women who have not yet graduated to reading the *Wall Street Journal*, and there's always *Time* and *Newsweek* to read on the loo.

Last but not least there are the **comics**, including that whole stable of Marvel heroes (Captain America, Spiderman, The Hulk) who express the variety of American neuroses, or those old standbys from a more innocent, confident age, principally Superman and Scrooge McDuck.

ON THE ROAD

ACCOMMODATION

Let's face facts: accommodation in North America is going to absorb at least one-third of your travel money. So how can you keep that figure to a minimum while enjoying your trip to the maximum? Here are eight pointers:

1. *Learn your accommodation options*. You'll constantly hear about the visible and well-advertised options: chain hotels and motels, lodgings close to freeways and tourist attractions, National Park accommodation and the conventional rock-bottom suggestions—YMCAs and youth hostels. But a wealth of inexpensive and almost invisible alternatives exist in North America. Examples: guest and tourist homes; bed and breakfast in

private residences; farms and ranches; resorts and retreats; residence clubs, *casas de huespedes* and other pension-style lodgings; free campsites on Indian lands; non-hostel accommodations which honour hostel rates and philosophies; university-associated places to stay, many open to the general public; and self-catering digs, from apartments to rustic cabins to housekeeping/efficiency units in standard hotels/motels. (You will see lots of specific examples of these choices throughout this Guide.)

2. *Choose a lodging that also gives you a taste of North America.* Want to stay in a New York City brownstone, a San Francisco painted Victorian, a Maui condo, a solar-heated A-frame near a ski slope? How about spending a few days on a Mississippi River houseboat or riding through Kansas prairies with a covered wagon train? Maybe you'd rather tent-camp in a Sioux teepee, explore a Mennonite farm, visit a Southern plantation, sleep in a goldminer's cabin, gain a few pounds at a Basque boarding-house, beachcomb near a lighthouse hostel or stay in a 400-year-old Mexican mansion. It's all here. And by integrating your sleeping (and sometimes eating) arrangements with an offbeat experience, you'll receive double value. In the process, you'll get acquainted with everyday North Americans from many walks of life.

3. *Rent a room the way you shop for a car.* If tourism is down and vacancy rates are up, you'll have added leverage and bargaining power. Use it! Don't be afraid to haggle—hotel/motel rates in the US are extremely fluid and based on what the market will bear. (Unlike Mexico, where they are government regulated.) Rooms within a building are never identical—ask to see the cheapest. It may be small, viewless or noisy. It may also suit your needs very well. If you're willing to share a bath, sleep in a dorm, or take a room without air-conditioning or TV, *say so*. Most clerks (in the US anyway) will assume you require a private bath and colour TV to sustain life, and won't mention other accommodation. 'Ask for a room that is out of service and then offer a price for the night. You may be lucky.'

4. *Use impeccable timing.* Plan ahead to take advantage of special offers and slow times. Do your travelling on weekends so you arrive to catch the midweek (Sunday through Thursday) rates. Alternatively, look for higher-priced hotels at your destination that offer low-cost weekend or 'getaway' packages—often very good value. If you can possibly swing it, travel in May or September: best weather, fewest crowds and significantly lower off-season prices. Another timing tip: the later in the evening it gets, the more likelihood you have of a reduced rate on a room. You may be tired and worried about a place to lay your weary head but remember: the hotel/motel owner is even more worried about filling that room, which goes on costing him money whether empty or full. But caution, in resort areas and big cities at peak holiday times desirable accommodation fills by 4-5pm.

5. *Always ask about discounts and special rates.* You'd be amazed at the discount categories that exist in North America. A partial list: senior, student, youth hostel card-holder, bus/train/plane passholder, rental car user, member of AAA or other auto club, YMCA/YWCA member, Sierra Club or other environmental club members, military, family, group, foreign visitor, government employee, airline employee and corporate or

commercial rates. Incidentally, hotel/motel people sometimes grant 'commercial rates' as a face-saving way to fill rooms, so it pays to flash your company identification or business card and ask for them. Throughout this edition, you'll notice specific discount offers where known. 'Being a British student was worth a $2 discount to many motel owners'. Being a *Moneywise Guide* holder sometimes gets you a better deal too!

6. *Ask other travellers for accommodation leads.* When travelling in the US most Americans tend to stay with families/friends, at chain motels/hotels, or in campgrounds or RV (recreational vehicles). Thus they are often oblivious to the unsung lodging opportunities around them.

7. *Double up. Better yet, triple up.* US lodging (with the exception of hostels, YMCAs and a few hotels/motels that give the lone traveller a break) has a Noah's Ark, two-by-two mentality. Your best bet is to travel with one or more companions. Relish your independence? Then split up and rendezvous with friends every couple of days—you'll still save money. 'Five of us crammed into a $60 double room with owner's consent. Try any motel.'

8. *Learn about local variants and accommodation nomenclature.* Lodging traditions vary around North America. For instance, the best bargains in Hawaii are called hotel apartments—Honolulu is full of them. In Colorado, ski lodges with dorms (ask for 'hiker' or 'skier' rooms) are popular. San Francisco is a mecca for congenial residence clubs which offer superlative weekly rates for room and board. Parts of the South and New England are full of small guest houses. In Canada, low-priced B&B digs are called tourist homes. When you enter an area, ask the Visitors Centre or librarians, or look in the Yellow Pages; if there's a local variant, you should spot it. Second, learn what lodging descriptions really mean. In the US, the cheapest and simplest accommodation is variously described as 'economy', 'budget', 'no frills', 'rustic', 'basic' or 'European-style rooms'. The breakfast portion of bed and breakfast may vary from a continental roll-and-coffee to a full meal; ask. Unlike Europe, many US B&Bs offer (for a modest fee) other meals, transportation, tours and worthwhile goodies from free bike loans to use of libraries, saunas and tennis courts. Beware of lodging descriptions that include the words 'affordable', 'quaint', 'Old World charm' (evidently it costs a fortune to drag charm from the Old World to the New), and 'standard' or 'tourist class' (travel agenteese for mid-price range).

Hotels and motels. Thanks to the great success of the Motel 6 chain, the American travel industry has reluctantly concluded that no-frills lodging is not just a ploy for the pathologically frugal. Thus dozens of budget chain motels have emerged in the last decade. Except for Motel 6, however, they tend to be regional in scope and with prices that vary from unit to unit and season to season. To be fair: many of them offer more for the money (eg. pool, larger rooms, bath, phones, TV, etc.). See the Appendix for a list of budget hotel chains in the US.

Budget motels work out cheapest with three or more people. Unfortunately, they are often difficult to reach without a car, but do call to ask about bus connections, if any. As a rule, cheapie motels (chain or non-chain) provide better, cleaner and safer accommodation for the money than do cheap downtown hotels.

Finding a hotel with the ideal mix of low price and reasonable quality is an art. Besides the suggestions in this Guide, you could try: (1) comparing notes with other travellers; (2) asking the Greyhound bus driver and at the terminal—but be careful with this; in small towns or out west maybe, but in New York, Detroit etc, forget it; and (3) check at the Travelers Aid kiosks in transit terminals. It's also wise to leave your luggage in a locker so you can check out your prospects. Ask to see rooms and don't settle for bad-news facilities (eg. doors that don't lock or that have signs of forced entry, unclean linen, etc.). If you are a woman alone, we strongly advise you to arrive in big cities during daylight hours.

YMCAs and YWCAs. Most YMCAs offering accomodation are located in the often run-down heart of big city downtowns. Y lodgings have no membership or age restrictions and the use of rec facilities is often free. Two-thirds of them are coed; the rest, men only.

The economics of desperation bring in a mixed clientele; that, coupled with the grimy streets outside and steadily rising prices sometimes make the YMCA less and less of a bargain especially if there is more than one of you. For the single traveller the Y can still be the best bargain in town. You may do even better with prepaid reservations (valid at 124 YMCAs in the US, Canada and Mexico), and better still with an AYH card—many Ys give hostel rates. Contact the Y's Way, 224 E 47th St, New York NY 10017, (212) 756-9600.

The women-only YWCAs are concentrated in the Northeast, the Midwest and Texas. They tend to be smaller, more cheerful and better bargains than their YMCA counterparts—if you can get in.

Hostels. American Youth Hostels (AYH) has adopted the International Youth Hostel Federation blue triangle symbol and become Hostelling International—American Youth Hostels. Some 200 US hostels are already re-affiliated to the new HI-AYH, and members can now make reservations through the International Booking Network (IBN) for a $5 fee per hostel, (202) 783-6161 or through the free 800 number: 1-800-909-4776. Refer to HI-AYH *Handbook* for details on how this works. Most major USA gateway hostels are part of the network.

All in all, the hostel situation in the USA is pretty good and is especially bright in the Northeast states and in Ohio, Michigan, Minnesota, Colorado, Arizona, California, Oregon, Washington and Alaska (along the ferry route) but pretty thin elsewhere. There are hostels near Yellowstone and Yosemite, and in expensive cities like Chicago, Houston, Los Angeles, New York City, San Francisco, Minneapolis, Miami Beach and Washington DC. Mexico has 20 hostels in Mexico City, Acapulco, Cancun and elsewhere. Canada has opened hostels in Montreal and Toronto and there are many others in major cities as well as in recreation areas.

If you belong to an overseas Youth Hostel Association, you're entitled to use HI-AYH and AAIH (see below) facilities. Annual fees in the US are $25 (age 18-54). Write to AYH, Membership Dept., 733 15th St NW, Suite 840, PO Box 37613, Washington DC 20003-7613, or phone: (202) 783-6161. Overseas visitors who are not members in their own country must make use of the introductory pass most hostels offer so you can try it on a one-time basis. Get your pass stamped each time you use it, and after 6 times you become a 'guest member'—although you will not be entered onto the database, which may cause complications. It is recommended that if you plan to do a lot of hostelling you get the handbook published jointly by HI-AYH and the Canadian Hostelling Association which lists all hostels in both countries. In the US it comes free.

In addition to AYH-affiliated hostels there are a growing number of independently run hostels in the US. The American Association of Independent Hostels (AAIH) has hostels, or else provides hostel-type (ie. dorm.) accommodation within large hotels in several cities. Aimed primarily at the young, international traveller, they are generally located in downtown areas near to the bus terminal. Then there are many other smaller independents which seem to spring up like mushrooms, mostly in the large cities such as Los Angeles (a prime hostel spot) and New Orleans. In some cases they last one season and then disappear! So be careful.

The accommodation provided by independent hostels can be a bit of a mixed bag. Some are very good, but others aim simply to cram in as many people as possible regardless of standards of cleanliness, safety or sanitation. If you are on a budget, of course, you may feel you don't really have a choice. The majority of the hostels listed in this book have been recommended by previous users.

Two useful associations for travelers are the Pacific Rim Network and Backpackers Hostels Canada. These groups link independent hostels, ranging from farms to city hostels. Call or fax (800) 9-RIMNET for California listings, and as much free advice as you could want on hostelling in North America! Also write to Thunder Bay Int Hostel, RR 13, Thunder Bay, Ont, Canada P7B 5E4, (807) 983-2042, or email: *david.burgess@fyberstore.ca*, for info on these hostels and general advice on hostelling/travel-planning.

Pluses of North American hostelling: often in locales of great scenic beauty; a growing number are housed in buildings of historic or architectural interest (from decommissioned lighthouses to adobe haciendas); many offer special activities free or at low cost, from wilderness canoe or cycling trips to hot-tubbing. Reader comments show that US hostels are generally more relaxed and friendly than their European counterparts. 'I found youth hostels most convenient places to stay. Full of young people of all nationalities, the hostels were a nucleus of information and I met many travelling partners. Whilst not boasting of exceptional comforts, the hostels generally proved to be very good value and certainly took a lot out of the loneliness of travelling on one's own.'

Drawbacks? Uneven distribution make hiking or biking itineraries impractical, except for certain regions. Remote locales make it tough to use public transport to get to many of them. And hostel curfews and customs can cramp your style, particularly if you plan to do much urban or nighttime sightseeing. 'Most US hostels insist on your having (or renting for 50¢) a sheet sleeping bag.' 'On the whole American hostels were very good indeed.'

University-associated lodging. Over 230 universities in the US and Canada offer on-campus housing in dorms and residence halls. Points to consider: usually available summer only (exceptions noted in listings); rates vary widely and definitely favour doubles and weekly stays; facilities often heavily booked; campuses can be far from city centres. It's always worth trying the local student union or campus housing office when in the vicinity. Many of these offerings are open to the general public.

You can also find off-campus residences, fraternity and sorority houses with summer space to rent, all of which tend to be looser, friendlier and cheaper than on-campus options. Fringe benefits: use of kitchen facilities (sometimes) and entree into the thirsty social life of local students, including the infamous TGs or kegger parties.

Camping. Camping provides the cheapest and one of the most enjoyable means of seeing the best parts of North America, the national and state parks and other preserves. Your choices are almost infinite—free campgrounds in the US alone total over 20,000! State park camping fees range from zero to $8 and are indicated with the state listings. National parks (same price range) are given considerable attention in this Guide; for further information, write to the National Park Service, US Department of the Interior, P.O Box 37127, Washington DC 20013-7127 Room 1013. Other excellent Sources for campgrounds info are the AAA books, Rand McNally's *Campground and Trailer Park Guide* (17,000 US and Canada listings) and the tourism offices of each state.

You should be aware that the biggest drawback for the on-foot traveller is access. Ironic as it sounds, you really need a car to get to numerous campgrounds and trailheads to backcountry camping, especially those sites located on National Forest or Bureau of Land Management property. Once you have wheels it is possible to zig-zag your way across America camping in some of the loneliest, loveliest spots in the world. It might even be worth investigating hiring a camper vehicle (VW or the dreaded RV) for an extended trip. For a group of 3 or more it could be worth the extra expense.

Campground facilities vary from fully developed sites with electricity, bunk-equipped cabins and hot showers to primitive sites where you're expected to bury your wastes and pack out your rubbish. Tent campers are advised to avoid RV-oriented campgrounds. They may offer a pool, laundromat, store and other amenities but the noise, asphalt and vehicle fumes sadly dilute the 'wilderness' experience. Although more expensive, private campgrounds can be good. A number of readers have recommended KOA (Kampgrounds of America). In general, while their sites are not always the most scenic, their facilities are luxurious in camping terms. 'We used the KOA campgrounds the whole time—they have the best facilities available. And get a KOA discount card; this allows a 10 percent reduction on the cost of a campsite, plus gives a "free" guide.' Sites cost $12-$20. For the hiking/biking camper, many state parks offer a few sites designated as 'hiker/biker' for 50¢-$1 per night on a first-come, first-served basis.

In the north, the camping season lasts from mid-May to mid-September or sooner, depending on weather. In the Rockies and other mountainous areas, temperatures drop dramatically in the evening, making warm clothing vital. In the warm dry Southwest, you probably won't have to put up a tent, although You might want to exclude any unwelcome wildlife! At Yellowstone and other Northern parks, you may encounter bears who roam the campground for food. Wear a bell! These bears are not interested in campers as nourishment and will not harm you as long as you leave them well alone. Do not leave food in the tent, in ice chests, on picnic tables or near your sleeping bag. Lock it in the trunk of your car, or use park-recommended 'bear cables'. Bring along a generous supply of insect repellant and calamine lotion to combat mosquito bites, chiggers (a maddening insect that burrows beneath your skin) and poison ivy/poison oak (glossy three-leaved plants).

Popular national and state parks get very crowded from Memorial Day through to Labor Day, making May and September the ideal months for visits. In summer, you may want to book through TICKETRON, the national ticketing service, to ensure a place. To get the best site, try to arrive by 5 pm or earlier. Beware that some campgrounds keep the 'No Vacancy' sign up all summer so always ask. At the most popular parks queuing all night for space is not unheard of.

Native American campgrounds and other Indian-run lodging facilities are a first-rate way to get acquainted with North America's first people. Most sites are located on reservation land which, if you remember your history, has traditionally been located about a million miles from nowhere. Although the whites did their best to fob off nothing but marginal lands on the Indians, what they ended up with is often superbly scenic. A car is nearly imperative as you'll find little public transit to and from reservation land. Besides campgrounds, Native American owned facilities range from simple motels to sumptuous resorts. Some offer traditional dancing, crafts and native food. For a detailed and loving look at the Indian nations, read Jamake Highwater's *Indian America* (Fodor).

Bed and breakfast. An old concept in Europe, B&B crossed the Atlantic a few years ago and has now hybridised in several directions. Most visible are the 'too cute to be true' B&B Inns, widely written about and gushed over and punitively expensive in most cases. Least visible but most moneywise are the private homes in the US, Canada and Mexico which only rent rooms through an agency intermediary. (This is partly for security reasons, partly because of US zoning laws.) Most agencies concentrate on a given city or state; you'll find their names and addresses under the appropriate listing. Their rates run from $35-$45 single and from $45-$90 double. (NB: higher rates are for incredibly lavish digs.) Booking procedures, type of breakfast, length of stay and other conditions vary from agency to agency. The common denominator is the need to book ahead. If in the US, this can often be handled with a phone call. Only rarely can you breeze into town and get same-day accommodation.

If you are planning to do a lot of B&Bing you should consider buying one of the many books on the market which list hundreds of guest houses or tourist homes on a national or regional basis. A good guide will also list the various reservation services, their rates and how they work.

Is the lack of flexibility worth it? Most people think so. Foreign visitors who want to meet locals, see American homes and eat home cooking are particularly enthusiastic. Private home B&Bs are an inexpensive, warm and caring environment for women travellers on their own, too. Bonuses: many B&Bs serve meals other than breakfast and a large number are willing to pick up and deliver guests (sometimes a small fee). Hosts often speak other languages, so make your needs known at booking time. Canadian B&Bs are called hospitality homes. In Mexico, the B&B programme is known as Posada Mexico.

There are several B&B umbrella agencies which cover a number of states (and countries) and which cater to foreign and US travellers. They can book you into one B&B or work out a whole itinerary of B&Bs for you. Write for details and brochures. A few of the better known agencies:

1. B&B California, PO Box 282910, San Francisco, CA 94128-2910, call (800) 872-4500 or (415) 696-1690, www/bbintl.com/ Outstanding host and guest matchups; fees from $65 for single or double; full breakfast; many homes throughout California and Nevada.
2. Northwest B&B Inc, 1067 Hanover Court S, Salem, OR 97302. Call (503) 2243-7616. As the name implies, homes in Washington, Oregon, British Columbia, California, Hawaii, Alaska, Idaho, Nevada and Victoria. Full breakfasts. Around 400 B&Bs are listed starting at around $65 per night. Also: Pacific B&B, PO Box 46894, Seattle, WA 98146; (206) 784-0539. Rates from $45 single (shared bath). Homes in Washington and British Columbia.
3. B&B League Ltd, PO Box 9490, Washington DC 20016. Phone: (202) 363-7767. Recommended primarily for travellers in pairs, since rates are $35-$115 single, $50-$130 double plus $10 booking fee. Continental breakfast. Makes rsvs for B&Bs in DC and area.

Like every other business in America, new organisations mushroom all the time. Some of them are very localised so it is always worth checking in the immediate vicinity (eg. Yellow Pages) for local listings.

Other accommodation possibilities. If you're planning to bicycle around the US, it makes sense to contact Adventure Cycling, a national non-profit organization, at PO Box 8308, Missoula, Montana 59807. Tel: (406) 721-1776. they provide books and maps to help you. Hostelling International offers special tours for cyclists and of course accommodation. Many individual hostels arrange their own bike rental and tours. Also recommended is a series published by Ballantine—*Cyclist's Guides to Overnight Stops*.

Two mutual hospitality exchange programmes also exist. The Globe trotters' Club, BCM/Roving, London WC1N 3XX (postal address only; there is no office) and in the US, Box 9243, North Hollywood CA 91609, has a $10 membership fee, magazine and directory. Members have the option of choosing to offer hospitality or not. The Traveler's Directory, 6224 Baynton St, Philadelphia PA 19144: an informal, mutual hospitality exchange system listing people worldwide who can stay in each others' homes free of charge when travelling. To be listed, you must complete an application form, giving a brief summary of your interests and what hospitality you can offer.

Only those who have been listed can obtain a copy of the directory.

Should you decide to (or be reduced to) crash out it is a good idea to ask locally whether or not your chosen spot is safe. The local police, or students, are probably the best people to ask but it's not a good idea to just crash out by the side of the road or on the beach without checking first. Some readers have suggested highway rest areas as good sleeping places but sometimes this is not allowed and you should only do this if other people are clearly doing so already—never alone.

If you're totally stranded and penniless then Travelers Aid or the Salvation Army may help.

FOOD

To eat cheaply and well in America is easy once you realise that menu prices have more to do with restaurant decor and labour costs than with food quality. Everyone will quickly develop his or her own game plan depending on available funds and taste. However you should plan to get at least some of your meals from non-restaurant sources: supermarkets, open-air farmers markets, roadside stands and farms.

When possible, avoid higher-priced outlets like 24-hour stores, bus station canteens, street vendors, beach stands, airport restaurants and liquor stores. 'Some supermarkets, especially 7-11s, have microwaves, so a hot stew can be eaten for the price of the can and if you are on the road this is generally also true of some gas stations.' In general the food you buy and prepare yourself will always be the cheapest. At least one meal a day should fall into this category.

Keep away from endless soft drinks; even at supermarkets, they're 75¢ and up, double that elsewhere. Accompany your dining-out meals with ice water or lower-priced multiple refills like coffee or tea.

If you can eat a good meal in the morning then you'd be wise to start with a big breakfast (best food bargain in the US) and/or to stay in bed and breakfasts, hotels, hostels and other lodgings which include it as part of the price. Everywhere you will find excellent breakfast 'specials' for as little as $1.25 for eggs, toast etc. At lunchtime, again look for daily 'specials'—usually the tastiest/freshest and cheapest choice available.

In the evening, plan to eat early (to take advantage of lower-priced 'sunset' or 'early bird' specials) or eat in a non-restaurant setting.

Wherever you are, check out the Happy Hour situation. States and cities with liberal liquor laws often honour a daily discount period (usually 4pm-7pm) with cheap drinks and free food, sometimes a stunning array of it. Fittingly, California is the Happy Hour paradise.

No matter where you are, ethnic restaurants are invariably the cheapest. Chinese, Mexican and Italian can be found in profusion. In larger areas, look for Vietnamese, Greek, German, Indian and other specialties. Cafeterias offer cheap if sometimes insipid food; besides downtown, look for them on campuses, around hospitals, in large museums, in department stores and at YMCAs. 'Anyone can eat in university cafeterias—all you want for the price of a burger, fries and soft drink at McDonalds.' The good old American diner, now unfortunately in decline, is another reasonably inexpensive option, usually with an amazing choice of dishes on the menu and enormous portions.

Regional and local specialties are usually wonderful, or at the very least a worthwhile cultural experience. As you work your way around the country sample Key Lime pie, Virginia ham and redeye gravy, Chicago-style deep-dish pizza, California guacamole dip, Texas chili, Southern grits, Hawaiian poi and roast pig, Wisconsin bratwurst, Maryland crabcakes, Navajo tacos.

In the West, salads and salad bars are generally excellent. Large sand-wiches (often with local nomenclature like grinder, submarine, po' boy, blimp, hero, hoagie, etc.) on rolls with meatballs, sausage, corned beef, you name it, are available everywhere for a couple of dollars.

Many readers have suggested the salad bars now available in some fast food chains or as sold by the pound in supermarkets and grocery stores. For about $3 you can eat as heartily as any well-to-do rabbit. Those on a budget will inevitably find themselves eating from time to time at McDonald's, Burger King, Boston Market, Pizza Hut, Kentucky Fried Chicken and the rest. At least you know what you're getting. Coast to coast it's always the same! The Taco Bell chain has been recommended for a good, filling, cheap vegetarian meal eg. 89¢ for bean burritto. And there's always pizza!

Americans are ice cream fanatics and eat it year-round in more flavours and combinations than you've ever dreamed of. Lots of the ice cream par-lours will give you free samples until you hit on the one you want most.

Wherever you eat, portions are invariably enormous—you'll soon under-stand why Americans invented the doggie bag for leftovers! 'Forget doggie bags—nobody objected to our ordering one portion and two plates and sharing—portions still bigger than at home.'

'Nowhere have I found it difficult, and usually I've found it fun, hunting out a place to suit my quite small pocket. I do feel that discovering food, rather than following a map to it, is part of the holiday.'

TRAVEL
The means you choose to travel around North America will depend on your budget, your time, your adventurousness and a number of other factors. Since there are certain discounts available to travellers who buy their tickets outside North America, it is a good idea to give careful consideration to travel plans *before* you go. Also, when you buy your tickets outside the US, you save the eight percent sales tax. Basically, travel is like everything else in America—you have to shop around for the best buys. Never be afraid to ask for the cheapest fare. There are always variations and the clerk selling you a ticket is not necessarily about to offer you the cheapest one.

'Canada and the US cater for wheelchairs much better than the UK does. Theatres, museums, pavements, airports, bus stations, even buses are all usually equipped with either lifts or ramps.'

Bus. Travelling long distances cross-country by bus has become a part of American mythology and for natives and overseas visitors alike bus remains the most popular method of cheap travel in North America. Despite competition from comparatively inexpensive air fares which has resulted in the cutting back of bus routes and facilities in recent times, the major nationwide company, Greyhound, and the many regional, smaller companies, survive and flourish and will no doubt still be the chief means of inter-city transportation for most budget travellers to North America for the forseeable future.

It is possible to travel comfortably all over North America whether it be on Greyhound or one of the many other bus lines. Bus terminals provide restaurants, ticket, baggage and parcel services, travel bureaux, restrooms and left-luggage lockers, although you should be aware that bus stations are often in the seediest areas of downtown and therefore not a place to actually plan on spending a lot of time. Periodic rest stops are made every three to four hours enroute and if you are on a very tight budget you can save by travelling at nights and sleeping on the bus.

Currently, advance reservations on Greyhound are not accepted, it is advised to turn up at the relevant bus station several days before departure to purchase your ticket. More usual perhaps is to turn up at least an hour before departure on the day of travel, before all spaces are gone. Greyhound's central information number is (800) 231-2222.

When travelling by bus from point A to point B, always ask about the cheapest available fare. Fare reductions are made and usually depend on the time of travel, how long away, when returning etc. Available to overseas visitors are the various Greyhound Ameripasses. These are the 5-day Pass for £85; the 7-day Pass for £110; 15 days for £170; 30 days at £230 and 60 days at £340. You can no longer buy extra days while on the road. A 4-day Pass is also available for £75. It is non-refundable and valid for travel only on Monday to Thursday—ie. it is not possible to use the pass at weekends although you can interrupt useage and restart again after the weekend. The Ameripass is not valid for travel in Canada except for direct journeys from Seattle to Vancouver, Fargo to Winnipeg, Buffalo/Detroit to Toronto, and Boston or New York to Montreal. (*For further information on Greyhound fares in Canada, please see the Background Canada section of this book.*) It is also possible to buy the Ameripass from Greyhound International (only) office in New York City, Port Authority Bus Terminal. The 4-day pass costs $119, 5-day pass costs $139, 7-day pass $179, 15-day pass $279, 30 days, $379, and for 60 days of non-stop adventuring, a pass costs $549.

Time on all the passes starts ticking away when you start your journey. The passes offer unlimited travel on Greyhound routes (and those of participating carriers) for the duration of the pass. They represent excellent value for the cross-country traveller. For approximately £200 more, you can purchase a Go Hostelling Pass combining pre-paid accommodation at youth hostels with bus travel.

Some Tips. Whenever possible, take your bags on to the bus with you, otherwise get a check-in ticket, make sure they are labelled and watch them like a hawk—it is not uncommon for you and your bags to set off in different directions, and without the check-in ticket you may never get them back. If you have to put your bag underneath the bus it is recommended that at each stop en route to your destination you get off the bus and watch to make sure that your bag stays there and continues with you—on the same bus. 'If all lockers are taken, luggage can be stored for up to 24 hours at an approximate cost of $1.50 per piece, in the bus depot luggage store.'

'Bus pass coupons have to be validated each time for further travel. As ticket lines can be very long, it's good to have your ticket stamped for the next journey as soon as you arrive.'

If planning to sleep on the bus, get a cheap inflatable pillow. It can make all the difference to your comfort, though some readers say a sleeping bag is better 'and doesn't puncture'. Malleable wax ear plugs are also a good idea for lighter sleepers. Always have a sweatshirt or pullover with you. Bus drivers seem to be impervious to cold. 'Even at 3 am on a chill night the air conditioning is set to combat the climate of Death Valley.'

The bus passes often entitle you to discounts at station restaurants, nearby hotels and on various sightseeing tours. It's in fact cheaper to eat away from the stations, but you might not always have the time to do so.

Most bus routes are meant solely to get you from A to B; scenic considerations rarely come into it.

The Green Tortoise. A kind of alternative bus/tour combo designed to get the budget traveller across country cheaply, but in a fun, laid-back way. Time is not of the essence here. No effort is made to get there fast. The idea is to meander gently with the route changing at the request of the passengers. The coast to coast trips begin and end in either New York or Boston and San Francisco, depart weekly, last 10-14 days and at present cost between $299-$379. You will need extra money for meals en route. Other tours are available—to Yosemite, the Grand Canyon, Mexico, Alaska and New Orleans for Mardi Gras. Green Tortoise also provides a cheap way of travelling down the West Coast—Seattle to LA, $79; San Francisco to LA, $35, San Francisco-Seattle $59.

Buses accommodate 28 to 44 people and have most of their seats removed and replaced by wooden platforms covered with foam rubber padding. They also have stoves and refrigerators. Often cross-country tours are accompanied by a cook. Passengers can put about $9 or so a day into a kitty and get two full meals cooked on the bus but often eaten at some scenic place such as a Louisiana bayou or the banks of the Rio Grande. Smoking is banned on the buses.

'A wonderful trip. I made many new and lasting friends and saw many places I might otherwise have missed.' 'Don't do it if you're an insomniac, a loner, need a shower more than once every three days, or a moaner.'

Reservations should be made through Green Tortoise, 494 Broadway, San Francisco CA 94133. Or for information phone (800) TORTOISE (867-8647); when in the bay area call (415) 956-7500; when at your screen call up, www.greentortoise.com/.

Car. The car overwhelmingly remains the most popular form of travel and the vast system of super-highways—'monuments to motion'—enables you to cover great distances at high average speeds, despite the nationwide imposition of a 55 mph speed limit (although 65 mph on some rural interstates). 'The National System of Interstate and Defence Highways is designed for maximum efficiency. For enjoyment, try state and country roads, even for a lengthy trip. The additional time spent will be more than compensated for by the increased intimacy with American culture and scenery.'

Buying a car. For a group of three or four it can be worthwhile buying a second-hand car. Try to buy and sell privately, utilising the notice boards of universities, and the local press.

Be sure to obtain a 'title' or, in states such as New York, a notarised bill of sale. If stopped by the police, 'proof of ownership' will be required. (In some states it is illegal to drive without this.) Allow for a delay while the title comes through. If you buy from a dealer he can issue temporary licence plates on the spot.

You can have your car checked over at a gas station at a very low cost. If you have to buy new parts get them at one of the nationwide stores like Montgomery Ward or Sears, or from major gas stations like Shell and Mobil. They will give you guarantees and have the advantage of being readily available all over the continent. Garages are efficient and friendly, and if you are from out-of-state, will usually do repairs, however major, on the spot.

Prices of second-hand cars vary very much from place to place and tend to be higher on the West Coast. Prices fall in September when the next year's new cars come on to the market. Leave several days for selling your car and if possible try not to do it in New York. Automatic cars are easier to sell.

'Two of us bought a large station wagon for $800 and drove it 12,000 miles in two months. We slept in it often, and sometimes ate in it too. We sold it back to the dealer we bought it from at half-price. Worst problems: two $50 repair bills and finding places to park.' 'We bought a car. It cost $400 among seven. I personally paid $50 and to travel 5000 miles it cost me $60 in gas. Well worth it and it gave us freedom to visit so many places.'

Insurance. Although insurance cover is not obligatory in every state, you are strongly advised to take out at least third-party cover—and full comprehensive coverage is preferable—as insurance claims can be very high and inadequate insurance can lead to financial ruin. Expect to pay at least $450 for six month's coverage. 'State Farm Insurance, found in all states, offers good service and very good short-term policies.'

Insurance premiums are generally high, particularly for males under 25. Women are considered better risks and their premiums are lower. Premiums are lower if you are resident outside large urban areas. Allow time for your policy to come through.

In states where insurance is compulsory it is necessary to have it before you can register your car. 'We bought a car in Colorado and had trouble insuring it with an International Drivers' License. So be prepared to take a test and get a state license!'

Licences. All states and provinces of the US and Canada now officially recognise all European licences and those of Japan, Australia and New Zealand among others. However, an International Driving Licence is recommended since it provides you with photographic ID. Also police are more familiar with them and this could save you time and embarrassment (but don't forget to bring your *original* licence too—you may not be able to hire a car or get a drive-away without it). In addition, your own licence can be validated by the AAA office in the USA. Although not a legal requirement, it's a good idea to have it done particularly if your licence is not in English. You won't encounter many multi-lingual patrolmen along the way. You must always have your insurance certificate, car registration certificate and driving licence with you in the car—there is no grace period; you will simply be done for driving without the legally required documents.

Road Tips. Traffic regulations vary from state to state, so familiarise yourself with them in each. The 55mph speed limit is standard, however, except on an increasing number of rural interstate highways, where it is 65 mph. Many readers recommend buying the Rand McNally *Interstate Road Atlas*, useful even for non-drivers. Maps from gas stations cost around $3.

'Most truck drivers have CBs. When driving, follow the example they set. If they adhere to the speed limit it means they've picked up the police lurking in the locality.

If you have a breakdown, raising the hood is the recognised distress signal. Also switch on your flashing warning lights.

Never pass a stopped and flashing school bus (they are usually yellow) no matter which side of the road it is on: it is not only against the law, but could easily result in death or injury to young children.

AAA Membership. Benefits include: helping with car rental, hotel reservation, towing service, $5000 bail if arrested, excellent and free maps and regional guide books, and a comprehensive information and advisory service. For example, the AAA will plan your journey for you, giving the quickest or most scenic routes, and provide detailed maps of the towns you will pass through.

Touring membership varies depending on which state you join. In New York for example it costs $55 for the first year and $45 thereafter. In Florida costs are $64 for the first person and $37 for each additional person. Apply to: AAA, 1000 AAA Drive, Heathrow, FL 32746, or to AAA, Broadway and 62nd St., in New York, 212-586-1166, or to the Club in whichever state you happen to be.

Membership of your own national automobile association entitles you to AAA benefits, eg. Allstate Motor Club, (800) 347-8880, $60.

Gasoline. Depending on which part of the country you are in, expect to pay as much as $1.65 per gallon, or as little as about $1.20. (The American gallon is one-fifth smaller than the imperial gallon used in Britain and Canada and is equivalent to 3.8 litres.) Self serve is cheaper.

When driving in remote areas, always keep your tank topped up. Gas stations can be few and far between. Keep a reserve supply in a container for emergencies. Shop around and use self service pumps for cheapest gas.

Automobile Transporting Companies—Driveaways. Americans change homes more often than any other people, and may live for a few years in New York and then move off to California. When they do move they sometimes put their car (or one of them) into the hands of an automobile transporting company which does no more than find someone like you to drive the car from A to B.

Most movements are from east to west, major starting points being New

York, Detroit and Toronto. 'East-west is the easiest route to get; otherwise New York-Florida or New York-Atlanta. The cheapest way to travel bar hitching'. Even on the popular routes you may have to wait a couple of days for a car, particularly in summer.

Conditions regarding age limitation, time schedules, routing, gas and oil expenses, deposit, insurance and medical fitness vary considerably and should always be carefully checked. And another thing: 'The car trunk may be full of the owner's belongings, leaving no room for yours.' A fair example would be for a driver 21 years or over, with character references, to be charged about $300 deposit, refundable on safe delivery. 'A superb and cheap way of travelling. I went with three others in a van and it only cost us $70 each in gas to get from New York to San Francisco via the Grand Canyon.' 'Beware. We had a series of bad experiences. Each office acts independently and sometimes against what the same company's office elsewhere tells you.' 'You have to take a reasonably direct route, but the time limit (after which you are reported to the FBI) allows a fair amount of sightseeing. I was given nine days for the coast-to-coast trip and made it in six. It's certainly a great way to see America.'

'I drove a new Cadillac with only two thousand miles on the clock. It was air conditioned, everything electric—really unbelievable, and we slept in it at night. Good places to sleep are truck-stops run by Texaco, Union 76, etc. They have 24 hr restaurants and free showers, and the truckers themselves, though rough-looking, are often interesting people to talk to.' 'Try and have more than one driver in the car.'

'When asking for your deposit back and before handing the keys over, hold out for cash. American cheques are a bugger to cash.' And a word of warning: 'It is essential to check the car thoroughly for dents and scratches before taking it. We lost $135 because the owner complained about scratches and we could not prove they were there before we took it.'

The names of companies can be found in the *Yellow Pages* under 'Automobile and Truck Transporting'. It is a good idea to shop around, go to the office in person, and make sure you do not sign away your insurance rights—ie. make sure you personally are covered and not just the vehicle. Try Auto Driveaway, 310 S Michigan Ave, Chicago, IL 60604, (800) 346-2277. The addresses of some other companies are listed under many towns and cities below.

Car Rentals. The biggest national firms are Hertz, Avis, National, Budget, Thrifty and Dollar. The last two are generally cheaper, but even Hertz can offer some amazing deals. It's important to phone around. Always compare costs per day against costs per mile and other variations, such as unlimited mileage or so many miles free, within the context of your specific needs. Many rental companies offer discount rates to foreign visitors, though sometimes only when bookings are made abroad.

The renter must usually be 21 or over, sometimes over 25 (Sears has been mentioned as one hire company which may rent to someone under 21). If you don't have a credit card then a hefty cash deposit will be required, and for foreigners a passport may also have to be deposited as security. 'It's very difficult to rent a car without a major credit card, and in many cases it's not possible to leave a deposit.' 'Small companies generally ask drivers to be 25 or over; large companies usually accept drivers from 18 provided they have a major credit card.' 'Younger the driver, higher the surcharge'—in some cases as high as $45 per day!

Insurance is not usually included in the cost, or often it's only third-party. It's essential that you take out full coverage; the alternative may be a lifetime of paying off someone's massive hospital bills.

Greyhound operates one of the cheapest rental companies, though it concentrates mostly on Florida and California. Alamo and Amerex are also recommended. Then there are the companies renting out older cars, eg. Rent-a-Wreck, Rent-a-Heap, Rent-a-Junk and Ugly Duckling. But they are not always the cheapest or most flexible, eg. in some instances you must stay within a 50- or 100-mile radius of the point of rental. Worth checking out, though. 'Phone the national company number as well as the local agent's number. One may well offer a better deal than the other.'

'Ask a travel agent for good deals; I found them to be in the know.' 'It's a good idea to check with the airline you're travelling on for special arrangements. Sometimes these can only be booked before the flight.' 'Don't entertain a firm that charges for mileage and drop-off; there are plenty that don't.' 'If you want unlimited mileage you must usually go to a large company.'

'We found car rental easiest, most convenient and, for groups of three or more, the cheapest way of getting to see National Parks and other areas where transport, other than tours, is minimal.'

Air. The vast distances of the North American continent have resulted in the popularity and relative cheapness of domestic air travel, and since government deregulation there has been a bewildering and ever-changing scramble to offer more for less. There are air travel bargains to be had but it is often hard to keep track of what is available. If you plan to fly check with a travel agent, phone around the airlines and keep an eye on newspaper and television advertising—and always ask for the cheapest available fare.

Some possibilities: night flights are sometimes cheaper than day flights; some airlines from time to time offer off-peak, cheaper, fares. Other airlines make discounts if you travel on a flight making stops en route and, if planning to travel great distances, it may pay to investigate the air passes (see below). There may be considerable price competition on major routes such as New York to Florida and New York to the West Coast. Once again, the clear message is shop around!

Additionally there are two Visit USA bargains available only to non-US residents and offering incredible value for cross-country travel. The terms and prices vary from airline to airline, but the principles are the same and the tickets have to be purchased BEFORE leaving for America.

The first (VUSA fares) offers a discount on all flights on the airline's system though the itinerary must be worked out and paid for prior to departure for the US. Reservations can be made at any time. This scheme may be preferable if you know in advance where you want to go and if you're not stopping at many places. Discounts are usually up to 40 percent.

Delta Airlines offer 'Discover America' coupons which can be bought in conjunction with Delta or British Airways trans-Atlantic flights. For example, 3 coupons costs $359, 4 coupons are $519, and 10 coupons $1249. 1 coupon equals 1 stopover. It is possible to buy coupons even if the trans-atlantic flight is on another airline. Not surprisingly it costs more: $559 for 3 coupons, $669 for 4 and $1,389 for 10 of them.

Northwest Airlines have several pass-type options, but only in conjunc-tion with a transatlantic flight on Northwest, KLM, BA or Virgin. Visit USA coupons are purchased with the transatlantic flight. There is a minimum of 3 coupons. 1 coupon represents 1 flight. Travelling from the UK, prices cur-rently range from $359 for 3 coupons to $1249 for 10, depending on when you fly. Once you begin using your coupons there is a maximum stay of 60 days permitted. One of the advantages of travelling by air is that careful timing can get you free meals and night flights save on accommodation expenses. Air passes can be bought from most travel agents. Check the Sunday papers for special deals to the Caribbean, sometimes as low as $399 for four days.

Rail. The railroads played a major role in the history of the United States, but over recent decades declined in service, increased in price, lost money and saw much of their former business go to cars and airlines. Part of the reason for this may have been the great number of competing railways and the inability of the individual companies to undertake the new investment necessary to improve service and efficiency. But then in 1971 Amtrak was established. All the major lines now operate under the one Amtrak board, and though the railways remain privately owned, losses on passenger ser-vices are made up for by government subsidy.

RIDING SCENIC RAIL

North America, especially the Rockies, is full of scenic narrow gauge rail-ways, where restored steam locomotives backtrack to bygone days. These are some of the more interesting rides.

Cumbres & Toltec Scenic Railroad in Antonito, CO, is North America's highest narrow-gauge steam railroad. Full-day, 64-mile tour, $50; (719) 376-5483. **Great Smoky Mountain Railway**, Bryson City, NC (near Asheville). Trips through Nantahala Gorge and Fontana Lake, 9 am & 2 pm Wed-Sun; $18 for 4 hr r/t. To reserve call: (704) 586-8811. **Mt Washington (NH) Railway Co**, (800) 922-8825. Historic route with steep grade, highly scenic trip to highest point in Northeast; 3 hr trip, $35. **Royal Hudson Steam Train**, Vancouver, British Columbia, (604) 68-TRAIN, follows the coast of Howe Sound to small mining town; $56 for full day. **Narrow Gauge Railroad**, Durango, CO, (303) 247-2733. Along Animas River Valley to Silverton. Old fashioned. $42 r/t, 4 trips daily. **Pikes Peak Cog Railway**, Manitou Springs, CO, (303) 685-5401. Several trips daily from Manitou Springs to Pikes Peak, the highest route in the US. $21 r/t. **Skunk Train**, Ft Bragg, CA, (707) 964-6371. Half day $21, full day $26. Scenic route through Redwoods. **Strasbourg Railroad**, Strasburg, PA, (717) 687-7522. 45 min route through Amish country 10 am-7 pm on the hour, $7. America's oldest short-line steam locomotive.

On long-haul Western routes, outdated equipment has been replaced by new double-decker Superliners, variously fitted up as lounges, dining cars (restaurant upstairs, kitchen below), sleeping cars (with bedrooms) and open-plan coaches. On shorter routes and generally in the East, cylinder-shaped Amcoaches are used, their interiors like luxury airliners.

In the East, frequency, time-keeping and the large number of destinations served permit comparison with European railways. From Chicago westwards it is the trans-Siberian railway that comes to mind. There are only four east-west routes, but all except one operate daily. Delays are common. But for the traveller that should not matter: the scenery is often spectacular, the service is better than on any railway in the world, the seats recline and have foot rests, you can eat and drink well and inexpensively, and the company is congenial. The Western railways are the last stronghold of graceful travel in America and many readers have written in to praise Amtrak and the standard of its services. 'Ideal for the student traveller going from city to city.' 'Very comfortable.' 'The best way to see a wide variety of scenery. On occasions we felt less worn from 20 hours on a train than four hours on a bus.' 'A wonderful window on to the USA.'

A rundown on some of the more interesting routes:

The Empire Builder runs between Chicago and Seattle via Milwaukee, Minneapolis/St Paul, Fargo in North Dakota, Glacier National Park and Spokane. Majestic scenery. Takes about 46 hours; operates daily.
The Coast Starlight, between Los Angeles and Seattle, offers superb coastal, forest and mountain scenery. 'Attracts many young people. A highly social train: spontaneous parties and lust.' Takes 33 hours; operates daily.
The California Zephyr, formally operated by The Denver & Rio Grande Western Railroad, is now operated by Amtrak three times a week. The journey, between Denver and Salt Lake City, takes 14 hours, almost all in daylight, and climbs 9000 feet over the Rockies for what is considered the greatest railway ride in America. It then runs on to Las Vegas and LA.

Also special are the *Pioneer* between Seattle and Salt Lake City, the *Adirondack* between New York and Montréal, and the crack *Broadway Limited* between New York and Chicago with the best onboard dining service.

Amtrak passes for 15/30 days unlimited travel are available to overseas visitors outside the US and are available in most cities at the Amtrak station. Check first however. High season rates (1 June-1st Sept) are: $425/$535 Nationwide, $315/$395 Western Region, $250/$310 for either the East or Far West Region. The Northeast Region pass is $195/$230. For the 30-day Coastal Pass (east or west) it's $275. Once you have bought the pass you can make reservations by phoning (800) USA-RAIL. 'Excellent value, great way to travel. Trains spacious and comfortable. Staff friendly and helpful.' 'Disadvantages—trains slow and often late.' 'It is essential to make reservations for the busy East Coast routes to Florida.' 'One drawback is the early morning (4 am!) arrival time at some mid-west stations.' 'Every time you phone, you get different information! Be pushy if need be.'

In Britain contact: Long Haul Leisurerail, PO Box 113, Peterborough PE1 1LE; 0733 51780. In the US call (800) 872-7245, Amtrak Vacations (800) 321-8684, or look up some interesting routes on www.amtrak.com/.

Boats. 'If you want to take a longer trip on the Mississippi, you can try to get on a towing boat. But you'll have to work hard. Look in the *Yellow Pages* under "Towing—Marine".'

How about paddling your own canoe? The Appalachian Mountain Club publishes three books of interest to canoeists and kayakers including: *AMC River Guide Maine; AMC River Guide Massachsetts; AMC River Guide New Hampshire and Vermont, Sea Kayaking in the Mid Atlantic and Sea Kayaking in the New England Coast.* They're available by mail from AMC Books, 5 Joy Street, Boston MA 02108, or PO Box 298 Gorham, NH 03581, (800) 262-4455.

The Chicagoland Canoe Base Inc, 4019 N Narragansett Avenue, Chicago IL 60634, can provide you with all the information you need on canoes, kayaks, rafts, accessories, rentals, books and maps, (312) 777-1489.

Hitchhiking. Hitchhiking in the United States can vary from state to state, but generally it can be 'superb, simply due to the long rides'. However, we strongly recommend that women, or even men, do not hitch alone.

'A sure way of getting long rides in relative comfort and at speeds in excess of the general 55 mph limit is to ask for rides at truck stops. At Union 76 truck stops there will often be hundreds of trucks going to all parts of America. Just ask the drivers in the canteen. By using this method I managed to cover over 1000 miles from Mexico to New Orleans with only two rides.' 'Don't try truck stops unless on your own. Even then, due to new insurance regulations, it's difficult.' 'I had better luck at truck stops at night when drivers like passengers to keep them awake.' 'Truck stop directories can be obtained free at truck stops.'

Hitching is forbidden on freeways and interstates, so get your rides on the ramps, at rest areas, or at service areas. With regard to other roads, the laws vary from state to state, but even when hitching is technically illegal you can usually still get away with it if you are standing on the shoulder or sidewalk, and sometimes even if you are walking with the traffic, regardless of the fact that you might be walking backwards. 'I had no problems except the usual ones. The police are okay, though they may ask to see your identification.' 'Police in New York warned me, "Ten days in jail if we see you again". The next day I was given a ride by a policeman.'

Never carry any dope. Display your national flag. Always carry a sign saying where you want to go. 'We carried two signs: one stating our destination, the other saying PLEASE. Fantastic results.' 'Female hitchhikers should not use destination signs; that way you have a chance to look over the driver before accepting.' Avoid getting off in cities if you don't want to stay there. 'People who gave us lifts often gave us meals and even a bed for the night.'

'Warning to female hitchhikers: don't hitch overnight trucks unless willing to satisfy the driver. No malice intended but "payment" is expected. At least that's what I found, and I was hitching with my boyfriend.' 'I often got rides with truckers and found them nice and helpful people. I slept in a cab of a truck three times without having to grant any favours, and I was a female alone. I'm not recommending overnight rides with truckers nor hitching alone for that matter, but I had no bad experiences.'

Holidays, especially Labor Day, are good times to travel as there are millions of cars on the road. If you don't want to thumb, try radio stations or look in the local (especially the freaky) papers. 'For hitching long-distance, or if you're prepared to share the driving, try the ride boards at universities—either advertise yourself or go to see what's offered. I got from Chicago to San Francisco this way in one car.'

'When crossing the US-Canadian border do not say you're a hitchhiker.' 'Beware the heat in the Southwest, ie. anywhere between LA and mid-Texas. In this area hitchers should carry a large container of water and some salt tablets. Hitchers have been found dead on the side of the road due to dehydration.' 'People are usually very congenial and offer accommodation and food.' 'I hitched from San Francisco to New York in four and a half days and could have done it in less. I experienced no more hassles than I have in Europe: The Southern states are populated by a different breed of people who are proud to be rebels and consider the Civil War to be still on, but they are still cool for hitching, especially if you are European. By the way, they call you Euro-penises.' 'I hitched 9500 miles with over 130 lifts and all but two were very friendly and helpful. I got beds, showers, endless meals, and made friends while hitching. Far more rewarding than bus travel.'

Hitching by air is another possibility. America is dotted with thousands of *small airfields* (ie. not JFK or LA International) located outside most towns from which people fly in *small aircraft* for pleasure or business. Those are the people you ask. 'Difficult across US/Canada border.' 'Air hitching is really difficult but saves so much time it's worth a try.' 'I walked into an air freight company office in San Francisco and got a free ride back to New York with the overnight packages.' Not a good idea to carry much luggage though—*small*, light, aircraft remember.

Bicycle. There's a 4450-mile TransAmerica Trail stretching from Virginia to Oregon, divided into five shorter routes. Five sectional booklets are available, with detailed maps and details of flora, fauna, campsites, eateries, bike shops and gradients enroute. Free leaflet from Adventure Cycling, PO Box 8308, Missoula, Montana 59807, (406) 721-1776. Also, some hostels do bicycle tours; information is available from local regional offices and the hostels themselves.

A strong bicycle lock is advisable for security when parking in towns, plus a helmet (US drivers are not attuned to looking out for bikes). Bicycles are cheaper in the US than abroad. It's possible to ship a bike around the US with Amtrak or the bus companies provided it's dismantled and boxed. Bikes can sometimes be taken free on flights to and from the US as part of your baggage allowance and again must be boxed. The cost, if any, varies from airline to airline.

Walking. Yes it is done. Mostly by mad dogs and Englishmen. Like John Lees of Brighton, England, who in 1972 walked from City Hall, Los Angeles, to City Hall, New York, a distance of 2876 miles, in 53 days 12 hours 15 minutes, averaging 53.75 miles per day.

'When asking for directions, remember that most people think you are on wheels. I was directed to one place along a roadway that took me 15 minutes to negotiate in the boiling hot sun, an excursion I could have avoided by cutting—in one-third the time—through a leafy forest. Unfortunately, the guy I asked thought I was a Chevy, so I had to go the long way round.'

A list of more than 25 hiking clubs along the East Coast can be obtained by writing to the Appalachian Trail Conference, Box 807, Harpers Ferry WV 25425, (304) 535-6331. The Conference manages the 2000-mile Maine to Georgia Appalachian Trail in conjunction with the National Park Service. For 50¢ they'll send you information about the trail, membership, etc. Be sure to ask specifically for the list of clubs.

On the West Coast there's the Sierra Club. They can provide information about the Pacific Crest Trail, 2400 miles along the Pacific Coast from Canada to Mexico, but also offer backpack and camping advice as well as trips which last 6-10 days. 730 Polk St, San Francisco CA 94109, (415) 923-5522.

Tours with a difference. If young and on your own and looking for fun and adventure, one of the proliferation of alternative tours or treks would be worth considering. Typically they either load up a van full of young people and tour chunks of the country or else they operate a roughly scheduled service allowing the traveller to get off and on when they please. One of the longest running companies (so to speak) is **TrekAmerica**. They run camping expeditions such as 25 days up the Alaska Highway, or six-week coast-to-coast journeys, stopping at the most interesting cities, towns and national parks enroute.Trek America offers offers 38 different itineraries from 7 days to 9 weeks, covering virtually every area of North America. During July and August a 14-day tour costs between $800-$900 plus $35 per week for food. There is a 15% discount for all BUNAC members. Extras such as riding and sailing are available at additional cost.

In Britain, contact TrekAmerica, Worldwide Reservation, 4 Waterperry Court, Middleton Road, Banbury, Oxon, OX6 8OG. Tel: 01295-256777. In the USA: TrekAmerica, PO Box 189 Rockaway, NJ 07866. (973) 983-1144 or (800) 221-0596. 221-0596. Email: hhp//www.trekamerica.co. 'An excellent way to see America if you don't mind camping and long drives. For a girl travelling on her own who didn't want to Greyhound or hitch, it enabled me to see a terrific amount in three weeks.'

Operating up and down the west coast and east to Las Vegas is **ANT**, Adventure Network for Travelers, (800) 336-6049, (415) 399-0880 in San Francisco. You can get on and off along the way. Departures are regularly scheduled and it costs about $60 to ride (one way) from Los Angeles to San Francisco, about $30 from LA to Las Vegas. Each ANT ticket is valid for 6 months.

New on the road is the **US BUS** which runs a travel pass system across America in 15-seat maxiwagons. Their routes take in interesting cities and scenic places. A 5-day 'travel America pass' costs $99, or $110 with an open start date. For 10 days it's $179/$199; for 30 days, $349/$379. In the UK: 64 Mount Pleasant Avenue, Tunbridge Wells, Kent TN1 1QY. Tel: 01892-512700. In the US, call (617) 984-1556.

See also a source book called *Adventure Travel North America* which lists all kinds of outdoor-type vacations including a wide range of 'Cowboy

Vacations'. $16.95 plus $3 postage.The book is available from Adventure Guides Inc., 7750 E. MacDonald Drive, Scottsdale, Arizona 85250, (800) 252-7899.

Urban Travel. City buses and subway systems generally offer good services throughout North America. Usually, a flat fare is used which can make short hops expensive but long rides very reasonable. Many cities have a transfer system allowing you to change from one bus line to another, or even from bus to subway, without paying extra. Stick-ups have meant that bus drivers will not carry any more money than is absolutely necessary, so you must always have the exact fare.

Taxis can be pretty expensive unless shared. The ubiquitous Gray Line company ensures that nearly every city has its bus tour, and some have boat tours as well.

For further details on all forms of urban travel, see under city headings throughout the Guide.

FURTHER READING

Fiction

Bonfire of the Vanities,   Tom Wolfe
Catcher in the Rye,   J. D. Salinger
Changing Places,   David Lodge
The Color Purple,   Alice Walker
Elmer Gantry,   Sinclair Lewis
Ethan Frome,   Edith Wharton
Gone with the Wind,   Margaret Mitchell
Glitz,   Elmore Leonard
The Grapes of Wrath,   John Steinbeck
The Great Gatsby,   F. Scott Fitzgerald
Huckleberry Finn,   Mark Twain
Lake Wobegon Days,   Garrison Keiller
Light in August,   William Faulkner
The London Embassy,   Paul Theroux
A Month of Sundays,   John Updike
Native Son,   Richard Wright
Ninety-Two in the Shade,   Thomas McGuane
On the Road,   Jack Kerouac
Southern Discomfort,   Rita Mae Brown
Stepping Westward,   Malcolm Bradbury
Trout Fishing in America,   Richard Brautigan
USA,   John Dos Passos

Other Works

Blue Highway: A Journey into America,   William Least Halfmoon
Democracy in America,   Alexis De Toqueville
Fear and Loathing in Las Vegas,   Hunter S. Thompson
New York Days, New York Nights,   Stephen Brook
The Nine Nations of North America,   Garreau
Old Glory,   Johnathan Raban
The Lost Continent: Travels in Small Town America,   Bill Bryson
Vagabonding in America,   Ed Buryn (if you can get hold of it)
Walk West,   David Jenkins

NEW ENGLAND

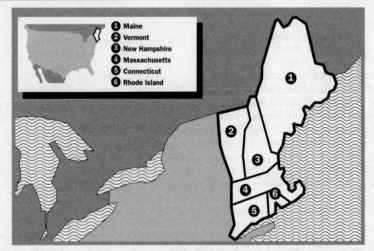

1. Maine
2. Vermont
3. New Hampshire
4. Massachusetts
5. Connecticut
6. Rhode Island

The upper northeast corner of the United States is sometimes called the nation's attic. One of the first areas in the New World to be colonised by Europeans, the Pilgrim Fathers, it is the old historical ties, more than any other, which bind these New England states together. It was here that American independence was born, embodied by such patriots as Paul Revere and Sam Adams. The region's size does not match its great historical significance. Its six states are together smaller than Oklahoma.

New England is a melting pot, spiced with a rich diversity gained from the British, Irish, Italians, French Canadians, Portuguese, Jews and many others who now make up the population. Cultural contrasts abound: contemporary, cosmopolitan Boston stands alongside peaceful country towns—revered reminders of early American society. To 'Southerners', however, New Englanders are still Yankees.

This compact region offers a great variety of scenery, from the rugged White Mountains of New Hampshire to the rolling green hills of Vermont, Massachusetts and Connecticut and the often spectacular coastline varies in its moods from state to state. Coastal roads stretch for miles weaving around jagged points and hidden inlets. Lush green countryside becomes weather-beaten and sun-bleached as it meets the Atlantic.

Politically, New England is important; the world's first written 'constitution'—the Mayflower Compact—was signed by the Pilgrim Fathers here in 1620. The American revolution was hatched in Boston, and in modern times, ex-President Bush and the Kennedys hailed from the area.

The seasons are distinct in New England: a long, cold, winter followed by a short blossom-filled spring, a hot, often humid summer, and best of all, a glorious autumn when the leaves turn the hillsides gold, scarlet and amber.

Hard-core hikers may like to tackle the 2000-mile long Appalachian Trail—the longest marked trail in the world. Beginning north of Bangor in Maine it winds more than 2000 miles from Baxter State Park to the mountains of Georgia.

CONNECTICUT *The Nutmeg State*

Connecticut has historically regarded itself as part of New England, although the area abutting New York State along Long Island Sound has far stronger ties with New York City than it has with Burlington, VT, or even Hartford, the state capital. Greenwich, Stamford and Bridgeport make up a significant commuter-belt and many people here look to the New York media for their news and entertainment.

Away from the coast, Connecticut is a state of broad rivers, farms, forests, rolling hills and placid colonial villages. In particular, the Litchfield Hills in the northwestern part of the state offer pretty scenery and have several excellent state parks good for camping and walking.

Connecticut is the third smallest state in the Union and one of the most densely populated.

The submarine was invented here in 1776 and Connecticut is also the birthplace of the lollipop and the payphone. The insurance industry has its roots in Connecticut and the Constitution State is home to America's first law school. Some of the oldest university art collections are at Yale, in New Haven. www. yahoo.com/regional/us states/connecticut/.

The telephone area code for the south western corner of the state is 203, elsewhere it is 860.

HARTFORD The state capital is home to a the nation's insurance industry, and thanks to the dark-suited image this presents, the city is not ordinarily known for its sparkling social scene. Recently, efforts have been made to turn the city into a livelier regional attraction. The Civic Center and State House Square provide shopping, restaurants, and entertainment, and should be added to a list of more antique sights, such as Mark Twain's House, the pre-World War One carousel in Bushnell Park, and, in the nearby suburbs of Wethersfield and Farmington, some of the oldest colonial houses in the US.

While here, pick up the *Hartford Courant*, founded in 1764 and the newspaper with the oldest continuous name and circulation in the nation, possibly in the world.

ACCOMMODATION
Most hotels downtown are $50 and up for doubles.

Days Inn, 207 Brainard Rd, 247-3297, D-$49, XP-$5. A bargain for four sharing!

Hartford Hostel, 131 Tremont St, 523-7255. Rambling Victorian house preserved in its natural state. $13 AYH, non-AYH $13+$3 stamp (towards membership), $1 linen. Private rooms $28-$36, rsvs required. Kitchen, dining room, picnic area, bike storage, laundry. Friendly, enthusiastic staff, open 24 hrs, 365 days a year. Tours available for Mark Twain House which is only a block away.

Windsor Home Hostel, 126 Giddings Ave, Windsor (north of Hartford on I-91), 683-2847. $15 AYH; $18 non-AYH, $1 linen rental. Rsvs required.
YMCA, 160 Jewel St, 522-4183. $18, coed. Close to Civic Center.

FOOD/ENTERTAINMENT
City Steam Brewery Cafe, 942 Main St, 525-1600. Lunch around $8, dinner around $12. Very popular with the locals. Live comedy on weekends, cover varies.
Russian Lady Cafe, 191 Ann St, 525-3003. In a wonderful old building topped with a statue of a royal Russian lady, hence the name. Live bands Tue-Sat. Drinks special offered every night. Check out the rooftop garden! Behind Civic Center.
The Municipal Cafe, 485 Main St, 527-5044. 6.30 am-2.30 pm, good meals and a diverse American menu, soups $2, speciality burgers $5.95. This popular cafe then re-opens at 7 pm with a cheap bar menu and Weds-Sat there's live local music too.

OF INTEREST
Bushnell Park, adjacent State Capitol, 246-7739, has a 1914 carousel; you can ride one of its 48 horses or a chariot to the tunes of a Wurlitzer Band Organ for 50¢. Tues-Sun 11 am-5 pm.
Hartford Festival of Jazz, Bushnell Park, 293-0131. Last weekend in July, free.
Harriet Beecher Stowe House, Nook Farm, Farmington Ave at Forest St, 525-9317. This charming Victorian cottage was the home of HBS after the publication of *Uncle Tom's Cabin*, from 1873 to her death in 1896. Same hours as Mark Twain House next door, Sun noon-5 pm, closed Mon in winter, tours $6.50.
Mark Twain House, 351 Farmington Ave, 493-6411. Calling all lovers of American literature—MT lived here for almost 20 years, publishing *Huckleberry Finn* and other major works from this quirky Victorian-Gothic style mansion. Summer: Mon-Sun 9.30 am-5 pm, closed Tue in winter; 1 hr tour $7.50. Bring a picnic to a free Twain by Twilight' concert evening held in the grounds during July, includes free admission to first floor of house. Call for dates and details.
Old State House, 800 Main St, 522-6766. Formerly the State Capitol, recently restored and refurbished back to its 1796 appearance. Information centre, Mon-Sat 10 am-5 pm.
State Capitol, Capitol Ave and Trinity St, 240-0222, exit 48 off I-84. A dazzling Gothic monolith capped by a gold dome. Contains lots of Connecticut historical memorabilia. Be sure to see the dramatic Hall of Flags. Tours available hourly Mon-Fri, 9.15 am-1.15 pm, Sat 10.15 am-2.15 pm, free.
Wadsworth Athenaeum, 600 Main St, 278-2670. One of New England's best art collections with 45,000 works; it is the country's oldest public art gallery. Tues-Sun, 11 am-5 pm; $7, $5 w/student ID. Free all day Thurs, and Sat before noon.

INFORMATION
Convention and Visitors Bureau, Civic Center Plaza, 728-6789/(800) 793-4480. Mon-Fri, 8.00 am-4.30 pm.
Hartford Guides, 101 Pearl St, 293-8105. Goodwill ambassadors on duty throughout the town, ready to serve the lost and the curious. Easily recognisable in their red,white and khaki uniforms.

TRAVEL
Greyhound, (800) 231-2222. NYC ($14, 3 hrs), Boston ($14, 2 hrs).
Amtrak, (800) 872-7245, at Union Place. NYC ($21, 3 hrs, time restrictions apply).
Connecticut Transit Information Centre, behind old State House, btwn Main & Market Sts, 525-9181, has info on public transport within the city (basic fare $1) and a map of downtown area. Mon-Fri 7 am-6 pm.
NB. Only regular transport available from downtown to Bradley International Airport is via shuttle service from downtown hotels. Cost: about $10.

LITCHFIELD HILLS In the northwestern corner of the state, this is an area of rolling hills, with woods, rivers, streams and lakes. The town of Litchfield is a movieman's epitome of New England, with its white wooden churches, fine colonial houses, and of course, picket fences. The town centre itself is a National Historic Site. Harriet Beecher Stowe and Ethan Allen were born here: the **Litchfield Historical Society**, 567-4501, has all the facts, historical and art exhibits. Those of a judicial frame of mind may wish to stop at the **Tapping Reeve House**, 82 South St, 567-4501, America's first law school. Tues-Sat 11 am-5 pm, Sun 1 pm-5 pm. $3 to visit both.

Nearby is **Bantam Lake**, good for water sports, including ice yachting in winter. The **White Memorial Foundation**, a wildlife sanctuary and museum, takes up about half of the lake's shoreline, with 35 miles of trails for hiking.

Southwest of the lake via Rte 109 & Rte 47 is the village of **Washington**, another 'jewel of a colonial village', home to many artists and writers. The **American Indian Archaeological Institute**, 38 Curtis Rd, 868-0518, is also here. Take Rte 47 to Rte 199. The Institute is home to a replicated Algonkian village complete with wigwams and a traditional longhouse, a walking trail and museum. Mon-Sat 10 am-5 pm, Sun noon-5 pm, $4.

Lime Rock Park, Lakeville, 435-2571, (800) RACE-LRP. Although 50 miles from Hartford, nestled in the scenic Berkshire Hills, the Park is a great day out if you can get there; you might even catch Paul Newman on the track! Bring a picnic and stay all day at one of the vintage car festivals, or take a look behind the scenes at a professional road race. Amateur races $12, up to $75 for a full access weekend pass, with free on-site camping.

The Litchfield Hills are a good area for walking and camping. Three of the nicer state parks, where you can do both, are **Housatonic Meadows**, **Lake Waramaug** and **Macedonia Brook**, none of which is far from Kent. For more information on parks, historic sites, accommodation and restaurants in the area contact **Litchfield Hills Visitors Commission**, P.O Box 177, New Preston, CT 06777, 567-4506. For camping permits in the State Parks write to the **Bureau of State Parks and Forests**, 165 Capitol Avenue, #265, Hartford, 06106, 424-3200. Mon-Fri 8.30 am-4.30 pm.

BRISTOL As you meander through picturesque landscapes and tiny hamlets on your way to New Haven, stop off in Bristol, the one time clock-making capital of the US. Arrive at the **American Clock and Watch Museum**, 100 Maple St, 583-6070, in time to hear the midday chimes! A horologist's delight, brimming over with 3500 timepieces past and present, comic and stately, grand and miniature. April-Nov, 10 am-5 pm, $3.50.

Step back in time and visit the **New England Carousel Museum**, 95 Riverside Ave, Bristol, 585-5411, Mon-Sat 10 am-5 pm, Sun noon-5 pm, $4. Some 300 carved horses, cats, elephants, chariots, etc., of intricate and occasionally bejewelled design. Guided tours include two hurdy gurdy organs, and a workshop restoring working carousel figures and parts. Magical.

Lake Compounce Theme Park, 822 Lake Ave, 583-3631, (exit 31 off I-84). At 150 years old, this is the country's oldest running theme park. A beautifully handcarved 1911 Carousel is the main attraction, but for a real bone-shaking ride, try the 'Wildcat,' a wooden roller-coaster built in 1927. Other attractions include a water park, paddleboats, mini-golf. Mid-June-mid-Aug, Weds-Mon 11 am-10 pm. $18.95 admission and rides all day, general admission $3.95, includes swimming and shows.

NEW HAVEN   The city grew up around its harbour and Yale University (boola, boola). This Ivy League university, one of the best and oldest in the United States, currently enjoys recognition for graduating President Bill Clinton, Hillary Rodham Clinton, *and* former president, George Bush.

Sadly, however, New Haven has failed to uphold its 19th-century reputation as one of America's most beautiful cities. While some areas are undergoing renovation, the nicest parts by far are still found on and around the Green. On the credit side, however, theatre and music thrive in New Haven, and there are numerous enjoyable bars, cafes, and restaurants patronised by the student population.

Going east along Long Island Sound, you come to New London, from where you can catch a ferry to Long Island and Block Island. Further still, there's Mystic, en route to Newport, RI, and the Massachusetts seacoast.

ACCOMMODATION
Duncan Hotel, 1151 Chapel St, 787-1273. Downtown, right next to Yale, well-appointed for the price. S-$40, D-$60, XP-$10, TV.
Regal Inn, 1605 Whalley Ave, (Exit 59 off rte 15), 389-9504. S-$40, D-$45, TV.
Three Judges Motor Lodge, 1560 Whalley Ave, 389-2161. S-$46 king-size bed, D-$65, TV.

FOOD
The most popular restaurants in town are on Wooster St, in the attractive Italian district.
Archie Moore's, 188½ Willow St, ½ mile north of Peabody Museum, 773-9870. Named 'best watering hole in state,' great buffalo wings, nachos, burgers, pasta, baseball on the tube, popular with grad students and locals. Moderately priced, $2.50-$7.50.
Atticus Bookstore, 1082 Chapel St, 776-4040. Relaxing coffee shop in the Yale Center for British Art. Mon-Sat til midnight.
Clerks, 74 Whitney Ave, 777-2728. Grab fast food at great prices from this busy lunch-spot. Sandwiches from $2, deli sandwiches with fries $6, hot dogs $2.50,. Mon-Sat 7 am-10 pm, Sun 9 am-10 pm.
Louie's Lunch, 263 Crown St, 562-5507. Enjoy breakfast cooked in a 250-year-old frying pan. Lunches are good, and worth the wait, at this reputed birthplace of the hamburger, $2.90 and up. Unique, antique, friendly atmosphere.'
Pepe's Pizzeria, 157 Wooster St, 865-5762. Try their specials, clam and garlic, broccoli and sausage or invent your own! Small cheese and tomato $5.50.
Thai Taste, 1151 Chapel St, 776-9802. Appetizers from $4, entrees from $7.50. Pad Thai a speciality. Downstairs from Duncan Hotel. Evenings only. 'Extremely good.'
Yankee Doodle Coffee Shop, 260 Elm St, 865-1074. The 'Doodle' serves good breakfasts ($1.40), cheeseburgers ($1.60), steak sandwiches, BLT's. Their speciality is a Pig-in-a-Blanket ($1.80)! Mon-Sat 6 am-2.30 pm. 'One of the best deals in America.'

OF INTEREST
The Green, once a wild, swampy forest trodden by Indians, is now a shaded park. Despite encroaching modern buildings, the Green still retains much of its original flavour, flanked as it is on the north side by the impressive, ivy-clad halls of Yale.

In August, New Haven plays host to world tennis champions in the **International Tennis Tournament**, The Connecticut Tennis Center at Yale University, I-95, exit 44. Call 776-7331/(888) 997-4568 for details of this prestigious annual event when the world's top players, such as Agassi or Stich compete. If you missed Wimbledon, this is a must! Tickets $15-$30; don't forget your strawberries!

Peabody Museum of Natural History, 170 Whitney Ave, 432-5050. Dinosaurs and Connecticut flora and fauna. Mon-Sat 10 am-5 pm, Sun noon-5 pm, $5.

Shore Line Trolley Museum, East Haven, 5 miles from New Haven, 467-7635. Summer: daily 11 am-5 pm. Admission and 3-mile ride, $5.

Yale Center for British Art, 1080 Chapel St, 432-2800. Hogarth, Constable, Turner, Pre-Raphaelites and contemporary art, including the work of Damien Hirst. Most comprehensive collection of British works outside Britain. Tues-Sat 10 am-5 pm, Sun noon-5 pm; free. Will re-open Jan 1999. www.yale.edu/ycba/ provides a fascinating and informative tour through the permanent collections.

Yale University, 432-2300. Free tours around the old spires and cobbled courtyards of the university, mostly built in the thirties, and meticulously designed to look effectively ancient, are available in summer, Mon-Fri 10.30 am & 2 pm, Sat & Sun 1.30 pm, starting at Phelps Gate. Highlights include the Old Campus through Phelps Gate off College St, **Connecticut Hall** (the oldest building), the **Art of Architecture Building** designed by Paul Rudolph and the **Beinicke Rare Book Library**.

Yale University Art Gallery, 1111 Chapel St, 432-0600. Home to a good collection of French Impressionists, an excellent assortment of contemporary American paintings; Hopper, Aitkins and Homer, and Van Gogh's *Night Cafe*. Tues-Sat 10 am-5 pm, Sun noon-5 pm, closed Aug, free.

ENTERTAINMENT

In summer try the *New Haven Advocate*, (Thurs) a free arts and news weekly.

Anchor Bar, 272 College St, 865-1512. Authentic fifties bar with intimate booths, orange lighting, and good food at moderate prices.

Picnic Performances. Enjoy free outdoor concerts, R&B, Jazz and ethnic bluegrass, Latin, rock, folk and Cajun, in parks around the city, from mid-July—mid-Aug on Friday evenings at 6.30 pm. Call 773-1777 for details.

Toad's Place, 300 York St, 624-8623. Dance club and concert venue. David Byrne and Dogstar have both played here recently. Box office 11 am-6 pm daily, tkts around $12.50.

Look for current productions at the **Long Wharf Theater**, 222 Sergent Dr, 787-4282. Season runs Oct-June. Closed Mon. Discount tkts available for students on day of performance (not Sat). Pay what you can system Tues-Fri, 4 pm at the box office.

The excellent **Yale Repertory Theater**, 222 York St, 432-1234, boasts Meryl Streep, Henry Winkler among others as alumni. Offers drama, comedy, classics Oct-May. $25-$32, half price w/student ID except Sat night.

INFORMATION

Maps and guides from the **University Information Office**, 14 Elm St, 432-2300. Mon-Fri 9 am-4.45 pm.

Traveler's Aid, 1 Long Wharf Dr, 495-7437. Mon-Fri 9 am-5 pm. Phone messages monitored at weekends for crisis situations.

New Haven Convention and Visitors Bureau, #7, One Long Wharf Dr, 777-8550. Mon-Fri 8.30 am-5 pm.

TRAVEL

Amtrak, Union Ave, (800) 872-7245. Newly renovated station but unsafe at night. NYC ($21), Boston ($32).

Connecticut Limousine Service, Sports Haven Complex, 600 Long Wharf Dr, (800)

472-5466. Frequent runs to JFK, Newark and La Guardia Airports. $37 to JFK and LGA, $40 to Newark. Also runs from other CT towns.
Greyhound, 45 George St, (800) 231-2222. NYC ($14), Boston ($18).
Metro-North Commuter Railroad, Union Station, (800) 638-7646/in NYC (212) 532-4900. Fares are cheaper to NYC than Amtrak, $11 off-peak, $14.75 rush-hour.

CONNECTICUT RIVER VALLEY

The lower river valley, where river meets sea between New Haven and New London, is one of the state's loveliest, most unspoilt and peaceful areas. Once an important seafaring commercial centre, this is now an area for gentle sailing, pottering around the small towns, or watching the wildlife at Selden Neck State Park or on the salt marshes around Old Lyme.

ACCOMMODATION

Unless you feel like treating yourself to a night at one of the expensive old inns here you will have to search out a motel or campground somewhere off I-95. Some worth trying are;
Heritage Motor Inn, 1500 Boston Post Rd, exit 66 off I-95, 388-3743. From $60 for two, free local calls, outdoor pool, 2 miles from downtown.
Liberty Inn, 55 Springbrook Rd, exit 67/68 off I-95, 388-1777. From $68 for two, bfast included, 1 mile from downtown.

OF INTEREST

Essex: Main St is lined with white clapboard homes of colonial sea captains. America's first warship, *Oliver Cromwell*, was built here. At the **Ivoryton Playhouse**, Katharine Hepburn 'found out what theatre was all about'.
Gillette Castle State Park, across the river from Essex, off Rte 82, 526-2336. Once the estate of actor William Gillette who made his name playing Sherlock Holmes. The castle was built and furnished like a Victorian stage-setting. 'Weird.' Daily in spring & summer 10 am-5 pm, Sat & Sun in fall, 10 am-4 pm, $4. Reached by the **Chester-Hadlyme ferry**, which has been in service since 1769. The trip across the river costs $2.25 for a car and driver, XP-75¢.
Old Lyme, Rte 156. Summer artists' colony and home of the **Nut Museum**, 434-7636, dedicated to a greater awareness of nuts. Owner Elizabeth Tashjian, artist and visionary, collects art, music, and lore on the nut and has appeared on the Johnny Carson and David Letterman shows singing her 'nutty' songs. May-Oct, Wed, Sat, Sun 1 pm-5 pm, otherwise call for appointment; admission is $3 plus one nut (no, your friend doesn't qualify). 'Indescribably bizarre.'
A one-time boarding house and centre of the Old Lyme art colony is now the **Florence Griswold Museum**, 96 Lyme St, 434-5542. The bohemian antics of Miss Griswold and her fellow impressionists were considered somewhat shocking by the locals. You can see their work Tues-Sat 10 am-5 pm, Sun 1 pm-5 pm; Jan-Jun, Wed-Sun 1 pm-5 pm; $4, $3 w/student ID.
Valley Railroad, Exit 3 off Rte 9, 767-0103. Scenic 2½ hr combined train/boat ride along the Connecticut River past Gillette Castle and Goodspeed Opera House, $15. Train only, $10. Daily in summer, otherwise Wed-Sun, closed in winter except for special Xmas trains.

INFORMATION

Connecticut River Valley & Shoreline Visitors Council, 393 Main St, Middletown, 347-0028. Daily 8.30 am-4.30 pm.

NEW LONDON

Off I-95, on the River Thames (pronounced as it looks),

the town, once an important whaling port, had the distinction of being burnt to the ground by Benedict Arnold and his troops in 1781. Today it is the home of Connecticut College and the US Coast Guard Academy. There are some well-restored houses on Star Street and on Green Street is the Dutch Tavern once frequented by Eugene O'Neill. 'The best bar in the US; unique atmosphere.'

ACCOMMODATION
Motel 6, west of New London, in Niantic, exit 74 off I-95, 739-6991. S-$50, D-$55, XP-$3.

FOOD
Bangkok City, 123 Captain's Walk, 442-6970, Thai food at cheapish prices. Spice-rating allows you to go as hot as you dare.

For picnic table informality, the **Sea Swirl**, 536-3452, in Mystic, at the junction of Rtes 1 & 27, is an ice-cream stand much favoured locally for really good clam strips ($7.75) and clam bellies ($12.95). Daily 11 am-10 pm.

In **Groton** there is **Paul's Pasta**, 223 Thames, 445-5276. A favourite with students, it has churning pasta machines in the window and a view of the ships in New London harbour from the terrace. Offers classics such as lobster ravioli ($8 95) and spaghetti pie ($7.95).

OF INTEREST
The *Argia*, a replica of a 19th-century gaff-rigged schooner, will take you cruising to Fisher's Island on half-day adventures, full-day sailing odyssees or sunset cruises. Departs from Steamboat Wharf, 10 am, 2 pm, & 6 pm. $30, $32 w/ends, refreshments included. **Argia Cruises**, 73 Steamboat Wharf, 536-0416.

Connecticut College Arboretum, Williams St, 439-5020. 425 acres of hiking trails and ponds, open daily early am 'til dusk. Call 439-2787 for details of 'Shakespeare in the Arboretum' during July and August, $10, $7 w/student ID.

Groton, across the Thames, on Rte 12. Investigate WW2 paraphernalia and climb aboard the world's first nuclear-powered sub launched from the Electric Boatyard here in 1954. **Nautilus Memorial**, 449-3558, daily 9 am-5 pm, free.

Lyman Allyn Art Museum, 625 William St, near the arboretum, 443-2545, specializing in furniture and silver, also includes outstanding collection of dolls and dolls houses. Tues-Sat 10 am-5 pm, Sun 1 pm-5 pm. $3, $2 w/student ID, guided tours $3.50.

Monte Cristo Cottage, 325 Pequot Ave, 443-0051, boyhood home of Eugene O'Neill, inspired sets for *Ah, Wilderness* and *Long Day's Journey Into Night*; named after the Count of Monte Cristo, his actor-father's most famous part, $4. Summer: Tues-Sat 10 am-5 pm, Sun 1 pm-5 pm.

Mystic Marinelife Aquarium, just off I95, 536-3323. Whales, sea lions, dolphins, seals. Daily 9 am-6 pm, gates close at 5 pm, last mammal demo at 4.30 pm, $11. Call the aquarium collect if you see a marine mammal stranded on the beach.

Mystic Seaport, 572-0711. A re-created mid-19th century coastal village and maritime museum on Rte 27. Some of the fastest clipper ships were built in Mystic and the last of the wooden whaling ships, the *Charles W. Morgan* (which celebrated its 150th anniversary in 1991) awaits inspection. Daily 9 am-6 pm in summer; $16 (ticket valid for two days). Seasonal events include a lobster festival over Memorial Day weekend, and an October Chowderfest.

Ocean Beach Park, foot of Ocean Ave, 447-3031. Recreation area offering swimming in Olympic size pool, triple water-slide, mini-golf, food concessions. Summer: Daily 9 am-midnight, gates close 10 pm. Parking $2 first hr, $7 max, $14 max w/ends. Rides cost extra.

MAINE *Pine Tree State*

As big as the other five New England states combined, Maine has a modest population similar to that of Rhode Island. In some areas the wildlife outnumbers the human inhabitants which means it is the perfect place to get away from it all. Maine offers a variety of spectacular environments and unspoiled natural wonders, from rugged coastline, to mountains and clear lakes to breathtaking whitewater.

Especially recommended is the drive 'down east' (northeast) along the rocky coastline. On a straight line, the coast of Maine is 250 miles long, but all the bays, harbours and peninsulas lengthen the shoreline to some 2400 miles. Inland are acres of unexplored, moose-filled forests and huge lakes, remote and seldom visited, 2,500 in all. While in Maine, look out for blueberry festivals, clambakes, and lobster picnics—the state annually harvests millions of pounds of fish and shellfish, and fertile farmlands mean Maine is also among the top spud producers in the US.

In addition to hiking, boating, and swimming, Maine offers great opportunities for biking and white water rafting. Thousands of miles of peaceful, scenic secondary roads—good for biking—wind through the interior and along the coast. Bike rentals are widely available, and two guidebooks list scenic routes and travel tips: *25 Bicycle Tours in Maine*, by Howard Stone (Back Country Publications, PO Box 175, Woodstock, VT 05091), and *Bicycling*, by DeLorme Publishing Company.

White Water Rafting in Maine is an adventure not to be missed. You'll find both water and outfitters to be plentiful at **The Forks** (named for the confluences of the **Dead** and **Kennebec** Rivers in the upper Kennebec Valley) and the **West Branch of the Penobscot** between Moosehead Lake and Baxter State Park in the Katahdin/Moosehead Region. *Great Rivers of the East*, P.O Box 442, Jim Thorpe, PA 18829, (800) 828-7238, provides recommendations and a brochure on reputable East Coast outfitters.

For more information on camping and access rules write to the **Bureau of Parks and Recreation**, Maine Department of Conservation, State House, Station #22, Augusta, 04333, or call on (207) 287-3821. Camping fees $11-$16 per site, $2 rsvs fee.

If all that exercise is not for you, then Maine has one other main attraction: **factory outlet stores** 'headquartered' in the Kittery area, 1 hr north of Boston, and south of Portland, exit 3 off I-95, call 1-888-KITTERY. There are real bargains to be found with products often having 20%-75% off.
www.yahoo.com/regional/us states/maine/
The telephone area code for Maine is 207.

SOUTH COAST If you're in a hurry to head 'down east', hop on I-95, but if you have the time to meander try coastal Rte 1. This winding road, which can be busy during the summer, provides easy access to a variety of seaside towns and attractions.

Though actually beginning further south, the Maine section of Rte 1 begins in **Kittery**. Known historically for its shipbuilders, this town is buzzing with bargain hunters at the factory outlets mentioned above. If relaxing on a long, sandy beach is more appealing, head for **Ogunquit** about 10 miles north. Centuries after the Indians named this 'beautiful place by the sea,' it is still an attractive and popular resort. You'll find a quieter spot a few miles off Rte 1 on Rte 9 at the **Rachel Carson National Wildlife Refuge** in **Wells**, 646-9226. Here, solitude and rare birds among 1600 acres of shady wetlands combine to delight ornithologist and picnicker alike.

Continuing up Rte 9 brings you to **Kennebunkport**, vacation residence of former president, George Bush. Though beautifully maintained, this one-time ship-building village is sadly falling victim to 'quaint disease'. Avoid downtown at rush hour.

Try **Dixon's Campground**, 2 miles south of Ogunquit on **Cape Neddick**, 363-2131, free shuttle to beach 5 times daily. Sites for two, $28 with hook-up, XP-$7.50, rsvs recommended.

PORTLAND   The gateway to northeast Maine, Portland is the largest city (pop. 64,000) in a state where cities and towns are few and far between. Here the coast changes from long sections of beach to a hodgepodge of islands, bays and inlets. Portland had an early history of Indian massacres and British burnings. The city has recently been revitalised and restored and is now a commercial and cultural centre, as well as being home to the University of Southern Maine.

Take a ferry to one of the hundreds of islands in Casco Bay. Inland there is vast Sebago Lake for summer swimming, sailing, waterskiing and sunning.

ACCOMMODATION
Hotel Everett, 51A Oak St, 773-7882. S-$42, D-$53. Off-season rates lower. 'Clean and only 5 minute walk from scenic Old Port area.'
Portland Summer Hostel, 645 Congress St, 874-3281 (in season) (617) 731-8096 (off season). Downtown, close to Greyhound station, Portland Hall in Southern Maine University. Double rms private bath $14 AYH, $17 non-AYH, bfast and linen included. Kitchen, TV, laundry and storage facilities. Check-in 5 pm. Rsvs recommended.
Inn at St. John, 939 Congress St, 773-6481. S-$35, D-$55, shared bath, bfast included, XP-$6. 20 min walk from downtown. 'Excellent location opposite Greyhound.' 'Exceptionally clean and pleasant.'
YMCA, 70 Forest Ave, 874-1105. S-$27 night, $87 week. Single rooms, men only. Turn up at 11 am for the best chance of a room.
YWCA, 87 Spring St, 874-1130. S-$25, D-$20 per person. Women only. Free use of pool in morning. 'A clean, friendly place, very handy for Old Portland.' Rsvs recommended in summer.

FOOD
Carburs Restaurant and Lounge, 123 Middle St, 772-7794. *Huge* sandwiches from $4-$10, tackle the Down East Feast—ten rounds of bread piled high! 'I have never eaten so well so cheaply.'
Great Lost Bear, 540 Forest Ave, 772-0300. Choose from over 100 items on the menu and 54 varieties of draft and bottled beer! Burgers and veggie specials $6-$7. Mon-Sat 11.30 am-11.30 pm, Sun noon-11.30 pm. Best place to drink in Maine.'
Silly's, 40 Washington Ave, 772-0360. Burgers, pizza, seafood, homemade ice-cream shakes. Try their famous Jamaican jerk chicken $6.50, or their creative roll-up sandwiches,' $2.25 upwards. Daily 10 am-10 pm.
Three Dollar Dewey's, 241 Commercial St, 772-3310. Pub-style eatery. 36 beers on

tap, 50-plus bottle beers, three alarm chilli, lots of seafood and ethnic veggie dishes. Nothing on menu over $8.

OF INTEREST

For memorable boat trips and best views of the rugged coastline try **Casco Bay Lines** (America's oldest ferry service), CBITD Ferry Terminal, Commercial & Franklin Sts, 774-7871. Year round service to Peaks, Chebeague, Long, Great and Little Diamond and Cliff Islands. $5.25-$8.60, or take the Mailboat for $9.50.

Farmers Market: sells local produce; some organic food. Weds 9 am-5 pm, in Monument Sq.

Henry Wadsworth Longfellow House, 485 Congress St, 772-1807. Was the poet's childhood home. June-Sept, Tues-Sun 10 am-4 pm, $4, includes tour.

Old Orchard Beach, south of Portland. 'Maine's answer to Blackpool. Large water slides, good beach. Lots of French Canadians frequent this place.' Biddeford/Saco Shuttle Bus, 282-5408, leaves Portland for Old Orchard Beach six times daily, from corner of Elm & Congress on Monument Sq, $3 o/w.

Higgins, **Crescent** and **Scarborough** beaches are also good, and **Prout's Neck** is where artist Winslow Homer did much of his painting.

Old Port Exchange, on the waterfront. Reconstructed in Victorian style with cobblestone streets, gas lamps, boutiques and restaurants. Favourite haunt for locals as well as visitors.

Portland Head Coastguard Station and Lighthouse, follow road to Cape Elizabeth south from Portland, off US 1. Commissioned by George Washington and built in 1791, Portland Head light is Maine's oldest lighthouse. Small museum and picnic facilities. 'Great views.'

Portland Museum of Art, 7 Congress St, 775-6148. Painting, sculpture and decorative arts, including works by Homer and Wyeth. July-Oct, Mon-Sat 10 am-5 pm, Thurs & Fri 'til 9 pm, Sun noon-5 pm, $6, $5 w/student ID.

INFORMATION

Greater Portland Convention and Visitors Bureau, 305 Commercial St, 772-4994. Sells maps for self-guided walking tours; $1. Daily 9 am-6 pm, w/ends 10 am-6 pm.

TRAVEL

Concord Trailways, 161 Marginal Way, (800) 639-3317. Boston ($16, 2 hrs), Bangor ($20, 2 hrs).

Greyhound, St John & Congress Sts, 772-6587/(800) 231-2222. Be careful at night. Boston $12 (three day advance tkt $10).

Peter Pan Trailways, 828-1151. Run buses from Boston to Portland ($16), and Brunswick ($8).

Prince of Fundy car ferry to Yarmouth, Nova Scotia, 775-5616, (800) 341-7540. Runs nightly May-Oct, 11 hr trip. Call for prices and schedule.

Continuing on up the coast will bring you to **Freeport**, a haven for over 100 factory outlets, chief of which is *THE* sporting and outdoor goods store, L.L. Bean. Open 365 days, 24 hrs, Bean's is a Mecca to middle America, and the pilgrims come here at all hours. 'It was really strange to be shopping at 3 am.' In case you're feeling overly verdant, there's relief just around the corner at the **Desert of Maine**, Desert Rd, Freeport, exit 19 off I-95, 865-6962. A natural phenomenon, $6.50 includes guided tour (daily 9 am-5 pm) and tram rides (9 am-4 pm) through the dunes. Watch the unusual art of sand-sculpting using the 100 different shades of sand in the desert. Acres and acres of sandy glacial (not ocean) remains create dunes up to 80 feet high. You have to feel it to believe it. Shuttle bus available from Freeport.

MAINE 55

MID-COAST Brunswick is home to small, but lovely **Bowdoin College**, alma mater of writers Hawthorne and Longfellow and explorers Peary and MacMillan among others. The college hosts **Bowdoin Summer Music Festival** featuring nationally renowned artists and low-priced concerts, call 725-3000 for details. Also on campus are the Peary-MacMillan Arctic Museum, Hubbard Hall, 725-3416, polar exploration, ecology and Inuit culture. Tues-Sat 10 am-5 pm, Sun 2 pm-5 pm; and the Museum of Art, Walker Art Building, 725-3275, featuring Baskins as well as old masters and Greek and Roman artefacts. Hours as above.

You can camp among the tall pines at **Thomas Point Beach Campground**, off Rte 24, Cook's Corner, Brunswick, 5 miles from downtown, 725-6009. Sites $17 for two, $21 w/hook up. Home to an annual **Bluegrass Festival**, Labor Day weekend, the **Maine Highland Games** in August, and the nearby, **Maine Arts Festival** which takes place in July and August, and features folk arts, workshops and local foods. Tkts $10. Contact WCSH TV, 828-6666. **Brunswick Chamber of Commerce**, 725-8797.

Dipping off Rte 1 onto Rte 27 takes you into **Boothbay Harbor**, a bit touristy but a good taking off point for quiet, isolated **Monhegan Island** where cars are prohibited, and artists take refuge. This is not an island for wild nights (no bars or discos in town), but if you're in the mood for rocky cliffs, ocean spray, and hiking amid 600 varieties of wildflowers it's worth the 1½ hr ferry ride into Muscongus Bay. Daily from Pier 8, 63 Commercial St, 633-2284, $28 r/t, rsvs recommended.

Getting back onto Rte 1 and continuing north you hit **Rockland**, which hosts an annual **Maine Lobster Festival** in early August, call 596-0376 for details. Generations of artists have found this coast an inspiration; Andrew Wyeth spent much of his life in nearby Cushing, and the **William A. Farnsworth Museum and Library** in **Rockland**, 596-6457, $5, has a large collection of paintings by the Wyeth family. Just north of Rockland is **Camden**. Picturesquely situated with a busy little harbour, the town has a Cornish-like charm, despite the tourists, and although the trash-trend emporia fast encroach, there are still genuine and attractive local craft shops. If it's not foggy, the observatory atop **Mount Battie** affords a spectacular view of Camden harbour, the sea and the surrounding hills. It's an enjoyable two-mile hike from the town. Try camping at **Camden Hills State Park**, 1½ miles north of town on Rte 1, 236-3109. Sites $16. Rsvs recommended, apply to the Park Bureau in Augusta, 287-3824, 14 days in advance (but arrive btwn 10 am & 4 pm and you'll probably get a pitch). Hot showers, stone fireplace and picnic table at each site, take-out store within walking distance. A free shuttle bus operates from downtown Camden to the park, daily 9 am-6.30 pm, if you see it coming, stick out your thumb! Concord Trailways also pass by here en route from Portland to Bangor.

If you have your own transport, spend a few relaxing days at the beautiful wooded **Megunticook Campground By-The-Sea**between Camden and Rockland at Rockport on Rte 1, 594-2428. Sites $25 w/hook up, rsvs recommended in summer. Tents can be hired ($15) but call first. Small store, bathrooms and free showers, laundry and heated outdoor pool. Rent kayaks, canoes and bikes, on site ($15 per day) or nearby.

Feeling adventurous? Contact **Maine Sport**, Rte 1, (P.O Box 956)

Rockport, 236-7120; ask about their guided kayaking trips. The Camden harbour trip ($30) takes 2 hrs. The Megunticook Lake day-trip ($45) takes 4 hrs where you can try navigating a keowee! Equipment provided, no experience neccessary, rsvs required. For energetic landlubbers, bikes are available to rent; $15 full-day, includes helmet and lock, cheaper weekly rates available.

For tourist info on Rockport and Lincoln, contact **Camden Chamber of Commerce**, PO Box 919M, Camden, Maine 04843, 236-4404.

With a name said to be derived from an old hymn tune, **Bangor** is socially about that exciting. The best time to be in Bangor is during the Bangor Fair, one of the oldest in the country, held annually the first week in August.

Otherwise, by-pass the town and continue on your way to **Bar Harbor** via the coastal route, or else head inland where thousands of lakes make this a popular area for canoeists. **Moosehead Lake**, 40 miles long and 10 miles wide, is the largest. P.S., fans of *Murder She Wrote* should note that there is no Cabot Cave in Maine; the TV series is shot in Mendocino, California.

ACADIA NATIONAL PARK/BAR HARBOR

The park encompasses a magnificent wild, rocky stretch of coast and its hinterland. The granite hills of Acadia sweep down into the Atlantic where the ocean has carved out numerous inlets, cliffs and caves. At every twist and turn of the roads around the coast a new and spectacular view of the sea becomes visible.

For the best view of all, it is an easy walk or drive to the summit of **Cadillac Mountain** (1530 ft), the highest place on the Atlantic coast north of Rio. Beneath the 'mountain' lie lakes, cranberry bogs, quiet spruce forests, and the Atlantic itself. The dramatic Loop Road, cars $5 per week, $3 pp, from the Park Visitor Center takes about 1½–3 hrs (depending on the number of stops you make) and offers incredible views. A stop right on the Loop, and not to be missed, is tea and popovers ($6.50) at Jordan Pond House, 276-3610. The House is an easy drive from Seal or Bar Harbor and accessible by several hiking trails.

Bar Harbor is the most popular resort on the **Mount Desert Island** part of Acadia National Park. This was a town of fashionable summer homes owned by the wealthy, until 1947 when a great fire destroyed most of them. More recently, chic boutiques and restaurants have moved in, forcing prices up. Come and enjoy The Bar Harbor Music Festival in July and August, a whalewatching tour or an excursion on a working lobster boat. The *Bluenose Ferry*, 288-3397, also leaves from here on its way to Nova Scotia. The less-frequented **Isle au Haut** is the other half of Acadia; a good place for walking, it can be reached by ferry from Stonington on the southern tip of Deer Isle.

Further inland lies **Bangor**, a good stopping off point before heading into the interior. In early summer **harness racing** is held at Bass Park on Main St, 866-7650, $1 admission. The Park is also home to the Bangor State Fair held at the end of July.

ACCOMMODATION
Bass Cottage in the Field, off Main St, downtown Bar Harbor, 288-3705. From S-$55 for two. Rsvs required in summer.
Bar Harbor Youth Hostel, 27 Kennebec St, 288-5587. Summer only, $12 AYH, $15 non-AYH, rsvs recommended.

YWCA, 36 Mt Desert St, 288-5008. Women only. S-$30, D-$25 pp.

Camping. Within the park there are sites at Black Woods and Seawall, 288-3338. Both areas can be reached by car, Black Woods costs $14/night, Seawall $10/night, walk-ins at Seawall $8. Rsvs are essential in peak season, apply two months in advance to be sure of a pitch. (800) 365-2267 is the number to reserve pitches in parks nationwide—persevere, the line is always busy! There are also more expensive private campgrouds near the park.

OF INTEREST
Bike rentals are available from **Bar Harbor Bicycle Shop**, 141 Cottage St, 288-3886, $9 half-day, $14 full-day. **Acadia Bike and Canoe**, 48 Cottage St, 288-5483, bikes $11 half-day, $16 full-day, and organise kayaking trips $34 2½hrs, $43 half-day, $65 full day.

Whale Watcher, Frenchman Bay Co, 1 West St, Harbor Place, 288-3322, (800) 508-1499. A 3½hr cruise costs $28 and leaves three times daily from the pier, rsvs recommended. www.acadia.net/whale/ detailed information and photos of various cruises offered.

INFORMATION
Jekyll and Hyde, 70 Main St, 288-3084. Sells complete camping gear.
Chamber of Commerce, 93 Cottage St, 288-5103. 'Extremely helpful.'
Park Visitors Center, 288-3338, just off Rte 3 at Hulls Cove. Short film about the park shown every hour, offers audio cassette tours and all the information you'll need. Daily 8 am-4 pm.

TRAVEL
Bay Ferry to Yarmouth, Nova Scotia, (888) 249-7245. 6 hr crossing, leaves daily at 8 am, June-Oct. $42 pp, $55 car.
Greyhound/Vermont Transit run a very limited service to Ellsworth, 20 miles away, ($4.50).

THE APPALACHIAN TRAIL/BAXTER STATE PARK About 100 miles north of Bangor is **Baxter State Park**, where **Mount Katahdin** (5267 ft) marks the northern starting point of the Appalachian Trail. This is wild, remote country where moose out-number humans. (Best time to see a moose: early morning/late afternoon, late spring to early summer. Best place: near bogs and ponds, keep yourself unobtrusive.) The park can be reached via **Millinocket** on Rte 11 off I-95, or **Greenville**, a small lumber town, on Rte 15, at the southern end of Moosehead Lake. There are ten campgrounds in the park, only two of which are inaccessible by car. For all information on camping and for detailed area maps call in or write to the **Baxter State Park Headquarters**, 64 Balsam Drive, Millinocket, 04462. Tel: 723-5140.

Just to the north of Baxter lies the **Allagash Wilderness Waterway**. This is a canoeist's paradise, a 100-mile-long stretch of lakes and rivers preserved in their primitive state to provide white-water and backwoods experience for the modern canoeist.

For the bargain price of $23, **Allagash Wilderness Outfitters** in Greenville, (May-Nov) radio contact (207) 695-2821, will provide complete equipment for your adventures (right down to an axe!) including two-person tent and canoe. For a few days, a week or longer, explore the lakes or accept the challenge of the thundering rapids, fish for your salmon-supper then camp ($5 pp) under the stars with moose and deer as your companions. For around $23 you might prefer a log cabin on the shores of Frost Pond in Maine's North Woods. Call 695-2821 for details.

If you are staying near Greenville, contact **Folsom's Air Service**, Greenville (207) 695-2821, about their Floatplane adventures; it costs $30 to take in the local sights and the vast Moosehead Lake.

INFORMATION
Write to the **Appalachian Trail Conference**, P.O Box 807, Harper's Ferry, WV 25425; or the **Appalachian Mountain Club**, 5 Joy St, Boston, MA 02108.
Greenville Chamber of Commerce, Main St, 695-2702. Summer: daily 9 am-5 pm, otherwise Mon-Fri only.

MASSACHUSETTS   *The Bay State*

The Bay State is rivalled only by Virginia in the richness of its history. Massachusetts was the colony where the loudest and most open protests were raised against the British prior to 1777. After the initial skirmishes, the war switched to the other colonies, yet Massachusetts contributed the largest number of troops to the war.

Presidents John Adams, John Quincy Adams, John Kennedy and George Bush all came from Massachusetts, as did Daniel Webster; in the field of literature Robert Frost, John Whittier, Emily Dickinson, Louisa May Alcott, Nathaniel Hawthorne, Henry David Thoreau and Ralph Waldo Emerson were either born or came to live here. Just to show that there is a lighter side to the Bay state, Massachusetts is also the birthplace of sewing machines, frozen food and roller skates.

Massachusetts takes its name from the Massachuset Indians who occupied the Bay Territory, including Boston, in the early 17th century. An annual Indian pow-wow is still held at Mashpee in July.
www.yahoo.com/regional/us states/massachusetts/
The telephone area code for the eastern part of the State is 617, for mid-Massachusetts and the Cape it's 508, and in the west it's 413.

BOSTON   Capital of Massachusetts and, undeniably, of New England, Boston is a proud Yankee city and seaport thick with reminders of its past. Bostonians are fiercely loyal, regarding their city as the hub of New England, and in colonial times of the whole New World. Boston was the spiritual heart of the Revolution, the birthplace of American commerce and industry, and leader of the new nation in the arts and education. These days, the original WASPs (White Anglo Saxon Protestants) have been joined by successive generations of Blacks, Irish, Poles and Italians, and the city has developed a more cosmopolitan feel (although compared to New York City, Boston feels positively provincial).

Known as 'America's Walking City', Boston has a cosier feel to it than most major US cities, and also something of a European flavour. Within a comparatively small area you can stroll through 18th century cobbled streets, or on the Common where the colonists grazed their cattle, down by the harbour or river, or around such fine examples of modern architecture as in the Back Bay or the impressive Government Center.

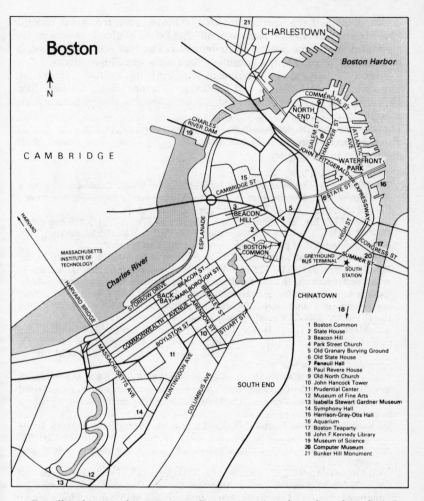

Boston

N

CHARLESTOWN

Boston Harbor

CAMBRIDGE

MASSACHUSETTS
INSTITUTE OF
TECHNOLOGY

Charles River

HARVARD

HARVARD BRIDGE

MASSACHUSETTS AVE

STORROW DRIVE

BACK
BAY

BEACON ST
MARLBOROUGH ST
COMMONWEALTH AVENUE
BERKELEY ST
CLARENDON ST
BOYLSTON ST
STUART ST

HUNTINGDON AVE

COLUMBUS AVE

SOUTH END

CHARLES
RIVER DAM

ESPLANADE

CAMBRIDGE ST

BEACON
HILL

BOSTON
COMMON

COMMERCIAL ST

NORTH
END

SALEM ST
HANOVER ST
ATLANTIC AVE

JOHN F FITZGERALD
STATE ST
JOHN F FITZGERALD EXPRESSWAY

WATERFRONT
PARK

HIGH ST
CONGRESS ST
SUMMER ST
SUMMER ST

GREYHOUND
BUS TERMINAL

SOUTH
STATION

CHINATOWN

1 Boston Common
2 State House
3 Beacon Hill
4 Park Street Church
5 Old Granary Burying Ground
6 Old State House
7 **Faneuil Hall**
8 Paul Revere House
9 Old North Church
10 John Hancock Tower
11 Prudential Center
12 Museum of Fine Arts
13 Isabella Stewart Gardner Museum
14 Symphony Hall
15 Harrison-Gray-Otis Hall
16 Aquarium
17 Boston Teaparty
18 John F Kennedy Library
19 Museum of Science
20 **Computer Museum**
21 Bunker Hill Monument

For all its historical associations, Boston is a city of youth and vitality. In addition to prestigious Harvard and MIT, there are 70 accredited colleges in Greater Boston, and many of the city's businesses and amenities cater to the young and diverse population.

Boston acquired its nickname, 'the Athens of America', by the 19th century and continues to earn it as a centre for music, literature and the arts. At any time it is possible to see good theatre, modern dance, and hear classical, jazz, folk and pop music. Sport too has its place. In summer, when the Boston Red Sox baseball team is battling it out in the race for the American League title, the only real place to be is at Fenway Park, eating Fenway franks, shelling peanuts, and drinking cold beer. In winter the mania transfers itself to basketball with the Celtics, football with the New England Patriots, and to ice hockey with the Boston Bruins.

One of the nation's finest examples of creative urban renewal is Faneuil Hall Marketplace. Once a rundown building on the blighted waterfront, its revitalization became Boston's bicentennial gift to itself and to everyone, it now houses over 150 shops, boutiques, food stalls and 23 restaurants.

Boston is particularly convenient for visits to nearby Cambridge, Concord, Lexington, Salem and Gloucester. Further afield, the Berkshire Hills and sun-drenched Cape Cod are unforgettable destinations for an expedition.

The telephone area code for Boston and Cambridge is 617.

The hotel occupancy tax in Boston is around 9.7%—one of the lowest of all major cities in the country.

ACCOMMODATION

The Information Center at the Tremont St side of the Boston Common provides a list of low-cost accommodation. Budget chain hotels can be expensive in summer, but call for details of special offers; see appendix for details.

Abercrombie's Inn, 23 Farrington Ave, Allston, (800) 767-5337, UK toll free (0800) 896-040. Beds $20, private room/apt share $35, bfast, free local calls, parking. Rsvs recommended. 'Good part of town, very friendly.' Real luxury!'

Boston International Youth Hostel, 12 Hemenway St, 536-9455, in Back Bay. 24 hrs, check-in 8 am. $19 AYH, $22 non-AYH, $10 cash deposit. Individual lockers in room, will rent locks. E-mail facilities. Must have photo ID for security records. 'Superb kitchen facilities. Very friendly staff.' 'Excellent hostel, launderette, clean, good value, maximum stay 5 nights, take subway to Hynes Convention Center then 2 blocks.' 'Good for meeting people. Go early to reserve a bed.'

Brookline Manor Guest House, Coolidge Corner, 32 Centre St, Brookline, 232-0003/(800) 201-9676. S-$45, D-$64 sleeps three, up to six sharing, XP-$10. TV, phone. 'Beautiful room, clean and close to centre. Lovely staff. Should ring in advance.' 'Well worth it.'

Greater Boston YMCA, 316 Huntington Ave, 536-7800. Co-ed, S-$38, D-$56, plus $5 key deposit; includes breakfast, free use of pool and well equipped gym. Mixed reviews. 'Clean, friendly, safe.' 'Unpleasant clientele, be careful, seems to have a bad atmosphere.'

HI-Back Bay Summer Hostel, call 536-9455 year round for details and rsvs. Venue changes yearly, but usually on Beacon St. AYH $17, $22 non-AYH; D-$24-AYH, $27 non-AYH. Check-in after 2 pm, check-out 10 am, 2 am curfew. 'Clean and comfortable.'

Irish Embassy Hotel, 232 Friend St, 973-4841. Dorm $15, kitchen, free bands and BBQs, 24 hrs. Rsvs recommended. 'Very friendly, safe, clean and great location.'

Longwood Inn, 123 Longwood Ave, Brookline, 566-8615. Green Line subway, downtown 10 mins. S-$53-$63, D-$74 for three, $93 for five. Kitchen, parking, TV and laundry. 'Clean and safe.' 'Old-fashioned style guest house, staff pleasant and helpful.'

YWCA, Berkeley Residence Club, 40 Berkeley St, 482-8850. Women only, 2-week max stay. S-$32, D-$46, T-$51, XP-$10 plus $2 temp. membership. 'Very safe, clean, canteen, laundrette and roof-deck. Access to pool and gym $3, dinner $6.50, bfast $2.50. 'Absolute bargain despite women in their night attire!'

HOUSING INFORMATION

Meegan Services, 569-3800, located in Logan Airport, has lists of hotels, guest houses, etc). Daily 8 am-11 pm. Free.

Roommate Connection Referral Agency, 24 hr info 262-4679 or www.opendoor.com/RoomateCo/TRC.html. If you're staying for the summer it might be cheaper and safer to pay the $75 fee rather than advertise. 'Shared accommodation, short/long term Boston & suburbs. From $500/month depending on location. By appointment. 'Very helpful.'

Townhouse Realty Co, 272 Newbury St, 267-1344. Short-term rentals, one-room studio apts, $100-250/week. 'Friendly guys.'

FOOD

In addition to clam-bakes and seafood, Boston is home to many diverse restaurants. Small family owned eating places occupy every corner of the North End. Thai, Vietnamese and Polynesian foods are available in Chinatown, while the South End offers American Southwestern fare and cafes. Other nearby neighbourhoods tempt the hungry and the curious with Indian, Japanese, Mexican, Hungarian and Greek delights.

Blue Diner, 178 Kneeland St, 695-0311, 2 mins from South St Station. 'For THE BEST bagels (95¢) you'll ever have and a great bottomless cup of coffee (95¢). Like walking onto the set of "Happy Days".' 'Very friendly.'

Bull & Finch, 84 Beacon St, 227-9605, by the Public Garden. An English pub; burgers, sandwiches, etc from $6. Only the exterior has anything to do with *Cheers* (the series was filmed in LA), but at least you can imagine that Sam or Rebecca are going to walk in the door. Great wings!' Very disappointing.'

Country Life, 200 High St. (Financial dist., across from Rowes Wharf, Aquarium subway), 951-2462. 'Supreme veggie food.' All you can eat lunch $6 (10% off before noon), dinner $7, (Sun, Tues, Weds, Thurs) Sunday brunch $8.

Durgin Park, 390 Faneuil Hall in Quincy Market, 227-2038. Known for its good food, great prices, long bar, and wisecracking waitresses: 'They throw food in front of you, spill water on your head and insult you. Hilarious. An excellent act.' An *act*? Family-style eating. Ribs, seafood; famous for its prime rib and great Chowder. Go for lunch for the best buys. Daily 11.30 am-10 pm.

No-Name Restaurant, 15½ Fish Pier, near southeast end of Northern Ave, 338-7539. In old warehouse. Seafood from $8. Expect queues. 'Vibrant atmosphere.' 'Hard to find; a bit of a walk, but the best seafood for the price in Boston.' 'A shouting match and a shoveling session, but great.'

The Purple Shamrock, 1 Union St, 227-2060. A favourite among sports fans, it has long been Boston's place to warm up and cool down for Boston Garden events. TV, live bands cover $3, chow down on supreme Chowder from $4 and large beers.

Quincy Market has plenty of foodstalls of great variety: Chinese, Italian, Greek, health foods and of course, the requisite pizzas, burgers, doughnuts etc.

Warburton's Bakery and Cafe, Government Center (and other locations). 'Great muffins; politicians eat here for breakfast.' Also good sausage rolls and pasties.

OF INTEREST

Back Bay, southwest of the common is a lively, beautiful 19th century development project built on land reclaimed from the Charles River. In this area is **Trinity Church**, Copley Square, 536-0944. Daily 8 am-6 pm. Designed in 1877 by HH Richardson, this church is French Romanesque style on the outside. Inside its highly decorated walls and flamboyant mosaics give it more the feel and look of Greek Orthodox. The IM Pei designed **John Hancock Tower**, 572-6429, stands behind the church. This is the tallest building in New England, the observatory on the 60th floor offers unparalleled views of Boston and beyond. Daily 9 am-11 pm Mon-Sat, 10 am-11 pm Sun, last admission 10 pm; $4.25, $3.75 w/student ID. 'A must. Sets you up for the whole city.' 'There are two interesting audio-visual presentations in the observatory on the city and its history.' There is one small problem with the building, hundreds of the 10,344 panes of tempered glass have fallen out onto the street below. Pei has had to replace them all, costing millions of dollars. The problem has never been solved but fortunately up to now no one has been hurt.

Boston Common. Boston is the only large American city still to have its common, but the flower-filled **Public Gardens** have more to offer; enjoy gliding around the lagoon on the world-famous Swan Boats in summer. Both areas are unsafe at night.

Beacon Hill, especially Louisburg Square, is Boston's old residential section to which every visitor must make a pilgrimage. Louisa May Alcott, William Dean Howels, the Brahmin Literary Set and many other famous Bostonians lived here.

Christian Science Center, 175 Huntington Ave, 450-2000, world HQ of the Christian Science religion, is a conglomerate of stunning buildings including the Mother Church; the Publishing Society, which produces among other literature the highly respected *Christian Science Monitor*; and the **Mapparium**, a beautiful 40-foot stained glass, walk-thru globe with unusual acoustics. 'You walk *into* the world! Tremendous visual and sensory delight.' Free guided tours. Tues-Sat 10.30 am-4 pm.

Faneuil Hall, Merchants Row, Faneuil Hall Sq, 242-5642. Built in 1742 and given to the city of Boston by Peter Faneuil. Known as the 'Cradle of Liberty' the hall was the scene of mass meetings during the pre-revolutionary period. Daily 9 am-5 pm. And what is that up there? A bird, a plane, superman? No, it's a weathervane in the form of a grasshopper that sits atop Faneuil Hall, placed there at the request of Peter Faneuil himself. 'Grasshopper' was the symbol of the Boston port and during the War of 1812, was the password used to weed out spies: if you couldn't identify it as the symbol of Boston, you were in trouble.

The Freedom Trail is a walking tour through the heart of old Boston, beginning in the Boston Common at the Visitors Center. On it you can visit nearly all Boston's associations with the American Revolution. The Trail is clearly marked by a path of red bricks set in the sidewalk; few visitors to Boston escape it. The Trail tends to be a tad dull, and unless you have a passionate interest in American revolutionary history, forget it.

Institute of Contemporary Art, 955 Boyleston St, 266-5152. Weds-Sun noon-5 pm, Thurs 'til 9 pm, tours on Sat & Sun at 1 pm & 3 pm. $5.25, $3.25 w/student ID, free after 5 pm on Thurs.

Isabella Stewart Gardner Museum, 280 Fenway, 566-1401. Italianate villa built by the eccentric Mrs Gardner to house her art collection in 1903. It lost many fine works in a 1989 robbery but still has a lot to see, including the house itself. Retreat to the cool sanctuary of the Venetian courtyard. Tue-Sun, 11 am-5 pm, $9, $3 w/student ID on Weds. 'Excellent.'

Museum of Fine Arts, 465 Huntington Ave, 267-9300. One of the finest art collections in the US, with outstanding Asiatic and 'marvellous Egyptian' sections. Also some fine American watercolours, wonderful Gaugins and Degas and the largest collection of Monets outside of France. Entire museum Tues, Sat, Sun 10 am-4.45 pm, Wed-Fri 10 am-9.45 pm; West Wing only Thurs-Fri, 5 pm-9.45 pm. $7, $6 w/student ID; West Wing only, $5, free Wed 4 pm-9.45 pm. 'Well worth the money; allow at least a whole day.' 'Inexpensive cafeteria.'

Old Granary Burying Ground, in the location of a 17th century granary. An interesting graveyard with many 18th century heroes including Paul Revere, Sam Adams and John Hancock. A grave marked 'Mary Goose' is supposedly the final resting place of Mother Goose.

Old North Church, Salem St, in the north end. Built 1723, gave Revere the signal to ride. 'Perhaps the most elegant and historic church in the USA.'

Old South Meeting House, School & Washington Sts, built 1729, was where Samuel Adams gave the signal that launched the Boston Tea Party in 1773.

Old State House, Washington & State Sts. Built 1713 as the seat of British colonial government; the *Declaration of Independence* was read from the East Balcony in 1776. Has an important display of Americana. Daily 9.30 am-5 pm.

Old Town Trolley shuttle bus, 269-7010, goes everywhere of historical note; you get on and off and on again when you like (9 am-last re-board at 4.30 pm), tkts $18, $16 w/student ID, from **Boston Common Visitors Center**, 536-4100. The Trolley Tours also operate a 3 hr jaunt around Boston providing an 'insiders' look at the city and it's favourite son—JFK ($22). On Fri, Sat & Sun at 9.30 am, from corners of South Charles and Boyleston Sts. National Park Service tours leave from Visitors Center at 15 State St, last 1½hrs; 10 am-3 pm—Old South Meeting House, Old State House, Paul Revere's house, and Old North Church.

Park St Church, 523-3383, at Brimstone corner, built 1809. Where *America* was first sung, in 1832. Daily in summer 8.30 am-4.30 pm.

Paul Revere House, in the North End on the Freedom Trail, 523-1676. Paul Revere lived here from 1770 to 1780 and set out from here on his famous ride to inform the nation the British were about to attack. Probably the oldest wooden structure in Boston; built 1670s. Daily in summer 9.30 am-5.15 pm, otherwise 9.30 am-4.15 pm; $2.50, $2.00 w/student ID.

Prudential Center, 859-0648. A daring, $150 million urban renewal project of the 1960s, with apartments, offices, and countless shops. On the 50th floor is an observatory, **SkyWalk**, which has a 360 degree viewing deck. Daily 10 am-10 pm $4.

State House, 727-3676, with its large gold dome, is the seat of the Massachusetts State Government. Charles Bulfinch, greatest American architect of the late 18th century designed the central part of the building. Free guided tours weekdays 10 am-4 pm. Enter on Beacon St.

On the waterfront:

Bay State Cruise Co, 723-7800 runs **ferries** to Boston Harbor Islands State Park, 30 islands with colorful names such as Grape, Bumpkin, and Gallops. 90 min sightseeing historical tour, $10. 'Go in the morning, stop off at Georges Island and get picked up later.'

Boston Harbour Cruises, leaving from Long Wharf, 227-4320. 1½hrs around the Boston Harbour, $10; cruise to the *USS Constitution*, $6 and St. George's Island, $7.50. Sunset cruises, at 7 pm last 1½hrs, $10. Take warm clothing.

Boston Tea Party Ship & Museum, Congress St Bridge, 338-1773. *Beaver II*, replica of ship whose dumped cargo brewed rebellion in 1773. Daily 9 am-6 pm. $7, $5.50 w/student ID, or AYH card/Old Town Trolley tkt. 'A rip-off. Makes you feel proud to be British.'

Computer Museum, Museum Wharf, 300 Congress St, 426-2800 (call even if you don't need info—the museum's hilarious computer answers the phone). The world's first and only computer museum. Test drive the information superhighway! Daily 10 am-6 pm; $7, $5 w/student ID; Sun 3 pm-6 pm, half-price. 'Hands-on.' 'Hats off.' www.tcm.org/galleries/ accept the robot challenge, and through interactive screens, control a robot over the Internet.

Earth Bikes, 35 Huntington Ave at Copley Sq, 267-4733. Rent a bike and explore Boston's hidden places in Beacon Hill, along the bike paths of the Charles River and to quaint side-streets in the North End and the Waterfront. $9 for 4 hrs; includes bike, lock and helmet.

John F Kennedy Library and Museum, Columbia Point, overlooking harbour, 929-4523. Another IM Pei building, it houses momentoes and memorials to not only JFK but also his brother Robert. Daily 9 am-5 pm; $6. Take T to U Mass then take free shuttle bus (runs every 20 mins).

Museum of Science, on the Charles River Dam in Science Park, 723-2500. The $10 million large-screen theatre is worth a visit—so big it can project a lifesize image of a whale. 'Could spend 2 days here and still not see it all.' Daily 9 am-7 pm, Fri til 9 pm; como tkts to theatre, planetarium and museum vary from $12, $8 for museum only.

New England Aquarium, Central Wharf, off Atlantic Ave, 973-5200. World's largest collection of sharks and 2000 other specimens in a 187,000 gallon tank.

Dolphin and sea lion shows daily. 'Excellent! Could spend the whole day there.' Mon-Fri 9 am-5 pm, Sat & Sun 9 am-6 pm, $10.50. 'One dollar less after 4 pm but you miss all the shows.'www.neaq.org/explore/ is great for landlubbers who want to try virtual whale-watching!

USS Constitution, a frigate from the war of 1812, preserved in Charleston Navy Yard, 242-0543. Daily 9 am-6 pm, $4, $3 w/student ID, free July-Sept. Interesting tours conducted by members of Navy. Nearby is the **Bunker Hill Monument** commemorating the first set battle of the Revolution. The battle was actually fought on a different hill, but all the good stuff is here; **Bunker Hill Pavilion**, 241-7575; $3, $2 w/student ID: An audio-visual programme, *The Whites of Their Eyes*, gives the background to the battle with dramatic effects (every $1/2$ hour from 9.30 am-5 pm).

Whale-watching trips, 973-5281, organised by the Aquarium April-Oct, $24, $20 w/student ID. Also qualifies for half price entrance to Aquarium. Rsvs recommended.

ENTERTAINMENT

For who, what, where and when read the *Boston Phoenix* or check the Thursday edition of the *Boston Globe* for '*Calendar*' section. The **Bostix** booth in Faneuil Hall has half-price tickets on day of performance. Look for free jazz concerts in Copley Square, lunchtimes in summer.

Axis, 13 Lansdowne St, near Fenway Park, 262-2437. Techno, House, Funk & Soul. British bands and videos. Cover $5-$15. Sun is gay night. Over 21s only.

Rathskeller, 528 Commonwealth Ave, Kenmore Sq, 536-2750. A legendary night spot, grungy atmosphere, live bands in the basement (Weds-Sun), cover $5-$10. Over 18s only.

Sevens, 77 Charles St, 523-9074, 'Authentic British pub atmosphere; serves both local and imported beer. Friendly.' Most expensive item on the menu is $5.50!

Symphony Hall, 301 Massachusetts Ave, 266-1492. Discount available Fri 9 am, Tues & Thurs at 5 pm for evening performances in the fall/winter. Home of the Boston Symphony and the popular 'Pops'. During the first week in July, the 'Pops', which were for many years led by John Williams, of *Star Wars* music fame, play at the **Hatch Memorial Shell** by the Charles River. The free outdoor concerts, including Jazz, start at 8 pm, so get there early if you want to get good places. 'Take a picnic, lots of fun.'

Wang Center for the Performing Arts, 270 Tremont St, 482-9393. If you don't manage to 'catch a show' at this old vaudville theatre make a visit anyway, the building is an historic landmark and the architecture is more than worth it; the lobby was used as the interior of Jack Nicholson's mansion in *The Witches of Eastwick*. See the world renowned **Boston Ballet** here. Best available seats for $12.50 (Oct-May) with a 'student rush' ticket, 1 hr before the curtain. Call 695-6950 for details.

Tune into WGBH, the city's non-commercial TV channel and reputed to be one of the best in America.

Closest beach is Revere. 'Scruffy but only 85¢ (to Airport Station) on the Blue Line.' Further afield is Ipswich, only a short train ride away for a splash in the sea; orange line to North Station, then commuter rail, $3.50, for schedules and info call 722-3200.

SPORT

Boston's four professional sports teams inspire devotion in the city and fans nationwide. In summer the **Boston Red Sox** play at historic **Fenway Park**, 267-1700, one of the most beautiful ball parks in the States. The fall and winter see the **New England Patriots** play American football at **Foxborough**, (800) 543-1776, an easy train ride from South Station. 'A fantastic day out.' The **Boston Garden** is the home of both the **Celtics** for basketball, 523-3030, and the **Bruins**, 227-3200, for ice-hockey.

Biking: A 14 mile loop follows both banks of the Charles River, from the museum of Science to Watertown, and may be entered at any point on the Cambridge or Watertown sides. Call Earth Bikes for rentals, 267-4733.

Canoeing: **Charles River Canoe & Kayak**, 965-5110, kiosk located on the bank of the river across Soldier's Field Rd from Harvard Stadium (head upstream from Elliot Bridge). Canoes $9 p/hr, $36 p/day, double kayaks $12 p/hr, $48 p/day.

Inline skating: Paths along both banks of the Charles River are good for novice rollerblading'. Start from Memorial Dr at Harvard, call 890-1212 for rentals.

SHOPPING
Filene's Automatic Bargain Basement, 426 Washington St. A Boston institution. Amazing bargains to be had—everything from designer clothes to luggage.

The **Boyleston Street** area in Back Bay, is good for books, records and lively evenings.

INFORMATION
Boston Common Visitors Center, the Common on Tremont St, 536-4100; and **Greater Boston Convention and Tourist Bureau**, west side of Prudential Plaza, 536-4100. For $3.10 you can purchase the *Official Guidebook to Boston*, 100-plus pages with numerous maps of city and discount coupons. Both offices open daily 9 am-5 pm.

Massachusetts Office of Travel and Tourism, 100 Cambridge St, 13th floor, 727-3201.

National Park Service Visitor Center, 15 State St, 242-5642, centrally located. Has short slide show of Freedom Trail, books, pamphlets and brochures on Boston and surrounding areas. Free guided tours of the trail in the summer, hourly, 10 am-3 pm. Office open daily 9 am-6 pm.

TRAVEL
American Auto Transporters, Inc, 981 Providence Highway, Norwood, MA, about 18 miles south of Boston, 821-4660. Over 21s, must have good driving record, international licence and deposit $200.

Amtrak, (800) 872-7245, Back Bay and South Station (Red Line, main station) and Back Bay Station (Green Line, Copley; Orange line, Back Bay). NYC ($43, 4½ hrs).

Bonanza Bus Lines, Back Bay and South Station, (800) 556-3815, buses to Portsmouth, Newport ($14).

East Coast Explorer, outside of New York (800) 610-2680, inside NY (718) 694-9667. Offers specialised intercity bus-travel, Washington DC-NYC-Boston, at budget prices ($29). Take a day to explore the real America via the scenic back roads, with stops at places of natural, historical and cultural interest. Max 14 people per trip, rsvs essential, door to door service.

Green Tortoise, (800) 227-4766. Camper bus touring company which offers interesting, economical 1-4 week trips all over North America. (Leave from Boston to west coast but no travel between east coast cities—see New York section for more details.)

Greyhound, South Station, (800) 231-2222. NYC ($39, 4½ hrs).

Logan Airport is across the bay only 3 miles from downtown: Blue Line T' to Airport station (85¢) from where there's a free shuttle bus to the terminals. Taxis from airport to downtown cost $10-$18.

You can take the **water shuttle**, (800) 235-6426, from Logan, across the harbour, to Rowe's Wharf for $8. Leaves every 15/30 mins Mon-Thurs 6 am-8 pm, Fri 6 am-11 pm, Sat & Sun 10 am-11 pm. 'A great way to see the city.'

Massachusetts Bay Transit Authority (MBTA), 722-3200, runs buses, trains and trolleys throughout Boston and surrounding towns. Flat fare subway 85¢, bus 60¢, no transfers. The **subway** is referred to as the 'T' comprises four intersecting lines: the Blue, Green, Orange and Red. The stations can be identified by a black T' on a white circular sign. Maps are posted in stations, you can pick up a free colour-coded pocket version at any station or visitors centre, where you can also buy the '**Boston Passport**' which provides unlimited travel on bus, trolley and subway lines: 1 day ($5), 3 days ($9) or 7 days ($18). Bus and subway services shut down around 12.30 am. MBTA also run a commuter rail system to Rockport and Salem.

Peter Pan Bus Line, South Station, (800) 237-8747, serves New England except Maine, Vermont and Rhode Island. For Maine/New Hampshire, try **Concord Trailways**, South Station, (800) 639-3317.

Plymouth & Brockton Bus Lines, South Station and Park Square, 773-9401, to Plymouth ($8), Hyannis ($11) and Provincetown ($20).

CAMBRIDGE Just across the river, Cambridge is often referred to as Boston's Left Bank'. Teeming with an eclectic collection of cafes, bookstores and boutiques, and nestling in the shadows of two of the world's premier educational institutions, Harvard and Massachusetts Institute of Technology (MIT), the lively streets and bustling squares are home to a young, diverse population. The lifestyle of the students here sets the pace for both sides of the Charles River, and Harvard Square is where it all happens. You will be amazed at the range of entertainment and activity to be found in such a small area. Over one hundred restaurants and cafes will satisfy any hunger and on warm summer evenings street entertainers fill the air with music, but for a cozier atmosphere head to one of the many blues bars and jazz clubs. For those interested in history there are some outstanding 19th century mansions.

You can take the 'T' to Harvard Square from Boston, but it's better to walk across Harvard Bridge, taking in the cityscapes, and the sailors, windsurfers and rowers on the Charles river below.

www.cambridge.ma.us/ provides informative introduction to the city.

ACCOMMODATION
Cambridge is a 10 min T-ride from the heart of Boston where accommodation is more readily available.

ABC Accommodations, 335 Pearl St, (800) 253-5542. Comfortable B&B accommodation in family homes, from $65. Rsvs essential.

Bed & Breakfast in Cambridge & Greater Boston, PO Box 1344 Cambridge, MA, 02238, (800) 888-0178. Rooms from $65 in Boston, Concord and Lexington.

Budget Chain Hotels: Before you call, check out the discounts available at the information booths off I-90, make rsvs from phones there to take advantage of the best deals.

Cambridge YWCA, 7 Temple St, Center Sq, 491-6050. Advance rsvs only; $35 pp.

The Missing Bell, 16 Sacremento St, 876-0987. D-$80, shared bath, bfast included. A short walk from Harvard Sq.

FOOD
An array of ethnic restaurants and sidewalk cafes will tempt even the most adventurous palate. Pick up the free *Square Deal* newspaper for special offers at local eateries.

Border Cafe, 32 Church St, 864-6100. Super tasty Tex Mex and Cajun cooking at this ever popular hot spot. Fabby fajita dinners for $9, Mexican specials $8-$10. Open late. Good, authentic food.'

Brookline Lunch, 9 Brookline St, 354-2983. Huge portions at super cheap prices, French toast $2.75, scrumptious veggie omelette with toast and special home fries, $3.50. Meaty dinner dishes $4.95. Mon-Fri 8 am-5 pm.

Cafe of India, 52A Brattle St, Harvard Sq, 661-0683. Good, hearty Indian food. Lunch $5-$8, dinner $10-$18.

Hong Kong, 1236 Mass Ave, 864-5311. Chinese. Lunch from $5, dinner from $6. Share a Scorpion Bowl,' a potent mix of fruit juices and secret ingredients sucked through long straws. 'Excellent drinking establishment (lounge upstairs). A Harvard/Tufts hangout.'

Pizzeria Uno, 22 Harvard Sq, 497-1530. Pizzas $5-$13, try their special Spinniccoli! 'Lively Italian restaurant. Good value.'

Tasty Sandwich Shop, 2 JFK St, Harvard Sq, 354-9016. Atmospheric all-night diner complete with fluorescent lighting guaranteed to bring on a hangover! Go drink coffee with insomniac Harvard students, entrees $2-$6. 24 hrs.

OF INTEREST

Cambridge Trolley Tours, 269-7010, depart from Harvard Sq on the hour 9 am-3 pm. Non-stop tours last 1 hr 20 mins, otherwise get off and on again when you like, $14.

Harvard University, founded 1636, is the oldest university in North America. Massachusetts Hall (1720) is the oldest building still standing. The **Harvard University Visitors Information Center** is at 1350 Mass. Ave, 495-1573 (in the Holyoke Center). Mon-Sat conducted walking tours are free. Walk from Harvard Square up Brattle St past **Radcliffe**, previously a women's college, now fully merged with Harvard, to **Longfellow's house**, 876-4491, where the poet lived between 1837 and 1882. The house is furnished with Longfellow's furniture and books. In earlier times George Washington used this house as his HQ. Daily 10 am-4.30 pm, $2. Also in the campus area is the **Fogg Art Museum**, Quincy & Broadway Sts, 495-9400; which has the largest collection of Ingres outside of France, and works by Rembrandt, Monet, Renoir, Picasso and Rothko. Tues-Sun 10 am-5 pm, $5, $3 w/student ID.

Le Corbusier's Carpenter Center of the Visual Arts and **Houghton Library** (housing the Keats collection), 495-3251, are opposite **Memorial Church**; the **Harvard Museums of Natural History**, contained in one building with entrances at 11 Divinity & 26 Oxford St include: **Peabody Museum of Archeology and Ethnology**, **Museum of Comparative Zoology**, **Botanical Museum and Mineralogical and Geological Museum**. 'It takes all day to see most of it.' There's a spectacular collection of glass flowers in the Botanical Museum.' For info on all Harvard museums: 495-3045. All museums (except Fogg) open Mon-Sat 9 am-4.30 pm, Sun 1 pm-4.30 pm; $3 w/student ID, small donation/free Sat 9 am-11 am.

MIT tours, 253-4795, include a look at the lovely chapel designed by Eero Saarinen. Student conducted tours Mon-Fri begin at 10 am & 2 pm at the information centre, 77 Massachusetts Ave. 'It's probably just as worthwhile to get a map and wander around yourself.'

Mt Auburn Cemetery on Mt Auburn St, contains the graves of Longfellow, James Lowell, Oliver Wendell Holmes and Mary Baker Eddy, founder of Christian Science. Both a cemetery and a park, with ponds, hills, footpaths, arboretum. 'Quiet relaxing place, great for birdwatching in spring.'

Walking tours, pick up a self-guided tour map ($2) from the info booth in Harvard Sq and discover the historic sites of Cambridge and Harvard Yard for yourself.

Book Stores: It's not surprising, perhaps, that America's academic capital plays host to one of the world's largest concentrations of book stores. A few of the more intriguing shops:

Grolier Poetry Bookshop, 6 Plympton St, 547-4648, oldest continuously operating poetry bookshop in US, more than 14,000 titles. Mon-Sat noon-6.30 pm.

Harvard Co-op, 1400 Mass Ave, 499-2000, books, posters, music, and more.

Revolution Books, 1156 Mass. Ave, 492-5443, anything you could want by Marx, Lenin, Stalin, Mao, etc.

Words Worth, 30 Brattle St, 354-5201, over 100,000 titles in 110 categories. Mon-Sat 9 am-11.15 pm, Sun 10 am-10.15 pm.

ENTERTAINMENT

Watch *Boston Phoenix* for details of concerts and lectures. Also, *The Harvard Gazette*, *Crimson* and *Independent* are good, though the latter is not published in summer. The active music scene is closely tied to Harvard and MIT; summer is therefore quieter.

Cantab Lounge, 738 Mass. Ave, Central Sq, 354-2685. Packed out with locals enjoying Little Joe Cook and his Blues band. Cover $3-$5.

Cybersmith, 36 Church St, 492-5857. Gourmet cafe and launching pad to the Internet. $9.95 p/hr, 16¢ p/min for on-line use, virtual reality sessions $3.75, video games, face-morphing stations $5. Mon-Sat 10 am-11 pm, 'til midnight Fri & Sat, Sun 11 am-9 pm.

John Harvard's Brew House, 33 Dunster st, 868-3585. Brewery restaurant serving good homemade ales, lagers and seasonal beers. Try a brewery sampler, five tasters for $4.75. Daily 11.30 am-midnight. Mon & Tues nights, free bands.

Ryles Jazz Club, 212 Hampshire St, Inman Sq, 876-9330, Sun Brunch $5 cover. Not cheap, but good jazz.

TT The Bear's Place, 10 Brookline St, Central Square, 492-0082, hard rock, beer. Live 'n' loud!

LEXINGTON/CONCORD Lexington and Concord are ideally situated for daytrips from Boston, and are easily accessible by public transport or pedal power (you can bike up the **Minuteman Commuter Bike Trail** from Arlington). Known as the 'Birthplace of American Liberty', the towns share the distinction of being the site of the first skirmish in the American Revolution. Near Concord's old North Bridge on 19 April 1775, local farmers took aim at advancing British redcoats and fired the 'shot heard round the world'.

The bridge is part of the **Minuteman National Historic Park**, 369-6993; park rangers give excellent historical talks here on request. Battle re-enactments are staged throughout both towns in April to mark Patriot's Day (closest Monday to April 19), and a special 'Colonial weekend' in early October.

Concord is also the home of the literary transcendentalist movement. Interestingly, all of the best-known transcendentalists, Ralph Waldo Emerson, Henry David Thoreau, Nathanial Hawthorne, Amos Bronson Alcott and his daughter, Louisa May, at one point lived within blocks of each other in this tiny, pristine town. Also here is **Sleepy Hollow Cemetery**, (3 blocks from town) where some of them have been laid to rest. Not far away is Thoreau's Walden Pond.

The telephone area code for Concord is 508, Lexington is 617.

ACCOMMODATION

Accommodation here is limited and rather expensive. See under Cambridge for local B&B options.

Col. Roger Brown House, 1694 Main St, Concord, 369-9119. D-$75.

Desiderata B&B, 189 Wood St, Lexington, 862-2824. D-$69, includes good bfast.

Red Cape B&B, 61 Williams Rd, Lexington, 862-4913. D-$70, XP-$10.

FOOD

Bertucci's, 1777 Mass Ave, Lexington, 860-9000. Pizza, pasta, salads; $7-$15.

Brighams, 15 Main St, Concord, 369-9885. Famous ice-creams! Hot Fudge Sundae $3.20, burgers from $4.50, breakfast specials from $2.50.

Concord Tea Cakes, 59 Commonwealth Ave, 369-7644. Homemade cakes, muffins, cookies and tea-time treats.

Sally Ann Food Shop, 73 Main St, 369-4558. Soups, sandwiches and bakery take-outs at reasonable prices.

OF INTEREST

Hancock-Clarke House, 36 Hancock St, 861-0928, is where Sam Adams and John Hancock were staying when Paul Revere came galloping by to warn them. Mid-April to Oct, Mon-Sat 10.30 am-5 pm, Sun 1 pm-5 pm (last tours 4.30 pm). A $10 combo ticket gets you into the house and the Buckman and Monroe taverns nearby, otherwise $4 for each building. **Monroe Tavern**, 1332 Mass Ave, was headquarters and hospital for British troops. Call 862-1703, opening times as above.

Lexington Green, where it all happened two centuries ago is lined with lovely colonial houses; on the east side, facing the road by which the British approached, is the famous Minuteman Statue. Over in the southwest corner of the Green is the Revolutionary Monument erected in 1799 to commemorate the eight minutemen killed here. Near the Green is **Buckman Tavern**, the oldest of the local hostelries and gathering place of the minutemen on drill nights.

INFORMATION/TRAVEL

Concord Chamber of Commerce, call 369-3120, or write 2 Lexington Rd, Concord, Mass 01742.

Lexington Information Centre, 862-1450, near Buckman Tavern at 1875 Mass Ave, has details and literature. Daily 9 am-5 pm. In summer guides give lectures on the Green.

To get there; take the commuter train ($2.75) from Boston's MBTA North Station, (617) 722-3200, to Concord, or the subway to Alewife in Cambridge, then the bus to Lexington.

THE NORTH SHORE Meandering north on Hwy 1 your first port of call should be **Salem**. The **Witch House**, 310½ Essex St, 744-0180, has tours ($5) of the judges quarters in what was the home of the famous witch trials in 1692 during which Puritan judges sent 19 suspected witches to the gallows and ordered a man to be crushed to death under millstones. The whole horrific turn of events is used by Arthur Miller in his play *The Crucible*, as a metaphor for the 1950's McCarthy communist 'trials'. The **Salem Witch Museum**, 19½ Washington Sq North, 744-1692, has an audio-visual programme with life-sized dioramas which tell the story of the witchcraft hysteria. Daily in summer 10 am-7 pm, $4.50. For a slightly more sensational rendition of history, visit the **Witch Dungeon**, 16 Lynde St, 744-9812. A witch trial is re-enacted for the audience's edification. Afterwards, visitors tour the lower dungeons. Daily 10 am-5 pm; $4. 'A rip-off. Lasts about 15 minutes and not very realistic.'

Nathaniel Hawthorne's birthplace, the **House of Seven Gables**, 54 Turner St, 744-0991, made famous in his novel, still stands complete with secret stairways, hidden compartments and beautiful period gardens. Daily in summer 9 am-6 pm; $7.

A prominent port in colonial days, Salem is a veritable museum of American architecture of the 17th and 19th centuries. Chestnut Street is lined with the lovely homes of Salem Clipper captains and owners. The **Pioneer Village** off West Ave in Forest River Park just outside Salem historic district, 745-0525, recreates typical homes of the Puritan community, *circa* 1630. Costumed guides take tours through the village, $5, Mon-Sat 10 am-5 pm, Sun noon-5 pm. House of Seven Gables combo tkt $10.

On **Cape Ann**, about 30 miles north of Boston, **Gloucester** a rugged port packed with fishing boats and seafood restaurants. Four miles north of Gloucester, off Rte 127A, is the typical fishing village of **Rockport**, now an artist colony and full of arty-crafty stores. 'Great for browsing and getting broke.'

On your way north from here to New Hampshire and Maine, there's the small town of **Newburyport**, the High Street is adorned with splendid early American mansions. 'While you're here, go whale watching; from Hilton's Fishing Dock, 462-8381. $24 for 4½hrs; money goes to finance research.' Daily 8.30 am & 1.30 pm.

The telephone area code for Salem and the North Shore is 508.

PLYMOUTH South of Boston, Plymouth marks the spot where the Pilgrims landed in 1620; the first Thanksgiving celebrations were held here in 1621. A few 17th-century houses still stand, and on Leyden St markers indicate where the very first houses stood. Moored by the Rock is *Mayflower II*, a full-size replica of the original. 'Worth a quick visit, but it's really for Americans.'

Today Plymouth County is known as **Cranberry Country**. Harvest in September is a colourful ritual; the dazzling crimson of America's native berry covers over 12,000 acres and seems to reach to the horizon.

The telephone area code for Plymouth is 508.

ACCOMMODATION
Guest houses are the cheapest option, but they become more coveted and expensive every year. Try looking in the area behind the Tourist Information Center.

Blue Anchor Motel, 7 Lincoln St, 746-9551. Rooms S-$50, D-$56.

In-Town B&B, 23 Pleasant St, 746-7412. D-$65 for three, full bfast. Good location. 'Lovely people.'

Camping: **Indianhead Campground**, 1929 State Rd, 12 miles south of Plymouth, 888-3688. Sites $20 for two w/hook up, XP-$10. Laundromat, showers, groceries; fishing, swimming and mini golf, boat rentals and amusement arcade.

Plymouth Rock KOA Kampground, Middleboro, 15 miles from Plymouth on Rte 105, just off US44, 947-6435. Laundromat, showers, pool, game room, food store. Sites $23 for two, no hook-up, $35 for a cabin, XP-$4. 'Friendly; great place.'

FOOD
There are many reasonably priced sub shops and good greasy spoons in Plymouth. Generally, the farther away from the water, the cheaper.

Cap'n Harry's Deli & Sandwich Shop, 170 Water St, 747-5699. Sandwiches $3.50-$5, try their Cajun turkey roll-ups. 8 am-9 pm.

Court Street Cafe, 39 Court St, 746-2057. Breakfast special $2.99 before 10 am. Nothing over $6. Mon-Fri 7 am-3 pm, w/ends 7 am-2.30 pm.

OF INTEREST
Cranberry World Visitor Center, Water St near *Mayflower II*, 747-2350. See how cranberries are grown and harvested, then view the cranberry bogs that produce the tart fruit for which Massachusetts is famous. Daily 9.30 am-5 pm; free. 'Nice facility and tour.' 'More than you ever wanted to know about cranberries.' Free samples.

Pilgrim Hall Museum, 75 Court St, 746-1620. Personal possessions and records of the Pilgrims. Daily 9.30 am-4.30 pm, $5, $4 w/student ID.

Plimouth Plantation. Rte 3 & Warren Ave, 746-1622. Re-creates the 1627 Plymouth community, 3 miles south of town square. Daily, 9 am-5 pm. Combo tkt: *Mayflower II* and Plimouth Plantation $18.50 valid for two days. Both staffed by American students dressed as Pilgrims speaking with 'English accents', pretending they are still in the 17th century. 'Less pro-American bias than elsewhere on the East Coast. Characters very knowledgeable.'

Plymouth Rock, on the harbour, supposedly the site of the pilgrims' arrival in the New World. Good for a chuckle, but don't make a special trip for it. Moored on the adjacent pier is *Mayflower II*, 746-1622. The replica of the original, built in England and sailed to America in 1957. $5.75 (but see above).

INFORMATION
Plymouth Information Center, Hwy 44 at the waterfront, 747-7525. General information on historical attractions. Daily in summer 9 am-9 pm.

TRAVEL
Plymouth & Brockton Bus Lines, 746-0378. Boston, $8.
Take the short cut to Provincetown with **Capt John Boats**, (800) 242-2469/746-2643, Town Wharf. Express ferry trip takes $1^{1}/_{2}$ hrs from Plymouth to the tip of Cape Cod. $22 r/t, $12 o/w.

CAPE COD
A 65 mile-long hook jutting out into the Atlantic, the Cape is a narrow string of sand from where, atop a dune, you can gaze over the ocean on one side and Cape Cod Bay on the other. Known for its distinctive architectural style of gable-roofed houses, their shingles weathered to a soft grey, the Cape can be an icey cold and blustery spot out of season, but in summer warm and sunny with a refreshing tang of salt in the air.

The Cape, with no less than 77 beaches, is home to many scientists who come to study the ocean's mysteries. The **Woods Hole Oceanographic Institute**, at the southern point of the Cape, is the most famous research group here. Be sure to see the **National Marine Fisheries Service's Aquarium**, 548-7684, daily 10 am-4 pm, free, home to many rare New England species of sea life. At the other end of the Cape, near the northeast tip, is the **Wellfleet Bay Wildlife Sanctuary** in South Wellfleet, a 1000-acre area operated by the Massachusetts Audubon Society.

Although the Cape is an extremely popular summer resort, it is still possible to avoid the crowds and escape to deserted sand dunes or down beautiful, sandy New England lanes leading to the sea: simply avoid Hyannis and the coast south of Cape Cod National Seashore.

Hyannis and environs is the part of the Cape most exploited by tourism and free enterprise, but over in the lower Cape, small towns like Sandwich, Barnstaple, Catumet and Pocasset remain relatively quiet, even in the high season. After Labor Day you can have the whole Cape to yourself. (Well, sort of; Cape Codders let you know in no uncertain terms, that it belongs to them. However, high unemployment in recent years means that the Cape's commercial community are depending on tourists more than ever for their livelihood.)

On the Cape you will come up against numerous private beaches, or public ones which extract heavy parking fees. The Chamber of Commerce booklet *Cape Cod Vacationer*, free and available everywhere, lists all beaches and their status and has other useful information. There is plenty of camping near Sandwich where there is also a free public beach. State run and private sites can also be found in Bourne, Brewster, and Truro. Near Brewster is Orleans—a favourite beach for surfers.

Aside from the tourist, the Cape's great source of revenue is the cranberry. Nearly three-quarters of the world's cranberry crop is produced here and in neighbouring Plymouth County.

The telephone area code for Cape Cod is 508.

ACCOMMODATION

Can be expensive, but there are several camping sites and also 3 youth hostels. For other listings, see Hyannis or Provincetown, or else consult *Yankee Magazine's Guide to New England* or the *Cape Cod Vacationer*.

Bed & Breakfast, Cape Cod, Box 341, West Hyannisport, MA 02672; 775-2772/ (800) 686-5252. Reservation service; in-season rooms from $75 incl. bfast, plus $10 one-time booking fee and 25% deposit.

Mid-Cape Hostel, Goody Hallet Dr, Eastham, 255-2785. Mid-May to mid-Sept; 7.30 am-10 am and 5 pm-10 pm. $14 AYH, $17 non-AYH, linen $2. Summer rsvs essential. 20 miles from Truro, ideal if you're working your way up the Cape.' 'Very strict.'

Camping: Shawme Crowell State Forest at Sandwich, 888-0351, and the **Roland C Nickerson State Forest** at Brewster, 896-3491, are both recommended. Sites at each are $6 per night; but be warned: 'Campsites are often full right up to Labor Day and you may need to drive right out to North Truro to find a vacancy.' Plan your summer Cape Cod accommodation as early as possible.

TRAVEL

See also under Hyannis.

The **Cape Cod Automated Travel Service**, 771-6191, offers 24 hr comprehensive info on fares and schedules for transport to, from and within the area.

Bonanza Bus Lines, 59 Depot Ave (old train depot), Falmouth, 548-7588/(800) 556-3815. Boston $13, New York $45, and Bourne.

HYANNIS The metropolis of the Cape, Hyannis is the main supply centre for the area and a busy summer resort. Main Street is an example of the typical all-American strip; for charm you want the outlying areas like Hyannisport and Craigville with its excellent beach for swimming.

More upper crust than most of the other Cape Cod towns, Hyannis is the home of wealthy trendies and is bathed in the aura of the Kennedy family sequestered in their Hyannisport compound.

ACCOMMODATION

Cascade Motor Lodge, 201 Main St, 775-9717. D-$62, XP-$6 (four can share) very close to bus station. 'Had large, luxurious room with bathroom and double waterbed!'

Ocean Manor, 543 Ocean St, 771-2186. D-$68-$74, private bath, comfortable rooms. Close to beaches, 1 mile from downtown. Summer rsvs recommended.

Sea Beach Inn, Inc, 388 Sea St, 775-4612. D-$50-$60, XP-$10. Bfast included.

FOOD

Hearth & Kettle, 412 Main St, 771-3737. Breakfast from $4, lunch from $5. Try a kettle of lobster chowder $3.50. 'Recommend the Early Bird Specials 12 pm-6 pm daily.'

Mooring, 230 Ocean St, on the harbour, 771-7177. Open into the wee hours, depending on the crowd. Lunch from $6, dinner from $10. 'Good food.'

Perry's, 546 Main St. 775-9711. Breakfast from $2, sandwiches from $3.50, stacked sandwiches with fries $5.50. Daily 5 am-9 pm.

INFORMATION
Cape Cod Chamber of Commerce, Rtes 6 & 132, 362-3225. Offers accomodation and entertainment information for the entire Cape area. Ask for *The Vacationer* booklet, *Resort Directory*, and the *Current Events* booklet. A good place to start learning about the Cape highlights. Summer hours; Mon-Fri 8.30 am-5 pm, w/ends 10 am-4 pm.
Hyannis Area Chamber of Commerce, Rte 132, Hampton Rd, 775-2201. Mon-Sat 9 am-5 pm, Sun 10 am-2 pm.

TRAVEL
Cape Cod Scenic Railroad, 771-3788, Hyannis to Sandwich, Tue-Sun, $11.50 r/t.
Ferries: During the summer, boats leave frequently from Hyannis South St Dock for Nantucket and Martha's Vineyard, r/t to either is $22, cars $180. R/t from Woods Hole $9.50. Contact **Steamship Authority**, 477-8600 for schedule.
Trips around the Hyannis Inner Harbour to gape at the Kennedy compound are also available for $8. Contact **Hy-Line Harbour Cruises**, on the Ocean St docks, 775-7185. Hy-Line give discounts with coupons available at any Cape or Island hostel.
Plymouth & Brockton Bus Lines, 17 Elm St, 746-0378. Provincetown $9, Boston $11.

PROVINCETOWN   P-town, as it's known locally, is at the very tip of the Cape, thus giving it its other nickname: Land's End. The Pilgrim Fathers' first landfall in North America was actually here. They stayed for four or five weeks before moving on to Plymouth. The town has made its name on tourism and fishing.

In summer the town is jam-packed with artists, playwrights and craftsmen (including a very large gay community) and the tourists and hangerson who come to watch them. All in all, swelling the off-season population of around 4000 to close to 40,000 people! P-town is an attractive spot with old clapboard houses, narrow streets and miles of sandy beaches. Commercial St, appropriately named, is the main drag, so to speak.

In the summer months, it's a perpetual street fair. For a special evening's entertainment, take a beach taxi ride over the sand dunes. 'Nightlife is very limited if you are looking for "straight" bars and there are very few college age students around.'

ACCOMMODATION
Alice Dunham's Guest House, 3 Dyer St, 487-3330. Victorian sea captain's house. Bunk n' Brew—D-$49-$57 plus a cold beer! One night free for each week you stay; 20% discount Sept-June. 'Nicest place in town.' 'Very friendly, interesting proprietor.' Rsvs recommended.
HI-Truro, N Pamet Rd, 349-3889, 10 miles from Provincetown. $12 AYH, $15 non-AYH, linen $2, kitchen. Rsvs essential. Two minute walk to beach.
Joshua Paine Guest House, 15 Tremont St, in the west end (quiet, non-commercial part), 487-1551. June 15-Sept 15. S-$40, D-$45, XP-$10. 'Friendly; nice place.'
The Outermost Hostel, 28 Winslow St, 487-4378. $14.95 per night. Dorm-style cabins, kitchen facilities, May-Oct 8 am-9.30 am, 6 pm-9.30 pm. Good location.'

FOOD
Stormy Harbor, 277 Commercial St, 487-1680. Italian, Portuguese, and seafood food. Bfast from $5, dinner from $12. Open April-Oct.

Surf Restaurant, 315 Commercial St on MacMillan Wharf, 487-1367. Eat on the deck overlooking the harbour. A drafthouse with jug band, washboard, and kazoos! Seafood menu $9-$20.

OF INTEREST
Art's Dune Tour, 487-1950, leaves from Commercial & Standish Sts. April-Oct. $9 for standard tour, $10 for sunset tour (need rsvs). From 10 am throughout the day. Interesting ride out to the site of dune shacks' once belonging to Tennessee Williams and Eugene O'Neill, then onto a cranberry bog before heading out to the ocean.

Provincetown Museum, at the base of the Pilgrim Monument, 487-1310. 'The Treasures of the pirate ship, *Whydah*. Artifacts from the ship of the pirate Samuel (Black Sam) Bellamy sunk in 1717 and identified in 1984.' Daily 9 am-7 pm, last admission 6.15 pm, until Sept; shorter winter hours. $5 admission to monument, museum and exhibit.

Whale Watching from MacMillan Wharf, $18 for 3½ hrs at sea (off season $16). Call Dolphin Fleet: (800) 826-9300, or Ranger Five: 487-3322 for savings on 8.30 am trips. 'Good, interesting commentary on board; we saw several whales, including one that swam under and around the boat; incredible and not to be missed.'

INFORMATION
Province Land's Visitors Center in Cape Cod National Seashore, 487-1256, off Race Point Road. Tour information, maps of seashore. Daily in summer 9 am-5 pm.

Provincetown Chamber of Commerce, 307 Commercial St, 487-3424. Offers maps and accommodation listings. Daily 9 am-5 pm.

Summer Shuttle Bus, will take you from the town centre to the beach, daily in summer 10 am-6.30 pm. The shuttle (a yellow school bus) may be hailed at intersections on Bradford St, or pick it up at the MacMillan Parking Lot behind the Chamber of Commerce. Buy tkts on board, $1.25 o/w.

NANTUCKET 'The Little Grey Lady of the Sea', as the island is known, provided inspiration for Melville's *Moby Dick*, and stepping off the ferry you will find yourself in another world. Thirty miles off Cape Cod, the island retains a certain charm with its weather-worn (though meticulously preserved) houses, cranberry bogs and salt marshes. Lobsterboats crowd the small harbour in the evenings, when they sell their catch to restaurateurs and passers-by. On every side of the island there are miles of open sand beaches terrific for swimming, surfing, fishing and all-night bonfire parties. Rent a bike near the ferryport and follow the purpose built bike paths or explore the island on the narrow streets and winding lanes. The 10 mile scenic ride to the beaches at Siasconset on the east coast will whet your appetite for a dip in the ocean.

The cobblestoned Main Street of Nantucket town and fine colonial homes testify to the past prosperity built on the blubber of the hunted whales. Today the money flows in with the flood of 'off-islanders' in summer; a crowded place then, but a lot of fun. For the pristine scene, come out of season when there's nobody there but the 'on-islanders', some of whom brag that they have never seen the mainland.

www.nantucket.com/ helpful introduction to the island, where to stay, eat, play.

The telephone area code for Nantucket is 508.

ACCOMMODATION

The island is generally a very expensive place to stay, and to maintain premium hotel rates any riff-raff caught camping will be fined $50, ie., what you would have paid for a bed. But all is not lost:

Nantucket Accommodations Bureau, 4 Dennis Dr, P.O Box 217, Nantucket, MA 02554, 228-9559. Lists most of the island's guest houses and inns. Charges $14 for service. Call or write early for best bargains.

Nesbitt Inn, 21 Broad St, 228-2446 in centre of town. S-$50, D-$70; T/Q-$90-$100. Bfast included. Rsvs required.

Star of the Sea Youth Hostel, Surfside, Nantucket, MA 02554, 228-0433. 3 miles from ferry wharf. $12 AYH, $15 non-AYH, linen $2. Two mins to beach. April-Oct 7.30 am-10 am, 5 pm-10 pm. Rsvs essential in summer.

FOOD

Captain Tobey's Chowder House, Straight Wharf, 228-0836. Winner of 'Best Chowder' award. Lunch from $9, dinner from $16, early bird special (5 pm-6.30 pm) $13, .'Good seafood.' Pricey but worth it. Daily 11 am-10 pm.

Henry's, on Steamboat Wharf, 228-0123, has the biggest, and some say the best, sandwiches on the island, $3-$6. Daily 9 am-10 pm.

OF INTEREST

Whaling Museum, Broad St, 228-1736. In the 18th and early 19th centuries, Nantucket was the best known whaling town in America. You can recapture something of the flavour of those times here. Has a good scrimshaw collection. Daily 10 am-5 pm; $5.

Whale Watching. Call 1-800-WHALING for details. About $65 for a day trip (9.30 am-5 pm), Tues only. Guarantee sighting or return visit. 'Saw more than 20 whales. Best part of our trip.'

Young's Bicycle Rental, 6 Broadstreet, 228-1151. $20 per 24 hrs, $12 for 2 hrs, sunset special available from noon; $6 until late evening.

ENTERTAINMENT

Gaslight Theatre, N Union St, 228-4435. Mainstream and art films, $7.

The Muse, 44 Surfside Rd (1 mile out of town), 228-6873. Best live entertainment on the island: rock and roll, reggae, blues, cover up to $10. Don't miss the lipsynching contest on Sundays!

Rose and Crown, S Water Street, 228-2595. Good pub-grub from $7. Live entertainment, karaoke, cover for bands $4-$6. 'Packed out but has a dance floor.'

INFORMATION

Chamber of Commerce, Pacific Club Building, Main St, 228-1700, maps, restaurant and accommodation information. Mon-Fri 8.30 am-6 pm.

Hub Board, Main St. Very useful for ads of jobs and rooms. 'We found two rooms from it on the first day.'

TRAVEL

See under Hyannis.

MARTHA'S VINEYARD Once you've experienced the Vineyard' as it is fondly called, you will never forget it. Just five miles off the Cape, New England's largest island boasts sandy beaches, pine forests, moorland, winding lanes and picturesque towns steeped in maritime history. It's a pleasure to visit at any time of year, although July and August are the most lively. In September, the island becomes a peaceful haven once again, basking in the warm gold of Indian summers.

Surfing, swimming and sailing are the attractions, although ever-increasing prices exclude such sports to anyone other than the jet-set who take over the island in the summer including Bill and Hillary Clinton, among others. Settle instead for a bicycle (rentals widely available) and pedal around Edgartown, the elegant yachting centre, where you can admire the fine old houses of the whaling captains, or make the strenuous 20-mile-trip out to Gayhead to watch the setting sun do its light show against the dramatic coloured cliffs. In summer it is possible to take a tour bus from the ferry terminals in Vineyard Haven and Oak Bluffs for a fascinating visit up-Island' (and down-Island').

If you long to ditch people for the gentler company of swans, lesser terns and mergansers, pay a visit to one of the Vineyard's three wildlife refuges: **Cedar Tree Neck** on the North Shore, 693-7233; **Long Point** on the South Shore, or **Wasque Point** on Chappaquiddick, 693-7662. Massachusetts Audubon Society run natural history tours to bird haven **Monomoy Islands**. 3hr tour $30, rsvs required, 349-2615.

The island is dry (no alcohol sold) except for Edgartown and Oak Bluffs. *The telephone area code for Martha's Vineyard is 508.*
www.mvol.com/ for all you need to know to have fun on the island.

ACCOMMODATION
Manter Memorial AYH, Edgartown Rd, PO Box 3158, W Tisbury, MA 02575, 693-2665. 7.3 miles from ferry terminal. April-Nov 7 am-10 am, 5 pm-10 pm. $12 AYH, $15 non-AYH, linen $2. Rsvs essential for summer; include SAE with first night deposit for confirmation. 'A long way from anywhere.'
Camping: Martha's Vineyard Family Campground, Edgartown Rd, Vineyard Haven, 693-3772. Sites $27 w/hook up. **Webb's Camping Area**, Barnes Rd, Oak Bluffs, 693-0233. Sites $29 for two, XP-$9.

FOOD
The Black Dog Inn, Beach St, Vineyard Haven, 693-9223. Breakfast, lunch and dinner at moderate prices, very popular with both tourists and locals.
Linda Jean's Restaurant, Circuit Ave, Oak Bluffs, 693-4093. Home cooking, breakfast $3-$7, lunch and dinner $5-$14, daily specials. Daily 6 am-8 pm.
90 Main Street Deli, 90 Main St, 693-0041. Gourmet sandwiches from $4.75, salads and subs. Daily 6.30 am-6.30 pm.

INFORMATION/TRAVEL
Visitor Center, at Ferry terminal in Vineyard Haven, 693-0085. Accommodation lists, maps and employment information available. Mon-Fri 9 am-5 pm, Sat 8.30 am-5.30 pm.
See under Hyannis for travel information.

NEW BEDFORD / FALL RIVER   On Rte 6 on the way from the Cape to Providence, RI, **New Bedford** was once the whaling capital of the world. It has recently been transformed from a dismal, rundown place to a cross between Mystic Seaport and Nantucket. There is a fascinating **whaling museum**, well worth visiting, and known for its exceptional collections of scrimshaw, 18 Johnny Cake Hill, 997-0046, daily 9 am-5 pm, Thurs til 8 pm, $4.50. Scrimshaw, perfected by New England sailors in the 19th century, involves carving and etching the surface of the teeth or jawbone of the whale.

Further west is the port town of **Fall River**, where the *Battleship*

Massachusetts, 678-1100, veteran of WWII Pacific battles, is moored. Daily 9 am-6 pm in July & Aug, $8.

THE BERKSHIRE HILLS   Only about two and a half hours from NYC and Boston, Berkshire County is an ideal escape from the hustle of the city. The Green Mountains of Vermont in the north slope down to become the Berkshire Hills, a sub-range of the Appalachians, that sneak south to leafy Connecticut, along the western border of Massachusetts.

A great area to venture off the beaten track, explore picturesque villages, such as **Lenox** and **Stockbridge**, or hike in idyllic countryside on the trails around Mt Greylock, at 3491 feet the highest peak in the state, or the 80 miles of the Appalachian Trail that winds through Massachusetts. Drive along The Mohawk Trail and feast your eyes on panoramic views of this green and pleasant land. Finish up in **Williamstown** (famous for its college), or make your stop in **Pittsfield** the county seat of the Berkshires, and from here canoe the Housatonic, investigate the many theatrical and musical events on offer around Lenox, Lee and Stockbridge or simply soak up the local history. The free *Berkshire Eagle* will keep you abreast of current happenings.

The telephone area code for the area is 413.

ACCOMMODATION
Susse Chalet Motor Lodge, Massachusetts Turnpike, exit 2, on Rtes 7 & 20, 637-3560. Summer S/D-$77 up. Bfast included. Rsvs recommended.
YMCA, 292 North St, Pittsfield, 499-7650. S-$28, $67 weekly plus $6 key deposit.

OF INTEREST
Pittsfield was the birthplace of writer Herman Melville of *Moby Dick* fame. The Atheneum has a room devoted to his effects, and you can visit his house, **Arrowhead**, at the edge of Pittsfield on Holmes Road 442-1793. Daily 10 am-5 pm, last tour at 4.30 pm; $5.
Hancock Shaker Village (5 miles West of Pittsfield), 443-0188. Earning their name from an early nickname 'Shaking Quakers', the Shakers originated in the late 18th century in Manchester, England and flourished for two centuries. Perhaps due to an avowal of celibacy, only a handful remain, living in Maine and New Hampshire. Known for their simple yet exquisite architecture, furniture and handcrafts, the Hancock Shaker Village, founded in 1790, displays many fine examples of their craftsmanship. Alas the Shakers abandoned their village to the tourists in 1960. Daily 9.30 am-5 pm, $12.50. 'Worth a visit.'
The Mount, Plunkett St, Lenox, 637-1899. Designed and built in 1901 by the writer Edith Wharton, author of *Ethan Frome, The Age of Innocence* and *The Buccaneers*. Wharton's opulent mansion was a source of inspiration for her writings. Summer: Daily 9 am-3 pm, $6.
Norman Rockwell Museum, Rte 183, Stockbridge, 298-4100. The museum houses a vast collection of original works and the studio of America's favourite illustrator. Daily 10 am-5 pm, $9.
The **Tanglewood Music Festival** held in Lenox late June-Labor Day, is the summer home to the Boston Symphony Orchestra. Sit out on the lawns with a blanket and picnic. Tkts from $14, for info call 637-1600. All kinds of music are performed, and many other fringe activities are available in the area.
Jacob's Pillow Dance Festival, 243-0745, with ballet, jazz and contemporary dance, held at the Ted Shawn Theater off US 20 east of Lee, late June-August. North of Lee is the **October State Forest**, with the Appalachian Trail running through it.

INFORMATION
Berkshire Visitors Bureau, 2 Berkshire Common, Pittsfield, (800) 237-5747/443-9186. Mon-Fri 8.30 am-5 pm.
Mount Greylock Visitors Information Centre, Rockwell Rd, Lanesborough, 499-4262, have free maps of the trails. Daily 9 am-5 pm.
Pittsfield Information Booth on the Rotary Circle for further info.
Williamstown Information Booth at junction of Rte 2 & Rte 7, staffed 10 am-6 pm June-Sept, but open 24 hrs for info. Will help find accommodation in local **B&Bs**.

TRAVEL
Amtrak's *Lake Shore Limited*, Boston-Chicago, stops here: Depot St between North & Center. Call (800) 872-7245. Boston-Pittsfield $27, $3^1/_2$ hrs, rsvs recommended.
Berkshires Regional Transit Association, 499-2782, covers the Berkshires from Great Barrington to Williamstown. Fares 75¢-$3.
Bike Rentals, from Main Street Sports & Leisure, Rte 7A, Lenox, (800) 952-9197/(413) 637-1407. Also rollerblading, canoeing, tennis.

NEW HAMPSHIRE   *The Granite State*

Many people consider the Granite State the most scenic state east of the Mississippi. The only state named after an English county, New Hampshire has a short but sandy Atlantic coastline, hundreds of lakes (the biggest is 72-square-mile Lake Winnipesaukee), the impressive White Mountain range, more than 60 covered wooden bridges and a 90 percent tree cover. The countryside, warm and green in the summer, seems to catch fire when the leaves change colour in the Fall Foliage Show. The long, cold, snowy winters make the state a popular and fashionable skiing centre.

Notice the granite walls everywhere. Built by the early settlers to enclose their fields, the walls remain even though most of the fields are forest again.

New Hampshire was the first state to declare its independence and also the first to adopt its own constitution. Nowadays it is regarded as a political barometer, the results of its early primary elections strongly influencing the choice of candidates in the presidential elections.

The inhabitants are mostly genuine, laconic Yankees, and the state motto 'Live Free or Die' reflects the tough Yankee spirit behind the Revolutionary War.

A good way to find cheap lodgings is to call New Hampshire Bed & Breakfast, P.O Box 146, Ashfield, MA 01330, 279-8348. They make reservations at B&Bs throughout New England, S/D-$40-$85. A hearty breakfast is included at most establishments. www.yahoo.com/regional/us states/ New Hampshire/
The telephone area code for New Hampshire is 603.

PORTSMOUTH   Its situation at the mouth of the Piscataqua River has always made Portsmouth a significant port, and it was the state capital until 1808. The only seaport on the state's modest 18-mile coastline, the city has numerous old and well-preserved colonial homes. Nearby, are several fine, sandy beaches, including those at Wallis Sands and Rye Harbor.

ACCOMMODATION/FOOD
Accommodation in town is invariably expensive, a better bet would be to try areas off US-1 instead.

Comfort Inn at Yoken's, on US-1, 433-3338/(800) 552-8484. Rooms from $60, pool. Adjecent to Yoken's, 436-8224, a popular and inexpensive ribs restaurant.

Pine Haven Motel, 6½ miles south of town on US-1, 964-8187. Prices from; S-$64, D-$80, XP-$5.

Muddy River Smokehouse, 21 Congress St, 430-9582, has live blues and good bar food.

OF INTEREST
Isle of Shoals, just off-shore, and the supposed haunt of Blackbeard the pirate. Boat trips are available from the harbour, call 431-5500.

John Paul Jones House, Middle & State Sts, 436-8420. Built 1758, house of the US Naval hero. Jones obtained the surrender of a British warship in 1779, as his own ship was sinking. Later, he became a Russian contra-admiral and died in Paris during the French Revolution. Mon-Sat 10 am-4 pm, Sun noon-4 pm, $4.

Old Harbor Area, Bow & Ceres Sts, once the focus of the thriving seaport, is now an area of craft shops and eateries.

Strawberry Banke Museum, just off I-95 on the waterfront, 433-1100. From this settlement, starting in 1623, grew the town of Portsmouth. Tour historic homes and period gardens dating from 1695. Craft demonstrations and exhibits. Daily 10 am-5 pm, $12.

INFORMATION
Portsmouth Chamber of Commerce, 500 Market St, P.O Box 239, 436-1118. Mon-Fri 8.30 am-5 pm, w/ends 10 am-5 pm.

CONCORD   The financial and political centre of New Hampshire, the State Capital, on the Merrimack River, is home to the third largest legislative body in the world.

While much of the region's character is shaped by the state's three largest cities—Concord, Nashua and Manchester, the Merrimack Valley is surprisingly rural. If you're about to tour the state, this is a reasonably central place to start. On the main highway from Boston, it has long been the main thoroughfare to the the lakes of central New Hampshire, the alpine-like White Mountains and further north still, to Quebec, Canada.

ACCOMMODATION
Brick Tower Motor Inn, 414 S Main St, I-93 Exit 12S, 224-9565. S-$64, D-$74. Large rooms, TV. Pool.

Dame Homestead, 203 Horse Corner Rd, Chichester, Rte 4 off 393E, 798-5446. $30 pp, shared bath.

Camping: Sandy Beach Campground, 677 Clement Hill Rd, Contoocook, 746-3591. Sites w/hook-up $20, XP-$4. Lake swimming.

FOOD
Thursday's Rest and Lounge, 6 Pleasant St, 224-2626. Southwestern food. 'Creative, homemade cuisine.' Daily 11 am-1 am, Sunday brunch 9 am-2.30 pm. Live entertainment, $3 cover, frozen drink specials .

Tio Juans, Bicentennial Sq, 224-2821. Eat Mexican food and massive Magaritas ($4.25), behind bars at this atmospheric watering hole in the old police station. Food $6-$15. Daily 4 pm-10 pm, Sun 1 pm-10 pm for food, bar open later.

OF INTEREST
America's Stonehenge, Mystery Hill, N Salem, 893-8300. Daily 9 am-7 pm. One of

the largest and possibly the oldest stone-constructed sites in the country. $7.

Anheuser-Busch Brewery, 221 Daniel Webster Hwy, Merrimack, 595-1202. Free tours of the world-famous Budweiser Brewery and Clydesdale Hamlet, complimentary beer samples with valid ID, sodas for those without! Tours daily 9.30 am-5 pm.

Christa McAuliffe Planetarium, I-93 exit 15E, 271-STAR. Take an expedition through space,' land on Mars or explore the constellations in the night sky. Shows (last 1 hr) 10 am-5 pm Tues-Sun, $6, $3 w/student ID, advance tkts recommended.

Coach and Eagle Walking Trail, a self-guided tour of 17 historic sights including the **State House**, where the Hall of Flags is worth seeing. Free brochures available from Chamber of Commerce.

Pierce Manse, 14 Penacook St, 224-5954. Restored home of President Franklin Pierce. Daily June-Sept, 11 am-3 pm, $3.

INFORMATION/TRAVEL
New Hampshire Office of Vacation Travel, P.O Box 856, Concord, NH 03302, 271-2666. Daily 8 am-4 pm.

Without a car getting around is difficult. Getting here is easy:
Concord Trailways, 228-3300. From Boston $11, 1½ hrs.
Greater Concord Chamber of Commerce, 244 N Main St, 224-2508. Mon-Fri 8.30 am-5 pm.

THE WHITE MOUNTAINS A popular destination year-round, with hikers in summer and skiers in winter, the range is dominated by **Mount Washington**, at 6288 ft the highest peak in the Northeast, where wind velocity has been recorded at 231 miles per hour! Climbing the mountain is quite a feat, but it can be done in summer, and the view is well worth the effort. Be warned: the weather can be nasty, even in July and Aug; take warm clothing, and seek local advice before setting off on a serious expedition. Most visitors ride the cog railway, 846-5404, to the top, from where six states and Canada are visible on a clear day. It's not cheap, though; the 3 hr round trip costs $39, discount available on 9 am & 4 pm trains. The auto (toll) road to the summit is equally costly: $14 per car plus $5 pp. $18 pp for a tour.

Loon Mountain, 745-8111/(800) 227-4191, provides summer and winter activities, with scenic chairlifts, mountain bike trails, rollerblading and horse riding. Similarly, **Ski Bretton Woods**, 278-5000/(800) 258-0330. North Conway is the best area for equipment rentals. Bikes are available from **Loon Mountain Bike Center**, on Kancamagus Hwy, Lincoln, 745-8111, and **Joe Jones**, Main St, N Conway, 356-9411.

At the base of Mt Washington, along Rte 302, is the resort of **Bretton Woods**, site of the conference which, in 1944, laid the ground work for a post-war financial structure and which created the World Bank and International Monetary Fund. Now it has a cosy ski resort.

Visit **Franconia Notch** and its 700-ft flume chasm with the **Old Man of the Mountain**, a natural stone profile, rising at the northwest end. **Cannon Mountain** in this area can be conquered by an aerial tramway. The **New England Ski Museum** is on Rte 3 in Franconia Notch State Park, 823-7177. Ancient skiing artifacts, from New England and elsewhere. Daily noon-5 pm, free.

Cranmore and **Wildcat Mountains** to the southeast of Mt Washington are more sheltered than most, with the best skiing facilities in the White Mountains.

During fine summer weekends, the area attracts crowds of people; anyone seeking a bit of peace and quiet is strongly advised to search elsewhere. Accommodation is plentiful and reasonably priced, although most facilities are generally expensive.

ACCOMMODATION

Hikers might consider staying at one or several of the **Appalachian Mountain Club's 8 huts**, spaced a day's hike apart; from $57 pp, depending on amenities and meals provided. Rsvs and deposit required. Call 466-2727 or write for brochure and to make rsvs at AMC Pinkham Notch Camp, P.O Box 298, Gorham, NH 03581. 'Clean, friendly and helpful. Hearty meals.'

Berkshire Manor, 133 Main St, Gorham, 466-9418. Hostel with private rooms from $30.

Bowman Base Camp, Rte 2, Randolph (north part of national forest), 466-5130. Bunks $10, tent site $5 pp.

Crawford Notch Youth Hostel, Rte 302, 846-7773, run by AMC. $10 AMC members, $15 non-AMC. Open year round. 'We went midweek after Labor Day and the hostel was almost empty. Avoid Fridays and Saturdays.'

Camping: campers may pitch their tents, for free, anywhere in the White Mountains National Forest, below the tree line, but there are strict rules for your safety; call the **U.S Forest Service**, 528-8721. For details and info on private campgrounds in the area, call 528-8727.

INFORMATION

White Mountains Attractions Center, exit 32, off I-93, in N Woodstock, 745-8720/(800) FIND-MTS.

White Mountain National Forest Information, 466-2713. Crawford Notch State Park, 374-2272. Trail & weather info 24 hrs, 466-2725. Franconia Notch State Park, 823-5563, visitor centre open daily 9 am-7 pm.

White Mountain Visitor Centre, Rte 112, (next to MacDonalds) in North Woodstock can provide maps, and help find accommodation.

LAKE WINNIPESAUKEE is New Hampshire's largest body of water. Set against a backdrop of tree-covered hills and the White Mountains, to the North, it is a popular summer spot. Come here for sunning, swimming and sailing. **Center Harbor**, **Laconia**, **Wolfboro** and **Meredith** are the main centres for accommodation and sightseeing. There are several campgrounds around the lake.

Winnipesaukee Railroad, 279-3196, operates 1 hr ($3) & 2 hr ($7) scenic trips along the lakeshore between Merdith and Weirs Beach, daily in summer.

RHODE ISLAND   *The Ocean State*

'Little Rhody' is the smallest state in the nation. With 400 miles of shoreline, it is dominated by the sea, and the Narragansett Bay, which cuts the state almost in half.

A colony founded by Roger Williams who dissented from the Puritan theocracy of Massachusetts, Rhode Island successfully developed by smuggling, slaving and whaling and for a while hesitated to sacrifice its post-Revolutionary War independence by joining the United States.

Little Rhode Island is home to some of America's biggest music events—the Newport Jazz and Folk Festivals.
www.yahoo.com/regional/us states/rhode island/
The area code for the entire state is 401.

PROVIDENCE Founded by Roger Williams in 1636, and named for the act of God that he believed led him there. Rhode Island's state capital and New England's fourth largest city, Providence is enjoying a renaissance as a modern industrial city and port. A college town, and home to the prestigious Brown University, it is fiercely proud of its success, its traditions and its historic past. Elegant Colonial homes and early nineteenth century commercial buildings survive on Benefit St, the mile of history'. Many of these are open to the public during the Festival of Historic Houses in May.

ACCOMMODATION
International House, 8 Stimson Ave, 421-7181. $50 pp, $35 w/student ID, XP-$10, rate drops for stays of five nights or more. Kitchen facilities. Advance rsvs essential on w/ends. Clean, friendly and cheap.'
Susse Chalet Inn, 341 Highland Ave, Seehonk, MA. (½mile south of I-95, exit 1, 5 miles east of town), (508) 336-7900. From S/D-$74, bfast included.

FOOD
Meeting St Cafe, 220 Meeting St, on College Hill, 273-1066. Pastries, soups, salads, sandwiches. Bfast $4-$7, lunch $5-$10.
Murphy's Delicatessen, 55 Union St (behind the Biltmore), 621-8467. Mountain High' sandwiches ($3-$5) are as big as Rhode Island. Daily 11 am-midnight.
Smith's Restaurant, 1049 Atwells Ave, 861-4937. Excellent Italian food (and lots of it) for great prices. Mon-Thur 11 am-9.30 pm, Fri til 10.30 pm, Sat 4 pm-10.30 pm.
Wes's Ribs, 38 Dike St, Olneyville Sq, 421-9090, ribs from $2, sandwiches, dinner special $4.95. Sun-Thur 'til 1.30 am, 'til 4 am Fri & Sat.

ENTERTAINMENT
The free weekly **Nice Paper** has complete entertainment listings.
Providence's nightlife is generally student-generated, though Thayer Street is always bustling, and in summer the influx of tourists ensures a lively atmosphere. A **party trolley**, 861-1385, shuttles clubbers around downtown. The $6 fee includes entrance to six nightclubs, and a half-price drink, Fri & Sat 8.30 pm-2 am.
The Cable Car Cinema, 204 S Main St, 272-3970 and the Avon Rep Cinema, at 250 Thayer St, 421-3315, show good independent and art films ($6).

OF INTEREST
Arcade, btwn Westminster & Weybosset Sts, a Greek Revival Building, the first enclosed shopping mall in America. Shops, fast food stalls, restaurants. 'Very small and expensive.'
Brown University, College Hill, 863-1000. A member of the Ivy League, has been here since 1764; interesting libraries and exhibitions (eg. pre-16th century books, and Renaissance through 20th century paintings in the **Annmary Brown Memorial**). For tours, stop by Admissions Office, 45 Prospect St, 863-2378.
Rhode Island School of Design, 224 Benefit St, contains a first-rate
Museum of Art, 454-6500. 19th century French and modern Latin American painters, 18th century porcelains and oriental textiles, and classical art; also the **Pendleton House**, faithfully furnished replica of an early Providence house. Thur-Sun noon-5 pm in summer, longer hours in winter. $2, free on Sat.
A Stroll Through Providence, a self-guided walking tour (brochure available from Visitors Centre) takes in all the sights including: the **Beneficient Congregational**

Church, an early example of Classical Revival, the First Baptist Church, dates from 1775 and stands where Roger Williams founded the first Baptist church in America in 1638, the Providence Athenaeum and the State House, which has the second largest unsupported marble dome in the world (St. Peter's in Rome has the largest). Inside is the 1663 charter granted by Charles II and a full-length Gilbert Stuart portrait of George Washington. Mon-Fri 8.30 am-4.30 pm.

INFORMATION/TRAVEL
Providence Preservation Society, 21 Meeting St, 831-7440. 1772 publishing house; plenty of info here on historical Providence, booklets ($1), free maps. Mon-Fri 9 am-5 pm.
Visitor Center, Waterplace Park, exit 22 off I-95, 751-1177. Mon-Fri 10 am-5 pm, w/ends 10 am-4 pm.
Visitor Information Center, 1 West Exchange St, 3rd floor, 274-1636, (800) 233-1636. 'Very helpful.' 8 am-6 pm Mon-Fri.
Bonanza Bus Lines/Greyhound, 102 Fountain St, (800) 231-2222. Boston $6, 1 hr.
Rhode Island Public Transit Authority (RIPTA), 265 Melrose, 781-9400. Fares from $1, $3 to Newport.

PAWTUCKET
If you're in the mood for a side trip of historic and contemporary dimensions, make the short (5-10 min) drive up I-95 to Pawtucket. Slater Mill Historic Site, Roosevelt Ave, 725-8638 features an 8-ton water wheel operating a 19th-century machine shop as well as exhibits of local history and fibre artists. Tues-Sat 10 am-5 pm, Sun 1 pm-5 pm, tours $6.

Travelling east across town on Armistice Blvd takes you to Slater Memorial Park, a fine place for a picnic and a tour through Daggett House, 333-1268, the Colonel's home built in 1645, which has an impressive collection of 17th and 18th century memorabilia. Summer w/ends only, 2 pm-5 pm, $2. The park has no less than 9 baseball fields, tennis courts and a merry-go-round. Daily 10 am-9 pm. Wind down your day as the pitchers wind up at McCoy Stadium. Eat hot dogs, drink beer and watch the AAA Pawtucket Red Sox play their hearts out to make the major leagues. 724-7300 for ticket and schedule info.

NEWPORT
Thirty miles from Providence on Narragansett Bay, Newport is a lively summer resort and home of such enchanting events as the Newport Bermuda Race, a tall ships regatta, and the famous Newport Folk, Jazz and Music festivals.

Although a rival of Boston and New York in colonial times, Newport really came into its own only around the turn of the century when the town became the place for millionaires to build their summer 'cottages'. Many of these ridiculously ornate relics of the Gilded Age are now open to the public. Find them close by Newport's fabulous beach and on Bellevue Avenue.

The new Americas Cup Ave has changed the feel of the waterfront. Somewhat sanitised bars and boutiques have recently appeared, but the twinkling lights of the harbour still make for a beautiful setting to sit and watch the world go by on summer evenings.

ACCOMMODATION
Hotels here are above average in price and fill up quickly, especially in summer, so

make plans for Newport as early as possible.

Gateway Visitor Center, 23 Americas Cup Ave, (800) 976-5122. Has some helpful accommodation listings. Sun-Thur 9 am-5 pm, Fri & Sat 9 am-6 pm.

Seaman's Church Institute, 18 Market Square, 847-4260. $15 per night or $100 per week. First come, first served with preference to seafaring folk, but 'if you're here and there's a vacancy, we'll take you.' People start arriving in May for the summer.

FOOD

Anthony's Shore Dinner Hall, 25 Waites Wharf, 848-5058, casual, family, picnic setting, inexpensive chicken and seafood with great view of Newport harbour, moderate prices from $6.95.

Dry Dock Seafood, 448 Thames St, 847-3974. Bring-your-own-booze. Inexpensive fish n' chips $5.95, lobster dinner $ 8.95. Sun-Thur 11 am-10 pm Fri & Sat 11 am-11 pm.

OF INTEREST

Belcourt Castle, Bellevue Ave, 846-0669, has a staggering collection of antiques and treasures from all over the world. Daily 9 am-5 pm. Self-guided tours $7.50, $6 w/student ID, guided tours $1 more, ghost tours $12.50, Thur 5 pm.

Cruising by ship or sailboat, around Narraganssett Bay is a pleasant introduction. **Spirit of Newport**, departing Newport Harbor Hotel, 49 Americas Cup Ave, 849-3575, offers 1 hr narrated cruises of the Bay, $7.50; **Newport Sailing School & Cruises Ltd**, departing Goat Island, 848-2266, offer 1 hr ($12) & 2 hr ($20) cruises aboard 23' & 30' sloops. Pure sailing, no motors! Rsvs only.

Viking Boat Cruises, depart Goat Island Marina, 847-6921, and offer 1 hr cruises, $7.50, as well as a 2½hr trip that stops and tours Hammersmith Farm, $14.

The Newport Preservation Society, 118 Mill St, 847-1000, maintains 7 of the mansions: **The Breakers, Marble House, Rosecliff, Chateau-sur-Mer, Kingscote, Hunter House**, and **The Elms** plus **Green Animals**, a topiary garden.

The Breakers , Cornelius Vanderbilt's, is unquestionably the most opulent. **Marble House** is thought to have been inspired by the Petit Trianon at Versailles. **Rosecliff** is where the *Great Gatsby* was filmed. The Breakers are $10; other houses are $6.50-$7.50. Combo tkts available. Open daily in summer, 10 am-5 pm, The Breakers 'til 6 pm on Sat. Other privately owned mansions of interest: **Mrs Astor's Beechwood**, 589 Bellevue Ave, 846-3772, is the most enjoyable to visit, with actors as servants and hangers-on of Mrs Astor leading you as her personal guests in a tongue-in-cheek tour of her home. (Most of the characters portrayed are British). Daily, 10 am-5 pm, $8.50.

Hammersmith Farm, on Ocean Dr, next to Ft Adams, 846-0420. This was the setting for Jack and Jackie's wedding reception, and the presidential hideaway during the early 60s. Kennedy memorabilia abounds. Daily in summer 10 am-5 pm, $8.

Newport Folk Festival. *The* folk festival of the sixties. Recently revived by Ben and Jerry of ice cream fame, it once again provides a forum for top talent. Held every year at Fort Adams State Park over two days in August, call 847-3700 for details.

Newport Jazz Festival. The oldest, and considered by many to be the finest, jazz festival in the world. Held outdoors in mid-August. For details write: Jazz Festival, PO Box 605, Newport, RI 02840, 847-3700, or ask at the Chamber of Commerce. 'Expensive but worth it.'

Block Island 12 miles south of the mainland and a peaceful summer resort with wonderful beaches, first settled in 1661; classified by the Nature Conservancy as one of the '12 great places in the Western hemisphere'. Has two interesting restored lighthouses, one featuring a 19th century newspaper story that tallied the value of ships wrecked around the island as greater than that of the island itself. Ideal for biking (plenty of rentals from $9 p/day). Day trips recommended since food and lodging prices tend to gouge the unwary; although **Maple Leaf Cottage**,

Beacon Hill Rd, 466-2065, a farmhouse in the remote interior of the island, is worth a try; D-$75 includes bfast.

Try lobster rolls at **Smugglers Cove**; **Cappizanos** for pizza; and clam chowder at **Harborside**. Ferries run by Interstate Navigation/Nelseco, 783-4613, go to the island from New London ($13.50 one way), Newport ($6.45), Port Judith (Galilee) ($6.60) and Providence ($7.40). The 4 hr trip from Providence is recommended. 'Great getaway.'

INFORMATION/TRAVEL
Both the *Newport Life* and the monthly *Pineapple Post* have details of what's on in and around Newport.
Newport Chamber of Commerce, 45 Valley Rd, in Middletown, 5 min drive from Newport, 847-1600. Mon-Fri 8.30 pm-5 pm. Very helpful.
Bonanza Bus Lines, 23 Americas Cup Ave, 846-1820. Boston $14, 1 hr 40 mins.

VERMONT   *Green Mountain State*

Vermont has always been known for its fiercely independent people, from the colonial days when it asserted its own independence in the form of a republic. The state remained that way for 14 years, operating its own post office and minting its own money. Vermonters have retained their independent spirit and protective sentiment for the state—their motto being Freedom and Unity'. They cherish the beauty of their Green Mountains, banning billboards and imposing the toughest anti-pollution laws in the US. An ardent defender of state rights, Vermont has supported only one Democratic presidential candidate and elected only one Democratic senator in over a century.

Vermont is famous for maple syrup, Cheddar cheese and the magnificence of its autumn foliage and winter ski trails. The autumn colours are at their best toward the end of Sept; this is also the time for foliage festivals and get-togethers. March is the season for syrup festivals, but there are a number of museums open year round devoted entirely to the history and manufacture of this state institution.

The state has many small, progressive schools and has always attracted artists, craftsmen and writers, including the painter Norman Rockwell who lived in Arlington, and Rudyard Kipling, who wrote *The Jungle Book* in Dummerston.
www.yahoo.com/regional/us states/vermont/
The area code for the entire area is 802.

BURLINGTON   This small city of approximately 40,000, a metropolis by Vermont standards, is set on the eastern shore of Lake Champlain, the beautiful 120-mile-long lake (the sixth largest in the US) which divides the New York Adirondacks from the Green Mountains of Vermont. Home of the University of Vermont, Burlington in 1981 became the first city in the US to elect a socialist mayor. The town's economy boomed as a result. Burlington hosts a number of festivals each year, the craziest of which has to be the 'Fools-a-Float' challenge each September.

ACCOMMODATION

Haus Kelley B&B, Old West Bolton Rd, Underhill Center, 899-3905. D-$22.50 pp, 'big breakfast.'
Howden Cottage B&B, 32 North Champlain St, 864-7198. S-$39, D-$49.
Midtown Motel, 230 Main St, 862-9686. S-$45, D-$55, XP-$5.

FOOD

Ben & Jerry's, 36 Church St, 862-9620. 'Best ice cream in the world,' according to *Time* magazine. A Vermont original; destined to reach the far ends of the earth.
Carbur's Restaurant, 115 St Paul St, 862-4106. A downtown landmark, richly decorated in Vermontabilia.' Best known for Grandwich' combinations. Over 150 sandwich variations! Moderate prices. Daily 11.30 am-11.30 pm.
Chicken Bone Cafe, 43 King St, 2 blocks from the lake, 864-9674. Popular with students and locals. Daily 11.30 am-2 am. Try Bone Chips,' $2.95, and homemade chilli, $3.50.
Daily Planet, 15 Center St, 862-9647. Good bar food, moderately priced. Bass and Guinness on tap ($4), student and yuppie hang out.
Five Spice Cafe, 175 Church St, 864-4045. Award-winning Asian food. Sumptuous feasts include Vietnamese Calamari, Evil Jungle Prince with chicken. Lunch $5-$8, dinner $9-15.
Henry's, 155 Bank St, 862-9010. In the heart of Burlington, a local hangout serving 'Americana', burgers and 'blue-plate specials'. 'Cheap and cheerful.'
Vermont Pub & Brewery, 44 College St, 865-0500. Indulge in Dr Walter's Wonder Pilsner, bangers n' mash $5.95. Free live entertainment. 'Best pint I had all summer.'

OF INTEREST

Boat tours of Lake Champlain aboard *Spirit of Ethan Allen*, 862-8300. Replica of a vintage paddlewheeler. Four daily cruises around the lake, $7.95, sunset trips $8.95.
Ethan Allen Homestead Trust, off Rt 127 N, 865-4556. Restored 1787 farmhouse home of Ethan Allen, Revolutionary War hero. 200-acre park with picnicking, fishing, canoeing. Mon-Sat 10 am-5 pm, Sun 1 pm-5 pm, $3.50.
Robert Hull Fleming Museum, U of Vermont, Colchester Ave, 656-2090. European, decorative and Native American art. Tue-Fri noon-4 pm (9 am-4 pm in winter), Sat-Sun 1 pm-5 pm, $3.
Shelburne Museum, 7 miles south on Hwy 7, 985-3344. Outdoor museum of early New England life. 45 acres of Americana, folk-art and architecture. Daily 10 am-5 pm, $17.50, $10.50 w/student ID, pass valid for two days. 'Worthwhile if you have a whole day.'

INFORMATION

Chamber of Commerce and Visitor Center, 60 Main St, 863-3489. Mon-Fri 8.30 am-5 pm, w/ends 11 am-3 pm.

MIDDLEBURY This small and beautiful New England town which borders on the Green Mountains has miles of hiking trails, including the Appalachian itself, with overnight shelters and various state parks for camping. One of the nicest state parks is not far from Middlebury, on beautiful **Lake Dunmore**.

The town is built around a village green and Otter Creek, flowing right through the middle of Middlebury. Picturesque, stone-built Middlebury College, founded in 1800, is famous for its excellent 'total-immersion' summer school of foreign languages, and gives a lively flavour to the town.

ACCOMMODATION

Accommodation in Middlebury itself is expensive but usually elegant and friendly.

Call ahead as most have limited availability.

Cream Hill Farm, near Shoreham, 20 mins southwest of Middlebury, 897-2101. 1100-acre sheep and cattle farm. Renovated 18th-century farmhouse, family atmosphere; S-$45, XP-$10, incl bfast.

Camping: **Branbury State Park** on east side of Lake Dunmore, 10 miles south of Middlebury on Rte 53, 247-5925. Swimming, fishing, boating, bath house. Sites $12 for four, XP-$3, lean-to $17 for four, XP-$4. **Lake Dunmore Kampersville**, south of E Middlebury on Rte 53, 352-4501. Sites $17-$26 depending on facilities.

Rivers Bend Inc Camping Area, 3 miles north of Middlebury, 1 mile off Dog Team Rd, 388-9092. Sites $18, $22 on the riverbank, all w/hook up. Small store and great swimming hole.

FOOD

Fire and Ice, 26 Seymour St, 388-7166. Friendly. Seafood, steak, great salad bar. Locals, students, and travellers. Tues-Sat lunch 11.30 am-4 pm, dinner 4 pm-9 pm, Mon from 5 pm, Sun 1 pm-8.30 pm. Entrees from $10.

Woody's Restaurant, 5 Bakery Lane, 388-4182. Outdoor dining. Seafood specials, steaks, pasta. Lunch $4-$7, dinner $8-$17, burgers etc. til late, Sunday brunch.

OF INTEREST

UVM Morgan Horse Farm, 74 Battell Dr, Weybridge, off Rte 23N, 388-2011, where the first American breed of horse is bred and trained. Tours $3.50.

Vermont State Craft Center at Frog Hollow, 1 Mill St, 388-3177. Craft gallery featuring the work of over 300 Vermont craftspeople, studios open to the public.

INFORMATION

Chamber of Commerce, 2 Court St, 388-7951. Mon-Fri 9 am-5 pm, w/ends 10 am-2 pm.

MONTPELIER This smallest capital in the nation is also surely one of the most beautiful. It was the granite industry which built Montpelier and nearby Barre. Today the economy is based on the state government and the insurance business, although a granite revival is afoot.

Montpelier is also a thriving centre for theatre, music, crafts and antiques, and boasts its own museum and Historical Society. If you want to get away from it all, wander the back roads and admire the scenery. 'Come here for a slice of 50s rural village community life!'

ACCOMMODATION

Econolodge, 101 Northfield St, ½ mile from downtown, 223-5258. S-$53, D-$62, XP-$5.

Montpelier Guest House, 22 North St, 229-0878. S-$32, D-$42, Q-$52. Victorian house, 10 min walk to downtown, no smoking. 15% discount on second night for those with bikes. Spacious deck and lovely gardens. Free use of cross-country skis and snowshoes for those adventuring to nearby Hubbard Park in winter.

Vermonter Motel, Barre-Montpelier Rd, 3 mi from Montpelier and Barre, 476-8541. S-$38, D-$45, XP-$4.

FOOD

Montpelier is home to the **New England Culinary Institute**, so quality, low-priced restaurants abound.

Ben & Jerry's Ice Cream Factory, Hwy 89 north to Waterbury, 1 mile north on Rte 100, 244-5641. The genesis of the ice cream made by two guys from Vermont. Taste for yourself during factory tours—ice cream cold off the dasher! Mon-Sat 9 am-9 pm, frequent tours, $1.50. Ask about their interesting management philosophy.

Horn of the Moon Cafe, 8 Langdon St, 223-2895. All-natural, wholefood bakery

and vegetarian food. Tues-Sun 7 am-9 pm, Sunday brunch from 9 am, $4-$8.
Hunger Mountain Co-op, 3 Granite St Extension, 223-6910. 1½ miles from Montpelier. Natural foodstore, open daily. 'Fantastic selection at great prices. Good place to stock up on food.'
Julio's, 44 Main St, 229-9348. Good Tex Mex food, $4-$8. 'The cheapest eats in town.' Open late on Fri & Sat.
Thrush Tavern, 107 State St, 223-2030. Lunch, dinner, seafood, burgers, sandwiches. Mon-Fri 11 am-11 pm, Sat 4 pm-midnight. $2-$6.

OF INTEREST
Morse Farm, Country Rd (3 miles from Montpelier; follow signs on Main St), 223-2740. Watch maple syrup being made here in March & April, and sample the end product! Daily 8 am-5 pm, til 8 pm in summer.

INFORMATION
Montpelier Chamber of Commerce, Stewart Rd & Paine Turnpike, 229-5711. Mon-Fri 9 am-5 pm.

STOWE   At the foot of Vermont's highest peak, Mt Mansfield (4393 ft), sits Stowe, one of New England's most popular resorts. Although predominately a skiing town, Stowe is gaining popularity in all seasons for its variety of outdoor activities—hiking, biking, canoeing and hang-gliding. It is also the home of the von Trapp Family, of *Sound of Music* fame, who operate a lodge and ski touring centre.

ACCOMMODATION
Anderson Lodge, 3430 Mountain Rd, 253-7336. Rooms from $48, including bfast.
Baas' Gastehaus B&B, 180 Edson Hill, 253-8376. D-$65 including bfast. Rsvs recommended.
Golden Kitz, 1965 Mountain Rd, 253-4217. Rooms $20-$28 pp.
Vermont State Ski Dorm, on Rte 108, 8 miles from the centre of Stowe, 253-4010. Independent winter hostel, $15-$25 pp. Sept-May. Bfast $4, dinner $6. 'The best in town.'

FOOD
Fox Fire, 1606 Pucker St, (Rte 100), 253-4887. Daily 5.30 pm-9.30 pm. Italian home-style cooking at moderate prices, from $9.
McCarthy's, Mountain Rd, ½ mile from centre of town, 253-8626. Sandwiches, grinders, soups, daily specials. 'Lots of homemade goodies.' Daily 6 am-3 pm.
Ye Olde England Inn/Mr Pickwick's Pub, Rte 108, 253-7558. English-style pub with pints of ale and darts. 'Great place.'

INFORMATION
Stowe Chamber of Commerce, Main St, 253-7321. Accommodation and travel info. Mon-Fri 9 am-5 pm, w/ends 10 am-5 pm.

THE NORTHEAST

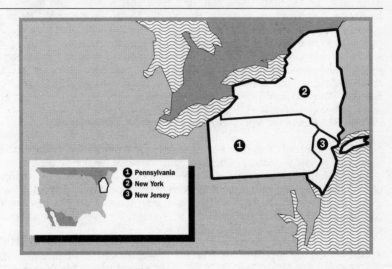

1 Pennsylvania
2 New York
3 New Jersey

Through the Northeastern region runs most of the 400-mile strip of that megalopolis known as 'Boswash' (Boston to Washington). This rates as the USA's most crowded urban concentration, containing the nation's largest city, New York, and heaviest industry. The region has been called the headquarters of Enterprise America for, from the time of the industrial revolution, much of the impetus for commercial and industrial expansion has stemmed from these states.

You would be cheating yourself if during your tour of the Northeast you did not veer away from the nasty highway, I-95, to visit the large tracts of unspoiled countryside within easy reach of the cities. Especially worth seeing are the mountainous Adirondacks in northern New York State and the rolling farmlands of western Pennsylvania; and there is greater variety still. A region rich in historical and cultural associations there is a wealth of places to visit and things to do. The climate varies as much as the geography. Winters are very cold and snow can be expected everywhere, while summers are marked by searing heat and sapping humidity.

NEW JERSEY   *The Garden State*

Sandwiched between industrial Pennsylvania and New York, New Jersey when first glimpsed after crossing the Hudson River from Manhattan seems an incredible wasteland, a lunar cesspool difficult to miss. Riding the **New Jersey Turnpike** (toll road) between New York and Delaware and seeing mile after mile of refinery pipes, gasoline storage tanks and smelly smoke-stacks, you may well ask yourself what happened to America The Beautiful!

What is hard to believe is that there really is some truth to the state's nickname, the Garden State. West from the New York suburbs and interstate highways that bisect the state lies the bucolic **Delaware River Valley** in a corner of the Appalachian mountains. To the east lies a virginal pine forest called the **Pine Barrens** and the **Jersey Shore** along the Atlantic, 150 miles of sandy beaches and boardwalks. From paved paths to muddy tracks, New Jersey has dozens of bike trails. *25 Bicycling Tours in New Jersey*, by Arline and Joel Zatz, is a useful book, available from Backcountry Publications, PO Box 748, Woodstock, VT, 05091, (800) 245-4151.

www.yahoo.com/regional/us states/new jersey/

There are three telephone area codes for New Jersey: 201, 609 and 908.

NEWARK In truth, this is one of America's most unpleasant cities, with a history of physical decay, political corruption, racial tension and plain old ugliness. Manhattan's poorer cousin, Newark even *sounds* like a corruption of *New York*, but the city has recently been redeveloping as its airport draws more commerce to the region. The busy international airport has made Newark a frequent first and last stop in America for overseas travellers—and is as much as the traveller need ever see.

There is no reason to go into downtown Newark. Accommodation is available near the airport but it is on the expensive side. It's better to catch the Olympia Airport Express ($10) for an exciting ride into Manhattan and stay there. (See New York City section for further accommodation and travel information.)

INFORMATION/TRAVEL
Travel and Tourism, Gateway Center, (201) 624-4462.
Greyhound, Penn Station & Market St, (800) 231-2222.

THE PALISADES are a 15-mile long line of granite cliffs rising as high as 500 ft above the Hudson. The most impressive view is from the George Washington Bridge when riding over from Manhattan, but on the New Jersey side you can enjoy the **Palisades Interstate Park** with it's picnic grounds and beautiful woods.

West from Newark, in an area of dense suburbs, is the residence and laboratory of American inventor Thomas A. Edison, creator of the phonograph, incandescent light bulb and other harbingers of modernity. From the Garden State Pkwy (toll) take exit 145 to I-280 W, then exit 10, turn right at light, go through two more lights, left at second one on to Main St, Edison's home, Glenmont, is at the corner of Main St & Lakeside Ave, (201) 736-0550. Daily 9 am-5 pm, $2.

Just across the Hudson river from lower Manhattan is the gritty port town of **Hoboken**, famous as the place where *On The Waterfront* was filmed, and where Frank Sinatra was born. PATH commuter trains from New York will get you there, and as you pass through the station, marvel at its intricate marble construction. One of the better technological universities, **Stevens Institute**, also calls Hoboken home, as does an aromatic Maxwell House coffee plant.

Two fine universities lie just off the New Jersey Turnpike (toll) southwest of Newark. **New Brunswick** is the home of **Rutgers University**, and 30 miles further is **Princeton**, a beautiful New England town that ran away to New Jersey. Both Albert Einstein and Thomas Mann lived here, while F. Scott Fitzgerald and Eugene O'Neill are among the more luminous alumni of **Princeton University**. Free tours of the campus start at the yellow Maclean House, (609) 258-3603, Mon-Sat 10.30 am-3.30 pm, Sun 1.30 pm & 3.30 pm. Highlights include Nassau Hall, built in 1756, where the Continental Congress met in 1783, and which was used as barracks during the Revolution by both American and British soldiers.

FOOD IN PRINCETON

Chuck's Spring St Deli, 16 Spring St, 921-0027. Daily 11 am-9.30 pm.
Yoko's Kitchen, 354 Nassau St, 683-9666. Chinese, average price $4. Mon-Fri noon-7 pm.
Small World Cafe, 14 Witherspoon St, 924-4377. Pastries and desserts at reasonable prices, small lunch menu. Mon-Sat 6.30 am-midnight, Sun from 7.30 am.

Fifteen miles west from Princeton is the point where General Washington crossed the Delaware River on a bone-chilling Christmas night in 1776 to deliver a special Christmas present to the British troops at Trenton. Eight days later he stormed the garrison at Princeton.

THE JERSEY SHORE begins south of Newark. Drive along the **Garden State Pkwy**, which follows the contour of the coast. Gritty **Asbury Park**, where it seems everyone works in a garage, is Bruce Springsteen country. Forty miles further south is the road to **Long Beach**. 'A great place to relax and enjoy sea, sun and sand. No usual boardwalk, but no usual commercialism.'

ATLANTIC CITY 'The playground of the world' was once the best loved seaside resort in America and the original model for the game of Monopoly, but Atlantic City saw its glamour wilt when better-off bathers made for hotter climes in the South and the West. The home of salt-water taffy (America's equivalent of Brighton Rock) and the Miss America contest, the town was revitalised in 1977 when casino gambling was legalised here.

With the arrival of the gambling resorts, a new game of monopoly has ensued (Donald Trump heading the list of players), with speculators razing entire city blocks in hopes of profit, and investors raising a dozen garish, neon-lit pleasure palaces. The result is an urban desert spotted with the casinos and linked to the rest of the world by hundreds of buses bringing the hopeful from Philadelphia, New York and Washington. Special Amtrak trains, with connecting buses to the casinos, go there too.

To escape the crowds and gaudy joie de vivre of Atlantic City, go north to the 2700 acres of **Island Beach State Park**, (908) 793-0506.
The telephone area code is 609.

ACCOMMODATION

Atlantic City is more expensive than the rest of the Jersey shore, especially during the summer season. If you're stranded and have to stay in town, try **AmeriRoom Reservations**, (800) 888-5825. Free reservation service for hotels, condos and casinos throughout the city; pricey, but efficient.

Inexpensive, family run motels can be found on the Whitehorse Pike in Abescon, Rte 30.

Beachside Hotel, 162 St James Pl, 347-9085. D-$100 p/week. Adjacent to the **Irish Pub**, S-$25, D-$65.

Camping: is the cheapest alternative. **Casino Campground**, Hwy 575 & Moss Mill Rd, 12 miles west of Atlantic City, 652-1577. Sites $24 for two XP-$2.

FOOD/ENTERTAINMENT

Baltimore Grill (Tony's to the locals), 2800 Iowa & Atlantic Ave, 345-5766. Cheap food in snug booths with your own personal juke-box. 'Pizzas are the best in city, especially topped with home-made sausage.' $5.50 up. Beer 95¢ a mug. Daily 24 hrs.

White House Sub Shop & Deli, 2301 Arctic Ave, 345-1564. World famous since 1946. $6-$8, half-subs $3-$4.

Many of the casinos serve breakfast, lunch and dinner buffets. Eat as much as you want, $4-$10.

OF INTEREST

Convention Hall on the Boardwalk, 348-7000, is the largest in the world, seating 70,000 in the main auditorium. It also has the world's largest pipe organ to match. Watch the Miss America Pageant here mid-Sept.

Lucy the Margate Elephant, 9200 Atlantic Ave, 822-6519. A building in the shape of an elephant, originally built of wood and tin in 1881. Tours $3, daily in summer, 10 am-8 pm, otherwise, w/ends 10 am-5 pm.

Renault Winery, 16 miles from Atlantic City on Breman Ave, off Rte 30, 965-2111. Tours of working winery which was built in 1864. Guide will show you bottling process, museum and take you through a wine-tasting, $2. Grape stompin' Festival at harvest time in September. Mon-Sat 10 am-4 pm, Sun noon-4 pm.

INFORMATION/TRAVEL

Chamber of Commerce, 1125 Atlantic Ave, Suite 105, 345-5600. Mon-Fri 9 am-5 pm.

Convention and Visitors Bureau , 2314 Pacific Ave, 348-7111. Daily 9 am-5 pm.

Many of the casinos run free or low-priced buses to Atlantic City from New York and Philadelphia. Check the *Yellow Pages* under 'Casinos' for information or look for billboard advertisements.

Greyhound, Arctic & Arkansas Aves, 345-6617/(800) 231-2222. Also, **New Jersey Transit**, same location, (800) 582-5946 (in state only), (215) 569-3752.

www.nj.com/navigator/ provides comprehensive transport information for the whole state.

OCEAN CITY 8 miles south, tee-total cousin to hedonistic Atlantic City. Alcohol cannot be bought on the island but the summer workers who flock here every year can walk a sobering 2.3 miles across 9th St bridge to find importable drink on the mainland. Plenty of casual jobs in 'America's greatest family resort' make this a popular destination for BUNACers and others who share the long, crowded beaches and lively nightlife. There is a wide choice of cheap rooms in boarding houses and old resort hotels, if you get there early enough (beginning of June if you're planning to stay.) Ocean City's 2.5 mile long boardwalk is known for its wacky contests and festivals, which reach a bizarre peak in July and August.

The telephone area code is 609.

ACCOMMODATION
Commodore Guesthouse, 701 Plymouth Place, 399-4761. D-$36-40, XP-$8.
Ocean City Guest House Association, P.O Box 356, Ocean City, NJ 08226, 399-8894. Rooms in private residences from D-$50. Brochure available.

OF INTEREST
Challenger Fleet, whale and dolphin watching, Ocean City Marina & Fishing Center, 3rd & Bay Aves, 399-5011. Sightseeing and mammal cruises, daily at 2 pm, 2 hr $12. Fishing trip, 4 hr $17. Speed boat rides daily.
Ocean City Boardwalk Art Show, over 500 artists, sculptors and photographers from the NorthEast display work for sale and compete for prizes. First w/end in August.
Miss Crustacean Hermit Crab Beauty Pageant, the world's only beauty pageant for hermit crabs. 2nd Aug, 6th St beach , free.
Weird contest week, includes french-fry sculpting. Mid Aug, free.

INFORMATION
Ocean City Information Center, Rte 52, 9th St Causeway, btwn Somers Point & Ocean City, 399-2629/(800) BEACHNJ, has info on beaches, hotels, restaurants. Help and information also available at bus station. Summer Mon-Sat 9 am-5 pm, Sun 10 am-2 pm.

WILDWOOD is a smaller, perhaps more wholesome, version of Atlantic City, practically at the tip of the southern peninsula of the state. The beach is 1000 ft wide in some places and there are 2 miles of boardwalk, six amusement parks, and plenty of wild nightlife. It's also a resort where families come for their traditional week by the sea. 'Lots of American students work here. Everyone works hard and plays hard. We had a fabulous time.'

ACCOMMODATION
'Accommodation easily found by walking around and asking. Wildwood Crest is the nicest area to live.'
Beachwood Hotel, 210 E Montgomery Ave, 729-0608. D-$65, pool, TV, refrigerators. 1 block from boardwalk and beach. 'Small, but friendly.'
Overbrook Apts, 216 E Roberts Ave, 729-2775. A bargain if you plan to stay the whole season, $60 pp p/week. Later in summer will accommodate one night stays for $15 pp.'Reasonable rates, family atmosphere. Likes overseas students.' Also recommended:
Clearview Hotel, E. Poplar Ave, 522-0985, **Holly Beach Hotel** on Spicer Ave, 522-9033, and **Mount Vernon Hotel**, 124-126 E. Lotus Rd, 522-7010.

FOOD/ENTERTAINMENT
Recommended for its 'good food and atmosphere,' is **Ernie's Diner** on Atlantic Ave, 522-8288. 24 hrs in summer.

CAPE MAY Family orientated Victorian beach resort where the 700-800 well-preserved houses date from the 1870-80s. The main attraction is the pristine beach where beach tags must be displayed if you plan to hit the sand, $3 from beach vendors or the Beach Tag Office, 884-9520. More secluded beaches, gentle dunes are located at Cape May Point, take Cape Ave off Sunset Blvd. At Sunset Beach you can join the hunt for the famous and elusive Cape May diamonds, milky stones which, when polished, glitter like precious gems.

For spectacular views of the coast walk for about 30 mins from the town centre and climb the curling stairs of the old lighthouse, built in 1859, which stands just inside the entrance gates to Cape May State Park. $3.50. If you're heading south, you may want to take the **Cape May Ferry**, 886-2718, to Lewes, Delaware. Frequent daily sailings, $18 car and Driver, foot passengers $4.50 o/w, same-day r/t $8.50. Bikes $8.

OF INTEREST
The East Creek Trail 10 mile long cycle path in the **Belleplain State Forest**, Woodbine, which may be accessed from country Rte 550, call 861-2404 for details. Bikes may be rented at **Village Bike Rentals**, Ocean & Washington Sts, in the Acme parking lot, 884-8500, $4 p/hr, $10 day, $35 week. Daily 7 am-7 pm.

INFORMATION
Welcome Center, 405 Lafayette St, 884-9562, has info on restaurants, accommodation, tours, etc. Free phones for calling guest houses. Mon-Sat 9 am-4 pm.

DELAWARE WATER GAP   Where the 'Garden State' comes into its own. Here the mountains diverge dramatically to make way for the Delaware River and a national recreation area which is a haven for outdoor enthusiasts, offering everything from swimming to rafting, canoeing to cross-country ski-ing, hiking to biking.

NEW YORK   *The Empire State*

Everything about New York State is big. It has the biggest industrial, commercial and population centre in the United States all rolled into one great metropolis, which together with the vast upstate area contributes mightily to the nation's manufacturing and agricultural output.

In colonial times New York was one of the most sizeable chunks of land in North America, hence its nickname, the Empire State. Although New York State was technically discovered in 1524 by Giovanni da Verrazano sailing for France, Henry Hudson (an Englishman employed by the Dutch) sailed through the Lower Bay of New York in 1609, and on up the river which now bears his name. The river was later fought over by the British and the Dutch, whilst the Brits also wrested the Northern area from the French.

Peter Minuit founded the Dutch Colony of New Amsterdam (renamed New York City by its conquerors in 1664) after buying Manhattan from the Indians for $24 worth of trinkets. Yet it says something about the vastness of the state, much of it still wilderness even today, that as late as 1700 the most formidable empire in New York was that of the Iroquois Confederacy of the Five Nations based in Syracuse and controlling the water routes to the coast and therefore trade. Their power was broken only in the middle of that century when the British defeated the Indians and their French allies at Ticonderoga, Niagara and Montréal. *www.states/new york/*.

NEW YORK CITY   'There are many apples on the tree, but when you pick New York City, you pick the Big Apple.' So said the jazz musicians of the roaring '20s, as fascinated by the lure and excitement of NYC as visitors are today.

More than 18 million people now live and work in New York, the USA's largest city, home to the United Nations and the business, entertainment and publishing capital of the nation. It isn't possible within this book to give more than the merest introduction to New York, so, if you plan to spend some time here, we recommend you buy the excellent *Michelin Guide*, *Fodor's* or *Let's Go/Rough Guide New York City*.

The greater metropolitan area, stretching out into New Jersey and Connecticut, is composed of five boroughs, Queens, Brooklyn, the Bronx, Staten Island and Manhattan. It's the last of these that you're really talking about when you say New York: that long stretch of stone lying between the Hudson and East Rivers, the place where skyscrapers tower over an intense mangle of social extremes.

New York's explosive variety and its appeal to so many different types of people make it an exciting place to visit. Chances are that whatever you are looking for, you will find, and so much more besides. In the words of President John F Kennedy, 'Other cities are nouns. New York is a verb.' New York offers the finest in theatre, cinema, music, museums, shopping, restaurants and general tourist attractions, as well as a riveting study in social contrast. Just watch the bag ladies huddle over a steam grating across the street from a row of limousines, and see the homeless slumped in the doorway of some gilded apartment block. Summers can be painfully hot and humid, and winters are bitterly cold and windy. It can be filthy, or dangerous, flashy, or funny, but it is a city which is always outrageous, alive, enthusiastic and, above all, resilient.

The Big Apple nearly went sour in the 1970s as it tottered on the brink of bankruptcy but it sprang back through the hot-shot 80s and is now going through another transitional phase. Whilst facing drug problems, escalating homelessness, deteriorating schools and hospitals, and the increasing overcrowding common to any modern metropolis, the violent crime rates in the city have actually dropped in recent years. Not to be complacent, New Yorkers are still looking to Republican mayor, Rudolph Guiliani who has promised, and delivered, a safer, cleaner city. The city's reputation is notorious. But, like most NYC natives, visitors can live there, travel by subway and move around perfectly safely by using caution and common sense. Whatever your approach to Manhattan, when you see the skyline, day or night, you will experience an unforgettable feeling of intimidation, enchantment and awe—this is New York! Welcome to the fastest-moving, most famous and fascinating city on earth.

The telephone area codes are 212 for Manhattan and the Bronx, 718 for Brooklyn, Queens and Staten Island. *www.yahoo.nyc.com/*

MANHATTAN NEIGHBOURHOODS

The Financial District: This is the oldest part of the city, a maze of narrow winding canyons that stand where Peter Stuyvesant once erected his wall to keep the Indians out. Hence *Wall* Street. The New York Stock Exchange is here on Broad St, and the American Stock Exchange is on Trinity Place. George Washington was inaugurated first President of the United States at Federal Hall, Wall and Nassau Sts, in 1789. From Battery Park you can take the ferry to Staten Island and the Statue of Liberty. Towering over everything are the second tallest buildings in the world—the 1350-ft twin towers of the World Trade Center, at West St. **Battery Park**

City: situated near Battery Park is literally a land-fill. Water was pumped out and the *roads dropped* to create this waterfront community. The district is a necropolis on Sundays, thus great for cycling or a picnic on the steps of City Hall. The thriving South Street Seaport area combines a museum, tall ships, a small shopping mall, and a cluster of seafood restaurants that collectively bear witness to New York's origins as a port.

Chinatown: The public telephones are housed in miniature pagodas, and the local grocery shops are great for snow peas or bok choy (Chinese lettuce). Restaurants are good, plentiful and cheap. Chinese New Year is celebrated with the explosion of firecrackers the first full moon after 21 January. Mott and Mulberry are the major streets.

Little Italy: Just northwest of Chinatown, in the area of Mulberry and Grand Sts. Good restaurants, bakeries and grocery shops, and a lively place in June with the Feast of St. Anthony, and again in September with the feast of San Gennaro, when you can ride ferris wheels in the middle of the street, eat lasagne and zeppoles, and buy large buttons that beckon, 'Kiss me, I'm Italian.'

SoHo: Formerly a warehouse and trading district, SoHo, the area south of Houston (pronounced HOW-ston) St and, increasingly, **Tribeca** (stands for triangle below canal), the area between Soho and the World Trade Center, is a haven for up-and-coming artists and musicians. Their artwork, music and theatre fill the old industrial lofts with the avant-garde of American culture. Chic (yet affordable) restaurants and designer stores are opening all the time, and excellent cheap clothing and electronic stores abound. Tribeca is also home to a wealth of nice restaurants (buy your coffees and brunches here) and, like Soho, there are many cast-iron buildings, dating from the turn of the century. Movie star Robert De Niro moved here in 1982 and opened his own film centre and grill restaurant (the TriBeCa Grill). Other celebrity residents include Dan Ackroyd and Bette Middler.

The Lower East Side: Orchard and Delancey Streets have attracted waves of immigrants, Eastern European Jews in the early part of this century, Puerto Ricans and Haitians today. Some older Jews still remain and Sunday is their big market day, a good time to swoop in for bargains. Note that many stores are closed on Saturdays—the Jewish Sabbath. The Lower East Side is slowly growing more fashionable, with poor immigrants being chased out by galleries and restaurants. Visit the **Lower East Side Tenement Museum**, 90 Orchard St at Broome St, 387-0341, to experience nineteenth century immigrant life, $8.

The East Village: St Mark's Place and 2nd Ave took the overflow from increasingly pricey Greenwich Village to become the hang-out for struggling artists, writers and students. It's also home to some of the more wasted punks, drug-users and drop-outs, who can make this a dangerous and intimidating area late at night, so tread carefully. However, as with the Lower East Side, the East Village is experiencing something of a renaissance, with an increasing number of trendy new bars, cafes and clothing stores attracting a vibrant young community with a style all of it's own. A recent influx of galleries, theatres and music venues has meant the East Village is becoming a hang-out for the cultural style-setters of the nineties. Former inhabitants of the East Village include WH Auden and James Fenimore Cooper.

Greenwich Village: New York's original bohemian quarter and one-time home of such figures as Edgar Allan Poe, e e cummings, Eugene O'Neill, Allen Ginsburg and Dylan Thomas, the Village is not what it used to be. Lots of expensive plastic cafes now cater to the tourists, but 10th, 11th and 12th Sts remain somewhat peaceful, lined with the brownstone homes of celebrities and the wealthy. New York University faces onto ever-lively Washington Square, with its version of the Arc de Triomphe. In the square listen to everything from casual guitar strumming to classical violin; watch the jugglers and break dancers, and compare strategy with the hustlers working the chess boards. During the summer, street fairs and markets are common up and down the Village streets. The area of the Village centered on Christopher Street is also home to New York's large gay community.

Chelsea: Home to the garment district, where one-third of all the clothes worn in the US are made or handled, Chelsea is a vast stretch of warehouses and lofts that is starting to gentrify under the pressure from Greenwich Village. The flower district is dug in around 27th St. To forget the grime of the city, walk along here among the ferns, tropical plants and examples of every imaginable flower in season. To the west stand the crumbling remains of the docks where the great steamships used to call. Better known as **Hell's Kitchen**, the hope is that the waterfront will revive now that the giant space-age Jacob K Javits Convention Center is complete. Further uptown, around Herald Square and 34th St, things are bustling around the large department stores like Macy's and A&S, as well as inside the nine-storey Herald Center shopping mall. Just a block away in either direction stand the Empire State Building and revamped Madison Square Garden. The Garden is where sports events, exhibitions and pop concerts happen; beneath it is **Penn Station** where you can catch trains out to Long Island, or Amtrak to Boston, Washington or Chicago.

Midtown: The core of the Big Apple. East and West, btwn 42nd & 59th Sts, is the heart of the theatre district, cinema district, shopping district and porno district, to name a few.

5th Ave splits midtown down the middle, marking the border between East side and West side. The swankiest shops in the city elbow for space along this justifiably famous street. Rockefeller Center and St Patrick's Cathedral are here, and when Britain decides to pawn the crown jewels, they'll be on sale at Tiffany's, corner of 57th St. The impressive Trump Tower, ritziest building in New York, packs five floors of astonishingly expensive boutiques around a rose marble waterfall. 'You won't be able to afford anything, but definitely worth a look.' The brotherhood of mankind fulminates daily in the United Nations Building on 44th St, by the East River. **Grand Central Station**, with trains to upstate New York and Connecticut dominates E 42 St.

Times Square, once home to pimps and tarts as well as the Broadway theatres, dominates W 42nd St. Until recently attempts to clean up the area, junkies, peep shows, porn cinemas and all manner of sleaze were in vain. However the Disney Corporation have acquired a massive block of real estate here and are forcing a sanitising transformation of the entire area, including Times Square itself. Renovation work is currently underway and several hotels and office buildings have sprung up: an indication that the area is gradually becoming more respectable.

Well policed, it's not as dangerous as it seems, but be on your guard—the action here goes on all night. Pleasant places in which to picnic or relax are the 'pocket parks' hidden away in Midtown: 57th St east of 5th Ave, and 47th St btwn 2nd & 3rd Aves.

Central Park: A huge, rambling green oasis which stretches for miles through the heart of Manhattan, the park extends from 59th to 110th St with ponds, gardens, tennis courts and zoo. On Sundays the streets are blocked off, and the park fills with New Yorkers roller-blading, walking, sailing, jogging, riding, cycling, skate boarding, playing baseball or reading the *Sunday Times*. Others contemplate Strawberry Fields, the international garden of peace named in memory of John Lennon. Nearby an imitation medieval castle, Belvedere, nestles in the park with climbable turrets and spires that offer an unusual view of the Manhattan skyline. Look for the Shakespeare Festival and free concerts, plays and opera in the summer; ice-skating in the winter. And don't forget to clear out at night; the park is unsafe after sundown.

The Upper East Side: The 60s, 70s and 80s in this area are among the most coveted addresses in New York. The vast Metropolitan Museum of Art and the spiralling

Guggenheim anchor Museum Mile along 5th Ave. East 86th St is the heart of Yorkville, the German part of town, with beer and Gemlichkeit on draught. Beginning at 96th St and running north to 145th is East Harlem, the largely Puerto Rican section called El Barrio. A sprinkling of Irish and Italian families remain, desperately trying to learn Spanish.

The Upper West Side: At the intersection of Columbus and Broadway lies the cultural hub of Manhattan, The Lincoln Center, which includes the Metropolitan Opera House and the New York State Theatre. At night it's pretty crowded; by summer's day it's a pleasant place to sit and eat ice cream. Around 72nd St and on Columbus Ave is a young, semi-posh and lively neighbourhood; on Central Park West is the impressive victorian Dakota building where John Lennon lived and died. Across the street, in the park, is the memorial to Lennon, Strawberry Fields. Further north on Central Park West is the Natural History Museum, and still further, in the Morningside Heights area, is Columbia University at Broadway & 116th St.

Harlem: This is the centre of New York's black community, stretching from the top end of Central Park up to 155th, and encompassing everything from miserable tenements to fashionable residential rows. A historic area in terms of religion and culture, Harlem is trying to get over its 'stay out' reputation and attract daytime visitors to its landmark churches and soul/gospel/jazz venues like The Cotton Club and the famous Apollo Theater. One of the best, if expensive, ways to see the district is by guided tour, (**Harlem Spirituals**, 757-0425, $33 or **Grayline Harlem Gospel Tour**, 397-2600, $33). Head for a tour which includes Sunday brunch if possible because this is the place to try tongue-tingling Cajun cuisine. Away from the tours Harlem can be a rough area where money for drugs is in short supply, especially on 125th St, and the night visitor should be wary.

ACCOMMODATION

To find cheap accommodation try the classified ads in *The Village Voice* newspaper, published late Tuesday evening in Manhattan. Shops near Columbia U are sometimes good for sub-lets and also try the fraternity houses around **NYU** and **Columbia** (NYU Loeb Student Center, Washington Sq, 998-4900).

New York Habitat, 307 7th Ave, Suite 306, New York, NY 10001, 255-8018. Finds accommodation from 1 bedroom shares to apartment sublets in safe areas and according to budget. Fee: less than 30 days 35% of one month's rent, 30 days-3 mnths, 50%. Call in advance for the best deals. www.nyhabitat.com/

'NY Information Center at Penn Station has price info on all hotels in New York. Very useful if you don't want to stay at a hostel.' Single accommodation can be astronomically expensive, but rates for doubles and triples are markedly less, so travel in herds where possible.

Big Apple Hostel, 119 W 45th St, 302-2603. $25 dorm, $65 for small private room. 'Excellent location.' 'Absurdly hot in summer—no AC.' 'No advance res.'

Broadway American Hotel, 2178 Broadway, 362-1100. 'Economy' hotel, conveniently situated. Fridge, TV, AC. S-$55-$80, D-$85-$110.

Carlton Arms Hotel, 160 E 25th St (at 3rd Ave), 679-0680. S-$49, D-$62-$69, T-$74-$84, Q-$78-$88, depending on shared or private bath. Flamboyant artwork makes each room a shrine to downtown New York style. Rsvs essential in summer.

Chelsea International Hostel, 251 W 20th St, 647-0010. On a leafy street btwn 7th & 8th Aves, directly opposite a police station. $20, private rooms $45, 7 days, one night free. $10 key deposit. The linen, showers and toilets are clean, as are the single-sex dorms. Will lock-up bags until 6 pm. Great location, within easy walking distance of the subway, Amtrak, Greenwich Village and midtown Broadway. Weds & Sun nights free beer and pizza. Non-AYH if space allows. Rsvs recommended. 'We made some great international friends here.' 'Good self-catering facilities.'

Chelsea Center, 313 W 29th St, 243-4922. $22 dorm style, bfast included. Kitchen, showers. $5 key deposit. German & French spoken. Check-in 8.30 am-11 pm. No curfew, rsvs required. 'Very cramped.' 'Safe, friendly, personal atmosphere.'

Gershwin Hotel, 7 E 27th St, 545-8000. $22 mixed dorms, $80-$120 private room with bath. Sundeck. Near Empire State Building. Check-in 3 pm. 'Basic, but clean and good security.' 'Nice, friendly staff.' 'Leave plenty of time for checking in and out.'

International AYH-Hostel, 891 Amsterdam Ave, and 103rd, 932-2300. Take #1 or #9 subway to 103rd St and walk 1 block east. Largest hostel in the USA. Kitchen, garden, daily activities, travel services. 24 hrs, $25 AYH, $28 non-AYH. –http://www.hostelling–wwwhostelling–com/ E-mail: hiAYHnyc@aol.com/

International Student Center, 38 W 88th St, 787-7706. $15 dorm-style. Kitchen, linen provided. Foreigners only. Check-in 10.30 am, 5 night max stay, 3 weeks in winter. 'Friendly place in heart of big city.' 'Good safe area but dirty rooms.' 'Cockroaches everywhere—take a spray for protection.'

International House, 500 Riverside Drive, 316-8400. Dorm, $35-$40. Summer only. Check-in after 1 pm. Close to Columbia U and subway. 'Clean. Excellent and cheap canteen.' Rsvs recommended.

Madison Hotel, 21 E 27th St, 532-7373. D-$91, Q-$110, $5 discount w/student ID. Check-in at mid-day. 'Good location, security and helpful staff.'

Martha Washington Hotel, 30 E 30th St, 689-1900. Women only. Rooms from S-$50, $175 weekly, twin bedded room with running water from $70, $280 weekly. Check-in 12.30 pm. 'Dark and dingy, not worth it.'

New York Uptown International Hostel, 239 Lenox Ave at 122nd St, 666-0559. $15 dorm. 'Need to be there early.'

Sugar Hill International Hostel, 722 St. Nicholas Ave, 926-7030. E-mail, infohostel@aol.com. Run by author of the *Hostel Handbook* (see background USA section for details) and staff who are keen to pass on knowledge of hostelling and NYC. Clean, spacious dorms $16. 'Very friendly staff, safe hostel (opposite 145th St subway stop),' for those who don't mind being uptown in Harlem. Check in 9 am-10 pm, 24 hr access. Lock-up available. Kitchen. Take A, B, C, or D train to 145th St. Rsvs required.

The Blue Rabbit Hostel, 730 St Nicholas Ave, 491-3892. Fax/E mail as above. New, sister hostel to Sugar Hill International. $16 dorm, D-$25.

Travel Inn Motor Hotel, 515 W 42nd St, 695-7171. Expensive, but Q-149, bath, TV, pool, roof deck. Secure indoor parking is free—'very useful in the city!' 'Can be quite cheap if several share a room—the floors are comfortably carpeted.'

YMCA—McBurney, 206 W 24th St, btwn 7th & 8th Aves, 741-9226. Co-ed. S-$43-$50, D-$59. $5 key depsoit. 25 day max stay. Café, gym, 24 hrs. 'Reasonable rooms, but mainly frequented by older people; handy for Washington Sq and Greenwich Village.'

YMCA—Vanderbilt, 224 E 47th St, 741-9226. Co-ed. S-$53-$66. $10 key deposit. TV in rooms. Two week advance rsvs required. Gym, pool. 'Great location—10 mins from Empire State.'

YMCA—West Side, 5 W 63rd St, 787-4400. Co-ed. S-$57-$80. D-$67-$90. Check-in 2 pm. Two week advance rsvs required.

FOOD

The spirit of adventure will keep you well-fed in Manhattan. With over 13,000 multi-ethnic eateries serving everything from bagels to Bratwurst, borscht to baklava, do not resist the temptation to try it all! Food can be expensive but for a budget alternative the all-American diner will provide endless coffee and pancakes drenched in maple syrup. Below you'll find two lists of places to try, one containing some tried-and-true favourites, the other, a list of neighbourhoods known to have a lot of cheap, good restaurants.

Abyssinia, 35 Grand St at Thompson St, SoHo, 226-5959. Delicious, spicy Ethiopian cuisine eaten off low wicker tables and stools. From $6.

Brooks Restaurant, 330 5th Ave, btwn 32nd & 33rd Sts, 947-1030. Next to the Empire State Building. Promises foreign visitors a 'royal welcome,' beer and cheap food (for 5th Ave). 'Muffins are a good bet and best cheesecake in New York, $3.' Bfast $2.50-$5, lunch $5-$8, dinner $9-$12. Daily 6.30 am-midnight.

Big Nick's, 77th and Broadway. Hamburgers, Greek food and pizza next door. Open 23 hrs, dinner from about $4; 'The best'.

Carnegie Deli, 7th Ave at 55th St, 757-2245. Sandwiches large enough to feed two, from $10.50. Other Jewish specialties. This was the restaurant featured in Woody Allen's *Broadway Danny Rose*. Staggering cheesecake and their corned beef and pastrami are rated no.1 in the country.

Dallas BBQ, 21 University Place, 674-4450. Friendly, spacious student favourite, right across from NYU. Mobbed in the evenings. 'Great early bird specials.' ($7.95 for two, Mon-Fri 2 pm-6.30 pm, w/ends 2 pm-5 pm). Filling bowl of home-made chili with corn-bread, $3. Veggie options. Mon-Thur 11.30 am-midnight, Fri, Sat & Sun 'til 2 am.

Eddie's, Waverley Pl & Broadway, 420-0919. NYU student eatery. Stir-frys and tacos good, burritto—enough for two—$5. 'Fresh, very cheap and enormous portions.'

El Cantinero, 86 University Place, 255-9378. Authentic Mexican food. Fajitas a specialty. Lunch average $6.50, dinner average $10.50. Large garden. Mon-Thur 5 pm-8 pm, happy hour. Mon nights $9 all-you-can-eat, Tues nights 15% off bill. Fri & Sat 'til 2 am, Sun 'til 10.30 pm.

H&H Bagels, 2239 Broadway, W 80th St, 595-8000, and smaller store at 639 W 46th St. Traditional American bagels. Great bargain snacks to hold off mid-sightseeing starvation. Unadulterated plain or cinnamon raisin are best, 75¢ each. 24 hrs.

Harley Davidson Cafe, 1370 Ave of the Americas, corner of SE 56th St & 6th, 245-6000. Yes, *another* Hollywood-style themed restaurant. But still a good place to sit back and lap up American culture amongst the gleaming Harleys and biker memorabilia. $7.50-$20, veggie options. Daily 11.30 am-midnight, Fri & Sat 'til 1 am.

Katz's Delicatessen, 205 E Houston St (at Ave A), 254-2246, Lower East Side. You can sample the meat before deciding which sandwich $5-$10 (average $8). After 103 years, a New York Jewish institution. Sun, Mon, Tues 8 am-10 pm, Weds, Thur 'til 11 pm, Fri & Sat 'til midnight.

Famous Ray's Pizza, 319 6th Ave, 645-8404, and 11th St & 6th Ave, 243-2253. Greenwich Village. One slice of pizza the size of Luxembourg costs less than $3 and is a filling meal. 'This is the best.' Regular cheese slice $1.70, six slices $9. 24 hrs.

West End Gate, 2911 Broadway, btwn 113th & 114th Sts, 662-8830. Bar/restaurant popular with CU students. Pasta and burgers from $4-$15. Occasional jazz nights. Daily 11.30 am-4 am.

Street vendors, for salty wheel-shaped pretzels, hot-roasted chestnuts and the quintessential New York 'dog' with everything on.

For cheap, spicy **Indian** food, visit Madison Ave around 27th St, also E Sixth St btwn 1st & 2nd Aves and other nearby streets. The number of hole-in-the-wall restaurants here has exploded recently. Dinner for $6 isn't a fantasy, but bring your own booze if you want a drink with dinner.

Chinatown justifies its reputation as a haven for good, inexpensive Chinese cooking. Walk along Mott, Bayard & Pell Sts, read menus, and look for the restaurant where the most Chinese people are eating. For oom-pah-pah bands and the wurst in **German** cooking, stroll through **Yorkville**, along E 86 St. **Little Italy**, next to Chinatown, has a number of good Italian restaurants, cafes and groceries, with waiters surlier than Rocky ready to push the pasta. Mulberry & Lafayette Sts, south of Houston, are especially fertile territory.

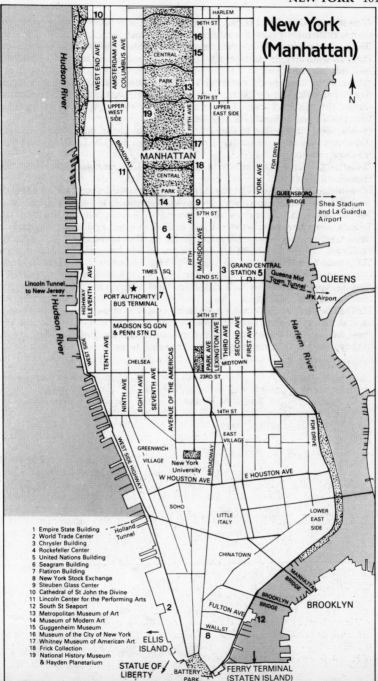

New York
(Manhattan)

N

HARLEM
96TH ST
79TH ST
57TH ST
42ND ST.
34TH ST.
23RD ST
14TH ST

HARLEM RIVER

Hudson River

WEST END AVE
AMSTERDAM AVE
COLUMBUS AVE
FIFTH AVE
BROADWAY

CENTRAL PARK

UPPER WEST SIDE

MANHATTAN

CENTRAL PARK

UPPER EAST SIDE

YORK AVE
FDR DRIVE

QUEENSBORO BRIDGE

Shea Stadium and La Guardia Airport

QUEENS

TIMES SQ.

MADISON AVE

GRAND CENTRAL STATION

Queens Mid Town Tunnel

JFK Airport

Lincoln Tunnel to New Jersey

HIGHWAY ELEVENTH AVE

PORT AUTHORITY BUS TERMINAL

MADISON SQ GDN & PENN STN

WEST SIDE HIGHWAY

TENTH AVE
NINTH AVE
EIGHTH AVE
SEVENTH AVE
AVENUE OF THE AMERICAS

CHELSEA

PARK AVE
LEXINGTON AVE
THIRD AVE
SECOND AVE
FIRST AVE

MIDTOWN

EAST VILLAGE

FDR DRIVE

Hudson River

WEST SIDE HIGHWAY

GREENWICH VILLAGE

New York University
W HOUSTON AVE

BROADWAY

E HOUSTON AVE

SOHO

LITTLE ITALY

LOWER EAST SIDE

Holland Tunnel

CHINATOWN

MANHATTAN BRIDGE

BROOKLYN BRIDGE

BROOKLYN

FULTON AVE

WALL ST.

ELLIS ISLAND

STATUE OF LIBERTY

BATTERY PARK

FERRY TERMINAL (STATEN ISLAND)

1 Empire State Building
2 World Trade Center
3 Chrysler Building
4 Rockefeller Center
5 United Nations Building
6 Seagram Building
7 Flatiron Building
8 New York Stock Exchange
9 Steuben Glass Center
10 Cathedral of St John the Divine
11 Lincoln Center for the Performing Arts
12 South St Seaport
13 Metropolitan Museum of Art
14 Museum of Modern Art
15 Guggenheim Museum
16 Museum of the City of New York
17 Whitney Museum of American Art
18 Frick Collection
19 National History Museum
   & Hayden Planetarium

The Bowery, east of Chinatown, is more famous for its bums (that's American for derelict) than for places to eat. But if your budget is rock bottom, walk along Bowery St by day for some of the lowest food prices in the city. Be careful at night. Try **MacDougall's**, 89 MacDougall, 477-4021. General American $4-$14, 9 am-2 am, w/ends 'til 4 am.

Upper West Side, btwn 60th & 90th Sts has an endless succession of trendy restaurants. Try **Victor's Cafe**, 236 W. 52nd, 586-7714 for Cuban food. $9-$25, noon-midnight, Fri & Sat 'til 1 am. Lots of new, trendy cafe-type places are opening, especially along Columbus & Amsterdam Aves.

SoHo, south of Houston to Canal, has a large number of interesting restaurants (although they can be expensive) squeezed between the galleries and second-hand clothing stores.

Veselka, 114 Second Ave at 10th St, 228-9682, a 24 hr Ukrainian café, has the best Borscht in the city.

Greenwich Village West and **East Village** are probably the most varied and exciting places to look for food. Walk btwn 14th St south of Houston, and west on 1st Ave to the river. Cheaper spots cluster around NYU, along 2nd Ave, and if you take a walk along Avenue A between E11th & E3rd, you will find an exciting array of temptations at very reasonable prices: including The Flea Market, 131 Ave A , 358-9282, **7A**, 109 Ave A, 475-9001, for 24 hr people watching, and breakfast specials $1.99, and **Two Boots To Go**, 36 Ave A, 565-5450, for festive Cajun pizza. St Mark's Place offers: **Stingey Lulu's**, 129 St Mark's Place, 674-3545, with drag queens to indulge your every whim, Yaffa Café, 97 St Mark's Place, 674-9302, for 24 hr kitsch, **St Dymphna's**, 118 St Mark's Place, 254-6636, for great Boston Scrod, and **Bel Air**, 110 St Mark's Place, 677-6563, for the best iced-coffee in the city! Also in this area, and definitely worth a visit; **Mission Burrito**, 91 E 7th St, 477-0773, for the very best, **Mama's**, 200 E 3rd St, 777-4425, for home-cooked delights, and Miracle Grill, 112 1st Ave, 254-2353, for bargain Cajun brunch at w/ends.

OF INTEREST

Brooklyn Heights. A neighbourhood of brick, brownstone and wooden houses, high up overlooking New York harbour. New York as it was 100 years ago. You can walk here across the **Brooklyn Bridge**, a hundred-year-old suspension bridge, from South Street Seaport, for a fine view of lower Manhattan.

Cathedral of St John the Divine, 112th St & Amsterdam Ave, 316-7540. The largest Gothic cathedral in the world, with an awe-inspiring vaulted roof that sweeps up as high as a 12-storey building. Otherwise known as St John the Unfinished. Work began in 1892, but was suspended in 1941 when America entered the war. Enthusiasm waned, funds dried up and Americans forgot how to build Gothic cathedrals. Magnificent, even with 100 years' work still to go. Now work is ongoing again. Free tours Mon-Sat, 11 am, Sun, 1 pm. 'Weird, wonderful, memorable.' Also, don't miss the **Peace Park** and its amazing fountain right next door.

Chrysler Building, 405 Lexington & 42nd St, 682-3070. An evocative landmark of the NYC night skyline, the famous Chrysler spire sits atop a building which typifies the art deco style inside and out. Built as a tribute to the great American automobile in the 1920s, some of its gargoyles are radiator caps. At 77 storeys, (1045 ft), it was the world's tallest building for one whole year until the Empire State Building snatched the record in 1931. No tours.

Chelsea Hotel, 222 W 23rd St, 243-3700. This hotel was once a haven for artists, writers and other fringe-elements in NYC. Expensive rates (D-$150) now mean it's better just to look at the landmark where Thomas Wolfe wrote, Dylan Thomas drank and Sid Vicious offered his honey.

Coney Island, (718) 372-0275, where generations of New Yorkers met, played, fell in love and screamed on the Cyclone roller-coaster (amusement park $13). Crowded beach. While here visit the **NY Aquarium**, (718) 265-3400/265-FISH.

Daily 10 am-6 pm, last tkt 5 pm, $7.75. See penguins, walrus, dolphins, sharks and Beluga whales. 'Fantastic.' Take F or D subway to W 8th St exit, Coney Island is directly opposite, a pedestrian bridge leads to the Aquarium. While there, take the boardwalk to amazing Brighton Beach where the Russians have really landed.

Ellis Island. Once the landing point for 15 million European immigrants entering the US between 1892 and 1924, and consequently a museum of enormous significance and poignancy for many Americans. The fortress like building can only be reached by an excellent ferry ride from Manhattan's Battery Park or Liberty State Park, NJ, (201) 435-9499. 'Highly recommended.' Mon-Fri 9 am-5 pm (extended summer hours). For info call **Circle Line**, 269-5755. Ferries leave Battery Park every 45 mins, 9.30 am-5 pm, $7 r/t.

Empire State Building, 5th Ave & 34th St, 736-3100. Not the tallest building any more, but the view, night and day, is still fantastic. If it's breezy, try the outdoor deck to really get the adrenalin buzzing. 'Go up at night, unforgettable views and less crowded.' Daily 9.30 am-11.30 pm, $6.

Flatiron Building, Madison Sq at 22nd St. The first iron-framed building and progenitor of New York's skyscrapers. An ornate wedge shaped building, it's still worth seeing.

Grand Central Station, 42nd St & Park Ave, itself a star of many movies. Take a look at the famously beautiful zodiac ceiling which depicts a Mediterranean winter sky with 2500 stars. Said to be backwards, it is actually seen from a point of view outside our solar system. A mammoth cleaning operation took place in 1997—using only soap and water!

Liberty Island. Info: 269-5755. Beware of hours of heated queuing with no shade: go to the dock early (arrive by 8.45 am; first boat leaves for Ellis Island directly, 9.15 am). Consider going by way of New Jersey (from Liberty State Park—75% of visitors leave from Manhattan.)

Lincoln Center for the Performing Arts, 62nd-65th Sts & Columbus Ave, 546-2656. Largest performing arts centre in the world, containing opera house, concert hall, theatre, museum, Juilliard School. 1 hr tour $8.25, $7 w/student ID, daily 10 am-5 pm. The **Metropolitan Opera House** has its own 90 min backstage tours, but closes early in the summer. Call 769-7020 for details and rsvs. Look for free concerts and other events during the summer.

NBC Television Studio Tours, 30 Rockefeller Plaza, btwn 49th & 50th Sts, off 6th Ave, 664-4444. 1 hr tour of studios, famous home to *Saturday Night Live* amongst other shows. Daily, 9.15 am-4.30 pm, $10. First come, first served at tour desk, 49th St entrance. 'Fantastic, definitely the best tour I went on. Free tkts for shows offered.'

New York Stock Exchange, 20 Broad St at Wall St, 656-5167. Free admission to the observation gallery and Visitors Center, Mon-Fri 9.15 am-4 pm. Arrive early to get a ticket.

Radio City Music Hall, 1260 Ave of the Americas (6th at 50th St), 632-4041. An art deco showtime palace, created by 30s impresario 'roxy' Rothafel. Home to the world's largest movie theatres, some two-ton chandeliers and 60 years of showbiz history. 1 hr tours every half hour, Mon-Sat 10 am-5 pm, Sun 11 am-5 pm $14. See the Great Stage and meet a Rockette.

Seagram Building, 375 Park Ave, btwn 52nd & 53rd Sts, 572-7000. Designed by Mies Van Der Rohe and Phillip Johnson as first 'anti-bourgeois' modern building. Brief free tour, Tue, 3 pm.

South Street Seaport, 732-7678, by Fulton St Fish Market. Historic waterfront district, just off Wall St, restored as it was 200 years ago. Now featuring a ship museum ($6, $3.50 w/student ID), and shopping mall with cheap fast-food outlets. Evening entertainments include Cocktail Cruises ($15). Also craft centre and 19th century printing store. Tours noon and 7 pm. Daily 10 am-5 pm.

Staten Island Ferry, (718) 390-5253. Nobody should miss what is certainly the best travel bargain to be found anywhere. It costs just nothing!! Frequent departures from Battery Park, at the tip of Manhattan. Passes close to the Statue of Liberty. Superb view of the Manhattan skyline, many people's (among them poet Walt Whitman's) favourite view of New York.

Statue of Liberty National Monument, Liberty Island, 269-5755. After getting the world's largest facelift, Lady Liberty is again open to the public. Daily, $7. Take Circle Line ferry ($7 r/t) from Battery Park, 269-5755. 'Can queue for two hours to climb to the crown—not worth it, take the lift to mid-way.'

Steuben Glass Center, 5th Ave & 56th St. Too expensive to buy but always superb to look at.

United Nations Building, 1st Ave & 46th St, 963-4475. 45 min tours every 30 mins, 9.15 am-4.45 pm. $7.50, $4.50 w/student ID. Expect an hour-long wait. Call in advance as hours vary depending on meetings of the General Assembly.

Woodlawn Cemetery. In the Bronx, and the last stop on the subway. The last stop for much of New York's high society, too. 400 landscaped acres of opulent mausolea and monuments to men who started from nothing and worked their way to a spot of turf at Woodlawn. Cast includes Westinghouse, Bat Masterson, associate of Wyatt Earp, Fiorello La Guardia, FW Woolworth, JC Penney, and A Bulova, the watch tycoon.

World Financial Center, across from the World Trade Center, Battery Park City, Hudson River & West St. Take the subway #1 or #9 to Courtland St. A gathering place of shops, restaurants and entertainment. Particularly relaxing (and free!) on a hot day is the **Winter Garden**, one of the most beautiful indoor spaces around, and a popular venue for free performances and recitals. Tall, elegant palm trees and AC, a superb view of the harbour and a flowing monumental staircase. Info: 945-0505. www.worldfinancialcenter.com/

World Trade Center, Church, Vesey, West & Liberty Sts, 323-2340. Miss this and you miss the best view anyone will ever get of New York. Make sure its not foggy. Stomachs plummet in the elevators up to the 107th floor, glassed-in observation deck, which offers a panoramic view of the city. Thrill-seekers can send their stomachs even deeper and venture outside onto the highest open-air observation platform in the world, at over a quarter mile high. Go just before sunset and the horizon will change colour as you walk round (it can take up to an hour) while night-time New York lights up before your eyes. Daily 9.30 am-11.30 pm, June-Sep, until 9.30 pm the rest of the year. $10. 'Breathtaking.'

MUSEUMS AND ART GALLERIES

American Museum of Natural History, Central Pk W btwn 77th & 81st Sts, 769-5000. Vast natural history collection from all continents and seas. Especially strong on Africa and North America. Meet Tyrannosaurus Rex and Velociraptor in the newly renovated dinosaur halls. Daily, Sun-Thur 10 am-5.45 pm, Fri & Sat 10 am-8.45 pm. Entry by donation, suggested $8, $6 w/student ID. In the same complex is the **Hayden Planetarium**, a new improved version will re-open in 2000.

The Cloisters, Fort Tryon Park, off Henry Hudson Pkwy, call 923-3700 for bus and subway info. A branch of the Metropolitan devoted to medieval European art and architecture. On top of a hill overlooking the Hudson, the museum gives the impression of a 12th-century monastery. One of the lesser known but more enjoyable galleries, it shelters magnificent medieval sculptures and the famed Unicorn Tapestries. Mar-Oct, Tue-Sun 9.30 am-5.15 pm; otherwise closes at 4.45 pm. $8, $4 w/student ID (includes admittance to Metropolitan Museum of Art).

The Frick Collection, 1 E 70th St at 5th Ave, 288-0700. Walk in to this Italianate villa, once Henry Frick's home, and there is a peaceful hush in the small courtyard. Walk round the rooms and see works by Titian, Velzquez, Whistler and a searing Rembrandt self-portrait; plus wonderful furniture and interiors. A small delight.

Tues-Sat 10 am-6 pm, Sun 1 pm-6 pm; $5, $3 w/student ID. 'Unsuspected highlight of New York.'

Solomon R. Guggenheim Museum, 1071 5th Ave at 88th St, 423-3500. After restoration the fantastic building is finally as architect Frank Lloyd Wright wished it. The spiral winds down taking you past the contemporary art collection. Now with a new wing for more permanent displays. Sun-Weds 10 am-6 pm, Fri & Sat 'til 8 pm, $10, $7 w/student ID. Second location downtown, with Impressionist, Surrealist and Minimalist collection, 575 Broadway at Prince St, $15, $5 w/student ID. Sun, Weds, Fri noon-6 pm, Sat 11 am-8 pm.

Intrepid Sea-Air-Space Museum, W 46th St & 12th Ave, Pier 86, 245-2533. Restored aircraft carrier with planes, also space exhibit and submarine. Daily 10 am-5 pm, $10.

Metropolitan Museum of Art, Central Park, 5th Ave & 82nd St, 879-5500. One of the world's greatest collections and the largest of its kind in the Western Hemisphere. There are over 3 million works tracing the evolution of art from the 13th century to the present day, plus the largest Egyptian collection outside Egypt. Particularly restful on a blistering summer's day is **Astor Court**, the Ming scholar's retreat. Stone, flora and a miniature waterfall are arranged in a yin and yang relationship, installed by 27 Chinese engineers in 1980. Tue-Sun 9.30 am-5.15 pm, Fri-Sat 9.30 am-8.45 pm, closed Mon. Suggested donation, $8, $4 w/student ID.

Museum of Modern Art, 11 W 53rd St, btwn 5th & 6th Aves, 708-9480. Set up in 1929 because the Met refused to acknowledge the existence of modern art so this is the place to see Picasso, Monet, and just about any other modern painter you can care to think of, plus superb photography. Rest those weary feet in the restful and heavily stocked sculpture garden. Daily 10.30 am-6 pm, Fri 'til 8.30 pm, $9.50, $6.50 w/student ID, pay what you can 4.30 pm-8.30 pm Fri. For evening jazz concerts call 708-9491. Films are shown daily except Weds, free tkts available at 11 am for afternoon shows and 1 pm for evenings. www.moma.org/

Museum of the American Indian, Smithsonian Institute, Alexander Hamilton US Customs House, 1 Bowling Green, near Battery Park, far southern end of Broadway, 668-6624. One of the finest collections of native American artifacts in the world. Scheduled to join the other Smithsonians on the Mall in Washington DC by 2001, this is a museum where contemporary issues receive as much attention as past history. Daily 10 am-5 pm, Thur 'til 8 pm, free. 'A treasure house.'

Museum of TV and Radio, 25 W 52 St, btwn 5th & 6th Aves, 621-6800. The computer library here holds over 40,000 TV and radio programs, commercials for listening and viewing. Popular, so reserve on arrival. Also special exhibits and screenings. Tue-Sun noon-6 pm, Thurs noon-8 pm. $6, $4 w/student ID.

Museum of the City of New York, 5th Ave at 103rd St, 534-1672. Fascinating story of city's growth from a small Dutch community. Free, although donations suggested, $5, $4 w/student ID. Wed-Sat 10 am-5 pm, Sun 1 pm-5 pm.

Whitney Museum of American Art, 945 Madison Ave, at 75th St, 570-3676. Devoted exclusively to 20th-century American art. Wed-Sat 11 am-6 pm, Thur 1 pm-8 pm; $8, $7 w/student ID, free Thur 6 pm-8 pm.

TOURS

Tours really worth taking include the boat trips around Manhattan and the guided bus/foot tours of Harlem. Other than these, one of the best and cheapest ways to explore New York is on foot.

Circle Line, Pier 83, 12th Ave & W 42nd St, 563-3200. 3 hr boat trips circumnavigate the island of Manhattan 10 am-4 pm, $20, 2 hrs $17. Bar onboard. Call for harbour lights cruises schedules, $17. 'Make sure you sit on left side of boat.' 'Can get chilly.' 'Great value.'

Grayline Tours, 900 8th Ave btwn 53rd & 54th Sts, 397-2600. Offers twenty different tours (including Harlem and Manhattan) daily. From 2 hrs to all day ventures, from

$19, departing from north wing of Port Authority bus terminal, W 42nd St & 8th Ave. See leaflets in hotel lobbies and tourist centres. The Grayline tours are probably not worth taking unless you're only in New York for a brief time—a 'hop on and off' tour starts at 9 am.

Harlem Your Way, 690-1687. Bus and walking tours of gospel churches and jazz venues.

Island Helicopters haul you aloft from their pads at 34th St on the East River, 683-4575. Tours start at $44 pp for 7 mins of booming and zooming over the UN and East River. Other longer, costlier tours available. 'A real experience if you've never been up in a helicopter before.' 'Try to sit next to the pilot.' Mon-Fri 9 am-6 pm.

New York Apple Tours, several locations, 944-9200. Sightseeing and shopping abord double-decker buses. May-Oct daily 9 am-10 pm, otherwise 'til 6 pm.

ENTERTAINMENT

No other American city can offer such a variety of amusements. Entertainment, however, can be expensive for the stranger who does not know his way around. Broadway theatres, most night clubs and some cinemas will put a strain on modest budgets. At the same time, free entertainment abounds. Read the *New Yorker*, *Village Voice*, *Where Magazine*, *Seven Days*, *New York Magazine*'s *Cue Magazine* section, or look for a free copy of *NY Talk*, for complete details of shows, jazz and cinemas. The New York Convention and Visitors Bureau, Times Square, (800) 692-84748/397-8222, can also provide useful information regarding shows, events and entertainments. There are free orchestral, pop, operatic concerts, dance groups, and theatrical performances in **Central Park** throughout the summer. These are popular, so try to arrive at least 2 hrs before the performance to stake your claim. Also, look out for local street festivals.

Greenwich Village and **SoHo** are two of the most interesting entertainment areas. Good jazz and folk music, as well as eating places, can still be found among the many tourist traps in the Village, although SoHo is definitely where New Yorkers go now. Go to the better places, even if there is an admission charge; you will find the best music. Beware of places that do not advertise an admission or cover charge but extract large sums for a required drink and offer inferior entertainment.

Washington Square is infested with pseudo folksingers on w/end afternoons.

JAZZ

Check the *Village Voice*, *New York Magazine*'s *Cue Section* and *Jazz Interactions* news sheet for all the gigs. Jazz remains one of New York City's biggest sounds and the action takes place all over town.

Apollo Theatre, 253 W 125th St, 749-5838, nearest subway stop: 125th St station on 8th Ave line. Historic 1930s jazz cabaret and theatre which featured Duke Ellington, Louis Armstrong and Ella Fitzgerald in its time. Now has shows from $20. Try the famous Wednesday Amateur nights, which gave so many their big break, for $10-$19. Book ahead at Ticket Masters, 307-7171. Look for some of the biggest names in contemporary music to play here. Remember to be careful in Harlem at night.

Cajun, 129 8th Ave at 16th St, 691-6174. Come here for the classic New Orleans sound. Jazz brunch on Sundays, $12, noon-4 pm.

Blue Note, 131 W 3rd St, 475-8592. Serves food and hot jazz. 'Small, but attracts some big names.' 'Jazz capital of the world.' Music $30 & $5 min at table/ 1 drink min & $20 at bar (drinks from $4).

Greenwich Village Jazz Festival. In Washington Sq. Free. 'Great atmosphere and big names, including Dizzy Gillespie.'

Sweet Basil, 88 7th Ave S, 242-1785. Smallish room with nice atmosphere and pleasant food; attracts the best bands; a steep $17.50 cover, $10 min food & drink.

Village Vanguard, 178 7th Ave S, 255-4037. Sleazy, unkempt, chaotic and cramped; the perfect jazz club, always worth going to, whoever's playing. Mon Big Band,

$12, Tue-Sun $15, $10 drink min all nights.

BLUES
Dan Lynch's, 221 2nd Ave at 14th St, 677-0911. A melting-pot of blues music in an atmospheric, faded dive.

Manny's Car Wash, 1558 3rd Ave at 87th St, 369-2583. Mostly local bands playing upbeat bluesrock. Interior is like *Budweiser* commercial; 45 rpm singles, photos and beer signs adorn the walls.

Tramps, 51 W 21st St, 727-7788. The *New York Times* bills it 'the most comfortable and refined place in the city to hear genuine blues.'

ROCK, POP & INDIE
Acme Underground, 9 Great Jones Street, 420-1934. A new and increasingly popular venture, the Acme is the latest haunt of A & R scouts looking for the next big hit. Great bands and good acoustics. Cover $7-$10.

Arlene Grocery, 95 Stanton St, 358-1633. Promotes an assortment of up-and-comers and established stars, always a good scene. No cover.

CBGB's, 315 Bowery at Bleecker, 473-7743. Starts new rock bands off on the route to fame and fortune. Blondie and Talking Heads both had their debuts here. Whilst still infamous, other clubs are now eclipsing its reputation.

CLUBS
Limelight, 660 6th at 20th St, 807-7850. Get hot and sweaty in a converted church. Popular, mainly techno. Closed Mon. Mon-Thur $15, Fri & Sat $20.

Midsummer Night's Swing, at the Lincoln Center, 546-2656. Take a 6 pm lesson then dance the night away to the music of a live band. Learn to salsa, fox trot, swing or jitterbug, for a bargain $9 pp.

Palladium, 126 E 14th St, 473-7171. 'The best and flashiest disco in town.' Very state of the art; includes 50 banks of TV monitors! Doors open 9 pm.

Spy, 101 Greene, 343-9000. More bar than club, Spy is a people-watcher's paradise. Dark, palatial and luxurious, not to mention intimidating—this is the place to see and be seen. Dress in your very best finery if you want to look like you belong! Free.

Webster Hall, 125 E 11th St, 353-1600. Mainstream mega-club with several floors spinning house, hip-hop, '80s and rock 'n' pop. Look out for stilt walkers and trapese artists, for more details visit www.websterhall.com/

COUNTRY/WESTERN
Lone Star Roadhouse, 240 W 52nd St btwn Broadway & 8th, 245-2950. The 'official' Texas Embassy in the Big Apple. Offers an authentic Western experience, with 'the best in modern country-music,' R&B, rock, Texas beer, hot chili, and a dance floor just right for two-stepping the night away.

Rodeo Bar/Albuquerque Eats, 375 3rd Ave at 27th St, 683-6500. Authentic Southwest cuisine with late night country & western entertainment.

COMEDY
In the past few years, the number of comedy clubs across America has exploded, led by New York City. Since these clubs are popular, call at least a day before to reserve a table and check out prices.

Caroline's, 1626 Broadway btwn 49th & 50th Sts, 956-0101, light snacks, cabaret, two drink minimum. 'The later the set the better the comedy.'

Catch a Rising Star, 1487 1st Ave btwn 77th & 78th Sts, 794-1906. Well-named. Tomorrow's famous names get up and practise their routines. The place really comes alive in the late hours when today's stars return to help them out. Sun-Thur $8 cover, Fri-Sat $12, plus two drink min.

THEATRE

Broadway prices are high, but tickets go on sale at half price ($4 service charge) on the day of performance at the **TKTS** booth, 47th St at Times Sq. 'Be prepared for very long queues.' Wed, Sat matinee sales 10 am-2 pm, Sun noon-2 pm, evening sales 3 pm-8 pm. Get there at least 1½ hrs in advance. Discounted same day tickets also available at 2 World Trade Center, where the lines are shorter (Mon-Fri 11 am-5.30 pm, Sat 11 am-1 pm, travellers' cheques accepted). There is also always something interesting happening 'Off-Broadway' and prices are lower. **La MaMa**, 74a E 4th St, 475-7710, and the **Brooklyn Academy of Music (BAM)**, (718) 622-4433, are always good for interesting and experimental theatre. Read the *Village Voice* or Passport (available in theatres) for 'Off-off-Broadway' plays, discounts and the best theatre buys. Keep a look-out in hotels, drugstores, coffee shops, news-stands and Visitors Bureau in Times Square for 'Two Fers' (two tkts for the price of one). If you hang around the outside of a show that is not sold out, right before it begins, and timing is critical, you can bargain your way into very cheap theatre seats. Standing room is often available at the most popular shows.

CINEMA

Movie houses around Times Square and along the Upper East Side start around $8. For both art house and mainstream movies, visit the **Sony Lincoln Square**, 1998 Broadway at 68th St, 336-5000, a lavishly decorated monster of a movie house with twelve screens, plus an eight-storey-high IMAX theatre. Also worth a visit is the enormous screen at the **Ziegfeld**, 141 W 54th St, 765-7600, but for independent films and a more intimate atmosphere, try the **Angelika**, 18 W Houston at Mercer St, 995-2000. There are many other smaller and cheaper neighbourhood cinemas, however. Look them up under 'Other Movies' in the *Village Voice*, or in *Time Out New York*. For a real New York summer experience catch a free Monday night movie at **Bryant Park**, W 42nd St east of 6th Ave, for info call 382-2323. Thousands take picnics and watch old classics under the stars. Pitch your site in the afternoon to be sure of a good view. 'A great atmosphere.' The Park is also a venue for music and dance throughout the summer, call 768-1818.

Info on tickets to TV shows being taped in Manhattan can often be obtained from the Convention and Visitors Bureau in Times Square. Or just call the TV stations.

SHOPPING

Department Stores: **Macy's**, (Broadway at 34th St). New York's biggest; **Bloomingdale's**, 705-2000 (Lexington Ave & 58th St), Sak's 5th Ave, 753-4000, and **Lord and Taylor**, 391-3344, are the epitome of American Style. **Century 21**, 227-9092, 22 Cortland St btwn Broadway & Church Sts, near the World Trade Center. Bargain-hunters in the know swing through the revolving doors of this enormous store to find discounts on everything from Armani jeans to Levi's and Chanel No 5. **F.A.O. Schwarz Fifth Ave**, 767 5th Ave at 58th St, 644-9400, opposite the Plaza Hotel. Magical toy store with several storeys of fantasy-fulfilling goods. Where actor Tom Hanks danced on a pavement-sized electric keyboard in *Big*. Worth a visit just to gawp at the amazing Lego and pedal-power Porsches that cost almost as much as the real thing.

Book Stores: **Strand Bookshop**, Broadway & 12th St, 473-1452. Huge second-hand bookstore. **Barnes and Noble**, 33 E 17th St, 253-0810, 675 6th Ave, 727-1227, and on Broadway at 82nd (and other locations all over the city). The world's biggest book store with almost 13 miles of shelving and reductions on best sellers and others. **Science Fiction Bookshop**, 214 Sullivan St, 473-3010. Stocks virtually every SF book in print. **Rizzoli Books**, 57th St off 5th Ave, 759-2424, beautiful, coffee table books. **Coliseum Books**, Broadway at 57th St, 757-8381; a BUNAC favourite, open until 11 pm (10 pm Mon).

Records: **Downstairs Records**, 35 W 43rd St, 354-4684. A great place to look for that lost Deanna Durbin single. J&R Music World, 23 Park Row, 238-9000. Enormous stocks of records and tapes. Venus Records, at 13 St Mark's Place, 598-4459. 'Good for old records, collector's items. Tower Records at 74th St & Broadway, 799-2400, and 2107 Broadway and nearby **HMV Superstore** at 72nd & Broadway, 721-5900. The **Virgin Megastore** is at Times Square.

Clothing: **Canal Jean Co**, 304 Canal St, 226-1130, & 504 Broadway at Spring St Jeans, etc. (Canal St is good for everything). Orchard St Market, Lower East Side, off Canal St, Sun mornings. 'Traditional Jewish street market, lots of bustle and colour.' For **vintage** classics visit **Screaming Mimi's**, 382 Lafayette St, btwn 4th & Great Jones Sts, 677-6464; or **Cheap Jacks**, 841 Broadway, 995-0403. If you yearn for a little designer number, take a look in the **Armani Exchange**, 568 Broadway near Prince St, 431-6000, for his 'diffusion collection'—labels at affordable prices.

Outlets: Woodbury Commons, Rte 32, Central Valley, junction of Rte 17 & I-87, Harriman exit. A mind-boggling massive collection of premium outlets, including Levi, Timberland, Calvin Klein, Gap, J. Crew, and every big name designer you can think of—spend a full exhausting day there and you still won't cover it all! For buses from Port Authority, call Shortline Bus Company, 736-4700, from $25 r/t .

Markets: The **Farmer's Market**, in Union Square every summer weekend is a not-to-be-missed experience. Fresh produce, pressed juices, homebaked pies, breads, fruit and flowers—wander amongst the bustling crowds, investigate the stalls and ask to taste, the stall holders are generally very willing. Listen out for interesting street musicians—jazz quartets frequently appear.

Flea Markets: **Annexe Antiques Fair & Flea Market**, 6th Ave, btwn 25th & 26th Sts, 243-5343. Sat & Sun only. For quintessential East Village style on the cheap, try the parking lot at Ave A & 12th St, also on Sat & Sun mornings.

OUT OF DOORS

The Bronx Zoo, properly the New York Zoological Park, Fordham Rd & Southern Blvd, (718) 367-1010. Take the #5 or #2 to E 180th St. Daily 10 am-5 pm, $6.75, Weds 'til 5.30 pm, free all day Weds. Shorter hours in winter. New York's biggest zoo. All rides have additional fees. www.wcs.org/

Central Park Zoo, 830 5th Ave at 64th St, north of Plaza Hotel, 861-6030. A compact collection of 100 species, with exquisite rainforest, arctic and other exhibits. The Bronx Zoo has larger wildlife. Mon-Fri 10 am-5 pm, w/ends 10.30 am-5.30 pm, $2.

Central Park offers so much to the visitor and resident alike—a zoo, skating rinks, pools, playgrounds, horse paths, and even a maze garden—that it is impossible to conceive of life in New York without it. Visit the information center at the Dairy, west of the zoo near 64th St, 794-6564, (daily 11 am-5 pm in summer) for an excellent map and orientation to one of the world's great parks. **Belvedere Castle**, 81st St, mid-park, 360-1311, also has information and an unusual view of the park from the ramparts. May-Nov. 'Extremely helpful staff.'

Rockefeller Centre, 48th & 50th St, btwn 5th & 6th Aves, 632-3975. At Christmas the Rockefeller Plaza has a gigantic, sparkling tree, gossamer angels and a cold bite rising off the ice-rink. In summer it's a place to sit and enjoy the free lunchtime concerts. Skating from Oct, 757-5730. $7 plus $4 skate hire.

Beaches: Coney Island and **Brighton Beach**, Brooklyn, reached by D Subway—both have interesting Russian communities. **Jones Beach**, by Long Island Railroad from Penn Station to Freeport, then local bus to beach. $11 r/t.

SPORT

Chelsea Piers, 23rd St on the Hudson River, 336-6666. Sports and entertainment complex incl in-line skating, basketball, roller hockey, soccer, golf range, ice-skating, wall-climbing, shopping, eating, etc. Built in converted historic piers.

New York Historical Ride, City Hall Park Fountain, Broadway & Park Row, 802-8222. Hordes assemble for this guided tour of Wall St-area sights on summer evenings. Skaters also welcome, free.

Pro-Sports NY, 987 8th Ave, 397-6208. Bike rentals close to Central Park, 2 hrs $12, 3 hrs $15, $20 daily. May-Oct, Mon-Sat 8 am-8 pm, Sun 'til 7 pm.

Skating: **Blades, Boards & Skate**, 120 W 72nd St, 787-3911 (and other locations). In-line skates $16 for 2 hrs, $27 daily. Staff will show you the basics, but you should also scramble towards Central Park for the free weekend clinic operated by the Skate Patrol.

Wallman Ice Rink, Central Park, 360-1311. Oct-April, ice-skating all day $7.50, skate-hire $3.50.

Roller-Hockey, St Catherine's Park, 68th St btwn 1st & 2nd Aves, all are welcome on weekend mornings, whether you want to watch or play in a pick-up game.

Spectator sports: baseball in summer: the Mets at Shea Stadium in Queens, the Yankees at Yankee Stadium in the Bronx. Basketball: the Knicks at Madison Square Garden, the Nets across the Hudson in the Meadowlands. The Islanders ice hockey team plays at the Coliseum, Uniondale on Long Island, and the Rangers skate in Madison Square Garden. For tennis devotees, the US Open takes place at Flushing Meadows in Queens in early September. The Jets and Giants American football teams play at the Meadowlands in New Jersey.

INFORMATION

New York City Convention and Visitors Bureau, Times Square btwn 7th & 8th Aves, has a freephone 24 hr help and information line, 692-8474/(800) 692-84748. Counsellors available Mon-Fri 9 am-6 pm, w/ends 10 am-3 pm. Free maps, list of tourist attractions, pamphlets with walking tours of the city. www.nycvisit.com/

New York Visitor Information Centre, 435-4170, located on the Mezanine floor of Two World Trade Center. Mon-Sun 9 am-5 pm.

Traveler's Aid, 944-0013, 145 Broadway. Mon-Fri 9 am-6 pm.

Post Offices: there are dozens around the city but the major ones are, 8th Ave at 33rd St (24 hrs), 340 W 42nd St, Lexington Ave & E 45th St, in Macy's, Herald Square, beneath Rockefeller Center (enter at 620 or 610 5th Ave), and 62nd St & Broadway.

TRANSPORTATION WITHIN MANHATTAN

Subways: One of the largest and most complex subway systems in the world—714 miles of track and 468 stations, the subway is one of the quickest, cheapest ways to get around NYC and contrary to popular belief, generally safe. The information/ticket booth in every station, distributes a useful leaflet called *Manhattan Transit*. It has maps, instructions on using the subway/buses and a guide on how to reach major tourist attractions. For travel info call Transit Authority at (718) 330-1234, 6 am-9 pm daily. Basic fare: $1.50. Buy tokens or Metrocards (an automated fare card, min $5, allows free transfers to metrobuses) at the kiosk or vending machines near the turnstiles. There are express and local trains; it is very important to know which you have to take to reach your destination. Since the whole system is very badly marked, alertness and a venturesome spirit are prerequisites. Women alone should avoid using the subway at night. 'Off-hour waiting areas,' visible to the clerks at all times, are marked by yellow signs which usually hang from the ceiling. There are information centres at Penn Station, Grand Central and the Port Authority. **PATH** trains link several subway stops with points in New Jersey, fare $1.

Buses: (718) 330-1234. 3700 blue and white buses will take you to just about anywhere within the five boroughs. Fare: $1.50 in exact change (no bills or pennies), token or metrocard. Free transfers available. Exit buses from rear doors only.

Taxis: Only ride in the bright yellow taxis, others are impostors. 'Insist that the meter is put on, "private deals" don't work.' Learn the meaning of fear, as your certifiable driver squeezes the cab between two buses at 45 mph. Always tip the driver

15 percent, if you arrive alive. Expensive for one, but for three or four, economical over short distances.

ARRIVING IN/LEAVING MANHATTAN

Buses : All inter-city bus lines, including Greyhound, (800) 231-2222, use the Port Authority Bus Terminal, 8th Ave & 41st St. Arrive at least one hour early to purchase tickets. It's worth shopping around, cheaper and faster travel can sometimes be found with Trailways. Ask at information desk on street-level floor if confused about where to go—don't accept offers of help or directions from 'friendly' strangers who sidle up as you walk through the door unless you want hassle. Most will expect a tip for showing you the way and can be offensive if you say no. Though the building is new, the inhabitants late at night are a bit run down. Be careful.

Green Tortoise, 431-3348 or (800) 227-4766. 14 day bus trips Westbound to SF, LA for $329-$379 plus $81-$91 for food. May-Oct.

Trains: Penn Station, 33rd St & 8th Ave, under Madison Sq Garden. Amtrak service, (800) 872-7245, between Boston, Washington, Chicago and further south and west. Amtrak north towards Montréal and Toronto. Also Long Island Railroad, (718) 217-5477, and PATH, (800) 234-7284, operates in Manhattan and New Jersey, fare $1.

Grand Central Station, 42nd St & Park Ave. Handles Metro-North Commuter Railroad (532-4900) to NY suburbs and Connecticut.

New Jersey Transit trains, (201) 7625100, can also take you to Princeton, and Philadelphia.

Car Rental: Difficult if you're under 25, or don't have a major credit card. Try bargaining and arguing. See *Yellow Pages* for companies. Thrifty, National and Rent-a-Wreck among the cheapest. 'Most companies want driver to have licence and credit card with a sufficiently large credit limit; they won't allow splitting the cost between several people. Cash is generally useless except at international airports in conjunction with a passport.'

Car Driveaways: Automobile transporting companies come and go quickly, check *Yellow Pages* for details. For **maps** try the Rand McNally Map Store, 150 E 52nd St btwn Lexington & 3rd Aves, 758-7488, or AAA, (800) 222-4357.

Car Rides. For rides with college students, check the bulletin boards at NYU, Loeb Center, Washington Sq, or at the Columbia University Bookshop, near Columbia U. Hitchhiking is illegal on major roads in New York State, discouraged by police and highly dangerous. Single men or women absolutely mustn't do it.

J. F. Kennedy Airport, (718) 244-4444. Allow at least $1\frac{1}{2}$ hrs travel. The cheapest way: subway to Howard Beach, $1.50, then free shuttle bus to airport terminals. Otherwise: take the E/F subway trains to Union Turnpike/Kew Gardens, then catch the Q10 bus to JFK. Total cost $1.50 with metrocard bus transfer, (718) 995-4700 for info. You can also take the Long Island Railroad train from Penn Station to Jamaica, $3.50, then the Carey bus to JFK, $5. Another quick, easy way: Carey Transportation, (718) 632-0500 $13 o/w from 125 Park Ave near Grand Central Station and GrayLine from the Port Authority to JFK/La Guardia. For general info: (800) AIR-RIDE.

LaGuardia Airport, (718) 533-3400. Allow at least 1 hr travel. The cheapest way in and out: Q47 or Q33 bus to Roosevelt Ave/Jackson Heights subway station, then E train to Manhattan. Easier: Carey Transportation—$10 to 125 Park Ave near Grand Central Station and GrayLine from the Port Authority. Also, bus M60 from 116th St and Broadway or 125th St direct for $1.50.

Newark Airport, (201) 961-6000. Allow at least 1 hr travel. Olympia Airport Express to Penn Station, Grand Central Station, or World Trade Center at West St, $10. (212) 964-6233. Also to New York Port Authority $10.

AMERICA'S AMAZING THEME PARKS

America's incredible amusement parks have evolved from trolley company-sponsored carnivals, a ploy to attract passengers, to the present megaparks that entertain over 129 million visitors annually in hundreds of versions of derring-do, spine-tingling, and otherwise. If you're looking for thrills, try these:

THEME PARKS: Coney Island, New York City, (718) 372-0275. Indulge in nostalgia, of the sort featured in Woody Allen's *Radio Days* and countless other films. **DisneyWorld**, Orlando, FL, (407) 824-4321. The largest and most visited in America features The Epcot Center, Magic Kingdom, Typhoon Lagoon Waterpark, Pleasure Island nightclub extravaganza. **MGM Studios** park is nearby (407) 824-4321, currently featuring *Star Tours* ('A ride to the moon of Endor') and *Here Come the Muppets!*, *Roger Rabbit's Hollywood*, and *Tower of Terror Hotel*. **Disneyland**, Anaheim, CA, (714) 999-4000. The original Disney park and 2nd most visited, includes Space Mountain Rollercoaster, Michael Jackson's amazing 3-D movie *Captain Eo*, Star Tours. **Universal Studios** (407) 363-8000. The Orlando branch has 444 acres of rides, shows and attractions from the movie world. Rides include the virtual reality *Back to the Future*, *ET* and *Kongfrontation* and there is an *Alfred Hitchcock—the art of making movies* show.

ROLLERCOASTER PARKS: The fastest, highest and biggest US rollercoasters are in the flat Midwest. Among the most well-known: **King's Island**, Mason OH, (513) 398-5600. Eight banked turns and 70 mph speeds make this wooden rollercoaster *The Beast*, the world's longest with 7400 ft of tracks (lasting a death-defying 3 mins 40 secs). Their *King Cobra*, a stand-up looping coaster, is described as 'the ultimate elevator nightmare in forward motion.' Also here, *Top Gun*, based on the film, a 2 mins 30 secs suspended adrenelin rush. The park is sometimes hired out to private groups so call ahead to check if open. Even more terrifying, according to the *New York Times*, is the Magnum XL-200 at **Cedar Point**, Sandusky OH, (419) 627-2350. This coaster climbs 20 storeys only to hurtle down a 60-degree drop with curves at 70 mph. Cedar Point's most recent addition is Snake River Falls, with 80 ft drops at 50 degree angles, this is the world's tallest, steepest and fastest water-ride. For true rush-junkies, there is also the horrifying 65 mph *Meanstreak*. **Six Flags Great America**, Gurnee IL (708) 249-1776, offers the double-track triple helix wooden *American Eagle* which reaches speeds of over 66 mph; *Batman*, a 2 min suspended outside looping thrill-of-a-lifetime; and the triple looping *Steel Shockwave*. **Six Flags over Mid-America**, Eureka MO, (314) 938-5300 features the *Ninja*, has spirals, drops, a sidewinder and 360 degree loop. **Worlds of Fun** (and Oceans of Fun water park next-door), Kansas City MO, (816) 454-4545, has two equally thrilling coasters, the *Timber Wolf* is faster but the *Orient Express* has twists and coils and even doubles back on itself. In the south, **Six Flags in Arlington**, TX, (817) 640-8900, features *Flashback*, a sky coaster that zips you forward and backwards in corkscrew spirals; the *Texas Cliffhanger* drops a sickening 128 ft in a free fall. The *Texas Giant* drops 137 ft at 62 mph and is the second in size only to the 166 ft drop *Rattler* at the **Texas Fiesta**, San Antonio (210) 697-5050. At **Six Flags Houston**, TX, (713) 799-1234, try the *Texas Cyclone*, a long-time favourite and the *Sky Screamer*, an elevator car simulates a free fall from 10 stories. Their newly-invented *Ultra Twister* is described as 'like riding inside a giant slinky, with a 9-storey free-fall to start.' At **Six Flags over Georgia** near Atlanta, (404) 739-3400, the *Free Fall* slowly climbs 10 storeys but descends at 50 mph. Here also is the world's first triple-loop roller coaster, the *Mind Bender*. **Six Flags Magic Mountain**, Valencia, CA, (805) 255-4111. The world's largest looping rollercoaster, the *Viper*, reaches 70 mph and achieves 7 inversions 'The initial drop is truly heart-stopping!' 'They even have cameras mounted on the cars.' Other rides include the latest addition, *Superman—the Escape*, the first coaster that will break the 100mph barrier, necessitating a drop of 40 storeys! Other ideas include the *Colossus*, one of the largest double-track, wooden coasters in the world; and the *Revolution*, who's track threads through tunnels 'A knee-wobbling experience.' For still more thrills—http://www.yahoo.com/entertainment/amusement-www.   yahoo.com/entertainment/amusement—and theme parks/

WATER PARKS: Of growing popularity and ingenuity, especially in America's warmer states, are America's 136 waterparks. In Florida, **Typhoon Lagoon** in Orlando, (407) 560-4141 has the largest wave pool in the US; **Adventure Island**, Tampa, (813) 987-5660 is home of the *Tampa Typhoon*, a slide that shoots down from a height of seven stories. **Waterworld's** *Tidal Wave*, in Denver CO, (303) 427-7873, releases mammoth waves. **Water Country USA**, Williamsburg VA, (800) 343-7946, boasts *Double Rampage*, a nearly-vertical water slide of 75 ft. On the body flume, *Jet Stream*, you'll reach up to 25 mph as you round a curve—on your back. New here is *Malibu Pipeline*, a totally enclosed (dark tunnel) flume ride over 3 stories high. **Wet and Wild** parks are located in Orlando FL, Las Vegas NV, (702) 734-0088, and Dallas TX, 9817) 265-3356, and feature, among other rides, fast, helical rides on water mats (Mach 2) and sensational 7-storey free fall. Professional surfing competitions can be witnessed at **Wild River Park**, Laguna Hills CA, (714) 768-9453.

LONG ISLAND   'The Island,' as New Yorkers call it, is a 150-mile-long glacial moraine, the terminal line of the last encroachment of the Ice Age. Extending eastwards from Manhattan, it includes two of the New York City boroughs, Brooklyn and Queens, and the built-up suburban county of Nassau, though more than half its length is occupied by the more rural county of Suffolk.

Long Island Sound quietly laps against its North Shore where hills, headlands, fields and woods have attracted some of the great houses of the wealthy. Scott Fitzgerald's Gatsby partied here, and **Sagamore Hill**, outside of Glen Cove, Nassau, was the home of President Theodore Roosevelt. In **Huntington**, further east, poet Walt Whitman spent his childhood (you can visit the house, 246 Old Walt Whitman Rd, 427-5240, hours vary, tours $3) and, nearby, the Vanderbilts had an estate which they connected to New York City with their own private motorway.

The South Shore, protected by Fire Island, receives a surprisingly gentle Atlantic breeze. Its beaches are generally flat and sandy. Except right out at the **Hamptons** (Southampton and East Hampton), this shoreline has always been less exclusive than the north, but it has certainly attracted those in search of magnificent beaches which stretch in a virtually unbroken line 100 miles out from the city.

All areas of Long Island are easily accessible from Manhattan via the Long Island Railroad from Penn Station, or via the Northern State and Southern State Parkways, and the Long Island Expressway, which at the city end is so often jammed with traffic that it's known as 'the longest parking lot in the world,' but which eventually sweeps beyond the pandemonium towards the remoteness of Montauk Point's majestic lighthouse.

Long Island is fraught with social experiments, and **Jones Beach** is one of the nicest of them. With millions unemployed during the Depression, President Franklin Roosevelt found work for many and fun for more by developing this four-mile stretch of the South Shore into an excellent sandy beach. On a hot summer's weekend, or the 4th of July, up to half a million people and their cars join the seagulls for a good splash in the sun and water. Go there during the week if you want more of the beach to yourself. The Long Island Railroad, (718) 217-5477/(516) 822-LIRR, offers train/bus service between the beach and Manhattan, $11 r/t.

Fire Island, on a long sandbar further east than Jones Beach, is nicer yet, being not so much developed as preserved as a National Seashore for its natural beauty and bird life. Here is an excellent place for swimming, surfing, sunbathing, fishing, cooking over an open grill and getting up to no good in the sand dunes. Take Long Island Railroad to Bayshore, $13 r/t, then ferry (665-3600) to Ocean Beach, $11 r/t

Facing the calm waters of Gardiners Bay, **Sag Harbor**, once a whaling port, is now a pleasant town where John Steinbeck chose to end his days, and where those wealthy enough to own sailing boats moor them. The **Sag Harbor Whaling Museum**, (516) 724-0770, is on Main St. Mon-Sat 10 am-5 pm, Sun 1 pm-5 pm, $3.

There are in fact several such salty and tranquil spots at the end of the island, as well as an Indian Reservation. A few days wandering is well worth it.

Many of the place names on Long Island derive from the Indians who once lived here fishing, planting or hunting deer: the Wantaghs, Patchogues and Montauks were a few of the tribes. **Montauk Point** marks the eastern extremity of Long Island where a towering lighthouse, 668-2428, built in 1792 by order of George Washington, looks over three sides of water and offers magnificent views of the rising sun.

Curiously enough, the oldest cattle ranch in the United States is also located out here: Deep Hollow Ranch in Montauk, where visitors can go horseback riding. 'Birthplace of the American cowboy.'

The telephone area code is 516.

INFORMATION

Long Island Convention and Visitors Bureau, 951-3440/(800) 441-4601. Offer a comprehensive, free Long Island travel guide and have information centres on the South State Pkwy btwn exits 13 & 14 and on Long Island Expressway btwn exits 52 & 53.

ACCOMMODATION

Camping: There are vast campsites scattered around the State Parks in Long Island. All advise rsvs at w/ends during the summer, tent sites $13. **Wildwood State Park**, 929-4314. Campsite on Long Island Sound with path to the beach. Picnic area, baseball/volleyball courts. By train, take Long Island Railroad to River Head Station, catch a bus, 360-5700, to the campsite. Rsvs (800) 456-CAMP.

HUDSON RIVER VALLEY   Though not the key to the Northwest Passage that many early explorers hoped it would be, the Hudson has gouged a considerable valley from the mountains of upstate New York past the chalk cliffs of the Palisades to the granite slab of Manhattan, and onwards even from there, forming a great underwater trench several hundred miles long out to the edge of the continental shelf.

Much of the scenery along the valley is very beautiful and contains several historical towns such as **Tarrytown**, **West Point**, **Hyde Park** and electrifying **Sing Sing State Prison** in **Ossining**.

About 16 miles north of the George Washington Bridge on the eastern side of the Hudson, **Tarrytown** was the home of Washington Irving, creator of Rip Van Winkle, and the model for his story *The Legend of Sleepy Hollow*. His books, manuscripts and furniture are still here, in his house, on West Sunnyside Lane. The creeper-covered, white brick cottage is open to visitors, Weds-Mon 10 am-5 pm. Both Irving and Andrew Carnegie, the American Steel magnate, are buried in Sleepy Hollow Cemetery. Also worth a visit are two restored (with Rockefeller money) Dutch colonial manors, the **Philipsburg** and **Van Cortlandt Manors**. The Philipsburg Manor has a working gristmill. Entrance to the Washington Irving House, **Sunnyside**, and each of the manors is $8. For information call (914) 631-8200.

If your feet can't take any more punishment then **NY Waterway**, (800) 533-3779, offer a 2 hr cruise along the Hudson River, departing from Tarrytown ferry dock on W Main St, May-Oct Thur-Sun 1.15 pm, $12.

West Point is the site of the US Military Academy, founded in 1802 to train military officers. The Academy is the alma mater of such architects of victory as Robert E Lee, General Custer and William (sue the media) Westmoreland. Visitor Center, 938-2638, Mon-Sat 10 am-3.30 pm, Sun 11 am-3.30 pm, 1 hr guided tours, $5.

If you like brass bands and cadets walking in straight lines, this is the place for you. Museum and grounds open daily. Parade schedules can be obtained by calling the information officer at 938-2638. Close by is the 5000-acre **Bear Mountain State Park**, good for camping and hiking. Park office, 446-4736, Bear Pond Campground 947-2792, tent sites $13, $2 registration fee, rsvs recommended.

Hyde Park, a small village 80 miles north of New York City, lies on scenic Rte 9 overlooking the Hudson River. It was the home of President Franklin D Roosevelt and both he and Eleanor lie buried in the Rose Garden of the FDR Library and Museum. Nearby is the **Frederick W Vanderbilt mansion**, a Beaux-Arts-style house set in 600 glorious acres, formerly country retreat of the industrialist/philanthropist Vanderbilt. See how the big-time million-aires lived. For information call (914) 229-9115, Weds-Sun 9 am-5 pm, $8. **Hyde Park Trail**, 229-9115 is an 8.5 mile hiking and biking trail which snakes along the banks of the Hudson River, linking historic sites such as the Roosevelt Home and the Vanderbilt Mansion. Bikes are only allowed on the 2.5 mile Val-Kill section of the trail which starts at the Roosevelt Home.

Just a little further up the Hudson is the quaintish, stockade city of **Kingston**, founded as a Dutch trading post in 1614. In 1777 it became the first state capital and you can visit the restored **Senate House** on Fair St, where the senators met before fleeing for their lives in the face of a British attack. Call 338-2786, April-Oct Mon-Sat 10 am-5 pm, Sun 1 pm-5 pm, $3. There are several Colonial buildings in the area, including the Old Dutch Church on Main St.

Woodstock, a magic name from the 1960s, is nearby off Rte 28. Many an aging hippy can be seen making a nostalgic pilgrimage to the village which came to symbolise the Age of Aquarius youth movement after the rock concert to end all concerts in 1969. Imagine their surprise upon learning that the festival was actually held 57 miles south on Rte 17-B in the town of Bethel! Promoters intended to hold the festival in Woodstock but as its pop-ularity became more apparent were forced to move it to a more spacious location. Today Woodstock, the town, is as it has long been, an arts colony with lots of boutiques and summertime craft and theatrical festivals. **Hudson River Valley Tourism**, (800) 232-4782.

The Catskill Mountains, just to the west of Kingston, is reputedly the spot where Rip Van Winkle dozed off for 20 years. It's an area of hills, streams, hiking paths and ski trails. The Catskills used to be the place where wealthy New Yorkers took their holidays and there is just a touch of decay and nostalgia at the resorts, an air of having seen better days. The resorts still operate, catering to a more Eastern European Jewish clientele, hence the nickname for the area, the Borscht Belt. The area remains a marvellous retreat for walking and getting away from it all. **Catskills Regional Tourist Office**, (800) NYS-CATS.

The telephone area code is 914.

ALBANY Capital of the State of New York and named after the Duke of York and Albany who later became James II of England. Not the greatest place for the casual visitor but downtown does have some interesting architecture in the shape of the Rockefeller Empire State Plaza, a massive shopping, office and cultural complex that cost a billion dollars to build.

Situated near the juncture of the Hudson and Mohawk Rivers, and on a line with the boundary between western Massachusetts and southern Vermont, the city is a convenient halting place before visiting these states, or before exploring the local New York attractions of Saratoga, Lake George and Ticonderoga, the Adirondacks and Ausable Chasm.
The telephone area code is 518.

ACCOMMODATION
The most inexpensive accommodation during the summer is likely to be at the residence halls of the **State University of New York at Albany** (SUNYA), 442-5875, the **College of St Rose, 454-5295. Call ahead to see if a room is available.**
Ramada Inn, 300 Broadway, (800) 333-1177. S-$69, D-$79, includes full bfast. Pool, TV. Conveniently located in downtown. 'Will pick up from Amtrak.' 'Quoted one price over the phone and a more expensive one when we got there.'
Pine Haven B&B, 531 Western Ave, 482-1574. Family run Victorian house in safe neighbourhood. S-$25 w/AYH card. 'Friendly; excellent breakfast!'
YMCA, 13 State St and Connecticut, 374-9136. Men only. $23.50, $60 weekly, plus $5 key deposit.

OF INTEREST
Albany Institute of History and Art, 125 Washington Ave, 463-4478. Oldest museum in the state, some say the country. Dutch period and Hudson River School landscape paintings, 18th and 19th century furniture, etc. Wed-Fri 12 pm-5 pm, Sat-Sun noon-5. Free.
Gov Nelson A Rockefeller Empire State Plaza, btwn Madison & State Sts, centre of town. 12-building complex housing 30 state agencies and cultural facilities. The most striking feature of this ultra-brute-modern affair is the 44-storey state office tower with **observation deck** up top, panoramas 9 am-3.30 pm, free.
New York State Museum, Empire State Plaza, 474-5877. Geology, history, Indians and natural history. In the New York Metropolis Hall is a vast display of the NYC urbanisation process, including a 1940 subway car, 1929 Yellow Cab, 1930 Chinatown import-export shop and mock-up of Sesame Street stage set. Daily 10 am-5 pm. Free. 'Superb.'
Schuyler Mansion State Historic Site, 32 Catherine St, 434-0834. Built in 1762, home of Gen Philip Schuyler, revolutionary luminary. Gentleman Johnny Burgoyne was a prisoner and Schuyler's daughter Betsy married Alexander Hamilton here. Tours $3, April-Oct Wed-Sat 10 am-5 pm, Sun 1 pm-5 pm.
State Capitol, northern end of Empire State Plaza, 474-2418. Free 1 hr tours Mon-Fri 9 am-4 pm, w/ends 10 am-noon, 2 pm-4 pm. Begun in 1867, the building includes the Million Dollar Staircase. The stonecarvers of the staircase reproduced in stone not only the famous, but also their family and friends. Also Senate and Assembly Chamber. Free.

INFORMATION
Albany County Visitors Bureau, 52 Pearl St, (800) 258-3582. Mon-Fri 9 am-5 pm.
Albany Urban Cultural Center, 25 Quackenbush Sq, 434-6311. Offers walking tours around historic area of the town. Daily 10 am-4 pm.
Visitors Assistance, #106 on the Concourse, Empire State Plaza, 474-2418, 8 am-5 pm daily. Has information of free events taking place in the plaza.
Chamber of Commerce, 540 Broadway, 434-1214. Mon-Fri 9 am-5 pm.

TRAVEL
Greyhound, 34 Hamilton St, 434-8095/(800) 231-2222.

Amtrak, Albany-Rensselaer station, East St, (800) 872-7245/462-5763. The scenic *Adirondack* train passes through btwn NYC & Montréal.

SARATOGA SPRINGS   About 30 miles north of Albany, this favourite resort with its mineral springs bears a Mohawk name meaning 'place of swift water.' The waters, high in mineral content, are on tap at the Spa State Park. Abraham Lincoln's son, Bob, came here to celebrate his graduation from Harvard and found a town agog with its new racecourse. Now the nation's oldest thoroughbred racing track the **Saratoga Race Track**, 584-6200, (called America's Ascot when it opened 100 years ago) runs races every August. The **National Museum of Racing**, 584-0400, is located in town on Union Ave and Ludlow St. During August, accommodation is therefore more expensive and less available than at other times of the year. However, the **Saratoga Downtowner**, 413 Broadway, 584-6160, is a good deal D-$65, includes bfast. Pool. Read Damon Runyon's short stories before you go.

Saratoga Springs is also the summer home of the **New York City Ballet** in July, the Philadelphia Orchestra in August, and various transient rock and roll bands, all of which play at the outdoor **Saratoga Performing Arts Center**, 587-3330. Lawn seats cost $10-$12, depending on event. The Arts Center also hosts the **Saratoga Jazz Festival** in June.

Saratoga claims to have more restaurants per capita than any other American town, so finding good food won't be hard. Finding cheap food may be harder, so to savour the essence of Saratoga cuisine, buy a bag of crisps called *Saratoga Chips*, which were invented here 100 years ago.

Saratoga City Chamber of Commerce, (800) 526-8970, Mon-Fri 9 am-5 pm.

The telephone area code is 518.

LAKE GEORGE   Another 25 miles north of Saratoga Springs is the town of Lake George and the lake itself, running to Fort Ticonderoga where it constricts before opening out again as Lake Champlain.

Lake George is billed as the resort area with 'a million dollar beach,' but that refers less to the shore's quality and more to how much it probably costs to clean the place up after the tourist hordes have been by. Best to keep going through the area and on to the Adirondack Park.

Fort Ticonderoga at the other end of the lake is accessible by road or by boat from Lake George town, and is of interest to those who would know the methods by which the British Empire grew great. Constructed by the French in 1755, the British waited just long enough for it to be made comfortable before taking it over in 1756. Perhaps requiring some repairs to be made, the British then let rebel Ethan Allen grab it in 1775, and when suitable again for officers and gentlemen, Burgoyne took it back in 1777. The Yanks got the place in the end and now conduct guided tours for $8. Includes the museum and displays inside the fort where 'non-stop action' is promised all summer. Call 585-2821 for information. Daily 9 am-5 pm mid-May to mid-Oct. There is a car ferry service from Ticonderoga to Vermont.

The telephone area code is 518.

THE ADIRONDACKS   This 101 year old state park encompasses the year round resort area of the Adirondack Mountains, an enormous expanse of mountains (including the state's highest peak, Mt Macy at 5344 ft), forests and lakes stretching thousands of square miles west of Lakes George and Champlain.

Lake Placid is the sporting centre of the area and hosted the original Winter Olympics in 1932. The games came back in 1980 and left behind an Olympic ski-jump platform which still offers the best view of the area. Call 523-2202, daily 9 am-4 pm, $7. The landscape, with cross-country and downhill ski trails, large lakes and chairlifts is equally suitable for summer and winter excursions. 'Worth it for the view alone.' **Lake Placid Visitor Center**, (800) 447-5224, Mon-Fri 9 am-5 pm, w/ends 9 am-4 pm. www.lakeplacid.com/

Ausable Chasm lies on the western shores of Lake Champlain where the Ausable River has cut a vast canyon through the rock. Boats, bridges and footpaths allow the visitor to explore it. By boat, $19. 'Not worth it.' Angling fanatics can obtain **fishing licences** for the river from the Town Hall on Main St (523-2162). $11 day pass $20 five days, $35 season pass. **Adirondacks Regional Information**, (800) 648-5239. Mon-Fri 8 am-5 pm.

ACCOMMODATION
Lake Placid is generally expensive. These are the best deals:
Hotel St Moritz, 31 Saranac Ave, 523-9240. D-$50, XP-$10, includes bfast.
Northway Motel, 5 Wilmington Rd, across from junction of Rts 73 & 86, 523-3500. S-$52-$58, D-$68-$78.

OF INTEREST
Ausable Chasm, 834-7454. The tour by foot, raft and return bus costs $19. Available mid-May-mid-Oct, daily 9.30 am-4.30 pm. 'Not worth the effort. Big tourist trap full of little English grannies.'
Blue Mountain Lake, about 40 miles southwest of Lake Placid en route to Utica and Syracuse. Lake and mountain scenery, and the **Adirondack Museum**, 1 mile north, 352-7311. Shows life in the Adirondacks since colonial times, with 1890 private railroad car, log hotel, 1932 Winter Olympics memorabilia. Daily 9.30 am-5.30 pm, $12. 'Allow 4 hrs to see it all.' 'Excellent.' Lake Placid: **John Brown Farm State Historic Site**, 2 miles out of town on Rte 73; 523-3900. This is where he lies amouldering in the grave (see Harpers Ferry, West Virginia). Summer: Wed-Sat 10 am-5 pm, Sun 1 pm-5 pm, free.

THE FINGER LAKES   These slender lakes splay like the fingers of an open hand across midwestern New York. Their names Canandaigua, Seneca, Cayuga, Owasco and Skaneateles, still speak of the Indian legend that the lakes are the impress of the Great Spirit who here laid his hand upon the earth.

The region is the oldest wine-producing district in the East and offers plenty of opportunities to sample the local product. 'Very pleasant area. Go to wineries for short tour and a booze up on terrible wines.' The **Cayuga Wine Trail** will take you on a tipsy tour through 8 vineyards which sit on the lake's edge. Call the **Finger Lakes Association**, (800) 548-4386, Mon-Fri 8 am-4 pm, for this and other tourist information.

En route be sure to pitch up to the **National Baseball Hall of Fame** in the pleasant summer resort **Cooperstown**. The Hall of Fame is open May-Sept

9 am-9 pm, 607) 547-7200, $9.50. www.cooperstown.net/

Syracuse, to the east of the Finger Lakes, was the site Chief Hiawatha chose about 1570 as the capital for the Iroquois Confederacy. Around the council fires of the longhouse met the Five Nations which for two centuries dominated northeastern North America. Salt first brought the Indians and later the French and Americans to the shores of Lake Onondaga. Syracuse was founded in 1805 and for many years most of the salt used in America came from here. The New York State Fair is held annually in Syracuse from late August through Labor Day. Well-regarded Syracuse University was founded here in 1870. **Downing International Hostel, AYH**, 535 Oak St, (315) 472-5788. $10 AYH, $13 non-AYH, linen $1. Check-in Sun-Thur 7 am-9 am, 5 pm-10 pm, Fri & Sat 'til 11 pm. Rsvs recommended. 'Arrive early.'

ITHACA As the bumper sticker saying goes 'Ithaca is gorges'. Situated at the southern end of **Cayuga Lake**, Ithaca has within its boundaries many deep river gorges and spectacular waterfalls as well as hills that rival those of San Francisco in their steepness.

Perched high atop a hill overlooking Cayuga Lake is Ivy-Leaguer **Cornell University** (on a campus considered by many to be the most beautiful in the US) and also in town is well regarded, liberal arts Ithaca College. This high concentration of students (18,000 or so at Cornell) make the campus and town a fun, lively place to visit.
The telephone area code is 607.

ACCOMMODATION
Elmshade Guest House, 402 S 0lbany St, 273-1707. S-$35, D-$45-$50. Includes bfast.
Hillside Inn, 518 Stewart Ave, 272-9507, S-$45, D-$55. AC, TV, continental bfast. Rsvs recommended.
Super 8 Motel, W Clinton St at Rte 13, 273-8088. D-$55-$61.
Camping: Buttermilk Falls State Park, 273-5761, 1 mile south on Rte 13, $11.50 first night, $10 extra nights. Rsvs on (800) 456-2267.

FOOD/ENTERTAINMENT
Cornell is reputed to have the best campus food in the US. **The Ivy Room, Willard Straight Hall**, is open to all. Cornell also makes its own ice cream. The **Collegetown area** on the edge of campus is also good for eating and is the place to be when the sun goes down. Try **The Nines**, 311 College Ave, 272-1888, for live bands, beer and cheap pizza and **Collegetown Bagels** for 'cheap, yummy bagels'. Big student hang-out.
Ithaca Commons downtown has various inexpensive eateries and student bars, recommended is **The Haunt**, 273-3355, with live music on Sat.
Hal's Delicatessen, 115 N Aurora St, 273-7765. Old fashioned, but cheap, filling sandwiches ($4) etc. 'Well fed for $5.'
Moosewood Restaurant, Seneca & Cayuga Sts, 273-9610. Famous vegetarian restaurant. The owners have written several very popular vegetarian cookbooks, to be found on the kitchen shelf of every self-respecting college student. Lunch $4-$7, dinner $12-$15.

OF INTEREST
Hiking and biking are the ways to get around the area. There is a 30-mile hiking trail which loops around Ithaca and this may be a good way to start.
Cornell University: On the northeast side of town and can be reached by local bus from downtown. Take a guided tour (2556200) or just wander. Climb the **McGraw**

Tower (162 steps) for a glorious view of the lake and hills. Further vistas can be had from the **Herbert F. Johnson Museum of Art**, University Ave, (255-6464). Designed by I M Pei and dubbed 'the sewing machine,' the museum also offers excellent collections of Asian, graphic and modern art. Tues-Sun 10 am-5 pm. Free.

Cornell Plantations: The campus covers some 4000 acres including the main campus buildings, experimental farms, nature trails, Beebe Lake and **Sapsucker Woods**, a bird sanctuary. The Plantations are one of the nicest things on campus and comprise an arboretum, specialised plant collections in the botanical gardens, and a network of forest trails. Nice to wander and picnic. Off Judd Falls Rd, 255-3020.

Taughannock Falls State Park, 10 miles N on Rt 89, 387-6739. A mile-long glen with 400 ft walls and 215 ft high falls (higher than Niagara).

Buttermilk Falls State Park, south on Rte 13, 273-5761. Waterfalls and quiet pools are the main features. Good for swimming, hiking and a picnic.

INFORMATION/TRAVEL

Ithaca City Convention & Visitor Bureau, 904 East Shore Drive, (800) 284-8422.

Tompkins County Tourist Info, 272-1313. Tompkins County Transport: T-CAT 277-RIDE.

Greyhound, W State & N Fulton Sts, 272-7930/(800) 231-2222.

Local Ithaca Transit, 277-7433, covers Ithaca, Tompkins County and Cornell campus. Fares 50¢-$1.50.

Still within the Finger Lakes region is **Corning**, 50 miles southwest of Ithaca. Corningware and Steuben Glass originated here, and it's well worth spending several hours at the amazing **Corning Glass Center**, watching glass being cut, moulded, blown into any shape for every conceivable use. For information phone 974-8271. Daily 9 am-5 pm. $7. Midway between Ithaca and Corning is **Elmira** where Mark Twain wrote *Huckleberry Finn*. He is buried here—in Woodlawn cemetery.

North of Corning at the extremity of Seneca Lake is **Watkins Glen** famous for a lovely park, motor racing and discount shopping. For info on international motor racing events phone 535-2481. Various car and go-kart meets are held throughout the summer. The small town of **Hammondsport**, at the southern end of Keuka Lake, has its own salute to another form of high speed travel flying. This is the birthplace of pioneer aviator, **Glen H. Curtis** and you can visit the aviation museum named after him here.

Northeast of the Finger Lakes, on the shores of Lake Ontario, **Rochester** is a grimy, crowded city encircled by insipid flowery suburbs. But one mile east of downtown is the **George Eastman House**, (716) 271-3361, abode of the founder of Kodak and now the **International Museum of Photography**, 900 East Ave, sure to fascinate amateur and professional alike. Tue-Sat 10 am-4.30 pm, Sun 1 pm-4.30 pm. $6.50, $5 w/student ID.

The telephone area code for the whole region is 607.

NIAGARA FALLS A traditional destination for honeymoon couples in search of the awesome, and including Marilyn Monroe in *Niagara*. Mere tourists also flock to Niagara to see one of the most outstanding spectacles on the continent.

On the US side are the American Falls and the Bridal Veil Falls with a drop of 190 ft and a combined breadth of 1060 ft in a fairly straight line; the Horseshoe Falls, belonging half to the US and half to Canada, describe a deep curve 2200 ft long though with a slightly lower drop of 185 ft. About 1,500,000 gallons of water would normally plummet over the three falls each second, but the use of the river's waters to generate electricity reduces that flow by half in the summer and by three-quarters in the winter.

The Canadian side offers the better view (see Niagara Falls, Ontario), but (or therefore) it's more commercialised.

The telephone area code is 716.

ACCOMMODATION
Coachman Motel, 523 3rd St, 285-2295. Rates vary, w/ends in summer are the most expensive times, S-$69-79, D-$79-$89. 'Very good location near falls.' 'Clean and comfortable, but quite noisy, rough area of town.'

Frontier Youth Hostel (AYH), 1101 Ferry Ave, corner of Memorial Pwy, 282-3700. $11 AYH, $16 non-AYH. Rsvs recommended. 'One of the friendliest and most helpful hostels in America; clean small dormitories; 20 mins from falls.' 'Very cramped.' Closed 9.30 am-4 pm. Check in 5 pm-11 pm. 11.30 pm curfew.

Olde Niagara House, 610 4th St, 285-9408. D-$55, XP-$10, includes bfast. Check-in 7.30 am-9.30 am, 4 pm-11 pm. 'Brilliant.'

Rainbow Guest House, 423 Rainbow Blvd S, 282-1135. D-$65-$95, Q-approx $95, includes 'wonderful breakfast.' Rsvs essential. Less than 10 mins from falls. 'Friendly and welcoming.'

Scottish Inn, 5919 Niagara Falls Blvd, 283-1100. Mon-Fri July-Aug flat rate S/D-$69. Discount $5 if staying more than 1 night. TV, pool, rsvs advised. $45 tour of falls. Taxi from Falls $6. 'Clean, bright and friendly ... some rooms have waterbeds.' 'Free coffee and donuts.' 'Very cheap for a group of 4/5 people.'

YMCA, 1317 Portage Rd, (716) 2858491. $15, co-ed with a sleeping bag on a dorm room; mattress, private room $25 for men only, $10 key deposit sleeping hrs 10 pm-6 am. Exact change only for check-ins after 9 pm.'Wonderful showers, incredible security.' 30 min walk to the falls.

FOOD
'Rainbow Blvd N, variety of quite cheap places to eat Chinese, Italian, American, etc.'

OF INTEREST
Beware of tours offered by various information centres charging anything up to $60, the ones listed below see the same sights.

Aquarium, 701 Whirlpool St, 285-3575. World's first inland oceanarium, using synthetic seawater. Sea lions in summer, Dolphins and sharks in winter; $6.25. Daily summer 9 am-7 pm, otherwise 'til 5 pm.

Cave of the Winds Tour, 278-1770, on Goat Island is not really a cave. Don oilskins for a trip to the base of Bridal Veil Falls, $5.50. Daily 9.30 am-7.30 pm. 'A must see.'

Old Fort Niagara. About 6 miles north in Fort Niagara State Park, 745-7611. The fort saw service under three flags—British, French and American, and contains some pre-revolutionary buildings. Displays of drill, musket firing, etc. $6.75.

Prospect Point Observation Tower, 50¢. Deck overlooking falls adjacent to Maid of the Mist.

Seeing the Falls. Walk from the US to Canada via the **Rainbow Bridge**. Cost 25 cent each way, and don't forget your passport. If you have a restricted visa, check in with the customs people on the US side to make sure you won't have any problems returning. On either side you can don oilskins for a trip on the **Maid of the Mists** boat, 284-8897, which will carry you within drenching distance of the Falls. Cost $7.75, mid-Apr-mid-Oct until 8 pm. Boat leaves every 15 mins. 'Youth Hostel provides people staying there with a discount voucher.' 'Excellent.'

Niagara International Factory Outlets, 1900 Military Rd, (716) 297-2022. Huge 'fabulous' mall stocked to the roof with discounted name brands.

INFORMATION
Niagara Falls Convention and Visitors Information Line: 285-2400/(800) 338-7890. Mon-Fri 9 am-5 pm. Ask about the festival of lights in Nov.
Visitors Center at 4th & Niagara Sts, adjacent to bus station, 284-2000, daily 8.30 am-8.30 pm.

TRAVEL
Amtrak, twice daily, (800) 872-7245/683-8440. NB: station is two miles out of town.
Greyhound, 343 4th St, not actually a Greyhound stop, but you can get Greyhound tkts and a bus to Buffalo Greyhound Station for $1.85 (in exact change).
From/to Buffalo Airport, 632-3115, #24 bus to downtown ($1.70—$2.00 transfer), then #40 to Falls.

BUFFALO is better known for its cold snowy winters than for its tourist attractions. This is not a city to dawdle in, but it is near enough to the Falls, and is an important travel centre. If fate should cast you into the city, be sure to enjoy one nice thing Buffalo is famous for—spicy chicken wings, $3 and up for 10 at many restaurants, especially along the Elmwood strip.
The telephone area code is 716.

ACCOMMODATION
Buffalo Hostel International, 667 Main St, 852-5222. $15 p/night. Kitchen, laundry. 'Clean, well-equipped.'
Lord Amhurst, 5000 Main & High Sts, (800) 544-2200. From D-$69, Q-$83 includes bfast. Pool, laundry, game room. Rsvs advised.

FOOD
Anchor Bar, Main & High Sts, 886-8920. Where the chicken wings originated. $5-$20.

INFORMATION/TRAVEL
Convention and Tourism Division of Greater Buffalo Chamber of Commerce, 107 Delaware Ave, 852-0511/(888) 228-3369. Will advise on accommodation. Mon-Fri 8 am-5 pm.
Amtrak, 75 Exchange St, (800) 872-7245. Bus to Falls from here is $15. No public transport into Buffalo.
Greyhound Station, 181 Ellicott St, (800) 231-2222/855-7531. Bus 40 to Falls, $1.75.
Buffalo Bus and Metro. Information: 855-7211. Basic fare $1.25.

PENNSYLVANIA   *The Keystone State*

The 'Keystone State' seemed at one time destined to become one of the most powerful states in the nation, bridging the gap between North and South. The Civil War, one of the worst battles America has known was fought in the centre of the state. During the Industrial Revolution, Pennsylvania retained its prominence, with Pittsburgh as the steel-producing capital of the country. Today, as industry has migrated south, Pennsylvania's economy and population have shifted. Pittsburgh and Philadelphia, the two major cities, are enjoying a renaissance and renewed economic growth, and tourism in all parts of the state is now second only to health services in contribution to Pennsylvania's economy.

Pennsylvania is also known for its lush scenery: rolling hills; rich, meticulously cultivated farmlands; and the Appalachian Mountains, which provide good hunting, hiking, and camping.

PHILADELPHIA English Quaker William Penn founded Philadelphia in 1682, on New World land given to him by Charles II in payment for a debt. By the time of the American Revolution the City of Brotherly Love had become the second largest in the English-speaking world—it is currently the fifth largest city in the country. Both the Declaration of Independence and the Federal Constitution were signed here. For visitors interested in pursuing the Liberty Trail, Philadelphia rivals Boston in historical reminders.

In the early 1800s, when the commercial and political power moved to New York City and Washington DC, Philadelphia's stature began to wane. The early 1900s were dreary for the city, which gained the nickname 'Filthy-delphia' and became the brunt of jokes by W C Fields, who quipped that he 'spent a month in Philadelphia one day.' Asked by *Vanity Fair* magazine what he would like to have on his epitaph, he replied, 'I'd rather be in Philadelphia.'

Today Philadelphians are having the last laugh. The city is once again an important manufacturing and cultural centre, and some glamour has returned, the result of a recent urban and riverside face lift. Although one of the country's oldest cities, Philadelphia has one of the youngest populations; 40% of which is aged between 25-54 years; in addition, there are numerous universities and colleges in the area, hence plenty of restaurants, bars, pubs and clubs; and the Italian Market and Chinatown provide a special ethnic flavour. Philadelphians refer to downtown as Center City.'

Valley Forge and the Pennsylvania Dutch Country lie just to the west, and New York City is only an hour and a half away.

The telephone area code for the Philadelphia area is 215.

ACCOMMODATION
Major hotels in the city centre are worth checking for seasonal special offers which allow three or four people to take a double room for around $90, (eg. Holiday Inn, 923-8660 or City Center Hotel, 568-8300).

Bank Street Hostel, 32 S Bank St, 922-0222. $15 dorm, plus $2 for sheet sleeping bag (must use one). AC, TV, laundry, kitchen. Closed 10 am-4.30 pm. Within walking distance of all major attractions. 'The perfect hostel.' No rsvs over the phone.

B&B Connection/B&B of Philadelphia, P.O Box 21, Devon PA, 19333, (610) 688-1437 (in Philly) or (800) 448-3619 (out of Philly). email, bnb@bnbphiladelphia.com/ Rooms in and around Philadelphia, some hosts fluent in European languages. From S-$35/D-$50. Deposit of one night's rent, plus 6% required at booking. Some hosts require a two night stay. Be sure to ask about cancellation fees.

Chamounix Mansion International Youth Hostel, W Fairmount Park at end of Chamounix Dr, 878-3676. $15, plus $5 deposit and $2 sheet rental-AYH. 'Excellent, but out of the way.' 'I cannot speak highly enough of this place.' Take #38 bus from Market St. Get off at Ford & Cranston, continue on Ford, left at Chamounix to the end. 'Take food with you.'

Divine Tracy Hotel, 20 S 36th near U of Penn, 382-4310. Long list of rules: no smoking, no alcohol, no meals in rooms; women required to wear dresses or skirts w/stockings, and shorts are prohibited for either gender. But if the limitations don't bother you, the price is right: S-$33-$40, D-$20-$23 pp, shared bath, all rooms on single-sex floors. Cash or travellers cheques only.

Old First Reformed Church, 4th & Race Sts, 922-9663, central downtown. $15, mats and pillows provided, laundry, AC. July-Sept only. 'Clean, very friendly, peaceful and quiet; breakfast provided.' Doors open 5 pm-10 pm.

Several fraternity houses at the **University of Pennsylvania** offer housing to transient students. Call 898-5263 for information.

Camping: West Chester KOA, in **Embreville** on Rte 162 (just west of West Chester), 30 miles from Philadelphia, (610) 486-0447, laundry, showers, store, swimming, fishing, miniature golf, daily van trips into Philadelphia with minimum of 5 people. Tent site $22; camper cabin, $36 for two.

FOOD

The local specialities are 'hoagies,' cold subs of all kinds; 'Philly steaks,' thin slices of steak on an Italian roll with onions, catsup, mayo, green peppers, cheese ... and you name it; and soft pretzels, gigantic twists of dough freckled with salt crystals, zigzagged with mustard. All these and many more are sold everywhere on the street, especially in neighbourhoods filled with fast food stalls.

The Bourse, 111 S Independence Mall East, 625-0300, certainly the most convenient collection of eateries, in the heart of the historical area—opposite the Liberty Bell. A restored building full of interesting shops and a large variety of food stalls, including a good one for your mandatory Philly Cheesesteak. Closes at 6 pm.

Famous 4th St Delicatessen, 7005 S 4th St, (4th & Bainbridge), 922-3274. Traditional, Jewish delicatessen established in 1923. Award-winning chocolate-chip cookies.

Gold Standard Cafeteria, 3601 Locust Walk, 387-3463, on U Penn campus and near the International House. Good prices and a good place to meet people. Sept-May 8.30 am-3 pm.

Jim's Steaks, 400 South St, 928-1911. A local tradition, features mouth-watering Philly Cheesesteaks, $5, served cafeteria-style. Open into the small hours, daily.

Reading Terminal Market, 12th & Arch Sts, 922-2317. Huge Farmers Market where you can satisfy your heart's desire—from Pennsylvania Dutch breakfasts to Southern Soul Food. Try 'shoo-fly pie', a heavy, molasses-packed Pennsylvania Dutch concoction and 'the best blueberry pancakes ever!' Mon-Sat 8 am-6 pm.

Southeast China Restaurant, 1000 Arch St, 629-1888. In the centre of Chinatown. 'Good for vegetarians.' Lunch $4.50-$6, dinner $7-$10, Mon-Thur 11.30 am-11 pm, Fri & Sat til midnight, Sun noon-10 pm.

OF INTEREST

The best way to begin a tour of Philadelphia is to go first to the **National Parks Service Visitors Center**, 3rd & Chestnut Sts, 597-8974, in the 'Most Historic Square Mile in America.' Here you can arm yourself with the *Visitors' Guide Map of Philadelphia* and other free maps and literature on the city and surrounding area. Daily in summer, 9 am-6 pm. In the heart of the heritage city is the **Independence National Historical Park**, the four-block area near the Delaware River. It includes: **Carpenters Hall**, home of the first Continental Congress, and **Independence Hall**, Chestnut St btwn 5th & 6th Sts, is where the Declaration of Independence was signed. Here also is the **Liberty Bell Pavilion**, at Market St btwn 5th & 6th Sts. Independence Hall: in summer Mon-Thur 9 am-5 pm, Fri-Sun 9 am-8 pm, Liberty Bell Pavilion: daily in summer 9 am-8 pm; Carpenters Hall: Tue-Sun 10 am-4 pm; the other buildings are open daily 10 am-6 pm. After Labor Day, all buildings are open daily 9 am-5 pm. Admission to colonial buildings in the area is free.

Other historic sites within or close to the park include:

Afro-American Historical and Cultural Museum, 7th & Arch Sts, 574-0380. Tues-Sat 10 am-6 pm, Sun noon-6 pm, $4, $2 w/student ID.

Atwater Kent Museum, 15 S 7th St btwn Market & Chestnut Sts, 922-3031. Depicts Philly's growth through the centuries. Weds-Mon 10 am-4 pm; free.

Philadelphia

← N

1 Army and Navy Museum
2 Congress Building
3 Old City Hall
4 Second Bank of the United States
5 Philosophical Hall
6 Franklin Court
7 Thaddeus Kosciuszko National Memorial
8 Edgar Allen Poe National Historical Site
9 Graff House
10 Betsy Ross House
11 Atwater Kent Museum
12 Carpenters Hall
13 Independence Hall
14 Liberty Bell Pavilion

Delaware River

Schuylkill River

POPLAR STREET

FAIRMOUNT AVENUE

SPRING GARDEN

BENJAMIN FRANKLIN PARKWAY

Museum of Art

FAIRMOUNT PARK

VINE STREET

CHINA TOWN

FRANKLIN SQUARE

RACE STREET

THE GALLERY

ARCH STREET

INDEPENDENCE MALL

CHRIST CHURCH BURIAL GROUND

INDEPENDENCE NATIONAL HISTORICAL PARK

INDEPENDENCE SQUARE

WASHINGTON SQUARE

SOCIETY HILL

Academy of Fine Arts

★ GREYHOUND BUS TERMINAL

CITY HALL

BROAD STREET

CHERRY STREET

MARKET STREET

CHESTNUT STREET

WALNUT STREET

SPRUCE STREET

RITTENHOUSE SQUARE

UNIVERSITY OF PENNSYLVANIA

3rd St
4th St
5th St
6th St
7th St
8th St
9th St
10th St
11th St
12th St
13th St
15th St
16th St
17th St
18th St
19th St
20th St
21st St
22nd St
26th St
27th St
34th St

Betsy Ross House, 239 Arch St, 627-5343. Betsy Ross is said to have put together the first American flag from strips of petticoats. Tues-Sun 10 am-5 pm, free. Near this house, off 2nd Ave is **Elfreth's Alley**, 574-0560. The oldest continuously occupied residential street in America, lined with Georgian homes. House No 126 is a museum, daily 10 am-4 pm, $1.

Christ Church, on 2nd St above Market St, 922-1695, Mon-Sat 9 am-5 pm, Sun 1 pm-5 pm. Franklin and six other signatories to the Declaration of Independence are buried at **Christ Church Burial Ground**, 5th & Arch Sts.

Congress Hall, Chestnut & 6th Sts next door to Independence Hall, is where the legislature met when Philadelphia was the nation's capital.

Franklin Court, at Market btwn 3rd & 4th Sts, 592-1289. Interesting collection of buildings. A working print shop, showing Franklin's trade; a post office (daily 9 am-5 pm), where you can get your letters hand cancelled with a colonial style stamp; an underground museum which features a diorama of Franklin's life and inventions and a phone bank (you can call up Thomas Jefferson and find out what he thought of Ben).

Graff House, 7th & Market Sts, is a reconstruction of the house where Thomas Jefferson drafted the Declaration of Independence.

Penns Landing, East of Columbus Blvd, btwn Market and South Sts, 923-8181. Re-vitalised waterfront area with restaurants and shops. Free concerts in summer. Also here; **Independence Seaport Museum**, 2115 Columbus Blvd & Walnut St. 925-5439. Museum telling the story of the city's port and maritime history. Daily 10 am-5 pm. $7.50, includes tours of historic ships and working boat-building shop, museum only $5.

Old City Hall, 5th & Chestnut, was the first home of the US Supreme Court. Daily 9 am-5 pm.

Philosophical Hall, the home of the American Philosophical Society, founded by Benjamin Franklin in 1743.

Second Bank of the United States, Chestnut btwn 4th & 5th Sts, a beautiful Greek Revival building looking somewhat out of place here, has an interesting portrait collection.

Society Hill, restored colonial town houses around Spruce & 4th Sts. The name comes from the Free Society of Stock Traders, a company formed here by William Penn.

Thaddeus Kosciuszko National Memorial, 3rd & Pine Sts, where Mr K, who helped the colonists win the revolution, stayed 1797-98.

Todd House, 4th & Walnut Sts. A house that figured prominently in Philadelphia society of the 1790s and the home of Dolley Pane, who later married James Madison. Sign up at the Visitors Center, 3rd St btwn Walnut & Chestnut Sts for a tour. Free.

United States Mint, 5th & Arch Sts, 597-7350. Small museum, self-guided tour along viewing balcony, free unless you want to mint your own souvenir coin for $2. Daily 9 am-4.30 pm. No cameras.

Elsewhere in Philly: **Academy of Natural Sciences**, 19th St & Benjamin Franklin Pkwy, 299-1000, big dinosaur exhibit and tropical butterflies. Mon-Fri 10 am-4.30 pm, w/ends 10 am-5 pm, $7.75.

Edgar Allen Poe National Historic Site, 532 N 7th St, 597-8780, where Poe lived when his short stories *The Black Hat*, *Gold Bug*, and *The Telltale Heart* were published, 1843-1844. Daily 9 am-5 pm, free.

Fairmount Park, west along Benjamin Franklin Pkwy towards the Schuylkill (pronounced 'Skoo-kill') River. A beautiful riverside park of nearly 9000 acres. No less than 73 baseball diamonds, 115 all weather tennis courts, and 75 miles of walks, bike and bridle paths. Outdoor concerts, and a 90 min ride on a recreated turn-of-the century trolley to see it all. Within the park are several colonial mansions, and other attractions:

Japanese House and Gardens the grounds of the Horticultural Center, 878-5097. Visitors required to wear socks and no shoes. May-Sept Tues-Sun 11 am-4 pm, Sept & Oct w/ends only 11 am-4 pm, $2.50, $2 w/student ID.

Rodin Museum, 22nd St & Benjamin Franklin Pkwy, 763-8100. Somehow, they prised *The Thinker* and *The Burghers of Calais* away from the French. Tue-Sun 10 am-5 pm. Suggested donation, $1.

Philadelphia Museum of Art, in the centre of Fairmount Park, 763-8100, ranks as one of the world's greatest, with more than 500,000 works of art. (It's the third-largest museum in the US). See the arms & armour collection. Tue-Sun 10 am-5 pm, til 8.45 pm Weds, $7, $4 w/student ID. Sun free until 1 pm. 'Worth every penny.'

Philadelphia Zoo, 34th & Girard Sts, 243-1100, America's first, open daily 9.30 am-4.45 pm (w/ends 'til 5.45 pm), $7.50, treehouse $1 extra. www.phillyzoo.org/—a whistle stop tour of the zoo and animal houses.

Fairmount Water Works, right next to the art museum, 685-0144, home of **Philadelphia Ranger Corps Visitors Center** with info on all the sights in the park as well as trolleys and shuttles to get you there. Mon & Tues 7.30 am-4 pm, Wed-Sun 'til 7 pm.

Franklin Institute Science Museum and Fels Planetarium, 20th St & Benjamin Pkwy, 448-1200. Worth a visit. Daily 9.30 am-5 pm; planetarium show 2.15 pm daily, $7.50. $12.50 combo tkt. The complex now includes the **Mandel Future Center** and the **Omnibus Theater**, one of the world's most modern cinemas with a 4-storey screen and 3D sound, $7.50. www.fi.edu/

Germantown, 6 miles northwest of Center City and originally settled by German folk. Many old houses and fine mansions, some of distinctive German design. Among the best is **Cliveden**, dating back to 1763. Thur-Sun noon-4 pm, $6, $4 w/student ID.

Mummers Museum, 2nd & Washington Aves, 336-3050. Tue-Sat 9.30 am-5 pm, Sun noon-5 pm (Sun closing Jul & Aug), $2.50, $2 w/student ID. Hypnotic and hilarious, the Mummers—a Philly original—are hard to explain; you just have to *see*. Their New Years Day parade is legend. They also hold outdoor string band concerts Tue at 8 pm.

Pennsylvania Academy of the Fine Arts, Broad & Cherry Sts, 972-7600. Nation's oldest art museum and school. Good collection of American art dating from 1750. Mon-Sat 10 am-5 pm, Sun 11 am-5 pm. $6, $5 w/student ID, free 3 pm-5 pm Sun.

University Museum of Archaeology/Anthropology, University of Pennsylvania Campus, 33rd & Spruce Sts, 898-4000. Outstanding archaeological exhibits. Tue-Sat 10 am-4.30 pm, Sun 1 pm-5 pm, closed Sun during summer; $5, $4 w/student ID.

Curtis Center Museum of Norman Rockwell Art, 6th & Sansom Sts, 922-4345. Over 600 works including some of the famous Saturday Evening Post covers. Mon-Sat 10 am-4 pm, Sun 11 am-4 pm, $2. **Audio Walking Tour of Historic Philadelphia**, headsets and cassettes available here, $9 pp, for nicely narrated walking tour through the **Independence National Historical Park**, from 10 am daily; from 11 am Sun.

ENTERTAINMENT

Check the *Weekend* section of the Friday *Philadelphia Inquirer*. Call the Cultural Affairs Council, 972-8500, or the **Performing Arts Hotline**, 573-ARTS, for information on all types of music, theatre and dance. Half price day of show tkts are available from **Upstages**, at Liberty Place, 16th & Chestnut Sts, 893-1145. Mon-Sat 9 am-5 pm, Sun noon-5 pm.

Shampoo, 417 N 8th St, 928-6455. Unique club, cutting-edge dance music until 2 am, avant garde art and stylish jazz lounge. $5 cover.

South St, from Front to 7th and from South to Market, the old city area, is the funky end of town, with many restaurants, pubs and clubs. The area around Walnut and 38th Sts is also good for pubs.

INFORMATION

Visitors and Tourist Information Center, 16th St & JFK Blvd, 636-1666. Daily in summer 9 am-6 pm, otherwise 'til 5 pm.

Philadelphia Convention and Visitors Bureau, 1515 Market St #2020, 636-3300. Mon-Fri 8 am-5.30 pm.

National Parks Service Visitors Center, 3rd & Chestnut, 597-8974. www.liberty net.org/

Thomas Cook Currency Services, 1800 JFK Blvd, (800) 287-7362. Mon-Fri 9 am-5 pm.

Travelers Aid, 311 S Juniper St, 546-0571. Mon-Fri 8.45 am-4.45 pm, Sat 9 am-5 pm at Greyhound terminal, 238-0999.

TRAVEL

Amtrak, for intercity trains, 30th St Station, 824-1600/(800) 872-7245. To and from NYC, DC, Boston.

Greyhound, 10th & Filbert Sts, 931-4014/(800) 231-2222. To NYC, DC, $25 o/w.

PHLASH buses, 636-1666, are purple buses which run in a loop from Logan circle through center city, to waterfront, to South St and all major attractions. Bus stops are all along Benjamin Franklin Pkwy, Market St and Old City, marked by signs with PHLASH wings. $1.50 per ride or $3 all day pass. Buses run May-Sept 10 am-midnight, Sept-May 10 am-6 pm.

SEPTA, 580-7800, operates trains to suburbs from Market East Station, buses and street cars in the city. Exact fare, $1.60, transfer 40¢. Tourist-friendly day-pass available from Visitor Center, 16th St & JFK Blvd, $5 for unlimited travel on all city transit vehicles, plus o/w on the airport line. SEPTA **Welcome Line**, bus route through heart of city via a mix of historical landmarks, shopping areas and cultural attractions, 50¢. Bus #76 goes via Society Hill/South St, along Market St, to Philadelphia Museum of Art, and the Zoo in Fairmont Park, 50¢.

VALLEY FORGE/BRANDYWINE RIVER VALLEY Just east and south of Philadelphia, this is a region steeped in history and art. **Valley Forge National Historic Park**, 1-888-VISITVF, one of the nation's most solemn memorial grounds, is 20 miles west of Philadelphia. (Inquire at Visitors Bureau about buses, tours.) General Washington hibernated here along with his half-starved troops through the bitter winter of 1777-78. Loaded with Americana, including Washington's headquarters, cabins modelled after those in which the troops were billeted, and a few museums. Dogwoods blooming in spring enhance the pastoral air.

South of Valley Forge, the **Brandywine River Valley** has inspired three generations of Wyeths—NC, Andrew and Jamie—to produce a uniquely American brand of art. The **Brandywine River Museum** in **Chadds Ford**, (610) 388-2700, holds the world's largest collection of Wyeth paintings. Daily 9.30 am-4.30 pm, $5, $2.50 w/student ID. 'Highly recommended.'

PENNSYLVANIA DUTCH COUNTRY While most of the original settlers of Lancaster County have long since been absorbed into modern society, the Amish and Mennonites have retained their traditional identities in this stretch of country west of Philadelphia. Eschewing electricity and modern machinery, the 'plain people' still speak a form of Low German ('Dutch' is a derivation from 'Deutsch,' the German word for 'German'). The women in their long dresses and small caps and the bearded menfolk in sombre black suits and broad-brimmed hats continue to live as simply and contentedly as they did centuries before in southern Germany.

The Pennsylvania Dutch have always fascinated visitors, and the 1984 award-winning film *Witness* only increased the interest. In order to really understand what you are seeing, try reading *Amish Life*, by John A. Hostetler, and *A Quiet Peaceable Life*, by John L. Ruth, which provide an excellent introduction to the area and its people; another highly informative book, recommended by the Amish people themselves, is *Twenty Most Asked Questions about the Amish and Mennonites*, by Merle Good, $6.95. All are available at the **Peoples Place**, Main Street, Intercourse, 768-7171. *Note*: Restrain your cameras; the people here consider photographs to be 'graven images'.

The area lies on Hwy 30, but to avoid an excess of tourists, take to the sideroads. One good excursion is the 3 mile jaunt from **Paradise** to **Strasburg**, equally enjoyable on foot or via the old railroad. **Lancaster**, US capital-for-a-day (the day was 27 September, 1777), was a prominent city in the late 18th century; the well-preserved downtown reflects the town's colonial heritage. If you're looking for **Intercourse**, you'll find it signposted at the junction of Hwys 772 & 340 east of Lancaster.

Keep an eye out in late June and early July for the **Kutztown Folk Festival**: soap making, sauerkraut shredding, pewtering, square dancing and folklore sessions. 'The festival is a real hoe-down, straw-in-the-hair fun affair.' Call (800) 963-8824 for details.

The telephone area code is 717.

ACCOMMODATION

Accommodation is relatively inexpensive here, but in summer prices rise and the best deals go quickly. The best places to stay are the farm homes: they're cheaper, serve hearty breakfasts, and you'll learn more about your hosts. For the best information on accommodation, contact the **Mennonite Information Center**, (see below).

Benner's Home For Tourists, Bird-in-Hand, 299-2615. On main bus route from Lancaster, 2 miles from Intercourse. $22 per room (can squeeze 5 in) with private bathroom. Rsvs required.

Countryside Motel, 134 Hartman Bridge Rd, on Hwy 896, 6 miles east of Lancaster, 687-8431. S-$35, D-$40.

FOOD

Amish austerity does not extend to eating. Many restaurants in the area serve bountiful communal feasts of sausage, scrapple, pickles, beef, chow-chow, schnitz and knepp, noodles, homebaked bread, apple butter, funnel cakes and molasses shoo-fly pie.

Lancaster's **Central Market**, King & Queen Sts, 291-4723, sells produce and goodies; it's one of the best places to see what Pennsylvania Dutch food is all about. Tue & Fri 6 am-4 pm & Sat 6 am-2 pm.

OF INTEREST

Amish Village Inc., on Hwy 896, 7 miles southeast of Lancaster, 687-8511. See the Amish way of life, and tourists seeing the Amish way of life. Summer daily 9 am-6 pm, otherwise 9 am-5 pm, $5.50.

Ephrata Cloister, 12 miles north of Lancaster on Hwy 272, 733-6600, was founded and later forsaken by a German community of Seventh Day Baptists. Living as sisters and brothers, they stooped through low doorways to learn humility and walked down narrow hallways to assure themselves of the straight and narrow path. Many of their original structures of unpainted wood, now gloomy-grey with time, still stand. Mon-Sat 9 am-5 pm, Sun noon-5 pm (last tour at 4 pm), $5. There are candlelit tours on Fri & Sat evenings, in August, from 6 pm-8 pm, $5. Call 733-4811.

Historical Lancaster Walking Tours, 100 S Queen St, 653-8225. Interesting walking tour of colonial Lancaster. 1½ hr tours daily at 10 am, Tues, Fri, Sat at 10 am & 1.30 pm, $4.

Pennsylvania Farm Museum, in Landis Valley on Hwy 272, 3 miles north of Lancaster, 569-0401. Museum village with the buildings, homes, trades and tools of three centuries. Tue-Sat 9 am-5 pm, Sun noon-5 pm, $7, free w/student ID.

People's Place, Main St, Intercourse, 768-7171. Mon-Sat 9.30 am-8 pm. The self-guided tour, 'Twenty Questions,' $4. Award-winning 25 min slide documentary, *Who are the Amish?*, shown every 30 mins, 9.30 am-6.45 pm. $5.50, $4.50 combo ticket for tour and slide show. 'Worth every penny.'

Railroad Museum of Pennsylvania, Rte 741 east of Strasburg, 687-8628. Historic locos and rolling stock. Mon-Sat 9 am-5 pm, Sun noon-7 pm, closed Mon in winter, $6.

Strasburg Railroad, Rte 741 1 mile east of Lancaster on Rte 896 south, 687-7522. America's oldest short-line steam locomotive goes to and from Paradise, 45 mins. Summer Mon-Sat 10 am-7 pm, Sun noon-7 pm, $7.75.

INFORMATION/TRAVEL

Mennonite Information Center, 2209 Millstream Rd, 4½ miles east of Lancaster off Rte 30, 299-0954. Go here first. Very helpful and friendly staff who can assist you in finding accommodation, tours and background on Mennonites and Amish. Informative introductory film of the area and people. The center also has the most non-commercial tour of the area, which is a treat in this overly exploited area. Here you can hire a local Mennonite guide (2 hr min.) for a fascinating country tour of homes, barns, factories. 'Not to be missed.'

Pennsylvania Dutch Convention and Visitors Bureau, 501 Greenfield Rd, Lancaster, 299-8901. Brochures and maps. Daily 8 am-6 pm.

Amtrak, McGovern Ave, (800) 872-7245.

HARRISBURG The undistinguished capital of Pennsylvania has two out-standing features: heading west, the landscape becomes beautiful, even dramatic, where the broad Susquehanna River cuts a gap through granite bluffs and green forests; and the city is crowned with a stunning Italian Renaissance capitol dome modelled after St. Peter's in Rome (and built on graft; get the scandalous scoop from a local resident). Rockville Bridge, 4 miles west of Harrisburg, spanning the Susquehanna, is the longest and widest stone arch bridge in the world.

The Harrisburg area sprang to international attention in 1979 after the nuclear accident at nearby **Three Mile Island**, which brought into question the safety of nuclear reactors. The accident didn't scare away tourists, of course not. Tourism, in fact, increased fourfold in the area. The **TMI Visitors Center**, across from the plant near **Middletown** on Rte 441 south, 367-0518, has a fascinating description of what happened and what steps have been taken to keep it from happening again. Thurs-Sun 12 pm-4.30 pm.

Further north up the Susquehanna River lies the **Pine Creek Gorge**, otherwise called the Grand Canyon of Pennsylvania, and said to be one of the last and most extensive wilderness regions between New York and Chicago. This once industrial area has been reabsorbed into nature and, with its free-flowing river and creek-side track, is now a haven for hikers, bikers, canoeists and horseback riders alike. **Wellsboro** is the nearest town for the area and a good base for activities. Call Pine Creek Outfitters, (717) 724-3003, for more info.

East of Harrisburg, in **Hummeltown**, are the **Indian Echo Caves**, 566-8131, with impressive natural formations. Daily 9 am-6 pm; $8 for a 45 min guided tour. You can pan for gems at Gem Mill Junction, $4 a bag. There are also carriage rides for $2.

The telephone area code is 717.

HERSHEY   A company town built in 1903 by a Mennonite candy bar magnate of the same name who came up with the inspired concept of milk chocolate. The air is thick with the aroma of chocolate and almonds; the two main streets are Chocolate and Cocoa Aves, and even the streetlamps are shaped like Hershey's famous 'kisses.' A beautiful Spanish-style resort hotel, the Hotel Hershey, sits atop the town; luscious gardens surround it. **Hershey's Chocolate World** near the park entrance takes you on a 12 min ride from the cocoa bean to the candy shop (but not into the factory). May-Oct daily 9 am-7.45 pm, otherwise 9 am-5 pm. Free, plus sample, and you never leave without spending money on chocolate (there are worse fates). Call 534-4903 for more information.

Also here is **Hersheypark**, (800) 437-7439, an English, German and Pennsylvania Dutch theme park with 50 rides and enough entertainment to keep you occupied all day. Daily, 10.30 am-10 pm, $28 for the day.

GETTYSBURG   The quiet peaceful town that Gettysburg is today belies its history as the site of 51,000 casualties in 3 days in the most significant battle of the worst war America has ever known, the Civil War. On 3 July, 1863, General Robert E Lee was defeated here, and the tide turned irrevocably against the South. Lincoln came later to give his famous Address at the dedication of the National Cemetery. The battlefield is now preserved as a national military park where visitors may follow the struggle of both sides on maps and displays.

The telephone area code is 717.

ACCOMMODATION
Gettysburg has many 'Ma and Pa' motel/guest house operations, so with a little bit of searching you can find good, central, and relatively inexpensive accommodation even in the summer, the peak season.
Budget Host, 205 Steinwehr Ave, 334-3168, Bus rt 15. D-$55. Pool, morning coffee, walk to all major attractions. For rsvs call (800) 729-6564.
North of Gettysburg: Ironmonger's Mansion Youth Hostel, on Rte 223 in Pine Grove Furnace State Park, 486-7575, $10, $13, $1 sleeping sheet. Check-in 5 pm-10 pm; rsvs essential. Built in 1762, the building was an ironworks which manufactured cannonballs during the Revolutionary war. It was also part of the underground railway which sheltered escaped slaves.
Round Top Campground, south on Rte 134, 334-1565. Showers, laundry, pool and mini-golf. Tent site $15 for two, XP-$5, $20 w/hook-up.

OF INTEREST
Go directly to the **National Park Visitors Center**, on Business Rte 15, 334-1124, for complete introduction and information. Park staff are extremely knowledgeable and helpful. Here you can make arrangements for touring. You can hire a local

licensed battlefield guide for $30 for 2 hrs (AutoTour cassettes, $10.50 for 2 hrs, are available from the Wax Museum in town). Here also you can see the **Electric Map**, showing troop movements during the battle; daily 8 am-5 pm, $2. The **Cyclorama**, next door to the Visitors Center, is probably the most dramatic rendition; view this dioramic painting of Pickett's charge, augmented by a sound-and-light show, daily from 9 am-5 pm, $2.

A. Lincoln's Place Theater, 213 Steinwehr Ave, 334-6049. Here James Getty, a Lincoln scholar and look-alike, gives an intimate talk in which he, as Lincoln, recounts memories, describes events and answers any question you could possibly have about the man. Not to be missed. 'Unbelievable!' (As far as anyone knows, Getty is not related to J Gettys, the town's founder.) Summer shows Mon-Fri 8 pm; $6, $5 w/student ID.

Civil War Heritage Days, last w/end in June—1st week in July. When the town comes out to commemorate the Battle of Gettsyburg with concerts, shows and fascinating battle re-enactments involving thousands of 'troops.'

Eisenhower National Historic Site (take shuttle bus from Visitors Center), 334-1124 (same number as Gettysburg), is a farm where the President retired and died. Daily 8.30 am-4 pm; $5.25, includes shuttle, admission and tour.

National Tower, 334-6754. Daily 9 am-6.30 pm. $4.60. Let the high speed elevators whisk you up 300 ft to the top for a spectacular view of the area.

INFORMATION
National Park Visitors Center, Business Rte 15, 334-1124. Daily 8 am-6 pm.
Gettysburg Convention & Visitor Bureau, 35 Carlisle St, 334-6274. Daily 8.30 am-5 pm. Very helpful; has accommodation information.

PITTSBURGH   When Rand McNally named Pittsburgh 'the nation's most liveable city' in 1985, everyone was surprised but the Pittsburghers, for they have always had fierce pride in their city. Famous for steel and home of much of the nation's industry, Pittsburgh coughed its way through the Industrial Revolution in a perpetual cloud of smoke. After World War II it began a clean-up campaign and in recent years has emerged, blinking, into the sunlight. And an amazing transformation it is: Pittsburgh's skyline of blast furnaces, open hearths, steel mills and dramatic bridges is imposing, and the city's air is reportedly now cleaner than that of any other American Metropolis. There is some exciting architecture down at the Golden Triangle, where the Allegheny and Monongahela Rivers join to form the Ohio River. Pittsburgh's terrain is an appealing mix of plateaux and hill-sides, narrow valleys and rivers; with elevations ranging from 715 ft to 1240 ft; expect to do some climbing.

As a bizarre footnote, the former nation of Czechoslovakia was founded in Pittsburgh, of all places. In 1918, the leaders of the Czechs and the Slovaks met in the Moose Club (now the Elks Club) at Penn & Scott Place to hammer out the Pittsburgh Agreement uniting these peoples.
The telephone area code for Pittsburgh is 412.

ACCOMMODATION
Hotel and motel accommodation is expensive in the Pittsburgh area; if you have a car, you would do better to stay on the outskirts in the Monroeville and Green Tree areas. Wherever you stay in Pittsburgh reservations are advisable, particularly at the guest houses.
Days Inn, I-79 & Steubenville Pike, 922-0120. S-$46, D-$54.
Pittsburgh International Hostel—HI, 830 E Warrington Ave, 431-1267. New hostel

in a renovated bank, 10 mins to downtown and South Side. $17 members, $20 non; also some family accom. available. Closed betw 10 am and 5 pm

Point Park College, 201 Wood St, 391-4100. $15, check-in 2 pm-midnight. Students only. Ring in advance.

FOOD
The local brew is Iron City Beer, available at any bar that knows it's in Pittsburgh.

Benkovitz Seafood, 23rd & Smallman Sts, 263-3016. A market and one-time truckers' joint in the wholesale district, now moved up several pegs but keeping down its prices. Daily 9 am-5 pm.

Big Z Hamburgers, 961 Liberty Ave, 1½ blocks from Greyhound (turn right out of terminal), 566-2600. $2-$4.

Parmanti Brothers, 3 outlets in Pittsburgh on Cherry, Forbes & 18th Sts (24 hrs), 263-2142. Unique recipe grilled cheese sandwiches served with fries and coleslaw. $4-$5.50. Also soup and chili.

OF INTEREST
Pittsburgh culture was once severely neglected by the city's big-money steel magnates, who couldn't wait to get out of town to the refined air of Europe and New York's 5th Ave. The cultural life has picked up considerably since then, and Pittsburgh now boasts several fine museums and universities as well as the world-class Pittsburgh Symphony Orchestra.

Carnegie Institute, 4400 Forbes Ave, Oakland, 622-3131, wwwcipgh.org/ Encompasses two internationally-known museums: the **Museum of Art** includes masterpieces of the French Impressionists and contemporary works as well as decorative arts of the ancient world; and the **Carnegie Museum of Natural History** tells the story of the earth and man in hundreds of displays of arts, crafts and natural history, including minerals, gems and Egyptian mummies. An impressive herd of prehistoric monsters towers over strange skeleton birds. The institute is open Tue-Sat 10 am-5 pm, Sun 1 pm-5 pm; $6, $4 w/student ID. Open Mondays Jul-Aug. Plus there's the new **Andy Warhol Museum**, 117 Sandusky St, 237-8300, which is the biggest single-artist museum in the US. Wed & Sun 11 am-6 pm, Thurs-Sat 11 am-8 pm. $6, $4 w/student ID.

Carnegie Science Center, 1 Allegheny Ave, W of Three Rivers Stadium, 237-3400. This includes the former Buhl Science Center and Planetarium. Don't miss the Van de Graaf generator which spits indoor lightning several times a day (announced over loudspeakers). The new **Henry J. Buhl Jnr Planetarium** gives sky shows daily, and the **Omnimax Theater** with shows on the 79 ft domed ceiling drawing the audience into the action. $4, 40 mins. There are also tours around the WW2 *Requin* (meaning 'shark') submarine in front of the Center. Sun-Fri 10 am-6 pm, Sat 'til 9 pm. $6-$12 depending on what you opt to see.

Duquesne Incline, 1220 Grandview Ave, 381-1665, a vertical trolley from 1877 carries you 400 ft into the air for a bird's eye view of the city and its three rivers, daily 'til 12.45 am, $1 each way.

Fallingwater, southeast of Pittsburgh, 329-8501. This futuristic home-over-a-waterfall is a paragon of Frank Lloyd Wright design. Take Hwy 51 South to Uniontown, Rte 40 East to Farmington, 381 North for 12 miles (through Ohio Pyle Park) to Fallingwater on left. Tours every half hour, Tue-Sun 10 am-4 pm, $9, w/ends $13. Rsvs essential.

Frick Museum, 7227 Reynolds St, Pt Breeze, 3710600. French, Italian and Flemish Renaissance paintings. Tue-Sat 10 am-5.30 pm, Sun noon-6 pm; free. Free jazz and chamber concerts Oct-April, offers free lectures on temporary exhibits. Also the recently-restored **Clayton House** (call 371-0606 for rsvs), $6, $4 w/student ID and **Clayton Greenhouse** and **Carriage Museum**.

Nationality Classrooms at University of Pittsburgh, in the Gothic masterpiece, the

Cathedral of Learning, 624-6000. Impressive conglomeration of 23 classrooms designed in different international designs with authentic furnishings from all over the world. 'Worth a visit.' Mon-Fri 9 am-4 pm, Sat 9.30 am-3 pm, Sun 11 am-3 pm. Classrooms are locked on w/ends, but tape-recorded tour includes key; during week they are empty and quiet in the afternoon. $2.

Pittsburgh Zoo, Hill Rd, Highland Park, 665-3640. 55 acres of natural habitat show off animals that include 16 species of endangered primates. A new tropical rain forest exhibit covers 5 acres inside and 5 acres open air. 10 am-6 pm, $7.50.

White-Water Rafting on the Youghiogheny River. Day trips last 5-6 hrs and cost $35-$65 during the week, more at the w/ends. Includes orientation, lunch and guide, at **Laurel Highlands River Tours**, 329-8531, or **White Water Adventurers Inc**, 329-8850, for more info. 'A spectacular experience.'

ENTERTAINMENT

For students, **Oakland** is the place, although the **Shadyside** area still has its fair share of swing. Read *Rock Flash* and *In Pittsburgh* free from around town, to find out what's going on. Rock and pop concerts, ice shows, sports events at the **Civic Arena**, Center and Bedford Aves, downtown at Washington Plaza, 642-1800s. The arena has a vast, retractable, dome-shaped roof.

Heinz Hall, 600 Penn Ave, downtown, 392-4900/642-2062 (info line). Elegant hall named after the ketchup king. Home to the Pittsburgh Symphony Orchestra.

Shakespeare in the Park. Three Rivers Shakespeare Festival offers free outdoor performances in city parks throughout the summer, call 624-0102/624-7529 for details.

Three Rivers Stadium is home turf for the Pirates (baseball) and the Steelers (football); 321-0650 for schedule info.

INFORMATION/TRAVEL

Convention and Visitors Bureau, 4 Gateway Center, 281-7711, (800) 366-0093. Mon-Fri 9 am-5 pm.

Amtrak, Liberty Ave & Grant St, near bus terminal, 471-6170/(800) 872-7245.

Greyhound, 11th & Liberty Ave, (800) 231-2222.

TITUSVILLE The oil well business got off to a picturesque start out here in northwestern Pennsylvania. In 1859, Col Edwin Drake, right here in Titusville, sunk the first oil well in the world. The site is now **Drake Well Memorial Park**, with a working reconstruction of the original rig and a museum containing photos and artifacts of the early boom days, (814) 827-2797, daily May-Oct, 9 am-5 pm, $4.50. Park daily 8 am-dusk, Sun noon-5 pm.

THE MID-ATLANTIC

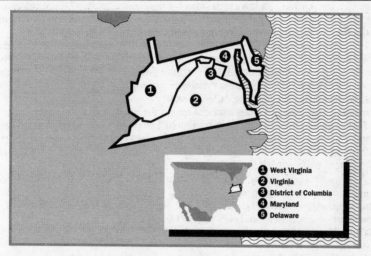

1 West Virginia
2 Virginia
3 District of Columbia
4 Maryland
5 Delaware

A visit to this region, where North meets South historically and climatically, reveals not only America's past but the shape of its future: decisions made here are the stuff from which history books are written. Focused on Washington DC, the area features politics, colonial and civil war history, legions of lawyers, and growing federal research. The nation's governmental heart has spawned technology, research and information industries in neighbouring Maryland and Virginia where there are such notable federal establishments as NASA's Goddard Spaceflight Center, the National Cancer Institute at Frederick, the Agricultural Department Research Center at Greenbelt, the National Security Agency at Fort Meade, the National Institute of Health in Bethesda, and the Smithsonian Institution in Washington. The I-270 'Technology Corridor' from Washington to Frederick now outpaces growth in California's 'Silicon Valley.'

The region has a varied climate (snowy in winter, almost monsoonal in July), brilliant springtime flora (azaleas, dogwoods, flowering cherries), and its natural resources offer recreation in all seasons. You can sail and fish on the Chesapeake Bay, hike, raft and ski in the Appalachians of Virginia and West Virginia.

DELAWARE   *The Diamond State*

This skinny triangle of a state should have been named, in all fairness, 'du Pont': it was built on the success of the du Pont empire. (The family traces its roots in Delaware soil back 200 years when Pierre Samuel du Pont de

Nemours, a counselor to Louis XVI at the time of the French Revolution, decided to visit his friend Thomas Jefferson and take an extended vacation in the US for his health.) The state is instead named for the British Lord de La Warr, who never set foot on his namesake's soil. The second smallest state in the Union, Delaware is known fancifully as the Diamond State because of its value in proportion to its size. And Delawareans proudly call it the First State, as it was the first to ratify the US Constitution in 1787.

If you're like most travellers, you will probably only pass through the northern tip of the triangle—across the Delaware Memorial Bridge (the world's largest twin span bridge) and on to Baltimore, Philadelphia, or New York City. Between the state's northern metropolis, Wilmington, and the southerly Fenwick Island lie miles of sandy coastline. Great beaches offer a variety of sporting activities and cheap camping.

Flat coastal plain covers 94 per cent of Delaware's three counties (New Castle, Kent and Sussex); there's even a cypress swamp, the most northerly in the US. Ponds and tidy farms are sprinkled across the wooden backbone of the peninsula, which levels out towards the Maryland border.

A former slave-holding state, Delaware sided with the North in the Civil War, and ran an 'underground railway,' a clandestine escape route from house cellar to house cellar that brought 3000 blacks to Northern freedom.
www.yahoo.com/Regional/US states/Delaware/
The telephone area code for the entire state is 302.

WILMINGTON   The 'Chemical Capital of the World,' and the lucky spot where Eleuthere du Pont decided to build his powder mill in 1802. Wealth, labs, factories and eyesores followed, though downtown renewal has restored the Grand Opera House. There are several other imposing or otherwise interesting historical relics to see before pushing on to Dover, 45 miles south.

ACCOMMODATION/FOOD
The Fox, 900 N Market, Wilmington, 654-9700. Cafeteria-style breakfasts, lunches and daily specials.
Red Rose Inn, 1515 N du Pont Hwy, New Castle, 328-3500. S-$40, D-$42.
Tallyho Motor Lodge, 5209 Concord Pike, N Wilmington, (800) 445-0852. S-$42, D-$48.

OF INTEREST
Brandywine Park, 571-7713. One of Delaware's 13 state parks. Along the river between Augustine and Market St Bridges. Zoo and landscaped gardens with 118 Japanese cherry trees.
Grand Opera House, 818 Market St Mall, 652-5577. Built in 1871 with an ornate cast iron facade, it now houses the **Delaware Center for the Performing Arts**.
Hagley Museum, Barley Mill Rd & Brandywine Creek, 658-2401. 225-acre complex on the site of the original du Pont black powder works, with restored granite buildings amidst wooded hillsides and huge trees; pleasant walks along the Brandywine. Exhibits, demonstrations and museum. Daily 9.30 am-4.30 pm. $9.75; $7.50 w/student ID. 'Very interesting and worthwhile.'
Longwood Gardens, 12 miles west of Wilmington at US 1 & Rte 52 near Kennett Square, PA, (610) 388-1000. Yet another du Pont hangout, formerly the country estate of industrial magnate Pierre S du Pont. Spectacular gardens 9 am-6 pm, Tue, Thur & Sat 'til 9.30 pm; conservatories 10 am-5 pm, Tue, Thurs & Sat 'til 10.15 pm.

$10, Tue, $6. Admission includes concerts and choreographed fountain displays. 'Beautiful.'

Nemours Mansion and Gardens, 3¹/₂ miles northwest on Rockland Rd, 651-6912. 102-room Louis XVI chateau look-alike with all the gear: furniture, tapestries, French gardens, built in 1910 by Alfred I duPont. Tours Tue-Sun by appt., $8, May-Nov.

New Castle, 6 miles south of Wilmington on Rte 9, is a small town full of the atmosphere and architecture of the colonial and early republic periods. Near Strand and Delaware Sts, William Penn, of Pennsylvania fame, entered his vast colonial lands. Here, a round border separates the states of Pennsylvania and Delaware; the spire of the New Castle courthouse was used as the compass point to create this odd configuration.

The Rocks, at the foot of 7th St, 1 block south of Church St. A monument marks the site of **Fort Christina**, built by the Swedish-Dutch expedition which landed here in 1638, making it the site of the first permanent settlement in the Delaware Valley. Also an 18th century log cabin survives. Free.

Wilmington & Western Railroad, Greenbank Station, off Route 41, 998-1930. Ride through historic red clay valleys on this turn-of-the-century steam train. 1 hr trip $8.

Winterthur Museum, 6 miles northwest on Rte 52, 888-4600. Once the home of Henry Francis du Pont, Winterthur now houses one of the world's greatest antique collections—nearly 200 period rooms display American decorative arts from the 17th-19th centuries. 1 hr tour, $13; 2 hr decorative arts tour, $21. Mon-Sat 9 am-5 pm, Sun noon-5 pm.

INFORMATION/TRAVEL
Statewide Delaware Visitor Information, 99 King's Hwy, Dover, (800) 441-8846.
Visitors Bureau, 1300 Market St, Suite 504, 652-4088.
Amtrak, Martin Luther King Jr Blvd & French St, (800) 872-7245.
Greyhound, Wilmington Bus Station, 101 N French St, 655-6111/(800) 231-2222. Open 24 hrs.

DOVER One of the oldest state capitals in the nation, Dover was founded in 1683 when William Penn decided to build those amenities of civilised life on the site—a prison and county courthouse.

ACCOMMODATION
Econo Lodge, 561 N du Pont Hwy, 678-8900. Pool, TV, laundry. S-$50, D-$55.
Super Lodge, 246 N du Pont Hwy, 678-0160. Pool, TV, laundry, fridge in room. S-$35, D-$45.

OF INTEREST
Delaware State Museum, 316 S Governors Ave, 739-4266. Three galleries house fascinating range of Americana. Tue-Sat 10 am-3.30 pm.
Legislative Hall, capitol building on Court St.
Old State House, the Green, 739-2466. Built in 1792, a fine example of American Georgian architecture with portraits of Delaware celebrities inside. Tue-Sat 10 am-4 pm, Sun 1.30 pm-4 pm. Go to visitor center for tickets.

INFORMATION/TRAVEL
Delaware Visitor Information, 99 King's Hwy, (800) 441-8846.
Dover Information Center, 406 Federal St, 739-4266. Information on accommodation, restaurants and museums. 'Very helpful.'
Trailways, 650 Bay Court Plaza, 734-1417. Mon-Fri 9 am-4 pm, w/ends 11 am-4 pm.

THE DELAWARE COAST Much of the coastline follows Delaware Bay out towards the Atlantic, but even the southern shore is protected from the open ocean by Fenwick Island. **Lewes** (pronounced 'Lewis') is one of the earliest European settlements in the New World. First inhabited by the Dutch, Lewes is now the traditional home of pilots who guide ships up Delaware Bay—and a charming town to explore by foot. Further south near Delaware Seashore State Park, **Rehoboth Beach** is popular with Washingtonians fleeing the US capital's cruel summer heat. 'Rehoboth', Hebrew for 'enough room' will seem ironic to anyone visiting the body-blanketed beach on a hot weekend. Nearby **Dewey Beach** and **Bethany Beach** are nearly as popular.

ACCOMMODATION/INFORMATION

In **Rehoboth**, summer rates are very high. Try searching on foot away from the ocean or contact the **Chamber of Commerce**, 73 Rehoboth Ave in the Train Station, 227-2233, for room listings.

Camping: Near Lewes, **Cape Henlopen State Park** on Rte 9, 645-8983. Sites $14 for four, XP-$2. Between Dewey and Bethany Beaches,

Delaware Seashore State Park on Rte 1 at the Indian River inlet, 227-2800. Sites $14, $24 w/hook-up. 'Friendly proprietors.'

FOOD

Rehoboth Beach is paradise for junk-food junkies, e.g. pizza at **Nicola's** on 1st St, and french fries at **Thrasher's**, on Rehoboth Ave.

DISTRICT OF COLUMBIA

WASHINGTON DC The Federal Capital lies on the Potomac River between North and South. This was Thomas Jefferson's idea, a seat of government free of regional interest, while Congress, which oversees the district, entrusted the design to Frenchman Pierre L'Enfant. In 1791 L'Enfant began work on a city he envisioned would rival the capitals of Europe, at the same time reflecting the bold qualities of the new America.

Washington today does indeed have a monumental quality, with its broad avenues, magnificent memorials, and great granite buildings in the classical style. It is only in recent, years, however, that Washington has overcome its backwater past, progressing from the days when John F Kennedy wryly described it a city of 'Northern charm and Southern efficiency,' to become the nation's focal point as it is today.

A formerly transient town, which once changed populations with every new presidential administration, DC has become a highly desirable place to live.

This is particularly evident in Georgetown, whose quaint brick houses, once quarters for slaves, poor labourers and free blacks, now command million-dollar sums. Georgetown's M and Wisconsin Streets buzz with cosmopolitan diners, flutter with art galleries and expensive boutiques. Its quiet townhouse-lined neighbourhoods are best explored on foot, and its waterfront enjoyed on warm evenings.

While Georgetown caters increasingly to well-heeled tourists and suburbanites, another section of town known as Adams-Morgan attracts a more diverse, local crowd. 'Flavour' is the password to this buzzing, international community just a few minutes walk from Dupont Circle. From Cajun to Caribbean, Ethiopian to Hispanic, you name it and you're likely to find it (at bargain prices) along 18th St at Columbia Rd. Primarily a night-time neighbourhood, things change every September on Adams-Morgan Day when the streets explode with music, dance, ethnic food and thousands of Washingtonians who, for one day at least, exchange their pinstripes for T-shirts and let it all hang out.

Indeed, despite its bureaucratic image, DC is surprisingly youthful, due in part to a large student population (Georgetown U, George Washington U, American U, Catholic U, Howard U and Johns Hopkins) and a probably larger international community that includes, besides embassies, the 6000-person World Bank, its sister the International Monetary Fund (IMF), the Inter-American Development Bank, and the Organization of American States (OAS), plus sizeable immigrant groups. Crime in DC is concentrated in the northeast, southeast and southwest quadrants. Fortunately for the traveller, the majority of attractions, accommodation, and restaurants are located in the northwest quadrant, an area that is unusually safe for a city. Even so, it is always advisable to travel with caution, especially at night.

Washington is a pleasant city to visit. There is a tremendous amount to see (mostly free), and it's cleaner and greener than most US cities, with a subway system which is graffiti-proof, efficient and safe. Some parts of the city now buzz with recently revitalized activity around the Old Post Office, the Georgetown waterfront, and 18th St in Adams-Morgan. During the summer there is a constant stream of interesting events on the huge village green known as the Mall and other locations, but beware the great heat and humidity. The most agreeable times to visit are spring, when daffodils, cherry trees, tulips, azaleas, and magnolias bloom in orderly succession; and autumn, when the air is crisp and clear, and the museums are not overflowing with tourists.

www.yahoo.com/regional/us states/washington dc/
The telephone area code for Washington is 202.

ACCOMMODATION

Housing, like most things in DC, is more expensive than in other US cities and less abundant for the budget traveller. For longer, summer stays, be prepared to search long and hard as you will be competing with the hoards of interns that descend on the Capital from May to September. The classified section of the free *City Paper*, out every Thursday evening, is packed with temporary/shared housing and summer sublets—move fast to get the one you want. Available from most convenience stores and street corner vending machines. It's also worth checking the Friday and weekend classifieds in the *Washington Post*.

Braxton Hotel, 1440 Rhode Island Ave NW, (800) 350-5799. $55 for 2. TV, easy walk to White House, Metro. 'Good value for money.'

Connecticut Woodley Guest Home, 2647 Woodley Rd NW, 667-0218. S-$49, D-$52, shared bath. Metro: Woodley Park Zoo.

Davis House, 1822 R St NW, near Dupont Circle, 232-3196. Run by Quakers, limited, bare accommodation, single $35, sharing with other $30. No smoking or drinking.

George Washington University Off-Campus Housing Office, Marvin Center, 800 21st St NW, 994-7221. Advertises apartments and shared houses available for the summer period.

Georgetown University publishes a good weekly listing of summer accommodation for rent; contact the student housing office at the Leavey Center on campus, 687-1457. You will have to go in person to get a copy of the list. In general, campus accomodation is only available to students taking summer courses at those universities—and these are usually full by the end of May. Try the notice boards at local cafes (**Chesapeake Bagel Bakery** and **Food for Thought**, both on Connecticut Ave, have boards brimming with ads), and at Union Station.

Harrington Hotel, 11th & E NW, 628-8140. Downtown, between Capitol and White House. $92 for up to 4. 'Crowded.' 'Clean, safe & central location, near all tourist attractions, self-service cafeteria downstairs.''Brilliant.'

International Guest House, 1441 Kennedy St NW, 726-5808. 4 miles from downtown. D-$25 pp, includes breakfast and tea and cookies at 9 pm. Rsvs. 'Very kind people; you can meet travellers from all over the world here.'

Kalorama Guest House, 1854 Mintwood Pl NW, 667-6369. D-$50, XP-$5 shared bath. 'We were very well looked after.'

Washington International AYH Hostel, 1009 11th St NW, 737-2333. $17 AYH, $20 non-AYH. $2 sheet rental. Open all day; organises tours and outings. Rsvs. 'All the facilities you could need—the red jelly baby of the hostel world.'

Washington International Student Center, 2451 18th St NW, 667-7681. In the heart of lively, trendy, Adams Morgan, this is the place to stay for the newly arrived foreign traveller. $15 for clean and 'cozy' dorms. Kitchen, free linen. 'Cheapest but very crowded.' 'Not a nice place for women to stay.'

William Penn House, 515 E Capitol St, 543-5560. A Quaker Seminary Center open to travellers when there are no conferences. $35 p/night (students), dorm-style room, includes a hearty breakfast. 'Clean and friendly, no smoking or alcohol.'

Camping: Greenbelt Park, Greenbelt, MD, (301) 344-3944. 6 miles north of Washington along I-95, off at exit 23. Sites $10, no showers.

HOUSING INFO:

For B&B listings: **The Bed & Breakfast League**, and **Sweet Dreams and Toast**, PO Box 9490, DC 20016, 363-7767, From S-$35, D-$50.

Bed & Bread, 3918 W St NW, north of Georgetown, 338-8163. Information and referral service for women and their families only (couples OK). From $15 a night for a shared room; can find you a room immediately in safe neighbourhood (Glover Park, above G'town). 'Excellent, people very friendly and kind.'

Foreign Student Service Council, 1930 18th St NW #21, 232-4979, has a directory of local families offering a three-day homestay to foreign students for the cultural exchange—they are not hotels! Around $20 per night. Free telephones for enquiries. 'Worth a try.' Office open Mon-Fri 9.30 am-5 pm.

FOOD

NEAR THE MALL: Restaurants are scarce around the Mall, and the distance between them can be daunting to a hungry stomach-on-legs. Most museums have a (crowded, noisy, smoky) cafeteria with some awful, overpriced, plastic food. A few government cafeterias are open to the public during working hours: '**Dept of Commerce** building cafeteria—good food at reasonable prices.' Here are some inexpensive eating alternatives, but be aware that, in the summer, all the other visitors to the nation's capital are going to head for them, too.

Au Bon Pain, at locations all over DC. Choose from a variety of different breads and design your own sandwich at little cost, half sandwiches available. Good places for BUNACers.'

The Cascades Cafe, in the basement of the **National Gallery of Art** between the old and new wings. Sat 11.30 am-4.30 pm, Sun noon-3.30 pm. Buffet (right next to the cafe) Mon-Sat 11 am-4.30 pm, Sun noon-4 pm. 'Tourist food, tourist prices, but it's beside a fabulous waterfall—it's like being a part of a sculpture. Worth a cup of coffee.' (The gallery also contains two other decent cafeterias).

International Square, 19th & K Sts, 223-1850, French, Italian, Chinese, US, etc. Sit next to indoor fountain. Mon-Fri 7.30 am-6.30 pm, Sat 10 am-6 pm.

Old Post Office Pavilion, 1100 Pennsylvania Ave. 'Large selection of reasonably priced places to eat—American, Greek, Indian, Chinese, etc,' plus entertainment. Mon-Sat 10 am-9.30 pm, Sun noon-8 pm.

Scholl's Colonial Cafeteria, 1990 K St NW in the Esplanade Mall, 296-3065, is THE place to eat for those on a budget. Good, homecooked food at unbelievably low prices. 'Try the rhubarb pie, in fact, any pie!' Mon-Sat 7 am-8 pm. Closed between meal times.

Shops at National Place, 14th St & Pennsylvania Ave, 783-9090. Plenty of inexpensive cafes. Mon-Sat 10 am-7 pm, Sun noon-5 pm.

Union Station, 1st Ave & Massachusetts, houses a wide variety of eating places, everything from bagels to rice bowls to gourmet frozen yoghurt. Easy access by Metro.

US Senate Cafeteria, 224-4249, in the basement of the Dirkson Bldg, Capitol Hill. Famous for its Bean Soup. 'Try it—you'll know where they get their wind.' Open to public 7.30 am-3 pm. Noon-1.30 pm is feeding time for congress people alone.

ETHNIC FOOD: DC excels at cheap, authentic ethnic restaurants. Generally speaking, look for **Vietnamese** food in the Vietnamese enclave in Arlington, VA (take the blue/orange metro line to the Clarendon stop); good **Ethiopian** and various types of **Hispanic** eateries in the Adams-Morgan 18th St & Columbia area; and **seafood** at Eastern Market (7th St) at the Capitol South metro stop on the blue/orange line, especially for crab cakes, and on Maine Ave along the Potomac River in SW Washington. If you're feeling spontaneous, go to Adams-Morgan and look around; it would be hard to go wrong, no matter which restaurant you stumble into. Unless otherwise noted, assume Georgetown restaurants are a rip-off. Some recommendations:

Burrito Brothers, 332-2308, 1524 Connecticut Ave. Carry-out your quesadillas, tacos, etc, a few southward steps to Dupont Circle for a Mexican picnic amid an ever-changing crowd of bike messengers, chess players, musicians, protesters. Delicious and filling for a good price. Mon-Sat 11 am-11 pm, Sun 'til 8 pm.

Cactus Cantina, 3300 Wisconsin Ave, 686-7222. The best value Mexican in DC, look for the big plastic cacti outside. Daily 11.30 am-11 pm 'til late on Saturdays.

City Lights of China, 265-6688, 1731 Connecticut Ave. Absolutely the best Chinese food in Washington; even the fortune cookies are delicious! Try pan-fried dumplings and vegetable curl. $9-$12, 'moderately expensive and worth it.'

El Tamarindo, 1785 Florida Ave NW, 328-3660. Salvadorean and Mexican dinners, $6-$9. By all accounts the cheapest and best in Adams-Morgan. Free tortillas and salsa; wash it all down with a Mexican beer.

Human Gourmet, 726 7th St NW, 783-6268. 'Amazingly friendly, reasonable Chinese restaurant.'

Meskerem, 2343 18th St NW, 462-4100. Ethiopian restaurant renowned for quality cuisine and affordable prices. Eat upstairs sitting on floor cushions, and soak in the ambience. Be warned, though; you'll struggle to your feet after filling up on a plate of *injera* and *wats*! Friendly staff and bright decor. Appetizers $7-$11, dinner $9-$12. Worth it: 'You won't have to eat for a week!' Noon-midnight daily.

Paru's, 2010 S St just north of Dupont Circle, 483-5133. Informal setting, tasty Indian food; specials $6.

Thai Room, 5037 Connecticut Ave NW at Nebraska, 244-5933. Mingle with over-landers over real Thai food. Don't get this mixed up with the more expensive and not-as-good Thai restaurant down the street.

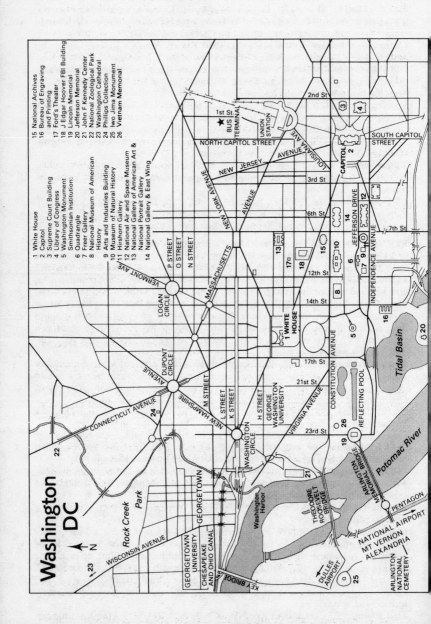

Washington DC

←N

1 White House
2 Capitol
3 Supreme Court Building
4 Library of Congress
5 Washington Monument
Smithsonian Institution:
6 Quadrangle
7 Freer Gallery
8 National Museum of American History
9 Arts and Industries Building
10 Museum of Natural History
11 Hirshorn Gallery
12 National Air and Space Museum
13 National Gallery of American Art & National Portrait Gallery
14 National Gallery & East Wing
15 National Archives
16 Bureau of Engraving and Printing
17 Ford's Theater
18 J Edgar Hoover FBI Building
19 Lincoln Memorial
20 Jefferson Memorial
21 John F Kennedy Center
22 National Zoological Park
23 Washington Cathedral
24 Phillips Collection
25 Iwo Jima Monument
26 Vietnam Memorial

PLAIN OLD AMERICAN: Plenty of these in DC, too.
The Brickskellar, 22nd St NW, btwn P & Q Sts, 293-1885. Over 600 different beers from all over the world. Good, cheap food includes (genuine) buffalo. 'Tastes like beef.' Beers from US microbreweries more potent than US domestic beers—you have been warned! Sun-Thur 11.30 am-2 am, Fri-Sat 'til 3 am.
Lindy's, 2040 Pennsylvania Ave, near Tower Records, 452-0055. Perfect for lunch. Choose from the 22 different varieties of burgers, each with vegetarian equivalent, and lots of sandwiches, $2-$6. Tempting ice-cream store in the arcade next door.
Town House Food Store, 2060 L St NW and 20th & S Sts, 659-8784. 'Substantially cheaper than People's Drug if shopping for meals. Good salad bar.' **Safeway** 2000 Wisconsin. Gigantic supermarket otherwise known as Social Safeway'; full of shoppers picking up ice-cream and each other.
Trios Restaurant, 17th & Q Sts NW, 232-6305. 'Very friendly little restaurant, serving good food. Frequented by locals. About $10 per head.'
Coffee shops have sprung up all over DC in recent years. You'll find, **Starbucks**, **Dean & Deluca**, **Foster Brothers** and **Hannibals**, to name but a few, at locations citywide.

BREAKFAST: Chesapeake Bagel Bakery, Connecticut Ave just above Dupont Circle, and at several locations throughout DC, for great coffee and bran muffins, as well as 60¢ bagels (also open for lunch and supper).
The Florida Avenue Grill, 110 Florida Ave NW, 265-1586. Taxi drivers originally frequented this small corner cafe near Howard U when it opened in the 1940s. Today it is visited by all walks of life. Breakfast is highly recommended; country ham, eggs, grits, sweet fried apples and hot biscuits. All meals under $10.
Sherrill's Bakery, 233 Pennsylvania Ave SE, Capitol Hill, 544-2480, bee-hive coiffed waitresses are pros at moving food and people. Don't cross them!

ATMOSPHERE: Au Pied de Cochon, 1335 Wisconsin Ave, NW, 333-5440, Georgetown. Site of real-life spy hi-jinks involving KGB defector (or not?) and flabbergasted CIA agent. Ask a bartender for a commemorative 'Yurchenko shooter' and for the *true* tale behind the events of 4 Nov 1985. Open 24 hrs..
Food for Thought, 1738 Connecticut Ave NW, 797-1095. Vegetarian food; wholeearth music nightly. Bargain prices for substantial meals.
Kramerbooks and Afterwords Cafe, 1517 Connecticut Ave NW, 387-1400. Bookshop and cafe with jazz, folk and bluegrass music; the place to book-browse or people-watch. Order margaritas and split the atomic nachos, or chill out with a smoothie (blended ice-cream, fruit and liqueur—delicious!) 24 hrs at weekends.

SWEET TOOTH: The best ice cream in DC is **Max's Best Ice Cream**, 2416 Wisconsin Ave NW. Featuring the bestseller Orange Chocolate Chip.
Winners in the variety stakes are: **Ben & Jerry's**, Columbia & 18th St, 667-6677, and M St & Wisconsin Ave in Georgetown. Flavours include environmentally-conscious *Rainforest Crunch*.
A cool place to hang out. Open daily 8 am-11 pm, weekends 'til 1 pm.
Thomas Sweets, Wisconsin Ave & P St, Georgetown, 337-0616. Try their cinnamon ice cream if you like 'Cheerios'! No longer do 'skinny dip'.

OF INTEREST
GOVERNMENT BUILDINGS:
Botanic Garden, 1st & Maryland Aves, btwn Air and Space Museum and Capitol, 225-7099. Tired feet will enjoy a respite as you lounge on benches amid 500 varieties of orchids and other tropical flora. Daily 9 am-5 pm. Free. Metro: Federal Center SW.
Bureau of Engraving and Printing, 14th & C Sts SW, 622-2000. Manufactures money—not only all denominations of paper bills, but government bonds and

stamps as well. Free guided tours Apr-Sep, Mon-Fri 9 am-2 pm. Long wait for tour. No free samples.' Metro: Smithsonian.

Folger Library, 2nd & East Capitol Sts, behind the Jefferson Building, 544-4600. Here you'll find America's finest Shakespeare collection, including 79 copies of the First Folio (the first published edition of Shakespeare's collected works)—more copies than anyone else has. At least one is always on display. Mon-Sat 10 am-4 pm. Metro: Capitol South.

J Edgar Hoover FBI Building, Pennsylvania Ave btwn 9th & 10th Sts NW, 324-3447, named after the man they couldn't get rid of because he had the goods on them all, even though, as it turns out, the Mafia had the goods on *him*. The only way to enter the building is to go on the free 1-hr guided tours which run every 15 mins, Mon-Fri 8.45 am-4.15 pm starting from the E entrance. See various FBI labs, a fire-arms demo and mildly impressive displays of riches recovered from bad guys. 'Ugliest building in DC.' 'Disappointing.' 'Hour long queues.' Metro: Center.

Library of Congress, 1st St & Independence Ave SE, opposite Capitol, 707-5000. The largest library in the world is made up of three buildings, but the one you'll want to see is the astounding **Jefferson Building**: walls, ceilings and floors are covered with inspiring, allegorical scenes representing such popular subjects as 'Truth, Beauty,' etc.' The cumulative effect is overwhelming (west entrance on 1st St, is open for viewings of the Great Hall, 10 am-5.30 pm, Mon-Sat. Tours available, 707-8000). Among the library's holdings are a perfect copy of the Gutenberg Bible (1450), first book to be printed from moveable type; Jefferson's rough draft of the Declaration of Independence; Lincoln's drafts of the Gettysburg Address; a vast folk music collection you can listen to (by appt.); and a major portion of the books published in the US since the Civil War. Metro: Capitol South.

National Archives, 8th St & Constitution Ave NW, 501-5402. Daily from 8.45 am, Mon & Weds 'til 5 pm; Tues, Thurs, Fri 'til 9 pm, Sat 'til 4.45 pm, free. Preserves and makes available government records of enduring value, eg. Declaration of Independence, Bill of Rights, Constitution and Watergate Tapes. Metro: Archives/Navy Memorial.

Supreme Court Building, 1st St, btwn Maryland Ave & E Capitol St NE, facing the Capitol, 479-3000. Where the country's highest judicial body holds its sessions. You can see the court in session by waiting in line, but the court is usually adjourned from the last part of June until October. Mon-Fri 9 am-4.30 pm, tours 9.30 am-3.30 pm. Metro: Capitol South.

The Capitol, 225-6827, on Capitol Hill, the central point of Washington, from which the city is divided into quadrants. The city's most familiar landmark, it holds the chambers of the Senate and the House of Representatives. Of particular note are the works of Brumidi in the Great Rotunda and corridors. Introductory tour covers only the Rotunda and the Crypt, then you're left to your own devices. 'Very interesting tour, certainly worthwhile.' Most interesting part is the Senate Chamber-much smaller than you'd expect.' Summer: Mon-Fri 9.30 am-8 pm, Sat 'til 4.30 pm; otherwise 9 am-4.30 pm. Free guided tours are available from the Rotunda, daily 9.30 am-3.45 pm. When the Senate or House are in session, you need a pass to enter. Passes for the Senate Gallery can be obtained from the Appointment Desk, Senate side; for the House apply to the Doorkeeper's Office on the House side of the Capitol. Passports or photo ID required. The underground train linking the Capitol and the Senate Office Buildings is available to all. Metro: Capitol South.

Voice of America, 330 Independence Ave, 619-4700. Watch and listen to live broadcasts. 'Fascinating; not just another radio station.' Tours Tues-Thurs 10.40 am/1.40 pm/2.40 pm.

White House, 1600 Pennsylvania Ave, 456-7041. Although he chose the site, George Washington is the only president never to have slept here. The White house has been rebuilt or redesigned inside and out many times, most memorably in 1814, courtesy of the British Army who burnt it down. The structural integrity may have been most severely tested in 1829 15 years later, during Andrew Jackson's inaugural carouse (the new president's backwoods buddies nearly destroyed the place). On a tour you'll be shuffled through a few of the well-proportioned rooms and furnishings supplied by successive Mrs. Presidents. Free tours Tue-Sat 10 am-noon. 'Long, slow lines.' Tickets are only issued on the day of the tour, from the White House Visitor Center on 15th & E Sts. They start issuing them at 7 am and you *must* get there early. Metro: McPherson Sq.

MONUMENTS: The National Park Service, which runs all of DC's monuments and major parks, has an amazing web site, www.nps.gov/

The new **Franklin D Roosevelt Memorial**, 426-6841, is situated near the cherry tree walk on the Tidal Basin, W Potomac Park. Each of FDR's four terms in office are represented by a landscape of four outdoor rooms with inscribed walls and sculpted figures, surrounded by a profusion of waterfalls, trees and plants. Metro: Foggy Bottom.

Jefferson Memorial, 426-6841, on Tidal Basin south of Mall. The dome, based on Jefferson's home at Monticello, and the quiet serenity of the ionic columns create an intimate monument. See it at night, floodlit, for best effect.

Korean War Memorial, adjacent to **Lincoln Memorial Reflecting Pool**, 619-7222. Built at a cost of $18m. A sculptured row of 19 ft soldiers ready for combat, and a 164 ft mural etched with over 2000 photographic images, depicts in detail the hardship and tragedy of a war in which 54,000 Americans lost their lives. Daily 8 am-midnight. Metro: Foggy Bottom.

Lincoln Memorial, 426-6841, at the foot of the Mall, open 8 am-midnight, free. The large brooding figure, sculptured with mastery and affection, flanked by two Lincoln addresses, is an impressive sight which no visitor to the city should miss. Rather than becoming an overgrown tombstone, this memorial has evolved into a living symbol of freedom and human dignity. The **Vietnam Veterans Memorial** is just next door, a sombre granite slash in the ground that, by listing the names of all 58,000 American dead on its walls has a shockingly direct power. The faces of the visitors tell more than the memorial does. Metro: Foggy Bottom.

Theodore Roosevelt Island, Potomac Park NW, (703) 285-2598. This peaceful isle is accessed by footbridge from the car park off the northbound lane of the George Washington Pkwy. The 17 ft bronze statue of Roosevelt, champion of nature and wildlife conservation, can be seen in the Statutory Garden. The island is also home to a wildlife refuge with over 2 miles of trails. Daily 8 am-midnight. Free. Metro: Rosslyn.

Washington Monument, on the Mall at 15th, 426-6841. A 555 ft obelisk, by law the tallest structure in DC. The view at the top is splendid, but the observation room is grungy, small and usually overcrowded. Queues year round to take the ride up. Don't believe anyone who tells you that the line about ¾ of the way up the side of the monument is the 'high water mark' from spring floods (it's the point at which construction was halted during the Civil War and later resumed with a different colour of stone), and don't let anyone sell you an 'elevator pass' (it's *free*). 'Closes during thunderstorms!' Summer: daily 8 am-midnight, otherwise 9 am-5 pm. Walk down, tours of inside at 10 am and 2 pm. Metro: Smithsonian.

SMITHSONIAN INSTITUTION. The world's largest collection of museums begun by British scientist, James Smithson, who left his entire fortune (105 bags of gold) to finance it. Fifteen museums plus the National Zoo, most of these museums are on the Mall between the Capitol and the Washington Monument. There are millions of catalogued items ranging from Lindbergh's plane to Glenn's capsule, from fossils to the Hope Diamond, from moon rocks to the First Ladies' gowns. All museums are free (nominal charge for films). General hours 10 am-5.30 pm (some museums extend their hours in summer). 357-2020 for 24 hr info on new displays and museum events; for general info 357-2700. The **Arthur M. Sackler Gallery** and the **National Museum of African Art**, both 357-1729, 10th St & Independence Ave SW. Underground museums behind the Smithsonian Castle. The former houses a collection of Asian art and artifacts, while the latter is the only museum dedicated to the African arts in the US. The **Freer Gallery**, 12th St & Jefferson Dr SW, has a wonderful collection of Asian and Asian-inspired art, with an underground link to the Sackler. The **Smithsonian Castle**, the museum's original building, houses a Visitors Center with info on all there is to see and do.

Arts and Industries Building, 9th St & Jefferson Dr, has the Centennial collection from the World Exposition in 1876. Funky old place, full of old machinery, trains and stuffed stuff. Metro: Smithsonian.

Hirshhorn Museum and Sculpture Garden on the Mall at Independence Ave, has a modern art collection not to be missed. The upper floors of the controversial, donut-shaped Hirshhorn display a fine permanent collection of 20th century art (1930-1970ish); the lounge has a nice view of the Mall. But the changing exhibits in the basement are where the avant-garde action is. The theatre in the basement occasionally screens free cutting-edge films. Metro: L'Enfant Plaza.

Museum of Natural History, 10th St & Constitution Ave, is truly 'the nation's attic'— some 118 million artifacts—it even *smells* like mothballs and formaldehyde. Among warrens where you could wander for ever are wildlife dioramas, dinosaur bones, the Hope Diamond, a scale model of a blue whale, a functioning coral reef, live insects, Indian skulls with partially-healed holes, a perfect crystal ball and the world's largest stuffed elephant. Metro: L'Enfant Plaza.

National Air and Space Museum, 357-1686, next door to the Hirshhorn, is the world's most popular museum, with everything from space capsules to U2 photographs of Soviet missile sites, to the earliest planes. 'Best thing we did in Washington, take a tape-recorded tour for most benefit.' 'A must.' See the 'mind-blowing' films such as *To Fly* and *The Dream is Alive* on a 5-storey screen that gives you the impression you are riding through a forest in a coach, zooming over the desert in your fighter jet or hovering outside your space capsule above the earth. Highly recommended,' check out the award-winning 'Cosmic Voyage,' $3.45, $2.20 w/student ID. Good cafe.' Metro: L'Enfant Plaza.

National Gallery of Art, 737-4215, sprawls magnificently along Constitution Ave at the upper end of the Mall. The old wing houses one of the world's great collections of Western European painting and sculpture, from the 13th century to present, and American art from colonial times. Rembrandt, French Impressionists, Flemish, Spanish, German and British artists are all represented, plus one proudly-displayed Da Vinci, the sole work by that artist on the North American continent. Connected via an underground walkway, **IM Pei's east wing** is a work of art in itself. This modern structure, formed by unexpected juxtapositions of triangles, displays the gallery's modern art. Picasso, Mondrian, Rothko, Motherwell and O'Keeffe line the walls, and magnificent changing exhibitions keep things lively. Mon-Sat, 10 am-5 pm, Sun 12.30 pm-4 pm. Metro: Archives/Navy Memorial.

National Museum of American Art & National Portrait Gallery, in the Old Patent Office Bldg, bounded by 7th & 9th, G & F Sts NW. Greek Revival architecture with beautiful vaulted galleries. The permanent collections include 200 years of American art, plus portraits of famous Americans. Also displays important photography exhibits. Free jazz/blues concerts in the summer. Metro: Gallery Place/Chinatown.

National Museum of American History, 357-1300, across the Mall at 12th St & Constitution Ave, has all sorts of Americana including Dorothy's ruby slippers, Fonzie's leather jacket, and Archie Bunker's chair. The original 'Star-Spangled Banner,' immortalized by Francis Scott Key, comes out to the blare of trumpets every hour on the half hour. 'A delve into the realms of American culture!' Don't miss the Information Technology exhibit. Metro: L'Enfant Plaza.

National Postal Museum, City Post Office Building, Massachusetts Ave & North Capitol St NE, 357-1729. The newest addition to the Smithsonian empire is a fascinating paeon to not only the lowly stamp, but also the way the postal system has helped to define the country. Metro: Union Station.

National Zoological Park in Rock Creek Park, entrances along the 3000 block of Connecticut Ave NW, 673-4800. Giant pandas are the pride of the zoo, along with Golden Lion, Tamarinds, and a fabulous wetlands exhibit. Check out the recently opened Amazonia exhibit. Summer: 6 am-8 pm, winter 6 am-6 pm (animal houses 10 am-6 pm). Metro: Woodley Park—and follow the trail of families pushing prams.

Museum Hopping, a museum bus service is available, a $5 ticket allows unlimited travel on museum bus, free admission, and 10% discount in museum shops and some restaurants. Call 588-7470 for details.

MORE OF INTEREST

Capitol River Cruises, (301) 460-SHIP. Cruises along the historic DC waterfront start on the sweeping curve of the Potomac river at Washington Harbour Pier in Georgetown. 12 pm-9 pm daily on the hour, from pier at 31st & K Sts, $10. Also contact Spirit Harbour Cruises, 554-8000, who provide an alternative way to view the city. Two hour cruises, $24, depart at 9 am (be there at 8.30 am) from Pier 4, 6th at Water St. There is also a pleasant cruise to **Mount Vernon**.

The **Chesapeake & Ohio Canal** passes through Georgetown, and the towpath makes for good cycling, walking or jogging. Free folk and jazz concerts at the **Foundry Mall** alongside the canal on alternate summer Sundays at 1.30 pm, 866-6984. Summer barge trips from Georgetown, (301) 299-2026/(301) 413-0024 $4, 3 trips daily. Upriver the **Great Falls of the Potomac**, (301) 413-0721, are worth a look from either the MD or VA side.

Corcoran Gallery of Art, 500 17th St btwn E St & New York Ave NW, 639-1700. Extensive collection of 18th-20th century American art; European paintings, sculpture, tapestries and pottery; changing exhibits of modern art and photography. Wed-Mon 10 am-5 pm, Thur 'til 9 pm. Metro: Farragut West.

Dumbarton Oaks, 31st St btwn R & S Sts, 339-6400. Hidden away above **Georgetown** sits a discreet wonder. The museum ia a great collection of Byzantine and Mayan art, some of it in a Phillip Johnson-designed extension with truly bizarre acoustics. The gardens are simply heavenly, the design making every corner private, romantic and relaxing. The one real "must see" in DC.' Tue-Sun 2 pm-5 pm, donation asked for the gardens open daily 2 pm-6 pm.

Ford's Theater, 511 10th St NW, 347-4833. Where Lincoln was shot by John Wilkes Booth in 1865. Beautifully restored; call first to avoid rehearsals and performances if just looking. Daily 9 am-5 pm, free. Interesting talks on the half hour. Excellent museum in basement. Opposite is the house where Lincoln died the next day, open daily 10 am-5 pm, free. Metro: Metro Center.

The Harbour Front in Georgetown, a collection of expensive restaurants and bars, is interesting for its architecture and for people watching. The 'living' statues are always a talking point and access to the Potomac is most welcome, especially lovely at night, when the orchestrated fountain gushes in a colourful symphonetta. Water taxis stop here.

Holocaust Museum, 100 Raoul Wallenberg Place SW (formerly 15th St, south of the Washington Monument), 488-0400. Intense, moving, thought-provoking record of the Holocaust and its victims between 1933 and 1945. Recommended. Daily 10 am-5.30 pm, free (passes available at 10 am—get there early). Highly recommended.' Very moving, it will stay with you for the rest of your life.' Metro: Smithsonian.

John F Kennedy Center for the Performing Arts, at the bottom of New Hampshire

Ave on the Potomac, 467-4600. The finest music, drama, dance and film from the US and abroad. Some students discounts. Many free events including daily tours, 10 am-1 pm. Terrace views of the Mall, Georgetown and Rosslyn across the Potomac are gorgeous, especially at night. 'Excellent tours.' Metro: Foggy Bottom.

National Geographic Society, Explorer's Hall, 17th & M Sts, 857-7588. The world famous magazine displays some of its work with interesting exhibits showing some breathtaking photography. The world's largest free-standing globe—brings geography to life. Mon-Sat 9 am-5 pm, Sun 10 am-5 pm, Free. 'Quality museum.' Metro: Farragut North.

National Museum of Women in the Arts, 1250 New York Ave, 783-5000. One of the few museums devoted entirely to art created by women, including Mary Cassat, Georgia O'Keeffe. Mon-Sat 10 am-5 pm, Sun noon-5 pm. $3 donation. 'Worth seeing.' Metro: Metro Center

U.S Navy Memorial and Heritage Center, 701 Pennsylvania Ave, NW, 737-2300/(800) 723-3557. The outdoor memorial features an enormous, granite map of the world and its oceans, overlooked by the Lone Sailor. Free Navy band concerts Tuesday evenings in summer. The Heritage Center includes interactive exhibits and the breathtaking At Sea' film shown hourly. Daily 9.30 am-5 pm, free. Film costs $3.75, $3 w/student ID. Metro: Archives-Navy Memorial.

Old Post Office Pavilion, 1100 Pennsylvania Ave, 606-8691, has a short tour that includes a free ride in an interior glass elevator to a tower overlooking the city. Not as high as the Washington Monument—but the lines are not as long, and the breezy arches afford a much less obstructed view. Daily 8 am-10.45 pm. Entertainment at the Pavilion daily. Also free jazz, dance and music at **Freedom Plaza** across Penn. Ave, call 724-9091 for info. Metro: Metro Center.

Phillips Collection, 1600 21st NW at Q St, 387-2151. In an unprepossessing house and gallery extension sits a treasurehouse of art. While its centerpiece of Renoir's *Luncheon of the Boating Party* attracts all the tourists, go and see the Cezannes, Picassos, Delacroixs, Goyas, and a room of Rothko. Tues-Sat 10 am-5 pm, Sun noon-7 pm. $4.50, $3.25 w/student ID at w/ends, suggested donations weekdays. 'Beautifully designed; superb collection.' 'A wonderful surprise.' Metro: Dupont Circle.

The Tidal Basin, is surrounded by a ring of cherry trees, a gift from Japan in the early 1900s. The Cherry Blossom Festival takes place the first two weeks in April. The Tidal Basin Boathouse, 479-2426, rents paddleboats daily 10 am-7 pm in spring and summer; $7 for two, $14 for four.

Washington Cathedral (Cathedral Church of St Peter and St Paul), Massachusetts & Wisconsin Aves NW, 537-6200. Take the best from all the Gothic cathedrals you have ever seen, mix, stirring occasionally, and you have Washington Cathedral. Teddy Roosevelt laid the cornerstone in 1907 and it was finally completed in 1990. It *is* beautiful despite being close to architectural pastiche; and it dominates the skyline from wherever you are in DC, perched as it is on one of the city's highest points. It has gargoyles of Washington lawyers and a moonrock embedded in one of its stained glass windows. Woodrow Wilson, Admiral Dewey, and Helen Keller are interred here. Carillon concerts and organ recitals weekly; tours Mon-Sat 10 am-3.15 pm, Sun 12.30 pm-2.45 pm. Tower is open until 9 pm in summer. Metro: Tenleytown-American University.

Nearby in Arlington, VA:

Arlington National Cemetery, (703) 692-0931, where more than 218,000 people are buried, including JFK and his brother Robert. Changing of the Guard Ceremony at the **Tomb of the Unknown Soldier** takes place every half hour May-Oct; otherwise once on the hour. 'Impressive!' 'Beautifully serene—hard to believe Washington could be this peaceful.' Apr-Sep 8 am-7 pm, Oct-May 'til 5 pm. Metro: Arlington Cemetery.

Iwo Jima Memorial. A sculpture of 5 marines and a sailor hoisting an American flag on to Mt Surabachi on the island of Iwo Jima, modelled after a famous World War II photograph by Joe Rosenthal. 'Stunning, as is the view from here to Washington.' Metro: Rosslyn.

The Pentagon, (703) 695-1776, nearby, gives desperately dull tours of its gargantuan facility. Foreigners require a passport for entry. Metro: Pentagon.

Alexandria, a few miles down the George Washington Memorial Parkway, is a mini-Georgetown, a delight with over 100 18th century buildings, including the church attended by George Washington and Winston Churchill. Follow King Street east toward the water to get to the heart of the Old Town. Don't miss the unique **Torpedo Factory**, whose original purpose has been subverted by artists in search of studio space. Metro: Alexandria/King St.

Mount Vernon, 8 miles south of Alexandria via the George Washington Parkway, (703) 780-2000. Home of George Washington and a fine example of a colonial plantation house, built 1740. Original furnishings, plus key to the Bastille, etc. George and Martha are buried here, too. Daily 9 am-5 pm 1 March-31 Oct, otherwise 9 am-4 pm; $8.

North of DC:

RFK Memorial Stadium is the home of the Washington Redskins, '88 and '92 Superbowl Champs, who play here August (pre-season) -January. Tkts around $40 available from Ticketmaster, 547-9077, or go to Hecht's dept store. 'Skins fever hits the city in early August.' 'Fans are fiercely proud.' Metro: Stadium-Armory.

SPORT

Evenings on **the Mall** are a treat for sports enthusiasts. Pick-up games of softball, hockey, football, volleyball, and ultimate frisbee,' are always on the go.

Biking: DC and surrounding area is home to hundreds of miles of trails for walking and biking.

Golf: DC has two public golf courses. **The East Potomac Golf Course**, 333-4861, offers 18-hole and two 9-hole courses year round.

The Rock Creek Golf Course, 882-7332, offers two 9-hole courses, may be played as 18-holes.

Ice Skating: the small **Sculpture Gardens Ice Rink** on the Mall at Constitution Ave & 7th St NW, 371-5340, offers skating Nov-March, daily 10 am-11 pm. $5, skate rental $2.50.

Swimming: Out of the 35 outdoor and 11 indoor free public pools in DC, the indoor **Capitol East Pool**, 724-4495, the **Marie Reed Pool**, 673-7771, and the **Georgetown Pool**, 282-2366, all come highly recommended.

Tennis: The city maintains more than 50 free public tennis courts. For info and a permit, call 673-7671. At Haines Point on the Mall, there are indoor/outdoor courts available at low cost, 554-5926.

SHOPPING

Department Stores, **Hechts** at 12th & G Sts (Metro: Metro Center) and **Lord and Taylor** are the two big stores—watch out for constant sales with huge savings. Pentagon City, easily accessible on the Metro. State of the art, multi-level mall. 'Worth it just to see the building—amazing.'

Georgetown is the place to be seen shopping. Levis, Timberland, Gap, Banana Republic and assorted more interesting stores (try Commander Salamander, Second Hand Rose, upstairs at 1516 Wisconsin, and The Green Barrel on M St) are here on Wisconsin Ave but the real bargains will be elsewhere. The weekend Flea Markets on Wisconsin Ave, if you can stand the blistering heat, are like walking into an unexplored old attic, full of **bargain** Levis, antique clothing, ethnic jewellery, Pentax cameras and even electric guitars. There are insipid malls accessible by metro such as **Mazza Galleria** (Friendship Heights) and **Ballston Commons** (Ballston).

Potomac Mills, 20 miles south of DC off I-95 near Woodbridge,1 (800)-VA-MILLS. An enormous shopping mall filled with 'outlet' stores of all the major chains. Levi Strauss, Calvin Klein, Nike, Macy's, Nordstrom and others offering merchandise at warehouse prices.'Levis 501's for $25.' Mon-Sat 10 am-9.30 pm, Sun 11 pm-6 pm. Shuttle bus from DC, (703) 551-1050.

TOURS

DC Ducks, 966-3825. A land *and* water tour in a WW2 amphibious landing craft. A tour is not really necessary; most Washington sights are easily reached on foot or metro, and Arlington is an easy walk across the Potomac. Vessels depart regularly from Union Station, 11 am, 1 pm, 3 pm. 1½ tour $23.

Gray Line, 550 Tuxedo Rd, MD, (800) 862-1400. Specialises in sightseeing tours of DC and surrounding areas. Catch the bus from most major hotels and Union Station. 2 hr tour around $18.Union Station.

Old Town Trolley Tour, (301) 985 3020. A loop of DC taking in all the sites, you can hop off and on again later. $20. Non-stop tour lasts 2 hrs.

Tourmobile, 554-5100/554-7950 (24-hrs), offers Washington and Arlington Cemetery tours for $12. Mt Vernon in the spring and summer $20. Combo tours for $25.50, admission included. Passes are good for a day of unlimited reboarding and you can begin at any sight. Look for Tourmobile Sightseeing Shuttle Bus Stop sign (main ones at Washington Monument, Lincoln Memorial); buses run every 20 min. 'Convenient and easy to use.'

Water Taxi, Washington Harbor, Georgetown. Travel from G'town to the Franklin D.Roosevelt and Jefferson Memorials, and Theodore Roosevelt Island, r/t $7. Pleasant, relaxing way to travel.'

ENTERTAINMENT

For the best, most comprehensive listings and reviews of what's going on in the area, pick up a free copy of the *City Paper* Thurs (in shops and from street-corner boxes); the *Weekend* section of Friday's *Washington Post* and the NW neighbourhood paper, *The InTowner*, a free monthly paper available around Dupont Circle and Adams-Morgan.

Festivals: two major yearly events, the **Smithsonian Folklife Festival**, held around 4 July on the Mall; and **Adams-Morgan Day** (mid-Sept) on 18th St, 332-3292: Ethnic music, dance and food plus blues and gospel sounds. DC's most prominent park, a huge village green known as **the Mall**, is the grassy stage for all manner of summer entertainment. Over July 4, fireworks and fun concerts are held there (for best viewing of fireworks from the Mall, get there early or barge in at the last minute, call for times 254-3760, and take a blanket.) Weekends on the Mall see sports events, including polo.

Nightlife: In DC, much of it centres on drinking in dingy bars. Although such establishments can be good places to meet people and sample the character of Washington.

Childe Harold, 1610 20th NW, 483-6702, a center of activity in DuPont Circle; **Sign of the Whale**, 1825 M St NW, 785-1110, Wednesday night drink specials, **The Big Hunt**, 1345 Connecticut Ave, 785-2333, pizza, beer and pool.

Eclectic music/spectacles abound:

Blues Alley, off Wisconsin between M & K, Georgetown, 337-4141, showcases best jazz artists in the country. Expensive and reservations necessary, but worth the entrance charge of $10-$30. Also serves Creole cuisine.

Cafe Lautrec, 2431 18th St, 265-6436. Chic, French-style cafe/bar, easily located by the huge Lautrec painting outside. Always busy; often queues to get in.

Comedy Cafe, 1520 K St NW, 638-JOKE, attempts to provide laughs and often succeeds. $5-$10.

Dance Place, 3325 8th St NE (2 blocks from Brookland stop on the metro red line), 269-1600. Innovative modern dance performances.

The Front Page, 19th St NW, near DuPont Circle, 296-6500. 'Popular bar for Happy Hour.' (Mon-Fri 4 pm-7 pm). Cheap beer and free food. 'Good atmosphere, especially on Fridays.' Full of interns and would-be politicians.'

Kelly's Irish Times, 500 N Capitol St NW, 543-5433. The place to go for those feeling homesick—full of Brits and Irish! A fair number of Americans too: fraternity boys ('sigma chi 'til I die!'), marines, firefighters . . . the world is here. Live music; place your requests and sing along—but keep your eye on the bill. Has downstairs pub theatre, ID needed. Also worth a visit—**The Dubliner** just down the road at 4 F St or enter through the Phoenix Park hotel.

One Step Down, 2517 Pennsylvania Ave NW, 331-8863. Great jazz just over the bridge from G'town. No cover for jam sessions on weekend afternoons. Much cheaper than Blues Alley and more intimate, too. $10 cover plus two drink minimum.

The Tombs, 1226 36th St, NW, at Prospect in Georgetown, 337-6668. College bar—rowing blades on the wall—food under $10.

For dancing:

Cafe Heaven & **Cafe Hell**, 2327 18th St NW, 667-HELL. In the heart of Adams-Morgan, this two tier club/bar is heaven upstairs, hell down. Infamous '80s retro night on Thursdays—packed with interns.

Fifth Column, 915 F St NW, 393-3632. Huge converted bank with two dance floors and open air bar in between. A poseurs' paradise; come here to see and to be seen. Mon $7 cover, under-21s admitted Mon, Wed, Thurs, Fri. Thurs-Sat cover $6-$8. Expect to queue if you come late (club opens at 10 pm). House, 'industrial' and European dance music.

Babylon nextdoor, $10, Euro-techno.

The Insect Club: 627 E St, NW, 347-8884. Insect decor and cuisine (fried worm anyone?), bar/dancing/pool tables.

Kilimanjaro, 1724 California St NW, 328-3838. African dance music, calypso, reggae—with some rap thrown in. Live music at weekends; cover jumps to $10 or more. Strict dress code; no shorts, caps, etc.

9.30 Club, 930 F St NW, 3-930-930 (concert-line). It smells, it's dark, dingy and small but if indie's your thing, then this is it. Has great live music, SuperGrass, Blur, and The Charlatans have all played here, $10 at the door, local bands $5.

Trax, 80 M St SE, 488-3320. Great club, horrific area. Indie/Euro-dance. Thurs-Sun, $10 cover.

Theatre in Washington gets better and better. Look for the **Washington Theater Festival**, in July, 462-1073. Call **Ticketplace**, 1100 Pennsylvania Ave NW, 842-5387, for half price tkts on the day of a show, or on Sat for a Sun show. Cash only.

The Arena Stage, 6th & Maine Ave SW, 554-9066, has one of the finest repertory companies in the nation.

John F. Kennedy Center for the Performing Arts on the Potomac River south of Georgetown, 467-4660, has several theatres: the Opera House (ballet, plays, opera); the Eisenhower Theater (plays); the Terrace Theater; the Concert Hall, home of the world-class National Symphony; and the movie house of the American Film Institute (AFI). Students half-price for some performances.

National Theater, 1321 E St NW, 628-6161, also has some of the best performances in the city, direct from—or heading for—Broadway.

Source Theatre Company, 1835 14th St NW, 462-1073, does some powerful productions on small stages. Prices are reasonable, but be careful in this area at night. See *Washington Post* for listings. In addition, **DC Arts Center**, 462-7833, **Church St Theatre**, 265-3748, **The Shakespeare Theatre**, 393-2700, and the **Studio Theatre**, 332-3300.

Wolf Trap Park, 1624 Trap Rd, Vienna, VA, (703) 255-1868, the only US national park devoted to the arts. You can sit on the lawn or in the open-air theatre for top-notch ballet, symphonies, opera or popular music. Lawn tickets are cheaper, and you can picnic during the performance, but come early and bring a blanket. Metro: orange line to West Falls Church and pick up a shuttle to Wolf Trap for $3.50. For info call **Ticketplace**, 12th & F Sts NW, 842-5387, to purchase discount tickets on the day of a show or on Sat for a Sun show, you must pay cash.

INFORMATION
For current information on events around the city, the following numbers are useful:

Dial-a-Museum, 357-2020, info on current exhibits at the Smithsonian.

Dial-a-Park, 619-PARK, info on activities at memorials and park areas. www.nps.gov/

Travelers Aid, 1015 12th St NW, 347-0101. Also at National Airport, 684-3472, and Dulles Airport, 661-8636.

Washington DC Convention and Visitors Bureau, 1411 K St NW, 789-7038. Distributes information by mail or from its sixth floor office.

White House Visitor Center, 15th & E Sts, 7 am-5 pm, 456-7041. Stop here for maps etc. Ask for leaflets on attractions other than the White House.

TRAVEL
Confusion over the street lay-out here is forgiveable. The same address may have four different locations, one in each quadrant. Just remember that NS streets are numbered, EW streets are lettered, and the Parisian-style diagonal avenues are named after US states, one of the focal points being the Capitol, another obvious one is the White House.

Metro, 637-7000, Washington's space-age subway system is an experience in itself. Never-ending escalators descend below ground to reveal cavernous, museum-like vaults—'something out of 2001.' It whisks you in minutes to shopping and other developments that have sprung up around town. The system is clean, efficient and safe; platform walls are protected from graffiti by deep dry-moats and trains are carpeted (vacuumed daily). Cynics claim that everyone in DC could have been given a car for the money! Most places are within easy reach of a station which are identified (rather obscurely) by brown posts marked with a white 'M.' Lines are denoted by colour and end-of-line destination. Farecards cost $1.10 (more during rush hours and for longer journeys) obtained from machines before you reach the platform. One-day pass $5. Dollar bills are accepted, change given, and transfers to buses are free, get them before you board. Trains run Mon-Fri 5.30 am-midnight, Sat 8 am-midnight, Sun 10 am-midnight.

Metrobus, 673-7000, is a complex but extensive system integrated with the Metro—practically every block in the city is reachable by bus. When stuck, ask any bus-driver for assistance, they are willing to help. All buses stop every couple of blocks on their route. #30, 32, 34 & 36 are very useful for Penn Ave, Georgetown and Wisconsin Ave. Exact fares are required—'carry a wad of $1 bills.' Flat fare is $1.10.

Taxicabs are relatively inexpensive, but the system is complicated, based on a 'zone system.' For that reason, visitors are vulnerable to the small minority of cabbies who may try to overcharge. Be savvy. Ask the driver to tell you how much a ride will be, especially from the airport. By law, rates and zone information must be posted in the cab—study this to learn the system. There's a surcharge at afternoon rush-hour (4 pm-6.30 pm). Also, be sure the driver understands English before you get in the cab.

Airports: **Baltimore Washington International Airport (BWI)**, (410) 261-1000, one hour north of Washington, is served by Amtrak, (800) 872-7245, $12 o/w.

National Airport, (703) 611-2700, is close to the city and easy to get to on the Metro blue and yellow lines. Domestic flights only.

Washington Dulles International Airport, (703) 611-2700, is located about 26 miles

AMERICAN MUSIC—THE SOUND OF SURPRISE

BLUEGRASS: Washington, DC is called bluegrass capital, but this very ethnic American music is heard throughout the Midwest too. **The Birchmere**, a premiere showcase of folk music, bluegrass, country. Catch *Seldom Scene* Thur night in **Alexandria, VA**, (703) 549-5919. **The Station Inn**, Nashville, TN, (615) 255-3307, plays bluegrass six nights a week. Live bands most evenings, for progressive style, hear the *New Grass Revival*. Most bluegrass action happens at some 400+ festivals across the country. For a listing refer to *Bluegrass Unlimited*, Box 111, Broad Run, VA 22014, (703) 349-8181.

BLUES: There are good local blues bands all over the US, but **Chicago** is the blues center. Pick up a copy of *The Reader* for info. Don't miss **B.L.U.E.S**, (312) 528-1012, with low-down blues, fresh acts; hot, smoky, and cramped, or sister club **B.L.U.E.S etcetera**, 525-8989, for bigger names. Try also **Rosa's**, (312) 342-0452, small, not as well known, but great music. Don't miss the free **Blues Fest** in early June, (312) 744-3315. If appearances count for anything, **Benny's, New Orleans, LA** , a bare-bones shack, wins hand-down for inspiring the blues. For general current info, read *Living Blues*, published by the University of Mississippi. **City Blues**, DC, (202) 232-2300, for atmosphere or **Madam's Organ**, 667-5370. Raunchy live blues, jazz and eclectic clientele.' Oakland, CA is also filled with blues bars.

COUNTRY: Branson, MO, has become the new center for country. The **Grand Palace**, (800) 572-5223, has been host to big names like Johnny Cash and Kenny Rogers, and if you ever wondered what happened to the **Osmonds**, they're still crooning at the **Osmond Family Theater**, (417) 336-6100. Also not to be missed, the **Andy Williams Show**, (417) 334-4500, and the **Ben Tillis Show**, (417) 335-6653. The legendary **Broken Spoke, Austin, TX**, (512)-442-6189, once frequented by Willie Nelson and Ray Price, is one of the last honky-tonks. Continues to showcase bands just on the edge of hitting big time. **Rodeo Bar**, (212) 683-6500, NYC, southwestern food, country and western entertainment. **Crazy Horse, Santa Ana, CA**, (714) 549-1512, is billed as the top country and western entertainment spot; top names perform here. For two-stepping and hot chili, go to **Lone Star Cafe**, New York City, (212) 245-2950. **Jimmy Driftwood Barn, Mountainview, Ark**, (501) 269-8042, hosts the best Ozark country bands. You never know what legend will turn up next at the **Bullpen Lounge**, (615) 255-6464, in **Nashville, TN**. Want more big names? **The Legends of Western Swing Festival**, Scurry County Coliseum, Snyder, TX, late June. For reading, try *Music City News*.

FOLK: Smithsonian Folklife Festival, Washington, DC, late-June-early July, has authentic folk and ethnic music, dancing. Excellent performers grace the back room of this guitar shop at weekends: **McCabe's, Santa Monica, CA**, (310) 828-4403. Try the **New Orleans Heritage Fest**, (504) 552-4786, for an eclectic mix of gospel, zydeco, progressive rock, jazz and more. The **Aspen Music Festival**, Aspen, CO, late June-Aug, 9 weeks, (303) 925-3172. As good as **Tanglewood Music Festival** in Lenox, MA, in terms of prestige and importance. Open rehearsals and other free events.

GOSPEL: Two million people fill the streets of **Harlem** during its massive week-long fest of gospel, rhythm & blues, and jazz. To hear gospel at its best, go to church in Detroit, Chicago or Harlem. In Washington DC, superb, uplifting gospel music can be heard each Sunday at **St Augustine's Catholic Church**, 15th & V Sts NW, 265-1470.

JAZZ: There are good jazz clubs in most North American cities. **The Baked Potato** near Universal Studios in LA, (818) 980-1615, is the oldest major jazz club in the US and launching pad for many famous performers. **Preservation Hall**, hub of **New Orleans** jazz, hosts pioneers of Dixieland, (504) 523-8939. In **Washington, DC**, **Blues Alley**, (202) 337-4141, has attracted such greats as Dizzie Gillespie and Ahmand Jamal and recently Wynston Masalis. There's no place like **New York City** for jazz: try **Blue Note**, (212) 475-8592; downstairs in the **Time Cafe**, is the **Fez Club**, (212)533-7000; **Sweet Basil's**, 242-1785, 'Village temple of jazz'; the venerable **Village Vanguard**, 255-4037; or newer **Visiones**, 673-5576. Don't miss **JVC Jazz Festival**, NYC, June 23-July 1, (212) 397-8222. More than 40 events and 1000 performers at different locations including Lincoln Center and Carnegie Hall. All the best including Ella Fitzgerald, Ray Charles and many others. Other essential festivals: **Chicago Jazz Fest** is exceptional, Labor Day weekend, (312) 744-3315; **Monterey, CA, Jazz Festival**, mid-September, (408) 373-3366; and **Montreux/Detroit Festival**,in Michigan, early Sept, (313) 259-5400. More than 100 performers play their licks in Burlington, VT, in June, call DISCOVER JAZZ, (802) 863-7992. See magazines *Jazz Times* or *Downbeat* for the latest on the jazz scene nationwide.

RHYTHM & BLUES: The tradition rooted in Bo Diddly, Jerry Lee Lewis, Chuck Berry, Carl Perkins and others still survives at the **Rum Boogie Cafe, Memphis, TN**, (901) 528-0150, or catch blues legend B.B King at his own club, **B.B.King's Blues Club**, (901) 527-5464.

ALTERNATIVE: Lilith Fair is a travelling Lollapalooza-style festival celebrating women in music, as envisioned by Canadian songstress Sarah McLachlan. Tours the US in July & Aug.

Lollapalooza. Originally conceived in 1991 by Perry Farrell as an alternative music and political travelling roadshow, the 27-odd shows are now as mainstream as Genesis. **House of Blues Smokin' Grooves Tour**. This recently established event has featured such artists as The Fugees, A Tribe Called Quest, The Pharcyde, and has been described as 'the most comprehensive sampling of the diversity of Hip-Hop culture in the 90s.' Touring North America Jun-Aug. **The Vans Warped Tour**, combines skateboarding and rock n' roll creating a global event that hits most major US cities throughout the summer. Info on all the above music genres, www.excite.com/xdr/Entertainment/Music/Genres/

Festival info, www.yahoo.com/Entertainment/Music/Events/Festivals/.

from downtown Washington. Flights are generally cheaper here. Sharing a cab out may be cheaper than the shuttle, about $47, (703) 661-8230.

Washington Flyer, (703) 685-8000, run airport shuttles from 1517 K St NW. Metro: Mc Pherson Sq, to National and Dulles airports. Buses run every ½ hr weekdays, 6 am-10 pm, hourly at w/ends, 7.30 am-10 pm. National, $8 o/w, $14 r/t. Dulles $16 o/w, $26 r/t, cash only.

Greyhound, 1005 1st NE, (800) 231-2222. Terminal behind Union Station. 24 hrs. Not an area to be alone in at night.

Union Station, 1st & Massachusetts NE, 484-7540, serves Amtrak, B&O, Virginia Express and metro. 8 mins from downtown. Day trips and overnights from here to Baltimore, Harpers Ferry, Fredericksburg, etc 24 hrs. Beautifully renovated, lots of eateries, shops and multiplex cinema. Look in the *Washington Post* for *shared expense rides*, especially late August/early Sept when students are returning to college.

MARYLAND   *Free State, Old Line State*

That Maryland is 'America in miniature' is the local boast. Perched precariously on the Mason-Dixon line, Maryland shows northern influences in its western mountainous area, settled heavily by British and Germans, and southern character along the eastern shoreline famous for hunting, old antebellum mansions, and delicious Chesapeake Bay crab and oysters. Maryland credits itself with the second largest steelworks in the world, the Bethlehem Steel Corporation at Sparrow's Point.

If you have time, visit the tobacco auctions in Hughesville, La Plata, Upper Marlboro, Waldorf or Waysons Corner; the auctioneer's patter is riveting. Or, attend a tournament of the official state sport—jousting!

The telephone area code in the west of the state is 301, in the east it's 410.

www.yahoo.com/Regional/US states/Maryland/

BALTIMORE   One of the nation's major seaports and not long ago, considered the ugly step-sister to Washington, DC and other major east coast cities. Today it sparkles from one of the most successful urban renewal programs in America. The city's Inner Harbor, the center-piece of Baltimore's rebirth, was designed by the prolific Rouse Company, also responsible for Faneuil Hall in Boston and the entire city of Columbia, Maryland, a pleasant stop-over near Baltimore.

On Baltimore's seafront, recently re-discovered (though trying hard not to be) **Fells Point** offers an unpretentious step back into the city's colonial and sea-faring past. The country's oldest waterfront has for the most part avoided both development and tourism, resulting in a setting strikingly unchanged for some 200 years. But don't think this is an old-fashioned area; 'real' people live and work here, and in addition to history, the Point has a great food market, bars, restaurants and summer festivals.

It is a city that is fiercely proud of its baseball team, the Orioles, and of its heroes, which include baseball star Babe Ruth, journalistic curmudgeon H L Mencken, and author and poet Edgar Allen Poe. While you're here, don't miss tasting fresh crab; and use correct pronunciation when referring to city or state: 'Bawlmer, Merlind' is quite acceptable.

ACCOMMODATION
Travellers on a tight budget may find the **Baltimore Quick Guide** helpful. Available at tourist offices.

Baltimore International Hostel, 17 W Mulberry St, 576-8880. $13 AYH, $16 non-AYH, free linen. 'Close to Inner Harbor area; 4 blocks from Greyhound. Clean; nice staff.' Check-in 10 am-11 am.

Schaefer Hotel, 723 St Paul St at Madison, 332-0405. S/D from $40. 'Rough but cheap.'

Wellington Hotel, 9th St & Baltimore Ave, (410) 289-9189. Clean, bright, fully equipped apartments sleep 6-8, $85 pp/per week. Close to boardwalk, amusement park and local attractions. Excellent location.'

FOOD
Crab, Baltimore's speciality, is available anywhere there's salt water. The scrumptious crustaceans are served by the dozen hot from the pot, peppered with volcanic Old Bay seasoning. Your only implements will be a mallet and a newspaper. Soft shell crabs are delicious too. Also, try **Phillip's** crab cakes at **Harbor Place**, Pratt & Lombard, a giant Inner Harbor pavilion with countless fast food stalls and a few restaurants. Don't miss **Ostrowski's** Polish kielbasa there. 'Beautiful view of harbor.'

Bertha's Dining Room, 734 S Broadway, Fell's Point, 327-5795. The restaurant's catchphrase is 'EAT BERTHA'S MUSSELS!' and you can for about $7.50. Wash it down with one of 90 different beers.

Ikaros, 4805 Eastern Ave, 633-3750. Greek, $8-$15. Closed Tues.

Jimmy's, 801 S Broadway, Fell's Point, 327-3273. Good, solid breakfasts and lunch at low prices, specials $3, a whole meal for $5. 'Usually crowded, especially Sun mornings.'

Lexington Market, Lexington & Eutaw, is a little United Nations of people, languages and food, food, food in endless display.

Louie's Bookstore Cafe, 518 N Charles, 962-1225. Seafood and literature, live classical music every night, local art exhibits. Lunch $6-$7, dinner $10-$12.

Mencken's Cultured Pearl Cafe, 1114 Hollins, 837-1947. The neon sign in the window says, 'EAT ART.' Jokes about starving artists aside, eat good Mexican food and gaze upon the work of local artists. Entrees $8, margaritas $3.50.

Pete's Grille, 3130 Greenmount Avenue, 467-7698. A real diner with good, cheap food and a great atmosphere.' Winner of local Best Breakfast' award, $1-$7. Mon-Sat 6 am-2.30 pm, Sun 7 am-1.30 pm.

OF INTEREST
Babe Ruth Birthplace and Maryland Baseball Hall of Fame, 216 Emory, 727-1539. Memorabilia of America's favourite slugger and other Maryland heroes. Daily 10 am-5 pm (7 pm when Orioles are playing), $5.

Baltimore Museum of Art, Charles & 31st Sts, 396-7100. Owes its wonderful Matisse collection to the shrewd purchases of the Cone sisters from the artist himself. Plus good Modernism section. Wed-Fri 10 am-4 pm; Sat-Sun 11 am-6 pm. $5.50, $3.50 w/student ID, free Thurs.

Edgar Allen Poe House, 203 N Amity, 396-7932. Winding staircase leads to the tiny garrett where Poe wrote 1832-1835. Sporadic hours: Jun-July Wed-Sat noon-3.45 pm, Aug-Sept Sat only noon-3.45 pm, closed mid-Dec to March; $3. Phone to check. NB: Poe was never wealthy, and his former home is in a rundown area. Use caution.

Flag House, Pratt & Albermarle Sts, 837-1793. The house where Mary Pickersgill sewed the flag that inspired Francis Scott Key to write the *Star Spangled Banner*. Tue-Sat 10 am-3.30 pm, $4, $2 w/student ID. The **Maryland Historical Society**, 201 W Monument St, 685-3750, has the original manuscript of that poem which was later (1931) adopted as the national anthem.

Fell's Point, a revamped harbour area around Aliceanna, Lancaster, Ann and Thames Streets. Shops and good places to eat. Can be reached by the water taxi which ferries people around the harbour.

Fort McHenry, end of Fort Ave, 962-4290. Successful defense of the fort in the War of 1812, over which the flag flew, was the inspiration for Francis Scott Key to write what was to become 'Star Spangled Banner.' Today, ancient cannons still cover the harbour. Daily 8 am-8 pm, $5. 'Catch the boat across to the fort, leaves every ½ hour from Inner Harbor, 685-4288. $6.60 r/t ticket allows you to get on and off at various points en route. Very worthwhile.'

Maryland Science Center and Davis Planetarium, 601 Light St on the harbour, 685-2370. Hands-on exhibits; computer games, Chesapeake Bay and Baltimore City displays. The 5-storey IMAX theatre overwhelms your senses, $9 includes IMAX film. 'Not worth it.'

Mount Clare Station, Pratt and Poppleton Sts, 237-2387. The first railroad station in the US. Erected 1830. From here Samuel FB Morse sent the first telegraph message 'what hath God wrought'. Tues-Sun 10 am-5 pm, $5.

National Aquarium, Pier 3, E Pratt St, 576-3810. Take the elevator to the 4th floor, then the escalator to the rain forest where piranhas glower, sloths dangle, and free-flying birds practically land on your head. Then walk along a spiraling aquarium tank to the friendly, schmoo-like Beluga whales, who laugh at the crowds around their 1st-floor tank. 'Expensive, but worth it. Modern and interesting design; the shark tank is amazing.' Summer: Sun-Thurs 9 am-6 pm, Fri & Sat 9 am-8 pm, $11.50.

Peale Museum, 225 N Holiday St, 396-3523, and the **Walters Art Gallery** , 600 N Charles St at Center, 547-9000. One of the largest private collections in the world with something of everything from across the ages. With a new floor to house the Oriental decorative arts. Tues-Sun 11 am-5 pm, $4, w/student ID, free to all Sat 11 am-noon.

Poe's Grave at Westminster Hall, Fayette & Green, 706-2072. The tombstone marking his grave is near the front gate. Take a fascinating tour -1st & 3rd Fri (at 6.30 pm) & Sat (at 10 am) in each month—of the church's catacombs and grounds for $4 (rsvs required). Cemetery open daylight only, free. On Halloween the local historical society hosts a weirdly funny party in the graveyard, during which 'Frank the Body-Snatcher' lectures on the perils of his profession. On the anniversary of Poe's death (Oct 7th), fans come from around the world for a midnight celebration that began in 1949, 100 years after Poe's death. It continues to this day unchanged: a mysterious man clad in black appears after midnight to offer a toast of French cognac to Poe's memory; after the ceremony he leaves roses and the open bottle at the grave and vanishes into the night.

Top of the World at the top of the **World Trade Center**, 401 East Pratt St, Inner Harbor, 837-4515, the world's tallest pentagonal building, designed by I M Pei. Offers panoramic views of harbour and city and exhibits on Baltimore's history. $2.50.

Washington Monument, Charles St and Mt Vernon Pl. 178 ft high, the monument was built between 1815 and 1842, long before the one in DC.

ENTERTAINMENT

Harbor Place may seem the logical hot spot, especially the enormous factory here converted into an adult Disneyland with corresponding steep tariff, but it's best avoided. Instead head for **Fell's Point**, east of Harbor Place, where the real fun is. Around 9 pm or 10 pm, serious drinking and dancing get underway in the numerous little bars filled with local rowdies, yuppies, bohemians, unrepentant pirates and assorted lowlifes, all in good fun. Most places here charge a buck or two cover, if that, on weekends. Tourists invariably get lost trying to find it, not because it's difficult to find—just take the trolley from Inner Harbor or follow Broadway toward the harbour till you run out of street—but because locals intentionally give them the wrong directions, ha ha.

SPORT
Baltimore Orioles, Orioles Stadium, Camden Yards, 685-9800. 'Great baseball in an electric atmosphere. Highly recommend. THE place to go for a good time. Watch out for 'Wild Bill' the beloved taxi driver/cheerleader. 'Tasty roast beef sandwiches made on outdoor grills. Amtrak and MARC run special trains from DC to Camden Yards on game days, $10.25 r/t, from Union Station, (800) 325-7245. Return train leaves Camden 20 mins after last out. 'Great value and a real Oriole atmosphere even before you reach the ground.'

INFORMATION
Baltimore Area Convention and Visitors Association, 301 East Pratt St, 837-4636, info on accommodation, restaurants, attractions.
Travelers Aid, 111 Park Ave, 685-3569/685-5874, and at Baltimore-Washington International Airport.

TRAVEL
Amtrak, Penn Station, 1515 N Charles St, (800) 872-7245.
Baltimore Trolley Works, 563-3901. Stopping at major downtown attractions including the inner harbour, Fells Point and Fort McHenry. Three trolleys run daily 'til 7 pm.
Baltimore/Washington International Airport, 10 miles south of Baltimore. Take the #17 Mass Transit bus, or light rail, from downtown.
Greyhound, 210 W Fayette and Howard Sts, 752-0908/(800) 231-2222.
Mass Transit, 539-5000, for bus and light rail schedules for downtown and suburbs; $1.35-$1.65.
Water Taxi service, Constellation Dock, Pratt St, (410) 563-3900. Calls at all major attractions around the harbour. $3.25 all-day unlimited use, 11 am-11 pm, 'til midnight Fri & Sat, Sun 10 am-9 pm.

ANNAPOLIS
Situated on Chesapeake Bay, the city of Queen Anne is the capital of Maryland. At the State House, George Washington resigned his command of the Revolutionary Army after his victory over British forces. The waterfront is 18th century and clustered behind it is one of the most beautiful of America's colonial towns.

Annapolis is synonymous with sailing and the United States Naval Academy; now coed, it's still 'where the boys are' and acts as a magnet for young women, especially on weekends. The bars on the wharf are good for a beer and overhearing the fish stories of Chesapeake Bay. Treat yourself to a basket of hot crab, delicious and cheap, and catch the Clam Festival in late August. A trip round the harbour is a must. The movie, *Patriot Games*, was shot here.

ACCOMMODATION
Accommodation tends to be expensive in this trendy little town.
Bed and Breakfasts of Maryland, (800) 736-4667, can arrange accomodation in Annapolis.
Capital KOA Campground, 11 miles from Annapolis on Rte 3 north in Millersville, 923-2771. April-Nov; sites $24 for two, $29 w/hook-up, XP-$4, cabins available $40-$48, rsvs required.

FOOD
Chick and Ruth's, 165 Main, 269-6737. Down the street from the state capitol, this 24 hr deli has politically-named specials, $3-$6, in a homey, memorabilia-crammed atmosphere.

Market House, Market Space, City Dock. Restoration of an 1858 building with tons of fresh seafood and various other foods. 'Best value, tastiest seafood in town!' 'Best oysters in the east!'

Maryland Inn, Church Circle, 263-2641. Well-known early 18th century inn, houses **King of France Tavern**, 'excellent' jazz. Thurs-Sun, cover $5-$20.

OF INTEREST
A **Boat trip** round the harbour is the pleasantest way to experience the many facets of Annapolis; **Chesapeake Marine Tours** , Slip 20, City Dock, 268-7600, 40 min harbour cruises $6, 90 min Severn River cruises, $12, and 'A Day on the Bay' for $35.

Maryland State House, State Circle, 974-3400. Oldest US State House in continuous legislative use. 9 am-5 pm daily, free tours. 'Interesting tour.'

US Naval Academy, bordered by King George St & Severn River, 263-6933. Large, beautiful chapel has sarcophagus of John Paul Jones. Guided walking tours, $5.50, depart from Ricketts Hall. Free admission to grounds, Mon-Sat 9.30 am-3.30 pm. 'Excellent, interesting tour.'

Walking Tours, Historic Annapolis Tour, 267-8149, covers major sights. Mon-Fri meet at Old Treasury, State Circle; Sat-Sun at Victualling Warehouse, Maritime Museum, foot of Maine St. $7 for 1½ hr tour of colonial Annapolis.

ASSATEAGUE ISLAND   Situated off Maryland's Atlantic coast, the island is the home to the threatened peregrine falcon and the snow goose. Roaming the island are the Chincoteague wild ponies, descendants of shipwrecked horses. Assateague is a 37-mile long narrow barrier island. Maryland's **Assateague State Park** sits at the northern end, 641-2120, **Assateague Island National Seashore** is in the middle, 641-3030 and **Chincoteague National Wildlife Refuge**, belonging to Virginia, is in the south, (804) 336-6122. Limited camping is available in both Maryland parks, $9-$18 site, rsvs required. The refuge has hiking trails. 'Delightful area.'

OCEAN CITY   Maryland's only major oceanside resort. The town has a lively boardwalk and a wide beach, but gets crowded in the summer. This is the place to go if you want a wild time. Plenty of boarding house accommodation and good for summer jobs. 'Packed with British and Irish students. Anticipate bumping into your enemies from home.'

ACCOMMODATION
Accommodation can be reasonable here during the off season, but in summer months even the tackiest dives can get away with outrageous rates. A rule of thumb is the farther away from the boardwalk, the better. Accommodation is available—you just have to walk around to find it, particularly around 5th St. 'Beware of those selling "cheap" accommodation at the bus terminal and realtors who are out to make money from summer employees.'

Harbor Lights Townhouse Apartments, PO Box 622, Ocean City, MD 21842, 289-6626. Furnished, well equipped apartments. Long-term only. Perfect if you are staying for the summer, approx. $1000-$1200 for 3 mnths.

Jarman House, 105 Talbot St, 289-7678. 'Low weekly rates. Great for working students.' Approx. $80 per week.

Ocean City Convention and Visitors Bureau, 4001 Coastal Highway, 289-8181, can provide accommodation information.
Periwinkle Apartments, 11 & 79th Sts, Nov-April (301) 649-4172, April-Oct (410) 524-6481. All units 3 bedrooms, kitchens, TV, ideal for international students.' $15 pp.
Summer Place Youth Hostel, 104 Dorchester St, 289-4542. Cheapest place in town.' $15 per night, $80-$150 per week. Kitchen, BBQ, sun-deck and hot tub.
Whispering Sands Aptmts, 45th St, Ocean City, MD 21842, 289-5759. Approx. $15 per night. 'Reasonable; friendly.' 'Ace.'

FOOD/ENTERTAINMENT
Ocean City has a league of bars, clubs and eateries. Many restaurants close after Labor Day, but even so, you'll never starve here.
The Angler, 312 Talbot St, 289-7424. Lively bar and restaurant with drinks specials on Sundays & Weds, $3 cover, 50¢ drafts. 'Excellent!'
Bull on the Beach, 12th St at Boardwalk, 289-3744. 'Excellent sandwiches.'
La Hacienda, 80th St at Coastal Hwy, 524-8080. 'Great Mexican food.' Most dishes under $10.
Seacrets, 542-4900, 49th St and the Bay. Huge cpmplex of bars constructed on and around the Bay. Live reggae, great atmosphere.' Mon-Sat 11 am-2 am, Sun 2 pm-2 am, cover $3-$5.
Tavern-by-the-Sea, 16th St and Boardwalk, 289-8444. Very popular bar/restaurant, always packed!' Infamous Import night' on Weds, $3 cover, $1 for imported beers. All-you-can-eat Crab, $13.

ANTIETAM BATTLEFIELD An interesting side-trip from Baltimore heading west on Rte 70—the site of the Civil War's bloodiest battle which resulted in 23,000 casualties in 1862. The scene of the battle is now a National Park, with an excellent museum and diorama at its Visitors Center, 432-5124, near Sharpsburg, off Rte 65 (Hagerstown Pike). Daily 8.30 am-6 pm, $2.

CHESAPEAKE & OHIO CANAL Until the advent of the railways, America made use of a considerable system of canals throughout the Northeast and Midwest, one of these being the Chesapeake & Ohio, running along the Maryland border from Washington, DC to Cumberland via Harper's Ferry. The canal is now a National Historic Park extending for 185 miles, the longest of all national preserves. Mostly disused but leafy and beautiful, the banks of the canal are well worth a hike or bicycle ride (bikes can be rented in DC).

VIRGINIA   *The Old Dominion, Mother of Presidents*

Famed for its colonial heritage, for the statesmen it has produced, its historic homes and estates, and the great battlefields on which the fate of the nation was decided in both the 18th and 19th centuries. Seven of the 15 pre-Civil War Presidents were born in the state.

Virginia is the least southern, both geographically and in attitude, of the old Confederate states and suffers least from their usual social problems. It is a state that has a great deal to offer both from the scenic and the historic

point of view. In the east, sandy beaches and the amazing 17½ mile Chesapeake Bay Bridge Tunnel linking Virginia to Maryland, in the west, the Skyline Drive and the Shenandoah National Park, while everywhere there are countless well-preserved links with the past.
www.yahoo.com/regional/US States/Virginia/

RICHMOND The capital of Virginia and of the old Confederacy, Richmond was largely destroyed by retreating southern troops. Today, old and new meld forming an attractive, bustling city with plenty of history and entertainment. Richmond also makes a good base for visiting nearby landmarks, but—'it's dead at weekends.'
The telephone area code is 804.

ACCOMMODATION
Days Inn North Motel, 1600 Robin Hood Rd, 355-1287. Downtown area. S-$30-$39, D-$34-$45. Pool and restaurant.
Holiday Inn, 301 West Franklin St, 644-9871. D-$65, XP-$5.
Massad House Hotel, 11 N 4th St, 648-2893. S-$43, D-$50, T-$56 (3-5 people). Recommended by YMCA, which does not have overnights. 'Good accommodation.'
Motel 6, 5704 Williamsburg Rd, 222-7600. Six miles east on Hwy 60, near airport. S-$30, D-$34.Good value for money.'
Pocahontas State Park, 10301 Beach Rd, 796-4255. Ten miles south of Richmond, Exit 61 off I-95 to Rte 10, take country road 655. Sites $12, showers, boating and biking. 'Nice place.'
Radisson, 555 East Canal St, (five blocks from the Capitol), 788-0900. Rms from $59/week, $69/w/end, pool, jacuzzi, mini-gym.

FOOD
Aunt Sarah's Pancake House, 2126 Willis Rd, 747-8284, and other Virginia locations. Real old-time Virginny cooking. Daily 24 hrs
Farmer's Market, on 17th St in Richmond's old town Shockoe Bottom near Shockoe Slip, 780-8597. Oldest continuously operating farmer's market in the country. Mon-Sat 6 am-9 pm.
Mamma Zu, 501 South Pine St, 788-4205. Huge pasta dishes $6-$9, large pizza will feed three for $8.
Oceans, 414, East Main St, 649-3456. Stop off here for refueling at breakfast and lunch. All meals under $5. Daily 7 am-2.30 pm.
The Strawberry Street Cafe, 421 North Strawberry St, 353-6860. Boasts the best burger in town,' $5.50. Famous for its bathtub salad bar, a cast-iron claw-foot tub stocked with salads, homemade soup and fresh fruit for $6.95.
3rd Street Diner, 3rd & Main Sts, 788-4750. Popular with locals, fantastic sandwiches,' $3-$5, breakfast special $2.25. Daily 24 hrs.

OF INTEREST
Take a historic walk through Richmond. Starting from the Court end, many attractions within 8 blocks—national landmarks, museums and other notable buildings. Discount block ticket $9, admission to most museums, valid for 30 days.
City Hall Skydeck, 9th & Broad, 643-9524, for a view of the city. Daily 9 am-5 pm, free.
Hollywood Cemetery, Albemarle and Cherry Sts, US Presidents James Monroe and John Tyler, and Confederate President Jefferson Davis, are buried here, along with some 18,000 Confederate soldiers.
Monument Avenue, a beautiful tree-lined boulevard with statues commemorating, among others, Arthur Ashe, JEB Stuart and Matthew Fontaine Maury, scientist and oceanographer.

Science Museum of Virginia, 2500 W Broad St, 367-0000. Has 'hands-on' exhibits and the excellent Universe Space Theater, where films are shown on a large planetarium dome providing sight and sound from every direction. Mon-Thur 9.30 am-5 pm, Fri-Sat 9.30 am-7 pm, Sun 11.30 am-5 pm. $5 exhibits only, $4 IMAX films.

St John's Church, 24th & Broad. Built 1741, this is where Patrick Henry made his famous 'Give me liberty or give me death' speech. Nearby is a **'Poe Museum '** in a house Poe never lived in. You would be well advised to skip it. The museum's only attraction is that it is across the street from a cigarette company—Poe would have been amused.

The State Capitol, Capitol Square, 786-4344, neo-classical domed building designed by Thomas Jefferson. Daily 9 am-4.15 pm, free tours.

Valentine Museum, 1015 E Clay St, 649-0711, on the life and history of Richmond. Mon-Sat 10 am-5 pm; Sun noon-5 pm. $5.

Virginia Aviation Museum, 5701 Huntsman Rd, near the International Airport, 236-3622, houses an extensive collection of vintage flying machines. Daily 9.30 am-5 pm, $3.50.

Virginia Museum of Fine Arts, Boulevard and Grove Sts, 367-0878. A panorama of world art from ancient times to the present. Entry by donation ($4). Tues-Sun 11 am-5 pm, Thur 'til 8 pm, Sun 1 pm-5 pm.

White House and Museum of the Confederacy, 1201 E Clay St, 649-1861. Mon-Sat 10 am-5 pm, Sun noon-5 pm, $5 museum, $5.50 White House, $5 both on same day. There is a block ticket available for all the city's main museums—$11.

ENTERTAINMENT
King's Dominion, north on I-95 (20 miles north of Richmond), 876-5000, $30 all day. 'Great rides'—don't miss the Anaconda—a looping roller-coaster featuring an underwater tunnel.'

Shockoe Slip, Carey St btwn 12th & 14th Sts, old warehouses now store galleries and eclectic craft shops, hip restaurants, bars, and nightclubs.

Sixth St Market, btwn Coliseum & Grace St, live music, beer and dancing Friday afternoons in summer.

SPORT
Biking and Hiking: There are over 200 miles of trails to explore in the Richmond-Petersburg area, many cut through surrounding battlefields. **Golf**: Several courses in the metropolitan area, check out **Glenwood**, 3100 Creighton Rd, 226-1793, $15 weekdays. Also **The Crossings**, 800 Virginia Center Pkwy, 226-2254, $37.

Skating: **Hampton Bike & Skateboard Park**, 9 Woodland Rd, Hampton, (757) 825-4805. Outdoor park with vert, mini and street course.

Whitewater Rafting: One of only a few 'urban' whitewater runs in the country rages right through the heart of historic Richmond. Contact, **Richmond Raft Company**, 4400 E Main St, 222-7238, or **James River Runners**, 286-2338. Trips cost $30-$45.

INFORMATION
Visitors Information Center, 1710 Robin Hood Rd, exit 78 off I-95, 358-5511. Has short video on Richmond and Virginia and info on accommodation, restaurants, travel, and attractions. Daily, summer 9 am-7 pm, winter 9 am-5 pm. Another **Visitors Center** is located at Sixth Street Marketplace, 782-2777.

TRAVEL
Amtrak, 7519 Staples Mill Rd, (800) 872-7245. About five miles from downtown, no buses available. Taxi fare $15. (Charlottesville $16, 1 1/2 hrs).

Greyhound, 2910 N Blvd, (800) 231-2222. Then take GRTC bus to town. (Charlottesville $18, 1 1/2 hrs, Williamsburg $10, 1 hr).

Richmond International Airport, 226-3052. Buses to and from the airport are few and far between; call Grooms Transportation, 222-7222, for pick-up service to downtown Richmond, $13.50 one person, $17.75 for two, $21.25 for three, after that $6.50 a head. Prices depend on which zone in Richmond you are travelling to.

FREDERICKSBURG   One hour north of Richmond off the I-95, the place where four great Civil War battles were fought. You can tour the Fredericksburg Battlefield where Lee's army fought off wave after wave of charging Federals from Marye's Heights.

The town itself has several interesting old houses, among them the home of Mary Washington, George Washington's mother; **Kenmore**, the home of George's sister, Betty Washington Lewis; and the **Rising Sun Tavern**, owned by George's brother, Charles. Antique shops selling overpriced Americana line the quaint streets, but there are some good, inexpensive, places to eat; **Goolrick's Pharmacy**, 901 Caroline St, 373-3411. Original soda fountain, milkshakes, soup and sandwiches will satisfy for under $5, or try Sammy T's on Caroline St, 371-2008, where delicious vegetarian fare costs around $5.50.

The telephone area code is 703.

INFORMATION
Fredericksburg Battlefield Visitors Center, Lafayette Blvd, 373-6122. Museum exhibits, guided walking tours (in summer), and slide show describe the four battles of Fredericksburg. Summer: Daily 8.30 am-6.30 pm, otherwise 9 am-5 pm.

WILLIAMSBURG   As state capital between 1699 and 1780, Williamsburg played a significant role in the heady days leading up to the American Revolution. Nowadays there is Colonial Williamsburg, hundreds of houses painstakingly restored to create the look of earlier times with actors dressed up to give an air of reality. It even tries to address the subject of slavery— Virginia was the first slave state—with the actors 'living' a slave's life. Even so this is, as one reader put it, 'a sort of colonial Disneyland.' Major tourist area.

www.visit Williamsburg.com/
The telephone area code is 757.

ACCOMMODATION
Williamsburg is loaded with hotels, but even the modest ones charge high rates.
The **Colonial Williamsburg Visitors Center**, 229-1000, has a list of guest houses from about $50.
The College of William and Mary, fraternities and sororities sometimes have rooms. Check at the housing office, 221-4314.
Johnson's Guest Home, 101 Thomas Nelson Lane, 229-3909. Rooms from $26. Kind, friendly landlady will pick up from train or bus station. 'Excellent place.'
Mrs H J Carter Guest House, 903 Lafayette St, 229-1117. S-$25, D-$30, T-$35, Q-$38. 1 mile from downtown. Further afield is **Sangraal By-The-Sea Hostel**, in **Wake** (south of Urbanna, VA), 776-6500. Actually, it's by the Rappahannock River where it meets the Chesapeake Bay, but a lovely location all the same. Urbanna is almost due north of Williamsburg (30mi); take Hwy 17. $15 AYH, $18 non-AYH, linen $3, meals available; rsvs rec.
Williamsburg Hotel/Motel Association, (800) 446-9244 (out of state), (804) 220-3330 (in state).
Camping: **Kinkaid Campsite**, exit 37 off I-64. Sites $12, 'basic but adequate.' 5 miles from Busch Gardens.

FOOD

Authentically decorated Taverns in Colonial Williamsburg offer 18th and 20th century fare at 21st century prices.

A Good Place to Eat, 410 Duke of Gloucester St, 229-4370. A wide variety of good food from $3, $6.50 complete meal.

College Deli, opposite William and Mary College, 229-6627. 'Best sandwiches in North America.' Dinner $6-$10, 10.30 am-2 am daily.

Paul's Deli Restaurant and Pizza, 761 Scotland St, 229-8976. Popular student hangout. Huge subs from $4, pasta and seafood specials. Half price Happy Hours, Wed-Sat 7 pm-9 pm. Daily 10.30 am-2 am.

Sal's Pizza, 1242 Richmond Rd, in the commercial part of town, 220-2641. 'Best pizza in town.'

OF INTEREST

Busch Gardens, 3 miles east of Williamsburg on Hwy 60, 253-3350. A fanciful re-creation of old world Europe and action packed theme park operated by the Anheuser Busch Brewing Company. Authentically-detailed European hamlets alongside wet, dry and mind-erasing rides with such fear-inducing names as 'Atomic Breakers' and the 'Drachen Fire,' one of the fiercest roller-coasters in the world! Free beer samples await at the brewery, but have ID ready. Summer: open 10 am-10 pm, Fri-Sat 'til midnight, $30. 'Loads of fun. Don't miss the Big Bad Wolf.'

College of William and Mary. Founded 1693, the second oldest in the nation. The **Sir Christopher Wren Building** at the west end of Duke of Gloucester St, is purported to be the oldest academic buildingf in continuous use in the US. Also part of the college, the **Muscarelle Museum of Art**, 221-2703. Fine Arts Museum, permanent collections feature old master paintings, contemporary works and colonial Virginia portraits. Mon-Fri 10 am-4.45 pm, w/ends noon-4 pm.

Colonial Williamsburg. Perhaps the best buildings are the Capitol, jail, Raleigh Tavern, Governor's palace, and various colonial craft shops. Tickets are priced according to the number of buildings and craft shops visited—basic admission, 12-bldgs, $25, a Patriot's Pass provides unlimited admission to all exhibits for $33. Daily 9 am-5 pm. Call 229-1000 for more info. Finally, you can just wander for free without going into the houses at all. Go first to the **Visitors Center**. You can see a documentary film here which may make the visit more meaningful. Daily **James River Plantations**. Take Rte 5 along the river to visit several plantation homes of early American leaders; then Hwy 60 to **Carter's Grove** (also to Busch Gardens), often called 'the most beautiful colonial home in America.'

Jamestown, first permanent English settlement in America. Not that much has been restored: the visitor must often be content with looking at foundations. Plagues, Indians, starvation and fires hindered its development, and when finally the penninusula became an island, Williamsburg and Yorktown prospered in its stead. The original settlement is about a mile from the more recent **Jamestown Settlement Park**, 229-1607. In the park are replicas of three ships, a re-creation of the first fort, an Indian village and a museum. Daily 9 am-5 pm, $9. 5 min from Williamsburg on Hwy 31 south.

Walking Tour. As cars are banned from the historic district, this would seem a logical option. Start at Merchants Sq and continue in a rough counter-clockwise direction. Buildings in the historic district are open daily, Apr-Oct, 9 am-6 pm. 8.30 am-6 pm, historic area open 9 am-5 pm.

Yorktown is the least restored of the James River historical areas. The battlefield and 67 18th century structures remain.The surrender of the British at Yorktown ended the War of Independence, although the final peace treaty wasn't signed until two years later. **The Yorktown Victory Center**, in Yorktown on Rte 238, 887-1776, sits on a 21-acre tract overlooking the York River. Built for the Bicentennial, it is a permanent museum dramatising the military events of the Revolution. Daily 9 am-5 pm, $3.75.

INFORMATION
Colonial Williamsburg Visitors Center, on State Hwy 132-Y, (800) HISTORY. Daily 9 am-5 pm. Runs shuttle bus (9 am-10 pm) to Historic section, free with admission ticket.
Williamsburg Chamber of Commerce, 201 Penniman Rd, 229-6511. Mon-Fri, 8.30 am-5 pm.

TRAVEL
Greyhound, 229-1460/(800)231-2222; and **Amtrak**, 229-8750/(800) 872-7245, at Lafayette & N Boundary St.

VIRGINIA BEACH
Continuing southeast from Williamsburg and past Norfolk, you come to this fast-growing resort with a 28-mile beach running from the landing dunes of America's first permanent colonists on Cape Henry to Virginia's Outer Banks. From here you can get on the amazing Chesapeake Bay Bridge Tunnel for the northern drive up the Atlantic coastline, stopping off to visit Assateague National Seashore (see also Maryland).

ACCOMMODATION
All prices skyrocket from June to Labor Day. $59 for a double passes for 'economy' at the tackiest hotel or motel. It's cheaper to rent an 'efficiency apartment' and cram everyone you know into it. For starters, go to or call **Angie's Guest Cottage**, 302 24th St, 428-4690; $12 AYH, $15 non-AYH, rates drop $3 off season. B&B $42 pp, D-$78 fits four, XP-$10. Camping $3 less than hostel prices. If they don't have space, they'll recommend others that might, although no one's prices come close to matching Angie's.
Coral Sand Motel, 23rd & Pacific Ave, 425-0872. Close to beach, rooms from $45 for two, includes breakfast. (Predominantly gay resort.)
Sundial Motel, 308 21st St, 428-2922. Rooms from D-$59, close to beach.
Camping: Seashore State Park, 5 miles north of town on US 60. (800) 933-7275. Pitch your tent ($10.50) in the dunes or under a cypress tree; $19.25 w/hook-up, cabins for four $82.

FOOD
Junk food heaven! Fast food joints crowd the boardwalk which at night becomes loud and luminous!
Giovanni's Pizza Pasta Place, 2006 Atlantic Ave, 425-1575. Inexpensive Italian food. Lunch and dinner $5-$8. Daily noon-11 pm.
The Jewish Mother, 3108 Pacific Ave, 422-5430. Burgers, sandwiches, etc. $6 average meal price. 'Friendly place, and while waiting you can crayon on the walls and menus!' At night a popular bar with live music.

OF INTEREST
Poe wasn't the only Edgar around these parts with a finger on the pulse of the paranormal: the work of Edgar Cayce, the 'best documented psychic of modern times' is explained in exhibits, lectures, movies and tours at his **A.R.E. Library and Conference Center**, 67th & Atlantic, 428-3588. You can learn about life after death and have your ESP tested too. Mon-Fri 9 am-8.00 pm, Sat 8.30 am-5.00 pm, Sun 11 am-8 pm. Free.
The **Viva Elvis Festival**, (800) 446-8038, in early June has Elvis impersonators, Elvis films, Elvis food (fried peanut-butter-and-banana sandwiches) and a 'Flock of Elvi' skydiving to the beach (!) not to mention four days of Elvis karaoke contests, so if you've ever fancied yourself as a bit of a hound dog, here's your chance!
Virginia Beach is amusement park paradise. If you're looking for thrills, try **Ocean Breeze Fun Park**, 422-6628, **Fun Spot Action Park**, 422-1401, or **Atlantic Fun Center**, 422-1742.

SPORT
Virginia Beach is host to a leg of the annual **Bud Surf Tour**, attracting pros world-wide. If you fancy your chances, **Wave Riding Vehicles**, (757) 422-8825, provide local surf reports and info on main surf areas. Cycling, jogging and skating are popular along the boardwalk, and there are a couple of fishing piers for those wishing to take things easy.
Skating: Lynhaven Skatepark, Great Neck Rd & First Colonial Rd, 422-5122, or **Mount Trashmore Skatepark**, South Blvd & Edwin Dr, 490-0351.

INFORMATION
The Virginia Beach Visitor Information Center, 2100 Parks Ave. Free publications full of useful info and accommodation directories. Daily 9 am-8 pm.

CHARLOTTESVILLE Located in central Virginia and surrounded by beautiful dogwood-laden countryside and old estates, Charlottesville is one of the most interesting and charming places in the state. Recent celebrity converts to the gentleman-farmer lifestyle, for which the area is renowned, include Sissy Spacek, Sam Shepherd and Jessica Lange. Much of the architecture is either directly Jefferson's or influenced by his example. The elegant University of Virginia is testimony to his humanism and architectural genius.
The telephone area code is 804.

ACCOMMODATION
Budget Inn, 140 Emmet St, 293-5141. Near University and CSXT railway line. Rooms from S-$36, D-$38.
Econo Lodge, 2014 Holiday Dr, 295-3185 & 400 Emmett St, 296-2104. S-$45, D-$47, XP-$5.
Town and Country Motor Lodge, Rte 250E, 293-6191. S-$36 D-$42. 'Very friendly and clean.'

FOOD
Baja Bean Co, 1327 W Main St, 293-4507. Californian-style Mexican food washed down with a choice of 12 Mexican beers and 15 different Tequilas. 'Cheap and delicious.'
Big Jim's Barbeque, 2104 Angus Rd, 296-8283. Huge burgers that you can't finish, Cajun-style, $1.60-$4.25.
Macado's, 1505 University Ave, across the street from the University Lawn, 971-3558. Downstairs it's wonderful sandwich time; upstairs it's the bar, 9.30 am-2 am daily.
White Spot Restaurant, 1407 W Maian St, 972-9746. Small, basic diner food.Try the Gus,' an egg-cheese-cholesterolburger, with fries and a soda for $3.50. Friendly, helpful staff.'

OF INTEREST
Ash Lawn, 2½ mi beyond Monticello on Rte 53, 293-9539, 535-acre estate of the 5th US president, James Monroe. The site was chosen by his close friend Thomas Jefferson. Daily 9 am-6 pm. $7.
Historic Court Square, E Jefferson St, self-guided tour info available free at visitors center and historical society.
Michie Tavern, ½ mile from Monticello on Rt 53, 977-1234. Re-creates 18th-century tavern life. Story has it that Jefferson, Monroe, Madison and Lafayette met here. Converted log-house next door serves all-you-can-eat 18th-century southern-style lunch 9 am-5 pm. $6 museum. Lunch and museum combo tkt $11.
Monticello, 3 miles southeast of the town on Rte 53, 984-9800. The architectural

masterpiece where Thomas Jefferson lived and experimented. Built from his own design, this Palladian villa has many ingenious extras such as the clock that sits over the front door. Daily 9 am-5 pm Mar-Oct, $9, frequent tours. 'Magnificent, with fine views of the surrounding countryside.'

ENTERTAINMENT
Durty Nelly's, 2200 Jefferson Park Ave, 295-1278. Bar/deli, choose from over 50 beers. Happy Hour specials, live music at weekends, cover $2-$4. Daily 11 am-2 am.
Friday After Five, on the mall, live entertainment, festive atmosphere, every Friday during summer.
Millers, 109 W Main St near the mall, 971-8511. Bar with live music Mon-Sat, $2-$4 cover. 'Cheap food.'

INFORMATION
Albemarle County Historical Society, 220 Court Square, 296-1492, brochure on historic sites, museum features law in Virginia and local history. Walking tours leave from the McIntire Bldg, 200 Second St, Saturdays at 10 am, suggested $3 donation.
Charlottesville Visitors Center, at intersection of Rte 20 and I-64 on the way to Monticello, 293-6789, has info on places to eat and stay, and things to do in Charlottesville; also has exhibit 'Thomas Jefferson at Monticello.' Daily 9 am-5.30 pm.

TRAVEL
Amtrak, 7th & W Main Sts, 296-4559/(800) 872-7245, for fare and schedule info.
Greyhound, 310 W Main St, 295-5131/(800) 231-2222. (Richmond $18, 1 hr 15 mins).

SHENANDOAH NATIONAL PARK Though only 80 miles from Washington DC, the park remains a wilderness area. The 105-mile long Skyline Drive runs along the crest of the Blue Ridge Mountains, following the old Appalachian Trail, with an average elevation of over 3000 ft. The southern end of the drive meets the Blue Ridge Parkway which takes the traveller clear down to the Smokies.

The route affords a continuous series of magnificent views over steeply wooded ravines to the Piedmont Plateau on the east, and across the fertile farmlands of the Shenandoah Valley to the west. Check the weather before doing the Skyline Drive. If it's bad, you'll just drive through clouds.

There are over 500 miles of foot trails for every grade of hiker. Campgrounds, lodges and shelters can be found throughout the park (see below). Look out for pioneer dwellings and homesteads. **Skyline Drive Entrance**: (North to south) Front Royal off Hwy 340; Thornton Gap near Luray off Hwy 211; Swift Run Gap near Elkton off Hwy 33; Rockfish Gap near Waynesboro off Hwy 250 or I-64. $5 per vehicle.
The area code is 540.

ACCOMMODATION
Bear's Den AYH-Hostel, just off Rte 601 S, near Bluemont, 554-8708. A stone lodge that sits on the Appalachian Trail, overlooking the Shenandoah River. Office hours 5 pm-10 pm, front gate locked at 10 pm. $12 AYH, $15 non-AYH, linen included. Rsvs recommended. Camping $6 pp.
Lodges: Skyland Lodge at milepost 41.7 or 42.5. Room with 2 D beds $74 weekdays, $140 w/end; **Big Meadows Lodge** at milepost 51, easy access to hiking trails

WHITEWATER

North America is home to some of the worlds most beautiful and spectacular rivers making it ideal for whitewater rafting: a mind-blowing experience you'll remember for years. These are some of the most fun whitewater rivers: **EAST: Chattooga, Long Creek, SC**. 50 ft/mile drops through most inaccessible canyons in Southeast, site of movie *Deliverance*. Day trips $78-$96, call Wildwater Outfitters (803) 647-9587. **Cheat, Albright, WV**. Try 'Big Nasty' and 'Coliseum' rapids, part of largest natural watershed in East; mainly rafted April-May. Half-day trips from $45; for more info call WV Visitors Center, (800) 225-5982. **Gauley, Summerville, WV**. 2-day autumn trip rated 'the best', experience or deathwish needed for Upper section. Day trips from $75, for more info call (800) 225-5982. **James, Richmond, VA**. Raft past commuters in metropolitan Richmond. Day trips from $45 include nature refuge, or raft through evening rush hour for $30. Call Richmond Raft Co, (804) 222-7238 for details.

New, Beckley, WV, is the world's second oldest river after the Nile. Lower section is known as 'Grand Canyon of the East,' with spectacular view of the longest, highest single-span bridge on earth. Day trips from $86, for more info call Class VI River Runners (800) 252-7784. **Youghiogheny** (The 'Yough,' pronounced Yock'), **Ohiopyle State Park, PA**. Splendid, challenging rapids , prices depend on season and difficulty. Wilderness Voyageurs Inc, (800) 272-4141. **Upper Yough, Friendsville, MD**. Ranks among most challenging in world with rapid names including 'Meat Cleaver' and 'Double Pencil Sharpener' (!); an experienced rafter's dream, a beginner's night-mare.

Penobscot, Maine, through the steep-walled granite Ripogenus Gorge, one of the most scenic whitewater stretches in east US. But no time for the view if you ride the 'Exterminator' Class V rapid—'intense.' Call Wilderness Expeditions, (207) 534-2242, $75-$90 for w-end trips. USA Raft, (800) 624-8060, is the reservation company for several outfitters. They can help you choose from among 30 different outings, to suit all skill levels, on ten of the best whitewater rivers in the east. More info, www.hps.gov/neri/w-water/htm.

WEST: Colorado, Grand Canyon, AZ. Over 150 world-class rapids between Badger Creek and Lava Falls, surrounded by canyon walls a mile high. Arizona Tourist Board (800) 666-2877. **Middle Fork of Salmon, Boise, ID**. Whitewater of unforgettable intensity and beauty, natural hot springs and waterfalls. Idaho Outfitters and Guides Association (208) 342-1438.

Snake, Boise, ID. Rafting through Hell's Canyon, the deepest gorge in the world, on 'reorganizer' rapids and warm water. Idaho Outfitters and Guides Association (208) 342-1438. For more information on Eastern whitewater, consult *Whitewater Rafting in Eastern North America* by Lloyd D Armstead, Pequot Press, Chester, CT. For extended trips on Western rivers, contact the *American Wilderness Experience*, Boulder, CO, (800) 444-0099. Also check out www.westernriver.com/and www.travelsource.com/rafting.

Tips: Wherever you decide to go, bear in mind the following: look for an established outfitter that has been in business for a number of years and has a current licence. Decide what you want and know the level of ability required (Class IIII for first-timers, IV-VI more advanced, difficult rapids). Plan ahead—deposits may be required; w-ends are more expensive than weekdays; find out what the price includes, meals, equipment, etc. Finally, if you fall out of the raft, point your feet DOWNstream.

and restaurants. Rsvs required (months in advance for fall), contact ARA Virginia Skyline Company Inc, 743-5108. All campgrounds and lodges have rangers-in-residence who provide info on trails, natural history, etc. Shelters for day hikers, and huts for backpackers with *3-night* or *Appalachian-Through-Trail-Permits* only are scattered throughout the park. Be sure to talk to rangers about location, availability and permits.

Campgrounds: **Mathews Arm** at Skyline Drive milepost 22.2 (no showers); **Big Meadows** at milepost 51; **Lewis Mountain** at milepost 57.5; **Loft Mountain** at milepost 79.5. Tent sites $14. All on first-come, first-served basis, except Big Meadows which requires reservations—(800) 365-2267.

INFORMATION
Shenandoah National Park Visitors Centers: Byrd Center at Big Meadows (milepost 51), 999-2243 (has info on camping within the park); and Dickie Ridge Center (milepost 4.6), 635-3566.

OF INTEREST
Luray Caverns, 743-6551, with stalactites and -mites, and organ. Daily 9.00 am-7 pm, $13, 1hr tours. 'Excessive.' 'Worth every cent.'

WEST VIRGINIA *Mountain State*

A common image people have of West Virginia is of a poor but proud population struggling to make a living from coal mining and enduring a hard life between business cycles as up-and-down as the Appalachian mountains that cover the state.

Though this image is partly accurate, 50 years of federal programmes, a growing tourist economy, and industries flourishing in other, less mountainous parts of the state have combined to alter the economic picture of West Virginia. The most striking (and most lucrative) aspect of the Mountain State, however, remains its natural beauty. Tree-covered mountains, raging rivers, caves, waterfalls and gorges offer the visitor a variety of scenic vistas and wilderness adventures.

The state was formed during the Civil War when people in the western part of Virginia refused to join the rebels and seceded from the Confederacy and not from the Union. The mountain people, who still speak a form of Elizabethan English, are authentic hillbillies and local bluegrass musicians can be heard in small town and big city alike.

www.yahoo.com/Regional/US States/West Virginia/
The telephone area code for the entire state is 304.

CHARLESTON Not to be confused with Charleston, South Carolina. This is the state capital and an industrial town; not much to look at, but there are nice hills nearby, and the city is a good base for a more interesting visit to the countryside.

ACCOMMODATION
Dunbar Super 8 Motel, 911 Dunbar Ave, 768-6888. S/D-$48-$88.
Night's Inn, 6401 MacCorkle Ave, I-77 exit 95, 925-0451. S-$44, D-$49, XP-$5.
Red Roof Inn, 4006 MacCorkle Ave, I-64 exit 54, 744-1500. S-$46, D-$49, XP-$5.

FOOD

Charleston Town Center Picnic Place and Restaurants, Clendin, Court, Lee and Quarrier Sts, 345-9525. 160 stores and restaurants, one of the largest downtown enclosed malls in the US. Mon-Sat 10 am-9 pm, Sun 12.30 pm-5 pm.
Kanawha Mall, 57th St & MacCorkle Ave SE, 925-4921. Mall with food court and restaurants. Mon-Sat 10 am-9 pm, Sun 12.30 pm-5 pm.

OF INTEREST

Cultural Center, Greenbrier & Washington Sts, 558-0162. Free exhibits of West Virginia arts, crafts and history. Mon-Fri 9 am-5 pm, Sat & Sun 1 pm-5 pm.
State Capitol, Main rotunda, Washington St E, 558-3809, free tours daily 9 am-3.15 pm.

INFORMATION/TRAVEL

Convention and Visitors Bureau, 200 Civic Center Dr, Suite 2, 344-5075.
Amtrak, 350 MacCorkle Ave SE, (800) 872-7245. Baltimore $92, Washington DC $85.
Greyhound, 300 Reynolds St, (800) 231-2222. Baltimore $53, Washington DC $53, Richmond $57.

NEW RIVER GORGE   In the southernmost part of the state, the New and Gauley rivers churn some of the most exciting rapids anywhere. The Gauley, in fact, is billed as one of the top ten whitewater rivers in the world. The major city serving the region is **Beckley**, where accommodation and hiking equipment can be found. The area can be reached by following I-77, the West Virginia Turnpike (toll).

ACCOMMODATION

Budget Inn, 222 S Heber St, 253-8318. S-$35, D-$38. 'Convenient.'
Days Inn, off I-77 exit 44, 255-5291. Rooms from $54.

OF INTEREST

Exhibition Coal Mine, New River Park in Beckley, 256-1747. Learn about coal mining by going down into a real coal pit. April-Nov, daily 10 am-6 pm, $7. 'Take a sweater.'
Honey-In-The-Rock Theater, in Grandview State Park near Beckley, 256-6800. Classic and modern drama by local repertory companies. June-Sept, Tues-Sun, 8.30 pm. Includes play about Hatfield/McCoy feud. Tkts $12, Fri/Sat $15.
New River Gorge, every Friday, the Amtrak *Cardinal* between Chicago and New York, offers a narrated trip through the gorge between White Sulphur Springs and Montgomery.
Whitewater Rafting. The Chamber of Commerce in Beckley, 500 N Valley Dr, 252-7328, has brochures of many organisations that run whitewater rafting tours along the New and Gauley Rivers at various prices. $75 could buy you the thrill of a life-time.
   New River Gorge is surrounded by numerous State Parks, including; **Babock**, **Bluestone**, **Carnifex Ferry**, **Hawks Nest**, and **Pipestream**. All offer exceptional recreational facilities and camping.

MONONGAHELA NATIONAL FOREST   Sounding like the name of a monster from a Japanese sci-fi flick, the Monongahela is actually a charming and beautiful forest covering much of eastern West Virginia. Unusual geological formations beneath the mountains have resulted in the creation of some of the largest caverns in the world, as well as warm mineral springs that bubble up in several valleys. There's coal under the mountains too, and many of the back roads are made bumpy by the giant coal trucks that roll in convoy all day and all night.

Within a few miles of the town of **White Sulphur Springs** are the **Lost World Caverns**, filled with amazing rock formations and bats. Lost World, in Lewisburg, 645-6677. Self-guided tour $7, daily 9 am-7 pm. Also along Hwy 219 is the **Droop Mountain State Park**, site of a Civil War battle. Two hours northeast of White Sulphur Springs town is **Cass Scenic Railroad**, 456-4300, where a coal-fired locomotive hauls visitors along old logging railways through the remote corners of the National Forest late May through early Oct. 1¹/₂ hr rides at 11 am, 1 pm, 3 pm; $11; 4¹/₂hr trip at noon (not Mon), $14.

Green Bank National Radio Astronomy Observatory, on Rte 28, 456-2011, is 10 miles away from the Cass Railroad. This is a major radio telescope which American scientists are using to map the universe and study its chemical composition. Free daily tours from mid-June-Sept between 9 am-4 pm.

ACCOMMODATION
Allstate Motel, Hwy 60, 1¹/₂ miles east of White Sulphur Springs, 536-1731. S-$36, D-$42.
Budget Inn, Hwy 60, 536-2121. Rooms from $55.
Camping: There are no camping restrictions in the forest, so if you have some of that pioneer spirit, just find a spot and camp down. State parks with campgrounds: **Greenbrier**, near White Sulphur Springs, 536-1944, has cabins suitable for groups; from $72 first night, $52 per night thereafter. Tent sites are $11, $14 w/hook-up. **Watoga**, near Hillsboro, Rte 28, 799-4087. Rates as above, but all prices vary with the seasons.

NORTHERN PANHANDLE The section of the state that sticks up between Ohio and Pennsylvania, has two things worth visiting: **Grave Creek Mounds**, at Moundsville, 843-1410, the largest pre-historic, conical Indian burial site in the US. Mon-Sat 10 am-4.30 pm, Sun 1 pm-5 pm, $3, $2 w/student ID. **Prabhupada's Palace of Gold** in New Vrindaban, south of Wheeling on Hwy 250, 843-1600. This glittering gold complex is a Hare Krishna tribute to their departed leader. Future plans include a theme park called 'City of God,' proving that it's not *all* spirituality, after all. Daily 9.30 am-8 pm, $5 donation.

HARPERS FERRY The National Park Service preserves this small, historic town where in 1859 John Brown raided the government arsenal, freed a few blacks and hoped to spark a general slave uprising. He was captured the following evening by Col Robert E Lee and two months later was tried and publicly hanged in neighbouring Charles Town.

Highly recommended for Civil War buffs—Harpers Ferry changed hands 17 times during the war—the area also appeals to nature lovers for the view from Jefferson Rock. Park Service tours throughout the day, 8 am-6 pm in summer; in winter, talks are few and far between, but exhibits and orientation films are open 'til 5 pm. 535-6298 for more info. Pedestrian bridge connects into C&O Canal Towpath over the river.

Nearby **Shepherdstown**, the oldest town in West Virginia, home of Shepherd College, offers shops, higher priced accommodation and restaurants (**Betty's Pharmacy Cafe, Mecklenburg Inn**).

Charles Town has a race track with nearby motels and cheap eats (**Sadler Cafe, Stuck and Alger**, both on W Washington St) as well as country fairs, carriage rides and charming old houses. The first rural postal delivery service in the US began here.

ACCOMMODATION
Bear's Den, 25 miles south of Harper's Ferry in Bluemont, VA, (540) 554-8708. $12 AYH, $15 non-AYH. Office hours 5 pm-10 pm. See also 'Virginia.'
Harpers Ferry AYH Hostel, on Sandy Hook Rd, in MD, (301) 834-7652. $11 AYH, $14 non-AYH; $4 AYH camping, closed 9.30 am-5 pm. Overlooking the Potomac and Shenandoah Rivers, this is a great location for hiking and rafting. A shuttle service operates from the train station to the hostel ($5 o/w), call (301) 834-7653.

OF INTEREST
Whitewater Rafting on the Shenandoah, a tamer ride than the New River Gorge. Blue Ridge Outfitters, Hwy 340, 2 mi from the Harpers Ferry National Park, (304) 725-3444. Raft and canoe trips, Mar-Oct, $50 half day, $75 full day. Rsvs recommended.

INFORMATION/TRAVEL
Harpers Ferry is readily accessible by car from Washington DC, Baltimore, and Harrisburg.
Amtrak, (800) 872-7245, from Washington's Union Station once a day, $17 o/w.
MARC Line Trains, (800) 325-7245, also run from DC, Mon-Fri only, $7.25 o/w. You might also want to pass through here if you're on your way to the Skyline drive through Virginia's Shenandoah National Park.

THE MIDWEST

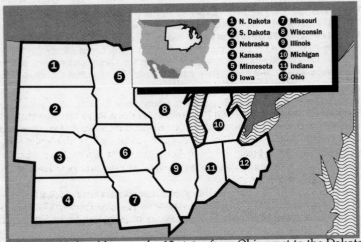

1 N. Dakota	**7** Missouri
2 S. Dakota	**8** Wisconsin
3 Nebraska	**9** Illinois
4 Kansas	**10** Michigan
5 Minnesota	**11** Indiana
6 Iowa	**12** Ohio

The Midwest (defined here as the 12 states from Ohio west to the Dakotas) is the rich, flat underbelly of the US, its glacier-scoured fertile lands yielding massive quantities of corn, soybeans, hay, wheat and livestock. It's also the manufacturing, transportation and industrial heart of America; the Chicago-Gary area alone once poured more steel than all of France. The region boasts the world's most powerful and fastest computer, CRAY-2 (in Minneapolis), the highest-energy particle accelerator (near Batavia, Illinois), and the largest manufacturer of farm equipment (in Moline, Illinois).

But the recession of the early 1980's hit the Midwest hard. From some it earned the nickname 'the rust belt' for its deteriorating and closed-down factories. Falling prices and excessive debts trapped many farmers in a downward spiral toward bankruptcy, causing unprecedented suicides that tore at the fabric of a settled life. However, industry has recently revived somewhat; farm prices and the value of land have also risen.

The essential quality of Midwestern life is its smalltown character, and that's where you should seek it out. Take time to meet its friendly and generous people, to get to know the prairie villages and the slow drawl of fields between them. Listen to the charming Scandinavian brogue of the northern states. And try to find time to read the novels of Nobel Prize winner Sinclair Lewis (*Babbitt, Main Street, Elmer Gantry*), each of which was carefully mapped out by Lewis in quintessential midwestern cities.

Mother Nature provides much of the drama here, from tornados in spring-summer to the fantastic electrical storm displays that light up summer evenings. The area is also seismically active: in 1811-1812, the biggest quakes in recorded history rolled through one million square miles, causing the Mississippi and Ohio Rivers to flow backwards.

The region's mighty rivers and Great Lakes serve as liquid highways for its products, just as they did in paddlewheeler days; they also create liquid disasters such the great floods of 1993 that caused way over $10 billion in damage and left millions of people homeless and (ironically) without water. Itself once 'the West', the Midwest in turn became the staging area for pioneer trails like the Santa Fe, Oregon and Mormon. With the advent of the railroad, the region became the distribution link between cattle ranch and consumer, a role it continues to play today.

ILLINOIS   *The Prairie State*

Illinois takes its nickname from the prairie, the original ground cover for the vast region lying east of the Mississippi River. On it, the grasses grew nine feet or more, which is why Illinois' corn can get as high as an elephant's eye today. West of the Mississippi, the land gradually turns from prairie to plains which are just as flat but receive less rain, more sun, and have thinner soil—prime wheat-growing land.

Illinois has a tradition of plain-spoken eloquence, from Lincoln, Sandberg and Hemingway to the Grange Movement farmers of the 1870's, who took as their slogan: 'Raise less corn and more hell!' Its premier city, Chicago, is also the birthplace of the only truly American architecture and the earthy Chicago blues. In the countryside, you'll taste Midwestern hospitality at its best, as sweet and honest as an ear of young corn.
www.yahoo.com/Regional/U_S__States/Illinois/

CHICAGO   In the aftermath of the Great Fire of 1871, a Chicago realtor put up a sign that read: 'All gone but wife, children and energy!' That unquenchable jauntiness is still Chicago's trademark. The place hurls superlatives at you: tallest buildings, largest grain market, greatest distribution point, busiest airport and train terminal, biggest Polish populace outside Warsaw, highest concentration of practicing psychics—the list is endless.

Chicago, which is where Ferris Bueller took his day off, has two popular nicknames, Second City and The Windy City. For decades it was the nation's second most populous region, after New York, but that title has since passed to Los Angeles. It's the politics, not the breeze sweeping in off Lake Michigan, that explains Chicago's other nickname.

Volatile is the word for Chicago's politics, particularly for the periods following the deaths of Mayor Richard Daley and more recently, of the much admired black mayor, Harold Washington. The ruthless Mayor Daley ran one of the last great political machines in America for a generation after World War II. He made Chicago 'the city that works'. His son, Richard M Daley, elected in 1988, is a man of the 90s. He's captured the affection and trust of Chicago's crazy quilt of ethnic and political groups.

Built on a swamp the Indians called 'place of the stinking wild onions', Chicago is the fount of architectural innovation in the United States, a vital communications and trading centre, and the hub for both industry and

Chicago

1 Archicentre
2 Robie's House
3 Sears Tower
4 Adler Planetarium and Museum
5 Art Institute of Chicago
6 Musuem of Science and Industry
7 Field Museum of Natural History
8 Shedd Aquarium
9 Chicago Historical Society
10 Museum of Contemporary Art
11 Market Street
12 Water Tower
13 John Hancock Tower

Lake Michigan

Lake Michigan

O'HARE AIRPORT

ZOO

NORTH AVE
SCHILLER AVE
BANKS AVE
EVANSTON
DIVISION ST
CEDAR AVE
OAK ST BEACH
DELAWARE AVE
CHICAGO AVE
ONTARIO AVE
OHIO AVE
HUBBARD
MICHIGAN AVE
FAIRBANKS CT
Chicago River
LAKE AVE   THE LOOP
RANDOLPH   AVE
ILLINOIS CENTRAL STATION
MADISON ST
ADAMS AVE
JACKSON AVE
VAN BUREN DR
EXPRESSWAY
BALBO DR
COLUMBUS
WACKER DR
LA SALLE DRIVE
STATE STREET
GRANT DRIVE
PARK
LAKE SHORE DRIVE
Chicago River
MILWAUKEE AVE
CONGRESS
DAN RYAN EXPRESSWAY
UNIVERSITY OF ILLINOIS
ROOSEVELT RD
14TH ST
16TH ST
ACHSAH BOND DRIVE
SOLDIER'S FIELD
BASEBALL & FOOTBALL STADIUM
MEIG'S FIELD
CERNAK ST
STEVENSON EXPY
35TH ST
47TH ST
51ST ST
55TH ST
57TH ST
DAN RYAN EXPRESSWAY
WABASH AVE
INDIANA AVE
MARTIN LUTHER KING AVE
COTTAGE GROVE
WASHINGTON PARK

N

agriculture in the Midwest. Both the true skyscraper, where the stress falls on the metal skeleton rather than the walls, and balloon framing, a cheap breakthrough in housing construction, were born here. At various times Chicago was the home of Louis Sullivan, Frank Lloyd Wright, Daniel Burnham, Helmut Jahn and Mies van der Rohe. The city possesses the finest architectural tradition in the country and had the good sense to preserve its lakeshore as recreational land, giving it an extraordinary skyline along 27 miles of parklands and clean beaches.

Always pugnacious, Chicago in its gangland heyday (1920's-1940's) had wide-open criminal activity and hundreds of unsolved mob murders. The 1988 movie, *The Untouchables*, reveals the morbid underworld of the infamous criminal, Al Capone, and his gang. One public official tried to divert attention from his Capone connections with an anti-British Empire campaign. He periodically offered to punch King George V 'in the snoot' if the monarch ever ventured near Chicago. Mob action may be gone, but the city still has an exceptionally high murder rate. As a natural corollary, Chicago also has more practising lawyers than all of England. With this in mind, visitors should remember that the Loop and lakeshore areas are the safest. After dark, stay clear of parks and poorly-lit streets. These cautions hold particularly true for women. The South Side is very risky at night.

The telephone area code is 312.

www.chi.yahoo.com.

ACCOMMODATION

AAIH-Chicago International Hostel, 6318 N Winthrope Ave, 262-1011. S-$13 AYH, $15 non-AYH, $5 deposit, bike rental $8. Take Howard St train to Loyola Station, walk 3 blocks S on Sheridon Rd to Winthrop. Closed 10 am-4 pm, curfew 12 am Mon-Fri. 'Sunny, safe location'.

Acres Motel, 5600 Lincoln Ave, 561-777. Free parking, S/D-$35, w/end $40.

Arlington House Hostel, 616 W Arlington Pl, 929-5380. $15 AYH, $18 non-AYH, $2 linen rental. Private room from $30. 'Excellent hostel, but dirty bathrooms.' Close to Chicago nightlife. Mixed reports.

Blackstone Hotel, 636 S Michigan Ave, across from Grant Park, 427-4300. S/D-$69-$99 w/student ID on non-convention days (Fri, Sat & Sun). Near museums, State St shopping. 'Area can be dodgy.'

Cass Hotel, 640 N Wabash Ave, 787-4030. S-$50, D-$55. 2 blocks off Michigan Ave. 'Excellent, clean rooms, recently refurbished.' 'Good breakfast café'. Popular with BUNACers. $5 off with ISIC.

HI-Chicago Summer Hostel, 1414 East 59th St, 753-5350. $16 AYH, $19 non-AYH (inc. shared suite and bath). Private room D-$48, $2 linen rental, $5 key deposit. Packed with students, 2 blocks from Chicago's free summer festivals in Grant Park. Rooms sleep 2-3. Kitchen, laundry, small gym. In downtown business area.

Hotel Wacker, 111 W Huron, 787-1386. Close to downtown, easy to find (look for the big green sign on the corner). 'Clean rooms,' TV, phone, 24hrs. S-$40, D-$45.

International House, 1414 E 59th, 753-2270. Take Illinois Central RR to 59th St, walk ½ block W. Open mid-June-August. $21 AYH, $35 non-AYH. Rsvs essential. Cheap in-house cafeteria. Near science museum. 'Good place'. 'Part of Uni of Chicago, neighbourhood can be dangerous.'

Lawson YMCA, 30 Chicago Ave, 944-6211. Coed, S-$33–$5 key deposit, D-$44–$10 key deposit. Price lowers with additional nights. Pool. 'Convenient and safe neighbourhood, if squalid.'

Ohio East Hotel, 15 E Ohio, 644-8222. Month: S-$325, and (on request) D-$365 ($50 deposit). 'No AC or TV but clean and with excellent views.' 'Full of weirdos.'

Parkway Eleanor Club, 1550 N Dearborn Pkwy, 664-8245. (For less than 28 days) $40, $5 key deposit. If you plan to stay longer than 28 days you must go through an application process to join the club. Both include bfast. Women only. 'Full of American students, located by Lake Michigan.'

Three Arts Club of Chicago, 1300 N Dearborn Pkwy, 944-6250. Check-in, noon-11 pm, out, noon. Coed conference centre and summer hostel. Located on the 'Gold Coast', one of Chicagos most beautiful neighbourhoods. Bus and subway 1 block, close to 'Magnificent Mile' shopping district. Courtyard, art studio, pianos, TV lounges, laundry. $40 includes bfast and dinner. Also try **Northwestern Uni**, Accommodation Office, Goe McClellan Bldg, 850 Lakeside Dr, 908-8514. $16-$20, June-July only, call for application.

FOOD

Local specialties: Chicago-style deep-dish pizza, stuffed pizza, kosher all-beef hotdogs and el-cheapo hamburgers called sliders. Pick up *Chicago Magazine* from most tourist offices for an extensive, comprehensive guide to eating out.

Ann Sathers, 929 W Belmont, 348-2378, take the El to Belmont. Bakery and Swedish diner. Homemade cinnamon rolls, pies and bread. Sun-Thu 7 am-10 pm, w/ends 'til 11 pm. Bfast served all day.

Berghoff"s, W of State at 17 W Adams, 427-3170. German menu, a Chicago tradition, big helpings. Closed Sun.

Billy Goats, 430 N Michigan, 222-1525. Cheap rib-eye steaks. 'Run by Greeks who holler your order across the Midwest: 'Cheezebooga, Cheezebooga, Pepsi, Pepsi! No fries, Cheeps!'

Ed Debevic's, 640 N Wells at Ontario, 664-1707. 50's-style diner. 'Great American food. The most fun you can have eating out—you have to go in there just to read the outrageously rude messages posted around the restaurant'.

Edwardo's, 8 locations including 1212 N Dearborn, 337-4490, on the near North Side; 521 S Dearborn, 939-3366, downtown; and 1321 E 57th St, 241-7960, in Hyde Park. Pizza, pasta & salads.

Gino's East, 160 E Superior, 943-1124. 'Most well-known pizza house in Chicago.'

Giordano's, 747 N Rush St, 951-0747, and about thirty other locations. Voted best pizza by *Chicago Magazine*. 'The best pizza ever.'

Jacob's Deli, 185 N Wabash Ave, inside the food-court at Wabash and Lake. Chicago hotdogs for $1.25. Jacob's Bfast Special (4 eggs, bacon, ham, sausage, hash browns, toast, butter, jelly, coffee) $3. 'Amazing value.'

John Barleycorn Memorial Pub, 658 W Belden Ave at Lincoln Ave, 348-8899. Free slide show set to classical music. An English-style pub with artsy intellectuals.

Hamilton's Bar, Broadway and Sheridan, 764-8133; good cheap food.

Lou Mitchell's, 565 W Jackson, 939-3111, 1 block from Union Station. A family operation since it opened in 1923, this venerable eatery gives free Milk Duds to the 'ladies', donut holes and a prune to all. Fresh-ground coffee, baked goods, Greek toast. 'Wonderful atmosphere.'

For ice-cream lovers: try the luscious **'frango mint'** at Marshall Fields 3rd floor ice-cream parlour, State and Randolph.

Mitchell's Original, 101 W North at Clark, 642-5246. Good filling bfasts for under $6.

Miller's Pub, 134 S Wabash Ave. 'Good for breakfast, with friendly service, moderate prices and a good atmosphere.'

Nookies, Tree, 2114 N Holland, 248-9888 . Run by a talkative Irish ex-pat, you can get 3 course meal with refill coffee for under $7. 'Very wide selection from quality burgers to gourmet.'

Oodles of Noodles, 2540 N Clarke, 975-1090. Great choice of different types of noodles, $4-$9. 'Friendly.'

Pete's Restaurant, 742 W Fullerton, 880-5730. Bfast for under $6. 'Good value and filling—keeps you full to lunch.'

Rocky's, south of Navy Pier. 90 years of tradition behind this restaurant on the riverfront, with a mural of the late Rocky looking out over the water.

Thai Star, 660 N State, 951-1196. Charming, inexpensive, one of the first of its kind in Chicago.

White Castle, several locations around Chicago. Home of the slider, so called because its grease content helps it slide down the throat easily. Order 4 or more for a meal.

West Egg on State, 1139 N State, 951-7900. Wide variety, excellent.
www.chicagorest.com/—also has good club listings.

OF INTEREST

Adler Planetarium and Museum, 1300 S Lake Shore Dr, 322-0329. $4 sky shows. Free on Tues. 'Good show, interesting photos.' 9 am-5 pm daily, 9 pm Fri.

American Police Center and Museum, 1700 S State St, 431-0005. All you've ever wanted to know about police and FBI work from forensics to an exhibition of death masks (including Dillinger's) to their authentic electric chair for visitors to try. Indulge your obsession with the macabre. Mon-Fri 8.30 am-4.30 pm; $3.50.

Archi Center, 224 S Michigan, 922-3432, offers tours of outstanding Chicago architecture. 2 hr walk around the Loop costs $10, Mon-Sat at 10 am &1.30 pm, Sun 1.30 pm. 'Good way to see a variety of Chicago architecture. Wear comfortable shoes.' Bus tour departs Sat at 9.30 am in spring, summer and fall, for 30 mile 4 hr tour including Frank Lloyd Wright's **Robie House**, $25. (Rsvs essential). For a panoramic view of the city you can ascend **Sears Tower**, 875-9447, the tallest and one of the ugliest buildings in the world, at Wacker Drive and Adams. On a clear day you can see across the lake to Michigan—60 miles. Go at night for a truly spectacular view of the city but forget the audio-visual show beforehand, it's a waste of time. Open 9 am-10.30 pm, $6.50. Or take a **boat trip**—Chicago is at its best from the lake. 'Best thing I did in Chicago.' Mercury, 332-1353, and Wendella, 337-1446, boats leave from opposite sides of the Chicago River at Michigan and Wacker Dr: $1^1/_2$hr trip, $18; 2hr trip $20. The longer the better as you sail further and proportionately less of your time is taken up with passing through the locks into Lake Michigan (which is 8 ft higher than the river). Best of all is the 2 hr night-time trip (7.30 pm departure) for the dazzling lights. 'Boat stops in front of Buckingham Fountain—spectacular lights and colour show.'

Art Institute, Michigan & Adams St, 443-3500. A magnificent collection of Impressionism, post-Impressionism—great Cezanne and Gaugin, modern American art and the Thorne Rooms: a series of minutely detailed period rooms—in miniature. Mon-Fri 10.30 am-4.30 pm, Tues 'til 8 pm, Sat 10 am-5 pm, Sun 12 pm-5 pm. $7, $3.50 w/student ID, Tues free. Good basement cafe. 'Wonderful, well worth six bucks.' 'Fantastic art collection. Give yourself a whole day if you want to see everything.'

Capone's Chicago, 605 N Clark St. Free entry to small Capone museum. Worth paying $5 to hear the 30 min talk on Chicago's Prohibition era and gangster history through a series of 'talking waxworks' and special effects. Daily 10 am-10 pm.

Chicago Board of Trade, 141 W Jackson Blvd, 435-3500. 'This is the commodities exchange, there is a free visitors' gallery with an audio-visual presentation.' An incredible $25 billion changes hands here each day, in grain contracts, treasury bonds and other commodities. Mon-Fri 8 am-1.15 pm. Free.

Chicago Historical Society, Clark St & North Ave, 642-4600. An impressive collection of exhibits centred on Chicago and Illinois. Outstanding on Lincoln with notebooks, letters, fashions, photos, manuscripts, furnishings. Mon-Sat 9.30 am-4.30

pm, Sun noon-5 pm; $3 w/ student ID, free Mon. Library open Tue-Sat only.

Chicago Mercantile Exchange, 30 S Wacker St, 930-1000. The largest financial futures exchange in the world handles over 400,000 contracts each day, including those of pork bellies and other livestock. From the visitors centre, you can observe the colourful, madcap behaviour on the floor below. Mon-Fri 7.30 am-3.15 pm, main floor; 8th floor for foreign currency, 7.15 am-2 pm.

The Cultural Center at Michigan and Randolph, is the best place to plan your sight-seeing. Before hitting the streets, wander around the changing exhibitions (modern art, photography, aspects of Chicago, etc.) situated on the ground floor. Everything is free.

Field Museum of Natural History, Roosevelt Rd & Lake Shore Dr, 922-9410. Anthropology, botany, zoology, geology. Daily 9 am-5 pm; $5, $3 w/student ID, free Wed. 'There are interesting exhibits on American Indians and Eskimos.'

Frank Lloyd Wright houses. There are 25 in the suburbs; the Art Institute bookshop has good guidebooks. You need a car to see many of them, but FLW's own house and studio at Chicago and Forest Aves in Oak Park is reachable by El—to Harlem. From here, some of the houses are within walking distance. **Visitors Centre**, 158 Forest Ave, (708) 848-1500.

John Hancock Center, 875 N Michigan, 751-3680. Tallest residential building in the world. Cocktail bar skywalk. Views of the city at night; $7.75, observation hall. Open 9 am-midnight. Try the 95th floor restaurant for lunchtime buffet $8.

The Loop, a 5-by 7-block city core, is defined by the steel tracks of the elevated subway ('El'), a transit system with a voice like a giant trash compactor yet strangely lovable. Besides being fast and cheap, this dotted line of noise gives free rein to voyeurism, letting you virtuously peep at a thousand fleeting tableaux as you flash past. Within the Loop are theatres, smart hotels and shopping districts, including the once pre-eminent **Marshall Fields** department store (still has the best Christmas windows anywhere).

Marina City, 300 N State St, a prototype self-contained 'vertical city' of residences, offices and spiral car port; resembles two upended corncobs.

Michigan Ave, 20's and 30's facades, mortared with money, opulent restraint, shops for ogling only.

Museum of Contemporary Art, 220 E Chicago ave 280-2660. The MCA's new building, located near the historic **Water Tower**, holds exhibits of fine art dating from 1945, as well as permanent collections featuring the works of Kline, Magritte and Warhol. 'Good Café'. Tue,Thu, Fri 11 am-6 pm, Wed 11 am-9 pm, w/end 10 am-6 pm. $4, free first Tue of each month.

Museum of Science and Industry, E 57th St & Lake Shore Dr, 684-1414. Visit the Apollo 8 spacecraft, go for a simulated space shuttle ride, or see the latest Omnimax presentation. Free; fees for coal mine, U-boat sub. Sun-Thu 9.30 am-5.30 pm , Fri 9 am-9.30 pm, shorter hours in winter. $6, plus extra for Omnimax Theater. Free Thurs. 'Best I've ever been to—easily spend a whole day here.' 'Magnificent place.'

Shedd Aquarium, next to Field Museum, 939-2426. One of the worlds largest indoor aquariums. Over 6000 species of fish occupy 206 tanks. Daily 9 am-6 pm year-round; $5, free Thur. Also an oceanarium with Beluga whales, dolphins, penguins, etc. $10 combo tkt. 'Very disappointing—save your money for the coastal aquariums in Boston and Baltimore.'

State Street, running north-south, and **Madison**, east-west, bisect within the Loop at what's called the world's busiest intersection. (At 1 S State, take a peep at the delicate ironwork, by Louis Sullivan, F L Wright's mentor.) All street numbers in Chicago begin here, each block representing increments of 100. One block east of the Loop is Michigan Ave; its most elegant stretch, the **Magnificent Mile**, gives a glittering, often windy view of Lake Michigan.

University of Chicago, 7 miles south of the Loop on the Midway. Dominating the Hyde Park neighbourhood, this beautiful campus holds one of Americas best universities. 'Wonderful examples of Gothic architecture', and the "Nuclear Energy" sculpture, marking the site of the first sustained nuclear chain reaction. Although patrolled by Uni police, surrounding areas are dangerous, especially at night.

Water Tower Pumping Station, 806 N Michigan Ave at Pearson St. This fanciful Gothic Revival station conceals a very utilitarian pump—it distributes over 72 million gallons of water each day. One of the few public buildings to survive the 1871 fire, consequently revered by Chicagoans. Mon-Thurs 9.30 am-5.00 pm, 7 pm Fri. **Visitors Center** with maps, discount coupons in booklet 'Chicago's Got It' in the lobby, 9.30 am-5 pm daily.

There is enough to see without having to spend a dime:

Beaches: 18 sandy miles of 'em—free! Try **Oak St** beach just NE of John Hancock Center. 'The best beach we found in America. Clean, safe and a nice place to relax after seeing the city.' Or **Lincoln Park** beaches. The area is pleasant and relatively safe, with bars, cafes, and restaurants. 'Makes Chicago seem like the seaside.' 'Quite pleasant walking along waterfront—a park all the way to Museum of Science.'

Buckingham Fountain: set in Grant Park along Chicago's lake front, the fountain is outlined against the skyscrapers of the Loop. At night a light show transforms the fountain into a dazzling, many-coloured sculpture.

Great Ape House, Lincoln Park Zoo, 2200 N Cannon Dr, 742-2000. More than 2,000 exotic and endangered species, including special exhibits on big cats, primates and others. Daily 9 am-5 pm, free. Ingenious glass cylinder arrangement lets you see monkeyshines at close hand. NB: Keep out of park after sunset.

Outdoor Art

The skyscrapers in Chicago are amazing. **The Standard Oil Building**, 200 E Randolph St, the world's fourth tallest; the **Hancock Tower**; the **Chicago Tribune Tower** with its ornate faux-Gothic design, 435 N Michigan Dr, and the **Wrigley Building** opposite; the elliptical, mirrored offices that look out onto the river, 333 W Wacker Dr; the wedge-shaped **Illinois State Center**, 100 W Randolph St, with its light, airy atrium; and, of course, the black monolith that is **Sears Tower**.

Sculpture fills the city. Outside the State Center sits Alexander Calder's *Flamingo*, a huge set of pink interconnecting girders; *The Picasso*, Daley Center Plaza at Washington and Dearborn, is a 63 ft steel woman with typical abstraction; *Untitled Sounding Sculpture* by Bertoia outside Standard Oil; *Batcolumn*, Claes Oldenburg's huge baseball bat in full erection at 600 W Madison; Miro's *Chicago*, a smaller homage to the city than most, Brunswick Plaza, 69 W Washington; and finally Marc Chagall's *Four Season's* 70 ft mosaic wall that looks like graffiti, First National Bank Plaza.

Tomb-hopping. Al Capone has two graves, one at Mt Olivet ('qui reposa'), another at Mt Carmel ('My Jesus mercy').

The industrial Chicago suburb of **Des Plaines** is the birthplace of that most American of eateries, McDonald's. The original is now the **McDonald's Museum**, 400 Lee St, (847) 297-5022. Tues-Sat, 10 am-4 pm. Lots of 50's McDonald's memorabilia—but you can't eat here! Go to the *operating* McDonald's across the street for your Big Mac instead. In Oak Brook, the nation's only **Hamburger University** trains McDonald's managers.

The Chicago Motor Coach Company, 922-8919 ($12), and the **The Chicago Trolley Company**, 738-0900 ($15) both provide near identical tours of the downtown area. They depart every 10-15 mins; pick-up at **The Sears Tower** and various locations. 1 hr narrated tours cover a 9-mile route stopping and picking up at the major sights. Unlimited boarding. 'Plenty of seats but so noisy it's impossible to hear the commentary!' . 'Only for people with limited time and sore feet.'

ENTERTAINMENT

Chicago is the centre of the blues world, has one of the strongest folk scenes in America and boasts an impressive amount of jazz activity. Pick up a free copy of *The Reader*, published Fri and available at record shops, to find out where it's happening. Also check the listings in *Chicago Magazine* or buy Hargrove and Snooks' *500 Things to Do in Chicago for Free*. NB: Stick to Old Town, the Rush Street area, and the North Side at night, even if you are in an armoured car.

Avalon, Belmont and Sheffield, 472-3020. El stop is Belmont. Local bands. $3-$6 cover. 'New wave.'

B.L.U.E.S., 2519 N Halsted, 528-1012. 'The people—exhilarating. The blues—totally overpowering.' 'Crowded, small, hot.' A larger sister club, **B.L.U.E.S etcetera** is now in existence and is the place to go to see big names such as Bo Diddley, Albert King and Dr John. Cover for both $5-$8. 9 pm-1.30 am.

Club 720, N Wells St, 397-0600. Recently opened, 4 levels, 14,000 sq ft. Live jazz main floor, DJ and dancing downstairs, cigars/billiards 2nd floor, Big Band upstairs. Mon-Fri 5 pm- 2 am, w/end 6.30 pm- 2 am.

Club 950, 950 Wrightwood, 929-8955. Alternative and new wave. $4 cover after 10 pm w/ends. 'Lots of English music.' Experience 'slam' poetry at the **Green Mill Lounge**, 4802 N Broadway, 878-5552. Every Sun at 7 pm, local poets recite their work, one-on-one, for up to $50 in winnings at this 80-year-old mobster hangout.

Crobar, 1543 N Kingsbury Ct, 587-8574. 'Futuristic industrial warehouse dance club'. 'Bladerunner meets Batman'. Boasts the largest dancefloor in the city. Wed-Sun 9 pm-4 am.

Downtown Thursday Night, every Thursday 5 pm-8 pm from the river to Roosevelt Rd. Mingle with locals and take advantage of the many specials offered on downtown accommodations, dining, entertainment, services and shopping. 'Something for every taste and budget'.

Hot Tix, 108 N State St, 977-1755. 'Half-price tickets for same day performances—theater, dance, the arts.' Mon-Sat, 10 am-6 pm, Sun 12 noon-5 pm. Must buy tkts personally. Show up 15-20 mins before booth opens for your pick.

Jazz Andy's, 11 E Hubbard, 642-6805. A great place to hear jazz, blues and Rock 'n' Roll. Free shows at noon Tue-Fri; daily shows at 5 pm, w/end shows 9 pm. Cover $3-$5

North Pier Chicago, a restored warehouse on the Chicago River with shops, restaurants and **Dick's Last Resort**, a large jazz bar. Close by is **Navy Pier**, stretching into Lake Michigan. If it's still untouched by redeveloper's hands, have a pleasant, uncommercial walk.

Second City Comedy Revue, 1616 N Wells, 337-3992. 'The place to see great comedians with a twisted sense of humour.' John Belushi, Jim Belushi and Bill Murray are among the egregious graduates of this wellspring of irreverent American comedy. Two sets of revues Fri & Sat, one show Tue, Wed, Thur & Sun. $11-$16.

Shelter, 564 W Fulton, 528-5500. Surround yourself with 'phat' beats and lava lamps. Sweat it out 'til the sun comes up on one of 7 dancefloors. Open 10 pm, cover $8-$10.

Sluggers World Class Sports Bar, Inc., 3540 N Clark, 248-0055. Has acres of screens with all sports and a games room with an indoor baseball batting cage! Cheap beer too. 'A right laugh.'

Wise Fools Pub, 2270 N Lincoln, 9291510. Blues and jazz greats, $5-$10 cover. *www.barsonline.com/chicago.htm*

Chicago Blues Festival (in early June) and **Chicago Jazz Festival** (in late August), Grant Park, 744-3315. Largest free blues and jazz festivals. To hear who's playing, call 744-3315. Afterwards there's more jamming at the clubs.

Two Chicago theatres are especially well-known, and have prices to match their fame. **The Steppenwolf Theater**, 1650 N Halsted, 335-1650, where Malkovich and Mamet grew up, and **The Goodman Theater**,2005 Columbus Drive, 443-3800. Both provide consistently good original work. Tkts $20-$30. The monthly *Chicago* and the weekly *Chicago Reader* give thumbnail reviews of all major shows, with times and ticket prices. Also, the monthly edition of *Where Chicago* is available from the Visitor Center.

SPORT
Chicagoans are sports mad. After the Chicago Bulls basketball team won the NBA title for the second time in 1992, the celebrations became a riot. See the Bulls and their all-star team at the **United Center**, 1901 W Madison, 455-4000, in the summer, tkts, $15-$30. The Blackhawks play ice-hockey there in the winter, 733-5300. NFL action can be viewed at **Soldier Field**, McFetridge Dr and S Lake Shore Dr, 708-651-2327. **Wrigley Field**, 1060 W Addison, 404-2827, is the home of the Cubs and one of the most beautiful baseball parks in the country. Intimate and packed to the rafters with people and atmosphere, it was the last park in the leagues to introduce flood-lights: night games didn't arrive until 1988. An ideal way to taste the most American thing this side of apple pie. The White Sox play at **Comiskey Park**, 924-1000, and have equally fervent supporters. Tkts range from $8-$20. Tkts from Ticketmaster, Bulls and Blackhawks 559-1212, White Sox 831-1769, Cubs 831-2827. For current sporting events call Sports Information 976-1313.
Cycling: Bike Chicago, locations at Oak St Beach, Navy Pier, Buckingham Fountain, Lincoln Park Zoo, (800) 915-2453. 'Great way to tour the city.' Service includes free bike route maps, free guided tours, free delivery to your hotel for daily rentals. 18 mile Lakefront Bike Tours depart Navy Pier, Mon-Fri 1.30 pm. Bikes $8 hr, $30 daily. In-line skates also for hire $7 hr, $24 daily.
Skating: Skank Skates Skatepark 1101 South Grand Ave E, 9217 0 522-7267. Mini-ramp complex featuring hip, bowl and spine, 4 ft-6 ft, $3 hr, $5 day. Mon-Fri 6.30 pm-10.30 pm, w/end 1 pm-midnight.

INFORMATION
Chicago Office of Tourism, (800) 226-6632. **Travelers Aid** , 327 S LaSalle, 629-4500; at **Greyhound**, (800) 231-2222; and airport, Terminal Two 686-7562. Maps, brochures. 'Extremely helpful.'
State of Illinois Tourism, 310 S Michigan, 814-4732, Mon-Fri 9 am-5 pm.
Visitors Center: 806 N Michigan at Pearson, 9 am-5 pm daily, 280-5740. Good map of the Loop.

TRAVEL
Amtrak, Union Station, Canal & Adams Sts, 655-2354/(800) 872-7245. Hub of the Amtrak intercity system. Think *The Untouchables*. Think Kevin Costner standing atop of a set of steps, gun in hand. Think pram going down the steps between bullets. Now walk up the steps in the station and relive it.
Auto Driveaway, 310 S Michigan, 939-3600. 'Friendly.' 'Very helpful.'
Greyhound, 630 W Harrison St, 781-2900/(800) 231-2222. 'Public library nearby, with free art exhibits—good place to go if between buses.' Local bus CTA/RTA, 836-7000, for fare and schedule info..
O'Hare International Airport 668-2200, the busiest airport in the world. The Northwest El line takes you directly to the airport for $1.50. There are buses, but congestion is horrific, it'll take forever.

SPRINGFIELD The pleasant state capital has one main attraction: Abraham Lincoln. At the age of 28, 'The Great Emancipator' arrived in the city to practice law and stayed for twenty years. See the only house he ever owned, 426 S 7th St, 789-2357. Recently beautifully restored, it has a useful visitors bureau; you can also visit Lincoln's old law offices, 6th & Adams, 785-7289; the **Lincoln Depot**, Monroe & 9th, 788-1356, where he boarded the train to go to DC for his inauguration; the **family tomb**, Oak Ridge Cemetery, 782-2717; and the **Old State Capitol**, Capitol Plaza, 785-7960, where he was a member of the Illinois House of Representatives. There are other 'highlights' such as walking the same route as Abe did when he worked at the post office, the family pew in the church, and his bank ledger. Northeast of the city on Rte 97 is **New Salem Historic Site**, 632-4000, a reconstruction of the 1830's village where Lincoln lived as a young man. All this is free. The state's other adopted golden boy, Frank Lloyd Wright, is also on show in Springfield. The **Dana-Thomas House**, 301 E Lawrence, 782-6776, was built in 1903 for a local socialite. This prime example of the 'Prairie Style' that Wright pioneered also has furnishings by the man himself. 8 am-6 pm, may vary, call ahead.

The telephone area code is 217.

ACCOMMODATION
All-Star 8 Inn, 2224 E Cook, 789-0361. S-$24.
Best Rest Inn, 700 N Dirksen Pkwy, 522-7966. Laundry, TV, fridge available. S-$28, D-$38.
Capitol City Motel, 1620 N 9th, 528-0462. Near the fairgrounds and with kitchenettes. S-$38, D-$50.
Mr Lincoln's Campground, 3045 Stanton Ave, 529-8206. 4 miles E of downtown, take bus #10. Free showers, tent space $7 pp. Cabins $23 for 2, XP $3.
Nights Inn, 3125 Widetrack Dr, 789-1063. S-$33, D-$42.

FOOD
Try around the Vinegar Hill Mall, 1st and Cook Sts, for cheapeats, there are lots of places to quell those hunger pangs. **Capitol City Bar and Grill**, 753-5720, in the mall. Lots of lunchtime specials. Homemade lager for 50c on Wed. Mon 11 am-2 pm, Tue-Fri 11 am-9 pm, Sat 12 pm-1 am. No food after 9 pm.

INFORMATION/TRAVEL
Springfield Convention and Visitors Bureau, 109 N 7th, 789-2360. Mon-Fri 8 am-5 pm.
Greyhound, (800) 231-2222, take the #10 bus into town from the nearby shopping centre. Ticket Office Mon-Fri 5 am-2.30 pm, w/ends 6 am-10 am.

GALENA   Once an opulent riverboat and lead-mining town in northwest Illinois, Galena is now a beautiful backwater of stately homes and small-town friendliness. Galena produced a clutch of Civil War generals, including Ulysses S Grant; each year, the townspeople re-enact a battle or two.

If you have a car, by all means take the Great River Road south from Galena, which follows the Mississippi all the way to New Orleans. A lovely drive.

METROPOLIS   It's a bird, it's a plane, it's Clark Kent's 'home town' in southern Illinois on the Ohio River. Giant mural of Superman in the park, free kryptonite from the Chamber of Commerce, and for entertainment and the comics—the *Daily Planet*. No, this isn't where Superman was invented, or even where he was supposed to have lived ('Metropolis' in the comic book was a big city; this Metropolis is a small town of a few thousand friendly souls). Nonetheless, locals hold a 'Superman Celebration' each year on the 2nd w/end of June, complete with bank robbery foiled by you-know-who; (618) 524-2714 for more info.

INDIANA   *The Hoosier State*

Indiana has a wholesome, almost cornball ingenuousness about it, so it's not surprising to learn that it's the home of Notre Dame, Johnny Appleseed, Orville Wright (Wilbur was born in neighbouring Ohio), Studebaker, Cole Porter, Amish villages of *Friendly Persuasion* fame and David Letterman of late-night TV show notoriety. The rural portions have most to offer: rustic landscapes of country roads, covered bridges (notably in Parke County west of Indianapolis), round barns (in Fulton County) and even a 'Steamboat' Gothic mansion (in Vevay on the Ohio River).

Indiana cranks out lots of steel and more band instruments than any place on earth. Most of the heavy industry is in the northwest corner of the state, near Chicago, so don't let the atrocity called Gary colour your opinion of the rest of the state.

Several rebels, with and without causes, are buried here: Eugene Debs in Terre Haute, and James Dean in Fairmont (whose gravestone behind Friends Church is walking away in ghoulish bits and pieces). For a more mundane type of rebellion, check out Sunny Haven Recreation Park, a 20-acre nudist camp and site of sunbathing conventions.
www.yahoo.com/Regional/U_S__States/Indiana/

INDIANAPOLIS   Foursquare in the centre of the state, Indianapolis is state capital, national headquarters for the American Legion, home of the Indy 500 auto race and crossroads of America, so-called because a dozen or so major routes meet here. The city is as exciting as mashed potatoes except during the month of May, when the '500' Festival, the Indy time trials and other pre-race madness stir things up a bit. It's almost impossible to get seats for the race itself on Memorial Day Sunday (you must write for them a year in advance), but standing room and scalpers' tkts are available closer to race day. Time trials and qualifying runs begin 2-3 weeks before the main event and provide nearly the same level of thrills, decibels and mayhem as the big race, so bring beer, lunch and make a day of it. At night, party with the racing fans along Georgetown Ave. Call 481-8500 for an application form, or write to: Tkts, Indianapolis Motor Speedway, PO Box 24152, Speedway, IN 46224.

During spring, summer and fall, folk festivals take place by and around the Monument Circle area downtown.
The telephone area code is 317.

ACCOMMODATION
Basic Inn, 5117 E 38th St, 547-1100. S-$24, D-$28.
Indianapolis Motor 8, 3731 Shadeland, 545-6051. S-$28, D-$32
Motel 6 Inn, 5241 W Bradbury St at Lyndhurst, 248-1231. S-$34, D-$40.
Skyline Motel, 6617 E Washington St, 359-8201. S/D $35-$45 (Sun-Thur), $45-$50 (Sat and Sun).
YMCA, 860 W 10th St, 634-2478. S-$25, $70 weekly, w/student ID $60, ($5 key deposit). Higher during 500 Festival. 'Raunchy area.' Take #13 or 6 bus to get there. Reserve 2 weeks ahead.
For the more adventurous (ie with strong legs and country hearts) there are

numerous campgrounds throughout the state. Few rent tents/trailers so bring your own.

The Indianapolis State Fair Recreational Vehicle Campground, 1202 E 38th St, 927-7510. 6 miles from downtown. Can be reached by bus. Tent space-$11. All amenities.

Kamper Korner, 1951 W Edgewood Ave, 788-1488. A 7 mile hike from downtown. Tent space-$18, $21 w/hook-up. Fishing facilities.

Indianapolis KOA, 5896 W 200 North, Greenfield, 894-1397. 14 miles from downtown. Tent space-$16, $18 w/hook-up.

FOOD

Between Bread, 136 N Delaware, 638-4174. Great sandwiches.

Broad Ripple Village, north of city centre at 62nd St, is a mall full of ethnic restaurants and quaint shops.

Fireside South, 522 E Raymond St, 788-4521. Enjoy sizzling steaks, German entrees, spirits and a wide selection of seafoods. Heart-healthy menu available. 'Quality food in a comfortable, relaxed atmosphere.'

Pacos Cantina, 737 Broad Ripple Ave, 257-6200. Tacos $1.25, burritos $3, 'til 4 am.

Renee's French Restaurant, 839 E Westfield Blvd, 251-4142. 'Cheap, friendly with a really pleasant atmosphere.'

Shapiro's Deli, 808 S Meridian, 631-4041. Cheap and good cafeteria style food.

Yorkshire Rose Pub and Deli, 1168 Keystone Way, 844-4766. Large selection of imported beers, soup, sandwiches, sides, salads and entrees, $3-$11. Mon-Thu 11 am-midnight, w/end 11 am- 1 am.

OF INTEREST

Benjamin Harrison House, 1230 N Delaware, 631-1898. Home of the 23rd President of the US. Mon-Sat 10 am-3.30 pm, Sun 12.30-4 pm. $1 w/student ID.

Conner Prairie Pioneer Settlement, 6 miles N of Indianapolis, is a restoration of a 30-building pioneer village *circa* 1836. Visit typical homes and work-places of the era, eat frontier cooking, celebrate various festivals and meet inhabitants. Allisonville Rd exit off I-465, 773-06066. Tue-Sat 9.30 am-5 pm, Sun 11.30-5 pm, $9.

Children's Museum, 3000 N Meridian, take 29th St exit off I-65, 924-5431. Mon-Sat 10 am-5 pm, Thurs 'til 8 pm, Sun noon-5 pm; $7. World's largest kiddie museum: puppets, films, mummy, Tyranosaurus Rex, huge toy and antique train layout.

Harrison Eiteljorg Museum, 500 W Washington, 636-9378. A private collection of American art, both Native and Western, in a lovely atmosphere. Mon-Sat 10 am-5 pm, Sun noon-5 pm; $5, $2 w/student ID.

Indiana State Fair, Meridian St and Rte 37. Two weeks of Hoosier hoopla in mid-August, with an audience of almost a million. 'Huge, mad, big name groups.'

Indianapolis Motor Speedway, 4790 W 16th St, 481-8500. Tkts for the time trials are sold at the gates the day of the trials. Gates open at 7 am the opening day; 9 am other days. You can park in the infield. Tkts range from $30 to $150.

Indianapolis Zoo, 1200 W Washington, 630-2030. One of the newest and therefore well planned. $9, 9 am-5 pm daily.

Museum of Art, 1200 W 38th St, 923-1331. Major permanent exhibitions include one of the largest collections of Turner prints outside Great Britain, and the W J Holliday collection of neo-impressionist. Tue-Sat 10 am-5 pm; Sun, noon-5 pm, free.

Union Station, 200 S Illinois St. Built in 1888, one of the finest examples of Romanesque Revival architecture in the US. Galleries, restaurants, boutiques and passenger trains.

Speedway Museum, located in the infield of the Speedway, has a collection of Indy racers and memorabilia. Daily 9 am-5 pm, $2.

ENTERTAINMENT

City Taproom, 28 S Pennsylvania St, 637-1334. Live jazz, no cover. Closed Sun.

The Chatterbox, 435 Massachusetts Ave, 636-0584. Divey bar but good jazz.

Crackers Comedy Club, 8207 Keystone Crossing, 846-2500. Tue-Fri, shows at 8.30 pm, extra show Fri at 10.30 pm, Sat at 8 pm/10 pm, Sun at 8 pm.

Ike's and Jonesy's, 717 W Jackson, 632-4553. 50's and 60's music. Open until 3 am, no cover. Closed Sun.

The Slippery Noodle, 372 N Meridian, 631-6968. Live blues 7 nights a week.

Sports Bar and Grill, 231 S Meridian, 631-5838. Near Union Station, famous for its 'lingerie lunches'.

The Vogue, 6259 N College, 255-2828. Music for the masses, $2-$7 cover.

INFORMATION

Amtrak, 350 S Illinois St, 263-0550/(800) 872-7245.

Chamber of Commerce: 464-2200.

Greyhound, Union Station, 1 block S of Pan Am Plaza, (800) 231-2222. Open 24 hrs.

Indianapolis International Airport, 7 miles NW of downtown; hop on the #9 'W Washington' bus to get there, basic fares apply.

Metro Bus, 36 N Delaware, 635-3344. Runs the city buses; off-peak rate 75¢, rush hour $1.

Visitors Information: Indianapolis City Center at Pan Am Plaza, 201 S Capitol Ave, (800) 323-INDY or 237-5200 direct. Mon-Fri 10 am-5.30 pm, Sat 'til 5 pm, Sun noon-5 pm.

AMISH COUNTRY An hour north and east from Peru, lands you in the heart of Amish country in the counties of **LaGrange** and **Elkhart**. The town of **Shipshewana**, SR 5 off US 20, is a centre of Amish culture, with an auction and fleamarket every Tuesday and Wednesday in the summertime (phone 768-4129 for info). **Yoder's Department store** also carries Amish crafts and goods for those who miss the market days. For info about Mennonite and Amish history visit **Menno-Hof** across from the flea market on SR 5, 768-4117. At the **Buggy Wheel Restaurant and Bakery** try German sausage or roast pork and for dessert eat outrageous wet-bottom shoo-fly pie.

In the town of **Nappanee** on US 6, tours of an Amish farm and buggy rides are available, 773-4188. Nappanee is also home to the **Pletcher Art Festival** in early August and the **Apple Festival** in late September. **Amish Acres** is home to the **Round Barn Theater**, 1600 West Market, US6 West, 773-4188, where you can see a live Broadway musical classic about Amish life and love in a 400-seat restored round barn theater. Tues, Thur, Fri-8 pm; Wed and Sat-3 pm and 8 pm, from $20. The **Essenhaus Restaurant** in Middlebury, at the intersection of SR 13 and US 20, serves up Amish cooking. NB: Watch out for slow-moving Amish buggies on back roads. For info: **Chamber of Commerce**: 743-7812.

The telephone area code is 219.

BLOOMINGTON is a pleasant college town, home of Indiana University, an hour's drive southwest from Indianapolis on Rte 37. The movie *Breaking Away* was filmed here, and featured a bike race called the little 500. The race is an annual event in mid-April. Look too for the numerous abandoned stone quarries, also featured in the movie, which now serve as swimming holes on hot summer days.

An hour southwest from Bloomington takes you to the Wabash River town of **Vincennes**, site of **Grouseland**, 882-2096, the home of the shortest-lived US president—William Henry Harrison. At his inauguration, doubtless ignoring his mother's advice, Harrison gave a 2 hr speech in freezing rain, contracted pneumonia and died 31 days later, never having made a major decision as president. His 32-day term lasted from 4 March-4 April, 1841.

Seventy-five miles downstream from Vincennes lies the town of **New Harmony**, where two Utopian communities were set up in the early 19th century. In 1814 a grumpy Lutheran named George Rapp quit Germany to found New Harmony and await the coming of the Lord. Being delayed for some reason, the Lord never appeared, and Rapp departed after having waited ten years. Rapp left his village to expatriate Robert Owen, a Welshman, who founded a community of equality based on education. Kindergarten, coed public education and other new ideas in education were first tried here, and what remains is an historic district of 20 buildings and a dramatic 'roofless church' designed by Philip Johnson.

The telephone area code for the region is 812.

ACCOMMODATION
Lake Monroe Village Campground, 8107 S Fairfax Rd, 824-2267. 8 miles N of Bloomington. Free showers, pool. $18, w/hook-up $23, cabins available $42 for two.
Motel 6, 1800 N Walnut St, 332-2267, clean, spacious rooms and pool. S-$32, D-$37.

FOOD
The **Downtown Sq**, an abundance of restuarants within 2 blocks. Most found on Kirkwood City Ave, near College and W Walnut St.
Garcia's Pizza, 114 S Indiana Ave, 3340404. Good pan pizza by the slice.
Nick's, 423 E Kirkwood Ave, 332-4040. Cheap hamburgers and beer.

TRAVEL/INFORMATION
Visitors Bureau, 2855 N Walnut St, 339-8900.
Greyhound, 535 N Walnut St, 332-1522/(800) 231-2222.
Chamber of Commerce: 336-6381.

IOWA   *The Hawkeye State*

Imagine this: a state that produces unthinkable quantities of corn, soybeans and cattle and quarter of the nation's porkers and generates over $10 billion annually from its agriculture, is hit by the worst flood in history; a flood that leaves the whole state a National Disaster Area and hundreds of thousands of people homeless and without water. This was Iowa's fate in 1993 when heavy rains and already full rivers combined to leave the state as one huge muddy pond.

The weather has always been famous in Iowa—with its nature of instant changes (such as the freak blizzard that resulted in the serendipitous development of the Golden Delicious apple) and amazing electrical storms. Herbert Hoover, 31st President, is the most well-known of the strong Quaker community that resides here and which was a vital link in the underground

railway that was the road to freedom for thousands of slaves. It was to Iowa that black scientist and inventor George Washington Carver fled to escape persecution. Every four years Iowans are remembered by the rest of the country when they have first shot in the choice of the next President.
www.yahoo.com/Regional U_S_States/Iowa/

DES MOINES Trisected by rivers, Iowa's capital (population 193,000, excluding hogs) is a green and friendly place to catch your breath and take advantage of good food and lodging. Like Minneapolis, the city has a (carpeted) skywalk connecting major downtown buildings. 'A really beautiful city.' Worth seeing is the **Living Farms** complex, whose visitors have included Nikita Krushchev and Pope John Paul II (the latter delivered mass—shades of *Animal Farm*).
The telephone area code is 515.

ACCOMMODATION
A-1 Motel, 5404 SE 14th St, 287-5160. From S-$29, TV.
Iowa State Fairgrounds Campgrounds, E 30th St at Grand Ave. Site $10, $12 w/hook-up. Open mid May-mid Oct.
Motel 6, 4817 Fleur Dr, 287-6364. Close to airport. S-$30, D-$36.
Village Inn, 1348 Euclid at 14th St E, 265-1674. 'Large, clean, comfortable rooms.' S-$30, D-$36.
YMCA, 101 Locust, 288-0131. Men only. $25 ($5 key deposit).
YWCA, 717 Grand, 244-8961. Women only. Large, grand. S-$10, $48 weekly.

FOOD
Bishop's Cafeteria, in the Merle Hay Mall (largest shopping mall in Iowa), off I-80, 276-1534.
To eat **downtown**, go to the Court Ave district: **Julio's** , Tex-Mex, 244-1710; **Kaplin Hat**, a renovated hat factory with inexpensive steaks, 243-1414; and **Stella's Blue Sky Diner**, 4th and Locust, 246-1953, with cheese frenchies and vintage rock n' roll.
The Tavern, 2058 5th St, 255-9827. 'The best pizza in town', with some of the most obscure toppings, $7-$15.

OF INTEREST
Adventureland, east of city, 142A exit off I-80, 266-2121. Over 100 thrill rides including the Tornado rollercoaster: 'largest and fastest in the Upper Midwest'. Daily, Memorial Day-Labor Day, Fri-Sun 10 am-9 pm, Mon-Thurs 10 am-9 pm; $20.
Iowa State Fair, 10 days in late Aug, one of the oldest and largest in the country attracting thousands of visitors. Top-notch. Camping at fairgrounds at Dean Ave, 262-3111. Huge, good amenities, wooded area;$8-$10 site. For more info call (800) 545-3247.
Living History Farms, I-35 and I-80 at Hickman Rd exit, 278-5286. Four operating farms: 1700's Indian, 1850's pioneer, 1900's farm and farm of the future; also 1870 town of Walnut Hill. Lots of special events, exhibits. May-Oct, Mon-Sat 9 am-5 pm, Sun 11 am-6 pm; $8.
Science Center of Iowa, 4500 Grand Ave, 274-6868. Home of the Digistar Planetarium, 'fabulous laser shows', and simulated shuttle flights. Mon-Sat 10 am-5 pm, Sun noon-5 pm, $5.
White Water University Water Park, 5401 E University Ave, 265-4904. Enjoy the wave pool, tubing rides, water slides, The Lazy River and twin-engine go-carts on an over/under track. Open 11 am-8 pm. $15, $11 after 5 pm.

INFORMATION/TRAVEL
Central Iowa Tourism, 832-4808/ (800) 285-5842.

Des Moins Convention and Visitors Bureau, 286-4900/ (800) 451-2625.
Visitors Bureau, 309 Court Ave, 242-4705, in Saddlery Bldg, 2nd Floor, and at Des
Moines International Airport, 286-4960.
MTA city bus, 283-8111. Serves downtown, the fairgrounds. 75¢. There is a bus
service to the airport, but it is rather erratic and takes a tortuous route; take a cab to
be sure, $10-$12.

EFFIGY MOUNDS NATIONAL MONUMENT In northeast Iowa, 1500
acres along Mississippi River bluffs, dotted with prehistoric burial mounds
shaped like birds and bears, some of which date back to 1000BC. In the north
unit, 'Great Bear' stretches 120 ft from head to tail. Museum with artefacts,
interpretive history 3 miles N of Marquette on Hwy 76, open daily 8 am-5 pm
summers, 873-3491. 'The March of Bears' lies in the south unit, where ten bear
mounds and three bird mounds are strung together in one line. Most impressive when outlined by snow; area has lovely autumn colours also. Greyhound
goes no closer than Dubuque, IA or LaCrosse, WI, so car rental or hitching a
must. 12 miles SW of Dubuque, the Trappist monastery of **New Melleray
Abbey** allows free overnight stays (offering encouraged) Sun-Thur, a nice
counterpoint to mound exploration. Often full, call to make rsvs, 588-2319.
The telephone area code is 319.

AMANA Settled by German mystics in 1854, the Amana Colonies (7
villages located one hour apart by oxen) became the longest-lived commune
in the US. Reorganised along corporate lines in 1932, Amana residents no
longer practice communal living but instead produce microwave ovens and
other appliances along with woollens, wine and other hand-crafted goods.
You can walk past the houses, factories and workshops (built along traditional German lines) and visit museums but the main attraction is the solid
food (heavy on pork and carbohydrates).
The telephone area code for Amana, Williamsburg, Brooklyn and Iowa City is 319.

ACCOMMODATION/FOOD
Super 8 Inn, Rte 2, Box 179H, Williamsburg, 668-2800. Rooms from $38-$51.
Wesley House Hostel (HI-AYH), 120 N Dubuque St, Iowa City, 338-1179. $12 AYH, $24
non-AYH. Check-in 7 pm-9 pm, check-out 9 am. Kitchen and lounge, all day lockout.
Colony Inn, 741 47th Ave, Amana, 622-6270. 'Great breakfast—$7 for fruit salad,
pancakes, eggs, sausage, hash browns and more.'!

OF INTEREST
Heritage Museum of Johnson County, 310 Fifth St, Coralville, 251-5738.
Illustrating the culture and heritage of eastern Iowa and Johnson County. Wed-Sat
1 pm-5 pm, Sun 1 pm-4 pm. $3. Free on Weds.
Museum of Natural History, on Clinton and Jefferson Sts, Iowa City, 335-0480.
Exhibits include a wide variety of displays interpreting Iowa's geology, early
Native American cultures and ecology. Mon-Sat 9.30-4.30 pm, Sun 12.30-4.30. Free.
Tanger Factory Outlet Center, Exit 220 on I-80, 668-2811 or (800) 1-TANGER. More
than 60 brand-name manufacturers and designer outlet stores. Save 30%-70% off
regular retail prices. Mon-Sat 9 am-9 pm, Sun noon-6 pm.

INFORMATION
Amana Convention and Visitors Bureau, 622-7622/ (800) 245-5465
Eastern Iowa Tourism, 472-5135/ (800) 891-3482.
Iowa City Area Convention and Visitors Bureau, 337-6592/ (800) 283-6592.

KANSAS   *The Sunflower State*

Kansas is America's heartland. Although a prairie state in quintessence (think of *Little House on the Prairie*) with all the home sweet homeyness you could want, there's still a wildness in the air here: namely, the wind. For all its landlocked glory, Kansas seems mysteriously powered by oceanic forces—full of wheat fields rippling under the caress of constant breezes.

This same, unceasing wind has played a hand in the state's history—kicking up deadly dust storms and twisters (one of which sucked up poor Dorothy in *The Wizard of Oz*), driving lonely pioneer women insane with its howling. The survivors, however, must have been of good stock, for Kansas boasts the first woman mayor (1887), the first female US senator (Nancy Landon Kassebaum), the most famous aviatrix (Amelia Earhart) and the most fanatical and annoying prohibitionist, Carry Nation.

Carry began by singing hymns to saloon idlers, but soon found it more effective to turn saloons into kindling with a hatchet. Besides being anti-booze, Carry's vendetta encompassed tobacco, corsets, barroom paintings and foreign foods. Her last 'hatchetation' ended in ignominy: she unwisely took on a female saloonkeeper, who thrashed her soundly. Carry's zeal kept Prohibition alive in Kansas until 1948.

Kansas' bid for statehood was the fuse for the outbreak of the Civil War, and ferocious anti-and pro-slavery factions gained it the epithet 'Bleeding Kansas'. In the riproaring cattle and railroad era of mid/late 1800's, cowhands drove one million cattle a year to Abilene, and 'blew' their $1-a-day wages on cards, rotgut and fancy 'wimmin'. The cow capital eventually moved west from Abilene to Wichita and Dodge City. As the 'breadbasket to the world', Kansas sells much of its surplus wheat to needy Russia. Ironically, the original seeds for 'Turkey Red', a hard winter variety, were brought here from Russia in 1874 by Mennonite settlers.

'A remarkable state, well worth making an effort to discover.' 'At night, a magnificent and fulfilling stillness falls over the plains.' *www.yahoo.com/Regional/U_S__States/Kansas/*

ABILENE   Considering its associations with the Chisholm Trail, Wild Bill Hickok and all, Abilene's lack of westernness disappoints. Abilene is really Ike's Kansas—grain elevators, porch swings and funky little cafes; and is the unlikely subject of the affectionate chorus, 'prettiest town I've ever seen'. The Eisenhower buildings are pompous but do stop for a look at Ike's simple boyhood home. Check out the Abilene City Guide at *www.history.cc.ukans.edu/heritage/abilene/abilene.html*
The telephone area code is 913.

ACCOMMODATION
Best Western, 1709 and 2210 N Buckeye, off I-70, (1-800) 701-1000. Year-round, S-$39+, D-$42-$48, $4 XP. Free continental bfast.
Diamond Motel, 1407 NW 3rd St, Abilene, 263-2360. Year-round S-$22-$30, D-$26-$34. Sml refrigerator in room.
Super 8, 2207 N Buckeye, 1 mile from downtown, 263-4545. S-$40, D-$45, $5 XP.

FOOD

For an entertaining read and a look at what people have to say about local restaurants, go to www.ict.feist.com/Restaurants/

Leona Yarbrough Restaurant, 2800 W 53rd St, Shawnee Mission, 722-4800. 'Has been a long time bastion of heartland cooking with a feminine touch.' From homey chicken noodle soup and fresh-baked bread to old-fashioned lattice-top apple pie, dinners of braised lamb shank, turkey divan and excellent fried chicken. Menu printed daily.

Paolucci's Restaurant and Lounge, 113 South Third St, 367-6105. 'A casual, cosy restaurant and bar with panelled walls, where a hamburger, $2.25, and glass of Merlot, $2.25, hit the spot.'

OF INTEREST

Amelia Earhart Birthplace Museum, 223 N Terrace St, 367-4217. Earhart amassed a long list of breakthroughs for women: first to fly Atlantic as a passenger, first to fly solo across Atlantic and first to fly solo across US. She was out to become the first woman to fly around the world when she disappeared somewhere in the Pacific on July 2, 1937. Daily guided tours 9 am-noon, 1 pm-4 pm from May thru Sept; open w/ends at other times. $2.

Great Plains Theatre Festival, 263-9574. Kansas' premiere professional regional theatre.

The Garden of Eden-yes, you read it here first-is in **Lucas**, 22 miles E of Paradise, west of Abilene on I-70, off Hwy 272. An eccentric by the name of SP Dinsmoor built this statue garden in the 1920's in his front yard, using 113 tons of concrete, among other things. A Civil War veteran, Dinsmoor held a cynical and rather prophetic view of the 20th century, particularly toward crooked bankers and lawyers. Daily 10 am-5 pm in the summer, 525-6395. $4. 12 miles from the geodetic centre of the US.

WICHITA Meaning 'painted faces' in Indian, Wichita has Kansas' most worthwhile cowboy mockup in its Cow Town ('authentic, much better than Dodge City'), with five original and 32 replica buildings. Boeing, Cessna and Beech—three major aircraft producers—make Wichita the 'Air Capital of the World'. 'Great place to hitch-hike by air.' *www.prairielink.com/* is an internet jumpstation and directory which maintains links of particular interest in the High Plains.

The telephone area code is 316.

ACCOMMODATION

Inn at Willowhead, 3939 Comotard, (800) 533-5775. W/end room special D-$59. Bfast included. Complimentary videos and cocktails.

Motel 6, 5736 W Kellogg St, 945-8440. S-$33, D-$38. Winter: S-$28, D-$33.

Red Barn, 6427 N Greenwich Road, 744-0866. Rooms from D-$65-$80. Privately owned house. Features the *Pioneer Room, Sunflower Room, Americana Room*, and the *Heritage Room*. Own bathroom. Shared hot tub. Bfast included. Rsvs req.

Super 8, 6075 Aircap Drive, 744-2071. S-$40, D-$48.

Town Manor Motel, 1112 N Broadway at 10th, 267-2878. S-$25, D-$30. Winter: S-$23, D-$28.

FOOD

La Galette Bakery, 1017 W Douglas Ave, 267-8541. Mon-Fri 8 am-5 pm, Sat 8 am-4 pm..

Miller's Bar-B-Que, 4601 E 13th St, 684-8080. Plentiful ribs, brisket and baked beans.

New York Bagel Shop & Deli, 101 N Market, 267-8800. Bagel and sandwich shop serves bfast and lunch. Mon-Fri 7 am-4 pm.

Panama Red's Café and Roadhouse, 608 E Douglas, 263-0669. Real cajun food and 'hickory smoked Bar-B-Q second to none', with local/regional blues acts at w/end.

The Artichoke, 811 N Broadway, 263-9164. 'Cold beer on tap, great acoustic music at w/end and a Nancy's #8 on your plate! Exceptionally cool lunch stop.'

The Chinese Express Buffet, 123 E Douglas, 262-8882. Mon-Fri 8 am-5 pm, Sat 8 am-4 pm. 'All you can eat' Chinese Buffet (including salad bar), $4.75. 'All you can eat' salad bar, $2.85. 1 trip Chinese buffet, $3.85. Mon-Fri, 11 am-2 pm.

OF INTEREST

First National Black Historical Society of Kansas, 601 North Water, 262-7651. This museum and cultural centre was established to give recognition to black participation in early Wichita. Their contributions in the fields of sports, government, entertainment, medicine, education and the military are depicted in the museum. Also exhibited are African artifacts, wood carvings, jewellery and dress. Mon, Wed, Fri 10 am-2 pm, Sun 2 pm-6 pm. Free.

Kansas Bike Trails: Shawnee Mission Park, Dornwood Park, The Levee, The Bowls and Clinton Park (from Kansas City, take K-10 which switches to 23rd St. Go west until you arrive at park. One of the largest trails in area. Lots of hills, rocks, and hikers to watch out for!)

Old Cowtown Museum, 1871 Sim Park Dr, 264-6398. A 'living' historic village. Mon-Sat 10 am-5 pm, Sun noon-5 pm; $6.

Pipe Dreams skateboard/in-line/BMX park, 2915 W Mary, Garden City, (316) 275-1073 and **No Bust Street Spot**, Wichita, (310) 267-2950. Latter is under the Douglas St bridge downtown. Features ledges, small walls and curbs. There are several good (free!) art museums, including the **Ulrich Museum** at the Univ of Wichita, 689-3664, which has on its outside wall an exquisite Miro mosaic with over one million pieces of glass. Closed summers, Wed-Sun during school year. Kansas skyscrapers hold wheat, not people, and you'll find the tallest **grain elevators** in the world in **Hutchinson**, 45 miles NW on SR 96. They hold 20 million bushels of grain. Annual **Wichita Beerfest** is held at the beginning of June, at the **Kansas Coliseum Pavilion**, 1-5 pm. Sample over 150 beers, try a selection of foods. Live bands, booths, exhibits and bagpipes! Meet the brewers personally! Must be 21yrs+ and present ID. Call (316) 687-2222.

INFORMATION

Chamber of Commerce, 265-7771.

Kansas B&B Assoc, 1-888-8-KS-INNS.

Kansas State Tourist Bureau, (913) 296-5403.

Visitors Bureau, 100 S Main, #100, 265-2800. Stop here first for map and information.

For sport and recreational activities, in and around Kansas, try Bill's Bike Rack, *www.sunflower.org/~billhh/*. For more info on Kansas, try Kansas Community Networks: *www.history.ac.ukans.edu/heritage/towns/*

THE SANTA FE AND OTHER TRAILS Because of its geographic position, Kansas was crosshatched with trails: the Santa Fe, Chisholm, Oregon, Smoky Hill and others. Whether travelling across Kansas, or settling it, pioneers needed grit and resilience. South of Colby (60 miles from Colorado), near I-70, you can examine an authentic sod house at the Prairie Museum. **Fort Larned** (6 miles from Larned off Hwy 154) and graffiti-covered **Pawnee Rock** (NE of Larned on 156) still stand as trail markers. Along US 50, 9 miles W of Dodge City, wagon ruts of the Santa Fe trail can be seen.

MICHIGAN *The Wolverine State*

Which state has 3000 miles of shoreline and the nation's largest sand dune yet touches no ocean? Which state has more than 10,000 lakes and isn't Minnesota? Michigan, that's who. Rich soil and surprisingly friendly climate (considering it's Canada's neighbour) make the state tops in cherry, blueberry and other fruit growing. The wine country is centred around Paw Paw in southeast Michigan.

A campers' and hikers' dream, Michigan has youth hostels, thousands of campsites (including the unspoiled northern pleasures of Isle Royale National Park) and a rich network of farm trails and roadside produce markets on its two peninsulas.
www.yahoo.com/Regional/U_S__States/Michigan/
National park: Isle Royale.

DETROIT Forget car manufacturing, Motown and race riots—as elsewhere, you can still get mugged in Detroit but auto assembly lines and good soul music are both disappearing. A bustling inland port, the city is working to revitalise a decaying downtown (with emphasis on flashy complexes like the Renaissance Center to snare those lucrative convention gigs). However, parts of downtown still look like bomb sites and it is a desperately sad place to be. The natives of course live out in the suburbs and that's probably, if you have to come here at all, where *you* should stay too!

The Motor City came by its name and fame quite by accident, and largely because Henry Ford, Ransom Olds and other auto innovators happened to live and work in the area. The auto industry brought thousands of blacks to Detroit; one of them was Berry Gordy, founder in 1959 of the Motown sound (Smokey Robinson, the Supremes, the Temptations, etc), who used to make up songs on the Ford assembly line to relieve the monotony. *Meet Me In Detroit*, at *www.milner-hotels.com/dtravel.html* is a comprehensive city guide providing travellers with convenient hot links to airlines, car rental companies, dining and local attractions.
The telephone area code is 313.

ACCOMMODATION
Bali Hi Hotel, 10501 E Jefferson Ave, 822-3500. A short drive from downtown. S-$29 w/days ($34 w/ends); $5 key deposit. Dubious area.
Cabana Motel, 12291 Harper Ave, 371-1220. Located near Connor off I-94. S-$35 for two, D-$55, $5 key deposit.
Country Grandma's Home Hostel, 22330 Bell Rd, 753-4901. Located halfway between Detroit and Ann Arbor, surrounded by 3 parks. The hostel is 1hr from Toledo and 30 mins from Windsor, Ontario. $10 AYH, $13 non-AYH.
Falcon Inn Motel, 25125 Michigan Ave, Dearborn, near Telegraph on US 12, 278-6540. Convenient for the Henry Ford Museum and Greenfield Village. S-$30, D-$30-60.
Mercy College of Detroit, 8200 W Outer Dr, 592-6170, 11 miles from downtown off Southfield Fwy (Rte 39). S-$24, D-$22 pp.
Park Avenue Hostel, 2305 Park Ave, 961-8310. Located in heart of the theatrical district. Close to art and Motown museums. $12.

Tea House of the Golden Dragon Home Hostel, 8585 Harding Ave, Center Line, (810) 756-2676; $5 AYH. 'Amazing place.'

Village Motel, 21725 Michigan Ave at Oakwood Blvd in Dearborn, off Southfield Fwy, 565-8511. Near the Henry Ford Museum and Greenfield Village. D-$55.

YMCA, 1601 Clark St, West side, 554 2136 and 10100 Harter, East side, 921 0770. Men only. Pool. 'Very clean rooms. A bargain.' Weekly $55,–$10 key deposit; book ahead.

FOOD

Strong ethnic communities here, so head for Greektown, Chinatown and the Polish community (called Hamtramck—actually an independent city within Detroit).

Doug's Body Shop, 22061 Woodward Ave, Ferndale, 318-1940. Done in late and early American cars. Check for your favourite Chrysler.

Edmund Place, 69 Edmund Pl, 831-5757. 'Succulent fried chicken, luscious pork chops with mashed potatoes and corn bread. Pleasant African-American staff. A worthy destination for anyone seeking true urban American soul food.'

Elias Brothers Big Boy, 400 Renaissance Center, 259-0606. Try the sandwiches and homemade desserts.

Ham Heaven, 70 Cadillac Sq, 961-8818. Ham dishes that are baked, fried, sandwiched, folded into an omelet, ground up for hash, or diced for salad. Try the hamlet.

Jacoby's, 624 Brush St, 962-7067. Open 11 am, kitchen closes 9 pm. Near Greyhound, 2 blocks N of RenCen, has landmark status. **Markets: Hart Plaza** btwn the RenCen & CivicCenter holds w/end ethnic festivals all summer long. **Eastern Market** on Russell St has produce bargains. Open year round.

Lafayette Coney Island, 118 Lafayette St, 964-8198. Open nearly round the clock, serves wieners smothered in chili and raw onions with a cup of bean soup on the side.

Pizza Paplis Tavern, 553 Monroe in Greektown, 961-8020. Open 11 am-1 am. Deep-dish Chicago pizza, fresh pasta and large sandwiches.

Soup Kitchen Saloon, 1585 Franklin, 259-2643. Mon-Fri 11 am-midnight, 5 pm-2 am w/ends. Known as 'Detroit's home of the blues'. Pasta, creole and fresh fish specials. Cover $5-$15.

OF INTEREST

Belle Isle, 267-7115, is an island park in the Detroit River (bridge at E Jefferson), has 5 sections: an aquarium (free), conservatory, a safari-like zoo, and the **Dossins Great Lakes Museum**, (donation).

Cobo Hall and the **Joe Louis Arena**, 600 Civic Centre Dr, 567-7444, where sporting events, ice capades, concerts and the circus come to town.

Detroit Grand Prix, Indy Cars World Championship race takes place in mid-June. The course follows the city streets by the RenCen.

Detroit Institute of Arts (DIA), 5200 Woodward Ave (off I-75, 1 miles W), 833-7900. Wed-Fri 11 am-4 pm, w/ends 11 am-5 pm. $4, $1 w/student ID. From fine primitives to Andy Warhol, plus Diego Rivera's famous and scathing mural on factory life. Also: has one of the best African art collections in the country, and *Quilting Time*, a mosaic by black modern artist Romare Beardon. Cafe in Renaissance decor.

Detroit Kool Jazz Festival, 961-6289. This is the US half of the Swiss Montreux International Jazz Festival, one of the most prestigious and widely recognized festivals. Most of the concerts are free. Runs from 1st—4th Sept.

Greenfield Village and adjacent **Henry Ford Museum** in **Dearborn**, W of Detroit. Greenfield Village is 240 acres containing 100+ genuine historic buildings amassed by Henry Ford and set up in sometimes curious juxtaposition: Abe Lincoln's courthouse, Wright Brothers' cycle shop, Edison's lab (complete with vial said to contain Edison's dying breath). Almost everything runs or ticks or does something—a stunning microcosm of the roots of technological Americana. Fee rides for horse carriages, steam trains, Model-T Fords, steamboats, horse-drawn sleighs. The fantastic 12-acre Ford Museum has huge transportation collection, antique aircraft. Daily 9 am-5 pm; $12.50 to village and museum, 2-day pass to both for $22; 271-1620.

Graystone International Jazz Museum, 3000 E Grand Blvd, 963-3813. Museum specialising in jazz memorabilia from 1920 to the present. The collection includes musical instruments from the Graystone Ballroom, as well as artifacts of such great jazz artists as Count Basie, Duke Ellington, and others. The museum also organises travelling exhibits. The **K-Zoo Skate Zoo**, is Michigan's oldest indoor skatepark. Located at 1502 Ravine Rd, Kalamazoo, (616) 345-9550, it has the best spine ramp and a great street course with 6800 sq ft of skating area for all skateboarding, inlining and BMX enthusiasts! **Also: Airborne** is on the corner of Martin and Hayes Sts; 5 1/2 spine ramp, fun box, launches, rails, quarter pipes, 2x11 ft half pipes.

Motown Museum, 2648 W Grand Blvd, 875-2264. It all began here, Hitsville USA, as Berry Gordy Jr. called it. Motown sound was introduced to the world in the 1960s from this small home. Offices and recording studios remained here until the company moved to LA, California in 1972. Museum filled with gold discs, rare photos, vintage clothing, memorabilia and artifacts recapturing the history of this seminal era in American music. Exhibits feature musicians, songwriters and black singing groups such as Diana Ross and the Supremes and The Temptations. Mon noon-5 pm, Tues-Sat 10 am-5 pm, Sun 2 pm-5 pm, last tour at 4.30 pm; $6.

Renaissance Center, the 'RenCen' on the river, 568-5600, is a mirrored fortress of four 39-story towers protecting an 83-story hotel. The glass-fronted elevator ride is certainly worth it for the view ($3.50), if the costly drinks at the top are not. 'Fantastic views of Detroit, Windsor, the river.' 100+ shops, restaurants. Across the street is **Mariner's Church**, 1848 shrine for lake sailors, whose bells still toll each time a life is lost on the lake.

SPORT
On the professional scene, the excellent Detroit Tigers play in the American Baseball League, the Pistons are the city basketball team, the Detroit Lions (Amercan football) and the Redwings (ice hockey) keep everyone jumping in winter.

Winter sports: For info on events, sports and activities, call **Michigan Travel Bureau**, (800) 5432-YES. Skiing resorts around the Michigan state include Big Powderhorn Mountain, Bessemer (800) 222-3131 and Blackjack, Bessemer (906) 229-5115. Boyne Highlands, Harbor Springs, and Boyne Mountain, Boyne Falls (800) GO-BOYNE. Crystal Mountain, Thompsonville (800) 968-7686, Indianhead Mountain Resort, Wakefield (800) 3-INDIAN, Shanty Creek, Bellaire (800) 678-4111.

Windsor, Canada: this city which gets mixed reviews is *south* of Detroit. It is reached via bridge or tunnel and recommended, but with a few warnings: 'I was given a difficult time because I was backpacking and had only $100 plus ticket home. Plenty of trucks outside immigration to ask for a ride though.'

INFORMATION
Michigan Travel Bureau, (800) 543-2937.
Travelers Aid, at **Greyhound** and 211 W Congress, 962-6740; at **Metro Airport**, 941-3943.
Visitors Bureau, Hart Plaza on E Jefferson St, 567-1170, or 100 RenCen, Suite #1900, 259-4333. Both are centrally located and helpful.
Visitor Hotline, 567-1170.

TRAVEL
Amtrak, 2601 Rose St, 336-5407/(800) 872-7245. Not the best station or area to be stuck in at night.

Greyhound, 1001 Howard St, 961-8011/(800) 231-2222.
Detroit Department of Transportation (DOT), 933-1300. Runs buses in the down-town area; $1.
Southeastern Michigan Area Regional Transit (SMART), 962-5515. For buses to the 'burbs.
Metropolitan Wayne County Airport, 942-3550. Detroit's main airport, about 21 miles from downtown. To get there by bus, take a SMART bus #200 from Michigan Ave to Middlebelt, change there and take the #285 to the airport, takes about 90 mins-2 hrs, $1.60. Alternatively, Commuter Transportation, 941-3252, runs a shuttle bus from major downtown hotels; rsvs req, $13 o/w. Taxi approx $30.

FLINT Midway between Detroit and Lake Huron's Saginaw Bay, has what Motor City lacks nowadays: **auto plant tours**. Buick City has hi-tech and robotics tours on Tue & Thur. You'll need to book tours far in advance during summer. Call the Flint Area Convention & Visitors Bureau, 400 N Saginaw St, (800) 288-8040, for more information. Flint's own homepage may be accessed at *www.flint.org/*
The telephone area code is 313.

ANN ARBOR An hour's bus ride west of Detroit, Ann Arbor is thor-oughly dominated by the University of Michigan and loves it. As a conse-quence, lots of good hangouts, live music including excellent bluegrass, cheap eats, support services, and events like the July Art Fair. For info on the **Ann Arbor 36th Film Festival**, held at the Michigan Theater annually every March, go to *www.citi.umich.edu/u/honey/aaff/*
The telephone area code is 313.

ACCOMMODATION
Ann Arbor YMCA, 350 S 5th Ave, 663-0536, downtown at William St. Clean dorm rooms for men and women, $92.50 weekly, $325 mnthly + security deposit. Rsvs essential.
Lamp Post Motel, 2424 E Stadium Blvd, 971-8000. S-$55, D-$60. Friendly management.
U of M, Conference & Catering Services, 603 Madison, 764-5325. Summer dorm rooms; S-$40, D-$49. Air conditioned. Rsvs required.

FOOD/ENTERTAINMENT
Afternoon Delight, 251 E Liberty St, 665-7513. This place has all-natural muffins and pitta sandwiches. Try the yoghurt shakes. Open 8 am-8 pm.
Rick's American Cafe, 611 Church St, 996-2747. Reggae and blues bands, $3-$6 cover, closed Sun. Serves burgers, burritos, nachos and more; dinner only. Best bar in Ann Arbor, according to the locals.
Zingerman's Deli, 422 Detroit St, (313) 663-3354. Serves every kind of sandwich; the menu is a good hour's read. Also stocks a tremendous inventory of cheese, smoked fish, meats, breads, coffees etc.

OF INTEREST
Ann Arbor Summer Festival, in July. Offers a variety of performances and exhibits every day.
Gerald R Ford Presidential Library, 1000 Beal Ave, 741-2218. Mon-Fri 8.45 am-4.45 pm. Not a museum.
Museum of Art in Alumni Hall, S University, 525 State St, 764-0395. First-rate col-lection of Asian and Western art. Tue-Sat 11 am-5 pm, Thurs 'til 9 pm, Sun noon-5 pm; free.

Nichols Arboretum and Gallup Park are next to the Huron River on the city's northeastern edge. You can canoe, fish and swim. Daily 6 am-10 pm. Call the Ann Arbor Recreation Dept, 994-2326, or Park and Recreation Dept, 994-2780.

INFORMATION/TRAVEL
Amtrak, 325 Depot St, 994-4906/(800) 872-7245. Services to Detroit and Chicago.
Ann Arbor Convention and Visitors Bureau, 120 W Huron, 995-7281.
Greyhound, 116 W Huron St, 662-5511/(800) 231-2222, at Ashley St, 1 block off Main St.

NATIONAL LAKESHORE/UPPER PENINSULA Michigan has two special wilderness areas, the **Upper Peninsula** and the **Sleeping Bear Dunes National Lakeshore**. The Upper Peninsula is above Wisconsin. This multi-million acre forest is bordered by three of the Great Lakes. It provides a rare retreat into untouched wilderness; hiking, cross-country skiing, fishing and canoeing are available. For more information, contact the Upper Peninsula Travel and Recreational Association, PO Box 400, Iron Mountain, MI 49801, or 618 Stevenson Ave, Iron Mountain, 774-5480. Also, the US Forestry Service, Hiawatha National Forest, 2727 North Lincoln Rd, Escanaba, MI 49829, 786-4062, can supply you with guides and maps.

Sleeping Bear Dunes, 45 mins from **Traverse City**, is known for its magnificent sand dunes and polar-bear swimming (Lake Michigan never seems to warm up). In Traverse City, catch the **Bing Cherry Festival** in mid-July, an excellent festival.

The telephone area code for the Upper Peninsula is 906; for Sleeping Bear Dunes, 616.

ACCOMMODATION/FOOD
Northwestern Michigan Community College, East Hall, 1701 E Front St, Traverse City, (616) 922-1406. About 1 mile from the bus station. Accomodation provided on limited basis. S-$25, D-$35.
Dale's Donut Factory, 3687 South Lakeshore Dr, St Joseph, (616) 429-1033; also at 607 Broad St in St Joseph, (616) 983-1007. The donut factory of donut fans' dreams!

MACKINAC ISLAND An island in time as well as space, Mackinac (pronounced Mackinaw) permits no motor vehicles—your choices are horseback, bicycle, surrey or shank's mare. Restful, beautiful Victorian, especially nice during the June Lilac Festival. Chocoholics Note: island specialty is homemade fudge. Boat runs every hour in summer.

Don't miss at least a look at the elegant 1880's Grand Hotel, which starred in the movies *This Time for Keeps* and *Somewhere in Time*. It has a porch that never ends, the longest in the world. Check out the Mackinac Island pages, created on the island by the islanders themselves. Rich in pictures, info, news and stories, the web site is *www.mackinac.com/*
The telephone area code is 906.

ACCOMMODATION
Unfortunately, accommodation is rather expensive here and no camping is allowed on the island. Also, there are few lockers to be found here, or on the mainland at St Ignace and Mackinaw City, so you will be carrying your rucksack with you—'an exhausting bind if you go over to the island intent on walking'. The moral of this is: if you plan to go here, plan ahead. The Chamber of Commerce is helpful, 706 S Huron, 847-3783/6418.

Bogan Lane Inn, PO 482, Mackinac Island, ³/₄ mile E of the boat docks, (906) 847-3439. S or D-$72, T-$80. All include bfast. Rsvs req. Open year round. There are the usual motel chains along I-75; they are probably your best bet.

TRAVEL/INFORMATION
Arnold Mackinac Island Ferry, Box 220, 847-3351. Departures from Mackinaw City and St. Ignace, $12.50 r/t.
Mackinac Island Chamber of Commerce, 847-3783/6418.
Shepler's Mackinac Island Ferry, Box 250, Mackinaw City, MI 49701, (616) 436-5023. Serves Mackinaw City and St Ignace, also $12.50 r/t.

ISLE ROYALE NATIONAL PARK This is the roadless, wild and beautiful 'eye' in Lake Superior's wolfish head. Free camping by permit only, including use of screened shelters around the island. 'Boil surface water at least 5 mins.' Carry salt along—inland lakes on the island have leeches. Island closed in winter.

MINNESOTA *Land of 10,000 Lakes*

Driving through Minnesota, you may well wonder if you took a wrong turn somewhere and wound up in Scandinavia. The countryside, fertile farmland in the south, covered with pine forests in the north and dotted with 15,000 glacier-scoured lakes, almost duplicates the Nordic landscape. Doubtless this is why so many immigrant Swedes and Norwegians moved here earlier this century; to them, the state looked like home and had frigid winters so everyone could keep their skis on.

Vikings may have learned of Minnesota's Nordic delights early on, if a Viking runestone dated from 1000AD proves authentic. Much of the population still appears Nordic, and the countryside and cities are among the cleanest and most well-preserved in the US.

The land also seems to attract giants, both literal and figurative. It's the birthplace of J Paul Getty, Bob Dylan, Charles Lindbergh, F Scott Fitzgerald, Sinclair Lewis and the Mississippi River, as well as the home of Paul Bunyon the woodsman and the Jolly Green Giant of canned pea fame.

The state is especially lovely during Indian summer; highway markers often point out the most vivid colour displays. Free maps of the fall colour routes are obtainable from the Minnesota Tourism Bureau, 375 Jackson, Room 250, St Paul, MN 55101. Or call toll-free within the state, (800) 652-9747, for guidance. Any time of year, **North Shore Drive** (US 61) along Lake Superior north to Canada is a top contender for the most beautiful camping and gawking route in America. Miles of well-kept biking paths criss-cross the state. **The Heartland Trail**, a 27 mile paved bike trail in north-central Minnesota, is one of the loveliest. Call (800) 657-3700 for more information. While here be sure to go canoeing, a peculiarly Minnesotan tradition passed down from Chippewa Indians and French-Canadian trappers to present day. You can disappear into the north country wilderness and not see another person for days on end. Fishing is the other biggie sport up here. *www.yahoo.com/Regional/U_S__States/Minnesota/*
National Park: Voyageurs.

MINNEAPOLIS/ST PAUL Laced together by the curves of the Mississippi River, Minneapolis and St Paul are 'Twin Cities' only in geographic terms. It's said that Minneapolis was born of water, St Paul of whiskey.

Minneapolis is young, Scandinavian, modern and relaxed, a working-class city freckled with lakes and home base of 15 Fortune 500 companies, headed by electronics. As in San Diego and Seattle, residents here sensibly take advantage of their versatile setting; many spend their lunch hour sailing in summer. Minneapolis was and is Mary Tyler Moore territory, as bouncy and clean as the Pillsbury doughboy, another local product.

St Paul began as an outpost with the uncouth name of Pig's Eye, described in 1843 as 'populated by mosquitoes, snakes, Indians and about 12 white people'. Perhaps to compensate for these rough beginnings, St Paul has become a conservative capital city of Irish and German Catholics, doting on history and Eastern refinement. F Scott Fitzgerald is St Paul's native son. (So is Charles 'Peanuts' Shultz, but he was evidently too brash for St Paul; in high school his cartoons were rejected by the school yearbook.)

To the south is the younger sibling of **Bloomington**, where lurks the gigantic "Mall of America" (#7 bus). Out of the three metropolitan areas, Minneapolis offers most for the visitor: friendly, outgoing locals, a handsome downtown with mall, skyways, parks, a meandering waterfront and swimmable lakes. Stick to downtown, however: 'I am astonished—could other US downtowns be like this, given a chance? The rest of Minneapolis that I've seen is as ordinary and soulless as anywhere else in America.' Check out the Yahoo! Twin Cities Metro city guide at *www.minn.yahoo.com The telephone area code is 612.*

ACCOMMODATION
City of Lakes International House, 2400 Stevens Ave, Mpls, 871-3210. Located in the historic mansion district. Living room with piano and fireplace, outdoor patio. Clean and relaxed. Close to major attractions, downtown, bus lines and lakes. No smoking, drinking, drugs. 'Not a party hostel.'! Bike hire $3 daily, $17 weekly ($30 deposit req). Private room $32, dorm $15. 'Friendly, helpful staff!'
Fraternities in the 16-1700 block of University Ave can sometimes offer room to travellers. 'Very cheap and plenty of lovely half-naked men wandering around—just what you need after two months in camp.'
Hi-Caecilian Hall, 2004 Randolph Ave, St. Paul, 690-6604. 1 June-14 August. S-$14/20, D-$28/30, T-$35. (Cheaper if AYH member).
Hillview Motel, Hwys 169 & 41, 445-7111. S-$32-89, D-$39-89.
Student's Coop, 1721 University Ave SE, 331-1078. $10, available only in summer. Kitchen, laundry, colour TV. 'Smashing place to live—full of friendly lunatics. Great social life.'
Super 8 Motel, 7800 S 2nd Ave, exit at Nicollet Ave off I-494, 888-8800. S-$57-64, D-$64. Close to airport, shops, and zoo. Several around the twin cities. Call 738-1600.
Camping: Lebanon Hills Regional Park Campground, 12100 Johnny Cake Ridge Rd, Apple Valley, (612) 454-9211. Tent site $10.

FOOD
Be sure to try Minnesota specialties: wild rice, walleyed pike, sweet corn and Fairbault blue cheese. St Paul's soul dish is *boya* , a Hungarian stew served on the slightest pretext. For cheap munchies try some of the downtown and college bars during happy hour.

Al's Breakfast, 413 14th Ave, SE, 331-9991. Mon-Sat 6 am-1 pm, Sun 9 am-1 pm. 'Best morning meal in town! Good things happen here; people's lives change. If you want a car, or an apartment, or a sweetheart, come in, have coffee, and chat a while.'

Big City Bagels, Lasalle Plaza, 825 Hennepin Ave, Mpls, 305-4880. 'Café-cum-bakery, serves a wide selection of bagels and spreads, sandwiches, bakery and cream cheeses at reasonable prices.'

Cafe Latte, 850 Grand Ave, St Paul, 224-5687. Located in Victoria Crossing. Energetic urban cafeteria. 'Seductive sprawling triple-layer turtle cake.' Bring a friend so you can try more than one. Choice of four interesting soups every day.

Cossetta, 211 West Seventh St, St Paul, 222-3476. An Italian market and deli. Fresh meats, cheeses and salads are served cafeteria style. Lunch or dinner for two with wine is about $15.

Ediner, Calhoun Square, Mpls, 925-4008. Trendy '50's-style diner.

Green Mill, 2626 Hennepin Ave, Mpls, 374-2131. Excellent burgers, good pizza. Mon-Thurs 11 am-11 pm, Fri-Sat 'til midnight. Bar open 'til 1 am.

It's Greek to Me, 626 W Lake St, Mpls, 825-9922. Gyros are cheap and even moussaka is reasonably priced. Mon-Sun 11 am-11 pm.

Keys Café, 1007 Nicollet Mall, Mpls, 339-4499. 'Small and friendly café which serves good food at reasonable prices. All day bfast and daily specials are a good deal.'

Lotus, 313 SE Oak St, Mpls, 331-1781, and 3037 Hennepin Ave, near Calhoun Square, 825-2263. Vietnamese food in a stylish setting.

Mickey's Diner, 36 West Seventh St, St Paul, 222-5633. Living-history museum of this American eating tradition. Meal for two costs about $15.

Mudpie, 2549 Lyndale Ave, Mpls, 872-9435. Natural food. Mon-Fri 11 am-10 pm, w/ends 'til 2 am.

North Country Co-op, 2129 Riverside Ave, 338-3110. Full grocery with fresh produce and bread—even pickled Japanese vegetables. Mon-Sat 9 am-9 pm, Sun 9 am-8 pm.

Sawatdee, 607 Washington Ave, S Mpls, 338-6451, and 285 E 5th, St Paul, 222-5859. The one in St Paul is the older and better restaurant. Some of the best Thai food.

Seward Community Cafe, 2129 Franklin Ave, Mpls, 332-1011. 'The Sunday bfast is very cheap and filling.'

OF INTEREST: MINNEAPOLIS

Besides being the longest pedestrian walkway in the US, the **downtown mall** along Nicollet Ave is one of the most agreeable and attractive. It's full of flowers, fountains, friendly conversation, strollers, sandwich-eaters, bus stop shelters, wafting classical music, boutiques and smart shops. Overhead an enclosed

Skyway system (designed for Minnesota winters) lets pedestrians cross in comfort from building to building across 45 downtown blocks.

Focal point of the Mall and Skyway complex is the 57-storey **IDS Center** at Nicollet and 8th St. The **Crystal Court**, a 3-level arcade within the IDS complex, has a 'ceiling' of crystal pyramids and shapes which nicely diffuse the sunlight, creating a dappled effect as though one were strolling beneath trees. Both the lighting and the vivacious cafe/meeting-place ambiance are best absorbed mornings until lunchtime. Cafe has reasonable lunch specials, and there's an info center in the Crystal Court. Suggestions of scenic walks around the Twin Cities can be found in free leaflets from the info center in the IDS Complex and Minnesota Convention and Visitor Commission, 1219 Marquette Ave, Suite 300, Mpls, MN 55403; 348-4313.

Recommended: cross the Hennepin Ave bridge to the far side of the Mississippi and then return to downtown via the 3rd Ave/Central Ave bridge. The area immediately across the river is called **Riverplace & St Anthony Main**, restored warehouses on the original cobblestone Main Street of Minneapolis. The 3rd Ave bridge takes you across to St Anthony Falls; the Minneapolis side is lined with fine old warehouses and flour mills (walk along S 1st St to Portland Ave), eg. the Crown Roller Mill built in 1879. Between these mills and S Washington Ave is the **Milwaukee Road Station**, a handsome complex which the city has decided to preserve. A favourite walk or bike ride is along the Mississippi on either side. Others are around Lake of the Isles, Cedar Lake, Lake Harriet or Lake Calhoun, all in south Minneapolis. This is a city with 153 parks and 45 continuous miles of bike paths.

American-Swedish Institute, 2600 Park Ave, 871-4907. Shops, fine art, 33-room mansion with exhibits on Minnesota's Scandinavian heritage. Tue, Thur and Sat noon-4 pm, Wed 'til 8 pm, Sun 1 pm-5 pm; $3.

Historic Fort Snelling, junction of Hwys 5 and 55 near airport, 726-1171. Daily May-Oct 10 am-5 pm. Reconstruction and preservation of 1827-era fort. Film, exhibits, fort tours; $4.

Historic Orpheum Theater, 910 Hennepin Ave South, Mpls, 339-7007. Pop, jazz and rock events. Also shows such as *42nd St* and *Riverdance*. 2,200-seat facility. Located in the LaSalle Plaza. Call 989-5151 for tkts.

Lake of the Isles, reached via Lake of the Isles Pkwy btwn 25th & 26th Sts, 348-4448. Maintains four and a half acres of ice for skating from mid-December to late Feb. Skating is free, no rentals.

MC Gallery, 400 1st Ave N, 339-1480. One of 9 galleries located in the Wyman Building. Features good contemporary American arts.

Minneapolis Institute of Arts, 2400 3rd Ave S, 870-3046. Tue-Sat 10 am-5 pm, Thur 10 am-9 pm, Sun 12-5 pm; free, special shows $5, $3 w/student ID.

Minnehaha Falls and Park, south of city. 144-acre woodland with 53-foot cataract popularised (though never seen) by Longfellow in his *Song of Hiawatha*.

University Theater, 120 Rarig Center, 330 21st Ave South, 625-4001. Musicals, comedies and dramas (Shakespeare/Classics/Contemporary), featuring student and professional actors, designers and directors.

Walker Art Center, 725 Vineland Pl, 375-7600, a modern collection, Tue-Sat 10 am-5 pm, Thurs 'til 8 pm, Sun 11 am-5 pm; $3. Free on Thurs. On the grounds is the **Sculpture Garden**, including the enormous Spoonbridge and Cherry.

OF INTEREST: ST PAUL

Alexander Ramsey House, 255 S Exchange St, 296-0100. Victorian home of early Minnesota governor, run by Minnesota Historical Society. 1 hr tours Tue-Sat 10 am-3 pm, Sun 1-3 pm, $4.

Indian Mounds State Park, Dayton's Bluff, east of downtown. A pleasant picnic spot overlooking the Mississippi, believed to be a Sioux burial site.

James J Hill House, 240 Summit Ave, 297-2555. 45-room Romanesque mansion and private art gallery that once belonged to the builder of the Great Northern Railway. 1/2 hr tours Wed-Sat 10 am-4 pm, rsvs recommended; $4.

Jonathan Padelford Packet Boat Co, 227-1100, Harriet Island, downtown St Paul. Paddlewheel boat tours of Mississippi River. 2 daily 1 1/2 hr cruises in summer (noon and 2 pm), less often in May & Sept, $8.50.

Landmark Center, 75 W 5th St, 292-3225. The old Federal building, now an art gallery. Worth going for the architecture alone. Mon-Fri 8 am-5 pm, Thurs until 8 pm, Sat 10 am-5 pm, Sun 1 pm-5 pm; free.

Science Museum, 30 E 10th St (corner of Wabasha Ave), 221-9488/44. Mon-Sat 9.30 am-9 pm, Sun 10.30 am-9 pm. Omnitheatre, a huge, domed screen, 221-9400. Buy ticket for $6 and enter the museum for $2.

State Capitol, near the Science Museum, 297-3521. 45 min tour of building, governor's quarters, golden horses on top and base of dome for panoramic view. Tours Mon-Fri 9 am-4 pm, Sat 10 am-3 pm, Sun 1 pm-3 pm; free; go to info desk.

Summit Avenue District. The Victorian mansions get grander as you work your way up Laurel, Holly, Portland and Summit Aves—just the way the family of F

Scott Fitzgerald did. Born at 294 Laurel, FSF and family lived in 4 successively posher homes before ending up at 599 Summit, where he wrote his first novel in 1919. On the **University of Minnesota campus** is the **Goldstein Gallery**, MacNeal Hall; displays on fashion, housing, and interior design.
Nearby: Lake Pepin, 1hr S of the Twin Cities on Hwy 61. Good swimming beaches.
Mall of America, 60 E Broadway, Bloomington, 883-8850, about 15 mins from St Paul; take MTC bus #54 or #7. The largest shopping mall in the States with the usual feast for shopping gastronomes and also for added piquancy: a seven acre indoor theme park with a rollercoaster and Golf Mountain—a two level 18 hole 'golf course'!
Minnesota Zoo, in Apple Valley south of St Paul, 432-9000. Buses from Twin Cities' downtowns. 5 zones, from tropics to oceanic, with Siberian tigers, wolves and caribou. May-Sept Mon-Sat 9 am-6 pm, Sun 'til 8 pm. Other months, daily 10 am-4 pm, $8.
Sauk Center. Sinclair Lewis' hometown and the setting for his book, *Main Street*. Located 2 hrs NW of St Paul on 94 West, (320) 352-5201. Interpretative Center and museum Mon-Sun 8.30 am-5.00 pm, June-Aug; Mon-Fri 8.30 am-4 pm, Sept-May, free. Lewis' boyhood home open May-Sept only; Mon-Fri 9.30 am-5 pm, Sat/Sun 9 am-5 pm, $3.
Taylor's Falls, located on the St Croix River near Wisconsin border. Spectacular falls and great rock climbing. On your drive up, stop in Stillwater.

ENTERTAINMENT: MINNEAPOLIS
First Avenue and **7th St Entry**, 701 1st Ave N, 332-1775. First Avenue was made famous by Prince in the movie *Purple Rain* . You probably won't see Prince, but you can see good rock groups. 7th St Entry is around the corner: cheaper, lesser-known groups.
Festivals: summertime noon concerts throughout downtown Mpls, esp Nicollet Mall. Peavea Plaza has Thur night jazz in June, 5 pm-7 pm; 338-3807 for more information. Activities of the lakes are featured in the **Aquatennial** in July, and the **Minnesota State Fair** is held in Aug at Snelling Ace, St Paul; 642-2200.
Guthrie Theater, 725 Vineland Pl, 377-2224, was founded in the 1960's by Sir Tyrone Guthrie and has one of the finest repertory companies in the US. Excellent discounts for students week nights and Sunday. Low cost previews; enquire.
Hayes' City Stage Theater, 1430 Washington Ave S, 338-5534. Excellent satires and stand-up improvs.
Orchestra Hall, 1111 Nicollet Mall, 371-5656. Home of Minneapolis Orchestra. Cabaret in summer; jazz, pop and other concerts.
The Quest Club, 110 N 5th St, 338-0632. $5-$8 cover. 'Great nightclub. Thursday night is all ages (18+) $7 entry.'
U of Minnesota. 17th and University Ave SE, 627-4430. The **Dinkytown** area near campus on the east side of the river is liveliest at night. On campus: 'the Film Society often has free or cheap screenings of recent flicks. See notice board in Student Union'. Good country rock groups perform at many bars in the metropolitan area.

ENTERTAINMENT: ST PAUL
Ordway, 345 Washington St, near Landmark Center, 224-4222. The St Paul Chamber Orchestra and Minnesota Opera perform here.
Winter Adventure Family Festival, Minnesota History Center, 345 West Kellogg Blvd, (800) 657-3773. On Jan 25th, 1-4 pm; offers family activities, music, hands-on crafts and outdoor activities (cross-country skiing).
Winter Carnival, Rice Park, btwn 4th & 5th Sts and Market & Washington. 10 days of parades, parties, sporting events and fireworks; $3 button, available throughout Twin Cities, entitles holder to participate in most activities. Check out Grande Day Parade, torchlight parade and ice-carving competitions. Call (800) 488-4023 for info.

World Theater, 10 E Exchange St, 290-1221. Once home of *A Prairie Home Companion*, now hosts a Saturday night radio show featuring some of the finest in American folk music. Box Office Mon-Fri 11 am-4 pm.

INFORMATION

Check the free newspapers (available from street boxes and stores downtown), *Skyway News*, *Twin Cities Reader* and *City Pages* for events, accommodation and job tips.

Minneapolis Convention and Visitor Commission, 1219 Marquette Ave, #300,611-4700, or Info Center at Crystal Court in IDS complex. Get free 'Do It Yourself' brochure, map of downtown and Skyways from either source.

Minnesota Tourism Bureau, 121 7th Place E, #300, Metro Square, St Paul, 296-5029.

St Paul Chamber of Commerce, 332 Minnesota St, Suite #N205, (800) 657-3700.

Travelers Assistance, 726-5500. Located at airport, inside security area.

TRAVEL

Amtrak, 730 Transfer Rd, (800) 872-7245. On the 'Empire Builder' route that connects Chicago and Seattle/Portland. 'Located on an industrial estate, no accommodation nearby.'

Greyhound, in Mpls: 29 N 9th St; in St Paul, 25 W 9th St, (800) 231-2222.

Metropolitan Transit Commission (MTC), 349-7000, runs the two cities integrated bus systems. Basic fare $1.10.

Minneapolis/St Paul International Airport, about 9 mi from both downtowns. Take the #7 C,D,E, or F bus from 6th St, Mpls, basic fares on boarding and then 25¢ on disembarking; Airport Express runs a limousine service to downtown hotels, $7 o/w, $11 rtn to St Paul; $9 o/w, $13 r/t to Mpls.

DULUTH Situated on a steep hillside overlooking Lake Superior, the city is the world's largest fresh-water port and is known for its unbelievably cold winters, with the wind whipping off the lake. The mines that used to provide the city with much of its income have all but disappeared and now it's you, the happy tourist, who helps keep the place moving. It's access to the lake that most people come for; there is a beautiful new 1 mile walkway that takes the visitor along the shore of the lake and across the harbour. Accommodation can be a problem in the summer when it's busier and the motels bump up their prices, but try **Best Western Downtown Motel**, 131 W 2nd St, (218) 727-6851, S or D-$62 (Sun-Thurs), S or D-$92 (Fri and Sat), XP-$5. Visit the **Convention and Visitors Bureau**, 100 Lake Place Dr, 722-4011/(800) 4-DULUTH, for information on the best current deals. For special events, pictures, lodging, attractions, dining and shopping, check out *www.visitduluth.com/*

The telephone area code is 218.

HIBBING Famous for three things: Mesabi Range iron ore, the birthplace of Greyhound buses and also of Bob Dylan. The US Hockey Hall of Fame is nearby, on US 53 one hr north of Duluth—web site is *www.ushockeyhall.com*. For those interested in digging up more knowledge about mining, the Minnesota Museum of Mining in Chisholm and the Iron Range Interpretive Center may be worth visiting. Hwy 73 takes you through a multicoloured mini-Grand Canyon, the mined-out maw of the Pillsbury open pit. Along the way are several vista points for viewing other gaping holes, some as much as four miles long and two miles wide.

NORTHERN MINNESOTA is known for the beauty of its wild areas. Among the best: **Chippewa National Forest**, a 650,000 acre wilderness that contains nearly 500 lakes and rivers with broad vistas of beautiful large and small lakes. Hiking trails have been developed and maintained for visitors. Bald eagles are the star attractions. For information call (218) 335-8600. Try *www.paulbunyan.net/users/blawler/chipp.htm* for recreation opportunities and a complete list of campgrounds.

North Shore, Lake Superior, (218) 626-4300. If you have about a week, you can drive all the way around Lake Superior into Canada and Wisconsin. Otherwise, go to Duluth to see this beautiful shore line.

There is a plethora of campgrounds scattered throughout the area. The best include **Grand Marais Municipal Campground**, 387-1712. Camp site-$15, $20 w/hook-up. Right on Lake Superior. Near pool; and **Lamb's Campground**, 663-7292. 60 wooded acres and 1 1/2 miles of beach. Fishing, hiking, boat facilities. $18, $21 w/hook-up. On lake sites-$20/23.50.

Superior National Forest stretches across Minnesota's northeastern area from the Canadian border to the north shore of Lake Superior. It is especially known for the **Boundary Waters Canoe Area**, a million-acre protected wilderness area honey-combed with rivers. There are bugs, bears and a lot of portaging, but, if you come prepared, this adventure is well worthwhile. For information write to the Forest Supervisor, PO Box 338, Duluth, MN 55801, or call the **Minnesota Tourism Bureau** in St Paul, 296-5029.

VOYAGEURS NATIONAL PARK On the Minnesota-Canadian border, this 219,000 acre expanse of forested lake country is just beginning to be developed for public use. The park takes its name from the French Canadians who plied this network of lakes and streams in canoes, transporting explorers (some seeking the Northwest Passage), missionaries and soldiers to the West, and returning by Montreal with vast quantities of furs. You can reach the park by car, but inside there are only waterways and you'll need to rent a boat. Free primitive camping in designated area. Other lodgings at nearby private resorts. No park entrance fee. A new visitors center is located 11 miles E of International Falls on Black Bay off County Road 96. Houseboats can be rented on **Rainy Lake, Crane Lake** or the **Ash River**. For more information write **Voyageurs National Park**, Box 50, International Falls, MN 56649 or call (218) 283-9821. **Voyagaire Lodge and Houseboats**, Crane Lake, has a website at *www.voyagaire.com* and its hosts Bill and Deena Congdon can direct you to the places where decades ago Native Americans etched their stones into the granite walls along the park's bluffs.

MISSOURI *The Show-Me State*

Mix equal parts of the Old South, the Wild West and the modern Midwest and you've got the flavour of the Missourian: shrewd, salt of the earth, slightly cantankerous—nobody here believes anything unless they see it with their own eyes. The flat landscape is dominated and divided by the Big

Muddy, the Missouri River, a wilful, sediment-laden powerhouse. Missouri produces more tents, lead, Missouri mules, corncob pipes and space vehicles than anyone else. Missouri has also produced Harry S Truman, Mark Twain, TS Eliot, Jesse James and Generals Pershing and Bradley.

In the southwest begins the Ozark Plateau, wooded, full of springs, unspoilt rivers and caverns like Fantastic near Springfield, which has seen service as a speakeasy and a KKK meeting place. Other interesting caves include Meramec (55 miles NW of St Louis), a five-storey cave variously used as a Civil War gunpowder mill, an underground railway station, and a hideout for Jesse James' gang. A portion of the Cherokee Trail of Tears runs through NE Missouri and has been made into a scenic camping and recreational area. *www.yahoo.com/Regional/U_S__States/Missouri/*

ST LOUIS Founded in 1764 by French traders, its associations are as American as apple pie. Home of both the ice cream cone and the hot dog, the latter first devoured in 1893 by hungry St Louis Browns baseball fans. St Louis is where W C Handy wrote and sang the blues, where slave Dred Scott sued for freedom, where one-time resident Tennessee Williams set his *Glass Menagerie* and where Charles Lindbergh got the bucks for his trans-Atlantic venture.

Huge, humid, full of unsavoury slums and heavy industry from meat-packing to beer-brewing, the city nevertheless has a vital cultural life, lots of free attractions and the elegant Gateway to the West arch. St Louis Convention & Visitors Commission has a website, *www.St-Louis-CVC.com* with links to a calendar of events, attractions and nightlife.
The telephone area code is 314.

ACCOMMODATION
Huckleberry Finn Youth Hostel, 1904-1906 S 12th St, 241-0076. $15. 'Oldest facilities but good place to stay.' Get there by downtown #30 bus then #73 bus from Locust St/Tucker Blvd Market/4th St. Alternatively take taxi from Amtrak/Greyhound for safety.
Washington University, 6515 Wydown, 935-4637. 1 June-7 Aug, open to public. S-$17, D-$15-20.
To reserve a **B&B** place write: B&B of St Louis, River Country, MO & IL, 1900 Wyoming, St Louis, MO 63118, 771-1993. Over 40 B&Bs. Willing to work within budget restraints and they'll also pick you up at the rail and bus stations.

FOOD
Crown Candy Kitchen, 1401 St Louis Ave, 621-9650. A 1913 ice cream parlor with a blend of shakes and sundaes. Drink 5 malts in 30 mins and pay nothing!
Jimmie's Deli & Restaurant, 415 N 9th, 241-8760. Any kind of meal, 24 hrs a day. A favourite with truck drivers.
McDonald's, on riverboard along the Mississippi. Built along lines of a riverboat, complete with Mark Twain at the helm!
Noah's Ark, 1500 S 5th St, St Charles (across the river from St Louis), 946-1000. 'Dinner is pricey, but the restaurant is a scream—all they need is a good storm, and it's a cruise ship!'
Old Spaghetti Factory, 727 N 1st St, 621-0276. 'Massive helpings, good atmosphere, spaghetti dinners with dessert, coffee from $4-$8.'
Ted Drewes, 6726 Chippewa St, 481-2652, and 4224 Grand, 352-7376. 'Naughty-

but-nice frozen custard desserts. Take-away/'drive-up' only. Always draws a crowd—be prepared for large queues esp in eves and w/ends'.

There are also many inexpensive ethnic restaurants around **Laclede's Landing** and on the 4th flr of **St Louis Center**, Locust & 6th St.

OF INTEREST
Gateway Arch, 425-4465. A unique 40-person tram ('don't go if you get seasick') mounts the core of each leg of this 630-ft stainless steel arch designed by Eero Saarinen, in response to a competition in which the architect would best represent St Louis as 'The Gateway to the West'. Once there, you overlook the city and the Mississippi. 'Awesome.' Get there before 11 am to avoid long lines. Daily 8 am-10 pm during summer; 9 am-6 pm, winter. $4 for tram ride; $3 to enter the grounds of the arch and the **Museum of Westward Expansion** complex beneath the arch. 'The museum is very atmospheric, giving vivid impressions of frontier life.' $1 for film depicting the construction of the arch. **The Old Court House**, west of Arch at 11 N 4th St, was scene of slavery auctions and the unsuccessful attempt by slave Dred Scott to win his freedom in court; the ramifications of his case helped ignite the Civil War. Trial room no longer exists, but you may see **Dred Scott's** grave in Section 1, Calvary Cemetery.
Forest Park, midtown, 5 miles W of Gateway Arch. A large and well laid-out park with numerous attractions; in 1904 the site of the centennial Louisiana Purchase Exposition and World's Fair. An electric signal from the White House simultaneously unfurled 10,000 flags, while fountains flowed, bands played, 62 foreign nations exhibited, and 19 million people visited, there to sample iced tea and ice cream cones for the first time. Of the 1576 buildings erected for the fair, only one was permanent; it's now the **St Louis Art Museum**, 1 Fine Arts Drive, 721-0072; one of the most impressive in the US.
Nearby: Anheuser-Busch Brewery, 13th and Lynch St, 577-2626. World's largest brewery gives free 1 1/2 hr tours (every 10 mins) with beer and pretzels. Mon-Sat 9 am-5 pm.
Grant's Farm, Gravois Rd at Grant Rd (outskirts), 843-1700. Free look at the largest group of lovably huge Clydesdale horses anywhere, with a few deer, buffalo & birds thrown in. Rsvs essential. Tue-Sun 9 am-3 pm June-Aug; Thur-Sun, spring and fall.
Missouri Botanical Gardens, Tower Grove & Shaw Ave, 577-5100. 479 acres. See the Climatron, first geodesic-domed greenhouse with computer-controlled climates maintained within. Summer hrs: 9 am-8 pm daily; closes at 5 pm in winter. $3.
Outdoor Municipal Opera (1500 free seats at the back of the 12,000-seat amphitheatre) holds operettas, ballets, musical comedies and concerts most nights in summer. Call 361-1900 for schedule.
Six Flags Theme Park, St Louis, PO Box 60, Eureka, 938-5300. 30 miles NW of downtown St Louis on I-44. $30 includes all rides and attractions. Daily April-October. 'The inverted looping thrill ride Batman is totally awesome!' Tip: go in evening; less humid and possibility of discount.
St Louis Science Center, southeast corner of Forest Park, 289-4444. Daily Mon/Wed/Thur 9 am-6 pm, Tue-Fri 'til 9 pm, Sat 10 am-9 pm, Sun 11 am-6 pm; free.
The Jewel Box is a floral conservatory.
The Magic House, 516 S Kirkwood Rd, 822-8900. Mon-Thur–Sat 9.30 am-5.30 pm, Sun 11 am-5.30 pm. $4.50. 'Illusions, tests and games meant for children. Just as many adults go.'
Union Station, recently completed restoration of 19th century Gothic train station. Now full of—surprise!—shops and restaurants and old railroad cars.

ENTERTAINMENT

Gateway Riverboat Cruises, below Gateway Arch, 621-4040. The oldest excursion company on the Mississippi offers sightseeing trips of varying duration and price on one of its three boats, *Huck Finn,Tom Sawyer* and the *Belle of St Louis*; 1 hr sightseeing tour $7.50; $32 for the cruise, including prime-rib dinner and band.

Laclede's Landing, a 1-block area of re-developed mills and warehouses along the river just north of Gateway Arch, is focus of nightlife; there is a massive **Blues Festival** in September. Call **St. Louis Blues Society** on 241-2583 for details.

Paddlewheel steamboat trips are easy to find in St Louis, most of the boats dock in front of the arch. Check out the last authentic showboat, the *Lt Robert E Lee*, 241-1282.

INFORMATION

Fun Phone, 421-2100. Gives a roundup of events and entertainment.

Missouri Tourism Bureau, 869-7100/ (800) 877-1234.

St Louis Convention and Visitors Commission, 10 S Broadway, Suite 300, 421-1023 or (800) 247-9791.

Travelers Aid, 809 N Broadway, 241-5820.

Visitors Center at Gateway Arch, 425-4465.

TRAVEL

Amtrak, 550 S 16th St, (800) 872-7245. Service to Chicago, New Orleans, Dallas, Denver and Kansas City; station closes at midnight.

Bi-State Transit, 231-2345, runs the city buses with basic fare of $1.

Greyhound, 801 N Broadway, (800) 231-2222. Open 24 hrs.

Metrolink, also run by Bi-State, is the new light railway that can take you to most of the major sights. $1 basic fare, 10¢ transfer; day pass valid for both bus and Metro, $3.

Lambert/St Louis International Airport, 426-2955. About 10 miles from downtown and serviced by Bi-State buses and Metrolink: the easiest way is to take the Metro to the new airport station or catch the 'Natural Bridge'
#4 bus on Broadway and Locust, journey time of about 1¹/₂ hr, $1 for both. Greyhound also runs buses from their terminal, $6, approx 20 mins.

HANNIBAL   Although born down the road a piece, Mark Twain (*ne* Samuel Clemens) spent his boyhood in Hannibal, and this is the place that flogs Twainiana for all its worth. Its good-natured hucksterism for the most part. The old rogue would no doubt approve, being no stranger to exaggeration himself: 'Recently someone sent me a picture of the house I was born in. Heretofore I have always stated that it was a palace but I shall be more guarded now.'

Eschew Tom Sawyer's cave (2 miles out of town and decidedly unspooky) and take a 1hr boat trip on the Mississippi: departures at 11 am, 1.30 pm and 4 pm (boards ¹/₂ hr before), $8; 221-3222. 2 hr dinner cruise tours are also available for $26 (inc. band). Bar extra.

Mark Twain's home and museum, 206 Hill Street, 221-9010, is worth a look-in especially if you like Norman Rockwell. 8 am-6 pm daily. $5.

Twilight Zone time: MT's birth coincided with the appearance of Halley's Comet. Throughout his life, Twain predicted he would go out as he had come in. In 1910, right on cue, the comet reappeared and Twain snuffed it. *www.webcom.com/twainweb/* provides historical and current city info as well as in depth details and guides. Hannibal Convention and Visitors Bureau, 221-2477.

The telephone area code is 573.

KANSAS CITY Envelope-maker for the world, international headquarters for Hallmark, and home base of the baseballers, the Kansas City Royals, Kansas City is also an important cattle market, which leads us unerringly to Arthur Bryant's, the Holy Grail of barbequedom and a reason for visiting the city. In fact, *www.rbjb.com/rbjb/ab2.htm* takes you to Bryant's personal homepage, with an amusing read of the history behind the restaurant and even photos of the renowned Arthur Bryant's barbecue sauce!

Once part of a great blues and jazz triangle with New Orleans and Chicago, KC nurtured the careers of Count Basie, Duke Ellington, Charlie 'Yardbird' Parker. KC's sister city is Seville, Spain, which explains the preponderance of Moorish arches, Spanish tiles and ornamental fountains around town. The effect may not look like Spain to a Spaniard, but it sure does to a Missourian.

The telephone area code is 816.

ACCOMMODATION
Kansas City Motel 901 W Jefferson St, 228-9133. From S-$30, D-$36. XP-$3.
Rockhurst College, 926-4125, has cheap digs June-July, open to the general public. Available only by the week: S-$21, D-$18 pp. Call or write for an application, 1100 Rockhurst Rd, KC, MO 64110.
Super 8 Motel, 6900 NW 83 Terrace, NW Kansas City, 587-0808. From S-$48, D-$60. 5 miles from airport. One of several Super 8s in the area. Another is **Super 8 Motel**, 4032 S Lynn Court Drive, Independent, 833-1888. From S-$42, D-$54.

FOOD
Arthur Bryant Barbecue, 1727 Brooklyn Ave at 17th, 231-1123. A sensational place to eat barbecue. Hot, grainy opaque sauce (which you'll see aging in the window). Get lots of sauce. 'World class BBQ ribs, swooning beef brisket sandwiches. Go on, stuff yourself!' *www.rbjb.com/rbjb/ab2.htm*
Dixon's Chili, 9105 E 40 Hwy, 861-7308. Many locales in KC. Harry Truman loved KC chili—cheap and savoury.
Fric and Frac, 1700 W 39th St, 753-6102. Special deals each night; tacos, shrimp dinners, 2-for-1 burger meals, bfast. 'Ideal place for mixing with the locals'.
Otto's Malt Shop, 3903 Wyoming, 756-1010. Built in a vintage 1930's gas station with 50's and 60's decor and music. The definitive milk shake/malt/pancake shop in KC. Cheap food, bfast, lunch and dinner specials all day and nearly all night. 'With a good atmosphere, make this the perfect place to hang out.'

OF INTEREST
Country Club Plaza, btwn Main St & SW Expressway. Oldest shopping mall in the US. Huge Spanish-style plaza with fountains, genuine Iberian art, beautiful night lighting, interesting food and shops (200 of 'em). At **47th & Nicholas**, a copy of the Giralda Tower in Seville.
47th and Central: Spanish murals, exquisite sevillano tilework depicting the bullfight. Splendid display of lights at Christmas.
Crown Center, Main and Pershing Rd. 'City within a city,' built by those friendly people at Hallmark Cards. Hotel, shops, 5-storey waterfall, indoor gardens, restaurants, etc. 'Go Sat mornings when woodcarvers, artists, etc are at work.' Attached to it is the **Hallmark Visitors Center**, 274-5672. Mon-Fri 9 am-5 pm, Sat 9.30 am-4.30 pm. Lots of exhibits showing how the company grew big, peddling sentiment and gushing rhymes.
EarthRiders: Bring people who enjoy riding mountain bikes together. Organised off-road rides and sponsors regional mountain biking events. Call Stan Gaskill (316) 468-4591 for more info.

Independence, a few miles east of KC and one-time home of that well-known haberdasher Harry Truman. The library and museum contain presidential papers; his grave is in the courtyard. Free 30 min slide and sound show, *The Man From Missouri*, hourly at the Jackson County Courthouse.

Museum of History and Science, 3218 Gladstone Blvd, 483-8300. Tue-Sat, 9.30 am-4.30 pm, Sun noon-4.30 pm; $2.50. Housed in the 72-room mansion of lumber king RA Long, are exhibits on natural, regional history, and anthropology. Crawl-through igloo, other good native American stuff.

Nelson Atkins Museum of Fine Art, 45th Terrace & Oak Sts, 561-4000. Huge variety, especially of oriental art and crafts. Outdoor sculpture garden is great with its fine Henry Moore collection. Tues-Thurs 10 am-4 pm, Fri 10 am-9 pm, Sat 10 am-5 pm, Sun 1 pm-5 pm; $5, $2 w/student ID.

The Livestock Exchange and Stockyards are at 12th & Genessee. If the smell doesn't remove your appetite, the **Golden Ox** next door has good if somewhat pricey steaks.

ENTERTAINMENT

Westport, original city heart btwn 39th & 45th Sts, is famous for good taverns and nightlife. Or try **Grand Emporium**, 3832 Main St, 531-1504; good bands. With luck, you may catch the **Jazz Pub Crawl** in May or Sept, a night of hopping in and out of 30 clubs with hot live jazz. Shuttle buses transport you safely from one to the next at your leisure.

Jazz hotline, 931-2888, gives the lowdown on what's playing all around town.

Kelly's Irish Pub, 500 Westport Rd, 753-9193. Cheap drink and a friendly atmosphere.

River City USA, River City Drive on the Kansas side, (913) 281-5300. Missouri River's largest and newest riverboats feature 1hr afternoon excursions, $7.50, Sunday brunch, $20 and moonlight cruises, $10.

Stanford and Sons, 504 Westport Rd, 561-7454. Great music, and 2-for-1 drinks.

INFORMATION/TRAVEL

Amtrak, 2200 Main St, 421-3622/(800) 872-7245. For trains to St Louis, Chicago, and even LA.

Convention and Visitors Bureau, 1100 Main, Suite #2550, 221-2424.

Greyhound, 1101 Troost St, 221-2835/(800) 231-2222.

Kansas City Area Transportation Authority (Metro), 221-0660.

Kansas City International Airport, 243-5237, about 18 miles from the city. Take the #29 Metro bus from downtown ($1.10 for express), about 1hr. The KC Shuttle picks up from major downtown hotels and costs $10 o/w; a taxi will cost you about $30.

Kansas City Trolley, 221-3399, $4 will get you a day of unlimited rides. 'Drivers are very friendly and give an interesting commentary.'

KC Funline, 691-3800.

ST JOSEPH 'Wanted: young skinny wiry fellows, not over 18. Must be expert riders willing to risk death daily. Orphans preferred. Wages $25/week. Apply Central Overland Express.' Over 100 young masochists applied and thus on 3 April 1860, began the Pony Express, a 2000 mile Missouri to California mail delivery system. Only in operation 18 months, it left a lasting impression on the world. **St Joseph Museum** at 914 Penn Street, (816) 232-8471, preserves the original stables and other interesting memorabilia, well worth a visit; Mon-Sat 9 am-5 pm, free on Sun 1 pm-5 pm, $2. Same day, different year in St Joe, Bob Ford shot Jesse James for a $10,000 reward. The house where the shot was fired is now the **Jesse James Home Museum**, 12th & Penn, (816) 232-8206, which is full of original

Jamesabilia and even has the hole left by the bullet in the wall; Mon-Sat 10 am-5 pm, Sun 1 pm-5 pm, $3. The telephone area code is 816.

CAVES Of all things, Missouri is blessed with more known caves than any other state, many with guided tours to keep you from getting lost and driving up the owners' insurance premiums. For more information, write Missouri Division of Tourism, PO Box 1055, Jefferson City, MO 65102, or call (573) 751-4133. Some examples: **Bluff Dwellers' Cave**, 2 miles S of Noel, (417) 475-3666. A 45 min tour includes stalactite curtains, corals, 10-ton balanced rock, as well as a 54-foot rimstone dam; $6. **Fantastic Caverns**, 4 miles N of Springfield, (417) 833-2010. They are as good as their name implies, and you don't even have to walk! Propane-run jeeps transport visitors through the caves in modern comfort; $13.50. **Marvel Cave**, Branson, (417) 338-2611, has a huge waterfall at a depth of 500 ft and a main chamber that is 20 storeys high. Back on the surface is **Silver Dollar City**, an 1880's theme park. $28 gets you into the park and Marvel Cave, call (800) 952-6626 for info. **Meramec Caverns**, Stanton, (314) 468 3166 and *www.mobot.org/stateparks/ meramec.html*; '1 1/2 hr tour, lots of stunning formations in calcite and onyx including a very large botryoidal formation and 70 ft high stalactite; $10, well worth it!' For more in-depth details about each state park, check out the official state parks listing at *www.mobot.org/stateparks/parklist.html*

NEBRASKA   *The Cornhusker State*

A huge, tilting plate of a state, Nebraska rises from 840 ft at its Missouri River eastern border to nearly 5000 ft as it approaches the Rockies. Through it runs the feeble Platte River, 'a mile wide, a foot deep, too thick to swim and too thin to plow', along which countless buffalo roamed until done in by kill-crazy Buffalo Bills. As shallow as 6 inches in places, the Platte nonetheless made an excellent 'highway' and water supply for the 2.5 million folks who crossed Nebraska in Conestoga wagons, 1840-66. Even today, the most worthwhile things to see in the state are those connected with the pioneer trails west.

Like other plains states, Nebraska has perfectly miserable weather summer and winter. Its specialty is hailstones, which occasionally reach the size of golfballs. A leading producer of beef cattle, TV dinners and popcorn, Nebraska specialises in silos, both grain and ICBM missile. *www.yahoo.com/Regional/U_S__States/Nebraska/*

OMAHA Once a jumping-off place for pioneers, Omaha is the Union Pacific train headquarters and has taken over the noisome title of 'meat packer for the world' from Chicago. Friendly yes, but about as lively at night as a hog carcass, except around Old Market.

Hometown of Fred Astaire and Malcolm X, Omaha nowadays is site of Boys Town and also the underground Strategic Air Command (SAC) headquarters. A collection of aerial photos of Omaha, Omaha links and a photo map can be accessed thru *www.novia.net/~sadams/Omaha_Pages/*

OMA_Pics.html. Well worth it!
The telephone area code is 402.

ACCOMMODATION

The Bellevue Campground, Haworth Park, 291-3379, on the Missouri River 10 miles N of downtown at Rt 370. Use the infrequent 'Bellevue' bus from 17th and Dodge to Mission and Franklin, and walk down Mission. Right next to the Missouri. Camp sites-$5 w/hook-up.

Excel Inn, 2211 Douglas St, 345-9565. Not the best of areas, but very convenient to downtown. From S/D-$34. Stay 5 nights and next 2 nights are free. Weekly rate S-$175.

Motel 6, 10708 M St, 331-3161. From S-$37, D-$43.

Satellite Motel, 6006 L St, 733-7373. S-$34, D-$45.

YMCA, 430 S 20th, 341-1600. S-$9 (+ $10 key deposit). Weekly rate of $58 (+ $10 key deposit). Pool, 5 mins from Greyhound. An extra $3.50 for use of athletic facilities.'New, clean, pleasant.'

FOOD/ENTERTAINMENT

Try the cobbled streets of the Old Market, on Howard St, btwn 10th & 13th Sts, for shops, restaurants and bars.

Bohemian Cafe, 1406 S 13th St, 342-9838. 'Czech food and atmosphere—the duck is superb.' Lunches for $4, dinners $6-$8.

Coyote's Bar and Grill, 1217 Howard St, 345-2047. Try the 'holy Avocado' ($5.75), salads, chili and humongous burgers ($4-$5) at this fun Tex-Mex restaurant. Mon-Sat 11 am-1 am, Sun noon-10 pm.

The Diner, 12th & Harney Sts, 341-9870. For a true diner experience for under $3 for lunch. Open 6 pm-4 am.

Dubliner Pub, 12th & Harney, 342-5887. A good place to shoot darts. 150 imported beers. Open 11 am-1 am.

Garden Cafe, 72nd Dodge, Crossroad Mall, 390-2040. 'Wholesome breakfast' for $3, dinners for $6.

The Great Wall, 1013 Farnam St, 346-2161, has good Chinese food. Weekday lunch buffet ($5), w/end dinner buffet ($7). Sun-Thurs 11.30 am-10 pm, Fri-Sat 11.30 am-11 pm.

Johnny's, 4702 S 27th St, 731-4774. Omaha's Stockyard's steak house for three-quarters of a century. Every cut of steak available.

Spaghetti Works, 502 S 11th St in Old Market, 422-0770. $4.50 lunch, $6 dinner buys pasta, garlic bread and salad bar. Also one in suburban Ralston, off I-80 at 84th St and Park Drive.

OF INTEREST

Boys Town, 136th St and W Dodge Rd, 498-1140. Includes Hall of History, stamp and coin museum. May-August. Tours daily 8 am-5.30 pm; free. 'Very interesting.'

General Crook House, 30th & Fort, 455-9990, Italianate brick mansion, with beautiful Victorian gardens stands on the site of Fort Omaha; built in 1879 by the outpost's first commander, General George Crook. Tue-Fri 10 am-4 pm, Sun 1 pm-4 pm, $3.50. Closed Mon. Tours of city arranged from the house.

Henry Doorly Zoo, 10th and Dear Park Blvd, 733-8400. Contains rare white Bengal tigers and a 4½ acre aviary, the world's second largest, and 'Lied Jungle', a simulated tropical rainforest with the accompanying wildlife. 9.30 am-5 pm daily summers; 'til 6 pm Sun/hol. Visitors can remain in the park for two hrs after the park has closed; $7.25.

Joslyn Art Museum, 2200 Dodge St, 342-3300. Housed in Art Deco building, Indian and other art; pictures painted during the Maximillian Expedition up the Missouri River in 1833-4 are worth seeing. Free jazz Thur eves in July/August. Tue-Sat 10 am-5 pm, Thur until 8 pm, Sun 1-5 pm; $4.

Old Market, 10th & Howard. Cobbled streets, warehouses recycled into smart shops, galleries, restaurants. 'Most interesting place in Omaha.' See where oft eulogised and misrepresented black leader **Malcolm X**—ne Malcolm Little—was born, 3448 Pinkey St. Then see the wider picture, **Great Plains Black Museum**, 2213 Lake St, 345-2212, has extensive exhibits on the black experience, including black cowboys, athletes and soldiers; Mon-Fri 8.30 am-5 pm, $2.

Orpheum Theater, 409 S 16th St, 444-4750. An ornate theater featuring concerts, ballet, plays.

Strategic Air Command Museum, 2510 Clay St, Bellevue, 10 miles N of Omaha, off Hwy 75, 292-2001. Bombers, missiles, a *red phone* (hear the end of the world!) and the *Red Alert* slide show, shown in winter only. 'Nuclear nightmare at its *finest*! A must-see!' 8 am-8 pm summer; 8 am-5 pm winter; $4.

Union Pacific Historical Museum, 801 S 10th St (now part of **Western Heritage Museum**), 444-5072. Lots of Lincoln memorabilia including replica of his funeral car with original furnishings, plus oddments. Mon-Fri 9 am-3 pm, Sat 9 am-noon; free.

Union Stockyards, 29th & O Sts, 734-1900. Cattle auction on Wed.

Western Heritage Museum, 801 S 10th St, 444-5071. Housed in the wonderful Art Deco old Union Station, worth a look in itself, this museum has displays on Omaha and Nebraska history. Tues-Sat 10 am-5 pm, Sun 1 am-5 pm, $3. Closed Mon.

INFORMATION/TRAVEL

Amtrak, 1003 S 9th St, (800) 872-7245.

Events Hotline, 444-6800.

Greyhound, 16th & Jackson, (800) 231-2222.

Nebraska Tourist Information, (800) 228-4307.

Student Center, U of Nebraska, 60th and Dodge Sts, 554-2383. Helpful with accommodation, rides, general info.

Visitors Bureau, 6800 Mercy Road, #202, (800) 332-1819.

LINCOLN The Nebraska State Capitol dominates this cow town and many miles of surrounding plains. This is home of the Unicameral, Nebraska's unique one-house, non-partisan legislative body—an improvisation made during the Depression to save money.

The capitol, 'Tower on the Plains', was not blown in by tornado, despite what its incongruent appearance may suggest, but architect Bertram Goodhue did come all the way from New York City in 1920 to design this early 'skyscraper'. The broad base of the building represents the plains; the tower the aspirations of the pioneers.

Lincoln was home to William Jennings Bryan, a populist who three times was the Democratic Party's presidential candidate around the turn of the century, and who finally made a monkey of himself at the notorious Scope's Monkey Trial in Tennessee. His house stands at 4900 Summer Street. For a virtual tour of downtown Lincoln, click on *www.db.4w.com/lincolntour/*
The telephone area code is 402.

ACCOMMODATION

Visit the Nebraska Association of B&Bs at *www.bbonline.com/ne/nabb* or call (402) 843-2287.

Cornerstone Youth Hostel, 640 N 16th St, on U of Nebraska campus, 476-0355. $10. 11 pm curfew.

The Great Plains Motel, 2732 O St, (800) 288-8499; large rooms w/small fridges. S-$38/40, D-$46.

The Town House Motel, 1744 M St at 18th, (800) 279-1744. Super-suites with full kitchen, bath, living room and TV. S-$43, D-$48.

Camping: Nebraska State Fair Park Campground, Exit #399, 1402 N 14th St, 473-4287. April-October. Sites $15 for two w/hook-up; **Camp-A-Way**, 1st & W Superior, Exits #401 & #401-A, 200 Ogden Rd, (402) 476-2282. Open year round. Sites $10.

Cheap motels abound on **Cornhusker Hwy**, around the 5600 block (E of downtown).

FOOD

The Coffee House, 1324 P St, 477-6611, is a favourite hangout for locals. Muffin mania for $1, and a great 'capalpacino' ($1.50)! Mon-Sat 7 am-midnight, Sun 11 am-midnight.

PO Pears, 322 S 9th St, 476-8551. A college hangout with cheap beer, good burgers, and live music. Open 11.30 am-1 am.

Rock 'n' Roll Runza, 210 W 14th St, 474-2030. Roller-skating waitresses, and their infamous foot-long chili cheese dogs ($5). Mon-Thur 10.30 am-10 pm; Fri/Sat 'til midnight; Sun 10 am-10 pm, serving brunch 10 am 'til 2 pm.

OF INTEREST

Roller-Skating Museum, 4730 South St, 483-7551. See the world's largest collection of roller skates, including skates on stilts and skates worn by dancing bears, horses. Free; Mon-Fri 8.30 am-5 pm.

Sheldon Memorial Art Gallery, 12th and R Sts, 472-2461. Houses a fine collection of 20th century American art and sculpture garden. Tues-Sat 10 am-5 pm & 7 pm-9 pm; Sun, 2 pm-9 pm; free.

State Capitol, located btwn 14th & K Sts, 471-0448. In Art Deco style with a bit of everything inside. Mon-Fri 8 am-5 pm, Sat 10 am-5 pm, Sun 1 pm-5 pm; guided tours (every 1/2hr w/days in summer) on the hour.

ENTERTAINMENT

There are several nightspots in Lincoln, among them the notorious **Barry's Bar and Grill**, 235 N 9th St, 476-6511. Mon-Sat 11 am-11 pm, Sun noon-1 am. For good music try **The Zoo Bar**, 134 N 14th St, 435-8754, with a cover charge of $4. Mon-Fri 3 pm-1 am, Sat noon-1 am. **The Panic**, 2005 18th St, 435-8764, at N, is a great gay dance/video/patio bar. Mon-Fri 4 pm-1 am, Sat noon-1 am.

Check out some of these annual events: **Annual Boat, Sport, Travel Show**, Nebraska State Fair Park. Displays of outdoor fun-boats, fishing, camping and other sporting activities. Admission charged. Thurs & Fri 6 pm-10 pm; Sat 11 am-10 pm; Sun 11 am-5 pm. Call (402) 466-8102; **Chocolate Lover's Fantasy**, Ramada, 9th & P St. This festive event features Lincoln celebrities, chefs, and fabulous chocolate in every form with a live and silent auction. Begins 5 pm. Call (402) 434-6900; **Jazz in June**, Sheldon Sculpture Garden. Free outdoor concerts featuring well known jazz vocalists and musicians each Tue in June, 7 pm-9 pm. Call (402) 434-6900.

INFORMATION/TRAVEL

Amtrak, 201 N 7th, (800) 872-7245.

Chamber of Commerce, 1221 N St, #320, 476-7511.

Greyhound, 940 P St, (800) 231-2222.

Lincoln Convention and Visitors Bureau, 1221 N St, 434-5335.

Tourist Information Center, 301 Centennial Mall S, 471-3796.

ALONG THE PIONEER AND PONY EXPRESS TRAILS   The Oregon, Mormon and other pioneer trails plus the Pony Express routes followed the Platte River, which today is paralleled in large part by I-80 and by Hwys 30 E & 26 W.

The land outside of Omaha lies flat and covered with farms. If you like corn, you should be in heaven here. Two and a half hours west from Omaha, in the town of **Grand Island** on Hwy 34, is the **Stuhr Museum of the Prairie Pioneer**, (308) 385-5316, a preservation of a small frontier village of the late 1800's. $6.40. Picnic area.

Going east to west: at **Gothenburg** in midstate, you can see two original Pony Express stations (one at 96 Ranch St) and an old stagecoach stop with bullet holes still in the walls. At **Lafayette City Park**, free camping. **North Platte**, long-time home of scout and show biz personality Buffalo Bill Cody, offers a free look at his ranch house—a pretty but prissy-looking Victorian affair. At **Scout's Rest Ranch State Park**, $2 per vehicle entrance fee, (308) 535-8035. Nightly rodeos are held across from the park at 8.30 pm in the summer; B Bill got his nickname for killing 4280 buffalo in 17 months while employed by the railroad to supply meat for its crews.

At **Bayard** further west, the Oregon Trail Wagon Train company offers 1-and 4-day treks which circle **Chimney Rock**. Meals (including pioneer items like vinegar pie and hoecakes), wagon driving or riding, and other activities from an Indian 'attack' to prairie square-dancing for about $150 a day. They also do 3 hr covered wagon tours to Chimney Rock and back, for $8 pp; leaving at 8 am, returning noon. Book through Oregon Trail Wagon Train, Rt 2, PO Box 502, Bayard, NE 69334 or call (308) 586-1850.

Scotts Bluff and **Chimney Rock**, off US 26 in western Nebraska, are two rock formations that served as landmarks for the frontier families. Both are climbable with poignant pioneer graves and clearly defined wagon ruts. The park rangers at Scotts Bluff give daily lectures in summer and the pioneer campsite can be visited. Spectacular views from the bluff.

NORTH DAKOTA *The Peace Garden State*

Virtually border to border farmland, interspersed with missile sites, North Dakota grows lots of wheat, sugar beets and cattle. Its superlatives aren't exactly the kind to make you rush up here: it has the world's largest concrete buffalo (in Jamestown), concrete Holstein (in New Salem) and steel turtle with movable head (40,000 lbs in Dunseith). Not to mention the longest road without a curve—110 miles of tedium on Rte 46. But do explore the Badlands and the simple pleasures of what Teddy Roosevelt called 'the roughrider country', in the west, accessible by bus to Medora.
www.yahoo.com/Regional/U_S__States/NorthDakota/
The telephone area code for the state is 701.

BISMARCK   Capital and craftily named by the Northern Pacific railway after Otto von B in the hope of getting German marks to capitalise railroad construction (it worked!). The state's capital city newspaper is located online at *www.ndonline.com*

OF INTEREST
State Capitol Building, 328-2480. Famous sons and daughters in the Roughrider gallery: Eric Sevareid, Peggy Lee, Lawrence Welk, Roger Maris. Take the elevator to the 19th floor to the observation deck and see for miles and miles over the plains. Mon-Fri 8 am-4 pm, Sat 9 am-4 pm, Sun 1-4 pm; free.

North Dakota Heritage Center (on Capitol grounds), 328-2666, has an Indian collection called one of the finest in the world. Many personal effects of Sitting Bull. Not to be missed: the Indian crafts store—outstanding and authentic artifacts for sale. Mon-Fri 8 am-5 pm, Sat 9 am-5 pm, Sun 11 am-5 pm; free. United Tribes International performs a **pow-wow** in early Sept, where you can see native Americans dance, play drums and chant in full costume. Others take place sporadically at Indian reservations, check with tribal offices at Ft Totten, Turtle Mountain and others.

INFORMATION/TRAVEL
Amtrak, 400 1st Ave SW, Minot, (800) 872-7245. The nearest station to Bismarck; lies on the 'Empire Builder' Chicago-Seattle route.
Bismarck Visitors Bureau, 107 West Main St, 222-4308.
Greyhound, 1237 W Divide Ave, (800) 231-2222.
North Dakota Tourism Dept, Liberty Memorial Building, near State Capitol, (800) 435-5663.

LEWIS AND CLARK TRAIL   By auto or on foot, you can retrace the explorers' route of 1804 south along the Missouri River. Points of interest include: **Ft Yates** (Sioux national headquarters), **Ft Lincoln** (from which Custer and the 7th Cavalry rode out to defeat), **Ft Mandan** (where Sakakawea joined Lewis and Clark), buffalo wallows, **Knife River Indian Village**, and **Sitting Bull Historic Site**, where the leader was originally buried. Great hunters, 600 Sioux braves once killed over 6000 buffalo in three days in 1882. An excellent Indian campground one mile W of Ft Yates at **Long Soldier Coulee Park**, open year-round. *www.glness.com/tourism/ html/west/WestTrails.html* takes you to *Trails In The West*, detailing trails, hiking, biking and backpacking options.

BADLANDS AND ROOSEVELT NATIONAL PARK   There are three units, spread over 75 miles of rough terrain. Described as 'grand, dismal and majestic', the Badlands formations are best seen early morning and late afternoon. (Not to be confused with South Dakota's Badlands, which are bigger and badder.) The south unit near Medora has a 36 mile loop with scenic overlooks, buffalo and prairie dogs, and a campground at Cottonwood. Teddy's **Elkhorn Ranch** is very remote; the ranch ultimately showed a net loss of $21,000 but he loved the area, saying: 'I owe more than I can ever express to the men and women of the cow country'. Sully Creek Campground, two miles from Medora: 'Primitive, can get cold but very convenient to Roosevelt if one has a car.' For online photographs of Badlands National Park, visit *www.udri.udayton.edu/personal/klosterm/adakota.htm*

INTERNATIONAL PEACE GARDENS   On the US/Canadian border— the world's longest unfortified border. The formal gardens commemorate years of peace between the countries. Enter via **Dunseith**. Daily 7.45 am-9 pm; $7 per vehicle. Tel: (701) 263-4390. For details on the newest and most scenic route to the Peace Gardens, surf the *www.tradecorridor.com/stjohn* website.

OHIO *The Buckeye State*

Ohio makes everything and more of it than anybody else: comic books, coffins, Liederkranz cheese, bank vaults, vacuums, false teeth, playing cards, rubber, jet turbine engines, soap, glassware—you name it. Small wonder that Ohio also produced America's first billionaire: John D Rockefeller. They're always tinkering in Ohio, birthplace of the cash register, the fly swatter, the menthol cigarette and the beer can, not to mention one of the Wright brothers, Thomas Edison, John Glenn and Neil Armstrong.

Get out of its highly industrialised cities and you'll discover a surprising amount of green and gentle countryside, full of lakes, wineries (50 of them), farms with roadside produce and local colour from Amish villages to oddities like Hinckley, buzzard capital of the world (where you can satisfy that craving for a buzzard cookie). Sinclair Lewis used Ohio as his model setting for small town America in *Babbit*, a novel written in 1922 about a businessman whose individuality is eliminated by Republican pressures to conform.

The state also has some of America's best roller coasters and amusement parks, the largest state fair in the US, over 1000 festivals (including Twinsday at Twinsburg) and is birthplace of eight presidents. No wonder Ohio ranks third in tourism, behind New York and California. *www.yahoo.com/Regional/U_S__States/Ohio/*

CINCINNATI Probably unique in being a place which grew to cityhood on steamboat traffic, as many as 8000 boats a year docked at Cincinnati to take on passengers, lightning rods and lacy 'French' ironwork destined for New Orleans bordellos. Besides their practical value, steamboats were raced incessantly, causing huge sums of money to change hands and equally astonishing losses of life—in one five-year period, 2268 people died in steamboat explosions. Settled by Germans, the 'City of Seven Hills' became a leading producer of machine tools, Ivory soap, beer, gin and a variety of ham favoured by Queen Victoria, all without losing its livable, likeable essence. Check out Cincinnati events such as the Oktoberfest Zinzinnati (Sept) and the Queen City Blues Festival (July) under *www.gccc.com/oktfest.htm*
The telephone area code is 513.

ACCOMMODATION
Anna Louise Residence for Women, 300 Lytle St, near the Taft Museum, 421-5211. S-$20.
Calhoun Residence Hall, University of Cincinnati, Calhoun St, 556-8596. Near Clifton Ave, south side of campus, 23 miles N of downtown. Take buses #17, #18, #19, from downtown. AC rooms available; call ahead. $23 per room (for 2), discounts for longer stays. Mention BUNAC.
College of Mount St Joseph, 5701 Delhi Road, 244-4327, 8 miles W of downtown off Rt. 50 on Fairbanks St (it turns into Delhi Pike). Clean rooms in quiet location. S-$25, D-$30. Call for rsvs.
Denizen Hotel, 716 Main St, 241-7035. Rooms begin at $37.
Evendale Motel, 10165 Reading Road, 563-1570. Take a ride on the Reading bus 43 North to Reading and Columbia; then walk 1/2 hr north on Reading. Dark, but clean rooms. S-$26 for two.

Camping: Camp Shore Campgrounds, Rt 56 Aurora, (812) 438-2135, 30 miles W of Cincinnati on the Ohio River. $14/site, includes swimming and tennis. Also, **Rose Gardens Resort—KAO Campgrounds**, I-75 exit 166, (606) 428-2000; 30 miles N of Cincinnati. Tent sites $16 w/hook-up. and cabins $28 w/hook-up. **Yogi Bear's Camp Resort**, I-71 exit 24 at Mason, (800) 832-1133. Close to King's Island. Camp site $35 for two, w/hook-up, XP-$5). An extra $3 gets you a shaded site.

FOOD

Cincinnati's Germanic tradition means it has a number of beer gardens. It's also noted for local chili, served '3-, 4-or 5-way'; eg with spaghetti, beans, meat, onions, Cheddar cheese. Chili parlours abound, each with a secret recipe. It's accepted that they all contain cinnamon; rumour has it that **Skyline Chili** adds chocolate too. Here are just a few around town (meal approx $4 with soft drink):

Camp Washington Chili, Hopple and Colerain, 541-006. 'Prime source of 5-way Cincinnati-style chili: thick, spicy meat sauce atop a bed of plump spaghetti, garnished with beans, shredded cheese and chopped onions.'

Gold Star, 8467 Beachmont Ave, 474-4916.

Hartwell's Empress Chili, 8340 Vine St, 20 min N of downtown, 761-5599. For a filling $2 bfast, try **Reba's Diner**, 588 Cheviot Rd, 385-4833.

Skyline Chili, 643 Vine St, 241-2020 and at 6th & Walnut, 381-4244.

Also: Findlay Market, Findlay & Elm St, 352-3282. Produce and picnic items. Mon-Wed 7 am-1.30 pm, Fri-Sat 7 am-6 pm.

Izzy's, Elm & 9th, 721-4241. A Cincinnati tradition.

OF INTEREST

The Beach, 2590 Waterpark Dr in Mason, 20 miles N of Cincinnati on I-71, 398-7946. One of the ten largest water parks in the US, with a 25,000 sq ft wave pool, as well as speed, giant inner-tube and body slides, $19. Daily 10 am-9 pm to July, August-September 10 am-7 pm.

Carew Tower, 5th and Vine Sts. From the 49th floor, take a gander at Cincinnati, the Ohio River and Kentucky opposite.

Cincinnati Art Museum, Eden Park Dr, 721-5204. Tue-Sat 10 am-5 pm, Sun noon-6 pm; $5, $4 w/student ID.

Cincinnati Zoo, 3400 Vine St, 281-4701. Called 'the sexiest zoo in the US' for its successful breeding programme: lots of gorillas, rare white Bengal tigers, an insectarium. Celebrating its 150th anniversary. Daily 9 am-6 pm, grounds close at 8 pm; $8.

Contemporary Arts Center, 115 E 5th St, 721-0390. Mon-Sat 10 am-6 pm; Sun noon-5 pm, $3.50, $2 w/student ID.

King's Island, in Mason, off I-71, 398-5600. The Midwest's largest and often busiest theme park and the world's longest coaster, 'The Beast'. Over 100 rides and live shows; fireworks nightly. Daily 8 am-10 pm Memorial Day-Labor Day; $31. 'Need a car to get there.'

Krohn Conservatory, Eden Park, 421-4086. One of the largest public greenhouses in the world. Seasonal floral displays. Daily 10 am-6 pm; donation encouraged.

Meier's Winesellers, 6955 Plainfield Pike, 891-2900. Ohio's oldest and largest winery. Free hourly tours of wine making and wine aging, ending with wine tasting. Mon-Sat 10 am-3 pm; bar and garden open 'til 4 pm.

Taft Museum, 316 Pike, 241-0343. Federal 1820 mansion houses collection of paintings (including Rembrandt and Whistler), Chinese porcelains, French enamel, portraits. Mon-Sat 10 am-5 pm, Sun 1-5 pm; $4, $2 w/student ID. 'Exquisite. Marred only by poor taste in carpets.'

Tyler Davidson Fountain Square. The centre of downtown activity is around here. Lunchtime concerts, pre and post-ballgame celebrations; shops and businesses.

Union Terminal, 1301 Western Ave, 287-7000. The newly renovated building, an Art Deco gem with the world's highest unsupported dome, now houses 'Museum

Center', which includes **Museum of Natural History** where a cavern full of bats and the Ice Age (simulated) awaits; the **Cincinnati Historical Society** has a mock-up of a 1860's street to wander in; and finally pop over to the **Omnimax** to see those films on the big screen. Museums open Mon-Sat 9 am-5 pm, Sun 11 am-6 pm; to one museum $5.50, to two $9 and for everything $12 (inc. Omnimax). Call to check Omnimax showtimes.

Riverboats: At public landing, foot of Broadway. Revitalised riverfront area, including seating at the Serpentine Wall for pleasant boat-watching. Cruises heavily booked and rather pricey, but you can take in arrivals, departures and attendant hoopla and steam calliope-playing for free.

Cincinnati is home base for the *Delta Queen*, genuine relic on the National Register of Historic Landmarks. This is a real paddlewheeler as opposed to the ignoble beasties that ply the waters in hundreds of US cities and towns. *Showboat Majestic*, (513) 241-6550, also docks here, with live theater nightly; $12, $11 w/student ID. On the Covington, KY, side is the *Mike Fink*, a riverboat restaurant with a delectable New Orleans-style seafood bar. Not cheap but you may feel like splurging on catfish, crab legs and chocolate chip pecan pie. For information about year-round cruising, sightseeing, lunches and dinners aboard boats here contact BB Riverboats, at the foot of Greenup St, (800) 261-8586. 1hr sight-seeing cruises at $8. Located at **Covington Landing**.

ENTERTAINMENT

Mt Adams, Cincinnati's answer to Greenwich Village, is where the yuppies are. The students hang out in the **Clifton area**, where the University of Cincinnati is. The place to go in this college town is **Calhoun St** or **Short Vine** (1 block off Vine St). Many bars and clubs, ranging in musical style, dress code, and price in the U district. Try to time your visit for the **Oktoberfest** in mid-Sept; lots of dancing, eating, and beer drinking in downtown area. Check out *www.gccc.com/oktfest.htm*

Arnold's, 210 E 8th St, 421-6234, btwn Main & Sycamore Sts downtown. Has jazz, ragtime and swing music along with sandwiches and dinners. Cincinnati's oldest bar.

Blind Lemon, 936 Hatch St, Mt Adams, 241-3885. Old-fashioned decor. Pop, acoustic guitar music at 9.30 pm, no cover.

Music Hall, 1241 Elm St by Lincoln Park Dr, 721-8222. Classical music; discount w/student ID 10 min before performances. Call **River Bend**, 348-2229, for tkt info on these concerts; pop, rock and more.

Playhouse in the Park, 962 Mt Adams Circle, 421-3888. Two theaters with plays Oct-June, cabaret in the summer. Student rush tkts on sale 15 mins before performances. For updates, call **Dial The Arts** on 751-2787.

SPORT

Cincinnati Reds games, 421-REDS, at Riverfront Stadium. America's first professional baseball team. The Bengals football team also play at Riverfront Stadium, 621-3550.

INFORMATION/TRAVEL

Amtrak, 1901 River Rd, (800) 872-7245.

Cincinnati Convention and Visitors Bureau, 300 W 6th St, (800)344-3445.

The Greater Cincinnati International Airport is actually in Kentucky, about 13 miles away. Jetport Express, (606) 283-3702, runs shuttle buses there from downtown hotels for $10 o/w every ¹/₂ hr, $15 r/t.

Greyhound, 1005 Gilbert, (800) 231-2222. A long walk from city centre.

Queen City Metro Buses, 6 E 4th, 621-4455 for info and schedules. Rush-hour fare of 80¢, 65¢ off peak.

State Information, (800)-BUCKEYE.

Visitors Information Center on Fountain Square, in the heart of town, 421-4636.

COLUMBUS Writer O Henry once did three years for embezzlement in a Columbus cell, while in confinement he produced some of his best stories. Local humorist James Thurber attended Ohio State University briefly and set his play *The Male Animal*, there. This capital city sits in a region intriguingly called Leatherlips, the name of a Wyandot Indian chief who was executed by his people for siding with palefaces. Discover Columbus, Ohio, with Columbus InfoPages at *www.fpsol.com/infopages.html*
The telephone area code is 614.

ACCOMMODATION
German Village offers the best value motel accommodation. Student-style accommodation is also available close to the State University.
Heart of Ohio Hostel, 95 E 12th Ave, 294-7157. $12. 'Superb. Highly recommended.' Take #2 bus.
Ohio Stater Inn, 2060 North High St, 294-5381. More of a long-term accommodation solution. Approx $150 weekly. Private rooms across from the Ohio State University campus.
Village Inn Motel, 920 South High St, 443-6506. D-$46. 1mile from downtown.
YMCA, 40 W Long St, 224-1131. Men only; weekly rates depending on income!
The Greater Columbus B&B Cooperative, (800) 383-7839. Includes 30 B&Bs with rates around $45-$75 a night.

FOOD/ENTERTAINMENT
Try the **Short North Area,** between downtown and the Ohio State Campus, for real bohemian atmosphere. The hippest shops, galleries, restaurants and night clubs are to be found here.
Blue Danube, 2439 N High St, 261-9308. Good, cheap restaurant with generous portions.
The French Market/Continent, 6076 Busch Blvd. All kinds of European restaurants and food-stalls. Good eating places in the **German Village**, bus from High St. Also at **North Market**, 29 Spruce, a century-old centre for produce. For nightlife, try **North High St**, 2 miles N of downtown. This is where the Ohio State University students go.
   Some of the better restaurants are to be found in the **Brewery District/German Village**, Busch Blvd, and in rather off-beat places like **Grand Ave** (NW of downtown). Bar bands are Columbus' specialty. Almost all have live music on w/ends.
Grand Avenue in the NW is a hidden treasure with it's 'bijou' cinema, open air coffee houses and bookstores. Try
Nickleby's Bookstore Cafe, 1425 Grand Ave, (800) 723-7323. Over 50,000 titles, in-store cafe, 'coffee of the day' and special events (live music, author talks etc) Daily 8 am-10 pm. 'This place is a find. A very relaxed atmosphere.'

OF INTEREST
Center of Science and Industry (COSI), 280 E Broad St, 228-2674. 4 flrs of science, health, industry and history exhibits. Mon-Sat 10 am-5 pm, Sun noon-5.30 pm; $6. 'Worth it.'
Columbus Zoo, 9990 Riverside Dr, 645-3550. Exit 20, Sawmill Rd, off I-270 outer belt. 100-acre zoo. Impressive collection of great apes, including the first gorilla ever born in captivity; only zoo in the world housing four generations of gorillas. Daily 9 am-6 pm, Wed 'til 8 pm. $6. Some activities involve additional charges.
Dodge Skatepark: Concrete snake run, three bowls, pyramid and other obstacles suitable for skateboarding and inlining; free.
German Village, 624 S Third St, 221-8888. Open daily. Restored 19th century community containing private homes, shops, restaurants.
Ohio State University library: largest collection of Thurber's works, drawings.

Thurber is not easy to get to—held under tight security and not generally accessible.
Ohio Theater, 55 E State St, 469-0939. A 1930's cinema with wonderful Titian red, gold-spangled baroque interior. Show classic movies all year round. 'Amazing decor; organist rises through the floor.'
Topiary Garden, 408 E Town St at Washington Ave, 645-3300. Topiary depiction of Georges Seurat 'A Sunday Afternoon ...' complete with 52 topiary people, 8 boats, 3 dogs, and a monkey!
Wyandot Lake Amusement Park, adjacent to the zoo, 889-9283, has 43 rides. Mon-Thur 10 am-8 pm, Fri-Sun 10 am-9 pm, $17 ($10.50 after 4 pm).

INFORMATION/TRAVEL
Central Ohio Transit Authority (COTA), 1775 High St, 228-1776, runs the local buses; $1.35 express routes, $1.10 basic fare.
Chamber of Commerce, 221-1321.
Greyhound, 111 E Town St, (800) 231-2222.
Port Columbus International Airport, E of downtown. Take the COTA bus #16 'Long St' from Broad & High, approx 30 mins, $1.
Visitors Bureau, 10 W Broad St, Suite 1300, 866-4888 and **Visitors Center**, 3rd floor of the City Mall, (800) 345-4386.

CLEVELAND   Superman was born in Cleveland in 1933, brainchild of 2 teenagers who in 1938 sold all rights for $130 and commenced upon a life-time of generally fruitless litigation. This earthly urban version of Krypton, like the doomed planet, is an entirely suitable birthplace for the 'Man of Steel'—at once an industrial powerhouse, but looking like Dresden after the war. Iron and steel were once the big money-earners; also shipbuilding, for Cleveland is on Lake Erie—the Great Lakes a great fissure through the core of America—with ocean-going ships tied up along its waterfront. John D Rockefeller spun his oil business here into one of the largest personal fortunes the world has ever known. Downtown is thick with corporate head-quarters, while the symphony orchestra and municipal art museum and other cultural endeavours rank amongst the finest in the US.

Cleveland is the site of the Rock 'n Roll Hall of Fame designed by IM Pei, an honour won after an arduous battle with Philadelphia and San Francisco. Opened in 1995, it has good credentials: one of its disc jockeys coined the phrase 'rock & roll' and the city hosted the very first rock concert in 1952. Check out the Cleveland web site, *www.cleveland.oh.us/* detailing the city's remarkable renaissance.
The telephone area code is 216.

ACCOMMODATION
There is no downtown hotel accommodation for less than $80. Better to stay at one of the many motels near the airport. The airport is connected to Tower City (down-town) by the 'Rapid' ($1.50 o/w fare).
Brooklyn YMCA, 3881 Pearl Rd (W 25th St), 749-2355; $31, $90 weekly, $84 three weekly, $70 four or more weeks .
Cleveland Private Lodgings, 321-3213, finds accommodation in private homes around the city. From $55 for B&B; from $175 weekly; from $350 monthly.
Cleveland YMCA , 2200 Prospect Ave, 344-7700. 15 min. walk from downtown, at the corner of Prospect and E 22nd. Must have proof of employment. S-$28 or $94 p/w.
Knight's Inn, I-90 at SR 306, exit 193, 953-8835. S-$50-62; D-$52-70.
Lakewood Manor Hotel, 12020 Plympton Ave, 226-4800. 3 miles W of downtown

in Lakewood. Take bus 55 CX. TV, AC. Free coffee daily, and donuts on w/ends. Rooms range $60-70.

Ramada Inn-Cleveland Airport, I-480 Exit 12, 13930 Brookpark Rd, (800) 2-RAMADA. From D-$59. Complimentary bfast/airport shuttle, coin laundry.

Red Roof Inn, I-90 & Crocker Rd, exit 156, Westlake, 892-7920. From $54-$74.

Camping: Woodside Lake Park, 2256 Frost Rd, (330) 626-4251. 35 miles E of downtown, off I-480, in Streetsboro. Sites $23 for two w/hook-up.

FOOD

Hungarian restaurants are Cleveland's pride: various along Buckeye Rd; the best is **Balaton**, 921-9691. Cleveland is also the home of the '**National Rib Burn-off**' held Memorial Day weekend, bringing in best ribs from all over the world. As one would guess, a restaurant in this host city has even won the competition; **Geppetto's**, 3314 Warren Rd, 941-1120. And the prices are reasonable. The gastronomic cross-section at the **West Side Market**, 25th and Lorain Ave, has old world vibes, inexpensive and mouth-watering selection.

The Arcade, Euclid Ave, east of Public Square. 5-level mall, filled with a wide variety of ethnic restaurants.

Coventry Road area in Cleveland, interesting stores and food shops.

OF INTEREST

Cleveland Indoor Skatepark, close to Ohio turnpike. Approx 32,000 sq ft area for skateboarding/inlining/BMX. Heated and dry with a smooth tile floor. Spine ramp, 8 ft decks, hip ramp on one deck, jumpbox w/dual rail slides, 16 ft wide wallride ramp, assorted funboxes, launches and railslides. Helmets req. Large stage for an assortment of fun shows. Sml shop inside with vital bike/skate parts; **Lorain Skatepark**, Lorain near Cleveland, has a concrete vert ramp.

Museum of Art, 11150 East Blvd at University Circle, 421-7340. Free and first-rate, second only to the NY Metropolitan. Tue/Thurs/Sat/Sun 10 am-5 pm; Wed/Fri 10 am-9 pm.

Museum of Natural History, Wade Oval University Circle, 231-4600. Mon-Sat 10 am-5 pm, Sun noon-5 pm; $6, $4 w/student ID.

NASA-Lewis Research Center, 21000 Brookpark Rd, adjacent to Cleveland Hopkins Airport, 433-4000. Exhibits of NASA work. Mon-Fri 9 am-4 pm, Tue 'til 8 pm, Sat 10 am-3 pm, Sun 1 pm-5 pm; free.

Rock and Roll Hall of Fame and Museum, 1 Key Plaza, North Coast Harbor, 781-7625. The world's greatest repository of R'n'R memorabilia, incl Lennon's Sgt Pepper outfit, Madonna costumes, Michael Jackson's glove, a myriad selection of lyric sheets and guitars, and other entertaining historical artefacts/exhibitions. Daily 10 am-5.30 pm, Wed 'til 9 pm; $15. Takes 3-4 hrs to tour. *Check out website www.rockhall.com.*

Sea World, 995-2121, take Solon Exit off I-480 E from downtown. A 90-acre marine life park with the only Tsunami wave pool in Midwest, 20 miles NE of Cleveland. $28; $17 after 6 pm in summers. $4 parking. Busiest July/Aug. Open 10 am 'til 7 pm/11 pm depending on season. New 3D *Pirates* movie adventure.

Shaker Historical Museum, 16740 S Park Blvd, Shaker Heights, 921-1201. Tue-Fri 2 pm-5 pm, Sun 2 pm-5 pm. Once the site of a rural commune begun by the Shakers, a religious sect who turned their backs on industrialization for 10 mins—and along came Cleveland! Today's Shaker Heights is a ritzy suburb with good (and not always expensive) restaurants.

ENTERTAINMENT

Cleveland Ballet, 1375 Euclid Ave, 1 Playhouse Sq, 621-2260. Professional repertory ballet, featuring modern and classical work. Tkts $15-$55 (30% off w/ID).

Cleveland Orchestra, Severance Hall, 11001 Euclid Ave, 231-7300. World-famous symphony orchestra established in 1918, presenting a variety of concerts. Tkts $26, $20, $14 ($11 w/student ID)

Cleveland Playhouse, 8500 Euclid Ave, 795-7000. 3-theater complex. The season runs Jan-June, Oct-Dec.

The Flats, NW of Public Square, where the Cuyahoga River meets Lake Erie. Many rock bars and good eating establishments including **Fagan's**, 996 Old River, 241-6116 ('live music and excellent food'); **The Nautica Stage**, at the Flats, plays host to a number of outdoor summer concerts (rock, jazz, classical etc). Call 621-3000 for details.

INFORMATION/TRAVEL

Amtrak, Lakefront Station, 200 Cleveland Memorial Shoreway, 696-5115/(800) 872-7245. Like the Greyhound Station, this is not a safe part of town. Most trains arrive in the early hours, so use caution when leaving the station. Either take a taxi or wait until daylight before venturing out.

Chamber of Commerce, 621-3300.

Cleveland Convention and Visitors Bureau, 621-4110.

Cleveland Hopkins International Airport, 265-3729. About 11 miles from downtown, the easiest, cheapest and quickest way to get there is to take the #66X—Red Line train; $1.50 o/w.

Greyhound, 1465 Chester Ave, (800) 231-2222. 'High crime area—take extreme care, especially at night, even in restrooms.'

Regional Transit Authority, 621-9500, runs buses and the rapid rail system. Basic fare on buses, $1.25; express buses/rail, $1.50.

Visitors Information Center, 50 Public Square, Tower City Center, Suite #3100, 621-4110.

TOLEDO   A must-see in Ohio is the **Toledo Museum of Art**, 2445 Monroe Street at Scottwood Ave, Toledo, (419) 255-8000. Houses the finest collection of glass in the US; founded by Edward Libbey, who brought the glass industry to Toledo in 1888. Tue-Sat 10 am-4 pm (Fri 10 am-10 pm), Sun 1 pm-5 pm, closed Mon; free. A good day trip from Cleveland or Detroit.   Toledo's past, preserved through time in magnificent photographs, drawings and documents dating back to the 1860s, comes alive in the Local History and Genealogy Department's collection of over 150,000 images. Check out this pictorial history at *www.library.toledo.oh.us/history/*

SERPENT   MOUND   STATE   MEMORIAL   and   MOUND   CITY NATIONAL MONUMENT   South of Chillicothe near Locust Grove and 3 miles N of Chillicothe are these two Indian sites in south central Ohio. The first is the largest Indian effigy mound in the US, built by the Adena culture circa 1000 BC. 'Unforgettable, majestic and truly amazing that it's still around at all.' In summer, green grass covers the enormous coils, making them even more sinuous. **The Mound City Group**, Hopewell Culture, 16062 State Rte 104, Chillicothe, (614) 774-1125, dates back 2000 years; the 23 burial mounds are described as 'the city of the dead'. One contains a window through which you can view a mica grave, four cremation burials and numerous artefacts. Daily in summer 8.30 am-6 pm; $2, $4 per car load.

SOUTH DAKOTA *The Mount Rushmore State*

South Dakota is living proof that bad weather (from 40 below zero to a blazing 116 degrees) can't be all bad. To look at its tourist brochures, you'd think the place was full of nothing but jolly Anglo hunters, ranchers and fishermen. It has, however, a large (mostly Sioux) Indian population on nine reservations, regarded as 'uppity Injuns' (and worse) for their quixotic determination to win back more of their traditional lands. It was the discovery of gold in the Black Hills (verified by that catalytic figure, General Custer) that spelled doom for the fierce Sioux nations: today gold continues to be South Dakota's leading mineral.

Concentrate on the scenic western section: Mt Rushmore, the Black Hills, the Badlands. Because of distances and lack of public transit, it's difficult to sightsee without a car. Wyoming's Devil's Tower is only 35 miles from the South Dakota border, but you'll need a car to reach it as well.

The state's newest tourist attraction is what Kevin Costner left behind, namely the sets from his earnest and politically correct epic, *Dances With Wolves*. It's possible to visit Ft Hays, a whole faux fort, through **Prairie Adventures**, 342-4578; the camp by the river where the tribe celebrates its buffalo hunt and where Costner gets married, **Dakota Vistas**, 347-3138; the Sioux winter camp that ends the film is in Little Spearfish Canyon in the Black Hills National Forest.

For info: *www.yahoo.com/Regional/U_S__States/SouthDakota/*
The telephone area code is 605.

RAPID CITY A strategic spot for exploring the Black Hills and Badlands, itself a hodgepodge of tourist claptrapery. Visit the city guide compiled by the Rapid City Convention & Visitors Bureau at *www.rapidcitycvb.com/*

ACCOMMODATION/FOOD
Bunkhouse Lodge in nearby Custer, 673-3029. Q-$50. Call for individ rates.
College Inn Motel, 123 Kansas City St (part of National College), 394-4800/(800) 752-8942 within the state. Rooms begin at $45. 6 blocks from bus depot. 'Clean, well furnished.' Pool, laundry, cafeteria. Tally's, 530 6th St, 342-7621. Downtown; good food for not much money. 'Nice food and good locale.'
YMCA, 815 Kansas City St, 342-8538. $10 AYH. Summer only. 12 singles (no bedding) in co-ed room. You can reserve by postcard, zip code 57701, or phone ahead. **JB Big Boy Restaurant** around the corner.

OF INTEREST
Sioux Indian Museum and Crafts Center, West Blvd btwn St Joe & Main Sts, 394-2381. Wonderful collection of historical objects, excellent crafts, all the contemporary Sioux artists from Oscar Howe to Herman Red Elk. Sioux are noted for beadwork, stone pipes, quillwork. Mon-Sat 8 am-6 pm, Sun 11 am-4 pm; $6.50.
Caves in the Rapid City region: Sitting Bull Crystal Caverns, 342-2777, 9 miles N on Hwy 16 (heading toward Mt. Rushmore), has calcite dog-spar crystals. Daily 8 am-7 pm, $6.50. **Diamond Crystal Cave** is closest: 'Quite long but very pleasant walk.' '**Bethlehem Cave Drive** is superb though bumpy. Best cave in Black Hills.'

INFORMATION
Chamber of Commerce, Rushmore Plaza Civic Center, 343-1744. Useful maps. Ask

for the South Dakota Vacation Guide, with a dandy section on panning for gold and rockhounding. 'Very helpful people.'
South Dakota Tourism, Capitol Lake Plaza, Pierre, (800) 487-3223.

TRAVEL
Gray Line Tours, (800) 456-4461. Different itineraries of Black Hills, Rushmore, Devil's Tower, Custer Game Refuge: June 'til mid-Oct. Leaves daily at 9 am, returns 5 pm, pickup from various hotels. $28 and up for the day. The fully narrated 9hr Black Hills tour is 'quite extensive; well worth the money'.
Stagecoach West, 343-3113. An alternative to Gray Line for tours to the Black Hills and Mount Rushmore.

DEADWOOD Twenty-eight miles NW of Rapid City via I-90, Deadwood calls itself 'where the West is fun!' but 'where the West is wax' might be more like it. Once the stomping ground for Calamity Jane, Wild Bill Hickok, Deadwood Dick and the rest, but amazingly ordinary today. For links to Deadwood, the stomping grounds of the wildest western characters, and Old West related sites, click on *www.deadwood.net/*

ACCOMMODATION
Super 8 Motel, Hwy 85 S, 578-2535. Reasonable for groups of 4 or 5; around $80 nightly. Jacuzzi suite Q-$130. From S-$65 (summer), S-$50 (Oct onwards). 'Pool, sauna, friendly, very clean.'

OF INTEREST
Number 10 saloon, Main St. See the chair where Wild Bill Hickok was gunned down while holding a poker hand of 2 aces and a pair of eights—still called 'a dead man's hand'. Hickok was never punished for any of his killings, several of which were clearly murders; *his* killer was hanged, however.
Adams Memorial Museum, Sherman St downtown, 578-1714. Gold-mining train, Wild Bill's marriage certificate and a sea of other nonsense. Open summer Mon-Fri 9 am-6 pm, Sun noon-5 pm; free. 'Interesting.'
The Ghost of Deadwood Gulch, corner of Lee and Sherman St, 578-3583. A wax museum where a play called *The Trial of Jack Mccall* is performed Mon-Sat in summer. Starts with dramatic capture of Hitchcock's killer, continues with trial in town hall. 'A laugh.' Daily 9 am-6 pm, tours every 15 mins; $4.
Mt Moriah 'Boot Hill' cemetery. Good place to do gravestone rubbings: Calamity, Wild Bill are here.
Nearby: Lead (pronounced Leed), a steep little mining town with the largest gold mine in the western hemisphere, the **Homestake**, 584-3110. Surface tours May Sept, $3.25 w/student ID. Half a million ounces of gold are mined each year; about 13 million tons remain. 'Free ore sample.' Open 8 am-5 pm in summer (Mon-Fri 8 am-4 pm only in May, Sept 10 am-5 pm w/ends)
Spearfish, (800) 457-0160, for 56 years home of the *Black Hills Passion Play*. June-Aug, at 8.15 pm on Tue, Thur & Sun; $14, $12, $9, $7. Huge cast in outdoor setting.

THE BLACK HILLS They are poorly named: picture instead high and ancient mountains cloaked with spectacular pine forests, a green citadel above the vastness of tawny plains and considered sacred ground by the Sioux. For links to everything in Black Hills and South Dakota, search thru *www.rapidweb.com/bhlinks/*

OF INTEREST
Custer State Park, 255-4515. Free if you drive through on Hwy 16A, otherwise $8 for a 7-day vehicle permit; $13 per camp-site (Center Lake-$10). Rsvs recom-

mended. Over 1600 buffalo, around which you can take a thrilling $1^1/_2$ hr jeep ride for $17, daily in summer, by appointment otherwise; horseback riding, $14/hr. Any tour through the Black Hills should include **Needles Hwy**, past spectacular volcanic pinnacles. Someone once wanted to carve these into Wild West heroes, the genesis of the Rushmore idea. There are two concessions here: the **State Game Lodge** (jeeps), 255-4541; and the **Blue Bell Lodge** (horses), 255-4531.

Crazy Horse Monument, N of Custer on Rte 385. A great Oglala Sioux leader, Crazy Horse resisted white encroachment on Indian lands and at 33 was stabbed in the back by an American soldier under a flag of truce. If ever finished, this completely 3-dimensional monument to him will dwarf Rushmore, ultimately standing 563 ft high and 641 ft long. Korczak Ziolkoski logged 36 yrs and blasted away some 7 million tons of rock before dying in 1982. His family has carried on and you can see work in progress 7 am-8.30 pm, daily. Check with Gray Line tours or drive through, $6 pp, $15 per car.

Jewel Cave National Monument, 673-2288. Dog-tooth crystals of calcite sparkle from its walls in the 2nd longest cave system in the US. Park hours and tours are decided each season depending on available federal funds; take the historic tour for $6, more strenuous but fun, if it's offered.

Mt Rushmore, 574-2523. Free, includes a 12 min film, evening amphitheatre programmes at 9 pm. It took 14 yrs to create the 60-ft-high granite faces of Washington, Jefferson, Teddy Roosevelt and Lincoln, carved by Gutzon Borglum and partly paid for with South Dakota schoolkids' pennies and it is still not finished. Most beautiful in morning light and when floodlit, summer eves. Visitors Center, 8 am-10 pm. Sculptor Studio, where models and tools are displayed, 8 am-7 pm, summer only.

Wind Cave National Park, 11 miles N of Hot Springs, 745-4600. 28,000 acres. Discovered in 1881, the cave, some 10 miles deep, is named for the winds that whistle in and out of it, caused by changes in barometric pressure. Daily, 60 mins-90 mins tours; $4-$6. The 2hr candlelight tour ($7) is recommended, as is the 4hr caving tour at $15. Dress warmly. Above ground and free, superb animal watching and photographing: deer, buffalo, antelope, prairie dog towns. Dawn and dusk are the best times. 'The candlelight tour is great.'

BADLANDS NATIONAL PARK Like hell with the fires put out, as the locals used to say, 207 square miles of weird and beautiful buttes, canyons and brilliantly coloured rock formations of clay and sand washed from the Black Hills. At sunset the sandstone slopes turn all shades of pink and purple. Bones of sabre-toothed tigers, three-toed horses and Tyranosaurus Rex have been found in this arid land once covered by swamps. 'Absolutely amazing—the surprise package of our tour. Come into it at dawn with the sun at your back—it'll blow your mind, it's that good.' 'Well worth the 10 mile hike along rough track to watch the sunset and spend the night at Sage Creek primitive campground. No water on site.' Previous travellers' reviews of Badlands can be accessed through: *www.chicweb.com/Domain/dnl/Badland_index.html*

OF INTEREST

Kodoka, an authentic Western backwater town east of the Badlands on I-90, is the best place to stay overnight to make the favoured dawn drive through the Badlands, emerging at **Wall** . Excellent visitor centre at the **Cedar Pass Badlands entrance**, includes video. To stay, **West Motel**, Hwy 16 and I-90 Business Loop, 837-2427; D-$35. 'Clean rooms, friendly staff.'

Wall, notorious for **Wall Drug**, 279-2175, a drug store that mutated into a tourist-trap-run-wild. Roads leading to and from Wall are peppered with some of the 3000 billboards hawking the place; other signs can be found at the North and South Poles, a Kenyan rail station and in the Paris Metro, informing potential customers of the number of miles it is to Wall Drug. Sip free ice water and nickel coffee, buy a rattlesnake ashtray and puzzle over a jackalope, a cross between a jackrabbit and an antelope.

MITCHELL   If passing through, take time to see the **Corn Palace**, a vaguely Russian fantasy of onion domes, dazzling pointillistic murals formed of 3000 bushels of coloured corn cobs. Watch artists construct new murals each summer on the outer wall of the civic auditorium. Extraordinary. (Find details of the Corn Palace Stampede Rodeo and a link to Corn Palace's own website at *www.mitchell.net/rodeo/*). In Mitchell also, the **Oscar Howe Art Center**, 119 W 3rd Ave, 996-4111, housing work by the most noted Sioux artist of present times. Tue-Sat 10 am-5 pm; donation. Area lodging: **Skoglund Farm** near Canova off I-90, 247-3445. They will pick you up from bus depot at Salem. $30 includes two full meals plus coffee at a friendly family operation. Horses to ride, animals to pet on a working cattle ranch.

WOUNDED KNEE   'I did not know then how much was ended. When I look back from this high hill of my old age, I can still see the butchered women and children lying heaped and scattered all along the crooked gulch as plain as when I saw them with eyes still young. And I can see that something else died there in the bloody mud, and was buried in the blizzard. A people's dream died there. It was a beautiful dream. The nation's hoop is broken and scattered. There is no centre any longer, and the sacred tree is dead.'—Black Elk.

The symbolic end of Indian freedom came at Christmas-time, 1890, at the so-called Battle of Wounded Knee when the US Cavalry opened fire with rifles and field guns on 120 Indian men and 230 Indian women and children. Most were murdered instantly; some wounded crawled away through a terrible blizzard. Torn and bleeding, many did not crawl far: a returning army burial party found numerous bodies frozen into grotesque shapes against the snow.

A shabby monument marks the spot 100 miles SE of Rapid City, a few miles off Rte 18 near Pine Ridge.

But their unquiet mass grave nearby continues to serve as a rallying point for this century's Indians. In 1973, at the second battle of Wounded Knee, two Indians died in the 71-day siege of the American Indian Movement, and the chapter is far from over.

NB: although the reservation has a motel, museum and other tourist facilities, don't expect uniformly friendly attitudes toward white faces. The Wounded Knee homepage is located at *www.dickshovel.netgate.net/ WKmasscre.html* with excellent links to related Native American sites and images.

MOBRIDGE   On a high hill across the Missouri from Mobridge in north-central South Dakota is Sitting Bull's grave. One of the events preceding the massacre at Wounded Knee was the murder of Sitting Bull, the great Sioux leader, organiser and victor at Little Bighorn. It was carried out by Indian policemen under the eye of the US Cavalry.

The authorities always felt uncomfortable with Sitting Bull alive, regarding him as a subversive figure. In death, however, he became something of a commodity. Originally buried in North Dakota, Sitting Bull's body was snatched by South Dakotans, who planted him in Mobridge. A large stone bust was placed over the grave, just to be sure Sitting Bull stays put. Mobridge has a sculpture of Sitting Bull by Korczak Ziolkowski and ten fine murals by Sioux artist Oscar Howe in the municipal auditorium. Mobridge Chamber of Commerce has a fantastic city guide at *www.sodak.net/~rfrey/ Mobridge.html* detailing events, campgrounds, fishing, parks and maps.

WISCONSIN *The Badger State*

A liquid sort of place, Wisconsin: famed for beer, milk and water of all sorts— Wisconsinites gave names to 14,949 of their inland lakes before giving up in despair. On Lakes Michigan and Superior, the state sports no less than 14 ocean-going ports. Other places had gold rushes: Wisconsin had a 'lead rush'.

Politically, it has swung from the rapaciousness of early lumber barons to the progressive decades of the 'fighting LaFollettes', from Commie witch-hunter Joseph McCarthy to present-day liberal Gaylord Nelson.

Unlike other Midwest states, the cities here are clean, amiable and altogether charming. Of course, so is the countryside, but watch out for mosquitoes the size of aircraft carriers (the price you pay for all those lakes).

Many old railroads have been converted into trails for bicycling, running, hiking and skiing. *www.yahoo.com/Regional/U_S__States/Wisconsin/*

MILWAUKEE   There's a comfortable, old-shoe feeling about Milwaukee, enhanced by its reputation for good beer, 'brats' and baseball. Remarkably short on grime and slums, long on restaurants and festivals, the city is a good-natured mix of ethnic groups, especially Germans, Poles and Serbs. In quantity of beer produced, Milwaukee has now been aced out by, gasp, Los Angeles, but for quality this is still Der Platz. Check out the Cityzine: Guide to Milwaukee at *www.cityzine.com/milwaukee*
The telephone area code is 414.

ACCOMMODATION
The **Wisconsin B&B Assoc**, 108 South Cleveland St, Merrill, W 54452, (800) 365-6994, will assist with info on motels, B&Bs and country inns. Also, **The Wisconsin Innkeepers Assoc** has an interactive website at *www.lodging-wi.com*. Excel Inn, 115 North Mayfair Rd, Wauwatosa, 257-0140. Rooms from $50.
Red Barn Youth Hostel, 6750 W Loomis Rd, 10 miles NW of downtown, 529-3299. $10 AYH.
Red Roof Inn, 6360 S 13th St, Oak Creek. Call 764-3500; rates fluctuate often.
Sonnenhop Inn, 13907 N Port Washington Rd, Mequon 53097, (414) 375-4294. From $40. Non-smoking rooms, TV/movies, tennis.
Camping: For a free copy of the **WACO Campground Directory**/info on campgrounds across the state, call (800) 432-TRIP.

TAKE ME OUT TO THE BALLGAME

Baseball may be more American than apple pie. First played in modern form, it's said, by Abner Doubleday in Cooperstown, New York, 155 years ago (in 1839), America's national sport is an inexpensive (from $5) treat not to be missed. The pleasure of watching a game on a warm summer evening, beer and hot dogs in hand, cannot be beaten. Along the way, brush up on your ballgame terms, such as steal, chopper, pop-up, fly, walk, bunt, line-drive, slider, RBI, ERA, ball four, bottom-of-the-ninth, watermelon, strikeout, etc. There are two major leagues, each divided into three divisions and each including a Canadian team. The league champions meet in the end-of-season World Series in October:

NATIONAL LEAGUE (est 1876): **East**—Atlanta *Braves*, Florida *Marlins*, Montreal *Expos*, New York *Mets*, Philadelphia *Phillies*.
Central—Chicago *Cubs*, Cincinnati *Reds*, Houston *Astros*, Pittsburgh *Pirates*, St Louis *Cardinals*.
West—Arizona *Diamond Backs*, Colorado *Rockies*, LA *Dodgers*, San Diego *Padres*, San Francisco *Giants*.

AMERICAN LEAGUE (est 1900): **East**—Baltimore *Orioles*, Boston *Red Sox*, New York *Yankees*, Tampa Bay *Devil Rays*, Toronto *Blue Jays*
Central—Chicago *White Sox*, Cleveland *Indians*, Detroit *Tigers*, Kansas City *Royals*, Milwaukee *Brewers*.
West—Anaheim *Angels*, Oakland *Athletics*, Texas *Rangers*, Seattle *Mariners*.

BALLPARKS: 3 Com Park (formerly Candlestick Park) (415) 468-2249, **San Francisco Giants**, where 60,000 fans were rocked by the October '89 earthquake as they waited for the start of Game Three of the World Series against the Oakland 'A's.
Comiskey Park/Chicago Whitesox, (312) 674-1000. Has craziest fans who staged 'Disco Sucks Night' in 1979 and craziest organist Nancy, a jokester who cranks out an appropriate song for every situation and player. As host to the 'Black Sox Scandal', this is where the World Series was fixed in 1919. 'Say it ain't so, Joe,' they asked of Joe Jackson, one of the eight players involved. See the movie *Eight Men Out*.
County Stadium/Milwaukee Brewers, (414) 933-9000. Known for the best stadium food and beverage including bratwurst, barbecued chicken and steak with secret sauce. Hank Aaron wound up his career here in 1976 with the major league lifetime home run record of 755.
Dodger Stadium/Los Angeles Dodgers, (213) 224-1301. Most palatial of the stadia, and probably the only one with as many celebrities in the bleachers as on the field. 1988 World Series opened here, during which Kirk Gibson of LA hit a 2-run homer in the final inning with two outs, giving the Dodgers a 54 victory over the Oakland Athletics.
Pro-Player Stadium/Florida Marlins (954) 792-8793. In North Miami off the Florida Turnpike, and where the Marlins beat the Cleveland Indians in the World Series in 1997 in only the 5th year of their existence.
Fenway Park/Boston Red Sox, (617) 267-8661. Home of the 'Green Monster' in left field, intimate atmosphere lets you be a part of the game like in the good ol' days. The Red Sox were the first team to win the World Series when it was established in 1903.
Jack Murphy Stadium/San Diego Padres, (619) 283-4494. Baseball la California, complete with sunny skies, warm temperatures, and fans in their bathing suits tossing giant beach balls.
Orioles Stadium, Camden Yards/**Baltimore Orioles**, (410) 685-9800. The $105 million, 48,000-seat ballpark downtown opened in 1992. Only 4 blocks from Baltimore's inner harbour, it has a wonderful barbecue-soaked atmosphere.
Oakland Alameda Stadium/Oakland Athletics, (510) 639-7700. Here baseball combines with the finest sound and video system in the league to create baseball-

rock. The team isn't half bad either, though they lost the 1988 World Series to Dodger neighbours.

Royals Stadium/Kansas City Royals, (816) 921-8000. More than one baseball player has conceded that this is their favourite away stadium. KC barbecue, baked beans and baseball make for a great game.

Toronto Skydome/Blue Jays, (416) 341-1111. New in 1989, this space-age ballpark has the largest retractable roof in the world, and the first non-US world champions. They won in 1992 and again in 1993.

Wrigley Field/Chicago Cubs, (773) 404-2827. Oldest in league, and most traditional with ivy-covered walls and hand-turned scoreboard. Join legendary Ronnie in shouting 'Go Cubs, Go Cubs'.

Yankee Stadium/New York Yankees (718) 293-6000; World Champions in 1996 and wellspring of many baseball legends, including Yogi Berra who, once when a game was poorly attended, is reported to have said, 'if the people don't want to come out to the park, nobody's gonna stop them'. Fans voted unfriendliest by baseball players. The 1927 'Murderers' Row Team' included Lou Gehrig, Bob Meusel, Tony Lazzeri, and Babe Ruth who hit a home run every nine trips to the plate that year. Catch Yankees fans at their most partisan during a game with archrivals Boston Red Sox.

FOOD

Besides Wisconsin's famous cheeses, Milwaukee is noted for 'beer and brats', the latter a particularly succulent variety of German bratwurst, served boiled in beer and tangy with sauce. If you don't go to a Brewers baseball game and gorge in the sun on beer'n'brats, you've blown it. Also try local frozen custard at places like **Kopp's Frozen Custard**, 5373 N Port Washington Rd, Glendale, 961-3288. Other locations include 18880 W Bluemound Rd, Brookfield, 789-9490; and 7631 W Layton Ave, Greenfield 282-4312. All open 10.30 am-11.30 pm. Always mobbed, sundaes are the speciality of the house, each with their own blueprint detailing exact ingredients and their place in the architecture of each concoction! Call 282-4080 for your 3-day flavour forecast!

German and Serb restaurants are best bets ethnically, but also check to see if Milwaukee is celebrating one of its ethnic feasts at the lakefront.

Crocus, 1801 S Muskego, 643-6383, Mon-Fri. This neighbourhood Polish restaurant offers the strange brew Czarnia—'a sweet brown syrup, thick with little dumplings, beans, shreds of duck, and plump raisins'. One full meal under $10.

Jessica's, 524 E Layton Ave, 744-1119. 1950's-theme burger-and-malt shop. 'Gorgeous creamy shakes and malts. Turtle sundaes recommended!'

Karl Ratzsch's, 320 E Mason St, 276-2720. An early dining menu, 4 pm-6 pm, is under $15 pp. Famous for its German food, there are five German beers on tap, a whole array of liquors and a non-German food menu too.

Real Chili, 419 E Wells, Milwaukee, 271-4042. Green Bay-style chili for under $10. Lunch and dinner served.

OF INTEREST

The **DASL (Door County Amateur Skateboarding League) Skatepark**, Sturgeon Bay. Across the street from the Palmer Johnson building (the big one where they build the ships). Indoor 2 half pipes, a big one (about 6-7 ft) and a little one (2-3 ft), 3 quarter pipes, a fun box and other fun street obstacles. Free to get in! Helmets must be worn at all times and knee pads rec when skating the big halfpipe. Inliners must wear helmet, kneepads and wristguards.

Discovery World Museum, 818 Wisconsin Ave, 765-9966. Mon-Sun 9 am-5 pm; $5. free. Science and interactive technology exhibits.

Miller Brewery Tour, 4251 W State, 931-2337. Mon-Sat 10 am-3.30 pm. Free indoor/outdoor tour, ending with courtesy suds. Take umbrella!

Milwaukee County Zoo, 10001 W Bluemound Rd, 771-3040. Mon-Sun 9 am-5 pm; $7.50.

Milwaukee Art Museum, 750 N Lincoln Memorial Dr, 224-3200. Tue/Wed/Fri/Sat 10 am-5 pm, Thur noon-9 pm, Sun noon-5 pm; closed Mon; $4, $2 w/student ID. Strong in Haitain primitives, 19th century German and American contemporary works/pop art such as some Warhol soup cans.

Mitchell Park Conservatory, 524 S Layton Blvd, 649-9800. Three 7-storey glass domes with different luxuriant botanical gardens: arid, tropical and a seasonal display. Daily 9 am-5 pm; $3.25.

Public Museum, 800 W Wells St, 278-2700. Walk-through European village of Milwaukee's 33 ethnic groups—charming. The Polish and Serbian houses are beautiful. Also a huge hand-made Costa-Rican rain forest, constructed with wood and other natural materials. Remarkable effect. Daily 9 am-5 pm; $5.50, $3.50 w/student ID.

Washington Park, NW from downtown. *Music Under The Stars* concerts in July & Aug; free. Call 278-4391 for details.

ENTERTAINMENT

African World Festival: Held in August, this ethnic event showcases the best in African garb, jewelry, authentic foods, heritage, gospel, blues, R&B. Held at Henry Marer Festival Park, noon-midnight. Call (414) 372-4567 for more info.

Bombay Bicycle Club, 509 W Wisconsin Ave, 271-7250. Bar and music videos; open 4 pm 'til 2 am.

Fun Line, 799-1177. Sample the 6000+ taverns—most are rollicking, unpretentious good fun. **Summerfest**, two week festival June & July, by lakefront. 'Groups, beer, funfair, massive.' **Festa Italiana** in July, one of the biggest pastafazools anywhere: 'delicious'. Jul-Aug: **German, Irish, Polish Feasts**.

The Great Circus Parade rolls out in full grandeur in July, downtown.

Milwaukee Repertory Theater, 108 E Wells St, 224-9490. First-class plays; from $6. Season runs Sept-May.

Performing Arts Theater, 929 W Water St, 273-7206. The Milwaukee Symphony.

INFORMATION/TRAVEL

Amtrak, 433 W St Paul Ave, (800) 872-7245.

General Mitchell International Airport, 5300 S Howell Ave. Take the #80 bus from 6th & Wisconsin, $1.10. Takes about 30 mins.

Greyhound, 606 N 7th St, (800) 231-2222.

Milwaukee County Transit System, 344-6711. Runs the metro area buses, $1.25 basic fare (or pass allowing 10 rides for $10).

Visitors Bureau, 510 W Kilborn, 273-7222/747-4808 at airport.

MADISON   To some, Madison, wrapped picturesquely around two lakes, is the bastion of enlightened civilization. A famous college town; it is similar to Ann Arbor and Berkeley in its radical activism. It probably has the highest under-employment anywhere; your taxi driver no doubt has a PhD in Medieval Philosophy and your waiter one in Set Theory Topology. The east side has the alternative community, the west side has all those liberal democrats who belong to the ACLU and the Women's Political Caucus. There's a lot packed into this pretty town, plus cheap eats starting at 2 open-air farmers' markets. Rent a bike to get around. The City of Madison city guide can be found at *www.ci.madison.wi.us/* including the 'MAD about MADison' site which is entertaining and helpful.

The telephone area code is 608.

ACCOMMODATION

Abendrun B&B Swisstyle, 7019 Gehin Rd 53508, (608) 424-3808. $50-$70. TV/movies, non-smoking rooms.

Excel Inn, 4202 E Towne Blvd, 241-3861. S-$42 ($51 w/ends), D-$50 ($62).

Wisconsin Center Guest House, 610 Langdon, 256-2621. S-$49, Q-$72. On fraternity row. Great frat parties in the vicinity. In **Dodgeville**, 40 miles W of Madison on Hwy 18: **Folklore Village Farm**, Rt 3, 924-4000. $8 AYH, $3 one-time membership fee.

Spring Valley Trails Home Hostel, RR 2, PO Box 170, Dodgeville, WI 53533, 935-5725. A-frame house available, $10. Write for rsvs.

FOOD

Best eateries are on or near campus.

Brat Und Brau, 1421 Regent, 257-2187. Good, cheap burgers, brats and salad bars.

Cafe Palms, in the Club de Washington, 256-0166. After hours, has 'killer muffins and amusing waiters.'

Ella's Kosher Deli, 425 State St, 457-8611. A real deli, standby of natives; sit and shmooze for hours.

The Fess, 123 E Doty, 256-0263. 'Sat and Sun brunch will leave you stuffed for a week. Never-ending stream of fresh baked goods.'

Gino's, 540 State St, 257-9022. Known for its stuffed pizza.

Dane County Farmers Market, Capitol Sq, 6.30 am-noon. There's no shortage of fresh fruit and veg at this market, held every Sat, April-Nov. 'Beautiful local produce with a festival atmosphere.'

Sunprint Cafe and Gallery, 638 State St, 255-1555. Original photographs in cafe setting. Specialties are coffee, soups, sandwiches and pastries.

Willy St Co-op, 1202 Williamson St, 251-6776. A well-run co-op on Madison's east side. You'll be at the heart of Madison's alternative culture while you buy veggies. Daily 8 am-9 pm.

OF INTEREST

It all revolves around the campus—a must for briefing yourself on social action, people, and activities throughout the town. Pick up a copy of *Isthmus*, be sure to read 'Dear Ursula'.

American Players Theater, in Spring Green, 45 miles W of Madison, 588-7401 (Box office: (608) 588-2361). Quality Shakespearean and classical drama performed in the open air. Bring a picnic and enjoy the beautiful countryside. Performances on Tues-Sun evenings mid-June-Oct; from $14.

Concerts on the Square: Capitol Square, every Wed eve, June-July.

Lakeshore path, start behind the Union terrace and walk out to Picnic Point. You'll meet many joggers and Madisonians talking over their problems.

State Capitol, 266-0382. The story goes that it is just a foot shorter than the one in Washington, DC. Mon-Sat 9 am-4 pm, Sun 1 pm-4 pm.

Vilas Park Zoo, Drake & Grant. This is not the world's greatest zoo, but Vilas Park has lovely beaches and is a nice place to take a walk. Daily 9.30 am-8 pm.

Nearby: Wisconsin Dells, 53 miles N of Madison. 'Magnificent rock and river scenery but terribly commercialised. Only visible by boat.' Inexpensive all-you-can-eat ($6.79) for breakfast, lunch and dinner at the **Paul Bunyan Lumberjack** restaurant, 254-8717.

Baraboo, about 40 miles N of Madison. In May 1884, the five Ringling Brothers began their world-renowned circus in a modest way, behind the Baraboo jail. Their former winter quarters is now the site of the excellent **Circus World Museum**, 426 Water St, 356-8341. Daily 1-ring performances, 152 rococo circus wagons, 19th century sideshow, calliope. Daily 9 am-6 pm; $12.

Taliesin, near Spring Green, 45 mins W of Madison. A walk through Frank Lloyd

Wright's Wisconsin estate is a journey through his evolution as an architect. Seven different tours, through Hillside Studio (designed as a school in 1902) and Theater, the grounds or through the House. Seasonal tours run May 1-October 31 (April/November Tours, Off-season Tours and Group Tours available). From $8, discount on House Tour every Tues and Thurs w/student ID. Call 588-7900 to reserve tkts. Also, **Riverview Terrace Café** looking out over Wisconsin River at **The Frank Lloyd Wright Visitor Center**, 588-7937. FLW may have been more famous, but the prize for sheer originality has to go to Alex Jordan for his spectacular **House on the Rock**, south of Taliesin in Rt. 23, 935-3639. Described by *Roadside America* as 'the Palace of Versailles converted into a Tussaud wax museum by a Kuwaiti sheik,' House on the Rock is a mind-boggling conglomeration of mermaids, angels, antiques, enormous things (fireplace, steam locomotive, carousel, theater, organs), catwalks, bisque dolls, and the heart-stopping 'Infinity Room', a horizontal glass-enclosed needle stretching 140 ft out into the clear Wisconsin air with no visible means of support. *See it!* Daily 9 am-8 pm for tkts; $15.

LAKE SUPERIOR REGION In northwestern Wisconsin, 2 areas to explore: **Indian Head Country**, extending from the shore of Lake Superior to the Mississippi River; and the **Apostle Islands**, a national lakeshore known for its peaceful beauty. Call 266-2621 or write Wisconsin Dept of Natural Resources, PO Box 7921, Madison, WI 53707, for more info. The **Turtle Flambeau Flowage** alone offers 19,000 acres of angling and wildlife watching opportunity.

In these parts, fishing has become a sort of pagan religion. See a testimonial to Wisconsin fish-worship at the **National Fresh Water Fishing Hall of Fame**, on Hwy 27 in **Hayward**, (715) 634-4440. Icons include gigantic fibre-glass statues of beloved sports fish, including a muskie the size of a blue whale (in which you can be Jonah—observation deck inside the muskie's mouth). Daily 15 April-1 Nov, 10 am-5 pm; $4. The museum also has a website at *www.oldcabin.com/freshwater* with the opening greeting, 'A kid hooked on fishing won't get hooked on drugs'!

THE MOUNTAIN STATES

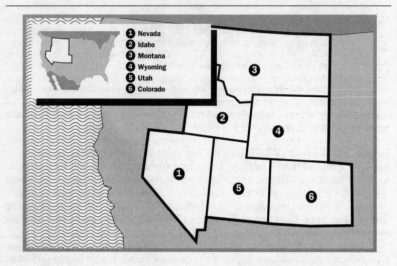

After the endless horizontality of the Midwest, the carefully manicured patterns of fences and townships and agriculture, the landscape of the Mountain States bursts upon you, young and rangy and wild as a colt. These are exuberant mountains, still in their teens: the Rockies, the San Juans, the Grand Tetons. Even now, crossing them is a pilgrimage, an event; just imagine how their sharp white beauty must have made pioneers' hearts sink into their boots.

The topography doesn't limit itself to mountains, either. In this six- state cluster, you are treated to geysers, glaciers, buttes, vast river chasms, vivid canyons in paintbrush colours. The greater portion of this beauty is protected in National Parks and Monuments, among them: Rocky Mountain, Yellowstone, Craters of the Moon, Glacier, Devil's Tower, Zion and Bryce Canyon. In stark contrast to all this natural grandeur are Las Vegas, Reno and Hoover Dam/Lake Mead, without a doubt the most wondrously artificial trio of spots on earth.

Organized outdoor adventures are one way to explore the area. Llama trips, white-water rafting and trekking can be compared and booked at no extra cost through American Wilderness Experience (AWE). Write PO Box 1486, Boulder, CO 80306 or call (800) 444-0099 for a catalogue, which lists various outfitter agencies and trips in the Mountain States, Arizona, New Mexico, California, Oregon, Hawaii, Alaska, Canada, Mexico, Minnesota and West Virginia.

Las Vegas excepted, weather throughout the region is dry and hot in summer, cold and snowy in winter. Even summer evenings can be cold, and violent thunderstorms are common, so plan accordingly.

COLORADO   *The Centennial State*

Horace Greeley, the newspaper editor famous for his advice 'Go West, young man', in truth found the West a bit raw for his tastes. In 1860, he described what he saw on the frontier: 'They had a careless way of firing revolvers, sometimes at each other, at other times quite miscellaneous—so I left'.

Like other mountain states, Colorado had a lusty, shoot-em-up past filled with gold seekers, gold diggers, cattlemen and con men. Many former mining towns remain, some recycled into ski resorts, others tarted up for tourism but still in settings of unparalleled grandeur.

Manufacturer of components for the Hubble telescope and second largest employer of federal government workers, Colorado is a prime tourist destination—and with good reason. Known as the nation's backbone, the state has 54 peaks over 14,000 feet. Over 75 percent of US land over 10,000 feet is concentrated in Colorado.

The eastern section up to the Rockies has little to offer, being a monotony of rangeland, strewn with dun-coloured tumbleweeds and fenced 'hog-tight, horse-high and bull-strong', as the cowpokes put it. Concentrate instead on the western half, where you find two national parks, awesome scenery and an extraordinary display of summer wildflowers (some 5000 species).

Colorado's many youth hostels, among the best in the US, include ranches, historic hotels and ski lodges. www.state.co.us/colorado.html & www.state.co.us/visit_dir/visitormenu.html.
National Parks: Rocky Mountains, Mesa Verde
There are three telephone area codes for Colorado: 303, 719 and 970.

DENVER   Impressively situated against a backdrop of snowy peaks, Denver has grown to be the single most important metropolis in an area larger than Western Europe. Much of the unpleasant urban sprawl, crime and pollution that plague other American cities has arrived in Denver. Despite this and an ugly decade of rapid development, Denver now sports a modern, well-finished look, befitting its role as banking, government, and industrial capital for the Rocky Mountains.

In 1858 you couldn't see Northern Colorado for dust as thousands of miners left in search of a different kind of dust—gold. As a result, Denver—complete with Colorado's first saloon—emerged and became the state's capital. Today, people pour into Denver by the million, many in transit at the first major, new airport in the US for 20 years—Denver International Airport which opened in February 1995. The largest in the world (53 acres), and looking like a tented Bedouin city, it can handle around 32 million people a year.

With a median age of 30, over 200 parks and more days of sunshine (300) than San Diego or Miami Beach, the 'Mile High' city is teeming with sports-mad enthusiasts. Its undying love of the Broncos football team has reached saturation point; games from Sept-Dec are sold out for an undetermined number of years and plans are afoot to find a stadium to hold in excess of 76,000. Coors Field, built in 1995, packs crowds of 50,000 Colorado Rockies baseball fans from March-Sept, while the McNichols arena hosts the Nuggets (basketball) from Nov-Apr and the Avalanche (ice-hockey) from Sept-Apr. Denver also boasts possibly the world's largest sporting goods store—Gart Sports—where you can shop from a golf cart.

Denver was also once a centre of counter-culture, a mecca for spiritualists, faith healers and radical thought. Though the politicized coffeehouses that populated Jack Kerouac's *On the Road* are gone, a lively cultural life still throbs in Denver when the sun goes down. Most likely you'll find the nation's most educated downtown workforce at the movies, as the city leads the nation in attendance.

Downtown Denver revolves around 16th St Mall, a mile-long promenade lined with up-market shops. The building of so many office blocks around the city centre has meant that the Mall is very lively around lunchtime but virtually devoid of activity after 6 pm. 'Denver is dead after 7 pm. Not the sort of place to walk alone at night.'

The telephone area code is 303.

www.denveronline.com/ & www.downtown-denver.com/

ACCOMMODATION

Denver International Youth Hostel, 630 E 16th Ave at Washington St, 832-9996. Houseparents are good guides to the area. No curfew. $8.50 per night. Laundry, TV, sundecks. Also serves as a general travel and hostel information centre with discounts on many activities.

Franklin House B&B, 1620 Franklin St, 331-9106. S-$25, D-$35 shared bath, D-$45 private bath. Incls bfast.

Hostel of the Rocky Mtns, 1530 Downing St, 861-7777. $11 dorm, D-$20 shared bath. 'Clean, comfortable and well equipped.' 'Owners very knowledgeable about sights and attractions.'

Motel 6, 3050 W 49th Ave, 455-8888. S-$42, D-$49. AC, pool, TV, phones. Bus stop 1 blk away. 'Friendly staff, good service.' Also on Wadsworth Blvd, 232-4924.

Melbourne Hotel and Hostel, 607 22nd St, 292-6386. $11 AYH, $14 non-AYH, private rms D-$29 AYH, $32 non-AYH. 6 blocks from bus stn. If arriving at airport call for directions. 'Brilliant.' 'Good, clean rooms. Staff very helpful.' 'Reservations strongly recommended.'

Standish Hotel, 1530 California St, 534-3231. S-$20 shared bath, D-$32 private bath. XP-$2. TV, laundry. 'Quiet, pleasant, simply furnished. Staff and clientele obviously regarded young people as quite a curiosity.' 'Not for a woman alone.'

YMCA, 25 E 16th Ave, Denver, CO 80202, 861-8300. Coed. Across from city bus stn. Write to make rsvs. S-$26-$29 shared bath, S-$34 private bath, D-$49 private bath, $12 key deposit. Full use of sports centre incl. gym and pool. 'Very limited bathroom facilities.'

FOOD

Try Rocky Mountain trout, the local speciality. This is also the home of 'Rocky Mt oysters' or 'swinging steaks', an indelicate dish made of French-fried bull testicles. *The Official Visitor's Guide* (avail. at Visitors Bureau) lists dozens of places to eat in Denver, and includes an extensive ethnic restaurant guide. 'Larimer & 17th Sts, variety of quite cheap places to eat—Turkish, Greek, Chinese, French, pizza.'

Casa Bonita, 6715 W Colfax, 232-5115. The all-you-can-eat Mexican platter for $8.39 is not the half of it. This isn't a restaurant, it's a Mexican carnival—with gun fights,

cliff divers, mariachi bands. Watch out Casa Bonitas in Tulsa. 'Disappointing.'
Duffy's Shamrock, 1635 Court Place near YMCA, 534-4935. 'Good service, excellent value.' 'A godsend for the traditional boozer. Longest bar west of Mississippi - 78ft. $6 specials, home-made red and green chili.' 'All-American food.'
The Market, 1445 Larimer St, 534-5140. 'A trendy place to sit and drink coffee, buy health foods, watch people.' $5.50-$6, self-service deli.
Observatory Bar and Cafe, El Rancho and Evergreen, (take exit 252 off I-90 West), 526-1988. Open-air dining overlooking the Continental Divide. Free use of telescopes on weekends by arrangement.
The Old Spaghetti Factory, 18th & Lawrence St, 295-1864, dinners with drink and dessert, $5-$8 with antique surroundings incl. tables made out of beds.
20th St Cafe, just behind Greyhound bus station at 1123 20th St, 295-9041. $2-$4; chicken-fried steak a speciality. 'Good cheap breakfast and lunch in clean and friendly surroundings.'

OF INTEREST
Art Museum, 100 W 14th Ave Pkwy, 640-4433, $4.50, $2.50 w/student ID, free on Saturdays. Striking, fortresslike building covered with a million sparkling tiles. Seven floors of well-displayed art from totem poles to Picasso, incl. Native American and European collections. 'Exhibits on Indians more interesting and paintings better than in many small US galleries.' Tue-Sat 10am-5 pm, Sun noon-5 pm.
Black American West Museum, 3091 California St, 292-2566. Black pioneer history. Founded by Paul Stewart, now in his 70s, who as a child was told he could only play the Indian -'there are no black cowboys'. Wrong again, as his museum proves. Also pays homage to western black women. Winter Wed-Fri 10am-2 pm, w/end 12 pm-5 pm; summer Mon-Fri 10am- 5 pm, w/end 12 pm-5 pm. $3 w/stud ID.
Colorado History Museum, 13th and Broadway, 866-3681. The 112-ft time line spans 150 years of Colorado history, with documents, maps, photos, and artifacts. Library and Native American exhibits. Open Mon-Sat 10am-4.30pm, Sun noon-4.30pm; $3. $2.50 w/student ID.
Governor's Residence Tours, 400 E 8th Avenue. Free tours 12 pm-2 pm, every Tues in June, July and August. No need to book.
Larimer Square, 14th to 16th Sts. Denver's restored Victorian and highly commercial 'heart', with gaslit lamps and horse-drawn carriages. Bring brass or take a pass. Larimer Square runs into **16th Street Mall**, Denver's $76 million pedestrian path with more shops and eateries and free shuttle buses. Nearby is the glittering **Tabor Center** , a completely glass-enclosed shopping complex, named after an 1890s gold rush bonanza king.
Denver Center for Performing Arts, 125 Champa St, 2 blks southeast of Larimer Square, 893-4000. Call to arrange free tour of scene shops, theatres and Metro Concert Hall where high-tech sound is controlled by dozens of 'floating' discs suspended from the ceiling.
Museum of Natural History, 2001 Colorado Blvd in City Park, 322-7009. Recommended for its detailed dioramas, meteorite and mineral collections, dinosaur displays. Laser and rock shows at planetarium, $6. IMAX giant screen cinema, $6. 'Exhilarating experience.' Open 9 am-5 pm.
Museum of Western Art, 1727 Tremont Place, 296-1880. Tue-Sat 10am-4.30pm; $3, $2 students w/ID. Russell's classic cowboy sketches, sculpture and paintings by Remington and many other western artists are housed in this former gambling hall and brothel. An underground tunnel connected this house of ill repute to **Brown Palace**, a beautiful grand dame hotel with stained-glass roof.
The Molly Brown House Museum, 1340 Pennsylvania St, 832-4092. The Titanic sunk, but Molly didn't, earning her fame & the name 'unsinkable Molly Brown'. 'Interesting story, uninteresting museum.' $5. In summers, open Mon-Sat 10am-

3.30pm & Sun noon-4pm; in winter, closed Mon and at 4pm other days.

State Capitol, 14th St and Broadway, 866-2604. This dome has been gold-leafed 3 times since 1907, but of true value is the Colorado onyx (the world's entire supply) used in the interior of the Capitol. As you ascend to the top, pause at step 15—it's exactly 5280 feet above sea level. On the deck, a brass marker identifies surrounding peaks. Free 30-min tours Mon- Fri 9 am-3.30pm, Sat 9.30pm-2.30pm. Closed Sun.

US Mint, 320 W Colfax Ave, entrance on Cherokee St, 844-3582. Free 20-min tours Mon-Fri 8 am-2.45 pm (9am on last Wed of month). Production stops at the end of the fiscal year; there are no tours from 25th Aug-2nd Sept. Long queues, get there early. Stamps out 35 million coins a day; 'no free samples'.

Nearby: Coors Brewery, 13th and Ford, Golden, 277-2337. Free 30-min tours and suds, Mon-Sat 10am-4.30pm. Bring proper ID. 'Very nice people.' Overlooking Coors, high above on Lookout Mt, is **Buffalo Bill Grave and Museum**, 526-0747. Open daily 9 am-5 pm. Lots of Wild West show and Pony Express artifacts of this flamboyant figure who symbolised the make-believe West. Among other things, you learn here that scalping was unknown to most Plains Indians until introduced by white scalp hunters. $3.

ENTERTAINMENT

Pick up a copy of *Westword*, a free weekly, for info about the arts in Denver.

Buckhorn Exchange, 1000 Osage St, 534-9505. Pricey downstairs restaurant ($30-$40) with buffalo and elk entrees. Stick to upstairs, Denver's oldest western bar. Outdoor covered patio Wed-Sat, live music in cocktail lounge (incl folk music and 'old ballads').

El Chapultepec, 20th and Market, 295-9126. 57-year-old jazz bar. $4-$6. 'A real dive, but good jazz.'

Elitch Gardens, 2000 Elitch Circle, CO 80201. 1-800-ELITCHS. This 1995 amusement park has more than 21 dare-devil rides including 'Mind Eraser' and 'The Tower of Doom'. Open weekends April-May and daily from Memorial Day to Labor Day. $15; seasonal discounts available. 'Not for the faint-hearted.'

Glendale is Denver's 'singles scene' with over a dozen discos, saloons and restaurants crammed into a small area. Bars with discos, outdoor volleyball courts, saddles for bar stools ... you name it.

Mercury Cafe, 2199 California, 294-9281. Charismatic and bohemian entertainment; open stage on Wed for poetry, song and acrobatics, swing bands on Sun and Thurs at 7.30pm, dance classes, jazz nights Fri-Sat. Open Tues-Fri 5 pm-11 pm, w/ends 9 am-3 pm and 5 pm- 11 pm. 'Laid back and popular with locals.'

Red Rocks Amphitheater, SW edge of Greater Denver in Morrison. Listen to summer rock, country & western, pop and classical concerts surrounded by 440-ft red sandstone bluffs. 'Any concert here is a must—the most beautiful setting in the world with spectacular views over the prairies and Denver.' For tckts, phone 640-7334. Park admission is free; shows up to $30.

Wazee Supper Club, 1600 15th St, 623-9518. Great pizza and downtown neighbourhood bar. Live music Sat nights, no cover. 17 beers on tap, $2-$3.50 per glass.

Wyncoop Brewing Company, 1634 18th St, 297-2700. Eleven beers on tap at all times, all brewed on premises. Stout, porter, light and medium ales, bitter beers. Tours of brewery Sat 1 pm-5 pm.

SHOPPING

Tattered Cover, 2955 East 1st Ave, 322-7727. Reputedly one of the nation's most outstanding bookshops (so says the *NY Times*). Four storeys with reading lamps and comfy chairs to aid browsers. Will mail books anywhere in the world. Open Mon- Sat 9 am-11 pm, Sun 10am-6 pm.

INFORMATION
Visitors Bureau, 225 W Colfax Ave, 892-1112. Internet: www.denver.org. Also at airport. Summer, Mon-Fri 8 am-5 pm, Sat 10am-4pm, Sun 10am-2 pm; winters, Mon-Fri 8 am-5 pm, Sat 9 am-1 pm.
State Tourism Dept, 1625 Broadway, (800) 433-2656.

TRAVEL
Greyhound, (800) 231-2222, 1055 19th St & Curtis. Bus service to Salt Lake City is one of the most scenic routes in America. 'The best part is the first 3 hours out of Denver.' 'Do not do it at night, fantastic scenery, too great to sleep through.'
City Bus, RTD, 299-6000, $1 during rush hours, 75c mid-day and evenings. $3 to Boulder.
Amtrak, Union Station, 17th and Wyncoop Sts, (800) 872-7245. The 'California Zephyr', Chicago-Oakland,CA route runs through Denver and the stretch to Salt Lake City is one of the best in the US, with the train running slowly up into the mountains, through one of the longest tunnels in the US, into beautiful gorges otherwise inaccessible to humanity. 'Get off at Glenwood Springs to see natural steam rising behind the station.'
Car rental: Rent-A-Heap-Cheap, 4205 Colorado Blvd, 393-0028.
Auto Driveaway, 5777 E Evans, 757-1211.
Interstate Transportation Inc, 9485 W Colfax, Lakewood, 232-1522.

HEADING NORTH TO THE ROCKIES
Leaving Denver on I-70 west, one of the most scenic routes north—the Peak-to-Peak Highway—begins near **Central City**, a well-preserved Victorian town with honky-tonk saloons. The discovery of gold in Central City in 1859 turned fledgling Denver into little more than a revolving door, when everyone cleared out overnight to strike it rich. You can still pan for gold in what was 'the richest square mile on earth'.

The final leg of this road, Highway 7, leads to the east entrance of the Rocky Mountain National Park. An alternate route to this entrance at Estes Park, Highway 36, passes through Boulder.

BOULDER
Although it's become too popular for its own good, Boulder still makes a scenic and lively alternative to Denver for explorations in northern Colorado. The anti-smoking laws are fiercely debated by the middle-class professionals and hippy spiritualists who live here but it's largely a laid-back student mecca, at its grooviest along the Pearl Street Mall: 'fun on Sundays, clowns, magic shows, good eats, lots of young people'. 'Quite a magical place and altogether more interesting than Denver.' 'One of my favorite places in the whole USA. A medium-sized university town, full of life and young people.' *visitor.boulder.net*
The telephone area code is 303.

ACCOMMODATION
Boulder International Youth Hostel, 1107 12th St, 442-9304. Dorm $13 with $5 deposit. S-$27, D-$34, $10 deposit, both shared bath. Kitchen, laundry; deposit for fans, phones, refrigerators. 20 mins to mountains. 'Friendly, relaxed.' 'Ill-equipped kitchen.' 'Rather cramped.'

FOOD
Boulder is the only city in the US to own its own glacier, which once served as a delicious water supply. **Alfred Packer Memorial Grill**, U of Colorado, University

Memorial Bldg, 16th and Broadway, 492-6578. Named after the only man ever convicted of cannibalism in the US. Alf's orgy took place in 1886, when he and 5 others were trapped by blizzards at Slumgullion Pass for 60 days. Alf got 17 years from the judge, who said: 'There were only 6 Democrats in Hinsdale County and you, you son-of-a-bitch, ate 5 of them!' Postscript: Packer became a vegetarian after his release from prison.

Buchanan's Coffee Pub, 1301 Pennsylvania on The Hill, 440-0222. Pastries, sandwiches and flavoured coffees from $1.15.

Buffalo Burgers, 1310 College, 444-8991. All buffalo menu; low-fat, healthy and free-range. Baked french fries, cheap burgers and chilli; combo meals $3.99. 'Best tasting meat I've ever eaten—try it!'

Colacci's, 816 Main St, 673-9400. Excellent Italian food, huge portions $6—shared.

CreativeVegetarian Cafe, 1837 Pearl, 449-1952. Exclusively veggie menu, whole wheat pizza dough, barbecued tofu on the patio. $5-$8 for large portions.

Old Chicago Pizza Parlour, 1102 Pearl, 443-5031. Huge selection (110) of beers. Beer monsters can try the 'World Tour of Beers Special' in the bar: drink 25 or more and become a member of the *Foamers* club. Prizes! But don't forget the food: 'Best pizza I've ever tasted.'

Tra Ling's Oriental Cafe, 1305 Broadway, 449-0400. Cheap and cheerful Chinese dishes from $1. Hip with students.

Trident Cafe, 940 Pearl, 443 3133. Voted 'Best Coffeehouse' by Boulderites in 1997. Browse in the adjoining bookstore, then sip gourmet coffee from $1 with free refill. 'All it lacks is *Ellen*.'

OF INTEREST

Arapaho Glacier, 28 miles west. 1 mile long and 100-500 ft thick, the Arapaho moves at a sedate 11 to 27 inches per year. Nothing to worry about.

Colorado Chautauqua, 9th and Baseline, 440-7766. Founded to provide recreation, education and the arts, the centre hosts music festivals and other events in its 100 yr old dining hall and auditorium. Call for events list. A variety of hiking trails start near here at Flatirons. 'Great views over Boulder—but take plenty of water!'

Eldorado Springs, just off Hwy I70, 499-1316. Fresh water pool, slide and towering mountains above, $5. 'Scenic place to cool off or rock-climb but you need transport.'

U of Colorado, 4921411, ersatz Spanish architecture, big party place. **Fiske Planetarium**, 492-5002, on campus, Regent Drive: 'Worth a visit, especially the laser show'. Opening times and shows vary, esp during summer. Call to check. Laser show $4.

ENTERTAINMENT

The Mall, along Pearl St. 'Superb spectacles any summer evening—all free.' Near the mall is **The Walrus**, 1911 11th St, 443-9902. Good mix of students and locals. 'Cozy, friendly atmosphere.'

Catacombs Bar, 2115 13th St, 443-0486, has good bands, pool tables. Sundown Saloon, 1136 Pearl, 449-4987 has a wide selection of microbrews. 'Plenty of pool tables downstairs. 'On University Hill, **Tulagi**, 442-1369 is a popular fraternity bar with cheap eats and drinks, occasional music.

Colorado Shakespeare Festival, at U of Colorado. Rates 3rd in nation. Call 492-0554 for tickets, $10.

Rockies Brewing Company, 2880 Wilderness Pl, 444-4796. Pub open Mon-Sat from 11am. Free tasting tours of handcrafted Boulder beers at 2 pm daily (exc. Sun).

INFORMATION

Boulder Convention and Visitors Bureau,2440 Pearl St, (800) 444- 0447/442-2911.

ESTES PARK A hairbreadth away from the park entrance to Rocky Mountain National Park, Estes may be the most convenient place to lodge if you're without wheels. Commercial campgrounds here have showers and are nearer to everything.

ACCOMMODATION

Estes Park Welcome Centre, 1850 Fall River Road, CO 80517, 586-0320; http://www.estes-park.com. Comprehensive guide to lodging and recreation in Estes Park and Rocky Mountain National Park.

H-Bar-G Ranch Hostel (AYH), 6 miles from Estes Park at the head of Devil's Gulch, 586-3688. $9 per night. Memberships for sale at hostel for $18 to foreign nationals. Former dude ranch with splendid views. 'Lou, the warden, takes hostellers into town every morning at 7.30am and picks people up from the Chamber of Commerce at Estes Park at 5 pm.' 'Lou will rent out cars.' 'Best hostel I stayed at.' 'My favourite hostel of the summer.' Open 25 May to 12 September.

FOOD/ENTERTAINMENT

Estes Park Brewery, 470 Prospect Village Drive, 586-5421. Open daily 11am-midnight. 'Pool tables, pinball, basic food and free tasting tours anytime.'

MacDonald Coffee and Paper House, 150 East Elkhorn, 586-3451. Enjoy a relaxed coffee on the patio or, on Fridays, a 30 min massage for $9.

Poppie's Pizza and Grill, 342 E Elkhorn, 586-8282. Pizzas from $3. 'Nice cheap restaurant with big patio, frequented by locals.'

Prospect Peak. Visible from anywhere in the centre. Catch the tram to the top for stunning views, chipmunk-feeding, and the odd wedding! $8. 'Good hiking trails.'

The Stanley Hotel, 333 Wonderview Avenue, (800) 976-1377. A must-see if you're in Estes; this striking 1909 building is where *The Shining* was filmed. 'Creepy.'

The Wheel Bar, 132 E Elkhorn, 586-9381. Cheap liquor, steaks under $11.50.

ROCKY MOUNTAIN NATIONAL PARK To the Indians and early trappers, these were the Shining Mountains, gleaming with silvery lakes, golden sunrises, blue-white glaciers and snowpacks. Later settlers prosaically dubbed them 'Rocky', but there is nothing prosaic about this wildlife-rich range of mountains and valleys crowned by a cross-section of the Continental Divide. Over 70 peaks in the park are 12,000 feet or more and even the untrained eye can see the clear traces of glacial action and the five active glaciers that remain. **Longs Peak** at 14,255 feet is highest.

Be sure to take the **Trail Ridge Road** (Hwy 34), which follows an old Ute and Arapaho trail along the very crest of a ridge. Along its 50 miles, you actually overlook 10,000 ft peaks, alpine lakes, spruce forests and wild-flower-spangled meadows. Particularly delightful when the flowers are at their peak, in June and July; indeed, snow keeps this and other park roads impassable until the end of May and from late October on. Look out for elk, moose, hawks, coyote, bighorn sheep and mountain lions.

Other routes lead hikers to a variety of long and short trails. One excellent trail is the 5.6 mile hike from **Glacier Gorge Junction** to **Bear Lake** and **Lake Haiyaha.** At the end of the hike, catch the free park bus back to Glacier Gorge (runs mid-June to Labor Day). Horseback riding is also popular; horses can be rented at Estes Park and Grand Lake. (Also at Glacier Creek and Moraine stables in the National Park.) The entrance fee is $10 per car for seven days, $20 for one full year. The park has hundreds of trails; for good maps visit the main visitors' centre 2 miles west of Estes Park on Highway 36.

Open daily summers, 8 am-9 pm. Other centres are scattered throughout the park. For info, call Rocky Mountain National Park Office: 586-1206.
www.nps.gov/romo/
The telephone area code is 970.

ACCOMMODATION
Campgrounds near east entrance cost $14 per night: **Moraine Park, Glacier Basin** require booking (through DESTINET, call (800) 365-2267). **Aspen Glen, Longs Peak** and **Timber Creek** are first-come, first served and cost $12. $15 back country camping permits for the entire park are available at Back Country Office, Rocky Mtn National Park, Estes Park, CO 80517, 586-1242. 'Glacier Basin has a free bus to the main hiking area. Campsites have no shops or showers so it is difficult without a car.'
Near southwest entrance. Excellent lodging at **Shadowcliff AYH, Grand Lake**, 627-9220. $8 AYH, $10 non-members. S/D-$25 plus XP $5, up to six per room with shared bath. 'Brilliant Scandinavian-style hostel on cliff overlooking lake.' During summer, try **Arapahoe Ski Lodge**, 78594, Hwy 40, 726-8813 for B&B; D-$54; four people sharing, $84. For pastries, homemade bread and more, go to the British-owned **Carver's Bakery**. **Moffat's Bagel** behind Conoco gas station in Winter Park do great bites for very little.

TRAVEL
The best way to get to the park is by car; see car rentals under Denver. **Gray Line** offers daily 10-hr tour of the park for $39, leaving from Denver, 289-2841. Hitching to the park is described as 'very easy'.

COLORADO SPRINGS
Founded by bonanza kings and intended as a resort and retirement centre, the Springs grew to become second largest city and a military headquarters for the US Air Force Academy, NORAD and Ft Carson. Trash features like motel sprawl cannot dim the glory of its setting at the base of Pike's Peak. Constant winds at the Peak blow the snow like a banner, an exhilarating sight. The city makes a good base to explore Garden of the Gods, Cripple Creek and Royal Gorge.
The telephone area code is 719.

ACCOMMODATION
Buffalo Lodge, 2 El Paso Blvd, 634-2851. S/D-$48, D-$68 for 4. AC, pool, TV, telephones, laundry facilities, continental bfast, bus stop 2 blks. Trolley to Colorado Springs every hour.
Garden of the Gods Campground (AYH), 3704 W Colorado Ave, 475-9450. Summers only; pool. Cabins $14. Camping $23 for 2.
Golden Eagle Ranch Campground and May Museum Centre, 710 Rock Creek Canyon Road, 576-0450. 5 mls south on Hwy 115. Camping: $15.50; $17.50 for 2 w/hook-up. Museum houses large insect displays, space wing, NASA movies; $4.50 ($1 disc for campers).
Motel 6, 3228 N Chestnut St, 520-5400. S$46, D$52. AC, pool. View of Pike's Peak from rooms.

ENTERTAINMENT/FOOD
Barney's Diner, 1403 South Tejon St, 632-1756. Open 6 am-3 pm; special roast dinners and hearty breakfasts from $3.30.
Poor Richard's Feed & Read, 324 N Tejon St, 632-7721. Part of an entertainment complex with restaurant, toy and bookstore as neighbours. Poor Richard's has an art gallery and excellent vegetarian dishes for $6.

OF INTEREST

The Cheyenne Mountain Complex incorporates the North American Aerospace Defence Command (NORAD) and Airforce Space Command; it sits 1800 ft below Cheyenne Mountain in its own cavern, designed to withstand even a direct nuclear hit. Free tours of the base are very popular and have to be booked 6 months in advance through the tour scheduler, 554-2241(info line); 474-2238/9 to speak to tour scheduler or make resv. Cancellation places are available; passport number needed. Call for more info or look them up on www.spacecom.af.mil.

US Olympic Complex, 1750 E Boulder St, 578-4618. Home of the US Olympic Committee HQ, 15,000 potential Olympians come and train here every year. Free 1 hr tours from the Visitor Center (includes a film). The velodrome is in Memorial Park, 4 blks from main complex. Open Mon-Sat 9 am-5 pm, Sun 10am-5 pm.

Pike's Peak, Lon Chaney of horror movie fame was once a guide to this 14,255-ft peak. Hike the Barr National Recreation Trail or take the 18-mile auto highway that climbs 7039 ft—nearly to the top of the mountain, $6 all yr. For experienced mountain drivers only. This is the course of one of the most harrowing and oldest car races in the world, held in July. At the top is the view that inspired Katharine Lee Bates to write *America the Beautiful* in 1893. Pike's Peak **cog railway**, 685-1045, open May-Oct is $22.50 to the summit. Follow one of the trails for as long as you like and then walk down. 'The view is breathtaking.' 'Take a sweater.'

Cave of the Winds, off Hwy 24, 685-5444. Year round horseback riding and nightly laser show during summer; $10.

Garden of the Gods, NW of Colorado Springs off Hwy 24. 940 acres of stunning red sandstone formations, especially striking at sunrise or sunset. Free. 'Outstanding scenic beauty—next thing to Grand Canyon.' 'Well worth a visit.'

Nearby: Canon City and **Royal Gorge**, the town from which Tom Mix launched his cowboy career and also known through the films *Cat Ballou* and *True Grit*. Little of interest except the art shop at the Colorado State Penitentiary and Royal Gorge, site of the highest suspension bridge in the world, an acrophobe's nightmare. Lousy with tourist claptrap of all sorts (including the sickening aerial tram), but the viewpoint is stupendous. $10.50 for either tram ride or train ride to bottom of the gorge, open daily. You can also find the **Prison Museum** along Rte 50—free admission.

Cripple Creek, on the opposite side of Pike's Peak. The picturesque, but difficult route is via Gold Camp Road (follow Old Stage Road then join up with Gold Camp to avoid the tunnel cave-in) - 3 to 4 hrs of gravel and curves (Teddy Roosevelt called it 'the trip that bankrupts the English language'). Far easier is the route by Hwys 50 and 9 (an hr). In its heyday, Cripple Creek yielded more than $25 million in gold in one year and had the honour of being called a 'foul cesspool' by Carry Nation for its brothels and 5 opera houses. Despite tourism the place has considerable charm. Don't miss the salty cemetery (wry epitaphs, heart-shaped madame's tombstone, wooden headstones, etc) and the superlative melodrama, twice daily Fri/Sat, once daily Wed/Thurs, June-Aug. Stay overnight at the Victorian relic **Imperial Hotel**, 689-2922, with shared bath, D-$65, to partake of the melodrama downstairs and the excellent buffet dinners. The **Mollie Kathleen Gold Mine**, 689-2465. $8—'very worthwhile—free gold ore' and takes you 1000ft down. Open daily 9 am-5 pm.

INFORMATION

Colorado Springs Chamber of Commerce, (800) 888-4748; Internet: www.coloradosprings-travel.com. Cripple Creek Chamber of Commerce, (800) 526-8777.
Greyhound, 120 S Weber St, Colorado Springs, 635-1505. $11.25 o/w to Denver.

ASPEN 210 miles west of Denver on Highway 82, Aspen is a tasteful, beautiful ski resort and classical music festival site, set amid National

Forests and more recently the multi-million spreads of Jack Nicholson, Don Johnson, Melanie Griffith, Cher and others. Most things cost the earth in Aspen but reasonable accommodation can be found here, unlike the case with its patrician sister resort, Vail.

The telephone area code is 970.

ACCOMMODATION
NB: rates are highest in winter, lowest in spring and autumn.

Alpine Lodge, 1240 E Cooper Ave, 925-7351. Summer rates: S/D- $49 shared bath; $68 private bath. Incls bfast.

Alpen Hutte, 471 Rainbow Dr, PO Box 919, Silverthorne, (on I-90; get off bus at Silverthorne), 468-6336. $13, $12 AYH ($23, Dec-March). Nr Breckenridge ski area. Strict midnight curfew, laundry, TV lounge, smoking room, kitchen, no spirits. 'Really nice, clean kitchen.'

St Moritz Lodge, 334 W Hyman, (800) 817-2069/925-3220, fax 920-4032. Dorms $30 summer, $45 winter, shared bath. Incls linen, coffee and tea in the summer, bfast in winter. Partial kitchen. Sauna, pool, off- street parking.

In nearby Breckenridge:
Fireside Inn, Wellington & French Sts, 453-6456; fax: (970)453-9577. Email: fireside@breknet.com. Internet: http://www.colo.com/summit/Fireside-Inn. Summer dorms: $13 AYH, $15 non-members; winter dorms $28/$30. Hot tub, cable TV.

Camping, free wilderness camping w/running water in **White River National Forest**, which covers nearly all of Pitkin County. Closest: E Maroon, 1 mile NW of Aspen on Hwy 32.

FOOD
Recommended: **Pour la France**, 411 E Main, 920-1151. 'Sit on street and watch the world go by'; **Hickory House** on W Main, 9252313. 'Good breakfast, lunch, reasonably priced.' $5.95 specials.

Little Annie's Eating House, 517 East Hymen, 925-1098. Lunchtime specials from $6.95.

OF INTEREST
Aspen Music Festival, 9 weeks late June-Aug. Rivals Tanglewood's Berkshire Festival, in prestige and importance. 'The combination of setting, fresh air and music blew my mind.' Many open rehearsals and other free events. Call 925-9042 for tickets.

Gondola up Aspen Mt to 11,000 ft, 925-1220; $18.

INFORMATION
Aspen Central Reservations and Visitors Center, 425 Rio Grande Place, (800) 262-7736. The airport lies 5 miles from town; take the county bus from the highway that runs outside the airport, 75c; it will take you downtown.

ACROSS WESTERN COLORADO The northernmost route will take you through **Steamboat Springs**, an expensive ski resort ('fun and friendly— great skiing'), and ultimately to **Dinosaur National Monument**, which overlaps into Utah. The monument presents striking and lonely canyon vistas (used by Butch Cassidy and Co as a hideout) and the fossil remains of stegosaurus, brontosaurus and other big guys, exposed in bas relief on the quarry face, with more being excavated before your eyes. 'Not at all gimmicky; fascinating to anyone even vaguely interested in paleontology or geology.' NB: quarry, visitor centre is in Utah; see that section.

The major route west is the Interstate 70, which passes through the

Eisenhower Tunnel, Eagle and **Glenwood Springs**, an invigorating place to pause for a dip in the world's largest open-air thermal pool. Wyatt Earp's sidekick at the OK Corral, Doc Holliday, lies buried here, his headstone reading: 'He died in bed.' The Interstate continues its scenic paralleling of the Colorado River all the way to Grand Junction. This is the last town of any size in Colorado and gateway to the towering spires and canyon wilderness of **Colorado National Monument,** which is on the eastern edge of the **Colorado Plateau**. Call 858-3617; $4 per car for 7 days, $2 on foot, camping available, $10 a site.

Further south is the **Black Canyon** of the **Gunnison National Monument** ('a very special place—deer wander regularly through campsites') near Montrose, and the high adventure of the journey through Ouray and Telluride to Silverton and well south to Durango. **Ouray**, the 'Switzerland of America', is noted for the Camp Bird Mine, which produced $24 million for the Walsh family and remains productive today. With some of the loot, papa Walsh bought his daughter the Hope Diamond.

'Try getting a ride in the back of a pickup truck between Ouray and **Telluride**. The views are spectacular, the road, hair-raising.' Dizzy Gillespie once said, 'If Telluride ain't paradise, then heaven can wait,' as wait it did for Butch Cassidy, who pulled his first bank job here. Interesting buildings from the mining era have earned Telluride national historic landmark status. Telluride is also well-known as a ski resort (inexpensive, too) and festival centre, including the remarkable Labor Day Film Festival (now ranked second only to Cannes) and summer music events from bluegrass and jazz concerts. *The telephone area code is 303.*

ACCOMMODATION
Camping at **Dinosaur National Monument**, 374-2216, $5 entrance fee, $10/site with bath and running water; motels at nearby Dinosaur, CO and Vernal, UT. See also *Utah.*

Glenwood Springs Hostel, 1021 Grand Ave, Glenwood Springs, CO 81601, 945-8545. Private rooms, S-$18, D-$24. Large record collection and taping facilities. Will pick up from bus or train with advance notice. Kitchen, laundry, free bedding. 'Comfortable'. Organises half-day white-water rafting trips $25; caving $22; disc for ski areas and Vapour Caves; mountain bike rentals $12 and free transport to 'No Name' for hiking. Local bus to Aspen, $6 return.

At Grand Junction: Hotel Melrose, 337 Colorado Ave, 242-9636. With shared bath, S-$22, D-$26, dorms $12 AYH, $15 non-AYH. Walking distance to bus and rail stns. Also have 3 hiking tours, incl Colorado National Mounument. $25-$35 each tour, $75 all three.

At Montrose: Mesa Hotel, 10 N Townsend, 249-3773. S/D$35. Mainly residential hotel but will take over-nighters if there are any empty rooms. Kitchenettes. Discounts for multiple night stays, no rsvs. Bus station in same blk.

At Telluride: New Sheridan Hotel, 231 W Colorado Ave, 728-4351. S/D-$70-$120. Incls bfast. Restored hotel with a bar that appeared in *Butch Cassidy and the Sundance Kid* (but not the version which starred Robert Redford).

At Silverton: French Baker Teller House, 1250 Greene St, 387-5423. S/D-$48 shared bath, S/D-$68, private bath, incls bfast. 'Town worth visiting, price incl. b'fast.'

OF INTEREST
Glenwood Springs Hot Pool, Glenwood Lodge, 945-6571. 'Exhilarating.' 'Especially superb at night.' $7.25 for all-day pass, 7.30am-10pm; 9 pm-10pm, $4.75.

Million-dollar highway, between Ouray and Silverton. A 6-mile stretch, numbered among the most spectacular in the US.

TRAVEL/INFORMATION

Amtrak: Glenwood Springs, 413 7th St, 872-7245; Grand Junction, 339 S 1st St, (800) 872-7245. Both stops on the beautiful 'California Zephyr' route.

Greyhound: Glenwood Springs, 118 W 6th Ave, 945-8501; Grand Junction, 230 5th St, 2426012, (800) 231-2222.

Grand Junction Tourist Information Center, 759 Horizon Dr, 244- 1480.

Glenwood Springs Chamber Resort Association, 1102 Grand Ave, 945-6589. Visitor information centre open Mon-Fri 9 am-5 pm; w/ends 9 am-3 pm in summer.

Dinosaur National Monument. No direct transit, but take bus or Frontier Airlines to Vernal, Utah, where you can rent a car or hitch.

Glenwood Springs: 'Day trip from Denver; take 8.40am bus service to Glenwood Springs. Glorious Rocky Mt scenery along the way. If the bus is not late, you arrive at lunchtime. Swim, eat strawberry waffles at Rosie's Bavarian Restaurant behind bus station and catch 4.10pm bus back to Denver, arriving at 7.55 pm. A long day, but worth it.' Alternatively, the 'California Zephyr' gets in at 1.40pm from Denver and leaves at 3.15 pm.

Ouray and south: bus route from Grand Junction to Durango passes through Montrose, Ouray and Silverton. 'Unparalleled scenery; exceeds the Denver-Salt Lake City run. Canyons through 11,000 ft red rock mountains. Best from mid-Sept when aspens have changed to gold.' 'Wrecked cars 500 ft below, left as warning to other motorists.'

Telluride: jeep trail to Ouray over 13,000-ft Imogen Pass. 'Astounding' in a jeep, a truly remarkable accomplishment when covered on foot-as many people do each summer in a 19-mile race.

DURANGO   Located in the southwest corner of the state, Durango is as authentically western as a Stetson hat (which incidentally was invented in Colorado in 1863). Billy the Kid and other outlaw types used to make Durango their headquarters; before that, the Spaniards came looking for gold, found it and lost it again when local Ute Indians got fed up with them.

Western hospitality is common currency here, markedly so at the local youth hostel. Durango's location 40 miles east of Mesa Verde makes it a natural base for sightseeing.

ACCOMMODATION

Youth Hostel, 543 E 2nd Ave, 247-9905. $12 AYH and non-AYH $15. 2nd oldest hostel in Colorado, good base for hiking and mountain biking. 'Olsons' very friendly, willing to help.' 'Without a doubt the best hostel I've seen—clean, well-equipped, nice garden and BBQ.'

OF INTEREST

The main local attraction is the circa 1882 **narrow-gauge railway to Silverton,**479 Main Ave, 2472-733. The coal-fired train runs 45 miles one way and climbs 3000 ft through the sawtoothed San Juan Mts. Round trip takes all day, costs $50 (more if you reserve seat in the elegant parlour car). Runs 24 times daily and takes 3hrs 15mins, early May through mid-Oct. It is recommended that you book 'at least 6 weeks in advance'. Others say arriving at 6.30am the day before suffices, but the odds are against you. Alternatively, take the am bus to Silverton and then catch the train back to Durango (but the price is still the same). 'Plenty of seats on south-bound journey.' 'Beautiful scenery, worth every dollar.'

FOOD/ENTERTAINMENT

'If you're feeling flush, try fresh trout at the **Palace Restaurant**,' 3 Depot Place, 247-2018.

Diamond Belle Saloon, in the Strater Hotel, 699 Main Ave, 247- 4431. 'Authentic saloon atmosphere with ragtime piano.' Also in hotel: **Diamond Circle Theater** has melodramas in the summer every night but Sun, $14.
Prontos, 2nd Avenue, 247-1510. Cheap and cheerful; Wed night pizza specials, all-you-can-eat spaghetti from $5.95.

INFORMATION
Durango Area Chamber Resort Association, PO Box 2587, CO 81302, 247-0312. Free visitor's guide and information.

MESA VERDE NATIONAL PARK   'Far above me, set in a great cavern in the face of the cliff, I saw a little city of stone, asleep.'—Willa Cather.

No matter how limited your tourist plans for the West might be, a visit to Mesa Verde, the finest of the prehistoric Indian culture preserves, is a must. The 80-square-mile area is at 6,200ft and rises 2000 feet above the surrounding plain, gashed by many deep canyons. On the surface of the tableland now covered in junipers and pion trees, the Indians once tilled their squash, beans and corn, while from the depths of the canyon they drew their drinking water from springs. Originally they built their pueblos on the surface, but later for security dug their homes into the sheer canyon walls.

There are two loops to the park: one leads to **Cliff Palace** built by the Anasazi tribe in 11001275AD, which is a large medieval-looking town containing 200 living rooms, 23 kivas and eight floor levels, all within a single cave. You can climb on parts of it. The other loop, to **Mesa Wetherill**, provides good vantage points for viewing the hundreds of ruins scattered throughout the canyons. The dwellings were occupied for about a century beginning in 1200 and were vacated for unknown reasons, though probably due to drought.

To really enjoy the park, leave yourself at least a day and read the park service pamphlet on the centuries of human habitation here. A visit to the museum, with its extensive exhibits of tools, clothing, pottery and dioramas depicting the Anasazi way of life, is also a must for understanding the culture. Admission to park, $10; tour of Cliff Palace and a balcony house $1.35. www.nps.gov/meve/

ACCOMMODATION
In Cortez: El Capri Motel, 2110 S Broadway, 565-3764. S/D$47. Cheaper in winter. AC, TV.
In Mesa Verde Park: Mesa Verde Campgrounds, 529-4400, $9, $17 w/hook-up. Showers, store, snack bar, laundry. 'Gets very cold at night; need warm sleeping bag as well as tent.' Call (800) 449-2288 for info alternative accommodation.

TRAVEL
ARA Tours from Farview Lodge in the park, save non-drivers the 6-mile hike to Cliff Palace. Buses leave at 9.30am for a full day tour, $22; half-day tours of the Mesa-top dwellings leave at 9am and 1 pm, $17. Call 529-4421. Hitching is not allowed in the park, though you can discreetly ask for rides in parking lots.

OF INTEREST
Four Corners. The meeting of Colorado, Utah, Arizona and New Mexico is commemorated with a slab of inscribed concrete where you can sprawl to have your picture taken performing the amazing feat of being in 4 states at once! In summer, Indians from Navajo and other tribes come in their pickups and sell their hand-

crafted wares, often at much better prices than you'll find in the tourist centres or trading posts.

Toh-Atin Galleries, 145 W 9th and Main Ave, 247-8277. Native American and Southwestern art gallery with fine Navajo weavings, jewellery, sculptures and origninal paintings. Free admission Mon-Sat 9 am-9 pm, Sun 9 am-6 pm.

IDAHO

Rugged with mountains (50 peaks over 10,000 feet), slashed with wild rivers and deep chasms (including the Snake River and Hell's Canyon, deepest in North America), dappled with fishing lakes and hot springs, Idaho is like Colorado without the people or the public transit.

The state was settled by French trappers, later by a mix of Basques, Mormons and WASPS who came to run livestock, mine silver, log timber and grow lots of delicious Idaho spuds. Idahoans are a taciturn lot; interesting, then, that the most famous figures associated with the state were noted for eloquence. One was Chief Joseph of the Nez Perce Indians, who surrendered by saying: 'From where the sun now stands, I will fight no more forever'. The other, writer Ernest Hemingway, was an adoptive Idahoan who chose to live, write (parts of *For Whom the Bell Tolls*), commit suicide and be buried in Idaho.

The most scenic section is the panhandle, located along the northern route taken by Greyhound and crowned by the shattering beauty of Lake Coeur d'Alene—well worth a stop. The southerly route takes you within 80 miles of the Craters of the Moon and near Sun Valley, but is minimally interesting otherwise. city.net/countries/united_states/idaho.

National Park, Yellowstone (though this is mostly in Wyoming). For main entrances to park, see Montana.

The telephone area code for Idaho is 208.

CRATERS OF THE MOON NATIONAL MONUMENT   Located at the northern end of the Great Rift system, this grotesque grey landscape of extinct cones, gaping fissures and cave-like lava tubes is the largest basalt lava field in the lower 48 states. Since it was only formed a relatively short time ago—within the last 10,000 years—no vegetation has yet grown. The area erupted 2000 years ago; another eruption is expected at the end of the next millennium, but that fact shouldn't trouble visitors for a few generations!

The most extravagant formations can be seen from one 7-mile loop road in the 83-square-mile preserve; $4 per car, good for 24 hrs. US moon astronauts spent a day in training here, rockhounding; free guided walks explore the extensive caves here about six times/day. **Camping**: $10/night on loose rock, mid-April to mid-October only recommended, 527-3257. No public transport to park; Salmon River Stages runs to **Arco**, 19 miles outside the park. If you have a car, pitching a tent on BLM (Bureau Land Management) tracks outside the park is free.

This chilling region, which looks like the day after an atomic attack, is appropriately the home for much nuclear testing and tinkering. 30 miles east is the Idaho National Engineering Laboratory. Nearby **Arco** was the first town lit by atomic power. The area has more nuclear reactors per citizen than anywhere else in the world, and Atomic City needs no introduction. Keep within park limits!

TWIN FALLS   Set on a pretty stretch of the Snake River, Twin Falls is near sights of interest and a starting point for a journey into Sun Valley and Sawtooth National Forest. West off US 30, the **Balanced Rock** rests on a base only a few feet in diameter. No sneezing. Five miles northeast of town are thundering **Shoshone Falls**, 52 feet higher than Niagara Falls. Most spectacular in winter. As you head north to Sun Valley on Rte 75, cool off at **Shoshone Ice Caves**, a lava tube spanning three blks, with naturally frigid temperatures and fascinating ice formations. Open daily 8 am-8pm from May-end Sept; $5, 886-2058. 'Bring your coat.'

ACCOMMODATION
Gooding Hotel and AYH, 112 Main St, Gooding, 934-4374. Head west from Twin Falls, 10 mls from exit Hwy 46. Dorms (AYH members only) $11, D-$27. B&B rooms: S-$40, D-$49. Full kitchen and lounge. Located near Snake River—rafting, boating, waterskiing, rock-climbing.

OF INTEREST
Hagerman, 35 mls north of Twin Falls on Hwy 84, was the site of discovery for 3-toed horse fossil in the early 1990's, now housed in the Smithsonian; you'll find the replica in the museum on Main Street. Take a day to enjoy the natural hot springs and beautiful trout-fishing.

Hell's Canyon, on the Snake River, stretches 50 miles and is the deepest chasm in North America (up to 7,900ft deep). To see it by car, Rim View Drive (Rd 241 out of Riggins) is one of the rough roads cut through Hells Canyon Nat. Recreation Area. NB: Some areas are restricted by the Forest Service. White Water tours are available, but are generally expensive. Contact Idaho Outfitters and Guides Association, PO Box 95, T- 9, Boise ID 83701, (208) 342-1919 for information 8 am-4pm Mon-Thurs or (800) VISIT-ID for a brochure.

Jerry Lee Young's Idaho Heritage Museum, Rte I-2390, Hwy 93 S, 655-4444. Jerry has collected over 40,000 artifacts which chronicle the natural and man-made history of Idaho, ranging from pre-historic fossils, to ancient Indian peace pipes and the 'guns that tamed the West.' Open Tues-Sun 10am-6 pm.

SUN VALLEY/KETCHUM   World-class skiing on ol' Baldy has attracted world-class spenders, their thirst for ultra-resort fare in tow. So for fun go to nearby Ketchum, more congenial and much less ostentatious—but still expensive.

ACCOMMODATION
Ski View Lodge, 409 S Hwy 75, 726-3441. 8 individual cabins, w/3 double beds, kitchens, showers, TV, gas heating. $40-$70 for 1-4 people. Cheap camping by the creek. Pitch a tent for free in designated areas in **Sawtooth National Recreation Area**, north on Rt 75. $5 user fee (for hiking, white-water rafting etc.). Camping outside designated areas from $6-$10. Call (800) 280 2267.

ENTERTAINMENT
Desperado's, 4th & Washington, 726-3068. Tacos for $2.95 and a selection of 15 Mexican beers.

Louie's, 331 Leadville St, 726-7775. In remodeled church building, serving 15 kinds of pizza from $7. Extremely popular.

Pioneer Saloon, 308 N Main, 726-3139. Prime ribs, fresh fish and prices from $6.50. Cheap beer and *the* place to go in town.

OF INTEREST
You're in one of the best kept secrets of the West, so spend some time hiking in **Sawtooth**. After hiking, relax in one of the many hot springs in the area: the closest is **Warm Springs** near Baldy Mnt ski lift, but go three miles further to **Frenchmen's** for a free dip. The ski lift is open in summer; $12, but trip down is free if you hike up (you can even take a mountain bike).

Ice shows at the **Outdoor Resort Ice Rink**, off Sun Valley Road, 622-2194, feature Olympic athletes on Fri-Sat eves, mid- June to mid-Sept. The rink is open to the public all year; $7.50 plus $3 for skates. July 4th and Labour Day are big events here; catch the arts and crafts shows, Sun Valley Symphony, motorised parades, rodeos and bull riding. 24 **jazz bands** from the US, Canada and Europe arrive in mid October for a huge festival; tickets from $15.

The Chamber of Commerce Visitor Centre, 4th & Main St, 726-3423, (800) 634-347, has maps, info and details of events as does **Redfish Visitors Center**, 774-3376, at the northern end of Stanley Lake, Wed-Sun 9 am-5 pm.

BOISE   If you've spent the last few hours rendered comatose by the serial passing of small farmhouses either east or west of Boise, you'll probably experience a jolt of hope upon arriving here. Boise, capital of Idaho, is a very pleasant and liveable town, and a good place to plan a white-water rafting trip on the Salmon River.

ACCOMMODATION
Cabana Inn, 1600 Main St, 343-6000. S-$35, D-$42. Free ice, cable TV.
Capri Hotel, 2600 Fairview, 344-8617. S-$32, D-$38. Outdoor spa.

FOOD
Noodles, 8th and Idaho, 342-9300. Lunchtime slice of pizza and salad for $3.50; $4.95-$7.95 pasta dishes w/salad and garlic bread.At **8th Street Marketplace** are several small cafes and shops, such as **Cafe Ole**, 344-3222, with $5.95 Mexican lunch specials.

TRAVEL/INFORMATION
Amtrak, (800) 872-7245 and **Greyhound**, 343-3681 (800) 231-2222 are both at 1212 W Bannock. Amtrak no longer operate trains out of Boise but contracts Greyhound buses to get passengers to Portland train station (9 hrs).
Idaho Travel Council, 700 W State St, (800) 635-7820.
Boise Convention and Visitors Bureau, (800) 635-5240. There is a visitor centre at 2739 Airport Way; Mon-Fri 8.30-5am.

COEUR D'ALENE   This utterly lovely lake, whose depth and fire remind one of sapphires, is considered one of the most beautiful in the world. In the keeping of such glamorous company, the city of Coeur d'Alene inevitably went for a facelift, in 1988 tastefully revamping downtown and building a huge resort and the world's largest floating boardwalk.

ACCOMMODATION
Down motel row (Sherman Ave) are several similarly-priced rooms:
Alpine Inn, 667-5412, S/D-$38-$45; **Bates Motel**, 6671411, S/D-$30; **Lakedrive Motel**, 316 Canada Lake Drive (end of Sherman Ave), 667-8486, S-$35, D-$45.

FOOD
Idaho Rubys, 206 N 4th St, 664-8522. Homemade muffins, soups, salads and fresh

bread. 'Half' sandwiches are filling enough in themselves - $2.95. Specials (sandwich and soup) - $5.

Rustlers Roost, 819 Sherman, 664-5513. Good food all day long. Serves the city's only barbeque at dinner. Sandwiches w/fries from $4.25.

OF INTEREST
Be sure to take the 1¹/₂ hr **lake excursion**, $12, leaving from Independence Point near the resort.

Fishing permits are $7.50 per day, available at any marina or tackle shops. **Digging for rare star garnets** at Emerald Creek south of St Maries ranks somewhere between gardening and an Indiana Jones adventure. (Follow Hwy 3 south 25 miles to Rd 447; SE 8 miles to Parking Area, then 1/2 mile hike to 81 Gulch.) All-day digging permits are issued at the campground for $10; call 245-2531. They have very limited equipment, bring a container and shovel if possible! Guides will show you what to do. These black and blue garnets are found only in Idaho and India. Wear old shoes and clothes—it's wet and muddy.

Coeur d'Alene Visitors Information, 105 Sherman, 9 am-5 pm daily—walk-in centre only.

Coeur d'Alene Convention and Visitor Bureau, 202 Sherman Ave, 664-0587.

Chamber of Commerce, PO Box 850, Coeur D'Alene, IH 83816, 664- 3194.

MONTANA

Touted as the 'Big Sky' country, Montana is an immense, Western-feeling state, rich in coal, sapphires and chrome, a grower of wheat and cattle, and a major centre for tourism. A regular record-breaker when it comes to the hottest, coldest, windiest and snowiest weather in the lower 48 states, Montana achieved a mind-numbing 76°F below in the early 1980's. And wouldn't you know it—Gary Cooper was born here. Yup.

Its only sizeable minority are the Indians—about 30,000 Crows, Northern Cheyennes, Blackfeet, Flatheads, Grox Ventres, Chippewas and Crees. And Montana's the place where the Indians put paid to the whites, not only at the Little Bighorn but at the Battles of Big Hole and Rosebud as well. Indians on the seven reservations offer numerous events and facilities to non-Indians and are generally very friendly.

While in Montana, try to catch a rodeo, and don't overlook the work of artist Charles M Russell, whose cowboy days are brilliantly depicted in oils and bronze in the museum in Great Falls, Helena's Capitol Building and other towns. Helena is also the starting point for the **Gates to the Mountains** boat trip, 458-5241, which retraces Lewis and Clark's early 1800's expedition along the wild and scenic Missouri River.

One of America's great train journeys is the *Empire Builder* route across northern Montana, especially the portion that loops around Glacier National Park—both east and westbound trips are in daylight or at dusk.

National Parks: Glacier, Yellowstone (mostly in Wyoming). For information on volunteer-guided walks in the parks, and maps of designated wilderness areas and National Forests, contact the Montana Wilderness Association, Box 635, Helena, MT 59624, or call 443-7350. For a recreation guide and accommodation listings, contact **Montana Travel** at the Dept of Commerce, Helena, MT 59620, or call (800) 541-1447.

Important note: while most of Yellowstone lies in Wyoming, three of the main entrances and the gateway towns of West Yellowstone and Gardiner are in Montana and are best reached via Greyhound from Montana cities or from Idaho Falls, Idaho. Read *both* Montana and Wyoming sections when trip planning for the park. www.olcg.com/mt/index.html.
Telephone area code for the whole state is 406.

BUTTE   A company town one mile above sea level, dominated by a giant copper mining company. Its locale in southwestern Montana makes it a good base to explore the ghost towns and Indian battlefields roundabout. 'Road from Butte to Helena is great—lots of cliffs, narrow canyons, etc.' The white madonna-like figure of 'Our Lady of the Rockies' stretches 80 feet upward, adding watchful presence to the Continental Divide and Butte.

ACCOMMODATION
Capri Motel, 220 N Wyoming St, 723-4391. S-$40, D-$45, incls bfast.
Finlen Motor Inn, Broadway & Wyoming, downtown, 723-5461. S- $37, D-$40.
Kings, 307 S Main, Twin Bridges, (Hwy 41 S from Butte), 684-5639. S/D$45 w/kitchenette.

OF INTEREST
Visit the **mining museum at Montana Tech** or the **World Museum of Mining**, on a shaft-mining site, Park St. Plenty of antique mining equipment. At the same location, **Hell's Roaring Gulch** is a replica of a pioneer village including a sauerkraut factory, Chinese laundry and general store at same location; both museums and village are free.
Copper King Mansion, 219 W Granite, 782-7580. 34-room mansion of copper baron W A Clark. Open daily 9 am-5 pm; $5. Or visit his son's home, **Arts Chateau**, 723-7600, at 321 Broadway, for more art and antiques, $3.75. Tues-Sat 10am-5 pm, Sun noon-5 pm.
Ghost Towns. About 60 miles SE of Butte is **Nevada City**, a restored village of 50 buildings and a museum. 'Don't miss the deafening collection of organs, pianolas, etc, and the old RR carriages.' To pan for gold and garnets in nearby streams, visit the **River of Gold** in Nevada City, 843-5526; share a $12 bucket of 'dirt' to pan for gold with. 'Takes lots of patience to pan for gold outside RR station to end up with a few tiny specks of the yellow stuff.' Restored in 1997, the **Alder Gulch Short Line train** covers a two-mile stretch to Virginia City, a 'working ghost town,' more restored buildings, shops, restaurants, daily Western shootouts, etc.
Our Lady of the Rockies, an 80ft statue on East Ridge overlooking Butte. Finished in 1985, it was built by volunteers from many religious sects, with donated materials. Between Virginia City and **Bannack** (Montana's first boom town and territorial capital) was the 'Vigilante Trail'. In 6 months, 190 murders were committed here and gang activity got so notorious that miners secretly formed a vigilante committee; when they caught up with the gang leader, it turned out to be their sheriff, who was duly hanged on his very own gallows. 'Bannack: the best old Western town I've seen. Still has gallows, jail. View from top of Boot Hill unbelieveable.' **Castle** (Calamity Jane's home town) and **Elkhorn** (300 old buildings still standing) are other interesting destinations.
Big Hole National Battlefield. Site of the Nez Perce victory over US troops in 1877. Chief Joseph and his band were in flight to Canada, having refused to accept reservation life. Pursued by troops, they fought courageously and intelligently under Joseph's masterful military leadership. Despite their win, they were pursued and ultimately beaten at Bear Paw, less than 30 miles from the Canadian border. For info, call the National Parks Service in Wisdom, 689-3155.

Greyhound, 101 E Front, 723-3287, 8 am-8pm daily; (800) 231-222, 24hrs.
Chamber of Commerce, 2950 Harrison Ave, 723-3177. 8 am-8pm daily.

BILLINGS Montana's largest and most sophisticated city, Billings is on the Yellowstone River and makes a good stopover point for travellers from North or South Dakota en route to Yellowstone. This is a good route to the park, via the scenic Cook City, Hwy 212. 'A spectacular mountain view—pass 10,000 feet up & lots of elk & buffalo along the way! Don't go before mid-June, though—otherwise, snowed in.'

ACCOMMODATION
Billings Inn, 880 N 29th St, 252-6800. S- $42, D-$46, incls bfast.

FOOD
King's Table, 411 S 24th St W, 656-7290 (phone/fax). Take exit 446 off I-90. Enormous buffet of salad, homemade soups, roast beef, ham, breads and much more; $7 dinners, $6.50 lunches. There are several Chinese and Mexican restaurants in town, some with reasonable lunch specials.

OF INTEREST
Foucault Pendulum, First Citizen's Bank Building, 1st Ave N and Broadway. Two storeys tall, this pendulum is modelled on the same principles that account for the earth's rotation. Free. **Western Heritage Center**, 2822 Montana Ave, 256-6809. Exhibits change twice a year, but the theme in general is an 'Interpretive program reflecting on the history of the Yellowstone Valley River region'. Open Tue-Sat 10am-5 pm, Sun 1-5 pm; suggested donation.
Yellowstone Art Center, 401 N 27th, 256-6804. Museum of modern and Western art housed in 1916-vintage jail; 2 new wings added 1997. Tue-Sat 10am-5pm, Thurs 11am-8pm, Sun noon-5 pm in summer; free.
Chief Black Otter Trail. N of the city: spectacular views, Indian scout grave, and a monument to settlers. **Sacrifice Cliff**, on the trail, is said to be the place where Indian braves, distraught over the loss of their families to smallpox, rode their ponies and themselves into oblivion. In **Pictograph Cave State Park**, you can also see Indian drawings. $3 per vehicle. 50c pp.
Pompey's Pillar, 30 miles east of Billings. A National Landmark along the Lewis and Clark trail. 150ft tall sandstone formation 'signed' by Capt William Clark in 1806 and named by him in honour of Sacajawea's son Pompey. Renovated 1996 to include staircase to top!

TRAVEL/INFORMATION
Greyhound, 2502 1st Ave N, 245-5116, (800) 231-2222. 24 hrs.
Chamber of Commerce, 815 S 27th St, 252-4016. Daily 8.30am-6 pm (summer).

CUSTER BATTLEFIELD NATIONAL MONUMENT Here on the Little Big Horn River, just under 60 miles east of Billings, General George Custer imprudently attacked the main camp of the Sioux, Hunkpapas and others. The date was 25 June 1876. 'I did not think it possible that any white man would attack us, so strong as we were,' said one Oglala chief. A Cheyenne recalled that after he had taken a swim in the river he 'looked up the Little Big Horn toward Sitting Bull's camp. I saw a great dust rising. It looked like a whirlwind. Soon a Sioux horseman came rushing into camp shouting: 'Soldiers come! Plenty white soldiers!'

Before they could be moved to safety downstream, several women and children were killed, including the family of warrior Gall. 'It made my heart bad. After that I killed all my enemies with the hatchet.' Brilliantly led by Sitting Bull and Crazy Horse, the Indians routed the soldiers and surrounded Custer's column, killing them all. Who killed Custer is not known. Sitting Bull described his last moments: His hair 'was the colour of the grass when the frost comes. Where the last stand was made, the Long Hair stood like a sheaf of corn with all the ears fallen around him.'

GREAT FALLS   Home base for Charles M Russell and an outstanding collection of his work; also home base for a fearsome array of Minuteman missiles at Malstrom AFB. This is a likeable hick town, home of the state fair in August and a useful stopover if heading north towards Canada or Glacier National Park. (Kalispell, the western gateway, is actually a better way to the Glacier.)

ACCOMMODATION
Super 8 Motel, 1214 13th S, 727-7600. S-$48, D-$57.

OF INTEREST
C M Russell Museum, 400 13th St N, 727-8787. Outstanding collection of his Western paintings, bronzes and wax models. Other famous painters on show include Remington and George Montgomery. Mon-Sat 9 am-6 pm, Sun 1 pm-5 pm, $4, $2 w/stud ID. Russell's **house and studio** are at 1300 4th Ave N, open in summer, free with museum ticket.

TRAVEL
Greyhound, 326 1st Ave S, 453-1541, (800) 231-2222.

GLACIER/WATERTON NATIONAL PARK   'Nothing that I can write can possibly exaggerate the grandeur and beauty of their work.' So wrote naturalist John Muir about glaciers, and nowhere are his words truer than here, surely one of the contenders for the title of 'most beautiful place on earth.' The joining of Glacier in Montana and Waterton in Alberta created this 'International Peace Park', the first in the world to cross national boundaries.

The Glacier section is traversed east to west by the **Going-to-the-Sun Highway**. Open mid-June to mid-Oct (snowed in the rest of the year), these 50 miles of remarkable beauty are most impressive coming from the west: hugging the side of a cliff for dear life, the road grinds its way up a dizzy precipice along a fantastic hanging valley backed by angry peaks to **Logan Pass**. From the visitors center at the pass, there are day hikes—either along the **Garden Wall** to the north, or up **Mt Oberlin**, an easy peak by Glacier standards that pays off with an eagle's eyrie-view of the park. Nearly 1000 miles of trails wind among rugged mountains and cirque glaciers, leading to encounters with wildflower-scattered alpine meadows, trout-splashed lakes and quizzical mountain goats. Glacier's dangerous and unpredictable grizzlies are *not* one of the tourist attractions; wear bells on your toes (or boots) to avoid surprising a browsing bear. Park naturalists lead parties to **Grinnell** and **Sperry Glaciers**; one trail goes over the **Triple Divide**, a unique point from which water trickling through tiny streams must choose its ultimate destination: west to the Pacific; southeast to the Gulf of Mexico; or northeast to Hudson Bay.

When it comes to scenery, the Canadian side is no slouch, either. To reach **Waterton**, you must leave Glacier Park at the east entrance (**St Mary**), and re-enter just at the US-Canada border. The Canadian park, much smaller than its sister to the south, centres on Waterton Lake. The cruise from the north shore to the south is wonderful, and the hike around the lake's east side has been called Canada's best.

Generally warm in summer with occasional storms and invariably cold nights; by Oct, some of the park is liable to be snowed in. Excellent trout fishing; if you don't fancy catching your own, **Eddy's**, in **Apgar**, 888-5361, (at the foot of Lake McDonald), is famous locally for good $12 trout dinners; 7.30am-9.30pm (summer). www.nps.gov/glac/.

ACCOMMODATION

Glacier Park makes reservations at the 4 hotels and 3 motels within the park. They recommend rsvs 6 months in advance, (602) 207-6000. Last minute cancellations may make space available. Rooms start at $35 for a basic wood cabin, $70 w/bath.
Backpackers Inn, 29 Dawson Ave, East Glacier, 226-9392. Hostel accommodation in cabins $10, linen $1; outdoor BBQ grill, check-in noon-10pm. 'Good bulletin board.'
Brownie's Grocery and AYH Hostel, 1020 Montana Hwy 49, 226-4426. (800) 662-7625 rsvs. 6 blks from Amtrak station—will pick up. $12 AYH, $15 non-AYH, rooms $23-$33 non-AYH. Check-in 7.30am-9 pm. Kitchen, linen and info provided. Park is 8 miles away.
North Fork Hostel, 80 Beaver Dr, 862-0184, in Polebridge on the western border of the park. In a remote old log house, no electricity, $12 AYH. Many lodges at **East and West Glacier**, just outside park. Best prices for doubles, triples or quads, so it pays to bunch up.
Super 8 Motel, 1441 1st Ave E, (800) 800-8000 or 755-1888, D- $59-$68.
Park Campsites cost $12. If you are in a car, $10 buys you a 7-day pass. Back country camping free with permit from park office; $20 if you want to book in advance. Watch out for bears. Call the park office, 888-7800, for information.

TRAVEL

In summer Amtrak, (800) 872-7245, stops at Glacier Park. The railtracks through the park have no joints and so the ride is silent, except for the park ranger who gives a commentary about the sights and history of the park. **Greyhound** only goes as far as Great Falls. There is no bus service to the park, but the hitchhiking is easy and safe. Horses can be rented in East and West Glacier. If you enjoy exotica, the **Great Northern Llama Company** offers 4-day llama pack trips. Cost is $165 pp per day, incls meals. Call 755-9044 or write 1795 Middle Rd, Columbia Falls, MT 59912. River rafting trips by **Glacier Raft Co** and others, 888-5454, (800) 332-9995, all equipment provided; $36 half-day, $69 whole day—incls BBQ steak lunch. Blackfoot Indians will take you on a cultural tour of the park, incl short hikes,for $35; call Sun Tours, 226-9220, (800) 786-9220.

GATEWAY CITIES TO YELLOWSTONE: BOZEMAN, GARDINER, WEST YELLOWSTONE

Of *Zen and the Art of Motorcycle Maintenance* fame, Bozeman is a college town and agricultural centre. It lies on the Butte to Billings Greyhound route; south from Bozeman, Hwy 191 dips in and out of Yellowstone Park, coming at length (90 miles) to West Yellowstone.

Gardiner, a small village on Yellowstone's central north border, has the only approach open year-round. West Yellowstone, a few blocks from the western entrance to Yellowstone, has numerous lodgings, shuttlebus service to Old

Faithful, bike rentals, car rentals and other amenities for exploring the park. Hitching is also good and relatively safe. $20 entrance fee for 7 days.

ACCOMMODATION

In Bozeman: Rainbow Motel, 510 N 7th Ave, 587-4201, S-$50, D- $68, pool.
Royal 7 Motel, 310 N 7th Ave, 587-3103, S/D$42-$47, 4 people $58.
Sacakawea International Backpackers Hostel, 405 W Olive St, 586-4659. $12.
In West Yellowstone: Madison Motel, 139 Yellowstone Ave, 646-7745. $17 AYH, non-AYH $18, S-$26-$31, shared bath; D-$39-$45, private bath. Hotel part circa 1912, reflects early, pre-auto days of Yellowstone. 'Romantic old loghouse.' 'Very friendly.'
Wagon Wheels RV Campground, Gibbon and Faithful Sts, 4 blks from Greyhound, 646-7872. $20 per camping site, XP-$4. 'Very generous host. Shower block is palatial.' 5-min walk to **Running Bear Pancake House**.

TRAVEL

GrayLine bus tours, 646-9374, of the park leave from West Yellowstone; Upper/Lower Loop tours cost $36, plus $4 first time park entry. 'A fascinating day tour. Lots of chances to get out and view the sights.' Tetons tour $46 all day.
Car rental: 'If traveling from Bozeman and returning, try hiring a car for a round trip in 24 hours. Four of us did and it worked out cheaper than busing.'
AmFac, (307) 344-7901. Bus tours, Upper/Lower Loop $25-$27, and Grand Loop $29, leave from Mammoth Hot Springs and Gardiner once daily. Rsvs 2 days in advance.
NB: Chamber of Commerce operates as a **Greyhound** stop.
Park Information, (307) 344-7381.

NEVADA

'Stark' describes the Silver State. It's a flat and monochrome universe of sagebrush, raked with north-south mountain ranges that rise like angry cat scratches from the dry desert floor.

Nevada's the place for misanthropes. About 800,000 people rattle around in a state that measures 110,000 square miles, and 50 percent of them live in and around Las Vegas. Despite its small population, Nevada became a state in 1864 on the strength of the gold and silver from the Comstock Lode, which helped finance the Union side of the Civil War. After several boom-and-bust cycles, Nevada got on a permanent roll when three things happened: the building of Hoover Dam in 1931, which drew thousands of workers into the state; the legalisation of gambling the same year, which grew to become the largest single source of revenue; and government nuclear testing in the 1950s, which provided good jobs (and generous amounts of irradiation). Today Nevada produces 60 percent of the gold mined in the US and 10 percent of the world's supply.

Nevada's trademarks may be glitter, fallout and quickie marriages, but it's also a land of ranches, Indian PowWows, Basque and Mormon communities and natural wonders like the Valley of Fire, weirdly beautiful Pyramid Lake, and (unofficially) the oldest tree in the world, in Great Basin National Park. The past and the future also meet here; there are ghost towns—such as Belmont, built in 1865—and a newly designated *Extraterrestrial Highway*, so-named because of its proximity to the top-secret Area 51 Air Force Base.

Legend has it that more UFO's have been spotted here than anywhere else in the world. Keep your eyes peeled. www.travelnevada.com/.
The telephone area code for the state is 702.

LAS VEGAS   There is a point at which overwhelming vulgarity achieves a certain grandeur, and Las Vegas is living proof. Just remember to see it at night. In the blue velvet hours, it's an opulent oasis of neon jewels, endless breakfasts and raucous jackpots, a snug clockless world that throbs with totally unwarranted promise and specious glamour. As daylight approaches, the mirage wavers and melts away and the oasis becomes a banal forest of overweight signs, tacky and oppressive.

Best approaches for nighttime views: coming from Boulder City, through Railroad Pass gives you a brilliant view of the entire city, as does the *Desert Wind* train from Los Angeles.

The splashiest casino-hotels are along The Strip, where it all began in 1941 with El Rancho Vegas. It didn't all start with gangster Bugsy Siegel and *The Pink Flamingo* as Hollywood said in the movie *Bugsy*; like the movies however, the scenery is ever- changing. The latest mega-resorts include a re-created New York skyline, complete with Statue of Liberty at **New York, New York**, a 55-storey replica of the Eiffel Tower at the **Paris Casino Resort** and a 'Star Trek Experience' at the **Hilton** in which 'Trekkies' can beam up to a simulator ride and virtual reality stations.

Three miles from The Strip lies 'Glitter Gulch', the downtown area, a high-wattage cluster of 15 casino-hotels where Dustin Hoffman played his special trick in *Rainman*. The Gulch tries harder with looser slots, cheaper eats and a more tolerant and friendly attitude towards newcomers and low-rollers. However: lots of cheap lodging and food deals on The Strip, so it's a toss-up. A word of warning for those under the magic State-side age of 21, the casinos will let you in, will let you gamble, will let you lose but if you win they'll dispatch the security guards to 'card' you. So if you're under 21, say adieu to that money. Finally, a little advice from *Fear and Loathing in Las Vegas* and the Doctor, Hunter S. Thompson: '... this is not a good town for psychedelic drugs. Reality itself is too twisted'.
www.lvol.com/

ACCOMMODATION
Since the casino owners want to encourage visits by unwary tourists, cheap lodging is the rule in Las Vegas. Lodgings are cheaper in winter than summer, cheaper midweek than on weekends. Avoid public holidays if you can. Sometimes there are some astonishing bargains, even at big flashy hotels on The Strip on Las Vegas Blvd. 'Don't be afraid of bargaining.' If you find it difficult to get a room on a summer weekend, try one of the big places—more likely to have vacancies and it can still work out cheaply for 2 or more people. Beware of booking agents, 'they tell you the city is fully booked, just one free room. They then charge you $20 to book it. Don't be fooled by the free fun books they offer—you can get them anywhere'. Also, compare freebies (eg coupons for gambling, shows, meals) between hotels—they can make a big difference to your overall expenses. Local radio and giveaway papers advertise the latest bargains, as do the *LA Times'* classified ads.
Downtown (close to bus, train stations):
Budget Inn, 301 S Main St, 385-5560. Across the street from Greyhound. 'Spotless.' S-$30-34, D-$39-52.

Las Vegas Airport Inn, 5100 Paradise Rd, 798-2777. S/D-$45, $85 w/ends. 2 pools, 24 hr shuttle service to the strip.

Las Vegas Independent Hostel, 1208 S Las Vegas Blvd, 385-9955. $12 AYH, $14 non-AYH, $5 key deposit. TV, video, free coffee and tea. 'Real friendly.' 'Ants a problem in summer.'

Lee Motel, 200 S 8th St, 382-1297. S/D-$20, $-33 w/ends, incls key deposit. 'Clean.'

Victory Hotel, 307 S Main St, 384-0260. 12 blocks from Greyhound. S-$24, $35 w/ends, D-$28, $40 w/ends. 'Cheap, helpful.'

On the Strip:

The Aztec Inn Casino, 220 Las Vegas Blvd S, 385-4566. S/D-$25- $35, $35-$45 w/ends, $5 deposit. Prices go up sharply certain w/ends, call to check. 2 pools, slot machines. 'In easy reach of all casinos, safe, with brilliant rooms.'

Circus Circus, 2880 Las Vegas Blvd S, 734-0410. Hundreds of AC rooms, TV, pool, amazing themed amenities including acrobatics. S/D-$29-79, $59-99 w/ends. Payment of first night req in advance; phone (800) 634-3450 for reservations. 'Excellent.'

King Albert, 185 Albert Ave, 732-1555. Behind Maxim Hotel. S/D- $39 all week.

Sahara Hotel, 2535 Las Vegas Blvd S, 737-2111. S/D-$28-$135. Moroccan themed resort. 'First class. Amazing pool.'

Stardust Hotel, 3000 Las Vegas Blvd, 732-6111, (800) 634-6757. Possibly the most garish on The Strip, with 1,034 AC rooms and a motel annex, S/D$36-$300(!) weekdays, $65-$300 w/ends, with frequent specials advertised in newspapers and elsewhere. 2 pools. 'Sparkling room.'

FOOD

As a ploy to keep you gambling, many casinos dish up cheap and/or free meals to keep your strength up. You don't have to gamble to take advantage, either. Do read the fine print, however; some of the largesse has strings attached. Free or cheap breakfasts are commonplace. Many of the cheapie 'lunches' and 'dinners' actually serve breakfast food, so be prepared to like eggs and toast. The local paper prints a list of the all-you-can-eat buffets and other cheap deals at all hotels and casinos; you shouldn't spend more than $4 at breakfast, $4-$8 at lunch/dinner. Don't expect quality (some of it is barely edible), just quantity. Most frequently mentioned: **Freemont Hotel; Circus Circus**, the Strip, 734-0410, with all-you-can-eat buffets, bfast for $3, brunch for $3.99, dinner for $4.99. 'Best you could want.' Free or cheap drinks are another casino attraction. If you are gambling, waitresses are glad to serve all manner of libation. 'To get free drinks, go to casinos where they are playing 'Keno'. Sit down and pretend to play by marking sheets provided. The waitresses then come and take your drink order for free!'

OF INTEREST

For a change of scene, try the **Barrick Museum of Natural History**, Uni of Nevada, 4505 S Maryland Parkway, 895-3381. Local archaology, anthropology and natural history of Mojave Desert and Southwest. Mon-Fri 8 am-4.45 pm, Sat 10am-2 pm. Free.

Binion's Horseshoe, 128 Freemont, 382-1600, has glass elevator to Skye Rm, worth a ride for the views of Glitter Gulch, The Strip, the desert and mountains beyond.

Caesar's Palace, The Strip, 731-7110. Outrageous fixtures—Cleopatra's Barge, a Temple of Diana with moving sidewalk, etc. Superb Omnimax theatre next door; 11am-11 pm, $5/1 film, $8/two. Call 369-4008. If nothing else, visit the **Liberace Museum**, 1775 E Tropicana Ave, 798-5595, a memorial to an entertainer who personified the Las Vegas way of life. Open Mon-Sat 10am-5 pm, Sun 1 pm-5 pm, $6.95, $3.50 w/stud ID, to look at all 3 bldgs full of glitz (the world's largest rhinestone is here as well).

Red Rock Canyon, about 12 miles west of Vegas. Gray Line, 384-1234, has an all-day tour Tues-Thur. Leaves at 10am from downtown hotels, returns at 5 pm; $30.75 incl lunch—look out for discount coupons. 'Very beautiful.' **Cowboy Trail Rides**, 387-2457 at Red Rock Canyon stables offer horse-back riding, mustang viewing and cowboy poetry; 8 am-9 pm daily; $25.

ENTERTAINMENT

Las Vegas is famous for big-name superstar shows featuring comedians such as Bill Cosby, George Carlin and Joan Rivers, as well as entertainers such as George Burns, Diana Ross and Frank Sinatra. Championship boxing matches, golf tournaments and other sporting events also take place here. Paris-style revues, soft-core sex shows and lounge singers are all Las Vegas standards. Few shows are free, but like the restaurants and lodgings, they are less expensive here than most places, and the drinks are usually cheap. **The Luxor Hotel**, 3900 Las Vegas Blvd, has the city's first IMAX 3-D theatre; call (800)288-1000 for listings. **Wet 'N Wild Water Park**, 2601 Las Vegas Blvd, 734-0088. $21.95; opens 10am, closing time varies. For a simple, free way to relax in Las Vegas, hop into any of the fancy pools in the hotels along the strip. Several readers have written to say that no one asked if they were guests at the hotel. The key is to look like you belong there.

INFORMATION

Las Vegas Convention and Visitors Bureau, 3150 Paradise Rd, in the Convention Center, one blk from the Strip, 892-0711.
Nevada Visitors Bureau, 5151 S Carson, Capital Complex, Carson City, 687-3636, gives info on state attractions.
Las Vegas Entertainment Guide: 225-5554.
What's On guide lists weekly entertainments: 891-8811.

TRAVEL

Greyhound, 200 S Main St, downtown, (800) 231-2222. Also at the Tropicana and Rivieria Hotels.
Amtrak, Union Plaza, 1 Main St, (800) 872-7245. The **Desert Wind** no longer serves Las Vegas: catch the **California Zephyr** from Oakland to Reno, then bus it to Vegas.
Auto Driveaway, 252-8904, 4410 North Rancho.
McCarran International Airport, 5 miles south of downtown. Lavish, carpeted. 'Large couches, ideal for dossing.' Don't play slots here. Take the CATRIDE #1 'Maryland Pkwy' bus from 300 N Casino Ctr, $1, takes about 45 minute (CATRIDE: 228-7433). Many of the big hotels also have free airport shuttles.
Scenic Airlines, 739-1900 or (800) 634-6801, does 4 different trips from Las Vegas to the Grand Canyon. Best value probably the 7-hr air-ground tour over Hoover Dam and all along the Canyon in a small plane. Expensive at $214, but well worth it for a unique experience. Shorter flight-only tours cost between $111-$162. Book in advance. Las Vegas, according to one traveller, is 'hell to hitch out of'.

HOOVER DAM and LAKE MEAD Proof that engineering can be elegant as well as massive, Hoover's 726-foot vaguely Art Deco wall holds back miragelike Lake Mead, irrigates over one million acres, and keeps the lights on in LA and elsewhere. 'You can see the best of it by just driving past.' 'Fantastic value. Don't just drive past!' 20 min tours 8.30am-5.45 pm, $5; 293-8367. 'Tour goes right inside the workings of the dam.' 'Probably absorbing for the student engineer but not for the artistically inclined.' An oasis of trees and shade by the shore of Lake Mead is the **Boulder Beach Campground**, 293-8906, $10 a night for a tent space. NB: do *not* stay here in summer, when the temperature is 100°F at 4am and the air is wall-to-wall

insects! 'You'd have to camp in the lake to get a decent night's sleep.'
www.hooverdam.com/service/index.html

RENO Although it tries hard to peddle greed, instant gratification (eg quickie marriages/divorces) and fantasy like Big Brother Las Vegas, Reno doesn't quite make it. Despite the worst of intentions, little glimpses of culture, humanity and scenic beauty keep peaking through: its treelined parkway along the Truckee River; its friendly university; its jazz festivals; its good Basque restaurants. Close to the beauties of Lake Tahoe and a day's drive from San Francisco, 'the Biggest Little City' makes a pleasant base to explore Virginia and Carson Cities. For an outstanding view of the lake take the Mt Rose Hwy, south of Reno on Rte 431; it climbs 8,911ft up the highest pass in the state before descending into the Tahoe Basin. www.reno.net

ACCOMMODATION/FOOD
El Cortez Hotel, 239 W 2nd St, 322-9161. S/D-$29, $34 w/ends.
Motel 6, 866 N Wells Ave, 786-9852, (800) 466-8356, S/D$ 35-40.

OF INTEREST
National Automobile Museum, 333-9300. 10 S Lake St in downtown. $7.50. Mon-Sat 9.30am-5.30pm, Sun 4pm. Mind- boggling collection of over 200 classic autos: Bugattis, an 1938 Phantom Corsair Coupe, entertainers' custom vehicles, plus rail cars, boats.
Nevada Historical Museum, 1650 N Virginia St, near campus, 688-1190. Washoe Indian Dat-So-La-Lee was one of the finest weavers of Native American baskets in the country. Her work, as well as mining history and the development of casino industry, is on display Mon-Sat 10am-5 pm. $2.
Nearby: Virginia City. A $25/week reporter for the local *Territorial Enterprise*, Mark Twain wrote of this semi-ghost town in its boisterous prime: 'It was no place for a Presbyterian, and I did not remain one for very long'. The **Territorial Enterprise Building**, 54 S C St, 847-0525, still owns the original printing and editorial rooms of the paper where Samuel Clemens first used his pen-name in 1863. The museum is open 10am-5.30pm daily (4pm in winter), $1. The Sundance Saloon, now a T-shirt shop, still houses the city's oldest bar. The city also has a melting pot of **cemeteries**, from Masonic and Catholic to Chinese and Mexican. Explore also the museums on C St—one of the best being **The Way It Was**, full of mining and local history and don't miss the annual camel, ostrich and water-buffalo races, held on the weekend following Labor Day. The Chamber of Commerce can tell you more, 847-0311.
Carson City. Loaded with Victorian gingerbread and refreshingly situated in the green Sierra foothills, this is the smallest capital city in the lower 48. Mark Twain lived at 502 N Division St with his brother, who was the first territorial secretary of state. Free sights include a rare collection of natural gold formation at the **Carson Nugget**; the former mint (now the **State Museum**); and the **Nevada State RR Museum** on 600 N Carson St, 687-4810. $3, w/stud ID. 8.30am-4.30pm daily. Call the **Carson City Chamber of Commerce** for local events, 882-1565.

TRAVEL
Amtrak, E Commercial Row & Center, (800) 872-7245.
Greyhound, 155 Stevenson St, 322-2970, (800) 231-2222.

GREAT BASIN NATIONAL PARK Opened in 1987, Great Basin was the first new national park in the lower 48 in 15 years. The youngest of the parks is also the least-visited, due mainly to its location near Route 50, the 'loneliest road in the country' (287 mls through nine mountain ranges, mostly over

10,000ft); Reno is 300 miles west, with Salt Lake City a further 250 miles to the east. The nearest town to the 77,100-acre Great Basin is the miniscule **Baker** whose population of 50 boasts half a dozen houses, a gas station, a two-room school, post office, two bars and a convenience store.

Scenery within the park varies from spectacular mountains topped by the 13,063ft **Wheeler Peak**, to sagebush-studded desert, alpine lakes, deep limestone caves, lush meadows and groves of gnarled bristlecone pines, the oldest living trees. The vistas are said to be 'unbelievable, absolutely outstanding'. Explorer John C. Fremont, who travelled through the area in the early 1800s is credited with the name Great Basin for the region. The idea for a national park here is more recent, however, having been under consideration for a mere 50 years.

Park headquarters and visitor centre is at **Lehman Caves**; 90 min ranger-guided tours of the caves run from 8.30am-4.30pm, $4. To camp free, go to Upper or Lower Lehman, Wheeler or Baker Parks; other campgrounds with drinkable water cost $5/site. For park information phone 234-7331.

UTAH

Although the US government owns 70 percent of Utah's land, the Beehive state is, for all intents and purposes, under Mormon control, a unique situation indeed considering the American insistence on separation of church and state.

The Church of Jesus Christ of the Latter-Day Saints (LDS) began in 1827 when New Yorker Joseph Smith was led by an angel named Moroni to some gold tablets. Translated (with Moroni's help and two seer stones called Urim and Tummim) into English, the writings became the scriptures of the *Book of Mormon*. The fledgling sect was pushed from New York westward but didn't encounter any significant antagonism until Smith introduced polygamy at Nauvoo, Illinois. A hostile mob promptly killed Smith and his brother. The mantle fell to Brigham Young, who ably led his band west to the bleak wilds of northern Utah in 1847, in which no one, not even the local Ute Indians, seemed terribly interested.

The industrious Mormons established their new state of Deseret and applied repeatedly to the US government for admission to the Union but were turned down over the issue of polygamy, which was still going strong. (Brigham himself ultimately had 27 wives and 56 children.) After years of wrangling, in 1890 the Mormons gave in and banned polygamy among themselves. A number of dissenters left and their descendents can be found living quietly and polygamously in Mexico, Arizona and elsewhere.

The importance of Mormonism makes Utah—especially Salt Lake City and environs—sharply different and in many ways better than other states. Hardworking Mormons have built clean, prosperous, humanistic cities and settlements. From early settlement days, Utah has supported the arts; it is home not only to the world-famous Tabernacle Choir but galleries, museums, opera, theatre and the Sundance Film Festival. On the negative side, it's hard to find a drinkable cup of coffee anywhere. Mormons discourage the use of coffee and stimulants and apparently feel the same way about seasonings. Liquor laws, once extremely stringent, have eased somewhat but getting a drink in a restaurant can still be a baroque procedure.

All of Utah's five National Parks are in the south, an area studded with magnificent monuments of the greatest historical, geological and scenic importance. Take a tour or rent a car, allowing yourself ample time for exploration and reflection. Utah makes a good point from which to explore attractions on the UtahArizona border and further south, such as Monument Valley, the Navajo reservation and the north rim of the Grand Canyon (via Kanab). A boat trip through the flooded canyons of the Glen Canyon National Recreation Area is also an unforgettable (albeit pricey) experience. www.utah.com

National Parks: Zion, Bryce Canyon, Canyonlands, Capitol, Reef Arches.
The telephone area code for the whole of Utah is 801.

SALT LAKE CITY Not just a state capital but the Mecca/Vatican/Jerusalem for Mormons worldwide, Salt Lake City has a joyful, almost noble air about it. Founder Brigham Young had a sharp eye; the city is cradled by the snowy Wasatch Mountains, a setting of remarkable grace. Add to that streets broad enough for a four-oxen cart to turn in, a tree for every citizen, clean air and ecclesiastical architecture that succeeds in being impressive without being dull, and you have quite a place.

'The beauty of this city is that nearly everything worth seeing is within ten minutes walk of the Greyhound terminal. I managed to see a great deal in the four hours' break I had between buses. I found Mormonism really interesting but it's easier to stomach if taken with a pinch of salt.'

Not hard to do, since the Great Salt Lake lies just 18 miles west of the city. The lake is a mere remnant of Lake Bonneville, a vast prehistoric sea that covered much of Utah and parts of Nevada and Idaho. The outline of the ancient sea is still visible from the air.

ACCOMMODATION
Avenues Residential Center, 107 F St, Salt Lake City, UT 84103. 359-3855, (800) 881-4785. AYH $12, non-AYH $14 dorm; S-$25, D-$30. No telephone rsvs. 1 night's cash in advance req (at least 3 days notice). 'Spacious, well-equipped, kitchen, launderette.'
Carlton Hotel, 140 East South Temple St, 355-3418. S-$55-$69, D- $74. Nr bus depot. 'Super place with lovely bathrooms, restaurant.'
Deseret Inn, 50 W 500 South, 532-2900. S/D-$39, D/Q-$43.
Kendell Motel, 667 N 300 W, 355-0293. 9 blks from bus stn. S/D-$40, Q-$45. Kitchens; check in any time if call first.
The Avenues Hostel, 107 F St, 359-3855, (800) 881-4785. 5 blks east of Mormon Temple. Dorm $10-$14, S-$25, D-$35.
Ute Hostel, 19 E Kelsey Ave, 595-1645. Opened 1994, friendly hostel; dorm $15, D-$35, shared bath.

FOOD/SHOPPING
Marianne's Deli, 149 West 200 South, 364-0513. Genuine ethnic servicing SLC's German population. Good salami, sausages, sauerkraut, sandwiches from $3.95.
Lotsa Hotsa Pizza, 50 South Main (basement of Crossroads Plaza Mall), 363-0353. 'Succulent pizza slices $2.15, other specials around $3-$4.'
Union Cafeteria, 581-4741, on the university campus is about the cheapest place in town with good choice.

NATIONAL PARKS—SOME TOP CHOICES

It can take a lifetime to visit all of North America's National Parks. If you're planning to go to several, think about buying a *Golden Eagle Pass* ($50, valid for a year) from any one of the parks charging entrance fees. Before you go check the National Park Service homepage at www.nps.gov/parklists/byname.html. If you only have time to see a few, here are some of the best:

Acadia/Maine, (207) 288-3338. America miniaturized with beaches, forests, lakes, and Mt Cadillac, the highest point on the Eastern seaboard.

Banff and Jasper/Alberta, (403) 762-1550. Banff, Canada's oldest park, offers mountain grandeur and hot mineral springs. Alongside is Jasper with more mountains, glaciers and lakes. Colombia Icefields, between the two, is the place to spot various big-horned sheep, moose, bears and wapiti (elk). Breathtaking.

Everglades/Florida, (305) 242-7700; $10/vehicle. 2nd largest in US, with panthers, bobcats and alligators; a 50-mile wide river that's only 6 inches deep. Bug spray essential.

Fundy/New Brunswick, (506) 887-6000. Has the highest tides in the world.

Glacier National Park/ Waterton Lakes/Montana and Alberta, together making the **International Peace Park**, (406) 887-7800. 10,000 years ago glaciers carved peaks, valleys, ripples here. 50 glacier crumbs remain.

Grand Canyon/Arizona, (520) 638-7888. Deeper, wider and more colourful than thought possible; you cannot prepare yourself for this one.

Great Smoky Mountains/Tennessee, (423) 436-1200. Highly accessible. Home of Clingman's Dome, highest point in the Smokies. Try any of the 900 miles of trails along the Appalachian Trail.

Olympic/Washington, (360) 452-4501. Boasts rain forest, Mt Olympus at 7,965 ft and grey whales along the coast; best seen in Sept-Oct or Mar-Apr. Isolated from the mainland for so long, the park has several unique species of plant and animal, eg. Roosevelt elk and Olympian chipmunk.

Yellowstone/Wyoming, (307) 344-7381. World's 1st national park and largest in Lower 48. Its myriad attractions include Old Faithful and other geysers, wildlife, mudpots and much more.

Yosemite/California, (209) 372-0200. Home of the superlative El Capitan, Half Dome, Bridalveil Falls, Glacier Point, redwoods you can drive through and more.

OF INTEREST

Visitors Centers in Temple Square, in the north and south parts of the square, 240-2534. Run by the Mormon Church, the visitor centers offer a number of free tours on Temple Square. Excellent walking tour maps are also available. 'Guided tour conducted by Mormons who must have been trained to sell insurance. Intimidating.'

LDS Church office building, 50 East North Temple, 240-2190. Free guided tours Mon-Sat 9 am-4pm plus 'fantastic view from 26th floor'.

Genealogical Library, 35 NW Temple, 240-2331. Because Mormon doctrine recommends the baptism of adherents' long-dead ancestors, the church has been accumulating and organizing genealogical records from all ages and all corners of the earth. With more than 2 billion on record, the library has become a major world centre for genealogical research. If you know the birthdate and birthplace of an ancestor before 1900, the library can probably help you trace your family tree back for generations (they have a separate section for British ancestry). Open Mon 7.30am-6 pm, Tue- Sat till 10pm. Free tour and help.

Mormon Temple on Temple Square. This monumental structure in Mormon Gothic took exactly 40 years and $4 million to build. Notice the golden statue of the angel Moroni on one of the towers; according to LDS doctrine, this was the being who appeared to church founder Joseph Smith. 'Even if you're only passing through, go to see the temple. Fantastic the way it's lit up.' Not open to non-church members.

Mormon Tabernacle, home of the Mormon Tabernacle Choir. To witness the weekly radio and TV broadcasts, be in your seat by 9.15am Sun morning to be sure of a place. 'An acoustic wonder.' This is one place where if you stand in the back you can still hear a pin drop in the centre. Call Visitor's Centre, 240-2190 for more information.

Additional Mormonabilia: 'This is the Place' monument at Pioneer Trail State Park, Emigration Canyon, at east edge of city. Also restored pioneer settlement, etc. 'Mormons are obsessed with the pioneers but they don't try to convert you—in fact, I found Mormonism quite fascinating.'

Brigham Young's grave in the cemetery on 1st Ave between State and A Sts.

Beehive House, 67 E South Temple, 240-2671. BY's first residence. Free 30 min tours Mon-Fri 9.30am-6.30pm, Sat 9.30am-4.30pm, Sun 10am-1 pm. The adjoining **Lion's House** was home for 19 of BY's wives, where they lived in tiny dorm rooms in the upper hall and main floor. Legend has it that after supper the great man would climb the stairs and chalk an X on the door of his lady for the night. Sometimes a rival would erase the X and chalk another on her door before the absent-minded stud came back upstairs. In this fashion, BY brought 56 new Mormons into the world.

Abravanel Hall, at **123 W South Temple**, 533-5626; a glorious glass wedge of a place which houses the Symphony. Close by is the **Salt Palace** which houses the **Capitol Theater** and the **Delta Centre**, home to the Utah Jazz (NBA basketball) and Salt Lake Golden Eagles (hockey) teams. 128,000 crowd capacity—free self-guiding tours of both the Palace and Abravanel Hall are available.

Utah Museum of Fine Arts (free) and Utah Museum of Natural History, $3, are both at 1530 E South Campus Drive, University of Utah, 581-7049.

Shopping: Brigham Young established the first department store in the US, the Zion Cooperative Mercantile Institution (ZCMI). Now a huge affair, and at one time it was the biggest covered mall in the country. Also good browsing at Trolley Square and Crossroads Plaza.

Great Salt Lake, 18 miles west. 1500 square miles and 10 percent saline, the Mormons used to put joints of beef in the water overnight, retrieving them tolerably well pickled. Then the lake was saltier, but more fresh water is added each year when the snow melts off the mountains.

ENTERTAINMENT

Days of '47 Festival, 3rd week in July. Rodeo, parades, free concerts, dances, and a sunrise service by the Mormon Tabernacle Choir. 'Fun.'

Raging Waters, 1200 W 1700 S, (801) 977-8300. Utah's largest water theme park. Open Mon-Sun 10.30am- 7.30pm. Avoid visiting Aug 14th. $9.95.

Utah Winter Sports Park,649-5447; try a bobsled run with the professionals or watch luge and ski-jumping events. 'Hairy but exhilarating!'

INFORMATION

Salt Lake Convention and Visitors Bureau, 90 South West Temple, 521-2868; website: www.saltlake.org.

Utah Travel Council, Council Hall on Capitol Hill, 538-1030. Info on attractions in rest of Utah, open Mon-Fri 8 am-5 pm.

TRAVEL
Amtrak, 320 S Rio Grande, (801) 531-0188. Catch the **California Zephyr** between Oakland, CA and Chicago; the desert scenery between Salt Lake City and LA is stunning.
Greyhound, 160 W South Temple, (800) 231-2222. Not a good area.
Gray Line Tours, trip to Bingham Canyon and the Great Salt Lake, $27. Leave 2 pm, about 4 hrs. Departs from Shilo Inn, 206 SW Temple, or call 521-7060. 'Bus to San Francisco drives along the lake anyway.'
Utah Transport Authority (UTA), 287-4636, runs the buses; $1 basic fare.
Salt Lake City International Airport, 776 N Terminal Dr, about 4 miles west of downtown. Catch the #50 bus from Main St outside the ZMCI Center, $1; goes straight there.

PROMONTORY About 80 miles north of Salt Lake City is the **Golden Spike National Historic Site**, 471-2209, marking the spot where North America's first transcontinental railroad was completed in 1869. After a symbolic gold-spike ceremony, Leland Stanford and Thomas Durant, the heads of the railroads thus joined, attempted to pound in the final iron stake. Both missed, and a professional spike-pounder standing nearby was called on to do the job. The gold-spike ceremony is reenacted (hopefully without mishaps) each 10 May, the 2nd Sat of August and on w/ends at 1 pm and 3 pm during the summer.

DINOSAUR NATIONAL MONUMENT This park overlaps two states (see also Colorado) but the major attractions lie mostly in Utah. **Vernal** has a superb **Field House of Natural History**, 789-3799; nearby is dinosaur quarry, where you are on eye level with half-exposed brontosaurus and other remains. See Indian Petroglyphs as you look down into the gorge beside the quarry. The road from Vernal to Daggett is called 'the Drive through the Ages' for the billion years of earth's history that lie exposed on either side. Numerous campgrounds in and around the Dinosaur National Monument, emphasis on RVs though. **Dinosaur Gardens**, 235 E Main, 789-7894. Mineral hall, educational explanations of ancient fossils plus 14 life-sized dinosaurs incl a new Raptor, unveiled 1997. Open summer 8 am-9 pm, winter 8 am-5 pm; $2, $1 w/stud ID. $5 per carload (up to 8 people).

ZION NATIONAL PARK Though not as famous as Yosemite or the Grand Canyon, tiny Zion ranks with those giants in outstanding land-scapes. Zion has a huge, painted gorge of magnificent and constantly changing colours, its floor is an oasis of green. At one point the North Fork of the Virgin River pours over the 2000 ft drop of the **Narrows Abyss**, whose walls are just 20 ft apart. Cottonwoods grow on the lush canyon floor, where you can camp. So delightful was the sight that the first Mormons called it Zion, later corrected by Brigham Young, who proclaimed 'It is not Zion', and 'Not Zion' it remained for some years.

The 6-mile drive into the canyon passes the *Great White Throne, Weeping Rock* and the trail to the *Emerald Pools*, but for a better look you are advised to walk. There are numerous short trails, sometimes dotted with guide boxes containing leaflets on local flora and geological features. You can do any of these on your own, though a ranger leads hikers along the **Gateway to the Narrows Trail** in summer. Before setting off on any trail, long or short, check with rangers for advice on availability of drinking water in certain areas, sudden summer cloud-bursts with attendant flash flooding, and rock-falls.

'We liked the **Emerald Pools footpath**, a gentle stroll for a hot day—beautiful waterfall, a cool and welcome swim.' 'Try walking up to **Angels' Landing**, 5-mile round trip rising 1488 feet. Incredible views.' 'Angels' Landing walk—strenuous but very rewarding.' (NB: sheer drops along path - *not* for acrophobes.) The best view of the **Great White Throne**, a colossal multicoloured butte, is from the **Temple of Sinawava**. $5 park entry fee, good for 7 days; back country passes are required prior to hiking. For further info call the Parks Office, 772-3256, 8.30am-6 pm.
www.nps.gov/zion/

ACCOMMODATION
Park HQ: 772-3256. **Camping**: 375 sites, unreserved; arrive by noon to snag one, $8 each. Fuel, running water, toilets. No showers. Motels, groceries, and gas station at **Springdale**, 2 miles from south entrance. **Cedar City**, 40 miles north of Zion, 16 miles from Cedar Breaks National Monument (called 'Little Bryce' for its spires, perhaps more intensely coloured than anywhere else—good camping) makes a good base.
Astro Budget Inn, 323 S Main, 586-6557. S-$33, D-$36, T-$40. AC, cable TV.
Dixie Hostel, 73 S Main St, Hurricaine, 635-9000. Very central—2 hrs from Bryce, Vegas and the north rim of the Grand Canyon, 20 mins from Zion. Dorm $15, D-$35, shared bath. Incls linen and bfast.
Economy Motel, 443 S Main St, 586-4461. S-$27, D-$35-$37. AC, TV.
At Kanab: Canyonlands International Hostel, 143 E 100 South, (801) 644-5554. $9, kitchen, TV, launderette. Camping $9 when house is full. Also good for Grand Canyon, AZ.

TRAVEL
Greyhound, 355-4684, (800) 231-2222, from Salt Lake City and Las Vegas to Cedar City.
Within Zion: 45 mins tram rides into main canyon from Zion Lodge, 772-3213. $2.95, daily 9 am-5 pm. Hitching between Cedar City and Zion is slow.
Car rental: National Car Rental, Town and Country Inn. 50 W 200 N, Cedar City, 586-9900. Must be over 25.

BRYCE CANYON NATIONAL PARK Bryce's landscape belongs to God's Gothic period—delicately chiselled spires, colonnades and crenellated ridges in vivid to pastel pinks, madders, oranges, violets. Most stunning when seen against the sun: west rim in morning, east rim in afternoon. Named for Ebeneezer Bryce, an unpoetic soul who described the canyon as 'a hell of a place to lose a cow'. From the pine-covered clifftops (site of the visitors centre and other facilities), the horseshoe-shaped amphitheatres reveal surreal formations that have been likened to houses, sunburned people and pertrified sunsets. For hiking, descend the canyon to the **Peekaboo Trail** or for a short trip along the **Navajo** and **Queen's Garden trails** which link at the bottom. About 1½ hours for a quick trot. There is a 16-mile auto road but the views are less spectacular. On full-moon nights, take the free 'moon walks' down Navajo Trail or try a star walk on w/ends of dark-moon nights at 8.30pm. 'Wall Street is more spectacular than Queen's Garden.' Park HQ: 834-5322. Entrance fee $10, good for 10 days.

ACCOMMODATION
Most accommodation is in Panguich, 24 miles southwest of Bryce.
Bryce Canyon Pines Motel, outside Panguitch on Rt 12, 6 miles from Bryce entrance, 834-5441. S-$65, D-$75; lower in winter. AC, pool, cafe, homey dining room with good home cooking. Horseback riding $8; $85 full day.
Rocking Horse Inn, 2762 N Hwy 89, (801) 676-2287. Free minature golf, kitchenettes. S-$22, D-$ 27.
Camping in park, $10/night for up to 7 people per site. 'Arrive by noon to be sure of a place.'

TRAVEL
Bryce Zion Trail Rides, 834-5219, has horseback trips in both Bryce and Zion National Parks. Make rsvs at lodges or on phone. $26 for 2-hrs.

MOAB A former uranium mining town on US 163 in east-central Utah, Moab makes a convenient centre from which to visit Canyonlands, Arches and Capitol Reef National Parks.

It's also a place to book a tour to one of these parks. Lin Ottinger's land tours are recommended: 600 N Main, Moab, 259-7312. Mining/fossil tours, $45-$65. Other operators in town offer bike rentals and tours, horseback riding and white-water rafting. The Visitors Center at Center and Main can help you sort out options. Open daily 8 am-5 pm summers, (800) 635-6622. For rafting ($40 per day) contact Tag-A-Long Tours, 452 N Main St, Moab (801) 259-8946.

ACCOMMODATION
Inca Inn Motel, 570 N Main, 259-7261. S/D-$38 private bath, T-$47. Cable TV, AC, pool.
Lazy Lizard Hostel, 1213 S Hwy 191, 259-6057. Dorm-$7, S/D$20. Separate bath/shower room and hot tub in the back; kitchen and laundry facs. Not affiliated w/AYH, same prices for all. 'Nice atmosphere.'
The Virginian, 70 E 200 St S, 259-5951. S-$59, D-$64, XP-$5. Fridges, cable TV, AC, rsvs essential.
Camping in Arches National Park, a mere 2mls from town, 259- 8161. $8 Apr-Oct; otherwise free.

ARCHES, CANYONLANDS, CAPITOL REEF Arches contains water-hewn natural bridges and over 2000 arches of smoky red sandstone carved by the tireless wind in a 73,000-acre area. 'Our most memorable national park.' $5 entrance on foot, $10/vehicle for 7 days. **Natural Bridges** is noted for three rock bridges, the foremost a 268-foot span—the 2nd largest in the world. Less well-known features are the hundreds of Anasazi cliff ruins and the world's largest photovoltaic solar generating plant (free viewing), which runs the park's electrical system.

The outstanding characteristic of **Canyonlands** is its variety of colour and forms: towering spires, bold mesas, needles, arches, intricate canyons, roaring rapids, bottomlands and sandbars. The park is rich in petroglyphs, pictographs and ruins: the Maze district with its Harvest Scene and the Needles district south of Squaw Springs campground are particularly good. Call 259-4711 for Needles info or check out the Canyonlands web page:

www.nps.gov/cany/visctr.htm. If you enter Canyonland Park at the **Maze** Visitors Center, 259-2652, there is no entrance charge but you will need a back country camping pass, $25, good for 14 days. There is a $10 admission fee if you enter in the south-eastern corner; camping permits cost $10 for 14 days. 'Superb view from **Dead Horse Pt**, just outside park.'

Capitol Reef, rising 1000 feet above the Fremont River and extending for 20 miles, is the most spectacular monocline (tilted cliff) in the US. The bands of rock exposed along its length are luminous, rich and varied in their colour, and often cut with petroglyphs of unusual size and style. Its formations were named 'sleeping rainbows' by the Navajos. For lodging, try **Rim Rock Resort Lodge**, 7 minutes from Capital Reef on Hwy 24, 425-3843. Summer: D-$55. Book horse tours, fishing trips, other expeditions here; 'Good restaurant.'

GLEN CANYON, MONUMENT VALLEY   The soaring pink sandstone arch of Rainbow Bridge and the beauties of boating in Glen Canyon can be undertaken from Moab, but closer bases would be **Page**, Arizona, and **Kanab**, Utah.

On Navajo land, **Monument Valley's** landscape of richly-coloured outcroppings was the scene of many a John Ford western. Two campsites: 'the best is in the Tribal Park among the mesas—quiet, hot showers'. Call (520) 608-6404 for info.

WYOMING

'The foothills of heaven' to Buffalo Bill, who first saw this land in 1870, 'Wyoming' means 'wide prairie place' in an Indian tongue, Algonquin Indian, paradoxically, for Algonquin-speaking tribes lived thousands of miles away on the East Coast. The name, in fact, was first given to a valley in Pennsylvania, later re-applied much more appropriately to this section of the continent.

Cowboy machismo and women's rights might seem an odd mixture, but Wyoming is nicknamed the Equality State for good reason: it had the first women's suffrage act, the first female voter, governor, justice of the peace and director of the US Mint. (Buffalo Bill was among the early feminists of Wyoming, declaring 'if a woman can do the same work that a man can do and do it just as well, she should have the same pay').

A horsy, folksy, gun-totin' state, home of the notorious Hole-in-the-Wall Gang in the 1890s, Wyoming has ranches so huge they're measured in sections instead of acres. Everyone knows about the twin treasures of Yellowstone and Grand Teton National Parks, but Wyoming also contains Devil's Tower, now imprinted on the world's retina as an extra-terrestrial landing pad; and Salt Creek, world's largest light oil field and site of the infamous Teapot Dome scandal in 1927. www.state.wy.us/state/tourism/tourism.html.

National Parks: Grand Teton, Yellowstone (largely in Wyoming but slivers of the park are in Montana and Idaho; see Montana section for additional information).

The telephone area code for the whole of Wyoming is 307.

CHEYENNE Formed in 1867 when Union Pacific Railroad tracks were laid, and named after the Indian people who inhabited the area, Cheyenne was once fondly called 'hell on wheels' for its volatile mix of cowpokes, cattle rustlers and con men. Capital city Cheyenne now contents itself with having the purest air and the most frequent hailstorms in the US. A little of the old buckaroo flavour returns each July during the week-long Frontier Days rodeo, largest in the US.

ACCOMMODATION
Big Horn Motel, 2004 E Lincolnway, 632-3122. S-$22, D-$26, TV, AC.
Home Ranch Motel, 2414 E Lincolnway, 634-3575. S-$28, D-$30 summers.
Motel 6, 1735 Westland Rd, 635-6806. S-$43, D-$48, less in summer.
Super 8 Motel, 1900 W Lincolnway, Hwy 30 West, 635-8741. S-$45, D-$50.

FOOD
Albany Cafe and Restaurant, 1505 Capitol Ave, 638-3507. Open 11am-10pm Mon-Sat, dinner from 4.30-9 pm, meals from $4.55. Bar is good for meeting people. 'Not a pickup bar, not gay, not expensive, good music. Can this be true?'

OF INTEREST
Frontier Days, 'Daddy of 'em All' rodeo, last full week in July. 778-7200. 4 parades, chuckwagon race, free pancake breakfasts, and perhaps the best rodeo in the US. Tickets are pricey: $8-$20. 'During rodeo, the whole town goes wild on Saturday night but forget it at other times'; 'Cheyenne is dead as a doorpost on Saturday night'. However, there are planned entertainments every evening, eg. country music, Indian dancing at an Indian village. Livestock auctions on first w/end following Frontier Days events.
State Museum, Central Ave & 23rd St, (800) 778-7290. Worthwhile cowboy, Indian and pioneer museum. Free tours available on request (48 hrs notice req). Open Mon-Fri 8 am-5 pm, w/ends noon-5 pm, $3. Also the **Old West Museum**, Frontier Park, 778-7290 has splendid collection of horse-drawn vehicles, Oglala Sioux beadwork. Open Mon-Sat 8 am-5 pm, Sun 10am-5 pm; $3.

TRAVEL/INFORMATION
Greyhound, 634-7744, at 120 N Greeley Hwy.
Cheyenne Area Convention and Visitors Bureau, 309 Lincoln Way, 778-3133.

DEVIL'S TOWER NATIONAL MONUMENT Accorded inter-galactic notoriety in *Close Encounters of the Third Kind*, Devil's Tower was declared the nation's first national monument in 1906 in recognition of the special part it played in Indian legend. A landmark also for early terrestrial explorers and travellers, the monolith is a fluted pillar of sombre igneous rock rising 865 feet above its wooded base and 1280 feet above the Belle Fourche River. Open year-round, $10 entrance fee per vehicle.

NB: 'Tower can be climbed safely *only* by experienced rock-climbers and takes about 4 hours. Descent 1 hour.'

The scene is 'creepily impressive, much more so than the movie.' In the park are prairie-dog villages, an outdoor amphitheatre and ranger programmes in summer (talks, demos and guided walks on the subject of wildlife, rockclimbing or the monument, 9.30am-4.30 pm). Park Visitors' Center: 467-5501; open 8 am-7 pm.

ACCOMMODATION
Campsites at the monument open year- round; $8 per night.

Arrowhead Motel, 214 Cleveland St in **Sundance**, 283-3307. S/D$55, T-$60. 'Most clean and attractive. Friendly, helpful and bright.'

YELLOWSTONE NATIONAL PARK   Established in 1872, the oldest and perhaps the most well-loved of the national parks, Yellowstone comprises 2.2 million acres, covering the northwest corner of Wyoming and dribbling over into Idaho and Montana. Three of the five entrances are in Montana; they and the gateway cities of Gardiner, Bozeman and West Yellowstone are discussed in the Montana section. Wyoming park entrances are from the east via Cody, from the south via Jackson/Grand Teton National Park.

Drought and 40- to 70-mile-per-hour winds set the stage for the uncontrollable forest fires of 1988. The fires burned a mosaic pattern throughout nearly 800,000 acres, but only half of this acreage was blackened, and much of this is quickly rejuvenating. None of the major attractions were disturbed.

Yellowstone is one of the world's most impressive thermal regions. Besides Old Faithful (which blows over 130-foot, dispelling 5,000-8,000 gallons of water every 79 minutes or so), there are some 10,000 thermal features including geysers, hot springs, colourful paint pots and gooey mud pools—an uncanny array of colours, temperatures, smells, disquieting sounds and eruptions. Old Faithful is the most famous, but many others erupt more frequently nearby and also in the **Norris Junction area**. There you can see hundreds of geysers and pools on a walk of less than two miles.

Another priority should be the **Grand Canyon** of the **Yellowstone River**, whose 1,540 foot gorge is 'one wild welter of colour', as Rudyard Kipling put it. 'Breath-taking—even better than the Arizona one.' The river tumbles into the canyon through the **Lower Falls**, twice the height of Niagara Falls. **Artist Point** gives possibly the most scenic view of Yellowstone—look over the sheer drop of 700 feet to the canyon below. Also do not miss **Yellowstone Lake**, famous for its trout, and 110 miles of shoreline and sublime scenery, nor '**Morning Glory**', a deep turquoise lake rimmed with gold along the Firehole River.

A wildlife sanctuary, the park is home to over 200 species of birds and over 60 species of mammals including deer, moose, bison, and bear. Because so many people fed the bears (often being hurt in the process by these naturally wild, 3ft tall, 300-400 pound animals), the park has removed many of them to remote areas. Over 100 who had become real menaces over the years had to be shot—all due to human meddling. If you do sight bears, do not feed them, get close to them, or come between an adult and cubs. The bears are wild, and meant to stay that way.

Cars were not admitted to the park until 1915; today, about 800,000 of them enter, with attendant traffic jams, accidents, pollution and parking problems. But as in other parks, visitors tend to congregate in the same places, leaving the rest of the park refreshingly empty.

Challenging hikes include the $3^1/_2$-mile walk to the summit of **Mt Washburn** (but stay on trails, don't take shortcuts). If you have more time, rent a canoe at West Yellowstone and canoe/camp the **Lewis River** to the **Shoshone Lakes** - a pristine, wildlife-filled journey. Many campsites (free permit required) along the route and at the lake. 'Don't forget Canyon and Upper Falls—on a par with Grand Canyon!'

The park is open year-round ($20 per car, good for 7 days), but the official season runs May to September, after which bus service and other facilities cease and there is a real chance of snow. Offseason months, the only roads and entrance open are via Gardiner. However, you can take a snow coach from West Yellowstone. Yellowstone in winter is enchanting: the wildlife move in close to the warmth of the geysers and thermal springs—awesome to see them in the swirling mists. You can actually ski or snowshoe close to bison and elk. www.nps.gov/yell/.
Park Information: 344-7381.

ACCOMMODATION
Lodging outside the park is discussed under West Yellowstone and Gardiner, Montana. See also Cody.
Within the Park: 9 different lodges and cabin clusters are available for individuals and small groups. Prices range from $26 a night for a cabin without linens or running water up to $88 for fully equipped lodges. **Roosevelt Lodge** is the cheapest, $29-$74, 'only place worth the money'. Other bargains are **Old Faithful Snowlodge**, $49-$95, and **Old Faithful Lodge and Cabins**, $27-$44. Lodges open and close at different times in spring and fall. Call 344-7311 to reserve space.
Camping: 12 campgrounds with more than 2300 sites are available for $8-$22 a night. Usually filled before noon in summer, first-come first-served. 'If you are prepared to sleep in the car, you can use the high bear-risk campsites.' 'Arrive before 8pm if you want a shower—or use hotel as we did.' Camping can be very cold, even in July, so bring a warm sleeping bag. To camp outside the developed sites and away from all the RVs, obtain a free permit at one of the park's visitor centres, where you can also buy a necessary hiking map. Do not sleep with food near you. At night some bears can't distinguish between bags of crisps and bags of people! Winter camping at Mammoth Campground only.

FOOD
Six concessions in the park, none particularly cheap. If you can manage, bring in groceries from West Yellowstone.

TRAVEL
AmFac Parks and Resorts, 344-7901, tours Lower and Upper Loops of the park, $25-$27. 'Clerks at West Yellowstone very helpful with advice.' 'You can make your own combinations.' Hitching within the park is rated 'very easy'. Greyhound: see W Yellowstone, MT.

GRAND TETON NATIONAL PARK Twenty miles due south of Yellowstone and 15 mins from Jackson lies the totally different world of the Grand Teton Mountains. As awe-inspiring as Yellowstone, this 500 sq ml park reminds one of Alpine Europe rather than the American West. The Tetons rise without preliminaries from a level valley to sharp pinnacles more than 13,000 feet high, separated by deep glaciated clefts. On their crags and flanks, you see remnants of the last great glaciation that once covered North America, 10,000 years ago. Besides peaks, valleys like Jackson Hole, the lakes and the winding Snake River add up to a stirring environment. Jackson Hole, Jenny Spring and Solitude Lakes make good if icy swimming.

Warm clothes and tough shoes are essential here. There are many excellent hiking trails and this is mountaineering country; several schools have their headquarters in the area. Free permits for climbing must be obtained from a park ranger, and it's not for novices.

One of the best ways to absorb the Tetons is to float down the Snake River on a large rubber raft steered by boatmen. In the forests at river's edge you may see some of the wapiti (elk) which form the largest herd in America. Commercial river rafting tours abound, but depending on your karma you may meet up with a group of locals who are already going. Join in—but remember Snake River rapids require skillful handling.

Admission to the park is combined with Yellowstone: a $20 pass is good for 7 days in both areas. Visitor centres are located in Colter Bay and Moose, 739-3399. www.nps.gov/grte/

ACCOMMODATION
Lodging both in the park and in nearby Jackson tends to be more costly than at Yellowstone and vicinity. Call 543-2811 for details of **Colter Bay Village Cabins** in the park, and **Jackson Lake Lodge.** Both very reasonable. At Colter Bay, one room (8 people) in a tent cabin w/shared bath is $18pp; $60-$84 for two people in a log cabin. The tent cabins are cheaper and more 'adventurous', constructed of canvas and logs, with outdoor grill and woodburning stoves. Bring own bedding for bunks. Cabins at Jackson Lodge are from $99 for two people. Try also **Signal Mountain** cabins in Moran, 543-2831, D-$75.

JACKSON   A cross between Aspen and Boulder, pretty and gentrified Jackson draws crowds of boisterous tourists in summer, but in winter the tiny village entices gentler, more noble visitors when 10,000 elk come to graze at the edge of town. Capture some of this magic on a sleigh ride through the elk refuge, 733-9212, $7.50. In the spring, local boy scouts collect and sell antlers, some of which end up as aphrodisiacs in the Far East. Look out for the nose, mouth and folded arms of the 'Sleeping Indian' on the horizon.

ACCOMMODATION
Bunkhouse, 733-3668, 2 blks N of town square, 215 N Cache St, PO Box 486, WY 83001. $15 dorm. The hostel has lounge with TV, kitchen.
The Hostel 'X', Box 546, Teton Village, 12 miles north of Jackson, 733-3415. $20 in small dorms. Game room, lounge with fireplace.
Grand Teton Lodge Co. has tent cabins, with canvas-covered patio, double-deck bunks, outdoor grill, picnic table, woodburning stove, $26 for two, XP-$3. 45 miles N of Jackson on Hwy 89. Write to reserve: PO 240, Moran, WY 83013; or call 543-2811.

FOOD
Bubba's, 515 W Broadway, 733-2288. Good home cooking; breakfast $3.85, sandwiches $3.80.
Mountain High Pizza Pie, 120 W Broadway, 733-3646. Traditional, deep-dish and whole wheat crusts, $6.25-$10. Outdoor seating; plays Dead music.

ENTERTAINMENT
For good reading, pick up a copy of *Jackson Hole News* or *Jackson Hole Guide*. Both have been awarded 'best weekly in the nation' over the years, and the competition continues. Try **JJ's Silver-Dollar Bar**, with 2,000 silver coins embedded in the counter; or the **The Rancher**, 733-3886, facing the town square. Large pool hall, open 11am-2 pm, bar food from $2-$6. The **Mangy Moose**, in Teton Village, 733-9779 has live bands, $1-$5 cover. The **Jackson Hole Brew Pub**, 265 S Millward, 739-2337 has 12 beers incl stout, porter and largers; free tours. For good music, try

Stagecoach, 733-3451; disco on Thurs nights, bluegrass on Sun.
Jackson Hole Llamas, 739-9582, (800) 830-7316. 5-hr trek with llamas (by group request only) includes lunch and a spectacular view of the Tetons, $500 an outing (ie. 10 people - $50 each). Also available: longer guided trips in Teton, Yellowstone, and Wind River areas, but they're expensive.
Teton Village, 12 mls northwest of Jackson offers skiers the largest vertical rise in the USA—4139 ft to **Rendevous Peak**. A 63-passenger aerial tram services the peak year round.

TRAVEL/INFORMATION
Start Buses, 733-4521, runs a service between Jackson and Teton Village twice a day, $1.
Jackson Hole Airport, about 8 miles from town. **Allstar Transportation** runs a shuttle service from the town's hotels to the airport, $12, or a taxi for $16. Phone ahead to request service.
Jackson Hole Chamber of Commerce, 532 N Cache St, 733-3316. For all local information and help. Hitching is described as 'very easy'.

CODY It may look like endless motels, but be not dismayed. Cody possesses a superlative, four-in-one museum complex and an Old Trail Town that are well worth your attention. About 60 miles east of Yellowstone, Cody is of course the namesake of William F, also known as Buffalo Bill, bison hunter/army scout/Pony Express rider turned showman. His Wild West show was one of several that earned their players a living by touring the US, Canada and Europe with a mawkish morality play of brave cowboys and savage redskins—very popular at the time. Royalty loved it; Queen Victoria gave Cody a diamond brooch, saying his show was so exciting she found it 'almost impossible to sit'. Annie Oakley and Sitting Bull were among Buffalo Bill's prize 'exhibits'; the mythology created thereby was later recycled by Hollywood.

East of Cody, the vividly coloured strata of **Shell Canyon** along the winding stretch of Highway 14 between Shell and Sheridan is highly scenic; to reach Custer's Last Stand in Montana, turn north at Sheridan.

ACCOMMODATION
Irma Hotel, 1192 Sheridan Ave, 587-4221. Luxurious and expensive, S/D-$80-$90 (annex rooms-$63-69), but a grandly historic place built by Buffalo Bill and named after his daughter. If you don't stay, at least stop by for a drink at the incredible French cherrywood bar, a gift from Queen Victoria after BB's command performance in England. Lunches ($4.95-$6) and even dinners are very good value at the Irma Grill.
Pawnee Hotel, 1032 12th, 587-2239. S-$28-$32, D-$32-36.
Rainbow Park Motel, 1136 17th St, 587-6251. S/D-$47, T-$60.

OF INTEREST
Buffalo Bill Historical Center, 720 Sheridan, 587-4771. Daily 7 am-10 pm, June through August, 8 am-8pm thereafter; $8 ($6.50 w/stud ID). Contains 4 museums: The **Buffalo Bill Museum** holds Cody memorabilia, BB's boyhood home. The **Plains Indian Musuem** is huge, imaginative and head-and- shoulders above most Indian collections. The **Whitney Gallery of Western Art** has bluechip Western painters: Remington, Catlin, Russell and Bierstadt's work on Yellowstone. Recently opened in a new gallery is the **Cody Firearms Museum** (formerly the Winchester Gun Museum), with over 5,000 firearms from America and Europe.
Old Trail Town, 587-5302, 2 miles west in Shoshone Canyon. A well-conceived collection of historic buildings and relics from all over Wyoming from Cassidy and

Sundance's hideout to Jeremiah Johnson's grave. 'Non-gimmicky.' Open mid-May to mid-Sept, $3. Open 8 am-7 pm.

Buffalo Bill Dam Visitors Centre, 13 mls west of Cody on Hwy 14, 16-20 miles from Yellowstone, 527-6076. Exhibits, natural history; interactive displays show how this beautiful dam was built. Mon-Sun 8 am-8pm, free.

Rodeos early June-Aug, nightly on the west side of town. Enquire locally. The **Cody Stampede** is held annually from 1st-4th July.

INFORMATION
Cody Chamber of Commerce, 836 Sheridan Ave, 587-2297. Mon-Sat 8 am-7 pm, Sun 10am-3 pm.

THE PACIFIC STATES

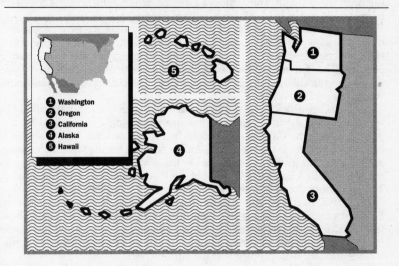

1. Washington
2. Oregon
3. California
4. Alaska
5. Hawaii

The Pacific states have everything and more. From ancient redwoods to modern cities, from lumbermen to film stars, from Polynesian huts to Arctic igloos, and in every state much of the most exciting scenery in America. The Russians, British, French, Spanish and Mexicans have all had claims here, and though Americans swept west under the conquering banner of Manifest Destiny, some of the old influences survive.

But the Pacific is also where the rainbow ends, where expectations must finally prove themselves. Enthusiasm reigns, and that is probably the region's most enjoyable quality—though the final results are still awaited.

ALASKA   *The Last Frontier*

Aleut for 'great land,' Alaska has a penchant for superlatives: biggest, coldest, costliest, highest peak, longest coastline, richest animal life, longest *and* shortest days.

Alaskans are proud people who are Alaskans first, and, by the way, Americans. The contiguous states, known as the 'lower 48' are far, far away, and Alaskans seem quite glad about that.

The state was jeered at as 'Seward's Folley' when President Lincoln's Secretary of State bought it from the Russians for 2¢ an acre in 1867. But no one laughed for very long, for gold was discovered only a few years later, inspiring a deluge of opportunists and virtually creating such towns as Skagway, Fairbanks and Juneau.

After becoming the USA's 49th state in 1959, Alaska proved fruitful again when one of the world's richest caches of petroleum was discovered in Prudhoe Bay in 1968. To tap its potential a consortium of oil companies financed the 800-mile Trans-Alaska Pipeline, which now brings 1.5 million barrels daily to Valdez, on Prince William Sound.

In an attempt to spread the oil profits equitably among native people and other Alaskans, the 1971 Alaska Native Claims Settlement Act puts emphasis on money and land ownership, concepts foreign to the state's native peoples. The Act has consequently had a devastating impact: you'll see many downtrodden and misplaced Indians, particularly in Fairbanks and Anchorage.

Alaska is breathtakingly beautiful and well worth visiting, particularly in summer when daytime temperatures are surprisingly warm and there's plenty of daylight. Campers and hikers be forewarned however: the unofficial state bird here is the mosquito. And watch out for the wildlife: humans are expected to give way to bears on trails and pathways. According to travel writer Erik Sandberg-Diment of the *Washington Post*, 'that part is easy. The part about doing it slowly, without running, is more difficult.'

The land route of the Alaska Highway from British Columbia to Fairbanks and Anchorage is an adventure, but the finest approach is by boat from Seattle or Prince Rupert. State-run, inexpensive ferries ply the Inside Passage year-round, allowing closeup looks at glaciers, islands, fjords, whales and stopover privileges at the various ports of call.

Prices in Alaska range from 'tolerable' in the SE panhandle to double those in Seattle, San Francisco and elsewhere. 'Some things are not much more than the lower 48, but be prepared for some nasty shocks.' Bus passes aren't valid in Alaska, but various tours are available Gasoline prices are on par with or slightly higher than California. Conventional lodging is very costly, but spartan youth hostels do exist, and there are campgrounds everywhere. (Come prepared for plummeting temperatures at night, although one reader notes that the American tourists simply wear their shorts over thermal underwear during the day.) Stick to locally grown produce and seafood to keep food costs down.

National Park: Denali (formerly Mt McKinley).

www.AlaskaOne.com/travel/alaska.htm. The telephone area code for the state is 907.

THE INSIDE PASSAGE and THE PANHANDLE Warmed by the Japanese Current and protected from the open sea by a necklace of islands, this southeastern waterway enjoys the state's mildest weather (a relative term meaning it rarely gets below zero in winter). Besides access by cruise ships, the state operates an extensive ferry system called the Alaska Marine Highway, an appropriate name since five of the seven ports in the Panhandle have no overland highway access to the outside world. 'Just the sight of a humpback whale breaching is enough to make the journey a memorable one.' 'Good vessels, interesting places to stop over, many opportunities to meet people.' 'In summer, Tongass Forest interpreters give free talks, film shows, on board. An imaginative and interesting service.'

First port of call is **Ketchikan**, still a salmon centre, now more dependent on cruise ship traffic. Weatherbeaten houses on stilts and the harbour give it a New England flavour, but it never rained like this in Massachusetts. The record here is 223.8" a year.

Sitka, once capital of Russian America and beautifully situated at the foot of Fuji-like Mt Edgecumbe, has a reconstructed Russian cathedral full of icons, plus interesting gravestones from this period. There is also a large and well-preserved collection of totems. James Michener spent much time here researching his book, *Alaska*.

Capital city, **Juneau**, climbs steep wooded hillsides with wooden stairways and a kaleidoscope of architectural styles. It's a great irony and a bone of contention among many Alaskans that the capital city is not reachable by highway, only by air or water. The once impassioned-campaign to move the capital city is on hold because of the expense involved. **Mendenhall Glacier**, 14 miles away (and accessible by car) has camping. From Haines, the old Dalton Trail leads off to the **Klondike**, several ghost towns and the amazing overhang of Rainbow Glacier.

In its sourdough heyday, **Skagway** was big-city size. Now down to a population of 767, it's reaping a new gold rush of tourists to photograph its well-preserved wooden sidewalks, false-front buildings and memorials to Soapy Smith, the local bad guy. 'On his birthday, locals urinate on his grave.' Best during the oldtime fervour of Sourdough Days, celebrated in September. *www.alaskainfo.org* specifically focuses on Alaska's Inside Passage and provides useful links to Inside Passage communities.

ACCOMMODATION
Alaska B&B Assoc, Juneau, 586-2959. Can help find you a room downtown from $65.

Alaskan Hotel, 167 Franklin, **Juneau**, (800) 327-9347. S-$55, D-$65 w/shared bath. S-$77, D-$80 w/private bath. Sauna, jacuzzi, some kitchenettes. On National Register of Historic Places, built 1913. Good bar!

Bear Creek Camp & Hostel, PO Box 1158, **Haines**, 766-2259. 1½ miles from Haines; located in pristine wooded area 1 mile from beach, hiking, fishing. Small store on premises. Free pickup/drop off from ferry. Summer: $14pp, wood-heated cabins. Private cabins, $38 for two, XP-$4. Hot showers, kitchen. Winter: cabins $25/$30. Camping from $5.

Eagles Nest Motel, 1183 Haines Hwy, **Haines**, 766-2891. S-$74, D-$84. TV, private bath.

Gilmore Hotel, 326 Front St, **Ketchikan**, 225-9423. Rooms from $70. Next door to **Annabel's Keg and Chowder House**, 7 am-10 pm (lunch $5-$10; dinner $20-$50).

Inn at the Waterfront, 455 S Franklin, 586-2050. Once a Gold Rush brothel! S-$51; D-$60. Bfast included.

Juneau Youth Hostel, 614 Harris St, Juneau, 586-9559. 3 blocks from downtown; $10 AYH. Kitchen, showers, large common room with fireplace. Year round, daily 7 am-9 am, 5 pm-11 pm. Rsvs req by mail, with $10 deposit included. 'A beautiful facility in a prime location.'

Ketchikan Reservation Service, 225-3273, provides info on B&Bs (S-$50-75). Ketchikan Youth Hostel, First United Methodist Church, Grant and Main Sts, 225-3319. June 1-Sept 1. $8 AYH, $11 non-AYH. 4-night limit, extendable by manager. Clean kitchen, common area, piano, hot showers, open for late-arriving ferries if call beforehand.

Sitka Youth Hostel, United Methodist Church, 303 Kimsham St, 747-8775. 1 June-31 Aug. $7 AYH, $10 non-AYH.

Skagway Inn, 7th and Broadway, 983-2289. B&B, 'delicious bfast.' Rooms begin $55, prices are reduced in winter. Shared bath, restaurant open May-Sept.

Camping: SEAVC, 228-6214, provides info and rsvs for Forest Service campgrounds, including **Signal Creek Campground**, 6 miles N of ferry terminal on Tongass Hwy, featuring attractive views and pleasant nature trails. Approx $10 at all state parks. In **Ketchikan**, 225-2148, US Forest Service manages **Ward Lake** area campgrounds, $20; 2-week limit June-Aug.

Also: Mendenhall Lake Campground near **Juneau**, on Montana Creek Rd. Sites $8; beautiful views of glacier. For rsvs call (800) 280-CAMP. Free camping on steep **Chilkoot Trail** from Skagway (no permit needed), but check-in with the Klondike Gold Rush National Park office, Broadway, 983-2921, first. Historic and breathtaking route—one of the most beautiful passes in Alaska—worth lingering.

FOOD
Armadillo Tex-Mex Café, 431 S Franklin St, 586-3442. 'Fantastic food,' serving locals and tourists alike. Mon-Sat 11 am-10 pm, Sun 4 pm-10 pm.

Channel Bowl Café, Willoughby Ave across from Juneau A&P, 586-6139. Get your $5.50 pancake bfast feast here! Daily 7 am-2 pm.

5 Star Café, 5 Creek St, 247-7827. Serves soup for $2.50 and delicious scones for $2. Mon-Sat 7.30 am-5.30 pm, Sun 9 am-5 pm.

Tatsuda's, 633 Stedman at Deermount St, 225-4125. The most convenient supermarket to downtown. Daily 7 am-11 pm.

OF INTEREST
Ketchikan: Salmon Capital of the World: see **Deer Mountain Fish Hatchery**, 225-6760, next to the Totem Heritage Center (see below). A self-guided tour explains artificial sex, salmon style. Daily 8 am-4.30 pm.

Historic Creek Street is the old red-light district with renovated stores and galleries and a colourful stretch of houses.

Dolly's House, 24 Creek St, 225-6329. A brothel turned museum. Antiques are set amid secret hideaways where Dolly kept money, bootleg liquor, and respectable customers during police raids. $3.

Tlingit (pronounced Klinkit!) **Totems** at Saxman Native Village (2 miles south by bus) have a woodcarver on site, 9 am-5 pm; Totem Bight State Park (10 miles north), and Totem Heritage Center, 601 Deermont St, 225-5900. It is the largest collection of authentic, pre-commercial totem poles in the US. Daily 8 am-5 pm, $3; Sun afternoon free. Go see Totems 160 yrs old as well as more contemporary ones.

Ketchikan Museum, 225-5600, 629 Dock St, downtown, with displays on local history, art, native heritage and fishing. Mon-Sun 8 am-5 pm; $2.

Sitka: Sitka National Historical Park, Lincoln St, at the other end of which is **Castle Hill**, the actual spot where the sale of Alaska from Russia to US occurred. Daily 8 am-6 pm, free.

Russian Bishops' House, Lincoln St, 747-6281. Largest and last remaining Russian-built home in Alaska. Daily in summer 8 am-5 pm ; otherwise by appointment only, $3, free w/student ID.

Sheldon Jackson State Museum, 104 College Dr, 747-8981. Impressive collection of artefacts, representing all four native groups of Alaska: Eskimos, Aleutians, Athabaskans and NW Indians. Jackson began the Indian Trading School, a boarding school for natives in Alaska. Building itself is a National Historical Site, the first concrete building in Alaska. Daily in summer, 8 am-5 pm; Tue-Sat 10 am-4 pm after Sept 15, $3.

Southeastern Alaska Indian Cultural Center, 106 Metlakatla St (in park), 747-8061. Tlingit Indian craftsmen and artists at work. Daily 8 am-5 pm in summer, Mon-Fri 9 am-5 pm in winter.

St. Michael's Cathedral, 747-8120, Russian Orthodox, in middle of street in centre of town. Stunning, built during Russian period, burned in 1966 and since restored. Mon-Sat 11 am-3 pm.

Juneau: Alaska Historical Society and Museum, 4th and Main. Exhibits on mining and city history. Also see the **State Museum**, 465-2907, on Whittier St for good artefacts; $2, free w/student ID. In summer, nightly salmon bakes, self-guided walking tours of historic Juneau, through the Division of Tourism at 33 Willoughby St, 9th floor, 465-2010.

Alaskan Brewing Co, 5249 Shaune Dr (in Lemon Creek), 780-5866. The beer has been awarded prizes galore and been featured in *Northern Exposure*. $1/2$ hr tours of the brewery: Tues-Sat 11 am-4.30 pm summer; Thurs-Sat 11 am-4.30 pm winter. The slopes of the **Eaglecrest Ski Area**, 155 S Seward St, Juneau 99801, 586-5284 on Douglas Isl, offer alpine skiing in winter. Call for prices. Glacier Bay National Park, 50 miles NW of Juneau, 697-2225. Beautiful and untouched wilderness of seals, whales, bears and 20 glaciers. Access by boat or plane only; expensive. 'Awesome.'

Hiking in Juneau: If you're looking for the best view of Juneau, go to the end of 6th St and head up the steep, 4 mile trail to the summit of **Mt Roberts** (3576ft). Haines: Old Ft Seward, 766-2202, now a centre for the Chilkat dancers. Don't miss Indian artists at work on totems, masks, and soapstone, Mon-Fri 9 am-5 pm, Memorial Day-Labor Day. Near Haines is the world's largest concentration of **bald eagles**; best months Oct & Nov.

Skagway: Klondike Gold Rush National Park, 983-2921. The 7-block historic Broadway Street contains many restored structures, leftovers from the Gold Rush days. Daily 8 am-6 pm.

Trail of '98 Museum, 983-2420, Arctic Brotherhood Hall, btwn 2nd and 3rd Ave on Broadway. Gold Rush and Native artefacts on display. Fascinating stuff. 9 am-5 pm daily. $2, $1 w/student ID.

INFORMATION

Ketchikan: Southeastern Alaska Visitors Center (SEAVC), on waterfront, 228-6214. Provides info on Ketchikan an entire Panhandle, esp good on outdoors. May-Sept daily 8.30 am-4.30 pm; Oct-April Tues-Sat same hrs.

Visitors Bureau, at the City Dock, 131 Front St, (800) 770-3300. May-Sept daily 7 am-5 pm, limited winter hrs.

Sitka: Visitors Bureau, 303 Lincoln, 747-5940.

Juneau: Davis Log Cabin, 134 3rd St at Seward St, 586-2201/586-2284. Visitors centre Mon-Fri 8.30 am-5 pm.

Division of Tourism, 33 Willoughby St, 9th Flr, 465-2010. Mon-Fri, 8 am-5 pm and Sat & Sun in summer.

National Forest and National Park Services, in Centennial Hall, 101 Egan Dr at Willoughby, 586-8751. Provides info on/rsvs for Forest Service cabins in **Tongass National Forest. Skagway: Visitors Bureau**, 2nd & 3rd at Broadway, 983-2854. 8.30 am-noon and 1-5 pm daily.

TRAVEL

Alaska Marine Highway, PO Box R, Juneau, AK 99802-5535, 225-6181. Contact for rsvs, schedules and other info. Alternatively, place a rsvs by filling out an online form via *www.alaska.alaskan.com/~ams/ferry/*. Bellingham, WA — Skagway, $246; Juneau-Haines $20; Juneau-Sitka, $26. Meals, staterooms cost extra, run at or below hotel prices. 'Tolerates camping out and sleeping bags on top-deck solarium for those who have the gear and can't sleep on reclining seats.' 'Board early if you want a place on the solarium.' 'Boat deck is heated, has camping beds, showers, lockers provided free.' 'Cafeteria good value, but taking your own food definitely advisable.' Only one ferry makes the complete Bellingham-Skagway run, once a week in summer. 'Very crowded.' 3 ferries work Prince Rupert-Skagwag, runs Sun, Tues, Thurs & Sat, $124. Rsvs necessary on all services.

Allstar Rent-a-Car, 9104 Menden Hall Mall Rd, 790-2414. Provides shuttle from airport or ferry terminal to their office.

Gray Line, (800) 544-2206. Runs buses from Haines to Anchorage, Tues,Wed, Fri and Sun at 8.15 pm, takes two days, $190. Also Skagway-Whitehorse daily at 7.30 am, $52. Both services only run 'til mid-September.

THE ALASKA HIGHWAY For years nearly all gravel or dirt-surfaced, the highway nowadays is paved from top to bottom. Beginning at Dawson Creek, British Columbia, it's 915 miles to Whitehorse in the Yukon and a total of 1,420 to its official end in Delta Junction. To reach Fairbanks, take the Richardson Hwy, a continuation of the Alaska Highway. The Glenn Highway out of Tok leads to Anchorage.

ACCOMMODATION
Plenty of expensive motels along the way. Also numerous campgrounds; bring a tent. In and near Tok:
TOK International Youth Hostel, PO Box 532, Tok, AK 99780, 883-3745. Hrs away from any large city, offers clean air, solitude and starry skies. Clean and comfortable, kitchen, beds, all in a big tent. Fishing in the Tanana River; Eagle Trail is 3 miles from hostel. Summer only; $7.50.

TRAVEL
'Make sure your car is in good running order and carry a few of the more essential spare parts. Garages charge what they like for spares.' Gas stations are every 20-50 miles, occasionally as far apart as 100 miles. Hitching: long waits. Don't get let off at Tok Junction (which gets below-zero temps in Sept): 'horror stories abound of people getting stuck.' Alaskan law requires motorists to pick up hitchhikers when it is very cold out, but we don't recommend you put this to the test. As always, be careful.
Greyhound: year-round, fewer schedules in winter. Informative drivers; informality reigns. Call (800) 231-2222.

INFORMATION
Tok Information Center, Alaska Public Lands Info Center, PO Box 359, Tok, AK 99780, 883-5667. 'Friendly, helpful.' Before setting out on your journey, pick up a copy of the free pamphlet *Help Along the Way* at a visitors bureau, or contact the **Department of Health and Social Services**, PO Box 110601, Juneau, AK 99811, (907) 465-3030. Includes exhaustive listing of emergency medical services and emergency phone numbers throughout Alaska, the Yukon, and British Columbia, plus tips on preparation and driving. Also: *Milepost* ($19.95 + $4.50 shipping in US, more for UK), is an essential mile-by-mile guide to the Hwy, both Alaska and Canada portions. To order: Vernon Publishing, 300 Northrup Way #200, Bellevue, WA 98004 or call (800) 726-4707 in Seattle. Free, useful literature about Alaska from **Division of Tourism**, PO Box E, Juneau, AK 99801, 465-2010.

ANCHORAGE Largest city (250,000) in Alaska and unremarkably modern since its rebuilding after the 1964 earthquake, Anchorage makes a good excursion base for Mt McKinley, the peninsula and the islands of southwestern Alaska. The quake sunk some of the land around here below sea level, inundating the ground with salt water. The result is an eerie vista of sodden, sterile land and skeletal trees.

Besides its transportation links and a fairly rambunctious nightlife, Anchorage also dabbles in the business of love: its *Alaskamen*, published every two months, provides profiles and photos of eligibles for women in the lower 48, and is so far credited with 170 engagements and marriages. Single men outnumber single women in Alaska by 7-1, ripe conditions for match-making. *Alaska scenes* at *www.alaska.net/~design/scenes/* provides scenery and events in Anchorage, including photo essays about the Fur Rondy, State Fair, wildlife and seasons.

ACCOMMODATION
Both **Alaska Private Lodgings**, 1010 W 10th Ave, 258-1717, and **Stay With A Friend**, 3605 Arctic Blvd #173, 278-8800, can refer you to B&Bs.

Anchorage International HI Hostel, 700 H St at 7th, 276-3635. 7.30 am-noon, 2 pm-12 am. $15 AYH, $18 non-AYH. Laundry, kitchen. 'Good place, easy to meet people.' 'Very crowded July-Aug.' Lockout noon-5 pm. Curfew 1 am; check-in 'til 3 am. 3-night max in summer. Rsvs rec 1 day before.

Inlet Inn, 539 H St, downtown, 277-5541. No-frills budget chain; D-$65, cheaper in winter. South of Anchorage on the New Seward Hwy, in **Girdwood**: **Alyeska Home Hostel**, PO Box 104099, Anchorage, AK 99510, 783-2099. $9 AYH, $12 non-AYH. Wood-burning stove; 6 bunks, no laundry or bathing facilities. Rsvs req. **Note**: All hostel rsvs may be booked through Alaska AYH Council, 562-7772. North of Anchorage on Hwy 1 (btwn Palmer and Glennallen): **Sheep Mountain Lodge**, HC03 Box 8490, **Palmer**, AK 99645, 745-5121. Summer only; $14 AYH, $17 non-AYH. Cabins also available, D-$60, including sauna. Free showers with both. Hot-tub, jacuzzi extra. Restaurant with home-cooked meals. Hiking. In **Seward**: **Snow River International Home Hostel**, HCR 64, Box 425, Seward, AK 99664. $12 AYH, $15 non-AYH. Kitchen, bathroom. Must have sleeping bag.

Camping: Chugach State Park, 354-5014; two of the best areas are **Eagle River**, 688-0998, $16, and **Eklutna**, 694-2108, $11, respectively 12½ miles and 26½ miles NE of Anchorage along Glenn Hwy.

FOOD/ENTERTAINMENT
Blondie's Café, at corner of 4th and D St, 279-0698. All-day bfast includes 3 hot-cakes, $4.25. Daily 5 am-midnight.

Mr Whiteky's Fly-by-Night Club, 3300 Spenard Rd, 279-SPAM. Even in darkest Alaska, you can satisfy that unquenchable craving for Spam! This 'sleazy' place has Spam entrees in every imaginable configuration, as well as great nightly entertainment ('adult' musical show 'Whale Fat Follies,' from $10, pokes fun at Alaska and its tourists, 8-10.30 pm). Menu has now been 'expanded' to include desserts, sandwiches and seafood. Also serves fine champagnes, the rec accompaniment to spam. (Your spam is free when you order Don Perignon.) Tue-Sat, 4 pm-2.30 am.

Twin Dragon, 612 E 15th Ave (near Gambell), 276-7535. Lunch buffet of marinated meats and vegetables, $6.25. A favourite among Anchorage's knowledgeable diners. Daily 11 am-midnight.

OF INTEREST
Alaska Experience Theater, 705 W 6th Ave, 276-3730. 40 mins of Alaskan adventures on the inner surface of a hemispherical dome. Every hr, 9 am-9 pm; $7.

Earthquake Park, close to town off Northern Lights Blvd. Recalls the 1964 Good Friday earthquake. The quake was the strongest ever recorded in North America; 9.2 on the Richter scale.

Museum of History and Art, 121 W 7th Ave, 343-4326. Historic and ethnographic art from all over Alaska, as well as national and international art exhibits. A traditional dance series runs 3 times daily in summer ($4) and a summer film series shows at no extra cost. Daily 9 am-6 pm in summer, Tues-Sat 10 am-6 pm, Sun 1-5 pm, from Sept thru winter. $4. Walk, bike or skate along the **Tony Knowles Coastal Trail**, an 11 mile paved trail that skirts **Cook Inlet** on one side and the backyards of Anchorage's upper crust on the other.

Nearby: Ekoutna Burial Grounds, 26 miles N on Glenn Hwy. Indian cemetery with spirit houses that look like doll houses, interesting gravesites. Get info from visitors bureau. 'Fascinating.' There are still regular earth tremors—'one of 5.5 while we were here'—but nothing to compare with the 1964 monster quake—yet.

Must-see: the magnificent **Columbia Glacier**, 440 square miles of ice over a half-mile thick surging into Prince William Sound east of Anchorage. No overland access, but West Grey Line Tour, 547 W 4th Ave, 277-5581, operates the expensive **Glacier Queen** to the glacier's edge, where the Columbia 'calves' (breaks off) into the sea. Incipient icebergs are born with a thunderous roar and fountains of salt water and ice; the seals sunning themselves on ice floes nearby remain unperturbed. '*Go*—you'll never forget it.'

Portage Glacier, 53 miles S of Anchorage. Gray Line, 277-5581, offers several tours: 1 hr cruise leaving from dock on Portage Lake, $21; 7¹/₂-hr tour includes transport to Portage Glacier and 1 hr cruise, $55. Gray Line and other tours available from Anchorage call at Alyeska Ski Resort, 40 miles S, on the way. Award winning film *Voices of the Ice* shown at Portage Glacier Visitors Information Center (end of Portage Hwy), 783-2326, 9 am-6 pm daily, by donation. 'Superb.' 'A must.'

INFORMATION
Log Cabin Visitor Information Center, W 4th Ave at F St, 274-3531. Dispenses lots of maps, including **Bike Trails** guide. Daily 7.30 am-7 pm (summer); 8 am-6 pm May-Sept; 9 am-4 pm (winter).

Alaska Public Lands Information Center, 605 W 4th Ave, 271-2737. Daily 9 am-6 pm. (Camping and shuttle rsvs for Denali National Park stop at 6 pm.) Info on state and federal recreational lands. 'Helpful; friendly people.'

TRAVEL
Anchorage International Airport, 266-2525. Serviced by 8 international and 15 domestic carriers: **Delta**, (800) 221-1212; **Northwest Airlines**, (800) 225-2525; **United**, (800) 241-6522, and **Alaska Airlines**, (800) 426-0333. Nearly every airport in Alaska can be reached from Anchorage, either directly or through a connecting flight in Fairbanks.

The 80-yr-old **Alaska RR**, (800) 544-0552 runs btwn Anchorage and Fairbanks via Denali National Park ($135 one-way); call 456-4155, daily 7 am-5 pm. One train daily each way. Anchorage to Seward train ($80 r/t) passes within 800 ft of a glacier. In winter, 1 p/wk to Fairbanks; no service to Seward. Also daily bus from Anchorage to Portage, **Alaskon Express**, (800) 544-2206. Tip: take $16 train, departs 11 am and 3 pm, to Whittier, then $20 bus to Portage; several times weekly to Seward. 'Not a good town to be without a car.'

Affordable Car Rental, 4707 Spenard Rd, 243-3370. Charges $35 daily with unlimited mileage. You must be at least 21 w/major credit card.

DENALI NATIONAL PARK   Mount McKinley has twin peaks, the south being higher at 20,320 ft. Although native Indians originally named the mountain (and the park) Denali, meaning 'the tall one,' it was renamed for US president William McKinley while he was campaigning. A later president, Jimmy Carter, had the mountain officially renamed Denali in 1979.

This giant, tallest in North America, surveys a vast kingdom of tundra, mountain wilderness and unusual wildlife (caribou, Dall sheep, moose, grizzlies). The highway over **Polychrome Pass** into the valley of Denali is astonishing: a huge bowl, rimmed with frozen Niagaras of clouds tumbling over the encircling cliffs, spreads out before you. And in the distance, Denali itself, shrouded in cloud cover 75 per cent of the time in summer.

Eighty-six miles of gravel road allow you to see much of the park by bus (you can go into the park only 12 miles by car, unless you have a campsite reserved), but hiking one of the trails radiating from McKinley Park Hotel is the best way to enter into the spirit of the place. Best views of the mountain-top at **Wonder Lake**—'have to go at least 8 miles into the park to see the mountain.' Visitors Center ½ mile up Park Rd, 683-1266/1267, daily 8 am-8 pm 'til late September, then 7 am-6 pm. Pick up info on shuttle buses to Wonder Lake here. 'Fantastically situated; caribou come right up to the centre.' No food or gas in the park except at Park entrance. Don't overlook a trip to **Yentana**, the 'Galloping Glacier'—most beautifully coloured on earth. $3 entrance fee good for 7 days. Denali's National Park's website is at *www.nps.gov/dena/*

ACCOMMODATION
Denali Hostel, PO Box 801, Denali Pk, 683-1295, about 9½ miles N of park entrance. Friendly hosts will pick up from park (Visitor Centre) if you call ahead. Offer bunks, showers, kitchen and morning shuttles in/out park; $22. Seven **campgrounds** within the park line Denali Park Rd. Sites $6-12. Must have permit to camp inside park. For rsvs, call (800) 622-7275/272-7272; arrive early! Hikers waiting for a backcountry permit or a campsite can find space in **Morino Campground**, $6, next to hotel.

Grizzly Bear Cabins, 6 miles S of main entrance, 683-2696. Tent cabins, D-$23, T-$25, bath with showers with hot water nearby. Other cabins $52-$99 (subject to change). Rsvs rec (by VISA only), closed by Sep 10th.

TRAVEL
Free and frequent **shuttle bus** service to all 7 campgrounds in park 'til Labor Day, reduced after that. Booked up quickly but stand-bys available from 5.30 am. Shuttle buses leave **Denali Visitor Center**, 683-1266, daily, 5.30 am-2.30 pm.

Wildlife coach tours from the hotel rec; $45 with box lunch; lasts approx 7 hrs. Mid-May to mid-Sept. 'Interesting—*the* way to see wildlife and the park.' Rail, bus and air service from Anchorage and Fairbanks.

Camper buses, $15, move faster, transporting *only* people with campground permits/backcountry permits. Leave visitors centre 5 times daily. The final bus stays overnight at Wonder Lake, returns 7 am. You can get on/off bus anywhere along the road; flag the nxt one down. Good strategy for dayhiking/conv for Park explorers.

FAIRBANKS   Warmest place in Alaska in summer and one of the coldest in the winter, Fairbanks was once a frontier town with 93 saloons in one three-block stretch. Today the second largest city, a direct result of the Pipeline and oil boom, it is 150 miles S of the Arctic Circle. Try to time your visit for one of its many festivals: the Eskimo/Indian Olympics (dancing, blanket toss, etc) each July and the Solstice Festival, 19-21 June, are among the wildest. Play or watch midnight baseball at the latter. 'Definitely the rough frontier town—drunken Indians everywhere.' 'Surprisingly nice—lots of trees.' The Fairbanks Summer Arts Festival Home Page, *www.alaskas-best.com/festival/*, offers info on a wide range of musical, visual, skating and fine art courses in a two week festival.

ACCOMMODATION
For info on B&Bs, go to Visitors' Bureau, or call/write **Fairbanks B&B**, 902 Kellum St, Anchorage, 452-4967.

Ah! Rose Marie, 302 Cowles St, 456-2040. From D-$70. 'Loves students.' Close to bus line, centrally located.

Alaska's 7 Gables Inn, 4312 Birch Lane, 479-0751. From S/D-$75, XP-$10. Upmarket, special-treat inn with such delights as VCRs in every room and mouth-watering bfasts (peachy pecan crepes and raisin bran muffins.) Inclusive: 'gourmet' bfasts, bikes, canoes, jacuzzis, TV, phones.

Alaska Heritage Inn Youth Hostel, 1018 22nd Ave, (907) 451-6587. Outfitted canoe and raft trips, wildlife viewing, horseback riding. $12 dorm; $30-60 private room.

Billie's Backpackers Hostel, 2895 Mack Rd, 479-2034, near Univ of Alaska. $15 a night; linen charge. Will collect from train station/airport.

Cripple Creek Resort Hotel, Ester City, 6 miles from Univ of Alaska, 479-2500. June-Labor Day. Group transport available from major downtown hotels. S-$46, D-$60. Former mining camp with traditional, family-style meals, saloon, nightly entertainment. Unusual and popular. Home to the Malemute Saloon, notorious in Alaska. 'Awesome Northern Lights show here.'

Delta Junction Youth Hostel, btwn Tok and Fairbanks (from Fairbanks take mile-post 272 on Richardson Hwy), PO Box 971, Delta Junction, 99737, 895-5074. $7; sleeping bags req, no smoking.

Fairbanks Backpackers Hostel, 2895 Mack Rd, (907) 479-2034. Next to Univ of Alaska. Great $5 bfast available: 'Best sourdough pancakes in Alaska!' Beautiful floral areas, volleyball and picnic area; $14-20.

Fairbanks International Youth Hostel, 400 Arcadia at the top of Birch Hill 456-4159, $15. If full, will help you find other accommodation in area. Will collect from airport/bus station.

Grandma Shirley's Hostel, 510 Dunbar St, 451-9816. Beats all other hostels to earn the title of uberhostel of Fairbanks! Showers, common room, free bike use; co-ed room with 9 beds; $15.

Camping: Tanana Valley Campground, 1800 College Rd, 456-7956. Grassy and secluded for its in-town location, sites from $12, tentsites for travellers on foot $6.

Chena River Campground, off Airport Way on University Ave, tent sites $15 for two.

OF INTEREST

Alaskaland, Airport Way and Peger Road, 2 miles outside city near airport, 459-1087. The 44-acre site, developed to commemorate the Alaska Centennial in 1967, portrays state history with gold rush cabins, a sternwheeler, Indian and Eskimo villages and a mining valley. Free, closes Labor Day. Food pricey, but gets praise: 'Alaska Salmon Bake—all you can eat; salmon, halibut, ribs, etc—lovely!' New 36-hole miniature golf course—the farthest north in the world! Old-fashioned carousel and train; various nightly shows. Also: **Fairbanks Summer Folk Fest** is held here in July, 457-6939. The **Large Animal Research Station**, is also worth a visit, and its tours offer a chance to see baby musk ox and other animals up close. Tours Tue/Sat 11 am and 1.30 pm; Thur 1.30 pm. $4 w/student ID. You can also grab your binoc-ulars and view the big beasts from the viewing stand on Yankovitch Rd.

Univ of Alaska Museum, 4½ miles NW of city, 474-7505. Features exhibits ranging from displays on the aurora borealis to a 36,000 yr old bison recovered from the permafrost; Eskimo arts and crafts. Daily 9 am-7 pm summer; 9 am-5 pm winter. $5. 'Superb, don't miss it.' 'Definitely one of Alaska's highlights.'

Eagle Summit, 108 miles along the Steese Hwy, from where you can watch the sun fail to set on 21 and 22 June.

INFORMATION

Alaska Public Lands Information Center (APLIC), 250 Cushman St #1A, Fairbanks 99707, 456-0527. Has exhibits and info on different parks and protected areas of Alaska. Daily 9 am-6 pm (summer); Tues-Sat 10 am-6 pm (winter).

Convention and Visitors Bureau Log Cabin, 550 1st Ave, nxt to Golden Heart Park, (800) 327-5774. Distributes the free Visitor's Guide. Daily 8 am-8 pm (summer), 8 am-5 pm (winter).

Univ of Alaska Student Union: info board for digs, rides, etc.

TRAVEL
Air (see Anchorage)
Alaska Railroad, 280 N Cushman St, 456-4155/1 (800) 544-0552. Runs one train daily from mid-May to mid-Sept; (once a week from mid-Sept, i.e. Sun to Anchorage; Sat r/t journey to Fairbanks), to Anchorage ($135), and Denali National Park ($50). Depot; Mon-Fri 7.30 am-430 pm, Sat-Sun 7.30 am-noon.
Municipal Commuter Area Service (MACS), 6th and Cushman St, 459-1011. Runs 2 rtes thru downtown and surrounding area. 'Very limited, most journeys $1.50.' Day pass $3. Transfers good within 1hr of stamped time. Daily 6.45 am-7.45 pm.'Fairbanks very difficult without a car.'
Parks Hwy Express, 479-3065, runs 6 buses p/wk to Denali ($20 o/w, $40 r/t) and Anchorage ($40 o/w, $75 r/t).

CALIFORNIA   *The Golden State*

California. The word beckons, like an incantation: the Far West inspires images of sun, sand, surfing, Hollywood, adventure, health foods, healthy people and easy life. But California is much more complex than its popular image implies. You could spend a lifetime in the Golden State and still not see it all. It has the natural beauty of several states combined: rich redwood groves containing the tallest trees on earth; the stark superlatives of Death Valley; and the dizzying glacier-carved heights of Yosemite Valley. Like Shangri-La, California is cut off from the rest of the world by uninviting terrain: the volatile Trinity Alps in the north and the Sierras in the east; the Mojave Desert in the south; and to the west, over 100 miles of sunny beaches and rocky precipices on the Pacific Ocean coast.

When pioneers crossed the prairie to California, they found a land with potential for riches beyond mere gold, a promise that has since been ful-filled. There's more of everything in California—more people (over 30 million) more money (it's the world's 6th largest economic power), and more science activity (a disproportionate share of the US's pure science research and more Nobel laureates than the former Soviet Union). A key partner in the emerging Pacific Basin economy, California leads in both agri-cultural and industrial output, from avocados to aerospace, from Silicon Valley to Sunset Strip.

Recently, however, the golden image has become a little tarnished. As unemployment figures rise, crime rates climb, LA riots and burns and is then hit by a killer earthquake. All the while the state gets more and more crowded, a certain disillusionment is apparent. The result: a *reverse* immi-gration trend, as Californians head *east* to seek the wide open spaces of states like Montana and Wyoming.

The major regions and cities of California are listed below, roughly from north to south. www.yahoo.com/Regional/U_S__States/California/
National Parks: Kings Canyon, Lassen Volcanic, Redwood, Sequoia, Yosemite

ACCOMMODATION OVERVIEW
Perhaps in response to its popularity, California offers a great variety of lodging options, many of them dead cheap. This is but a brief summary to supplement specific information listed under *ACCOMMODATION* for each region or city.

Youth Hostels: number about 40, with new ones opening all the time. Others are in a state of flux because of precarious funding. Always enquire locally—even the AYH handbook cannot keep pace with developments. There are also independent hostels—with private ownership, each hostel manager and houseparent has a great deal of interest in the hostel being operated to your satisfaction and for your safety, comfort and pleasure.

Motel 6: The chain began here, in the state that invented the motel. This mega-chain offers basic rooms at very reasonable rates. Call (800) 440-6000 to reserve a room anywhere in California. No pampering: their 6 pm 'show up or lose your rsvs' policy is extremely firm; if you book ahead, be sure you'll be able to arrive on time. If you pre-paid and can't get there, you need to cancel the rsvs before 6 pm or no money back. If you're stuck, **E-Z Motels**, have been recommended as a similar budget alternative. Call (800) 32-MOTEL

B&B Inns: A new comprehensive directory of Golden State B&B Inns is available on the Net or in printed form, produced by the **California Association of B&B Inns**. From San Diego to the Oregon border, the directory showcases more than 268 California inns. Contact California Association of B&B Inns, 2715 Porter St, Soquel, CA, 95073, (408) 462-0402, or *www.innaccess.com*.

University lodgings: Many universities throw their dorms open to travelling students in the summer; also, most have housing offices that may list information on temporary housing. Accommodation in university towns is often easy to get in the summer, when all the students are gone; it may be more difficult if the university town is also a resort town (eg. Santa Barbara, Santa Cruz, San Diego).

Camping: National Park and monument fees are from $6-$12 (in addition to an entrance fee of around $5 per vehicle.) Primitive campsites are often much less, sometimes free; most require permits for back country use. 'State campsites are a good deal if you have a carload of people. Very good facilities.''Police will allow sleeping on Southern Cal beaches (for foreign tourists anyway) but be careful—many are hangouts for gays with attendant queer-bashers.' Also, be advised that some coastal communities respond with hostility to car-or beach-sleepers—even those who are just passing through. Some local ordinances actually prohibit sleeping in any sort of vehicle within the city limits. To reserve campsites: For rsvs and campsite availability in CA state parks: call (800) 444-7275, $5-25 per site plus $6.75 service charge, sites can accommodate up to 8 people. For national forests throughout the West Coast, call (800) 280-CAMP, $5-$20 per site plus a ghastly $6 service charge. Most campsites at national parks are first come, first served; however, sites at Yosemite and Sequoia can be reserved 8 weeks in advance in person through MISTIX, call (800) 436-7275 or (800) 365-2267 for info, but be patient, the line is always busy.

NORTHERN COAST

The Northern Coast region is a land of rugged shoreline and pounding surf, of towering redwood forests and rushing rivers, of verdant hills and bountiful vineyards. Time spent here is time spent in Paradise.

Redwoods were plentiful on the American continent around the age of the dinosaurs. During the Ice Age, these trees barely escaped the fate of their old contemporaries. A narrow strip, stretching nearly 400 miles N of San Francisco to the Oregon border, was all that survived of the coastal species of *sequoia sempervirens*, this remnant was further repleted by logging early in this century.

You can see these majestic survivors in the very northwesternmost corner of the state along two stretches of Hwy 101: **Humboldt Redwoods State Park**, *www.northcoast.com/~hrsp/* (take a detour off the hwy north of

Garberville to see the **Avenue of the Giants**); and **Redwood National Park**, which stretches from Orick to Crescent City and encompasses three state parks. In this park—a 'UNESCO World Heritage Site'—are the world's tallest trees, two over 367 ft tall. The *North Coast Redwoods* brochure gives an idea of what each park has to offer; available from Humboldt Redwoods State Park and other hostels.

The telephone area code is 707.

ACCOMMODATION

This area is saturated with pricey bed and bfast inns, however, a variety of inexpensive local motels and interesting hostels means affordable accommodation should not be difficult to find.

Eel River Redwoods Hostel, 70400 US 101, Leggett, 925-6469. Closest hostel to world-famous Ave of the Giants. A small price for a slice of paradise; $13-$15. Sauna, jacuzzi, hiking, self-guided 'eco' and history tours, own pub (Friday night linguini specials), free bfast; $13-15. Stay 6 days, 7th free. Ask the bus driver to stop at the hostel. Check out web site at *www.hostel.com/~ebarnett/eelriver.html*

Humboldt Redwoods State Park, 946-2409. 3 campgrounds, $16 for up to 8 people, extra vehicle $5.

Klamath Redwood Hostel, at Wilson Creek Rd (12 miles S of **Crescent City**), 482-8265. Newly restored 19th century home; $9 AYH or non-AYH. Close to beach and Redwood Forest. Greyhound will stop here, local buses will not. Arrive before 9.30 pm.

Prairie Creek Motel, 488-3841, 2 miles N of **Orick** on Hwy 101, at the entrance to the Park. 1pp-$30, 2pp-$38. 'Friendly Swiss and German couple. Can't recommend highly enough.' Restaurant next door.

Redwood HI Hostel, 14480 US 101, Klamath at Wilson Creek, 482-8265. The northernmost link in the California coastal chain of hostels, this one is located in mist-shrouded Redwood National Park, a World Heritage Site and International Biosphere Reserve. The hostel promotes sustainable living concepts through recycling and conservation of natural resources. $12-14. Private rooms available. Linen $1. Dining room, laundry, kitchen, 2 sundecks overlooking ocean, staple foods for sale. Curfew 11 pm, out by 9.30 am. Rsvs recommended by mail 3 weeks in advance.

Camping: Redwood National Park, 464-6101, encompasses 3 state parks that offer campsites with showers, $12-14 p/night.

FOOD

Alias Jones, 983 3rd St, 465-6987. Known for serving hearty bfast portions. Mon-Fri 7 am-5.30 pm, Sat 7 am-3 pm.

Eureka's Seafood Grotto, 605 Broadway, Eureka, 443-2075. Choose your own seafood at reasonable prices. 'We ketch 'em, cook 'em, serve 'em!'

Mousse Cafe, corner of Alban and Kasten 937-4323, in **Mendocino**, has excellent black-out cake with layer upon layer of chocolate for $5.50. Daily for lunch 11.30 'til 4 pm, dinner and brunch on Sundays, closed 4 pm-5.30 pm.

Orick Market, 488-3225, daily 8 am-7 pm to stock up on supplies.

Palm Café, Rte 101 in Orick, 488-3381. A locals' joint with delicious homemade fruit pies. Daily 9 am-8 pm.

Prairie Creek Park Cafe, 2 miles N of **Orick** on Hwy 101 (take Fern Canyon exit), 488-3841. Chow down on elk, buffalo and boar as well as traditional American food for bfast, lunch or dinner, at the only gourmet restaurant in the area; $7-$16 dinners. Daily 8 am-9 pm. Close Nov-Mar.

Samoa Cookhouse, west of **Eureka**, across the Samoa Bridge spanning Humboldt Bay (turn left on Samoa Rd, take 1st left turn), 463-1424. This, the 'last of western cookhouses,' is worth searching for. Loggers ate here once, and food is still served lumberjack-style: dish after dish arrives at long, communal tables, and everyone digs in. You'd have to be a lumberjack to finish it all. Lunches around $6, dinners around $10.

OF INTEREST

The Northern Coast offers dozens of parks and beaches strung like pearls along the way; here you can experience nature at its most diverse and best. Take a leisurely cycle through vineyard country, hike in primeval forests, or ramble along clifftops for spectacular views of the ocean. Raft down racing rivers, soak in hot mineral springs or luxuriate in the ultimate mud-bath! In Eureka: **Carson House Mansion**, 2nd & M Sts, said to be the most photographed residence in America, you can only look at the exterior of this quintessential Victorian-Gothic style mansion. Many other examples of Victorian architecture can be found both here and in nearby Arcata. The town's old bank is home to the **Clarke Memorial Museum**, E St, 443-1947; a local history museum with an interesting collection of Victoriana and Indian baskets. Tue-Sat noon-4 pm, donations accepted. Heading south: The **Pacific Lumber Company**, 125 Main St, Scotia, 764-2222. A working Redwood sawmill and historic logging museum. Hear how a sawmill *can* be environmentally friendly; tours Mon-Fri 8 am-2 pm, free. 'Fascinating.'

Rockefeller Forest in **Humboldt Redwoods State Park** contains the largest grove of old-growth trees, some over 200yrs old; nearby, in **Founder's Grove**, is the The Tree World Hall of Fame, home to the tallest, widest and oldest trees in the world.

Not to be missed is the **Avenue of the Giants**, just north of **Garberville** off US 101. A 33 mile scenic hwy winds its way through majestic redwoods. 16 miles S of Garberville, in Leggett, is the **Drive-Thru-Tree**, 925-6363, where for a $3 park entrance fee, you can do just that (as many times as you wish!)

Skunk Train, 964-6371, Laurel St, **Ft Bragg**. Steam engine (diesel in winter) takes you 40 miles through tunnels and trees on an old logging run btwn Ft Bragg and Willits. $26 for full day, $21 for half, June-Sept. Rsvs rec.

Pygmy Forest, btwn Navarro and Noyo Rivers on Hwy 1; particularly visible around Jug Handle Creek, south of Ft Bragg. A 3 hr hike will take you back five hundred thousand years in time to see how the ocean has shaped this countryside. The 5 mile (r/t) trail dubbed **The Ecological Staircase** meanders through terraces carved by the Pacific. The fifth terrace is the Pygmy Forest, a land of stunted cypress and Bolander pine unique to this area. A 50 yr old tree may grow to no more than an inch in diameter and two to five feet in height. The town of **Mendocino** on Hwy 1, an artists' colony by the sea, is a wonderful place to stop, stretch and stroll. Artisans show & sell at Gallery Faire (crafts) and Studio 2 (jewellery), among others. The town appears as Cabot Cove in the TV series *Murder, She Wrote*. Be sure to visit **Mendocino Headlands State Park** while you're there. When they shot the movie, *The Russians are Coming* along the Mendocino coast, they were wrong: the Russians have been here and gone. See the well-restored proof at **Ft Ross**, a 19th century seal-hunting outpost, and the only genuine Russian military installation in the lower 48 states.

TRAVEL/INFORMATION

Crescent City Area Visitors Center (in Chamber of Commerce), at 1001 Front St, 464-3174. Daily 8 am-7 pm.

Gaberville Chamber of Commerce, 733 Redwood Dr, 923-2613. Daily 10 am-5 pm.

Greyhound, 1125 Northcrest Dr, 464-2807/(800) 231-2222, in Crescent City passes through the park, stopping near park entrance,. Two buses daily going north and two going south. **Tall Trees Shuttle** from ranger station to grove is a 40 min ride each way with 3 miles of walking through the trees; count on 4-5 hrs total. 'Superb walks through the redwood forest.'

Orick Visitors Center, 1 mile W of Orick on US 101, (707) 464-6101 ext 5265. Daily 10 am-2 pm.

Prairie Creek Visitors Center, 464-6101 ext 5300. Daily 10 am-2 pm.
Redwood Information Center at Orick Ranger Station, PO Box 7, Orick, CA 95555, 488-3461. 9 am-6 pm daily in summer, otherwise 9 am-5 pm.

MOUNT SHASTA and LASSEN VOLCANIC NATIONAL PARK   Some

160 miles NW of Sacramento lies one of the country's most beautiful and unspoiled regions—the Shasta Cascade; towering mountains, stunning waterfalls, dense forests and glistening lakes create a dramatic landscape, itself dominated by the 14,162-ft **Mt Shasta**, the white-haired patriarch of Northern California. Sharing the crest of the mountain is Shasta's slightly smaller mate, **Shastina**. Nearly overwhelmed by the massive pair is baby **Black Butte**, a pile of volcanic ash that attests to its parents' vigour.

Younger, shorter, hotter-headed sister to Mt Shasta is **Lassen Peak**, which last erupted in 1917—a wink of the geologic eye. Brilliantly bizarre moon-scape, nasty mudpots, pools of turquoise and gold, sulphurous steam vents reveal volcanic activity, especially in the **Bumpass Hell** area. You are free to climb the $2^1/_2$ miles to the three craters of Lassen: main road takes you near, trail is easy, fine views of Shasta and the devastation to the northeast. Excellent summer programmes: Ishi, the last Stone Age man in America, was found near Lassen, and the Manzanita Lake info centre has photo displays of him. Open year-round but snows keep most sectors inaccessible from late Oct to early June. Passes are valid for 7 days, $5 per car, $3 on foot. 'Yosemite is tame by comparison.' Park Info, 595-4444, 8 am-4.30 pm. **Cool Mountain Nights** in Mount Shasta at the end of August, features an outdoor concert, street fair, classic car show, blackberry bluegrass festival, Tin Man Triathlon and community bfast. Call (800) 926-4865. In **Yreka** there are several interesting museums, showing exhibits of native Americans, gold mining and local history. Call **Yreka Chamber of Commerce**, 842-1649, (800) ON-YREKA, for details.
The telephone area code is 916.

ACCOMMODATION
Pine Needles Motel, 1340 S Mt Shasta Blvd, 926-4811. S-$37, D-$42.
Swiss Holiday Lodge, 2400 S Mt Shasta Blvd, 926-3446. Pretty chalet, Tremendous view of Mt Shasta. S-$44, D-$46.
Camping: Lake Siskiyou, 4239 WA Barr Rd, Mt Shasta City, CA 96067, (916) 926-2618. A popular recreational lake featuring boating, swimming, fishing, sailing. Campground, RV park, grocery/deli.
Lassen Volcanic National Park, PO Box 100, Mineral, CA 96063, (916) 595-4444. Volcanic lava flows, hot springs, mud pots and old emigrant trails. Season is June 7 thru Oct 6; call Park Info 595-4444.
Trinity Lake, USDA Forest Service, PO Box 1190, Weaverville 96093, (916) 623-2121. Officially known as Clair Eagle lake, includes secluded bays and coves ideal for camping, fishing, houseboating, swimming and other water sports.

TRAVEL
Amtrak, serves Redding and Dunsmuir, (800) 872-7245.
Greyhound, 1321 Butte St, (800) 231-2222, serves Redding.

SACRAMENTO   In 1839 Swiss immigrant John Augustus Sutter landed

on the banks of the American River intending to create a trading post and haven for European immigrants; and was granted land by the Mexicans, within a decade a sawmill was built in nearby foothills. A foreman inspecting the mill one morning made a discovery that was to change history—a gold nugget glinting in the sun.

Sacramento mushroomed into prominence as a supply dump for Gold Rush miners. Today, the state's capital, at the confluence of the Sacramento and American Rivers, the city has a pleasant, midwestern feel. If the Gold Rush is your thing, then this is the place for you! All its sights are downtown; the best way to see them is on foot.

The telephone area code is 916. For listings of places to go, things to see and restaurants to dine at, look up *www.worldofweb.com/sacsite.html*

ACCOMMODATION

Alpenrose Cottage Hostel, 204 Hinckley St, 926-6724. Located in grounds of herb gardens. $13 p/night or $75 weekly. Rsvs rec.

Berry Hotel, 729 L St, 442-2971. Rooms from $45. 'Threadbare but friendly.' Weekly & monthly rates available. $2 key deposit.

Capitol Park Hotel, 9th & L Sts, 441-5361. 1$^{1/2}$ blocks from Greyhound. From S-$33, D-$40. 'Very central, very clean.'

Gold Rush Home Hostel, 1421 Tiverton Ave, 421-5954. $10.

Motel 6, 1415 30th St, 457-0777. Close to Sutter's Ft, accessible by bus. S-$45, D-$52, 2nd XP-$6, 3rd XP-$3. Pool, AC, noisy (freeway nearby).

Sacramento HI Hostel, 900 H St, 443-1691. 1885 Victorian mansion within easy walk to Amtrak, Greyhound and public transportation. Patio, gardens, veranda, recreation rm, videos, library, info centre, kitchen, laundry, linen rental, bike storage. $11-13. Private rooms available.

FOOD

Delta King Restaurant, Hotel and Saloon. 1000 Front St, Old Sacramento, 441-4440. Located right on river, providing food and entertainment. *www.deltaking.com/*

Fanny Ann's Saloon, 1023 2nd St, 441-0505. Philly, turkey sandwiches, salads. 'A pleasant change from burgers.' Daily 11.30 am-2 am.

Fox and Goose, 1001 R St, 443-8825. Real British pub fare, meals under $10. Daily 7 am-12 am, Fri & Sat 'til 2 am.

OF INTEREST

California State Railroad Museum, 125 I St, Old Sacramento, 445-7387. Steam train excursions along the scenic Sacramento river depart from the Central Pacific Freight Depot on Front & K Sts, summer w/ends, 10 am-5 pm, $5.

Crocker Art Museum, 216 O St, 264-5423. Stately old mansion with staid old paintings; catch the sometimes-wild modern art exhibits upstairs. Wed-Sun 10 am-5 pm, Thurs 'til 9 pm, closed Mon & Tue. $4.50.

The Grind Skatepark, for all skateboard, in-lining and BMX Evel Knievels is located at 2709 Del Monte, West Sacramento, 372-7655.

Old Governor's Mansion, 16th & H Sts, 323-3047. Charming wedding-cake Victorian building, now a state museum with furnishings donated by 13 former state governors, including Ronald Reagan. Daily 10 am-4 pm, $2. 'Best sight in city,' 'good tour and stories.'

Old Sacramento, 28-acre historic district on Sacramento River. The riverfront encompasses 26 acres of shops and restaurants in 1849 to 1870-vintage buildings, of which over 100 have been renovated and 41 of them are actual 19th century originals. Especially evocative at night. Includes **Sacramento History Center, Old Eagle Theatre, Pony Express Monument** and **California State Railroad Museum**.

Old Sacramento Riverboat Cruises, 110 L St Landing, 552-2933, (800) 433-0263. Sightseeing cruises, 1hr from $10.

Self guided walking tours of historical Sacramento, free maps available from Visitors Centre.

State Capitol, 10th St at Capitol Mall. Magnificently restored to its ornate, domed 19th century grandeur. Eat lunch in the reasonably-priced basement cafeteria (a pleasant enough dungeon) or picnic on the lawn under massive deodar cedars (the species originated in the Himalayas). Mon-Fri 9 am-5 pm; Sat/Sun 10 am-4 pm; hourly tours. Stroll the surrounding **Capitol Park** filled with thousands of varieties of plants.

Sutter's Ft, 2701 L St, 445-4422, the bane of Sacramento schoolchildren, should fascinate anyone interested in history; self-guided tours through exhibit rooms which include a blacksmith's shop, a bakery and prison. **State Indian Museum**, on the same park-like grounds, displays examples of an Indian sweathouse and a teepee. Both daily 10 am-5 pm; $5, in summer, $2 after Labor Day.

Thursday Night Market, on K, btwn 7th & 13th Sts. Featuring street theatre, arts and crafts and food, 5 pm-9 pm, May-Sept.

Festivals: California Railroad Festival, June 13-15th. Colourful railroad circus cars, model train displays, performers, circus lore, games, exhibits, activities and entertainment. Call 327-5252. **Living History Days** is a historic Sutter's Fort event held June 14th, which includes reenactement of frontier life in 1846 with militia drills, open hearth cooking, spinning, hand sewing and carpentry. Call 445-4422. Also, from Aug 2nd-Nov 30th the **State Indian Museum Art Show** is a juried show featuring California Native American artists. Call 324-0971.

Nearby: You can trace the path of the '49er miners on their way through **Gold Country** by following Hwy 49 which links many of the 19th century mining communities in the Mother Lode. The flavour of the Gold Rush still lingers in rustic ghost towns, especially **Coloma**, where James Marshall found the nugget that set off the Rush.

Nevada County is dotted with historic landmarks. Nevada City claims to be the most complete gold town left in California. Victorian houses and flat-topped 'false front' buildings, popular in western frontier towns, line the streets, lending the town a feeling of a living museum. Head north on Hwy 49 to **Empire Mine State Historic Park**, in **Grass Valley**, this was the largest and deepest of California's mines; restored buildings, exhibits and an illuminated mine shaft are included on park tours, call 273-8522. Head south on 49 to **Coloma** and the **Gold Discovery Site State Park**. Nearby is **Placerville**, where Studebaker began making wheel-barrows for miners in 1848 and home to a typical Mother Lode mine, in Gold Bug Park, which remains untouched by the cave-ins and flooding that destroyed others. 10 am-4 pm, daily in summer, $1 admission, audio tour tape $1. While in this area, read up on the amazing Lola Montez, sample the wonderful gold rush tales of Bret Harte and read Mark Twains story, *The Celebrated Jumping Frog Of Calaveras County*.

Huge tracts of thick forests invite hikers, state parks offer meandering streams to pan for gold, white-water rivers to raft and breathtaking Sierra mountains to conquer!

INFORMATION
Nevada County Chamber of Commerce, 248 Mill St, Grass Valley, 273-4667.
Travelers Aid, 717 K St, Suite #217, 443-1719. Mon-Fri 9 am-4 pm, closed noon-1 pm.
Visitors Bureau, 1421 K St, 264-7777. Also at 1104 Front St, Old Sacramento, 442-7644. 8 am-5 pm daily.

TRAVEL
Amtrak, 4th & I St, (800) 872-7245.
Greyhound, 715 L St, (800) 231-2222. 'Gambler's buses to Tahoe, Reno—if you can afford to lay out the fare. On arrival several casinos give you money in chips and food vouchers. Details in local papers—a great day out.' To main terminal in Reno $25 o/w. Lake Tahoe $26 o/w, if you reboard in less than 4 days r/t is free, otherwise $41.

Regional transit: buses and a new light rail system, 321-2877. $1.25 basic fare, valid for 90 mins from purchase, $3 day pass. You can walk from 6th and K to Old Sacramento (3 blocks).

Sacramento Airport, 8 miles NW of town, is served by numerous shuttle bus companies who pick up from downtown areas. The journey takes 20-30 mins, $10-$18 o/w, XP-$5-$9. Call **Gold Dust Shuttles**, 944-4444, credit card rsvs only.

LAKE TAHOE For two adjacent states, California and Nevada seem worlds apart: one is verdant, varied and mellow; the other, desiccated, monotonous and frantically on the make. Nowhere is the contrast greater than on the shores of the lake the states share, Lake Tahoe, a sapphire in a mountain setting two hrs east of Sacramento. On the California side, South Lake Tahoe is a ski-bum village in winter, a granola filling station for hikers in summer. Across the border in Stateline, Nevada, casino-dwellers pump the one-armed bandits year-round, rarely venturing out into the light of day. Both sides have natural beauty to spare, although the area gets ridiculously crowded in mid-summer and during the ski season.

Lake Tahoe's homepage can be found at *www.yaws.com/LakeTahoe/tahoe.shtml* includes a Lake Tahoe winter guide.

The telephone area code is 916 in California and 702 in Nevada.

ACCOMMODATION

For a guide to ski areas and accommodation, look up *www.highsierra.com/ltahoeac/*.

Dave's Lake Tahoe Hostel, 3787 Forest, South Lake Tahoe, no phone. Skiing, boating, hiking, casinos. Small hostel with friendly ambience. $12.

Econolodge, 3536 S Lake Tahoe Blvd, 544-2036. S-$45, D-$55 during the week. More expensive at w-ends and during the ski-season.

Shenandoah Motel, 4074 Pine Blvd, **South Lake Tahoe**, 544-2985. Summer rates: S/D-$45-$55, XP-$5. Colour TV, 4 blocks from Nevada casinos.

Tahoe Mountain Lodge, 3868 Hwy 50, **South Lake Tahoe**, 541-6380. W/days: From S/D-$25; 'variable' on w/ends, which means they stick it to you.

Value Inn Motel, 2659 S Lake Tahoe Blvd, 544-3959. S-$35 and upwards during the week.

Camping: Bayview is the only free campground, 544-5994; June-Sept, 2 night max stay. For up-to-date info on other camping in state parks and forests around Lake Tahoe, contact the Forest Service or **Destinet**, (800) 365-2267.

OF INTEREST

Go to *www.yaws.com/101/index.shtml* for 101 fun things to do. Take a **sunset cruise** on Lake Tahoe any night during summer on the trimarran boat, by calling MS DIXIE2 on (702) 588-3508. Unlimited champagne all for $25! Discounts available through Visitors Bureau. At the end of Feb in Tahoe City, **Snowfest** is the largest winter carnival in the West showcasing downhill and cross-country skiing, skating, street dancing, a polar bear swim and zany contests! Call 583-7625. Also, the annual **Artour**, also held in Tahoe City in July, features dozens of local artists who choose to open their studios to the public. Call 581-2787.

South Tahoe Ice Center (STIC)1180 Rufus Allen Blvd, South Lake Tahoe, 542-4700, caters to figure skaters, hockey leagues and recreational skaters of all ages.

Truckee near Donner Pass on Hwy 80: wooden buildings and a frontier atmosphere. 2 miles W of Truckee is **Donner State Park**, where in the winter of 1846-47, the 89-member Donner party was trapped by 22-ft snows (memorial statue there is as tall as the snow was deep that year). Only 47 survived the ordeal, many of them resorting to cannibalism.

INFORMATION

South Lake Tahoe Visitors Center, 3066 Lake Tahoe Blvd, 541-5255. Mon-Fri 8.30 am-5 pm, Sat 9 am-4 pm. For lodging info call (800) 288-2463.

TRAVEL

Anderson's Bike Rental, 645 Emerald Bay Rd, 541-0500. Deposit (ID) req. Daily 9 am-6 pm.

Enterprise Rent-a-Car, (702) 586-1077.

Greyhound, 1098 Hwy 50 (in Harrah's Hotel Casino in Stateline, NV), (800) 231-2222. Daily 8 am-noon, 2.30 pm-6 pm. LTR bus line also in terminal.

Sierra Taxi, 577-8888, 24 hrs.

Tahoe Area Regional Transport (TART) public buses, 581-6365. Connects the west and north shores from Tahoma to Incline Village. 12 buses daily 6.10 am-6.30 pm, $1.25.

WINE COUNTRY Both **Napa Valley** and its neighbour **Sonoma Valley** are noted for superlative viticulture; these areas produce everything from world-class cabernets to sassy jug wines. Just two hrs by car from San Francisco, the scenery alone is worth the trip. Bus service to both valleys is good, but renting a car is a capital way to tour. That way, you can alternate wine-tasting with stops at farms, roadside stands, cheese factories, delis and other tasty locales.

Besides wine, you can taste the sparkling mineral water that bubbles out of the ground at **Calistoga** and visit the spas there; watch gliders and hot air balloons over the vineyards; visit Jack London's Beauty Ranch near old-worldly **Glen Ellen**; and maybe even pause a moment at the Tucolay Cemetery near Napa, where Mammy Pleasant is buried. A 19th century black civil rights advocate who owned a string of San Francisco brothels, Mammy Pleasant gave more than $40,000 to finance John Brown's raid on Harper's Ferry and travelled around the South to raise sentiment for Brown among the blacks. Her headstone reads: 'Mother of civil rights in California, friend of John Brown.'

Travel on a virtual visit to Napa Valley for the latest on wineries, lodging, events, and local attractions, *www.napavalley.com/cgi-bin/home.o.*

The area code here is 707.

ACCOMMODATION

Budget accommodation in the wine country is hard to find; B&B prices hover around $60-$225, tending towards the high end of the scale! Best to stay in Santa Rosa, Sonoma or Petaluma for budget accommodation' otherwise you are advised to camp.

Bothe-Napa Valley State Park, 3801 St Helena Hwy, 942-4575. For rsvs call Destinet at (800) 444-7275. Sites $16, $5 each additional vehicle. Hot showers and pool, $3. Daily 8 am-dusk.

Calistoga Spa Hot Springs, 1006 Washington St, Calistoga, 942-6269. D-$74-$87, w/days. Discounts for 4 days (10%), 7 days (15%). Rsvs advised.

Napa County Fairgrounds, 1435 Oak St, Calistoga. Dry grass in a parking lot with showers and elec. $18 for 2pp. Closed late June-early July.

Triple-S Ranch, 4600 Mountain Home Ranch Rd, Calistoga, 942-6730. These all-wood cabins are a good deal: 2 pp-$54. Rsvs recommended on w/ends.

FOOD

Restaurant fare tends to be dauntingly expensive in most instances, but there are numerous delis and stores with picnic makings (i.e. numerous Safeways!), and many wineries have pleasant picnic areas. Get suggestions for good grocery stores and bakeries from the locals. Some good ones are the Sonoma and Vella Cheese Factories; the Sonoma French Bakery (San Franciscans come *here* for sourdough bread); the Twin Hill Ranch near Sebastopol (applesauce bread); and the Oakville Grocery in Oakville. Calistoga has at least 7 all-different bfast places. Affordable restaurants with good food include:

Curb Side Cafe, 1245 1st St, **Napa**, 253-2307. Sandwich place, serving up delicious bfasts and tasty pancakes. $5-$7 sandwiches. Mon-Sat 8 am-3 pm, Sun 9.30 am-3 pm.
The Diner, 6476 Washington St, **Yountville**, 944-2626. Heavenly wine country hash house serving good bfasts (served all day) and fine Mexican food. Try the flautas and sample a Mimosa.

OF INTEREST

Wineries: Over 250 in Napa Valley alone. The tiny ones tucked away on side roads are informal and fun, but you need a car to get to them. The big 7 wineries, from north to south, are: **Christian Brothers**, housed in a castle with catacomb-like cellars where the wine ages in gargantuan barrels; **Mondavi**, Cliff May building, 'technical tour,' picnics on the lawn; **Inglenook** , mix of old and new buildings (the winery in back is owned by Francis Ford Coppola); **Beaulieu**, good tours; **Martini** ; **Beringer**, whose Gothic Rhine House is a landmark; and **Krug**, the oldest in the valley. Other good wineries: **Sterling**, 1111 Dunaweal Ln, 942-3300, near Calistoga. 10.30 am-4.30 pm daily, $6 includes tasting and aerial-tram to 'spectacular view.' **Stag's Leap** , 5766 Silverado Tr, Napa, has superb wine that measures up to the Continent's best; call 944-2020 to arrange a tour, $3 for a tasting includes complimentary wine glass. For champagne, hit **Kornell Brothers** in Calistoga. Around Sonoma are 4 more standouts, from **Sebastiani** to **Buena Vista**. The latter is the original winery of Agoston Haraszthy, the Hungarian 'count' who brought European vinestock to the US. Green Hungarian is good; Mozart Festival here in summer. Most wineries have tasting at the end of tours, 10 am-4 pm or so. 'Christian Brothers' last tour of the day is more like party-night than wine tasting-you get half glasses to taste!' 'Christian—one of the best—lets you try as many wines as you like.'

Jack London State Historic Park, off Hwy 12 in **Glen Ellen**, 938-5216. Contains ruins of Wolf House, built by author of *Call of the Wild*. Museum 10 am-5 pm; Park 9.30 am-7 pm, $5 p/vehicle. Check out **Napa Skatepark**. Lots of concrete banks; free. The annual **Napa Valley Wine Festival**, 252-0872 takes place in November. In August, **Napa Valley Fairgrounds** hosts a summer fair that includes wine-tasting, rock music, juggling, a rodeo and rides. Call Napa Parks and Recreation office, 257-9529 for more info.

Robert Louis Stevenson Park, in **St Helena**, 7 miles NE of Calistoga on Hwy 29, 942-4575. Free, day use only, wonderful picnicking and hiking (new trail leading to former site of RLS house). Bring your own water or wine.

Sonoma is still centred around its lush plaza, where in 1846 Yankee rebels raised a grizzly-bear flag and established the short-lived Republic of California. The republic gave way 40 days later to US control, but the flag, and its symbol, stuck. Remnants of Spanish control still exist here, including the **mission** and **Lachryma Montis**, home of General Vallejo, who once governed much of California. If you have the chance, take the hwy from Sonoma to Hwy 80; it's a beautiful drive any time of year.

INFORMATION

The local **Napa Visitor Center** is helpful. Be sure to pick up their farm trails brochures, including *Inside Napa Valley* for maps, winery listings and a weekly events guide. Also, **Chambers of Commerce** in:
St Helena, 1010A Main St, , 963-4456. Daily 10 am-noon; and **Calistoga**, 1458 Lincoln Ave, 942-6333. Daily 10 am-3 pm.

Wine Institute, 425 Market St, Suite #1000 (1¹/₂ blocks E of Union Sq in San Francisco), (415) 512-0151. Offers free guide to Napa Valley. Mon-Fri 9 am-5 pm.

TRAVEL
Golden Gate Transport, 544-1323, to Santa Rosa ($4.50) and then #80 bus to the vineyards.
Greyhound, (800) 231-2222 serves Napa to St Helena, Calistoga twice daily; but the trip requires an overnight stay. If you get off at St Helena, it's an easy walk to 3 wineries immediately north of town. Service also to Sonoma.
St Helena Cyclery, 1156 Main St, 255-3377. Mon-Sat 9.30 am-5.30 pm, Sun 10 am-5 pm.

MARIN COUNTY   Linked to San Francisco by the slender scarlet bracelet of the Golden Gate Bridge is Marin County, whose predominant hues are two shades of Green—green hills and green money. The western edge, facing the Pacific, is wild, windblown, solitary and beautiful. Among its treasures is the 70,000-acre **Pt Reyes National Seashore**, which has an earthquake trail along the San Andreas Fault. At the very point of Pt Reyes is a lighthouse; from December to February, migrating gray whales can sometimes be seen from here. Further up the peninsula is **Tomales Bay State Park. Drake's Beach** is another gem, where Sir Francis may have landed when he claimed all of Nova Albion for Elizabeth I.
   Near Pt Reyes are other public wilderness sanctuaries, among them popular **Stinson Beach** (closest swimming beach to San Francisco, enquire locally about the sea serpent) and **Muir Woods** , 6 mi of cool trails through a hushed and fragrant cathedral of *sequoia sempervivens*, some as tall as 240 ft. **Mt Tamalpais**, favourite of hikers and bicyclers, commands fantastic views; its trails link up with Stinson's, Muir Wood's and others.
   Inner Marin is stuffed with plush communities that line the northwest shore of San Francisco Bay. From **Tiburon** you can take a ferry to nearby **Angel Island**, which has seen several incarnations as a duelling field, military staging ground for three wars, quarantine station for Asian immigrants and a missile site. The island is now a state park with campsites, friendly deer, bicycling trails and the ghostly ruins of Civil War officers' houses to explore. Former whalers' harbour **Sausalito** has the best view of San Francisco, lots of costly, cutesie bars and boutiques, and a houseboat colony, the last vestige of its bohemian past. 'A fantastic way to get a feel for the area is to take a ferry to Sausalito and walk back across the Golden Gate Bridge. Once across, you can catch a bus back to downtown.'
   The Marin County Visitors Guide is located at *www.marin.org/mc/parks/mconvis/indexvg.html.*
The telephone area code for Marin County is 415.

ACCOMMODATION
The hostel and camping situation in Marin:
Angel Island camping, $9 per site (8 people max). To stay in one of the island's 9 camps, call (800) 444-7275 for rsvs, or write to MISTIX, PO Box 85705, San Diego, CA 92138-5705. Rsvs are accepted up to 8 wks in adv by phone, 9 wks by mail, which is just about how far ahead you'll have to reserve a place if you want to stay on Sat night. Fireplaces, water, chemical toilets. Also see **San Francisco** section *Housing Information.*
Marin Headlands, 941 Fort Barry, **Sausalito**, CA 94965, 331-2777. Hostel sits on a

hillside in the serene Marin headlands, just across the Golden Gate Bridge from San Francisco in the Golden Gate National Recreation Area. Surrounded by beaches, forests and rolling hills, wildlife, native plant life and scenic trails. Rec room, well-equipped kitchen, laundry, bicycle storage. 'Very spacious hostel. You'll need a car to get into the city 12 miles away, no public transport. 'Popular but far from centre of town.' Open year-round; $12-14.

HI-Marin Highlands, 331-2777. Game and common rooms, kitchen, laundry, pool table. Sumptuous location. $12.

Point Reyes HI Hostel, Box 247, Point Reyes Station, CA 94956, 663-8811. Hostel is spread btwn 2 cabins on a spectacular site. Hiking, wildlife and Limantour beach all within walking distance. $10-12. Write to rsvs beds.

FOOD/ENTERTAINMENT

This area has many organic groceries where you should buy supplies then picnic in one of Marin's countless parks. For one of the best people-watching places, try **The Depot Bookstore and Café**, 87 Throckmorton Ave, 383-2665. Food and drink at reasonable prices. Daily 7 am-10 pm.

Gray Whale Pizza, 669-1244, off Hwy 1 in **Inverness**, en route to Pt Reyes. 'Huge, excellent pizzas.' $5-20! Daily 10.30 am-9 pm.

Greater Gatsby's, 39 Caledonia, **Sausalito**, 332-4500. Come see Marin mellow out in this restaurant/bar. Bar opens at noon, food served from 5.30 pm w/ends only, closes midnight.

Marin County Fair, San Rafael, July 2-6th. This annual fair includes pig races, pie competitions, fireworks, high-tech exhibits, music and carnival rides! Call 499-6400.

Mayflower Inn, 1533 4th, near Shaver, **San Rafael**, 456-1011. Genuine British pub with darts and raucous singing. Bangers, pasties, fish & chips, and pints of Guinness in front of a blazing fire. Guaranteed to cure any case of homesickness. Lunch Sun-Fri, dinner daily, all meals around $7. Mon-Fri 11.30 am-2 am, Sat-Sun 9 am-2 am.

OF INTEREST/INFORMATION

Ferries from Tiburon to Angel Island, 21 Main St, Tiburon, 435-2131, leave four times daily. $5, $1 for transporting bikes. Sunset cruises $8 from 6.30 pm on Fri & Sat. Call (415) 435-1915 for more info on Angel Island.

Marin County Civic Center, 3501 Civic Center Dr, 499-7404, San Rafael. Reminiscent of a Roman aqueduct, the civic center is a riot of pink and turquoise against emerald hills and azure California sky. Some people love this Frank Lloyd Wright structure; some call it the Bay Area's biggest sore thumb. Whatever your opinion, you shouldn't miss seeing it—and if you travel through Marin County on Hwy 101, you won't. Tours on request.

Rainbow Tunnel, Hwy 1 northbound from Golden Gate Bridge to Marin County. A monument to a Cal Trans engineer's whimsy. You'll know it when you see it.

San Francisco Bay Model, 2100 Bridgeway, 332-3871. Constructed by the Army Corps of Engineers, the hydraulic model simulates tides, oil spills, etc. Tue-Fri 9 am-4 pm, Sat & Sun 10 am-6 pm in summer, otherwise Tue-Sat 9 am-4 pm.

SAN FRANCISCO   Big, beautiful Baghdad-by-the-Bay, San Francisco is a city that flows like a magic carpet of images: hills, bridges, cable cars, fog, ferryboats, gays, painted Victorians, earthquakes, movie car chases. Known to all simply as 'the City' ('Frisco' warrants the death sentence), San Francisco occupies a peerless setting on the tip of a green and hilly thumb separating ocean from bay. A narrow strait, fraught with dangerous under-

tows, is spanned with a sense of drama by a shimmering Golden Gate Bridge. Seen from afar, the city is by turns a citadel shining in the sun, a bank of diamonds glittering in the night, a coquette peeking over a ruff of fog, heartbreakingly lovely. Closer examination reveals imperfections: slums, cold corporate canyons, porno districts and boxy tract homes and, with memories of the 1989 earthquake still fresh, the ever-present fear of the 'big one.' Never mind; even with its flaws, San Francisco is still way ahead of whoever's in second place.

History and geography have conspired to make San Francisco a city of neighbourhoods in the European manner. Ethnic differences are not assimilated but encouraged, imparting a cosmopolitan flavour that comes as a welcome relief after the monotony of much of urban America. This western most of Western cities, paradoxically, is America's door to the East—to China, Hong Kong, Japan, and the rest of Asia—with which California does more business than with Europe.

It's hard to have a bad time here. The wealth of things to see and do, the diverse and delicious foods, and most of all, the San Franciscans themselves, make visiting a delight. People migrate here not to be successful but to be (or learn to be) happy and human. Their efforts make San Francisco a city of good manners, full of little kindnesses and occasional gallant acts, whether saving whales or cable cars, that speak of altruism and love.

Temperatures are mild year-round. Spring and autumn offer the most sunshine, but come prepared for brisk winds and chilly weather at any time. Unexpectedly, summer is when the city's famous fog crosses the line into infamy. Mark Twain, it is said, once complained that the 'coldest winter I ever spent was a summer in San Francisco.'

San Francisco's central location is perfect for daytrips to nearby attractions. Berkeley, Santa Cruz, Marin County and the Napa and Sonoma wine country can be reached within two hrs by public transport. It's more likely that, when it comes time to leave, you'll have to tear yourself away. When in San Francisco, remember three things: wear strong shoes, watch for seagulls and keep an eye on your heart at all times; otherwise as the song says, you'll probably leave it here.

Check out the Yahoo! SF Bay Metro at *www.sfbay.yahoo.com*.
The telephone area code is 415.

SURVIVAL

San Francisco's Greyhound depot is located in a scruffy-to-rotten district, predictably worse at night. When seeking accommodation, bear in mind that the large triangle formed by Market, Divisadero and Geary is a high crime area which spills over to the other side of Market, where the Greyhound depot is. The worst section is the Western Addition, bounded by Geary, Hayes, Steiner and Gough. Stay out, day or night (no reason to visit, anyway). Other dicey streets at night are the first four blocks of Turk, Eddy and Ellis. That doesn't mean you shouldn't stay here—just be aware and exercise caution, particularly after dark.

ACCOMMODATION

NB: The best accommodation goes quickly, especially in youth hostels, so check in early. If arriving late, phone ahead. Accommodation info also available at Greyhound. See also hostel listings for Marin County.

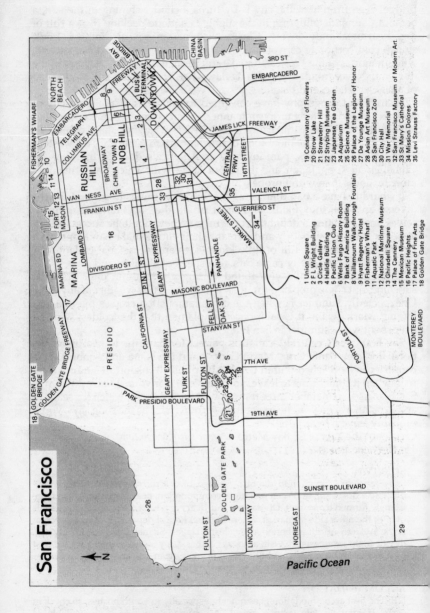

San Francisco

←N

Pacific Ocean

1 Union Square
2 F L Wright Building
3 Circle Gallery
4 Haldie Building
5 Pacific Union Club
6 Wells Fargo History Room
7 Bank of America Building
8 Vaillamount Walk-through Fountain
9 Hyatt Regency Hotel
10 Fisherman's Wharf
11 Aquatic Park
12 National Maritime Museum
13 Ghiradelli Square
14 The Cannery
15 Mexican Museum
16 Pacific Heights
17 Palace of Fine Arts
18 Golden Gate Bridge
19 Conservatory of Flowers
20 Strow Lake
21 Strawberry Hill
22 Strybing Museum
23 Japanese Tea Garden
24 Aquarium
25 Science Museum
26 De Younge Museum
27 Palace of the Legion of Honor
28 Asian Art Museum
29 San Francisco Zoo
30 City Hall
31 War Memorial
32 San Francisco Museum of Modern Art
33 St Mary's Cathedral
34 Mission Dolores
35 Levi Strauss Factory

Adelaide Inn, 5 Isadora Duncan, 441-2261. From S-$35, D-$43, w/shared bath, XP-$6. Continental bfast included.

Alexander Hotel, corner of O'Farrell/Taylor, (800) 843-8709. Own shower, TV, A/C. Easy access to China Town/Market St. 'Friendly staff, clean.' Rooms from $35.

Allison Hotel, 417 Stockton St, 2 blocks N of Union Square, 986-8737. From S-$50, D-$60 up with shared bath, XP-$10. Rsvs req.'Very friendly, ideal for Chinatown and Fisherman's Wharf.' 'Excellent, safe, clean if dull.'

Ansonia Hotel and Residence Club, 711 Post St, 673-2670. S/D-$55 w/shared bath, $73 w/private bath. XP-$15. Bfast included. International clientele. 'Very clean.'

AYH Travel Services, 308 Mason St, Powell BART Stn, 788-2525, provides hostel info, travel services, books, supplies and all membership facilities. Mon-Sat 10 am-6 pm in summer.

Castor Hotel, 705 Vallejo St, 788-9709. S-$15 pp, mention BUNAC. 'Central location. Given outside key so no curfew.'

Central YMCA, 220 Golden Gate Ave, 885-0460. From S-$30, D-$42.

Gates Hotel, 140 Ellis St, 781-0430. From S-$35, D-$38, $5 key deposit. 'Handy location. Always has beds.'

Golden Gate Hotel, 775 Bush, btwn Powell and Mason, 392-3702. S/D-$65, shared bath, $92 w/private bath. Excellent location, within walking distance to just about everything; safe and clean. 'Very friendly and helpful staff.' Continental bfast and afternoon tea included.

Grand Central Hostel, 1412 Market St, 703-9988, S-$20, D-$30, 4-bed dorm $14, free tea, coffee, linens, laundry, TV rm, pool table, jukeboxes. 'Mixed reports.'

Grant Hotel, 753 Bush St, btwn Powell and Mason, 421-7540/rsvs (800) 522-0979. 'Excellent location in a safe central part of the city. Our double rm was $65 p/night; we asked for an extra bed and fridge and got them. Large common room. Very comfortable hotel!'

Green Tortoise Guest House, 494 Broadway, off Kearny, 834-9060. $15 dorm plus $20 key deposit, $5 sheet deposit. 'Very friendly, clean hostel on edge of Chinatown.''A bit cramped.''Free tea and bfast if you get up early enough!'

Harcourt Residence Club, 1105 Larkin St, 673-7720. Weekly rates only; $130 shared bath, $145 w/private bath. Includes bfast and dinner, maid service. Sundeck, lounge with 40" colour TV, $20 key deposit. 'Excellent for meeting friends.'

India House Hostel, 1430 Larkin St, 673-7790. 24 hr reception, big kitchen, friendly staff, TV room. Dorms $12, $5 key deposit. Tip: catch trolley on Sacramento—it stops at Larkin ($2 o/w)

Interclub Globe Hostel, 10 Hallam Pl, 431-0540, on Folsom btwn 7th & 8th. From Greyhound take bus #14 or 15 min walk. $17 shared dorms, in nightclub district, no curfew. $10 key deposit. 'Brilliant atmosphere—best hostel I stayed in.' 'Druggy area.' 'Good food from cafeteria. Mostly "alternative" crowd.'

Olympic Hotel, 140 Mason St, 982-5010. '1 block from AYH, rec for hostel overspill. Will look after your bags for a few hrs after checkout.' 'Friendly, helpful.' D-$30.

Pacific Tradewinds Guest House, 680 Sacramento St, 433-7970. Converted apartment owned and run by two former backpackers. $16 per night in clean, comfortable dorms ($5 key deposit). Centrally and conveniently located in Chinatown, close to Market St and public transport. For $4 *they* will wash your laundry! No curfews. Rsvs recommended in summer. 'Very friendly and homely atmosphere.' 'Best accommodation I stayed in.''Mattresses and bunks and mixed dorms.' 'Not very clean.'

San Francisco Downtown HI Hostel at Union Square, 312 Mason St, 788-5604. $16-19. A block from the excitement of Union Sq, in the theatre district, this hostel provides double and triple rooms. Union Sq is a great place to people-watch or enjoy a picnic under the palm trees. Outside hostel is a variety of restaurants, shops and art galleries. 'Excellent on-site information desk, central location.' Kitchen, library, free linen and vending machines. 24hrs, 14 nights max stay. Rsvs rec for summer.

San Francisco European Guest House HI Hostel, 761 Minna St, 861-6634. Run by former Greyhound driver and 15 mins walk from Greyhound. Kitchen, TV rm, lockers. No curfew, 24hrs. 'Very friendly; totally mixed.' 'Don't seem to turn anyone away so very hot and crowded.' 'Not a safe area at night.' 'Excellent staff.' 'We arrived at 7.15 am and it was already full (for males).' 'Shared a bathroom with 20 others.' Meals available. Roof garden. Tours to Napa wine country. Dorms from $12-$14, private rooms available.

San Francisco Fisherman's Wharf HI Hostel, Bldg 240, Ft Mason, on Bay & Franklin, 771-7277. Take # 42, # 47 or # 49 bus from Van Ness. Located in the Golden Gate National Recreation Area, an urban national park on the Bay. Dorm overlooking the bay. 'Arrive early—fills very quickly.' Fort Mason is also home to museums, galleries and theatres. Fisherman's Wharf, Chinatown and Ghirardelli Sq all nearby. 'The abundance of British students makes it a good place to head for if you're alone and want to share costs.' $14-16, 3 nights max.

The Original San Francisco Roommate Referral Service, 610A Cole St, 558-9191. A $34 fee gets you lists of rooms to rent—shared housing only. 'Very helpful, found somewhere straight away.' Mon-Fri 10 am-6 pm, Sat 11 am, Sun 11 am-4 pm.

FOOD

Food is one of the things San Francisco does best; sampling the amazing variety of local cuisines is a top priority. The city grew as a seaport, so eat like a sailor: Dungeness crab and sourdough bread, Irish coffee and Anchor Steam, the local beer. Move on to other cultures in one of the many excellent and cheap ethnic Restaurants—Persian and Basque, Salvadorean and Greek, Sichuan and Russian, Italian and Vietnamese. The Bay Area Restaurant Guide, *www.sfbay.com/food* contains almost 14,000 SF Bay Area restaurants with 8,000 reviews, including several photographs!

Atmosphere: **Buena Vista Cafe**, 2765 Hyde St, 474-5044. Go on a foggy night and listen to foghorns moan and cable cars clang while you nurse an Irish coffee (introduced to the US in 1953 by SF newspaperman Stanton Delaplane). 'Extremely crowded.' **Hamburger Mary's**, 1582 Folsom, 626-5767. 10 am-10 pm daily. 'Best hamburgers, good live music, friendly atmosphere.'

Seattle St Coffee, 456 Geary St, 922-4566. 'Exceptionally friendly and welcoming coffee shop in an area with very few affordable options.' Bagels, scones, muffins $1-2. Sandwiches from $3-6. Great selection of coffees. Daily 7 am-midnight, 'til 7 pm Sun/Mon. **Specs' 12 Adler Museum Cafe**, 12 Adler St, off Columbus, 421-4112. Finding this seedy and wonderfully authentic North Beach bar can be a challenge, but its location (down an obscure alley called Saroyan) keeps it safe from the hordes of conventioneers swarming along Columbus. Don't bring your little dog, Dorothy.

Tommy's Joynt, Van Ness and Geary, 775-4216. 'Great decor, huge buffalo stew ($5.75).' Daily 11 am-1.45 am.

Breakfast: Brother Juniper's, 1065 Sutter St, 771-8929. Homemade breads, muffins, peaceful atmosphere. 7 am-2 pm Mon-Fri, Sat 'til 1.30 pm. 'Best bfast in town, original dishes, $6 or less.' Proceeds go to family shelter behind restaurant. Lunch also: **Doidges**, 2217 Union, at Filmore, 921-2149, serves brunch 'til 1.45 pm w/days, 2.45 pm w/ends. Need rsvs. **Economy Restaurant**, 18 7th St, 552-8830. '2 eggs, 3 sausage, hash browns, toast—$4.' Bfast all day. Daily 6.30 am-8 pm.

Pinecrest Restaurant, Mason and Geary. 'Dinner and bfast served, all day. 24 hrs. **Sears Fine Foods**, 439 Powell. Try French toast made from sourdough bread. 'Excellent bfast, go extra early.'

Burritos: La Cumbre, 515 Valencia, near 16th, 863-8205. Mon-Sat 11 am-10 pm, Sun noon-9 pm. Mouth-watering at $2.75.

Greek: Athens Greek Restaurant, 39 Mason. Daily, 11 am-midnight, Sat 'til 1 am.

Hamburgers: Hayes Street Grill, 320 Hayes St, 863-5545. Intimate, small-restaurant cooking up the finest modern California cuisine. **Hot 'N Hunky**, 4039 18th, 621-6365. Just like it sounds. **Original Joe's**, 144 Taylor, btwn Turk & Eddy, 775-4877, serves 12-ounce burgers—regular or charbroiled (after 5 pm)—for around $7. 'Only Brits can finish them,' so they've invented a 'junior' for wimps. (European soccer teams eat here). Mon-Fri, 10.30 am-1 am.

Italian: Little Joe's, 523 Broadway, 982-7639. Spectacular chefs, huge portions—ask to split spaghetti con pesto or roast chicken. Lunch $6-$11, dinner $8-$14. Daily 11 am-10.30 pm, Fri & Sat 11.30 pm. **Tommasso** 1042 Kearny, 398-9696, for pizza. Daily 5 pm-11 pm, Sun 4 pm-10 pm.

Oriental: Best tempura at **Sanppo**, 1702 Post, 346-3486; best Szechuan at **Tsing Tao**, 3107 Clement, btwn 32nd & 33rd, 387-2344.

Sourdough bread: Boudin Bakery. Several locations (Pier 39, Fisherman's Wharf, Ghiradelli Square), 928-1849. Best sourdough (from $2.25) outside Sonoma, CA.

Steaks: Tad's Steak House, 120 Powell, 982-1718. Steak, salad and bread for $6. 'Excellent food.' Daily 7 am-11 pm.

Sweet tooth: Gelato Classico, 576 Union, 391-6667. The standard of excellence in Italian ices. **Just Desserts**, locations on Buchanan, Church St and Embarcadero. 'Best cheesecake, chocolate cake in the city.'

Vegetarian: Green's at, Bldg A, Laguna St at Marina Blvd, 771-6222. 'Culinary experience for vegetarians.' Lunch $7-$10, dinner $10-$13. 'View of the bay very beautiful.'

OF INTEREST

Don't go looking for 'sights' and miss the best one: San Francisco itself. The best way to take it all in is to alternate walking with cable car or bus riding. Spend at least half your time away from the tourist ghetto of Fisherman's Wharf, The Cannery, Pier 39, Ghiradelli Square, etc, all of which are aimed squarely at your wallet. You've missed an essential part of the city's heart if you don't do one or more of the following: take a ferry to Sausalito past Alcatraz, the infamous prison; inch up and down the near-cliffs locally known as 'hills' while dangling from the downslope end of a cable car; hop on a MUNI tram for a tour of the peninsula; or stand on the Marin headlands north of the Golden Gate Bridge in the evening, watching the lights of the city come on. Unlike LA, San Francisco is fairly compact, easy to comprehend and well equipped with public transport to give your legs a much-needed break on its 43-plus hills. Check out *Things to do in the Bay Area* on the Net, *www-leland.stnaford.edu/~yaelp/hotlist.html*

Union Square: City centre, named on the eve of the Civil War. In 1906, the square served as emergency camp for earthquake refugees. Nearby is **Maiden Lane**, once a red-hot red-light district, now a charming cul-de-sac with the only Frank Lloyd Wright building in the city—the **Circle Gallery**. A striking tunnel entrance and interior ramp leads to this art gallery, the prototype for the Guggenheim Museum in New York City. The Gallery is at 140 Maiden Lane, 989-2100, Mon-Sat 10 am-6 pm, Sun noon-5 pm, free. North at 130 Sutter is the progenitor of the modern glass skyscraper, the 1917 **Hallidie Building**. Superb stores abound; even Woolworth's is nice, although **Gump's** is the local landmark among them. You'll also find **theatres** on Geary and **cinemas** on Market. At Market and New Montgomery is the **Sheraton-Palace Hotel** , whose lacy skylighted garden court was the sole remnant in this luxurious structure after the 1907 earthquake. Singer Enrico Caruso was staying in the Palace when the quake hit; he rushed out, said 'Give me Vesuvius!' and left SF in haste.

Alcatraz, Pier 41, ferry is $11 (including audio tour). Day trip to 'the Rock,' where the likes of Al Capone, Machine Gun Kelley and the 'Birdman' were incarcerated from Civil War times to 1963. 'Dress warmly.' Tours year-round, 9 am-5 pm, every ½ hr. 'Must pre-book tkts but well worth it.' 'Long queues—get there early.' 'Best tour I went on in whole of US.'

Bank of America Building. This building, the second tallest in the city, is pretty obvious, but for the record it's at 555 California St. The Carnelian Room, 433-7500, a posh restaurant on the 52nd floor, offers an excellent view along with prices you can't afford. Plebs are tolerated 3 pm-5 pm, but don't wear shorts. Restricted viewing is also possible from the 27th floor of the **Transamerica Pyramid**, at Montgomery St, a $34 million corporate symbol that has, amazingly, given the Golden Gate Bridge a run for its money as the City's symbol as well. The view of the Bay and hills beyond is nice, but it's more fun to go right up to the edge of the plate glass window—a plate glass wall, really—and just look down.

Chinatown: more Chinese live here than in any other Chinatown in the states. Inhabiting Grant and Stockton btwn Bush and Broadway, SF's Chinatown can be a crowded confusion of sights, smells and sounds. 'Do yourself a favour and spend a couple of hrs just wandering around taking it all in, especially the seafood shops.' All the tourists go to Grant; you should explore Stockton, Washington and little side streets to see: herbal shops at 837 and 857 Washington; fortune cookies being made at Mee Mee, 1328 Stockton; and T'ai-Chi practiced in the morning at Portsmouth Sq, RL Stevenson's old hang-out btwn Clay and Washington, where the City began.

City Lights Bookstore, 261 Columbus Ave, 362-8193. It's not the best bookstore in the city but not every store has the history of this one. This was the mecca for the Beat writers, such as Jack Kerouac, to come and be arty, and the owner published Alan Ginsberg's seminal poem, *Howl*. Open late every day, come in the evening and spend hrs! The alley next to the store is named in honour of Kerouac.

Civic Center: Btwn Franklin, Larkin, McAllister and Hayes. Its centre is **City Hall**, unhappy scene in 1978 of the dual murder of the mayor and gay supervisor by a former supervisor; both the crime and minimal punishment provoked rioting, outrage, and jolted SF's image as a tolerant mecca for gays.

Cruises around **the Bay:** from Piers 39 and 41, the Red and White fleets, 546-2700, and the Blue and Gold fleet, 781-7877, $16 but ask for student discount. Lasts about an hour. Frequent departures. Dress warmly and wait for clear weather. Better still, ride the Red and White ferries to Sausalito ($12 r/t) and Tiburon, departing from Fisherman's Wharf; Golden Gate ferries to Sausalito ($5 o/w) and Larkspur, departing from the Ferry Building on Embarcadero, 332-6600.

Embarcadero: **Vaillancourt walk-through fountain**, a 710-ton assemblage of 101 concrete boxes, unveiled in 1971 to cries of 'loathsome monstrosity,' 'idiotic rubble,' etc. A must-see. Also, overlooking one of the most famous and photogenic skylines in the world is the **Skydeck**, the *only* outdoor observation deck in San Francisco. It offers a show-stopping 360-degree view of the City by the Bay. Located on the 41st floor, the indoor/outdoor observatory also offers multimedia presentations of San Francisco history and culture, and original artwork. 'A visual delight for photographers and visitors.' Contact 1 Embarcadero Center, (800) 733-6318.

Financial District: **Montgomery St** is the 'Wall Street of the West.' **Wells Fargo History Museum**, 420 Montgomery, 396-2619. The bank whose symbol is a stagecoach pays homage to its worst enemy, Black Bart, who robbed Wells Fargo 28 times in 7 years (successfully all but once). Also includes other mementoes of the Old West. Free, Mon-Fri 9 am-5 pm.

Fisherman's Wharf/Pier 39: Minuscule amount of wharf, surrounded by a frightening quantity of souvenir rubbish, overpriced seafood, dreary wax museums and bad restaurants. The working wharf is a series of 3 finger piers, just past Johnson and Joseph Chandlery. A fair walk from the Wharf is **Pier 39**, a carefully hokey construct of carnival and commerce. Dive among sharks and fishes under San Francisco Bay at **UnderWater World**, (800) 325-7437, America's first 'diver's-eye view' aquarium. A 30 min headphone narrated dive journey guides visitors along moving walkways through a 400ft long, 16ft deep transparent tunnel. Inches away is a spectacular array of 10,000 rays, salmon, crabs, jellyfish, and other underwater wildlife. Highlights include 'Rocky Surge Pool' exhibit, an octopus and more than 150 sharks.

Aquatic Park, 3 blocks left of Fisherman's Wharf. The 6 vessels moored here as well as the nearby **National Maritime Museum** (daily 10 am-5 pm), 929-0202, are charming, 'especially the restored ferry.' $4 to enter **Hyde Street Pier**, where you can board 3 of the ships, including the 1886 *Balclutha*. Elsewhere is docked the liberty ship *Jeremiah O'Brien* and the WWII sub *Pompanito*, all with boarding fees. Also at the Aquatic: free swimming beach, cold but fairly clean, with free showers. Nearby is open-air seating where wonderful conga and jam sessions take place on fine Sat-Sun afternoons. Btwn Aquatic and the Wharf are **Ghiradelli Square** and **The Cannery**, both mazes of specialty shops, restaurants and contrived street colour with a thin veneer of history overall.

Golden Gate Bridge: It's painted orange-red but glows gold in the afternoon sun. Perhaps the most famous suspension bridge in the world, the 1¹/₂ mile Golden Gate links SF with the green Marin headlands (honeycombed with war fortifications). You can walk or bike across for free (dress warmly); pedestrian walk closes at sunset. At midpoint, you'll be 220 ft above the water, a drop that has drawn over 700 suicides. By car, the bridge is free northbound, $4 southbound. 'Take bus to bridge, then walk down through wooded area with lovely plants, stroll along beach all the way back to Fisherman's Wharf. Lovely way to spend a day.' Other ways to do the bridge: walk from SF to Marin on the Bay side, and once across, keep going down Alexander Dr to Sausalito (about a mile, downhill all the way) and catch the ferry back to SF—the best of both worlds.

Golden Gate Park and West SF: An exceptional park of 1017 acres, filled with a vast array of plantings, foot and bridle paths. Lots of free events and admissions, especially on first Wed of every month; Sunday concerts on music concourse (call (707) 253-2908 for details); lovely **Conservatory of flowers; Stow Lake** and **Strawberry Hill**; scruffy buffalo in the west end; occasional outstanding Sunday jugglers in the park near Conservatory; **Strybing Arboretum**. Get to the enchanting **Japanese tea garden** early or late to miss tour bus hordes. For info on places and events within the park, call the San Francisco Recreation and Parks Department, 666-7200. Within the park: The **California Academy of Sciences**, $7, $5.50 w/student ID, includes admission to the **Aquarium**, 221-5100, which has huge, open tanks, and the **Science Museum**, 750-3600, with its Hall of Man; the **de Young Museum**, $6, 'not worth the price or time'; and **Asian Art Museum**, 668-8921, $7.50. All free 1st Wed of the month, closed Mon, Tue. 'Don't walk to the park from the bus station unless you want to find out what it is like to be mugged or raped (local police advice).'

Haight-Ashbury, south of the Golden Gate panhandle, was famous in flower-power days, now being spiffed up in what is sometimes called the 'creeping gentrification' of the City. Take a stroll down Hashbury Lane: **Janis Joplin's pad at** 112 Lyon, now home of a charitable organization, and **Jefferson Airplane's hangar** at 2400 Fulton. SE of Haight is **Noe Valley**, a sunny version of Greenwich Village, whose main drag, **Castro St** is synonymous with gaydom. **Twin Peak** provides (on clear days) a fine view of San Francisco.

Hyatt Regency Hotel, Embarcadero Plaza, 788-1234. Glittering seven-sided pyramid, its lobby filled with trees, birds, flowers and fountains. Ride the twinkly elevators to the 18th floor for costly drinks in Equinox, a restaurant that revolves, with a magnificent view of the Bay Bridge. 'Romantic, delightful—$10 cocktails.' 'Req to buy drink.'

Marina Safeway, 15 Marina Blvd, 563-4946. Locally infamous pick-up joint and grocery store. Visit the produce department for proof that San Franciscans love their fog so much that they create it artificially indoors, too.

The Marina/Pacific Heights: The flat Marina district gives way to hills, climbing to Union St, now a trendy shopping and social district. From here on up is **Pacific Heights**, with its surpassing collection of **Victorian mansions**, many of them colourfully painted. Webster, Pine and the 1900 to 3300 blocks of Sacramento contain many charming examples.

Mexican Museum, Bldg D, Ft Mason, 441-0404. $4, $3 w/student ID. Don't pass up this rich panorama of folk, colonial and Mexican-American works, from masks to pottery to Siquieros lithos. Outstanding special exhibits. Get in free 1st Wed of every month. Tue-Sun noon-5 pm, Wed 'til 7 pm.

The Mission District: w/end eves, Chicano youth strut their mechanical stuff with their highly customised vehicles in the phenomenon known as low riding. On Mission btwn 16th and 24th or so; enquire locally. The area is rich in **murals**. See for yourself at the mini-park btwn York and Bryan on 24th; in Balmy Alley btwn 24th and 25th; and on Folsom at 26th. **Mission Dolores** at 16th and Dolores (621-8203) is a simple, restored structure with an ornate basilica peering over its shoulder. May-Sept, daily 9 am-4.30 pm, $2 donation. Interesting cemetery; drop in any time for free. The first **Levi Strauss Factory** , 250 Valencia, 565-9159, gives good tours every Weds. Ten people min in group. Call on Tues if individual to join school group.

Nob Hill: Cable car lines criss-cross here; transfer point. **Cable Car Museum**, Washington & Mason, 474-1887: 'The cable cars are powered from here, see how they work, very interesting.' Daily 10 am-6 pm; free. North of Union Square is the grande dame of SF hills; prior to the quake it was crowded with mansions, of which only the **Pacific Union Club** was left standing. If you're dressed for it, take the elevators to the view bars atop the **Fairmont** and **Mark Hopkins Hotels**. (The Fairmont features in the TV soap *Hotel.*)

North Beach: This, the birthplace of the beat movement, fends off Greenwich Village's claim to the same by maintaining even now a certain junkyard style. Once the centre of the rip-roaring Barbary Coast, the area now hosts topless, bottomless, seemingly endless clubs along Broadway's 'mammary lane.' Clashing crazily with this gaudy neon fleshpot are clubs, coffeehouses and bookstores that reek of intellectual prestige or pretense, depending on your point of view. Among the greatest (and not the latest) are **City Lights Bookstore**, 261 Columbus, still owned by Lawrence Ferlinghetti, still stocked with Alan Ginsberg. Look for **29 Russell St**, where Jack Kerouac wrote *On the Road*. Get *triste* at **Cafe Trieste**, 609 Vallejo, at Grant, 3926739, to the tune of an aria from a tragic Italian opera (Sat 1 pm), and drown your sorrows in a cafe latte; 'the highlight of my trip'! Pay your respects at **Vesuvio Bar**, 255 Columbus, 362-3370. When the beat movement bit the dust, the detritus gravitated here. Once, Kerouac and Dylan Thomas bent elbows at Vesuvio; the drinks are still cheap.

Palace of Fine Arts, 3601 Lyon St, 563-7337. Built for the 1916 Panama-Pacific Exposition out of plaster of Paris, the palace was not expected to hold up, as it did, for fifty years. It was restored with cement in 1967 and now houses the **Exploratorium**, a carnival of science and art that explains principles of physics and human perception through hands-on exhibits. To see the super-popular Tactile Dome: rsvs are essential, 1 week ahead for w/days, 4-6 weeks for w/ends. Admission to the rest of the Exploratorium is free the first Wed of every month, otherwise $9, $7 w/student ID, $12 will get you into both. Tues-Fri, Sat & Sun 10 am-5 pm, Wed 'til 9.30 pm, closed Mon. 'Don't miss it!'

San Francisco Museum of Modern Art, 151 3rd St btwn Mission and Howard, 357-4000. All the bluechips: Miro, Klee, Jasper, Pollock, etc. Free 1st Tue of every month, 10 am-5 pm, otherwise $7. Tue-Sun 11 am-6 pm, Thur 11 am-9 pm ($3.50 from 6 pm). Closed Mon. $4 w/student ID.

San Francisco Zoo, Sloat and 45th, 753-7061. $7, 10 am-5 pm daily.

Seal Rocks area: **Cliff House**, a spooky, Gothic-style reconstruction of a seaside resort on a cliff above the crashing sea. It offers a panorama from a walk-in *camera obscura*, and on the lower level, the **Musee Mechanique**, 386-1170, a droll collection of vintage arcade machines, from Fatty Arbuckle to zee French flasher! Free, but bring dimes and quarters. Daily 10 am-8 pm.

SoMA (South of Market): **Anchor Brewing Company**, 1705 Mariposa, 863-8350. See how SF's own Anchor Steam Beer is created. Tasting follows 30-40 min tour, Mon-Fri early afternoons. Rsvs 1 wk in advance, free.

St Mary's Cathedral, Geary & Gough. Almost extra-terrestrial in feeling, with a free-hanging meteor shower over the altar. 'Well worth seeing.' Free.

Telegraph Hill/Russian Hill: Romantic **Telegraph Hill** is topped by **Coit Tower**. Does it look like the nozzle of a firehose to you? $3 for the elevator to the top.

Russian Hill was the gathering place for bohemian writers, artists and poets, from Ambrose Bierce to George ('cool grey city of love') Sterling. It boasts not 1 but 3 steep streets that make it the most vertical district in SF: famous

Lombard, with its 8 switchbacks and 90-degree angles (almost impossible to photograph but featured in movies such as *What's Up Doc?* and *Foul Play*); **Filbert** btwn Hyde and Leavenworth; and **Union** btwn Polk and Hyde.

War Memorial Opera saw the signing of the UN charter on 25 April, 1945.

ENTERTAINMENT

Whatever your sexual proclivities, it takes quite a bit of cash (and often a smart appearance) to explore the singles bars, meat-rack taverns and gay watering holes of SF. Some tips: go at happy hour, when drinks are cheaper and hors d'oeuvres available; Union St is hetero, Castro-Polk is gay. A better tip: SF has a high VD and herpes rate, and the action has calmed down considerably since the advent of AIDS. Emphasis is now on 'safe sex,' but sex that's safe hasn't been invented. In unfamiliar environs, your best tip is to relax, enjoy the atmosphere and music, and save your hunting for your home turf. The City's 'happening' nightlife scene is constantly changing due to fashion and nightclubs changing names or going bust (as in any city). The area south of Market is usually quite lively. The best sources of info for events, clubs, music are the BAM monthly, the free *Bay Guardian* (comes out Weds) and the *Pink Datebook* section of the Sunday *Chronicle Examiner*. Also, you can call the City Guide Hotline, 332-9601, for answers to questions on entertainment as well as dining, accommodation, shops and services. Look under *www.sfbay.yahoo.com/Entertainment_and_Arts/* for the latest on bars, pubs and clubs, events, movies, music and theatre.

Cadillac Bar, 1 Holland Court, 543-8226. Mexican restaurant and bar with live Latin music where seafood specialities are cooked over Mesquite wood fires; entrees under $15. 'Great atmosphere and good fun.' 11 am-11 pm, Mon-Thurs, Fri & Sat 'til 12, Sun 'til 10.

DNA Lounge, 375 11th St, 626-2532. Subterranean disco-club open for all-night dancing.

Johnny Love's, 1500 Broadway, 931-8021. Live music nightly—jazz, dance, rock, funk, blues *ad infinitum*. Where the baseball players hang-out. Daily 5 pm-2 am. Cover Sun-Tue $2-5, Sat & Sun $9. Also has a restaurant.

Pier 23 Cafe, The Embarcadero, 362-5125. Newly remodeled cafe/nightclub, has Bay view, funky atmosphere. Cover $5 after 9 pm on Fri & Sat. Tues-Sat 11.30 am-1 am.

Plowshares, Ft Mason Center, Laguna St at Marina Blvd, 681-7966. Traditional, modern folk music.

Rasselas Jazz Club and Ethiopian Restaurant, 2801 California St, 567-5010. Jazz, blues and cabaret-style evenings. Restaurant opens at 5 pm, live music 8 pm-midnight Sun-Thur, 9 pm-1 am Fri & Sat.

Rock & Bowl, 1855 Haight St, 826-BOWL (for Fri & Sat) 752-2366 (other nights); check out the message even if you don't intend to bowl! Combine disco and bowling, add 12ft video screens, and there you have it. The young and hip place to be on a Thurs (around 9 pm), Fri or Sat night. Fri and Sat operate on a shift system—2 per evening, $7-10. Call ahead to rsvs. 'Good for a laugh.'

Slim's, 373 11th St, 255-0333. No age limit, over 21's get a stamp entitling them to a drink. 'Good for local bands.' Daily from 8 pm, cover $3-$25, depending on band.

Sigmund Stern Grove Concert Series, 19th Ave and Sloat Blvd, 252-6252. Bring a picnic and listen to opera/jazz/classical in a bower of eucalyptus and redwood trees. Free, Sun 2 pm, mid-June-mid-Aug. Serious music, dance, theatre offerings are abundant; see the *Datebook*. The symphony has inexpensive (around $11.50) open rehearsal seats; enquire at 431-5400. Also: 'You can usually get a standing ticket for $8 at the Opera House; after 1st act, grab a free seat. Productions of a high standard.'

Festivals: International Film Festival, March 7. More than 100 feature and short films from throughout the world. Call 863-0814. San Francisco's largest free blues festival, the **Blues and Art on Polk**, held July 12-13, features three stages of outstanding music, arts & crafts, gourmet food and drink. Call 346-4446. Also, **Union St Spring Festival**, June 1st. Arts and crafts, gourmet food, outdoor cafes and beer gardens. Call 346-4446.

SHOPPING

Tower Records, Columbus and Bay, 885-0500. Vast selection, daily 'til midnight. For deeply discounted records and rare stuff, go to **Rasputin's** in Berkeley; for second-hand records try **Reckless Records**, 1401 Haight St. Try along **Clement**, at the Thrift Town on Mission, and in Haight-Ashbury for **vintage clothing** and factory overruns: many marvellous shops.

SPORT

For professional baseball lovers: the **SF Giants in 3-Com Park**, Gilman Ave, and the **Oakland A's** at the **Alameda Stadium**. Later in the year, football action takes over, with the **SF 49ers at 3-Com**. Try looking under *Sports and Recreation* at *www.sfbay.yahoo.com* to find a wealth of online information on amusement/theme parks, baseball, basketball, outdoors, skating, skiing and snowboarding.

INFORMATION

General: SF is a Moonies mecca; they are friendly, may invite you to their camp, 120 miles N, or to dinner. Nip their overtures in the bud with a forthright, 'piss off.' 'Very convincing, hard to get away from.' 'Also watch out for hit artists around North Beach.'

Redwood Empire Association, 2801 Leavenworth, 2nd floor of Cannery at Fisherman's Wharf, 543-8334 (also at airport). Helpful organisation, friendly staff with info on all 'Redwood' counties—SF and north. Free guide. Mon-Fri, 9 am-5 pm, Sat 10 am-4 pm.

San Francisco Convention and Visitors Bureau, 201 3rd St, 974-6900. Mon-Fri 8.30 am-5 pm.

Visitors Information Center, 900 Market at Powell in Hallidie Plaza, 391-2000. Multilingual, helpful, Mon-Fri 9 am-5.30 pm, Sat 'til 3 pm, Sun 10 am-2 pm. MUNI passes available, 1 day $6, 3 day $10. Events message on 391-2001.

Travelers Aid, 877-0118, general information booth at the airport.

TRAVEL

'Parking can be very expensive, rely on local public transport.' Pick up BART or Golden Gate Transit maps for free, or a MUNI map for a fee. 'Wonderful but incomprehensible, even with regional transport guide; eg. trains become street cars. Transfers and cheap deals exist. Ask. Even the natives kept asking us questions in BART stations.'

A/C Transit services East Bay from Transbay Terminal, (510) 839-2882. Often faster than BART in rush hours.

Amtrak, (800) 872-7245. Free shuttle from Ferry Building to Emeryville and from Transbay to Oakland depot where you get daily service on *Coast Starlight* and *San Joaquins* (to Merced, Fresno, near National Parks). Also commuter train, 700 4th St at Townsend, 495-4546. Frequent trains, SF-San Jose only. Open 5 am-8 pm.

BART, 788-BART in SF, (510) 465-BART in East Bay. Sleek, carpeted, comfortable 'Bullet-Beneath-the-Bay,' connecting SF with Oakland, Berkeley, etc. Fares 90¢—$3.45. Long waits during rush hours and on Sun. Transfers valid btwn BART and MUNI. 'Worth it just for the experience.' Mon-Sat 6 am-midnight, Sun 9 am-midnight.

Express Airporter bus, 923 Folsom, 673-2433. Daily service from 5.20 am-11 pm, every 20 min in daytime. $9 o/w; $15 r/t. Also leaves from The Hyatt Regency in the financial district, hotels around Union Sq and Fisherman's Wharf.

Golden Gate Transit, 332-6600. Operates bridge, ferries to Sausalito and Larkspur from Ferry Bldg, about $5 o/w, and buses to Marin and Sonoma counties from Transbay Terminal, at 1st & Mission.

Green Tortoise Bus, 285-2441 or from outside CA, toll-free (800) TORTOISE. Counterculture service to East Coast, Baja, Alaska, Seattle, New Orleans, the Grand Canyon, Yosemite and just about anywhere, in diesels with sleeping platforms. To everything there is a season—and the Tortoises migrate accordingly: Mexico in winter, Alaska in summer, California anytime.

Greyhound, 425 Mission St, (800) 231-2222. Daily 5 am-12.30 am.

MUNI local transit, 673-MUNI. 700 mile network of buses and trains with frequent service, friendly drivers and good transfer system; $1 allows travel for 1½hrs anywhere on system, part of which is underground, a free transfer allows two more journeys. MUNI also runs the fabled cable cars; $2. MUNI passes $6 all day, $10 for 3 consecutive days available at Visitors Information Center at Fisherman's Wharf and the cable car ticket booth at Pier 39, Victoria Park. With the 1- or 3-day pass, discounts are available at museums and other attractions. MUNI map available and advisable $2.

San Francisco International Airport, 12 miles S, 761-0800; customs information (is downtown), 744-7742. Moonie-infested. For airport bus service see above.

San Mateo Transit (Samtrans), Burlingame, (800) 660-4287. SF to Palo Alto, San Mateo. To complicate matters some routes do not accept luggage—to get you and your luggage **to the airport** take bus #7B (local service which stops everywhere and takes 1hr—leave plenty of time!) from 5th and Mission. The express bus, #7F, *will not under any circumstances* allow luggage, it takes ½ an hour, $3.

Thrifty car rental: 928-6666, seems to offer the best value. There are massive daily surcharges for insurance, and under 25s must pay an extra $20 per day, rsvs at least 1 week in advance during summer.

For tours: **Gray Line**, 558-7300. City tours, Muir Woods, Sausalito, cruises. From 3½ hrs to all day; from $26, Alcatraz tour $10, daily 7.30 am-11 pm.

BERKELEY and OAKLAND

Like Siamese twins, these two neighbour cities blend imperceptibly into one another physically, while each demonstrates a personality of its own. Easily reached by BART or bus, this area—the East Bay—offers good day trips; Berkeley for its university and accompanying cultural and social dividends, Oakland for its Jack London Square, excellent lakeside museum, blues clubs and baseball team known as the 'Athletics.' Both cities are short on cheap lodgings and long on streets that are unsafe to walk at night.

Concentrate on the area in and around the university, the closest you'll

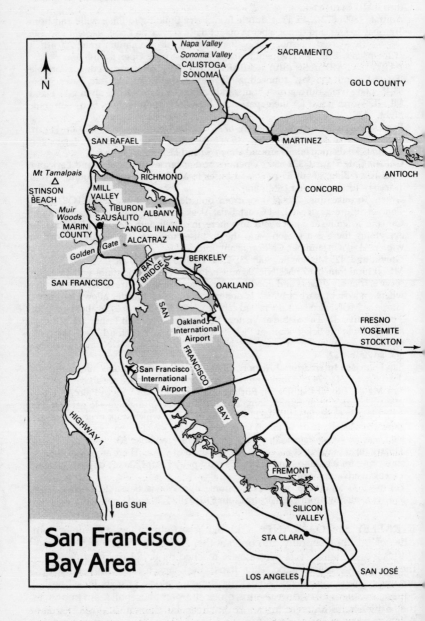

Napa Valley
Sonoma Valley
CALISTOGA
SONOMA

SACRAMENTO

GOLD COUNTY

N

SAN RAFAEL

MARTINEZ

ANTIOCH

Mt Tamalpais
STINSON
BEACH
MILL
VALLEY
Muir
Woods
MARIN
COUNTY

RICHMOND

CONCORD

TIBURON
SAUSÁLITO
ANGOL INLAND
ALCATRAZ

ALBANY

Golden Gate

BERKELEY

SAN FRANCISCO

BAY
BRIDGE

OAKLAND

FRESNO
YOSEMITE
STOCKTON

SAN

Oakland
International
Airport

San Francisco
International
Airport

FRANCISCO

HIGHWAY 1

BAY

BIG SUR

FREMONT

San Francisco
Bay Area

SILICON
VALLEY

STA CLARA

LOS ANGELES

SAN JOSÉ

come to the fabled Berzerkley of free speech, anti-war, radical fame. 'Rather bohemian atmosphere, good for buying secondhand rare books, homemade trinkets or discussing Marxist ideology with a stranger in a coffeehouse.'
The telephone area code is 510. www.berkeleystyle.com/ is a guide to movies, dining out, community resources and everything else in Berkeley. *www.oaklander.com/* provides info about the Oakland area.

ACCOMMODATION
Easily the greatest challenge to visitors is trying to find somewhere cheap to sleep in the East Bay. One source is housing advertised in the *Daily Californian*, the newspaper of the University of California, Berkeley. Also, try UC Berkeley fraternities—easy access to city and inexpensive if not free. 'Filthy but at the price who cares?' Each fraternity determines for itself whether or not to accept guests, and policies are subject to change. If the frats turn you down (or vice versa), here are some more possibilities:
Berkeley Hotel, 2001 Bancroft, Berkeley, 843-4043, S-$32, D-$43.
Motel 6, 8484 Edes, at Oakland airport, 638-1180, S-$39, D-$45.
YMCA, 2001 Allston Way, Berkeley, 848-6800. $27 includes use of facilities. $2 key deposit, 14-day max stay.

FOOD
Blondie's Pizza, 2340 Telegraph, 548-1129. Delicious slices for $2.50.
Brennan's, 720 University Ave, Berkeley, 841-0960. Downtown bar with Guinness, cheap and simple foods—a local hangout. Daily 11 am-9.30 pm (food), bar 'til 12.30 am. Fri and Sat 'til 2 am.
Cafe Milano, 2522 Bancroft, 644-3100. Nicknamed 'Cafe Pretentious.' 'This is a must if you're going to sample the atmosphere of Berkeley properly.' Daily 7 am-midnight.
Flint's Barbecue, 3114 San Pablo Ave, Oakland, 658-9912, and 6609 Shattuck, Oakland, 653-0593. 'Best ribs in town'—around $15. Mon-Thurs 11 am-11 pm, Fri & Sat 'til 2 am.
Pasand, 2286 Shattuck, Berkeley, 549-2559. Indian food, excellent and cheap.
Spenger's, 1919 4th, Berkeley, 845-7771. Forget Fisherman's Wharf, this is *the* Bay Area institution for seafood. Sun-Thur 7 am-11 pm, Fri & Sat 'til midnight; $10-$15.
University cafeterias on campus ('except the main one—expensive'), 'til 3 pm in summer. **International House** is also recommended.

OF INTEREST
On campus: Black Oak Books, 1491 Shattuck, 486-0698. 10 am-10 pm daily. New and used books on all subjects. Readings most evenings at 7.30 pm, often given by some very well-known authors and poets. 'A gem. Go!' **Lawrence Hall of Science**, Centennial Dr, 642-5132, sits above campus in the Berkeley hills, take buses #8/65 from downtown. Daily 10 am-5 pm, $6.50, $4.50 w/student ID. 'Top of the mountain, excellent view, amazing museum, spent whole afternoon playing computer games.' The football stadium sits directly on the Hayward fault, a branch of the San Andreas; a large vertical crack may be seen through the upper tier. Both the **Campanile (Sather Tower)** in the centre of campus and the **Lawrence Hall of Science** on the hill above (take bus) have excellent views of Berkeley and the Bay.
Main Library (where Mario Savio and Joan Baez addressed the first major student demonstration against the Vietnam War in 1964) has world's largest collection of Mark Twain materials. 'Try the browsing room (Morrison Room)—British newspapers, headphones to listen to records.'
Phoebe Hearst Museum, corner of Bancroft and College, 643-7648. Excellent Indian costumes and crafts, $2. Mon-Fri 10 am-4.30 pm, Sat & Sun from noon, free on Thur. **University Art Museum**, 2626 Bancroft Way, 642-0808. Video, perfor-

mance art, modern works, $6. Wed-Sun, 10 am-4.30 pm; free Thur 11 am-noon, 5 pm-9 pm. 'Not worth it.' Located in the museum building is **Pacific Film Archives**, 2621 Durant, 642-1124. Nightly showing, more at term time. $5 for the first show, $2.50 for additional features. Runs gamut from Japanese samurai flicks to vintage 1930s classics.

Off campus: Tilden Park, above city in the Berkeley Hills.

Moe's Bookstore, 2476 Telegraph, 849-2087. Huge and politically hip—4 floors of books. Daily 10 am-11 pm.

Sake Takara USA Inc., 708 Addison at 4th, Berkeley, 540-8250. 10 min slide show and free tastings of wine and sake, noon-6 pm daily.

Oakland: Jack London Sq, 10 mins from BART City Center station. Visit Jack London's cabin from his Klondike days, have a drink at the First and Last Chance Saloon, where London and RL Stevenson used to tipple. 'Village is excellent reconstruction of the wharf area.'

Lake Merritt, downtown Oakland, is the largest saltwater lake within a US city; overlooking it is the **Oakland Museum** at 1000 Oak St (Lake Merritt BART Stn), 238-3401. Art, history and natural science of California—interesting. $5, $3 w/student ID. Wed-Sat 10 am-5 pm, Sun noon-7 pm, free Sun 4 pm-7 pm.

ENTERTAINMENT

Ashkenaz, 1317 San Pablo, 525-5054. Multi-ethnic folk dancing. 'Cheap fun.'

Cafe Bistro, 2271 Shattuck, 848-3081. Fun bar with live jazz (no cover) serving country French food, prix fix $10. Upstairs is the **Metropole Restaurant**, larger menu at prices your parents could afford! Tues-Sun 7 pm-1 am, Fri & Sat from 5 pm.

Freight and Salvage, 1111 Addison St, 548-1761. Mixed bag of country, bluegrass, ethnic groups and comedy. Free, but no alcohol or smoking! Daily 7 pm-midnight.

Larry Blake's, 2367 Telegraph, 848-0886. Big-name blues, funk and rock bands. 'Lively restaurant/bar with good local bands.' 'Lively part is downstairs.' Daily 11 am-2 am. Food served 'til 1 am; $4-10 a dish. Cover $2-8, free Sun.

Triple Rock, 1920 Shattuck, 843-2739. Great bar with a redwood deck. Beer brewed on premises. For punk, go to Berkeley Square. Daily 11 am-12.30 am/1.30 am.

SURVIVAL

Berkeley Free Clinic, 2339 Durant, 548-2570 (24 hr). Mon-Thur from 7 pm, call at 6.45 pm.

Berkeley Support Services, 2100 Martin Luther King Way, 848-3378. Has info, plus rough and ready crash pad (emphasis on rough!). Not rec for women. 'This is designed for the truly homeless, so use only in emergency.' Donations.

INFORMATION/TRAVEL

A/C Transit also serves the campus, take buses #7, 8, 40, 51, 52.

Oakland International Airport. Take the Freemont bus to the Colosseum station ($2.15), AirBART bus from there ($2). Leaves every 10 mins from 6 am 'til midnight, $2. Call 465-BART.

UC/Berkeley Shuttle, 643-5708. From Berkeley BART stations to campus, Botanical Gardens, Hall of Science, etc. 25¢ o/w, 7 am-6 pm w/days only.

SANTA CRUZ-MONTEREY This stretch of coast rivals the section north of San Francisco in its scenic beauty. Not nearly so unpopulated, though—tiny hamlets and larger towns line Hwy 1 (also known in this area as the Cabrillo Hwy). The first major city, **Santa Cruz**, is 90 miles S of SF and similarly suffering considerable damage in the October '89 earthquake. Jumping nightlife, lots of movies and bookstores, surfers aplenty and a rowdy beach and boardwalk scene earn the town its name, as pronounced by natives:

'Sanna Cruize.' The **University of California campus**, home of the 'Battling Banana Slugs,' is a special jewel. Eight colleges, independent of one another are hidden in the redwoods on a hill above the town; can you find them all?

Nearby is **Capitola-by-the-Sea**, a doll's village of Victorian houses and beach bungalows; its name comes from the days when this sleepy seaside resort was California's capital. Catch the Begonia Festival if you're here in September. Further south are the towns of **Soquel/Aptos**. Around the curve of the **Monterey Bay**, the towns of **Pacific Grove**, **Monterey**, **Pebble Beach** and **Carmel-by-the-Sea** cluster on a knob of land jutting out into the Pacific. Here, the cheap glitz of the Santa Cruz boardwalk gives way to much more expensive glitz, and the soft warm beauty of the coast turns angular, dramatic and cold. You don't need to shell out $5 for the **17-Mile Drive** to see it, though—bike it for free, or just north of the drive is an even more beautiful stretch, beginning at Ocean View Blvd and 3rd St in Pacific Grove: **Sunset Drive**, which also happens to be the best time to see it. And it's also free.
The telephone area code is 408. www.santacruz-ca.com/ has links to restaurants, clubs and more.

SURVIVAL
This is a resort area, which means the necessities of life—food and shelter—tend to be treated as luxuries here: you can spend exorbitant amounts on either. Fortunately, Santa Cruz has a culture that generally welcomes students, transients or people who combine both qualities at once; the Monterey and Carmel area can be hostile to same.

ACCOMMODATION
Bill's Home Haven, 1040 Ceilo Lane, Nipomo, 929-3467. 50 miles NW of Santa Barbara just off the I-101. Get a map from the Mobil Station in Nipomo for directions. 12 beds, non-smoking, $10.

The Parmelee Victorian HI Hostel, Monterey. Victorian house with a spectacular view of the Monterey Bay, this hostel is a short walk from Cannery Row, Fisherman's Wharf and Monterey Bay Aquarium. Whale watching, fishing, boating, scuba diving, sunbathing and explore nearby historic Spanish adobes.

Point Montara Lighthouse HI Hostel, 16th St at Hwy 1, 25 miles S of San Francisco, (415) 728-7177. Restored lighthouse in an exceptionally beautiful place; including an outdoor hot tub. Explore the coastline and watch the annual migration of gray whales btwn Nov and April. There are several great beaches for swimming, surfing, jogging, horseback riding and windsurfing. $12-14.

Pigeon Point Lighthouse HI Hostel, 210 Pigeon Point Rd, Pescadero (Hwy 1, 50 miles S of San Francisco), (415) 879-0633. Perched on a cliff on the central California coast, the 115 ft Pigeon Point Lighthouse, one of the tallest lighthouses in America, has been guiding mariners since 1872. From the boardwalk behind the fog signal building, watch for gray whales on their annual migration. Walk through the tide-pool area or through the amazing 1,000 yr old redwoods nearby. $12-14. Outdoor hot tub, kitchen; rsvs essential.

Santa Cruz HI Hostel, 321 Main St, Santa Cruz, 423-8304. 15 min walk from Greyhound. Hostel is located at the Carmelita Cottages (restored 1870's cottages), on Beach Hill. Only 2 blocks from beach, boardwalk, amusement park, and wharf; 5 blocks from downtown. Steamer Lane is one of the best West Coast surfing spots. Capitola Village 4 miles away; Monterey is less than 1 hr by car. Extensive bus system makes this a great starting point to state parks in the nearby mountains. Outside lockers store bags of early arrivals, garden, fireplace, barbecue, free evening snack. $13-15. 3 night minimum stay. 11 pm curfew.
www.cse.ucsc.edu/~peter/yh/schs.html.

AMERICAN BEACHES

From the rugged and lonely north Pacific shoreline to the crowded, hedonistic playgrounds of Florida's coasts, America's beaches have something for everyone. Even to the landlocked, the scent of coconut oil strikes a deeper chord than that of traditional apple pie. For a truly American experience, try these beaches:

WEST COAST—The best: Redondo Beach, south of Los Angeles. Hawaiian George Freeth introduced the Polynesian art of surfing to the mainland here. **Most beautiful:** 17 miles of seals and sea lions, pink and purple ice plants between **Pacific Grove** and **Carmel**

See the surfers at sunset. **Most fashionable: Malibu**, with its bleached sandy beaches, celebs' homes dotting the hills above. A close second is **La Jolla**, near San Diego, CA, a ritzy, cove-lined beach frequented by upscale beachcombers, divers and surfers. **Strangest: Venice Beach**, near LA, has rollerskating grannies, graffiti, and a lot of muscle. **Snorkelling: Hanauma Bay**, Oahu, Hawaii. The best. **Surfing: Maui Island** in Hawaii boasts incredible surfing. NB: all the beaches in Hawaii are public. Try the local sport of 'Boogie-boarding', so-called because participants 'boogie' down the beach on rectangular boards, riding on the tail end of the surf. **Windsurfing: Hookipa Beach Park, Maui**—unrivalled as the world's No. 1 location due to constant trade winds and exceptional wave conditions. 'Fun just to watch.' 'If everybody had an ocean, across the USA, then everybody'd be surfing, Californ-I-A,' sang the Beach Boys, most likely with **Long Beach** in mind, *the* place for surfing and site of Howard Hughes' *Spruce Goose*. **Most forgotten: Santa Catalina Island**. Accessible by ferry. No cars, just scuba diving and swimming.
Most peaceful: Long Beach, on Vancouver Island's west coast, BC 12 miles of sea, sand and solitude.

THE EAST COAST—Hampton Beach, New Hampshire, has boardwalk, arcades, and waterslides. **Virginia Beach**, Virginia, fast growing resort with 28m beach. **Brunswick**, Maine, hosts excellent Beach Bluegrass Festival over Labor Day weekend. **Ocean City**, Maryland, crowded with Washingtonians, wild. **Myrtle Beach**, South Carolina, 3rd most-visited spot on East Coast behind Disneyworld and Atlantic City. Nearby **North Myrtle** becomes a student mecca in early mid-May. **Atlantic City**, New Jersey, birthplace of salt water taffy and showplace of Miss America. **Asbury Park**, decaying but still can lay claim to Bruce Springsteen. **Brighton Beach**, Brooklyn, New York, the only American beach where Russian is the native language!

FLORIDA—Sanibel Island, for the best seashells, starfish; **Cocoa Beach** has cosmic surfing and the added attraction of being the blast-off site for Space Shuttle flights. **Fort Lauderdale**, midway between Palm Beach and Miami is a glut of beer, raw lust and sports cars.

San Jose Sanborn Park HI Hostel, 15808 Sanborn Rd, Saratoga, (408) 741-0166. This log house hostel is tucked away in a forest of redwoods and madrones in Sanborn County Park. Excellent starting point for hiking in the Santa Cruz Mountains as is nearby Winchester Mystery House, Rosicrucian Egyptian Museum and Technology Center Museum. $9.
Townhouse Motel, 1106 Fremont Blvd, Seaside, 394-3113. 1 block from Monterey,

close to beach. From S-$50, D-$80. 'Good accommodation.'
Camping: Big Sur Campground and Cabins, 667-2322. $22 for two, $25 w/hook-up, XP-$3. Cabins S/D-$40-$150. Rsvs essential in summer. 2 miles N of Pfeiffer-Big Sur State Park on Hwy 1, 26 miles S of Carmel.

FOOD
Generally, be wary of any restaurant that caters too obviously to the tourist trade. Plenty of places, particularly in Santa Cruz, have a reputation with the locals for serving overpriced, mediocre food; the restaurants in Monterey and Carmel are merely overpriced. Here are some eateries that are more in line with a hungry budget traveller's needs:

Georgiana's, behind Bookshop Santa Cruz, 1520 Pacific Ave, 423-0900, Santa Cruz. In a Mediterranean-style courtyard that becomes the town square on Sunday afternoons. Each of the 8 colleges of the university has its own coffee house, where you can mix and mingle with students; the best is **Banana Joe's** at Crown College. Closed in summer.

Mike's Seafood Restaurant, Fisherman's Wharf, **Monterey**, 372-6153. 'Cheap for the area, good seafood.' Delicious deep-fried calimari and linguine Alfredo with shrimp, $8.50. Daily 9 am-10 pm.

Mr Toots, 221A Esplanade, **Capitola**, 475-3679. Grab a bran muffin ($1.95) and watch the seagulls from the outside deck. Everything under $4. 'A bargain!' Daily 7.30 am-midnight.

Seychelles, 313 Cedar, **Santa Cruz**, 425-0450. 'Quintessential Californian vegetarian meals.' Daily 10.30 am-4 pm, 5.30 pm-midnight

Village Corner, Dolores & 6th, **Carmel**, 624-3588. Greek food from $8, good bfasts around $7, 'try the eggs Benedict,' informal setting. Daily 7.30 am-10 pm.

Whole Earth Restaurant, UC Santa Cruz campus, 426-8255. An oversized treehouse with politically-conscious cuisine. Closed w/ends in summer. Mon-Fri 7.30 am-4 pm. 'World food.' African specialities, from $5.

Zachary's, 819 Pacific, **Santa Cruz**, 427-0646. Huge, good bfasts for cheap; under $10. Try Mike's Mess (if you dare!) $6.50. Go early unless you're keen on queues! Tue-Sun, 7 am-2.30 pm.

OF INTEREST
Coming down Hwy 1 from SF, you get to **Pt Ano Nuevo** (pronounced 'An-yo Noo-ey-vo') **State Beach** before Santa Cruz. If it's winter, you may be able to see breeding elephant seals lazing in the rookery there. Critters of another sort romp on the area's nude beaches; best known is the 'red, white and blue' beach, marked by a mailbox sporting stripes of those colours 4 miles S of Davenport on Hwy 1. Coming into town, glimpse **UC Santa Cruz** on the swelling green hills to your left; from roads leading to its colleges nestled in the trees, you can get spectacular views of Monterey Bay. The vista from **Cowell College** is particularly good. Of the Coney Island-type boardwalks that once lined California's coast, only one remains, and here it is: the Santa Cruz **beach and boardwalk** . The municipal wharf is also worth a stroll. If you get weary of squishing discarded hot dogs btwn your toes, wander over to the **Pacific Garden Mall**, which has organic restaurants, organic clothing stores and organic people roaming the streets. Just north of the boardwalk is **West Cliff Drive**, which leads to **Natural Bridges State Beach**, (408) 423-4609, ($6 car); though only one of the sandstone bridges still stands. If you have time and transportation, take Hwy 17 (drive carefully) to San Jose to see the **Winchester Mystery House**, 525 S Winchester Blvd, 247-2101. Tours $12.50, 65 mins. Sara Winchester, the story goes, was directed by the ghosts of people killed by Winchester Rifles to build additions onto her home haphazardly and continuously. The resulting jumble of 160 skewed rooms, staircases that go up and down, and doors leading to nowhere is seen by some as the architectural analogue to development in the sur-

rounding Silicon Valley. Daily 9 am-8 pm. Also, stick around for a number of festivals around the beginning of July. July 5-6th features the annual **Tahiti Fete**, a Polynesian dance competition with arts & crafts, music and dancing. Call 486-9177. The **San Jose America Festival**, is held annually July 3-5th. There is local and international music and dance groups, arts & crafts, food and fireworks. Call 457-1141.

Cannery Row, Monterey. Rows of defunct sardine canneries immortalized by John Steinbeck make wonderful homes for little shoppes. Daily 8 am-7 pm.

Kalisa's Coffee House, 851 Cannery Row, 372-3621, is a reformed brothel, with belly dancing on 2nd Sat of the month; across the street, the more cerebral **Monterey Bay Aquarium**, 375-3333, displays species native to the Monterey Bay in huge tank settings so natural that visitors get the impression that they are the ones behind glass. Daily, 9.30 am-6 pm in summer; $12.75. 'Great value for money. Fantastic for biologists and non-biologists alike.'

Carmel is an acquired taste. The town draws hordes of curiosity seekers, all of whom want to catch a glimpse of actor and one-time mayor, Clint Eastwood at his **Hog's Breath Inn**, at San Carlos and 5th. You won't, but stop by anyway for a look, maybe a drink—in a setting that would make Bilbo Baggins feel right at home. Carmel has been accused of calculated cuteness but is worth seeing, if only for the experience of wandering down an alley and discovering a greenhouse in a hidden courtyard.

Derby Skatepark, near Natural Bridges. Concrete snakerun built in the mid-70s, bowls at either end. Roll-out deck added in late 80s; suitable for skateboarding/inlining. Also, **Monterey Bay**, 1855 E Ave, and **The Skate Station**, Sand City (right next door to Monterey Indoor Park) has an 11½ ft vertical ramp, street course includes trannies to wall, a corner bowl, a 6 ft mini rampw/spine. Small but fun, also has a board shop. Daily. *www.TeamAdventures.com*

The Mission, ½ mile from downtown, has a star-shaped window framed by vines, fountains and flowers. It's free (donations are 'nice'). The white sand beach nearby is great for running barefoot on; don't attempt to swim in the cold and treacherous surf, though.

Point Lobos State Reserve, 624-4909, 2 miles S of Carmel. Monterey-Salinas Transit stops here several times a day, on its way to Big Sur. $6 p/car, walkers get in free. (You can park your car on the hwy and walk in to avoid the fee!) 450 acres of natural beauty: coves, islands, fearless animals and birds. Best of all are China Cove and the beach beyond (take lunch). Daily 9 am-7 pm.

Pfeiffer-Big Sur State Park, 667-2315, is only one tiny part of the 90 mile stretch of scissored coastline btwn Carmel and San Simeon known as 'Big Sur.' The stretch is almost pristine and wholly soul satisfying. Free with ticket from Point Lobus, otherwise $6. Do stop for the obligatory open-air quaff and sea-gazing at **Nepenthe**, 667-2345; Cafe Amphora on the lower deck actually has the better view. Big Sur was home to the beats and Henry Miller and today continues to be inhabited (sparsely) by rugged individualists.

INFORMATION
Carmel Tourist Information Center, on Mission btwn 5th and 6th Sts, 624-1711. Mon-Fri 8 am-4 pm.

Monterey Convention and Visitors Bureau, 380 Alvarado St, 649-1770, has a self-guiding walk brochure for the city's old buildings. Mon-Fri 9 am-5 pm.

Santa Cruz Convention and Visitors Center, 701 Front St, 425-1234. Mon-Fri 9 am-5 pm, w/ends 10 am-4 pm. Also open at w/ends 9 am-6 pm is the **visitors centre** at 401 Camino El Estero by the Lake.

TRAVEL
Greyhound, 425 Front St (downtown Santa Cruz), (800) 231-2222 has service from SF to Monterey. Daily 7 am-6.45 pm.

Monterey-Salinas Transit, 899-2555/424-7695. $1.25 per zone, free transfers. All downtown routes stop at Munras/Tyler/Pearl St triangle. Serves Monterey, Pacific Grove and Carmel; spring and summer service to Big and Little Sur as far as Nepenthe ($2.50 o/w).

Santa Cruz Metro, 425-8600. Lots of routes, runs late. $1 or $3 day pass, for bus or summer shuttle to Santa Cruz beach.

SAN LUIS OBISPO and SANTA BARBARA COUNTIES Called the central coast, this region stretches from Big Sur south to Santa Barbara. Among its highlights are **San Simeon**, site of **Hearst Castle**, built by William Randolph Hearst, newspaper magnate and the *Citizen Kane* of Orson Welles' film. This Spanish-style castle houses Hearst's $75 million art collection, which includes now-priceless tapestries, rugs, jade, statuary, even entire antique ceilings and fireplaces and assorted loot from all over Europe, including Cardinal de Richelieu's bed. 'A two-hour trip into paradise.'

Further down the coast, **Morro Rock** makes a monolithic landmark at water's edge, the first in a series of volcanic peaks that march picturesquely through San Luis Obispo County. You can follow them along Hwy 1 (also the bus route). Beaches and camping opportunities abound; the amiable character of the inland town of **San Luis Obispo** adds to the area's appeal.

90 miles S of Morro Bay on Hwy 101 is **Solvang**, a charming coastal replica of a Danish town, 'worth a visit with its reasonably priced accommodation and restaurants.' Further south, **Santa Barbara** beckons. Far and away the loveliest coastal cities, from its setting against the Santa Ynez Mountains to its beautiful Spanish adobe architecture. Despite its wealth, Santa Barbara is a non-stuffy, youthful city, with a big UC campus, sophisticated nightlife and the best sidewalk cafe idling anywhere in the US. 'Beautiful unspoilt beaches.' 'Elegant little town with a lot happening.'
The telephone area code is 805.

ACCOMMODATION
Farm Hostel, PO Box 723, Ojai, CA 93024, (805) 646-0311. An independent backpackers lodge located in the beautiful Ojai Valley, gateway to the Southern California outback. 50 miles N of LA; 40 mins drive from Santa Barbara; 20 mins from Ventura beach and ocean. Cable, video, music, A/C, hot showers, near hot springs. Free pick up from Greyhound/Amtrak. Non-smoking, passport and rsvs required $12.

Hotel State St, 121 State St, Santa Barbara, 966-6586. 'Excellent; staff very nice and helpful.' From S/D/T-$52, includes bfast.

San Luis Obispo SLO Coast HI Hostel, 1292 Foothill Blvd, 544-4678. Perfect stopover for travellers along California's spectacular Central Coast. Serving as gateway to Big Sur, the hostel is within walking distance of downtown shops, restaurants and theatres. Don't miss the downtown Farmer's Market every Thur night! With its ideal year-round climate, San Luis Obispo is a mecca for bicyclists, hikers and other outdoor enthusiasts. From $14, $2 less for cyclists. Hot tub, laundry, patio and barbecue, sports equipment, garden. *www.internetcafe.allyn.com/SLO*

Santa Barbara Banana Bungalow, 210 E Ortega St, 963-0154. Excellent bars and shopping. Mountain hiking, organised yacht trips to Channel Island and 3 day winery bike rides. $15-17.

Camping: Morro Bay State Park info line: 772-7434 and (800) 444-7275 for all parks in the area. $16 w/out hook-up. For Hearst Castle, **camping** at San Simeon and Atascadero Beach.

OF INTEREST

Giant Chessboard, Embarcadero at Front, Morro Bay, 772-1214. The local chess club plays each Sat noon-5 pm, on a 16'16' board with redwood pieces that weigh as much as a small child! Possible to rent other days. $17 all day.

Hearst Castle, State Hwy 1, 927-2000. Incredible palatial over-indulgence of 1930s. The influence for Xanadu in *Citizen Kane*, and where William Randolph Hearst entertained presidents, kings and Hollywood stars. 'Absolutely fascinating.' Book at least a day in advance through MISTIX, (800) 444-7275. $14 for one of four tours covering different aspects of the castle; $25 for evening tours. 'Take Tour 2 or 3—smaller groups, more personal and informative.' Each tour lasts about 1¹/₂ hrs, daily 8.20 am-3.20 pm.

Morro Bay State Park, Hwy 1, 772-7434. Bird sanctuary, heron rookery. Daily 8.30 am-10.45 pm.

Old Mission Santa Barbara, upper end of Laguna St, Santa Barbara, 682-4713. Noble facade with columns and towers, many unusual touches, from Moorish fountain to Mexican skulls in the 1786 'Queen of the Missions.' Daily 9 am-5 pm, self-guided tours $3. More beautiful still is the **County Courthouse**, 1120 Anacapa St: a 1929 Hispano-Moorish treasure, inside and out. Check out **San Luis Obispo SLO Skatepark** on the corner of Oak St and Santa Rosa St where there is a street course and mini ramp for all avid skateboarders, inliners and BMXers.

Festivals: Robert Burns Night in San Luis Obispo, January 25th. Celebration features Scottish foods, music and dancing! Call 238-7860 for more details. Also in January is the **Annual Garden Festival**, San Luis Obispo. Colourful displays of flowers and exotic plants, contests, and demonstrations. Call 781-2777.

In Santa Barbara, the International Film festival, March 7-16th has premieres and screenings of international and American films with city-wide festivities. Call 963-0023. Later on in the year in July, the **Santa Barbara County Fair** in Santa Maria is a 6 day celebration including nightly performances by nationally-known musicians, arts & crafts, carnival and food. Contact (800) 549-0036. Don't miss the **Santa Barbara PowWow** in early Aug, where more than 300 dancers represent 40 tribes in a Native American dance competition. Also, traditional arts & crafts. Call 496-6036. The **Ojai Music Festival**, June 6-8th, is an outdoor classical music festival featuring world-renowned musicians and arts and crafts show. Call 646-2094. Nearby is the **Presidio Cafe**, 812 Anacapa St, 966-2428. One of SB's great places for lolling on the patio. Also try **Joe's Cafe**, 536 State, 966-4638: 'bustling atmosphere, lashings of food at low prices; a favourite student meeting place.' Mon-Thurs 11 am-11.30 pm, Fri and Sat 'til 12.30 am, Sun noon-9 pm.

FOOD

In Santa Barbara: McConnell's Ice Cream, 853 E Canon Perdido St, 963-8813. 'Best ice cream in America—and we sampled quite a few!' 17% butterfat. 8 am-5 pm daily.

The Natural Café, 508 State St, 962-9494. Healthy sandwiches and delicious smotthies. Sun-Thurs 11 am-10 pm, Fri-Sat 11 am-11 pm.

RG's Giant hamburgers, 922 State St, 963-1654. Voted for the best burgers in Santa Barbara 7 yrs running! Daily 7 am-9 pm.

In SLO: Your best bet for food is to head for **Higuera**. Try **Big Sky Café**, 1121 Broad St, 545-5401; and **Woodstock's Pizza Parlor**, 1000 Higuera St, 541-4420, for good chow.

YOSEMITE   An Oxford don once said, 'Think in centuries.' In Yosemite, it's inescapable. Cut in jewel facets by a glacial knife, the park encompasses nearly 1,200 square miles of incredible beauty—luminous lakes and dashing streams; groves of redwood elder statesmen and aged incense cedar; salt-

and pepper boulders comically abandoned in boggy alpine meadows by the retreating glaciers of past millennia.

People bemoan the popularity of Yosemite, but not even 3 million visitors per year can ruin it. One-third of them choose to jam the park btwn July and August, and 80% of those content themselves with a stay in Yosemite Valley (just call it 'nature's parking lot'), leaving vast areas untrampled. Despite its congestion, you shouldn't miss Yosemite Valley's supreme vistas of **Bridalveil Falls** and **Glacier Point**, as well as the steel-blue shoulders of **Half Dome** and **El Capitan**. A mountaineers' mecca, Half Dome is the sheerest cliff in America (the back way up isn't exactly flat, either), and El Capitan, the biggest block of exposed granite in the world, so huge you need binoculars to see the climbers taking a week to scale it.

A fine way to see the park is to travel up Hwy 41 from Fresno to the south entrance near **Mariposa Grove of Big Trees**; the exit from Wawona Tunnel into the valley is absolutely spine-tingling. You may even walk through a grove of Giant Sequoia redwoods after paying the initial park entrance fee of $20 p/car or $5 if hiking. If you have the time, don't leave the park right after seeing the valley; instead, take the high road, Hwy 120, over **Tioga Pass** to shimmering, endangered **Mono Lake**. Continue south on Hwy 395 through **Owens Valley**, a neglected gem in a dusty corner of the state; **Mt Whitney** is visible from the highway.

Open year-round, Yosemite Valley is at its best in spring and early autumn; in summer visitors pay for the balmy weather by watching the spectacular waterfalls fade to a trickle. But winter is the time hardy souls and true Yosemite afficionados love best. With the season's first dusting of snow, the valley becomes a stark, eerie, white-on-black tableau—a living Ansel Adams photograph.

For a complete guide to Yosemite, with virtual photos and weather reports, check out *www.sierranet.net/yosemite*.

The telephone area code is 209.

ACCOMMODATION

Within the park: More than any other spot in California, you must book cabin, lodge or camping accommodation in advance to avoid disappointment. 'Urbanised' campsites can be reserved through MISTIX, (800) 365-2267.

Outside Park: Motel 6, 1983 E Childs Ave at Hwy 99, **Merced**, 384-3702. From S/D-$35; 'We got 5 in a room after paying only for two. Best to get a taxi from Amtrak, $7.'

Yosemite Bug Hostel, 6979 Hwy 140, Midpines, (209) 966-6666. So-called because of the owner's collection of various mounted insects, this hostel is 20 miles E from Yosemite on several forested acres. The area is great for cycling and mountain biking, skiing, rafting and hiking (organises snowboard/hiking/biking treks). 'Clean, comfortable and set in a beautiful location.' At the end of the day, relax in front of the fireplace or at the hostel's café and coffee house on the deck. 'Fantastic! Can't recommend this place enough!' $12. *www.yosemitebug.com*

Yosemite Merced Home HI Hostel, , 725-0407. Experience a typical American home. Shop at Farmer's Market every Thurs eve (May-Sept), visit the nearby Applegate Park and zoo or just relax at Lake Yosemite. Breathtaking views of mountains and large, old sequoia trees of Yosemite national Park, 80 miles (2 hrs) from Merced. Sleepsack provided. $12. Rsvs essential. Will pick up from Greyhound and Amtrak.

Campsites: Sunnyside: $2 for a walk-in, and your only hope if you haven't booked in advance. Call 372-8502. Also possible to take the shuttle to **Backpacker's Camp**, a quiet retreat behind **North Pine's campground**, $2. 1 day max stay.

Other cabins: at Curry Village, Yosemite Lodge and **White Wolf Lodge**. Tent cabins at **Curry Village**, $42 for 2 pp, wood cabins $65, XP-$5. 'Pay for 2, fit 6 in!' 'Was too cold to get undressed when I was there in Sept.' Showers nearby, often overtaxed. For rsvs call 252-4848. Housekeeping units have a stove (sometimes outside), cost a little more. No bedding. Also at **Housekeeping Camp**, 1 mile S of Yosemite Village, $42 for 4 pp, mattress beds provided in three-wall concrete shelter. Summer only.

FOOD

Food is costly and often poor in the park. Readers recommend Yosemite Valley's burger shop and pizza house. **The Recovery Café** offers bfast, pack lunches, dinners, espresso drinks, beer and wine on tap, pool table and games in the rustic Main Lodge with view decks. Grocery stores, restaurants, cafeterias are located at Yosemite Valley, Curry Village, Wawona, Tioga Lake, White Wolf, Fish Camp, El Portal and Tuolumne Meadows.

OF INTEREST

Everything! If you're adventurous, climb Half Dome by hiking around to the *back* via a 17-mile round-trip trail and hauling yourself up a cable-and-slats 'stairway' to the top. The payoff is the view: the panorama of Yosemite Valley and beyond, and the dizzying drop-off from the cliff. 'Hike Yosemite Valley, Glacier Pt, Illilouette Falls, Panorama Trail, Nevada Falls, Vernal Falls, Happy Isles for best photos. 14 miles, 3200-ft ascents and descents. Walk up to Nevada Falls via John Muir Trail and then down by Mist Trail. Take a swimsuit—icy mountain pools. (Do not swim above waterfalls.) Good for those with less time. Met a bear—terrifying.'

INFORMATION

Park Information, 372-0265/454-2088 has info on lodging in the park. Park open year-round except Hwy 120 at Tioga Pass. $20 cars, $5 per hiker/bus passenger. 'Keep your ticket—checked on exit.'

Visitors Center, 372-0299 at village mall in Yosemite Valley. Shuttle bus stop 6 & 9. 8 am-8 pm daily.

TRAVEL

Round-trip service to Yosemite from Merced: Via Bus Line, from the **Greyhound** Depot, 722-0366/(800) 231-2222, $30 r/t plus park admission $3.

Greyhound, 710 W 16th St, 722-2121/(800) 231-2222, serve all cities along Hwy 99. Hitching: 'a bit slow btwn Merced and Yosemite.' Yosemite is 67 miles E of Merced. Yosemite Park Tour Co, 1 mile from visitor centre in Yosemite Valley, 372-1240. Various tours 2-8 hrs, $15-$40. Rsvs a day in advance.

Incredible Adventures, PO Box 77585, San Francisco, CA 94107, (415) 759-7071/(800) 777-8464. Run one and three day tours to Yosemite from San Francisco. $75/$169.

SEQUOIA-KINGS CANYON NATIONAL PARKS These two parks, established around 1890 and administered jointly since WWII, straddle a magnificent cross-section of the high Sierras, including 14,495-ft **Mt Whitney** , highest peak in the lower 48 states. Here you'll find the beautiful and impetuous **Kings River**, remnants of Indian camps, and wildlife that may venture into view in early morning or at dusk. Here, too, are stands of giant sequoia; like their redwood cousins along the coast, these trees are survivors of the Ice Age and lumber companies both. One of their number, the 2500-year-old **General Sherman**, is the world's most massive living thing, in all his 275-foot-high, 2145-ton glory. The two-mile **Congress Trail** into the heart of the **Great Forest** begins at the Sherman tree.

Access to the parks is by road from the west and southwest or by foot from the east. Bus service is available from Visalia to trailheads on both sides of the Sierras. 'Road to Owens Valley gives very pretty views and climbs to about 4000 ft above sea level.'

The homepage is located at *www.nps.gov/sekil* which has its own virtual visitor centre.

The telephone area code is 209.

ACCOMMODATION

Dow Villa Hotel, 310 S Main, **Lone Pine**, (619) 876-5521. Hospitable place, good rooms, from $60 for two, XP-$5. Use of jacuzzi, pool. 'Centrally located.'

Hotel Burgess, 1726 11th St, **Reedley**, 638-6315. About 57 miles from park entrance. Wildly furnished hotel, no two rooms alike! From S/D-$37.

Motel 6, 933 N Parkway Dr at Hwy 99, **Fresno**, 233-3913. S-$31, D-$35.

Willow Motel, 138 Willow St, **Lone Pine**, (619) 876-5655. S-$52, D-$65. $8 extra for use of facilities including TV, shower, kitchens.

Camping: Buckeye Flat Campground—pleasant, rustic. We saw a bear in camp.' Rustic cabins without baths from $35 for 2pp, XP-$7, at **Giant Forest**, in Sequoia, and at **Grant Grove**, in Kings. Book ahead by calling 561-3314; rsvs for camping, cabins and cottages rec.

In Parks: $12 per site, no rsvs as getting a site 'shouldn't be a problem,' according to rangers. Free backcountry camping with permit. Also free camping on Sequoia National Forest lands near park.

INFORMATION/TRAVEL

Sequoia and Kings Canyon National Park Information, 565-3134, gives general information for both parks. For recordings on **weather** call 565-3351/on **backpacking** call 565-3708. 'Helpful and informative.' Daily 8 am-6 pm. Parks open year-round. $5 p/vehicle/ $2 pp covers entrance to both parks. Access in winter via hwys 198 and 180. In summer: park bus tours; horse rentals available.

DEATH VALLEY Covering two million acres, most of them about a million miles from nowhere, Death Valley has cornered the market on hottest, driest and lowest (282 ft below sea level) place in the US (ironically, less than 100 miles from Mt Whitney, highest point in the lower 48 states). High peaks ringing the valley prohibit moisture, and white sand and hills reflect light in a blinding glare. But the definition of Death Valley is heat: one July day in 1972, Furnace Creek lived up to its name with a ground reading of 201 degrees (that's not a typo), while the air was a balmy 128 degrees.

Late October to early May is the sanest time to gaze at the tortured landscapes of **Zabriskie Point** and **Dante's View**, climb the **Ubehebe Crater**, explore **Scotty's Castle**, and slide on the sensuous sand dunes at **Stove Pipe Wells**. Scotty's Castle is no prospector's shack but a $2 million, 18-room Spanish fortress with an 1100-pipe organ, a large waterfall in the living room and other astonishing features built by colourful con-man Walter Scott. Tours 9 am-5 pm last 1 hr and cost $8; call 786-2392, 60 miles from Furnace Creek. Always dramatic, the desert can bring forth storms of wildflowers in March and April as suddenly as it does storms of water or sand.

Visitor Information at Park headquarters, **Furnace Creek**, 786-2331, has a museum of geological interest mainly, descriptive literature, food and a cool oasis of date palms. Free rangers' hikes and programmes daily, less often in summer. Daily 8 am-6 pm. Visitor Information also located at Scotty's Castle.

The telephone area code is 619.

ACCOMMODATION

Death Valley lies 300 miles NE of Los Angeles and 135 miles NW of Las Vegas; the only bus is from Las Vegas. Park lodging boils down to **camping** for $5 per site (western campsites are free in summer to escapees from mental institutions), the costly **Furnace Creek Ranch**, (619) 786-2345 (from $98 for four), and the **Stove Pipe Wells Motel**, (619) 786-2387 (not much better; from S/D/Q-$55). 'During summer, arrive by 6 pm. Otherwise no key.' A better bet is the gas station/motel at **Panamint Springs**, 10 miles W of the park. 'A welcome relief in the middle of nowhere.' Also try:

Desertaire Death Valley HI Hostel, 2000 Old Spanish Trail Hwy, PO Box 306, Johannesburg, CA 92389, 852-4580. Only 1 hr drive from Death Valley National Monument, the hostel is an excellent base to explore desert peaks and canyons. Don't miss the free Tecopa Hot Springs Baths—107 F natural mineral water located just 3 miles from hostel. Also, hiking, biking, patio, watch tower deck, laundry, volleyball. $12.

Johannesburg Death Valley HI Hostel, 316 Goler St, PO Box 277, Johannesburg, CA 93528, 374-2323. Situated in the Mojave desert country, 1½ hrs NE of LA, 1½ hrs from Death Valley and 3 hrs from Yosemite. Gold mining and ghost towns are nearby. Native American petroglyphs, Fossil Falls, Red Rock Canyon State Park and Sequoia National Forest are within an easy drive from hostel. Hiking, biking, kitchen, 2 covered patios, free bfast, $12.

PALM SPRINGS A flat desert town hugging snow-capped mountains, Palm Springs is a class act—from artfully weathered New Mexican adobes to its view of 10,831-foot Mt San Jacinto. Even the Indians are millionaires here, but don't let that put you off. During the hot, dry summer, prices melt like ice cubes and swimming pools can be reached within microseconds from air conditioned rooms.

Palm Springs homepage, *www.palmsprings.com/*
The telephone area code is 619.

ACCOMMODATION

Each hotel seems to set its own dates for low season, approximately June through Sept. Rates always lowest Sun-Thurs. To find the best deal, check newspaper specials, ask the Visitors Bureau, call around and don't be afraid to haggle. Except for Motel 6, winter rates are generally shocking.

Carlton Hotel, 1333 N Indian Ave, 325-5416. S-$24, D-$34, XP-$10 in summer. Weekly rates available, from $100.

Motel 6, 595 E Palm Canyon Dr, 325-6129 and 660 S Palm Canyon Dr, 327-4200. Lush setting, pools, book ages ahead. Summer rates: 1pp-$35, 2pp-$42 etc. Winter: 1pp-$38, 2pp-$45.

Sunbeam Inn, 291 Camino Monte Vista, 323-3812. 15 June—15 Oct. Summer rates from S/D-$45. Winter rates from S/D-$56. 'Cheerful, small, with pool.'

FOOD

In summer, they practically give the food away; check local paper, giveaway tabloids for 'early bird' brunch and other specials.

Las Casuelas, 222 S Palm Canyon, 325-2794. 'Great Mexican food.' Daily 11 am 'til whenever they feel like it! $5-$13.

Nate's Deli, 100 S Indian Ave, 325-3506. 'Dinner specials good if you're hungry. A local institution.' Early-bird specials 4 pm-6.30 pm—attempt the 9 course meal for $10! Gulp! You'll be stuffed for days! Daily 8 am-8 pm.

OF INTEREST

Aerial Tramway, off Hwy 111, 325-1391. 18 mins, 8516 ft, and 5 climatic zones later, you're on **Mt San Jacinto** and it's 30-40 degrees cooler (in summer); you may even need a jacket. At the top: restaurant ('ride and dine' for $22), mule rides, backpacking, events and free camping. 'Can see part of San Andreas fault from top.' Mon-Fri 10 am-9 pm, 8 am-9 pm w/ends, $18.50.

Cabot's Indian Pueblo Museum, 67616 Desert View Ave, in Desert Hot Springs (N of I-10 on Palm Drive), 329-7610. Eccentric 5-storey pueblo, built of found objects by Cabot Yerxa. Inside are the prospector/packrat's mementos of the Battle of Little Bighorn and Eskimo and Indian relics. Open w/ends only in July & Aug; otherwise daily Wed-Sun 10 am-4 pm; $2.50.

Desert Museum, 101 Museum Dr, 325-7186. Impressive modern art, Indian basketry. Daily 10 am-5 pm. Closed July-Sept. $6.50.

Living Desert Reserve, 47900 Portola Ave, Palm Desert (E of Palm Springs off Hwy 111), 346-5694. 1200 acres of native plants, gazelles, Bighorn sheep and other desert denizens. 'After sundown' room displays with nocturnal beasties. Sept 1-June 15; daily 7 am-4 pm; $7.

Palm Springs International Film Festival, January 9-26. More than 150 films; awards gala honours film makers' careers. Call 322-2930 for more info.

INFORMATION

Chamber of Commerce, 190 W Amado Rd, 325-1577; and at airport. Mon-Fri 8.30 am-4.30 pm.

Palm Springs Visitors Bureau, off Hwy 111 in the Atrium Design Center, # 201, 770-9000. Pick up the *Palm Springs Desert Guide*, the *Desert Weekly* and the **Calendar of Events** put out by the city: all are free and packed with info, special offers. Mon-Fri 8.30 am-5 pm.

TRAVEL

Greyhound, 311 N Indian Ave, (800) 231-2222. On the Phoenix-LA route. Daily 6 am-5 pm.

Sun Bus Transit, 343-3451. Local buses; also has cheap shuttle (750) around town, transfers 25¢. Daily 7 am-5 pm.

JOSHUA TREE NATIONAL MONUMENT In the high desert 54 miles E of Palm Springs is this 870-square-mile sanctuary of startling rock formations, mountain lions and kangaroo rats, colourful cacti and giant 50-foot agave trees with manlike arms and twisted bodies. These odd plants were named in the 1850s by Mormon pioneers, who recalled a line from *The Book of Joshua*: 'Thou shalt follow the way pointed for Thee by the trees.'

Entrance to the monument and all **campsites** is free in the summer 'til Aug 31st (two charge $5 in the winter, reserve through TICKETRON); you need to bring food, water and firewood. Good exhibits, museum and ranger-guided tours (in autumn/winter only) from park headquarters at **Twentynine Palms**, (619) 367-7511, and the visitor centre at **Cottonwood Springs**, 8 am-5 pm daily. From 5185-foot **Salton View**, you get a splendid panorama of the Coachella Valley, the Salton Sea and Palm Springs. On a clear day you can see Signal Mountain in Mexico. Also, don't miss the annual **Village Street Fair**, held annually in September, featuring food, beer garden, games and entertainment. Call (800) 364-4063 for details.

LOS ANGELES   Everything you have ever heard about LA is true. The place is so large and diverse that it will become whatever you wish to make it. There is urban angst and alienation downtown, and sun-seeking hedonism at Zuma beach. There is Greek sculpture in Malibu and a Cadillac stuck into a Beverly Hills roof. There is the film director sipping Perrier in Venice and the Vietnamese fisherman angling for dinner off the Santa Monica Pier. Remember that this city specializes in creating fantasy. The only way to find your own LA is to jump in with both feet.

Whatever you find, you'll be in good company. Thirteen million Angelenos speak 100 languages, and it's true—most do say 'have a nice day,' some even mean it. Its part climate, and part culture—LA has always drawn more from the Far East and Latin America than from New York and the grimy East Coast. The pace is a bit slower here, and the attitudes more tolerant. Easterners may deride LA as shallow and vain, but there is little doubt among Angelenos that theirs is a city struggling with social, economic and artistic questions difficult for outsiders to appreciate.

Most difficult to grasp is the great fear that one day the California Dream may be over. The place where people came to live a dream is slowly becoming less than that. The freeways are clogged, the air is smoggy and there is a constant worry about water. When in May 1992 four white police officers were acquitted of beating black motorist Rodney King, the riot that ensued did not just leave more than 50 people dead but left the city with a profound sense of identity crisis. Then came the massive earthquake on the 17th January, 1994. More than 50 died and many people were left homeless and stranded. The dream had become a nightmare.

Despite the growing congestion, the youthful LA sense of unlimited possibilities is easily restored with a trip among Mulholland Drive. Named for the engineer of LA's first aqueduct, Mulholland twists along the spine of mountains separating LA from the San Fernando Valley. A drive here offers sweeping vistas out over the enormous possibilities of the LA basin. At night the city lights stretch down to the sea, covering a seemingly limitless expanse. Clearly this was a city meant to dream dreams.

If you haven't acquired a car, it is surely now or never. You will no doubt get lost, spend countless hours looking for parking, but there's a sly exhilaration to driving LA freeways. It's like urban surfing. Once you've experienced the silken pull of seamless traffic, conquered a complex exchange as cars confidently curl on and off into new trajectories, and got a taste of life in the fast lane, you'll probably agree.

Area code for LA is 213, for Santa Monica and Venice 310, for the San Fernando Valley 818, and for Long Beach and Orange County 714.

Check out LA Yahoo! Metro at *www.la.yahoo.com/*.

GEOGRAPHY

LA is immense and the first thing you need to do is get a sense of how to find your way round. For convenience sake, we'll assume that you have landed at the airport, and you're looking at a map. The airport is on the coast, in the middle of the **Santa Monica Bay**. Moving south along the coast you come to **Long Beach** (the *Queen Mary* is moored here, and Disneyland is about 10 miles inland from here in Anaheim) and then the resort areas of **Huntington Beach**, **Newport Beach**, **Laguna Beach** and finally **San Diego** about 125 miles S of LA.

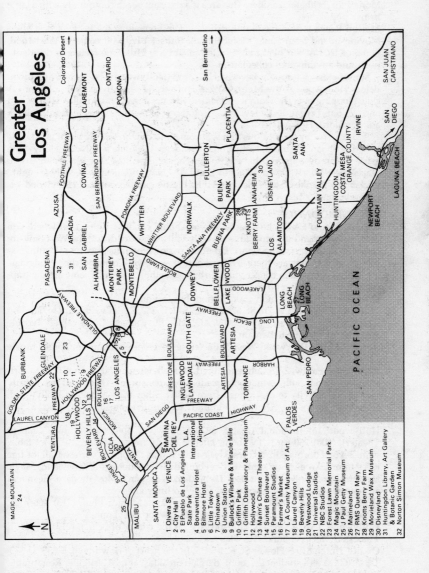

Greater Los Angeles

1 Olvera St
2 City Hall
3 El Pueblo de Los Angeles State Park
4 Bonaventura Hotel
5 Biltmore Hotel
6 Little Tokyo
7 Chinatown
8 Union Station
9 Bullock's Wilshire & Miracle Mile
10 Griffith Park
11 Griffith Observatory & Planetarium
12 Hollywood
13 Mann's Chinese Theater
14 Sunset Boulevard
15 Paramount Studios
16 Farmer's Market
17 L A County Museum of Art
18 Laurel Canyon
19 Beverly Hills
20 Westwood Lodge
21 Universal Studios
22 NBC Studios
23 Forest Lawn Memorial Park
24 Magic Mountain
25 J Paul Getty Museum
26 Marineland
27 RMS Queen Mary
28 Knotts Berry Farm
29 Movieland Wax Museum
30 Disneyland
31 Huntington Library, Art Gallery & Botanic Garden
32 Norton Simon Museum

Moving north along the coast from the airport, you first come to **Marina Del Rey**, the largest man-made marina in the world, and then to the beach community of **Venice**, a bohemian hang-out on the beach. When LA people let it all hang out, this is where it hangs. Moving along, you come to **Santa Monica**, also called Soviet Monica for its liberal leanings. This area is a pleasant beach community with a large British population.

Malibu Beach is about a 25 min drive N from here along the Pacific Coast Hwy. Moving inland from Santa Monica along **Sunset Blvd** you come to **Westwood**, home of UCLA. Further along Sunset, in **Beverly Hills**, the feeling is decidedly posh, and anything but collegiate.

Sunset passes through Beverly Hills and **Hollywood** and into **Downtown**. Below Hollywood is the **Melrose/West Hollywood** area, the cutting edge of LA chic. Hopping over the Hollywood Hills to the north, you enter **North Hollywood** and the **San Fernando Valley**. The TV and movie studios are located in Burbank and the North Hollywood area.

If you arrive by train or bus you will come into downtown. By bus it is possible to arrive at Santa Monica, Hollywood, Pasadena, Glendale and North Hollywood stations, but by train you have no other choice. Of course, LA is a tough city in places, particularly Downtown and East LA—'Never go near, especially at night.' Sticking to the West Side—Beverly Hills, Westwood and parts of Hollywood—is generally safe.

ACCOMMODATION

Getting around LA can be a battle, so you should choose lodging near where you will want to spend the most time. Beverly Hills, Westwood, and the West Side are centrally located to many sights. Do not stay downtown just because it sounds as though all the sites are there. They're not. Downtown has many cheap lodgings, but unless you want a concentrated urban and ethnic mix with some artistic trappings, you'll be better off elsewhere.

Downtown (close to Union Train Station/bus station):

Motel de Ville, 1123 W 7th St, 624-8474. S-$42, D-$47, $2 daily discount w/student ID if you stay 4 nights or longer. TV, AC, pool. Busy street. 'Good value.' 'Terrible area.' 'Don't hesitate to bargain.'

Beverly Hills/Hollywood/West Side (close to entertainment, shopping, movie sites):

Banana Bungalow, 2775 Cahuenga Blvd, W Hollywood, 1-800-4-HOSTEL. Resort-style facility. TV, bath, gym, pool, arcade, store, restaurant. Theatre w/free nightly videos. $30 LA city tour arranged from hostel/other trips including Hollywood, Universal Studios etc. 'Quite hard to find.' $5 shuttle to airport. 'Fantastic.' $15-18 mixed dorm, D-$45.

Hollywood International Hostel, 6820 Hollywood Blvd (across from Chinese Theater), (800) 750-6561. TV room, kitchen, linen, free coffee, arcade, pool table, gym. 3-4 bed dorms, $14. $85 weekly. Private rooms D-$35. No curfew. Call for free rides from LAX airport/Amtrak/Greyhound. Tours offered to Disneyland, Magic Mountain and Universal Studios. 'Dubious rsvs system.' 'Most modern, clean and airy hostel we stayed in. Easy access to sights, bus routes etc.'

Hollywood Vine Motel, 1133 Vine St, near Santa Monica Blvd, (213) 466-7501. From S-$42, D-$47. 'Friendly and near to Hollywood Greyhound.'

Hollywood YMCA, 1553 N Hudson Ave on the corner of Selma, (213) 467-4161. 4 blocks from Greyhound. $15. Has reasonably priced cafe.

Orchid Hotel, 819 S Flower St, 624-5855. In the heart of downtown. S-$38, D-$43, T-$45. 'Gave us a student discount. Bargain breakfast at the Gaslighter Restaurant.'

Student Inn International Hostel, 7038 Hollywood Blvd, (800) 557-7038. All rooms en suite, hot showers, complete kitchen, BBQ parties, free pickup. Call for rsvs. $10-$15 in 2/4 bedded rm. Kitchen and free bfast. Free tkts and tours.

The Valley (Area code: 818): El Patio Motel, 11466 Ventura Blvd, corner of Tujunga, near studios, 760-9602. S/D-$49, $62 for four.

La Tura Motel, 11745 Ventura Blvd, in Studio City near Universal Studios, 762-2260. Only two rooms, at $30 each. 'Need a car.'

Along Coast, near Airport: Airport Interclub Hostel, 2221 Lincoln Blvd, (310) 305-0250. Closest hostel to the airport. $14-16 plus $5 deposit, passport req. 24 hrs. Take shuttle bus C from airport to Lot C, then blue bus #3 (500) to Victoria Ave, or any 'Apollo' bus from all terminals.

Backpackers Paradise at Adventurers Hotel, 4200 West Century Blvd, Inglewood, (800) 852-0011 in CA/(800) 852-0012 elsewhere. S-$18, D-$35; dorm $14 includes free morning bfast java and muffin. Shuttle to and from airport and organised trips to places of interest. 'Excellent.' 'Mixed area, fun place.'

Cadillac Hotel, 401 Ocean Front Walk, Venice B, (310) 399-8876. S/D-$79, w/private bath, dorm $20. Gym, sauna, laundry and sun deck. Will pick-up from airport. Free coffee. 'Really friendly.'

Colonial Inn Hostel, 421 8th St, Huntington Beach, about 20 miles S of airport, (714) 536-3315. From airport take the #232 bus to the Long Beach Transit Center, board the #95 to the Hostel, not far from the Huntington Beach Pier, Laguna Beach Art Colony, Sawdust art festival and barbecue and beach parties! Run by a self-described 'funky old lady having a good time.' TV, nice garden and porch, kitchen etc. $15. 'Telephone rsvs made but we were disappointed on arrival.' 'Full of Aussie surfers. Bit awkward to get to on public transport.'

Hacienda Hotel, 525 N Sepulveda Blvd, El Segundo 90245, (800) 262-1314. 'Expensive but safe, excellent facilities—ensuite bathrooms, TV, swimming pool. Most important factor is the free shuttle to LA Airport. $70.'

LA South Bay HI Hostel, 3601 S Gaffey St, # 613, San Pedro, (310) 831-8109. Take # 446 bus to Korean Bell from 6th and Los Angeles Sts. Last bus leaves downtown at 2.45 pm. This seaside hostel has a panoramic view of the Pacific Ocean and Catalina Island, and features spectacular sunsets. Prime location for whale watching cruises to observe gray whales on their annual Alaska-Baja journey (Christmas to April). 'Clean and friendly.' $11-13.

Santa Monica HI Hostel, 1436 2nd St, Santa Monica, CA 90401, 393-9913. Library, kitchen, TV room, open courtyard, laundry, travel store. 2 blocks from beach. 'Fantastic facilities, but too many rules.' Call hostel upon arrival for free shuttle pick-up or take #33 bus from downtown. $16-18.

Share-Tel International Hostel, 20 Brooks Ave, (310) 392-0325. $18 p/night, $117 p/wk. After Labor Day, $16, $93 weekly. Show passport or student ID. Kitchen, linen, no curfew, safe area.

Venice Beach Cotel, 25 Windward Ave, Venice, 399-7649. Private rooms from $50, dorm from $15, $5 key deposit, lockers, trips and tours available. On the beach. 'Great. Very clean and super friendly/helpful staff.' Airport shuttle $7.

Venice Beach Hostel, 701 Washington St, (310) 306-5180. Take bus #33 from Spring St near Greyhound terminal as well as Bus Plaza at Union Station, $1.50. $12 p/night and $70 p/wk in a relaxed atmosphere. Kitchen, lounge. 'Very sociable hostel but not for those who need privacy.' 'Staff have lots of info on what to do in LA, just ask.' 'Sharing bathroom with at least 14 people!' Walking distance to beach, bars, restaurants and nightclubs. Surfboard rental.

Venice Marina Hostel, 2915 Yale Ave, Marina Del Rey, (310) 301-3983. $14 p/night, $91 weekly, kitchen, lockers, laundry, near beach. Will pick up from airport. 'Best place I stayed!'

Near Disneyland: Anaheim Inn, 1630 S Harbour Blvd (1 block S of Hwy 5), (714) 774-1050. 'Good location, just across Disneyland Themepark. Free transportation to and from hotel.'

Fullerton Hacienda HI Hostel, 1700 North Harbour Blvd, Fullerton, (714) 738-

3721. Closest hostel to Disneyland (5 miles N; 15 min drive). Hostel is situated in Brea Dam Park with a picnic area and golf driving range. Quiet, restful place to relax while in LA area. Kitchen, linen rental $1, tours available. Take the 'Golden Star' or 'Airway' super-shuttles from airport to the door, $18.

FOOD

The greater LA area has over 25,000 eating establishments. Does this city love to eat out, or what? In fact, during the 1982 recession, people in Los Angeles ate out more often than they had before the downturn. One reason for this obsession may be the mobile lifestyle, and the rich mix of ethnic cultures. Don't be surprised to find kosher burritos, Thai Tacos and more. Share the scoop on the best (and worst!) eats and drinks by searching **Bars and Clubs Message Boards** online at *www.la.yahoo.com/Entertainment_and_Arts/Restaurants/*

Downtown: Cassell's, 3266 W 6th St, (213) 480-8668. Beautiful hamburgers but too crowded any time after noon, cafeteria-style dining.

Cole's PE Buffet, 118 E 6th St, (213) 622-4090. Oldest restaurant and saloon in LA since 1908. 'Atmosphere hole-in-the-wall cafeteria.' Try the house speciality French dip, a west coast sandwich.

Clifton's Cafeterias, 648 S Broadway, (213) 627-1673; 515 W 7th St, (213) 485-1726. Vast array of cheap dishes ($6-7), soothing decor from a redwood forest with real waterfall to the Art Deco touches at 7th St. Daily 7 am-7 pm.

Dupar's, 6333 W 3rd St at the Farmer's Market (also at 12036 Ventura Blvd), (213) 933-8446. Old-style coffee shop specialising in savory pot pies and desert pies, legend bfast pancakes, with the option of buying batter ready to take home!

El Tepayac, 812 N Evergreen, (213) 268-1960, is home to the *Manuel Special*, an enormous burrito requiring two people to finish. This barrio hang-out draws an unusual mix of police, locals and Mexico food junkies. Weds-Mon 6 am-9.45 pm. Meals around $8 'til 11 pm Fri & Sat.

Kosher Burrito, 110 1st St, (213) 626-0998, cleanest burritos in town, $3! Daily 7 am-4 pm.

La Luz Del Dia, W 1 Olvera St, (213) 628-7495. Mexican food mecca. Cheapest deal going ($8.50 and under). Tues Fri 11 am-9 pm, later at w/ends.

Mandarin Deli, 727 N Broadway in Chinatown (in the food center), (213) 623-6054. You know its authentic because no-one here speaks English! Try the *jiao tzi* (fried dumplings), $5 for eight plates. Daily 11 am-9 pm.

Maurice's Snack N Chat, 5549 Pico Blvd, (213) 931-3877. Friendly, unpretentious soul-food landmark where Hollywood celebrities rub elbows with ordinary Angelenos. Fried chicken and pan-fried fish meals vary btwn $10 and $25. Rsvs req.

Pantry Cafe, 877 S Figueroa, (213) 972-9279. Huge helpings of basic meat and potatoes fare for less than $12. The Pantry is famous, not for its food, but because it is so unassuming and has been here forever. An anomaly in trendy LA. 24hrs.

Pho Hoa, 640 N Broadway, (213) 626-5530. 'Good Vietnamese restaurant. Large portions, reasonably priced, average $6.' Daily 7 am-7 pm.

Pink's Chili Dogs, 709 N La Brea Ave, (213) 931-4223. Bfast, lunch and dinner served. Experiment with the Guadalajara dog, cheese dogs, dogs wrapped in tortillas and chopped dogs in a cup of baked beans.

West Side: Apple Pan, 10801 W Pico Blvd, (310) 475-3585. Unassuming burger $5 and apple pie $2.50. Great food with the locals lining up behind the counter stools (no tables) waiting for a spot at the trough! Tues-Sun 11 am-12 am.

Barney's Beanery, 8447 Santa Monic Blvd, (213) 654-2287. Things haven't changed too much since Janis Joplin used to hang out here. The pool tables still need new felt, the vinyl in the booths is still bright, and the action at the bar is still pretty fierce. Excellent chili $6. A great place to meet locals, daily 10 am-2 am.

Canter's Deli, 419 N Fairfax, (213) 651-2030, 24hrs. In LA's old Jewish section close to CBS Television City. There is no better deli or bakery in town, especially at 3 am; recently awarded 'Best Pastrami in Town' by *LA Times*.

CC Brown's Hot Fudge Shop, on Hollywood Blvd near Mann's Chinese Theater, (213) 464-7062. Pressed tin roof, dark-wood booths, this ice cream store takes you back to the days when ice cream was still made by hand. Claims to be the originator of the hot fudge sundae $5.50. Daily 1 pm-10 pm; closed Sun.

Dolores' West Restaurant, 11407 Santa Monica Blvd at Purdue, (310) 477-1061. 24 hr old-fashioned burger joint. Bottomless coke and the renowned JJ Burger, $4.50

Ed Debevic's, 134 N La Cienega at Wilshire, (310) 659-1952. '50s-dressed staff dance on tables—totally wild.' Daily 11.30 am-3 pm & 5.30 pm-10 pm, Fri & Sat 'til midnight, Sun 'til 10 pm. Everything under $8, meatloaf $7.

Farmers' Market, 6333 W 3rd St, 100 block of Fairfax, (310) 933-9211. California is an agricultural engine, and this farmers' market is an impressive cornucopia. Stop here for Bob's coffee and donuts on your way to the big time at nearby CBS TV City or the county museum (LACMA). Gray Line Tours of Hollywood leave near here.

Musso And Franks, 6667 Hollywood Blvd, (213) 467-5123. This old bar and grill dates from 1919 and is the oldest restaurant in Hollywood. Once a haunt of Fitzgerald, Hemingway and Faulkner it is now a regular for film industry types. It offers a touch of the golden era of Hollywood elegance at prices that match ($20-$30). Closed Sun & Mon.

Nate 'n' Al's, 414 N Beverly Dr, (310) 274-0101. The Beverly Hills power schmooze takes place here early in the am. $5-$15. Daily 7.30 am.

Tail O' the Pup, 329 N San Vicente at Beverly, (310) 652-4517. A hot-dog shaped stand complete with bright yellow mustard oozing out of the sides! $2-$3.

The Valley: Adam's Restaurant, 17500 Ventura, (213) 990-7427. Great for ribs. Daily 5 pm-11 pm.

Dupar's, 12036 Ventura Blvd (also at 6333 W 3rd St), (818) 766-4437, great pies and one of the best coffee shops in town. Coffee $1, pies $2.50. 'This is a real hang-out late on a Friday or Saturday.' Open 'til 1 am.

Along the Beach: Alice's Restaurant, Malibu Pier, 23000 Pacific Coast Hwy, (310) 456-6646. Right on the beach. Good place to stop for brunch or dinner on a trip up the coast to Malibu. Seafood under $20. Daily 11.30 am-11 pm.

Patrick's Roadhouse, 106 Entrada just off Corner of Pac Coast Hwy and Entrada Dr (across the street from Will Rogers State Beach), 459-4544. Mon-Fri 8 am-3 pm; 'til 4 pm w/ends. Make rsvs for w/ends. Where Arnie had his bachelor party, and where everybody who's anybody comes to feed. 'Good homemade fish and chips.'

Rose Cafe and Deli, 220 Rose Ave in Venice, (310) 399-0711. Pretty place serving healthy food to beautiful people. Visitors are greeted by a mural of a bright red rose. Daily 7.30 am-10 pm, Sunday brunch 8 am-3 pm $7. Reasonable prices.

Wildflour Pizza, 2807 Main St in Santa Monica, (310) 392-3300. *LA Times* says its the best pie in town. Daily 11 am-10.30 pm, Sun from noon.

Ye Olde King's Head Pub, 116 Santa Monica Blvd, (310) 451-1402, a real ghetto for expatriate Brits, complete with darts, chips, everything!

OF INTEREST

For convenience, sites have been grouped geographically. It would be wise to plan day trips around one important site, rather than, say, attempt to get from Universal Studios to Disneyland, 2 hrs away by car, in one day. The RTD has an excellent self-guided tour booklet for people using the bus. *La Weekly*, the weekly events calendar, is the online source to check for cafes, clubs and comedy, *www.la.yahoo.com/external/laweekly/index.html/*

Downtown: Despite rumours to the contrary, downtown LA does exist. In fact, film producers use it as a double for Manhattan. Old and graceful structures survive, especially around the beautiful **Pershing Square Park**, but the area is dominated by soaring skyscrapers. To get oriented take DASH, (213) 972-6000, a bus system which covers all of downtown, 250 each time you board.

City Hall, 200 Spring St was 'til quite recently the tallest building in LA. It features an eclectic style of Babylonian and Byzantine architecture, and has an observation deck on the 27th floor. The *Los Angeles Times* is across the street and offers free tours at 11.15 am on w/days. You can see the editorial offices, press and production rooms of this major newspaper. You'll also get a free replica of the first edition in 1881. Just a few blocks from City Hall around First and San Pedro Sts, is **Little Tokyo**, a bustling area which has grown like mad in the last few years. LA has had an important Japanese community since the 1880s, although they were unconstitutionally rounded up during WWII and herded into camps. The community has rebuilt since that shattering experience. This is a good place to walk around. Be sure to visit the **Japanese American Cultural And Community Center gardens**, 244 S San Pedro, the koi pool at the **New Otani Hotel** and the many Japanese speciality shops. Walking along Broadway away from Little Tokyo towards **Pershing Square**, you would think you were in Mexico. This bustling Hispanic area becomes the garment and diamond districts near 7th St. If you turn west on 5th St off Broadway you come to Pershing Square—a graceful park in the middle of downtown. On the site of an Indian (later Spanish) trail, the **Biltmore Hotel**, 506 S Grand, is the square's most charming and sumptuous hotel complete with a fountain and wood-beamed ceiling in the Spanish-style entrance. JFK stayed in the $2400-a-day suite when he won the Democratic presidential nomination in 1960. A graceful architectural counterbalance to the skyscrapers is the Byzantine style **Los Angeles Central Library**, 630 W 5th St btwn Flores and Grand Ave, 612-3200. Mon, Thur, Fri, Sat 10 am-5.30 pm, Tues & Wed noon-8 pm, Sun 'til 5 pm.

Each of the enormous skyscrapers surrounding the Library—the **Arco Towers**, the **Citicorp Center**, and the **Bonaventure Hotel**—are small cities in themselves. They house underground shopping, parking and restaurants and are connected to one another by skywalks and underground passages. LA was the first city in the country to develop the concept of such skyscrapers, that function as self-contained shopping, entertainment and office complexes. The idea fits LA well, for it provides a centralized environment in a very decentralized city. The Bonaventure in particular offers a stunning atrium and impressive glass elevators that whisk you along the outside of the building to a restaurant at the top. On clear days the view is remarkable.

Hop on the DASH bus, or walk north along Broadway to get to **Chinatown and Olvera St**. Just off Main St, in the preserved Olvera St area, is the original Spanish settlement of Los Angeles, now the **El Pueblo de Los Angeles State Historic Park**, 628-7164. The small original Mexican settlement lead by Felipe de Neve adopted that big name of El Pueblo de La Reina de Los Angeles de Porciuncula. Olvera St, and the **Iglesia de Nuestra Senora** across the street are the oldest and most colourful reminders of LA's Spanish roots. This is a good area to have a Mexican lunch (try **La Luz Del Dia**) and to shop among the colourful Mexican and Central American stalls. Since the Spanish-style **Union Train Station** is nearby on Alameda St, you may want to save Olvera St 'til your last day in LA. Walk up Main St to Ord and head left to Broadway, and Mexico gives way to China, and **Chinatown**—not as classy as Little Tokyo, but full of good places to eat. The street life is perhaps a bit more old-fashioned here. Btwn crates of live chickens stacked helter skelter on the sidewalk, merchants still hold live birds upside down while old Chinese women poke the breast bones to check for tenderness. Your best orientation to the rest of LA is to take **Sunset Blvd** west away from Downtown (RTD #2).

Beginning in El Pueblo Park, Sunset shoots out towards Hollywood, banks in to the **Sunset Strip**, wends through the posh areas of **Beverly Hills** and **Bel Air**, and finally dips down to the Ocean. Sunset Blvd cuts a grand path through LA's many attractions. It is central to the city, and indeed, people measure their success in life by whether or not they have managed to acquire a home on the fashionable 'North Side' of 'The Boulevard.'

Hollywood: At Sunset and Los Feliz Blvd, head north to **Griffith Park**. The largest city park in America, Griffith offers trails, bridle paths, a zoo, the Greek Theater, three golf courses, and an observatory and planetarium. Performances in the Greek Theater from June through September; for info call 480-3232. The park observatory is free, and the 65' long, 12' wide refractor telescope is open to the public, from sundown 'til 9.50 pm. The ocean breeze generally blows the smog away, and visibility is good. There is also a free **Hall of Science**, a **Planetarium**, $5, and **Laserium**, $8.50, featuring shows about different topics in astronomy. For info call 664-1191, for astronomical info dial Sky Report, 663-8171. From the Planetarium you will not need a telescope to see the famous Hollywood Sign. The 50 foot letters were built by a real estate developer, and originally spelled out Hollywoodland, the name of his development. Not far from the observatory you'll find the stars are on the street along **Hollywood Blvd**. Over 2500 names of stars are laid into the terrazzo sidewalk above bronze symbols of microphones, cameras, television sets or records denoting the craft which brought them fame. Do not expect Hollywood to glitter as brightly as her sidewalks. The area has been a somewhat shabby, red-light district since the 50's. Children who run away from home for the glamour of Hollywood are often suckered into prostitution and worse. The Art Deco **Pantages Theater**, recalls the glamour of by-gone days. Built in 1929, the Pantages for many years housed the Academy Awards, and today draws many Broadway musicals. **Fredericks of Hollywood**, 6608 Hollywood Blvd, 466-8506, is LA's original, and uninhibited, sexual image-maker. Mon-Thur 10 am-8 pm, Fri 'til 9 pm, Sat 'til 6 pm, Sun noon-6 pm.

The most popular Hollywood attraction is **Mann's Chinese Theater**, 6925 Hollywood Blvd, 464-8111. The theatre opened in 1927 with the premiere of DeMille's *King of Kings*, and was christened by Norma Talmage who accidentally stepped in wet cement that night, the birth of a Hollywood tradition. Some of the world's most famous anatomy is imprinted here, including Michael Jackson, Donald Duck, R2-D2, Trigger and Marilyn Monroe. The building itself is a strange blend of Polynesian and Chinese Imperial architecture. Mann's offers one of the best sound systems, and largest screens in LA. Mon-Fri from 11 am, $8.50, $5.50 w/student ID. Just steps from Mann's is **Hollywood Entertainment Museum**, 7021 Hollywood Blvd, (213) 469-9151, a state-of-the-art museum featuring original sets and a collection of famous Hollywood memorabilia. Experience behind-the-scenes 'magic' as you create sound effects, record in the recording studio and edit film in the editing suite. Hollywood offers several other architectural styles than the bizarre Chinese at Mann's. Frank Lloyd Wright designed two homes near here— **Hollyhock House**, 662-7272, open to the public, and **Sowden House**. **Hollywood Bowl**, 2301 N Highland Ave, a large ampitheatre with near-perfect acoustics. The bowl hosts major jazz, classical and rock concerts. Call 480-3232 for tkts. Mon-Fri 8 am-9 pm, Sat-Sun 9 am-7 pm.

Off Hollywood, on Vine St is the **Capitol Records** office, designed to look like a stack of 45s with a huge 92' needle on top. The red beacon on the needle spells out Hollywood in morse code. After leaving Hollywood, but just before Beverly Hills, Sunset Blvd banks into the famous **Sunset Strip**—an exciting night spot lined with inventive, hand-painted billboards, and the best rock clubs in LA. At the other end of the frenzied Sunset Strip, Beverly Hills is as calm as a bank vault on Sunday. Everyone who has seen *Beverly Hills Cop* knows how rich and bizarre the residents are here. Actually, there are more attorneys and businessmen than Arabs, movie stars and drug lords. **Rodeo Drive** (pronounced Row-DAY-o) near Wilshire Blvd is the most expensive retail strip in the world. The Gucci side is the most fashionable. If you want to see the nearby homes of the stars—Gene Kelly lived at 725 Rodeo,

Carl Reiner at 714—you'll need to rent a car, take the bus or a Gray Line tour.
For a more affordable shopping experience head to the massive **Beverly Center**, corner 3rd and La Cienega. Next to the center, the Cadillac sticking out of the roof marks the spot of the **Hard Rock Cafe**. Be sure and stop in at the **Beverly Hills Hotel**. The bright pink decor is hard to miss. The film industry does its business at the Hotel bar called the Polo Lounge. Bring your wallet and don't forget to have yourself paged. Sunset continues on past the Polo Lounge along the northern edge of **Westwood Village** and **UCLA**. Tucked in with the campus, Westwood Village is a huge and handsome mall, one of LA's few walking districts, and chockful of cinemas, shops, street buskers and socialising places. 'Fri and Sat nights are like a circus with sword-swallowers, dancers, musicians, and even fortune-telling cats!' Celebs also frequent Westwood. The campus area is a live party spot. 'Frat parties along Gayley from 21 Sept on. Free beer, spirits, food, entertainment and the best-looking women in the world.' 'On a quieter note, **Westwood Village Cemetery**, 1218 Glendon, has the most visited grave in LA, that of Marilyn Monroe; Natalie Wood is also buried here. Continuing past Westwood, Sunset winds through miles of exclusive **Pacific Palisades** real estate (Ronald Reagan lived here) finally reaching Pacific Coast Hwy just above Santa Monica.

The Valley: Made famous by the song *Valley Girl*, (sung by Frank and Moon Zappa) the **San Fernando Valley** is really like a totally cooooool bedroom community for like kids who drive really bitchen Camaros. The shopping is like totally excellent at the **Sherman Oaks Galleria**, just er... over the hill from Westwood. The most totally kickin' part of the valley fer shur is near the studios in the North Hollywood area. Other than like, those, the major sites are like the **LA Zoo** in **Glendale**, and the famous **Forest Lawn Memorial Park**, 1712 S Glendale Ave, Glendale, open 8 am-5 pm, 254-3131, (its like totally freakin' an' fulla dead folks!). Also friendly branches in the Hollywood Hills, near Artesia and in West Covina, each with its own artwork, patriotic themes and style. This is the American way of death as depicted in Evelyn Waugh's *The Loved One*: odourless, spotless, artistically uplifting, almost fun, at least for the survivors. It's hard to keep from giggling at the crass wonder of it all, from repros of the Greatest Hits of Michelangelo and Leonardo da Vinci to the comic-book approach on the 'Life of Jesus' mosaics. Take a copy of Ken Schessler's *This is Hollywood* along (but keep it out of sight—park officials won't allow the book on the grounds) to find where the notables are planted. Free, daily 8 am-5 pm.

Museums and art galleries:
Downtown: Exposition Park, corner of Exposition & Figueroa Blvds. Was built in the early 1900s and houses LA's oldest museums and a beautiful rose garden.
LACE, Los Angeles Contemporary Exhibitions, 6522 Hollywood Blvd, (213) 957-1777, is devoted to artists who are still alive. The primary alternative space to the burgeoning traditional museum scene, LACE offers everything from performance art to video art, for free. If there is an avant-garde in LA, it stays one step ahead by coming here.
Museum of Science and Industry (MoSI), 744-7400, contains the Halls of Economics & Finance and of Health. Admission is free, except for the IMAX theatre, 744-2014. The airplane collection is impressive. $7.50, w/student ID $5.50. Daily 10 am-5 pm.
Natural History Museum of LA County, 744-DINO. Main exhibits include 'battling dinosaurs,' habitat halls with stuffed animals placed in natural settings, and the American History Halls covering the Revolutionary War to 1914. Also impressive are the California and Southwest History Halls and the Pre-Columbian—Meso American Hall covering Maya, Inca, and other civilisations. The Hall of Gems and Minerals includes the 102-karat Ashberg Diamond, thought to have been a part of the Russian crown jewels. 10 am-5 pm Tue-Sun. $7, $4 w/student ID. Nearby is the

Coliseum, site of the 1932 and 1984 Olympics, and **USC**. Best known for its football team, USC is affectionately called the University of Spoiled Children, although its real name is the University of Southern California.

MOCA, Museum of Contemporary Art, 250 S Grand Ave btwn 2nd and 4th, 62-MOCA-2. Famous Japanese architect Arata Isozaki designed this newest museum on the LA scene. The building itself is a work of art, integrating primary shapes into abstract patterns. The prime materials are rough finished red sandstone, gray granite and green panelling with a pink diamond pattern. The trim is in polished granite. Most impressive is the large polished onyx gable window above the ticket booth. The collection includes many modern artists from the 1940s to the present—Louise Nevelson, Robert Rauschenberg, David Hockney and others. Thur 11 am-8 pm; 'til 5 pm other days. $7.50, $5.50 w/student ID. Thurs after 5 pm is free. Closed Mon. MOCA's second building is the **Temporary Contemporary**, 152 N Central Ave. Tkts can be used for both buildings on the same day.

West Side: Los Angeles County Museum of Art, mercifully abbreviated to **LACMA**, 5905 Wilshire Blvd, 857-6111. LACMA has grown impressively in the last few years. A recent building houses the collection of 20th century works by Picasso, Braque and Matisse. The older Armand Hammer Building houses an impressive collection of Far Eastern works. Tues-Thur 10 am-5 pm, Fri 'til 9 pm, Sat & Sun 11 am-6 pm. LA has been developing the good sense to look west, to Japan and Asia for its artistic inspiration. The proof is found in the new **Pavilion for Japanese Art** which opened in mid-1988. The pavilion houses the Shin'enkan collection of Edo period screens and scrolls. Widely regarded as the most outstanding collection of its kind, the 32,100-square-foot pavilion instantly became a world-class centre for Japanese art. $7.50, $5.50 w/student ID.

La Brea Tar Pits are nearby. An ancient source of natural tar, the pits were often covered with a light layer of dust and water. Ice Age animals seeking water became ensnared in the tar and their bones were preserved for history, making the Tar Pits the single richest fossil find in the world. The **George C. Page Museum of La Brea Discoveries**, 5801 Wilshire Blvd, 936-2230, exhibits of fossils in atrium. Open pit to watch excavating in summer months. Still millions of fossils. Tue-Sun 10 am-5 pm. $7, $4.50 w/student ID.

Beach: J Paul Getty Museum, 17985 Pacific Coast Hwy, (310) 458-2003. The richest man in the world never lived in the painstaking reproduction of a Roman Villa at Herculaneum he built overlooking the Pacific to house his stunning art collection. Apparently Getty was afraid of flying from London across the Atlantic. The Getty houses a strong collection of French 18th century art. The museum is free, but you will hear many different rumours about the difficulty of getting in. Parking space is limited and cars need rsvs which are hard to get in the summer (apply at least a week in advance). Tue-Fri you can park at the nearby Charthouse Restaurant for $4 and take a shuttle bus to the Museum. RTD bus #434 stops nearby and you can walk up to the museum—but you must ask the bus-driver for a pass to enter—*you will not be allowed in without one*. If you are on a bike or motorcycle, you can get in without a rsv. Tue-Sun 10 am-5 pm.

Pasadena: Huntington Library, Art Gallery and Botanical Gardens, 1151 Oxford Rd in San Marino, (818) 405-2275. An impressive and well-housed collection of Gainsborough and Guttenburgs. English tea is offered every Friday afternoon, $14.50 for limitless buffet, call 683-8131 for rsvs. 'The gardens are mind-blowing.' Tue-Fri 1 pm-4.30 pm, Sat & Sun 10.30 am-4.30 pm. Suggested donation.

The Norton Simon Museum of Art, Colorado and North Orange Blvd, 681-2484. The worst day in the history of the LACMA was the day that Norton Simon got mad and decided to take his ball and go and start his own game. Simon had been on the museum's board, but decided to open his own museum in Pasadena. Simon's extensive collection includes Degas and Rodin (the *Burgers of Calais*) and a garden graced by Henry Moore's sculptures arranged along a fountain. $4.50, w/student ID $2.50. Thur-Sun noon-6 pm.

Amusement Parks (and tips):
Best to go in **off-season** (as it is cheaper and less crowded), or on a **school day**, or when everyone else is somewhere else, e.g. watching the Superbowl, shopping. **Arrive early** before gates open. Check for **discounts**.
Disneyland, 1313 S Harbor Blvd, Anaheim, (714) 999-4000. This is the original **Magic Kingdom** and the culmination of Walt Disney's dream. Disney designed the 57 attractions to provide wholesome entertainment for adults & children in this flawlessly clean park. Attractions are grouped into 7 theme parks: you enter the park through Main Street, a re-creation of an old American town. New Orleans Square houses one of the most elaborate rides, the *Pirates of the Caribbean*. Adventureland is devoted to the explorer spirit of African safaris. Fantasyland recreates the magic of the animation classics; the entrance is through Sleeping Beauty's castle, right next to the Matterhorn roller coaster. In Frontierland, you can journey through the old west on an incredible mining train roller coaster. A visionary himself, Disney took special interest in the future. You can do this at Tomorrowland, which includes the legendary Space Mountain roller coaster, the 3-D *Captain EO*, starring Michael Jackson; Star Tours, the original motion simulator set to a *Star Wars* theme; and newer delights such as *Indiana Jones Adventure: The Temple of the Forbidden Eye*. Aboard jeeps, fearless wannabes can revisit the perils of the Indiana Jones movies, evading serpents, spiders and explosions! Finally, Critter Country features the popular Splash Mountain, a water flume attraction themed around *Song of the South* adventures.

There is year-round entertainment (e.g. Big bands, the Videopolis Dance Club) but the Electric Light Parade (9 pm) with hundreds of light-bedecked floats and fireworks, is only available summer evenings. Since all this is available for the $35 admission fee ($60 for 2-day pass, $82 for 3-day), you really have to ask yourself why you should see any of the other parks in town. For specific opening hours call (714) 999-4000. 'Get there as early as possible. Lines for good rides become enormous by noon.' 'Avoid Saturday!' 'Take a full day.' 'Don't miss the parade of Disney Characters.' 'Don't leave luggage at Greyhound—station closes at 9 pm, Disneyland at midnight.' For transport, try RTD, 635-6010, from downtown (2hrs): take #460 E on 6th—$3.35 (runs as late as 1.20 am in summer); local Orange County Transit (OCTD), (714) 560-6282 from Greyhound terminal at corner of Harbor and Orange Wood, #43 on Harbor, every 15 min; and Greyhound—Anaheim, 999-1256/(800) 231-2222, $7 o/w. 'Tomorrowland is best—see it first.' 'Don't miss *America the Beautiful* 360-degree film.'
Movieland Wax Museum, 7711 Beach Blvd, Buena Park, 1 block N of Knott's, (714) 522-1154. Go see 200-plus movie and TV stars captured (not always successfully) in wax. The big event is the Chamber of Horrors, based on 13 scary movies, including *Werewolf in London*, *Dracula* , *The Exorcist* and *Psycho*. Here you can also be fooled by moviestar look-alikes of Clint Eastwood, Michael Jackson, Marilyn Monroe, Bette Davis. Box office daily 9 am-7 pm, $15.50.

Knott's Berry Farm, 8039 Beach Blvd, Buena Park, (714) 220-5200. The gift shops outnumber the rides and attractions 10 to 1 but its Montezooma's Revenge (with 360-degree upside-down loops) is nauseatingly effective, allowing you to meet yourself (and possibly your lunch) coming back. 'Hurts, but must be tried.' Rides include The Boomerang, a 54 second reverse looping roller coaster; XK-1, where you are launched as from an aircraft-carrier and you do the steering in a cockpit seven stories up; the Whirlpool, an indoor ride with sound and light show; and the Bigfoot Rapids. Great waterworks show at lake. Lots of special celebrations, rock concerts, discount promotions. Check the papers. Open 9 am-midnight, $32/$17 after 4 pm. Only 20 mins to Disneyland.
Movieland Wax Museum, 7711 Beach Blvd, Buena Park, 1 block N of Knott's, (714) 522-1154. Go see 200-plus movie and TV stars captured (not always successfully) in wax. The big event is the Chamber of Horrors, based on 13 scary movies, including *Werewolf in London*, *Dracula* , *The Exorcist* and *Psycho*. Here you can also be fooled by moviestar look-alikes of Clint Eastwood, Michael Jackson, Marilyn Monroe, Bette Davis. Box office daily 9 am-7 pm, $15.50.

RMS Queen Mary, (714) 522-1155. On Pier J, Long Beach, #7 at south end of Long Beach Freeway. Daily 10 am-6 pm; $5.

Six Flags Magic Mountain, Valencia, N of LA, (805) 255-4111. Alton Towers has nothing on this place. Experience some of the biggest rollercoaster rides in the world: The Viper, Collossus, The Revolution and the Ninja are all here. 'Thrilling to the extreme.' Superman: The Escape, is the world's tallest and fastest coaster. Also, extreme adventure is in store for those who experience the *Dive Devil*, a 60mph 50ft skydive/bungee jump freefall! 'Arrive early, by the afternoon 2 hr queues are not uncommon.' Accessible only by car (remember where you parked—huge car park) or shuttle—Magic Line, (213) 937-3851, from any downtown hotel, $68 r/t including basic admission of $35.

Universal Studios and Tour, 100 Universal City Plaza, (818) 508-9600. $36 for a 2½ hr tour taken by tram through the 420 acre lot. Shows include *Conan the Barbarian*, a *Star Trek* adventure (you'll be in the show), *Jaws* and a 30' King Kong attempting to derail the tram. Tours leave from 9 am-7 pm summers; varying hours in off-season. Get there early to avoid crowds. 'Get right-hand seat on tram—most scenes, Jaws, etc, to the right.' Catch a tidal wave of action and an ocean of thrills in the more recent attraction *Waterworld*. Or journey deep into the Jurassic Jungle on a turbulent water ride to face a towering T-Rex in *Jurassic Park—The Ride*, where you are thrust into the living, breathing, 3-dimensional world of Jurassic Park. 'Not on a par with Disneyland.' 'Better than Disneyland.' Take RTD # 424 from downtown heading north on Broadway. Near Universal is the 18-theater **Cineplex Odeon Universal City Cinema**, (818) 508-0588. If a movie isn't playing there, it isn't playing. Hardcore movie fans will head to **Eddie Brandt's Saturday Matinee** , 6310 Colfax, (818) 506-4242 home to 4 million movie stills from $8. Tue-Fri 1 pm-6 pm, Sat 8.30 am-5 pm.

The Industry: —what the cognoscente call the movie business. To get a feel for it, read the trade magazines *Hollywood Reporter* and *Variety*. More hands on experience can be gained by hanging out at the Polo Lounge, or Ma Maison Restaurant, but for those without the necessary wallets, TV shows are free, and you can watch them being taped at any of the major studios. Tkts are available from the Visitors Center ('We got tkts to Jay Leno') ; from the TV reps in front of Mann's Chinese Theater in Hollywood; or try calling LA Film and Video Permit Office on (213) 957-1000 for more information about studio tours and location film shooting. For most sitcoms, the best bet is Audiences Unlimited, (818) 506-0043, although beware it can take up to 4 hrs to get one 22 min episode wrapped up.

ABC Television, 4151 Prospect St. Mon-Fri 9 am-5 pm. Taping only, no tours. Only morning talk shows. Tkts (818) 506-0067.

CBS TV City, 7800 Beverly Blvd, (213) 852-2455. Talk shows and game shows include *The Price is Right*. Arrive before 8 am. Take your passport. Tkt office 6.30 am-5 pm daily.

NBC Studio Tour, 3000 W Alameda, (818) 840-4444. To see a show taped, arrive early at the ticket office on the west side of the NBC complex off California St. Mon-Fri 8 am-5 pm, 9.30 am-4 pm on w/ends. For a more low-key, history-oriented walk around the only studio still active in the heart of old Hollywood, there is the **Paramount Studios** tour. Paramount is the last of a string of studios that once lined the corridor along Gower St and Melrose Ave and is a big part of where the industry began. 'A visit to Paramount is an appealing step into both past and present.' $15 walking tour; 2 hr tours leave w/days on the hour 9 am-2 pm from the studio's pedestrian gate at **5555 Melrose Ave**, (213) 956-1777. Depending on production schedules, you may get a peek at tapings of shows.

Other Attractions

Beverly Hot Springs, 308 North Oxford Ave (north of Beverly Blvd), (213) 734-7000. Separate spas for males and females, each featuring a giant tiled pool filled with piping hot water, a cool pool to calm down in, a steam room perfumed with fresh-cut eucalyptus branches and a dry sauna. The main spa treatment is a 45 min shiatsu massage ($60), the quintessential Japanese acupressure technique; there's a good deal of stretching, tweaking, twisting and even pounding! Daily 9 am-9 pm.

Descanso Gardens, 1418 Descanso Dr (off Angeles Crest Hwy exit off the 210 Foothill Freeway), (818) 952-4400. Park nestled in 165 acres in the San Rafael Hills in La Canada-Flintridge. 100,000 camelias in 600 varieties fill winding walkways under a grove of ancient Cal live oaks, five-acre rosarium and a canyon filled with ferns, a lake, a bird observation station and a blue-tiled Japanese teahouse, tucked away in a garden of arched bridges and ponds, which serves tea and cookies on w/ends. $5. Daily 9 am-4.30 pm.

ENTERTAINMENT

The **Sunset Strip**, with new clubs and restaurants opening in the past few years, is once again becoming LA's cultural epicenter and a destination of choice for both visitors and the truly hip residents. The Strip is divided into three loosely defined zones. **Laurel Canyon West** to **La Cienega Blvd** is a largely pedestrian-free stretch that includes some of the Strip's newer clubs such as the **Bar Marmont, Roxbury, The House of Blues** and Dublin's **Irish Whisky Pub**, a sports bar. West of La Cienega is one of the few enclaves tailored for pedestrian traffic, **Sunset Plaza**; two blocks of upscale open-air cafes. From here, the Strip winds toward **Doheny** where there is an abundancy of commercial take-away eateries. The six blocks here are also home to the last of the area's clubs, the **Viper Room, Roxy, Whiskey** and **Billboard Live**. *BAM*, free monthly paper, lists gigs up and down the West Coast. Also pick up *The Reader* and *LA Weekly*, free, full of entertainment listings. All available at record/bookstores, newstands. New issues on Thursdays.

Anti-Club, 4658 Melrose, 661-3913. Everything from cow-punk, video poetry and South African. Cheap beer.

The World Famous Baked Potato, 3787 Cahuenga Blvd (near Universal), (818) 980-1615. Oldest major contemporary jazz watering hole. Tiny, but Lee Ritenour, Larry Carlton, among others established themselves here. Get there early for enormous spuds stuffed with whatever you want (served 'til 1 am). Showtimes 9.30 pm & 11.30 pm.

The Palace, 1735 N Vine St, (213) 467-4571. Rock out in a restored old theatre; cover under $15. Famous LA club owner Filthy McNasty's latest is called **FM Station**, 11700 Victory near Universal Studios, (818) 769-2220. A living room ambience from which to watch LA rock, and dance. Free before 9.30 pm, drinks specials $2.50.

The Troubadour, 9081 Santa Monica Blvd, (310) 276-1158. Ageing but legendary launching pad for top rock acts; small and smoky. Cover plus 1 drink min, cheaper on Mon hoot nights. Cover from $5 Sun-Thur; Fri-Sat $10.

Whiskey a Go Go, 8901 Sunset Blvd, (310) 652-4202. Cream of rock triumvirate and hang-out of the stars. Cover, naturally, $3-$15. Legendary Sunset Strip club where Jim Morrison and Van Halen have played.

Theatre/Comedy: LA comedy clubs not only feature some of the hottest up-and-coming comedians, they also enjoy routine surprise visits from comedy legends and almost always have entertainment industry types in the audience seeking the next superstar. Cover charges tend to range from $8 -$10, with a two-drink minimum. Besides **The Improv**, 8162 Melrose Ave, 651-2583 and **The Comedy Store**, 8433 Sunset, 656-6225, here are some of the other hot spots:

The Laugh Factory, on Sunset, (213) 656-1336. Hosts industry showcases and special benefits. Legends such as Rodney Dangerfield pop up from time to time.

The Ice House, Pasadena, (818) 577-1894. This place books star-powered headliners who do full, hour-long shows in comparison to the Hollywood-based clubs' 10 min specials.

LA has an enormous number of larger theatres, including the **Mark Taper Forum**, the **Shubert** and **Ahmanson**. The best theatre is often at the small equity-waiver houses where struggling actors hone their skills while waiting for the big break. Check the *Reader* and *Weekly* for listings. Best bets are usually the **Group Repertory** or **Odyssey**.

Los Angeles Theater Center, 514 S Spring, (213) 485-1681. LA's major regional theatre for new playwrights. $14-$23 w/student ID. Tkts (213) 660-TKTS.

Cinema: As you would expect from the world's film capitol, there are a lot of movies around town. Westwood is the place where most films premiere. Dial 777-FILM in the 213 and 310 area codes, to find the location and schedule of current movies, and purchase tkts in advance.

The Beverly Cineplex, in Beverly Center, Beverly and La Cienega, (310) 652-7760. 13 theatres featuring popular first-runs as well as art films.

The Nuart, 11272 Santa Monica Blvd, (310) 478-6379. Revival/art house par excellence.

Pacific Cinerama Dome, 6360 Sunset Blvd, (213) 466-3401/prog info 466-3347. This large-screen geodesic dome-shaped theatre housed the premiere of *Apocalypse Now*, among others. Daily 12.30 pm. $9.50 admission, $5.50 for first two shows of the day.

Festivals: Chalk It Up, June 6-8th, is the world's largest chalk mural festival featuring more than 300 artists, arts & crafts, music and food. Call (213) 850-4072. From mid-August 'til beginning September, don't miss the **African Marketplace and Cultural Faire**, a 10-acre global village featuring more than 40 cultures, 70 countries, 350 arts and crafts merchants, basketball and soccer tournaments and entertainment. Call (213) 217-1540.

OUT OF DOORS

Catalina Island, 26 miles off Long Beach. A romantic green hideaway, 85% in its natural state. Well worth a trip to see the perfect harbour of Avalon and its delightful vernacular architecture, plus the natural beauties of the place. Snorkelling is best at Lovers Cove, but look out for sharks. 'Beautiful.' Ships cost $35.50 r/t, depart (daily at 9 am) from Balbon Pavilion. Calll Catalina Passenger Service, (714) 673-5245 (Newport). Rsvs req.

Malibu Canyon, just north of Malibu offers one of the most stunning day trips in Los Angeles. Take this canyon road to the Malibu State Creek Park for trails into the rugged Santa Monica Mountains. Campground with hot showers, bathroom, biking/hiking trails. First come, first served, $17 per site. Call (800) 444-PARK for hiking and camping information/park info (310) 457-1324.

Rent-a-Sail, 13560 Mindanao Way, Marina Del Rey, (310) 822-1868. Rents sailboats from 14 to 25 ft, $20-$25 (2 hr min) and $36 per hr w/engine (4 hr min), $20 deposit. Cash or traveller's checks only. Takes about 25 mins to sail out into the open ocean. Advance rsvs for large boats suggested on w/ends.

SPORT

Southern California is a paradise for sports lovers. In professional sport you can catch the **Dodgers** baseball team at Dodger Stadium, 1000 Elysian Park Ave (213) 224-1400 or, also in major league baseball, the **Anaheim Angels** at Anaheim Stadium, 2000 Gene Autry Way, Anaheim (714) 937-6700. Mon-Sat 9 am-5.30 pm, $5-$11. Anaheim Stadium is home to the National Football League team the **LA Rams**, 937-6767, while the city's other football team, **The Raiders**, play at The Coliseum, 3939 S Figueroa, (213) 748-6131. **The Coliseum** hosted the Olympic Games in 1932 and 1984. For tkts (from $10) to the famous **LA Lakers** basketball, call (310) 412-5000.

INFORMATION

Bus and train info, (800) COMMUTE. 6 am-10 pm daily.

Human Services Hotline, 24 hr, 686-0950, locates doctors, emergency medical help.

LA Convention and Visitors Bureau, 685 S Figueroa St (downtown), (213) 689-

8822. Publishes *Destination Los Angeles*, including a lodging guide. Mon-Fri 8 am-5 pm, Sat from 8.30 am.

Travelers Aid, 1720 N Gower St, Hollywood, (213) 468-2500. Also information at airport. Mon-Fri 8.30 am-4 pm.

Visitors Information, Greater LA Visitors Bureau, 685 S Figueroa St, by the Hilton Hotel, (take DASH Bus A), (213) 689-8822. Mon-Fri 8 am-5 pm, from 8.30 am on Sat. Very helpful multilingual staff. Offers free maps, bus and rail information, TV taping tkts, and run-downs of special events. Also has a small branch in Hollywood in Jane's House Sq, 6541 Hollywood Blvd, 689-8822. Mon-Sat 9 am-5 pm.

TRAVEL

Amtrak, 800 N Alameda, (800) 875-7245. Also stations in Fullerton, Santa Ana, San Juan Capistrano, San Clemente and San Diego. The *Coast Starlight* to Seattle is highly recommended for socialising and scenery.

Auto Driveaway, 3407 6th St, #525, (213) 666-6100. Mon-Fri 9 am-5 pm. Ride board, Floor B, Ackerman Union, UCLA.

Car Rentals: Avon Rent-a-Car, (800) 822-2866 in-state, rents convertibles; call for special deals; **Alamo**, (800) 327-0400; **Thrifty**, (800) 367-2277. Call for rates. Rsvs required 1 week in advance; **Midway**, 4900 W Blvd, (213) 292-1239, 'Can bargain with them over rate and mileage.'

Gray Line Tours, (213) 525-1212. Picks up at Farmers' Market. $65 to Disneyland including admission, $35 for 6 hr tour of stars' homes. Daily 6 am-10 pm.

L.V. International Tours, 18147 Coastline Drive #1, Malibu, CA 90265. (800) 456-3050/(310) 459-5443; *www.lvint.com/*. Local LA tours—night club tour, city tour, Disney etc., plus further afield to Mexico, Las Vegas, Grand Canyon, etc. Specialise in small groups and give discounts to BUNAC members.

Greyhound-Trailways Information Center, 1716 E 7th St (downtown), (800) 231-2222. Call for fares, schedules and local ticket info. Inside, a huge, clean but cheerless terminal with no cafe; outside, the meanest streets anywhere—a zoo. Don't plan any overnights here. 'Friends twice approached by vicious druggies and tramps outside station—be careful.' 'Stay on the upper level.' See neighbourhood listings for other stations.

Hollywood Fantasy Tours, (213) 469-8184. 2 hr Beverly Hills tour ($32), 1 hr Hollywood tour ($18) by trolley. Runs Mon-Sun 9 am-4 pm.

Los Angeles International Airport (LAX), is located on the west side of town, just south of Venice. Transportation to and from downtown is fastest and least complicated using one of the numerous shuttle companies. Many accommodations offer free airport pick-ups so check beforehand. In general, shuttle companies will pick-up/drop-off from any major hotel, 24 hrs, req 1-day notice and cost $10-15. Take your pick: Super Shuttle, (310) 782-6600; USA Shuttle (310) 204-3100; Airway Shuttle, (800) 660-6042. Venice Beach is a $15 cab ride from LAX. Airport information (310) 646-5252.

MTA Bus Information Line for public transportation, (213) 626-4455. Mon-Fri 8.30 am-5 pm.

Orange County Transit District, (714) 636-7433.

LA Bus System (RTD) bus info: 626-4455. Bottom level of Greyhound terminal. Basic fare $1.30, $1.55 with transfers. Monthly pass ($45) can be purchased at RTD centres; try 6249 Hollywood Blvd, Mon-Fri 10 am-6 pm. 'Excellent value.' 'From the airport, change buses at Broadway.'

RTD Rail System Infoline: 972-6235. 20 mile Blue Line light rail south from 7th & Figueroa downtown to Long Beach, 22 stations, $1.10; 16-station Red Line E-W subway from Union Station/Civic Center downtown to Wilshire and Western to Hollywood and N Hollywood. Green line from airport to Norwalk.

Santa Monica City 'Big Blue' Bus, (310) 451-5444. Mon-Fri 8 am-5 pm. Basic fare

50¢, free transfers, #10 bus $1.25.

Taxis: Checker Cab, 482-3456; **Independent**, 385-8294; and **United Independent**, 653-5050. Best to call when you need a cab.

THE COAST TO SAN DIEGO: Huntington Beach. Surfer capital, a famed party beach. 'The local surfers love to take a complete novice in hand so don't hesitate to ask how it's done.' Also, check out **Huntington Beach Skatepark #2**: a little bigger and a little wider than its big brother it features concrete banks, ledges, rails and a curb. Located next to Huntington Beach High School on Main St near Yorktown. Absolutely free.

Laguna Beach, 30 miles S of LA, buffered against urban sprawl by the San Joaquin Hills, has a decided Mediterranean look, from its indented coves to its trees and greenery right down to the waterline. The long white sand beach has superb snorkelling, surfing (for experts) and safe swimming at **Aliso Beach Park**. In winter, whale watching and tidepooling are likewise excellent. Long a haven for artists, Laguna is famous for its 7-wk Pageant of the Masters each July-Aug, but the accompanying Sawdust Festival (crafts, live music, jugglers, food) is more accessible and more fun. While here, plan to eat at **The Cottage**, 308 N Coast Hwy, or **The Stand** on Thalia St, recommended by a Lagunian for its 'great Mexican food, smoothies and tofu cheeseless cake.' 'Laguna has excellent atmosphere, very picturesque.'

Newport Beach. Terribly yachty and formal except on **Balboa Island**, a mecca for boy/girl-watching. 'Try the Balboa bars and the frozen bananas at the icecream kiosks.' Also, **T-K Burgers** at 2119 W Balboa Blvd is the most popular hangout for the non-deckshoe set.

Orange County/Anaheim *(Area code: 714)*. **San Juan Capistrano**, 12 miles inland from Laguna and 22 miles S of Santa Ana. This mission town is well served by Greyhound, Orange County buses and Amtrak, so you have little excuse for passing up its mission, easily the best in California. The chapel, oldest building still standing in the state, is almost Minoan in proportions, feeling and colour. Also on the grounds are the romantic ruins of the great church tumbled by an 1812 earthquake and now a favoured nesting place for the famous swallows. Indian graveyard, jail, various interesting buildings. Well worth your dollar. Take a lunch.

SAN DIEGO One glimpse of San Diego, and it's hard to believe that when Juan Cabrillo first landed here in 1542, he found not a single tree or blade of grass. Today, this desert-defying city is green, green, green by a blue, blue sea. Developed as a naval port, San Diego is strategically (for the tourist) located 100 miles S of Los Angeles and as close to Tijuana as any sane person should want to get.

The town is breezy and casual, famous for top-notch Mexican and seafood restaurants, monstrous 'happy hour' spreads, a historic old town, and great beaches accessible by bus from downtown. Lavish sunshine and its citizens' personal wealth haven't entirely eliminated the small-town flavour of San Diego and it it is one of America's nicest and fastest growing cities.

Local Guy's Guide to San Diego, www.members.aol.com/localspage/index.html is a witty see-and-do guide, authored by an opinionated native. Places, entertainment, roadtrips and dining from a local's point of view.

The telephone area code is 619.

ACCOMMODATION
Capri Hotel, 319 West E St, 232-3369. S-$22, D-$27 or weekly S-$80, D-$95; $25

deposit (show ID and they might reduce deposit). 'Clean, friendly, TV, kitchen, washing facilities.'

Elliot HI Hostel, 3790 Udall St, 223-4778. 6¹/₂ miles from downtown; take 35 bus to Ocean Beach. San Diego Zoo, Mission Bay Park, Sea World, Balboa Park and Old Town are close by. 'Well equipped, nr cheap markets, 20 min walk from beach.' '2 am curfew but $1 late pass available.' Staff plan activities such as barbecues and beach nonfires. $12-16.

Golden West Hotel, 720 4th Ave, 233-7596 (near Horton Plaza). S-$21, D-$33 w/private bath. $2 key deposit.

Grand Pacific Hostel, 726 5Th Ave, 232-3100. In the heart of San Diego's Gaslamp District, this gateway-to-Mexico hostel is close to pubs, clubs and shops. Staff are experienced backpackers. Tons of info on travel, cheap fares and Mexico. 'If we don't have the info, we'll get it for you!' Day tours, free bfast, no curfew. $13 LAX airport shuttle. Dorms (summer) $16, private rooms $40; (winter) $15/$35; weekly rates available. BUNAC discount honoured.

Maryland Hotel, 630 F St, 239-9243. Near Gaslamp District. S-$27.50, D-$35.50. $5 key deposit.

Ocean Beach International Backpacker Hostel, 4961 Newport Ave, (800) 339-7263. Pick-ups from bus/train/airport. Free doughnuts at 9 am. Free dinners Tue & Fri. Laundry, TV & videos, lockers, free use of surf boards, no curfew, alcohol allowed. $14 dorm; private D-$18. 'Clean and well-kept.' 'Brilliant! Friendly, laidback, hostel located right on beach—easy bus route to downtown.' 'Well recommended!' Seaworld a 15 min walk, San Diego Zoo a 30 min bus ride.

Pickwick Hotel, 132 W Broadway, 234-0141. Next to Greyhound. From S-$43, D-$48, $10 key deposit. 'Clean.' 'Dangerous area.'

San Clemente HI Hostel, 233 Avenida Granada, San Clemente (Hwy 5 N of San Diego), (714) 492-2848. View beautiful sunsets off the pier, cruise the boardwalk shops or savor small town atmosphere every Sunday morning at the Farmer's Market. Hostel is near beach. $10-14.

San Diego Metropolitan HI Hostel, 521 Market, 525-1531. Second gateway hostel to Mexico, it is located in the soul of the city's historic Gaslamp Quarter (16 blocks of cafes and restaurants, clubs, shops, galleries and landmarks). Close by trolley, city bus, airport, Greyhound. Few miles from Balboa Park, the Zoo, Sea World and beaches. Laundry, kitchen, bike rental. $14-16, private rooms available.

FOOD

It's here that you're likely to find some of the best Mexican food in the US, and plenty of places to choose from. Some of the best are:

Big Kitchen, 3003 Grape St, 234-5789. A bfast-and-lunch place with characters. Bfast from $4, lunch from $5. Look for comedienne Whoopi Goldberg's graffiti contribution on the kitchen wall. Mon-Fri 7 am-2 pm, Sat-Sun 'til 3 pm.

Chicken Pie Shop, 2633 Oklahoma Blvd, 295-0156. Scrumptious chicken & turkey pies for $1.60 to go, $3 to sit down with side dish, $4 pie-dinner. Daily 10 am-8.30 pm.

Chuey's Cafe, 1894 Main St, 234-6937. String beef tacos, other outstanding Mexican dishes under $11. Nearby murals at Chicano Park on the Coronado Bay Bridge make a fitting post-comida stroll. Sat 'til midnight; closed Sun.

El Indio Tortilla Shop, 3695 India St, 299-0333. Situated in an artists' district. 'Heavenly chicken burritos ($4.75), 50 takeout items so park across the way and pop in!' Dishes under $8, daily 7 am-9 pm.

Filipe's Pizza, 4 locations in San Diego. 'Best Italian food in San Diego. Try the lasagne; really superb.'

Non-Mexican: Boll Weevil Restaurants, 17 locations around San Diego. Excellent, inexpensive burgers. 'More flavour than any other burger I had in three months.'

Old Spaghetti Factory, 275 5th St, 233-4323. 'Eat in a train, a change from

INLINE HEAVENS—WHERE TO PARK YOUR SKATES IN THE US

Skateboarding, in-line skating and BMX biking are currently three of the fastest growing sports in the world, but most skateparks are not listed in the yellow pages. These are some of the best, most likeable and renowned skateparks in the USA, so dig deep and pull out your best tricks.

EAST COAST & MIDWEST: Riverside Skate Park, NYC, 108th St & Riverside Park, Manhattan. Built by Andy Kessler, one of the original *Zoo York* skateboard company crew, the park has an 11 ft vert ramp, a bank, rail, little grindbox, 2 quarter pipes and a vert wall. Helmet and pads must be worn and it's a mere $3 to get in and shred it all up!

Skatepark of Tampa, FL: 4215 E Columbus Dr, Tampa, (813) 621-6793. This skatepark welcomes skateboarders, rollerbladers and BMXers from wherever. The facility includes 8,000 sq ft street course, hips, pyramids, quarterpipes, corners, banks, a 5ft x 24ft mini-ramp, and an 11ft x 32ft vert ramp; 'the best built ramps in the business!' No pads are required on the street course for boarders, only on vert. However, bladers are required to wear full pads hemlet/elbow/knee) at all times. There is also a pro shop in the park for your skateboarding necessities. Hours of opening vary, so do yourself a favour and call ahead. Membership may be purchased or alternatively, pay-as-you-skate; Mon-Fri $6, $8 w/ends for a full day's worth of blood and sweat!

K-Zoo Skate Zoo, MI: 1502 Ravine Rd, Kalamazoo, (616) 345-9550. Take I-94 N to US 131, exit on Westmain M43 eastbound to Nichols Rd. Turn left on Nichols, then right on Ravine and Skate Zoo is 1 mile up on left side. The K-Zoo, Michigan's oldest indoor skateboard park, open for over 8 years, brag they have 'the best spine ramp and a great street course' which incorporates 6,800 sq ft of skating area! The latest addition is a new bank-to-wall ramp. Daily 3pm-9pm Mon-Fri, Sat noon-9pm and Sun 'til 6pm. Helmet, elbow and knee pads are required, and skateboards, in-line skates and bikes are all permitted (no bikes at w/end). A two day membership pass is $5, $5 per session after this initial payment.

Rhodes Park (aka Boise Skatepark), Boise, ID: This public park is built under an overpass which makes it ideal for skating all seasons. A 2 ft high ledge borders the perimeter of this football-field sized facility. Fun objects to skate include a 6 ft steel halfpipe (situated directly underneath the overpass—watch you don't get too ambitious!), several jump ramps and quarter ramps. There are also 2 8ftx8ft dirt patches to ollie over with a 1 ft high bar running through the middle, suitable for boardslides, feeble-grinds and whatever else you can pull out of your bag.

WEST COAST: Burnside Skatepark, Portland, Oregon: Burnside is regarded as the cornerstone of skateboarding in the Pacific Northwest—broad, solid and permanent. Established in 1990 on public land beneath the eastern side of the Burnside Bridge, just across the river from downtown Portland. From I-5 take the Burnside exit. Pass the turn onto the bridge and turn right on Ankeny, 1 block south of the bridge. After 2-blks turn right and the park is on the right. Burnside is an ever expanding skater-built (unmalleable) concrete haven that initially began as a shoddily built bowl, which still stands as the centrepiece. Today there are new banks, spines, structures ranging from 3ft-9ft in height incl a 6ft sq bowl, a 9ft vert wall, 'and more hips, bumps, and lines than Liz Taylor' all connected and interwoven. The lines there are endless. Free.

The Grind Skatepark, California: 2709 Del Monte, W Sacramento, (916) 372-ROLL. From Hwy 80 take Harbor Blvd S, turn left (east) onto Del Monte. Park is on right. This park is open to boarders and in-liners but not to BMX—sorry! The facility consists of a 14,000 sq ft warehouse incl three big rooms, a 4ft mini ramp, a 7ft deep pool, an 11ft vert ramp, a 6ft spine ramp, plus one indoor and one outdoor street course. Phew! As usual, pads and a helmet must be worn at all times. $10 gets you an all-day skate pass (if you don't hold an annual membership).

Huntington Beach #1/#2, California: Next to Burnside, probably one of the most talked-about, skate parks and nr Los Angeles. The first skatepark, located nr the corner of Golden West and Warner Ave, was a runt first attempt at providing a place to skate, featuring concrete undersized banks, ledges and little room to push…Huntington Beach Skatepark #2, ah-ha now we're getting somewhere. A little bigger, a little wider, the big brother features concrete banks, ledges, rails and a curb. It is located next to Huntington Beach High School, on Main St near Yorktown. Both are free.

Encinitas (aka Magdalena Ecke Family YMCA Skatepark), nr San Diego, California: 200 Saxony RD, Encinitas, (714) 942-9622. From I-5, exit at Encinitas Blvd, go east to first traffic signal, turn left on Saxony Rd and park is at the top of the hill. This 23,000 sq ft street course has an array of quarterpipes, bank ramps, pyramids and manual/slider obstacles. The park also features a 70ft wide by 6ft high double-bowled, double-hipped L-shaped miniramp (gulp) as well as an 11ft high vert bowl ramp. Plenty to keep yourself and your wee wooden toy having fun, but only for the first lucky 75 or so before others are turned away. All of the ramps are surfaced with smoooooth masonite except the vert ramp which is covered in hard steel. Bring your own pads or loan them here (free of charge with valid ID). $10 p/session daily if not an annual member.

For a comprehensive roster of all skateparks in the States and relevant hot links, check out the following on-line Net sites: *www.skateboard.com/tydu/ skatebrd/parks/sk8parks/html*, *www.intensity.com/parks.html* and *www.bigdeal .com/sk8/parks.*

Greyhound.' Dishes for under $10. Daily 11.30 am-2 pm & 5 pm-10 pm, Sat & Sun noon-11 pm.

Roberto's. Wonderful greasy-spoon dives, popular with the locals; among the best for Mexican food. 'Great place. Try the rolled tacos.' Many locations in and around the city.

OF INTEREST

Old Town, a snippet of the city's original heart, along San Diego Ave. Free walking tours from the Plaza make the few historical remnants come to life. Up the hill is **Presidio Park**; its **Serra Museum**, 2727 Presidio, houses documents, maps, archaeological finds from the nearby dig.

Balboa Park. Take the bus or bike to this superlative 1074-acre park, whose pink-icing Mexican Churrigueresque buildings were designed by Bertram Goodhue for the 1915-16 Panama-California International Exposition. 'Beautiful. Worth going to just for the architecture.' The park has 11 museums and galleries (free Tues), a world-class zoo, a carousel complete with brass ring, pipe organ and other concerts, free sidewalk entertainment, free facilities for everything from volleyball to frisbee golf. Info Center: 1549 El Prado, 239-0512, 9 am-4 pm daily.

Inside the park: Museum of Art, 232-7931. Tue-Sun 10 am-4.30 pm, Fri 'til 8 pm in Aug. $8; **Natural History Museum**, 232-3821. Daily 9.30 am-4.30 pm, $6.50; **Aerospace Museum**, 2001 Pan American Plaza, 234-8291. Daily 10 am-4 pm, $5.50; **Museum of Man**, 1350 El Prado, 239-2001. Daily 10 am-4.30 pm, $5.50; **Space Theater/Science Center**, 238-1233, 'science portion is smallish, no great shakes, but the 360-degree films are exhilarating.'

Also at Balboa: summer light opera at the **Starlight Bowl**, free Sun afternoon music at the organ pavilion, and the Pacific Relations cottages.

Cabrillo National Monument, Pt Loma, 557-5450. Take a #6 bus from downtown San Diego. Splendiferous view of the site where Juan Cabrillo first touched land at San Miguel Bay. Excellent tidepools, nature walks, films on whales, exhibit hall. Open summer 9 am-sunset, winter 'til 5.15 pm. Fee $4.

Coronado/Hotel Del Coronado. Can be reached on **Trolley Tour**, 298-8687. Get on/off where you like; tours and Coronado are worthwhile.

Gondola Cruise in San Diego Bay: Gondola di Venezia offers a relaxing and romantic way to view the San Diego skyline and the beauty of Shelter Island's tranquil waters. A 1hr cruise includes Italian music, hors d'oeuvres, ice and wine glasses. Contact 1551 Shelter Isl Drive, 221-2999.

La Jolla, the jewel of San Diego, from sculptured rocks at Windansea to the St Tropez-like La Jolla Shores and limpid La Jolla Cove. On La Jolla Bvld, rent snorkels and roam in this fabulous underwater park and wildlife preserve.

Mission Bay Park, 2581 Quivira Ct, 221-8900. 4600-acre marine park, the largest facility of its kind in the world. Sailing, fishing, water skiing, wind surfing on 27 miles of beaches.

San Diego Wild Animal Park, 30 miles N of San Diego off Hwy I-15 near **Escondido**, 480-0100. 1800 acres of animals freely roaming in their natural habitats; view from a 50 min ride in a monorail. Spanish architecture. 'Lots to see—don't miss bird shows. Best monorail run is 4.30 pm for most animal activity.' 'Amazing.' Also, *Mombasa Lagoon* is an interactive attraction where you can climb inside a giant stork eggshell, hop across the water on extra large lily pads, or explore an oversized spider's web. $22 includes entrance, monorail, hidden jungle and all live shows. Daily 8 am-4 pm; gates close at 5 pm. Parking $3.

San Diego Zoo, off Park Blvd in Balboa Park, 2343153, is one of the world's best— a luxurious setting for the 3200 animals. General admission $14, $18.50—including the 35 min bus tour, $22 includes all this, the aerial tram, and zoo. Daily 9 am-9 pm ('til 4 pm after Labor Day); gates close at 4 pm. Don't miss the walk-through hummingbird aviary, the koalas and the primates. 'Good zoo but not quite as good as expected.' 'Need 5 hours to see it all.'

Sea World, 1720 South Shores Rd, 222-6363, on Mission Bay north of downtown. Expensive at $32, so you'd better like performing whales, dolphins, seals! Best part is the **Penguin Encounter**, with 300 penguins in their beloved refrigerated setting. 'Don't miss the seal and otter shows.' **Shamu Backstage**, a 1.7 million gallon killer whale habitat allows visitors to touch, train and feed the killer whales, even wading with them in their 55 degree water. 'An all-day affair.' Daily 9 am-11 pm in summer (10 am-6 pm after Labor Day).

Southern California Exposition, Del Mar Fairgrounds, north of San Diego, 755-1161. Some of everything: outdoor flower and garden show, arts, gems, minerals, hobbies, crafts, jams, jellies, 4600 animals and a carnival June 15-July 4. $7. Horse-racing takes place in summer months.

ENTERTAINMENT

Beachcomber, 539-9902, 2901 Mission Blvd. '2 min walk to Pacific Ocean.' Frequented by Brits and Aussies. Daily 7 am-2 am. Margaritas $2.50.

Blarney Stone Pub, 5617 Balboa Ave, Clairemont, 279-2033. Happy hour Mon-Fri, 4 pm-6 pm. Traditional Irish music Tues thru Sat.

In Cahoots, 5373 Mission Center Rd, Mission Valley, 291-8635. Popular Country and Western bar, 'Always a party! Something cookin' every day of the week.' $2.50 drinks 'til 9 pm. 5 pm-2 am daily.

Humphrey's, 2241 Shelter Island Dr, 224-3577. Great happy hours Mon-Sat 4.30 pm-7.30 pm, Sun 6 pm-7 pm. Live entertainment every day.

Princess Pub and Grille, 1665 India St, downtown, 238-1266. Saturday hosts live bands. '*Real* beers on tap. Biggest surprise is when you walk out of the door and back into California.' Daily 11 am-1 am, food served 'til 11 pm.

Schooner's, 959 Hornblend St, Pacific Beach, 272-2780. Cheap food, $7 dishes and under. 'Good atmosphere, worth the queue to get in.'

Festivals: National Whale-Watching Weekend, mid-January. Special speakers and presentations at the Cabrillo whale-watching station at Point Moma. Call 557-5450 for more details. **Fabric Fantasies Festival**, June 6-7. This wearable arts, crafts and design showcase offers fabric and finery from around the world. Call 296-3161. Also, **Street Scene** is an annual food and music festival held September 5-7th, featuring more than 100 blues, Cajun, zydeco, rock, jazz, and reggae bands. Telephone 557-8490.

SPORT
San Diego's Padres baseball team plays at Jack Murphy Stadium, 9449 Friars Rd, 283-4494; **National Football League** here also with the **Chargers**, 280-2121.
Mission Valley YMCA Skatepark, 9115 Clairmont Mesa Blvd, located in Missile Park (just off Missile Rd at General Dynamics). 14,000 sq-ft course which includes 11 ft vert ramp, mini ramp, fun box with two rail slides, pyramid, bank walls, quarter pipes, manual pads and more. Good for boarders, in-liners and bikers. All safety gear req. $10 'one-day' skate fee (includes pad rental) or $6 session (3 hrs).

SHOPPING
Bazaar del Mundo International Marketplace in Old Town, open 10 am-10 pm.
Horton Plaza, btwn Broadway & G and 1st & 4th Aves. Colourful, lively, shopping, eating, cinema complex. Opens 10 am.
San Diego Factory Outlet Center, 4498 Camino de la Plaza. 35 factory outlets. Mon-Fri 10 am-8 pm, Sat 'til 7 pm, Sun 'til 6 pm.
Seaport Village, 14-acre shopping complex at West Harbor Dr and Kettner Blvd; 75 shops and restaurants. Opens 10 am.

INFORMATION
Balboa Park Info Center, House of Hospitality, Balboa Park, 239-0512. Small info centres also in Old Town, at airport, and along the hwy. Daily 9.30 am-4 pm.
Council of American Youth Hostels, 500 W Broadway, 338-9981. Publishes a budget traveller's guide to San Diego.
Travelers Aid, 1765 4th Ave, #100, 232-7991. Mon-Fri 8.30 am-5 pm. Also information booth at airport, 231-7361. 8 am-midnight.
Visitor Information Center, 11 Horton Plaza (downtown), 236-1212. Multilingual staff on-hand. Mon-Sat 8.30 am-5 pm, Sun from 11 am summer only.

TRAVEL
Auto Driveaway, 4672 Park Blvd, 295-8060. Must be over 21yrs. $300 cash deposit, $290 refund when car is returned in same condition, must see passport and credit card. You pay all gas except first tank. Mon-Fri, 8.30 am-4.30 pm.
Amtrak, 1050 Kettner Blvd at Broadway, 239-9021/(800) 872-7245. Romantic 1915 depot with twin Moorish towers. Around 8 runs a day to LA, takes about 2 hrs 45 mins.
Bargain Auto Rentals car rental, 3860 Rosecans St, 299-0009. Must be one of the only places to rent to 18 year olds, although there is a $9 surcharge for drivers under 21-yrs. Credit card essential. Daily 8 am-6 pm.
Greyhound, 120 W Broadway, (800) 231-2222. 24 hrs.
San Diego International Airport (Lindbergh Field) lies at northwestern edge of downtown. Take #2 bus from Broadway downtown to reach it, $1.50. Last bus into downtown, 1 am. Cab fare to downtown, $7.50.
San Diego Regional Transit, 233-3004. Runs a 'very efficient and easy-to-understand' bus system. Basic fare $1.50; 'Daytripper' one-day pass, $5. Also operates **San Diego Trolley**, 233-3004, making breaks for the US border near El Cajon and Tijuana every 15 mins from Amtrak; $3.50 r/t. 'Buy a r/t ticket to Tijuana, you won't want to stay long.' 'Quick, comfortable' and cheaper than Mexicoach and Greyhound.

ANZA-BORREGO DESERT and EASTERN SAN DIEGO COUNTY The 600,000-acre state park is in San Diego's back yard, at the end of a scenic 90-

mile climb through forests, mountains and the charming gold mining village of **Julian**, ultimately spiraling down 3000 ft to the **Sonoran Desert** floor.

The route can be traversed by bicycle (tough) or car, but there's also a cheap bus service via the Northeast County Bus Service, 765-0145, several times weekly from **El Cajon**, east of San Diego, to Julian, Borrego Springs and other points. Mon-Fri 7 am-noon and 2 pm-5 pm.

At once desolate and grand, the Anza-Borrego Desert embraces sandstone canyons, rare elephant trees, pine-rimmed canyons, oases and wadis. Springtime brings wildflowers, which you can see year-round at the excellent sound and light presentation at the visitors center, 767-5311. Open only at w/ends during summer 9 am-5 pm. For rsvs: (800) 444-7275. Camping in the park is free at primitive sites, $12 w/hook-up at developed campgrounds (off-season). Best months are Nov-May; it's terribly hot thereafter. If you don't want to camp, stay in Julian at one of the B&Bs or cottages rather than in expensive Borrego Springs. Either way, don't miss out on the spectacular apple pie ($3) at the **Julian Cafe**, 765-2712. Around beginning of February, the **Native American Days Celebration** in Borrego Springs is an annual Cahuilla and Kumeyaay cultural celebration featuring demonstrations, lectures and nature walks. Call 767-4205.

Anza-Borrego Desert State Park Photos can be accessed through *www.olywa.net.hilliard/anza_borrego.html*

The telephone area code is 619.

HAWAII *Aloha State*

When your plane touches down, congratulate yourself—you've made it to paradise. But, as the song says, they've 'paved paradise and put up a parking lot'—particularly in Oahu, likely to be the first place you see. Japanese investors have fuelled real estate price increases, and prices in general are quite high. Hawaii has its poor and its homeless, but paradise still exists in this tourist-trampled state, if you know where to look.

For the real Hawaiians, this is actually Paradise Lost. Hawaii is the northern tip of the 'Polynesian Triangle'—a four-cornered triangle(!) with Fiji in the west, Easter Island in the east and New Zealand in the south. The spread of the Polynesian peoples (polynesia = many islands) can be charted, by archaeologists and philologists, from Malayan and Indonesian roots. It is believed that Hawaii was first inhabited sixteen hundred years ago by Polynesians setting out in their canoes from the Marquesas Islands in what is now French Polynesia. For centuries they grew their taro, hunted their pigs, and occasionally had each other over for dinner (one-way tkts only), undisturbed by 'civilisation.' Captain Cook, when he arrived at Kona in 1778, inadvertently brought an end to that, but the Hawaiians brought an end to him, which was irony, if not justice. Not for nothing did he name Hawaii the 'Sandwich Islands'; he had inside knowledge!

Polynesian-blooded Hawaiians now number about 250,000, and are well outnumbered by the descendants of the immigrants brought in to expand the sugar industry in the late 19th century: Europeans/Americans, Chinese, Japanese, Koreans, and, lately, Filipinos, Samoans and Vietnamese. The indigenous Hawaiians were powerless when American missionaries-turned-opportunists stole their lands and then their kingdom during the last century, just as they were when the US Government completed the process in 1959.

Just west of Kauai lies Niihau, the 'forbidden isle.' The family that owns Niihau, the western-most island of the archipelago, has prohibited outsiders in an attempt to preserve the culture of old Hawaii. Elsewhere in Hawaii the pure Hawaiian is almost, as Mark Twain put it, 'a curiosity in his own land'. The 'missionaries' also banned the teaching of the Hawaiian language (as well as removing some letters from the alphabet!), so that by 1987 fewer than 2000 people spoke the native tongue. Now, though, children can be taught in Hawaiian if they wish. There is a small but committed movement of Hawaiians still trying to regain their stolen sovereignty.

Hawaii's eight island chain has been formed (and is still being formed) by volcanic activity (mythically, Pele, the goddess of fire). The islands are actually the tips of the tallest volcanic mountains on earth (Mauna Kea on the Big Island is 13,796' above sea level, and over 19,000' below!). The oldest sizeable island (Kauai) is to the west, but the newest island (Hawaii itself, the Big Island) is still growing in the east as tectonic plate movement pushes the islands westward from the faultline. As of 1997, lava bubbling and sizzling into the sea sometimes adds metres per day to the eastern coastline. The Big Island is becoming the Even Bigger Island, and you can stand and watch it happen beneath your feet.

The main islands (from left to right: Kauai, Oahu, Maui and Hawaii) are readily accessible by air and are all worth visiting for their differing flavours, scenery and beaches. All beaches in Hawaii are public and most are excellent. They are home to obsessive hordes of young, tanned hedonists with sub-bleached hair, whose life is the surf, the board they ride on, and the beaten up old campervans they live in. Hippie-dom with a sporting purpose. (Many of those who 'dropped out' in the '60's found their way to Hawaii. The hair is still long, but it's turned grey.) The Big Island is not noted for its beaches, but it has its own spectacular volcanic scenery and '13 different climates'.

From **Oahu**, with its cosmopolitan capital, Honolulu, you can island-hop via the reasonably-priced local airlines to **Hawaii**, the Big Island, for its rural and volcanic scenery, and **Maui** or **Kauai** for beaches and tranquility. Don't be discouraged by the astronomical prices of the big resort hotels. Good, cheap motels and bed & breakfasts abound. (Pacific-Hawaii B&B, 1312 Oulepe St, Kailua, HI 96734, offers rooms on the four main islands starting from $54: call (800) 999-6026 from mainland; and B&B Honolulu, 3242 Kaohinani Dr, Honolulu 96817, (800) 288-4666, operates throughout the state, rooms from $44, include bfast). County, state and national campsites are available for overnight stays for a minimal fee; most popular state parks (with the exception of Maui and the Big Island) require an advance (free) permit. Camping is limited to five nights per 30 days. Sites open Fri-Wed on O'ahu, daily on other islands. Rustic cabins are available as well, but book way ahead.

National Park: Haleakala Hawaii Volcanoes
The telephone area code is 808. www.yahoo.com/Regional/U_S__States/Hawaii/

OAHU   Most urbanized and brutalised of the islands, but don't write Oahu off entirely. It absorbs the brunt of approx 4.5 million visitors a year. In doing so, it's won a few battles (billboards are banned, flowers are planted everywhere) and lost a few (highrise forests in Waikiki, plastic leis for tour groups).

Honolulu is the state capital, legally and touristically. But don't come looking for miles of beaches, Hawaiian village charm or quiet. You'll find Waikiki a postage-stamp sized beach covered with bodies in various shades of red. Honolulu's pace, while not quite the gallop of hypertensive Los Angeles, is nonetheless brisk. Crowded with traffic on foot and wheel both, Honolulu is a place to act the tourist, to shop at the International Market, to sip maitais and eat puupuus (Hawaii's hors d'oeuvres) and have a good time when the sun goes down.

For cheap food, the city offers huge and colourful produce and seafood markets as well as Japanese box lunch takeouts and noodle stands. If you like, join in the on-going debate over the merits of *poi*, a Hawaiian staple made of taro root. Packaged in plastic bags and sold in local stores, the squishy grey stuff looks remarkably like wallpaper paste. Some people say it tastes like it too, but be open-minded and decide for yourself. Although they are somewhat buried in the barrage of tourist ballyhoo, Honolulu's cultural attractions (from museums to Chinatown) are worth finding, and the city's historical sites, Pearl Harbor and Punchbowl Crater in particular, are tasteful and moving. Get a fantastic view of Honolulu from old war fortifications atop **Diamond Head**, a volcanic crater overshadowing the city. Local teens hang out in the smelly bunkers; note an eerie inscription memorialising a murder committed there. Go early—the hike up is as tiring as the view is rewarding, and the parking lot closes at dusk.

Good bus transit on the islands allows you easy access to the beautiful country outside Honolulu. Following Hwy 72 E, you come to **Koko Head State Park**; here, **Hanauma Bay** is snorkeling heaven. Coral reefs form tunnels and pools through which you can chase elusive, colourful fish and sea turtles. To the northeast of Honolulu on Hwy 61 lies the **Koolau Range**, which, like most Hawaiian ranges, is formed by steep, grooved ridges dripping with lush foliage. Cutting through the mountain, **Nuuanu Pali Pass** offers splendid views of the ocean. It was here that King Kamehameha the Great defeated the Oahuans in 1795, literally forcing them over the cliffs; the victorious king became the first ruler of the united Hawaiian Islands.

Near Hauula on the northeast coast, a tough one-mile climb along a rough mountain ravine brings you to the **Sacred Falls**, one of the loveliest sights on the island: 2500-foot cliffs form a splendid backdrop to the falls, dropping 87 ft into the gorge. Oahu's northern side boasts incredible beaches—**Sunset** and **Waimea Bay** among them—as well as some of the best surfing on earth (the infamous **Banzai Pipeline** is here). Further on is the **Puu O Mahuka Heiau**, where humans were once sacrificed to the gods (the practice has since been discontinued). Kick back, relax and explore Oahu by browsing *www.hshawaii.com/ovp/*.

ACCOMMODATION

Waikiki is crowded with low-cost digs, many with kitchens, most a couple of blocks from the beach. Rsvs advised year-round. NB: city buses take backpacks 'at the discretion of the driver.' Anything you can hold on your lap or load under your seat is fine. Otherwise, be prepared to take a cab to your hostel or hotel.

B&B Pacific Hawaii, 19 Kai Nani Place, 262-6026. Books rooms anywhere across island from $47 per couple.

Big Surf Hotel, 1690 Ala Moana Blvd (near boat harbour), 946-6525. From S-$40, suites $50 ($14 pp).

Central YMCA, 401 Atkinson Dr, across from Ala Moana Shopping Center, 941-3344. First come, first served; pool, weight room, 4 racquet ball courts. S-$30 + $10 key deposit men, 18+only. 'Convenient for all buses.'

Edmunds Hotel Apartments, 2411 Ala Wai Blvd, 923-8381. From S/D-$38. TV; homely, recommended.

Hale Aloha HI Hostel, 2417 Prince Edward St (2 blocks off beach), 926-8313. 3 night guaranteed stay. Dorm $16, D-$35; linen $1. Kitchen. Free use of snorkelling gear! No lockout or curfew. Rsvs advised.

Honolulu HI Hostel, 2323A Sea View Ave, 946-0591. Across the street from Univ of Hawaii; take #19 or #20; transfer to bus #6 to University. Small and peaceful. Kitchen, TV room, patio under coconut trees, laundry, clean single-sex facilities. 3 night guaranteed stay. $13-16. Check-out 10 am, lights out 11 pm. 'Very busy.' Rsvs essential.

Interclub Hostel 'Waikiki', 2413 Kuhio Ave, 924-2636. Laundry, BBQs, TV. Female or mixed dorms, $16 (stay 7 nights, pay for 6), or private D-$51, XP-$10.

Kim's Island Hostel, 1946 Ala Moana Blvd, Suite #130, 942-8748. Each room has A/C, bathrm, sink, fridge, TV. Cooking facilities available. $12 first night, $16 p/night additional or under $100 p/wk. Call for S/D rates.

NB: Camping is not recommended on Oahu; locals like to gather at campsites and may feel you are encroaching on their turf. Check out the grounds; if they are obviously being used by tourists, camping probably OK, particularly if the site seems to be patrolled regularly.

FOOD

In the local parlance, Hawaiians don't eat, they 'grind.' If it's a luau or all-you can eat smorgy, they 'grind to da max!' Grinding episodes usually start with puupuus (Hawaiian munchies), which reflect the state's ethnic diversity, from egg rolls to falafel. This is the home of the maitai, a nobly-proportioned ration of rum, pineapple juice, chunks of fruit and a baby orchid. Another local poison is the blue Hawaii, a toxic-looking concoction made from blue curacao and who knows what else? Good ethnic eating at Japanese delis, Chinese takeaway counters and noodle shops, especially on **Hotel Street**. If you're still not stuffed, tap into Honolulu's lavish happy hour spreads, or better still, a luau. When it comes to luaus, choices are plenty, but prices are high. Read the free *Waikiki Beach Press* and other local papers for Church luaus, generally cheaper and friendlier, with better food and entertainment, than those at the big hotels. Be sure to sample shave ice, Hawaii's better answer to the snowcone. And before you leave Oahu, don't miss the **McDonald's** in **Laie**. Regular old fast food, but the restaurant was constructed to resemble a Hawaiian longhouse, complete with tropical flowers and an indoor grotto. Try the variety of ethinic restaurants located btwn the 500 and 1000 blocks of **Kapahulu Ave. Kaimuki**, **Moili'ili** and **downtown** districts are thriving with good food and nightlife also.

Hamburger Mary's, 2109 Kuhio, Honolulu, 922-6722. Restaurant with w/end barbecues (ave plate $2). Building open 8 am-2 am.

Helena's, 1364 N King, Honolulu, 845-8044. Inexpensive Hawaiian specialties—butterfish, laulau, poi.

Queen Kapiolani, 150 Kapahulu Ave, Honolulu, 922-1941. Buffet lunch Fri-Sun 11 am-2 pm, under $15 all-you-can-eat.
Rainbow Drive-In, 3308 Kanaina Ave, 737-0177. Tasty cuisine at rock-bottom prices. Daily 7.30 am 'til 9 pm.

OF INTEREST

In Honolulu: Academy of Arts, 900 S Beretania, at Ward (take #2 bus from Waikiki), 532-8701. Tue-Sat 10 am-4.30 pm, Sun 1 pm-5 pm; closed Mon. Free; 30 galleries surrounding six garden courts. From Polynesian to avant-garde, including one of the finest collections of Asian Art in America. James Michener collection of Ukiyo-e woodblock prints is one of world's best. Academy also shows 'alternative' and foreign films ($4), and has concert and theatre programmes; call 532-8768.
Bishop Museum and Planetarium, 1525 Benice St, 848-4136. $8.50 includes gallery tours, dance performances, craft demonstrations and planetarium shows. Incredible feather cloaks (treasured as booty by the ancient kings), Hawaiian and Polynesian artifacts. Daily 9 am-5 pm.
Capitol District Walking Tour gives extensive coverage of Honolulu's historic district and may be picked up from the Hawaii Visitor Bureau.
Foster Botanical Garden, 50 N Vineyard Blvd, 522-7065. Cool oasis of rare trees, orchids and flowers. Wear insect repellent! Guided tours on Fri, call for times. Take #4 bus from Waikiki to corner of Vineyard Blvd. Daily 9 am-4 pm. $5.
Honolulu Zoo, 151 Kapahulu Ave, 971-7171. Daily 9 am-4.30 pm. $6. World's finest group of tropical birds.
Iolani Palace, King and Richards St, 522-0832. Only royal palace on American soil, used just 11-yrs by the Hawaiian monarchs. 45 min tours begin every 15 min. Queen Liliuokalani wrote *Aloha Oe*, easily the most famous Hawaiian song, while imprisoned here. $6. 9 am-2.15 pm Wed-Sat. Very popular; rsvs necessary.
Hawaii's postmodern State Capitol stands at the corner of Beretania and Richard St. Mon-Fri 9 am-4 pm; free.
Outside Honolulu: USS Arizona National Memorial at **Pearl Harbor**, 422-2771. Departures from Halawa Gate. 20 min film on Japanese attack on Pearl Harbor at the Visitors Center, followed by free Navy boat tours of the harbour and memorial. You can look down through the limpid water to see the ghostly outline of the Arizona, wherein lie 1000 of the sailors (some have been removed) who died on 7 Dec, 1941. Shivery. Take #20 bus from Waikiki, 1-hr bus ride, or shuttle bus (see TRAVEL). Daily 7.30 am-5 pm; tours 8 am-3 pm. Free; arrive early, queue forms at 7 am for same-day tkts. The **visitors center** is open Mon-Sun 7.30 am-5 pm.
USS Bowfin, nxt to Arizona Memorial, 423-1341. Self-guided tour (w/hand-held receiver) of this WW2 submarine. Daily 8 am-5 pm (last tour 4.30 pm), $8.50.
Sea Life Park, Makapuu Point (16 miles E of Waikiki on Hwy 72), 259-7933. The huge reef tank gives you skindiver's view of brilliant fish, coral, sharks. Various shows. Sat-Thur 9.30 am-5 pm; Fri 'til 10 pm. Bus service Fri back to hotels after Hawaiian entertainment (under $10) at 10 pm. $21.50, cheaper than mainland aquatic parks and better, too.
Beaches: Queen's Surf Beach is close to downtown and attracts swimmers, skate-boarders and in-line skaters. Als, try the **Sans Souci Beach**. If you seek more secluded beaches, head east on Diamond Head Rd until you reach **Kahala Ave.** *Aloha!* is a guide to Oahu's popular beaches, *www.aloha.com/~lifeguards/.*

ENTERTAINMENT

Kodak Hula Show, Waikiki Shell by Kapiolani Park, 627-3300. Array of Hawaiian, Tahitian dancing, costumes to blow colour film on; get there early for seats (some-times already filled by 9.30 am). Tue-Thur 10 am-11.15 am. Free. More free shows at: **King's Village**, on Kaiulani across from the Hyatt Regency, 944-6855, Sun, Wed, Fri at 6.15 pm.

The Wave, 1877 Kalakaua, Honolulu, 941-0424. Live rock music every night, 8.30 pm-4 am; free entry 'til 10 pm, then $5 cover. Mondays , DJ only. 21-yrs +.

World Café, 500 Ala Moana Blvd, 599-4450, has the best tunes and drink specials. Mon-Thurs 4 pm-3 am, Fri 'til 4 am, Sat 7 pm-4 am and Sun 8 pm-2 am.

Festivals: One of the best parades is held June 7th in Honolulu, from downtown Iolani Palace through Waikiki, to honor Kamehameha the Great, the warrior king who unified the island chain in the early 19th century. See floats festooned with countless tropical blossoms and *pa'u* riders. The **Pan Pacific festival**, June 12th in Honolulu, features folk dancers, artists and musicians from around the Pacific Rim, including a block party in Waikiki.

INFORMATION/TRAVEL

Camping and Parks, 1151 Punchbowl St, Rm #131, 587-0300. Info and permits for camping in state parks and trail maps. Mon-Fri 8 am-3.30 pm.

MTL, 848-5555, offers good bus service around the island; 60¢ gets you anywhere; free transfers. Runs airport bus also.

National Park Service, Prince Kuhio Federal Bldg #6305, 300 Ala Moana Blvd, 541-2693. Permits are given at individual park HQs. Mon-Fri 7.30 am-4 pm.

Visitors Bureau , 2270 Kalakaua, 7th flr, Waikiki Business Plaza, 923-1811. Mon-Fri, 8 am-4.30 pm.

24 hr surf report, 836-1952.

MAUI   Twenty-five flying minutes southeast of Honolulu is Maui, trendiest of the islands and famous for sweet onions, potato chips, humpback whales and Maui wowie, a potent variety of local marijuana. Formed by two volcanic masses linked by a wasp-waisted isthmus, Maui is marked by an extraordinary variety of terrain and climate, from the cold dryness of 10,023-foot **Haleakala volcanic crater** to the lush wetness of **Hana** (to describe it would require a new vocabulary for hues of green). The former whaling port of **Lahaina** is touristy and social; the upcountry eucalyptus land around **Makawao** is rural and mellow. Once past the endless condos of Kihei and Wailea, there are superb beaches and camping opportunities at **Makena** and further south.

At **Haleakala National Park**, 572-9306, $4 per car, the 'House of the Sun' has the largest dormant (for the last 200 years, anyway) volcano in the world, 21 miles in circumference. If you go there, you will be told repeatedly that the crater is big enough to swallow all of Manhattan (you might as well hear it here first). The terrain is magnificent: graceful cones and curves of deep red and purple punctuated by ethereal silversword plants. Huge cumulus clouds sometimes pour over the crater lip and pile up like whipped cream. At dawn and dusk you may see the Spectre of Brocken effect, where your shadow is projected gigantically against the clouds and encircled by rainbow light. Sunrise at Haleakala is like a slow-motion fireworks display, best seen near the Puu Ulaula observation centre. NB: Dress warmly! **Hookipa Beach Park**, on Maui's north shore, is the Mecca of the windsurfing world—a sport that is taking over the island and as much fun to watch as it is to do—well, almost. For an all-photo tour of Maui, get connected to *www.makena.com/lahaina/home.htm*.

ACCOMMODATION/FOOD

Flown-in food is costly on Maui, so stick to local products: seafood, pineapple, lettuce, tomatoes, fabulous sweet onions like nowhere else on earth (it's the soil), potato chips ('Maui Kitch'n Cook'd Potato Chips' is the one you want, accept no substitutes), and 'Maui blanc' (pineapple wine). While on the west side of Maui, seek out cheap hotels; on the east side, try the campgrounds.

Banana Bungalow, 310 N Market St, Wailuku, 244-5090. Uncrowded rooms and numerous facilities including TV rm, laundry, hot tub, hammocks, volleyball court and kitchen. Dorm $17, S-$34 with dble bed, D-$42. Cheap meals, airport and beach shuttles.

Camp Keanae, on East side of Maui (36 miles E of airport), 242-9007. Isolated, beautiful setting (bring food). 12 people $10 pp, (no linens). Kitchen, usual facilities. Check-in 4 pm-6 pm; out by 9 am. Rsvs in advance. Mailing address and rsvs through YMCA: 250 Kanaloa Ave, Kahuluihi, 96732.

Northshore Inn, 2080 Vineyard St, 242-8999. Relaxed place with kitchen, TV, laundry and fridges in every room. Movies daily at 9 pm. Dorm $16, S-$32, D-$43.

Camping: In Haleakala a small amount of free **tent camping** plus 3 **hiker cabins**, $22 for two; cabins are so popular they're booked by lottery. Access by foot or on horseback only. Worth enquiring about cancellations when you get there, call 572-9306. Rsvs attempts at PO Box 369, Makwao, 96768, but don't bother for 'lottery' cabins unless you can write 2 months ahead. Other **camping cabins**, from $10 for one, and from $30 for six. Free **tent camping** at **Waianapanapa State Park** , near Hana, 243-5354, or at **Oheo Gulch** (15 miles from Hana), 572-9306, no drinking water. Rsvs in advance, call 243-5354, then collect permit at office on 54 South High St, Wailuki.

OF INTEREST/TRAVEL

Top 10 things to do in Maui!—www.maui.net/~bikemaui/top10.html is guaranteed to give you some great adventure ideas!

In Hana: 54 miles of bad but beautiful road keep Hana private; Charles Lindbergh loved it, lived and is buried here. Lodging is exclusive, so day trips or camping near Seven Pools is just about it. 'Don't miss the **Oheo Gulch and Stream**; crystal clear, just like paradise.' The Shuttle runs btwn Lahaina and Kaanapali every 25 min, with stops at Royal Lahaina, Sheraton, Marriott, Kaanapali Beach and Hyatt, free.

Lahaina viewing for **humpback whales** who mate and calve in the channel Dec-Mar; lots of whale-watching tours from the harbour. Also see the **whaling museum** on the brig *Carthaginian*, 661-3262, at the harbour. Its A/V show has whale songs and birth of a whale. $4. Daily 10 am-4.15 pm.

In Kaanapali: Whalers Museum, Village on the Beach, 661-5992. Whaling artifacts, photographs, and antiques from 19th C. 'Small but stunning and poignant.' Daily 9.30 am-10 pm, free.

INFORMATION

Regency Rent-a-Car, Kahului Airport, 871-6147. Daily 8 am-8 pm.

Resort Taxi, 661-5285, offers an $11 ride into Kahului or Wailuku from airport.

Visitors Bureau, 1727 Pa Loop, Wailuku, 244-3530. Mon-Fri 8 am-4.30 pm.

Visitor Information Kiosk, 872-3893, at the Kahului Airport terminal. Daily 6.30 am-9 pm.

HAWAII Called the Big Island for its size (and to distinguish it from Hawaii, the state, which encompasses all of the islands). Also known as the Orchid Island for the 22,000 varieties that grow wild and in nurseries, this is the youngest and firiest of the archipelago. Unlike its sister isles, which draw crowds to their beaches, Hawaii's main attraction is inland—**Hawaii Volcanoes National Park**, a cracked and crumpled moonscape created by the living volcano Mauna Loa. Each day the volcano adds to the island's real estate, dumping 650,000 cubic yards of red-hot lava into the ocean, enough to pave a thin sidewalk from here to New York. Nearby **Mauno Kea** recently earned new fame. From its peak scientists discovered a galaxy 12 billion light years away, that began forming much sooner than was thought possible after the 'Big Bang.' This and **Kilauea** are two of the world's most active volcanoes. Mark Twain (when it was fashionable for 19th century writers, such as Somerset Maugham, Jack London and Robert Louis Stevenson, to visit the islands) wrote of Kilauea, 'The smell of sulphur is strong, but not unpleasant to a sinner.'

But there are other facets to the Big Island: the jungley mystery of the east side; the desert bleakness of the south; the commercialised carnival of the Kona Coast to the west, wafted with coffee-laden breezes; and the rolling hills of the north, Hawaiian cowboy country. Best of all is the comparative lack of crowding; the Big Island is big enough to comfortably accommodate all comers. This is a place where the aloha spirit hasn't frayed too much, and people still get together to 'talk story' and watch the sun set. 'Twenty years behind the times!' Search the Big Island online, *www.bigisland.com/*.

ACCOMMODATION

The **Kona Coast** on the western side is where the high-priced hotels are; **Hilo** on the east retains an unspoiled, if dilapidated charm. Cheap rooms can be found on either side of the island, however.

Arnott's Lodge, 98 Apapane Rd, Hilo, 969-7097. $18 bunk, S-$31, D-$40 or D-$20 (semi-private), suite for five from $80. Kitchen, TV lounge.

Dolphin Bay Hotel, 333 Iliahi, Hilo, 935-1466. From S/D-$50-$55, XP-$10. Wonderful garden with pick-your-own bfast. Kitchen.

Holo Holo Inn, 19-4036 Kalani Holua Rd, 967-7950. Large, clean rooms, dorm $16. Rsvs in advance after 4.30 pm.

Hotel Honokaa, PO Box 247, Honokaa, 775-0678. Dorm $16, from S-$33, D-$37, 'luxury' D-$65. Bathroom outside. Rsvs required. 'Very simple.' Has been going over 80 years.

Kona Tiki Hotel, 75-5968 Alii Dr, 329-1425, on the **Kona Coast**. Fridge, ocean view, freshwater swimming pool. D-$59 or $64 w/full kitchen, XP-$8.

My Island Volcano B&B, on Old Volcano Rd, 967-7216. Beautiful rooms in a historic mission-style home. From S-$37, D-$58.

Camping: The county runs beach parks where you can **camp** for $1 pp; permits required, from one of the four County Parks offices on the island. Call 961-8311 for info. In **Volcanoes National Park**, 967-7311, find free campsites at **Kipuka Nene**, **Namakani Paio** and **Kamoamoa**-each with shelters and fireplaces but no wood. Register with the visitors centre by 4.30 pm. Also, try the **Namakani Paio** cabins, in an *ohia* forest. From S/D-$33, with key deposit.

FOOD

Kona coffee and macadamia nuts are the indigenous items on the menu; restaurants seem to put the nuts in everything. Free samples and self-guided tours at, among others:

Hawaiian Holiday Macadamia Nut Company in Haina off Hwy 19 near Honokaa, 775-7743, daily 9 am-5.30 pm.

Royal Kona Coffee Mill and Museum, Hwy 160 on the way to Captain Cook's Monument, 328-2511, daily 9 am-5 pm.

OF INTEREST

Only in America—drive-in-volcanoes at **Hawaii Volcanoes National Park**, 967-7311, $5 per car, good for 7 days, via Hwy 11 from Hilo, Crater Rim Drive takes you through the **Kilauea Caldera**, almost into the gaping maw of the **Halemaumau Firepit**. Here lives Pele, the notoriously bad-tempered Hawaiian fire goddess. If you're lucky, you may see a sacrifice to appease Pele at the edge of the firepit. Nowadays, cookies, pineapples and even whole dressed chickens get tossed over the edge (park regulations prohibit virgins), with the result being something of a rubbish bin, as plastic bags and bottles are chucked in with the food. Pele makes her presence known at nearby **Mauna Loa** as well. Being a shield volcano (so-called because of its characteristic shape), Mauna Loa erupts in a relatively controlled manner, allowing the curious to get a closer look. Going south on Hwy 11, the magnificent vista of the island's desert comes into view.

You can visit the legendary **black sand beaches** at Kaimu and Punaluu, but be warned, the 'sand' is really volcanic rubble. Walking on it is a little like walking on broken glass, so bring shoes. The sand is green at **Ka Lae** (that is, if you can find any sand among the huge boulders that cover most of the shore). This is the most southerly point in the US, and the Hawaiian Plymouth Rock; here, Polynesian explorers first beached their canoes and established Hawaii's oldest known settlement, *circa* AD 750. Ka Lae is not developed for tourists and most car rental agencies prohibit customers from travelling this road. Further north on the island's western side is **Captain Cook's Monument**, accessible only by sea. Here the European discoverer of the Hawaiian Islands, once regarded by natives as a god, suffered a massive drop in popularity in 1779. The marker showing where he was killed (while intervening in a dispute) is under water.

Kahaluu Park Beach, south of **Disappearing Sands Beach** on Alii Drive. Amazing snorkeling among flashy fish, none of which is bigger than you are. It's like swimming through an aquarium. If you've forgotten your mask and fins, rent them from the park or at Jack's Diving Locker, just down the road from the Kona Inn Shopping Village in Kailua-Kona, at 75-5819 Alii Drive, 329-7585.

Manta Ray watching, Kona Surf Hotel. Nightly, the hotel spotlights the ocean where huge rays come to feed; free and thrilling. Taking Hwy 19 from Kailua-Kona, you pass through the verdant hills of northern Hawaii. Turn onto Hwy 24 at Honokaa to see the dreamlike **Waipi'o Valley**, a little green world captured by steep cliffs. The road goes all the way down to the valley, but the last part is too steep for cars. Jeep transport is available for a fee. Spare yourself the expense and the gear-grinding heart-attack ride down by hoofing it; if you're in reasonably good shape, you'll make it back up, too. Your reward: playing in the surf at the wonderful beach. The **Waipi'o Lookout**, offers one of the most striking panoramas in the islands. NB: A road to avoid is Hwy 200, the 80-mile saddle road with a high fatality rate btwn the twin behemoths Mauna Kea and Mauna Loa. Once you're on it, there's no turning back: attempting a U-turn on the narrow road lined with lava rock guarantees a flat tire or worse. Not to mention the debilitating fog. If you choose to traverse this or other questionable roads in a rented car, you must do so at your own risk. Check the contract for the company's policy.

INFORMATION/TRAVEL

Dollar Rent-a-Car , 961-6059 and **Avis Rent-a-Car**, 935-1290, in main terminal at Hilo Airport. Credit card essential.

Hele-on-Bus, 935-8241, takes you from Hilo to Kailua-Kona, Hawaii Volcanoes National Park, Pahoa and other points for 750 $6 o/w.

Visitors Bureau, 755719 W Alii Dr, 329-7787. Mon-Fri, 8 am-noon & 1 pm-4.30 pm.

Waipi'o Valley Jeep Shuttle, 775-7121. Catch it at the top of the valley; purchase tkts at the **Waipi'o Woodworks Art Gallery**, 775-0958. Rsvs rec.

KAUAI Once the 'Garden Island' was known as the 'undiscovered isle,' but no more. Now Kauai has its share of supermarkets, condos, huge resorts and canned tours. A constant stream of rent-a-cars flows along the highway that almost-girdles the island; crossing the street can be an adventure in itself. The landscape that lent the backdrop for the filming of *South Pacific* in the 1950s still endures: **Lumahai and Haena beaches** on postcard-perfect **Hanalei Bay**. But other patches of paradise are gone: the heavenly waterfall where France Nuygen cavorted with her GI beau has been closed due to tourist overload. Learn how you can experience Kauai on an exciting helicopter tour, an exhilarating boat trip and by driving past some of the most scenic spots imaginable, *www.jans-journeys.com/kauai*.

ACCOMMODATION
Garden Island Inn, 3445 Wilcox Rd, **Nawiliwili** (2 miles from Lihue), (800) 648-0154. Ocean views. From S/D-$58.
Hotel Coral Reef, 1516 Kuhio Hwy, **Kapaa**, 822-4481. Some rooms with ocean view, rsvs advised. Fruit in morning, car rentals available. Rooms from S/D-$63.
Kaua'i HI Hostel, 4532 Lehua St, (800) 858-2295. Located opposite beach and several restaurants, a great base for exploring island. Friendly backpacker crowd and staff. Full kitchen, TV, pool table, laundry, daytrips. Dorm $17, private rooms from $40.
Camping: Kaua'i County Parks Office, 4444 Rice St. Moikeha Bldg, Lihu'e, 241-6670, has permits for camping in county parks. Permits also available from rangers on-site.

FOOD/OF INTEREST
Kauai is the proud birthplace of **Lappert's ice cream**, available at not one but six Lappert's locations including the Coconut Marketplace, the Coco Palms Hotel and the Princeville Shopping Center. Now you know you're in paradise.
Green Garden, 13749 Kaumualii Hwy, Hanapepe, 335-5422, for mahi-mahi (dolphin fish) and lilikoi (passionfruit) pie. Closed Tues.
National Tropical Botanical Gardens, end of Hailima Rd (past 'Dead Entry' sign), 332-7361. Research centre and various collections of tropical, native and international plants, including award-winning Allerton Estate Garden, leading up to Ocean (palms, gingers, lilies and bamboo grove). Their Native Hawaiian Plant Project protects endangered species. Tours only; 9 am & 1 pm daily, 2½ hrs + 2 m walk, $15. Rsvs.
North from Lihue on Hwy 56: Turn off the road for a panoramic ocean view from **Kilauea Lighthouse**. Further north is the aforementioned Hanalei Bay; don't let its beauty distract you from the oriental splendour of **Hanalei Valley**, inland from the hwy. Wet and dry caves are right on the road; pull off and explore! Hwy 56 ends at **Ke'e Beach**, where the cliffhanging trail along the gorgeous **Na Pali Coast** begins. An easy hike takes you through some of the best scenery in the Hawaiian Islands: as you round one crucial corner, you get your first breathtaking view of a series of precipices plunging into the sea. The beach at the end of the hike is not for swimming, but that will be obvious. Breakers pound continually onto the boulder-strewn shore, sucking back with vacuum force.
South from Lihue on Hwy 50: Two historic sites of European contact with Hawaii: the **Old Russian Fort** (Ft Elizabeth), now a brush-covered rocky ruin; and **Captain Cook's Landing** (Jan 1778) at Waimea Bay. Take a side trip to see the **Menehune Ditch**, an ancient aqueduct built, some say, in a single night by Menehunes—Hawaiian leprechauns! All archaeologists know is that *someone* built the aqueduct years before the first Polynesian explorers arrived in Kauai.

INFORMATION
Division of State Parks, 3060 Eiwa St (in State Office Bldg), 274-3444. Has an abundancy of info on camping in state parks. Permits issued Mon-Fri 8 am-4 pm.
Hawai'i Visitors Bureau, Lihu'e Plaza Bldg, 3016 Umi St, 245-3971. Has the fun and informative Kaua'i Illustrated Pocket map. Mon-Fri, 8 am-4 pm.

OREGON *Beaver State*

In 1804-1806, Lewis and Clark explored this region, following the mighty Columbia River to its mouth. Their favourable reports brought pioneers along the 2000-mile trail—at first a trickle, swelling by the 1840s into a flood. A remarkably homogeneous bunch they were, too: farmers from the Midwest and South running from the economic depression of 1837-1840, looking for good soil, rainfall and an environment with neither malaria nor snow. Later, Astoria was founded near the mouth of the Columbia River to promote trade with China.

Oregon became a US territory the year of the California gold rush and promptly lost two-thirds of its males to the gold fever. A few struck it rich; more returned home and started selling wheat and lumber to the miners. At one point, Oregon wheat was actually made legal tender at $1 a bushel.

The heavily-forested Beaver State has suffered in recent years from a decline in the demand for lumber but still produces half the plywood in the US, the process having been invented here. Tourism is now the third-largest industry. Fortunately Oregonians work hard to preserve the state's natural beauty and like Vermonters, they have banned the construction of new billboards and kept crass tourist traps to a minimum (with noticeable exceptions along the coast). In 1991, Oregon was judged 'Greenest state in the US' by environmentalists.

The biggest magnet for visitors is the 400-mile coastline, protected as an almost-continuous series of state beaches. At times cold, foggy and windy, this region offers a kaleidoscope of magnificent sights: offshore rocks, driftwood-piled sands, cliffs, caves, twisted pines and acres of rhododendrons. Coastal villages seem to specialise in weatherbeaten charm.

Picturesque barns, covered bridges and historic villages make the area from the coast to the east Willamette valley fun to explore. Unless you're bent on speed, avoid the dull ribbon of interstate freeway that unseams the valley north to south.

Both the youth hostel and the bed and bfast networks are alive and well in Oregon. Biking is extremely popular here; just remember that it, like other outdoor activities can be rained out at any moment. Most of the time, it's a slow mournful drizzle, the kind that drove Lewis and Clark nearly crazy during their winter sojourn at Fort Clatsop.

Though many east coasters have drifted west to this state and find it much more beautiful that its more-popular neighbour to the south, Oregon has not drawn nearly the number of converts as California has. This makes Oregonians happy: while there you may spot one of the bumper stickers that define the 'Oregon attitude': 'Don't Californicate Oregon.' Furthering the wry underselling of the state, another slogan warns: 'In Oregon, you

don't tan; you rust.' Travellers are welcome, however, as long as they're passing through. The most popular bumper sticker reads, 'Welcome to Oregon. Now go home.'
www.yahoo.com/Regional/U_S__States/Oregon/.
National Park: Crater Lake
The telephone area code for the state is 503.

PORTLAND   In 1843, a couple of canoeists en route to Oregon City liked what they saw here and staked a 'tomahawk claim' by slashing trees in a 320-acre rectangle. The naming of the town was similarly impromptu: settlers flipped a coin (the losing name was Boston).

Portland modestly revels in its sparkling mountain and riverside setting, its luxuriant rose gardens (two-week Festival of Roses in June) and its low-key neighbourliness. Opportunities abound for good eating and social action in this city of booklovers, art lovers and ardent joggers.

Portland makes an ideal base to explore the Columbia River Gorge: take Hwy 84 E along the river to Troutdale and turn off onto the Columbia River Scenic Hwy. The old highway stops south of Bonneville Dam (its fish hatcheries are nice), but the scenic beauty doesn't. Further east on Hwy 84, the surrounding land dries up. Towns and farms line the river like oases, in stark contrast to the surrounding high desert cliffs. This is a drive that shows the state at its best. The Portland low-budget guide is an alternative offering to what the local Chamber of Commerce may typically offer. For a fun and very informative read, go to *www.orst.edu/~beauchav/lowrent/index.html.*

ACCOMMODATION
Ben Stark HI Hostel, 10225 Stark St, 274-1223. Charming but run-down, smoke-free hostel located close by restaurants, shopping, theatres, pubs, museum and local nightlife. Laundry and lockers downstairs. 40 mins to Mt Hood for snow sport action and the Henry Weinhard Brewery is just round the corner! Dorms $15-17, all bedding and bathrm items provided; $12, private rooms from $36-$45 up.
McMenamins Edgefield Hostel, 2126 SW Halsey St, (800) 669-8610. Converted farm, this lodge shares estate with a winery, brewery, movie theatre and two restaurants. Two single-sex dorms, showers, tubs. $18.
Portland HI Hostel, 3031 SE Hawthorne Blvd, 236-3380. Catch #5 bus from 5th St. Homey hostel with yard, BBQ, garden and covered porch. All-day van tours run year-round to Mt St. Helen's Volcano, Oregon Coast and MT Hood. Women's rooms fill up quickly in summer; rsvs or arrive at 5 pm for walk-ins. Coffeehouses, live music clubs and a $1 cinema-pub are within walking distance. No curfew. All-you-can-eat pancakes, $1. Baggage storage available if arriving before 10 am. Dorms $14-$16. AYH-members only July-Aug.
Portland Rose Motel, 8920 SW Barbur Blvd, 244-0107. TV, laundry facilities. Rooms from $35.
Camping: Ainsworth State Park, 37 miles E of Portland at Exit 35 off I-84. Close to noisy expressway but the drive through gorge is well worth it. Hot showers, flush toilets, hiking trails. $20 full hook-up. Also, **Champoeg State Park**, 8239 NE Champoeg Rd, 678-1251.Tent sites $16, 2-day advance rsvs required.

FOOD
The tastiest thing in Oregon is free—the drinking water. Grocery prices are high in town, even for local produce. You'll do better at the roadside produce stands, particularly along the Columbia River, where the peaches are huge and drip all over

your shirt when you bite into them. Don't miss local specialties: blackberry and boysenberry pie, razor clams (hideously expensive, but with a licence you can dig your own), scallops, smelt and Dungeness crab.

Bijou Cafe, 132 SW 3rd, 222-3187. 'A must for visitors. Great value for money with a friendly and relaxed atmosphere.' Daily for bfast and lunch.

Bread & Ink, 3610 SE Hawthorne, 239-4756. Local favourite for lunch. 'Best burgers.' Also pasta, fish specials, Vietnamese, Italian, Mexican and Jewish! Mon-Sat 8 am-late, Sun 9 am-2 pm. 'Nicest restaurant in town.'

Dan and Louis Oyster Bar, 208 SW Ankeny, 227-5906. Outstanding oysters, stew, marine atmosphere. Daily 11 am-10 pm, 11 pm w/ends.

Fuller's Coffee Shop, 136 NW 9th Ave, 222-5608. Bfast at this old-fashioned luncheonette on freshly made cinnamon rolls, four-star French toast, and omelets accompanied by classic hash browns. Try fried razor clams for lunch. Mon-Sat.

Jake's Famous Crawfish, 401 SW 12th Ave, 226-1419. A daily blackboard of sea creatures, hauled in fresh, choice includes salmon, crab and sole.

Old Wives' Tales, 1300 E Burnside, 238-0470. Multi-ethnic vegetarian, vegan, chicken and seafood; also soup and salad bar. 'New Age, classical and jazz music round out the eclectic atmosphere.' Daily for bfast, lunch and dinner, 8 am-10 pm, 'til 11 pm w/ends.

Papa Haydn's at two locations, 5829 SE Milwaukee, 232-9440 and 701 NW 23rd St, 228-7317. A Viennese coffeehouse with dynamite pastries. 'Milwaukee location hard to find.' Tues-Thur 11.30 am-11 pm, Fri& Sat 'til midnight, Sun 10 am-3 pm.

Saturday Market, under west end of Burnside Bridge, in Skidmore, SW 1st and Ankeny, 222-6072. 'Original buyers market.' Stalls with homemade everything. 'Wonderful.' Sat 10 am-5 pm, Sun 11 am-4.30 pm.

OF INTEREST

Niketown, 930 SW 6th, 221-6453. TVs in the floor, sculptures of famous sports stars and various artifacts such as jerseys and shoes. Mon-Thurs & Sat 10 am-7 pm, Fri 'til 8 pm, Sun 11.30 am-6.30 pm.

The **Oregon Museum of Science and Industry (OMSI)**, 1945 SE Water Ave (at the corner of Clay St), 797-4000, is open daily 9.30 am-7 pm, Fri 'til 9 pm, Sat & Sun 'til 7 pm. $7. Cheap planetarium shows. Don't miss 'state of the heart,' a human heart preserved through plastination; software that checks your cardio-vascular health; and a biofeedback train that goes faster as you get warmer.

Pioneer Courthouse Square, 701 SW 6th Ave, is an open-air city centre square paid for by the sale of 65,000 bricks used to build the square. The benefactors' names are inscribed on each one. Free performances and activities year-round. See the 'weather ball,' a meteorological glockenspiel. 'Silly noon-time fanfare.' In the summer the **Peanut Butter and Jam Sessions** attract huge amounts of jazz and folk music lovers, Tues & Thurs noon-1 pm.

Portland Art Museum, 1219 SW Park Ave, at the South Park Blocks, 226-2811. European, 19th and 20th century American, pre-Columbian, West African, Asian and Pacific Northwest Indian art. $5.50, $3 w/student ID. Tue-Sat 11 am-5 pm, Sun 1 pm-5 pm. The **Public Art Walking Tour** leaves from here too.

Portland Building, btwn Main and Madison, 4th and 5th. Architect Michael Graves, knowingly or not, has taken a page from Frank Lloyd Wright's notebook by designing a controversial pink and blue public building for a mid-sized American city (cf 'Marin County' in *California* section). Outside on the 5th Ave side is the *Portlandia* sculpture, a giant lady with hammered copper skin like the Statue of Liberty; she holds a trident instead of a torch.

Skidmore Old Town Historic District, New Market Block, SW 1st and Ankeny. Interconnected townhouses with open plaza, colonnade, outdoor stands. Old Town also marks the end of **Waterfront Park**, an excellent place to picnic, fish, stroll and enjoy community events.

South Park Blocks, a 12-block corridor of green grass, statues and tall trees, with Portland State University campus at the south end.

The Grotto, NE 85th & Sandy Blvd, 254-7371. Natural grotto in huge cliff, resembling grotto at Lourdes. Lower grounds are free, but it's worth $2 to see the monastery above (take elevator) for rose gardens, Marian art and one of the best views you can get of Portland, the Columbia River and Washington State beyond. 9 am-8 pm daily in summer, 'til 5 pm from mid-September. Some of Portland's most pleasant features are its **fountains**: the **Lovejoy**, SW 3rd & Harrison; the **Rose Ftn**, at O'Bryant Sq, 408 SW Park; **Ira Kellar Ftn**, 3rd & SW Clay and the **Skidmore Ftn**, 1888 SW 1st & Ankeny.

Washington Park, west of town, has **Japanese Gardens**, 223-1321, with 5 traditional styles, especially lovely with the white cone of Mt Hood framed by maple leaves and pagodas. $5.50; $3 w/student ID. Daily 10 am-8 pm 'til Sept; 10 am-4 pm after Oct. Also in the park is the **Rose Test Garden**, free, with over 8000 rosebushes. From here you can take 'the world's smallest railroad,' $3, through the forest to the **Zoo-OMSI** complex. The Zoo, 4001 SW Canyon Rd, 226-1561, daily 9.30 am-7 pm (last admission 6 pm), $6, has a huge chimp collection and large elephant herd. Free from 3 pm on the 2nd Tues of each month.

Outside Portland: The Columbia River Gorge, stretches east from Portland to The Dalles and offers truly magnificent scenery. Sailboard enthusiasts will know this place to be the most 'radical' location outside Hawaii due to the constant wind funnelled btwn the high cliffs. Take a car up and along the Historic River Hwy which parts with I-84 at Troutdale to enjoy spectacular views of the Gorge and see some of the numerous waterfalls en route (**Multnomah** is the biggest and most impressive). For real escapism, go up to the tranquil setting of **Lost Lake** and a close-up of **Mt Hood**, the state's tallest mountain. 'Spectacular, picture-book scenery.' Greyhound and Amtrak both serve the area; 'Amtrak is best for views.' **Bonneville Dam**, with its salmon farms and fish ladders is also worth a look.

Hwy 30, west. A beautiful 100-mile drive to **Astoria** that romps up hill, down dale, beside the Columbia and its wooded islands, and past roadside stands, houseboats, picturesque backwaters, juicy blackberries—there's even a pulloff to see **Mt St Helens**. **Westport**, with its Wahkiakum ferry across the river, makes a good lunch stop.

ENTERTAINMENT

The best entertainment listings are in Friday's *Oregonian* and various free handouts. Check the *Willamette Weekly* (put out each evening on street corners and in restaurants) for listings of good local blues and rock bands. There are 16 **microbreweries** in the state, many in Portland. A favourite, **Bridgeport Brew Pub**, 1313 NW Marshal, 241-7179, offers several cask-conditioned ales. Or watch free movies at **Mission Theatre and Pub**, 17th & Gleason NW, 223-4031, as you sample seasonal brews.

Bagdad Pub, 3702 SE Hawthorne, 236-9234. Great pizza, beer and movies.

Key Largo, 223-9919, 31 1st Ave, btwn Couch & Burnside, has rhythm & blues, rock & roll, jazz. Under $10 cover.

Festivals: Portland hosts excellent festivals: the **Blues Fest** in June, **The Bite** in mid-August, **Art Quake** in early September and others. 'Saw excellent African ballet for $2.'

INFORMATION

Chamber of Commerce , 221 NW 2nd St, 228-9411.

Portland/Oregon Visitors Association, 25 SW Salmon, (800) 345-3214. Mon-Fri 8.30 am-5 pm, Sat 9 am-3 pm. 'Maps and a bounty of info.' Pick up the *Portland Book*.

TRAVEL
Amtrak, 800 NW 6th Ave, 273-4865/(800) 872-7245.
Broadway Cab, 227-1234; and **Radio Cab**, 227-1212.
Dash Airport Shuttle, 246-4676 runs daily services every 30 mins from various downtown hotels and the Greyhound Depot. $8.50 o/w.
Gray Line, 4320 N Suttle Rd, 285-9845. Lots of tours: Mt Hood, the Columbia River, coast, around town. Pickup at local hotels.
Greyhound, 550 NW 6th Ave, next to Union Station, (800) 231-2222.
NW Auto Rental, 9785 SW Shady Lane, 624-1804. Over 21 only, need drivers licence and major credit card.
Tri-Met city bus and MAX rail, 231-3198 for rates and info. Free downtown zone, $1-$1.30 to other areas or $3.25 all-day pass.
Portland International Airport is located about 13 miles E of the city. To get there take bus #12 labelled 'Sandy Blvd to Airport' from SW 6th and Main. This will take around 20 mins and costs $1.30.
Tours: Green Tortoise, (800) 867-8647/(800) 227-4766. Approx $15 to Seattle, $39 to San Francisco, $59 to LA. Departs from SW 6th and College, outside the university deli.

THE OREGON COAST   Hwy 101 runs along the Pacific coast from the southernmost tip of California to the Canadian border, but the Oregon stretch, especially the pristine 225-mile section from the California boundary to **Newport**, is surely the loveliest. It's also the driest part of the Oregon coast (it gets about half the amount of rain as the stretch north of Newport), a definite attraction for those camping out. 'Best way to see this is by camping, buy a tube tent, light, compact, about $12.' The coast offers driftwood hunting, whale watching, clamdigging and rockhounding, from agates to jasper. While you're on the beach, nose-to-sand, look for glass floats, the ultimate beachcombing prize. The powerful combo of the Japanese Current and westerly winds wash these green, amber and turquoise buoyancy balls from Japanese fishing nets all the way across the Pacific. December through March is the best time to search; look for non-rocky beaches with moderate slope and go early to beat other float-hunters. Swimming is dangerous in many areas and cold everywhere; enquire locally.

Going north-to-south, the Oregon Coast starts at **Astoria**, a miniature San Francisco at the mouth of the Columbia River. Founded in 1811 by John Jacob Astor as a base for the Pacific Fur Company, the town survived as the first permanent US settlement on the Pacific Coast due to successful trading with China. While there, check out the rococo Flavel House and Shallon Winery; try scallops at Pier 11 and Finnish limpa bread at local bakeries. Also of interest is **Ft Clatsop**, where Lewis and Clark spent the winter of 1805. If you're in a car, cross the Megler Bridge to Washington, spanning 4.6 miles and barely skimming the surface of the water. Back on Hwy 101, turn west to **Ft Stevens**, a historic park with a picturesque shipwreck. **Seaside**, with its boardwalk, arcades and popular swimming beach, is a candyfloss sort of town, noted for cheap seafood at Norma's. **Cannon Beach** merits a pause: monolithic Haystack Rock, a charming art-village, and great windy walking at Ecola State Park are some of its pluses. Its annual **Sand Sculpture Derby** in spring is one of the most inventive anywhere.

Near **Tillamook**, take the **Three Capes Rd**, a 39-mile loop through a succession of scenic vistas, villages and lighthouses to **Three Arch Rocks National Wildlife Refuge**, with its herd of Steller sea lions. Tillamook provides tasting of its namesake cheese and others, along with wine, at the Blue Heron and Tillamook Cheese Factories. The lively little fishing and beach town **Newport**, on a sheltered and beautiful bay, is a good place to eat Dungeness crab and browse with other holiday makers. 'A friendly young community on NW cliff, where there are quaint wooden summer cottages facing the ocean.' Of interest here is the **Oregon Coast Aquarium**, 2820 SE Ferry Slip Rd, 867-3474, next to the Science Center. The aquarium offers various exhibit galleries of Oregon marine-life, including an outdoor animal park and sea-bird aviary. Open daily summer 9 am-6 pm (10 am-4 pm in winter), $9. Neighbouring **Depoe Bay** is noted as an excellent whale-watching spot, Nov-March; along its seawall, geyser-like sprays of ocean water often arch over the highway. **Beverly Beach** to the south is the nearest campground and has hiker/biker spots. South of Newport is a likeable tourist trap called **Sea Gulch**, a village of antic lifesize figures. The carving is done freehand—with a chainsaw!—and you can watch. **Yachats**(that's *Yah*-hots) is worth a stop, especially in smelt season May-Sept, or better yet, during the annual Smelt Fry in early July. It's nothing to eat a dozen of the silvery mini-fish and fun to watch the catch, too. Good non-fish offerings at the Adobe Hotel and others. Btwn rhododendron-happy Florence and Yachats are the **Sea Lion Caves**, 547-3111, reached via elevator and reeking of perennial, fishy sea lion halitosis. Open daily 9 am 'til dusk, $6.50; you can also see the huge creatures more distantly from various points near the caves.

Oregon Dunes, some as high as 600ft, stretch for 40 miles to Florence; duneside camping is possible but crowded at **Honeyman State Park**; the **Umpqua Lighthouse State Park** (hiker/biker section), 6 miles south of Reedsport, is better. Biggest town in SW Oregon, **Coos Bay** is a fishing and lumber port good for a night's stopover, with a grimy bar, good meals at the Blue Heron Bistro, and myrtlewood factories.

Hwy 101 turns inland at Coos Bay, but you can follow secondary roads nearer the coast to spectacular scenery at **Sunset Bay** (camping) and **Shore Acres State Park**. At cranberry-growing **Bandon** you have a cheese factory, the makings of an art colony, a youth hostel, and natural beauty all around. Further along, the panorama of **Humbug Mountain** and the rock-strewn coast are a worthwhile stop; 3-mile hike to the top. Excellent campground with low-cost hiker/biker section. **Gold Beach** is on the banks of the Rogue, an officially-designated wild river and prime spot for rafting and fishing. Good smoked salmon here. Explore the Oregon Coast from Astoria to Brookings Harbor through *The Wave, www.oregoncoast.com/*.

ACCOMMODATION
Adobe Motel, 1555 Hwy 101 N, **Yachats**, 547-3141. Fireplace, sauna, excellent bfasts and dinners, agate hunting and smelt fishing on their beach. D-$90 with ocean view, $62 without.
City Center Motel, 538 SW Coast Hwy, **Newport**, 265-7381. Rooms from $35.
Dexter Lost Valley HI Hostel, 81868 Lost Valley Lane, (541) 937-3351. Located on the grounds of the Lost Valley Educational Center, a conference and retreat centre

which focuses on living in harmony with the land. Lockers, self-guided interpretive trail, kitchen, linen rental. Dinner available most w/days. Centre is surrounded by 90 acres of woodlands, streams and forest hiking trails. Dorms $10.

Sea Star HI Hostel, 375 2nd St, **Bandon**, 347-9632. Located in the historic 'Old Town Waterfront District,' halfway btwn San Francisco and Seattle on the Oregon Coast Bicycle Route, see some of Oregon's most scenic coastlines: dunes, cliffs, rock formations and white sandy beaches. Hostel has bistro with everything made on premises from organic ingredients (they make their own pasta dough, smoke their own meats—even roll their own sausages). Lots of vegetarian options, open to non-residents. Skylights, wood stove, deck and courtyard overlooking harbor, day use, equipment storage area, information desk, kitchen, laundry facilities, linen. Dorms $14, private rooms available.

Seaside HI Hostel, 930 N Holladay Dr, **Seaside**, 738-7911. European style hostel on river, 4 blocks from beach; the town hosts festivals and events. Explore neighbouring Cannon Beach, an artists' town, and the historic maritime community of Astoria. Canoes available for use. Outdoor decks with river view and on-site espresso and pastry bar. Movies shown every evening; nature programs too. 5 night max stay, 10 min daily chore, bedding provided $1.50. Dorms $14-15 and private rooms from D-$30.

Camping: There are over 50 campgrounds in Oregon's state park system; approx $17-20 for a tent site with full hook-up. Many sites have hiker/biker sections for $2. Call (800) 452-5687 for rsvs and general info.

Tugman State Park: near Lakeside, 759-3604, open mid-April-Labor Day, comes highly praised: 'Best campsites in the US.' Greyhound will drop you where you like. Warm sleeping bag and tent advised, also food as parks are usually distant from shops. Tent sites from $17. **Free camping: near Florence** in the dunes—or try **Siuslaw National Forest**, from $8; and **Sunset Bay State Park**, 888-4902/(800) 444-PARK for rsvs, sites from $14.

CRATER LAKE NATIONAL PARK   Mt St Helens was a minor firecracker compared with **Mt Mazama**, which exploded some 6800 years ago to form **Crater Lake**. This inky blue well, in a densely forested part of southern Oregon's Cascade Range, cannot be bettered for dramatic settings: approached through a moonlike landscape and rimmed by 500 to 2000-ft cliffs (all that is left of 12,000-ft Mazama), Crater Lake descends to depths of 1932 ft, making it one of the deepest lakes in the world. Poking through the surface are **Phantom Ship Island** and **Wizard Island**, itself an extinct volcanic cone. Boat excursions visit Wizard, where you can hike to its 760-ft summit and down into its 90-ft-deep crater. The 33 mile **Rim Drive** is open mid-July to October; also recommended are the 1 mile hike down to the lake from Cleetwood Cove and the 1½ miles **Discovery Pt Trail**

From high points in the park, you can see Mt Shasta, 100 miles to the south. Wonderful bird-watching, wildflowers and nature programmes. Crater Lake is even more beautiful in winter, when snowcapped conifers are reflected in the deep blue iris of the lake. The unofficial guide to Crater Lake National Park is located at *www.halcyon.com/rdpayne/clnp.htm*.

ACCOMMODATION
Ft Klamath Lodge, Ft Klamath, Hwy 62 (about 22 miles S of Crater Lake), 381-2234. Restaurant and grocery nearby. From S-$33, D-$43.

Lodging also at Klamath Falls and **Medford**; try **Motel 6's**—884-2110 in Klamath Falls, and 773-4290 in Medford, rooms from $35, XP-$6.

Oregon Motel 8 and RV Park, Hwy 97 N, 3½ miles N of Klamath Falls, 882-0482. Sites $14.

Camping: Mazama Campground, 594-2511, at the junction of West and South Entrance Roads. Open mid-June to Oct, depending on snow conditions: sites from $15; and **Lost Creek Campground**, 594-2211 ext 402, at the SW corner of park has camping sites for $10.

Backcountry campsites are free; pay only $7 at **Lost Creek Campground**, on Pinnacles Rd, open July-Sept. The Nature Trail begins here. Grocery store at Rim Village; also excellent fishing.

FOOD
Best to buy food at the **Old Fort Store**, Ft Klamath, 381-2345. Open summer daily 9 am-7 pm. Also, try **Safeway**, Pine & 8th St; **Hobo Junction**, 636 Main St; and **Cattle Crossing Café**, on Hwy 62 in Ft Klamath for burgers and a filling bfast.

INFORMATION/TRAVEL
Amtrak, South Spring depot, (800) 872-7245.

Greyhound, 1200 Klamath Ave, Klamath Falls, 882-4616/(800) 231-2222.

National Park information, 594-2211. $5 entrance fee p/car, $3 cyclists/hikers. Rim Drive is closed in winter; enter the park via Hwy 62 south or west.

William G Steel Center, nxt to park HQs, 594-2211 ext 402. Provides free back-country camping permits. Daily 9 am-5 pm.

SOUTHERN OREGON   South and west of Crater Lake are a cluster of worthwhile destinations, made more appealing by well-placed hostels and other good lodging. **Ashland**, America's answer to the Old Vic, has three theatres (including a pleasant one outdoors) and an 8-month play schedule that specialises in Shakespeare but draws on other sources as well. Not far away is **Jacksonville**, an intelligently-restored gold mining town. Stagecoach rides are offered to the cemetery and 80-odd homes there. Nearby also are the **Rogue River** and **Oregon Caves National Monument**; the latter are set deep in the marble heart of **Mt Elijah** and full of stalagmites & stalactites, flowstone formations and strenuous hikes. Near **Cave Junction** is Takilma, a former hippy mecca which still has a hippy hospital. Nowadays the area is populated with 'survivalists'; apparently the natural convection of the land would eliminate the danger of radiation in the event of nuclear attack.

ACCOMMODATION
Ashland Hostel, 150 N Main St, **Ashland**, 482-9217. 3 blocks to Shakespeare Festival. Large kitchen, laundry; located in historic home. Open year round $14-16.

Cave Junction Fordson Home Hostel , 250 Robinson Rd, **Cave Junction**, 592-3203. Set on 20-acres of woodland with streams and garden. Large private room in addition to dorm rooms ($10). Solar showers (great fun), baths, kitchen, free use of bicycles, camping, river swimming and free berries in season. 13 miles to Oregon Caves, close to wineries (one is being built next door), bikes for use. Owner Jack Heald is a mine of information about the area and gives his guests 40 min tours covering sights from antique tractors to Douglas Firs. If you stay on a weekend he'll even take you rock' n' roll' dancing! Rsvs essential.

Manor Motel, 476 N Main St, **Ashland**, 482-2246. Downtown. From S/D-$60, TV, AC. Rooms with kitchen also available. Advance rsvs and deposit required.

WASHINGTON   *The Evergreen State*

Unofficially known as *The State of Nirvana*, there is a persistent legend has it that the original name proposed for Washington was 'Columbia'; the idea was dropped to avoid confusion with the nation's capital. True or not, Washington has always been haunted by its name, to the extent that the state once advertised itself to tourists as 'The *Other* Washington,' thereby selling itself short.

Like neighbouring Oregon, the Washington is mountainous, rainy and green in the west, and flat, dry and tawny in the east. Likewise, it has but one pre-eminent city, Seattle, which enjoys a pugnacious rivalry with Portland. Once a stronghold of the radical labour movement (the Wobblies were here in the 1930s), Washington now builds more Boeings, raises more apples, processes more seafood, stores more nuclear waste than just about anyone else and is the home of the world's most successful software company, Microsoft.

This is also David Lynch country. *Blue Velvet* and *Twin Peaks* were both filmed here, and there does seem to be a strange atmosphere invoked by the countryside that just might explain the bizarre nature of his work.

A large share of the state's scenic beauty is within reach of Seattle: **Puget Sound** and its hundreds of islands; the still, dark **Olympic rain forest**; omnipresent **Mt Rainier**; and the obtrusive upstart, **Mt St Helens**, 75 miles S. Other sights are further flung. **North Cascades National Park**, an expanse of alpine loveliness, with canyons, glaciers, peaks and grizzlies, lies along the British Columbia border. In the eastern part of Washington are **Grand Coulee Dam**, the Palouse River Canyon and the 'Scablands,' a weird, scarred landscape left thousands of years ago by a glacial flood that inundated much of the Columbia Plateau. The Long Beach peninsula, though part of SW Washington is more conveniently reached from Astoria, Oregon.

Rain is endemic to the Northwest, but Seattle gets most of its 34 inches per year btwn October and May; the Olympic rain forest gets up to 150 inches annually. *www.yahoo.com/Regional/U_S_States/Washington/*.
National Parks: Olympic, Mount Rainier, North Cascades.
The telephone area code for all places listed, unless otherwise stated, is 206.

SEATTLE Long before the advent of 'grunge,' before Nirvana, Soundgarden *et al*, the 'Emerald City' was a place to be. With becoming arrangements of hills, houses, water and mountains Seattle has long been a mecca for those who like life with a more laid-back attitude.

To the SW, the skyline is dominated by snowy Mt Rainier. To the west, the city's great deepwater harbour opens onto island-studded Puget Sound and the Olympic Mountains. Urbanisation is further subdivided by lakes and parks, from tiny to massive, girding the downtown district into a compact and pleasing shape. The look is an idiosyncratic mix of sleek and traditional, of contemporary ranch houses and bohemian houseboats. All this adds up to a city that feels similar to another great Pacific metropolis whose initials are 'SF.' Don't tell Seattlites that; they defend their city's individuality. And rightly so, Seattle does have a certain flair. It's not every city that would make a Wagnerian opera cycle (sung in German and English) its major cultural event, or outfit its waterfront with vintage 1927 Australian streetcars and its airport with a meditation room?

Considering that it's a major gateway to, and trade partner with, the Orient, Seattle shows few Asian influences of non-gustatory kind. Rather, at its core the city is boisterous, adventurous and optimistic, no doubt a legacy of its logging and Klondike gold rush past. America's richest man, Bill Gates, assessed at $36.4 billion, lives in nearby Bellevue near Redmond where his company (Microsoft) is based.

If coffee is your amour then Seattle is the place to get in some serious drinking. The city seems to run on caffeine, supplied by some of the strongest espressos you will ever taste. There are coffee bars and cafes everywhere all serving 'damn fine cups of jo,' as Agent Cooper would say. You'll be wired for weeks. *www.seattle.yahoo.com/*.

ACCOMMODATION

B&B's: lots of options including **B&B International** and **Northwest B&B**; details in *Accommodation Background*. Also: **Pacific B&B**, 701 NW 60th, Seattle, WA 98107 or call 784-0539; **Traveller's B&B**, Box 492, Mercer Island, WA 98040 or call 232-2345. Rates from S-$40, D-$48 (luxurious accommodations command the higher rates from $75). Traveller's reference service covers Seattle and most of the Northwest, including Puget Sound, Tacoma, Olympia, Spokane, Victoria and Vancouver Island, BC.

American Backpackers Hostel, 126 Broadway E, Seattle, (800) 600-2965. 'Helpful, cheap, excellent location...a must!' No curfew; free pick-up from Amtrak, Greyhound and downtown. Airport pick-up for 3+. Free bfast. Pool table. 'Clean and safe.' $14.

College Inn Guest House, 4000 University Way NE, 633-4441. Continental bfast plus all-day coffee, tea. Antique; registered as a historical landmark. From S-$50, D-$60, Q-$70, all shared bath.

Downtown YMCA, 909 4th Ave, 382-5000. Includes jacuzzi and gym. Excellent, very clean. '5th floor more comfortable, better facilties than 4th floor at same price.' From S-$43.50 ($35 AYH), D-$47.50 ($40 AYH). TV $2 extra.

Green Tortoise Backpacker's Hostel, 1525 2nd Ave, 340-0387. 1 block from Seattle's colourful Pike Place Market, within the free bus ride zone, close to Pioneer Sq, art museum and waterfront. All rooms have own wash basin. Kitchen, free bfast, laundry and discount cards. Call hostel for pick-up. $15 dorm, private rooms S-$30, D-$39. Also, **Green Tortoise Garden Apartments**, 715 2nd Ave North, 282-1222. Long-term accommodations suitable for travellers staying over 30 days. Charming building with a fantastic view of the Space Needle, 2 blocks from Seattle Center and convenient access to stores and bus lines. Lovely backyard and deck, barbecue, herb & veg garden, laundry, free bfast and friendly communal atmosphere. Beds $200/month, private rooms $500/month.

Moore Hotel, 1926 2nd Ave, 448-4851. 'Clean, modern, spacious—offered us the best deal.' 'Excellent hotel, warm and friendly.' From S-$40, D-$45.

Seattle HI Hostel, 84 Union St (near Pike Place Market), 622-5443. A former US immigration station, modern interior. The Seattle Art Museum And Pike Place Market-full of farmers' stalls, eateries and shops-are both only 1 block away. Walk down the waterfront, take a scenic ride on a Washington State Ferry, or stroll into Myrtle Edwards Park for a panoramic view of the Olympic Mountains across Puget Sound. Laundry, info desk, evening programs. Take bus #174 from bus station to Union & 4th Sts. $15-17. Private rooms D-$45 pp. Rsvs essential.

St Regis Hotel, 116 Stewart at 2nd, 448-6366. Situated in large gay community. 'Basic but comfortable.' Laundry and restaurant. 'Only hotel with vacancies just before Labor Day.' From S-$40-$48, D-$44-$60.

Vashon Island Ranch HI Hostel, 12119 SW Cove Rd, Rt 5, Box 349, **Vashon Island**, WA 98070, 463-2592. A ferry ride from downtown, this hostel offers a getaway from the city in a unique setting. Five Sioux Indian tepees offer couple and family rooms, or sleep in covered wagons surrounding a campfire. Get up early for free pancakes made from a family recipe, then enjoy beautiful, rural Vashon Island by bikes provided free at hostel. $10. Rsvs req.

Vincent's Guest House, 527 Malden Ave East, 323-7849. Historic capital hill location, within walking distance of tourist attractions including museums, galleries and live music. Free bfast (bagels, coffee). $13, private rooms $30-45.

FOOD

Washington is famous for superb fruit (especially peaches, apples and berries), Dungeness crab, Olympia oysters, razor and littleneck clams, and the indigenous candy, 'Aplets' and 'Cotlets,' a sort of jellied fruit bar covered with powdered sugar and guaranteed to be addictive. Seattle is a prime place to sample them all. Excellent Chinese, Thai, Japanese and Vietnamese restaurants, too.

Bakeman's, 122 Cherry St, 622-3375. Turkey or meat loaf; white or wheat; mayo or mustard. Make your mind up and move down the line! Open Mon-Fri only.

Café D'Arte, 2nd Ave (2 blocks from Commodore Hotel). The best coffee shop in Seattle! T-shirts, mugs etc., good to buy as souvenirs.

Cafe Loc, Seattle Center, 728-9292. 'Good Vietnamese food.'

China First Restaurant. 7 branches within city, but try 4237 University Way NE, 634-3553. Lunch 3-course special only $3.50; 'huge and delicious portions'. Also excellent service.

Elliott Bay Book Company, 1st and Main, 624-6600. Cafe and literary gathering place, with over 100,000 titles. Cafe Mon-Fri 7 am-10.30 pm, Sat from 9.30 am, Sun 11 am-5 pm.

Emmet Watson's Oyster Bar, 1916 Pike Place, behind the Soames-Dunn Bldg, 448-7721. Best oysters anywhere, three dozen kinds of bottled and draft beer, good ceviche (marinated fish). Savour hangtown fry (oyster omelet) for bfast. Inexpensive, under $10.

Gravity Bar, 415 Broadway E, 325-7186. A trendy, stainless steel decked juice bar serving things like 'Ginger Rogers,' a fruit and vegetable drink containing carrots, apple and ginger, $4.50. Drinks from $2.

Hi-Spot Café, 1410 34th St, 325-7905. Bfast is a must-eat Seattle meal here!

Iron Horse, 311 3rd Ave S, ½ block from King St Station, 223-9506. 'Burgers delivered by model trains! Great railroading atmosphere.' Mon-Sun 11 am-9 pm.

Ivar's Acres of Clams Restaurant, Pier 54, 624-6852. Seattle seafood tradition since 1938. Great old photos and waterfront view.

Pike Place Market is *the* place to purchase fresh produce, meat, fish and walkaway items; it's a warren of ethnic treats from Filipino lumpia to Spanish tapas.

Old Spaghetti Factory, Elliot and Broad, near Pier 70, 441-7724. Meals $6-10, daily specials.

Streamliner Diner, 397 Winslow Way, Bainbridge Island, 842-8595. Bfast and lunch only; American and Mexican food $6-10; reach the island via ferry from Seattle.

OF INTEREST

Mt St Helens. The Indians called it 'Loowelit-klah,' or 'smoking mountain,' and they knew what they were talking about. On 18 May, 1980, the mountain erupted, blowing away a cubic mile of earth, killing 57 people and 2 million mammals, birds and fish, and exhaling smoke and ash to 72,000 ft to circle the globe. Since then, Mt St Helens has erupted sporadically but on a smaller scale; quakes and ominous rumblings are commonplace. Plan on spending all day on your trip, whether from Seattle or Portland. 'A beautiful place.' To experience the mountain, options include: **air flyovers** from nearby Toledo, Cougar or Randle, which give the best views of flattened trees, debris-choked rivers and devastated landscape slowly regenerating itself; **bus tours** run from Seattle through a loop road leading to the mountain, also accessible by **car**. Check in with the Forest Service info center (turn W off I-5 on exit 49) or call 274-2100 to enter the volcano zone. **Hikers** can make a difficult but worthwhile trek from **Meta Lake** to **Independence Pass**, which overlooks ruined **Spirit Lake**, chilling views of desolation and crumpled human artifacts. The Norway Pass trail is also excellent. If you'd like to keep a respectful distance, you can take in the eruption and aftermath on the 100-ft screen of the **Omnidome**, Pier 59, in Seattle, 622-1868. $7. 'It's as if you're flying round the mountain during its eruption.' 'Do not on any account miss this extraordinary 30 min film.' Next to **Seattle Aquarium** at Pier 59, 386-4320, a fishbowl where you are in the bowl, and the fish swim overhead. 'Marvellous.' Daily 10 am-7 pm ('til 5 pm after Labour day); $7.95. Watch out for the 'Coconut Crab' exhibit.

Bainbridge Island Harbour ferries: Pier 51, 464-6400, $4.50 without car, r/t. Pubs and art galleries on the island, even a winery: **Bainbridge Island Winery**, 682 State Hwy 305 NE, 842-WINE. Free informal tours in Washington's second smallest winery, every Sun at 2 pm. Otherwise open Wed-Sun noon-5 pm for wine-tasting and self-guided tour around vineyards. 'Dirt! Corruption! Sewers! Scandal!' Sound good? Then take an **underground** tour, 610 1st Ave at **Doc Maynard's Public House**, 682-4646. When Seattle burned down in 1889, the city simply built the new on top of the old. What's left below is an odd warren of storefronts, brothels, speakeasies and tunnels where sailors are popularly supposed to have been shanghaied. Tour ends (naturally) at a gift shop. 'Highly amusing account of Seattle's early sewage system. Never thought crap could be so funny.' 'Interesting rip-off.' Tours last 1½ hrs; $6.50, $4.50 w/student ID. Rsvs req.

Government Locks, connecting Puget Sound, Lake Union and Lake Washington, were built in 1916 and at that time second only to the Panama locks in size. 'Best free sight in Seattle. Boats and leaping salmon passing through all day.' 'Some salmon nearly jump onto the footpath!' 'Interesting historical/ecological display in building.'

International District, btwn Main & Lane, 4th & 8th. Culturally-neutral official name for Seattle's Chinatown, bright with Buddhist temples, restaurants, herbal shops and the Bon Odori Festival in Aug.

Klondike Gold Rush National Historical Park, 117 S Main, 553-7220. Exhibits, free films and gold panning demos. 'Watch Chaplin's *The Gold Rush* free on 1st Sun every month.' Daily 9 am-5 pm; free.

Lake View Cemetery, next to **Volunteer Park**, at 14th Ave & E Prospect. Divided by nationality—Chinese, Japanese, Polish, etc. Also **Bruce Lee's grave**, covered with letters to him, martial arts trophies, mementoes, flowers, etc, left by devotees.

Museum of Flight, 9404 E Marginal Way S, 764-5720. Over 40 aircraft from the beginnings of aviation to an Apollo command module. Newest exhibit is a full-scale F-18 mock-up where you can sit in the cockpit. Daily 10 am-5 pm, Thur 'til 9 pm. $6.

Pacific Science Center, nxt to Space Needle, 443-2001, includes 6 buildings: spacerium, planetarium, computer rooms, seismograph, Indian longhouse, lots of science toys. Daily 10 am-6 pm. $7.50 entrance fee; $9 includes IMAX or laser shows. IMAX info line: 443-IMAX. 'Laserium *Rock It* is an exciting presentation.' The Center also has many shops, eateries and entertainment from opera to rock to folk festivals.

Pike Place Market, Pike & 1st, 682-7453. Begun in 1907, this multi-level maze of regional colour boasts over 250 permanent businesses (and a reserve of 200 arts and crafts and 100 farmers), includes dozens of restaurants, standup bars and takeaway places, plus local produce and seafood. Also bookshops, coffeehouses, bars, second-hand shops, crafts and 'excellent free entertainment by buskers and street musicians.' Daily Mon-Sat 9 am-6 pm, Sun 11 am-5 pm.

Pioneer Square, around 1st & Yesler, heart of old downtown. The original 'skid road,' so-named because logs were 'skidded' along the road in lumberjack days, gave rise to 'Skid Row,' a term widely imitated in several cities from LA to NYC. Nicely restored, but still a gathering place for bums and blots-on-the-town; good walking tour map available.

Seattle Art Museum, 100 University St, 654-3100. Newly-designed museum designed by Robert Venturi (the man who gave us the National Gallery extension in London) and it is his usual post-modern joke of differing styles from Egyptian to Neo-Classical. The building is better than its contents. Tues-Sun 10 am-5 pm, Thurs 'til 9 pm; $7, $4 w/student ID. First Tues of every month open 10 am-7 pm, free.

The Space Needle, 443-2111, a 605-ft relic of the 1962 Seattle World's Fair, has stunning views, best at night when the city is lit up. $7 for glass elevator ride to the top. 'Kitschiest souvenir shop in Seattle on top.' Revolving restaurant at 500 ft. On the grounds of **Seattle Center**, 90-second ride for 60¢. **Fun Forest** amusement park is there, too.

University of Washington, 15th Ave NE. 'Beautiful, like Berkeley.' On campus, an arboretum and Japanese tea garden, gift of Seattle's sister city, Kobe. Info centre on NE 40th.

The waterfront is the soul of any port town, and Seattle is no exception. The working piers for the Alaska halibut and salmon fleet and the large freighters are remote, but the tourist's waterfront is front and centre. Piers 48 through 70 have steamships to Victoria and also the Victoria Clipper Catamaran, a **waterfront park**; **Ye Olde Curiosity Shop**, 728-4050, is a delightfully macabre melange of shrunken heads, mummies, fleas wearing dresses, etc. ('must be seen'); and a **firefighting museum**.

Nearby: Boeing Aircraft Factory, 3303 Casino Rd S, **Everett**, 30 miles N of Seattle, exit 189 W off I-5. Call 342-4801 for tour info. See jumbo jets in the making in the building where the world's largest jetliners are manufactured. Very heavily booked in summer; free 90 min tours Mon-Fri 8 am-4 pm. Tkts available beginning at 7 am for the day but beware—can be sold out by 9 am.

ENTERTAINMENT

The 5th Ave, 1308 5th Ave, *circa* 1926 vaudeville house patterned after Imperial Chinese architecture of the Forbidden City, renovated in 1980 for $2.6 million, now hosts Broadway shows. Free tours for groups of 6 or more; call 625-1468. 'Absolutely smashing place.'

Gasworks Park: See beautiful kites being flown high up in the sky, or go get your own from **Gasworks Kite Shop**, 1915 N 34th St 1 block N of the park), 633-4780. On the other hand, if you feel inspired to go sailing on Lake Union, **Urban Surf**, 2100 N Northlake Way, 545-WIND, rents windsurfing boards for $35 daily, as well as in-line skates. During lunch hours in the summer, the free **Out to Lunch** series brings music and dancing to all parks, squares and offices downtown Seattle. Call 623-0340 for more info.

Pioneer Square, **Volunteer Park** and the **campuses of University of Washington and Seattle University** (downtown at E Cherry & Broadway) are all nuclei for daylight and after-dark activities. Plenty of good beer, live music and psyched crowds! For a joint cover ($8) you may wander from bar to bar. Read the *Post-Intelligencer* and the *Seattle Times' Tempo* mag for listings and the 'Hot Tix' column with discount and free stuff.

Seattle Opera, 389-7676, at the Seattle Center. Get there 20 mins before curtain up for 'student rush': leftover tkts sold at half-price, as low as $15. Occasionally, on selected performances, any leftover tkts are sold for $15, regardless of original price. Also performing at the Center, the **Seattle Symphony**, 443-4747. Rock and pop acts as well as legitimate theatre at the **Paramount Theater**, 911 Pine, 682-1414. Not cheap but good acoustics.

The Seattle Arts Festival, Bumbershoot, annually at the Seattle Center over Labor Day w/end. Bands, food, art, etc. 'Amazing, very popular.' Hotline 441-FEST. $8 in advance, $9 at gate.

INFORMATION

Park Service, Pacific Northwest Region, 915 2nd Ave #442, 220-7450. Mon-Fri 8 am-4.30 pm.

Travelers Aid, 909 4th (inside YMCA bldg), 461-3888. Free and useful maps from Dept of Transportation, Transportation Bldg, 420 Maple Park E, Olympia.

Seattle-King County Visitors Bureau, 800 Convention Pl (enter Union St side), 461-5840. Mon-Fri 8.30 am-5 pm, Sat-Sun 10 am-4 pm in summer.

TRAVEL

Alaska Marine Highway System Ferries: to Alaska and the Inside Passage. Departs approx 7 pm Fri from port in Bellingham, 89 miles N of Seattle. Call 676-8445 for info; rates vary (cheapest: $154 to Ketchikan). To islands, Olympic Peninsula, Bremerton, Vashon Island and other points: **Washington State Ferries**, Pier 52, 464-6400. 'Excellent way to see the Sound and the islands around Seattle.' Ferries for the **San Juan Islands** depart from Anacortes (north of Seattle), 293-8166. See 'San Juan' section.

Amtrak, King St Station, 3rd Ave & Jackson, (800) 872-7245. The *Pioneer* goes to Ogden/Salt Lake City; the *Coast Starlight* to Oakland/SF and LA, a beautiful ride down the coast; and the *Empire Builder*, a mammoth 42 hr trip to Chicago via Minneapolis.

Gray Line, 624-5813, from the Westin Hotel, Space Needle and other points.

Green Tortoise Bus Service, (800) 227-4766. Buses leave from 9th Ave & Stewart St, Thurs/Sun at 8 am, to Oregon, San Francisco and LA. Rsvs recommended 5 days in advance.

Greyhound, 8th & Stewart, (800) 231-2222. Serves Bellingham for ferry services north, daily to Sea-Tac Airport, Spokane, Portland, Tacoma and Vancouver, BC.

Metro Transit local public buses, 553-3000. Within the 'Magic Carpet' downtown area all buses free; 85¢ $1.60, depending on zone and rush-hour restrictions. All-day unlimited passes available only at w/ends and holidays, $1.70. For 24 hr schedules and directions call 553-3000/(800) 542-7876.

Seattle-Tacoma International Airport (Sea-Tac), about 12 miles S of the city. From downtown take #194 from the Metro Tunnel, Mon-Sat, $1.60 peak times, $1.10 off-peak; on Sun take M from 2nd and Union, $1.10.

OLYMPIC NATIONAL PARK Sparkling mountains and lush forests occupying 1400 sq miles in the centre and along the coastline of the Olympic peninsula, making this a crown jewel of US national parks. Hwy 101 circles the park, but only a few roads penetrate inward; its wilderness is further fortified by vast tracts of national forest around it. A hikers' park indeed.

Massive glacier-cut peaks are the park's signature. The highest at 7965 ft, was named **Mt Olympus** by an English sea captain in 1788. Use the **Port Angeles** entrance to get here. 'Don't miss the 18 mile drive from sea level to one mile high at Hurricane Ridge—what views of Mount Olympus and its glaciers!'

The park proves that rain forests are not solely a tropical phenomenon. West of Olympus in the Bogachiel, Hoh, Quinault and Queets river valleys is the great **Olympic rain forest**. Jewelled with moisture, tree limbs cloaked in clubmoss, this cool Amazon suffused by primordial light gets 150 inches of rain in an average year. Best access is via the 20 mile drive up the Hoh River. Don't overlook the intelligent displays at the visitor centre and the views along Quilcene River. Follow the **Hoh Rainforest Trail** which begins at the **Hoh Rainforest Visitor Center**.

Dense forest runs almost into the sea along the pristine, rocky coastal strip. The best view is at the southern end where Hwy 101 passes close to shore, but the best part is **Lake Ozette**, reached only by trails. Here the undergrowth is extravagant and the ground is boggy; much of the trail is bolstered by boards. Bears sometimes lumber down to the water in search of a meal. About 4 miles from the lake is beautiful **Cape Alava**, especially when silhouetted at sunset. 'Make every effort to see this park—fantastic.'

Admission to the park is $5 per vehicle (at the more built-up entrances), good for 7 days, and $3 per hiker/biker. **Campgrounds** in the park offer tentsites from $10. The really primitive sites are free. No food stores in the park, so purchase beforehand in Port Angeles. The unofficial guide to Olympic National Park, *www.halcyon.com/rdpayne/ onp.html*, includes highlights, maps and info on hiking, camping, fishing, scenic drives, biking and hot springs. *The telephone area code is 360.*

INFORMATION/TRAVEL
Greyhound, 1315 E Front, Port Angeles, (800) 231-2222.
Olympic National Park Headquarters, 600 E Park Ave, Port Angeles, and **Visitors Center**, 3002 Mt Angeles Rd, both 452-0330. Information on self-guided trails, camping, backcountry hiking, fishing and generally fields questions about whole park. Displays a map of locations of other park ranger stations. **NB: Backcountry camping** reqs a free backcountry permit, available at ranger stations. Daily 9 am-4 pm.

PORT TOWNSEND and THE SAN JUAN ISLANDS   Port Townsend shows you that western Washington isn't uniformly soggy; it lies in the 'rain shadow' of the great Olympic Mountains, and gets a mere 18 inches a year. Sunny weather, a vital cultural life, ebullient Victorian architecture and two nearby hostels make Port Townsend an excellent place to base for exploration. Seek out good food and friendly faces at the Lighthouse Cafe and occasional music at the Town Tavern.

In 1859 the US gained the 192-island chain of the **San Juans** in the great 'Pig War,' precipitated when a British pig recklessly invaded an American garden and was shot. The resulting squeal of outrage had US and British troops snout to snout on island soil, but diplomacy won out. With Kaiser Wilhelm the unlikely mediator, the US got the San Juans and the British got bangers, one supposes.

Connected by bridges to the mainland and each other are the islands of **Whidbey, Fidalgo** and **Camano**. The city of **Anacortes** on Fidalgo is a major ferry terminus. Despite their accessibility, these islands are quite rural. Further north and well served by ferry are **Orcas, Lopez** and **San Juan**. All have excellent camping, unsurpassable shorelines and scenery with good clamming and some fine beaches. Lopez is best for bicycling and has a good swimming beach at Spencer Spit, though water temperatures average a chilly 55 degrees. Call island information, 468-3663. The local Chamber of Commerce's Port Townsend net site is at *www.porttownsend.org/*.

ACCOMMODATION

Nordland: Fort Flagler HI Hostel, Ft Flagler State Park (on Marrowstone Island), 20 miles from Port Townsend, 385-1288. With 800 acres of forest and 7 miles of pristine beaches, the park is a wonderful place to enjoy hiking, biking, clamming, sea kayaking, fishing and deer grazing. Olympic National Park is only an hour's drive. Lrge common rm with wood stove, crab pots, info desk. Bikes to borrow. Not very well insulated, rural, and only 14 beds. 'The place to ebb out for a while.' May-Sept, otherwise by rsvs only. $11+ $3 linen. Rsvs recommended thru Sept.

Port Townsend: Olympic HI Hostel, Ft Worden State Park, 385-0655. The hostel affords outstanding views of the Cascade and Olympic mountain ranges and the Strait of Juan de Fuca. The 450-acre state park is host to music festivals (country, jazz, blues), kite flying and kayak gatherings, the Marine Science Center, and has miles of trails and beaches to explore. Near the town and a sandy beach, in the place where they filmed *An Officer and a Gentleman*. $11-14, private rooms available. **Palace Hotel**, 1002 Water St, 385-0755. From S-$54, D-$58. TV, brass beds, antique decor. Bus stops 1 block up street.

On the San Juans: Doe Bay Village HI Hostel, Star Rte 86, Olga, **Orcas Island**, 376-2291 or 376-4755. 'Used to be a '70s love-camp and is still like one in many ways. Not recommended.' Showers, fully-equipped kitchen, hot tubs $3/24hrs. 'Wonderful view over Otter coast.' $13-15. $16 camping.

Palmer's Chart House, PO Box 51, Deer Harbor, **Orcas Island**, WA 98243, 376-4231. Open year-round, warm place with private baths and entrances, decks, lots of amenities and pampering. Overlooks Deer Harbor. 1 hr ferry ride to Orcas from Anacortes; from Orcas 1 hr to Sidney. Morning or afternoon sailing for $32 pp on the Palmer's 33-ft yacht, *Amante*, weather permitting; rsvs essential. Highly rec for an unusual American experience. S-$45, D-$60, homecooked bfast included.

San Juan Island Camping: Snug Harbour Resort, 4pp-$22 per site, call 378-4762 to reserve; **Lakedale Campground**, $8 per site, call 378-2350. NB: a reader warns that San Juan island camping is crowded and full of American tourists, whereas the other islands are booked up in August. Rsvs early.

State Park Camping: Star Rte Box 22, Eastsound, WA 98245, 376-2326. $13 + $5 for rsvs for **Moran** on **Orcas**. Rsvs before Labor Day, in writing 2 weeks in advance only.

OF INTEREST

Two excellent guides to the area are *The San Juan Islands Afoot and Afloat* and *Emily's Guide*, with detailed descriptions of each island, both available at bookstores/outfitting stores on the islands and in Seattle.

San Juan Island: Jazz Festival. *www.rockisland.com/~jazz/* gives more details on the annual jazz and music festival held in July.

Whale Museum, 62 First St N, Friday Harbor, 378-4710. Exhibits of whale skeletons, brains; reading materials. Includes videos on Orcas and other whaling subjects. $5, $3.50 w/student ID. 'Small but very good.' Daily 10 am-5 pm in summer.

Whale watching at Lime Kiln Point, no entrance fee. From the cliff above the water you can see both Orcas and Minke whales come close to the rocks to feed on salmon. 'Usually arrive in afternoon.'

Wildlife: *www.karuna.com/san-juan-wildlife* is a wildlife guide with discovery maps and animal checklists.

Orcas Island: Moran State Park in Eastsound, 376-2326, has over 21 miles of hiking trails ranging from a light 1 hr stroll to a full day's adventure climbing Mt Constitution. Trail guides available from the registration station, 376-2326.

INFORMATION/TRAVEL
Greyhound, 401 Harris, Fairhaven, (800) 231-2222. Take Greyhound from Seattle to Port Angeles and connect with Jefferson County Transit to P.T. $1.10. Ferries from Anacortes daily to Shaw, Lopez, Orcas, San Juan and Sidney, BC. Westward journey to any island $5.20/foot passenger, then inter-island travel free. Orcas island to Sidney, BC, $2.25. Ferry and land combinations are extremely numerous; you'll do best to study the free ferry schedules and maps: call 464-6400 or (800) 542-7052 (in Washington).
Orcas Island Chamber of Commerce, 376-2273.
San Juan Chamber of Commerce, 378-5240.

MOUNT RAINIER NATIONAL PARK It was the enterprising 18th century British Admiral Rainier who got this 14,410-foot mountain named after himself. Today Mt Rainier, 80 miles S of Seattle and clearly visible from there, is surrounded by a national park that should interest the most jaded peak peeker. With 575 inches of snow piling up in an average year, little of the mountain shows beneath the glittering whiteness. More than 40 glaciers crown Mt Rainier, and lush conifer forests line its lower slopes, interrupted by meadows bright with wildflowers in July and August.

The **Wonderland Trail** wanders for 90 miles around the mountain, passing through snowfields, meadows and forests, with shelter cabins at convenient intervals. The full walk can take 10 days, but there are lesser trails for those with lesser ambitions. Near the park's SE corner is the **Trail of the Patriarchs**, leading through groves of massive red cedar and Douglas fir. The best place for seeing wildflowers is to march up from **Paradise Valley**. In the northeast, excellent hiking trails branch out from **Sunrise**, the highest point in the park that can be reached by road.

July through Sept are often warm and clear, sunsets and sunrises over the mountain are unforgettable. It rains even in summer, and cloudy, rainy or foggy weather is the rule the rest of the year. Always dress warmly and bring raingear. Entrance is $5 per car, $3 for hikers/bikers, or by bus.

The **Cascade foothills**, north of Rainier, are a closer alternative: 'Drive 30 miles E to North Bend, then follow south fork of the Snoqualmie River for 15 miles. Take dirt track marked Lake Talapus to car park. From there, a 2 mile hike to the lake. Gorge yourself on blueberries, swim and dive off rocks, kill bugs—on a sunny day, this beats any city tour. This is the real America.' The unofficial guide to Mount Rainier National Park is at *www.halcyon.comrdpayne/mrnp.html*.

ACCOMMODATION
Backcountry camping is free: with a permit hikers can use any of the free trailside camps scattered in the park's backcountry. Access to toilets and water.
Campgrounds (best option—that's what you're here for!): **Ohanapecosh** $10; **Cougar Rock and White River**, $8; **Sunshine Point** Ipsut Creek, $5. Open summers only except for Sunshine Point. Come equipped for cold. At higher altitudes, there will be snow on the ground, maybe some from the sky even in the dead of summer.
Mt Haven Campground & Cabins at Cedar Park, 569-2594. $12.50 per site with shower, laundry. Cabins: From D-$50 w/kitchen, bath, shower, fireplace.
Paradise Inn, 569-2413, at 5400 ft. Open mid-June to early Oct. From S/D-$69 ($98 w/bath). Suite for six $158. For rsvs write to Mt Rainier Guest Services, Attn: Reservations, PO Box 108, Ashford, WA 98304 or call 569-2275.

INFORMATION/TRAVEL

Henry M Jackson Memorial Visitors Center (largest centre in the park), ½ block from Paradise Inn, daily 8 am-7 pm.

Greyhound, 1319 Pacific Ave, Tacoma, (800) 231-2222.

Longmire Hiker Information Center, 569-2211 ext 3317. Distributes backcountry permits. Daily Sun-Thurs 8 am-4.30 pm, Fri 'til 7 pm, Sat 7 am-7 pm; closed in winter.

Mount Rainier National Park Headquarters, call 569-2211 for recording on weather and road conditions, food, lodging, camping, hiking, visitors centres and more. Mon-Fri 8 am-4.30 pm.

Ohanapecosh Visitors Center. Offers info and wildlife displays. Daily 9 am-6 pm.

Paradise Visitors Center, 569-2211 ext 2328. Offers food, pay showers and guided hikes. Daily Sun-Fri 9 am-6 pm.

Sunrise Visitors Center. Contains exhibits, snacks and a gift shop. June 25-mid Sept Sun-Fri 9 am-6 pm, Sat 9 am-7 pm.

NORTH CASCADES NATIONAL PARK Spectacular scenery in the Cascade Mountains: razor-backed peaks, plunging waterfalls, high snow-fields and deep lakes. From Seattle, take Hwy 5 N to Hwy 20 E. No entrance fee to park; most areas are wilderness, inaccessible by road. You can, however, drive to three **campgrounds** in the park: **Colonial Creek** and **Newhalen**, both $9; and **Goodell** , $6. Forest Service info 856-5700. **Visitors Center** on left side of Hwy 20. The unofficial guide to North Cascades National Park is at *www.halcyon.com.rdpayne/ncnp.html*.

LONG BEACH PENINSULA On its long sandy finger of land in extreme SW Washington, the Long Beach peninsula harbours an immense clam and driftwood-filled beach, covered with huge dunes (great for escaping the wind) and backed by pines hiding hundreds of old-fashioned beach cot-tages. Besides the windswept beauty of the area, visit the free **Lewis and Clark Interpretive Center**, 642-3029, 10 am-5 pm daily, near **Cape Disappointment Lighthouse**, a superb audio-visual evocation of the hard-ships and wonders of the explorers' epic journey. The display ramps lead you to the same magnificent ocean overlook that climaxed Lewis and Clark's trip in 1805. Long Beach Peninsula, *www.aone.com/~lngbeach/city-page.html* includes directions by car, lodging options and a link to the visi-tors bureau.

ACCOMMODATION

Ft Columbia HI Hostel, Box 224, **Chinook**, 777-8755. 7 miles from Astoria, Oregon, across a toll bridge (cars $2 o/w, 50¢ bicycles, hitchhikers free). April-Sept; at other times of year, send rsvs 1 month in adv. $11. The hostel is in an old army hospital in a lovely, isolated site in Ft Columbia State Park overlooking the mighty Columbia River in park with museum, and Pacific Ocean. Near Chinook Indian village. Good bathing. Convenient access to Washington's longest beach (26 miles), the site of many festivals and recreational activities. The Long Beach Peninsula, a short bike ride/drive away, is a great place to whale watch and hosts summer festivals for kite flyers, garlic and cranberry lovers and seafood connoisseurs.

THE SOUTHWEST

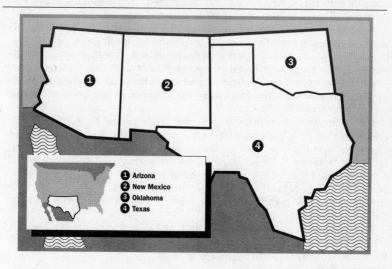

1. Arizona
2. New Mexico
3. Oklahoma
4. Texas

Much of this area is exactly as you would expect from seeing Westerns—whether shot in Spain or elsewhere. Purple mountains, searing deserts, cactus, cowboys and Indians inhabit Arizona, New Mexico and west Texas. Contrasting with this region are the lush farmlands of east Texas and Oklahoma and northern Arizona's and New Mexico's parks and ski resorts on the tailbone of the Rocky Mountains.

Hardly passing through an intervening industrial stage, the Southwest since World War II has leapt from a simple economy into the nuclear-industrial-aerospace age and is now the bright buckle of the Sun Belt. But the past has not been lost—old Indian and Spanish influences remain.

For several decades after it was blazed in 1822, the Sante Fe Trail served emigrants and traders between Missouri and the Southwest. Now the major thoroughfares are I-40 (the legendary 'Route 66') to the north and the cross-country I-10 to the south. To enjoy the natural splendour of the region and get a sample of day-to-day life here, stay off I-40 as much as possible.

ARIZONA *Grand Canyon State*

Once called the 'Baby State' (the words of one of the state's first senators) because it is the youngest of the lower 48, Arizona has slid comfortably into its mature role as a mecca for retirees and families on vacation. The low cost of living and unique quality of life are now also drawing younger residents in large numbers. A land of vast silences and arid beauty, the Grand Canyon

State (its new moniker) also contains sharp and sometimes troubling contrasts. One-quarter of Arizona is Indian land, containing the incredibly ancient and artistically advanced cultures of the Hopis, Navajos and others, and one in twenty inhabitants is a Native American. Yet Indians in this state were not allowed to vote until 1948.

Arizona's works of nature are among the grandest in the US, if not the world, beginning with the Grand Canyon and continuing through 17 other highly variegated national parks, monuments and recreation areas. But the works of man range from banal to short-sightedly destructive: water-greedy cities, a borrowed London Bridge, and dam-drowned canyons (even the upper portion of the Grand Canyon—the Marble Canyon—was threatened with a dam at one time!).

The southern section from Tucson east is the richest historically. It was once the stomping ground of Wyatt Earp, Billy the Kid, Apache chiefs Geronimo and Cochise and assorted prospectors, padres and gunslingers. Northern Arizona, with its stark mesas and richly coloured canyons (all could be called 'Grand') offers the greatest scenic drama. Glen Canyon and Monument Valley, both spilling over into Utah, and Canyon de Chelly should all be high on the visitor's list, after the mandatory pilgrimage to the Grand Canyon, of course.

The vast distances between cities and parks—not to mention the sprawl within Phoenix and Tucson themselves—make a car a smart acquisition. *www.yahoo.com/Regional/U_S__States/Arizona/.*
National Park: Grand Canyon.
The telephone area code for the state is 520, for Phoenix 602.

PHOENIX Huge, hot and horizontal, Phoenix is quite possibly the world's worst city for pedestrians. The city isn't a convenient gateway to anywhere—although at the rate it's sprawling, Phoenix may one day ooze right up to the lip of the Grand Canyon.

Actually the suburbs can be more interesting than the metropolis itself. **Tempe** is home to Arizona State U, with the largest student body in the west. **Scottsdale**, the destination for the moneyed traveller and the rich, boasts some decadent resorts. Go to *Phoenix At Your Fingertips* at *www.ci.phoenix.az.us/* which includes a calendar of events: arts, cultural and sports activities and programs.

ACCOMMODATION
NB: In general, expect much higher rates Oct-May in large Arizona cities like Phoenix and Tucson. In summer, check rates at the posh resorts—opulence can be had for less than $50 nightly. Check out the ranch-style motels on **Van Buren St** and **Main St** (aka **Apache Trail**).
In Phoenix: B&B Inn Arizona, 8900 E Via Linda #101, Scottsdale 85258, (800) 266-STAY. Matches you with rooms in private homes throughout Phoenix and general Arizona. Pref 2 night minimum stay. From S-$30, D-$40. Rsvs recommended.
Econo Lodge, 5050 Black Canyon Hwy, 242-8011. S-$54, D-$65. Off I-17 in downtown. Free coffee.
Metcalf House AYH, 1026 N 9th St btwn Roosevelt & Portland, 2 blocks E of 7th St, 254-9803. $12. 'Good for help and info. Common room (day use), no curfew, scheduled activities, kitchen, laundry. Glad to provide free sound advice when purchas-

ing a car esp if planning to resell. 'Very family style atmosphere promoted—liked everyone to have dinner together, etc.' 'Clean and quiet, the cheapest place to stay in Phoenix.' $5 taxi to Amtrak.

YMCA, 350 N 1st Ave, 253-6181. Co-ed, 1 floor for women. S-$20, D-$30; $10 key deposit. Pool, athletic facilities. 'Clean.'

Camping: KOA Phoenix West, 11miles W of Phoenix on Citrus Rd, 853-0537. 285 sites, heated pool, jacuzzi. $17 full hook-up.

Mi Casa-Su Casa, PO Box 950, Tempe, AZ 85281, 990-0682, (800) 456-0682. Rooms in 135 homes statewide, and also in Utah and New Mexico. From S-$35, D-$45. Loves foreign travellers.

In Tempe: Tempe University Travelodge, 1005 E Apache Blvd, 968-7871. From S-$37, D-$50, bfast included.

FOOD

Essentially an expensive gringo resort area, with fast food and a 24 hr convenience store seemingly on every corner. In **Tempe**, near the university, are low-cost bars and nosheries where students congregate. Most are along Mill Ave at University Ave.

Club Rio, 430 N Scottsdale Rd, (602) 894-0533. 'Huge burgers.' (Thurs burgers $3.75). For a splurge, try steaks cooked Indian-style, over mesquite, a technique that originated here.

Dash Inn, 731 E Apache at Rural, (602) 894-6445. Cheap Mexican food and pitchers of margaritas; closed Sun.

Jack's Original Barbeque, 5250 E 22nd St, 750-1280. Try the 'glorious' sloppy joe, a Thursday special. 'Super sweet potato pie. Taste the Wisdom!'

Pinnacle Peak Patio, 10426 E Jomax Rd in Scottsdale, (602) 585-1599, is where locals go for cheap and excellent mesquite-broiled fare. Mon-Sat 4 pm-11 pm, Sun from noon.

Los Dos Molinos, 8646 S Central Ave, 243-9113. Features live music at lunch and dinner. Huge menu offering enchiladas and burritos. Tues-Sat 11 am-9 pm.

OF INTEREST

Always phone first or check with visitors bureau; sights are far apart and the summer heat will make you believe that Phoenix has, like its namesake, risen from the ashes of some still-smouldering inferno.

In Phoenix: Camelback Pt Park, take Echo Canyon Park Rd. Phoenix' most visible landmark offers scenic views, picnicking, good trails.

Desert Botanical Gardens, 1201 N Galvin Pkwy, 941-1225. On the border of Phoenix and Scottsdale in Papago Park, by the zoo. Carefully maintained colourful collection of cacti and 10,000 desert plants that shows how desert ecosystem works. Daily 7 am-10 pm (summer), 8 am-8 pm (winter). $6. Also, within the confines of Papago Park, the **Phoenix Zoo**, 62nd and E Van Buren St, 273-1341. Specializing in Arizona wildlife; recently refurbished Arizona Trail is a 'zoo within a zoo,' covering indigenous species from the state. Walk around or take a guided tour via tram. Daily 7 am-4 pm, after Labor Day 9 am-5 pm; $7.

Heard Museum, 22 E Monte Vista Rd, 252-8840. Outstanding collections of Navajo handicrafts, silverwork, weavings, basketry, plus most of former Sen Barry Goldwater's collection of 450 Hopi Kachina dolls. Museum also promotes the work of contemporary Native American artists, and sponsors occasional lectures and Native American dances. Mon-Sat 9.30 am-5 pm (Weds 'til 8 pm), Sun noon-5 pm. $5, $4 w/student ID.

Mystery Castle, 800 E Mineral Rd, 268-1581. Bizarre mansion built by a man who felt guilty about deserting his wife and child. Tour the 18-rooms (none on the same level or in the same shape) for $3, $2 w/student ID. Tues-Sun 11 am-4 pm Oct-July 4th, then w/ends in July & Aug, closed Sept.

Paolo Soleri's gallery/studio, 6433 Doubletree Ranch Rd, Scottsdale, 948-6145. Daily 9 am-5 pm. **Arcosanti**, 632-7135, Soleri's futuristic vertical city in the making, is 65 miles N of the studio, exit 262 off I-17. Daily 9 am-5 pm, tours 10 am-4 pm, $5 donation. Must have a car.

Phoenix Art Museum, 1625 N Central, 257-1880. Exhibits art from medieval to Western and Latin American. Tue-Sat 10 am-5 pm, Wed 'til 9 pm, Sun noon-5 pm. $4, $1.50 w/student ID.

Phoenix Skatepark , 110th Ave and Glendale. Fri-Sun only.

Pueblo Grande Museum and Cultural Park, 4619 E Washington St, 495-0900. The Hohokam people—the ancestors of modern-day Pimas and Papagos—are thought to have built this irrigated city about 200 BC and disappeared about AD 1450. Visit both museum and dig site here. Mon-Sat 9 am-4.45 pm, Sun 1 pm-4.45 pm. $2.

Taliesin West, on Frank Lloyd Wright Blvd in nearby Scottsdale, 860-8810 (call for exact directions). Frank Lloyd Wright's winter home and workshop. Guided tours only. June-Sept daily; 1 hr tours; mornings hourly. (2¹/₂ hr tour at 7.30 am & 11 am, $20, Thurs only). Rsvs suggested. $8, $6 w/student ID.

The Annual Paysan Rodeo, Rodeo Ground, 474-4515. Said to be the world's oldest continuous rodeo (over 170 yrs old). 3rd w/end in August. $12.

In Scottsdale: Rawhide's 1880s Western Town, Scottsdale Rd (4 miles N of Bell Rd), 563-1880. Arizona's largest western theme attraction. Includes Old West shootouts, saloon, a steam powered locomotive *c.* 1880, a steakhouse (with deep-fried rattlesnake on the menu), rodeo country music and stage coach rides. Daily 5 pm-10 pm; free.

In Tempe:, the **Nelson Fine Arts Center**, 965-2787, built in 1989, is an avant-garde showcase housing a dance lab, playhouse and ASU Art Museum. The museum has 4 galleries of changing exhibits, Tue-Sat 11 am-5 pm, Sun 1 pm-5 pm. Free. **Gammage Center for Performing Arts**, 965-4050, designed by Frank Lloyd Wright, is also here. Free ¹/₂ hr tours, Mon-Fri, in winter, begins end Sept); to rsvs tkts (discount w/student ID) call box office: 965-8721. Elsewhere on campus: the **Matthews Center** (off Forest Mall) houses permanent collections including African and Latin American art, American crockery and ceramics, and a sculpture zoo and aviary. Tue-Fri 9 am-5 pm Sun 1 pm-5 pm, free. **Matthews Hall**, 965-6517 (next door), is a museum of photography with changing exhibitions. Mon-Thur 10 am-5 pm, Sun noon-4.30 pm. **Anthropology Museum**, 965-6213, **Planetarium** (rsvs required), 965-6891, and **Memorial Union** (SU) Art Gallery, 965-6822, are also free.

About 55 miles SE of Phoenix lies **Casa Grande Ruins National Monument** a 4-storey structure built by the Pueblo Indians AD 1300 and protected from further erosion by a hilarious 'umbrella,' courtesy of the US government AD 1936. Far more spectacular are the ruins at **Tonto National Monument**, 60 miles E. 'The **Apache Trail** follows Rte 88 to Tortilla Flats and Roosevelt Lake through superb desert scenery with views of Superstition Mountains and Weavers Needle. Make a day trip of it.'

ENTERTAINMENT

Sun Splash (plus **Adventure Island** and **Golf-land**), 1500 N McClintock Rd, Tempe, (602) 834-8319. The surf reaches 5ft on this 2¹/₂-acre, 450,000 gallon wave pool; no surfing any more but swimming still permitted. 10 giant water slides and waving palms complete the oasis illusion. Open mid-March through Sept, Mon-Sat 10 am-9 pm, Sun 11 am-7 pm. $13.50 ($9 after 4 pm) plus $2-$4 for raft rental. Lockers available. Discount coupons at 'Smithy's.' 'Most indulgent moment of my holiday.' For the after-hours scene, grab the free *New Times Weekly* and the *Cultural Calender of Events* guide. Check out **Char's Has The Blues**, 4631 N 7th Ave, 230-0205. Sports dozens of junior John Lee Hookers! 9 pm nightly; $3 cover w/ends.

INFORMATION

Arizona Office of Tourism, (800) 842-8257.

Casa Grande Chamber of Commerce, 575 N Marshall, 836-2125. Mon-Fri 9 am-5 pm, Sat 10 am-4 pm.

Phoenix & Valley of the Sun Convention & Visitors Bureaux, 400 E Van Burren St, 254-6500. Mon-Fri 8 am-5 pm. Also at 2nd St and Adams and at airport.

Scottsdale Chamber of Commerce, 7343 Scottsdale Mall, 945-8481. Mon-Fri 8.30 am-5 pm, Sat from 10 am, Sun from 11 am.

Tempe Chamber of Commerce, 51 W 3rd St, 894-8158. Mon-Fri 8.30 am-5 pm.

Weekly Events Hotline, 252-5588.

TRAVEL

AAA Driveaway, 4814 S 35th St, 468-1733. 'Good availability of driveaways both east and west. Cheap way to travel.' Mon-Fri 7 am-5 pm, Sat 9 am-noon.

Ace Taxis, 254-1999. Rent-a-Wreck, 1202 S 24th St (in Roadway Inn Hotel), 254-1000. Mon-Sat 7 am-3 pm.

Amtrak, Union Station, 401 W Harrison St, (800) 872-7245.

Greyhound, downtown, 525 E Washington St, (800) 231-2222, 24 hrs. Be careful in this area. Also at 2647 W Glendale Ave (near freeway), 246-4341. Use caution at night.

Horseback trail rides into the Superstition Mt Wilderness: Gold Canyon stables, 982-7822. 2 hr $32, 4 hr $53; and Peralta Stables, 982-5488, both in Apache Junction.

Sky Harbor International Airport, SE of downtown, 273-3300. Allow time to see the abundance of contemporary art exhibits depicting Arizona's cultural life. Showers and lockers available. From downtown; Mon-Fri take the 'Red Line' bus from Jefferson, opposite the American Arena and go east, $1.25; on Sat, take the 'Zero' bus from Jefferson until you reach Buckeye and then transfer to the #13 airport bus going east, $1.25, remember to pick up a transfer; on Sun and public holidays only, call Dial-a-Ride, 271-4545, trip about $4.

Valley Metro public transport, 253-5000. $3.60 all day pass, basic fare $1.25, free transfers. Most routes operate Mon-Fri 5 am-8 pm; no Sun service.

TUCSON   Once capital of the Arizona territory and now a university town, Tucson retains a Western informality as it grows past the half-million mark. Folksiness notwithstanding, Tucson is, like Phoenix, a big, tough town with its share of crime, poverty and drugs. Watch your step in downtown, particularly at night and especially if you are female.

Most worthwhile sights are well away from downtown: the Desert Museum, Mission San Xavier del Bac, Saguaro National Monument, Old Tucson and the interesting Yaqui Indian tribe. The Yaquis have been immortalised in the books of Carlos Castaneda, a renegade anthropologist who claims that members of this tribe possess ancient knowledge of true sorcery. Whether or not you buy this view, the Yaquis are a highly spiritual and musical people, whose rites combine native and Catholic traditions. Their public performances (around Pascua, a village south of Tucson) are especially magnificent during Holy Week and at Christmas.

Both Tucson and Phoenix are in the Sonora Desert, surrounded by giant saguaro forests, cacti and mountains—all within driving (not walking) distance. Tucson is 65 miles north of Nogales, an agreeable town on the Arizona/Mexico border. *www.ci.tucson.az.us/* takes you on a whirlwind adventure to the most popular city locations, even providing hot links for city job listings.

ACCOMMODATION
Motel row runs along **South Freeway**, the frontage road along I-10.

Hotel Congress & Tucson International Hostel, 311 E Congress St, 622-8848. Historic railroad hotel built in1919, conveniently located across from the Greyhound and Amtrak stations. AYH-$11, non-AYH $14. Private rooms: S-$29, D-$42 (summer); S-$45, D-$55 (Jan-Apr). 'Best value in USA.' 'Wild progressive nightclub in lobby. Great fun.' 'Only 40 miles to Mexico!'

Old Pueblo Homestays B&B, PO Box 13603, Tucson 85732, (800) 338-9776. Arranges homestays in private homes. From S-$40-$70, D-$65. Daily 8 am-8 pm. Winter rsvs required 2 weeks in advance.

Camping: Travel via the **Catalina Hwy. Mount Lemmon Recreation Area** in the **Coronado National Forest** offers beautiful campgrounds and free off-site camping in certain areas. For more info contact the **National Forest Service**, 300 W Congress Ave, 670-4552. 7 blocks W of Greyhound. Mon-Fri 8 am-4.30 pm.

FOOD
Tucson is the place to get great Mexican food, especially *chimichangas*, reportedly invented here. *Chimichangas* are essentially fried pastry stuffed with beef, chilies, onion, cheese and salsa. Follow your nose, or pick up a free *Tucson Weekly*.

Caruso's, 434 N 4th Ave, 624-5765. Entrees $6-$9. 'Great lasagna, $7.'

El Charro, 311 N Court, 622-5465. A fortress of Mexican-American food since 1922. Tasty carne seca (air-dried beef), a speciality of Mexican cattle country. Noisy and sociable, packed with tourists, Tucsonians, healthnuts and burrito hounds spooning it all up!

El Minuto Cafe, 354 S Main, 882-4145. 'Excellent and cheap Mexican food, basic decor.'

Food Conspiracy Co-op, 412 N 4th, 624-4821. Mon-Sat 9 am-8 pm, Sun 9 am-7 pm.

Little Café Poca Casa, 20 South Scott Ave, no phone. Closet-size café, chili colorado and chili verde. Horchata cooler drink made from rice; try!

Mamas, 831 N Park, 882-3993. Pizza, subs, beer and jazz. 'Very popular student joint.' Open 'til 1 am.

Sanchez Burrito Co, 2539 N 1st Ave, 622-2092. Huge helpings, low prices, eg $3.50 burritos, dinners $5.50. 'Authentic and excellent.'

OF INTEREST
Arizona-Sonora Desert Museum, 2021 N Kinney Rd (14 miles W of the city), 883-2702. A museum, zoo and nature preserve rolled into one. Detailed look at Sonoran desert, from tunnels that let you peer into snake and prairie-dog households to outdoor habitats of Gila monsters and mountain lions. Plants and rock of the desert are represented as well, in a museum that has been called 'the most distinctive in the US.' 'Don't miss this place.' Visit early am or late afternoon to see maximum animal activity; 7.30 am-6 pm daily, 'til 10 pm Sat. $8.95. At same site: **Congdon Earth Sciences Center** with a manmade limestone cave showing subterranean rock and life forms, and explanations of volcanic activity. 7.30 am-6 pm daily, $8.95 (rates subject to change). North of the museum, **Saguaro National Park**, 2 sections, one east and one west of Tucson, both open 24 hr. Found naturally only in southern Arizona and Sonora, Mexico (although pirated plants may be seen as far away as LA), giant saguaro cacti grow to 50ft tall and live for as much as 200 yrs. In late May, waxy white flowers sprout from the tips of cacti arms—a charming and improbable sight.

East Park, 3693 S Old Spanish Trail, 733-5153, has the oldest stands. $4 to drive the loop; $2 p/pedestrian. Gates close at 7 pm. 128 miles of trails and an 8 miles scenic drive lead through the cactus forest. Get a free permit from the visitors center for backcountry camping (before noon).

West Park 2700 N Kinney Rd, 883-6366, is free. Hiking trails, auto loop, and paved nature walk near visitors centre (daily 8 am-5 pm). **Gates Pass** is an excellent spot for watching the sun as it rises and sets.

Kitt Peak National Observatory, 56 miles SW of Tucson, on Rte 86, 318-8600. Centre for astronomical research. Daily 9 am-4 pm. Film at 10.30 am and 1.30 pm. Guided tours at w/ends (and weekdays after films). Free. 'Fascinating.'

Mission San Xavier del Bac, 9 miles SW on Papago reservation, 294-2624. Completed in 1797 and called 'the white dove of the desert' for its cool beauty, the mission has weathered 3 political jurisdictions, 2 explosions and 1 large earthquake and still serves as church and school for the Papagos, known formally as the Tohono O'dham nation. Mon-Fri 8 am-6 pm, donation.

Pima Air and Space Museum, 6000 E Valencia Rd near airport, 574-9658. Huge airplane cemetery. Tour plane used by Presidents Kennedy and Johnson. Daily 9 am-5 pm, $6.

Sabino Canyon, 749-2861 **and Seven Falls**, two of the area's most popular and breathtaking hiking, picnicking and biking areas (bikes before 9 am/after 5 pm only, not on Weds/Sat). Call Canyon folk for best directions. Either take a tram up the canyon ($5) or walk. The falls can be reached only by a 4½-mile hike. No overnight camping. Info: 749-3223, Mon-Fri 8 am-4.30 pm. **Visitors Center**, 749-8700.

Titan Missile Museum, exit 69 on I-19 in Green Valley, 791-2929. Don a hardhat and see the only ICBM (cruise missiles to the uninitiated!) silo in the world open to the public. Nov-April daily 9 am-4 pm, May-Oct closed Mon-Tues. $6. 'A chilling, frightening and all-powerful must see.' Rsvs recommended (call 625-7736).

Tucson Museum of Art, 140 N Main Ave, 624-2333. Outstanding collection of Pre-Columbian artefacts. Mon-Sat 10 am-4 pm, Sun noon-4 pm. $2, $1 w/student ID, free Tues. Worthwhile museums on UA campus: **Center for Creative Photography**, 621-7968, magnificent museum that houses 50,000 fine art photos, including the Ansel Adams and Richard Avedon archives. Three galleries (daily 11 am-5 pm, Sun from noon) with changing exhibits and a photo library; make appt to view archives. **Arizona State Museum**, Park Ave at Uni gates, 621-4895. Archaeology, Navajo, Apache, Pueblo artefacts. Mon-Sat 10 am-5 pm, Sun 2 pm-5 pm. The **Historical Society**, Park and 2nd, 628-5774. 'Free; excellent displays of Southwest history.' Mon-Sat 10 am-4 pm, Sun from noon. Donations appreciated. **Flandrau Planetarium**, free exhibits on space, astronomy. 'Part of tracking system for Voyager mission and space shuttle. Mineral museum; Mon-Fri 10 am-5 pm, w/ends from 1 pm; $2. Also laser shows with Nirvana vs Pearl Jam, Pink Floyd and others, $5 (Wed-Thurs $1 off).' Call 621-7827 for programme info. $4 w/student ID ($4.50 theatre).

ENTERTAINMENT

UA students are renowned for rocking and rolling on **Speedway Blvd**. Pick up a copy of the free *Tucson Weekly* or the w/end sections of *The Star* or *The Citizen* for current entertainment listings. Take a jaunt down **4th Ave**. Try **3rd Stone**, 628-8844, corner of 4th Ave and 6th St or head up 4th Ave to **O'Malley's**, 623-8600, which has food, pool tables, and pinball. During **Downtown Saturday Night**, on the first and third Sat of each month, Congress St is blockaded for a celebration of the arts with outdoor singers, crafts, and galleries.

Bum Steer, 1910 N Stone, 884-7377. Good lunch specials for around $4. 'A must. Good luck lads and don't forget Happy Hour.' Daily 'til 1 am. 'Try the house special "Jiffy Burger".'

Near UA Campus: The Shanty Cafe, 401 E 9th, 623-2664. 'Good friendly pub and student watering hole'; 'til 1 am daily. **Gentle Ben's Brewing Company**, 865 E University Blvd, 624-4177. You will need two forms of photo ID.

INFORMATION
Metropolitan Tucson Convention and Visitors Bureau, 130 S Scott Ave, (800) 638-8350. Ask for a bus map, the *Official Visitor's Guide*, and an Arizona campground directory. Mon-Fri 8 am-5 pm, w/ends 9 am-4 pm.

TRAVEL
Amtrak, 400 E Toole Ave (1 block N of Greyhound), (800) 872-7245. On the *Sunset Ltd* LA-Miami route. Open limited hours.

The Bike Shack bike rental, 835 Park Ave, 624-3663, across from the UA campus. Mon-Fri 9 am-7 pm, Sat 10 am-5 pm, Sun from noon.

Budget Car Rental, 3085 E Valencia Rd, 889-8800; **Rent-a-Ride**, 7051 Tucson Blvd, 294-4100; and **Care Free**, 1760 S Craycroft Rd, 790-2655.

Greyhound, 2 S 4th Ave, (800) 231-2222. 'Girls near depot should stay on the move. This is the local prostitutes' pitch—clients are very persistent and extremely unpleasant.'

Sun-Tran public buses, 792-9222, basic fare 75¢ exact change. Service runs Mon-Fri 5.30 am-10 pm, Sat-Sun 8 am-7 pm.

Tucson International Airport, 573-8000; south of downtown on Valencia Rd. Take the #8 bus east on Broadway as far as Alvernon, transfer to #11 'Tucson Airport' and go south, 75¢ (exact change) and free transfer. After bus hours, call Arizona Stagecoach, 889-1000, pick-up/drop-off at downtown hotels, $12.50. Rsvs.

Yellow Cab taxis, 624-6611. Open 24 hrs.

TOMBSTONE, BISBEE and APACHE COUNTRY   This rugged terrain, once subject to the raids of Mexican revolutionary Pancho Villa, was originally Apache territory. Cochise, who fought the US Cavalry until 1886, was never captured and lies buried somewhere in the **Coronado National Forest**, about 60 miles east of Tucson. (Fellow Apache chief Geronimo was imprisoned in Oklahoma and died there in 1900.)

Tombstone, was named as a bit of death-defying bravado by the prospector who founded the town. Told that in this wild Apache country, he would find 'only his own tombstone,' he struck silver instead. The silver was short-lived (1877-90), but the tombstones survive, in this city that lives off the tourists it traps. **Boot Hill Cemetery** (closes at dusk), one of the few sights in town that is free, displays the epitaph of the Clanton Gang, 'Murdered on the Street of Tombstone'—by Marshal Wyatt Earp, Earp's brothers and Doc Holliday at the shootout at OK Corrall, 457-3456. The shootout is re-enacted for visitors on Allen next to City Park, Mon-Sat 2 pm at 4th and Toughnut; $2.50. On the 2nd and 4th Sundays, you can see the 'vigilantes and vigilettes' have it out in downtown). 'Whole place is a little false but great fun.' Call Lou at the Legends of the West Saloon, 457-3055, to arrange with one of these groups to treat a friend or relative to a **public mock hanging!** The **Bird Cage Theater** where Lola Montez danced, is still standing and houses a museum.

South of Tombstone by 25 miles, **Bisbee** clings to the sides of steep hills—a mining town of great character and considerable charm. Over $2 billion in silver, gold and copper came from these hills, but today Bisbee is famous for a special variety of turquoise, on display at Bisbee Blue Jewelry. Don't miss the delightful Art Deco courthouse or the nearby 'Lavender Pit Queen Mine.' If you're here in the summer, take heart: Bisbee is 5500 ft above sea level, making it much cooler than Tombstone.

ACCOMMODATION
In Cochise: Cochise Hotel and Waterworks, Cochise, 384-3156. S-$25, D-$35. Booking mandatory for this authentic relic of the Old West: brass beds, quilts, chamberpots (plus modern plumbing) and chicken ($7) or steak ($12) dinners homecooked by the irascible proprietress. No AC, bring your own booze.
Hacienda Huachuca Motel, 320 Bruce St, (800) 893-2201, where John Wayne stayed (room #4)during the 1963 shooting of McLintock. S/D-$27.
Larian Motel, 457-2272, Rte 80 near Allen St on Fremont, is clean and close to downtown. S-$35, D-$40 (summer), $45/55 (winter).
Camping: free in **Coronado National Forest**, 826-3593.
In Bisbee: Bisbee Grand Hotel, 61 Main St, (800) 421-1909. Full bfast included from $44. Try **Jonquil Inn**, 317 Tombstone Canyon, 432-7371. Call ahead especially in winter. S-$33, D-$36.
Copper Queen Hotel, 11 Howell Ave, 432-2216. For From S/D-$69. Beautiful, regal, once the headquarters for everyone from Teddy Roosevelt to 'Black Jack' Pershing, hot on Pancho Villa's trail. Good sidewalk cafe, pool, saloon. 'Many rooms with antique furniture—a trip back in time when this was a bustling mining town.'

OF INTEREST/INFORMATION
Copper Queen Mine in Bisbee, 118 Arizona St, 432-2071. Daily tours, 1 hr, $8 at 9 am, 10.30 am, noon, 2 pm and 3.30 pm. 'Cold, so dress warmly.' 'Extensive, informative, good value.'
Tombstone Epitaph, the town local newspaper. Saved from bankruptcy by U of Arizona, now published by students. Pick up a copy or call 457-2211 for local info.
Visitors Center, 4th & Allen Sts, 457-3929. Daily 9 am-5 pm, 'til 4 pm at w/ends.

FLAGSTAFF Gateway to the Grand Canyon, a college town with character, Flagstaff is home of 'NAU' (Northern Arizona University, or otherwise, 'Not A University'). Other scenic splendours nearby are Oak Creek Canyon and Montezuma Castle to the south; Meteor Crater, Petrified Forest and Canyon de Chelly to the east; and Sunset Crater and Wupatki to the north. Somewhat closer to the Grand Canyon is **Williams**, which has some lodgings and good camping. *www.virtualflagstaff.com/* is a community based system which provides current info on events in the city.

ACCOMMODATION
'Worth getting into a casual conversation with a Northern Arizona University student. Tell them of your exploits and ask for a bed for the night. It worked for me and some others.' Alternatively, cruise historic Rte 66 to find cheap motels. *The Flagstaff Accommodations Guide* available at Visitors Centre, prices all area hotels, motels, hostels and B&Bs. Tip: If seeing the Grand Canyon, check the noticeboard in your hotel/hostel; some travellers leave their still-valid passes behind. Rates begin falling after Labor Day and are cheapest Nov-May. Summer rates given below.
Americana Motor Hotel, 2650 E Santa Fe Ave, 526-2200. S-$38, D-$54.
Chalet Lodge, 1919 E Santa Fe, 774-2779. From S/D-$40.
Downtowner/Grand Canyon International Hostel, 19 S San Francisco St, 779-9421/(800) 872-7245. 1 block from Amtrak. Dorm-$14, private rooms D-$30, T-$42; all include bfast. Free pickup/dropoff from airport/train/bus stations. No curfew. 'Day trips to Sedona Grand Canyon and the best staff anywhere in America!' 'Helpful staff.' 'Nice clean rooms; kept bags for us while we saw Canyon.'
Flagstaff HI-AYH, 23 N Leroux St, 774-2731. ¹/₂ block E from Greyhound. $12-$16. Two pubs with line dancing music. Rsvs essential.

Hotel du Beau Hostel, 19 W Phoenix, (800) 332-1944, directly behind Amtrak. $13 dorm, D-$30. A once famous motel, this friendly and fun hostel has free coffee, fruit and doughnuts for bfast. Runs an all-day tour to the Canyon, $29. Free use of bikes. Camper area out back $6 pp. Rsvs. 'Cheap, clean, friendly, but not the place for a good night's sleep—don't go if you're a light sleeper!' 'The best hostel I stayed in.' 'Looked after our rucksacks as we visited the Canyon.' 'Best night in America.' 'A real travellers' haven.'

Weatherford Hotel and Hostel (AYH), 23 N Leroux, 774-2731. Spacious rooms, bunk beds and funky furniture. Dorm beds $16, S-$30. Near Amtrak, buses. 'Lively area at night.' 'Excellent bar with good entertainment, English beer on draught.' Rsvs advisable. Free pick-up service from airport and bus station.

Western Hills, 1612 E Santa Fe Ave, 774-6633. S-$35, D-$47. Pool.

In Williams: try the **Red Lake Hostel**, Hwy 64, 635-9122. $11.

Camping: KOA Campground, 5803 N US 89, 526-9926, 6 miles NE of Flagstaff. Local buses stop nearby. Showers, free nightly movies. Tent sites 2 pp $17, cabins $29. XP-$4. For info on **campgrounds** and **backcountry camping** in the surrounding **Coconino National Forest**, call the **Coconino Forest Service**, 527-3600, Mon-Fri 7.30 am-4.30 pm. 'You'll need a car to reach the designated camping areas. Pick up a forest map ($6) at the **Flagstaff Visitors Center**.

FOOD

Alpine Pizza, 7 N Leroux, 779-4109, and 2400 E Rte 66, 779-4138. Praised for its Italian food. Popular spot for beer, pool and pizza. Daily 11 am-11 pm, Fri & Sat 'til midnight. Sun from noon.

Beaver St Brewery:, 11 S Beaver St, 779-0079. Fantastic menu and great beer. Dips and fondues and huge sandwiches. Daily 11.30 am 'til late!

Downtown Diner, 7 E Aspen, 774-3492. 'Excellent,' 'best value.' Daily 6 am-3 pm, Sun 8 am-2 pm.

Macy's, 14 S Beaver St, 774-2243 (behind Motel Du Beau). Hippy student hangout serves fresh pasta, veggie food, sandwiches, pastries and coffee. Sun-Wed 6 am-8 pm, Thurs-Sat 6 am-10 pm; food served 'til 7 pm.

Mary's Cafe, 7136 N Hwy 89, 526-0008. 24 hrs. 'Huge homemade cinnamon rolls.'

OF INTEREST

Flagstaff Festival of the Arts, NAU, 774-7750, (800) 266-7740. July through Aug. A variety of concerts (orchestral, chamber, pop, jazz), individual performers, dinner theatres and brunches.

The Festival of Native American Arts, Coconino Center for the Arts, Fort Valley Rd, 1 mile before Museum of Northern Arizona, Hwy 180, 779-6921. Free (donations accepted), Tues-Sat 10 am-5 pm. Contemporary art exhibits, dance, demonstrations, films, outdoor markets. In early June, the annual **Flagstaff Rodeo** comes to town with competitions, barn dances, a carnival, and the **Nackard Beverage** cocktail waitress race.

Near Flagstaff: Lowell Observatory, 1400 W Mars Hill Rd, 774-3358. Includes telescope through which Percivall Lowell 'discovered' canals on Mars; here also where Pluto was first sighted in 1930. Hands-on astronomy exhibits. 'Worth it if only for view over Flagstaff.' Daily 9 am-5 pm. Night sky viewings Mon-Wed and Fri-Sat 8 am, 8.45 am and 9.30 pm. Dec-Mar Mon-Sat 10 am-5 pm, Sun from noon; $2.50. Nearby **Mt Agassiz** has the area's best skiing. The **Arizona Snow Bowl**, 779-1951, daily 8 am-5 pm, operates its 30 trails from Dec to April.

Walnut Canyon, 10 miles E. Lush canyon filled with cliff-hanging ruins. The dayuse trail is strenuous in places (involving 240 steps over 185ft). Visitors' Center 7 am-6 pm daily, 526-3367. 'Wildlife and Indian relics, very worthwhile and not crowded.' Trail closes at 5 pm.

INFO/TRAVEL

Amtrak, 1 E Rte 66, (800) 872-7245. *Southwest Limited* btwn LA and Chicago stops here. USA Rail Pass holders can use shuttle bus to Canyon, free, otherwise $12. Leaves at 7.50 am but get there earlier. (Get a r/t ticket; no ticket office in Canyon).

Greyhound, 399 S Malpais Lane (across from NAU campus), (800) 231-2222. Open 24 hrs.

Peace Surplus camping equipment rental, 14 W Rte 66, 779-4521, 1 block from Grand Canyon Hostel. Daily tent, packs and stoves rental, plus a good stock of cheap outdoor gear. Mon-Fri 8 am-9 pm, Sat 8 am-8 pm, Sun 8 am-6 pm.

Pine Country Transit buses, 970 W Rte 66, 779-6624. Routes cover most of town; buses once every hour.

To get to Grand Canyon: NB: $4 entry fee.

Gray Line/Nava Hopi Tours, 114 W Rte 66, (800) 892-8687. Use caution in this area at night. Shuttle buses to the Grand Canyon (2 daily, $25 r/t) and Phoenix (3 daily, $43 r/t). Call for exact times.

Lloyd Taylor Tours, 526-2501. Full-day tours with very knowledgable driver offering flexible day-trips with plenty of freedom at destinations! Tours to various points in Arizona: $40 to Canyon, $25 w/student ID, Lake Powell, Petrified Forest, Indian Reservation and Sunset Crater. Free pick-up from downtown. 'If using a Delta pass, we suggest you fly to Flagstaff rather than Canyon airport. Difficult to get on the small commuter planes. Hire a car from Flagstaff, or hitch!' Hitching: reported as 'easy' to and from the Canyon. 'Just as quick as the bus trip.' Elsewhere, best to rent a car.

Budget Car Rentals, 100 N Humphreys St, 774-2763. Within walking distance of the hostels. Daily 7 am-9 pm. 'Push for a BUNAC student discount.' 'Probably the best way to see the Canyon, if you can round up three other people to split the cost.'

OAK CREEK CANYON and SEDONA   Going down Hwy 89A from Flagstaff, the road makes a switchback descent into this brilliantly tinted canyon carved by Oak Creek. From the **Oak Creek natural area**, a footpath takes you along the floor, through a dense growth of pines, cypresses and junipers, crossing repeatedly the swift-running brook. After the 16-mile descent you come to **Sedona**, a pretty artists' colony and setting for many of Zane Grey's Western novels. Take Hwy 179, south of Sedona, and the landscape opens up into striking vistas punctuated by mesas and serrated sandstone cliffs of red, pink, ochre and buff. Spend some time at the Frank Lloyd Wright Church of the Holy Cross, a stunning concrete shadowbox set against rust-coloured cliffs. The view from inside is nearly as moving, often accompanied by Gregorian chants.

ACCOMMODATION

The **Sedona Chamber of Commerce**, Forest Rd and Rte 89A, 282-7722. Distributes listings for accommodations and private campgrounds in the area. Mon-Sat 8.30 am-5 pm, Sun 9 am-3 pm. Both the **Star Motel**, 295 Jordan Rd (282-3641) and **La Vista**, 500 N Rte 89A (282-0000), can lodge you in comfy rooms with TV, S-$55-$60, D-$65-80.

Camping: There are a number of campgrounds within **Coconino National Forest**, 527-3600, along Oak Creek Canyon on US 89A (sites $10 p/vehicle). The largest, **Cave Springs**, 634-2859, 20 miles N of Sedona is a busy campground, administering 78 sites (for rsvs call 800-283-CAMP). $8 for unreserved sites so get there early. For more info on **Coconino**, call the ranger station, 250 Brewer Rd, 282-4119. Free **backcountry camping** is allowed in the forest, anywhere outside of Oak Creek and more than 1 mile from any official campground.

OF INTEREST

Sedona Arts Center, N on US 89A, Art Barn Rd, 282-3809. Free. Centre of the performing as well as visual arts. Touring exhibitions which change every 5 weeks; very diverse media and subject matter. Daily 10 am-4.30 pm. NB: Sedona is itself a centre for contemporary and traditional arts; galleries located throughout the city.
Slide Rock Park, 282-3034. 10 miles N of Sedona on US 89A. Takes its name from a natural stone slide into the waters of Oak Creek. Daily in summer 8 am-7 pm; closes earlier off season. $5 car, $1 pedestrian/cyclist.
Red Rock State Park, 282-6907, 15 miles SW of town on US 89A. Rangers lead dayhikers into the nearby red rocks, including nature and bird walks. Park open daily 8 am-6 pm (summer); Oct-April 'til 5 pm. $5 p/car, $2 p/pedestrian/cyclist.

INFORMATION

Sedona-Oak Creek Canyon Chamber of Commerce, 331 Forest Rd, 282-7722. Mon-Sat 8.30 am-5 pm, Sun 9 am-3 pm.

MONTEZUMA CASTLE NATIONAL MONUMENT Further south on

I-17 is **Tuzigoot National Monument**, a pueblo ruin atop a mesa overlooking the Verde River. But for a better example, cut across to Hwy 279 for **Montezuma Castle** (AD100-1400), far more picturesque and intact. Neither a castle nor connected with Montezuma, this was a cliff dwelling inhabited by Sinagua farmers. Visitors view the 'castle' from a paved path below. Daily 8 am-7 pm' $2. 'Ask at visitors centre for directions to Clear Creek campground. Friendly owners. You can swim in the nine-foot pool formed by the stream nearby.'

PETRIFIED FOREST NATIONAL PARK This 94,000-acre park actually

contains the varicoloured buttes and badlands of the **Painted Desert** as well as Indian petroglyphs at **Newspaper Rock**, pueblo ruins, two museums and a large 'forest' of felled and petrified logs. The trees date back to the Triassic period and were probably brought here by a flood, covered with mud and volcanic ash, preserved by silica quartz and laid bare once again by erosion. Most of the fossilised remains are jasper, agate, a few of clear quartz and amethyst. Like the red, yellow, blue and umber tones of the Painted Desert, these vivid colours are caused by mineral impurities. An excellent road bisects the park north to south. The park is open daily 7 am-7 pm; $5 p/vehicle, $3 p/pedestrian. **The Rainbow Forest** museum-restaurant, 524-6228, at the north end contains murals by noted Hopi artists, and serves as a visitors centre, open daily 8 am-7 pm, off-season 8 am-5 pm. Check out *www.wmonline.com/attract/pforest/pforest.htm* for hints on touring Petrified Forest National Park.

ACCOMMODATION

No lodging in the park. However, lodging is available in **Holbrook**, 27 miles from the museum, or **Gallup, NM** but prices are not always cheap. Budgeteers should return to Flagstaff. **Also: Brad's Motel**, 301 W Hopi Dr, **Holbrook** (3 blocks from Greyhound), 524-6929. S-$18, D-$26. **Camping:** There are no established campgrounds in the park, but free **backcountry camping** is allowed in several areas (hikers only) with a permit from the museum.

TRAVEL

There is no public transportation to either part of the park. **Nava-Hopi Bus Lines, Gray Line Tours,** and **Blue Goose Backpacker Tours** offer services from Flagstaff. Also: Greyhound operates along I-40 to Holbrook.

NAVAJO and HOPI RESERVATIONS The **Navajo** nation occupies the northeast corner of Arizona (plus parts of Utah and New Mexico), an area the size of West Virginia. On it dwell a shy, dignified, beauty-loving people, the largest and most cohesive of all Native American groups. Nearly all Navajos are fluent in their native tongue, a language of such complexity that Japanese cryptographers were unable to decipher it during the Second World War, when the US military used Navajos to send secret information. Originally a nomadic culture, the flexible Navajos adopted sheepherding and horses from the Spanish, weaving and sandpainting from the Pueblo Indians, and more recently such things as pickup trucks from the whites. The reservation, while poor, is a fascinating mix of traditional hogans and wooden frame houses, uranium mines and trading posts, all in a setting of agriculturally marginal but scenically rich terrain, anchored by the four sacred peaks of Mounts Blanca, Taylor, Humphrey and Hesperus.

Amidst the 150,000 Navajos is an arrowhead-shaped nugget of land upon which sit the three mesas of the **Hopis**, a strenuously peaceful and traditional tribe of farmers and villagers. The 6500 Hopis have planted corn and ignored Spaniards, Navajos and Anglos alike for nearly a thousand years, their religion and culture still poetically and distinctly non-Western.

Rte 264 crosses both reservations, allowing you access to the Hopi mesa villages and the Navajo settlements and capital at **Window Rock** on the Arizona-New Mexico border. Neither group is particularly forthcoming with whites, but you can bridge their suspicion by respecting their strong feelings about photographs, alcohol, tape recorders and local customs. Always ask permission to take pictures; if you are allowed, expect to pay for it and live up to your bargain. If you are lucky enough to witness dancing or healing ceremonies, behave as the Indians do to avoid giving offence.

Oraibi on the Third Mesa vies with the Pueblo Indians' Acoma as the oldest continuously inhabited settlement in the US. To enter the village, you must ask permission of the chief and pay a fee—absolutely no cameras, however. One of the most intriguing Hopi villages is **Walpi**, high atop the narrow tip of the Second Mesa. Dating from the 17th century, this classic adobe village of kivas and sculptured houses remains startlingly alien. 'Hire a four-wheel drive to get up very steep roads, dirt tracks.'

Monument Valley, scene of countless John Ford films and full of Navajo sacred places, sprawls across Arizona-Utah state lines and can be reached via Hwys 160 and 163 from the south. Perhaps easier is the access from the Utah side. Page, Arizona (also site of Lake Powell and its 90 flooded canyons) makes a good base for Monument Valley exploration. A car is almost a necessity, both here and elsewhere on the reservations. There is some bus service via Nava-Hopi from Window Rock to Tuba City, which stops at Kearns Canyon in Hopiland.

Besides looking at the masterful rugs, pottery, jewellery and other crafts, be sure to sample Indian food. Navajo specialties include fried bread, mutton stew and roast prairie dog. Interesting Hopi dishes are *nakquivi* or hominy stew and the beautiful blue cornmeal bread served with canteloupe for breakfast. The Hopi Cultural Center has accommodation, $55 pp, XP-$5 (rsvs recommended), and also a restaurant serving traditional Hopi food, 734-2401, on Rte 264; 7 am-9 pm daily. Read up on the Navajo and Hopi Nations through *www.infomagic.com/~natvrds/chapter.html*

ACCOMMODATION

Discover Navajoland, available from the **Navajoland Tourism Department**, PO Box 663, Window Rock 86515, 871-6426. Has a full list of accommodations, and jeep and horseback tours. Also, *The Visitors' Guide to the Navajo Nation*, $3, includes a detailed map. Mon-Fri 8 am-5 pm. Plan to camp at the national monuments or the Navajo campgrounds. Alternatively, you can make your visit a hard-driving day trip from Flagstaff or Gallup.

Greyhills Inn, 160 Warrior Dv, Tuba City, 283-6271. On a Navajo reservation; near Pature Canyon and several dinosaur tracks. 'Easy access' to Grand Canyon. $18 dorm (AYH), D-$50. Check-in 24 hrs. Tennis courts. Rsvs advisable.

CANYON DE CHELLY NATIONAL MONUMENT Surrounded by

Navajo land, Canyon de Chelly (about 30 miles N of Hwy 264 and pronounced 'Canyon de *Shay*') has the powerful beauty of a bygone Garden of Eden. Occupied successively by the Basket Makers, the Hopis and the Navajos, the canyon was just one of the targets in the 1863 US Army campaign to subdue or annihilate the Navajos. Kit Carson and his men eventually overwhelmed the stronghold at Canyon de Chelly, killing livestock and Indians, destroying hogans and gardens, even cutting down the treasured peach trees, a move which shattered the Navajos. Canyon de Chelly is again inhabited by Navajos, who live among 800-year-old pueblo buildings. Both are upstaged by the fantastic walls of the canyon itself, 1000 ft of sheer orange verticality.

A road runs along the rim with several lookouts to view **White House Ruin** and **Spider Rock**. The only descent you're allowed to navigate solo is the White House Trail; all others require a Navajo guide. The 1¼ mile trail to **White House Ruin** winds down a 400-ft face through an orchard and across a stream. The park service offers 3-4 hr tours three times per day during the summer, $10, or you can hire a private guide (minimum 3 hr, $10 p/hr). Rsvs recommended through visitors centre. Must provide your own four-wheel-drive vehicle and acquire a free permit from the visitors centre.

ACCOMMODATION

There is no budget accommodation anywhere in Navajo territory. **Farmington, NM**, and **Cortez, CO**, are the closest major cities with cheap lodging. **Free camping**: camp for free in the park's **Cottonwood Campground**, 1½ miles from visitors center, 674-5500. Facilities include restrooms, picnic tables, water and dump station

INFORMATION

Visitors Center, near Chinle, 674-5500. Daily 8 am-6 pm ('til 5 pm, winter). Although a National Monument, Canyon de Chelly is on Navajo land and is therefore subject to certain restrictions designed to limit intrusion into Navajo privacy.

TRAVEL

No public transport to either the monument or Chinle. Inside the monument, jeeps tour (six or more passengers) the canyon floor for a good look at ruins and pictographs, $31 p/p half day, $50 p/p full day (includes lunch), through Thunderbird Lodge, 674-5841 (rsvs recommended in summer).

Justin's Horse Rental, on South Rim Dr at mouth of the Canyon, 674-5678. $8 p/hr ride along the canyon floor; $8 for obligatory guide. 'My best experience in America—just like in the movies!'

SUNSET CRATER and WUPATKI NATIONAL MONUMENTS Hwy 180, the most direct route from Flagstaff to the Grand Canyon, is also the dullest. A better choice is to travel US 89 past Sunset Crater and Wupatki, turning off for the Canyon at Cameron.

Long a volcanic region, **Sunset Crater** erupted most recently about AD 1064, leaving a colourful cone on a jet black lava field. The crater rim makes an interesting hike although trips into the crater are no longer allowed. From the rim, over 50 volcanic peaks, including the San Franciscos, can be seen. Also: lava tubes to explore, although lava tube tours have been permanently discontinued due to falling lava. The self-guided **Lava Flow Nature Trail** wanders 1 mile through the surreal landscape surrounding the cone, 1¹/₂ miles E of visitors center. The volcanic ash from Sunset made good fertiliser, and a number of Indian groups built pueblos nearby at **Wupatki**. There are over 800 ruins on mesa tops, a ball court, dance arena, and a museum to interpret the finds at this long since abandoned settlement. $4 per car, $2 by foot, includes entry to both monuments, 8 am-dusk.

Before travelling, check out some amazing aerial views of Sunset Crater and useful links for further research, by clicking on *www.geo.arizona.edu/ Geo256/azgeology/sunsetcrater.html*.
Sunset Crater Volcano National Monument's Visitors Center, 15 miles N of Flagstaff on Hwy 89, 556-7042. Daily 8 am-5 pm. **Camping: Bonito Campground**, in the Coconino National Forest at the entrance to Sunset Crater, provides the nearest camping. Rents 44 sites, $8. Call 527-3600.

THE GRAND CANYON According to legend a Texas cowboy riding across the Arizona desert came to the edge of the Grand Canyon unprepared for what he would see, 'Good God,' he exclaimed, 'something happened here.'

This astonishment is probably repeated daily. Approached from a flat, sloping plain on all sides, the Grand Canyon is a startlingly abrupt gash. Wind, frost and the Colorado River have gnawed a magnificent, 217-mile-long canyon from the landscape, filled with 270 animal species and containing four of the seven known life zones. To the visitor on the rim, the colourful buttes amid early-morning mist appear as a dreamlike valley of palaces. The proportions of the 1-mile-deep canyon are deceptive; most people find it difficult to believe that it is never less than 4 times wider than it is deep. The cross-sectional prospect from **Grandview Point** helps set matters straight.

The Grand Canyon has 3 parts: the **South Rim**, open year-round, access via Hwy 64/180 from Williams and Flagstaff; the **North Rim**, open mid-May to mid-Oct, access via Hwy 67 from Jacob Lake; and the **Inner Canyon**, open year-round, access from the rim by foot, mule or boat only. To get from the North to the South Rim or vice-versa is 215 miles by car or an arduous 20-mile hike down and up. If you're not able to take your time in the park, you should choose early on which rim you want to visit.

The South Rim is easy to reach and has the best views as well as the lion's share of the lodgings and amenities. The North Rim boasts cooler temperatures, special autumn colours, an abundance of animal life and uncrowded serenity (a quarter-million tourists per year here versus 3 million on the south side).

If you're at all fit, you'll want to hike to the **canyon floor**, or at least part of the way. If you make it to the bottom, don't forget to touch an outcropping of black Vishnu Schist; this metamorphic rock, the lowest layer in the canyon, was formed when the Earth was half the age it is now. 'Hard work, but an awesome and breath-taking spectacle.' 'Do read the hiking tips under *Of Interest* before setting out; the heat, the stiff 4500 foot climb, the high altitude of the entire area and the need to carry large amounts of water are all factors you must prepare for.' 'No 2-D picture could ever do justice to this scene of nature at her most imposing form. Even if you have to go to great lengths to get here, that first sight of the canyon ... you'll have no regrets.'

Park entrance fee is $10 per car. It's $4 for someone on foot or on a bus! You will come across a wealth of info through any browser, but *www.kaibab.org* is a worthwhile site to explore for its virtual photo footage.

ACCOMMODATION

Most accommodations on the South Rim are very expensive. You are recommended to make reservations for lodging, campsites or mules well in advance—prepare to battle the crowds! Brisk weather and fewer tourists in winter, but most hotels and facilities close. TIP: Check at the visitors centre and the Bright Angel transportation desk after 4 pm for vacancies.

South Rim: Grand Canyon Lodges, 638-2631, books accommodation for 7 lodges and hotels within or near the park (book 6-9 months in advance). Prices start at $37 room w/out bath, $43 w/toilet, $53 full bath. **Bright Angel Lodge and Cabins** is usually the least expensive. **Maswik** and **Original** and **New Yavapai** are also reasonable. Book well ahead, even after Labor Day. Also! Try **Downtowner/Grand Canyon International Hostel**, 19 S San Francisco St, Flagstaff, 779-9421. **Camping: Mather Campground**, MISTIX (800) 365-2267, Grand Canyon Village, is open year-round, $10 a site; 7-day max stay. 'Always places reserved for people without own transport.' NB: Tent not needed in June and early July; later in summer, monsoons deluge the area. Campsites fill quickly June through Sept, so get there *very* early (ie. before 9 am). Other campsites on the south side at **Trailer Village** in Grand Village by entrance of park, 638-2631, 2 pp $18, XP-$1.50. Campground overflow generally winds up in the **Kaibab National Forest**, along the south border of the park, where you can pull off a dirt road and camp for free. OK as long as you remain within ½ mile of public telephone.' For more info, contact the **Tusayan Ranger District**, Kaibab National Forest, PO Box 3088, Grand Canyon 86023 (638-2443). Any overnight hiking or camping within the park requires a free **Backcountry Use Permit**, which is available at the **Backcountry Office** (638-7875), ½ mile S of the visitors centre.

Down the Canyon: Free camping at one of the 4 hike-in sites requires both an overnight wilderness permit and a trailhead or campground reservation. 'As soon as you arrive, go to the Backcountry Office by 7 am for a chance at unclaimed permits.' Keep in mind that there's a heavy fine for those caught camping without a permit.

Phantom Ranch, on canyon floor, 638-2401. Rustic cabins: D-$59; dorms $22. Booked up *long* in advance. 'Air conditioned, very comfortable.' NB: Anything you buy down here is bound to be expensive, and that includes food. Leave excess luggage on the rim for a fee.

North Rim: Grand Canyon Lodge, 638-2611. Late May to mid-Oct only. Cheapest are **Pioneer Cabins**, Q-$72. **Western Cabins** are D-$82, Q-$92, but have more comfort and unbelievable views. Can also reserve in Cedar City, UT for Bryce Canyon, (801) 586-7686. Campsite rsvs and trail info at Lodge, but no place to check luggage.

North Rim Campground, 638-2251, $10 per site. NB: Often necessary to camp outside park on National Forest land the night before, arriving at North Rim early am to nab site. Rsvs through MISTIX (800) 365-2267.

Outside park to the north: Jacob Lake Inn, 44 miles N, 643-7232. Open year-round: cabins: S/D-$59-$90. See also under 'Utah' for hostel accommodation at **Kanab**.

FOOD

Expensive and generally poor everywhere in the park, even at cafeterias, although it is possible to find meals for fast-food prices. **Best bets: South Rim: Babbitt's General Store**, 638-2262, (across from Visitors Center). Has a deli counter and reasonably priced super market. Stock up on trail mix, water and gear. Daily 8 am-8 pm; deli 8 am-7 pm.

Bright Angel Dining Room, in Bright Angel Lodge, 638-2631. Check out their hot sandwiches and specials. Daily 6.30 am-10 pm. Also! The soda fountain here chills 16 flavours of ice cream, daily 6 am-8 pm.

North Rim: The Grand Canyon Lodge, 638-2611. The restaurant serves dinners from $8 (rsvs only) and bfast $3-7. Sandwiches at buffeteria $2.50. There is also a bar and a jukebox at **The Tea Room** within the lodge, daily 11 am-10 pm. Dining room, daily 6.30 am-10 am, 11.30 am-2.30 pm, 5 pm-9.30 pm. Also, try **Jacob Lake Inn** for snacks, great milkshakes and $5 lunch dishes. Daily 6 am-9 pm.

OF INTEREST

Tips: Whether you descend the canyon or not, guard against heat exhaustion and dehydration by drinking the park-recommended juice mixture. Water alone will not satisfy your body's requirements, as the rangers will tell you. Other hiking tips: wear a hat, don't wear sandals, always check beforehand to make sure your trail is open. For hiking into the Canyon, plan to carry 4 litres of water per person per day. Also carry food, permit, pocket knife, signal mirror, flashlight, maps, matches and first-aid kit. Calculate 2 hrs up for every hr going down. (If you do get lost or injured, stay on the trail so they can find you.) The park service warns against hiking to the Colorado River and back in one day. Readers add: 'Do take notice of time estimates.' If you plan to camp at the bottom, you need a minimum of equipment—it reaches 100 degrees in summer.' Hardly worth the effort to carry tent.' A final recommendation: 'When camping at the bottom, start the ascent at 3 am, escaping the midday heat, seeing sunrise over the Canyon, and catching the 9 am bus back to Flagstaff.'

Along the South Rim: The most remarkable views are from Hopi, Yaki, Grand View and Desert Views points. A 9 mile trail from Yavapai Museum to Hermit's Rest follows the very edge of the Canyon. Pick up relevant leaflets from the visitors centres before setting out. The South Rim is also the starting point for the South Kaibab and Bright Angel Trails to descend into the canyon.

Bright Angel Trail has water at 3 points (May-Sept only) and is 8 miles to the river. 'A good one-day hike—Bright Angel to Plateau Point and back, 12 miles. Great scenery.' 'Try to leave yourself 8 hrs for comfort.' 'Water is essential.' **South Kaibab Trail** is 6 miles down, no campgrounds, no water and little shade: don't attempt in summer. 'Colorado River is nice to paddle in—too strong for anything else.'

From the North Rim: The North Kaibab Trail is 14 miles with water at 4 points. A good day hike would be to Roaring Springs and back, about 68 hrs. The entire Kaibab Trail is 21 miles and connects North and South Rims. Views from the North Rim include Cape Royal (nature talks in summer), Angel's Window, overlooking the Colorado River, and the much-photographed Shiva's Temple, a ruddy promontory of great beauty.

Grand Canyon Caverns, on Rte 66 in Seligman, 422-3223. Descend 21 storeys into the welcome 56-degree caves of coloured minerals, by elevator. 45 min tours, daily 8 am-6 pm, $7.50. For a special experience that few park visitors get to enjoy, hike in to **Havasupai Falls** from the Havasupai Indian Reservation adjacent to the park on the southwest side. The heavy calcium content of Havasu Creek has resulted in coral-like circular deposits that form a stairstep sequence of turquoise pools. Bathers can catch impromptu rides where the water bubbles over the top (watch out—the 'coral' is sharp!). A trail follows the creek downstream to the Colorado River. Ask around for directions, or call the Havasupai (whose land the creek is on) at 448-2121. You will have to be persistent calling this number, but it's worth it.

Ranger programmes, 638-7888, are highly recommended; they conduct guided hikes, do evening slide shows, etc. In winter, programmes are inside the Shrine of Ages building. Also recommended: the sunrise and sunset photo walks by the Kodak rep. Check at visitor centre for current topic.

Mule Rides into the Canyon: from South and North Rims (summer only). Outrageously popular and booked up for 6 months in advance, but many no-shows so try anyway. 7 hr trips $80 pp includes lunch, and overnight trips, $252 with 3 meals, cabin accommodation. The following restrictions apply: you can't be pregnant or handicapped or weigh more than 200 pounds, and you must be at least 4'7" tall, speak fluent English (the mules don't like people who talk funny), and not to be afraid of heights. To reserve, write to PO Box 699, Reservation Dept, South Rim, Grand Canyon National Park, AZ 86023, or call (303) 297 2757/for the North Rim call (801) 679-8665. Guaranteed rsvs require prepayment. For **whitewater boat trips** down the Colorado, the park office has list of companies. Rewarding trip but costs around $100 a day. **Air tours** depart from LA, Las Vegas, Phoenix, Flagstaff and Williams. Dozens of small companies offer tours; by day the sky above the canyon is filled with buzzing planes (much to the disgust of environmental groups and visitors who value serenity). Check Chambers of Commerce and *Yellow Pages* in those cities under Airline Tours. At the park, call 638-2407 to reserve a seat; $55 for 45 mins in an airplane. Helicopter tours, 638-2419, cost $90 for 30 mins, higher for longer tours. Copters and planes once flew below canyon rim, but this practice was banned after a 1986 crash in the canyon.

INFORMATION

South Rim: Equipment Rental from **Babbit's General Store**, 638-2262/2234, in Mather Center, Grand Canyon Village and Visitors Centre. Rents hiking boots (socks included), sleeping bags, tents etc. Deposits required on all items. Daily 8 am-8 pm.

Visitors Center, 6 miles N of the South entrance station, 638-7888. Daily 8 am-6 pm, off season 'til 5 pm. Ask for the free and informative *Trip Planner*.

Weather and Road Conditions, call 638-7888.

North Rim: National Park Service Information Desk, in the lobby of Grand Canyon Lodge, 638-7864. Info on North Rim viewpoints, facilities and some trails. Daily 8 am-8 pm.

TRAVEL

Transportation Information Desk: In **Bright Angel Lodge**, 638-2631. Rsvs for mule rides, bus tours, Phantom Ranch, taxis, backcountry camping etc. Daily 6 am-7 pm. For **bus service** to the South Rim, call **Nava-Hopi Bus Lines**, (800) 892-8687. Times vary by season, so call ahead. To and from the North Rim, call Gray Line in Flagstaff, Phoenix, Las Vegas and other large cities. Surprisingly reasonable tours. Also, **Transcanyon**, 638-2820, run buses to South Rim departing 7 am, arriving 11.30 am; returning 1.30 pm, arriving 6.30 pm. Call for rsvs. Open late May-Oct.

Hitching: 'Save your money by walking 3 miles out of Flagstaff and hitching. Will get a ride easily.' 'Hitching to North Rim is OK—we did it in less than 24 hrs from Zion in Sept.'

Within the Canyon: Bus tours from Bright Angel Lodge called 'a waste of money.' However, a **free shuttle bus** rides the West Rim Loop (daily 7.30 am-sunset) and the Village Loop (daily 6.30 am-10.30 pm) every 15 mins. A $3 **hiker's shuttle** runs every 15 mins btwn Grand Canyon village and South Kaibab Trailhead near Yalci Point.

LAKE HAVASU CITY If you wanted to hide London Bridge where no one would ever think of looking for it, where would you put it? That's right—in the middle of a big, fat desert! Specifically, at Lake Havasu City, spanning the Colorado river (at least the bridge isn't going to waste). A charmingly ersatz Tudor Village and double-decker bus, fast food restaurants make this a must for the discerning British visitor. Hwy 95 south to Parker traverses a beautiful stretch of scenery; if you continue all the way to **Quartsite**, you can visit the **Hi Jolly Monument**, a tribute to the Middle Easterner who tried to introduce camels to *this* desert, too. Chamber of Commerce, 1930 Mesquite Ave, suite #3, 855-4115, can direct you. Mon-Fri 8 am-5 pm. Free guided **Desert Walks**; contact John Kany, 855-7055. Recreationally, the city's lake is described as 'a lake to rent,' as all types of **water sports** are available here from paddle boats to jet-skiing and 'wave-runners.'

NEW MEXICO *Land of Enchantment*

Travel industry hyperbole aside, New Mexico *does* enchant. It possesses a dramatic landscape heightened by the scalpel-sharp clarity of the desert air; natural wonders like the Navajo's Shiprock and the Carlsbad Caverns; and the finest array of Indian cultures, past and present, in the country. In human terms, New Mexico is incredibly ancient, having been inhabited for over 25,000 years. More significantly, it is the only state that has succeeded in fusing its venerable Spanish, Indian and Anglo influences into a harmonious and singular pattern. You will notice the benign borrowings everywhere, from sensuous adobes tastefully outfitted with solar heating to the distinctive New Mexican cuisine, currently very chic.

New Mexico inspires awe for more than its beauty. On 16 July 1945, at the appropriately named Jornada del Muerto (Journey of the Dead) Desert, the world's first atomic bomb belched its radioactive mushroom into the air. (Physicist Enrico Fermi reportedly took bets on the chances that the test would blow up the state.) Today, the state is a leader in atomic research, testing, uranium mining and related fields. Blithe as locals may be about nuclear materials (the Alamogordo Chamber of Commerce still sponsors a twice-annual outing to Ground Zero the 1st Saturdays in April and October), think twice before visiting the Alamogordo-White Sands region. Your genes may thank you some day. Instead, concentrate on the fascinating and diverse Indian populations: the 19 pueblo villages, each with its own pottery, dance, arts and style; the Navajos, whose capital is at Window Rock; and the Jicarilla and Mescalero Apaches, noted for dancing and coming of age ceremonies. Celebrations open to the public are so numerous that you could plan an itinerary around them. *Viva New Mexico!* at *www.viva.com/* provides interesting information about New Mexico's writers and artists and how to buy Indian jewelry and pottery, etc.

National Park: Carlsbad Caverns.

The telephone area code for the entire state is 505.

ALBUQUERQUE   Named for a ducal viceroy of Mexico, and where Bugs Bunny didn't turn left, Albuquerque is not as pleasing as its euphonious name would lead you to believe. The state's largest city, Albuquerque contains one-quarter of the state's 1.7 million residents and although it has rather more of the state's trash features, from tacky motels to urban sprawl, it has a youthful feeling due in part to the large student population.

However, the setting and the scenery are spectacular and Albuquerque does make a good base for day trips to the Indian pueblos and to the Sandia Mountains. The best times to visit are during the June Arts and Crafts Fair, the September State Fair (the largest in the US), the October Hot-Air Balloon Fiesta and at Christmas, when city dwellings are outlined with thousands of *luminarias* (candles imbedded in sand, their light diffused by paper). For hints on what to see and do, go to *www.usacitylink.com//albuquer/default.html*

ACCOMMODATION
Central Ave is the northsouth divider; railroad tracks divide eastwest. 'Cheap hotels on Central SE. Walk to the other side of railroad, right side of Greyhound terminal to Central SE, then straight ahead.' 'Use caution; many are dangerous.'

Grand Western Motor Hotel, 918 Central SW, downtown, 243-1773. S-$32, D-$40, XP-$5. 'Very friendly and clean, but not in good side of town.'

Monterey Motel, 2402 Central SW, 243-3554. S-$42, D-$48, XP-$5. 'Small; friendly, helpful people.'

Route 66 (AAIH) Hostel, 1012 Central Ave SW, 247-1813. Beautiful, newly renovated private rooms. S-$16, D-$26, $5 key deposit, $1 linen. 'Friendly, no curfew.' Full kitchen. Free coffee, tea, snacks and cereal. Must help out with chores! Other hostel, **Oscuro**, call 648-4007, located on a ranch.

Sandia Mountain AAIH Hostel, 12234 Hwy 14 N in **Cedar Crest**, 20 miles E of Albuquerque (3¹/₂ miles N of I-40 on New Mexico Hwy N), 281-4117. $10. Kitchen, laundry and ping-pong!

Stardust Inn, 817 Central NE, 243-1321. S-$40, D-$52, XP-$3.

University Lodge, 3711 Central Ave NE, 266-7663. Has basic motel rooms and motel pool. S-$21, D-$29 (summer), $25, D-$32 (winter).

Camping: Albuquerque North KOA (off I-25), 867-5227. Tent sites $20, $25 for two. Rsvs required beginning of Oct (hot air balloon festival).

Coronado State Park Campground (Rte 44), 867-5589. Full hook-up $11, toilets, showers, drinking water. 1 week max stay, no rsvs.

FOOD
Check out the inexpensive eateries around the University of New Mexico.

Capo's Ristorante Italiano, 722 Lomas NW, 242-2007. Inexpensive, attractive place with good Italian food for $10 and less. Mon-Thurs 11 am-8.45 pm, Fri & Sat 'til 9.45 pm.

Jack's, 3107 Eubank NE, 296-8601, daily 7 am-2 pm, $2-$5; and **Rick's Kitchen**, 3600 Osuria NE, 344-4446. Homemade soups, salads, quiche, crepes; $5 lunch. Daily 7 am-2.30 pm, Sun 8 am-2 pm.

M & J Sanitary Tortilla Factory, 403 2nd SW, 242-4890. Neighbourhood chili parlour; excellent Mexican food, written up in the *New Yorker*; interesting art by locals on walls. Mon-Sat 9 am-4 pm.

Double Rainbow, 3416 Central SE, 255-6633, is a bakery, coffee shop and ice cream store. Salads and sandwiches under $7. Daily 6.30 am 'til midnight.

OF INTEREST
Old Town, 1 block N of Central NW. Shops, restaurants and occasional live entertainment. The only nugget of Spanishness left in the city. 'Well worth a visit.' On

the plaza is the **1706 Church of San Felipe de Neri**.

Indian Pueblos, all over the state. Religious and other dances are held throughout the year. Dances, fiestas and ceremonials are sacred and special to the Pueblo Indians. Tape recording, photography, sketching or painting may not be permissible. Please call ahead to verify dates and to obtain permission to visit the various pueblos.

Albuquerque Museum, 2000 Mountain Rd NW, 243-7255. Permanent and changing exhibits on history of Albuquerque and southwest US. Tue-Sun 9 am-5 pm; accepts donations. Tours of sculpture garden Wed & Sat 10 am. Entrance includes walking tour of town.

Albuquerque Museum Tours of Historic Old Town, 243-7255. 1 hr walking tours from museum, Tues-Sun, 11 am.

Hot Air Balloon Fiesta, International Balloon Fiesta Field, off I-25, 293-6800. About 650 balloons from around the world assemble for 9 days in early Oct. High points are the mass ascensions on opening and closing w/ends: get there 6 am-7 am.

Indian Pueblo Cultural Center, 2401 12th St near I-40, 1 mile E of Old Town, 843-7270. Excellent exhibit and sales rooms by the 19 Pueblo Indian groups allow comparison of techniques and styles. High quality, prices to match. 'Only thing of interest in this town.' Daily 9 am-5 pm, $3, $1 w/student ID. Also **Indian Pueblo dance performances**, Sat & Sun, 11 am and 2 pm, May early Oct; free, cameras allowed. Restaurant on premises serves traditional pueblo food—give it a try; 7.30 am-3.30 pm.

Maxwell Museum of Anthropology, west end of campus btwn Grand & Las Lomas, 277-4405, has exhibits on anthropology of Southwest US. Mon-Fri 9 am-4 pm; Sat 10 am-4 pm, Sun noon-4 pm. Free (but donations on the door).

National Atomic Museum, Building 358, Wyoming Blvd SE at Kirtland AFB (1 mile inside base), 845-6670. Free, daily 9 am-5 pm. Disquieting look at selection of nuclear weapons casings, plus 'oops' items like the A-Bomb the US accidentally dropped on Palomares, Spain, in 1966. Regular screenings of *Ten Seconds that Shook the World*. If driving to the museum, you need to show a driving licence, proof of car ownership, and insurance papers in order to gain a visitor's pass.

New Mexico Museum of Natural History, 1801 Mountain Rd NW, 841-2800. Evolutionary history of New Mexico presented through new hi-tec Dynamax Theater showing 3D movies, and an 'Evolator time machine,' unique to the museum, taking you millions of years back through time. 'Fantastic. Don't miss your chance to stand inside an "active" volcano.' Daily 9 am-5 pm, $4, $3 w/student ID.

Petroglyph National Monument, 6900 Unser Blvd NW, 873-6620. Formerly the Petroglyph State Park, it became a National Monument late 1990. 9 am-6 pm daily in summer. Parking $1, $2 at w/ends.

Rattlesnake Museum, 202 San Felipe, 242-6569. Mon-Sat 10 am-6.30 pm, Sun 1 pm-6 pm. $2 for everyone over 3ft tall! Living and artefact snakes from all over America. Gift shop includes such delights as *Snakebite Salsa* and *Poison Perfume*!

Sandia Peak Aerial Tramway, NE of town, take Tramway Rd off I-25, 856-7325. At 2.7 miles, the world's longest tramway, climbing to 10,378ft. Fantastic panorama which sometimes includes hot air balloons and hang gliders in the area. Daily 9 am-9 pm. 1½ hr ride, $13; $10 Wed 5 pm-9 pm.

University of New Mexico, Central NE & University, 277-0111. Pioneer in pueblo revival architecture, has free exhibits, often on Indians, in the **Maxwell Museum**, 277-4404. **Fine Arts Museum** in Fine Arts Center, 277-4001, has sculptures, photography and paintings. Tue-Fri 9 am-4 pm (Tue also 5 pm-8 pm), Sun 1 pm-4 pm. Free.

Christmas: Convention and Visitors Bureau does free night time bus tours of the outstanding *luminaria* displays, a medieval Spanish custom which began as small bonfires lighting the way to the church for the Christ Child.

INFORMATION
Visitors Information Centers: Albuquerque Convention and Visitors Bureau, 121 Tijeras Ave NE, 243-3696 (main office), Mon-Fri 8 am-5 pm; Old Town Plaza, 303 Romero NW; Albuquerque International Airport. Daily 9 am-9 pm.

TRAVEL
Albuquerque International Airport, south of downtown, next to the airforce base. **Amtrak**, 214 1st St SW, (800) 872-7245. Daily 9.30 am-6 pm.
Greyhound, 300 2nd SW, (800) 231-2222. Clean, safe depot with all-night cafe.
Sun-Tran Transit, 601 Yale Blvd SE, 843-9200. The local city buses, basic fare 75¢, includes two free transfers. After bus hours or on Sun, call 883-4888 for a **taxi**, about $10.

CARLSBAD CAVERNS Eighth deepest and very possibly the most beautiful caves in the world, the Carlsbad Caverns began their stalagtite-spinning activities about 250 million years ago. In contrast, the famous Mexican freetail bat colony has been in residence a mere 17,000 years. Once numbering seven million, give or take a bat, the colony reduced to 250,000, due in part to increased use of insecticides, but is now back to the 1 million mark. It was the eerie sight of bats pouring like smoke from the cave openings that led to Carlsbad's discovery in 1901.

The caves became a National Park in 1930, but the big bucks locally came from the sale of 100,000 tons of prime bat shit ('guano' to the genteel) to California citrus growers. No, the bats don't drink blood—and few harbour rabies, but the superstitious *should* keep the throat and other parts covered while the little boogers are zooming overhead.

Oh yes, the caves. The cross-shaped **Big Room** is 1800 ft by 1100 ft; nearby you'll see a formation called **The Iceberg**, which takes half an hour to circle. The cave's sheer size is not as impressive as the variety of colours and formations and the intricate filigrees (8 percent of which are still living and growing) these caverns house. Don't touch the formations, much as you might like to; a number of them have been turned black by ignorant handling. Carlsbad Caverns National Park homepage, *www.nps.gov/cave/* is a helpful resource for info on facilities and opportunities, recommended activities and adjacent visitor attractions.

ACCOMMODATION
Advised to drive to Carlsbad for cheap motels.
Carlsbad Caverns AAIH Hostel at Whites City, NM 88268, 785-2291. Part of **Cavern Inn**, near the caverns in Whites City. $16 AYH, $5 key deposit, non-AYH not accepted. Pool. Private rooms are pricey, but the campground here is $16 for up to six people, XP-$3. 7 miles from the caverns. Mixed reports.
La Caverna Motel, 223 S Canal, 885-4151. S-$22, D-$24; $2 key deposit. **Motel 6**, 3824 National Parks Hwy, Carlsbad, 885-0011. S/D-$32. 24 miles from caves.
Camping: The Park Entrance Campground, 785-2991, provides water, restrooms, and pool. Tent sites $16 full hook-up, up to six people. Also, **backcountry camping** is free in the park; get a permit from visitors centre.

OF INTEREST
Carlsbad Caverns National Park, 785-2233, is open all year. **Cave tours: Natural Entrance Tour**, walk in through natural entrance, elevator out; 3 miles, about 2 hrs. Open summer, 8.30 am-2 pm. **Big Room Tour**, elevator in and out; 1$\frac{1}{4}$ miles, about 1 hr. Both tours have plaques to guide you along. Open summer, 8.30 am-3.30 pm.

'Get there early—after 2 pm, you'll have to take the shorter 1¼ mile trip (Big Room Tour). Still worth seeing.' 'Rangers will not let you descend into the caverns unless you are wearing sensible shoes; ie not thongs, sandals, or anything with heels.' 'Free nature walks around cavern entrance at 5 pm, something to do while waiting for bats.' (Try to plan your visit to the caves for the late afternoon in order to see the nightly bat flight). Carlsbad costs $5, guided tours available, $6 for **Slaughter Canyon Cave**, more rugged and only for those in good shape. Advance rsvs and a flashlight required. Tours available twice daily, $8. Temperature inside the cave is 56 degrees, refreshing in summer but bring a jacket.

Bat facts: bats are in residence spring through mid-Oct only and are at busiest May-Sept, just before sunset. They leave the cave at dusk to fly up to 120 miles, consume an aggregate five tons of insects, return at dawn to spend the day sleeping in cosy bat-fashion, 300 per sq ft. Call Visitors Center, 785-2233, (open 8 am-7 pm summer) for more bat-data. 'No one should miss the incredible sight of a million bats flying a few feet over one's head. Just like Dracula, in fact.'

Bataan Recreational Area, below Lake Carlsbad is for sail boating, canoeing, picnicking and fishing.

Lake Carlsbad & Beach, a three-mile spring-fed water playground with free swimming, boat ramp and docks, water skiing, picnic area, tables, fireplaces, fishing and amusement parks.

TRAVEL
Texas, New Mexico and Oklahoma Coaches(TNM&O), 887-1108, runs two buses daily to Whites City from El Paso.

Hitching: 'There's about a 15 min wait 7 miles from Caverns while changing bus. Try hitching. If successful, get ticket refund in El Paso.' 'If you hitchhike to Cavern, get in free with whomever gave you a lift.' 'For girls, not worth the risk.'

SANTA FE That rarity of rarities, Santa Fe is a city for walkers, full of narrow, adobe-lined streets that meander round its Spanish heart, the old plaza where the Santa Fe trail ends. Long a crossroads for trade routes and the oldest seat of government in the US, Santa Fe has witnessed a remarkable amount of history. But the age of the place doesn't prepare you for its beauty, the friendliness of its locals, the vitality of its artistic and cultural life. The town has a strict architecture policy that requires that all the buildings must be in 17th century pueblo style and painted in one of 23 varying shades of brown, all of which gives the place a pleasing unity. 'Disappointing—caters too much to rich American tourists.' While here visit **Los Alamos**, where the first A-Bomb was built, and the ghost town of **Madrid**. *Santa Fe Online*, can be reached at *www.sfol.com/sfol/sfol.html*

ACCOMMODATION
For the low-down on budget accomodations, call the **Santa Fe Detours Accomodations Hotline**, 986-0038.

Motel 6, 3007 Cerrillos Rd, 473-1380. From S/D-$48, XP-$4. Far from downtown on 'motel row'; other cheapies along Cerrillos, too.

Santa Fe International Hostel, 1412 Cerrillos Rd, 988-1153. $14 AYH, $17 non-AYH; from S/D-$25-33 for private room. 'Excellent hostel; no curfew; friendly people, full of information.' 'More than adequate facilities: cooking, showers, library.' Organises occasional tours in summer. Linen $2. Rsvs required in Aug.

Outlying areas: Circle A Ranch, Box 2142, **Cuba**, NM 87013, 289-3350. Adobe hacienda in Sante Fe National Forest, remote area but near hiking trails and swimming hole; NW of Sante Fe. Rsvs strongly advised. Open May-Oct. Bunks: $10, D-$25-$40. 'Lovely adobe ranch, friendly people—felt part of the family.' The hostel is

40 miles from **Chaco Culture National Historic Park**, a massive 11th-century ruin, its largest pueblo containing 800 rooms and 39 kivas (sacred chambers). Contemporary with Mesa Verde, possibly more remarkable and certainly less visited.

Camping: Apache Canyon KOA, 11 miles SE of Santa Fe on I-25, exit 294, 982-1419. Free movies, showers, restrooms, store, laundry, rec room. $16, D-$26.95, XP-$2; stay 6 days, 7th free. Also, **Santa Fe KOA**, 466-1419. Full hook-up $21, Mar-Oct.

Black Canyon Campground, 8 miles NE of Santa Fe on Rte 475, $6 for tent site.

Camel Rock, 10 miles N of Santa Fe on Hwy 285, 455-2661. D-$16, XP-$2. 'Clean facilities, very cold at night in Sept.'

Santa Fe National Forest, 988-6940, has campsites and free backcountry camping in the beautiful Sangre de Cristo Mountains.

FOOD

Santa Fe is the home of southwestern cooking, a current favourite of American palates, and is based on humble indigenous ingredients—beans, corn and chilies, in imaginative combinations with other foods. Sample a bowl of *posole*, the hominy-based stew served with spicy pork that New Mexicans love. If you have a strong stomach and Teflon tastebuds, try the green chili stew. Prepare your mouth for a re-run of the Mt St Helens explosion.

Burrito Company, 111 Washington Ave, 982-4453. 'Tasty; not too chili-infested Mexican food at cheap prices. Varied clientele—many artists.' Mon-Sat 7.30 am-7 pm, Sun 10 am-5 pm. Nothing over $5! Cheap!

Josie's, 225 E Marcy, 983-5311. 'Very generous helpings of well-cooked Mexican food, $4-10, popular with locals.' Mouth-watering desserts. Mon-Fri 11 am-3 pm.

The Shed, 113½ E Palace in *circa* 1692 adobe, 982-9030. Good New Mexican lunches, crowded. Order their blue corn enchiladas and lemon souffle. Lunch Mon-Sat 11 am-2.30 pm; dinner Wed-Sat 5.30 pm-9 pm. Lunch under $10, dinner under $15.

Tia Sophia's, 210 W San Francisco St, 983-9880. A locals' hangout, the food is exceptional. Try the Atrisco ($6)—chile stew, cheese enchilada, beans, posole and a sopapilla! Mon-Sat for bfast 7 am-11 am, lunch 11 am-2 pm.

Woolworth's Luncheonette, an adobe on the plaza, 6062 San Francisco, 982-1062. Bfast from $3. 'A real anachronism—decor and prices right out of the 19th century. Cheapest place in town; clean.' 'Don't miss the frito pie.'

OF INTEREST

NB: Despite its compact size, Santa Fe can wear you out—its altitude is 7000ft. Pace yourself.

The Plaza de Santa Fe: city heart, popular gathering place since 1610, and terminus of both the Santa Fe and El Camino Real trails, the Plaza has seen bullfights, military manoeuvres and fiestas. Billy the Kid was exhibited here in chains after causing much trouble in the area. When the Kid vowed to kill territorial governor Lew Wallace, the intended victim hid out in the **Palace of the Governors**, fronting the north side of the Plaza (while cloistered, Wallace began *Ben-Hur*). The oldest public (1610) building in America and seat of 6 regimes, the Palace, 100 Palace Ave, 827-6483, houses historical exhibits; Indian craft and jewelry for sale under its portal (better quality than elsewhere in town). The four museums run by **The Museum of New Mexico**, 827-6451, have identical hours. A 3-day pass bought at one museum admits you to all 4. All open Tues-Sun 10 am-5 pm. Single visit $5, 3-day pass $8. Nearby is the **Museum of Fine Arts**, 107 W Palace Ave, 827-4468. Incls an amazing collection of 20th century Native American art and temporary exhibitions of more recent works. **Museum of International Folk Art**, 706 Camino Lejo, 827-6350. See the Girard Collection, miniature displays of cultures from around the world. 'Well worth the walk.' Call for special performing arts events. A gallery handout will help you appreciate the fascinating, though jumbled exhibit. **Museum of American Indian Arts and Culture**, 710 Camino Lejo, 827-6344. First state museum devoted to Pueblo, Navajo, Apache Indians, with exhibits on history and ethnology from the Laboratory of Anthropology.

A city of **churches** is Santa Fe. Among them: **El Cristo Rey**, noted for its size and stone reredos; the **San Miguel Chapel**, probably the oldest church in the US; the French Romanesque **St Francis Cathedral**, built by Archbishop Lamy (subject of Willa Cather's *Death Comes for the Archbishop*) to house La Conquistadora, a 17th century shrine to the Virgin Mary; the **Loreto Chapel**, a Gothic structure whose so-called 'miraculous' spiral staircase is of mild interest; and the charming **Sanctuario de Guadalupe**, where 18th century travellers stopped to give thanks after their hazardous journeys from Mexico City to Sante Fe.

Bandelier National Monument, ruins of Indian settlement. 'Need a car to get to, but well worth seeing.' Ask for directions in Santa Fe; easy to get to.

Fiesta de Santa Fe, early to mid-Sept, begun in 1692, the oldest non-Indian celebration in the US; great community spirit. 'Zozobra or Old Man Gloom, a 40ft dummy, is burned amidst dancing and fireworks. Most spectacular!' 'Fantastic.'

Indian Market, annually every 3rd or 4th w/end in August, 983-5220. The largest market of Indian arts and crafts in the world, with 1000 Indian artisans selling handmade jewellery, sculpture, pottery, baskets, beadwork, sand-painting, feather-work et al. Open 8 am-6 pm, but avoid the initial 8-deep crush in front of the stands by going after 11 am. Besides artists' wares there are practical demonstrations, Pueblo dance showcases and a fashion show of traditional and modern Indian dress. NB: Beware the non-authentic tourist-trap vendors who set up stalls in hotels, parking lots and side streets. Free, but $4 to see the dances.

Los Alamos, 30 miles N of Santa Fe: **Los Alamos National Laboratory**. First atom bomb was built here. Museum, 15th & Central, 667-4444, has replicas of 'Fat Man' and 'Little Boy' bombs. Tue-Fri 9 am-5 pm, Sat-Mon 1 pm-5 pm; free. 'Helpful, friendly staff. Fantastic scenery.'

Santa Fe Opera, 982-3855, one of America's truly great opera companies. Tkts for performances (July & Aug) run $18-70; standing room under $10. You can also take a 1 hr tour of the open-air **opera house**, set amid hills and white petunias 7 miles N of Santa Fe. Tours run daily at 1 pm in July & Aug, $5; call the box office. NB: Unless you have a tkt for a performance or are part of a tour, you won't be allowed in.

Wheelwright Museum of the American Indian, 704 Camino Lejo, 982-4636. This is the best museum in the area, and practically the only one that is still 'free' (dona-tion required). Designed to resemble a traditional Navajo hogan, the Wheelwright contains the artistry of many Indian cultures. Rotating displays. The gift shop is designed as a replica of a turn-of-the-century Navajo Trading Post. Mon-Sat 10 am-5 pm, Sun 1 pm-5 pm.

Interesting neighbourhoods: **Canyon Rd** for its adobe art galleries, studios and shops; **Barrio de Analco**, across the Sante Fe River and originally settled by Indian labourers; **Sens** and **Prince Plazas**, good shopping areas.

INFORMATION
Chamber of Commerce, 510 N Guadolupe, 983-7317. Very helpful with details of Pueblo Indian dances, ceremonials, etc. Good maps, booklets. Mon-Fri 8 am-5 pm.
Santa Fe Convention and Visitors Bureau, 201 W Mary St, (800) 777-2489. Pick up the useful *Santa Fe Visitors Guide*. Mon-Fri 8 am-5 pm. Also, an **information booth**, located at Lincoln & Palace, is open summer Mon-Sat 9 am-4.30 pm.

TRAVEL
Budget Rent-a-Car, 1946 Cerrillos Rd, 984-8028.
Capital City Taxi, 438-0000. Pick up coupons at hostel for Santa Fe discount cards.

Gray Line, 983-9491, picks up people where they are staying: Taos Indian Pueblo tour at 9 am, $55, and Bandelier National Monument tour at 1 pm, $50.

Greyhound, 858 St Michael's Dr, (800) 231-2222. Mon-Fri 7 am-5.30 pm, sporadic hours at w/end. NB: bus station is 3 miles outside town. Taxi to downtown around $8, citybus 50¢.

TAOS Set against the rich palette of the crisp, white Sangre de Cristo Mountains, the earth tones of soaring Indian pueblo and the turquoise sky of northern New Mexico, Taos has long been a haven for artists and writers like Georgia O'Keeffe, John Fowles and D H Lawrence. Given its powerful attractions, naturally the town has become a little precious and more than a little expensive. But get to know its traditional Indian and Hispanic communities and you'll glimpse the real Taos still. For a virtual glimpse at Taos, take a look at a photographer's representation of Taos through browsing his New Mexico photo gallery online, at *www.ourworld.compuserve.com/home-pages/david_giron/*

ACCOMMODATION
Abominable Snowmansion (HI-Taos), Arroyo Seco, 10 miles N of Taos, Rte 150, 776-8298. Kitchen, pool table, games in main bldg. Check-in 8 am-10 am, 4 pm-10 pm. $16 pp summer, $22 pp winter. Private rooms from $20.

Rio Grande Hostel (HI), 15 miles S of Taos on Hwy 68, Pilar, 758-0090. Plenty of diversions—in nature or in the hostel's cafe. Theatre and live music in summer. Located in Rio Grande Gorge; organised hikes available twice weekly, discounts available for Grand Canyon/whitewater rafting trips. Buses to/from Albuquerque & Santa Fe will stop here. $11-AYH, $14 non-AYH. Private rooms and bungalows available.

Camping: easy for those with a car. Check out the **Kit Carson National Forest**, which operates 3 campgrounds. Also, **La Sombra, Capulin** and **Las Petacas**. **Backcountry camping** requires no permit; call the **forest service**, 758-6200 for more info.

OF INTEREST
NB: Although Taos is small, its attractions are scattered, making a car very useful.

Art galleries. Best of local artists at **The Stables**, next to Kit Carson Park. For O'Keeffes, go to the **Gallery of the Southwest**. Navajo paintings of R C Gorman at the **Navajo Gallery** on Ledoux St.

Kit Carson Museums, 758-0505. Three museums: **Kit Carson Home**, ½ block E of Taos Plaza on Kit Carson Rd. Period rooms (1850s), Indian, gun and Mountain Man (how the fur-trappers lived) exhibits; **Martinez Hacienda**, 2 miles S of Taos on Ranchitos Rd, Hwy 240. A restored colonial fortress and living museum. Demonstrators show the Spanish way of life in New Mexico over the past 300 yrs; **Blumenschein Home**, 2 blocks S of Taos Plaza on Ledoux St. Built circa 1780, the pioneer artist moved here in 1898 where he started Taos' art colony. Furnishings and collectables from around the world; Indian and Taos artists' work. Entry $4 for one museum, $6 for two, $8 for all three, 9 am-5 pm daily.

Millicent Rogers Museum, 1504 Museum Rd, 4 miles N, 758-2462. $4, $3 w/student ID, daily 9 am-5 pm, May-Nov, closed Mon other months. Fascinating collection of death carts and *santos* (carved saints) of the Penitentes, New Mexico's fanatical religious brotherhood. Still active, the Penitentes once practised flagellation and other mortifications during Holy Week.

Mission of St Francis of Assisi, 4 miles S. A masterpiece of the Spanish Colonial period, the mission has a sculptural quality beloved by painters from O'Keeffe on down. The interior suffers from over-restoration but do see the reredos and Ault's mysterious painting, *The Shadow of the Cross*. Check locally for open hours before setting out.

Taos Pueblo, 1¹/₂ miles north. Best access via Hwy 64, 758-9593. This eye-satisfying 5-storey pueblo, punctuated with beehive ovens and bright *riatas* of curing corn and chilis, preserves an 1000-year-old architectural tradition. Its 200 families are equally traditional, having banned electricity, piped water, TV and other con-trivances. Noted almost solely for their dancing and devotion to ceremonials, the Taos Indians celebrate numerous fiestas, the biggest being the Sept Fiesta of San Geronimo (races, dancing). 'Craft market also with good prices.' Also of interest are the ruins of the old **Spanish Mission church**, burned by the Spanish in 1680 and again by the US army in 1847. Guided tours by request (tips).

Today visitors are tolerated 8 am-5.30 pm (but call before you go); private quar-ters not open to viewing. $5 p/car, $2 if walking. Photography permit is $5 and you must also ask permission to take individuals' portraits. No cameras at ceremonial dances. **Faust's Transportation**, 758-3410, sends taxis from Taos to the pueblo for $7 o/w from downtown. 'A spiritual experience—well worth it.' Feast days highlight beautiful tribal dances; **San Geronimo's Feast Days** (end Sept) also feature a fair and races. Contact the **tribal office**, 758-9593, for schedules of dances and other info.

Taos Ski Valley, (800) 776-1111 (lodging) /776-2916 (ski conditions). Offers powder conditions in bowl sections and short, steep downhill runs. Online Net site at *www.taoswebb.com/nmusa/skitaos*

INFORMATION/TRAVEL

Chamber of Commerce, 1139 Paseo del Pueblo Sur (Rte 68), (800) 732-8267. Distributes maps and tourist literature. Make sure you ask for a guide to Northern New Mexican Indian pueblos. Daily 9 am-6 pm.

Eight Northern Indian Pueblos Council, 852-4265, Main Church St, San Juan Pueblo, lies btwn Taos and Santa Fe on Rte 68; for info on all Pueblo activities and regulations.

Faust's Transportation, 758-3410, operates taxis daily 7 am-6 pm.

Greyhound, at the Chevron Food-Mart, 1137 Paseo del Pueblo Sur, (800) 231-2222. Two buses daily to Albuquerque, Santa Fe and Denver.

SILVER CITY Located in the southwest mining country, Silver City also sits in the Gila Wilderness, a wild and lovely terrain of blood-red gorges, ghost towns and Indian ruins. In this region, Geronimo eluded 8000 US Calvary troops for eight years. Amtrak and Greyhound go to Deming; from there take the **Silver Stage Lines** shuttle bus to city centre (rsvs essential: (800) 522-0162), $10 (they also go to El Paso airport). *Silver Web, www.zianet.com/silverweb/* is the unofficial homepage of Silver City, the Land of Enchantment!

ACCOMMODATION

Bear Mt Guest Ranch, PO Box 1163, Silver City, NM 88062, 538-2538. A wonderful room/board ranch with a year-round calendar of nature and arts events led by its owners, from wildflower tours to painting expeditions. From S/D-$42. Also house-keeping cottages available. Rsvs advised. Silver Stage Line comes to ranch.

HI-Carter House Hostel, 101 N Cooper St, (505) 388-5485. A spacious home with a wonderful front porch with views of the nearby mountains and Silver City's his-toric district. Experience great hiking and biking as well as the area's natural hot springs, diverse terrain and great Mexican food. $12 AYH, $15 non-AYH. Rsvs essential.

INDIAN GROUPS ELSEWHERE IN NEW MEXICO There are 19 Tewa-speaking Native American groups in all, called collectively the Rio Grande Pueblos. Among the most interesting of the Pueblos' cities is **Acoma**; the 'Sky City,' 60 miles west of Albuquerque, occupies a huge and spectacular mesa, the ground so stony that the Indians had to haul soil 430 ft for their graveyard. Inhabited since AD 1075, the pueblo vies with Oraibi in Hopiland as oldest settlement in the US. Noted for high quality pottery with intricate linear designs. Photo fee and restrictions. **Santa Clara**, between Santa Fe and Taos, is famous for its black polished pottery. More outgoing and open to visitors than other Pueblos, the Santa Clarans have fewer restrictions on photography. This is an excellent place to take in the dancing at the late August festival. Furthest west of the pueblos is the **Zui**, which figured prominently in the Spanish conquest. Spurred greedily on by the lies of an advance scout, Coronado thought he had 'the seven golden cities of Cbola' but instead found the Zui Pueblo. Renowned as silversmiths, stone crafts-men and dancers, the Zuis still measure their wealth in horses. Camping available on their lands. One of few places where outsiders can watch the masked dances.

The **Jicarilla Apaches** in the northwest and the **Mescalero Apaches** in the southeast have numerous tourist facilities, including camping on their lands. Their ceremonies are very striking, especially the female puberty rites which take place during Fourth of July week. Non-Indians may respectfully watch the principal activities.

OKLAHOMA   *The Sooner State*

Originally set aside as an Indian Territory, in 1893 Oklahoma was thrown open to settlers in one of the most fantastic landgrabs ever. One hundred thousand homesteaders impatiently lined up on its borders, and at the crack of a gun at noon, 16 September, raced across the prairie in buckboard, buggies, wagons and carts, on bicycles, horseback and afoot to lay claim to the 40,000 allotments drawn up by the federal government. Some crossed the line ahead of time, giving Oklahoma its nickname, the Sooner State. The territory was admitted to the Union in 1907.

Apart from prairies, the state has generous forests and low rolling moun-tains in the east. Agriculture, oil and the aviation and aerospace industries bring in most of Oklahoma's revenue. Oklahoma City installed the world's first parking meters way back in 1935. National Park: Platt *www.yahoo.com/ Regional/U_S__States/Oklahoma/*.

The area code for Oklahoma City and western Oklahoma is 405; for eastern Oklahoma and Tulsa it is 918.

OKLAHOMA CITY   Oklahoma City was established in a single day when 10,000 landgrabbers showed up at the only well for miles around in what had 'til then been scorched prairie-land. The city has become an insur-ance centre for farming and other enterprises in the area and like other parts of the state got rich on oil. Six oil wells slurp away in the grounds of the capitol building. Visit Oklahoma City on a virtual tour, *www.okconline.com*.

ACCOMMODATION
Accommodations in downtown OKC are scarce.

The Economy Inn, 501 NW 5th St, 235-7455. Downtown, near bus station. TV, S-$25, D-$35.

Motel 6 West, 820 S Meridian Ave (7 mins from airport), 946-6662. S-$34, D-$40, XP-$3.

Motel 6, 5th and Walker, 4 blocks from Greyhound, 235-7455. S-$25, D-$40, $5 key deposit. **Also located at** 4200 W I-40, in Meridian, 947-6550. Take bus #11/#38. Palatial rooms come with access to a pool and a spa, S-$34, D-$40. 'Positively luxurious!' **Camping: RCA**, 12115 NE Expressway (next to Frontier City Amusement Park, 478-0278. Has a pool, laundry room, showers, and fast-food restaurants nearby. Sites $18 w/full hook-up. A state-run campground is located on Lake Thunderbird, 30 miles S of OKC at **Little River State Park**, 360-3572. Swim or fish in the lake or hike the cliffs for a view. Showers available. Tent sites $6.

FOOD
Steaks and cafeterias, that's what Oklahoma City is famous for. Most places downtown close early in the afternoon. The best and cheapest steaks can be had near the stockyards at **Cattlemen's Cafe**, 1309 S Agnew, 236-0416, Mon-Fri 6 am-10 pm; Sat & Sun 'til midnight. Good **cafeterias** in the State Capitol building, the **Furr's** chain, and **Luby's** chain.

Flip's, 5801 N Western, 843-1527. An Italian restaurant and wine bar, food is served in an artsy atmosphere ($5-19). Daily 11 am-2 am.

The Split-J, 57th and N Western, 842-0331. A sports bar with TVs all around; serves weird and wonderful hamburgers such as the Caesarburger.

Sweeney's Deli, 900 N Broadway, 232-2510. Enjoy sandwiches and burgers in a friendly atmosphere. Pool too. Mon-Thurs 11 am-11 pm; Fri 11 am-midnight.

OF INTEREST
The Crystal Bridge is a glass-enclosed cylinder 70ft in diameter containing both a desert and a rainforest. Daily 9 am-6 pm; $3.

Indian City USA, near Anadarko, 65 miles SW of Oklahoma City on Hwy 62, 247-5661. Authentic re-creation of Plains Indian villages, done with help of U Oklahoma Anthropology Dept. Dancing, demonstrations, ceremonies, camping, swimming. Also **Indian Hall of Fame**, etc. $7 for village, including museum. ($1 entry to museum if not on walking tour).

The **Kirkpatrick Center Museum Complex**, 2100 NE 52nd St, 427-5461, houses 8 museums and galleries: **Air and Space Museum** has exhibits on the state's contribution to aviation and space; the **International Photography Hall of Fame**, holds examples of work by leading photographers around the world. Also the **Red Earth Indian Center and** Omniplex, a hands-on science museum with free planetarium shows on the hour. Admission to all 8 museums $6. Mon-Sat 9 am-6 pm, Sun noon-6 pm in summer; slightly shorter hrs weekdays in winter.

National Cowboy Hall of Fame and Western Heritage Center, 1700 NE 63rd, 6 miles N of downtown along I-44, 478-2250. $6.50, daily 8.30 am-6 pm summer, 9 am-5 pm winter. Sitting right on the Old Chisholm Trail, this complex, a joint venture by the 17 Western states, is magnificent. The art gallery includes many works by Russell, Remington, Schreyrogel, Bierstadt. 'Boring, and not worth it.'

Norman, home of **University of Oklahoma** (20,000 students), 30 mins from Oklahoma City. Student life dominates the town, so there's usually plenty to do. The university's housing dept is helpful in finding accommodation during the summer. The University of Oklahoma **Museum of Art**, 410 W Boyd, 325-3272, is worth a visit. Permanent collections of American, European, Oriental and African art. Tues-Sat noon-4.30 pm, free.

Oklahoma City Zoo/Aquaticus, 2101 NE 50th St, 424-3344. Daily 9 am-6 pm, $4.

Rated one of the top zoos in the nation with over 2000 animals from 500 species. Dolphin shows in the aquaticus $2 extra.

State Capitol, 2300 N Lincoln Blvd, 521-3356. Six derricks make politics pay; one of them is 'whipstocked' (drilled at an angle) to get at the oil beneath the Capitol, itself an unimpressive structure, one of the few state capitols without a dome. Daily, 8 am-4.30 pm; guided tours 9 am-3 pm. Free.

State Museum of the Oklahoma Historical Society, just south of the capitol at 2100 N Lincoln Blvd, 521-2491. Displays of Oklahoma history, from prehistoric Indians to the present. 'Interesting Indian relics.' Mon-Sat, 9 am-5 pm, both library and museum open 'til 8 pm Mon. Free.

Only in America: Enterprise Square, USA, on the campus of Oklahoma Christian College, 2501 E Memorial Rd, 425-5030. A sort of Disneyland-for-capitalists extolling the virtues of good old fashioned Adam Smith-ism. See the 'World's Largest Functioning Cash Register' with its singing dollar bills, the 'Hall of Achievers' (yay!), the 'Great Talking Face of Government' (boo!) and the 'Time Tunnel' and 'Economic Arcade Game Room,' where you'll find out whether you have the stuff it takes to survive in an open-market economy. Mon-Sat 9 am-5 pm, Sun 1 pm-4 pm; $5.

Festivals: Festival of the Arts, 236-1426, held annually every April at Myriad gardens, highlights visual, culinary and performing arts. **The Red Earth** festival, 427-5228, held annually every June, is the country's largest celebration of Native America, includes intense dance competitions in which dancers from different tribes perform for prize money.

ENTERTAINMENT

For nightlife ideas, pick up a copy of the *Oklahoma Gazette* or try the Bricktown district on Sheridan Ave, especially the **Bricktown Brewery**, 1 N Oklahoma St, 232-BREW. Dine on chicken dishes ($5-9) and watch the beer brew. The second floor houses live music. Cover $3-10, 21yrs+. Live music Tues and Fri-Sat 8 pm. Also, try the **Wreck Room at the Habana Inn** at 39th and Barnes St, 525-7610, for a good dance. Thurs-Sat 10 pm-5 am, cover $3-7.

INFORMATION

Chamber of Commerce Tourist Information, 123 Park Ave at Broadway, 297-8912. Mon-Fri 8.30 am-5 pm.

Norman Chamber of Commerce, 115 E Gray St, 321-7260. Mon-Fri, 8 am-5 pm.

Oklahoma City Convention and Visitors Bureau, 4 Santa Fe Plaza, 297-8912. Mon-Fri 8 am-5 pm.

Oklahoma City Tourist Information Centers, Oklahoma Tourism and Recreation Dept, 500 Will Rogers Building, 521-2409 at Capitol; and at 5101 N I35, 478-4637. Both open daily, 8.30 am-5 pm.

Travelers Aid, 412 NW 5th, 232-5507; Mon-Fri 8 am-4.30 pm. Also booth at airport.

TRAVEL

Miller's Bicycle Distribution, 3350 W Main, 360-3838. Bike rental $5 day, $54 month. In-line skates $10 day. Mon-Sat 9 am-8 pm, Sun 1-6 pm. Credit card essential.

Dub Richardson Ford Rent-a-Car, 2930 NW 39th Expressway, (800) 456-9288. Note: Oklahoma does not honor the International Driver's Permit.

Greyhound, Union Bus Stn, 427 W Sheridan & Walker St, (800) 231-2222. 24 hrs; crummy area, but station has security guards (until midnight). Also used by Jefferson; compare schedules and prices.

Oklahoma Metro Area Transit, offices at Union Station, 300 SW 7th, 235-RIDE. Bus service Mon-Sat approx 6 am-6 pm.

Royal Coach, 3800 S Meridian, 685-2638, has 24 hr van service to downtown ($9 pp, XP-$3). A taxi downtown costs approx $14.

Yellow Cabs, 232-6161 in OKC; 329-3333 in Norman.
Will Rogers International Airport, 7100 Terminal Dr, 681-5311. No buses run directly there. Take the #11 from 10th & Robinson to 29th & Meridian, about 40 mins, from there take a cab, $5-$6; or take a cab from downtown, $14.

TULSA Once known as the 'oil capital of the world,' Tulsa has slid tech-nologically sideways to 'aerospace capital of ... Oklahoma.' Its setting among rolling green hills on the Arkansas River is prettier than OKC but it's just as windy. (The whole state is notorious for wild weather). Check out Bret's Slightly Warped Tour o'Tulsa, *www.ionet.net/~bretp/index.html* where a lifetime resident takes a look at some of the things that make the city unique.

ACCOMMODATION
Try the budget motels on I-44 and I-244.
The Budgetel Inn, 4530 E Skelly Dr off I-44, (800) 428-3438. Free bfast delivered to your room; S-$43, D-$48.
Georgetown Plaza Motel, 8502 E 27th, 622-6616. TV, S-$26, D-$32.
Motel 6, 5828 Skelly Dr, 445-0223. S-$25, D-$29, XP-$2.
Tulsa Inn, 5554 S 48th W Ave, 446-1600. Take exit 222. S-$23, D-$33.
YMCA, 515 S Denver, 583-6201. $16 plus $10 key deposit; full use of facilities. No rsvs taken; men only.
Camping: KOA Kampground, 193 East Ave, 266-4227. Pool, laundry, showers, game room. Sites for two $17 (full hook-up). Also, **Heyburn State Park** on Heyburn Lake, 247-6695. Fishing, swimming, bike rentals. Tent sites $6 (full hook-up).

FOOD
Black-Eyed Pea, family style chain; 3 locations but none are downtown, 665-7435. $5-$8 dinner.
Both OKC and Tulsa have **Casa Bonitas**, 21st and Sheridan, 836-6464. A crazed mixture of Mexican village and dining area with waterfall, mariachis, puppets, dancers, etc. Sun-Thurs 11 am-9 pm, Fri & Sat 'til 10 pm. Good value, all-you-can-eat Mexican dinners; deluxe, $8.
Harvest Buffet, 3637 S Memorial, 663-9410. All-you-can-eat smorgies, b/fast $4, lunch $4.50, dinner $6. 7 am-9 pm daily, Sun 'til 8 pm.
Metro Diner, 3001 E 11th St, 592-2616. Salads, sandwiches, burgers, and pasta dishes, under $10. Daily 8 am-10 pm.
Po-Folks, 51st and Peoria in shopping centre, 749-6606. Mon-Fri 11 am-9 pm Sat & Sun 'til 10 pm, $6-$8.
Williams Center, 2 blocks from Greyhound. 'Amazing shopping centre overlook-ing ice rink. Cheap bfasts, better value than Greyhound.'

OF INTEREST
Cherokee National Museum, also in **Tahlequah**, 456-6007. Mon-Sat 10 am-5 pm, Sun 1 pm-5 pm. $2.75. Outdoor drama, the *Trail of Tears*, performed June through August, 8.30 pm in a lovely amphitheatre, telling the story of the tragic march 1838-39 in which 4000 of 16,000 Cherokees died of hunger, disease and cold, and were forced to begin life anew in the territory that would become the state of Oklahoma. Haunting music and dance. Tkts $10. **The Historic Trail**, est in Dec 1987, commem-orates this journey. For more info, contact Trail of Tears National Historic Trail, Southwest Region National Park Service, PO Box 728, Santa Fe, NM 87504, (505) 988-6888. Oklahoma in general and Tulsa in particular are in Bible Belt country; here you'll find **Oral Roberts University**, 7777 S Lewis, (800) 678-8876. Founded by the evangelist after a vision from God so specific that he was told what style to build the place in, ORU looks like a fifties version of the future, as seen in those

classic B movies. Campus tours, 495-6807. Visitors centre, Mon-Sat 10.30 am-4.30 pm, Sun 1-5 pm. When you are leaving Oklahoma, go by way of **Quapaw**, in the northeast corner of the state where Oklahoma cuts a corner with Kansas and Missouri. In this area, which some call the 'Bermuda Triangle of the prairie,' is the **Tri-State Spooklight**, described as a 'weird, bobbing light' along State Line Road. Scientific explanations (light refraction from an unknown source, underground quartz crystals) have been given for this phenomenon. But everyone knows the spooklight is really caused by UFOs on their way to North Dakota.

Creek Council Oak Tree, 1750 S and Cheyenne, 585-1201. Known as 'Tulsa's First City Hall,' the site of the Council Fire used by the first group of Creeks to come from Alabama to Oklahoma in 1828. For all skateboarding/inlining/BMX addicts, check out **Hoffman Bike Park**, Santa Fe, Edmonton.

Thomas Gilcrease Institute of American History and Art, 1400 Gilcrease Museum Rd, 596-2700. The treasurehouse of Western American art, plus 250,000 Native American-Indian artefacts, interesting maps and documents like the original instructions for Paul Revere's ride, the first letter written from the North American continent by Chris Columbus' son, Aztec codex, etc. $3 donation requested; summer Tues-Sat 9 am-5 pm, Thurs 'til 8 pm, Sun 1 pm-5 pm. Winter, closed on Mon.

Tsa-La-Gi Village, 70 miles SE of Tulsa near **Tahlequah**, 456-6007. Replica of a 17th century Cherokee village staffed by Cherokee who portray village life of their ancestors, including braves, kids and villagers; 45 min tour $4. Open mid-May through late Aug; Mon-Sat 10 am-5 pm, Sun 1 pm-5 pm.

Tulsa Ballet, Performing Arts Center, 3rd & Cincinnati St, 585-2573/595-7111. Box office, Mon-Fri 10 am-5.30 pm, Sat 10 am-3 pm.

Tulsa County Historical Society Museum, 1400 N Gilcrease Museum Rd, 596-1350. Collection of historic objects: unique photographs, rare historical books and letters, settlement period furniture. Tue-Thur & Sat 11 am-4 pm; Sun 1 pm-4 pm. There is another branch downtown with rotating, thematic exhibits: the **Philtower**, 427 S Boston Ave, 9 am-5 pm Mon-Fri. Both free.

ENTERTAINMENT

Pick up a free copy of *Urban Tulsa* at local restaurants. Bars on Cherry St (15th St, E of Peoria) and S Peoria. The intersection of 18th and Boston caters to the young adult crowd, whilst the college crowd flocks to **Hoffbtau**, 1738 Boston, 538-9520, where burgers, sandwiches and local bands are all served up! Fri-Sat 10 pm, cover $3-10.

TRAVEL/INFORMATION

Convention and Visitors Division, 616 S Boston, (800) 558-3311. Mon-Fri 8 am-5 pm.

Dept of Tourism and Recreation, US 66 and I-44 E of Tulsa near Will Rogers Turnpike Gate, 256-6748. Open 8.30 am-5 pm.

Greyhound, 317 S Detroit, (800) 231-2222.

Metropolitan Tulsa Transit Authority, 582-2100. Basic fare 75¢, transfer 5¢, runs 5 am-7 pm. Has 'ozone alert' days in summer when all buses are free.

River Trail Bicycles bike rental, 6861 S Peoria, 481-1818. Inline skates rental also. Mon-Thurs 10 am-7 pm, Fri-Sat 'til 8 pm, Sun 11 am-7 pm. Driver's license/major credit card required.

Thrifty car rental, 1506 N Memorial Dr, 838-3333. Open 24 hrs.

Tulsa International Airport, 838-5000, just off Hwy 11, about 6 miles NE of downtown. Mon-Fri take #13 'Independence-Barton' bus from 4th & Denver, 75¢. W/ends and after bus hours take a cab, approx $15.

Yellow Checker Cabs, 582-6161.

TEXAS *Lone Star State*

Texans may have had to pass the Stetson of 'biggest state' to Alaska but they haven't lost their talent for beer-drinking, braggadocio, BBQ and making Dallas-sized mountains of money. This state has the size, colour and raw energy of a Texas longhorn steer, and it'll wear you out if you try to cover it. As the old jingle has it, 'the sun is riz, the sun is set, and we ain't out of Texas yet'! Better to focus on its two cities of any charm—San Antonio and Austin—and perhaps the tropical coast around Galveston or Corpus Christi.

Always intensely political, Texas has seen six regimes come and five go, from Spanish, French and Mexican, to a brief whirl as the Republic of Texas and finally Confederate. Through it all, Texas remains good ole boy country, a terrain of hardbitten little towns and hard-edged cities whose icons are Willie Nelson, the Dallas Cowboys and LBJ. In recent years, with the downturn in oil prices, the state's energy-based economy has been depressed.

The Texan scenery may vary from desert to mountains to vast rolling plains but everywhere in the summer months there is one constant—the heat. Temperatures of 90-100 degrees are the norm and in Houston, especially, there is also high humidity—'Gulf weather' it's called.
www.yahoo.com/Regional/U_S__States/Texas/.
Texas telephone area codes: Dallas, 214; El Paso, 915; Ft Worth, 817; Galveston, 409; Houston, 713; San Antonio, 210; Corpus Christi & Austin, 512.

SAN ANTONIO   About 75 miles south of Austin sits thoroughly Hispanic San Antonio, the only Texas city to possess a proper downtown, much less one with attractions worth walking to. The action centres round the San Antonio River and its pleasant green Riverwalk, where fiestas, music and fun of one sort or another take place year-round.

This city of 800,000 began in 1691 as an Indian village with the wacky name of 'drunken old man going home at night,' which the Spaniards bowdlerised to San Antonio. Despite the early Spanish (and later Mexican) presence in Texas, settlement lagged and authorities began admitting Americans. By the 1830s, six of seven inhabitants were Anglo and the resultant friction caused skirmishes and ultimately the Battle of the Alamo. During its 13-day seige, 200 Americans gallantly fought to the last man against the 5000-man Mexican army of Santa Ana. Afterwards, the rallying cry of 'Remember the Alamo' helped Sam Houston and his troops defeat the Mexicans and establish the Republic of Texas, 1836-1845. *At Home in San Antonio* is a non-commercial view of a local's hometown, located on the net at *www.pages.prodigy.com/athome/index.html.*

ACCOMMODATION

For cheap motels, try **Roosevelt Ave** (an extension of St Mary's), **Fredericksburg Rd** and **Broadway** (btwn downtown and Brackenridge).
B&B Hosts of San Antonio, 8546 Broadway #215, San Antonio, TX 78217, (800) 356-1605. Finds rooms in private homes, From S-$50, D-$60.
Elmira Motor Inn, 1126 E Elmira, (800) 584-0800. Large, well-furnished rooms. TV/AC. 'Very caring management.' S/D-$38. Key deposit $2.

El Tejas Motel, 2727 Roosevelt Ave, 533-7123. Close to missions, 3 miles from downtown. Bus #42 to door. S-$25-$35, D-$40-45. AC, TV, pool.

Motel 6, 5522 N Panam, I-35 and Rittiman, 661-8791. S-$35, D-$45, TV, AC, pool. Also, **Motel 6**, at Starlight Terrace Exit off I-35, 650-4419, and at North WW White Rd off I-10, 333-1850, D-$41-$48.

San Antonio International Hostel/Bullis House Inn (AYH), 621 Pierce St, 223-9426. Private rooms with AYH discount, S/D-$33. Dorm rooms $14 AYH, $17 non-AYH. Sheets $2, bfast $4. Pool, kitchen. Fills quickly in summer. From bus station take #15 bus E from Houston St to Carson St, walk 2 blocks west or take #11 to Grayson St at Pierce. 'A friendly, ranch-style hostel in a quiet neighbourhood.'

Travelers Hotel, 220 Broadway, 226-4381. Downtown. S-$33, D-$56, + $2 key deposit.

Camping: Alamo KOA, 602 Gembler Rd, (800) 833-5267. 6 miles from downtown. Each site has a BBQ grill and patio. Showers, laundry, AC, pool, golf course, free movies. Open 'til 10.30 pm. $20 for two, XP-$2.

FOOD

San Antonio, with its 52 per cent Latin population, has far better Mexican food than most Mexican border towns. A directory of restaurants and other entertainment highlights of SA can be found at *www.food-leisure.com*.

Farmers' Market near Market Sq, 207-8600. Sells Mexican produce and candy. Haggle away with vendors and see prices drop! Daily 10 am-8 pm summer, 'til 6 pm winter.

Henry's Puffy Taco, 3202 W Woodlawn, 432-7341. Mon-Sat 10 am-9 pm, 'til 10 pm at w/ends, specials $5.

Hung Fong Chinese Restaurant, 3624 Broadway, 822-9211. The oldest Chinese restaurant in San Antonio, dishes under $10. Open 11 am-10.30 pm.

Kangaroo Court, 512 Riverwalk, 224-6821. 'Does Bass ale at $3.25 ¹/₂ pint/$4.75 pint, of very cold beer!' Seafood and sandwiches. Dinners under $15.

Maverick Cafe, 6868 San Pedro, 822-9611. Chinese and Mexican food. $5-$15. 11.30 am-9 pm, 'til 10 pm w/ends. 'One of a kind.'

Mi Tierra, 218 Produce Row in **El Mercado**, 225-1262. Open 24 hrs, dynamite Mexican food. Order the *Chalupa compuesta* and the supercheap *caldo* (soup), $6-$15.

Pig Stand, 1508 Broadway and 801 S Presa (off S Alamo), 227-1691. Diners offer cheap country-style food.

Taco Cabana, 101 Alamo Plaza, 224-6158 at Commerce. Best fast Mexican food in this area, 24 hrs.

OF INTEREST

The Alamo: Alamo Plaza near Houston and Alamo St, 225-1391. Texas' most visited tourist attraction, the restored 1718 presidio-mission is free and open daily 9 am-5.30 pm, Sun from 10 am (free). Mural inside of heroes Bowie, Crockett and Travis. Pass up the slide show across the way—ear-splitting and redundant. 'Boring—don't bother.' Also in Old San Antonio: **San Fernando Cathedral**, main Plaza, where Alamo heroes are buried. Behind city hall is the beautiful **Spanish Governor's Palace**, 105 Plaza de Armas, 207-8610. Mon-Sat 9 am-5 pm, Sun 10 am-5 pm, $1.

Brackenridge Park, 3900 N St Mary's St (3 miles NE of downtown on Hwy 281), 734-5401. Take bus #8. Two art museums, free Japanese sunken gardens, a skyride, riding stables, and the San Antonio Zoo (includes an extensive African mammal exhibit), 734-7183; $6—'worth the money but packed.' Park open daily 9 am-5.30 pm, Sat-Sun 'til 6.30 pm.

El Mercado, typical Mexican market with stalls of fresh fruits and meats, cheap clothes and crafts from Mexico. At junction of Santa Rosa and Commerce Sts.

HemisFair Plaza: The free **Institute of Texan Cultures**, 801 S Bowie at Durango, 558-2300, has displays on 26 ethnic groups; Tues-Sun 9 am-5 pm, (donation requested). The view from the 750ft **Tower of the Americas**, 600 Hemisphere Park, 207-8615, 8 am-11 pm, is worth the $3 fee. San Antonio has 5 missions, counting the Alamo. Unless you're mission-mad, skip the others and see **Queen Mission San Jose**, 6539 San Jose Dr, 229-4770. (Take the hourly S Flores bus marked 'San Jose Mission'). Interesting granary, Indian building, barracks. Try to time your visit for Sun mass when the mariachis play. Free. Every Sat morn, a national park ranger leads a 10 mile r/t bike tour from Mission San Jose along the historic corridor. Free; bring your own bike. Call 229-4700 for schedule.

La Villita, btwn Nueva & S Alamo Sts, downtown restoration of the city's early nucleus, with cool patios, banana trees, crafts demos and sales. Daily 6 am-6 pm.

Natural Bridge Caverns, 26495 Natural Bridge Caverns Rd, 651-6101. The caverns' 140-million-year-old phallic rock formations are guaranteed to knock your socks off! 1¹/₂ hr tours every ¹/₂ hr. Daily 9 am-6 pm summer, 'til 4 pm winter; $7.

Paseo del Rio or **Riverwalk**. The jade green river is echoed by greenery on both sides, cobblestone walks, intimate bridges at intervals, and lined with restaurants and bars with good Happy Hours and late hours. A civic as well as tourist focal point. 'Free lunch, evening concerts in summer.' 'Free dancing along the Riverwalk.' 'The hub of San Antonio's nightlife.'

River Boats—pick up across from the Hilton, and for $3 will take you on a 35-40 mins tour of the river. Call **Yanaguana Cruises**, (800) 417-4139, who have narrated boat tours along the Paseo del Rio. Tkts available at the **River Center Mall**, 849 E Commerce St, or outside the Hilton Palacio del Rio, 200 S Alamo St ($4).

San Antonio Museum of Art, 200 W Jones Ave, off Broadway, 978-8100. Housed in a restored turn-of-the-century brewery, the museum now exhibits Greek and Roman antiquities, Mexican folk art, 18th-20th century US art and Asian art. $4, $2 w/student ID. Mon & Wed-Sat 10 am-5 pm, Tues 10 am-9 pm, Sun noon-5 pm (summer); Tues only 'til 6 pm (winter).

Sea World of Texas, 15 miles NW of downtown, at Ray Ellison Dr and Westover Hills Blvd, 523-3611, (800) 722-2762. $170 million park—aquariums, flamingoes, waterfowl, a 12.5 acre lake for water skiers and two water rides (log flume and river raft). Daily 10 am-10 pm (summer), closed Dec-Feb. $26.

ENTERTAINMENT

For evening fun, any season, stroll down the **River Walk**. Also, the Friday *Express* or weekly *Current* is good for entertainment and what's on.

Arneson Theater, 207-8610. Showcases everything from flamenco to jazz to country; river separates you from stage. **Fiesta Noche del Rio** variety show is $8, June-August, Thurs, Fri, Sat at 8.30 pm.

Floore Country Store, 14464 Old Bandera Rd, btwn Old & New Hwy 16 in Helotes, 695-8827. One of the oldest Honky-Tonk hangouts and a favourite of Willie Nelson. Most Fri & Sats free dancing/cover from $5.

Jim Callum's Landing, 123 Losoya (in the Hyatt downtown), 223-7266. Happy Jazz Band Mon-Sat 9 pm-1 am, and the improv jazz quintet Small Worl performs on Sun nights.

Lerma's, 1602 N Arazmora, 732-0477. Conjunto music (Mexican accordian dance music). Also, for authentic *tejano music* (Mexican-country!) head to **Cadillac Bar**, 212 S Flores, 223-5533. Dancing frenzy heaven. Mon-Tues, 11 am-midnight, Sat 5 pm-2 am.

Mexican Festival, 3rd week in Sept, Riverwalk, and **Fiesta San Antonio**, 227-5191, April 18-27. Plenty of Tex-Mex action with concerts and parades, to commemorate the victory at San Jacinto and honor the heroes at the Alamo. Also, numerous fiestas, music events and blowouts (most free) throughout the year; during St Patrick's week, San Antonians dye both their beer and their river green!

INFORMATION
Convention and Visitors Bureau, 317 Alamo Plaza, (800) 447-3372. Daily 8.30 am-6 pm.

TRAVEL
Amtrak, 1174 E Commerce St, (800) 872-7245. For *Sunset Limited* LA-New Orleans-Miami and *Texas Eagle* to Chicago routes.
Greyhound, 500 N St Mary's St, (800) 231-2222. 24 hrs.
San Antonio International Airport, 821-3411. About 5 miles N of downtown; take #2 'Blanco-Airport' bus from Flores & Travis Sts, 75¢. Last bus to airport 8.30 pm.
Star Shuttle Service, 341-6000, travels from the airport to several locations near downtown, $6 pp. Cab fare $14. **VIA**, runs local buses, 227-2020. Basic fare 75¢, transfer 10¢, express $1.50, daytripper pass $4. Operates daily Sun-10 pm, but many routes stop at 5 pm. Also runs the El Centro old-fashioned trollies that circle downtown, 50¢.
Yellow Cab taxis, 226-4242.
Chuck's Rent-A-Clunker, 3249 SW Military Dr, 922-9464. Mon-Fri 8 am-6 pm, Sat 9 am-6 pm, Sun 10 am-6 pm.

AUSTIN Capital city, named after the state's 'founding father,' but Richard Linklater made his film, *Slacker*, here for a reason. With its laidback attitude it doesn't seem like 'real' Texas but it does seem like the most enjoyable city in the state. Truly an oasis, socially and culturally, in the middle of a desert, it has a huge student population that adds a vigour to the place. Austin is *the* place to go to see bands, hang out, drink too much and party hard. It's also, strangely enough, a centre for bats. In summer, a colony of the little critters roosts under the Congress Ave Bridge. Every evening, at around 8 pm, a crowd gathers to see them all leave to feed. *Austin 360* is an online newspaper with info on the Austin music scene, sports and news. *www.Austin360.com/*

ACCOMMODATION
Congress St is cheap hotel/motel row.
Austin International Hostel (AYH), 2200 S Lakeshore Blvd (near Barton Springs), (800) 725-2331. $12 AYH, $15 non-AYH. Extremely clean, well-kept hostel with a cavernous 24 hr common room overlooking town lake. Waterbeds available! Kitchen with individ cubbies plus laundry. Located near grocery store.
The Castilian, 2323 San Antonio St, 478-9811. Dorm-style rooms S-$30, D-$35. 1 June-17 Aug only. Private residence hall, coed, overlooking University. Cafe, AC, pool; very nice. Bus stop ¹/₂ block.
Motel 6, I-35 N Rundberg Ln Exit, (800) 440-6000. Pool, new AC, TV. S/D-$30-40, XP-$3. Rsvs required especially at w/ends
Pearl Street Co-op, 2000 Pearl St, 476-9478. Large rooms, laundry, kitchen, court-yard, pool. Friendly atmosphere. 3 square meals, shared bath, access to TV/VCR room. 2 week max stay. S-$13, D-$17.
San Jose Motel, 1316 S Congress St, 444-7322. S-$27, D-$35, + $3 key deposit.
Taos Hall, 2612 Guadalupe at 27th St, 474-6905. Hallway bathrooms and linoleum floors. 3 meals and a bed, $15.
21st St Co-op, 707 W 21st St, 476-1857. Carpeted suites, AC, common room, co-ed bathroom on each floor. $10 pp, plus $5 for 3 meals and kitchen access. Fills up quickly in summer. **Camping: The Austin Capitol KOA**, (800) 284-0206, 6 miles S of city along I-35. Offers a pool, clean bathrooms, game room, laundry, grocery store. Shady tent site, full hook-up $27; XP-$3. Cabins Q-$34, $44 for six. Get 3rd night free.

FOOD

Great pickings, but you'd better like Texas BBQ, Mexican food and Texas chili. Lots of student hangouts along Guadalupe.

The Filling Station, 801 Barton Springs Rd, 477-1022. Get 12oz ethyl-burgers or a gasket platter ($6). 'Try the high-octane speciality drink, the Tune-up, guaranteed to clean out your spark plugs!' $4. 11 am-midnight, Fri & Sat 'til 2 am.

Furr's Cafeteria, 4015 S Lamar, 441-7825. Two other branches in Austin. All-U-Can-Eat, $5, Delight plate $6. 11 am-8.30 pm.

GM Steakhouse, 626 N Lamar, 476-0755 serves T-bone ($7.95) and sirloin steaks ($8).

Hickory Street Bar and Grille, 800 Congress Ave, 477-8968. Array of speciality food bars (salad, soup, potato, bread and sundae); $1-$5, or All-U-Can-Eat for $5.50. 'Austin's best ¹/₂ pound hamburgers.'

Quackenbush's, 2120 Guadalupe St, 472-4477. A popular café/deli for espresso etc. Daily 8 am-11 pm.

Richard Jones Pit, 2304 S Congress, 444-2272, serves best BBQ in town.

Texas Chili Parlor, 1409 Lavaca St, 472-2828. World class chili joint and saloon, also serves $3 screwdrivers and Bloody Marys on w/ends.

Texas Showdown Saloon, 2610 Guadalupe, 472-2010. Small menu; 'Texas-style' atmosphere; average drinks $2, snacks $2.50.

Threadgill's, 6416 N Lamar, 451-5440. A stronghold of Texas food, and run by Eddie Wilson, a founding father of Austin's music scene, this soul-food joint has free seconds and was an early stomping ground of the original screamer, Janis Joplin. Eddie plays the place down, 11 am-10 pm. 'I've got easily the best restaurant in the history of the globe!' Kitchen's motto is 'we don't serve all you can eat, we serve more than you can eat.'

Trudy's Texas Star, 409 W 30th St, 477-2935. Fine Tex-Mex dinner entrees ($5-$8), margaritas and *migas,* a corn tortilla souffle ($4). Outdoor porch bar with picnic tables, open early morn 'til 2 am. Food served 'til midnight.

OF INTEREST

Austin Museum of Art, Laguna Gloria, 3809 W 35th St, 458-8191. 8 miles from the State Capitol. Blends art, architecture, and nature, overlooking Lake Austin. Also hosts a yearly arts & crafts festival with concerts and plays (in May). *Fiesta Laguna Gloria, 835-2385.*

Barton Springs, Zilker Park, 2201 Barton Springs Rd, 476-9044. Open-air swimming hole (not a chlorinated pool) fed by underground springs. 'Reached by lovely 40 min riverside walk, beautiful setting.' $3, 'but if you smile and ask for the loan of a swimsuit you might get in free.' Pool's temperature rarely rises above 60F though! Alternatively, walk upstream and swim at any nice-looking spot! Park is open Mon-Fri 5 am-10 pm, w/ends 10 am-6 pm, $2. Also **Hamilton Pool**—a favourite with Texan students (on Texas 71 West), 2642740. 60ft waterfall cascades into a jade green pool. Monitored—closed if bacteria levels are too high. $5 parking fee, $2 walk-ins, 9 am-6 pm daily.

Capitol building, Congress Ave & 11th St, 463-0063. 7ft higher than the national one! Free tours leave from Rotunda, unrestricted entry to public areas, including galleries from which you can observe debates.

Museums: O Henry Museum, 409 E 5th St, 397-1465, free. Personal effects of the popular short-story writer who lived in Austin from 1885-1895. Wed-Sun noon-5 pm. Also, **Daughters of the Republic of Texas Museum**, Anderson Lane, free. Indispensable museum for anyone interested in Texas or Civil War history.

University of Texas, Guadalupe and 24th St, north of Capitol. Huge, rich, highly social school. Has several museums and the **LBJ Library** at 2313 Red River St, 482-5279. Free, daily 9 am-5 pm. A/V displays, replica of the Oval Office and tapes of LBJ's twang. LBJ's birthplace, home, ranch and grave are west of Austin, in and around Johnson City. Also: **Harry Ransom Center**, 21st & Guadalupe on UT campus, 471-8944. Houses a good art museum, one of the world's four copies of the Gutenburg Bible, lots of Evelyn Waugh and the personal libraries of Virginia Woolf, James Joyce and the devil himself, Aleister Crowley. Mon-Sat 9 am-5 pm; free.

ENTERTAINMENT

Austin is a major music centre; check *The Daily Texan* and the free *Austin Weekly Chronicle* to see who's playing where. Guadalupe Ave, called The Drag, is a hot spot for student and non-student activity. For nightclubs and fancy bars it has to be 6th St, wall-to-wall music and a great Halloween street party. In the 6th St area, **Chicago House,** 607 Trinity, 499-8388, plays a different tune on w/ends and hosts poetry readings. $7 w/student ID. Toulouse's, 402 E 6th St, 478-0744, fills up to 5 stages with live music on the w/ends, ranging from relaxed acoustic to more hardcore. Cover $1-4, daily 8 pm-2 am. For a quiet evening, visit **Copper Tank Brewing Company**, 504 Trinity St, 478-8444, the city's best microbrewery. Pop along on a Wed for a freshly brewed pint, $1! Mon-Fri 11 am-2 am, Sat-Sun 3 pm-2 am. Lately, much nightlife has also headed to the **Warehouse Area** around 4th St, west of Congress. Also, check out: *Austin City Limits*, an excellent nationwide TV country show broadcast Weekly on public television in the US, 471-4811.

Antone's, 2915 Guadalupe at 29th St, 474-5314. Has drawn the likes of BB King and Muddy Waters. $3-8 cover charge admits you to a fine blues club. All ages welcome. Daily 8 pm-2 am.

Broken Spoke, 3201 S Lamar, 442-6189. Authentic C&W dive with live music, Texas two-step dancing, chicken-fried steaks. Cover, Wed-Thur, $4; Fri & Sat $6.

Liberty Lunch, 405 W 2nd, 477-0461. Has all sorts of good touring bands.

INFORMATION

Convention and Visitors Bureau, 201 E 2nd St, (800) 926-2282. Daily 9 am-5 pm; 125 pieces of free literature on the area.

University of Texas Info Center, 471-3434.

TRAVEL

Amtrak, 250 N Lamar Blvd, (800) 872-7245.

Austin Adventure Co Bike Rental, 706 B Simonetti Dr, 209-6880. $15 for 2 hr. Also, conducts 2-3 hr bike tours and full-day mountain bike tours. Rsvs required.

Capital Metro, (800) 474-1201. Local bus company; basic fare 50¢, free transfers. From 6th & Congress take #1 bus outbound to reach UT campus. The **Dillo Bus Service**, 474-1200, serves downtown area; green trolleys run Mon-Fri every 15 mins, 6.30 am-7 pm every 50 mins, 7-9 pm (free).

Greyhound, 916 E Koenig Lane, (800) 231-2222. 24 hrs.

Rent-A-Wreck car rental, 6820 Guadalupe, 454-8621.

Robert Mueller Municipal Airport, 4600 Manor Rd, 480-9091. About 4 miles NE of downtown; take bus #20 from 6th & Vrazos, 50¢; last bus out midnight in week, Sat 11.25 pm, Sun 9.15 pm.

Yellow Cab, 472-1111.

DALLAS/FORT WORTH Big D pushes culture but its finest achievements are Neiman-Marcus, the glittering emporium of the conspicuous consumer, and Tolbert's Chili Parlor, where the serious chiliheads go to eat a bowl of red before they die. 'Dallas is a hard-nosed business environment with entertainment geared to the relaxing businessman.' One of the world's largest permanent trade fairs is located here. The city seems to go on forever and attractions are not centralized. If you are not travelling by car, you may want to visit a city more accommodating to the pedestrian.

An airport larger than Manhattan is the umbilical cord linking Dallas with **Forth Worth**, its cattle-and agriculture-based sister city. Fort Worth, surprisingly, has a lot more of interest to see and do, with a number of top-notch museums and art collections, most free and conveniently clumped in Amon Carter Square. As befits an overgrown cowtown, the honky-tonk country and western scene is alive and well, more cowboy than urban. Forty miles and a heap of freeways separate these two behemoths, so don't plan to lodge in one and visit the other. *Do remember that Dallas (214) and Fort Worth (817) have different telephone area codes. Arlington also uses 817.* Check out the Yahoo! Town Cities online city guide at *www.dfw.yahoo.com*.

ACCOMMODATION

NB: Budget accommodation in either city does not exist in the downtown areas. We suggest you rent a car and schlepp out to one of the thirteen Motel 6s ringing the area, or make your visit a brief one.

In Dallas: Motel 6 locations, should be nearby wherever you are. Rates approx S-$28-38. Call (800) 440-6000.

B&B Texas Style, 4224 W Red Bird Lane, (800) 899-4538. Mon-Fri 8.30 am-4.30 pm. Rooms in private homes near town, from S-$50, D-$60.

Delux Inn, 3817 Rte 80E, 681-0044. Pool, restaurant. Must be 18yrs+. From S-$20, D-$25. XP-$2. Free bfast.

Market Center Boulevard Inn, 2026 Market Center Blvd, 748-2243. D-$50-$65, XP-$5, TV, bath, pool.

Red Crown Inn, Hwy 175 E, 557-1571. S-$33, D-$37, $1 key deposit. **Camping: KOA Kampground**, 7100 S Stemmons Rd, (817) 497-3353. Shady sites, free fire-wood, propane gas tanks, and a public hot tub and sauna. Site for two $24 (full hook-up).

FOOD

For the low-down on dining, pick up Friday's *Dallas Morning News*.

Celebration, 4503 W Lovers Lane, 352-5681. 'A real discovery for both its ambience and good food. Magnificent home cooking.'

Farmers' Produce Market, 670-5879, 1010 S Pearl Expressway, Downtown. Daily 5 am-6 pm. Best places to get fresh produce from local farms; 'veggie oasis.'

Gennie's Bishop Grill, 321 N Bishop Ave, 946-1752. Cafeteria-style, lines are short and functional. 'Garlic chicken is a must.' Note: **Rosemarie's**, the sister restaurant, is on Oak Cliff at 1411 N Zangs Blvd, 946-4146. 'Fabulous peanut butter pie!'

Mario's Chiquita, 4514 Travis, ground floor of Travis Walk, 521-0092. Mexican food, popular with Dallasites. 'Delicious, excellent service, not costly.' (Under $10; specialities change weekly.)

Mecca, 10422 Harry Hines Blvd, 352-0051. A happy-go-lucky roadhouse 'where a squadron of feisty waitresses rules the loose-jointed dining room/joint.' Chicken-fry and cinnamon rolls are specialities.

Natura Café, 2909 McKinney Ave, 855-5483. The menu is entitled 'New American Taste Indulgence with No Regrets!' Come here and experience high nutritional con-sciousness! Brunch Sat and Sun.

Norma's Café, 3330 Beltline Rd, Farmers Branch (near Dallas), 243-8646. Roadhouse with giant bfasts with everything from catfish to meatloaf on offer.

Sonny Bryan's, 2202 Inwood Rd, 357-7120. 'Best urban barbecue in Texas.' Funky, run-down atmosphere. Other Dallas locations are 302 N Market, 744-1610; 325 N St Paul, 979-0102; Plaza of the Americas Hotel, 871-2097; 4701 Frankford Rd, 447-0102; Macy's Food Court at the Galleria Mall, 851-5131. Mon-Fri 10 am 'til 4 pm, Sat 'til 3 pm, Sun 11 am-2 pm.

Tolbert's Chili Parlor, 350 N St Paul St, corner of Bryant St, 953-1353. Mon-Fri 11 am-7 pm, a primo chili shrine $5-$8.

In Fort Worth: Kincaid's, 4901 Camp Bowie Blvd, 732-2881. Feast your eyes (and mouth) on their world-renowned half-pound hamburger! Mon-Sat.
Paris Coffee Shop, 704 W Magnolia, 335-2041. Home-baking prepared daily, all under $6. Mon-Fri 6 am-3 pm, Sat 'til 11 am. 'The best breakfast and lunches in town.'
Pink Poodle Coffee Shop, 2516 NE 28th St, 624-1027. Homebaked pastries. Meals $4-$10, open 24 hrs. Under the Tower Restaurant, 5228 Camp Bowie, 731-6051. Chicken-fried steaks, burgers, sandwiches; $2-$6. Daily 11 am-6 pm, Sun noon-3 pm.

OF INTEREST
You have probably seen the Zapruder footage so often that there will be no problem in retracing the route that **John F Kennedy** took to his death on 22 Nov 1963. He was driven on Main to Houston and Elm where Lee Harvey Oswald is alleged to have fired the shot from the sixth floor of the **Texas School Book Depository**, 653-6666. Now a museum to the Kennedy life and legacy, it is easily reachable from the Greyhound station during a rest stop. Daily 9 am-6 pm, $4, audio tour $2. 'Very moving and sensitive.' Overlooking the scene is an **obelisk**. A Philip Johnson-designed **Cenotaph** is on Main St at Market. JFK spent his last night on this earth in the **Fort Worth Hyatt Regency**. Just across the street is **The Conspiracy Museum**, 110 S Market St, 771-3040. Exhibits, CD-Roms, maps and photos chronicle the deaths of famous figures including JFK and Lincoln. $7, daily 10 am-6 pm.
Dallas Museum of Art, 1717 N Harwood at Ross, 922-1200. Anchors the new **Arts District** with its excellent collections of Egyptian, Impressionist, modern and decorative art. Sculpture garden lies adjacent. Some pre-Colombian works. Tues-Wed & Fri 11 am-4 pm, Thurs 'til 9 pm, w/ends 11 am-5 pm. Free, except for special exhibits.
Neiman-Marcus Dept Store, Main and Ervay. Of it, Lucius Beebe said: 'Dallas, for all its oil, banks, insurance wouldn't exist without Neiman-Marcus. It would be Waco or Wichita, which is to say: nothing.'
Architecture: both the **Hyatt Regency** and **Reunion Tower** at 300 Reunion Blvd, 651-1234, get high marks: 'best things in Dallas,' 'especially beautiful at sunset'. There is an observation deck on the 50th floor of the Tower, $2, a good way to see and get a feel for the whole city before you start walking. Also worth a look is the c.1914 **Union Rail Station**, connected to the tower by underground walkway. The **Adolphus Hotel**, Commerce and Field, was built by a brewer and has a 40-ft beer bottle on top, which serves as a closet for a 19th floor suite.
Parks: Fair Park, SE of downtown on 2nd Ave, 670-8400. 277 acres, home to the Sept-Oct state fair, Cotton Bowl, and Big Tex fair. Inside park, **African-American Museum**, 565-9026, a multimedia collection of folk art and sculpture. Tues-Fri, noon-5 pm, Sat 10 am-5 pm, Sun 1 pm-5 pm; free. Nearby, **White Rock Lake** provides a haven for walkers, bikers, and inline skaters.
Ft Worth: Amon Carter Square: houses four free museums: the **Amon Carter Museum**, 738-1933, with its splendid Western Art Collection of Russells and Remingtons; the **Kimbell Art Museum**, 332-8451, itself an architectural tour de force by Louis Kahn, housing Oriental, pre-Columbian and late Renaissance works; the **Museum of Modern Art**, 738-9215; includes works by Andy Warhol, and the **Museum of Science and History**, 1501 Montgomery St, 732-1631, with sophisticated exhibits, and science movies in the Omni Theater, $5, $6 extra for films.
Fort Worth Stockyard District, along Exchange Ave and N Main St, on North side. Pungent and still active with Mon cattle auctions (free viewing). 'Original stalls and railway exist, storefronts and boardwalks renovated. Gives a feeling of the past.' For info on the Stockyards, obtain a copy of the *Stockyards Gazette* at the **Visitors Information Center**, 130 Exchange Ave, (817) 624-4741, Sun-Thurs 9 am-

6 pm, Fri 9 am-7 pm, Sat 9 am-8 pm. Every Fri pm, Sat and Sun, arts and crafts market, Stockyards Market Place, by Coliseum on Plaza. The Stockyards host Weekly rodeos, (817) 625-1025; April-Sept Sat 8 pm, \$8.

Billy Bob's Texas, 2520 Rodeo Plaza, the Yards, (817) 624-7117, the world's largest honky-tonk, a bull ring, a BBQ restaurant, pool tables, video games and 42 bars. Fri-Sat, 9 pm & 10 pm there is live professional bull riding. Free Texas waltz lessons, Thurs 7-8 pm. Cover \$1-9. Headliners at w/ends, \$5-\$25; local bands during week, \$1-\$3, daily 11 am-2 am (Sun noon-2 am). You can atone for your hangover at the **Cowboy Church** at the **Stockyards Hotel**, corner of Main and Exchange, Sun at 11 am. The **Chisolm Trail Round-Up**, (817) 625-7005, a 3-day jamboree in the stockyards, June 13-15 in 1997 commemorates the heroism of cowhands who led the Civil War-time cattle drive to Kansas, and the **Hog and Armadillo Races** are a must-see.

Frontiers of Flight Museum, Love Field, 2nd floor, 350-1651. Collection of aviation artefacts including the fur parka as worn by Adm. Richard E Byrd in 1929 on his first flight to the North Pole. Mon-Sat 10 am-5 pm, Sun 1 pm-5 pm, \$2.

Just outside of Fort Worth in Plano is **South Fork Ranch**, from the *Dallas* TV series. No longer tours of the house or oil rig, but free to view from outside.

SPORTS/ENTERTAINMENT

The free Weekly *Dallas Observer*, out every Wednesday, can help you assess your entertainment options. Also, for info on local entertainment, contact *www.pic.net/city-view/dallas.html* Check out **West End Market Place**, off Houston St. Shops, where there is a plethora of galleries, eateries, and dance clubs.

Six Flags Over Texas, 20 miles W of Dallas in Arlington, (817) 640-8900. \$28 includes all rides and shows. Open daily May-Sept; w/ends thereafter. The original of this ever expanding chain, the six flags referring to the six regimes that Texas has seen. Especially nauseating is the 'Texas Cliffhanger,' a 10 second free-fall from a 128 ft tower and 'Flashback' a looping rollercoaster with fast forward and reverse. The showpiece is a huge wooden frame coaster, the 'Texas Giant,' voted by those in the know the world's best. Also 5 hrs of air-conditioned shows.

Wet 'n' Wild, I-30 btwn Dallas & Fort Worth, exit Texas 360N, (817) 265-3356. \$20, see also 'Amusement Parks' box.

Sport: Football is the main religion in Dallas. Texas Stadium on the Carpenter Freeway is home to Superbowl champions, the **Cowboys**. Call 579-4800 for tkt availabilities (NB: tkts are scarce). The **Texas Rangers** play in btwn the two cities in Arlington. **Skateboarding/Inlining/BMX biking**: Rapid Revolutions Indoor Skatepark, 2551 Lombardy Lane #150, 358-0052.

INFORMATION

Dallas Convention and Visitors Bureau, Renaissance Tower, 1201 Elm St, suite #2000, 746-6700. The bureau also oversees two visitors centers: walk-in office at 1303 Commerce St, 746-6757, opposite the Adolphus Hotel and 603 Munger St, 880-0405, in the West End Market Place. Mon 8.30 am-5 pm; Tues-Fri 8 am-5 pm.

Fort Worth Convention and Visitors Bureau Information Center, 123 E Exchange, (817) 624-4741, at the Stockyards. Mon-Sat 9 am-6 pm, Sun from 11 am.

TRAVEL

Dallas: Amtrak, Union Station, 401 S Houston Ave, (800) 872-7245. The bars upstairs in terminal also worth a visit—cheap, and wonderful architecture.' Daily 9 am-6.30 pm.

Bicycle Exchange bike rental, 11716 Ferguson Rd, 270-9269. Mon-Fri 9 am-7 pm, Sat 9 am-5 pm. Also at 1305 S Broadway, 242-4209 (same hrs).

Dallas Area Rapid Transit (DART), 979-1111, The local buses, \$1. Routes radiate from downtown; serves most surburbs. Runs 5 am-midnight; to surburbs 5 am-8 pm. DART's downtown Dallas service **Hop-a-Bus**, 979-1111, has a park-and-ride system. 3 routes (blue/red/green) run Mon-Fri about every 10 mins. 25c, free transfers.

Greyhound, 205 S Lamar St (3 blocks E of Union Station), (800) 231-2222. 24 hrs.

Dallas-Fort Worth International Airport, 574-8888, btwn the two cities. Take #26 bus from Hines St downtown; at Parkland Hospital change to #409 'DFW-N Irving.' Free DFW shuttle will do the rest, and all for just $1. Or take a **Super Shuttle**, (817) 329-2000, from one of the main downtown hotels for $10 o/w. Rsvs only, 24 hrs in advance. At airport, in baggage claim area, dial (02) on 'ground transportation' phone.

Dallas LoveField Airport, 670-6080, in the north of the city, take #39 'Lovefield' bus from one of the blue bus stops on Commerce. Has mostly intra-Texas flights.

Fort Worth: Amtrak, 15th and Jones Sts, (800) 872-7245.

Greyhound, 901 Commerce St, (800) 231-2222. 24 hrs.

Yellow Cab Co, (800) 749-9422, 24 hrs.

HOUSTON The newer skyscrapers that crowd Houston's skyline have sleek skins of black sun-reflecting glass, the same material used for astronaut helmet visors. Seems appropriate, since this city of 1.6 million is inextricably linked with NASA and the first moon landing.

But space money is petty cash compared to Houston's real wealth, which comes from oil refineries and its port activities. A city of scattered satellite nodes, Houston has developed unconstrained by zoning—so it seems to go on for ever. Unless you have an air-conditioned car, ample time and money, skip humid and expensive Houston: 'Houston's wealth has taken a dive as the oil market has gone downhill. It is a huge modern city and has hardly any attractions. It is probably the most boring city I've been to. The tremendous humidity makes it even worse.' 'No car, no skates or bike? Forget Houston!' 'Downtown is dead!' For an interactive map and guide of Houston, click on *www.houstonet.com/*

ACCOMMODATION

Houston Downtown YMCA, 1600 Louisiana Ave, 659-8501. S-$17 + $5 key deposit. 'Basic.' Has cafeteria, TV and access to gym/health facilities. 'Usually full by noon.' Rsvs. Co-ed. Another branch, 7903 South Loop, 643-4396 is farther out but less expensive, S-$15.

Houston International Perry House Hostel, 5302 Crawford at Oakdale St, 523-1009. $11.25 AYH, $14.25 non-AYH. 'Friendly, clean and efficient with AC.' Laundry. Lock-out 10 am-5 pm.

The Morty Rich Hostel at Rice University, 6500 S Main St, 522-1096. Pool, small dorm rooms, modern facilities. Shopping and leisure sports are within walking distance, including university village and the museum district. Laundry, café, TV, computer room, games; $15.

FOOD

Diversity of ethnic restaurants due to city's large Indochinese population. Houston's cuisine mingles Mexican, Greek, Cajun, and Vietnamese food. Reasonably-priced restaurants along **Westheimer** and **Richmond Ave**, intersecting with **Fountainview**.

Bellaine Broiler Burger, 5216 Bellaine Blvd, 668-8171. 'Burgers are delicious, shakes are real!' Open Mon-Sat.

Goode Company Barbeque, 5109 Kirby, 522-2530/523-7154. Pig out on crunch-crusted pork ribs, melt-in-the-mouth brisket, chicken, ham, duck, or turkey with peppery pinto beans and luscious jalapeno cheese bread on the side. Busy at w/ends.

J Putty's Pizza, 500 Dallas, 951-9369. Also at 1910 Travis & 500 Jefferson.
Otto's BBQ, 5502 Memorial Dr, 864-8526. Serving best ribs in town since 1963. 11 am-9 pm Mon-Sat.

OF INTEREST

Astrodome, 799-9500, south of downtown. The first and still one of the largest indoor stadia in the world, modestly called 'Taj Mahal,' 'Eighth Wonder,' etc, in its literature. Tours $4, 3 times daily (except Sun), obligatory when no event. More worthwhile to combine a visit with a **Houston Astros** baseball game or other happening (from dog shows to dirt-bike races). Cheapest seats in the pavilion ($4, purchased day of game) but also: 'We recommend $6-$9 Upper Reserve seats, seven levels up, behind home base.' Take #15 bus from Main St.

Astroworld, opposite A-Dome, 799-8404. Six Flags clone with 100 rides, $28, open April-Labor Day, varying hours; thereafter w/ends only.

Take a drive by the **Beer Can House**, 222 Malone. Adorned with 50,000 beer cans, strings of beer-can tops, and a beer-can fence, the house was built by a retired upholsterer from the Southern Pacific Railroad. The **Anheuser-Busch Brewery**, 77 S Gellhorn Rd, 670-1695, offers free self-guided tours ending with a complimentary drink. Mon-Sat 9 am-4 pm. For all skateboarding/inline/BMX enthusiasts, there is an abundancy of skateparks, **Baytown Skatepark; Skatepark of Houston;** and **South Side Indoor Skatepark.**

Hermann Park. Zoo, gardens, paddleboats, golfing and the Museums of Natural Science.

Zoological Gardens, 525-3300. Gorillas, hippos, reptiles, and rare white tigers. Also hosts a macabre bat colony. You're allowed to see them quaff their daily blood—fascinating, repellent. Entry to zoo $2.50; 525-3300, 10 am-6 pm daily. **Natural Science Museum**, 639-4600, has moon-landing equipment. Also offers displays of gems and minerals, a planetarium, and an IMAX theatre ($9). Inside the museum's **Cockrell Butterfly Centre** in a tropical paradise of 80F, there are more than 2000 butterflies, $3.

Hundreds of shops and restaurants line the 18 mile **Houston Tunnel System**, which connects all the major buildings in downtown Houston, Civic Center to the Hyatt Regency. Also, try the **Galleria**, Westhiemer St, an enormous shopping mall with over 300 shops.

Museum of Fine Arts, 1001 Bissonet, 639-7300. Exhibition wing designed by Mies Van der Rohe. Renaissance art plus renowned Hogg collection of 65 paintings, watercolours by Frederick Remington. Tue-Sat 10 am-5 pm, Thur 'til 9 pm (free all day Thur), Sun 12.15 pm-6 pm. $3, $1.50 w/student ID. The museum's **Sculpture Garden**, 5101 Montrose St, includes pieces by artists such as Matisse and Rodin. Daily 9 am-10 pm, free. Across the street, the **Contemporary Arts Museum**, 5216 Montrose St, 526-3129, has multimedia exhibits. $3 sugg donation.

NASA-LBJ Space Center, 1601 NASA Rd 1 (20 miles S of downtown via I-45), (800) 972-0369. Limited bus service (#245), 6 hr Gray Line Tour, 223-8800, costs $29, leaving downtown 10 am daily. 'Cheaper to Rent-a-Heap, 977-7771, and take your time.' Also, 'hitching is worst I've ever come across, took us 2 hrs to get a lift.' daily 9 am-7 pm (summer), 10 am-5 pm (winter); $12. Or take free guided tour: see spacecraft, shuttle trainer, moon rocks, NASA films.'No need to book Mission Control tours. First come, first served basis.' 'Very exciting seeing Mission Control in action. We watched a test run for the next shuttle mission.' 'Very informative.' The complex also houses models of Gemini, Apollo and Mercury as well as countless galleries and hands-on exhibits. You too can try to land the space shuttle on a computer simulator!

Port of Houston. Now that a deep channel runs 50 miles S to the Gulf of Mexico, Houston is a major port. From the observation platform at Wharf 9 you can watch huge ships in the Turning Basin. 1½ hr boat trips, 670-2416, available Tue-Sun. A free look at the bayou and a stunning perspective of the skyline. Book well ahead in summer. Closed Sept.

Rothko Chapel, 3900 Yupon, in Montrose area, 524-9839. A multi-faith chapel, its walls bedecked with Rothko's exercises in controlled simplicity. Daily 10 am-6 pm; free.

Sam Houston Park, downtown at Allen Pkwy and Bagby St, 655-1912. Nice melange of historic Greek Revival, Victorian, log cabin and cottage against a canyon of office buildings. Daily guided tours $6. Not far away is **Tranquillity Park** at Bagby and Walker, named in honour of lunar landings. 'Truly an oasis in the desert.'

ENTERTAINMENT

For some chills and thrills, wander down **Richmond Ave**, btwn Hillcroft & Chimney Rock. **City Streets**, 5078 Richmond Ave, 840-8555 has 6 different clubs featuring country, R&B, disco, 80s etc. Tues-Fri 5 pm-2 am. $2-5 cover good for all 6 clubs. Also, the **Ale House**, 2425 W Alabama at Kirby, 521-2333 has a beer garden to chill in while you experiment some of the 130 brands of beer. Mon-Sat 11 am-2 am, Sun noon-2 am.

Astrodome (see Of Interest), Loop 610 at Kirby Dr, 799-9555, also features rock shows. Huge video screens afford a good view. 'During intermission girls often do impromptu strips (really!) when the video camera points at them.' Feb sees the Rodeo and Livestock Show, (naturally) the world's largest. Also home of the **Oilers** (799-1000), and the **Astros** (526-1709) baseball teams.

Miller Outdoor Theatre, Hermann Park, 520-3290. Free symphony, ballet, plays, drama and musicals most evenings, April-Oct. 'Get there 30 mins early for good position.' Tkts required for seats, box office 11 am-1 pm.

Annual Shakespeare Festival runs from late July to early Aug, 520-3290.

TRAVEL/INFORMATION

Amtrak, 902 Washington Ave, (800) 872-7245, near to main post office. In rough neighbourhood; at night call a cab.

Greater Houston Convention and Visitors Bureau, 801 Congress St across from Market Square, (800) 231-7799. Mon-Fri 8.30 am-5 pm.

Greyhound, 2121 S Main St, (800) 231-2222. Open 24 hrs—unsafe neighbourhood; call a cab, again!

Houston Intercontinental Airport (HIA), 25 miles N of downtown. Take Metro bus #102 (IAH Express)on Travis going north; last bus out 9.10 pm, last into downtown 9.10 pm; $1.20. No w/end service. Out of bus hours, catch an **Airport Express** bus, 523-8888, leaving from next door to Hyatt Regency on Louisiana, leaves every 1/2 hr from 7 am 'til 11.30 pm, $15-17, rsvs 1 day in advance.

Metro Transit Authority, 739-4000. Local METRO buses, basic fare $1, express $1.50, free transfers. Reliable service within the 'loop' of I-610, anywhere btwn NASA and Katy. Less frequent at w/ends.

GALVESTON   History rich, hurricane prone Galveston was once headquarters for pirate Jean LaFitte, who liked its 32 miles of sandy beaches (so handy for burying bullion). Houston's ship channel eventually siphoned off the big shipping business, leaving Galveston at its architectural peak: a resplendent little city of scarlet oleanders, nodding palms and fine 19th century mansions. Come here to gorge on bay shrimp, and imbibe the placid, slightly decayed Southern feeling of the place.

Unfortunately, the beach here isn't as fine as those further to the south. Nearby oil wells and refineries pollute the water with annoying globs of tar, and the shore is hard and flat. It reminds you of a parking lot by the seashore. Camping is permitted in the state park. Access via causeway and by free ferry from Port Bolivar to the East. Take a virtual tour of Galveston Island (includes photos), through *www.utmb.edu/galveston*

ACCOMODATION/FOOD

To save money make Galveston a day trip from Houston. However Galveston Island State Park on 13_ Mile Rd (6 miles SW of Galveston on FM 3005), 737-1222, has sites for $17. Along **Seawall Blvd**, check out the bountiful seafood and traditional Texas barbecue. Try **The Original Mexican Café**, 1401 Market, 762-6001, the oldest restaurant on the island. Tex-Mex meals with homemade flour tortillas. Daily lunch specials ($5). Mon-Fri 11 am-10 pm, Sat-Sun 8 am-10 pm.

OF INTEREST

Texas Seaport Museum, Pier 21 at end of Kempner (22nd) St, 763-3037. Home to *Elissa*, a Scottish-built square-rigged sailing ship restored to its 1877 condition. Daily 10 am-5.30 pm, $5. Some of the **architecture** worth seeing: **Ashton Villa**, 24th and Broadway, 762-3933, an elegantly restored 1859 Italianate mansion. Tour includes slide show about the 1900 hurricane that claimed 5000-7000 lives, $4, 10 am-4 pm daily. **The Bishop's Palace**, 762-2475, 1402 Broadway, extravagant 1886 home, $5, noon-5.30 pm summer, 4.30 pm winter. **The Strand** contains a fine concentration of over fifty 19th C iron front buildings, which house a pastiche of cafes, restaurants, gift shops and clothing stores. 'Rollerskate,' bike rental shops on Seawall Blvd. Useful shower/changing facilities on Stewart beach, $5 entry includes use of shower. Has lockers.

Stop by **Moody Gardens**, (800) 582-4673, an area although filled with touristy spas and restaurants, makes room for a l0-story glass pyramid which encloses a tropical rainforest, 2000 exotic species of flora and fauna, a 3D **IMAX Theater** with a six-story-high screen, and the **Bat Cave**. Rainforest and IMAX daily 10 am-9 pm Nov-Feb. Sun-Thurs 10 am-6 pm, Fri-Sat 10 am-9 pm. $6 each.

INFORMATION/TRAVEL

Galveston Island Convention and Visitors Bureau, 2106 Seawall Blvd, 736-4311; daily 8.30 am-5 pm. Provides info about island activities.
The Strand Visitors Center, 2106 Strand St, 765-7834. Mon-Sat 9.30 am-6 pm, Sun from 10 am.
Texas Bus Lines (affiliated to Greyhound), 714 25th St, 765-7731. Four buses daily btwn Houston and Galveston, $11 o/w.

CORPUS CHRISTI and THE SOUTH TEXAS COAST A large port city with a leaping population, **Corpus Christi** (translated as 'body of Christ') makes a good gateway to **Padre Island**, a long lean strip of largely unspoilt National Seashore that points toward the Texas toe. Once inhabited by cannibals, the shifting blond sands of Padre have seen five centuries of piracy and shipwrecks and no doubt conceal untold wealth. The natural wonders of the 110-mile-long island are quite sufficient for most people. However, it's a prime area for bird watching, shelling and beachcombing for glass floats. You can camp free at a number of idyllic and primitive spots. All are at the South Padre end, reached only via Hwy 100. Camp on the seaward side of the dunes; the grassy areas may have poisonous rattlesnakes. Besides Galveston and Padre, the South Texas coast has hundreds of miles of coastline and various other islands.

North and east of Padre Island and Corpus Christi is the **Aransas Wildlife Refuge** where you can go by boat from Rockport and see (in season and at a distance) the world's remaining 150 whooping cranes. In

Rockport, get down to marvellous seafood and gumbo eating at **Charlotte Plummer's**, 729-1185. Corpus Christi, South Padre and the entire area are rich in roadside stands that sell cheap, fresh boiled shrimp and tamales, the local speciality.

South Texas border towns with Mexico are numerous but not particularly appealing. Avoid **Laredo**: 'A dump with ripoff hotels.' **Brownsville/Matamoros** is probably the best and certainly most convenient to South Padre. 'Got free tourist card from Mexican consulate at 10th and Washington Streets in 5 mins.' For a directory to the most current events, places and services of Corpus Christi and Coastal Bend, check out *www.interconnect.net/connected*.

ACCOMODATION
Cheap accomodation is scarce downtown. For the best motel bargains, drive several miles south on Leopard St (bus #27) or I-37 (take #27 express). Campers should head for the **Padre Island National Seashore (PINS)**, (512) 949-8173, or **Mustang State Park**, (512) 749-5246. The latter offers elec, water, showers and picnic tables for $17. All must pick up a camping permit from the ranger station at the park entrance. **Nueces River City Park**, 884-7275, has free tent sites but portable restrooms, no showers.

FOOD
Best to check out the Southside, around **Staples St**, and **S Padre Island Drive**.
Buckets Sports Bar & Grill, 227 N Water St, 883-7776. An eclectic menu of American, Cajun, Italian and Mexican dishes. Daily 11 am-4 am.
Che Bello, 320 C William St, 882-8832. Homemade gelato, sorbets and pastries. Lunch up to $6, patio.
Howard's BBQ, 120 N Water St, 882-1200. Ample beef and sausage plate, salad bar buffet and drink ($5). Mon-Fri 11 am-3 pm.

INFORMATION/TRAVEL
Greyhound, 702 N Chaparral, (800) 231-2222. Daily 7 am-3 pm.
South Padre Tourist Bureau, 600 Padre Blvd, (210) 761-6433, 8 am-6 pm daily.
Visitors Bureau, 1201 N Shoreline, (800) 678-6232.

EL PASO Biggest Mexican border city, El Paso feels neither Hispanic nor Texan. Backed by mountains, El Paso's main focus is the Rio Grande River, where early Spanish expeditions used to cross. The river also serves as the border and a casual, non-bureaucratic one it is. Other than sampling the sleazy delights of **Ciudad Juarez**, there's little reason to tarry in El Paso. It can serve as a base for Carlsbad Caverns (in New Mexico) and **Big Bend**, 477-2251, and **Guadalupe Mountains National Parks**, 828-3251, which are all within easy driving distance. NB: Buses aren't very frequent—'you may get stranded in Whites City for 10 hrs!' The latter, 110 miles east, includes **El Capitan**, a 8085ft cliff, and 8749ft **Guadalupe Peak**, highest in Texas. The park has two main campgrounds; $6, no rsvs. 'Unless your journey necessitates going via El Paso, take another route.' The El Paso Infopage is a one stop information centre, located at *www.bestweb.com/elpaso/*

ACCOMMODATION
El Paso International AYH Hostel in the **Gardner Hotel**, 311 E Franklin Ave, 532-3661. Small dorms, beautiful, spacious kitchen, common room with pool table, TV and couches for lounging and socialising in basement. $14 AYH, $17 non-AYH. Linen

$2. Rsvs. Gardner Hotel: S-$25-30, D-$45. AC, kitchen, laundry, 24 hr check-in.

Gateway Hotel, 104 S Stanton St, 532-2611. Close to San Jacinto Sq. Clean, spacious lrge beds and closets. Diner downstairs. Check out 4 pm. S-$21, D-$33. Few dollars more for TV.

FOOD
Burritos are the undisputed local speciality!

Forti's Mexican Elder Restaurant, 321 Chelsea Dr close to I-10, 772-0066. The fajitas and shrimps are superb. $4-$12. Sun-Thur 11 am-10 pm, Fri-Sat 11 am-11 pm.

H&H Coffee Shop, 701 E Yandell, 533-1144. Adjoins H&H car wash; nip in for a quick cuppa! Renowned for its hangover cure of tripe and hominy stew (Sat only). Mon-Sat.

Leo's, 5315 Hondo Pass, 757-6612. 'Good Mexican food. Fast, helpful service.' 4 other locations in El Paso.

Smitty's, 6219 Airport Rd, 772-5876. Tender brisket, lunch and dinner served. Mon-Sat.

Tigua Indian Reservation, 121 Old Pueblo Rd, Ave of America's Exit off I-10, 859-7913. Daily 'til 5 pm. Besides its crafts and rather small restored mission, the reservation has a good eating place, 859-3916, in the museum, with excellent red and green chili, and other traditional dishes. Worth a stop, if only for the food.

OF INTEREST
Simply stroll through downtown to see the colourful remnants of El Paso's Wild West history.

Ciudad Juarez. Simply stroll across the bridge, 25¢ toll each way. 'Mexican immigration didn't even give us a glance.' 'You can also ride the bus over but why bother. If you do, hold on to your passport and don't surrender your IAP-66 to the US authorities.'

Ciudad Juarez, 4th largest city in Mexico, is poor by western standards, though wealthy by Mexican standards. The shopping for leather, rugs and clothing is excellent. Drinking Tecate Beer in the **Kentucky Club**, an old western bar, you can pretend you're Papa Hemingway as you wait for the bullfights to begin. Three bridges span the Rio Grande between El Paso and Ciudad Juarez. The main bridge is Cordova, which is free. Other bridges charge $1 there, $2 back (cars); on foot, 25¢ there and 50¢ back.

Americana Museum, Civic Center Plaza, under Performing Arts Bldg, 542-0394. Explores Native American and pre-Columbian America. Tue-Fri, 10 am-5 pm, free. Hop aboard the **Border Jumper trolleys**, departing every hr from El Paso, for a whirlwind exploration of the streets!

El Paso Museum of History, I-10 West and Ave of the Americas, 858-1928. Tells the story of the Indian, Conquistador, Vaquero (Mexican cowboy), cowboy, and the US Cavalryman, all of whom fought and bled to win the Southwest. Tue-Sun 9 am-4.50 pm, free/donations.

Fort Bliss Replica Museum, in north El Paso, 568-4518, houses several museums on the base exploring the history of the Civil War, the 3rd Armored Cavalry, and air defence, daily from 9 am-4.30 pm.

San Jacinto Plaza, plays host to street musicians. In Feb, El Paso hosts the **Southwestern Livestock Show & Rodeo**, 532-1401, and the **World's Finals Rodeo**, 545-1188 in Nov. Outside of El Paso, visit **Hueco Tanks State Historical Park** for rock climbing and Indian pictographs.

INFORMATION
Tourist Office, 1 Civic Center Plaza (small round building next to Chamber of Commerce), 544-0062.

Mexican Consulate, 910 E San Antonio St, 533-4082. Mon-Fri 9 am-4.30 pm.

TRAVEL
Amtrak, 700 San Francisco St, (800) 872-7245. On *Texas Eagle* route. Mon, Wed and Sat 11 am-6.30 pm, Tues, Thurs and Sun 9 am-5 pm.
El Paso International Airport, about 5 miles NE of downtown. Take #33 bus from the Plaza, 75¢; takes about 30 mins, last bus out to airport at 9.15 pm.
Greyhound, 111 200 W San Antonio, (800) 231-2222. 24 hrs.
Sun Metro, 533-3333. Local bus service, basic fare 85¢, departs from San Jacinto Plaza.
Yellow Cab Taxis, 533-3433.

LUBBOCK The link between Texas' heartland and coastal ports and called 'Chrysanthemum Capital of the World,' with over 80,000 plants throughout the city. However, it is perhaps better known as home of the **Red Raiders** (Texas Tech Football Stadium) and site of **Buddy Holly's Memorial and Walk of Fame**, 8th St and Ave A; a collection of plaques commemorating West Texas stars. Lubbock's state park, **Mackenzie**, is the most popular in Texas, off E Broadway and Ave A. BUNACers recommend the **Midnight Rodeo** (745-2813; closed Mon), a huge dance bar in the middle of town, for the traditional Texan two-step and lots of drinks specials.
The area code for Lubbock is 806.

THE SOUTH

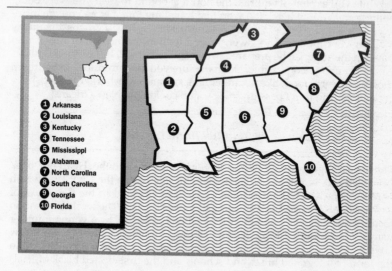

1. Arkansas
2. Louisiana
3. Kentucky
4. Tennessee
5. Mississippi
6. Alabama
7. North Carolina
8. South Carolina
9. Georgia
10. Florida

Although Northerners may hate to admit it, the South has given birth to much of the best American music, architecture and literature. The plaintive call of the blues rose up from the Mississippi Delta, and from the hills of Appalachia came the early strains of country music. Exuberant jazz echoed from the alleys of New Orleans; from Memphis burst rock n' roll. In contrast to the pristine architecture of Puritan New England, Spanish and French sensibilities contributed to the refined ante-bellum architecture of the deep South. Together, romantic notions of the plantation, the isolation of agricultural life, and the rigid social stratifications of slavery provided the setting for Southern writers such as Wright, Faulkner, Williams, Wolfe and Welty.

From a Southern perspective, the Civil War was a Northern attack upon a way of life based upon the misery of millions of slaves, but also upon agriculture and a planters' aristocracy. The passions the war unleashed are difficult to appreciate. The fight was to the death, and most of the old South was in fact destroyed. Although the United States had one-sixth the population in 1860 that it had in 1960, six times as many men died in the Civil War as in Vietnam. In defeat, Virginia General Robert E. Lee and Confederate President Jefferson Davis are still honored with statues and parades in the central square of every Southern city.

Only recently has the South begun to come out from under the economic and racial clouds of the war. The dream of equal rights, deferred since the Civil War, was brought closer by the hard-fought civil rights movement which forced legislative and social change in the 1960s. Today black mayors run many cities, economic success is open to all and schools and businesses are more integrated, but growing signs of a 'white backlash' reveal that ten-

417

sions still run deep. Meanwhile high technology in Alabama, banking in Atlanta, and research in North Carolina testify to the growing economic power of the 'New South.'

While you explore its quirks, the South is bound to treat you well. Being polite counts down here. You won't be travelling long before you are introduced to simple, but gracious 'Southern Hospitality.' Perhaps the sultry weather contributes to a slower, more Mediterranean pace of life. If you travel in the summer, be prepared to sweat it out. It will be hot and humid as you never imagined possible. Do make sure you are introduced to Southern cooking—hearty food, like pecan pie, chicken and catfish fried to crisp, juicy perfection. And don't pass up spicy Cajun cooking in New Orleans!

ALABAMA   *The Yellowhammer State*

Thirty years ago the ways of the Old South were dear to the 'Heart of Dixie,' (so called due to the old $10 notes issued here before the Civil War which bore the word 'dix,' French for ten). Governors stood in the doorways of white schools barring blacks; segregation was the law. The world's attention focused on Alabama's racism in 1955 when blacks, led by a young minister named Martin Luther King, Jr, began a peaceful revolt against the Jim Crow laws that walled them in. Today, the civil rights struggle has borne fruit in the form of integrated buses and schools and the first elected black officials since reconstruction.

Economic changes have been as far-reaching. Share-cropping and agrarian poverty still exist, but King Cotton no longer rules Alabama's economy as it did before the Civil War. Medical research in Birmingham, aircraft engines in Mobile, and rockets from Huntsville are major industries, closely followed by tourism, thanks to the Gulf Coast, the Tennessee Valley lake country in the north, and graceful touches of the Old South in Mobile and Montgomery. The humble peanut provides the base for another booming industry; there are acres of peanut fields in the southern Wiregrass area of the State, and each autumn the town of Dothan hosts the National Peanut Festival.

'The State of Surprises' is home to many of America's most prominent African-Americans, including Joe Louis, the boxer, Hank Aaron, the baseball home run king, W C Handy, father of the blues, George Washington Carver, scientist, Booker T Washington, educator, Jesse Owens, Olympic athlete, and Nat King Cole, singer.

With such diverse geography, mountains in the north and beaches in the south, Alabama is a perfect location for those who love the outdoors. With over 26 state parks and 4 national forests, spreading from the rugged wilderness to the Gulf Coast, there is no shortage of places to camp, hike, walk, fish, and even hunt. *www.nps.gov/.*
www.yahoo.com/Regional/U_S_States/Alabama.
The area code for Alabama is 334.

MOBILE   The flags of France, Spain, England and the Confederacy have all flown over this attractive port city on the Gulf of Mexico. The town's varied history is best reflected in the old quarter's architecture and is at its most beautiful when the azaleas bloom in March. The people of Mobile have been celebrating Mardi Gras since 1703, longer than anywhere else in the US, and people who have seen it say it is second only to the one in New Orleans, 150 miles west.

The area is not as attractive as it once was. Hurricane Frederick, which struck in 1979, destroyed many charming old buildings, now replaced by papermills and typical highway eyesores. Still, Mobile offers some of the most beautiful streets in the South.

ACCOMMODATION
Budget Inn, 555 Government St, Hwy 90, 433-0590. S/D-$35.
Family Inns, 900 S Beltine Rd, 344-5500. I-65 at Airport Blvd. S-$29, D-$36.
Holiday Inn Express, 255 Church St, 433-6923. S/D-$54. 'Right downtown. Rooms of a very good standard. Pool. Bfast included.'
Motel 6, 1520 Matzenger Dr, I-10 exit on Dauphin Island Parkway, 473-1603. S-$28, D-$32.
Olsson's Motel, 4137 Government Blvd, 661-5331. S-$29, D-$32.

FOOD
Rousso's, 166 S Royal St, 433-3322. Daily 11 am-10 pm. 'Good food, quite reasonably priced.'
The Lumber Yard, 2617 Dauphin St, 467-4609. Sandwiches, pizza, salad, soup, desserts. Bar happy hours, Mon-Sat, 4 pm-7 pm. Mon-Fri 11 am-10 pm, Sat until 11 pm.
Wintzell's Oyster House, 605 Dauphin St, 432-4605. Lunch under $7, dinner from $10. 'Very popular place.' Mon-Sat, 11 am-9 pm (Fri 9.45 pm).

OF INTEREST
February is a good time to visit Mobile, with the blooming of the 27 mile Azalea Trail and Mardi Gras filling the streets. Enjoy parades, floats, costumes, and the carnival atmosphere. Nice to wander around the old squares and streets, dating back to the 1700s when the French held sway in Mobile. **Bienville Sq, De Tonti Sq** and **Church Street** have been restored. Check with the Mobile Visitors Center at Fort Conde for walking and driving maps of the neighbourhoods. Among the houses open to the public are: **Condé Charlotte House**, 104 Theatre St, 432-4722. Tues-Sat 10 am-4 pm, $4, $3 w/student ID.
Richards DAR House, 256 N Joachim St, 434-7320. A $3 charge buys a tour of the 1845 period-furnished home as well as tea and cookies with the house staff. Tues-Sat 10 am-4 pm, Sun 1 pm-4 pm.
Oakleigh, 350 Oakleigh Place, 432-1281, 1833 antebellum mansion furnished by the Historic Society. $5, $2 w/student ID. Admission includes tours of the mansion and the nearby **Creole Cottage**. Mon-Sat 10 am-4 pm, Sun 2 pm-4 pm.
Museum of the History of Mobile, 355 Government St, 434-7569. 17th, 18th, 19th century artifacts. Tue-Sun 10 am-4 pm. Free.
U.S.S. Alabama Battleship Memorial Park, Mobile Bay, Battleship Pkwy, 433-2703. Roam around the historic WW II battleship moored here on the river along with the submarine U.S.S. Drum. See also the B-52 bomber 'Calamity Jane,' a SR-71 Blackbird spy plane and other military exhibits. The battleship is now a state shrine. 'Can be explored from bow to stern.' $8, flight simulator $3. Tkt office open 8 am-7.30 pm, ship closes 8 pm. 'Non-drivers must take a taxi to get there—cannot walk through road tunnel—about $4 each way.'
Cathedral of the Immaculate Conception, 4 S Clairbourne St, 434-1565. Designed by Claude Beroujon in 1835 and now named a minor basilica. Open 7 am-3 pm. 'Worth a look.'

Dauphin Island, 30 miles S of Mobile, is a quiet place where you can camp, swim and wander. Off the hwy just before the island, blooms **Bellingrath Gardens**, 973-2217, designed by the founder of Coca-Cola.

INFORMATION
Mobile Visitor Center/Fort Condé Welcome Center, 150 S Royal St, (800) 252-3862 or 434-7304. Inside reconstructed 1724 fort complete with canons and costumed guides. Open 8 am-5 pm.
Chamber of Commerce, 451 Government St, 433-6951.
Alabama Visitors Bureau, 968-7511. For general info call (800) 252-2262.

TRAVEL
Amtrak, 11 Government St, 432-4052/(800) 872-7245. Daily 5.30 am-midnight.
Greyhound, 2545 Government Blvd, (800) 231-2222.
Mobile Transit Authority, 344-6600. Major depots, Bienville Sq, Royal St parking garage, and Adams Mark Hotel. Runs Mon-Fri, 6 am-6 pm, $1.25, transfers 50c. NB: There is no service to the airport. For a taxi call 476-7711, around $24 o/w.

BIRMINGHAM   Once known as the steel town of the South, Birmingham is now a major centre for biomedical research, finance, manufacturing, wholesale/retail industries and engineering. The city scored a double in 1989 when it was named 'America's Most Livable City' by the US Conference of Mayors, and one of 'America's Hot Cities' by *Newsweek Magazine*.

The great civil rights marches of 1963 began here—protests that threw Martin Luther King, Jr. into the city's jail. Sixteen years later, Birmingham elected its first black mayor. Although the population is predominantly white, the city retains an ethnic diversity from the days when immigrants came to work in the steel industry. Birmingham stretches for 15 miles along the Jones Valley, and the best views are from the top of nearby Shades and Red Mountains.
The area code for Birmingham is 205.

ACCOMMODATION
National 9, 2224 5th Ave N, 324-6688, near downtown. TV, pool. S/D-$35-$41.
Oak State Park, 620-2527. 15 miles S of Birmingham, off I-65 in Pelham (exit 246). 10,000 acres of thick forest offer hiking, golf, horse-riding, and an 85 acre lake. Sites $8.50, w/hook-up $15.
Tourway Inn, 1101 6th Ave N, 252-3921. S-$33, D-$35. TV, pool. Downtown.
YWCA, for women only, 309 23rd St N, 322-9922, $10/night plus $15 deposit.

FOOD
Bogues, 3028 Clairmont Ave, 254-9780. Cheap diner serving southern fare. Mon-Fri 6 am-2 pm, w/end 11.30 am-2 pm.
Ollie's, 515 University Blvd, 324-9485. Famous for barbecued dishes. Meals under $6. Mon-Sat 10 am-8 pm.
Milo's, 509 18th St S, 933-5652. Unique hamburgers and fries. Mon-Sat 10 am-9 pm, Sun 11 am-9 pm.

OF INTEREST
Antebellum Arlington—the birthplace of Birmingham, is at 331 Cotton Ave SW, 780-5656. Home features an array of 19th century southern decorative arts. $2.50 w/student ID. Tue-Sat 10 am-3.30 pm, Sun 1 pm-4 pm. 'Something out of old Dixie.'

The **Vulcan Statue**, which dominates Red Mountain, is the largest cast iron statue in the world, and, in the US, is second only to the Statue of Liberty in height. Erected to honour the steel industry, Vulcan is 55 ft tall and stands on a 124-foot pedestal; his massive head alone weighs 6 tonnes. He carries a torch in his hand which burns green unless there has been a traffic fatality in the area, in which case the flame turns red: the world's largest traffic safety reminder! Elevator to observation deck at top; $1. 328-2863. 8.30 am-10.30 pm daily.

The Red Mountain Museum, 2230 22nd St S, 933-4104. Hands-on science museum with mineral and fossil displays as well as a free self-guided tour of the geology supporting Vulcan's craft. Don't miss the 14 ft mosasaur fossil or the 'discovery' section where you can explore body mechanics and the myths of modern technology. Mon-Fri 9 am-5 pm, Sat 10 am-4 pm, Sun 1 pm-4 pm. $2.

Birmingham Civil Rights Institute, 520 16th St N, in historic civil rights district, 328-9696. Documents the Civil Rights Movement since the 1920's. More than just a museum as it promotes ongoing research and discourse on human rights issues. Drama performances often held here at night. Tues-Sat 10 am-5 pm, Sun 1 am-5 pm. Free. **Alabama Sports Hall of Fame**, 2150 Civic Center Blvd, 323-6665, pays tribute to all-time greats such as Jesse Owens and Birmingham's own prize hitter, Willie Mays. Mon-Sat 9 am-5 pm, Sun 1 am-5 pm. $5, $3 w/student ID. 'Arrive early.'

Sloss Furnaces, 32nd St by 2nd Ave, 324-1911. Exhibits of iron and steel making. Free. Tue-Sat 10 am-4 pm, Sun noon-4 pm.

Botanical Gardens, 2612 Lane Park Road, 879-1227. Rose Garden, Japanese Garden with tea house and the largest conservatory in the Southeast. Open sunrise to sunset daily. Free. Across the road is **Birmingham Zoo**, 879-0408, the largest zoo in the Southeast which houses nearly 1000 mammals, birds and reptilea over 100 acres. 9.30 am-7 pm daily. $5.

Alabama Jazz Hall of Fame, in the historic, art deco Carver theater, 4th Ave and 17th St, 254-2731. Find out how a Birmingham native wrote jazz anthem 'Tuxedo Junction' and browse around this collection of memorabilia paying tribute to the jazz greats of Alabama. Tues-Sat 10 am-6 pm, Sun 1-5 pm. Free.

Alabama Museum of the Health Science, Lister Hill Library, University of Alabama Campus, 934-4475. Exhibits relating to history of medicine in the State. The adjoining **Reynolds Historical Library**, one of the top historical science libraries in the nation, has original letters from George Washington and Florence Nightingale. Mon-Fri, 8 am-5 pm.

INFORMATION/TRAVEL
Visitors Bureau, 2200 9th Ave North, 252-9825, (800) 962-6453. Mon-Fri 8.30 am-5 pm, Sun 1-5 pm.
Travelers Aid, 3600 8th Ave S, 322-5426. Mon-Fri 8 am-4.30 pm.
Chamber of Commerce, 2027 1st Ave N, 323-5461.
Greyhound, 619 N 19th St, (800) 231-2222. 24 hrs.
For a **taxi** to the airport call 788-8294, $8-$11.

MONTGOMERY   The capital of Alabama, Montgomery was capital of the entire Confederacy until the honour was transferred to Richmond. The Senate Chamber is kept just as it was the day secession was voted, and the tree-shaded streets lined with ante-bellum homes help carry you back a hundred and more years.

It was not until 1955, almost 100 years after the Civil War, that Rosa Parks, a black woman of tremendous courage, dragged Montgomery into the 20th Century when she refused to give up her bus seat to a white passenger.

Parks was arrested, and Montgomery blacks voted to stage a bus boycott on Dec 2, 1955, launching a new era in civil rights protest. A young preacher named King helped organize the boycott.

The area code is 334.

ACCOMMODATION
Fort Toulouse Jackson Park, 7 miles N of Montgomery on Rte 6 off US 231, 567-3002. 39 camp sites in woodland w/hook-up. Tents $8.
Motel 6, 1051 Eastern Blvd, I-85 to East Blvd Exit 6, 277-6748. S-$33, D-$38.
The Inn South, 4243 Inn South Ave, 288-7999. S-$29, D-$35.
Town Plaza, 743 Madison Ave, 269-1561, S-$22, D-$38.

FOOD
Chris's Dogs, 138 Dexter Ave, 265-6850. Famous for its chili sauce.
Martha's Place, 548, Sayre St, 263-9135. Recently opened. 'Country lunch,' entree with drink, sides, and dessert, $5.50. Sunday buffet $6.50. Mon-Fri, 11 am-3 pm, Fri 5 pm-9 pm, Sun 11 am-3 pm.
Montgomery Curb Market, 1004 Madison Ave, 263-6445. Sells home-made pies, fresh produce. Tue, Thur, Sat am. Also try **Montgomery State Farmers' Market**, 1655 Federal Dr, 242-5350, a 28-acre complex including cafe serving breakfast and lunch, garden centre and stalls selling farm produce, home baking, and crafts. Daily 7 am-6 pm.

OF INTEREST
State Capitol, Brainbridge St at Dexter Ave, 242-3935. A gold star marks the spot where Jefferson Davis was inaugurated as president of the Confederacy in February 1861. Note also the impressive murals depicting state history and the graceful hanging spiral staircases. Mon-Sat, 9 am-4 pm.
First White House of the Confederacy, 644 Washington Ave, across the street from the Capitol, 242-1861, contains memorabilia of Confederate President Jefferson Davis and family. Mon-Fri 8.30 am-4.30 pm. Free. 'Worthwhile.'
Designed by the architect of the Vietnam War Memorial in Washington, DC, the **Civil Rights Memorial** was unveiled during the fall of 1989. Visitors can view the outdoor memorial at the corner of Washington Ave and Hull St, 264-0286.
Dexter Ave King Memorial Baptist Church, 454 Dexter Ave. Where Martin Luther King, Jr. was pastor for 6 years. Mon-Fri, 10 am-2 pm, 263-3970. Donation appreciated.
Montgomery Museum of Fine Arts, 1 Museum Dr, in W M Blount Cultural Park off Woodmere Blvd, 244-5700. Tues-Sat 10 am-5 pm, Thur 10 am-9 pm, Sun 12-5 pm. Free.
W A Gayle Space Transit Planetarium, 1010 Forest Ave in Oak Park, 241-4799. Simulated space journeys. $3 for shows.
The **Alabama Shakespeare Festival**, 1 Festival Dr, 271-5353. Renaissance-style theatre which flies the flag of Britain's RSC. Performances running from Oct-Sep. Tkts from $15.
Scott and Zelda Fitzgerald Museum, 919 Felder Ave, 264-4222. Home to novelist F Scott and wife Zelda from October 1931 to April 1932, during which time Scott worked on *Tender is the Night*. Works of both writers on display. Wed-Fri 10 am-2 pm; Sat, Sun 1 pm-5 pm. Free.
About 40 miles northeast of Montgomery is the noted **Tuskegee University**, a co-ed university founded in 1881 by former slave Booker T Washington. One of the University's alumni was George Washington Carver, who became famous for his research on peanuts.
Grey Columns, the historical site's visitor center, is open Mon-Fri 9 am-5 pm with w/end hrs during the summer, 727-3200.

INFORMATION
Montgomery Visitor Information Center, 401 Madison Ave, 262-0013. Mon-Fri
8.30 am-5 pm, Sat 9 am-4 pm, Sun 10 am-4 pm.

TRAVEL
Greyhound, 950 W South Blvd, (800) 231-2222. 24 hrs.
Montgomery Area Transit System, 262-7321. Buses run morning and evening
rush-hours only, Mon-Fri. Sat only at noon. $1.50, transfers 15¢.
Yellow Cab, 262-5225. $1.50 first mile, $1.10 each additional mile.

HUNTSVILLE Founded by John Hunt in 1805 and the site of the first
English settlement in Alabama, this one-time sleepy town has become
rather more 'spaced out' as it is today host to one of the state's biggest
attractions. The **US Space and Rocket Center** was established here in 1960
and, thanks to the late German scientist, Wernher von Braun and his pioneering work on the Saturn V Moon Rocket, the Center is now the nation's
focal point for the research and development of the NASA Space Program.
Among its many public attractions is the only full-size model of the space
shuttle and a 67ft domed theatre screen showing breathtaking films of space
flight. Open 9 am-5 pm after Labor Day. $14 includes the Spacedome
Theater and NASA bus tour, 837-3400.

Back on earth, however, and for those seeking alternative and more cultural stimulation, Hunstville offers two historic areas downtown and east of
Court House Square. Many of the 19th century houses are inhabited by
descendants of the original owners. Located just north of the Tennessee
River and its numerous adjoining lakes, the area provides scope for water-
sport enthusiasts and is beautified with many parks such as Big Spring
International.

An hour's drive west of Huntsville is **Muscle Shoals**, a town known to
few people except the big names in the music business. *Time's better there*
according to Deep River Blues. Several recording studios are in and around
the town, and musicians ranging from WC Handy to Elton John to Doc
Watson have come here to play. Studio tours available free. Call Muscle
Shoals Sound, 381-2060, in advance.

ARKANSAS *Land of Opportunity*

Arkansas was named after the native Quapaw Indians, called 'Akansea' by
other tribes. The name (meaning 'South Wind') was misspelled by early
French explorers—hence its present form—which is pronounced 'Ark-an-
saw'. The Land of Opportunity was admitted to the Union in 1836 as the
25th state.

Eastern Arkansas, with its long hot summers and rich alluvial soil well
suited for the cultivation of tobacco, corn and cotton, became prime plantation country. Also known as 'The Natural State,' Arkansas has always
drawn its income from agriculture; only in the last two decades has industrial production increased substantially. A predominantly Democratic
domain, and home state of President Bill Clinton, Arkansas has only elected
5 Republican governors in its history—against 38 Democrats.

Western Arkansas, with its hills and forests, and the colourful Ozark Mountains to the north, smacked more of the frontier, and settler opinion caused the state to hesitate before seceding from the Union. The Ozark and Ouachitas areas retain a strong folksy flavour with a distinct mountain culture which has left its mark on national folk art, legend and music. Although Little Rock is the geographical, legislative and commercial centre of the state, look to Hot Springs National Park and the Ozarks for the truly rustic Arkansas. *www.yahoo.com/Regional U_S_States/Arkansas.*
The area code for the entire state is 501.

LITTLE ROCK   Named after a local landmark on the bank of the Arkansas River, this one-time hunter and trapper outpost is now the state capital. Known to its residents as the 'City of Roses,' Little Rock came to the world's attention back in 1957 with the attempt to ban nine black children from the segregated Central High School. It came to everyone's attention again in 1992 when former governor Bill Clinton moved to the White House and seemingly took half the town with him. Heady days in Little Rock! Don't neglect the surrounding countryside: west of the town is Hot Springs, and to the northwest lie the Ozarks.

ACCOMMODATION
Motel 6, 9525 I-30, 7 mile outside town, 565-1388, S-$29, D-$46. Pool, AC.
KOA Campground, in North Little Rock on Crystal Hills Road, 758-4598, 7 mile from downtown btwn exit 12 on I-430 & exit 148 on I-48. Sites $19, w/hook-up $25, cabins $28.

FOOD
River Market, btwn Commerce and Rock Sts on E Markham, 375-2552. Fresh crops, food stops and speciality shops by the Arkansas River.
The Minute Man, 322 Broadway, 375-0392. Cheap hamburgers and Mexican fare 'served up in seconds.' Mon-Fri 10.30 am-9 pm, Sat 11 am-8 pm.

OF INTEREST
The only city to have three capitol buildings. The hand-hewn, oak-log territorial capitol is in the **Arkansas Territorial Capitol Restoration**, a collection of 14 restored buildings dating to the 1820s, E 3rd and Scott Sts, 324-9351, hourly tours, $2. The aristocratic **Old State House**, 300 West Markham St, 324-9685, regarded as one of the most beautiful antebellum structures in the South, was used from 1836 to 1912. Mon-Sat 9 am-5 pm, Sun 1 pm-5 pm. The present **State Capitol**, Woodlawn and Capitol Ave, 682-5080, was based on the US Capitol in Washington. Don't miss the beautiful gardens and the brass doors made by Tiffany's of New York. Daily, self-guided tours with audio-headsets,10 am-6 pm.
The Quapaw Quarter, a 9 sq mile area, is the original Little Rock with many 19th century additions, both business and residential, including the **Governor's Mansion**; the **Pike Fletcher-Terry Mansion**, home of three colourful and famous Arkansans, and now a part of the **Arkansas Arts Center**, 372-4000. Mon-Thur and Sat 10 am-5 pm, Sun noon-5 pm; free. Also included in the quarter is the Old Arsenal in **MacArthur Park**, birthplace of Gen Douglas MacArthur and now the **Museum of Science and History**, 324-9231. Mon-Sat 9 am-4.30 pm, Sun 1 pm-3.30 pm. $3; free on Mon. Of the 49 State Parks in Arkansas, **Burns Park**, N Little Rock is one the county's largest, over 1,500 acres, offering camping, golf, tennis, hiking, and more.
Riverfront Park btwn the Statehouse Plaza and the Arkansas River has lighted

brick walkways, fountains, benches, a pavilion with a pictorial display of the city's history. The park is the site of Riverfest on Memorial Day Weekend, 376-4781, and various concerts throughout the year. The 'Little Rock' from which the city took its name is located here.

INFORMATION/TRAVEL
Little Rock Convention and Visitors Bureau, Markham and Broadway, 376-4781, has maps, info, and helpful staff. Mon-Fri, 8.30 am-5 pm.
Greyhound, 118 E Washington St in North Little Rock, (800) 231-2222.
Amtrak, 1400 W Markham & Victory Sts, 372-6841/(800) 872-7245.
Local Transit Authority, 375-1163. Basic fare 90¢, 10¢ transfer. To reach the airport, take the #12 bus from 4th and Louisiana, 6 am-6 pm. Taxis to the airport cost around $11. Call 374-0333.

HOT SPRINGS NATIONAL PARK   Pure and bubbling up from the ground at 143 degrees, the waters of the Hot Springs mix with cool water from natural reservoirs to create the ideal 100 degree bath. The hybrid town-national park is cradled between two peaks in the Ouachita Mountains, about an hour south of Little Rock on US 70. From February to April, lodging and bathing costs rise to match the demand of flocking tourists.

Although actual bathing is prohibited in the park, the Visitors Center does offer a free **Thermal Features Tour** during the summer, (mornings only in very hot weather), and information on private bathhouses during the rest of the year. Located at 369 Central, in the middle of Bathhouse Row, the center is open daily 9 am-4 pm, 623-1433. Elsewhere on the Row, look for baths for about $13-$16 and massages as well as a string of moderately-priced motels. Rooms start at around $25 but the prices double from Feb-April. Cheaper lodging can be had at the motels clustered on Hwys 7 and 88 or at one of several campsites, including two nearby state parks. Call (800) 643-3383 for info or contact the **Hot Springs Convention and Visitors Bureau**, 321-4378, (800) 722-2489. *www.nps.gov/hosp/index.htm.*

THE OZARKS   Although not especially high as mountains go, the Ozarks offer attractive wooded hills, rocky cliffs, gushing springs and rivers. It's a good area for white water canoeing, fishing, hiking, cycling and camping, or just getting away from it all for a few days. The **Ozark National Forest** is bounded on the east by the **White River** and to the west by the **Buffalo National River**, and includes **Blanchard Springs Cavern, Cove Lake** and **Mount Magazine**, the highest point in the state. Stop at the **Ozark Folk Center** in **Mountain View**, 269-3851, for Ozark music and crafts. Open 10 am-5 pm daily. Music show 7.30 pm-9.30 pm.

Summers are very hot and you will need mosquito repellent. Best months to visit are August and September when it's cooler, driest and bugless.

The small university town of **Fayetteville** is a good centre for visiting the area. Also worth a stop is the Victorian spa town of **Eureka Springs** in the northwest corner of Arkansas; it looks like a village in the Bavarian Alps and indeed has its own version of an Oberammergau passion play every year from April to October—just look for the 7 storey tall Christ that weighs in at 2 million pounds. Tkts $14-$16, 253-9200.

FLORIDA *The Sunshine State*

Beautiful, tacky, over-touristed and overflowing with Miami-sized vices, Florida draws sunseekers young and old from around the world. The climate is warm and gentle, the beaches broad and sandy, the citrus plentiful. Students from around the country flock here during Spring Break, making it easy to see why Spanish explorer Ponce de Leon believed the fountain of youth was in Florida. In 1513 he named his land after the Spanish for Easter—Pascua Florida.

Although Florida was one of the hard-core Confederate states, this followed from her plantation system along the panhandle; the southern part of the state remained tropical wilderness. During America's revolution, conservative Brits in the northern states began a now-familiar migration south to Florida. The state today dwells little on Dixie, but gets its impetus from tourists who have been piling in from the US and Canada since the Miami land boom of the 1920s, though more especially since the Second World War—and now from across the Atlantic, as Florida competes with Spain for northern Europe's summer holiday-makers.

Florida's youthful draw has given way to distinctly middle-aged problems. Rapacious real estate developers have lined the beaches with bland highrise hotels. The buccaneers who plied the coasts in the 1700s were pussy cats compared to the drug-kings of the 1980's, although authorities have reacted strongly and many localities have ultra-strict drug laws. Spanish is as common as English in Dade County where more than 50 percent of the population is now Hispanic, mainly refugees from Cuba and Haiti. Add to this the fact that most Floridians did not grow up in the state and have no developed sense of community and you have some real problems.

If you try hard, you may be able to ignore all the bronzed beach babes, the klatches of complaining New York retirees, and rowdy confederates. Once you catch a glimpse of Florida's stunning beauty—primeval Everglades, palms, mangroves, tropical vegetation and miles of sandy beaches groomed by warm seas, plus Cape Kennedy Space Center and the vast empire of Walt Disney World ... well, you'll be hooked.

Note: All hotel prices are for the summer/autumn season. Winter/spring rates are generally double. Shop around for cheap car rental deals, particularly off season, and also good air fares to and from the northern states. *www.yahoo.com/Regional/U_S_States/Florida.*
The Area Code for the Panhandle and the Northern Coast is 904, for the Space Coast and Central Florida it's 407 and 561; Ft Lauderdale 954; Miami and the Keys 305; and for Tampa and the Western Coast, use 813.

THE NORTHEAST COAST The most popular Florida coast begins unimpressively near the Georgia border in the port city of **Jacksonville**. The only site worth seeing is the **Fort Caroline National Monument**, 12713 Fort Caroline Rd, which marks the demise of the Huguenot Colony begun in 1564, daily 9 am-5 pm, free, 641-7155. However, nearby Amelia Island boasts nice quartz, white sand beaches at **Fernandina Beach** and **Fort Clinch State Park** as well as offering a haven for getting away from it all.

St Augustine, 40 miles further south, started as a Spanish colony in 1565, and was the survivor of the rivalry with the French to the north. The place is pointedly aware of being the oldest city in the United States and does much to commercialise its heritage. Try to ignore the billboard signs on the way in ('The Old Jail: Authentic and Educational') and give the history and atmosphere of the city a chance to make its mellow impact on you. By Florida standards, this is a tranquil town, picturesquely set on a quiet bay.

ACCOMMODATION

The different regions of Florida have different tourist seasons and St Augustine's is the hot and humid summer. Inexpensive hotels are difficult to find anytime, in summer especially. Your best bet here (and throughout Florida) may be camping.

St Augustine Hostel, 32 Treasury St, 808-1999. Near Greyhound Station. $12, linen $2. No curfew, check-in anytime. Bike rental $4 a day.

American Inn, 42 San Marco Ave, 829-2292. S-$40, D-$45, more at w/ends. **Monson Motor Lodge**, 32 Avenida Menendez, 829-2277. Downtown by historical area and waterfront. D-$55-$65, XP-$6. Pool, TV, AC, 1 mile from Greyhound. **Cooksey's Camping Resort**, 2795 State Rd 3, off A1-A south, 471-3171. Sites $23 for two w/hook-up. Walking distance to beach. Pool, laundry facilities.

North Beach Campground, 824-1806, 3 miles N of town, on west side of A1-A. $22 for two, XP-$4. 'Best campsite in the USA—jungle-type setting.' Rsvs nec at w/ends.

FOOD/ENTERTAINMENT

St George's Pharmacy and Restaurant, 121 St George St, 829-5929. 7.30 am-5 pm daily. Great homemade waffles and pancakes, lunch specials $4.25

Scarlet O'Hara's, 70 Hipolita St, 824-6535. The place to go for burgers from 11.30 am-1 am. Live R/B Tues-Sat and folk music nightly at 9 pm. Karaoke Mon & Sun.

OF INTEREST

Among the old Spanish buildings in the town are the **Castillo de San Marcos**, the **Cathedral of St Augustine**, **Mission of Nombre de Dios**, **Old Spanish Inn**, **Oldest House** and the **Old Slave Market**.

A 208 ft **stainless steel cross** marks the spot where the pioneer Spaniards landed in 1565, although the present mission church dates only from earlier this century.

The Spanish Quarter, 825-6830, is the restored area of the old city. Blacksmiths' shops, crafts shops, and morning cooking demonstrations can be had for the $5 admission, $2.50 w/student ID. 'A lot of it is disappointing, however, since a number of the lovely old buildings are now the home of junk and trash shops.' 9 am-5 pm daily. **Cross and Sword**. Florida's official state play depicting the settlement of St. Augustine by Spanish colonists in 1565, is presented from July 1st to Sept 1st at the St Augustine Amphitheater, 471-1965, in 're-organisation' in '97, should be running in '98. If you haven't had enough of Spain yet, you'll want to catch the **Days in Spain Fiesta**, held in the heart of the city every August, celebrating its birthday. Tourist-trap museums abound in St Augustine with the oddest of them all being the **Museum of Tragedy**, 7 Williams St, where tabloid followers can find the car Jayne Mansfield was decapitated in and various relics of President Kennedy's assassination. Open daily 9 am-dark, $4, $3 w/student ID.

Nearby on Hwy A1-A to the south is **Alligator Farm**, 824-3337. Established 1893, the farm seems to be trying to change from your standard man-vs-gator wrestling/souvenir stand into a place where people actually learn the difference between a crocodile and alligator. Open daily 9 am-6 pm, $11.

Marineland Ocean Resort, 9507 Ocean Shore Blvd, 471-1111. Open since 1938, this was the world's first oceanarium. Dolphin shows, 3-D movie, and some brave divers who risk life (and limb!) to hand-feed dangerous sharks. 9 am-5.30 pm daily. $14.95, $9.95 w/student ID.

INFORMATION/TRAVEL
Visitors Information and Preview Center, 10 Castillo Dr, 825-1000, 8 am-7.30 pm daily. Lots of free information and walking tour maps. Free 30 min movie on St Augustine.
Convention and Visitors Bureau, 1 Ribera St, (800) 653-2489.
Greyhound, 100 Malaga St, 829-6401/(800) 231-2222. St Petersburg, $42.

DAYTONA BEACH   Fifty miles south of Saint Augustine, following the old Buccaneers' Trail, Daytona Beach stretches out flat and hard. The fast ships of the buccaneers have been replaced by fast cars and fast romance. The **Daytona International Speedway** draws the best racers in the world, and during 'Spring Break' from mid-Feb to mid-Apr the beach draws thousands of students, all looking for a good time.

ACCOMMODATION
Rates are highest in summer and lowest after Labor Day. After Labor Day— 'Haggle.' There are many hotels on the beach, among those recommended:
Beachside Deluxe Inn, 1025 N Atlantic Ave, 252-6213. S-$20, D-$25 (no extra to share). TV, pool, laundry. 'Great location.' Discount for BUNACers staying a week or more. 'Good value motel.'
Candlelight Motel, 1305 S Ridgewood Ave, 252-1142. Rooms $38-$34, XP-$4. 'Loves having Brits.'
Daytona Beach Youth Hostel, 140 S Atlantic, 258-6937. Hostellers $14, $78 weekly. Private rooms $20, $5 key deposit. 'Two mins from the beach, very friendly.' 'Not very clean.'
Lido Beach Motel, 1217 S Atlantic, 255-2553. D-$30-$35 w/bath, shower, TV. 'Basic, clean rooms. Short walk to main pier and few seconds from beach.'
Majesty's Court, Fiesta Motel, 999 N Atlantic Ave, 252-5396. S-$25, D-$30, XP-$5, w/shower, AC, TV and pool—opposite beach. $5 discount for BUNACers.
Monte Carlo Beach Motel, 825 S Atlantic Ave, 255-0461. S-$25, D-$35, XP-$5. 'Clean and quiet, friendly atmosphere.' On the oceanfront. Pool.
Ocean Court Motel, 2315 S Atlantic, 253-8185. From $42 (no extra to share), great rates on efficiencies, balconies, ocean view rooms all the time and 10% discount for BUNACers, rates drop in Sept.
Skyway Motel, 906 S Atlantic Ave, 252-7377. S/D-$25, XP-$5, opposite beach.
Surfview Motel, 401 S Atlantic, 253-1626. From $28.
Camping: Daytona Beach Campground, 4601 Clyde Morris Blvd, 761-2663. From I-95, take exit 86A. Sites $20 for two, XP-$5. 5 miles from beach. Also **Tomoka State Park**, 676-4050. Tent site $8, $11 w/hook-up. **Nova Campground**, 1190 Herbert St in Port Orange, 767-0095. Tent site $16, $20 w/hook-up, XP-$2. Various other grounds at **Flagler Beach**.

FOOD/ENTERTAINMENT
Aunt Catfish, west end Port Orange Causeway, 767-4768. Name says it all. Seafood, burgers, BBQ, $7-$17. Sunday brunch $10. Mon-Sat 11.30 am-10 pm, Sun 9 am-10 pm
Ocean Deck, 127 S Ocean Ave, 253-5224. Reasonably priced menu, live reggae— plus beach volleyball court! Band 9.30 pm-2.30 am.
Oyster Pub, 555 Seabreeze Blvd, 255-6348. Sandwiches ($5-$7), seafood ($8-$12)— or try the raw oysters: $5.25 p/doz, $3 p/doz happy hr, 4 pm-7 pm or after mid-

night. 11.30 am-3 am daily. **Sweetwaters**, 3633 Halifax Dr in Port Orange, 761-6724. Lunch from $5, dinner from $8, daily 11.30 am-10 pm.

OF INTEREST
With major automobile and motorcycle races scattered throughout the year, **Daytona International Speedway**, 1801 Volusia Ave, seems to always be on the roar. The **Daytona 500** one of the premier races in the US, caps off 'Speed Week' in mid-February. Tkts to any of the races normally start at $45, 2 day pass for D500, $160. Call 253-7223 for race details. **Halifax Historical Society Museum**, 252 S Beach, 255-6976, Tues-Sat 10 am-4 pm, $3. Free on Saturday. But flying sand, not racing wheels, probably brought you to the **'World's Most Famous Beach**,' 23 miles of white sand along the Atlantic Ocean. Downtown Daytona is right in the middle, where the bulk of the crowds congregate, near Main St and Seabreeze Blvd; quieter spots can be found to the north and south. A variety of shops in the commercial district rent surf boards while shops along the community's western boundary, the Halifax River, rent sail boards and jet skis. Although overnight camping on the beach is illegal, drivers can take cars onto the beach and roam its length from sunrise to sunset; the fee is $5 per car. **Ponce de Leon Inlet Lighthouse**, 4931 S Peninsula Dr, 10 miles south of Daytona Beach, offers self-guided tours of the second tallest lighthouse on the eastern US at 175 ft. Call 761-1821 for info. Open 10 am-8 pm, close at 9 pm, $4.

SPORT
Daytona Beach offers a wide variety of sporting activities both on land and in the water. Sailing, surfing, scuba-diving, and jet-skiing are popular off-shore, while everything from skateboarding to karate can be found along the boardwalk and beyond. Baseball fans should head to the **Jackie Robinson Ballpark**, 105 E Orange Ave, 257-3172, home of the **Daytona Cubs**,, the Chicago Cubs Class-A affiliate in the Florida State League. Tkts $4.50 or less. The **Daytona Beach Breakers**, provide non-stop ice-hockey action Nov-Apr, at the **Ocean Center**, 254-4545. Public skating all other times.

INFORMATION/TRAVEL
Convention and Visitors Bureau, 126 E Orange Ave, 255-0415 or (800) 854-1234. Mon-Fri 9 am-5 pm.
Amtrak, 2491 Old New York Ave, (800) 872-7245. Station is in Deland, 24 miles to the west. Taxi to Daytona is $30-$35.
Greyhound, 138 S Ridgewood Ave, (800) 231-2222. A long way from the beach.
Voltran Transit Company, 761-7700, bus service around county and trolley through city. Fare 75¢.
Water Wheels, 255-2400. Take a historic 1hr narrated tour aboard the 'Nicholas James,' a 14,000lb amphibious vehicle, taking in historic sites, businesses, and local attractions. Departs daily from the city parking lot, Beach St and Int Speedway Blvd, $13.25.

SPACE COAST Midway along the Atlantic side of the Florida peninsula is considered America's final frontier, the home of the US space program. Because of its close proximity to Orlando and Daytona Beach, the area from Titusville to Melbourne has become a primary stop for anyone travelling through the state. And because it plays second to the other cities' better known attractions, the Space Coast is one of the better values in the state.

Visits to **Titusville**, where the **John F. Kennedy Space Center** and **Cape Canaveral** are located. Shuttle launches draw masses of people along US 1, some camping out nearly a week in advance to watch lift-off. For an up-to-date launch schedule, call (800) 572-4636 (in state only). *www.spaceportusa.com/main/htm.*

THE SCOOP ON AMERICAN ICE CREAM

There's nothing nicer than quenching the heat of an American summer day with an ice cream cone or a malted milk shake, an all-natural gastronomic experience you're unlikely to forget. No wonder Americans eat more ice cream than anyone, 47 gallons per person per year, there is even an Ice-Cream University (in Scarsdale, NY). The choice in the US is almost bewildering. The dieter's old vice, frozen yoghurt, has been replaced in popularity by low-fat ice creams, but the real thing is making a come-back. There has also been an explosion of new-fangled, mouth-watering ice cream bars, and fruit juice bars including **Baskin Robbins'** Jamoca Almond Fudge, Peanut Butter and Chocolate, and Pralines and Cream, but **Ben & Jerry's** are more imaginative with their 'Peace pops,' also look out for B&J's Coffee Heath bars – delicious and **Edy's** mouth-watering frozen apple bars

NATIONALLY AVAILABLE: The **Baskin Robbins** franchise, with its trademark 31 flavours, spearheaded the gourmet ice cream trend. Always new flavours, but standards Rocky Road and Chocolate Fudge are musts.
Ben & Jerry's Ice Cream. The pair of socially-aware Vermonters so famous they were parodied in the film *City Slickers* (remember those two bearded men on the cattle drive?). The most recent addition to their family is Phish Food, chocolate with nougat and caramel swirl, and fudge fish pieces, an absolute dream. The aptly named Chubby Hubby is a delicious vanilla malt ice cream rippled with fudge and peanut butter, loaded with fudge covered peanut butter pretzels. Dieters beware! Nut lovers should try Chunky Monkey with its fudge pieces and walnuts, Wavy Gravy for pistachios and brazils, or Rainforest Crunch with pecans and brazils, gives new taste to tired nuts. Don't forget the classics, World's Best Vanilla truly is, the Chocolate Cookie Dough is supreme, better than the Haagen Dazs variety, and the Chocolate Fudge Brownie is better than you'll ever taste. Also try their frozen yoghurt and sorbets, Purple Passion Fruit and Doosenberry come highly recommended. *www.benjerry.com*.
Haagen-Dazs offers, among other delectables, a decadent, deep, dark Belgian Chocolate flavour, a cool, crisp mint-choc-chip flavour, beautiful Butter Pecan and boozy Rum 'n' Raisin flavours. For an obscene treat try the Triple Brownie Overload, a melange of chocolate ice cream, brownie dough, fudge chunks and pecans—worth the calories. Haagen Dazs has also added its name to an innovative line of sorbets. To tingle your taste buds try Strawberry and Banana Margarita with a dash of real tequila, or classic Zesty Lemon. Their Vanilla Raspberry Swirl low-fat frozen yoghurt is divine.
Edy's/Dreyer's, offer a wide variety of ice creams, frozen yoghurts, sorbets and sherbets. Try Cherry Choc-Chip, and Chocolate Fudge Sundae ice cream and Strawberry Kiwi or Swiss Orange Chip Sherbet. *www.edy's.com*.
Starbucks have launched a range of sumptuous coffee ice creams. Double Expresso Bean, Café Latté and Biscotti Bliss are the tastiest. Also try juice-sweetened **Gourmet Ice-Cream**, available from health food stores. In Canada, **Laura Secord** is reputed to be the best. For a touch of the bizzarre visit Idaho, famous for producing potatoes and yep! You guessed it, they're making ice cream out of them now! Lobster flavoured ice cream has also appeared in Maine, but, for trendy Avocado, Beer and Rose flavours it has to be California. Not content with your local Safeway, **Out of a Flower** will have their ice cream flown to you, $40-$43 including freight, (800) 743-4696. **Graeters** of Cincinati will do the same. Choose from 22 standard as well as seasonal flavours, (800) 721-3323.

LOCAL PARLOURS: Max's Best Ice Cream, 2416 WisconsinAve NW, Washington DC, (202) 333-3111, makes huge sundaes and an orange choc chip ice cream that absolutely must be sampled. Seasonal flavour specialities include a potent Irish Cream. Also in DC: **Cone E.Island**, in Pennsylvania Ave 2000 Mall, which received the *Washingtonian* award for its 'Snapper' variety (butter-based ice cream with pecans, caramel and chocolate chunks), but their Marble Fudge and Tin Roof are also good. **Thomas Sweets**, on Wisconsin Ave, in Georgetown, 337-0617, is an institution and has a sinful Cinnamon ice cream, a heavenly Black Raspberry and a tropical tasting Coconut flavour among others. **Bob's Famous Ice Cream**, 4706 Bethesda Ave, MD, (301) 657-2963, features among many others a spicey Mozambique ice cream, a special blend of vanilla with cinnamon, cloves and nutmeg. Pop into **Old Pharmacy Cafe**, Shepherdstown, West VA, seemingly the only place in America stocking Edy's exquisite Capuccino Crunch. **CC Brown's Hot Fudge Shop**, in **Los Angeles, CA**, (213) 464-7062: creators of the hot fudge sundae, they make their ice cream by hand. **Chinatown Ice Cream, 65 Bayard St, New York City**, (212) 608-4170, delights the imagination and palate with its intriguing flavours, such as green tea, red bean and ginger flavours. **Emack and Bolio's**, 290 Newbury St in **Cambridge, MA**, (617) 247-8772: **Boston**'s best, serves Grasshopper, Orange Creamsickle and the patented Original Oreo Cookie. In **San Francisco, CA**, at 576 Union St, (415) 391-6667, **Gelato Classico**, (415) 989-5884, is unparalleled for Italian ices (this side of the Atlantic) and now has a Double Expresso Bean flavour, not to mention the '94% fat-free fresh Banana Walnut and Mocha Chip' which promises to be more of a mouthful than its title! Also worth a visit is **Swensen's**, at 1999 Hyde St, (415) 775-6818, for sticky chewy chocolate, swiss-orange chip or peppermint stick, guaranteed to tempt you back for more. **Great Midwestern Ice Cream Co**, 126 E Washington St, Iowa City, IA, (319) 337-7243, received the nation's #1 vote in *People* magazine. Try Blueberry and 'Sweet Iowa' (choc-blackberry). **King's Ice Cream, 1831 SW 8th St, Miami, FL**, (305) 643-1842, blends the cream of the Caribbean crop: banana, pineapple and coconut straight from the shell. The **University of Maryland** in College Park, the **University of Wisconsin** in Madison, and **Cornell University**, Ithaca, NY, produce award-winning ice cream with milk from their own cows.

Spaceport USA, (407) 452-2121, is NASA's tourist centre. Many of the exhibits and attractions are free while a spectacular film on a $5^1/2$ storey IMAX movie screen costs $7, and an interesting 2hr bus tour of the Space Center, which includes the world's largest scientific building—the 525-foot VAB (Vehicle Assembly Building), is $10. From I-95, take Rte 50 exit from N, 407 exit from S. The Spaceport is open daily from 9 am-8.30 pm. Cocoa Beach is the nearest Greyhound stop.

The rockets blast-off over spectacular wild-life on **Canaveral National Seashore** and **Merritt Island Wildlife Refugee**. The reserve's visitor center, 861-0667, is located on Rte 406 north of Titusville and is open Mon-Fri 8 am-4.30 pm, Sat 9 am-5 pm. The seashore's southern entrance at **Playalinda Beach** is at the end of Rte 406. Primitive backcountry camping is allowed. On summer evenings, marvel at the flying fish.
www.nps.gov/crweb1/nr/34.htm.

Cheap **accommodation** abounds along US 1. Rooms are hard to find in the winter and spring, but are one-half as much in the summer. In **Cocoa Beach**, be sure to stay at **Fawlty Towers**, 100 E Cocoa Beach Causeway, 784-3870. From S-$45 off-season, XP-$5. For camping, try **Jetty Park Campground**, 400 E Jetty Rd, 868-1108. Sites $17 for six, $20 w/hook-up. 'Best location of the campgrounds.' Further south, the **Melbourne Beach HI-AYH Hostel**, 1135 N Hwy AIA, Indianatlantic, 951-0004. $15, right on the beach.

Down the coast from **Melbourne** to **Jensen Beach**, 700 pound sea turtles lumber ashore. The **Jensen Beach Turtle Watch** offers late night (**Tue & Thur**) sea turtle egg-laying and hatching tours in June and July, suggested donation $5. Call **Hope Sound Wildlife Refuge** to see if the turtles are up to it, 546-2067, rsvs nec.

More info on the area is available through the **Cocoa Beach Area Chamber of Commerce**, 400 Fortenberry Road in Merritt Island, 459-2200 and the **Titusville Area Chamber of Commerce**, 2000 S Washington Ave, 267-3036.

FORT LAUDERDALE   Midway between Palm Beach and Miami, Fort Lauderdale is a double attraction, with a six mile beach on one side (probably the finest on the Gold Coast), and 250 miles of lagoons, rivers and canals on the other, hence the nickname, 'The Venice of America'.

A once popular 'Spring Break' destination, students from all over America would flock to Ft Lauderdale to write an American version of *Debauch in Venice*. Local authorities have cracked down on the revellers in recent years, causing somewhat of an exodus to Daytona Beach and Clearwater. Still, Mar and Apr can be crazy months, in this otherwise fairly sedate family vacation place and yachting mecca.

To the north in the little town of **Palm Beach** it is illegal to own a kangaroo, hang a clothesline, and it is impossible to find cheap lodging. A playground for the rich and merely tacky, Palm Beach is crowded with homes of Kennedys and lesser millionaires. You can look, but if you have to ask the price, you can't afford to shop in the posh stores of **Worth Ave**. For a real taste of the wealth that circulates here, walk through the **Breakers Hotel** and stroll down **Millionaire's Row**. The home of the man who built Palm Beach is now the **Henry Flagler Museum**, an impressive demonstration of what money can buy.

Ft Lauderdale is currently undergoing major re-development. By 2001, $1.5b will have been invested in tourism and recreation related facilities.

ACCOMMODATION
All Ft Lauderdale rates are for the off-season. Expect to pay more during winter and spring. Lodging information: **Broward County Hotel and Motel Association**, (305) 561-9333, 701C East Broward Blvd, for free directory of budget hotels. **Broward County Parks and Recreation**, 370-3755, for general info on camping in the county.
Days Inn Hotel, N Atlantic Blvd, 462-0444. S-$57, room w/kitchen $67. Pool, 2 mins from beach, laundry, kitchen. 'Absolutely gorgeous.'
Floyd's Hostel, 462-0631. Call ahead for address and free pick-up. $13, $88 weekly. Free food and laundry, central location, international students only. 'Excellent reports.'
Lafayette Motel, 2231 N Ocean Blvd, 563-5892, from $39, $42 w/kitchenette, weekly rates available. 'Bright, simply furnished rooms with very friendly and helpful staff.'
Lamplighter Motel, 2401 N Ocean Blvd, 565-1531. S-$29, D-$35, XP-$10. More at w/end.
Merrimac Hotel, 551 N Atlantic Blvd, 564-2345. Special BUNAC rate of $30 for four or from S/D-$49 room. Pool, right on the beach. Rsvs rec. 'Excellent.'
Ocean Way Motel, 1933 N Ocean Blvd, 566-8261. S/efficiencies from $35, XP-$4, 'owner can be haggled with.' Includes bath/shower, fridge, AC, TV; 'Beautiful apts just across the road from the beach; owner very helpful.' Will pick up at bus station for stays of 2 days or more.
Seagate Apt Motel, 2909 Vistamar St, 566-2491. D-$30, $40 w/kitchen. Pool, close to beach. 'Highly recommended.'
The Seville, 3020 Seville St, 463-7212. S-$30-$35 w/kitchen, XP-$5. 'Very clean, 5 mins from beach; ask for Linda.'

FOOD AND ENTERTAINMENT
Fast food joints and expensive restaurants prey on the students who flock to Fort Lauderdale. Lots of bars and discos along beach-front Atlantic Blvd. Some have happy hours with lots of free food.

Big Louies has the best pizza, 1990 Sunrise, 467-1166. Open daily 'til 1 am. Food $2-$15.

Chilli's, Powerline Rd, 776-6837. Open late daily. 'The best burgers ever!' Fajitas $9.

Hyde Park, 500 E Las Olas Blvd, 467-7436, best market in the middle of town, daily 7 am-11 pm.

Southport Raw Bar, 1536 Cordova Road, 525-2526. Cheap seafood and sandwiches. Open daily 'til 2 am. Friendly staff: 'Come on down: it's great!'

The Musician's Exchange, 729 W Sunrise, 764-1912, draws national name bands from reggae to blues Thur-Mon. Cover charge ranges from $2-$20. On w/ends cafe serves sandwiches, salads, burgers. It's not the best neighbourhood, though.

OF INTEREST

Tacky tours proliferate along the coast. Choose carefully.

Everglades Park, 21940 Griffin Road West, 434-8111. Free admission to park. 1 hr airboat tour for $12.50. Open 9 am-5 pm daily. To see the waterways through the city, the *Jungle Queen* sails twice daily (10 am & 2 pm) for 3 hr tours, $12, at the Bahia Mar Yacht Center on A1-A, 462-5596.

Hugh Taylor Birch State Recreation Area, 3109 E Sunrise, 564-4521. One of the few natural sights on the concrete beach, trails, fishing and canoeing. $3.25 per car, pedestrians $1. Open daily 8 am-8.15 pm.

Museum of Art, 1 East Las Olas Blvd, 525-5500. Largest collection of Cobra Art—post WW II artists from Northern Europe (Karel Appel, Asger Jorn and Joseph Noiret)—in the US. Tues 11 am-9 pm; Wed-Sat 10 am-5 pm and Sun noon-5 pm, $6, $3 w/student ID.

Museum of Discovery and Science, 401 S W 2nd St, 467-6637. The state's most widely visited museum. Hands-on and interactive exhibits, virtual reality, and 5-storey IMAX theatre. Check out 'Speed' and 'Rolling Stones at the MAX,' $9. Mon-Sat 10 am-5 pm, Sun noon-6 pm, $6.

INFORMATION/TRAVEL

Greater Florida Chamber of Commerce Visitor Information, 462-6000, 200 E Las Olas Blvd, Mon-Fri 8 am-5 pm.

Greyhound, 515 NE 3rd St, 764-6551/(800) 231-2222.

Amtrak, 200 SW 21st Terrace, 587-6692/(800) 872-7245.

Broward County Transit (BCT), 357-8400. $1 basic fare, transfers 15c. This stretch of coast is served by airports at Fort Lauderdale and West Palm Beach. The BCT runs regularly to and from Fort Lauderdale airport (#1) and connects with **Palm Beach County Transit** (233-1111) at the Boca Mall, and Dade County Transit at the Aventura Mall. From West Palm Beach airport, catch the #4 bus to downtown. Call (561) 272-6350 for times.

Tri-Service Commuter Rail, (800) 872-7245. See note under Miami *Travel* section.

MIAMI Miami's mayor once called his city 'the Beirut of Latin America'. He meant it as a compliment—Beirut was once the intellectual and economic trade centre for a region, as Miami is for Latin America. Unfortunately, most Americans believed the analogy to Beirut's violence was more appropriate for Miami's legendary crime problems. Boatloads of poor Haitians and Cuban criminals fed the legend. Miami still requires caution but not as much as television would have you believe.

Racial tension exists under the surface, but need not be intrusive: for the most part the Anglos, Hispanics and blacks live peaceably alongside one another. Add Nicaraguans to the list of exiled Hispanics living in Miami—there is quite a sizeable population. They and the Cubans give the city a very right-wing political flavour.

The city does sprawl—as one taxi-driver said, it goes out rather than up. While parts of the city are slums, other parts have the appearance of being very modern and high-tech; and other parts exhibit beautiful vegetation. The high-speed Metrorail, a people mover and excellent bus system, provide access to many areas of the city without the need for a car.

ACCOMMODATION/FOOD

Not many motels within Miami that are safe, clean and cheap. Smarter to stay at Miami Beach and commute to Miami attractions by bus or rail.

Kobe Trailer Park, 11900 NE 16th Ave, I-95 exit 14, 893-5121. Sites $20, $25 w/hook-up, XP-$2.

Miami Airways Motel, 5001 NW 36th St, 883-4700, S-$32, D-$37, pool, movie channel, restaurant. Pick up at airport.

Canton Too, 2614 Ponce de Leon Blvd, Coral Gables, 448-3736. Reputedly the best Chinese food in Miami. 11 am-11 pm daily.

The Versailles, 3555 S W 8th St, 444-0240. Cheap Cuban fare, bfast $2-$4, lunch from $2.50. Open daily 8 am-2 am.

OF INTEREST

Seaquarium, Rickenbacher Causeway on Key Biscayne, 361-5703. Oldest and best: dolphins, sharks and killer whales; home of TV star Flipper, Lolita the 10,000lb killer whale, Salty the Sea Lion. Also a wildlife sanctuary and rainforest exhibit. Open 9.30 am-6 pm, $20. Tkt office closes at 4.30 pm.

Bayside, Biscayne Blvd and 4th St, 577-3344. $95 million complex of shops, restaurants and night spots highlighting downtown. Mon-Thurs 10 am-10 pm, Fri and Sat 'til 11 pm, Sun 11 am-8 pm.

Little Havana, lies btwn SW 12th & SW 27th Ave with Calle Ocho (SW 8th St) housing most of the restaurants. Cigar and pinata manufacturers also. **Bay of Pigs Memorial** commemorates the failed US-backed invasion of Cuba in 1961, at SW 13th Ave and SW 8th St.

Vizcaya, 3251 S Miami Ave, 250-9133. An Italianate mansion created by millionaire James Deering in 1914/16, now the Dade County Art Museum. Open daily 9.30 am-5 pm, $10. Free tours of the home and formal Italian gardens.

St Bernard de Clarrvaux, the Spanish monastery was imported from Spain and reassembled in North Dade. Self-guided tours of the 'biggest jigsaw puzzle in the world,' Mon-Sat 10 am-4 pm, Sun noon-4 pm. Call 945-1461 for directions.

For wildlife try **Monkey Jungle**, 14805 SW 216 St, 235-1611. Monkeys run wild, you view them from cages: look smart and they might give you a cream bun. $11.50, daily 9.30 am-5 pm. Tkt office closes at 4 pm. $1 discount w/student ID. Also see **Parrot Jungle**, 11000 SW 57th Ave, near US 1, 666-7834. A huge cypress and oak jungle filled with exotic birds, some on roller skates. $12.95, daily 9.30 am-6 pm. Trained bird shows 10.30 am-5 pm. Tkt office closes 5 pm. $1 discount w/student ID.

Museum of Science and Planetarium, 3280 S Miami Ave, 854-4242. Open daily 10 am-7 pm (last tkt 5 pm); $9. Cosmic Hotline, 854-2222, for recording of everything you ever wanted to know and much more about what's going on in the sky. Rock 'n' Roll laser shows on Fri & Sat nights, $6.

Miami Jai-Alai Fronton, 301 E Dania Beach Blvd, 949-2424, $1 to stand, $1.50-$7 for rsv seating. Games begin at 7.15 pm, closed Sun, Mon, Weds. Betting on this fast-paced game is a prime Miami attraction.

Coconut Grove, in the southern suburbs, for a look at a 'Florida-style subtropical Chelsea scene'. Galleries, boutiques, boat hiring. Get there via bus 14 going south to Main Hwy. The bulletin boards in Coconut Grove are said to be good for rides going north. South of Miami in Homestead is **Coral Castle**, US 1 at SW 286th St, 248-6344. Designed by a jilted lover who waited for his fiancée by creating a 1,100-ton estate out of coral, the castle stood originally in Florida City; in 1939, it was moved in its entirety to its present location. Open daily 9 am-7.30 pm, $7.75 for self-guided tour.

Water Sports: surfing at Haulover Beach Park and South Miami Beach, but beware: the waves are small; good swimming at Cape Florida State Park, Matheson Hammock, Tahiti Beach, Lummus Park, etc. Sailing, jet skiing and windsurfing on Hobie Beach off Rickenbacher Causeway.

On land, 1997 baseball world champs, the **Florida Marlins** play at Pro-Player Stadium, (954) 792-8793, just north of Miami off the Florida Turnpike. They won in only the 5th season of their whole existence!

INFORMATION
Greater Miami Convention and Visitors Bureau, 701 Brickell Ave #2700, 539-3000, (800) 283-2707 (out of Fl), Mon-Fri 8.30 am-5.30 pm.

TRAVEL
Greyhound, 4111 NW 27th St, (800) 231-2222.
Amtrak, 8303 NW 37th Ave, 835-1221/(800) 872-7245.
Metro Dade Transportation, 638-6700. Extensive network of buses (Metrobus), subway (Metrorail) and downtown people mover (Metromover). Services airport. Bus and rail fare $1.25, 25¢ transfer. Metromover 25¢, 'Best tour of the city for a quarter.'
Tri-County Commuter Rail, 728-8445. Connects West Palm Beach, Ft Lauderdale and Miami. Trains run Mon-Fri 5 am-10 pm, Sat, 'til midnight. Sun, limited schedule.

MIAMI BEACH Situated on a long, narrow island, across Biscayne Bay from Miami, Miami Beach came to be regarded as the ultimate in opulence, the dream place for retirement, or a bar mitzvah. Seventy years ago this was a steamy mangrove swamp. Now it's a long strip of hotels of varying degrees of grandness, plus of course the beach.

It's still a favourite retirement spot but the really rich have moved further up the coast. In their wake have come the Cuban refugees and the North European package tours, making it harder to get the good hotel rates which used to be available here during the summer. Still worth bargaining, however. The peak season is from late Dec to Apr.

ACCOMMODATION
The **Beach Resort Hotel Association**, 407 Lincoln Rd, #10G, 531-3553, will assist you in finding accommodation. Mon-Fri 9 am-4.30 am.
Clay Hotel and International House (HI-AYH), 1438 Washington Ave, 534-2988. $12 AYH, $13 non-AYH, private rooms $28-$50, linen $5, $3 refund, bfast $2. In the heart of the Art Deco district, close to nightlife. Kitchen, laundry, TV. 24 hrs, no curfew. Take Bus C from downtown, Bus L from Amtrak takes you within 3 blocks. 'Outstanding.' 'Clean, safe area.'
Haddon Hall Hotel, 1500 Collins Ave, 531-1251, S-$35.
International Travellers Hostel, 236 9th St, 534-5862. $12 AYH, $14 non-AYH, linen $1. Kitchen, laundry and locker facilities. Private rooms from $31. In the heart of the Art Deco district, right on the beach. 24 hrs, no curfew.
Palmer House Hotel, 1119 Collins Ave, 538-7725, Art Deco hotel, S/D-$40.

FOOD
La Rumba, 2008 Collins Ave, 534-0522, serves cheap Cuban and Spanish fare. Open 7.30 pm-midnight daily.
Puerto Sagua, 700 Collins, 673-1115. Specializes in seafood and Latin food. Try the paella. $5-$15.

Wolfie's Restaurant, 2038 Collins Ave, 538-6626, is a New York deli transplanted to Miami Beach. An institution, it is open 24 hrs a day.

OF INTEREST
Whimsical and gaudy, the **Art Deco District** is as close to high art as Miami Beach comes. With the south half of the island designated a National Historic District because of 'Tropical Deco,' the truly impressive sights are along Collins Ave and Ocean Dr. The homes are part of a depression-era development, and can be seen on a Preservation League, 672-1836, tour. Only 2 guided tours a week, Thur at 6.30 pm and Sat at 10.30 am, $7. League office also has maps for self-guided tour, 10th St & Ocean Dr. Different areas of **The Beach** cater to different groups: punks and surfers stick to the area below 5th St, volleyball players at 14th St, gays to 21st St and the rich and famous to Bal Harbor near 96th St.
Miccosukee Indian Village, mile marker 20, Hwy 41, 223-8386. Guided tours show Miccosukee craftsmen at work. Museum has Indian artifacts. 9 am-5 pm daily, $5. Airboat rides $7.

THE KEYS The only living coral reef in America drapes itself along the Florida Keys, the scimitar-shaped chain of islands curving southwest from Miami to Key West.

You pick up the toll-free Overseas Hwy at Key Largo for the 100-mile run down to Key West. En route the road hops from island to island and at times you can travel up to 7 miles with only the sea around you. It's worth a brief stop in **Key Largo** to visit the **John Pennekamp Coral Reef State Park** and to pay a brief tribute to Humphrey Bogart. The *African Queen* now sits outside the Holiday Inn here and you can visit the rebuilt Caribbean Club Bar, 451-9970, open daily 7 am-4 am, where the movie *Key Largo* was filmed. Locations along the hwy are designated by milepost markers.

Key West itself is the southernmost and second oldest town in the United States. Hemingway once lived here and it remains a favourite place for gays, writers and artists—creative or otherwise. Key West is not typical America. Easy to imagine you've somehow made it to a Caribbean island; even the food—turtle steak, conch (pronounced 'conk') chowder, Key lime pie—suggests this.

Don't miss sunset over the Gulf of Mexico—the whole town turns out on Mallory Square to watch the show, both heavenly and earthly, for sundown here is usually accompanied by some kind of people-performance, a water-ski display, a magician or a folk singer.

'Key West was virtually deserted when we were there in September and October; very quiet and idyllic.'

ACCOMMODATION
Key Largo: **Bahia Honda State Park**, mile marker 36.5, 872-2353, $28 site. 'Well worth the stop but be prepared, as it is in the middle of nowhere.' 'White sands and crystal clear water.' Open 8 am-sunset, rsvs essential before Aug 20.
John Pennekamp State Park Campsite, mile marker 102.5, 451-1202, Sites $24-$26 w/hook-up. Rsvs rec.'Take more mosquito spray than you ever believe you'll need. Nice campsite, good swimming, it's just a shame the bugs spoil it.'
Jules Undersea Lodge, world's first underwater hotel, 57 Shoreland Drive, mile-post 103.5, 451-2353. A diver's dream; a pinch at $325 inc dinner, unlimited snacking and diving! Worth a peek, if you can scuba!
Key West: Angelina Guest House, 302 Angela St, 294-4480. D/T-$49-$79. 'Clean and simple. Very friendly.'

Boyd's Campground, Stock Island, milepost 5, 294-1465, $26 for two, XP-$6, $9 more for ocean site w/hook-up. Stay 6 nights, 7th night free. 'Worth it if enough people (more than two). Helpful owners, site has washing facilities, pool and TV.' Regular bus service to Key West, 75¢, bus leaves every ¹/₂ hr from 6 am-10 pm.

Caribbean House, 226 Petronia St, 296-1600 or (800) 543-4518. D-$49-$59, 4 people, w/bath. 'Excellent.' 'Very friendly and central.' TV & bfast.

El Rancho Motel, 830 Truman St, 294-8700, Rooms from $59, Q-$99. Prices change depending on day/month of arrival. Pool, within walking distance of downtown. 'Excellent, quiet.'

Jabour's Trailer Court, 223 Elizabeth St, 294-5723. $35, 2 in tent. XP-$5. 10% discount if you stay 4 days and pay cash.

Key West AYH, 718 South St, 296-5719. $14.50 AYH, $18 non-AYH. Private rooms available. Bikes for $4 daily. Bfast $2, dinner $1 'Highly recommended.' 'Good friendly atmosphere.' Organises snorkelling trips for $18—'a taste of paradise.'

Key West B&B, 415 William St, 296-7274, D-$59, XP-$10. 'Feels like home.' Rates drop in Sept.

FOOD

In Key West, the more expensive restaurants line Duval St while the side streets offer a more eclectic selection. Don't forget to try authentic Key Lime pie.

Sloppy Joe's, 201 Duval, 294-5717. Hemingway was an enthusiastic regular. Live entertainment seven days a week. Conch fritters $5.50. Mon-Sat 9 am-4 am, Sun noon-4 pm. Open 365 days a year! 'Don't miss it.' Nightlife is in abundance in Key West, take a walk along Duval St for some alternative choices.

OF INTEREST

Hemingway Museum, 907 Whitehead St, 294-1575. Papa left Paris and moved to Key West in 1928. This became his home in 1931 until he left for Cuba in 1940. He wrote *A Farewell to Arms* and *For Whom the Bell Tolls* among others in this 1851 house. On discovering that the house was as Hemingway left it, when he died the present owners decided to turn it into a museum. 'Full of the overfed descendants of Hemingway's cats.' Open daily 9 am-5 pm, last tour 4.30 pm, $6.50.

Conch Tour Train, 294-5161. Takes you about 14 miles in 1¹/₂ hrs and includes 65 points of interest such as Hemingway's house, **Truman's Little White House**, **Audubon House** where the artist stayed while sketching birdlife over the Keys, the **turtle kraals**, the **shrimp fleet**, etc. Tkt Office, 501 Front St or 3850 N Roosevelt, 9 am-4.30 pm, 294-5161, $15 for the whole island.

Tours of the area are also available by **glass-bottomed boat**. **Fireball**, 296-6293, **Glass Bottom Boat Tour**, $20 for 2 hr trip, $25 at sunset. Leaves 3 times daily, 451-4655. And try snorkelling trips over the coral reefs. 'Well worth splashing out $20 or so—and maybe even buying an underwater camera.' 'Explore the island by foot if you have more than one day in Key West, or rent a bike.' **Moped and Scooter Inc**, 523 Truman Ave, US 1, 294-4556. $4 for day, $20 for week. Mopeds are the most popular mode of transport on the island, $14, 9 am-5 pm, $23 for 24 hrs. Greyhound runs 3 buses daily from Miami. First bus leaves 7.45 am which gives you most of the day at Key West with time for the Conch Train Ride before catching the last bus back at 7 pm. R/t, $57, 4¹/₂ hrs.

INFORMATION/TRAVEL

Florida Upper Keys Chamber of Commerce, 451-1414, milepost 103.4 in Key Largo. Open daily 9 am-6 pm.

Key West Chamber of Commerce, 402 Wall St, 294-2587 open daily 8.30 am-5 pm, 9 am-5 pm w/ends.

Key West Visitors Bureau, (800) 352-5397.

Key West Welcome Center, 3840 N Roosevelt Blvd, 296-4444, (800) 284-4482. Mon-Fri 9 am-9 pm, Sun 'til 6 pm

Greyhound, 615¹/₂ Duval St in Key West, 296-9072/(800) 231-2222. For a taxi to the airport, call 296-6666, $14-$17.

EVERGLADES and BISCAYNE NATIONAL PARKS The Everglades lies further south than any other area of the US mainland and is the last remaining subtropical wilderness in the country.

World famous as a wildlife sanctuary for rare and colourful birds, this unique, aquatic park is characterised by broad expanses of sawgrass marsh, dense jungle growth, prairies interspersed with stands of cabbage palm and moss-draped cypresses, and mangroves along the coastal region. The level landscape gives the impression of unlimited space. *www.nps.gov/ever/index.htm.*

The western entrance to the park is near **Everglades City**on Rte 29, but the only auto road leading into the area is Rte 9336 from **Florida City**, 11 miles to the east. Admission is $5 paid at the entrance station, giving you up to 7 days access; the Visitors Center, 247-6211, which offers a free film, is open 8 am-5 pm daily. You will need to get out and walk along the paths to really understand the place. Try the **Anhinga Trail**, 2 miles past the entrance. The Royal Palm Visitors Center has great displays on the unique Everglades' ecology. At the northern end of the park off US 41, the **Shark Valley Visitors Center**, provides access to the **Tamiami Trail**, 15 miles which can be explored by foot, bike or 2hr tram, $8, 221-8455. Shark Valley entrance is $4.

Winter temperatures generally range between 60 and 85 degrees F. The rest of the year, the heat climbs over 90 degrees by mid-morning, and feels much hotter because of the high humidity. You are advised to bring sunglasses, suntan oil and gallons of insect repellent. Accommodation, restaurants, sightseeing and charter boats and other services are found in **Flamingo**, at the end of the main park road, about 50 miles from the park entrance. From the Gulf Coast of Florida, you can enter the park at Everglades City. Call (813) 695-3101.

Biscayne National Park is a jewel for snorkellers and scuba divers as most of the marine park's treasures are underwater in living coral reefs. Above ground, exotic trees, colourful flowers and unique shrubbery form dense forests. The main entrance is at the western side of the park at the **Convoy Point** Visitor Center, 230-1144, 9 miles E of **Homestead** on North Canal Drive, 247-7275, 8.30 am-5 pm daily. For snorkelling equipment and canoe rental or info on glass-bottomed boat tours, call the Biscayne Aqua Center in Homestead, 230-1100. *www.nps.gov/bisc/index.htm.*

ACCOMMODATION
Everglades Motel, 605 S Krome Ave, Homestead, 247-4117. D-$29, XP-$5, summer. AC, TV, coin laundry, small pool.
Flamingo Lodge, in Flamingo, 38 miles inside the park, (813) 253-2241. D-$66, XP-$11, Q-$72. Higher rates at w/ends.
Camping, $10 a site in winter, at **Lone Pine Key** and **Flamingo**. The Park office, (305) 247-6211, doesn't charge for camping in summer because they feel sorry for anyone who would brave the clouds of mosquitoes to do it. For the truly adventurous, 19 backcountry sites are accessible by motorboat or canoe. Just don't try swimming or paddling in the lakes or ponds—'unless ya' wanna 'gator to getya!' You

must have a backcountry permit, if you want to do your own canoe trip overnight. Note: in summer you'll need to bring food if you camp.

TOURS
Gray Line Tours from Miami and Miami Beach, but for a group of people it would be better and cheaper to hire a car for a day.
Flamingo Marina, (800) 600-3818, is the main departure point for most cruises. **The Sunset Cruise** takes you to Florida Bay, $9, or explore the mangrove forests of the southern Everglades on the **Back County Cruise**, $14. Call **Sammy Hilton Boat Tours**, (813) 695-2591, for tours in Everglades City.

ORLANDO Standing 35 miles from the east coast in the heart of the Florida lakes area, Orlando—hardly heard of a few years ago—is now perhaps the most visited place in the state owing to its access to the nearby Kennedy Space Center and especially the Walt Disney World complex. A favourite EU tourist spot, the chances are you'll meet folks from your home town. It has the mayhem atmosphere of a boom town, but choose carefully before you set out to see the sights—so many of them are waste-of-time, money-grabbing parasitical spinoffs. Cheap car rentals may be the best bet to visit these spaced out attractions.

ACCOMMODATION
A hundred zillion hotels have opened here in the last decade to lure the folks visiting all the nearby worlds. Most are expensive, but a few inexpensive chains like Motel 6 and Days Inn have staked their claim to the action. It may prove cheaper to stay in a more expensive motel nearer to Disney, etc. and get *free* shuttle to the attractions.
Airport Youth Hostel, 3500 McCoy Rd, 859-3165. $11, $55 weekly. 'Cheap, but shabby.' Take #11 bus from town, 75¢.'Clean and friendly.' Shuttle to Disney—$14 r/t.
Orlando International AYH Hostel, 227 N Eola Dr in downtown, 843-8888, $14, international passport gets same rate as AYH card. Private rooms $29, linen $1. Rsvs advisable. 'Very pleasant.' Free access to indoor/outdoor pools and gym at nearby YMCA. LYNX bus stops here every 2 hrs, 75¢ to Disney and all area attractions. Free van service to Greyhound and Amtrak.
Quality Inn Plaza, 9000 International Dr, 345-8585/(800) 999-8585. Rates vary but are based on room. $60 for four, $80 for seven. Same applies to **International Inn**, 6327 International Drive, 351-4444, (800) 999-6327. Both have pools and rsvs are advisable.
Travelodge, 409 Magnolia Ave, 423-1671. Pool, laundry room. Shuttles to Disney $15 r/t. 'Very friendly and helpful.' $65, 2 people, XP-$5. Rsvs rec in June/July. Pool.
Camping: Kissimmee Campground, 2643 Alligator Lane (5 miles from Disney World), 396-6851. $16 for two, XP-$2. Call for directions.
KOA Disneyworld, Bronson Memorial Hwy, off US 192 in Kissimmee, 396-2400. Cabins $42 for four, XP-$4. 'Basic, no electricity' but 'excellent' facilities—pool, store, laundry, showers, free shuttle to Disney. Also has tent sites, $21 for two. $30 w/hook-up, XP-$4.
KOA Orlando, 12343 Narcoossee Road SE (Hwy 15, 4¹/₂ miles S of Hwy 528), 277-5075. $16 for two, XP-$3, w/hook-up $23-$27. $2.50 shuttle to downtown/Disney.

FOOD
Church St Exchange offers a collection of shops and cheap places to eat from deli's to Mexican and Chinese. 'Fun atmosphere. Great bar downstairs.'

Duffs Smorgasbord, all-you-can eat; all over Orlando.

Fat Boys Bar-B-Q, 1606 W Vine St, Kissimmee, 847-7098. 'Good steak.' Juke Box. Daily 8 am-9 pm, 10 pm Fri.

Fox and Hounds Pub, 3514 W Vine St, Kissimmee, 847-9927. English/Irish decor and beer. Staffed by British. 'Worth a visit.' Mon-Sat 11.30 am-2 am, Sun 1 pm-2 am.

OF INTEREST

Prime your smile, open your wallet because a huge mouse with better name recognition than Bill Clinton is waiting for you at **Walt Disney World**. The huge complex of 3 theme parks, 2 water parks, an entertainment complex and thousands of hotel rooms sits glistening at Lake Buena Vista, about 15 miles S of Orlando on I-4. Some hotels and campgrounds offer free transportation to the complex while other commercial choices also are available. A day ticket for one of the major theme parks is $43, while multi-day tickets are usable for any combination of the parks on any of the days you use the ticket (4-day $142, 5-day $217). Prices fluctuate greatly, call on day you plan to visit. Tips to avoid the longest queues include getting to the parks when they open and hitting the most popular attractions first or wait until late afternoon and evening. General info number 824-4321. *www.disney.com/Disneyworld/index.html.*

Magic Kingdom.   The park that's the equivalent to Disneyland in Los Angeles and Tokyo, this is the place to venture on a ride through Space Mountain, to drift through the Pirates of the Caribbean or to watch all 41 US presidents come to life in one room. Exceeds Disneyland as a magnificent architectural, technological and entertainment achievement. 'You definitely need 2 days.' 'Great! I wish I was a child again.' 'Better than it's hyped up to be.' 'We thought the whole place was very artificial and plastic. Enormous queues for everything.' 'Visit after Labor Day to avoid queuing 1 hr for everything.' 'Food expensive, old and pre-packed.' 'Don't miss Space Mountain, but only if you like rollercoasters, 10,000 Leagues Under The Sea, Pirates of the Caribbean, and the amazing 3-D movie at the Kodak pavilion.'

Epcot Center (Experimental Prototype of Community of Tomorrow). Billed by some as an 'adult' amusement park and as 'dull' by others, the $1 billion Epcot is the second jewel in Disney's triple crown. Epcot has two worlds, Futureworld and the World Showcase. The former has exhibits and rides based on science and nature and don't miss the 3-D film **'Honey I Shrunk the Audience.'** In the **Wonders of Life** pavilion, **Cranium Command** explores the brain of a love-sick 12yr old boy in a simulator designed by George Lucas, the father of **Star Wars**. 'Hilarious.' The **World of Motion** is currently being updated to include exhibits on the future of transportation, and the **Universe of Energy** now features a new movie, *Ellen's Energy Adventure*, hosted by comedienne Ellen Degeneres. While some readers call some of the pavilions, like the one by GM, 'mind-boggling boredom,' others are described as 'wonderful,' eg. the incredible dinosaur ride in the Energy Pavilion. The World Showcase features pavilions from 11 lands, the most recent being Norway. All the employees in the showcase including the chefs come from their host countries and work at Disney for one year. Epcot has built a reputation as having the best food of any of the parks; visitors should make lunch and dinner reservations as soon as they enter the park at Spaceship Earth. Best bargain is the all-you-can-eat Norwegian smorgasbord. Be sure to view the park's nightly spectacular laser display, illuminations. 'Not worth the price; very modern and technical, no place to have fun like in Disneyworld.' 'Unique, contemporary—very good.'

Disney/MGM Studios Theme Park. Opened in 1989 to great reviews and huge crowds. The park, designed as a movie set, is inhabited by various Disney characters as well as 'directors' and 'stars.' In addition to the standard rides and attractions, there is a backstage Studio Tour which offers a behind-the-scenes look at film making. Production for some Disney and Touchstone (its adult subsidiary) releases takes place here, but the main goal of the park is to bring in tourists and their dollars. The Great Movie Ride, Catastrophe Canyon, Star Tours, the Animation studio and the Indiana Jones Stunt Spectacular are the main highlights. The action culminates at the **Twilight Zone Tower of Terror**, where you plunge 13 stories down a darkened elevator shaft, twice! Be sure also to catch the Muppet-Vision 3-D movie.

Other Disney Parks. Of the two water parks, **River Country** and **Typhoon Lagoon**, the latter is of the 'traditional' variety with water slides and a wave machine, while River Country bills itself as the land of Tom Sawyer, where visitors can spend a lazy day swinging into lakes. Neither of the parks is covered by the multi-day passports. River Country, $15. Typhoon Lagoon, $24. For a taste of Disney nightlife, venture to **Pleasure Island**. Seven distinct nightclubs, as well as numerous shops and restaurants, inhabit the island. Open 7 pm-2 am, one admission charge of $17 allows you to visit all of the clubs.

Sea World, on I-4 btwn Orlando & Disneyworld, 351-3600. $40. 9 am-10 pm. Features sharks, killer whales, walruses, multimedia fish and naked dolphins. 'One of the most spectacular aquatic animal displays I've ever seen.'

Wet n' Wild Amusement Park, off I-4 10 miles NE of Disney, 351-3200. Water park with slides of all degrees of daring including two 7 storey spectacular slides. 'Brilliant day out.' $25, half-price after 5 pm. 9 am-11 pm daily.

Universal Studios Orlando, near I-4 and the Florida Tnpk, 10 miles SW of downtown, 363-8000. Open since May 1990, the largest movie studios outside Hollywood stretch 444 acres and feature such attractions as *ET Adventure*, King Kong in *Kongfrontation* (no more said), a *Back to the Future* ride with seven-storey high OMNIMAX screens, and *Ghostbusters*. There is also a tour of famous film sets which include Jaws, and the Bates Motel from *Psycho*. Don't miss the new *Apollo 13* interactive motion picture attraction, the **Terminator 2, 'Battle Across Time'** ride, and display of dinosaurs used in the filming of *Jurassic Park*. Open daily 9 am-9 pm. 1-day pass $39.75, 2-day pass $59.75.

INFORMATION

Orlando-Orange County Visitors and Convention Bureau, 363-5871, several miles SW of downtown in Mercado, 8445 International Dr. Open daily 8 am-8 pm, tkt office closes 7 pm. Pick up *Orlando* for city info and ask for a free **Magic Card**, to receive discounts at various shops, restaurants, hotels and attractions.

TRAVEL

Orlando International Airport, 825-2001. 'Amazing airport, with fake monorail operated completely automatically.' #11 bus to town, 75¢.

Amtrak, 1400 Sligh Blvd, 843-7611/(800) 872-7245. Take bus #34 to downtown.

Greyhound, 555 N Magruder St, 292-3422/(800) 231-2222. Take bus #25 to downtown.

Tri-County Transit, 841-8240. Bus system serves downtown, airport and Sea World. Fare 75¢.

Orlando Airport Limousine, 423-5566, 324 W Gore St, 24 hrs. $13 to airport o/w. Also runs from hotels to Disney for around $16 r/t.

THE GULF COAST Broader, blindingly white and generally cleaner than those in the East Coast, the beaches of the West Coast are why many people vacation here. The area between Fort Myers and St Petersburg (St Pete), where the best beaches are found, is growing rapidly, though areas of relative isolation can still be found. The largest concentration of retirees also can be found here.

TAMPA/ST PETERSBURG Tampa, located 22 miles E of St Pete, best known for its cigars, is the area's business centre while **Clearwater** is the most popular beach destination among the under 25-set. But looks are deceiving. Tampa's only real draws are Ybor City, a unique Latin quarter, and Busch Gardens, an amusement park. Clearwater has not-so-pleasant crowds and tall nondescript hotels. The best finds on the Sun Coast, as the area is called, are tucked away and tough to get to. But once there, the beauty and relaxed atmosphere are supreme.

At the other side of the bay is sedate St Pete, the 'Sunshine City,' with a reputation for being a retirement community—*Cocoon* was filmed here—which helps obscure several interesting attractions as well as miles of excellent beaches.

ACCOMMODATION

Beach House Motel, 12100 Gulf Blvd, Treasure Island, 360-1153. D-$35, XP-$4.50. Rsvs rec. 'Right on the beach.'

Camping: St Petersburg KOA, 5400 95th St N, 392-2233. $21.95 for two, XP-$6. 'Great.'

Clearwater Beach International Hostel, at the Sands Hotel, 606 Bay Esplanade Ave, Clearwater Beach, 443-1211. $11 AYH, $13 non-AYH, private rooms $35, linen $2. AC, free bikes, pool. Rsvs rec. 'Excellent, friendly & fun.'

Days Inn, 2901 E Busch Blvd, on Rte 580, 1³/₄ miles E of jct I-75, exit 33, 933-6471. Rooms $49-$79, up to 4 people, depending on day of arrival. AC, TV, coin laundry, pool. 10 mins from Busch Gardens.

Dunedin Beach Campground, US 19 near Honeymoon Island, 784-3719. Sites $20 w/hook-up. 'Good campsite.'

Fort DeSoto Camp Grounds, 866-2662, near St Pete Beach, follow signs on Pinellas Bayway. Wildlife sanctuary composed of five islands. Sites $16.50. Call for availability but must make rsvs in person at camp grounds, or 150 5th St N, #146, in St Pete, or 631 Chestnut St in Clearwater.

Motel 6, I-275 and Fowler Ave Exit, 932-4948. From S/D-$28, XP-$6. AC, Pool.

Pass-A-Grille Beach Motel, 709 Gulf Way in St Petersburg Beach, 367-4726. Efficiency doubles from $45-$70. Hotel overlooks gulf.

St Petersburg AYH Hostel at McCarthy Hotel, 326 1st Ave N, 822-4141. $15 night in hotel room, $11 pp for four in bunk room, w/private bath.

Shirley Ann Hotel, 936 1st Ave N, 894-2759. D-$45, T-$59, Q-$64. 'Clean, comfortable. Owners are lovely people.' Near buses to Orlando.

Spanish Main Travel Parkway, 12101 US Hwy 301 N, 986-2415. Tent sites $14.50 for two, XP-$1, pool.

FOOD/ENTERTAINMENT

Cha Cha Coconuts, The Pier in St Petersburg, 822-6655. Mon-Sat 11 am-mid, Sun noon-10 pm. Sandwiches and ribs under $5. Live rock daily/evenings.

Gold Coffee Shop, 1st Ave N, next to St Pete Hostel, 822-4922. Open 6 am-4 pm. 'Amazing old-fashioned lunch counter. Really cheap food, full bfast for $3, main meal for $5.

Hurricane Seafood Restaurant, 807 Gulf Way in St Petersburg Beach, 360-9558. Right on Pass-A-Grille beach, famous for its grouper sandwich and other seafood selections from $5. Open daily for bfast, lunch and dinner as well as live jazz. Wed-Sun 8 am-1.30 am.

Carmine's, 1802 7th Ave in Tampa's Ybor City, 248-3834. Italian and Cuban fare, $7 for lunch, $8 for dinner. Live music on Sat nights.

Cafe Creole, 1330 9th Ave E in Tampa's Ybor City, 247-6283. Delicious Cajun cuisine from $8-$12. Live cajun music and Dixieland jazz Wed-Sat. Also check the music scene at **El Pasaje Plaza** next door, live cajun and zydeco played outdoors on the w/ends.

OF INTEREST

St Petersburg: Almost everything worth seeing in St Petersburg is located downtown but take caution after dark and stay in well-lit areas. The city's focal point and the centrepiece of the waterfront is **The Pier**, a recently renovated 5 storey upside-down pyramid in the middle of Tampa Bay. The Pier, 2nd Ave NE, 821-6164. Mon-Sat 10 am-10 pm, Sun 12 am-9.30 pm; houses a variety of shops, restaurants and the **University of South Florida Aquarium**, 895-7437, free. For miles in both directions of The Pier, you can walk through waterfront parks, beaches and marinas.

Salvador Dali Museum, 1000 3rd St S, 823-3767. Largest collection of surrealist works by the Spanish master. $8, $4 w/student ID, Mon-Sat 10 am-5.30 pm, Sun noon-5.30 pm. Across the street at 1120 4th St S is **Great Explorations**, 821-8992, one of the better 'hands-on' museums that appeals to adults, $5. Mon-Sat 10 am-5 pm, Sun noon-5 pm.

Sunken Gardens, 1825 4th St N, 896-3187, is a 5-acre sinkhole filled with tropical flora and fauna, 'gator wrestling and trained Macaws. Open 9 am-5.30 pm (last tkt 5 pm); $14. Also has **Biblical Wax Museum** depicting, amongst other things, the life of Christ. Open 10 am-4.30 pm. Free. 30 miles N of St Petersburg off the hellish Hwy US 19 is **Tarpon Springs**, a small colony of Greek fisherman who have been harvesting sponges for generations. Stroll through the village and dine on Greek fare.

The Museum of Fine Arts, 255 Beach Dr NE, 896-2667, is near the entrance to the Pier and boasts of having one of the largest photography collections in the Southeast. Tues-Sat 10 am-5 pm, Sun 1 pm-5 pm. $6, $2 w/student ID.

On the Beaches: Of the group, **Pass-A-Grille Beach** and **Caladesi/Honeymoon Islands** are 'supreme.' **Pass-A-Grille**, at the southern tip of St Petersburg Beach, combines the dunes, quaint shops, dolphins, and casual sun worshippers into a good mix. Take I-275 to the Bayway exit, the last exit before leaving the peninsula, then head west to the beach. **Caladesi Island State Park** and **Honeymoon Island State Recreation Area** have preserved the pristine state of the gulf shore while providing miles of white sand for beach goers. Side-by-side, one admission price admits you to both islands but the only way to get to Caladesi is by ferry, $6 r/t. Call 734-5263 for info. Ferry runs hrly 10 am-4 pm Mon-Fri, half-hourly 10 am-5 pm w/ends. When the gate keeper asks if you're from Florida, say yes—it's cheaper (otherwise $4 per car). Located between Tarpon Springs and Clearwater, take US 19 to State Road 586 and head west to the end of the road. Max length of stay on Caladesi, 4 hrs.

Tampa: Watch the **banana boats** dock and unload at Kennedy Blvd and 13th St. A stroll along Bayshore Blvd brings you a string of southern mansions.

Adventure Island, 4500 Bougainvillea Ave, 1 mile northeast of Busch Gardens, 987-5660, is one of the better water parks in Florida complete with water slides, rapids, wave pool, etc. $24. Open daily in summer, Mon-Thur 9 am-7 pm, Fri, Sat, Sun until 8 pm.

Busch Gardens—The Dark Continent, just off Rte 580, 987-5171. $39, open daily in summer although opening hours change monthly, call for details. Take an African safari to view more than 1000 animals, as well as dolphins and belly dancers, roller-coaster rides, shows, etc.

Museum of Art, 601 Doyle Carlton Drive, 274-8130. Ancient and contemporary art from Impressionism to photography. Tue-Sat 10 am-5 pm (Wed open 'til 9 pm), Sun 1 pm-5 pm. $5, $4 w/student ID.

Museum of Science and Industry, 4801 E Fowler Ave, 987-6100, Features a simulated hurricane. $7. Sun-Thurs 9 am-6 pm, 'til 9 pm Fri and Sat.

The Tampa Theater, 274-8286, a genuine old-time movie palace from the 1920s, designed in Rococco, Mediterranean and maybe other styles, the theatre shows old movies and art films at good prices, and when the show starts, watch the stars come out on the ceiling above. Franklin St in downtown Tampa. $5.50, $3.50 w/student ID. Before 6 pm, $3.50 for everyone.

Ybor City, which was once the 'cigar manufacturing headquarters of the world,' in the process of being gentrified, Ybor retains a stylish Latin influence. Learn of its history and that of the cigar industry at the **Ybor City State Museum**, 1818 9th Ave, 247-6323. Tue-Sat 9 am-5 pm, tours 10 am-3 pm, $2. Although several restaurants with live music and dance bars are in the area, take precaution when walking through Ybor at night. '97 saw the birth of the **Cigar Festival**, 23rd July, noon-11 pm, street shows, dancing, food, call 247-1434 for details.

INFORMATION
St Petersburg Chamber of Commerce, 100 2nd Ave N, 821-4069.
St Pete Beach Chamber of Commerce, 6990 Gulf Blvd, 360-6957.
Clearwater Chamber of Commerce, 128 N Osceola Ave, 461-0011.
Greater Tampa Chamber of Commerce, 401 East Jackson & Florida Sts, 228-7777.

TRAVEL
Tampa:
Amtrak, 601 Nebraska Ave, 221-7600/(800) 872-7245. Kissimee/Orlando $22 (bus service only), Fort Lauderdale $54, Miami $60.
Greyhound, 610 E Polk St, 229-2112/(800) 231-2222.
Hillsborough Area Regional Transit, 254-4278, $1.15, transfers 10-35¢. #30 btwn airport and downtown.
St Petersburg:
Greyhound, 180 9th St N, (800) 231-2222. Miami $52, Orlando $25.
Pinellas Suncoast Transit Authority, 530-9911. Runs 6 am-6 pm, $1 basic fare, free transfers.
BATS (bus service through the beaches), 367-3702. $1 basic fare.

THE PANHANDLE   The strip of land jabbing into Alabama, the panhandle has more in common with the states of the Deep South than it does with sub-tropical South Florida. Winter is distinctly cooler here and the terrain is broken up with that rarity in Florida, a hill.

Hidden away in the hills and forests is **Tallahassee**, the state capital. Much as the town seems able to resist the invasion of tourists today, it also avoided capture by the Union forces during the Civil War, the only Confederate capital east of Mississippi with that distinction. This is a city of real Floridians, not transplanted northerners, and there's still much of its 19th century architecture to see, and a slower way of life to appreciate.

Moving further west along the Panhandle, you come to **Panama City** and the commercialised resort of **Panama City Beach**. Panama City runs on Central Standard Time and so is one hour behind the rest of Florida. It used to be a peaceful fishing village and it remains quieter than most places along this coast. The developers are moving in, however, in the wake of their triumphs down the road at Panama City Beach. The beach really is lovely and the sea is clear and warm, but everything is over-priced and overpopulated.

Further west still, and the last city in Florida, is **Pensacola**. Since the first successful settlement here in 1698, Pensacola has flown the flags of five nations and has changed hands 13 times. The British used it as a trading post in the 18th century and business seems to have been good, for here Scotsman James Panton became America's first recorded millionaire. Here too, in 1821, Andrew Jackson completed the transaction whereby Spain sold Florida to the United States.

The white sand beaches near Pensacola are among the best in Florida; after a dip you're on your way west to **Gulf Islands National Seashore** (see Biloxi, Mississippi) and to New Orleans. **Information Center** in Gulf Breeze, (904) 932-1500, (800) 635-4803.

GEORGIA   *Peach State*

Georgia has seen rough times. Named after George II, the state began as an English debtor's colony, and many died before the swamps were cleared for cotton fields. Just when things were looking up, the final moments of the Civil War saw Union General Sherman break through rebel defenses at Chattanooga and devastate a 60 mile-wide swath to the sea.

But unlike some other states of the Deep South, the Peach State has chosen to look more to the future than to the past, and since the Second World War has been rising on the crest of an industrial boom. Atlanta is now the unchallenged capital of the 'New South.' Peanut farmer Jimmy Carter marched out of the anonymity of Plains to become president in 1976, and Savannah is still a strong rival to Charleston's claim as the most beautiful city in the South. *www.yahoo.com/Regional/U_S_States/Georgia.*
The area code for Atlanta is 404, for Savannah and Southern Georgia 912.

ATLANTA   Host to the 1996 Olympic Games, and home of CNN, Ted Turner, and Coca-Cola Atlanta's story has so far been one of fast-growing success. Founded in 1837 as a site for the South Western terminal of the Western & Atlantic Railroad, Atlanta was, by the time of the Civil War, the commercial and industrial centre of the South. In 1864, General Sherman 'drove old Dixie down', with his devastating march to the sea, during which Atlanta was bombarded and then burned to the ground, as immortalised in *Gone with the Wind.*

The city rose again, and has shown that progress counts more than prejudice. Atlantans elected their first black mayor in 1973, and it was here that Martin Luther King was raised and first preached.

Its skyscraper skyline, crisscrossing expressway system and ultra-modern airport (one of the 3 busiest in the world), while proclaiming perhaps Atlanta's leadership of the 'New South,' tend to be boring and charmless. However, Peachtree Street (be careful, there are 32 Peach Tree Streets in Atlanta), financial hub of the ante-bellum South, still retains some of its presence, and, away from downtown, the city's hills, wooded streets and numerous colleges—Atlanta University, Clark College, Emory University and the Georgia Institute of Technology—create a pleasant atmosphere. The Dogwood Festival here in April is the highlight of the year.

On the debit side, Atlanta has one of the worst murder records of urban America. After working hours, downtown is soulless, even uncomfortable. Tread carefully.

ACCOMMODATION

'Go to the Visitors Bureau. Lots of deals and discount vouchers.'

Atlanta Dream Hostel, 222 E Howard Ave, 370-0380. Located in a safe and fun downtown neighbourhood, 2 blocks from Decatur metro. $15, D-$41. 24 hrs, no curfew, kitchen/laundry, TV. Free linen, coffee, local calls, pick-up service (call for availability) and bike rentals, but surely it is the Elvis shrine, Barbie Doll girls dorm and other theme rooms that set this apart from other hostels! A dream come true, call for directions. 'Funky and friendly.'

B&B Atlanta, 1801 Piedmont Ave NE, 875-0525. Rooms in desirable neighbourhoods in and near Atlanta from S-$55, D-$60. Advance rsvs advisable and free of charge. Mon-Fri 9 am-5 pm. 'Southern hospitality in the European tradition.'

Hostelling International Atlanta (HI-AYH), 223 Ponce de Leon Ave, 875-2882. 4 blocks E of N Ave MARTA. $16.25 AYH, $25 non-AYH, student ID may get you the same rate as members depending on availability. 'Clean, safe and friendly.' Check-in 8 am-noon, 5 pm-midnight. Pool, free coffee and doughnuts.

Villa International, 1749 Clifton Rd NE, 633-6783. 'A ministry of the Christian community.' Situated near Emory U, pleasant, safe suburb, next door to the Center for Disease Control. 'Quiet with a very helpful staff, though a little shabby.' S-$30 w/shower, sm D-$20 pp, lrg D-$23 pp. No TV/tel.

YMCA, 22 Butler St NE, 659-8085. S-$16, $113 weekly, $5 deposit. Men only. No AC, 'stuffy and tatty rooms.'

Numerous budget motels, e.g. **Comfort Inn, Days Inn, Motel 6, Red Roof Inn**, in Atlanta area, but you'll need a car and they usually cost more here than elsewhere, from $34-$85. Look around Myrtle, Piedmont, Peachtree and Ponce De Leon.

FOOD

Atlanta's specialties are fried chicken, black-eyed peas, okra and sweet potato pie.

Aleck's Barbeque, 783 Martin Luther King Dr NW, 525-2062. Pork and beef ribs, chopped pork sandwiches and beef BBQ are bestsellers. Sandwich and sides for less than $6. 'Popular with locals.'

Barkers Red Hots, buy 'Atlanta's Best Hot Dog' from street vendors at various locations around town, from $2.50.

Mary-Macs, 224 Ponce DeLeon Ave NE, 875-4337. Good, cheap food (try the green turnip soup and corn muffins). Mon-Fri 7 am-9 pm, Sat 9 am-9 pm. 'Where the natives eat!'

Tortillas, 774 Ponce de Leon Ave, 892-0193. El cheapo Mexican food, popular with local student crowd, upstairs patio for *al freso* dining.

The Varsity, North Ave at I-75, 881-1706. World's largest drive-in, next to Georgia Tech campus. Serves 15,000 people with 8,300 Colas, 18,000 hamburgers, 25,000 hotdogs each day. 'Clean, fast, cheap and good.' Mon-Fri 8 am-12 am, Sat, Sun 8 am-2 am. Three large markets with cheap produce, meats, cheeses, etc:

Sweet Auburn Curb Market, 209 Edgewood Ave in downtown, 659-1665, Mon-Thurs 8 am-5.45 pm; Fri & Sat 6.45 pm; **DeKalb Farmer's Market**, 3000 E Ponce de Leon Ave outside Decatur, 377-6400, daily 9 am-9 pm; and **Atlanta State Farmer's Market**, 10 miles S of downtown off I-75, 366-6910, 24 hrs.

OF INTEREST

Atlanta Botanical Garden, Piedmont Ave at The Prado, 876-5859. A tranquil oasis with tropical, desert and endangered plant species. Tues-Sun 9 am-6 pm, $6, Free Thurs 1 pm-6 pm.

Memorial & Grave of Martin Luther King Jr, in Ebenezer Baptist Churchyard at 413 Auburn Ave NW, 524-1956. The inscription on the tomb reads: 'Free at last, free at last, thank God Almighty, I'm free at last.' Includes inter-faith Peace Chapel. Mon-Fri 9 am-5 pm. 'Be careful in this area.' Next door is the **ML King Jr. Center for Non-Violent Social Change**, 449 Auburn Ave, 524-1956. Free tour of his home and exhibits on the slain civil rights leader. Free film of his life. 9 am-8 pm daily in summer. *www.nps.gov/malu/*.

State Capitol, Washington at Mitchell, 656-2844. Modelled on the Washington DC capitol building and topped with gold from the Georgia goldfield at Dahlonega, brought to Atlanta by special wagon caravan. Houses **State Museum of Science and Industry, Hall of Flags** and **Georgia Hall of Fame**. 8 am-5 pm Mon-Fri, 10 am-4 pm w/ends. Tours on the hr, 10 am, 11 am, 1 pm, 2 pm, no tours at w/ends. Free.

Underground Atlanta, in downtown around Upper Alabama St. 12-acre complex housing more than 130 restaurants, shops and nightclubs. Impressive 10-storey light tower at main entrance. Shops open Mon-Sat 10 am-9.30 pm, Sun 'til 5.30 pm; restaurant/club hours vary.

World of Coca-Cola, 55 Martin Luther King Dr, 676-5151. Adjacent to Underground Atlanta; the pavilion includes historic memorabilia, radio and TV retrospective, a futuristic soda fountain and an 18 ft coke bottle! 'Watch the film and hear how Coca-Cola helped win World War II! ... Brilliant museum, brilliant value.' Mon-Sat 10 am-8 pm, Sun noon-5 pm; $6.

Science and Technology Museum of Atlanta (Sci Trek), 395 Piedmont Ave, 522-3955. Said to be one of the top ten physical science museums in America; over 100 hands-on science exhibits. Mon-Sat 10 am-5 pm, Sun noon-5 pm, $7.50, $5 w/student ID.

The Atlanta Historical Society, 3101 Andrews Dr NW, 814-4000. 34 acres of landscaped gardens and trails. Library, archives, exhibitions and films on Atlanta and its history. Mon-Sat 10 am-5.30 pm, Sun noon-5.30 pm. $9, $7 w/student ID, includes admission and guided tour of historic houses and grounds.

Atlanta Preservation Center, 84 Peachtree St NW, 876-2040. 1¹/₂hr guided walking tours of Atlanta's historic districts conducted 3 times weekly. $5, $3 w/student ID.

High Museum of Art, 1280 Peachtree St NE, 733-4200. Tue-Sat 10 am-5 pm, Fri 'til 9 pm, Sun noon-5 pm. $6, $4 w/student ID. Free, Thur 1 pm-5 pm 'Intriguing design. Excellent and varied temporary exhibitions, plus good American 19th century collection.'

Jimmy Carter Presidential Center, 1 Copenhill, 435 Freedom Parkway, 331-3942. Take bus #16 to Cleburne. Museum on the Carter presidency, also features other US presidents. Mon-Sat 9 am-4.45 pm, Sun noon-4.45 pm, $4. 'Well worth it.' *www.nps.gov/jica/*. Joel Chandler Harris, author of the Uncle Remus stories, lived at **Wren's Nest**, 1050 Abernathy Blvd, 753-7735. See the briar Brer Rabbit lived in, $6. Tue-Sat 10 am-4 pm, Sun 1 pm-4 pm.

Cyclorama, in Grant Park, 658-7625. 103-yr-old circular painting (one of the largest in the world) with 3-dimensional diorama complete with lighting and sound effects, depicting the 1864 Battle of Atlanta. Don't miss the *Texas*, of the Great Locomotive Chase of the Civil War (immortalised by Buster Keaton in *The General*). Open daily 9.30 am-5.30 pm: $4.50, $4 w/student ID. Further **Civil War memorabilia** in the area include the breastworks erected for the defence of the town—in Grant Park, Cherokee Ave and Boulevard SE—and Fort Walker, Confederate Battery, set up as during the siege.

Stone Mountain, Grant Park. In massive bas-relief the equestrian figures of Generals Robert E Lee, Stonewall Jackson and Confederate President Jefferson Davis have been cut from a 600-ft-high granite dome, the world's largest exposed mass of granite. Astride this mountain, looking down on Lee and Davis you can understand why King, in his 'I have a dream' speech said 'Let freedom ring from Stone Mountain in Georgia.' A cable car runs to the top, or you can climb it. Also in the 3200-acre historical and recreational park is an ante-bellum plantation, an antique auto and music museum, a game ranch, riverboat cruises, a 5-mile steam railroad and more. Park entrance $6 p/car, attractions must be paid for individually, $3.50 each. Dazzling nightly laser show at 9.30 pm at no extra cost. 'Worth waiting 'til dark: brilliant effects.' 'Take MARTA bus and you don't pay the $6.' 25 miles E of Atlanta off Hwy 78, (770) 498-5600. Gates open 6 am-midnight, attractions, 10 am-5.30 pm, 8.30 pm in summer.

Stone Mountain Family Campground, 498-5710. Tents $15, $17 w/hook-up. 'Beautiful sites on the lake.'

Marriott Marquis, 265 Peachtree Center Ave, 521-0000. One of a spectacular genre of hotels featuring a breathtaking atrium. A must-see if you are in Atlanta. Most expensive to construct and largest hotel in the southeast.

CNN Center, Marietta St at Techwood Dr, 827-2400. Tour the studios of this 24 hr all news network. $7. Daily 9 am-6 pm, every 10 mins. Next door is the **Omni Coliseum**, home of the Atlanta Hawks basketball team. Ticketmaster 249-6400.

Turner Field, 755 Hankeraaron Blv, the stadium built especially for the Olympics, is now the home of the **Atlanta Braves** baseball team, current National League champions and World-Series runners-up. Ticketmaster 249-6400. American football is played by the **Falcons** at the **Georgia Dome** which hosted the '94 Superbowl and was also host to some Olympic events in '96.

ENTERTAINMENT

Read the free, weekly *Creative Loafing, Atlanta Gazette* and *Where Magazine* to find out what goes on. 'Atlanta, especially midtown, is known second only to San Francisco for a large gay community.'

Piedmont Park, free open-air jazz and classical concerts, Atlanta Philharmonic Orchestra, throughout the summer. First week in Sep, Atlanta Jazz Festival. 'Not to be missed. People dance, drink; on a good evening it can be like the last night of the proms. Also watch the fireflies do illuminated mating dances.' Park also has an open-air swimming pool, 892-0117. 'Beautiful; great for a rest and a free shower. Friendly pool attendants.' 1 pm-7.15 pm daily, 11 am-7.15 pm w/ends, $2, free bwtn 1 pm and 4.15 pm. Keep eyes open at night; not too friendly neighbourhood.

Six Flags Over Georgia, 12 miles W on I-20, 940-9290. One of the nation's largest theme parks, home to the 'Georgia Cyclone' rollercoaster and such rides as 'Mind Bender' and 'Splashwater Falls.' Sun-Thur 10 am-10 pm, Fri, Sat 10 am-midnight. 1-day pass $30, 2-day pass $33. Take MARTA to Hightower Station, then bus #201. 'Don't go on Saturdays as you will spend the whole day in queues.'

The Fox, 660 Peachtree, 881-2100. Second largest movie theatre in America and now a national landmark. One of the last great movie palaces. Built in 1929; Moorish design. Now a venue for concerts, theatre and special film presentations. Call for listings. Atlanta Preservation Society, 876-2040, operate a history tour of the interior; Mon, Wed, Thurs, at 10 am, Sat at 11 am.

INFORMATION

Convention and Visitors Bureau, Harris Tower, 233 Peachtree St NE, Suite 2000, 521-6600. Mon-Fri 8.30 am-5.30 pm. 'Far more helpful than Chamber of Commerce.' Satellite locations in Lenox Square Mall and Underground Atlanta.

Chamber of Commerce, 235 International Blvd, across from Omni Building, 880-9000. 'Very helpful.'

TRAVEL

MARTA (Metropolitan Atlanta Rapid Transit Authority), 848-4711, combined bus and rail serves most area attractions and hotels. Free transfers btwn subway and buses. Basic fare $1.50, weekly pass $11, unlimited usage. Subway runs 5 am-1 am.

Greyhound, 81 International Blvd NW, (800) 231-2222. Use caution in this area. Savannah $43, Orlando $50.

Amtrak, Peachtree Station, 1688 Peachtree St NW, (800) 872-7245. The NY-New Orleans *Crescent* stops here daily.

Hartsfield International Airport is situated 12 miles S of the city, an impressive, innovative piece of building; 222-6688, general info. MARTA buses can take you downtown, 15 min rides run every 8 mins.

The Atlanta Airport Shuttle (525-2177) runs a van service to over 100 locations in and around the metropolitan area, $8-$30.Taxis downtown $10 o/w (530-6698).

SAVANNAH When Ray Charles sings *Georgia on My Mind*, it's surely Savannah and *not* Atlanta he's mooning over. Laid out in 1733 by English General James Oglethorpe, Savannah was America's first planned city and Georgia's oldest. In one of the earliest evangelical movements, Charles and John Wesley accompanied Oglethorpe as missionaries, later establishing in the city the Wesleyan Methodist Church. After seeing what Sherman had done to Atlanta in 1864, Savannah wisely decided to surrender, saving her charming gardens, public squares and old homes from certain destruction.

What Sherman spared, however, seemed almost doomed by declining cotton prices. The town was run-down until restoration efforts began on Trustees Garden in the 1950s. Today, the city (which has no less than 21 squares) echoes with reminders of its colonial past. Warehouses once housing stores of cotton and now shops and restaurants, line the cobble-stoned River Street which runs along the Savannah River. Here, monthly parades, concerts and other events take place; St Patrick's Day celebrations are said to rival those of New York. The first steamship (the *Savannah*, of course) crossed the Atlantic to Liverpool (in 1819) from here, the 10th largest port in the US. And an old seamen's pub referred to in Robert Louis Stevenson's *Treasure Island* still survives as the Pirate's House.
The telephone area code is 912.

ACCOMMODATION
Bed and Breakfast Inn, 117 W Gordon at Chatham Sq, 233-9481. In the heart of the historic district, an 1853 townhouse. 'Clean and well maintained.' From $55.
Savannah International Youth Hostel (HI-AYH), 304 E Hall St, 236-7744. Renovated Victorian Mansion in historic district. $14 AYH, $17 non-AYH, private rooms $25. Check-in 7.30 am-10 am and 5 pm-10 pm. Call ahead for late check-in. Maximum stay 3 nights.
Thunderbird Inn, 611 West Oglethorpe Ave, 232-2661. From S-$32, D-$38, XP-$5. Near bus station.
Camping: Bellaire Woods Campground, GA Hwy 204, 15 miles NW of downtown, 748-4000. $20.50 for two, w/hook-up.
Skidway Island State Park, 6 miles SE of downtown on Waters Ave, 598-2300, inaccessable by public transport. $17 1st night, $15 thereafter. Bathrooms and heated showers.

FOOD
Crystal Beer Parlour, 301 W Jones St, 232-1153. Hamburgers, chili dogs, seafood, gumbo. 11 am-9 pm Mon-Sat.
Morrison's Cafeteria, 15 Bull St, 232-5264. Good and inexpensive. 11 am-8 pm.
Shucker's Seafood Restaurant, almost at end of W River St, 236-1427. 'Recommended by the locals, it's casual, with a laid-back atmosphere and good food.' 11.30 am-10 pm daily.
Spanky's Pizza Galley and Saloon, 317 East River St, 236-3009. 'River Street's favourite good-time saloon.' Dinner $7-$15.
Toucan Café, 1100 Eisenhower Dr, #28, 352-223, serving all kinds of international food, sandwiches and salads, $4-$13.
Wally's Sixpence Pub, 245 Bull St, 233-3151. Mon-Sat 11.30-10 pm, Sun from 12.30 pm. 'A haunt of unusual and interesting characters.'

OF INTEREST

Old Savannah offers cobbled streets, charming squares, formal gardens and several beautiful mansions. Among the stately houses of the town is the **Owens-Thomas House**, at 124 Abercorn St, 233-9743, at which Lafayette was a visitor in 1825. Tue-Sat 10 am-5 pm, Sun 2 pm-5 pm; $7, $3 w/student ID.

Green-Meldrim House, Madison Sq, 233-3845, is where General Sherman enjoyed his victory, $4, $2 w/student ID. The Green-Meldrim serves as Parish house for the Gothic Revival Style **St John's Episcopal Church**, built 1852. Tue, Thur, Fri, Sat 10 am-4 pm.

Savannah Waterfront. Pubs, shops, restaurants and night spots housed in old cotton warehouses along cobblestone streets. 'Beware: it's a tourist trap with masses of souvenir shops and over-priced beer.' In the same vein is **City Market**, at St Julian and Jefferson Sts.

Ships of the Sea Maritime Museum, 41 Martin Luther King Blvd, 232-1511. Models and maritime memorabilia. Daily 10 am-5 pm, $4, $2 w/student ID .

Telfair Academy of Arts and Sciences, 121 Barnard St, 232-1177. The oldest art museum in the southeast and the home of a fine collection of portraits and 18th century masterpieces. Tue-Sat 10 am-5 pm, Sun 2 pm-5 pm. $5, $2 w/student ID; free on Sun.

Christ Episcopal Church, 28 Bull St, 232-8230. First church in Georgia; the present building was erected in 1840. John Wesley preached here in 1736-37, arousing extraordinary emotions in the congregation. He also founded the first Sunday school here. Tues & Fri only 10 am-3.30 pm.

Temple Mickve Israel, 20 E Gordon, 233-1547. Seeking religious freedom, a group of Sephardic Jews from England were among the first to settle here in 1733. The oldest congregation practicing reform Judaism. The synagogue looks like a church, complete with a steeple, choir loft, and gothic design. No one is sure why the Orthodox congregation built it this way. 2 of the Torahs, the oldest in America, are from the original congregation. Tours of museum and archives, Mon-Fri 10 am-noon, 2 pm-4 pm. Services Fri 8.15 pm, Sat 11 am, all welcome.

ENTERTAINMENT

Kevin Barry's, 117 W River St, 233-9626, Irish pub immortalised in a song, offering good, cheap Irish food, Guinness on draught (not so cheap!) and Irish folk music. Mon-Fri 4 pm-3 am, Sat 11.30-3 am, Sun 12.30-2 am. Also check out **Wet Willies**, 101 E River St, 233-5650, for 'irresistable frozen diaquiris.'

INFORMATION/TRAVEL

Chamber of Commerce Convention and Visitors Bureau, 222 W Oglethorpe Ave, 944-0456.

Savannah Visitors Center, 301 Martin Luther King Blvd, 944-0460. Literature, maps, a self-guided walking tour leaflet, slide show. Many tours start here. Open daily 8.30 am-5 pm.

Amtrak, 2611 Seaboard Coastline Dr, 234-2611/(800) 872-7245.

Chatham Area Transit (CAT), 233-5767. Public transportation system serving Savannah and surrounding area. Buses run 6 am-midnight, basic fare 75c, 1-day pass $1.50.

Greyhound, 610 W Oglethorpe Ave, 232-2135/(800) 231-2222.

Gray Line Bus Tours, 215 West Boundry St, 236-9604.

OKEFENOKEE SWAMP This large swamp area lies in southeast Georgia. 8 miles S of **Waycross** on Hwys US 1 and US 23, is the **Okefenokee Swamp Park**, 283-0583. This is a private park with an observation tower, 2-mi boat tour, $12 (special 1 hr 'Deep Swamp' also available $16), and walkways enabling you to take in the cypresses, flowers, aquatic birds, bears and alligators without getting your feet wet. There is also a museum telling the story of the 'Land of the Trembling Earth' (the old Indian name for the swamp). Entrance to the park is $8. 8 am-8 pm daily in summer, off season, 8 am-5.30 pm.. For info on the **Federal Park**, call 496-3331. The park offers 2-5 days canoe trips (reserve in advance), from $14.

KENTUCKY   *Bluegrass State*

A land of country pleasures, Kentucky's bluegrass hills have yielded bourbon whiskey, fried chicken, fast horses and even faster bluegrass music. Since 1769 when Daniel Boone cleared the Wilderness Trail to settle the first lands west of the Allegheny Mountains, Kentuckians have quietly elevated country living into an art form. Bluegrass Music features complex picking on guitars, banjos and fiddles, sometimes tedious in its traditional forms, but exhilarating in its progressive modes. Merle Travis, who initiated the famous Travis-style picking is from the state. Kentucky produces 87% of the world's bourbon (from Bourbon county) and bottles almost half of the nation's whiskey. The abundance of fertile bluegrass, which is not actually blue—it is green and blossoms blue in spring, attracted livestock farmers and in particular, horses. As a consequence the Kentucky equine passion has developed into a refined, multi-million dollar international obsession indulged annually at Louisville's Kentucky Derby.

Hardy country living has bred many proud Kentucky natives, among them Henry Clay, Jefferson Davis, Abraham Lincoln and Mohammed Ali. Kentucky's fighting spirit, important reserves of coal and strategic location made it a decisive factor in the Civil War. Even though the Constitution says nothing about allowing a state to be 'neutral,' that is what Kentucky tried to be. A worried Lincoln was said to have remarked that he hoped to have God on his side, but he had to have Kentucky. *www.yahoo.com/Regional/ U_S__States/Kentucky.*

The area code for Louisville, Frankfurt and western KY is 502, for Lexington and eastern KY, 606.

LOUISVILLE   The most prestigious horse race in the country, the Kentucky Derby, is held here the first week in May amidst a festival atmosphere of parades, concerts and a steamboat race.

Founded by George Rogers Clark as a supply base on the Ohio for his Northwest explorations, Louisville is now a commercial, industrial and educational centre specializing in things that are supposed to be bad for you. Fast food, bourbon whiskey and cigarettes are made here in abundance. This is also the hometown of the Louisville Lip, though the boulevard named after him is called Mohammed Ali.

Keep your eyes on the fountain in the Ohio River directly outside downtown. The tallest computerized floating fountain in the world, a series of 41 jets and 102 coloured lights create some spectacular effects.

En route from here to **Mammoth Caves** are various folksy attractions, including Abraham Lincoln's birthplace at Hodgenville, Stephen Foster's original 'My Old Kentucky Home' and the Lincoln Homestead nearby. Note: Louisville is pronounced Loo-AH-ville.

ACCOMMODATION

Junction Inn, 3304 Bardstown Rd, 456-2861. Exit 16 A off I-264. S-$30, D-$36. XP-$5.
Emily Boone Home Hostel AYH, 1027 Franklin St, 585-3430. $7, non-AYH $10, plus 20 mins of chores around the house. Rsvs essential, make sure you speak with the proprietor directly. 2 miles from bus station, near Farmers' Market.
KOA, 900 Marriot Dr, (812) 282-4474. I-65 N across bridge, exit Stansifer Ave. 'Very handy for downtown.' Free use of pool, mini-golf and fishing lake at motel next door. Sites $17 for two, $22.50 w/hook-up, XP-$4, cabins for two, $31.
Thrifty Dutchman Budget Hotel, 3357 Fern Valley Rd, 968-8124. Off I-65. S-$44.50, D-$50. XP-$6.

FOOD

Look along Bardstown Rd for budget cafes serving a wide variety of local. and international cuisine.
BBQ's, burgoo stew and cured ham are all Kentucky delicacies, unlike the famed fried chicken (see the Colonel Sanders Museum below).
Check's Cafe, 1101 Burnett, 637-9515. Local favourite where hamburgers start at $2. Oyster specialty. Open daily 11 am-11 pm.
The Old Spaghetti Factory, 235 W Market St, 581-1070. Full dinner with pasta, salad, bread and desert $5.50-$8. Mon-Thur 11.30 am-2 pm and 5 pm-10 pm. Fri & Sat 'til 11 pm.
Phoenix Hill Tavern, 644 Baxter Ave, 589-4957. 4 stages offering live blues, rock, and reggae every night 'til 4 am. Cover $3-$5. 'Cheap sandwiches."
The Rudyard Kipling, 422 W Oak St, 636-1311, 7 blocks S of downtown in Old Louisville. 'Hearty food and drink from all around the world.' Here you can eat anything from curry to crepes as well as a variety of national pasties! Try a bowl of Kentucky burgoo (a meat and veg stew) for $3. Mon and Wed nights offer folk and jazz music; theatre is performed on the in-house stage during Sept and Oct. 'If you eat one meal in Louisville, eat it here.' Mon-Sat 11.30 am-1.30 pm and 5.30 pm-midnight.

OF INTEREST

Churchill Downs, home of the **Kentucky Derby**, 700 Central Ave, 636-4400. On the morning of Derby Day, the first Sat in May, arrive around 8 am to claim a small piece of the track infield for $30 pp. The big race is in the afternoon, but the partying goes on all day. Potent mint juleps, the drink of the South, are available from vendors. Racing also takes place from late Apr-early Jul and late Oct-late Nov. At gate 1 stands the **Kentucky Derby Museum**, 637-1111, 9 am-5 pm daily, $5. Shows run twice hourly. Includes exhibits on horseracing and breeding, and an exciting 360 degree movie theatre that puts you in the middle of the race (hourly). Each August Louisville hosts the **Kentucky State Fair** which features the World Championship Horse Show for American saddlebreds—Kentucky's native horse breed.
JB Speed Art Museum, 2035 3rd St, 636-2893. One of the better mid-South galleries. Medieval, Renaissance and French works, a strong Dutch collection and a spacious sculpture court. The museum boasts an elaborately carved, oak-panelled English Renaissance room from 'The Grange,' Devon. Tues-Sat 10 am-4 pm, Sun noon-5 pm free Thomas Jefferson was the architect of the **John Speed Mansion**, Farmington, 3033 Bardstown Rd, 452-9920. Mon-Sat 10 am-3.45 pm, Sun 1.30 pm-3.45 pm. $4, $2 w/student ID. Shakespeare falls trippingly off the tongue in Louisville's **Central Park**. You will not have to pay a pound of flesh, it's free, 583-8738 for details. Curtain is 8 pm, Tue-Sun, early Jun-Aug.

Col Harland Sanders Museum, 1441 Gardiner Lane, 456-8300. Free museum records the life of the 'finger lickin' good' chicken purveyor who helped start the phenomenon of fast food. Mon-Thur 8 am-5 pm, Fri 8 am-3 pm. A pleasant way to spend an afternoon is to take a cruise on the Ohio River on the *Belle of Louisville*, 625-2355, an old sternwheeler. The boat runs from late May-early Sep and departs from the landing at 4th St and River Rd, Tue-Sun at 2 pm, $8. 'Sunset cruises,' Tue and Thur 7 pm, $8. 'Nightime Dance Cruises,' Sat 8.30 pm-11.30 pm, $12. The **Corn Island Storytelling Festival**, usually the third w/end in September, 245-0643, uses the *Belle* for a storytelling tour along the river. The most popular festival event is the **Long Run Park** ghost story event. Held near an old graveyard, thousands come out to hear the tales beginning at nightfall. Festival tkts for all the events are $50pp, $90 for two. Individual event tkts available, $10 pp.

Howard Steamboat Museum, 1101 E Market St, (812) 283-3728, Tue-Sat 10 am-3 pm, Sun 1 pm-3 pm, $4, $2 w/student ID. Billed as the 'only museum of its kind in the US,' models of steamboats, tools and pilot wheels are on display. Located across the Ohio River from Louisville in Jeffersonville, Indiana.

Jim Beam's American Outpost, 543-9877. 10 min movie and self-guided tour which shows you the joys of bourbon-making. (Bourbon is made using at least 51% corn and must be aged at least 2 yrs, preferably in a charred white oak container. Anything less is 'just' whiskey.) The tour is free, Mon-Sat 9 am-4.30 pm, Sun 1 pm-4 pm. Follow I-65, 22 miles S from Louisville, then E on Rte 245 toward **Clermont**. America hoards her gold at **Fort Knox**, 25 miles SW of Louisville on US 31 W-60. Don't expect to see the metal, but if you're in a military frame of mind, visit the **Gen Patton, KB, OBE, Museum of Cavalry and Armor**, Building 4554, Fayette Ave, in Fort Knox, 624-6350. 200 yrs of military history, from the old frontier fort to displays of weapons, equipment and uniforms dating back to the Revolutionary War. Also see the 'ivory-handled Patton pistols' and war booty that Old Blood and Guts gathered in WW II. Donation appreciated. Mon-Fri 9 am-4.30 pm, w/end 10 am-6 pm.

The Coca-Cola Museum, 1201 N Dixie Ave, Elizabethtown, 737-4000. Located 45 miles S of Louisville in the Elizabethtown bottling plant, this museum houses the world's largest collection of Coca-Cola memorabilia. Remnants of forgotten ad campaigns and items dating back to the 1880's, the dawn of the soft-drinks era. Mon-Fri 9 am-4 pm, $2.

INFORMATION
Kentucky State Dept. Of Tourism, (800) 225-8747.
Visitors Information Center, 400 S 1st St, corner of Liberty, (561) 582-3732/ (800) 792-5595. Mon-Fri 9.30 am-5 pm, Sat 10 am-4 pm, Sun 10 am-4 pm. Later in summer.

TRAVEL
TARC, 585-1234, local buses serving most of metro area. Daily 5 am-11.30 pm. Fare 75¢, $1 peak times. 30 min rides to the airport leave from 1st and Market St throughout the day. Limo service also available from outside the Hyatt and Goldhouse Hotels, $6-$10.
Greyhound, 720 W Mohammed Ali Blvd, (800) 231-2222.
Yellow Tours , 1601 S Preston St, 636-5664.

MAMMOTH CAVES NATIONAL PARK
Halfway between Louisville, Kentucky, and Nashville, Tennessee, above ground this is a preserve of forest, flowers and wildlife, below ground several hundred miles of passages, pits, domes, gypsum and travertine formations, archaeological remains and a crystal lake. The caves rival in size the better-known Carlsbad Caverns and may be explored on foot, or afloat during conducted boat trips.

Call the park office for details: (502) 758-2328.

Keep to the caves within the park and do not stray into the Trashy/commercial/privately-owned/exploited caves nearby. There are several campgrounds within the park. Various tours leave regularly from the Visitors Center. **Cave City** is the service centre for the Park. Lots of motels here. *www.nps.gov/*

A short drive N from Cave City is **Hodgenville** where you can visit the modest **Lincoln Birthplace and National Historic Site**. Nearby Knob Creek Farm was Abe's boyhood home, 549-3741, 10 am-6 pm in summer, earlier closing rest of year. $1 includes tour.

LEXINGTON Named in honour of its New England counterpart, Lexington was described by one traveller as 'an interesting historical town with a rich economy, not such a 'hillbilly' image as people say.' Sheik Mohammed bin Rashid al-Maktoum would certainly agree. He makes time for the annual horse sales at Keeneland Race Course. He has been known to snatch up prized thoroughbreds for $1 million plus. Lexington horse-traders have a certain shrewdness born of their unique trade. Luckily, the local industry leaves little non-organic pollution to spoil the rolling bluegrass hills of the countryside.

ACCOMMODATION
DIAL-ACCOMMODATIONS, for free assistance. Mon-Fri 8.30 am-6 pm, Sat 9 am-5 pm, 233-7299 or (800) 845-3959.
Kimball House, 267 S Limestone, 252-9565. S-$34, D-$38, $5 key deposit. Rsvs rec.
Hojo Inn, 2250 Elkhorn Dr, Exit 110 off I-75, 299-8481. S-$32, D-$44, XP-$5, more at w/end. Rsvs recommended.
Kentucky Horse Park Campground, 4089 Ironworks Pike, 233-4303. 9 miles N of downtown off Newton Pike. Showers, pool, ball courts, laundry, free shuttle to horse park. Sites $11, $15 w/hook-up.
YMCA, 239 E High St, 254-9622, $20, $85 per week, $40 deposit. Men only. The **University of Kentucky** has rooms and aptmnts available mid-May to Aug. Call the housing office at 257-3721.

FOOD
Alfalfa Restaurant, 253-0014, 557 S Limestone St, across from University Memorial Hall. Wide variety of seafood, meat and vegetarian dishes from $2. Lunch $4-$10, brunch $2-$7, dinner $6-$12. Live music Thur-Sat. No cover.
Central Christian Church Cafeteria, 205 E Short St, 255-3087. Filling Southern food; entrees $3-$4.50. Bfast 7 am-10 am, lunch 11 am-2 pm.

OF INTEREST
Some of the most magnificent horses in the world have been raised on **Three Chimneys Farm**, 873-7053. Seattle Slew and Affirmed are 2 of the most famous studs hard at work making future Derby winners. Tours 10 am and 1 pm daily by appointment only, with fillies going for up to $10.2 million, many of the farms have decided not to interrupt the horseplay with buses of gawking tourists. **Bluegrass Tours**, 252-5744, provides a twice daily tour of the area which takes you past the paddocks of the famous thoroughbred farms, 3 hrs, $18, Rsvs required. Famous farms include **Calumet**, **Darby Dan** and **King Ranch**. Also visit the **Kentucky Horse Park**, Iron Works Pike, 6 miles N on I-75, exit 120, 233-4303. 'Well worth a visit, especially for horse lovers.' Daily 9 pm-5 pm, $10. 50 min tour and riding at extra cost, $3.25. **Ashland**, Richmond Rd at Sycamore Rd, 266-8581, was the home of politician Henry Clay, the engineer of the great Missouri compromise on slavery.

The compromise allowed slavery below, but not above the 36th parallel. Ultimately proving unworkable, the compromise pushed the war back for years, $5 includes guided tour. Tues-Sat 10 am-4.30 pm, Sun 1 pm-4.30 pm.

The **Mary Todd Lincoln House**, 578 W Main St, 233-9999, built 1803, is where Abraham Lincoln's wife lived as a girl; Lincoln himself stayed here several times. Tue-Sat 10 am-4 pm (last tour 3.15 pm). $5. The first college west of the Alleghenies was **Transylvania University**. Folklore has it that the old administration building burned down and 10 students suffered nasty deaths because of a curse placed upon the school. Inside the new administration building at Old Morrison Hall lies the crypt of a professor named Rafinesque, which was placed there to remove the curse. Students celebrate the tale each Halloween. Tours of the crypt and the campus, W of Broadway and N of 3rd St, can be arranged by calling 233-8242.

The **University of Kentucky**, 257-3595, gives free campus tours aboard an English double decker bus; 10 am and 2 pm, Mon-Fri. Sat, walking tours only. **Visitor Center** open daily 9 am-4.30 pm. Also worth seeing is the **University Art Museum**, 257-5716, featuring over 3000 works including drawings, paintings and sculpture. Tue-Sun noon-5 pm; free. The **Museum of Anthropology**, Limestone St entrance (on campus), 257-7112, has exhibits ranging from the Native Indians to contemporary cultures. Mon-Fri 8 am-4.30 pm; free.

Outside Lexington: Shaker Village, in **Harrodsburg**, 25 miles SW of Lexington on US 68, this community was established by the Shaker sect in 1805 and by the middle of that century numbered 500 inhabitants. The Shakers have departed, but their buildings, with the help of some restoration, still stand. The museum preserves Shaker furnishings, $9.50, $13 includes river boat ride. To relive the Shaker life, you can stay in one of the buildings, furnished in the Shaker style, S-$40-$68 , D-$60-$78. Inexpensive Shaker meals as well (bfast from $7, lunch $5-$10, dinner $12-$19). Call (606) 734-5411 for rsvs. 7 miles from the original Kentucky settlement at Fort Harrod. In the SE corner of the state, the **Cumberland Gap National Historical Park** and the **Daniel Boone National Forest** provide a beautiful retreat into untouched wilderness. The Park Headquarters and Visitors Center, on Hwy 58, 248-2817 (daily 8 am-5 pm), has info on tours, camping and hiking in the Gap area. No rsvs. For info on hiking and camping in the Daniel Boone National Forest call 745-3100. *www.nps.gov/cvga/index.htm.*

INFORMATION/TRAVEL

Convention and Visitors Bureau, 301 E Vine St, 233-1221, (800) 848-1244. Mon-Fri 8.30 am-6 pm, Sat 10 am-6 pm, Sun noon-5 pm, in season.

The Visitors Center is in the same building, Suite 363. Mon-Fri 8.30 am-5 pm.

Greyhound, 477 New Circle Rd NW, 299-8804/(800) 231-2222. There are no buses serving the airport. For a cab, call 231-8294, $12-$15 o/w.

Lex Tran, 253-4636. Buses depart from the Transit Center, 220 W Vine St. Serves university, metro and surrounding area. Daily 6.15 am-6.15 pm, 'til 10 pm some routes. Fare 80c.

LOUISIANA *The Pelican State*

With its Voodoo, Jazz, Mardi Gras and Cajun cooking, Louisiana is anything but bland. The Creole State has given the United States some of its most varied ethnic cooking, its best party—Mardi Gras, and most flamboyant politicians (depression-era Huey Long vowed to 'Soak the Rich!,' former Governor Edwin Edwards claims that losing $1 million in Vegas was part of his hobby).

Louisiana's cultural heritage is a rich gumbo stew. The original French and Spanish settlers brought old world architecture and manners to the state, while their African and Caribbean slaves laid the musical foundations for what became jazz music. And, after the British expelled them from Nova Scotia in 1775, the French Acadians, now called Cajuns, brought fur-trapping, Cajun cooking, dialects and their special zydeco music to the bayous.

Caribbean pirates, Mississippi riverboat gamblers and plantation owners, have given way to a more respectable economy based upon offshore oil and trade, but Louisiana still beguiles visitors with a care-free, genteel atmosphere unlike anything else in America. *www.yahoo.com/Regional/U_S_States/Louisiana. The telephone area code for New Orleans is 504, for Acadiana, 318.*

NEW ORLEANS New Orleans is a party that never ends. First hosted by the French in 1718, followed by the Spanish, and the French again, the party finally passed to the Americans who bought out the last host, Napoleon, for $15 million in the Louisiana Purchase. Each culture has contributed an ingredient to the festivity: Spanish architecture, French joie de vivre, and a Caribbean sense of pace. A limitless supply of alcohol and music have contributed to New Orlean's reputation as the 'city which forgot to care.'

Visitors are drawn by the Vieux Carre above Canal Street, where gracious homes, walled gardens, narrow streets overhung by iron-lace balconies, and delicious Creole food struggle to retain a mellow atmosphere against encroaching plastic America. The 'grandfather' of the impressionists, Edgar Degas, captured the atmosphere of the city during his visit here in 1872-73 (his mother came from Louisiana) with some of his paintings, including *The Cotton Exchange of New Orleans.*

And of course there's jazz, though today Bourbon Street comes out with the wrong notes. The street is an over-commercialised strip of bars, drunks, prostitutes, skin shows, rip-off joints and gawking tourists in bermuda shorts. The locals usually avoid it, and the cognoscenti will at once make for the Jazz Museum and Preservation Hall, the place nonpareil for the traditional sound.

The New Orleans police have gained a reputation for brutality towards, and general ill-treatment of young foreign visitors. Be careful. *www.nawlins.com.*

ACCOMMODATION

Many of the rates given do not apply during Mardi Gras, the Jazz Festival and the Super Bowl. Check first. Off season rates prevail Memorial Day to Labor Day.

Campus accommodation available during summer; **Tulane U**, 27 McAlister Dr, 865-5426 (or 865-5724 after 2 pm), on streetcar line. Rooms S-$39 and aptmnts for rent through summer. **Loyola U**, 6363 St Charles St, 865-3735. 25 mins from downtown by streetcar. Jun-Aug. Dorms $21. Private rooms S-$30. Includes linen.

Friendly Inn, 4861 Chef Menteur Hwy, (800) 445-3940/283-1531. S-$30, XP-$5. TV, pool, transport to and from Amtrak. 'Excellent.' 'Cheap and comfy but 7 miles out of centre in dodgy area.'

India House , 124 S. Lopez St, 821-1904. $12, $15 during Mardi Gras/Jazz Festival, $5 key deposit. Mid-city area, mins from French quarter. Pool, tabletennis, kitchen, laundry, TV room. Pick-up from airport or bus station on request.

Hotel LaSalle, 1113 Canal St, 523-5831, (800) 521-9450. S-$29, $55 w/bath, D-$39-$59. 4 blocks from Bourbon St.'Absolutely excellent!' Near Vieux Carre. Clean, large rooms. TV, AC, laundry, safe-deposit boxes.'

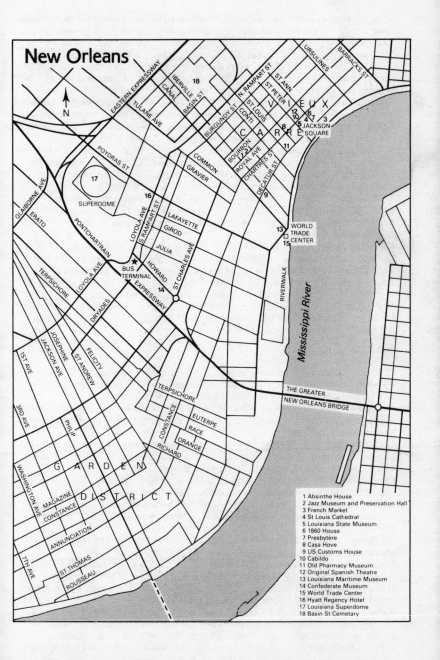

New Orleans

1 Absinthe House
2 Jazz Museum and Preservation Hall
3 French Market
4 St Louis Cathedral
5 Louisiana State Museum
6 1860 House
7 Presbytère
8 Casa Hove
9 US Customs House
10 Cabildo
11 Old Pharmacy Museum
12 Original Spanish Theatre
13 Louisiana Maritime Museum
14 Confederate Museum
15 World Trade Center
16 Hyatt Regency Hotel
17 Louisiana Superdome
18 Basin St Cemetary

Longpré House, 1726 Prytania St, 581-4540. $16, $12 w/student ID or overseas passport. S/D-$35-$40. ¹/₂ hr walk to French Quarter, 1 block off streetcar route. Free coffee and doughnuts in the morning. 'Dirty dorms, beautiful private rooms.'

Marquette House Youth Hostel, 2253 Carondelet St, 523-3014. $14 AYH, $17 non-AYH, private rooms $39-$45, $2 extra during Mardi Gras/Jazz Festival. Nr Garden District and St Charles streetcar. Rsvs recommended. 'Clean and comfy.' Nr laundry and supermarket. 'Very friendly and helpful.' 'Excellent.'

Prytania Inn, 1415 Prytania St, 566-1515. S-$29-$69, XP-$5. Rsvs required. Double rates during festivals.'Excellent; highly recommended.' 1 block from street car.

Prytania Park Hotel, 1525 Prytania St, 524-0427. S/D-$59-$89. AC, TV, includes bfast. Near French Quarter. 'Luxury.' Free parking.

St Charles Guest House, 1748 Prytania St, 523-6556. B&B 10 mins from French Quarter by streetcar, nr Garden District. Dorms $15-$25, D-$45-$65. Rsvs rec. Pool and sun deck. 'Near small supermarket and laundry. 'Free bfast and newspapers.' 'Owners are friendly and as kind and generous as anyone could be.'

YMCA, 920 St Charles Ave, 568-9622. Clean, air-conditioned, coed rooms. S-$33, D-$40. $20 deposit and $5 key deposit. Rsvs recommended. Free use of pool and gym and track. Shared bathrooms only. 'Relatively safe area in French Quarter, helpful travel info in lobby.'

Camping: New Orleans KOA West, 11129 Jefferson Hwy, River Ridge, 467-1792. Site $22, $26 w/hook-up , XP-$3, pool, laundry. Shuttle to French Quarter, leaves 9 am, returns 4 pm, $3. RTA bus and various tours also pick up from grounds.

Bayou Segnette State Park, 7777 Westbank Expressway, 736-7140. Bus service runs to park. Site $12, cabin up to 8 peope, $65. Rsvs essential for cabins.

St Bernard State Park, 682-2101. Follow I-10 to LA 47 S, then left on LA 39, 16 miles from French Quarter. Sites $12. 'Great camping.' Bus service 30 min away. Last bus 5.30 pm.

FOOD

www.neworleansonline.com/food-o.htm

Hot, spicy Cajun food abounds, as does old fashioned stick-to-your-ribs Southern cooking. Gumbo, jambalaya, and crawfish are specialities. Try chocolate pecan pie and beignets—a hot, square doughnut without the hole.

Café du Monde, 800 Decatur, 525-4544, in the French Market. Open 24 hrs. This is the place to get your beignets, 3 for $1.50. 'An experience not to be missed.' Begin and end every day here.

Café Mospero, 601 Decatur, 523-6250. Sandwiches, fried seafood. Open daily 11 am-11 pm, later at w/end. 'Good food—substantial meal $6.' All meals under $15. 'Expect to queue for a seat.' 'Low prices, big portions.'

Coops Place, 1109 Decatur, 525-9053. Cajun food, dinner around $6. 'The real thing, unpretentious local restaurant.' Open daily, 11 am-3 am.

Eddie's Restaurant, 2119 Law St, 945-2207. 'Excellent downhome cooking, gumbo recommended. 'All-you-can-eat' buffet every Thurs, 4 pm-9 pm, $7.' 'Great atmosphere.'

Fat Harrys, 4330 St Charles, 895-9582. Student atmosphere, cover $3-$6. Late night spot after the bars, on streetcar line, 11 am to 3 am. 'Excellent.'

Fudge Time in **Jax Brewery**, 620 Decatur, 524-8838. Delicious homemade fudge. 'Watch them make it right in front of you—yummy!' Open 10 am-9 pm daily.

Johnny's Po-Boy, 511 St Louis, 523-9071. 'Good sandwiches; excellent gumbo.' 'Friendly staff.' Mon-Fri 7 am-4.30 pm, Sat 9 am-4 pm.

Kaldi's Coffee House and Coffee Museum, 941 Decatur, 586-8989. Escape the tourists at this alternative hang-out. 'Delicious, real, fresh coffee.' 'Very reasonable; a must for coffee lovers.' Open 7 am-midnight w/days, 7 am-1 am w/ends.

K Paul's Louisiana Kitchen, 416 Chartres St, 524-7394, in the French Quarter, looks like a hole in the wall but is actually world famous, if you're there at dinner time, expect to see a looooong line waiting to get in. Chef Paul Prudhomme has made Cajun cuisine famous worldwide. Excellent, but expensive, $25-$35. Mon-Sat 11.30 am-2.30 pm (lunch), 5.30 pm-10 pm (dinner).

Mena's Place, 622 Iberville, 523-9071. Excellent seafood gumbo, $3.50, daily specials around $4. 'Very friendly.' Open 6.30 am-6.45 pm Mon-Sat.

Seaport Cafe, on Bourbon St, is a combo cafe and bar; not cheap, but has tasty food and a balcony—'fascinating way of viewing the Bourbon St characters.'

Shoney's, 619 Decatur, 525-2039, and other locations. Bfast special $4, salad bar from $4. 'Superb.' 7 am-11 pm, 'til 3 am on w/ends. You can learn to cook Cajun food from Chef Joe Cahn at the **New Orleans School of Cooking**, 620 Decatur, 525-2665 for info and rsvs. Crash courses Mon-Sat, $20.

OF INTEREST

French Quarter or **Vieux Carre** (Old Square), the heart and soul of New Orleans, includes about 70 blocks of the old city between the river and Rampart St and Canal and Esplanade Sts. Apart from the pleasure of simply wandering around the streets, and through back alleys, you will find in this area the city's most noteworthy buildings. Caution—do not wander down dark streets at night. As picturesque as they may be, the French Quarter's dark back alleys are good places for the foolish traveller to find trouble.

The Quarter is a National Historic District, within the **Jean LaFitte National Historic Park and Preserve**. Lafitte was a famous New Orleans pirate who also helped defeat the British at the Battle of New Orleans. Legend has it that his most audacious plan was to rescue Napoleon from his British captors. The park service **Folklife and Visitors Center**, 589-2636, 916-918 N Peters St in the French Market (enter through 914 Decatur) offers maps, informed rangers, and different tours throughout the area. A general 90 min **History Tour** covering New Orleans and Louisiana leaves at 10.30 am daily. The 90 min **Faubourg Promenade** explores the Garden District of the city. Tour starts 2.30 pm. Rsvs essential (589-2636). Meet on corner of Washington and Prytania. Tours of Garden District/French Quarter run 9 am-5 pm, daily, free. The **Tour du Jour** covers a different historic or cultural topic each day, depending on the Ranger's whim. A good starting point in the Quarter is **Jackson Square**. The old Place d'Armes parade ground, Jackson Square has been the central gathering place in the city since it was first laid out in 1721. The square is named after Andrew Jackson, the hero of the battle of New Orleans. The statue honouring 'Old Hickory,' as the scrappy populist was called, was erected in 1856.

St Louis Cathedral, 525-9585, Jackson Sq's exquisite centrepiece was rebuilt in 1794 after a fire destroyed the original and remodeled in 1850. It is a minor basilica and the oldest active cathedral in the United States. Free guided tours Mon-Sat, 9.30 am-5.45 pm, Sun 1.30 pm-5 pm. Sun mass 7.30 am-6 pm.

The Louisiana State Museum, 568-6968, includes several historical buildings in the Quarter which may be toured in combination. Individual museums $4, $3 w/student ID. Combo tkts, $10, $7.50 w/student ID. All Museum attractions open Tue-Sun 9 am-5 pm. Next to the Cathedral is the old Spanish governor's residence, **The Cabildo**, site of the US/French negotiations for the Louisiana Purchase. It was heavily damaged by fire in 1988, but restoration work is now complete. No 2 at the museum is **The Presbytere**, on Chartres St facing the Square. Dates to 1791 and houses portraiture, New Orleans architecture exhibit and changing collections.

The 1850 House, in a portion of the **Pontabla Apartments** (coincidentally also damaged by fire in 1989), facing the Square, offers a glimpse of elegant Southern living. Said to be the oldest aptmnts in the United States, the Pontabla Buildings were built for Baroness Pontabla and are furnished in the traditional antebellum style. Guided tours on the hr.

Finally, the **Old US Mint**, 400 Esplanade, houses historical documents and jazz and carnival exhibits. A working mint from 1838-62 and 1879-1920, it's 'O' mint-mark is a favourite among coin collectors worldwide. Other historic buildings of the French Quarter include:

Absinthe House, 240 Bourbon St, 523-3181. The house where the LaFitte brothers, Pierre and Jean, 'plotted against honest shipping.' Now a bar and literary landmark. Daily 9 am-4 am.

US Customs House, 423 Canal St, 589-6353. Dates from 1848; used as headquarters during Civil War Union occupation. Mon-Fri 8 am-5 pm. Free.

The Old French Market, 800, 900, and 1,000 blocks of Decatur St, 522-2621. Has been operating from the same spot since 1791. Many old colonnaded buildings have recently been restored and converted to shops and restaurants. The famous old vegetable market is still in operation 24 hrs. Other attractions open daily 9 am-6 pm. Flea Market daily. 'Wonderful. Lots of junk and good jazz in the air.'

Contemporary Arts Center, 900 Camp St, 523-1216. 'Visual arts, music theater; stunning interior to building.' $3, $2 w/student ID, some exhibitions are free. Mon-Sat 10 am-5 pm, Sun 11 am-5 pm.

Old Pharmacy Museum, 514 Chartres St, 565-8027. Was first used as a pharmacy in 1823 and is now an interesting museum of old apothecary items, voodoo potions, medical instruments and hand-blown pharmacy bottles and 'show globes.' Tue-Sun 10 am-5 pm, $2.

Voodoo Museum, 724 Dumaine St, 523-7685. If you are not too squeamish, learn about the magic and history of this ancient religion. Swamp and ritual tours offered for the strong of stomach and spirit. 'Recommended for the entire family', as advertised by the owner. Open daily 10 am-6 pm. $6.30, $5.25 w/student ID.

Historical Wax Museum, 917 Conti St, 525-2605, features a recreation of 'Congo Square,' the voodoo center of old New Orleans, as well as the popular Haunted Dungeon. Open 10 am-5.30 pm daily, $6.

Original Spanish Theater, 718 St Peter, built in 1791 was the first Spanish theatre in the US, later a private home, and has housed the well known Pat O'Brien's (of 'hurricane' fame) since 1942. Of note outside the French Quarter:

Confederate Museum, 929 Camp St, 1 block off Lee Circle, 523-4522. Has memorabilia of the Civil War. 'Ten out of ten.' Mon-Sat 10 am-4 pm. $5, $4 w/student ID. Take the St Charles St streetcar—one of only 2 remaining in the city—through the fashionable **Garden District** ($1, 10¢ transfer). The line is an excellent way to get to know the city. Once you reach the Garden District, get out and wander among the sumptuous houses built by rich antebellum whites to rival the Creole dwellings in the Vieux Carre. The District stretches from Jackson to Louisiana Aves between St Charles and Magazine Sts. Further down the streetcar line, you reach **Audubon Park** and the **Audubon Zoo**, 6500 Magazine, 861-2537. One of the 'top 10 zoos in the US.' Natural habitats for 1800 animals. Open daily 9.30 am-5.30 pm. Streetcar stop #35. Another prime attraction outside the French Quarter is **City Park**, at Esplanade and Carrollton Sts, 482-4888, site of the famous **Duelling Oaks**, where New Orleans society settled their differences 'under the Oaks at dawn.' The fifth largest park in the USA, 1500 acres. Enjoy its magnificent oaks, statues and fountains, sports and recreational facilities. Botanical gardens, sports stadium, tennis courts, carousel etc. More like a lifestyle than a park. Free, but charges for activities. **The New Orleans Museum of Art** , 488-2631, is located in the Park. The collection includes works by the Russian jeweller, Fabergé, a local decorative arts exhibit and a large collection of French impressionist paintings. 2 floors of the museum are dedicated to Asian, African and Oceanic art. Tues-Sun 10 am-5 pm, $6. More modern sites include the **Hyatt Regency Hotel**, Poydras and Loyola, with a free spectacular view. Not free, but still spectacular is the **Louisiana Superdome**, 1500 Poydras St, 587-3810. Host to the '97 Superbowl. Opened in 1975, and the world's largest indoor stadium with the largest single room in the history of man. 1 hr tours daily; 10 am-4 pm hourly, $6. 'The stadium is impressive but the tour is a rip-off;

better to pay to see an event. Nothing like it at home.'

Cruises on the Mississippi. A variety of companies offer all kinds of cruises, including buffets and parties, trips to Audubon Zoo, 2 hr port tours ('interesting only if you're into docks and Liberian freighters'), 5 hr explorations of nearby bayous and swamplands, and trips up the Mississippi into the heartland. For bayou, harbour, and zoo cruise info, call 586-8777 for the **New Orleans Steamboat Co**. The **Creole Queen**, 524-0814, offers a bayou, plantation, and battlefield cruise. Readership consensus is that the boat rides are generally 'boring' and 'not worth it,' but the Bayou trips by bus and boat are highly recommended if you want to see alligators 'au naturel.' Open since late 1989, the **Woldenberg Riverfront Park**, 17 acres of park land down by the Mississippi stretching from Canal Street through the French Quarter to the Moonwalk. You can ride to the top of the **World Trade Center** building, Canal St, for a view of the city and river. The **Old Algiers Ferry** crosses the river from here—and it's free! This is the first time for more than 100 years that residents have had direct access to the river. The **Aquarium of the Americas** on Canal St, 565-3006, recreates the underwater environments of the American continent. Sun-Fri 9.30 am-7 pm, Sat 'til 9 pm. $10.50.

ENTERTAINMENT

New Orleans *is* entertainment. This is a city that knows how to have a good time, and it's not only during Mardi Gras. Here you are likely to find a celebration of some kind at any time of the year. The French Quarter, one of the most European areas in the US, is always full of life and has been since Louis Armstrong, Bunk Johnson, Jelly Roll Morton, King Oliver, Kid Ory and other greats of traditional jazz stomped in Storyville.

Bourbon St, though somewhat sleazy, is a perpetual party, and a visit to this city would not be complete without at least one nightly stroll down this crazy stretch of decadence. Although the jazz revival in New Orleans has brought back many good musicians, there are also, on Bourbon St, scores of over-priced nightclubs, flashy restaurants, endless clip joints, and plenty of bad music. Choose carefully (always check prices before you buy a drink, as you are sometimes paying for the band with them) and carry ID. Check *Gambit* and *Wavelength* newspapers for current listings. New Orleans' temple of jazz is the **Preservation Hall**, 726 St Peter St, 522-2841 (days), 523-8939 (nights), where pioneers of jazz have always performed—and still do, hear jazz in its quintessential form. Doors 8 pm, arrive early. 8.30 pm-12 am nightly, $4 standing. 'An absolute must." 'I'd pay $10 to go and see it again—a magical experience.' 'Whatever you read/hear will never do it justice—Go!' In **Jackson Square**, Saturday jazz concerts are held 2 pm-6 pm during Oct-Nov, April-Aug. Most shows are free.

Annual Jazz and Heritage Festival. Takes place late Apr-early May, attracting musicians and fans worldwide. Listen to music played on 11 stages, or wander around cajun food and craft stalls. 'Fantastic day out.' Held at New Orleans Fair Grounds. 522-4786 for info.

Check Point, Decatur St past French Market. Bar, cafe and launderette all in one, plus live music and shelves of books. 'Where the alternative crowd hangs out.'

Monaco Bob's, 1179 Annunciation St, 586-1282. 'Excellent bar, live music most nights a must.' Stage and light-show. R 'n' B w/days, Blues on w/ends. Alternative music/film weeks. 40 different beers. Lunch entrees $6-$12, appetisers $3-$5. Bar food all night. $5-$20 cover.

Muddy Waters, 8301 Oak St 866-7174. See local blues and jazz favourites in this eclectic blues club. Live music every night, 10 am-2 pm.

Pat O'Brien's, 718 St Peter St, 525-4823. Reputed to be the 'busiest and the best' in the French Quarter. Popular with local students. 'Great atmosphere, no cover, closes 5 am.' 'Home of the Hurricane Cocktail. Don't miss it.' $5 ($7 w/souvenir glass) Also try **Snug Harbor** and **Storyville** for sweet soulful music. Uptown New

Orleans, around Maple, Oakand Willow Sts, down St Charles from Canal. 'Where the locals go. Good bars and clubs. Better music and cheaper.'

Tipitina's, 501 Napoleon, 895-8477. 'The real thing.' Dixie Cups, good music including zydeco and cheap drinks. Attracts both the best local talent and known artists such as Harry Connick Jnr. Learn how to dance Cajun-style on Sun evenings. 'The best part of our stay.'

Top of the Mart, World Trade Center, 2 Canal St, 522-9795. America's largest revolving bar/restaurant is 33 storeys high, seats 500 people and makes one revolution every 1¹/₂ hrs (3ft per min). 'Visit in the evening and watch the sunset over the city.' No cover but 1 drink minimum. Mon-Fri 10 am-midnight, Sat 11 am-1 am, Sun 2 pm-midnight.

INFORMATION
New Orleans Welcome Center , 529 St Anne Street, 568-5661. In the French Quarter, free city and walking tour maps.
Greater New Orleans Tourist Commission, 1520 Sugar Bowl Drive, 566-5011.

TRAVEL
New Orleans Regional Transit Authority (RTA), 700 Plaza Dr, 569-2700. City bus and streetcar, major lines run 24 hrs. $1, transfers 10¢. All-day pass $4, 3 days $8.
Louisiana Transit Authority, 737-9611. Bus from airport to downtown, $1.10, 'have exact change'. Last bus leaves airport at 5.40 pm.
Amtrak, 1001 Loyola Ave, 528-1610/(800) 872-7245. *Crescent* to NY, *City of New Orleans* to Chicago and *Sunset Limited* to LA originate here. Area not safe after dark.
Greyhound, 1001 Loyola in train station, (800) 231-2222. 'Bad neighbourhood.' Accommodation board here has been recommended. Try Tulane and Loyola for their ride boards.

BATON ROUGE During the first 150 years of its short history, Louisiana experienced considerable difficulty in deciding on a state capital. Ope lousas, Alexandria, Shreveport and New Orleans all previously enjoyed such status until 1849 when Baton Rouge was chosen over New Orleans due to concern over the state government being based in such a 'careless' city!

Situated in the heart of plantation country, 60 miles NW of the 'Big Easy' on the Mississippi, Baton Rouge was named after the cypress tree used by the Indians to mark hunting boundaries. Today it is the state's second largest city and one of the nations largest ports, profiting mainly from petrochemical and sugarcane production. However, the abundance of magnolia and cypress trees belies this industrial bias and the city still retains a small-town character. Of special interest are the 34 storey **State Capitol Building** (342-7317); the great white, **Old Governor's Mansion** and the two universities (Louisiana State and Southern). Call (504) 383-1825 for tourist info.

ACADIANA True bayou country—alligators, Spanish moss hanging from trees—begins in the Cajun area called Acadiana. The original French Acadians came to Louisiana after the British overran their native Nova Scotia. The British insisted that the Acadians swear allegiance to the British crown and renounce Catholicism. The Acadians refused, instead moving to Louisiana where they became known as Cajuns. Using their knowledge of fur-trapping, the Cajuns quickly adapted to the ways of the swamp. (One ingenious adaptation was the use of moths for bedding.)

Today's Cajuns still speak some Creole French, and the bayous of Louisiana continue to account for much of the fur-trapping in the United States. Cajun cooking and music are currently in vogue. Paul Simon's *Graceland* was heavily influenced by Cajun Zydeco music, a version of which makes for wonderful rock and roll. Modern Cajun life centers around **Lafayette**, **New Iberia** and **St Martinville**, about 120 miles NW of New Orleans. **Accommodation** is fairly inexpensive with most lodging centered in Lafayette. Try the **Lafayette Inn**, 2615 Cameron St, 235-9442 (S-$26, D-$30, $2 key deposit) or the **Lafayette Travel Lodge**, 1101 W Pinnhook Rd, 234-7402 (S-$45, D-$48). **Mulate's Cajun Restaurant**, 325 Mills Ave in Breaux Bridge, 332-4648/ (800) 422-2586, is arguably the most famous Cajun restaurant in the world. 'Not to be overlooked. Not cheap but meals can be split—worth it.' Open daily.

OF INTEREST
In Lafayette: Lafayette Museum, 1122 Lafayette St, 234-2208. With Mardi Gras costumes and LA heirlooms. Tues-Sat 9 am-5 pm, Sun 3 pm-5 pm, $3, $1 w/student ID. Just outside Lafayette, the **Acadian Village**, 981-2364, is a good place to learn about Cajun culture. Somewhat touristy, with authentic Cajun houses, tools, and furnishings. Open daily 10 am-5 pm, $5.50. The **Festival International de Louisiane**, 232-8086, is a 6-day fete celebrating music, art, theatre, dance, cinema, and southern cuisine and takes place in late Apr. 'Don't miss it.' Just N of the city lies the **Academy of the Sacred Heart**, 662-5494, the only known exact spot of a miracle in the US. It was here that St John Berchmans, a Jesuit novice, appeared in response to the prayers of a dying woman. She recovered and Berchman returned to heaven. Mon-Fri 9 am-4 pm. Tours Sun 1 pm-4 pm; other times call for appointment.

In **Eunice**, about 30 miles N on US-190, every Sat night a live Cajun radio show is staged at the Liberty Center for the Performing Arts featuring Zydeco music, humourists and recipes, $2, 6 pm-8 pm. Call Eunice Chamber of Commerce for more info 457-2565/ (800) 222-2342.

In New Iberia, St Martinville: Shadows on the Teche, 317 E Main St, New Iberia, 369-6446, a famous plantation on the banks of the Bayou Teche. H L Mencken stayed here as did Cecil B DeMille. Open daily 9 am-4.30 pm, $6.

Evangeline Oak on Port St at Bayou Teche marks the legendary first landing of the Acadians in bayou country. Nearby is statue of **Evangeline** beside **St Martin de Tours Catholic Church**, one of the oldest in Louisiana. Evangeline was one-half of the legendary pair of Acadian lovers immortalised by the Longfellow poem. The reputed home of Evangeline's beau, Gabrielle, is in the **Longfellow-Evangeline Commemorative Area**. A must-see quirk of history is the Roman-era **Statue of Hadrian** standing guard, appropriately, in front of a bank, on the corner of Weeks and Peters Sts.

Jungle Gardens, 369-6243, at end of Hwy 329 about 7 miles S of New Iberia, features a 1000 year old Buddha set in a swamp garden. Daily 8 am-5, $5. If you doubt that Cajuns like hot food, you should know that tabasco was invented nearby at the **Avery Islands Tabasco Pepper Sauce Factory**, 365-8173, free 20 min tours Mon-Fri 9 am-4 pm, Sat 9 am-noon.

In the bayou: Louisiana swampland is unique, and tours into the swamps abound. Choose carefully, though, as rip-offs exist. Call **Atchafalaya Delta Wildlife Area**, (504) 395-4905, they can refer you to tours. Try **Cajun Jack's Swamp Tours** of the Atchafalaya, the largest swamp in N America. See first hand how the Cajun people live as their ancestors did hundreds of years ago. If you are heading to Texas, try the drive along Hwys 82 and 27 through the **Creole Nature Trail**.

INFORMATION
Lafayette Convention and Visitors Commission, 1400 NW Evangeline Thruway, 232-3808/(800) 346-1958. Mon-Fri 8.30 am-5 pm, 9 am-5 pm at w/end.
Iberia Parish Tourist Commission, 2704 Hwy 14, 365-1540. Open 9 am-5 pm daily.

MISSISSIPPI *The Magnolia State*

The Blues, King Cotton, southern hospitality, southern pride, civil rights, and riverboat rides—Mississippi *is* the Old South—the embodiment of a tarnished American myth of polite Southern gentlemen and elegant plantation life.

Like any myth, parts of it are true—Mississippi folk are more polite than their Yankee neighbours. The graceful plantation homes that survived the Civil War do speak eloquently for the sensibilities of a lost time, before the last stand of the Southern gentleman on the battlefield of Vicksburg. And in the hot, humid Delta backwoods, the rhythms that once consoled the slaves have been pressed gradually into the modern blues by such Mississippi giants as John Lee Hooker, John Hurt, Son House, Elmore James and Muddy Waters.

The Old South begat other legends in the works of Tennessee Williams and William Faulkner, Mississippi's most famous literary sons. From the lazy beat of William's long, hot summer to the radical civil rights battles which exposed the ugly, violent underbelly of Southern life in the 1960s, the Magnolia State is the stage upon which an American myth lived and is surely dying.

The Natchez Trace Parkway stretches diagonally across Mississippi along the historic highway of bandits, armies and adventurers. You can drive along it, or else explore the old trails on foot. Along Mississippi's Gulf coastline there runs another old trail. This is the old Spanish Trail which ran from St Augustine, Florida, to the missions in California. US 90 from Pascagoula to Bay St Louis follows the trail through the state. *www.yahoo.com/Regional/U_S_States/Mississippi/.*
The telephone area code for Mississippi is 601.

JACKSON   Set on the west bank of the Pearl River, the capital city of the state began life as a trading post reputedly established by Canadian Louis LeFleur. But 'war is hell,' as General Sherman said on this very spot, and in 1863 his victorious Federal troops burnt the original Jackson to the ground, prompting locals to rename their devastated home 'Chimneyville.' It was not until early this century that Jackson recovered to become Mississippi's largest city and the discovery of natural gas in the area saved it from the economic ravages of the Great Depression.

ACCOMMODATION/FOOD
Parkside Inn, 3720 I-65 N at exit 98B, close to downtown. Must be 21 to rent, 18 and under free with adult. TV, pool. S-$30, D-$36.
Sun 'n' Sand Motel, 401 N Lamar St, 354-2501. Central location. From S-$33, D-$38, XP-$5. TV, pool, $5 lunch buffet.
Timberlake Campgrounds, 143 Timberlake Dr, 992-9100. Popular site with arcade,

pool, ball courts. Sites $9, $14 w/hook-up.

Primo's , 4330 N State St, 982-2064. Jazz and southern cooking; Open daily 11 am-10 pm

The Elite Cafe, 141 E Capitol, 352-5606. Homestyle cooking; lunch specials with 2 veg and bread from $5.25.

OF INTEREST

Mississippi Crafts Center, Natchez Trace Parkway at Ridgeland, 856-7546. Traditional and contemporary folk arts and crafts. Open 9 am-5 pm daily.

Mississippi Museum of Art, 201 E Pascagoula, 960-1515. Jackson's first art museum; opened in 1978. Presents as many as 40 exhibitions each year. Tue-Sun 10 am-5 pm. $3, $2 w/student ID, free Tue and Thur. Closed in Aug.

Russell C Davis Planetarium, 201 E Pascagoula St, 960-1550. The largest in the Southeast, and one of the best in the world. Shows Mon-Fri evenings and w/end afternoons. Call for times. $4.

The Oaks, 823 N Jefferson, 353-9339. Jackson's oldest house built 1746, occupied by General Sherman during the Jackson siege in 1863. Period antiques on display including original furniture from Abraham Lincoln's Office. Open Tue-Sat 10 am-3 pm. $2, $1 w/student ID.

The Old State Capitol, at the intersection of Capitol and State Sts, 359-6920. Houses the **State Historical Museum**. The building has survived 3 torchings and is Mississippi's second state house. Displays artifacts from Native American settlements and documents Mississippi's volatile history both before and after the Civil Rights movement. The 'magnificent' **New State Capitol**, at Mississippi and Congress, 359-3114, is where the state legislature currently gathers. 1 hr guided tours 9 am-11 am and 1.30 pm-3.30 pm. Mon-Fri 8 am-5 pm, free.

INFORMATION/TRAVEL

Jackson Visitor Information Center, 1150 Lakeland Dr, 981-2499. Located inside the Agricultural Museum. Mon-Sat 9 am-5 pm, Sun 1 pm-5 pm.

Amtrak, 300 W Capitol St, 355-6350/(800) 872-7245.

Greyhound, 201 S Jefferson St, 353-6342/(800) 231-2222. 'This area is best avoided at night.' No buses to/from the airport. For a taxi, call 355-8319, $13-$15 o/w.

OXFORD Literature has blossomed out of this small town which sits in corn, cotton and cattle country in the north of Mississippi. Pulitzer and Nobel Prize winner William Faulkner based his fictitious Yoknapatowpha County on Oxford as he wrote about the anguish of a decaying South and the plight of the blacks. Today, the mega-selling author of *The Client*, *The Chamber*, and *The Runaway Jury*, John Grisham, lives in Oxford, alongside some beautiful ante-bellum mansions. The University of Mississippi—*Ole Miss*—is where a courageous student called James Meredith shattered two centuries of white Southern tradition to be the first black graduate in 1963.

ACCOMMODATION/FOOD

Ole Miss Motel, 1517 E University Ave, 234-2424, 3 blocks from City Square. S-$25, D-$32, Q-$35.

The Hoka, 234-3057, just off City Square on S 14th St. Art movie theatre in the back and cafe in the front. Hoka features occasional blues bands and nightly jam sessions on the piano. Sandwiches from $3.50 (try the cheesecake!). For more mainstream music, try **The Gin**, 234-0024, across the street.

Smitty's Cafe, 208 S Lamar, 234-9111, just off the square. Southern cooking means fried chicken and catfish from $4-$8, most entrees under $6.

OF INTEREST

Annual Faulkner Conference in the first week of Aug draws scholars from around the world. 232-5993 for details and tkts. If you go, first read *The Sound and the Fury*, *As I Lay Dying* or *The Reivers*.

William Faulkner's Home, called Rowan Oak, Old Taylor Rd, 234-3284. Tucked back in the woods, unmarked from the street, Faulkner's home until 1962 can be reached by walking down S Lamar Street. Free, Tues-Sat 10 am-noon and 2 pm-4 pm, Sun 2 pm-4 pm.

Square Books, 160 Courthouse Sq, 236-2262, has impressive collection of Southern writers, and a cafe upstairs. Mon-Thur 9 am-9 pm, Fri, Sat 9 am-10 pm, Sun 10 am-6 pm. On the way to Vicksburg is the **Delta Blues Museum**, 624-4461, in the Carnegie Public Library at **Clarksdale**, 114 Delta St. Containing archives, books, records and instruments, the free museum is open Mon-Thurs 9 am-5.30 pm, Fri and Sat 9 am-5 pm. The museum hosts the **Sunflower River Blues and Gospel Festival** on the first w/end in Aug, with the best contemporary blues and gospel around. Free.

University of Mississippi, 232-7378. Self-guided tours of the 1848 campus, where a handful of the original buildings survive. Also on campus is the **Blues Archive 'N Center for the Study of Southern Culture**, which holds a huge amount of Southern music and literature, including B.B. Kings' personal collection of 10,000 recordings. Mon-Fri, 8 am-5 pm.

INFORMATION/TRAVEL

Tourist Information Center, in Oxford Square, 232-2419.
Greyhound, 2612B W Jackson, 234-0094/(800) 231-2222.

VICKSBURG   Lincoln had a simple, but brilliant two-part strategy for the Civil War. First, blockade Southern cotton from reaching European ports. Second, split the South in two by driving a wedge down the Mississippi river. The wedge fell upon Vicksburg, the heart of the South's defense of the Mississippi. After a campaign lasting more than a year and climaxed by 47 days of siege led by Gen. Ulysses S Grant, 'the Gibraltar of the South' fell to Union troops on Independence Day, July 4, 1863. The triumph effectively gave the Union control of the entire Mississippi River. Not surprisingly the city has many Civil War sites, and not a few antebellum mansions.

ACCOMMODATION/FOOD

Hillcrest Motel, 4503 Hwy 80 E, 638-1491. S-$24, D-$28. Pool.
Ramada Hotel, 4216 Washington St, 638-5750. S/D-$59.
Scottish Inn, 3955 Hwy 80 East, ¹/₄ mile from battleground, 638-5511. S/D-$39, includes $5 key deposit.
The Dock, East Clay St, ¹/₄ mile from National Military Park, 634-0450. All-you-can-eat seafood buffet, $11.95.
Walnut Hills Restaurant, 1214 Adams St, 638-4910. Southern cooking, sandwiches, soup, salads. From $3.50. Mon-Fri 11 am-9 pm. Look along **Washington St**, for cafes, bars and local flavour. **Millers Still Lounge**, a popular student haunt, hosts live blues and rock Thur-Sun. Tue-Sat noon-2 am, Sun 5 pm-2 am, no cover.

OF INTEREST

Old Courthouse Museum, 1008 Cherry St, 636-0741. Considered by many to be one of the finest Civil War museums in the South. Confederate troops operated from here during the seige of Vicksburg in 1863. Mon-Sat 8.30 am-5.30 pm, Sun 1.30 pm-5 pm, $2. Marble monuments, over 1,600 of them, recreate the fury of the battle at **Vicksburg National Military Park**, 636-0583. The Pantheon-like **Illinois**

monument is the largest. Entrance and Visitors centre on Clay St, about 1½ miles E of town on I-20, take exit 4B. Open daily 9.30 am-6 pm, off season 8 am-5 pm. A Civil War soldier's life is described by actors who dress in period costume and fire muskets and cannons. Guides provide a 2 hr tour for $20, or you can hire a cassette, $4.50. $4 p/car to enter the park. 'Need a whole day if you plan to walk the park. Bring water.' The **U.S.S Cairo Museum**, 636-2199, also on park grounds, houses the Union gunboat of the same name, sunk by the Confederacy in 1862, and raised 100 years later. A climb up to the **Vicksburg Bluffs** yields a great view of the Mississippi. Among several impressive ante-bellum mansions to see are: **Cedar Grove**, 2200 Oak St, 636-1605; **McRaven House**, 1445 Harrison, 636-1663; **Balfour House**, 1002 Crawford St, 638-3690; and **Martha Vick House**, 1300 Grove St, 638-7036. Most of the homes are open Mon-Sat 9 am-5 pm, Sun 1 pm-5 pm, and cost $4.50-$5.

Museum of Coca-Cola History and Memorabilia and the **Biedenharn Candy Co**, 1107 Washington, 638-6514. Where Coca-Cola was first bottled in 1894. $1.75. In the summer you can get cokes in antique soda fountain. To tour the Mississippi around Vicksburg, call *Mississippi Adventure Tours*, (800) 521-4363, 3 excursions daily departing from the pier at the end of Clay St, 10 am, 2 pm and 5 pm. $16. Old Man River is also the site of the **U.S Army Engineer Waterways Experiment Station**, 3909 Halls Ferry Rd, 634-2502, with working scale models of many of America's rivers, dams, harbours (including Niagara Falls) and tidal waterways. Open daily 7.45 am-4.30 pm. Guided tours at 10 am and 2 pm, self-guided tours 9 am-4.30 pm. S of Vicksburg, beautiful **Port Gibson** was considered by Union General Grant to be 'too beautiful to burn'. A good stop on the way to Natchez.

INFORMATION/TRAVEL
Vicksburg Convention and Visitors Bureau Clay St and Old Hwy 27 (exit 4B off I-20), 636-9421. Open daily 8 am-5.30 pm in summer.
Greyhound, 1295 S Fromtage, 638-8389/(800) 231-2222. Daily 7 am-8.30 pm.

NATCHEZ Natchez is the Old South. An important cotton trading centre, the port attracted some of the great fortunes of the 1850s. Cotton planters, brokers, and bankers settled in the small town named after the Indian tribes which first settled the area. Non-commercialised, Natchez is one of the finest historical towns in the US.

The favoured architectural style was Classical Greek and Roman as promoted by Palladio, Inigo Jones and Thomas Jefferson. Natchez families have carefully preserved, rather than modernised, their treasures, and for the visitor a block's walk off Main Street is to retreat a century and more back into time.

ACCOMMODATION/FOOD
Days Inn, 109 US Hwy 61 S, 445-8291. S-$44, D-$49, XP-$5.
Natchez Inn, 218 John R Junkin Drive, 442-0221. From S/D-$40.
Camping: Natchez State Park, 363 State Park Road, 442-2658, 10 miles N on US 61. Sites $6, $11 w/hook-up.
Traceway Campground, Hwy 61 North, 101 Log Cabin Ln, 8 miles from Natchez, 445-8278. Sites from $11, XP-$2.
Fat Mama's Tamales, 500 S Canal St, 442-4548. Mild or spicy tamales and other regional specialities. Mon-Wed 11 am-7 pm, Thur-Sat 11 am-9 pm, Sun noon-5 pm.
Mammy's Cupboard 555 Hwy 61 S, 445-8957. This unusual restaurant is shaped like a woman and the dining area lies under her skirt! Soup, sandwiches on home-made bread, and one hot Dixie lunch special every day. Everything under $10. Tue-Sat noon-3 pm.

OF INTEREST

There are so many truly stunning homes here, that one can easily see how Natchez housed one-sixth of America's pre-war millionaires. 30 homes and gardens are thrown open to visitors during the Pilgrimages each spring and fall while 12 residences are kept open year-round. The most impressive homes are **Dunleith** (Greek Revival style), **D'Evereaux** (Greek Revival), **Rosalie** (Brick Federal) and **Longwood** (Moorish style—octagonal with a whimsical cupola). The Pilgrimage Tours Headquarters, 446-6631, at the Canal St Depot, on the corner of Canal and State St, sells tkts for tours of individual houses at $5 pp and has maps and literature on the area. Tkts also available for 35 min horse-drawn carriage tour, $8, and 1hr bus tour, $10 The once notorious **Natchez-Under-the-Hill**, 446-6345, was the old cotton port and steamboat landing where gamblers, thieves and good-time girls scandalised the local residents. More respectable shops and a restored saloon fill the area now, against a spectacular backdrop of riverboats cruising along the Mississippi.

The Natchez Trace: *www.nps.gov/natc/index.htm*. Natchez is named for the Indian tribe which lived in the area before the white man came. The Trace was the centre of Indian activity from 1682-1729. An archeological site inside the city has uncovered the **Grand Village of the Natchez**. The Indians forged the Natchez Trace which winds its way north to Nashville. A beautiful drive, the trace is also full of history.

Emerald Mound, 445-4211, one of the largest Indian Burial mounds is 1 mile off the pkwy, 11 miles NE of Natchez. Built in 1300, the mound covers 8 acres and is the third largest such site in the US. Free. Davy Crockett travelled the trace, and the Bowie knife was forged at a campfire along the way. In 1812 Old Hickory (Andrew Jackson) led his troops against the British at New Orleans using the trace. The Visitor's Center Museum at the trace, 842-1572, at marker 266, has artifacts from the site. Free.

Elvis Presley was born along the trace in the little town of **Tupelo**. Elvis gave a benefit performance for his home town which raised enough money to create a park out of the King's first 'shotgun' (read hovel) home. Tours through the home, 306 Elvis Presley Dr on Tupelo's east side, 841-1245, Mon-Sat 9 am-5.30 pm, Sun 1 pm-5 pm. $1, museum, $4. Fans donated for the construction of a chapel in Presley's honour on the site. (The **Tupelo McDonald's**, 372 S Gloster, is a temple to the King.) The **Tupelo City Museum**, Hwy 6 W at James A Ball Park, 841-6438, houses a large collection of Elvis memorabilia, as well as Civil War artifacts. Tue-Fri 8 am-4 pm, w/end 1 pm-5 pm; $1.

INFORMATION/TRAVEL

Mississippi State Welcome Center, 370 Seargent Prentis Dr, 442-5849, 8 am-7 pm daily. Provides maps, lists of tours and homes.

Natchez Bus Station, 103 Lower Woodville Rd, 445-5849. Mon-Sat 8 am-5.30 pm. Vicksburg $14, New Orleans $35.

Natchez Chamber of Commerce, 205 N Canal, 445-4611. Mon-Fri 8 am-5 pm.

Natchez Convention and Visitors Bureau, 422 Main St, 446-6345. Mon-Fri 8 am-5 pm.

Tupelo Convention and Visitors Bureau, 399 E Main St, 841-6521. Mon-Fri. 8 am-5 pm.

BILOXI   The town is along the most populated area of the Gulf Coast and has commercialised on its white sand beach. Though tourism is important, this has been a shrimping community since the Civil War. In early June, the fleets are ritually blessed; at the harbour front down the end of Main Street, or in the Back Bay area, you can watch the fishermen get on with their lives oblivious to tourism.

At various times in the town's history, Biloxi has been under the flags of France, Spain, Britain, the West Florida Republic, the Confederacy and the US.

ACCOMMODATION
Beach Manor Motel, 662 Beach Bvld, 436-4361. Near Greyhound. D-$75.
Sea Gull Motel, 2778 Beach Blvd, about 7 miles from town, 896-4211. S/D-$30-$40, AC, TV, pool, near beach.
Camping: Biloxi Beach Campground, US 90 at 1816 Beach Blvd, 432-2755, 3 miles from town. Sites $10 for two. Across from beach and pier.

FOOD
Mary Mahoney's French House Restaurant, 138 Rue Magnolia, 1 block N of US 90, 374-0163. In a 1737 home, one of the oldest in America, not cheap, but excellent regional cuisine. Open 11 am-10 pm.
McElroy's Harbour House Restaurant, 695 Beach Blvd, 435-5001. Everything from local seafood to steaks and burgers, $5-$13. Bfast $3. Open daily 7 am-10 pm.

OF INTEREST
Beauvoir, on US 90 at Beavoir St, 388-1313. The last home of Jefferson Davis, President of the Confederacy. See the library where he worked, and the Tomb of the Unknown Soldier of the Confederate States. Open daily 9 am-5 pm, $6. The famous cast iron 65-ft **Biloxi Lighthouse**, built in 1848 and one of the few remaining iron lighthouses, on US 90. Open by appointment only; call 435-6293. Free.

Other than Biloxi's white-sand **beaches**, the most enticing site along the coast is the **Gulf Islands National Seashore**, 875-3962. The seashore stretches into Florida, but there are 4 islands off the Mississippi coast which can be visited—West and East Ship, Petit Bois (pronounced Petty Boy), and **Horn Island**. The islands have a unique ecosystem. They are anchored by sea oats which keep the sand from washing away. The islands are also great places to bird-watch. The *Biloxi* Excursion Boat runs to Ship Island from the Pier four blocks E of the lighthouse. $14 r/t, call 432-2197 for details. The main site there is **Fort Massachusetts**, a linch pin of Lincoln's effort to blockade the south.

Four miles from Biloxi, at the Visitors Center in **Ocean Springs**, 3500 Park Rd, 875-9057, shows a movie about the islands. Open 9 am-5 pm daily. Camping is allowed on East Ship, but there is no regular boat service to the island. You can camp out at the grounds near the visitors center in Davis Bayou. *www.nps.gov/guis/*
J L Scott Marine Education Center and Aquarium, 115 Beach Blvd (US Hwy 90), 374-5550. The state's largest public aquarium includes the 42,000 gallon 'Gulf of Mexico' tank which houses sharks, sea turtles and eels. Mon-Sat 9 am-4 pm. $3.50.

INFORMATION/TRAVEL
Biloxi Visitor Center, 710 Beach Blvd, 374-3105. Mon-Fri 8 am-5 pm, Sat 9 am-5 pm, Sun noon-5 pm.
Greyhound , 166 Main St, 436-4335/(800) 231-2222.

NORTH CAROLINA   *The Tarheel State*

American writer H L Mencken once described North Carolina as 'a valley of humility between two mountains of conceit.' Wedged between Virginia and South Carolina, this photogenic 'land of beginnings' was the birthplace of English America and powered flight but its people just don't seem to think it would be polite to boast of all their blessings: a rich heritage, unspoiled beaches, rugged mountains, and a stimulating cultural and intellectual life.

However, these blessings have not gone unnoticed by others. The state—first in the US in tobacco, textiles and furniture manufacturing—has attracted so many people that some native North Carolinians are now grumbling about an influx of 'Yankees.' Northern companies have flocked into the area around Raleigh-Durham, the so-called 'research triangle,' helping to make it an internationally renowned centre for science and technology.

In just a few years, the triangle has grown to house more PhDs per capita than anywhere else in the country. Outside of the triangle, especially in the Asheville area, the economy has not benefitted from high tech employment. Areas of the Appalachian Mountains are still some of the poorest in the land.

The approachable North Carolinians have welcomed film-makers to their celluloid-friendly state too. Parts of *Blue Velvet* were made here, as was the brutal tale of native Indians and colonists *Last of the Mohicans*. From Cherokee history to modern folk-art, diversity is one of North Carolina's greatest attractions. Whether you want to enjoy the mountains or the shore, a small town's tranquility or a big town's bustle, you'll find it here. *www.yahoo.com/Regional/U_S__States/North Carolina/.*

The area code for Asheville and Charlotte is 704, for Raleigh and the Coast, 919.

THE COAST The 'Outer Banks' is the name given to the three curving island strips, **Ocracoke**, **Hatteras** and **Bodie Island**, sheltering the North Carolina mainland from the Atlantic surf. The sandy beaches are relatively unspoiled and offer some of the best surfcasting in the country. *www.nps.gov/*

At the northern end of the Banks, fishing gives way to flying. The first power-driven flight was made near **Kitty Hawk** at Kill Devil Hills on 17 December 1903, by brothers Orville and Wilbur Wright. Now in the Smithsonian Institution in Washington, the plane was aloft for 12 seconds and achieved a speed of 35 miles p/hr. Orville later explained that he and his brother had remained bachelors because they hadn't means to 'support a wife as well as an aeroplane.'

From the popular sands of Kitty Hawk, the Banks stretch south past the large dunes at Jockey's Ridge towards the primitive wildlife refuges of the country's first National Seashore, **Cape Hatteras**. The deadly currents and frequent hurricanes off the Cape earned this strip of land the nickname 'graveyard of the Atlantic' and a range of ships from tankers to U-Boats lie buried under its waters. Two hundred years ago pirates used the currents to their own advantage and, legend has it, led unsuspecting ships to their doom by tying a lantern to a horse's neck and then walking up the beach towards Diamond Shoals. Before a navigator realized that the lighthouse he was steering by was moving, he had run aground. Cape Hatteras lighthouse, the tallest in the US (208 ft), now warns ships away.

Ocracoke Island was home to America's most famous pirate, Edward Teach, better known as Blackbeard. Teach enjoyed the protection of several colonial governors until he was done in by the Virginia Militia. Today, the hurricanes and treacherous waters seem to have scared off developers;

leaving the Banks' abundant wildlife in peace. **Pea Island National Wildlife Refuge**, 987-2394, shelters Great snow geese among others.

Further south along the coast the historical city of **Wilmington** is a good base for exploring the **Cape Fear River** and coastline. The name supposedly originates from sailors' battles with the strong currents at the river mouth. In any case, do not be put off by the movie!

ACCOMMODATION
Camping: There are 4 National Park Service campgrounds along the 125-mile national seashore. The first three, at Oregon Inlet (south of Nag's Head), Cape Point and Frisco (on Cape Hatteras) are filled up on a first-come, first-served basis for $12. The fourth camp is on Ocracoke Island which can only be reached by ferry and sites must be reserved in advance by calling 1-800-2267 and entering the password CAPE. All campgrounds open until Labor Day, Sep 2nd. Private campgrounds are also scattered around the area; for more info contact Hatteras National Seashore, 473-2111.
Kitty Hawk: Outer Banks Youth Hostel (HI-AYH), 1004 Kitty Hawk Rd, 261-2294. $15 AYH, $20 non-AYH, Private rooms $20.
Ocracoke: The following motels are located off Rte 12. **Blackbeard's Lodge**, 928-3421. From D-$50; **Sand Dollar Motel**, 928-5571. From $65; and the **Pony Island Motel**, 928-4411. From $60 (10% discount for stays of a week or more). **Wilmington: The Glenn Hotel**, 16 Nathan St on Wrightsville Beach, (910) 256-2645. S-$30, D-$40-$50. Basic, shared bath, no AC.

FOOD
Not far from the Wright Brothers Memorial is **Kelly's Outer Banks Restaurant and Tavern**, milepost 10 1/2, 441-4116. Seafood, steak, chicken, pasta. Open daily; food served 'til 10 pm, bar open 'til 2 am. At Nag's Head Causeway is **RV's**, 441-4963. Sandwiches, steak, seafood. Open noon-10 pm daily.

OF INTEREST
Just on the mainland side of the Banks, lies the mysterious small town of **Manteo**. Three hundred Englishmen led by Sir Walter Raleigh built a small fort and settled near here in 1587. When an expedition from Britain set out for the colony three years later, they found that the entire community had disappeared without a trace. The only clue to their fate was the word 'Croatan' scratched onto a tree trunk. Rebuilt **Fort Raleigh**, 473-5772, and **Elizabeth Gardens**, 473-3234, mark the likely site of the lost colony. Both are located at the N end of Roanoke Island on Rte 64. Fort open 9 am-dusk; free. Gardens open 9 am-8 pm, $3. *Lost Colony*, 473-2127, is an outdoor drama which tells the story of the Roanoke Island Colony late Jun-early Aug, $14, Mon-Fri and Sun. The *Elizabeth II*, a representation of the ship which brought the first English settlers to North America, is moored 4 miles S on Rte 400, Manteo St across from the waterfront. $4, $2 w/student ID, tours every 30 mins, 9 am-6 pm, 473-1144.
Nags Head Woods Preserve, 441-2525, 15 miles N of Manteo, is a nature preserve with two walking trails, open Tue-Sat 10 am-3 pm. Nearby in Kitty Hawk, the **Wright Bros Memorial and Museum** on Rte 158, 441-7430, pays homage to the great inventors. Open 9 am-6 pm daily. $4 p/car, $2 pp. What better way to celebrate a visit to the place where man first took flight than with an airplane tour from **Kitty Hawk Aerotours**, 441-4460, 30 min coastal tours. $19 pp for parties of four or less, $22 pp for six. Icarus fans may want to try the nearby hang-gliding operations: call **Kitty Hawk Kites**, 441-4124. $69 for a 3 hr lesson including training film, ground school and 5 flights.
Ramada Inn organises **dolphin tours**; $18 for 1 hr, 441-0424.
Lighthouses, at Cape Hatteras, Ocracoke, Corolla and Bodie. Visitors are not per-

mitted to climb up the Bodie tower, but are free to wander the grounds. Finally, the **Chicamacomico Life Saving Station**, on Hatteras Island near Rodanthe, records how private rescue companies of the 19th century operated.
Cape Fear Museum, 814 Market St btwn 8th & 9th St, Wilmington, (910) 341-4350. Dive into the background and history of the Lower Cape and learn how North Carolina earned its nickname, 'the Tarheel State.' Tues-Sat 9 am-5 pm, Sun 2 pm-5 pm. $2, $1 w/student ID.

INFORMATION
Outer Banks Chamber of Commerce, Ocean Bay Blvd, Kill Devil Hills, off milepost 8¹/₂, 441-8144. Mon-Fri 9 am-5 pm.
Aycock Brown Welcome Center on Bodie Island near Kitty Hawk, 261-4644.
Cape Hatteras Ntl Seashore Information Centers; Bodie Island, 441-5711; Hatteras Island, 995-4474; Ocracoke Island, 928-4531. All open daily 9 am-5 pm.
Cape Fear Coast Visitors Bureau, 24 N Third St, (800) 222 4757

TRAVEL
Car Ferry btwn Cedar Island and Ocracoke Island, daily, 2 hrs, $10 car (book several days ahead on summer w/ends), $1 pp. Call (800) 345-1665 in Ocracoke, (800) 865-0343 in Cedar Island or (800) BY FERRY. Free ferries across Hatteras Inlet btwn Hatteras and Ocracoke daily, 5 am-11 pm, 40 mins. Taxis to and from Wilmington airport cost around $15 o/w. Call 762-3322.

TOBACCO ROAD   A 150-mile-long arc of cities stretching between **Raleigh** and **Winston-Salem** is the backbone of North Carolina. Rolling through a region of gentle hills called the Piedmont, I-40 and I-85 pass the major tobacco growing farms and factories. The state capital is in Raleigh and the **Raleigh/Durham Triangle** area, home to three major universities, has the nation's highest number of PhDs per head of population.

ACCOMMODATION
In Durham: Carolina-Duke Motor Inn, 2517 Guess Rd, off I-85, exit in Durham, 286-0771/(800) 483-1158. S-$34, D-$40, XP-$3. Pool, AC, TV.
Budget Inn, 2101 Holloway St, Hwy 98, 682-5100. S-$32, D-$38, $3 key deposit. Pool, TV, laundry.
In Raleigh: Regency Motel, 300 N Dawson, 828-9081. S-$42, D-$50.
YMCA, 1601 Hillsborough St, 832-6601. $20 w/shared bath. Pool.
YWCA, 1012 Oberlin Rd, 828-3205. Women only. $22, $60 week. Rsvs essential, required to fill out application form in person.
In Winston-Salem: Days Inn North, 5218 Germanton Rd, (910) 744-5755. S-$45, D-$49, XP-$5.
Motel 6, 3810 Patterson Ave, (910) 661-1588. I-40 exit to US 52 N, exit Patterson Ave. S-$30, D-$35, XP-$4.

FOOD
In Durham: 9th Street Bakery, 776 9th Street, 286-0303. Cheap pastries and bakery items, sandwiches from $3. Live folk music at w/ends. Mon-Thur 7 am-6 pm, Fri-Sat 'til 11 pm, Sun 8 am-4 pm.
Satisfaction, Lakewood Shopping Center, 682-7397. Big Duke hangout. Pizzas, sandwiches, burgers. Lunch, dinner, Mon-Sat 11 am-2 am.
In Raleigh: Applebee's Neighborhood Grill & Bar, 4004 Capitol Blvd, 878-4595. American fare (burgers, chicken, steaks) $6.50-$10.

OF INTEREST
Durham: Duke Homestead State Historic Site, 477-5498, ancestral home of the Duke family, with early tobacco factories and historic outbuildings. **Duke**

University, 684-3214, also visitor centre, a gothic wonderland built with tobacco money, site of **Duke Chapel** boasting a 210 ft tower with 50-bell carillon, and over 1 million stained glass pieces fitted in 77 windows. **Duke Museum of Art**, 8681-8624, features Medieval sculpture, American and European paintings, sculpture, drawing and prints, Greek and Roman antiques. **Sarah P Duke Gardens**, 684-3698, 55 acres of landscaped and woodland gardens with 5 mile trail among waterfalls, ponds, pavilions and lawns. General tours of most attractions from visitor centre, 2138 Campus Dr, 684-3214, Mon-Sat. Call ahead as schedules change frequently.

Chapel Hill is a college town 15 miles SW of Durham on US 15501. Home of the **University of North Carolina**, the first public university in America. Visit the **Morehead Planetarium** on Franklin St, near campus, 962-1236. Star Theatre shows cost $3.50, $2.50 w/student ID. **Franklin St** is also the place to find cheap food and student bars and clubs. For those who have had enough of sight-seeing, **Cane Creek Reservoir**, 8705 Stanford Rd, 942-5790, offers boating, fishing, canoeing, swimming, picnic and sunbathing areas.

Raleigh: Mordecai Plantation House Historic Park, 1 Mimosa St, 834-4844. Birthplace of Andrew Johnson, features antebellum plantation house and other historic buildings. Mon, Wed-Sat 10 am-3 pm, w/end 1.30 pm-3.30 pm. $3, $1 w/student ID.

North Carolina Museum of Art, 2110 Blue Ridge Rd, 839-6262. European paintings from 1300, American 19th century paintings, Egyptian, Greek and Roman art. Tue-Thur 9 am-5 pm, Fri and Sat 'til 9 pm, Sun 11 am-6 pm. Free.

North Carolina State Capitol, 1 E. Edenton St, 733-4994. Greek revival style, built btwn 1833 and 1840. 'One of the best preserved examples of a Civic Building in this style of architecture.' Mon-Fri 8 am-5 pm, Sat 9 am, Sun 1 pm. Across the street is the **North Carolina Museum of History**, 715-0200. Explore the state's history through hands-on exhibits and 'innovative' programs. 'Check out the Sports Hall of Fame and Folklife galleries.' Changing exhibits provide detailed glimpses of the past. Tue-Sat 9 am-5 pm, Sun noon-5 pm. Free.

Winston-Salem: Reynolda House Museum and Gardens, Reynolda Rd, (910) 725-5325, houses 18th-20th century American paintings, sculpture, and prints associated with the founder of R J Reynolds Tobacco, including Church's *The Andes of Ecuador*. Tues-Sat 9.30 am-4.30 pm, Sun 1.30 pm-4.30 pm, $6, $3 w/student ID.

Historic Bethabara, 2147 Bethabara Rd, 924-8191. Reconstruction of 18th century Moravian Village, with 130 acre park, archaeological sites and other historic buildings. Settlers first came to this area in 1766.

Old Salem, 600 S Main St, 721-7300. Costumed interpreters re-create Moravian life. Daily demonstrations, bakery, restaurant and shops. Both are open Mon-Sat 9.30 am-4.30 pm, Sun 1.30 pm-4.30 pm. The newer art is at the **Southeastern Center for Contemporary Art**, 750 Marguerite Dr, 725-1904. Tue-Sat 10 am-5 pm, Sun 2 pm-5 pm; $3, $2 w/student ID.

Greensboro, on I-40 btwn Winston-Salem and Raleigh, was the birthplace of the 1960s national student sit-in movement for civil rights, when four local African-American students sat down in Woolworths and refused to move. 30 yrs on their courage and their legacy is chronicled in the **Greensboro Historical Museum**, Lindsay St at Summit Ave, (910) 373 2043. Tues-Sat 10 am-5 pm, Sun 2 pm-5 pm. Free. Greensboro also boasts one of the world's largest waterparks. **Emerald Point Waterpark**, 3910 S Holden Rd, (910) 852-9721, offers giant wave pool, tube slides, drop slides, drifting river and more. All day tkts $20. Mon-Thur 10 am-7 pm, Fri and w/end 10 am-8 pm. On I-85 at Asheboro, about 30 mins S of Greensboro, is the **North Carolina Zoological Park**, (800) 488-0444. The world's largest natural habitat zoo. Open 9 am-5 pm, $8.

INFORMATION
Chapel Hill: Chamber of Commerce, 104 S Estes Dr, 967-7075.

Durham: Convention and Visitors Bureau, 101 E Morgan St, 687-0288.
Raleigh: Capital Area Visitor Center, 301 N Blount St, 733-3456.
Winston-Salem: Chamber of Commerce, 601 W 4th St, 725-2361.
Winston-Salem Visitors Center, 601 N Cherry St, 777-3796.

TRAVEL
Durham: Greyhound, 820 W Morgan St, 687-4800/(800) 231-2222.
Durham Area Transit Authority, 683-3282. Public bus service runs daily, schedules vary, fare 60¢, 30¢ w/student ID.
Raleigh: Amtrak, 320 W Cabarrus St, 833-7594/(800) 872-7245.
Greyhound, 314 W Jones St, 834-8275/(800) 231-2222. Chapel Hill $8, Durham $7.
Capital Area Transit, 828-7228, public bus service runs Mon-Sat, schedules vary, fare 50c. Many hotels offer free shuttles to and from Raleigh-Durham airport to downtown, so ask around. Taxis cost around $25 o/w. Call 832-3228.

ASHEVILLE AND AREA   Travellers to this area find a simple, unhurried charm which is fading elsewhere in the busy 'New South'. The crafts and folklore of the Appalachian Mountains flourish in the shops and markets here, and the region's natural beauty is protected from overdevelopment. If you put your feet up anywhere in North Carolina, this is the place to do it.

ACCOMMODATION
Down Town Motel, 65 Merriman Ave, 253-9841. S-$35, D-$38.
Intown Motor Lodge, 100 Tunnel Rd, 252-1811, S-$29, D-$32, more at w/end.
Log Cabin Motor Court, 330 Weaverville Hwy, 645-6546. Cabins $31 for two.

FOOD
Boston Pizza, 501 Merriman, 252-9474. Popular student hangout; pizzas from $7. Try the 'Boston Supreme!' Mon-Sat 11 am-11 pm.
The Hop, 507 Merriman, 252-8362. Homemade ice cream in 50's style joint. Mon-Sat noon-9.30 pm.
Three Brothers Restaurant, 183 Haywood St, 253-4971, serves everything, over 40 types of sandwiches. Open 11 am-10 pm Mon-Fri, Sat 4 pm-10 pm.

OF INTEREST
Biltmore House and Gardens, 255-1776, built by the Vanderbilt family, is an opulent exception to the area's humble charms. Peter Sellers' last film *Being There* was filmed at this 250-room European style chateau. Includes garden, conservatory, winery, and two restaurants. Take exit 50 or 50B on I-40 south of Asheville. Tckt office 8.30 am-5 pm, house open 'til 6 pm, winery 'til 7 pm and gardens open 'til dark. $28 all inclusive.
Chimney Rock Park, (800) 277-9611, lies 25 miles SE of Asheville near intersection of US 64 and 74. A 26 storey elevator runs inside the mountain and ascends to 1200 ft. 'Spectacular views over the Appalachian Mountains.' Also various nature trails through the nearby **Pisgah National Forest**, natural rock slides at **Sliding Rock** and a 404 ft waterfall, 877-3265.
For literary interest head to **Flat Rock**, once home to poet Carl Sandburg, and current site of the **Flat Rock Playhouse**, North Carolina's State theatre, 693-0731. Sandburg's home for 22 years, **Connemara**, 693-4178, has books and videos of the writer-poet's life. His championship goat herd lives on. Tours of the home daily 9 am-5 pm, every 30 mins, $3. The **Thomas Wolfe Memorial**, 48 Spruce St (next to the Radison Hotel), 253-8304, honours Asheville's most famous son. Wolfe's best known novel, *Look Homeward Angel* (titled after Milton's poem of the same name), was inspired by childhood experiences; his father was the town stonecutter. Asheville is a prime spot to shop for **local crafts**. Traditions are lovingly preserved. The **Mountain and Dance and Folk Festival**, 258-6111, on the first w/end in Aug

has been going more than 60 yrs. The annual **World Gee Haw Wimmy Diddle Competition** is held annually in Aug at the **Folk Arts Center**, 298-7928, and includes demonstrations of this native Appalachian toy, made from laurel wood.

INFORMATION/TRAVEL
Asheville Chamber of Commerce, 151 Haywood St, 258-6111. 'A very helpful staff.'
Asheville Transit , 253-5691. Serves city and outskirts. Fare 60¢, 10¢ transfer.
Greyhound, 2 Tunnel Rd, 253-5353/(800) 231-2222. 2 miles E of downtown, served by Asheville Transit buses #13 & #14.

GREAT SMOKY MOUNTAINS NATIONAL PARK The name Great Smokies is derived from the smoke-like haze that envelopes these forest-covered mountains.The Cherokee Indians called this the 'Land of a Thousand Smokes'. Part of the Appalachian Mountains near the southern end of the Blue Ridge Parkway, the popular park has been preserved as a wilderness that includes some of the highest peaks in the eastern US and 68 miles of the Appalachian Trail. *www.nps.gov/gvsm/index.htm.old*

The **Great Smoky Mountain Railway** runs 4 hr trips through Nantahala Gorge and Fontana Lake, from $20. 'Waste of time. What mountains? Telephone cables obscured view of scrap yards.' 7 hour raft and rail trips, from $53 (includes picnic lunch and guided raft ride). All departures from Bryson City. Call (704) 586-8811 for rsvs.

The area near **Cataloochee** affords an excellent impression of the obstacles facing the earliest pioneers on their push into the west. Cabins, cleared acreage and other pioneer remnants dot this section of the park. Perhaps the most fascinating visit is to the **Cherokee Reservation**, (800) 438-1601. There's a recreated Indian village, and a production of *Unto These Hills*, an Indian drama about their land and the meaning it holds for them, and a museum.

The North Carolina entrance to the park is on US 441 at Cherokee with the visitor centre located at **Oconaluftee**, not far from the Indian reservation. Park info, including info of its 900 walking trails can be obtained by calling (615) 436-1200. Cherokee also offers numerous motels and campgrounds. Try **Oconaluftee Motel**, US 19 South, (704) 488-2950, D-$55.

SOUTH CAROLINA *Palmetto State*

In its semi-tropical coastal climate and historical background, the Palmetto State, first to secede from the Union, marks the beginning of the Deep South. South Carolina also typifies the New South. Since the Second World War, booming factories, based on the Greenville area, have replaced sleepy cotton fields and cotton itself has been replaced by tobacco as the major cash crop. Textile manufacturing and chemicals are the state's major industries, but industry has not developed at the expense of the state's traditional charm and lovely countryside.

South Carolina has, however, something of a split personality. Charleston beckons the visitor with its graceful streets and refined architecture. Myrtle Beach entices with all the subtlety of a tourist-howitzer. South Carolina has

her slower country charms, but other than Charleston, few compare favourably with her neighbours. The beaches are less cluttered in North Carolina and the mountains are grander in Tennessee. *www.yahoo.com/regional/U_S__States/South Carolina.*
The area code for the state is 803.

CHARLESTON   The curtain rose here on the Civil War to the cheers of society ladies and the blasts of harbour canon. Charleston's exuberance found a less violent expression in the 1920s when a dance dubbed the *Charleston* became a national obsession.   Dance was better suited to Charleston's nature which epitomises Southern graciousness. Settled by aristocracy, Charleston has always been concerned with architecture, art and the length of the family tree. More recently in 1989, this lovely old town was severely battered when hurricane Hugo roared through. Many of the historic buildings suffered severe damage, so much so that the town will never look the same again.

ACCOMMODATION
Bed, No Breakfast, 16 Halsey St, 723-4450. Guest house in Harleston Village near College of Charleston, S/D-$55, T-$60. 'Comfortable.' 'Limited space.'
Rutledge Victorian Inn, 114 Rutledge Ave, 722-7551, ground floor, also **King George Inn B&B**, 723-9339, upper floor. Located downtown. Shared hostel rooms $20, $15 thereafter, private room in B&B, D-$40. AC, TV. Favourite stop for BUNAC travellers and owners helpful in finding work in area. Rsvs essential, daily 9 am-5 pm.

FOOD
The Gourmetisserie in the City Market is junk food centre—hamburger, pizza stands. 'Great meeting place.'
Olde Towne Restaurant, 229 King St, 723-8170. Despite its name, it turns out to be Greek, with fish and meat specialities. Lunches from $6.50. Friendly.
Papillion's Pizza Bar, 41 Market, inside the church, 723-6510. All-you-can-eat lunch buffets daily $6, dinner buffet Mon and Tues $7.
Pinckney Cafe, 18 Pinckney St, 577-0961. Seafood etc. from about $4.50. 'A little gem. Sit outside and try the seafood gumbo.'

OF INTEREST
A tremendous city pride exists in Charleston, and there are excellent documentaries on the city shown in the downtown area. *Forever Charleston*, a slide show on the city, is shown at the Visitor Reception and Transportation Center, 325 Meeting St, 720-5678, from 9 am-5 pm daily; $2. The **Preservation Society**, 147 King St at Queen, 722-4630, is a useful place to learn about the history of Charleston and the volunteers welcome foreign visitors. Maps, pamphlets and walking books are available. Mon-Sat 10 am-5 pm.
    Charleston is famous for its fine houses, squares and cobblestone streets. Start your walk along **Church Street**, the vision Heyward and Gershwin used to create **Catfish Row** in *Porgy and Bess*. The **Battery**, along the Cooper and Ashley rivers, has blocks of attractive old residences. The only **Huguenot church** in the US is at Church and Queen streets while the **Dock Street Theater** is across the street. Topping the list of restorations is the **Nathaniel Russell House**, 51 Meeting St, probably the best house to visit. Dating from 1808, it has a famous 'free-flying' spiral staircase and lavish furnishings. Open daily 10 am-5 pm, $6. Basket-weaving traditions inherited from Africa, and handed down by generations of slaves can

still be seen at the **Market**, Meeting and Market Sts. Fruit, veggies, masses of junk and some beautiful handicrafts. Watch the ladies making baskets—and then buy one. 'Lively and colourful.'

Daughters of the Confederacy Museum, 723-1541. 'Rather higgledy-piggledy, but there are some unusual Confederate memorabilia at this place.' Sat and Sun 12 pm-5 pm, $2.

Gibbes Museum of Art, 135 Meeting St, 722-2706. Displays early art and portraiture of South Carolina and one of the finest collections of miniatures in the world. 'Worthwhile: some quite impressive early American paintings, and some even more impressive modern woodwork.' Tues-Sat 10 am-5 pm; Sun and Mon 1 pm-5 pm. $5, $4 w/student ID.

Kahal Kadosh Beth Elohim, 723-1090, founded by Serphadic Jews in 1749, the current temple was built in Greek-Revival style in 1841 and is the oldest synagogue in continuous use in the US, also an early centre of reform Judaism. Tours Mon-Fri 10 am-noon.

The Charleston Museum, 360 Meeting St, 722-2996. Started in 1773, claims to be the oldest museum in the country. Exhibits include a full-scale replica of the Confederate submarine, *HL Hunley*; you can peer into the open side of the sub. 'Creepy.' Mon-Sat 9 am-5 pm, Sun 1 pm-5 pm, $6.

The Old Exchange and Provost Dungeon, 122 E Bay at Broad St, 727-2165. Built btwn 1767 and 1771; delegates to the first Continenetal Congress were elected here in 1774. The dungeon was used as a prison by the British during the Revolution. Open daily 9 am-5 pm for self guided tours, $6. Charleston parades with military history: the **Citadel Military Academy**, 953-5000, is known as the West Point of the South. Female cadets have stormed and conquered West Point but the first woman who breached the staunchly male Citadel in August 1995 dropped out after a few days of 'hell week.' There are however, now several female cadets at the academy proving that they are every bit as tough as the boys! The college, at Moultrie Street on banks of Ashley River, offers tours and a free museum, open Sat noon-5 pm, Sun-Fri 2 pm-5 pm. Don't miss the dress parade every Friday at 3.45 pm when the cadets are in session. The Confederate bombardment of Federally-garrisoned **Fort Sumter**, just across the harbour, began the Civil War. Now Fort Sumter is a national monument, 883-3123, with its history depicted through exhibits and dioramas. There are as many as 6 boat tours daily to the fort, $10.50. Boats leave from City Marina and Patriot's Point, 722-1691 for schedules. Be careful to take a boat that actually lands on the fort!

Ft Moultrie, on Sullivan's Island but easily reached by car, has served as the bastion of security for Charleston harbour since the revolutionary war. Also just outside Charleston is **Boone Hall Plantation**, 884-4371, 7 miles N near US 17. Beautiful house and gardens; the stunning Avenue of Oaks leading to the mansion inspired the one seen in *Gone With the Wind*. . Mon-Sat 8.30 am-6.30 pm, Sun 1 pm-5 pm, $10.

Charles Towne Landing, 1500 Old Towne Rd, 6 miles outside Charleston, marks the site of the first permanent English speaking settlement in South Carolina. See the *Adventure*, a working reproduction of a 17th century sailing vessel. Also guided tram tours, animal forest, bike paths and walkways. Open 9 am-6 pm daily, $6. Summers can be close, but you can cool off at **Folly Beach**, off Rte 171, with public parking and showers. 'Excellent beach, very long, deserted and clean.'

INFORMATION

Charleston Visitor Reception and Transportation Center, 325 Meeting St, 720-5678. Open daily. Good maps available. 'Helpful.' Even the **Chamber of Commerce** is historic—it is one of the nation's oldest civic commercial organisations; 81 Mary St, 577-2510/853-8000.

TRAVEL

Amtrak, 4565 Gaynor Ave, 9 miles W of town on Hwy 52, 744-8263/(800) 872-7245. The *Silver Meteor* calls here from NYC. Taxi from downtown, $10-$14.

Charleston Airport is located 13 miles N of downtown. Taxis $15-$20, 577-7575. Limo shuttle $10, call 767-7111 for rsvs.

Greyhound, 3610 Dorchester Rd, 744-5341/(800) 231-2222.

Local Bus (SCE & G), 747-0922. Mon-Sat 5.30 am-midnight. Fare 75¢.

MYRTLE BEACH AND THE GRAND STRAND

The 60 mile stretch of South Carolina's northern coast, known as the Grand Strand, has seen almost frightening growth in the past two decades. It's loaded with countless amusements, fast food joints, and tacky boutiques with merchants selling the inevitable Myrtle Beach T-shirts and trinkets. In summer, the 30,000 population of Myrtle Beach swells to around 350,000.

Brookgreen Gardens, on US-17S, 20 min S of Myrtle Beach, 237-4218, seems out of place here. In a serene setting, the world's largest outdoor collection of American sculpture—over 400 works of art are on show, set against 2000 species of plants. The gardens also feature a wildlife park and aviary. 'Worth spending the whole day the sculptures are amazing.' Mon and Tue 9.30 am-4.45 pm, Thur 'til dark, $7.50.

Further south a short distance, is pretty and famous **Pawleys Island**. One of the oldest resorts on the Atlantic coast, this was originally a refuge for colonial rice planters' families fleeing from a malaria epidemic. Residents work hard to preserve its more elegant, less commercialised feeling. The well known Pawleys Island Hammock is hand-woven and sold here—you can watch them being made by local craftsmen.

Georgetown, on Hwy 17 at the southern end of the Grand Strand, was the first settlement in North America, established in 1526 by the Spaniards, and named 200 years later in honour of King George II. It became a thriving port in the 18th century, concentrating on the export of rice and in the early 19th century becoming the biggest exporter of rice in the world. Although this trade has now gone, there are still many signs remaining and things worth seeing, such as the old docks along the waterfront which have been converted into **Harborwalk**, a promenade of restaurants and shops.

ACCOMMODATION/FOOD/ENTERTAINMENT

Although hotels are everywhere, they are generally expensive in season, but you can find bargains.

Sand Dollar, 403 6th Ave N, 448-5364. Rooms w/baths, AC, TV. BUNACers welcome—special rate, D-$75 weekly pp for four. Pool. Fortunately Myrtle Beach claims 12,000 **campsites** and calls itself the 'Camping Capital of the World.' Try **Myrtle Beach State Park** on Rte 17 South, 238-2224, site $16, $12 Oct-Mar. Rsvs 2 weeks in advance. The Myrtle Beach Chamber of Commerce, 1200 N Oak St, 626-7444, has a complete guide to the area's campsites. For the **Myrtle Beach Reservation Referral Service**, call 626-7477.

Peaches Corner, 900 Ocean Blvd, 448-7424. 'Best burgers on the beach—try a famous 'Peaches Burger.'

The Filling Station, 626-9435. All-you-can-eat buffet for $5 lunch, $7 dinner. Salad, soup, sandwiches, pizza, desserts and more.

2001, 920 Lake Arrowhead Rd, 449-9434. Three clubs in one building. Choose from dance, country and 'shag'! Daily 8 pm-2 am, cover $6-$8.

INFORMATION/TRAVEL
Myrtle Beach Chamber of Commerce, 1200 N Oak St, 626-7444. Pick up copies of *Beachcomber* and *Kicks* for local events and entertainment listings. 'Also has useful accommodations directories.'

Greyhound, 508 9th Ave N, 448-2471/(800) 231-2222.

Coastal Rapid Public Transport Authority (CRPTA), bus service around Myrtle Beach area. Fare 75c.

COLUMBIA   In the middle of South Carolina at the joining of three interstates sits Columbia, the state's largest city and capital since 1786. Although growing rapidly, the city is mild by Charleston or Myrtle Beach standards. Lake Murray, with 520 miles of scenic lakefront, is less than 20 miles away.

ACCOMMODATION/FOOD
Along the interstates are the best places to find cheap and clean rooms.

Budgetel, 911 Bush River off I-26, 798-3222. S-$37, D-$40.

Masters Economy, 613 Knox Abbott Drive, 796-4300. S-$30, D-$36. Near the university campus.

Off-Campus Housing Office, Room 235, the Russell House, Green St, 777-4174, can direct visitors to people in the university community with rooms to rent. Open 8 am-5 pm. For food and entertainment, head to Five Points—a business district at Blossom, Devine and Harden Sts—frequented by students.

Columbia State Farmer's Market, Bluff Road across from the USC stadium, 737-4664. Fresh produce daily. Mon-Sat 6 am-9 pm.

Groucho's, 611 Harden St, 799-5708, Columbia's renowned New York-style Jewish deli. Cheap filling sandwiches, $4-$6.

Yesterday's Restaurant and Tavern, 2030 Devine St, 799-0196, is an institution. Open daily for lunch and dinner, lunch from $4-7, dinner from $5-14. 'Friendly manager!'

OF INTEREST
Many of the city's attractions are located in or around the **University of South Carolina**. A mall-like area lined with stately buildings built in the early 19th century and called the **Horseshoe** marks the campus centre. On the Horseshoe facing Sumter St is the **McKissick Museum**, 777-7251. Large collection of Twentieth Century Fox film reels and science exhibits.

Columbia Museum of Art, within walking distance from the McKissick at Senate and Bull Sts, 799-2810, houses Renaissance and baroque art as well as oriental and neoclassical Greek art galleries. Open Tue-Fri 10 am-5 pm, w/end 12.30 pm-5 pm. $2.50, $1.50 w/student ID, free on Wed. Adjoining **Gibbs Planetarium**, takes you on a journey 'Into The Future,' find out what it would be like to live on a space-station, or wander around on Mars. W/end shows only 2 pm and 4 pm, 'Carolina Skies' at 3 pm, what you'll see in the sky at night from the Carolinas. 50c.

South Carolina State Museum, 301 Gervais St, 737-4921, housed in a renovated textile mill, focuses on art, history, natural history, and science and technology. Mon-Sat 10 am-5 pm, Sun 1 pm-5 pm, $4, $3 w/student ID, free on the first Sunday of every month.

State Capitol, at Main and Gervais Sts, 734-2430. Built in 1855, the six bronze stars on the outer western wall mark cannon hits scored by the Union during the Civil War.

INFORMATION/TRAVEL
Greater Columbia Convention and Visitors Bureau, 1012 Gervais St, on corner of Assembly, 254-0479. Mon-Fri, 9 am-5 pm, Sat 10 am-4 pm, Sun 1 pm-5 pm.

Amtrak, 850 Pulaski St, 252-8246/(800) 872-7245.

Greyhound, 2015 Gervais St, 256-6465/(800) 231-2222.

TENNESSEE *The Volunteer State*

Tennessee is music country. Memphis has been fertile ground for blues musicians and rock and roll. Nashville brought country music down from the hills to mainstream America. The difference in music reflects deeper social differences within the state. The east is 'Hill Country,' backwoods and fiercely independent. The west is flat and more Southern, drawing life from the Mississippi River. The two cultures clashed violently during the Civil War, and several of the war's most costly battles were decided on Tennessee soil.

Tennessee's evolution from a backwoods state into the 20th century has not been easy. After a famous trial in 1925, a teacher named Scopes was fined for teaching the theory of evolution. The eastern half of the state is less isolated today thanks to the Tennessee Valley Authority (TVA) built by the Franklin Roosevelt Administration. TVA was a massive effort to both tame a river, and to civilise an entire region. People still argue over the proper role of government power in projects such as TVA. The state celebrated its 200th birthday in 1996. *www.yahoo.com/regional/U_S__States/Tennessee/.*
The area code for Nashville and the east is 615. For Memphis and the west dial 901.

NASHVILLE The Hollywood of the South, Nashville sparkles with the rhinestone successes and excesses of her country music stars. Bulging with moral character, Nashville is a centre of education and has more churches per capita than anywhere else in the country.

ACCOMMODATION
Most cheap motels are several miles outside town. 'Difficult to find cheap accommodation unless you have a car.'
Days Inn, 1400 Brick Church Pk, 228-5977/(800) 325-2525. D-$60 for four. TV, pool, bfast.
Knights Inn, I-65 and W Trinity Lane, exit 87B, 226-4500. 3 miles N of Nashville. S-$35, D-$42, XP-$6. AC, TV, pool.
Motel 6, 311 W Trinity Ln, 227-9696. Junction of I-24 east and I-65 north. AC. S-$38, D-$42.
Travelodge, 1274 Murphreesboro Rd, (800) 578-7878. Downtown. S/D-$45.
Camping: Many campgrounds are clustered around Opryland. Try **Nashville Travel Park**, 889-4225, site $18. or **Two Rivers Campground**, 883-8559. Take Briley Parkway north to McGavock Pike and take exit 12B onto Music Valley Drive. Sites $18.

FOOD
Bluebird Cafe, 4104 Hillsboro Pike, 383-1461. Mon-Sat 5.30 pm-midnight, Sun 6 pm-midnight. Live music and entertainment nightly, cover varies. Sandwiches, french bread pizzas.
Elliston Place Soda Shop, 2111 Elliston Pl, 327-1090. Mon-Fri 6 am-8 pm, Sat 8 am-8 pm. Home-cooked food.

OF INTEREST
The District. Broadway, 2nd Ave, Printer's Alley and Riverfront Park, make up the historic heart of Nashville. Renovated turn-of-the-century buildings house shops, restaurants, art galleries bars and nightclubs.

Country Hall of Fame and Historic RCA Studio B, 4 Music Square East, 256-1639. Number one on any tourist list. Where Elvis Presley cut 100 records from 1963-71. See the King's solid gold cadillac, alongside exhibits, rare artifacts and personal treasures of other legendary performers. Tours 8 am-6 pm daily, $10.75. 'Watch out for bogus Hall of Fame on next street.' 'Not worth it.'

Music Row, btwn 16th and 19th Aves S. The recording studios for Columbia, RCA and many others are here. For a taste of historic Nashville you can tour the 'mother church of country music,' the restored **Ryman Auditorium**, 116 Fifth Ave N, 254-1445/889-6611 for show info and tkt rsvs. The 100-yr old venue now offers daytime tours and live-performances every evening. Tours 8.30 am-4 pm, $5.50. The **Music City Queen**, 889-6611, docked at Riverfront Park offers daily sightseeing and Sun brunch cruises. Also host to blues and jazz events on Sat evenings, $12-$28, call for schedules. The recently opened 20,000-seat **Nashville Arena**, btwn 5th and 6th Aves, 770-2000, is home to the **Nashville Kats** football team and host to a variety of concerts and special events. Call for details.

Nashvillians are hot on reproductions. Their pride and joy is the **Parthenon Pavilion**, the world's only full-sized copy of the original and located in Centennial Park along West End Ave, 862-8431, Tue-Sat 9 am-4.30 pm, Sun 12.30 pm-4.30 pm, $2.50.

Fort Nashborough, 1st Ave N btwn Broadway and Church Sts, is a replica of the original fort from which the city first grew. For some real history, leave town on I-40 (Old Hickory Blvd exit) and head 12 miles E to the **Hermitage**, 4580 Rachel's Lane, 889-2941, the home of Andrew Jackson, a backwoods orphan who became US president (1829-1837). He is buried on the grounds. Open 9 am-5 pm daily, $8. **Belle Meade Mansion**, 5025 Harding Rd, 356-0501. Was the largest plantation and thoroughbred nursery in Tennessee. Mon-Sat 9 am-5 pm, Sun 1 pm-5 pm, $6.

ENTERTAINMENT

Topping the entertainment list is the show that made Nashville, **The Grand Ole Opry**. Radio WSU, and later television, broadcast this country music show out to a receptive nation. Tkts are tough to get during **Fan Fair**, the annual jamboree of country music held in June. The rest of the year you stand a decent chance. $17 admission to the 2 shows each Friday and Saturday nights with cheaper matinees in summer. You can ask to be on the waiting list. 'If you have up to number 15, you stand a chance.' 'Nothing quite like it.' The Opry's home is in **Opryland**, 2802 Opryland Dr, an entertainment park which offers 12 live music shows as well as rides and glitz. Open 10 am-9 pm daily. Closed Nov-March. 1-day tkts $30. Walk through the garish **Opryland Hotel** where tropical vegetation, southern architecture, a Liberace impersonator and a waterfall all co-exist under one enormous roof. The **Opryland River Taxi**, 2812 Opryland Dr, offers a shuttle service btwn the Opryland complex and Riverfront park via Cumberland River, taking in Opryland and downtown attractions, $12 r/t. For info on all Opry attractions call 889-6611.

Printer's Alley is Nashville's standard club strip. **Tootsie's Orchid Cafe**, 422 Broadway, 726-3739. Top Country/Western bar, springboard for future Oprystars. Merle Haggard and other country greats may drop in to see how things are going. Nightly 'til 3 am, no cover. Also try the **Station Inn**, 402 12th Ave S, 255-3307. Closed Mon. The area near Vanderbilt Campus has more student-oriented entertainment.

INFORMATION

Convention and Visitors Division, Chamber of Commerce, 161 4th Ave N, 259-4755. Mon-Fri 8 am-5 pm.

Visitor Information Centre at the Nashville Arena, corner of 5th and Broadway, 770-2000. Mon-Fri 8.30 am-5.30 pm.

Nashville Visitors Centre, 259-4747. 8.30 am-8 pm.

TRAVEL
Greyhound, 200 8th Ave and Demonbreun St, 2 blocks S of Broadway, 255-3556/(800) 231-2222. 'Use caution in this neighbourhood.'
Metropolitain Transit Authority (MATA), 862-5950. Runs Mon-Fri 5 am-midnight, minimal service w/ends. Murfreesboro Rd/Airport Bus, #18M. Fare $1.30

EASTERN TENNESSEE AND THE GREAT SMOKIES The **Great Smoky Mountains National Park** is one of the most heavily visited parks in the United States. Named by the Cherokee Indians for the haze which shrouds the mountain peaks, the 900 miles of trails offer an immense variety of wildlife and landscapes. You will have to travel through **Gatlinburg** to reach the park entrance. 'Commercialism at its worst,' Gatlinburg specializes in wax museums, Elvis memorabilia, UFOs and Jesus nicknacks, all for sale to the gullible tourist. The only things worth doing, perhaps, are to ride the ski lift or to climb the space needle from where you get a good look at the mountains. 10 miles E of Gatlinburg on US 321 N is the **Wa-Floy Retreat Hostel**, 436-7700, $10 AYH, $12 non-AYH.

N of Gatlinburg on US Hwy 441 is **Pigeon Forge**, home of **Dollywood**, 1020 Dollywood Lane, (800) 365-5996. The only Tennessee attraction to rival Graceland. The theme park is devoted to the life and career of Tennessee's own Queen of Country, Dolly Parton, and includes music shows, restaurants, rides and 'jukebox junction', devoted to the 50s—all with an 'old-time' atmosphere. 'You won't be disappointed!' Daily 10 am-6 pm, $29. For accommodation look towards **Smoky Mt Ranch Camp (HI-AYH)**, 3248 Manis Rd, 429-8563. 10 miles SW of Pigeon Forge on Rte 321. Situated in the mountains, 'great place to stay.' $13 AYH, $15 non-AYH.

The park has 3 Visitors Centers the main one being Sugarlands, 2 miles S of Gatlinburg, on Newfound Gap Rd, where you can get maps, and info on the park's unique history and wildlife. 436-1200 is the park info line which links all 3 centres, the others being at **Cades Cove** and **Oconaluftee**. You must get a permit at the center in order to stay overnight at any of the 100 back-country campsites which dot the park. For 3 of the 10 developed campgrounds at **Smokemont, Elkmont** and **Cades Cove**, you have to make rsvs, call (800) 365-2267 enter code GREA, sites $11. The other campgrounds are first-come, first-served, $6-$11. If you decide to stay over in the park, you will need to bring in your own food; there are no restaurants.

Getting around the park requires a car. The best way to see the mountain peaks is to drive along **Foothills Parkway** towards Walland, or along I-40 skirting the park's northeast flank. Only one road, Hwy 441, actually crosses the park, but it sometimes seems more like a superhighway than a drive through the country. Along the way there are numerous turn-outs and trailheads. A ranger can direct you to quiet walkways (trailheads with only one or two parking spaces) which offer more challenging and private trails, or you can stick to the more touristed, but impressive main turn-outs at the well-known vista points. **Cade's Cove** in the western part of the park offers some of the best wildlife, and a collection of historic buildings. Come early if you want to see the animals. Rangers offer guided tours in the evenings from most campgrounds in summer. *www.nps.gov/grsm/index.htm.old.*

CHATTANOOGA   In the southeastern corner of the state, this was the site of an important Civil War battle. Union troops were pinned down under siege here for two months before reinforcements allowed them to break free from the mountains and down into the plains of Georgia. 'A lovely city. One of the nicest places I visited in the USA.'

OF INTEREST
For both the view and the history, take the incline railway up **Lookout Mountain**, site of the famous Battle Above the Clouds. The mountain was an important signalling point for troops in the field. The gradient is 77.9% at its maximum; $7 r/t. There is a **Visitors Center**, 821-7786, at the top which has displays on signalling in the Civil War. Also a 13' x 30' painting, *The Battle of Lookout Mountain*. 'Cheaper to pay for bus right to top and back, $1.50. Bus leaves from near Greyhound.' 'While at the top, follow road to park and see the cannons and memorials, and imagine the battle. The view is still better from up here.' Just over the border with Georgia, on Hwy 27 is **Chickamauga** and **Chattanooga National Military Park**, (706) 866-9241. The Union forces were driven from here into Chattanooga after a fierce battle in which 48,000 men were wounded or killed. The **Battles for Chattanooga Museum**, (423) 821-2812, has an excellent slide and map show of the battle. Open daily 8.30 am-7 pm, last show 6.30 pm If you are heading to Chattanooga from Nashville, you may want to stop at the **Jack Daniel's Distillery**, Hwy 55 in Lynchburg, 759-4221. Free tours daily 8 am-4 pm but don't expect free samples, the distillery of the potent whiskey is in a dry county. 'Best tour in America; the smell of whiskey is all around!'

MEMPHIS   Chuck Berry, WC Handy, Carl Perkins, Jerry Lee Lewis, Elvis Presley and so many others have called Memphis home. Cradled in a bend of the Mississippi River, this city gave birth (via such legends as James Cotton, Howlin' Wolf and Junior Wells) to the urban blues and to rock 'n' roll. U2, Depeche Mode and Paul Simon all have a keen fascination with the place.

After a long spell of urban decay, Memphis has reconstructed its downtown waterfront. Beale Street, famous for its blues clubs, is once again worth visiting. And Mud Island, in the Mississippi River, has several river related attractions reached by monorail. The river connects Memphis with the Deep South, giving the city the most southern feeling of Tennessee's large cities. There are excellent views of the Mississippi as she makes a broad sweep away to the southwest just below the city.

Despite attempts to spruce up the city, however, vast sections remain depressed, reminding the visitor that this is a town where dreams have died. The number one attraction in Memphis is Graceland, where rock 'n' roll king Elvis Presley is buried. And in April, 1968, Martin Luther King, Jr was assassinated at the Lorraine Motel.

ACCOMMODATION
Admiral Benbow Inn, 1220 Union Ave, 725-0630. S/D-$36, $5 key deposit. TV, AC, pool. Take bus 13 down Union. 'In a rough area; not for someone travelling alone.'
B&B in Memphis, 327-6129. Helen Denton provides a listing of hosts who offer B&B services and makes rsvs. D-$95-$125. Advance rsvs of 2 weeks.
Kings Court Motel, 265 Union Ave, 527-4305. Downtown. S-$40, D-$50. TV, AC. Turn right out of station and it's on the right. Discount for longer stays. Mixed reports

GREAT AMERICAN BREAKFASTS

Breakfasts, and their Sunday cousin, 'brunch,' have a special place in American culture. For the great all-American breakfast, try: **Colony Inn,** in the main village, Amana, IA, (319) 622-6270, offers a plentiful spread of all the traditionals. A spicier wake-up call awaits at **Cisco's Bakery, 1511 E Sixth St, Austin, TX,** (512) 478-2420. Its Tex-Mex-breax include huevos rancheros, which will open even the most stubborn lids. **Em Lee's** best offerings are the huge blueberry waffles, Delores and 5th, **Carmel, CA,** (408) 625-6780. **Lou Mitchell's, Jackson St & Jefferson Chicago, IL,** (312) 939-3111, serves up unforgettable Greek toast. Also in **Chicago** the **West Egg Cafe,** 280-8366, does wonderful things with eggs, from breakfast burritos to the 'veggie benedict' special. Near Chicago in **Willmette, IL, Walker Brothers Original Pancake House, 153 Greenbay Rd,** (847) 251-6000, is noteworthy for pancakes of all kinds, with apple at the top of the list. **The Bunnery,** Cathe St in **Jackson, WY,** (307) 733-5474, boasts wonderful buttermilk coffee cake and much more. At **Original Pantry, Los Angeles, CA,** (213) 972-9279 (24 hrs), try hot cakes or French toast. **Sara Beth's, New York City,** (212) 496-6280, makes its own preserves, home-baked muffins, sticky buns and offers a wide range of other breakfast foods. It has 3 locations on Amsterdam Ave north of 80th St, on Madison and 92nd and in the Whitney Museum. In **San Francisco, Doidges,** on Union St, serves unique concoctions: peach and walnut chutney omelettes, and a breakfast casserole with meat, cheese, potato, tomato, sour cream and a poached egg. Open 'til 2 pm Mon-Fri and 3 pm w/ends, (415) 921-2149. For excellent coffee, try **Cafe Trieste** at **North Beach** in SF, where Kerouac probably began his day, (415) 392-6739. **Avignone Fréres,** 1773 Columbia Ave (off 18th St), Washington, DC, (202) 462-2050, serves continental, English and country breakfasts; great omelettes and good homemade muesli. North of the border in **Toronto, Ottawa** and **Montréal,** look for **Peel's Pubs** where you can still get eggs, toast, juice and a bottomless coffee pot for 99¢.

Super 8 Motel, 6015 Maccon Cove Rd, 373-4888. Exit 12C off I-40, 3 miles to airport. D-$59. Eating places nearby, about 12 miles to Graceland.
Motel 6, 1321 Sycamore View Rd, 382-8572. I-40 east exit on Sycamore View Rd South, 25 miles from train station. S/D-$41.
Memphis YMCA, 3548 Walker Ave, near Memphis State University, 323-4505. $69 weekly, $225 p/mth, $30 key deposit. Men only.
Camping: Graceland KOA, 3691 Elvis Presley Blvd, 396-7125. Pitch your tent right next door to the King's house. Sites $19, $21.50 w/hook-up.
T.O Fuller State Park, near Chucalissa Indian Village, 543-7581. $13 for two, XP-$1. 24 hrs. 'Very good.'

FOOD
Memphis is famous for pork BBQ, with over 100 BBQ restaurants.
Corky's, 5259 Poplar Ave, 685-9744, 30 mins from downtown. Renowned both nationally and locally, sit-in or drive-thru. BBQ platters with sides $6-$9.
The North End, 346 N Main St, 526-0319. Southern-style cooking; good, cheap vegetarian dishes. Open 11 am-3 am daily. Live music Wed-Sun.

OF INTEREST
The best sights in Memphis are her many musical shrines, the most holy of which

is Elvis Presley's home, **Graceland**, 3734 Elvis Presley Blvd, 10 miles S of town, 332-3322. Open daily 8 am-6 pm. The 'Platinum Tour', takes in the 23-room, 14-acre mansion, the *Lisa Marie*, a 96-seat airplane/penthouse in the sky, Elvis' tour bus, a stunning car museum, plus the Meditation Garden where Elvis and family are buried. $18.50. The 'Mansion Tour,' includes a 20 min video presentation and tour of the house only, $9, but you will not want to miss the costumes, gold-wrapped grand piano, and 'jungle' playroom. Walking through the amazing 80 ft long 'Hall of Gold' lined with the King's gold records is almost breathtaking. Only by walking down this hallway can you begin to comprehend the enormity of Elvis's success. Catch the #13 bus to Graceland from just outside Greyhound, $1.10. 'last bus on Sats leaves at 5 pm.' 'I toured house hurriedly with 15 middle aged fans brought to tears in midst of disgusting bad taste. Plastic souvenirs are everywhere." Worth it for the experience and insight into a great American icon.' *www.elvis-presley.com*.

Gray Line Elvis Tours, 346-8687. Comprehensive bus tour of Graceland and Elvis 'sites.' Pick up from most downtown hotels.

Audubon Gardens; and the 18 old buildings which make up **Victorian Village**, 680 Adams Ave, 526-1469, pleasant to stroll through and highly recommended, $5, $2 w/student ID. Mon-Sat 10 am-3.30 pm, Sun 1 pm-3.30 pm.

Chucalissa Indian Village, Indian Village Drive, T.O Fuller State Park, 785-3160. Reconstructed 1000-year-old Indian village. Choctaw Indians live on the site and demonstrate Indian crafts. Tue-Sat 9 am-4.30 pm, $4.

Dixon Gallery and Garden, 4339 Park Ave, 761-5250. Good collection of French and American Impressionist paintings. Tue-Sat 10 am-5 pm, Sun 1 pm-5 pm, $7.

Memphis Music & Blues Museum and **Hall of Fame**, 97 S 2nd St, 525-4007. 'Rare blues recordings, posters, guitars, video exhibits, photos and general memorabilia.' 'Not worth the money.' Mon-Thur 10 am-6 pm, Fri and Sat 10 am-9 pm, $7.50. The **Memphis Pink Palace and Planetarium**, 3050 Central Ave, 320-6320, is one of the largest museums in the Southeast, and specializes in science and history. Originally housed in the adjoining pink marble mansion. Mon-Wed 9 am-5 pm, Thur 'til 9 pm (free 5 pm-8 pm), Fri and Sat 'til 10 pm,Sun 12 pm-5 pm. $5.50 museum, $3.50 planetarium. Combo tkt $9.

Mud Island, 576-6595, situated offshore from main downtown area and accessible by a monorail. 52-acre park and entertainment complex devoted to life on the Mississippi River. Park entrance is $4, includes all attractions except **River Museum** $4. Tour a towboat, see a film about disasters on the river, and the Mark Twain talking mannequin that tells you about the river's history. The 5 block long **Mississippi River** scale model, complete with flowing water, follows the river's path to the Gulf of Mexico. Open 10 am-7 pm. Mud Island is also home of the *Memphis Belle*, the first B-17 bomber to successfully complete 25 missions in WW II, and subject of a Hollywood movie, 576-7241, and Tennessee's largest swimming pool. Concerts in the summer, call Ticketmaster, 525-3000 (10 am-5 pm) for details. Big names who have played in the past include Don Henley, Chicago, and Sheryl Crow.

National Civil Rights Center, 450 Mulberry St, 521-9699. Houses exhibits and films on the individuals who led the civil rights movement and has two constantly changing galleries. Adjoining the centre is the **Lorraine Motel**, site of the 1968 assassination of Martin Luther King, Jr. Mon-Sat 9 am-6 pm, Sun 1 pm-6 pm, $6.

The 32-storey, 6-acre **Pyramid**, which opened in autumn 1991, houses the American Music Hall of Fame, the Memphis Music Experience, College Football Hall of Fame and an arena seating 20,000. Tours Mon-Sat 9 am-5 pm, Sun noon-5 pm on the hr.

Sun Studio, 706 Union Ave, 521-0664, launched the career of many legends including Elvis Presley, B.B King, Muddy Waters, Roy Orbison and Johnny Cash. Tours daily 9.30 am-6.30 pm hourly, $8.50.

ENTERTAINMENT

Beale St, 4 blocks of nightclubs, galleries and restaurants. The place where WC Handy blew the notes to make him 'Father of the Blues.' His house is now a museum, 352 Beale St. Live music nightly and outdoor entertainment year-round. Call 526-0110 for festival schedule or check the Friday section of the *Commercial Appeal*. Try **Rum Boogie Cafe**, 182 Beale St, 528-0150, 11.30 am-3 am, $2-$5 cover. During the day, **Abe Schwab**'s, 163 Beale St, 523-9782, an eclectic and amusing drugstore, sells just about anything. 'Lively and bustling rapping, blues and loud records combine to create a unique atmosphere.' Listen to WDIA, 1070 AM, the famous black radio station where B.B. King used to spin records and an important station for the early growth of the blues, and R&B scene. Try to plan your trip for Elvis Week in August, 'in the week he died, there are Elvises everywhere!' 527-2583.

INFORMATION

Visitor Information Center, 340 Beale St, 543-5333. Mon-Sat 9 am-6 pm, Sun noon-6 pm.

TRAVEL

Greyhound, 203 Union Ave, 523-1184/(800) 231-2222. Use caution in this area at night.

Amtrak, 545 S Main St, 526-0052/(800) 872-7245. 'Surrounding area very dangerous, even during the day, watch out!'

Memphis Transit Authority (MATA), Union Ave & Main St, 274-6282. Buses to **Memphis International Airport** depart from 3rd and Beale, Mon-Fri 6.45 am-6.15 pm. Take the Showboat bus and transfer to #32 at the fairground, erratic service, fare $1.10. Hotel Express (HTS), 922-8238, is an airport shuttle and will pick you up from any downtown hotel, 8.30 am-11 pm, $8. For a taxi call 577-7777, $16-$20 o/w.

CANADA

BACKGROUND

BEFORE YOU GO

Citizens and legal, permanent residents of the United States do not need passports to enter Canada as visitors although they may be asked for identification (proof of citizenship or Alien Registration card) or proof of funds at the border. All other visitors entering Canada must have valid passports. Since Immigration officials have enormous discretionary powers, it is wise to be well dressed, clean cut, and the possessor of a return ticket if possible. The following persons do not need a visa if entering only as visitors:

1. British citizens and British overseas citizens who are readmissible to the United Kingdom.
2. Citizens of Andorra, Antigua and Barbuda, Argentina, Australia, Austria, Bahamas, Barbados, Belgium, Belize, Bolivia, Botswana, Costa Rica, Cyprus, Denmark, Dominica, Fiji, Finland, France, Federal Republic of Germany, Greece, Grenada, Honduras, Iceland, Ireland, Israel, Italy, Japan, Kenya, Kiribati, Lesotho, Liechtenstein, Luxembourg, Malawi, Malaysia, Malta, Mexico, Monaco, Nauru, The Netherlands, New Zealand, Nicaragua, Norway, Panama, Papua New Guinea, Paraguay, San Marino, Saudi Arabia, Seychelles Republic, Singapore, Solomon Islands, Spain, St. Kitts and Nevis, St. Lucia, St. Vincent, Surinam, Swaziland, Sweden, Switzerland, Tonga, Trinidad and Tobago, Tuvalu, United States, Uruguay, Vanuatu, Venezuela, Western Samoa, Zambia and Zimbabwe.
3. Citizens of the British dependent territories who derive their citizenship through birth, descent, registration or naturalization in one of the British dependent territories of Anguilla, Bermuda, British Virgin Islands, Cayman Islands, Falkland Islands, Gibraltar, Hong Kong, Montserrat, Pitcairn, St. Helena, or the Turks and Caicos Islands.

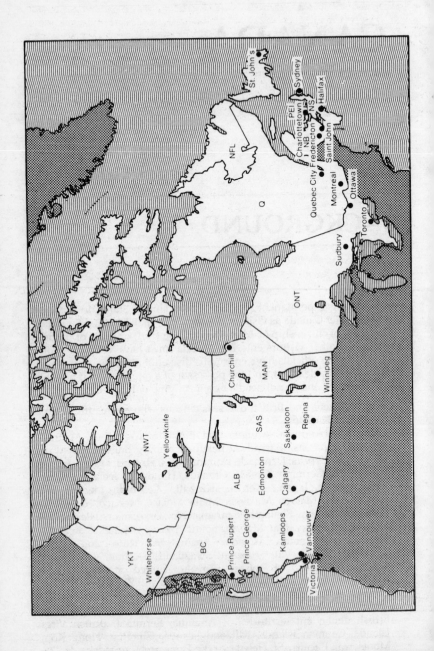

Nationals of all other countries should check their visa requirements with their nearest Canadian consular office. If there is no official Canadian representative in the country, visas are issued by the British embassy or consulate. Those requiring visas must apply before leaving home.

To **work in Canada**, a work visa must be obtained from the Canadian immigration authorities before departure. To qualify you must produce written evidence of a job offer. If you are a student, contact the **BUNAC** London office (0171 251-3472) for information about the *Work Canada* programme which gives eligible students (tertiary level or gap year) temporary work authorisation. Similar opportunities are open to students of a few other countries. Check with your nearest consulate. If you plan to **study in Canada** you will need a special student visa, obtainable from any Canadian consulate. You must produce a letter of acceptance from the Canadian college before the visa can be issued.

Visitors who plan to re-enter the United States after visiting Canada must be sure to keep their US visa documentation and passport to regain entry into the US. (*See Background USA chapter for information on the Visa Waiver programme.*)

Customs permit anyone over 18 to import, duty free, up to 50 cigars, 200 cigarettes and 1kg (2.2lbs) of manufactured tobacco.

Along with personal possessions, any number of individually wrapped and addressed gifts up to the value of $200 (Canadian) each may be brought into the country. Each visitor who meets the minimum age requirements of the province or territory of entry (19 in Newfoundland, Nova Scotia, New Brunswick, Saskatchewan, British Columbia, Ontario, the Yukon and Northwest Territories; 18 elsewhere) may, in addition, bring in 1.1 litres of liquor or wine or 8.5 litres of beer or ale, duty and tax-free.

Further details on immigration, health or customs requirements may be obtained from the nearest High Commission, embassy or consulate.

GETTING THERE
From Europe. Advanced booking charter (ABC) flights are available from London and other British and European cities, to various Canadian cities including Halifax, Ottawa, Toronto and Montréal, and Winnipeg and Vancouver. Also available are several different types of package deal. Canadian Airlines and Air Canada offer packages including anything from bus passes, hotels, coach tours, rail passes, to car and camper wagon rental. The only way to discover the best fare and route for yourself is to get all available information from your travel agent when you are ready to book and check with airlines directly for current promotions or seat sales.

Air Canada and Canadian Airlines offer 14-day advance purchase tickets. Currently the 14-day advance purchase fare from London to Toronto is £495 before July and £539 thereafter. Expect to pay about £495/639 to Vancouver or Calgary.

If you are not able to take advantage of the various advance booking fares, then it may make sense to fly into the USA and continue your journey from there. Using **VUSA fares** and booking before leaving for North America, you could fly on from New York for about US$137, and US$422 to Vancouver. Again, do your research before paying out your money, and bear in mind that travel from the USA, by bus, rail or air, into Canada is very easy and can be very inexpensive (see below). Travellers to Canada via the USA will of course need to obtain a US visa before leaving their home country.

From the USA. You have the choice of bus, train, plane or car, or of course you can simply walk across on foot. It is impossible, within the confines of this Guide, to give all the possible permutations of modes, fares and routes from points within the USA to points within Canada, but, as a rough guide to fares from New York to the major eastern Canadian cities, the current fares to Toronto are: by train, about US$65-$100 o/w, US$130-$195 r/t depending on when you travel; by bus, about US$83 o/w, $168 r/t. Airline prices vary from as little as US$80 to US$209 r/t, depending on dates of travel, even if you only need a one way ticket, buy a round trip, they are always much cheaper. Don't overlook the aforementioned VUSA fares.

Should you cross the border by car it's a good idea to have a yellow 'Non-resident, Interprovincial Motor Vehicle Liability Insurance Card' (phew!) which provides evidence of financial responsibility by a valid automobile liability insurance policy. This card is available in the US through an insurance agent. Such evidence is required at all times by all provinces and territories. In addition Québec's insurance act bars lawsuits for bodily injury resulting from an auto accident, so you may need some additional coverage should you be planning to drive in Québec. If you're driving a borrowed car it's wise to carry a letter from the owner giving you permission to use the car.

CLIMATE AND WHAT TO PACK

Canada's principal cities are situated between the 43rd and 49th parallels, consequently summer months in the cities, and in the southernmost part of the country in general, are usually warm and sunny. August is the warmest month when temperatures are in the 80s. Ontario and the Prairie Provinces are the warmest places and although it can be humid it is never as bad as the humidity which accompanies high temperatures in the US.

Be warned, however, that nights, even in high summer, can be cool and it's advisable to bring lightweight sweaters or jackets. Naturally as you go north, temperatures drop accordingly. Yellowknife in the North West Territories has an *average* August temperature of 45°F (7°C) for instance, and nights in the mountains can be pretty cold. Snow can be expected in some places as early as September, and in winter Canada is very cold and snowy everywhere.

When you've decided which areas of Canada you'll be visiting, note the local climate and pack clothes accordingly. Plan for a variety of occasions, make a list, and then cut it by half! Take easy-to-care-for garments. Permanent press, non-iron things are best. Laundromats are cheap and readily available wherever you go. Remember too that you'll probably want to buy things while you're in North America. Canadians, as well as Americans, excel at producing casual, sporty clothes, T-shirts, etc. But if you're visiting both countries plan to buy in the US, it's decidedly cheaper. The farther north you plan to go and the more time you intend to spend out of doors, the more weatherproof the clothing will need to be. And don't forget the insect repellent.

It's important too to consider the best way of carrying your clothes. Lugging a heavy suitcase is not fun. A lightweight bag or a backpack is possibly best. A good idea is to take a smaller flight-type bag in which to keep a change of clothes and all your most valuable possessions like passport, travellers cheques and air tickets as well, but always hand carry the bag containing your passport and money. For extra safety many travellers like to carry passport documents and travellers cheques in a special neck/waist pouch or wallet. When travelling by bus be sure to keep your baggage within your sights. Make sure it's properly labelled and on the same bus as yourself at every stop!

TIME ZONES
Canada spans six time zones:
1. Newfoundland Standard Time: Newfoundland, Labrador and parts of Baffin Island.
2. Atlantic Standard Time: The Maritimes, Gaspé Peninsula, Anticosti Island, Québec Province east of Comeau Bay, most of Baffin Island and Melville Peninsula.
3. Eastern Standard Time: Québec Province west of Comeau Bay, and all of Ontario east of 90 degrees longitude.
4. Central Standard Time: Ontario west of 90, Manitoba, Keewatin district of Saskatchewan and southeastern part of the province.
5. Mountain Standard Time: rest of Saskatchewan, Alberta, part of Northwest Territories and northeastern British Columbia.
6. Pacific Standard Time: British Columbia (except northeastern portion) and Yukon Territory.

Newfoundland Standard Time is 3 hours 30 minutes after Greenwich, Atlantic Standard Time, 4 hours, and, moving westwards, each zone is one hour further behind Greenwich, so that the Pacific Zone is 8 hours behind.

From the last Sunday in April through the last Sunday in October, Daylight Saving Time is observed everywhere except Thunder Bay and Essex County, Ontario, and the Province of Saskatchewan.

THE CANADIAN PEOPLE
Although Canada, like its neighbour to the south, is a comparatively young country, Canadians now feel that they have finally emerged as a major world power in their own right, and gone are the days when Canada can only function in the shadow of Great Britain or the United States.

It is a mere 131 years since the confederation of 1867. At that time Canada petered out into trackless forest to the north of Lake Superior, and no regular communication existed to the isolated settlements of the Red River in the west. The provinces of Ontario, Québec, Nova Scotia and Prince Edward Island made up the confederation. The other six provinces and two territories only gradually joined. Of the last provinces, Saskatchewan and Alberta were formed in 1905 and Newfoundland entered the federation in 1949, all amazingly recent.

The population of Canada is roughly 29 million, a relatively small population spread over a gigantic land mass. Practically everyone lives along the southern strip of Canada, which borders on the United States. Most of

Canada is still wilderness. The majority of the Canadian people are descendants of white European types, either Gallic or Celtic. There are also Native Peoples (Indians and Eskimoes) and, increasingly as Canada continues to open its doors to the rest of the world, late 20th century Canadian society is rich in cultural and racial diversity, Chinese, Eastern European immigrants, Tamils, Sikhs and other people from all corners of the world.

Canada is rich in natural resources and rich with money in the bank. There are five banks in Canada, and the influence of the big five is very strong, reaching far beyond banking. The Canadian dollar is for all intents and purposes pegged to the value of the US dollar, although, dollar for dollar, it is worth less (about 75%). All its natural wealth did not, however, prevent Canada from joining the ranks of nations suffering from economic recession in the early '90s. Such was the economic state of the nation, that it brought an end to the long rule of the Conservative Party when overwhelmingly, Canadians voted to transfer the economic future of Canada to the care of the Liberal Party.

Continuing to maintain its centre-stage prominence is the perennial problem of Canadian politics, Québec. The Bloc Québecois, formerly led by Lucien Bouchard, whose main pre-election aim was to prepare Canada for Québec's independence, still have the second highest number of seats in parliament. In Canada, the values and traditions of the individual provinces are strong and Canadian politics is renowned for its bitter interprovincial and provincial anti-federal rivalries. Ontario, the most wealthy province and the principal seat of the government, is often at the centre of the controversy, and one of the most bitter power struggles has been between Ontario and Québec.

There are more than 8 million French speaking Canadians; the majority live in Québec. You will notice the phrase 'je me souviens' on the license plates in Québec. This phrase (I remember) refers to the defeat of Montcalm on the Plains of Abraham by General Wolfe. This event signalled the end of a French power base in the New World. The French have felt besieged and encroached upon by the English world ever since, hence their sometimes desperate measures to protect their heritage and remain a 'distinct society' within Canada. Constitutional proposals designed to keep Québec within the federation and everyone else happy as well, have so far failed to gain approval. Though many bitter feelings still stem from the conflict, there is no doubt that this unsubtle blend of French and British influence adds an extra quelque chose to the Canadian cultural picture.

The Canadians have acquired something of a reputation for being puritanical, conformist, humourless and dull! Certainly there's a need there for more than a touch of Gallic charm and chic. Of course this image is largely the face of officialdom and bureaucracy. You will find the Canadian people charming, hospitable and anxious to share their land with you. They will also be most anxious to uphold Canada's uniqueness and to show that Canada is not the same as America—despite the apparent social similarities. Never call a Canadian 'American'!

Try and see something of the *real* Canada. Don't expect to find the stereotypical Mountie on every street corner; Native Indians don't live in teepees, and it doesn't start snowing on September 1st! Visit an Indian reservation, learn about Eskimo native arts and crafts, meet with Canadians as they celebrate at the numerous fairs, rodeos and festivals across the country. (Provincial tourist authorities can supply dates and locations of the various events.) 'Man-made 20th century Canada will impress you, but the Canadian way of life and the natural beauty of the land will really dazzle you.'

HEALTH
Canada does operate a subsidised health service, though on a provincial rather than federal basis. Most provinces will cover most of the hospital and medical services of their inhabitants, although three months' residency is required in Québec and British Columbia. The short-term visitor to Canada, therefore, must be adequately insured *before* arrival.

MONEY
Canadian currency is dollars and cents and comes in the same units as US currency, i.e. penny, nickel, quarter and a dollar, as well as a $2 bill. Canada also has a dollar coin with a great name, the 'loonie'. A loon (bird!) is featured on one side.

US coins are often found among Canadian change and are accepted at par. Most people will give you an exchange rate on US dollars. At present one Canadian dollar is worth US $0.72. To avoid exchange rate problems, it is a good idea to change all your money into Canadian currency or travellers cheques. (At the time of writing; £1 equals approximately CAN$2.23.) *Unless otherwise stated, all prices in this section are in Canadian dollars.*

Travellers cheques are probably the safest form of currency and are accepted at most hotels, restaurants and shops. As well as American Express, Thomas Cook and Barclays Bank (Visa) cheques, you can also purchase cheques issued by Canadian banks before you go. **Credit cards**, Barclaycard and Visa are reciprocal with Chargex, and Access or Eurocard with MasterCard.

Bank hours are generally 10 am-4 pm, Monday to Friday, and often with a later opening on Friday. If you are planning an extensive trip to Canada and the USA, you might consider opening a bank account that offers a cash card which works on both a Canadian and US bank system. The only reference you need to open an account in Canada is cash. It is a simple matter of filling out one form. Since opening an account with a Canadian bank means corresponding with them through the mail, you will want to look into it well in advance of your trip. The Royal Bank of Canada offers a 'client card' that is valid in Canada and at all 'Plus' system machines in the US.

Provincial **sales tax** applies on the purchase of goods and services. In Ontario for instance the rate is eight percent, although there are exceptions such as on shoes under $30, books, groceries, and restaurant meals costing less than $4. On the other hand if your meal costs more than $4, then the tax is ten percent. Canada also has a **VAT tax** of seven percent. Overseas visitors may be able to claim a rebate of this **GST** (Goods and Services Tax) paid on short term accommodation and on consumer goods. Details from: Revenue Canada, Customs & Excise, Visitors' Rebate Program, Ottawa K1A 1J5, 598-2298. Or, once in Canada, phone (800) 66-VISIT.

Tipping, as in the USA, is expected in eating places, by taxi drivers, bell-hops, baggage handlers and the like. Fifteen percent is standard.

COMMUNICATIONS

Mail. Postage stamps can be purchased at any post office or from vending machines (at par) in hotels, drug stores, stations, bus terminals and some newsstands. At present it costs 52¢ to send a letter to a US address and 90¢ to Europe and other overseas destinations. Within Canada the rate is 45¢. Canada Post is *very* slow. Post offices are not generally open at weekends.

If you do not know where you will be staying, have your mail sent care of 'General Delivery'. You then have 15 days to collect.

Telegrams. Not handled by the post office, but sent via a CP or CN telegraph office.

Telephone. Local calls from coin telephones usually cost 25¢. As in the USA (see earlier section, the two systems are very similar) local calls from private phones are usually free. You can direct dial to most places in Canada and the United States and to Europe from some areas of Canada. To check with the operator dial 0. Check local directories for the cheapest times to place a long distance call. Telephone cards are available in Canada.

ELECTRICITY

110v, 60 cycles AC, except in remote areas where cycles vary.

SHOPPING

Stores are generally open until 5.30 or 6 pm with late opening on Thursday or Friday. Usually, only shops located in tourist areas will be open on Sundays. Canada is big on shopping malls (the inventor of which was a Canadian). In the large cities there are huge underground shopping malls so that you do not need to go outside at all in the harsh Canadian winter, but can move underground from mall to mall, or mall to subway or train station.

Good buys in Canada include handicrafts and Eskimo products such as carvings, moccasins, etc. Casual, outdoors or winter wear is recommended too, but if you are visiting Canada and the USA, you will probably be able to buy more cheaply in the USA.

THE METRIC SYSTEM

As already noted above, Canada has gone metric. Milk, wine and gasoline are sold by the litre; groceries in grams and kilograms; clothing sizes come in centimetres, fabric lengths in metres; and, most important, driving speeds are in kilometres p/hour. See the conversion tables in the Appendix.

DRINKING

Liquor regulations come under provincial law, and although it's pretty easy to buy a drink by the glass in a lounge, tavern or beer parlour, it can be be pretty tricky tracking down one of the special liquor outlets which can be few and far between. Beer, wine and spirits can only be bought from a liquor store which will keep usual store hours and be closed on Sundays. The drinking age is 19, except in PEI, Québec, Manitoba and Alberta, where it is 18.

DRUGS

Narcotics laws in Canada are federal, rather than provincial, and it is illegal to possess or sell such drugs as cannabis, cocaine and heroin. Penalties (up to $1,000 or 6 months in jail for a first offence) are the same for offences involving marijuana as for heroin, etc.

CIGARETTES

Currently cost about $4 (perhaps this is a good time to give up the weed!) for a packet of 25. Foreign brands available.

PUBLIC HOLIDAYS

New Year's Day	1st January
Good Friday/Easter Monday	Variable
Victoria Day	3rd Monday in May
Canada Day	1st July
Civic Holiday	4th Aug in all provinces except Québec, Yukon and Northwest Territories
Labour Day	1st Monday in September
Thanksgiving Day	2nd Monday in October
Remembrance Day	11th November
Christmas Da	25th December
Boxing Day	26th December

INFORMATION

In *Britain* contact Canada House, Trafalgar Square, London SW1, 0171 629-9492. In *Canada* tourist information centres abound and are indicated on highway maps. Especially recommended is the information published by the provincial tourist offices. If you plan to spend any length of time in one province it is well worth writing to them and asking for their free maps, guides and accommodation information.
On the Internet: citynet/countries/canada or canada.gc.ca.

Provincial Tourist Offices

Northwest Territories Arctic Tourism, Governments of the Northwest Territories, Box 1320, Yellowknife, NWT X1A 2L9, (403) 873-7200 or tollfree (800) 661-0788.
Nova Scotia Department of Tourism, PO Box 130, Halifax, NS B3J 2M7, (902) 424-5000, from the US (800) 341-6096, or from Canada (800) 565-0000. Visitor Services Division of *Prince Edward Island*, PO Box 940, Charlottetown, PEI C1A 7M5, (902) 368-4444, in US (800) 565-0267, in Maritimes (800) 565-7421.
Ontario Travel, 9th floor, 77 Bloor St W, Toronto, Ontario M7A 2R9, (416) 965-4008, or tollfree from Canada and continental US, (800) 668-2746.
Super, Natural British Columbia, (800) 663-6000. Parliament Buildings, Victoria, BC, V8V 1X4. *Tourism BC*, Vancouver office, (604) 660-2861.
Newfoundland and Labrador Tourist Branch, Department of Tourism and Culture, PO Box 8730, St John's, Newfoundland A1B 4K2, (709) 729-2830 or from US and Canada (800) 563-6353.
Tourism New Brunswick, PO Box 6000, Fredericton, New Brunswick E3B 5HI, or (800) 561-0123.

Tourisme Québec, CP 979, Montréal, Quebec H3C 2W3, (514) 873-2015, from US and Canada (800) 363-7777.
Tourism Saskatchewan, 500/1900 Albert St, Regina, Saskatchewan S4P IL9, (306) 787-2300, (800) 667-7191.
Tourism Yukon, PO Box 2703, Whitehorse, Yukon Y1A 2C6, (403) 667-5340, (800) 661-0494 in Canada only.
Travel Alberta, 3rd Floor, 10155 102 St, Edmonton, Alberta T5J 4L6, (403) 427-4321, (800) 661-8888.
Travel Manitoba, 7th Floor, 155 Carlton St, Winnipeg, Manitoba R3C 3H8, (204) 945-3777, or from US and Canada (800) 665-0040.

THE GREAT OUTDOORS

Hardly surprising with all those wide open spaces, that Canadians are very outdoors minded. Greenery is never far away and the best of it has been preserved in national parks. There are many national parks in Canada ranging in size from less than one to more than 17,000 square miles, and in type from the immense mountains and forests of the west to the steep cliffs and beaches of the Atlantic coastline. In addition there are many fine provincial parks and more than 600 national historic parks and sites.

Entrance to the national parks costs $4-$5 for a one-day pass, $10-$12 for four days, or $35 for the season. All but the most primitive offer camping facilities, hiking trails, and facilities for swimming, fishing, boating and other such diversions. Most of the national parks are dealt with in this Guide. For more detailed information we suggest you write to the individual park or to: Parks Canada, Ottawa, Ontario K1A 1G2, for a copy of the free booklet *National Parks of Canada*, or visit their web site *parkscanada.pch.gc.ca/parks/main-e.htm*. A list of major parks follows:

Auguittuq, Quebec
Banff, Alberta.
Cape Breton Highlands, Nova Scotia.
Elk Island, Alberta.
Forillon, Québec.
Fundy, New Brunswick.
Georgian Bay Islands, Ontario.
Glacier, British Columbia.
Gros Morne, Newfoundland.
Jasper, Alberta.Wood Buffalo,
Kejimkujik, Nova Scotia.
Kootenay, British Columbia.
Kulane, Yukon.
La Mauricie, Quebec

Mount Revelstoke, British Columbia.
Pacific Rim, British Columbia.
Point Pelee, Ontario.
Prince Albert, Saskatchewan.
Prince Edward, Prince Edward Island.
Pukashwa, Ontario
Riding Mountain, Manitoba.
St Lawrence Islands, Ontario.
Terra Nova, Newfoundland.
Waterton Lakes, Alberta.
Western Territories:
Yoho, British Columbia.
Nahanni, Northwest Territories.

MEDIA AND ENTERTAINMENT

Canada until recently was viewed as a cultural wasteland. Even now, for preference, Canadians watch US or British television programmes and read US or European magazines. Traditionally, talented Canadians in order to succeed, moved from Canada to the USA. However, this has begun to change.

This is partly because the government has legislated a minimum level of Canadian content in radio and television and implemented a strict 'hire

Canadian' policy throughout the arts and entertainment business. Canadian culture is also flourishing more as a reflection of newfound Canadian pride. Visitors will be surprised at the high standards in ballet, the theatre and classical music. Folk music thrives too as do the visual arts and Canada boasts a number of exceptional museums and restorations well worth visiting for a glimpse of Canada past. There is also a huge annual festival scene in Canada. From major cities to small towns, from Shakespeare to jazz, you'll find a celebration of some kind wherever you go.

SPORT AND RECREATION

Sport has always played an important role in the life of Canadians, but only recently has Canada come into its own as a sporting nation, ranking among the top 15 countries in the world. Canada has hosted almost every major sports competition: the summer and winter Olympics, Commonwealth Games, Pan-American Games and World University Games. Winnipeg has officially submitted its candidacy to host the 1999 Pan-American Games, and Québec City is competing to host the 2002 winter Olympics.

Canadians love to camp, hike, fish, ski and generally enjoy the outdoors. Winter sports (naturally) are very popular from ice-skating to snowmobiling. Ice hockey is the biggie for watching. There is a Canadian version of American football and baseball is also very popular. In baseball, the Toronto Blue Jays won the world series in 1992 and 1993. Surprisingly perhaps, the national game is lacrosse.

ON THE ROAD

ACCOMMODATION

For general hints on finding the right accommodation for you, please read the 'Accommodation' section for the USA. The basic rules are the same.

All the provincial tourist boards publish comprehensive accommodation lists. These are obtainable from Canadian government tourist offices or directly from provincial tourist boards and have details of all approved hotels, motels and tourist homes in each town. These are excellent guides and are highly recommended.

Hotels and Motels: Always plenty to choose from around sizeable towns or cities, but if you're travelling don't leave finding accommodation until too late in the day. In less populated areas distances between motels can be very great indeed. The major difference between the hotel/motel picture here and in the US is that the budget chains like Days Inn and Motel 6 have not yet made it to Canada in force. The exceptions are Friendship Inns, Journey's End Hotels, Days Inns in Ontario, and Relax Inns in Alberta.

Many highway motels will often have restaurants attached. The local tourist bureau will usually have a list of local hotels and motels. However, for the budget traveller, it is likely that a tourist home will nearly always be a less expensive alternative.

Tourist Homes: A bit like bed and breakfast places in Britain and Europe, only without the breakfast. In other words a room in a private home. Usually you share a bathroom and your room will be basic but perfectly adequate. Such establishments are scattered very liberally all over Canada with prices starting around $25-$30. Certainly if hostels are not for you, and your budget doesn't quite stretch to a motel, then these are the places to look for. Again, the local tourist bureau will be able to provide you with a list of possibilities.

Bed and Breakfasts: There is now also the firmly established bed and breakfast circuit. Singles from about $35, doubles $35-$80. Several guides to bed and breakfast establishments (town and country locations) are published in Canada and can be picked up in bookshops everywhere. Otherwise, the local tourist office will provide listings. (See also under *Guest Farms and Ranches*). Bed and Breakfast is often your best bet for a cheap room in remoter areas where hotel/motel accommodation is expensive.

Hostels: The Canadian Youth Hostels Association (CYHA), has adopted the International Youth Hostel Federation blue triangle and become Hostelling International Canada. The association has over 80 member hostels across the country with at least one hostel in each major city. The National Parks in Alberta are well covered. You can save money with an International Youth Hostel Card from your own country since non-members usually pay about $2-$5 more. There is no limit to a stay.

For detailed information and lists of hostels write to: HI-Canada, 205 Catherine St, Suite 400, Ottawa, Ontario, K2P IC3, (617) 237-7884, or else enquire via the association in your own country. Annual membership is $27. For information on independent hostels contact Backpackers Hostel Canada, (807) 983-2047, (800) 663-5777. Or, write to Thunder Bay International Hostel, RR#13, Box 10-1, Thunder Bay, Ontario, P7B 5E4. *http://www.microage-tb.com/user/jones/hostel.htm*

YM/YWCAs: Y's have weight lifting machines, pools and aerobics classes for those in need of an exercise fix, but standards vary. Cheaper and often better, are tourist homes. Worth considering is the Y's Way travel voucher scheme. Contact the Y's Way, 224 E 47th St, New York, NY 10017 or phone (212) 755-2410 for information. For a complete list and information on Canadian Y's: YMCA National Council, 2160 Yonge St, Toronto, Ontario M4S 2A1, (416) 485-9447

University Accommodation: There is much campus housing available during the summer. Look particularly for student owned co-operatives in cities such as Toronto which provide a cheapish service, often with cooking facilities. University housing services and fraternities will often be able to help you also. In general, college housing starts at about $20 single but can be as high as $35 single. Staying on campus usually gives access to all the usual facilities including cafeterias, lounges, etc., and often a pool and gymnasium/athletic fields. The drawback about campus accommodation is that it is usually not available after mid-late August since that is when Canadian students begin returning to college.

Camping: Canadians are very fond of camping and during the summer, sites in popular places will always be very full. Usually, however, campgrounds are not as spacious as those in the USA and less trouble is taken with the positioning of individual sites. Prices are about the same, $8-$15 per site. There are many provincial park campgrounds, as well as sites in the national parks and the many privately operated grounds usually to be found close to the highways. Campgrounds are marked on official highway maps.

The Rand McNally *Campground and Trailer Park Guide* covers Canada as well as the USA. Also, the Canadian Government Office of Tourism publishes guides on camping across Canada: Canadian Government Office of Tourism, 150 Kent St, Ottawa, Ontario. The much recommended KOA now have about 50 campgrounds in Canada. Details from: KOA Inc, PO Box 30558, Billings MT 59114, (406) 248-7444. Both the provincial tourist guides and local tourist bureaux are other sources of information on where to find a campground. The government-run parks tend to have the more scenic tent sites. Most camp sites are open summer months only, July to September.

For real outdoor camping in Canada you need a tent with a flyscreen. Black flies and mosquitoes are a serious problem in June and July and the further north you go the worse the little darlings are. It gets cold at night too as early as August, so be prepared for colder temperatures and wetter weather than in the US. Other hazards of camping in Canada include bears and 'beaver fever', a rare intestinal parasite (*giardia lamblia*).

Guest Ranches and Farms: Many farms accept paying guests during the summer. Prices vary and in some cases guests are encouraged to help about the farm. For information write for *Farm, Ranch and Country Vacations*, Farm and Ranch Vacations Inc, PO Box 698, Newfoundland, NJ 07435, USA. For reservations and information (in the US) call (800) 252-7899 (sending US$17 from the UK), or Ontario Farm Vacations, Ontario Travel, 77 Bloor St W, 9th Fl, Toronto, Ontario M7A 2R9.

FOOD

How much you spend per day on food will obviously depend upon your taste and your budget, but you can think in terms of roughly $2-$5 on breakfast, from $4 on lunch, and anything from $6 upwards on dinner. It is customary in Canada to eat the main meal of the day in the evening from about 5 pm onwards. In small, out-of-the-way towns, any restaurants there are may close as early as 7 pm or 8 pm. Yes, McDonalds does operate in Canada, as do several other US fast food chains.

Canadian food is perhaps slightly more Europeanised than American and in the larger cities you will find a great variety of ethnic restaurants, any thing from Chinese through Swedish and French. In Québec, of course, French-style cooking predominates and in the Atlantic provinces sea food and salmon are the specialities. Remember to try Oka Cheese in Québec and wild, ripe berries everywhere in the summer.

CANADIAN WINTERSPORTS

Canada is a winter wonderland of sports. The country's vast, untamed wilderness offers over 300 ski areas and some of the world's best snowboarding, downhill and cross-country skiing. Canadians are also mad on ice hockey.

EAST Canada's eastern resorts are a paradise for both downhill and cross country enthusiasts and tend to be a good deal cheaper than those in the west.

Marble Mt, Corner Brook, Newfoundland, (709) 637-7600. Offers the best spring skiing east of the Rockies. Lots of trails and plenty of powder. Day pass $25. Ontario and Québec is where the real action is.

Blue Mt, Collingwood, Ontario, (705) 445-0231. This is the biggest and highest ski area in S Ontario. Great diversity of runs with new ones being cleared regularly. 'Check out Planet Collingwood, the hottest nightspot in town.' Day pass $10, $27 after Dec 19th.

Loch Lomond, Thunder Bay, Ontario, (807) 475-7787. One of the best hills in Thunder Bay with a good cross section of different skill level terrain. Day pass $27, $22 w/student ID.

Mt St Louis Moonstone, Coldwater, Ontario, (705) 835-2112. Downhill and cross-country trails, good spot for beginners. 'The hills are always groomed to perfection and lift lines are never too busy.' Day pass $30.

Horseshoe Resort, Barrie, Ontario, (705) 835-2790. This is the busiest resort in the Barrie area, quieter times are during the week and at night. Good skiing for all levels. 'Helpful staff and well maintained runs.' Day pass $33, $28 w/student ID.

Mt St Anne, Beaupre, Québec, (418) 827-4561. Great downhill, cross-country and 24hr skiing, plenty of variety and inexpensive. 'A hidden treasure'. Day pass $43.

Stoneham, Stoneham, Québec, (418) 848-2411. A medium sized resort with trails for every level. 'Great variety of terrain and great nightlife around the resort'. Day pass $36, $25 w/student ID.

Mt Tremblant, Mt Tremblant, Québec, (800) 461-8711. Tremblant is the ultimate definition for tons of snow, countless number of trails and variety of terrain. 'Peaceful, scenic cross-country trails'. Good employment opportunities. Day pass $46.

WEST The Rockies are *the* place to ski in the west.

Lake Louise, Lake Louise, Alberta, (403) 522-3555. Plenty of snow and plenty of challenge, huge diversity of terrain, beautiful scenery and well groomed runs. Good employment opportunities in surrounding hotels and restaurants. 'An absolute treat for skiers and snowboarders, their bowls are the best!' Day pass $46, $38 w/student ID.

Sunshine Village, Banff, Alberta, (403) 762-6500. Good powder and wide range of trails, excellent for beginners. Good employment opportunities. Day pass $42, $35 w/student ID.

Fortress Mt, Kananaskis Village, Alberta, (403) 591-7108. Heaven for snowboarders, lots of natural halfpipes, powder, trees and no one to bug you. 'Love it.' Day pass $32, $25 w/student ID.

Big White, Kelowna, BC, (250) 765-3101. Perfect for intermediates, one of the best mountains for powder with wide groomed runs. Recently expanded with lots of new facilities and fast lifts. Day pass $46.

Whistler/Blackcomb, Whistler, BC. Has been recognised as N America's best, most hard-core ski/snowboard resort. The most challenging peaks and the highest vertical rise in the north. Massive diversity of trails and outstanding facilities. 'Go to heaven and ski like hell.' 'Expensive but worth every penny.' Day pass $51, $38 w/student ID.

Silver Star Mt, Vernon, BC, (250) 542-0224. Home of the Canadian National Cross Country Team, with over 90 km of groomed trails. Challenging downhill runs for all levels and, of course, outstanding cross-country conditions. Day pass $45.

Red Mt, Rossland, BC, (250) 362-7384. One of Canada's oldest resorts, still challenging to both skiers and snowboarders. Good powder, tree skiing, quiet lifts. 'Radical expert terrain but most of it is unmarked'. Day pass $38, $31 w/student ID. For info on all mentioned resorts and more, *www.goski.com/canada.htm* or, *www.Skinetcanada.com/*.

ICE HOCKEY Hockey is by far Canada's most popular spectator sport and one of the country's most widely played recreational sports. The **National Hockey League (NHL)**, is a professional league comprising of 26 N American teams including 6 Canadian based teams. Although many teams are located in the US, the majority of NHL players are Canadian. The **Calgary Flames**, **Edmonton Oilers**, **Montreal Canadiens**, **Ottawa Senators**, **Toronto Maple Leafs**, and the **Vancouver Canuks**, slug it out among the top teams for the **Stanley Cup**, a trophy symbolic of hockey supremacy in N America. Hockey season runs from Oct-Jun. *www.nhl.com/*.

Ringette A relatively new sport that has attracted a large following in Canada is Ringette. More than 50,000 ringette competitors play on approximately 2500 teams. Played mostly by women, ringette is similar to hockey, but a rubber ring replaces the puck.

Skating Canada also excels at figure skating. A vast network of clubs across throughout the country has produced a long line of world and Olympic medalists including Barbara Ann Scott and Kurt Browning. As a spectator sport figure skating has steadily increased in popularity over the past several years. Although not as widely practised, speed skating has produced Canada's greatest Winter Olympian, Gaetan Boucher. For more general sports info, *http://.gc.ca/*.

TRAVEL
To be read in conjunction with the USA Background travel section.

Bus: Bus travel is usually the cheapest way of getting around, fares generally being less than half the airfare. Every region in Canada has different bus companies, Gray Coach, Acadian Lines, Greyhound and Voyageur are the largest.

The Greyhound Ameripasses are only valid in Canada on specific routes, eg. Buffalo or Detroit to Toronto. There are however two unlimited travel Greyhound Canada passes, the **Canada Pass** for travel west of Ottawa/Toronto and the **Canada Pass Plus** which covers the whole of Canada. Rates for the Canada Pass are: for a 7 day pass, £99; 15 days costs

£135; 30 days is £175 and 60 days costs £230. On the Canada Pass Plus, a 15 day pass is £165; 30 days is £215 and 60 days is £265. The passes must be purchased before departure for Canada and are non-refundable once any portion of the pass has been used.

As with the USA, Greyhound have combined with Hostelling International to produce the **Go Canada** and **Go Canada Plus Passes** combining coupons for bus travel and hostel accommodation for the period of travel. You have to purchase the pass before leaving for Canada and must be a member of Hostelling International. For 15 nights it's £310/£340 and for 30 nights it's £455/£495. Passes can be bought from travel agents, Greyhound or BUNAC in London.

Always check for the cheapest 'point-to-point' fare or excursion fare when making just one or two journeys without a bus pass. Toronto to the west coast, for instance, could cost about $212 (Canadian) one way.

One difference between the US and Canadian Greyhound operations worth noting is in baggage handling. Unlike the USA, the Canadian bus companies will never check baggage through to a destination without its owner. Bags cannot be sent on ahead, for instance, if you are simply seeking a way to dump them for a day or so while you see the sights. Lockers are usually available at bus stations, and don't forget to collect your bags from the pavement once they have been off-loaded by the driver.

Car: The Canadian is as attached to his car as is his American cousin. In general roads are better, speed limits are higher and there are fewer toll roads than south of the border. Canadian speed limits have gone metric and are posted everywhere in kilometres p/hr. Thus, 100 km p/hr is the most common freeway limit, 80 km p/hr is typical on two-lane rural highways, and 50 km p/hr operates most frequently in towns. Canadians, of course, drive on the right!

When considering **buying a car** for the summer, it may be as well to bear in mind that car prices are higher in Canada than in the US. Anyone planning to visit both countries by car would clearly be well advised to buy in the US first. You'll need to check that the US insurance policy is good for Canada too. It's a help to have a yellow 'Non-Resident Interprovincial Motor Vehicle Liability Insurance Card'. This is obtainable through any US insurance agent.

Note that the wearing of **seat belts** by *all* persons in a vehicle is compulsory in British Columbia, Manitoba, New Brunswick, Newfoundland, Nova Scotia, Ontario, Québec and Saskatchewan.

Car rental will cost from about $45 p/day, with free mileage up to a point and a cost p/km of about 5¢-20¢ thereafter. Or call Rent-A-Wreck, who charge $15 p/day plus kilometrage. To hire a Volkswagen camper would cost about twice as much, but of course you wouldn't be paying for accommodation. As always, shop around for the best available rates.

Third party **insurance** is compulsory in all Canadian provinces and territories and can be expensive. 'Insurance to cover a VW camper worth $1000 with a driver 24 years of age cost $155 for three months.' British, other European and US drivers licences are officially recognised by the Canadian authorities. Membership of the AA, RAC, other European motoring organisations, or the AAA in the US, entitles the member to all the services of the **Canadian AA** and its member clubs free of charge. This includes travel info, itineraries, maps and tour books as well as emergency road services, weather reports and accommodation reservations. (NB: The US AAA also publishes excellent tour guides for Canada.)

Gas is now sold by the litre and costs up to 50¢-60¢ a litre. Gas stations can be few and far between in remoter areas and it is wise to check your gauge in the late afternoon before the pumps shut off for the night.

One **hazard** to be aware of when driving in Canada is the unmarked, and even the marked, railroad crossing. Many people are killed every year on railroad crossings. Trains come and go so infrequently in remote areas that it's simply never possible to know when one will arrive. Be particularly alert at night.

Air: The two major Canadian airlines, Air Canada and Canadian Airlines, offer different discount fares. There are 14-day and 21-day advance fares, touchdown fares, and late night fares to name a few. Canadian Airlines offer an airpass with 3-8 coupons (on a confirmed basis only) in a range of $493-$850 for high season fares for those flying into Canada on Canadian Airlines. The rule is that when you make a stopover, you give up a coupon. If using another airline, it's called North American Unlimited and costs $545-$895 high season.

Air Canada offers **VUSA fares**, which offer discounts of 25-30% on fares, however, you must book in advance. Also available is the **Canada Regional Airpass** which covers Canada east of Winnipeg. The 7-day Pass costs £145, the 14-day pass costs £195 and a 3-week pass costs £245. A 7-day **National Pass** costs £189, the 14-day pass costs £249 and a 3-week pass costs £299. Both passes can be purchased from Airpass Sales, Enterprise House, 4 Station Parade, Chipstead, Surrey, CR5 3TE, (0173) 755-5300. These passes must be purchased before leaving the UK. BUNAC also sell the passes, as do **Horizon Airpasses**, which cover parts of western Canada and the USA. A 7-day pass costs £139, the 14-day pass costs £175 and a 3-week pass costs £259. U.K. students (with an ISIC card) may be able to get student discounts through Travel CUTS, The Canadian Universities Travel Service Ltd, 171 College St, Toronto, (416) 977-3703 or (800) 268-9044 (in Ontario), or at any of their other offices throughout Canada.

Rail: One of the conditions for the entry of British Columbia into the Confederation was the building of the Canadian Pacific Railway, and with the completion of the track in 1885, Canada as a transcontinental nation finally became a reality. Later came Canadian Northern and the Grand Trunk Pacific, nationalised into Canadian National in 1923 after both companies had gone bankrupt.

Until 1978, Canada possessed two rail systems, the privately operated but viable Canadian Pacific, and the state-owned, often floundering, Canadian National. With the formation of VIA Rail Canada in 1978, the routes and fare structures of both became totally integrated. To cross Canada by train was quite an adventure, one of the world's great railway journeys.

Unfortunately, the Canadian government has now scrapped the famous transcontinental track through the Rockies via Banff as part of a mammoth, more than 50 per cent cut in rail services nationwide. However, the more northern route via Jasper still operates but only three times a week. The one way fare coast-to-coast, is about $450.

The service cuts mean that many small, more remote communities can no longer be reached by train.

In the East, VIA Rail runs high speed *Rapido* trains along the so-called Ontario-Québec corridor connecting Montréal with Windsor, Ontario. The Toronto to Montréal trip takes less than 5 hours and costs around $65-$80. System-wide various discount fares are available. These vary according to the time of year, day of the week, length of stay, age of traveller, etc, so always enquire about the 'cheapest possible fare' when planning a trip. If you have a student ID card, be sure to show it.

Then there is the **CANRAIL Pass**. This gives unlimited travel on VIA trains and is good value for someone planning to do a lot of travelling. Currently, VIA offers a pass which is valid for 12 days within a 30-day period. During peak travel times (1st June-15th October), for the entire system a student pass costs $495 and an adult pass is $569. Extra days (up to 3), are $43 (student), and $48 (adult). Low season rates are: student, $339; adult, $369. At the time of writing VIA say that a combined VIA/Amtrak **North American Rail Pass** will be available in 1998. This would cover travel on both rail systems and the peak student fare is CAN$625 (adult – $895).

The trains are comfortable, civilised, have good eating facilities and are easy to sleep on. A much recommended way to travel. The pass can only be bought overseas and on production of a passport. Long Haul Leisurerail, PO Box 113, Peterborough PE1 1LE, (0173) 333-5599, are the main agents in the UK. Or call VIA up on the Internet: *www.viarail.ca.*

Hitching: Thumbing is illegal on the major transcontinental routes, but it is common to see people hitching along access ramps. Check the 'local rules' before setting out. In some cities there are specific regulations regarding hitching, but in general the cognoscenti say that hitchers are not often hassled and that Canada is one of the best places to get good lifts, largely because rides tend to be long ones—even if you do have to wait a long time on occasions.

The Trans Canada Highway can be rough going during the summer months so look for alternative routes, for example the Laurentian Autoroute out of Montréal, and the Yellowhead Highway out of Winnipeg. Wawa, north of Sault Ste Marie, Ontario, is another notorious spot where it is possible to be stranded for days. The national parks can also be tricky in summer when 'there are too many tourists going nowhere'.

Hiking and Biking: Trail walking is one of Canada's best offers. There is so much wilderness space that it really would be a crying shame to spend any length of time in the country without experiencing something of The Great Outdoors. Some of the best, of course, is in the national parks. A good guide to hiking trails in the national parks is *The Canadian Rockies Trail Guide: A Hiker's Manual to the National Parks*, by Bart Robinson and Brian Patton.

Information is also available from the individual parks. For information on the best routes for cyclists, contact the Canadian Cycling Association at 333 River Road, Vanier, Ontario K1L 8H9, (613) 748-5629.

Urban Travel: Town and city bus or subway fares are generally charged at a standard rate. Exact fares are generally required and are around 90¢-$1.10, and upwards. Transfers, allowing passengers to change routes or bus to subway routes, are generally available in cities.

Taxis usually are pretty expensive unless shared by two or three people. In rural areas (much of Canada outside the major population centres) there is little in the way of public transport and taxis (failing ownership of a car!) may be the only way. Check under individual towns and cities for more detailed information on local travel.

FURTHER READING

History
The very readable books of Pierre Barton including: *The National Dream, Klondike, The Promised Land* and *Arctic Grail*

General
My Discovery of the West, Sunshine Sketches of a Small Town, by Stephen Leacock
O Canada, Edmund Wilson
The Oxford Companion to Canadian History and Literature, ed. A. J. M. Smith

Fiction
Maria Chapdelaine, Louis Hémon
The novels of Margaret Atwood, Margaret Laurence, Carol White and Robertson Davies

Travel
For extended stays in Canada we recommend purchase of one of several available in-depth guides to Canada, e.g. *Lonely Planet*.

Want to know more? Check out these sites. *http/citynet/countries/canada* or *http://canada.gc.ca/*.

MARITIME PROVINCES AND NEWFOUNDLAND

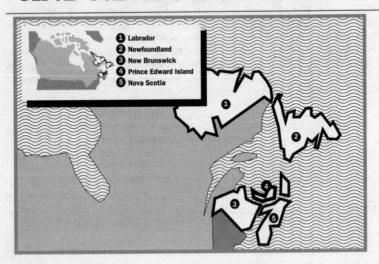

1. Labrador
2. Newfoundland
3. New Brunswick
4. Prince Edward Island
5. Nova Scotia

These Atlantic-lapped provinces were the early stop-off points for eager explorers from Europe and subsequently became one of the main battle-grounds for their colonial ambitions. The chief combatants were Britain and France and as a result, strong English, French, and Scottish threads run through Maritime culture and history. Indeed, the first recorded visitor from Europe to North America was Prince Henry St Clair, who arrived here from Scotland in 1398, almost a century before Columbus set foot on the continent.

Look for the 600th Anniversary celebrations of his voyage throughout the entire Maritime Provinces during the summer of 1998.

The story of the Maritimes is the story of a people who have fished and travelled and died at sea. The Grand Banks, the huge, shallow Continental Shelf ranging from Massachusetts to Newfoundland, is the most fertile fishing ground in the world. The economy of the Maritimes is based on forestry, tourism, and the Grand Banks, with more fishery-related PhDs per capita than almost anywhere in the world.

The region is beautiful in the summer, full of lake and sea swimming, excellent seafood, forest hikes and breathtaking scenery. Winters are long and hard with much snow, ice and general wintry chills to contend with! Spring comes late and Autumn, as elsewhere in northeastern North America, is colourful and spectacular. Summer or autumn are recommended as the best times to visit the Maritimes.

NEW BRUNSWICK

New Brunswick is bounded mostly by water, with over 1300 miles of coastline—a constant reminder of the importance of the sea in this Maritime province. To the west, it is bordered by Maine, Québec and part of the Appalachian mountain range. Inland, there is rugged wilderness accounting for the popularity of huntin', fishin', campin' and hikin'.

The Vikings are said to have come here some thousand years ago, but when French explorer Jacques Cartier arrived in 1535, the area was occupied by Micmac and Maliseet Indians. Later, the province became a battleground for French Acadian and British Loyalist forces. In 1713, by the Treaty of Utrecht, New Brunswick was ceded to the British along with the rest of Acadia (PEI and Nova Scotia). Many of the French fled south to the United States and settled in Louisiana. There, 'Acadian' was corrupted into 'Cajun', a word still used to describe the French in Louisiana. As a result of this early French influence, New Brunswick today remains 35 per cent Acadian, most in the north and the east of the province.

While in New Brunswick, be sure to sample the great variety of shellfish available, as well as the province's speciality—fiddleheads. Also, try a pint of the local Moosehead beer—although it is now available nationally, the sea air of New Brunswick itself is essential for a successful taste test.
The telephone area code is 506.

FREDERICTON The City of Elms is the capital city of the province and its commercial and sporting centre. Clean and green, this is 'a good Canadian town' which got started in 1783, when a group of Loyalists from the victorious colonies to the south made their home here, naming the town after the second son of George III. They chose for their new town a spot where there had previously (until the Seven Years War) been a thriving Acadian settlement. During hostilities the settlement was reduced by the British and the inhabitants expelled.

Fredericton's great benefactor was local boy and press baron, Lord Beaverbrook. His legacies include an art gallery, a theatre, and the university library. The latter is named Bonar Law Bennett Library, after two other famous sons of New Brunswick, one of whom became Prime Minister of Great Britain, and the other Prime Minister of Canada.

The town is situated inland on the broad St John River, the 'Rhine of America', once an Indian highway and a major commercial route to the sea. The whole area is one of scenic river valleys and lakes.

ACCOMMODATION
Elms Tourist Home, 269 Saunders St, 454-3410. S-$35, D-$45, XP-$10.
University of New Brunswick, Residents Admin. Bldg, Bailey Dr, (a red brick building with four clocks) 453-4891. S-$29, $18 w/student ID, D-$21pp, $15 pp w/student ID, $80 weekly, students only. 24 hrs. Close to downtown. 'Friendly and helpful.'
Camping: **Mactaquac Provincial Park**, 12 miles W on Hwy 2, 363-4747. Sites $17 for four, $19.50 w/hook up, kitchen shelters, showers.

FOOD
BBQ Barn, 540 Queen St, 455-2742. Inexpensive hot-spot, $4.25-$12. Daily 11 am-11 pm.

Boyce Farmers' Market, George St, 444-3885. Sat only 6 am-1 pm. Have breakfast or an early lunch in the market hall, then check out the fresh produce and local arts and crafts.

Café du Monde, 610 King St, 457-5534. Licensed cafe, seafood and good vegetarian food. Bfast $2-$6, lunch $4-$9, dinner $4-$15. Mon-Fri 7.30 am-10 pm, Sat 9 am-11 pm, Sun 11 am-10 pm.

Crispin's, King's Place Mall, King St, 459-1165. Deli, bakery with cafe. Great for cheap lunches, soups, salads, sandwiches, nothing over $4. Mon-Fri 6.30 am-5.30 pm, Thur & Fri 'til 9 pm, Sat 9 am-5 pm.

Lunar Rogue, King St, 450-2065. Good pub food and some interesting variations, $5-$10. Huge order of Rogues Nachos, $4.25. Live bands. Daily 11 am-midnight.

OF INTEREST
Beaverbrook Art Gallery, 703 Queen St, 458-8545. Has works of Dali, Reynolds, Gainsborough, Churchill, etc, plus good section on history of English china. A gift to the province from the press baron. Free tours daily Mon-Sat 10 am. Summer Mon-Fri 9 am-5 pm, Sat 10 am-5 pm, Sun noon-5 pm. Closed Mon in winter. $3, $1 w/student ID, 50¢ w/ISIC card.

Christ Church Cathedral, off Queen St at Church St, 450-8500. Worth a visit for its beautiful stained-glass windows. Free tours. Summer: Mon-Fri 9 am-8 pm, Sat 9 am-8 pm, Sun 12 pm-6 pm, otherwise 8.30 am-5.30 pm. Rsvs required.

Kings Landing Historical Settlement, at Prince William, 23 miles W of Fredericton on Rte 2, exit 259, 363-4999. Re-created pioneer village showing the life of rural New Brunswick as it was in the 1800s. Features homes, school, church, theatre, and farm. Daily 10 am-5 pm; $8.75, $7.25 w/student ID.

Mactaquac Provincial Park Golf Course, 363-4925. 12 miles W on Hwy 2. Beautiful 18 hole course, day passes week $30, w/ends $35, club rental $15.

Provincial Legislative Buildings, Queen & St John Sts, 453-2527. Includes, in Library, complete set of Audubon bird paintings and copy of 1783 printing of Domesday Book. Free tours include visit to legislative chamber. Summer: daily 8.30 am-7 pm, otherwise 9 am-4 pm.

University of New Brunswick, University Ave, 453-4666. Founded 1785, making it the third oldest university in Canada. Buildings on campus include the **Brydone Jack Observatory**, 453-4723, Canada's first astronomical observatory. Tours available in academic term, suggested donation.

York-Sunbury Historical Museum, 455-6041. In **Officers Square**, this military museum depicts the history of Fredericton and New Brunswick. Summer: Mon-Sat 10 am-6 pm, Mon & Fri 'til 9 pm, Sun noon-6 pm, otherwise Mon, Wed, Fri 10 am-6 pm. $2, $1 w/student ID. 'Kind of neat.'

INFORMATION/TRAVEL
Fredericton Tourist Information, 397 Queen St, City Hall, 460-2129. Summer: daily 8 am-8 pm, otherwise 8 am-5 pm. Very helpful.' Also another info booth on the Trans Canada Hwy btwn Rtes 640 & 101, same hours.

New Brunswick Tourism Information, (800) 561-0123. General telephone information; *web:www.go:nb.ca/tourism.*

TRIUS Taxis, 454-4444 To the airport, costs around $16 o/w.

MONCTON   This unofficial capital of Acadia is a major communications centre, but really has only two tourist sites of any importance: **Magnetic Hill** and the **Tidal Bore**. At Magnetic Hill, go to the bottom of the hill by car or bike, turn off the ignition, and by some freak of nature you'll find yourself drifting up the hill!

The Tidal Bore is at its highest when it sweeps up the chocolate banks of Petitcodiac River from the Bay of Fundy, reaching heights of 30 ft along the way. Bore Park is the spot to be when the waters rush in, all in 30 mins. Check the schedule published in the daily paper for the times when the tide is at its highest. Magnetic Hill is located at the corner of Mountain Road (126) and the Trans Canada. Bore Park is at the east end of Main St.

There is a nice beach with the warmest waters north of Virginia at **Shediac** on the Northumberland Straight. This is also the place to catch the annual lobster festival held in July. It's a short bus ride from Moncton and there is plenty of camping space nearby.

ACCOMMODATION
Ask at the Tourist Bureau, or call 856-3590/(800) 561-0123, daily 8.30 am-4.30 pm, for a list of local B&Bs, prices from D-$40.
Sunset Hotel, 162 Queen St, 382-1163. S-$30, XP-$5.
Univesite de Moncton, 858-4008. Lafebra & La France residence halls have accommodation. Lafebra S-$22, La France S-$32. Go to cnrs of Crowley Farm Rd & Morton St for best entrance.
Camping: Camper's City, 384-7867. Sites $18, $22 w/hook up.
Magnetic Hill Campground, 384-0191. Sites $15, $17 w/hook up. Both close to Magnetic Hill, and open May 1-Oct 31.

INFORMATION/TRAVEL
Tourist Bureau, 655 Main St, 853-3590. Daily 8 am-8 pm. *www.greater.moncton.nb.ca.*
Codiac Transit, 857-2008. Public transport system serving Moncton, Riverview and Dieppe.
See under Saint John for other buses.

CARAQUET Situated on scenic Baie des Chaleurs in the north of the province, Caraquet is the oldest French settlement in the area and just west of town is a monument to the first Acadian settlers who came here following their expulsion by Britain. On St Pierre Blvd there is an interesting museum of Acadian history, the **Acadian Museum**, and off Hwy 11 to the west of town is the **Village Historique Acadien**. The buildings here are all authentic, they were brought here and restored. There are also crafts and demonstrations showing the Acadian lifestyle.

SAINT JOHN Known as the Loyalist City, and proudly boasting a royal charter. Saint John was founded by refugees—those intrepid American settlers who chose to remain loyal to Britain after the American Revolution. The landing place of the Loyalists is marked by a monument at the foot of King Street, the shortest, steepest main street in Canada. Before the Seven Years War, however, Saint John was occupied by the French. The first recorded European discovery was in 1604 when Samuel de Champlain entered the harbour on St John's Day—hence the name of the town and the river on which it stands.

Largely as a result of its strategic ice-free position on the Bay of Fundy, Saint John has become New Brunswick's largest city and its commercial and industrial centre. Shipbuilding and fishing are the most important industries and Saint John Dry Dock, at 1150 ft long, is one of the largest in the world. The waterfront is a pleasant place to visit and the bustling downtown streets are dotted with shops, cafes and historic properties. Good times to visit are during the Festival-by-the-Sea in August and Loyalist Days, the third week in July. (Incidentally, Saint John is never abbreviated, thereby making it easier to distinguish from St John's, Newfoundland.)

ACCOMMODATION

Fundy Ayre Motel, 1711 Manawagonish Rd, 672-1125. S-$50, D-$56, XP-$6 all with private bath. Close to downtown and Nova Scotia ferry.

YM-YWCA, 1925 Hazen Ave, 634-7720. S-$30, $25 w/student ID or YH card, plus $10 deposit. Equipment storage area, parking. Friendly and helpful.'

Camping: **Rockwood Park**, off Rte 1, in the heart of the city, 652-4050. Sites $13, $16 w/hook-up. Two swimming lakes, horseriding at $15 per hr.

FOOD

Grannan's, 1 Market Square, 634-1555, is the place if you're a lover of raw oysters (half dozen $8.95), other seafood from $6. Mon-Sat 11.30 am-midnight, Sun 'til 10 pm.

Market Square, renovated building with 19th century exterior and trendy, modern interior; on the waterfront. Lots of places to eat and shop.

Old City Market, 47 Charlotte St, 658-2820. Fresh produce, crafts, antiques. Great for browsing and buying, a must. Closed Sundays and holidays.

Reggie's Restaurant, 26 Germain St, 657-6270. Imports smoked meat from Ben's, the famous Montréal deli. Inexpensive, filling meals $3-$7. Mon-Fri 6 am-8 pm, w/ends 6 am-6 pm.

OF INTEREST

There are four self-guided **walking tours** around Saint John: Prince William's Walk, the Loyalist Trail, a Victorian Stroll and the Douglas Avenue Amble. Each takes around an hour and a half, and shows you the highlights of the historic streets of Saint John. Among these are **Loyalist House**, 120 Union St, a Georgian house built in 1816; the **Old Loyalist Burial Ground** opposite King Square; the spiral staircase in the **Old Courthouse**, King Sq; **Barbour's General Store**, fully stocked as in the year 1867, with a barbershop. Pick up a map at Tourist Information, 1 Market Sq.

Carleton Martello Tower, Charlotte St Extension, 636-4011. Fortification erected during and surviving the War of 1812. Spectacular view of the city. Summer: daily 9 am-5 pm, $2.50.

Fort Howe Blockhouse, Magazine St. Replica of blockhouse built during 1777 in Halifax, then disassembled and re-built to protect Saint John Harbour. Good panoramic view of the city. Daily 10 am-dusk, free.

Guided walking tour, departs Barbour's Store, Market Slip at the waterfront, 658-2939, daily in summer at 10 am & 2 pm.

New Brunswick Museum, Market Sq, 635-5381. This museum, founded in 1842, was the first in Canada. It features a variety of historic exhibits, both national and international, a natural science gallery with a full-sized whale skeleton, artwork and Canadiana. Mon-Fri 9 am-9 pm, Sat 10 am-6 pm, Sun noon-5 pm. $6, $3.25 w/student ID, free Wed 6 pm-9 pm.

Reversing Falls Rapids. The town's biggest tourist attraction. Twice a day, at high tide, waters rushing into the gorge where the Saint John River meets the sea force the river to run backwards creating the Reversing Falls Rapids. There are two good lookouts for watching this phenomenon: the Tourist Bureau lounge and the sun deck on King St.

Rockwood Park, A beautiful park within the city limits. Fresh water lakes, sandy beaches, camping, golf, and hiking trails.

SPORT

Canoeing/Kayaking: Eastern Outdoors Inc., Brunswick Sq, 634-1530/(800) 565-

2925. The place to go for rentals, guided tours, and rock climbing.
Golf: Rockwood Park Golf Course, Sandy Point Rd, 634-0090. 18 holes $24, club rental $12.
Skiing: Poley Mountain Ski Area, in Sussex 51 miles E on Hwy 1. Information 433-3230. Also, **Crabbe Mountain**, in Lower Hainsville, 94 miles N on Hwys 7 & 2. Information: 463-8311.

INFORMATION
Saint John Tourist Information, Market Sq, 658-2855. Daily, summer 9 am-8 pm, otherwise 9 am-6 pm. In summer only: **Reversing Falls Visitor Centre**, 658-2937; **City Centre Seasonal**, on Hwy 1 west of harbour bridge, 658-2940. On the web: *www.city.st-john.nb.ca.*

TRAVEL
Saint John Transit, 658-4700. Local, city service.
SMT Bus Lines, 300 Union St, 648-3500. Bus to Moncton $21, 2hr 10 mins
VIA Rail, 300 Union St, 642-2916/(888) 842-7245.
There's a car ferry service from Saint John to Digby, Nova Scotia—a $2^1/_2$ hr trip. Nice scenery, but rather pricey, $50 per car, $23 for walk-on passengers. Crowded in the summer. Call 636-4048 for details.

CAMPOBELLO ISLAND   Going west on Hwy 1 from Saint John, you can catch a ferry from Back Bay which will take you, via Deer Isle and Campobello, to Lubec, Maine. On Campobello is the 3000-acre **Roosevelt Campobello International Park**. Visitors can see the 34-room 'cottage' maintained as it was when occupied by FDR from 1905 to 1921. Daily 10 am-6 pm (Atlantic time) June-Oct, free. Also here is the **East Quoddy Head Lighthouse**, the last working lighthouse with the St George's Cross facing east, the cross symbolises safety and peace to those at sea. The lighthouse stands on its own island, accessible only at low tide. In July and August, its a great spot for whale watching from land. The Public Library and Museum here has some surprising artifacts retrieved from the seabed in the Bay of Fundy. Call 752-7082 for details. Campobello is also linked to Maine by the Franklin D Roosevelt Memorial Bridge. For tourist info on the island, call 752-2997. Summer: daily 9 am-7 pm, otherwise 11 am-6 pm.

FUNDY NATIONAL PARK   The park is a vast area of rugged shore and inland forests, boasting unique ecosystems and rare birds, the Bay of Fundy has the world's highest tides (16 metres). This allows visitors the unique experience of strolling along the ocean floor at low tide. At Hopewell Cape on Rte 114, the Fundy tides have gouged four-storey sculptures out of the cliffs. The sculptures look like giant flower pots when the tide is low, and you can explore them from the ocean floor. At high tide the flower pots disappear, leaving little tree-topped islands in their place. The area offers a variety of impressive maritime scenery from fog-shrouded shores to sun-dappled forests, from steep coastal cliffs to tide-washed beaches, and from bubbling streams to crashing waterfalls. For info call 887-6000.
Centrally located, the park is just over an hour from Moncton and within two hours of Fredericton and Saint John. It is only a few hours from the Maine/New Brunswick border and within a day's drive from Montréal or Boston. Fundy National Park is a spectacular setting.

NOVA SCOTIA

Known as the Land of 10,000 Welcomes and the Festival Province, Canada's 'Ocean Playground' is famous for its attractive fishing villages, rocky, granite shores, and historic spots like Louisbourg and Grand Pré. The early Scottish immigration to Nova Scotia is manifested in such events as the annual Highland Games in Antigonish and St Ann's Gaelic College. It is said that there is more Gaelic spoken in Nova Scotia than in Scotland.

Although the French were the first to attempt colonisation of the area, it was James I who first gave Nova Scotia (New Scotland) its own flag and coat-of-arms when he granted the province to Sir William Alexander. The French preferred the name Acadia, after explorer Verrazano's word for Peaceful Land, however, and so the French thereafter became known as Acadians. By the Treaty of Utrecht in 1713, the province was finally ceded to the British for good. Cape Breton Island followed later, after the siege of Louisbourg in 1758.

Many Americans also emigrated to Nova Scotia in the late eighteenth and early nineteenth centuries, among them the Chesapeake Blacks and a group of 25,000 Loyalists—possibly the largest single emigration of cultured families in British history, since their numbers included over half of the living graduates of Harvard. They settled mostly around Sherbourne.

Driving is the best way of discovering Nova Scotia. There are eight specially designated tourist routes throughout the province which cover most of the points of interest. Among these, the Cabot Trail on Cape Breton Island is particularly recommended. Autumn is the most beautiful season; in summer, the ocean breeze always has a cooling effect. Although most people visit Halifax and the South Shore, Cape Breton Island is also worth a visit and has much to offer the nature-loving traveller.
The telephone area code is 902.

HALIFAX   Provincial capital and the largest city and economic hub of the Maritimes. The making of Halifax has been its ice-free harbour so that not only does it deal with thousands of commercial vessels a year but it is also Canada's chief naval base. Settled in 1749 by Govenor Edward Cornwallis, Halifax became Canada's first permanent British town, built as a response to the French fort at Louisbourg.

Although a thriving metropolis with the usual tall concrete buildings and expressways, the town does retain a certain charm with many constant reminders of its colourful past. The historic downtown areas of Halifax, and its twin **Dartmouth** across the bay, are perfect for discovering by bicycle or on foot (don't go alone after dark). Check with the Tourist Office for information on walking tours and the many festivals that go on in and around the town. **Citadel Hill** a hilltop fort in the middle of town is a good place to start exploring and to get your bearings.

Connected to Halifax by two bridges and two ferries (75¢), Dartmouth is known as the 'city of lakes' since there are some 22 lakes within the city boundaries. 'Walk across Macdonald Bridge, free, for a very good view of both cities.' The town is also home to the well-respected Bedford Institute of Oceanography, which collects data on tides, currents and ice formations.

ACCOMMODATION
Dalhousie University residences, 494-8840. S-$34, $18 w/student ID, D-$51, $30.50 w/student ID. Apartments also available. Pool and art gallery. May-Aug only.
Fenwick Place (off-campus residence), 5599 Fenwick St, 494-2075. Apartment-style accomodation, two bedrooms $46, three bedrooms $69, $18 pp for students willing to share. All apartments have kitchens and bathrooms. May-mid-Aug, rsvs recommended. Open 24 hrs.
Halifax International Hostel, 1253 Barrington St, 422-3863. YH-$15, non-members $18. Kitchen, laundry, no curfew. 'Very friendly.'
Inglis Lodge, 5538 Inglis St, 423-7950. Rooms from S-$29, D-$34.50, $85-$100 per week. Shared bathroom, kitchen and TV room.
Mount Saint Vincent University, 457-6286. About 15 mins from downtown. S-$28, $22 w/student ID, D-$39, $35 w/student ID. Gym and beautiful arboretum. May-Aug only.
Camping: **Laurie Park**, 12 miles N of Halifax on Old Hwy 2, in Grand Lake, 861-1623. Sites $10 for four. 'Very basic.'

FOOD
Athens Restaurant, Barrington & Blowers Sts, 422-1595. Greek and Canadian food, $6-$11. Daily 9 am-midnight. Good for breakfast.'
Midtown Tavern, Prince & Grafton Sts, 422-5213. Cheap pub-style food, nothing over $7. Mon-Sat 11 am-11 pm.
Satisfaction Feast, 1581 Grafton St, 422-3540. Good vegetarian food, lunch from $7, dinner from $10. People come from miles around for the homemade wholewheat bread and desserts ($3.50). Daily 9 am-10 pm, however, not an extensive breakfast menu .
Thirsty Duck, 5472 Spring Garden Rd, 422-1548. Irish and English beer; good music. Daily 11 am-1 am. Pub menu, very reasonable prices, $4.50-$7.

OF INTEREST
Art Gallery of Nova Scotia, 1741 Hollis St, 424-7542. Regional, national and international art. Tue-Sat 10 am-5 pm, Thur til 9 pm, Sun noon-5 pm. $2.50, $1.25 w/student ID. Free on Tues.
The *Bluenose II* sails from Historic Properties for a 2 hr cruise around the Harbour. This is the schooner stamped on the back of the Canadian dime. Many other harbour cruises are also available.
Citadel National Historic Park, 426-5080. This star-shaped fortress surrounded by a moat (now a dry ditch) was built in 1828-56, and is Canada's most visited historic site. There is a magnificent view of the harbour and the noon gun is fired daily. Free tours. 'Staff in uniform, friendly and well-informed.' There is an **Army Museum** recalling the military history of the fort. Grounds open year-round, Citadel mid-June-mid-Sept, daily 9 am-6 pm, $6.
Churches: **St George's Round Church**, Brunswick & Cornwallis Sts, 421-1705. An example of the very rare round church, built around 1800. In the summer, **Music Royale**, period music in historic settings, is presented. Tours available. **St Mary's Basilica**, on Spring Garden Rd, has the highest granite spire in the world. Daily tours in summer, 8.30 am-4.30 pm. **St Paul's Church**, Barrington & Duke Sts, 429-2240. Oldest Anglican church in Canada. Built in 1750, this is the oldest building in Halifax. **Old Dutch Church**, Brunswick & Garrish Sts, built in 1756, was the first Lutheran church in Canada.

Dalhousie University, Coburg Rd. An attractive campus with the usual facilities and guided tours. **The Art Gallery**, 6101 University Ave, 494-2403, is worth a look. Year round Tues-Sun 11 am-4 pm, suggested donation.

Halifax Public Gardens, on Spring Garden Rd & South Park St. 17 acres and 400 different varieties of plants and flora. Fountains and floating flower beds. Daily 8 am-dusk.

Maritime Museum of the Atlantic, Lower Water St, 424-7490. Exhibits on the 1917 Halifax explosion and relics from the *Titanic*. Docked behind the museum is CSS *Acadia*, one of the earliest ships to chart the Arctic Ocean floor. Don't miss the stunning view of the harbour. June-Oct, Mon-Sat 9.30 am-5.30 pm, Tues 'til 8 pm, Sun 1 pm-5 pm. Closed on Mon in winter. $4.50, $3.50 w/student ID.

Nova Scotia Museum of Natural History, 1747 Summer St, 424-7353, 424-6099 for 24 hr recorded info. Featuring the province's natural and human history, the spectacular quillwork of the Micmac Indians, and thousands of bees in glass enclosed hives. June-Oct Mon-Sat 9.30 am-5.30 pm, Wed til 8 pm, Sun noon-5.30 pm. $3.50, free 5 pm-5.30 pm, Weds 5.30 pm-8 pm. Closed Mon in winter (free Oct-May).

Point Pleasant Park is 20 min from downtown. Take South Park St, then Young Ave to the park. A good place to eat lunch.

Prince of Wales Martello Tower, located in Point Pleasant Park, the tower acted as part of the 'coastal defence network' set up by the British to protect against the French. June-Sept daily 10 am-6 pm. Free.

Province House, Hollis St, 424-4661. Canada's oldest and smallest parliament house. Built in 1818, called 'a gem of Georgian architecture' by Charles Dickens. 'The house has very detailed plasterwork and carving, very well kept.' Summer: Mon-Fri 9 am-5 pm, w/ends & hols 10 am-4 pm, otherwise Mon-Fri 9 am-4 pm.

York Redoubt, Purcell's Cove Rd, 15 miles W of Halifax on Rte 253. Site of historic fortification and magnificent harbour views. Daily in summer 10 am-6 pm; grounds 'til 8 pm. Picnicking facilities. Free.

Nearby: **Peggy's Cove**, **Liverpool**, **Lunenberg**, **Bridgewater** and the rest. Picturesque fishing villages but overrun by tourists.

SHOPPING/ENTERTAINMENT

Barrington Street and the Historic Properties are both good places to shop. The Scotia Square Complex has the usual shopping mall attractions.

Halifax International Busker Festival, 429-3910. Annual August festival of street performers in downtown Halifax.

The Nova Scotia International Tattoo, 451-1221, at the beginning of July, is a popular extravaganza featuring both Canadian and international performers of all kinds.

Shakespeare by the Sea, 422-0295, present the Bard's works outdoors in Point Pleasant Park, July-Sep.

INFORMATION

Check In Nova Scotia, 425-5781/(800) 565-0000; *explore.gov.ns.ca/virtua/ns*.

International Visitor Centre, 1595 Barrington St, 490-5946. Daily 8.30 am-7 pm.

Nova Scotia Travel Info Centre, near the airport on Hwy 102, 873-1223.

The Red Store, Historic Properties, Water St, 490-5946. Daily 8.30 am-7 pm.

TRAVEL

Acadian Lines Bus station, 6040 Almon St, near the Forum, in the south end of peninsula Halifax, 454-9321. Regular stops at the airport on the way from Halifax to Cape Breton and Amherst.

Ferry, to Dartmouth. Frequent departures from the foot of George St. $1.20 o/w. Bus transfers valid on ferry. Call 490-6600 for schedule.

Metro Transit, 490-6618. Basic fare: $1.50, transfers available.

Share-A-Cab, arrangements can be made 4 hrs in advance of travel time. Call 429-

5555/(800) 565-8669 for rates and schedules.
VIA Rail, 1161, Hollis St, (888) 842-7245.

GRAND PRÉ NATIONAL HISTORIC PARK The restored site of an early Acadian settlement. The nearby dykeland (*grand pré* = great meadow) is where the French Acadians were deported to in 1766 after failing to take an oath of allegiance to the English king, preferring to remain neutral.

Longfellow immortalized the sad plight of the deported Acadians of Nova Scotia in his narrative poem *Evangeline* (see under *Louisiana* in *USA* section). There is a museum in the park with a section on Longfellow and a fine collection of Acadian relics, everything from farm tools to personal diaries. Also in the park is the **Church of the Covenanters**. Built in 1790 by New England planters, this do-it-yourself church was constructed from hand-sawn boards fastened together by square hand-made nails. The similarly homemade pulpit spirals halfway to the ceiling.

The gardens are nice for walking and the whole park is open daily June-Sept, 9 am-6 pm, free. To get there from Halifax take Rte 101N, the park is three miles east of Wolfville. Call 542-3631 for park info. During the summer, accommodation is available in the residences of Acadia University in Wolfville, 542-2200.

ANNAPOLIS ROYAL Situated in the scenic Annapolis Valley, famous for its apples, this was the site of Canada's oldest settlement. Founded by de Monts and Champlain in 1604, and originally Port Royal, it became Annapolis Royal in honour of Queen Anne, after the final British capture in 1710. The town then served as the Nova Scotian capital until the founding of Halifax in 1749.

The site of the French fort of 1636 is now maintained as **Fort Anne National Historic Park**, and seven miles away, on the north shore of Annapolis River, is the **Port Royal Habitation National Historic Park**. This is a reconstruction of the 1605 settlement based on the plan of a Normandy farm. Here, too, the oldest social club in America was formed. L'Ordre de Bon Temps was organised by Champlain in 1606 and visitors to the province for more than three days can still become members. The park is open daily May-October, 9 am-6 pm, free. Thirty five miles to the south is **Kejimkujik National Park**, 682-2771, an area once inhabited by the Micmac Indians. The park entrance and information centre is at **Maitland Bridge**. Admission $3. The park is good for canoeing, fishing, hiking, and skiing in winter. Canoes can be rented for $4 per hr, $20 per day. Ask at info centre for details.

YARMOUTH The only place of any size on the western side of Nova Scotia, Yarmouth is the centre of a largely French-speaking area. During the days of sail this was an important shipbuilding centre although today local industry is somewhat more diversified.

A good time to visit is at the end of July when the Western Nova Scotia Exhibition is held here. The festival includes the usual agricultural and equestrian events plus local craft demonstrations and exhibits.

ACCOMMODATION
El Rancho Motel, Rte 1, Hwy 1, 742-2408. S-$39, D-$65, overlooking Milo Lake. Kitchen facilities.

TRAVEL
Ferries to Portland (10 hrs) and Bar Harbor, Maine (5 hrs). For info on the Portland run, call (800) 565-7900 (in Canada), (800) 341-7540 (in USA); for Bar Harbor info call (800) 565-9411 (in Canada), or (902) 742-5033 (in USA).

SYDNEY   Situated on the Atlantic side of the province, Sydney is the chief town on Cape Breton Island and a good centre for exploring the rest of the island. It is a steel and coal town, a grim, but friendly, soot-blackened old place. While here you can visit the second largest steel plant in North America.

Like the whole of Cape Breton Island, Sydney has a history of struggles against worker exploitation and bad social conditions. Since France ceded the island to Britain as part of the package deal Treaty of Utrecht in 1713, hard times and social strife have frequently been the norm.

A ferry goes to Newfoundland from North Sydney across the bay.

ACCOMMODATION
Garden Court Cabins, 2518 King's Rd, Sydney Forks, 564-6201, 14 miles W of Hwy 125 on Rte 4. S-$53 ($59 w/kitchen), from $42 for cabin for three ($55-$70 w/kitchen).

OF INTEREST
Highland Games, July, Antigonish or St Anne's. Kilts, pipes and drums, sword dancing, caber toss, etc.
Nearby: In Baddeck the **Alexander Graham Bell National Historic Park**, 295-2069, displays, models, papers, etc, relating to Bell's inventions. Bell had his summer home in the town. Summer 9 am-7 pm, otherwise 9 am-5 pm, $4.
Also in Baddeck, the **Centre Bras d'Or Festival of the Arts**, mid-July-mid-Aug, includes Music Fest with many famous artists, tkts from $10, 295-2787.
Glace Bay, 13 miles E, site of the **Miners Museum and Village**, 849-4522. Includes tour of underground mine running out and under the sea, and the village shows the life of a mining community 1850-1900. Ask about Tues evening concerts by the Men of the Deeps. June-Sept, daily 10 am-6 pm, Tues 'til 7 pm, Sept-June, Mon-Fri 9 am-4 pm, $3.25, mine tour, $6.

INFORMATION/TRAVEL
Visitors Information, 20 Kelpic Dr, Sydney River, 539-9876. Daily 9 am-5 pm.
Ferries to Argentia ($52.50, $118 car, 14 hrs) and Porte-aux-Basques ($19, $59 car, 5 hrs), Newfoundland, (800) 341-7981.

FORTRESS OF LOUISBOURG NATIONAL HISTORIC PARK   Built by the French between 1717 and 1740, this fortress was once the largest built in North America since the time of the Incas. Louisbourg played a crucial role in the French defence of the area and was finally won by Britain in 1760, but not before it had been blasted to rubble.

A faithful re-creation of a complete colonial town within the fortifications, with majestic gates, homes and formal gardens. There is a museum, and tours by French colonial-costumed guides are available.

The Louisbourg Shuttle, 564-6200, leaves from Sydney, 26 miles S, daily 8.45 am & 4 pm, $25 r/t, the park is open June & Sept, daily 9.30 am-5 pm, July & August, daily 9 am-7 pm, $11 (Visitors Information Centre, 733-2280).

CAPE BRETON HIGHLANDS NATIONAL PARK The park lies on the northern-most tip of Cape Breton sandwiched between the Gulf of St Lawrence and the Atlantic Ocean. It covers more than 360 square miles of rugged mountain country, beaches and quiet valleys. The whole is encircled by the 184-mile-long Cabot Trail, an all-weather paved highway on its way round the park climbing four mountains and providing spectacular views of sea and mountains.

In summer, however, it gets very crowded and the narrow, steep roads are jammed with cars. There are camping facilities in the park and good sea and freshwater swimming.

This is an area originally settled by Scots and many of the locals still speak Gaelic. There are park information centres at Ingonish Beach and Cheticamp, 224-2306. Admission to the park is $3.50. At **Cheticamp**, there is Trois Pignons, 224-2612, an Acadian Museum with craft demonstrations, French-Canadian antiques and glassware, and Coop Artisanal, a rug-making centre. Both are open daily in the summer. Visitor Information, 285-2329 (285-2691 off-season).

IONA On the way back across the Strait of Canso, a side trip here to the Nova Scotia Highland Village may be worthwhile. The village includes a museum and other memorabilia of the early Scottish settlers. A highland festival is held here in early August, 725-2272. Summer hours Mon-Sat 9 am-5 pm, Sun 10 am-6 pm, $4. The village is off Hwy 105, 15 miles E on Hwy 223 via Little Narrows, overlooking the Bras d'Or lakes.

PRINCE EDWARD ISLAND

Prince Edward Island—known primarily as the home of *Anne of Green Gables* and as a great producer of spuds—is Canada's smallest and thinnest province, being only 140 miles long with an average width of just twenty miles, and a population of a mere 128,000. PEI was originally named 'Abegweit' by the local Micmac Indians, meaning 'land cradled on the waves'. The French colonised the island and baptized it Isle St Jean, but when it was utlimately ceded to Britain as a separate colony, the British renamed it after Prince Edward, Duke of Kent. Now known as the 'Garden of the Gulf', PEI is a popular spot for Canadian family vacations because of its great sandy beaches and warm waters, perfect for lazy summer sunning!

Note the colour of the soil in PEI: it's red because it contains iron which rusts on exposure to the air. Limits are put on billboards here: you won't see any along the side of PEI's highways. The full effect of this constraint only hits you when you are bombarded with billboards back on the mainland. A note of caution: only camp in designated campgrounds—camping is prohibited everywhere else (including the beach).

In 1997, 124 years after the 1873 Terms of Union between Canada and PEI placed a constitutional obligation on the federal government to maintain 'continuous communication' between the island and the mainland, PEI has finally been linked to mainland Canada, by the 9 mile-long Confederation

Bridge which spans the Northumberland Strait. An engineering marvel, it is the longest continuous marine span bridge in the world. It takes ten minutes to cross the bridge by car.

Alternatively, you can reach this island paradise in the good old way by ferry from Caribou, Nova Scotia, to Wood Islands, east of the capital (75 min, $9.50, $45 car). Queues are long in the summer, particularly if you're taking a car. Schedules vary throughout the year but in summer the ferry runs every 1¹/₂ hours, 6 am-8 pm.

The telephone area code is 902.

CHARLOTTETOWN The first meeting of the Fathers of the Confederation took place in Charlottetown in 1864. Out of this meeting came the future Dominion of Canada (hence the nickname, 'The Cradle of Confederation'). In the Confederation Chamber, Province House, where the meeting was held, a plaque proclaims 'Providence Being Their Guide, They Builded Better Than They Knew'. The citizens of PEI were not so convinced however. They waited until 1873 before joining the Confederation. Even then, according to the then Governor General, Lord Dufferin, they came in 'under the impression that it is the Dominion that has been annexed to Prince Edward Island'.

These days things are quieter hereabouts, only livening up in summer when Canadian families descend en masse, and PEI's other tourist attraction, harness racing, gets going out at Charlottetown Driving Park. The restored waterfront section of town, Olde Charlottetown, offers the usual craft shops, eating places and boutiques. You can tour the town in a London double-decker bus, leaving from Confederation Centre (call Abegweit Tours, 894-9966).

ACCOMMODATION
Charlottetown Youth Hostel, 153 Mt Edward Rd at Belvedere, 894-9696. Near UPEI campus. $13, $16 non-members. Kitchen. 25 min walk from Charlottetown. Open June-Sept.
Univ of PEI residences: at University and Belvedere Ave, 566-0442. In **Blanchard Hall**, apartments sleep four, w/kitchenette, lounge and private bath, $65, S-$36, D-$45.
Marion Hall, S-$29, D-$38.
Bernadine Hall for female residents, S-$39, D-$44. All rooms include bfast, available July-Aug only.

FOOD
Cedar's Eatery, 81 University Ave, 892-7377. Large servings of Canadian and Lebanese food. Average price $8, lunch specials $4, dinner specials $5.
Olde Dublin Pub, 131 Sydney St, 892-6992. Specializes in seafood, moderate prices. Live Irish entertainment nightly in the summer. Daily 11 am-11 pm.

OF INTEREST
Abegweit Sightseeing Tours, 894-9966, operate guided tours of both the South and North Shores ($50), covering most points of interest including Fort Amherst National Historic Park and Pioneer Village. Daily from Charlottetown Hotel at Kent & Pownal Sts. 1 hr guided tours ($8) of Charlottetown depart six times daily from Confederation Centre.
Confederation Centre of The Arts, Queen & Grafton Sts, (800) 565-0278. The focal

point of the town's cultural life, it has an art gallery, museum, library and three theatres. In the main theatre, a musical version of the story of PEI's favourite orphan—**Anne of Green Gables**—is staged every summer. Tkts $16-$36, call for performance dates. A summer festival is held here annually.

Province House, Queen Square at Grafton St, 566-7626. The site of Confederation, Canada's founding fathers met here in 1864 to decide the fate of the Dominion. The provincial Legislature now meets here. June-mid-Oct daily 9 am-6 pm, otherwise Mon-Fri 9 am-5 pm, free tours.

Pioneer Village, on Rte 11 at Mont-Carmel, in the Acadian region of PEI, approx 1 1/2 hours from Charlottetown, 854-2227. A log reproduction of an Acadian settlement with homes, blacksmith's shop, barn, school, general store and church. June-late-Sept, daily 8 am-7 pm, $3.50.

INFORMATION/TRAVEL

PEI Tourist Information, (800) 463-4734. *www.gov.pa.ca.*
Be warned! There is no public transport on the island.
Acadian Bus Lines, 454-9321, operate from Halifax, Nova Scotia ($53).
Charlottetown is also accessible by rail from Moncton, New Brunswick and Amherst, Nova Scotia.
Ed's Taxi, 892-6561.

PRINCE EDWARD ISLAND NATIONAL PARK Situated north of Charlottetown, the Park consists of 25 miles of sandy beaches backed by sandstone cliffs. Thanks to the Gulf Stream the sea is beautifully warm. **Rustico** is one of the quieter beaches.

Ask about good places for clamming. Assuming you pick the right spot, you can just wriggle your toes in the sand and dig up a good meal.

At **Cavendish Beach**, off Rte 6, is **Green Gables**, 672-6350. Built in the 1800s, the farmhouse inspired the setting of Lucy Maud Montgomery's famous fictional novel *Anne of Green Gables*. The house has been refurbished to portray the Victorian setting described in the novel. Daily in summer 9 am-5 pm, til 8 pm July & Aug, $2.50. The beach here is very crowded during summer and probably best avoided. Camping sites and tourist homes abound on the island, call (800) 463-4734.

NEWFOUNDLAND

Officially entitled Newfoundland and Labrador, and with a population of just over 550,000, the newest Canadian province is a bit off the beaten track, but it's worth taking a little time and trouble to get here. It is a province rich in historic associations (the Vikings were here as early as AD1000) 'discovered' by John Cabot in 1497, it was the first part of Canada to be settled by the Europeans, and the first overseas possession of the British Empire. A society neither wholly North American nor yet European. Fishing is still the main industry, although mining is important and the oil industry has reached here too.

Labrador, the serrated northeastern mainland of Canada, was added to Newfoundland in 1763. Until recent explorations and development of some of Labrador's natural resources (iron ore, timber), the area was virtually a virgin wilderness with the small population scattered in rugged little fishing villages and centred around the now all but obsolete airport at Goose Bay.

Strikingly beautiful, Newfoundland has spectacular seascapes (and an estimated two million seabirds), long beaches, and picturesque fishing villages (some still with access only from the sea); vast forests, fjords, majestic mountains, and hundreds of lakes—Newfoundlanders call them 'ponds'—some of which are nearly 20 miles long!

Newfoundlanders' speech is unique: English interspersed with plenty of slang and colloquialisms. The curious nature of the province is also evident in the names of its towns, like Heart's Content, Come By Chance, and Blow-Me-Down. The people here are very friendly and helpful—well prepared to take a visitor under a collective wing. Newfoundland is probably the only Canadian province to celebrate Guy Fawkes Day; ask about the summer folk festivals also.

There is a daily car and passenger ferry service to Port-aux-Basques from North Sydney, Nova Scotia (794-5814, $19, $59 car). Once on the island the Trans Canada Highway goes all the way to the capital, St John's, via Corner Brook and Terra Nova National Park. There is a bus service from the ferry to St John's.
The telephone area code is 709.

ST JOHN'S A gentle though weather-beaten city, St John's overlooks a natural habour situated on the island's east coast, 547 miles from Port-aux-Basques on the southwestern tip. Nearby Cape Spear, is just 1640 miles from Cape Clair, Ireland, and the city's strategic position has in the past made it the starting point for transatlantic contests and conflicts of one sort or another. The first successful transatlantic cable was landed nearby in 1866; the first transatlantic wireless signal was received by Marconi at St John's in 1901; and the first non-stop transatlantic flight took off from here in 1919.

Lately, St John's has begun to develop more after the recent discovery of off-shore oil fields. Take a walk along Gower St to view the rows of historical old houses; downtown Water St has been the city's commercial centre for 400 years and is still the place to find interesting stores, restaurants and pubs.

ACCOMMODATION
Fort William B&B, 5 Gower St, 726-3161. Rooms from $45, XP-$15.
The Old Inn, 157 Le Marchant Rd, 722-1171. S-$35, D-$50, XP-$8. Bfast $2-$4. Close to downtown. Rsvs required.
Youth Hostel, Hatcher House, Paton College, on the campus of Memorial University of Newfoundland, btwn Elizabeth Ave & Prince Phillip Dr, 737-7933. S- $13, D-$18 non-students, D-$20, D-$30 non-students. Check-in 8 am-2 am. May-Aug only.
Camping: CA Pippy Park, Alandale Rd, Nagel's Place, $9-$14, $20 w/hook up.

FOOD
There is a good variety of reasonably priced places to eat on Duckworth St:
Bon Apetit, 73 Duckworth St, 579-8024. French bistro-style, crepes, pasta, meat and seafood all with a french twist. Lunch $6-$8, dinner $10-$18. Daily 11.30 am-3 pm, 5.30 pm-10 pm. Closed Sun in winter.
Chess' Snacks, 9 Freshwater Rd, 722-4083. Take-out fish. $4-$7, daily 10 am-2 am, w/ends 'til 3 am.
Harbourfront Pub & Eatery, 192 Duckworth St, 722-1444. 'A bit of everything.' All-day bfast $5-$7, entrees $5-$10. Daily 8 am-10.30 pm, Sun from 9 am.

OF INTEREST

Anglican Cathedral, Church Hill & Gower St, 726-5677. Said to be one of the finest examples of ecclesiastical Gothic architecture in North America. Begun in 1847, and following two fires, restored in 1905. Features sculptured arches and carved furnishings. National Historic Site. Mon-Sat 10 am-6 pm, Sun 1 pm-5 pm. Tours available by arrangement.

The annual **Royal St John's Regatta** on Quidi Vidi Lake takes place the first week of August. The province's event of the year. Call 576-9216 for details. The same week sees the **Newfoundland & Labrador Folk Festival**, 576-8508. Folk music, dancing and storytelling.

Memorial University Botanical Gardens, 306 Mt Scio Rd, 737-8590. Developed to display plants native to the province. Beautiful meandering walking trails. Guided tours May-Nov, Sun 3 pm. Summer daily 10 am-5 pm, $1.

Newfoundland Museum, 285 Duckworth St, 576-2460. St John's is rich in history and folklore and this particular museum has the only relics in existence of the vanished Indian tribe, the Beothuks. Mon-Fri 9 am-5 pm, w/ends 2 pm-5 pm. Free. Tours available by arrangement.

Newfoundland Museum at the Murray Premises, Water St. A second branch of the museum. Exhibits include the military, naval and marine history of the province. Same hours and phone number as the Duckworth location, above. Shops and a pub nearby.

Quidi Vidi Battery, (pronounced Kiddy Viddy), 729-2460. Just outside of St John's, the battery overlooks scenic Quidi Vidi village and is restored to its 1812 appearance. Staffed by guides in period costume. Daily in summer, admission free.

St John's Historic Walking Tours, 3 Fitzpatrick Ave, 738-3781. Guides will introduce you to the downtown area, historic landmarks, craft stores and local entertainment.

Signal Hill National Historic Park (accessible from Duckworth St), 772-5367, so named because the arrival of ships was announced from here to the town below through a series of flag signals, it also the site where Marconi received the first transatlantic wireless signal in 1901. Inside the park is **Cabot Tower**, built in 1897 to commemorate the 400th anniversary of John Cabot's discovery of Newfoundland and Queen Victoria's Diamond Jubilee. 'Million dollar view' of St. John's and the Atlantic, and an interesting visitors centre. Daily in summer 8.30 am-9 pm, $2.50.

Nearby: Trinity, on the Bonavista Peninsula, north of St John's. This town of 325 people has several national heritage sites, including the **Cape Bonavista Lighthouse**, 729-2460, and pretty streets lined with brightly coloured, saltbox-style homes.

INFORMATION/TRAVEL

Newfoundland Tourist Information, (800) 563-6353; *www.gov.nf.ca*.

St John's Tourist Information, City Hall, New Gower St, 576-8514.

Metro Bus, 495 Water St, 722-9400, covers downtown St John's, for further afield you will have to take a tour. Some recommended operators are;

Legend Tours 753-1497, **City & Outport Adventures** 754-8687, **All Season Tours**, 682-1644. A 2-3 hr tour costs $20-$30

The airport is situated north of town and is reached only by taxi. Call 726-4400, $11-$13.

TERRA NOVA NATIONAL PARK In the central region of Newfoundland, around three hours away from St John's, this area was once covered by glaciers 750 ft thick which left behind boulders, gravel, sand and grooved rock. The sea filled the valleys, leaving the hills as islands. The result is the incredibly beautiful **Bonavista Bay** a picturesque wilderness, with saltwater fjords, barrens and bogs. But it's certainly not swimming country. The cold Labrador Current bathes the shores and it's not unusual to see an iceberg.

Inland the park is thickly forested, hiking trails climb headland summits and follow the rugged coast. Moose are common sights in the park, and occasionally a fox or a bear may be spotted. Fishing, canoeing and camping are available inside the park, sites cost $14, $16 w/hook-up. For Park info, canoe rentals and camping rsvs, call (800) 563-6353.

Access to the park is easy since the Trans Canada Hwy passes right through it for a distance of 25 miles, admission $3.25, $6.50 car. Terra Nova Transport also provides bus transportation from St John's.

GROS MORNE NATIONAL PARK This is Newfoundland's second National Park, located on the island's west coast, 10 hours away from St John's. This park, about 65 miles wide, is the more popular of the two parks because of the rugged beauty of its mountains. The landscape here is very different from that of the eastern coast of the province—colossal collisions of tectonic plates created formations as barren as the moon: 'fantastic'. Flora and fauna are abundant, orchids thrive, over thirty wild species in all, and the park is home to giant atlantic hares, woodland caribou and moose.

You can wade along the sandy beaches of Shallow Bay, or look for 'pillow rocks' that formed along the coast as lava cooled under water. You can travel by boat winding up through the glaciated fjords of Western Brook or Trout River Ponds, and a serious hike to the top of Gros Morne Mountain will reward you with a spectacular view of Ten Mile Pond and the Long Range Mountains.

There are many campsites within the park; site prices range from $7-$10 per night. For groceries head for **Rocky Harbour**. For more info, call 458-2066. Entry fee $3.

ST PIÈRRE AND MIQUELON ISLANDS Off the southern coast of Newfoundland, these islands constitute the only remaining holdings of France in North America. Once called the 'Islands of 11,000 Virgins', these granite outcrops total only about 93 square miles. A French territory since 1814, the natives parlent Francais, mangent baguettes and pay for them in francs. You can reach the islands by ferry (daily 2.45 pm, $60 r/t) from **Fortune**, NF, on Rte 210. Canadians and Americans need to show proof of citizenship (driver's licence or birth certificate) and all other nationalities must have a passport. Accomodation on the island is reasonably priced, B&B $55-$65, Auberge $73. Tourist information, (800) 565-5118.

L'ANSE AUX MEADOWS At the northern tip of Newfoundland, and believed to be the site of the Viking settlement of AD 1000. According to legend, the Vikings defended this post against Indians until perils became too great and they withdrew to Greenland. No standing ruins of their buildings have survived, but excavations have disclosed the size and location of buildings, and many everyday objects have been found. Guides on site daily. Mid-June-August, daily 9 am-8 pm; otherwise, 9 am-4 pm, free.

ONTARIO AND QUÉBEC

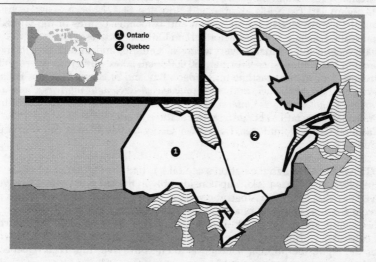

This section is devoted to those old enemies and still rivals, Ontario and Québec. Both provinces evolved out of vast wilderness areas first opened up by Indians and fur traders, only later to become the focus of the bitter rivalry between the French and British in North America as Québec was colonised by the French and Ontario by the British and American Loyalists. In 1791 Québec became Lower Canada and Ontario became Upper Canada. In 1840 the Act of Union united the two and finally brought responsible and stable government to the area.

Cultural differences between the two provinces remain strong, but one thing which is pretty similar is the climate. Summers can be hot and humid but winters long, very cold and snowy. Both Québec and Ontario also offer progressive, modern cities as well as vast regions of wilderness great for getting far away from whatever it is you're getting away from.

ONTARIO

The 'booming heartland' of Canada is the second largest province, claims one-third of the nation's population, half the country's industrial and agricultural resources and accounts for about 40 percent of the nation's income. Since Confederation, Ontario has leapt ahead of its neighbours, becoming highly industrialised and at the same time reaping the benefits of the great forest and mineral wealth of the Canadian Shield which covers most of the northern regions.

Ontario was first colonised, not from Britain, but by Empire Loyalists from the USA. Previously there were only sporadic French settlements and trading posts in what was otherwise a vast wilderness. The ready transportation provided in the past by the Great Lakes, all of which (except Lake Michigan) lap Ontario's shores, and now the St Lawrence Seaway, has linked the province to the industrial and consumer centres of the United States and has been a major factor behind Ontario's success story.

There is water virtually everywhere in Ontario, and in addition to the Great Lakes, Ontario has a further 250,000 small lakes, numerous rivers and streams, a northern coastline on Hudson Bay and of course Niagara Falls. *www.ontario-canada.com* and *www.yahoo.com/Regional/Countries/Canada/ Provinces_and_Territories/Ontario.* For a comprehensive list of cities in Ontario, try the latter net address, but at the end add */Cities.*

National Parks: Point Pelee, Pukashwa, Georgian Bay Islands, St Lawrence Islands.

OTTAWA Although the nation's capital has had the reputation of being a dull city, Ottawa has perked up considerably in the last few years. Dare we even say that Ottawa has become well, almost, a fun city to visit?! It has a lively student/youth emphasis and boasts a thriving cultural life, offering the visitor many excellent museums and art galleries, and top-notch theatrical performances. When the bars and restaurants start shutting down for the night, the popular solution is to cross the river into Hull, Québec, where everything is open until 3 am.

The most colourful time of year to visit is during spring when more than a million tulips bloom in the city and Ottawa celebrates its Festival of Spring. The tulip bulbs were a gift to Ottawa from the government of the Netherlands as thanks for the refuge granted to the Dutch royal family during World War II. In summer the city is crowded with visitors and there are many special festivals and activities.

A lively, fun atmosphere prevails. Even Ottawa in the winter has its charms. You can catch the Winterlude Festival in February or just enjoy the spectacle of civil servants, with their suits and briefcases, skating to work on the four and a half mile long Rideau Canal. The canal is known as the world's longest skating rink.

Champlain was here first, but didn't stay long and it took a further 200 years and the construction of the Rideau Canal before Ottawa was founded. Built between 1827 and 1831, the canal provided a waterway for British gunboats allowing them to evade the international section of the St Lawrence where they might be subject to American gun attacks. Queen Victoria chose Ottawa as the capital of Canada in 1857 because it was halfway between the main cities of Upper and Lower Canada—Toronto and Québec City—and therefore a neutral choice. *www.capcan.ca* is *Canada's Capital*, an online travel guide featuring a capital tour and activity zone covering Ottawa and surrounding areas.

The telephone area code is 613.

ACCOMMODATION

B&B places are abundant, except during May, and early June when student groups and conventioneers arrive for summer residence. A complete list of B&Bs can be found in the *Ottawa Visitors Guide*; information is available at the tourist office in the National Arts Centre. Also, from **Ottawa B&B**, 563-0161 and **Capital B&B Reservation Service**, 737-4129. From S-$50, D-$50-$75, includes cooked bfast, evening refreshments, shared bathroom, free parking.

Centre Town Guest House Ltd, 502 Kent St, 233-0681. Clean rooms in comfortable house. Free bfast in a cosy dining room. From S-$25, D-$35. Monthly rates from $400. Rsvs recommended.

Ottawa International Hostel (HI-C), 75 Nicholas St, 235-2595. Heritage building, a jail 1862-1972, and a hostel since 1973. The former Carleton County Jail is the site of Canada's last public hanging. 'Sleep in the corridors of a former jail and take a shower in a cell.' Centrally located. Laundry, kitchen, large lounges, 'Fantastic place; unique; friendly people.' Many organised activities including biking, canoeing, tours. $16-20.

Somerset House Hotel, 352 Somerset St West, 233-7762. Located btwn bus station and parliament buildings—10 min walk from downtown. S-$34, D-$45. 'Nice, clean rooms and very friendly staff.'

University of Ottawa Residences, 100 University St, 564-5400. Easy walk from downtown. Dorm rooms and shared showers. Free linen, towels. From S-$32, D-$40, cheaper w/student ID. Bfast $2. May-Aug.

YMCA/YWCA, 180 Argyle Ave, 237-1320. Close to bus station. 'Clean and bright.' Gym, TV, pool, kitchen with microwave. Cafeteria Mon-Fri 7 am-6.30 pm, Sat-Sun 8 am-2.30 pm; bfast $4. From S-$42, D-$49. Weekly and group rates available. Payment required in advance.

Camping: Gatineau Park, 456-3016 for rsvs/827-2020 for info, has 3 campgrounds: **Lac Philippe Campground; Lac Taylor Campground;** and **Lac la Peche.** All campgrounds are off Hwy 366 NW Hull, within 45 min of Ottawa. Map available at visitors centre. Also, **Camp Le Breton**, at Le Breton Flats, Booth and Fleet Sts, 943-0467. Summer $9 per night. 'Very convenient.'

On the Ottawa River: Outdoor Learning Centre, 1620 6th Line Rd, Dunrobin, 832-1234. 25 mins from Ottawa, exit Hwy 417 March Rd, then go E. For a break from the city madness, try canoeing, kayaking, rock climbing, skiing and camping, from $28, includes food.

FOOD

Bfast is cholesterol-rich here and a generous helping of eggs, potatoes, meat, toast and coffee is the norm!

Byward Market, north of Rideau. Local produce, cheese, meat, fish, fruit, clothing, bits and pieces; it's been here since 1846. 'Great.' 'Not to be missed.' The area around the market is good for eating places in general. Daily 8 am-6 pm.

Café Bohemien, 89 Clarence, 241-8020. Innovative menu and reasonable prices usually under $10.

Copacabano, 380 Dalhousie St, 241-9762. Homefries, bacon, ham or sausage, 2 eggs, toast and coffee all for $3! And open 24 hrs for your breakfast convience!

Father and Sons, 112 Osgoode St (at eastern edge of the U of O campus), 233-6066. Favoured by students, traditional tavern-style food and a variety of Lebanese specialties are served up. All served daily 'til midnight, generally Mon-Sat 7 am-2am, Sun 8 am-1 am.

Las Palmas, 111 Parent Ave, 241-3738. Hot hot hot Mexican cuisine heaped high! Meals under $15. Mon-Thur and Sat 11.30 am-10.30 pm, Fri 'til midnight.

Wringer's Restaurant & Laundromat, 151 Second Ave, 234-9700. Kill 2 birds with one stone. Mon-Sun 9 am-10 pm.

Yesterdays, 152 Spark St Mall, 235-1424. 'Good food at reasonable prices, $5-12.'

OF INTEREST

Canadian Museum of Caricature, 136 Patrick St, 995-3145. Smirk at cartoon

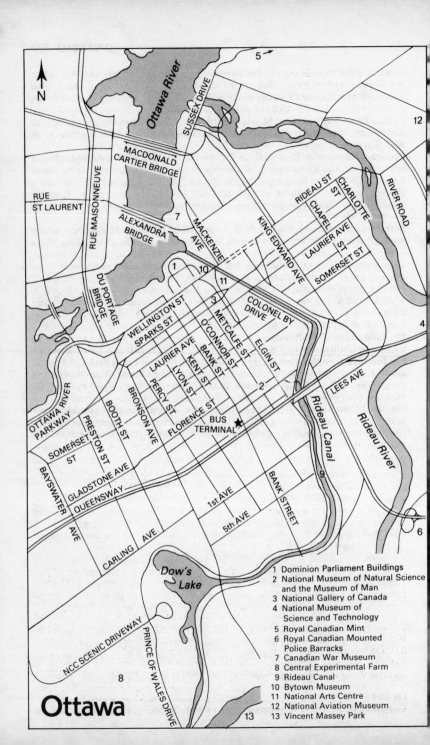

1 Dominion Parliament Buildings
2 National Museum of Natural Science and the Museum of Man
3 National Gallery of Canada
4 National Museum of Science and Technology
5 Royal Canadian Mint
6 Royal Canadian Mounted Police Barracks
7 Canadian War Museum
8 Central Experimental Farm
9 Rideau Canal
10 Bytown Museum
11 National Arts Centre
12 National Aviation Museum
13 Vincent Massey Park

Ottawa

impressions of famous people drawn by artists from all over the world. Sat-Tue 10 am-6 pm, Wed-Fri 10 am-8 pm. Free.

Canadian Museum of Civilisation, Laurier St & St Laurent Blvd, just across the river in Hull, (819) 776-7002. This impressive museum explores the history of Canada's cultural heritage. There are IMAX and OMNIMAX theatres here too, showing CINEPLUS films. Summer Fri-Wed 9 am-6 pm, Thur 'til 9 pm; otherwise Tues-Sun 9 am-5 pm. Closed Mon Sept-May. $5, $3.50 w/student ID.

Canadian Museum of Photography, 1 Rideau Canal, 990-8257. Take a glimpse at modern Canadian life. Summer Fri-Tues 11am-5 am, Wed 4 pm-8 pm, Thurs 11am-8 pm; Sept-May Wed 11am-5 pm, Thurs 'til 8 pm, Fri-Sun 'til 5 pm.

Canadian War Museum, 330 Sussex Dr, (819) 776-8600. Canada's military history from the early 1600s on. Daily 9.30 am-5 pm, May-Sept; otherwise Tue-Sun from 10 am. $3.50, free Thurs 5 pm-8 pm.

Central Experimental Farm, Maple Dr, 991-3044. Est 1886 and HQ for the Canada Dept of Agriculture. Flowers, tropical greenhouse, animals. Great place for a picnic—beautiful site on the canal. Daily sunrise-sunset. Horse-drawn wagon tours available. April-Oct, Mon-Fri 10 am & 2 pm, $2, $1 w/student ID.

Chateau Laurier Hotel, 1 Rideau St, 241-1414. Guided tours in summer, Wed-Sat, 10.30 am & 2.30 pm, Sun noon & 2.30 pm. A guide in historical costume will take you around this fairytale hotel. Among the many tidbits offered, you will learn that the original furniture bound for the Chateau Laurier went down with the *Titanic*. 'The art deco pool is wonderful.'

Dominion Parliament Buildings. The Gothic-style, green copper-roofed buildings stand atop Parliament Hill overlooking the river. Completed in 1921, the three buildings replaced those destroyed by fire in 1916. Conducted tours daily every 30 mins, 9 am-8.30 pm; w/ends 'til 6 pm. Go to Infotent located at the Parliament Buildings to make same day tour rsvs and avoid queues. Free. During the summer there are *son et lumière* displays. When parliament is in session you can visit the House of Commons. The best view in the city is from the 291-foot-high **Peace Tower** in the Square. The Tower has a carillon of 53 bells and during the summer the bells ring out hour-long concerts four times a week. In true Buckingham Palace tradition, the **Changing of the Guard**—complete with bearskins and red coats— takes place on Parliament Hill at 10 am, weather permitting, from late June to late Aug. The flame located in front of the Buildings burns eternally to represent Canada's unity. There is a white **Infotent** by the visitors centre; for public info call 992-4793. Note: Most museums in Ottawa are closed Mon in fall and winter.

National Arts Centre, Confederation Sq, 996-5051. Completed in 1969, the complex includes theatres, concert halls, an opera house and an art gallery. Year round 9 am-5 pm, tours available.

National Aviation Museum, Rockcliffe Airport, just off St Laurent Blvd, 993-2010. Offers special exhibitions in the summer, and displays over 100 aircraft. Discover the role played by airplanes in the development of Canada. Summer daily 9 am-5 pm, Thurs 'til 9 pm; closed Mon Sept-May. Free Thurs 5 pm-9 pm. $4 w/student ID.

National Gallery of Canada, 380 Sussex Dr (opposite Notre Dame Basilica), 990-1985. Canadian art of all periods in a modern glass building designed by Moshie Safdie. Worth visiting for insight into Canadian history and background. Open 10 am-6 pm daily, Thur 'til 8 pm. Free except for special exhibit. $8, $5 w/student ID (also: free with American Express card). 'Spectacular.'

National Museum of Science and Technology, 1867 St- Laurent Bvd, 991-3044. 'A must for those who like to participate.' Lets visitors explore the wonderful world of tech and transport with touchy-feely exhibits. Summer daily Sat-Thurs 9 am-6 pm, Fri 'til 9 pm; closed Mon Sept-May. Free Thur 5 pm-9 pm. $6, $5 w/student ID.

Rideau Canal. The 124 mile waterway which runs to Kingston on Lake Ontario.

The 'giant's staircase,' a series of eight locks, lifts and drops boats some 80 ft between Ottawa River and Parliament Hill. Cruises on the Canal and river are available. Cost $10. Contact Paul Boat Lines, 225-6781. Or hire a bike at **Dows Lake**, 232-1001 and ride along the towpath. Near the locks is the **Bytown Museum**, 234-4570. An interesting look at old Ottawa. May-Sept Mon-Sat 10 am-5 pm, $3, $2 w/student ID. Sun 1-5 pm, free. Close by, in Major's Hill Park, is the spot from where the **Noonday Gun** is fired. Everyone in Ottawa sets their watches by it. Can be heard 14 miles away.

Royal Canadian Mint, 320 Sussex Dr. Guided tours every half hour, Mon-Fri 9 am-5 pm, Sat-Sun from noon, $2. Tours in groups, rsvs essential, call 993-8990 the day before or early same morning.

Parks: There is a nice park at Somerset and Lyon and the Vincent Massey Park, off Riverside Dr, has free summer concerts. If you have transport, a trip to **Gatineau Park**, five miles beyond Hull, is worth a thought. Good swimming, cycling, hiking and fishing. 'The park gives one an impression of the archetypal Canada; rugged country, timber floating down the Gatineau, etc.' **Dow's Lake Pavilion**, 101 Queen Elizabeth Driveway, rents pedal boats, canoes and bikes. Open daily 11.30 am-1 am. Rentals by the hour with varying prices.

ENTERTAINMENT

Read *What's on in Ottawa*. For late entertainment cross the river to Hull where the pubs are open longer. Ottawa has several English style pubs. Recommended are: **Elephant & Castle**, Rideau Centre (fish 'n chips). **Marble Works**, 14 Waller St, and **Earl of Sussex**, 431 Sussex Dr, 14 English beers on tap. **Minglewoods**, York and Dalhousie is suggested for Canadian beer, pool and sport on big screen tv; **The Nax**, in the University of Ottawa Uni Centre off King Edward St often features live bands. Try **Reactors** in the Market, and **Hoolihans** on York for dancing.

Barrymore's on Bank St nr the Royal Oak is Ottawa's big venue for popular bands. **Bon Vivante Brasserie**, St Joseph, Hull. French Canadian music. At the **National Arts Centre**, 53 Elgin St, 996-5051, student standby (max 2 tkts pp) available for some performances.

If you are in town on Labour Day Sept w/end, don't miss the **International Hot Air Balloon Festival** which launches itself from the Parc de l'Abe in Gatineau and can be watched from Parliament Hill.

Odyssey Theatre, 232-8407, hosts open-air comedy at **Strathcona Park**. Annual **Summer Exhibition**, every August in Lansdowne Park, includes a fair, animals, crafts, concerts, etc. 'Good fun.' During the first 3 w/ends of Feb, **Winterlude**, 239-5000 lines the Rideau Canal with ice sculptures focusing on what it is like to be an Ottawan in winter!

SHOPPING

For Indian and Eskimo stuff try Four Corners, 93 Sparks St, and Snow Goose on Sparks St. Also, check out Sparks St Mall, a 3-block traffic-free shopping section btwn Elgin and Bank. Fountains, sidewalk cafes, good shopping, etc.

Arthur's Place, Bank, near Somerset. Second-hand books and records.

Rideau Centre, on Rideau, 5 min walk from Arts Centre. Ottawa's primary shopping mall.

INFORMATION

Capital Visitors and Convention Bureau, 65 Elgin St, in the Capital Square Building, 237-5150. Has accommodation and sightseeing advice, including *See & Do* brochure, maps, etc. Mon-Fri 9 am-5 pm. Read *Usually Reliable Source* and *Penny Press* for what's happening.

Hostelling International-Canada (HI-C), **Ontario East Region**, 75 Nicholas St, 569-1400. Youth hostel passes, travel info and equipment. Mon-Fri 9.30 am-5.30 pm, Sat 'til 5 pm.

Info Kiosk at National Arts Centre, Elgin & Queen, 237-5158. Daily summer 9 am-9 pm; otherwise Mon-Sat 9 am-5 pm, Sun 10 am-4 pm.
National Capital Commission Information Centre, 14 Metcalfe St, (800) 465-1867. Provides free maps and the helpful *Ottawa Visitors Guide*. Daily summer 8.30 am-9 pm; Sept-May Mon-Sat 9 am-5 pm, Sun 10 am-4 pm.

TRAVEL
One of the nicest ways of seeing Ottawa is by bike, and an extensive system of bikeways and routes is there for this purpose. Bicycles available for hire at Chateau Laurier and on sunny days, at Confederation Sq. For prices and info call: 241-4140. Daily 9 am-7.30 pm (credit card required). Real bike fanatics should go see one of the biggest bike-shops in North America, **Ottawa Bikeways**, on Carling St, 722-4470.
OC Public Transport, 1500 St- Laurent, 741-4390 (for all bus info). Excellent system with buses congregating on either side of Rideau Center. Rail station is 2 miles from city centre. To get there catch #95 bus on Slater St or Mackenzie King Bridge, every 15 mins; $1.85. For info on the blue **Hull City Buses** call (819) 770-3242.
VIA Rail, 200 Tremblay Rd, (800) 561-3949. Passenger train service throughout Canada.
Ottawa International Airport, 998-3151 (is six miles out of town). **Kasbury Transport**, 736-9993, runs shuttles btwn the airport and various hotels. Daily every 30 mins, $9 w/student ID.
Voyageur Colonial Coach, 265 Catherine St, 238-5900. Primarily services eastern Canada.
Greyhound, 237-7038, run buses bound for western Canada/southern Ontario.

MORRISBURG A small town on the St Lawrence whose main claim to fame is **Upper Canada Village**, a re-creation of a St Lawrence Valley community of the 19th century. The village is situated some 11kms east of Morrisburg on Hwy 2, in Crysler Farm Battlefield Park, 543-3704. The Park serves as a memorial to Canadians who died in the War of 1812 against the United States.

The buildings here were all moved from their previous sites to save them from the path of the St Lawrence Seaway and include a tavern, mill, church, store, etc, all of which are fully operational. Vehicles are not allowed. Daily 9.30 am-5 pm mid-May to mid-Oct; $10, $7.50 w/student ID.

KINGSTON A small, pleasant city situated at the meeting place of the St Lawrence and Lake Ontario. Early Kingston was built around the site of Fort Frontenac, then a French outpost, later to be replaced by the British Fort Henry, the principal British stronghold west of Québec. This was, ever so briefly, the capital of Canada (1841-44) and many of the distinctive limestone 19th century houses still survive.

The town is the home of Queens University, situated on the banks of the St Lawrence. The Kingston Fall Fair, which in fact happens in late summer, is considered 'worth a stop'. Kingston is also a good centre for visiting the picturesque **Thousand Islands** in the St Lawrence. For dining, drinking and entertainment links, try *www.Megahit.com/kingston.html*.

ACCOMMODATION
Donald Gordon Centre, 421 Union St, 545-2221. Good reasonably priced accommodation can be found here (part of uni). From D-$50. Dining room, lounge, bar and games room.

Hilltop Motel, 2287 Princess St, 542-3846. D-$48.

Kingston Area B&B Association, 542-0214. From S/D-$50, including bfast.

Kingston HI Hostel, 210 Bagot St, 546-7203. $14-18. Shower, lockers and kitchen. 'Super friendly hostel, 10 mins from bus route, shops, laundry, lake nearby. Highly recommended.'

Queen's University, 545-2529, has rooms May-Aug. Rsvs pref. $32, $17 w/student ID. Bfast available.

Camping: Lake Ontario Park Campground, 542-6574, 2 miles W on King St. May-Sept. Sites for two $18 w/hook-up, XP-$2.50. Also, **Rideau Acres**, 546-2711 on Hwy 15 (north of exit 104/exit 623 on Hwy 401). Sites $19, $23 w/hook-up.

FOOD

Chez Piggy, 68R Princess St, 549-7673. Brunch dishes all under $8, are interesting and different—lamb kidneys with scrambled eggs and home fries, Thai beef salad, along with the more typical brunch fare. Sun brunch served 11 am-2.30 pm. Rsvs recommended at w/ends. Mon-Sat 11.30 am-midnight, Sun from 11 am.

Kingston Brewing Company, 34 Clarence St, 542-4978. The oldest brewing pub in Ontario, with true British ale served from a hand-pump. Produces own lager and Dragon's Breath Ale. Burgers, sandwiches and main courses under $8. Locals come here for the charbroiled ghetto chicken wings served with spicy BBQ sauce and the smoked beef and ribs plus typical bar fare. Back courtyard garden and sidewalk patio. Tours of brewery available. Mon-Sat 11am-1 am, Sun from 11.30 am.

Farmer's Market, Market Sq, is open Tue, Thur, Sat.

Morrison's, 318 King St E, 542-9483. 'Best value set meals at $4-$7.' Daily 11am 'til 8 pm.

Pilot House, 265 King St E, 542-0222. Beautifully fresh fish and chips and expensive English beer (12 kinds of draft). Daily 11.30 am-1 am.

OF INTEREST

Fort Frederick, Royal Military College Museum, 541-6000, ext. 6652. On RMC grounds ($1/2$ mile E of Hwy 2). Canada's West Point, founded in 1876. The museum, in a Martello tower, features pictures and exhibits of Old Kingston and Military College history, and the Douglas collection of historic weapons. June through Labour Day. $2.50.

Murney Redoubt. At the foot of Barrie St, 544-9925. Now run by the Kingston Historical Society. Daily 10 am-5 pm May-Sept. $2.

Old Fort Henry, E on Hwy 2 at junction Hwy 15. The fort has been restored and during the summer college students dressed in Victorian army uniforms give displays of drilling. Daily 10 am-5 pm, $9.50, $6.75 w/student ID. The fort is also a military museum. For info call 542-7388. John A MacDonald, Canada's first Prime Minister, lived in **Bellevue House**, 545-8666, on Centre St. The century-old house has been restored and furnished in the style of the 1840s. Known locally as the 'Pekoe Pagoda' or 'Tea Caddy Castle' because of its comparatively frivolous appearance in contrast to the more solid limestone buildings of the city. The house is open daily, 9 am-6 pm. Free.

Pump House Steam Museum, on Ontario St, 542-2261. A restored 1848 pump house now housing a vintage collection of working engines. Also marine museum and coastguard ship. $3.75, $3.25 w/student ID. Mid-June-Sept, Tue-Sun 10 am-5 pm.

North of the city the **Rideau Lakes** extend for miles and miles. The Rideau Hiking Trail winds its way gently among the lakes. You can take a free ferry to **Wolfe Island** in the St Lawrence. Ferries leave from City Hall.

Once on the island it is possible to catch another boat (not free) to the US.

Thousand Islands Boat Tours. From Gananoque Quay, 20 miles from Kingston, on Hwy 2, 382-2144. Trip lasts 3 hrs. $15. There is a shorter cruise at $10. Tours 9 am-3 pm, mid-May-mid-Oct. Departing from Crawford Dock at the foot of Brock St in downtown Kingston, there are additional tours of the harbour and Thousand Islands. $12-$17. For info: call Island Queen, 549-5544.

ENTERTAINMENT/SPORT
Stages Nightclub, 390 Princess St, 547-3657. Bands and disco.
Canadian Olympic Training Regatta. Annual event, held during the last week in Aug; one of the largest regattas in North America.
International Hockey Hall of Fame, Alfred and York Sts. Daily 9 am-5 pm.

INFORMATION
John Deutsch, University Centre Union, University Sts. Ride board, shops, post office, laundry, etc.
Visitor & Convention Centre , 209 Ontario St, 548-4415. Summer daily 8.30 am-8.30 pm; otherwise 9 am-5 pm, Sun 10 am-4 pm.

TRAVEL
VIA Rail Station , Princess & Counter St, 544-5600.
Voyageur Colonial Bus Terminal , 175 Counter St, 547-4916. Daily 6.30 am-9 pm.

ST LAWRENCE ISLANDS NATIONAL PARK The park is made up of 17 small islands in the Thousand Islands area of the St Lawrence between Kingston and Brockville, and Mallorytown Landing on the mainland. The islands can be reached only by water-taxi from Gananoque, Mallorytown Landing and Rockport, Ontario, or from Alexandria Bay and Clayton in New York State. Park is open daily, mid-May to mid-Oct. Free.

It's a peaceful, green-forested area noted chiefly for its good fishing grounds. Camping facilities are available on the islands.

TORONTO 'Trunno,' or 'Metro' as the natives call their city, is the most American of the Canadian cities, having many of the characteristics of metropolitan America but without all of the usual problems. It's a brash, cosmopolitan city with some 25 different languages on tap around town, sprawling over 270 square miles, with many fine examples of skyscraper architecture, good shopping areas, excellent theatre, music and arts facilities, a vibrant night life, fast highways, and yet it's a clean city, with markedly few poor areas, and the streets are safe at night.

Perhaps out of envy, Toronto is also nicknamed 'Toronto The Good'; more like Switzerland than North America, remarked one reader. 'Good' in that the city has yearned to be as stylish as New York without the poverty and dirt, and has succeeded. You can get a great haircut, great clothes, great movies, great drinks, great music and a great job here. They also have a great polar bear section at the zoo where you experience a polar bear diving into the water two inches from your face.

Then take a look at the windows of the Royal Bank building. The golden glow emanating from them is real gold dust, mixed with the glass. That also is proof of how rich Canada is, and most of the wealth and power, the envy of the other provinces, is situated right here on Bay Street.

This is also a good centre from which to see other places in Ontario. Niagara Falls and New York State are an hour and a half away down the Queen Elizabeth Way (QEW), to the north there is Georgian Bay and the vast Algonquin Provincial Park, while to the west there are London and Stratford. *Toronto Life, www.tor-Lifeline.com/* includes restaurant guide, events calendar and the best of the city.
The telephone area code is 416.

ACCOMMODATION

For assistance on finding accommodation in Toronto, contact **B&B Homes of Toronto**, 363-6362; **B&B Registry**, 964-2566; **Downtown Toronto Association of B&B Guesthouses**, PO Box 190, Station B, Toronto M5T 2W1, 690-1724/368-1420; and **Econo-Lodging Services**, 101 Nymark Ave, 494-0541.

Chisholm Hospitality Home, 120 Leslie St, 469-2967. Dorm $19; ask for backpackers' rates.

Christiansen's Guest House, 183 College St, 979-2489. Renowned guest house, close to downtown. Dorm rooms, $26.

Karabanow Tourist Home, 9 Spadina Rd, at Bloor St W, 923-4004. Rooms with shared bath and free parking: from S/D-$24. Discounted weekly rates Oct-May. Rooms w/bath from $61. TV, next to subway. 'Clean and very helpful.' *email:* 7.1663.3131.@compuserve.com

Leslieville Home Hostel, 185 Leslie St, 461-7258. 'Run by British couple. Great atmosphere but a 15 min streetcar ride from centre.' 'Comfortable.' Rsvs essential in summer. Heavily discounted rates Nov-April. $16 dorm, S-$37, D-$47. Bfast $2.50.

Marigold Backpackers Hostel, 2011 Dundas St W, 536-8824. Closest hostel to the Canadian National Exhibition. Safe, clean, 'club like atmosphere,' TV room, free morning coffee and donut buffet. Dundas and Carlton street cars pass in front of door; close to Roncesvalles eateries. $20.

Neill-Wycik College Hotel, 96 Gerrard St E, (800) 268-4358. Try here first. Good facilities, baggage storage, central, 5 mins from subway. No AC in rooms but AC lounges and TV. Dorm $19; S-$34; D-$44 (10% weekly discount; also w/student ID, ask for backpackers' rates). Bfast $4. 'Recommended.' May-Aug only. Airport shuttle. 'High rise hospitality.'

Toronto HI Hostel, 90 Gerrard St W, 971-4440. Located a few blocks from bus station, centrally located with kitchen, laundry, linen, lockers, TV, swimming pool and gym. 'Fills quickly.' Rsvs advisable in summer. Dorms $23-$28.

University Residences: University College, 85 St George St, 978-8735. Summers only. From S-$40. Also suggested are **Trinity** and **Wycliffe Colleges** on Hoskin Ave, and **St Hildas** on Devonshire Place. About $80 weekly. 'Pleasant and clean.'

University of Toronto: Scarborough campus, Sir Dans, 73 St George St, 287-7367. 'Fantastic student residence.' Under $100 weekly (min 2 week stay). 17 May-25 Aug. 'Parties, sports facilities.' 'Basic uni accommodation, have to clean own rooms.' 'Excellent setting/location, full of other travellers/BUNACers in summer.' 90 mins from downtown; or try **University of Toronto Housing Service**, 214 College St, 978-8045. Has list of accommodations available in student residences, summer only. $30-50 range.

YWCA, 80 Woodlawn Ave E, 923-8454. Take Yonge-University subway to Summerhill, walk two blocks north. For women only. Dorm $18. From S-$45, D-$60.

Camping: Indian Line Tourist Campground, 7625 Finch Ave W, (905) 678-1233/off-season 661-6600 ext 203. This is the closest area to metropolitan Toronto. Sites $16-$20 (full hook-up). Showers, laundry. May-early Oct. Rsvs recommended July-Aug. Also, try **Glen Rouge Provincial Park**, 7450 Hwy 2/Kingston Rd, 392-8092. Near hiking, pool, tennis courts and beach. Showers/toilets. Full hook-up $22.

FOOD

Over 5,000 restaurants squeezed into this city! Fave dining areas to eat out in include **Bloor St W**, **Chinatown** and **Village by the Grange**, the latter being home of super-cheap restaurants and vendors.

Bergman's, on Yonge north of St Clair. Great brownies and cheese danish. For seafood lovers, **Coasters**, upstairs from the Old Fish Market on Market St near the St Lawrence Market, has inexpensive nightly specials in a cozy bar with a fireplace.

Druxy's Famous Deli Sandwiches, a cafeteria-style eating place with locations all over Toronto, is a good spot for salads and sandwiches.

Fran's Restaurants, 21 St Clair Ave W, 2275 Yonge, 20 College, 9239867. Spaghetti, fish and chips, burgers. 24 hrs. Under $12.

Ginsberg and Wong, McCaul and Dundas. Chinese and Jewish. 'Great food, reasonable prices.'

Hungarian Goulash Party Tavern, 498 Queen St W, 504-6124. Good, cheap Hungarian food. Entrees begin at $8.

Java Joe's, Gerrard St W (corner of Bay). Next to Toronto International Hostel, this coffee shop/bistro serves up bfast of bagel and coffee/tea for $1 (show hostel receipt). Lunch specials for $4-5. 'Good value, pleasant surroundings.'

Lick's Homeburgers and Ice Cream, on Yonge south of Eglinton and on Queen St E in the Beaches. For the messiest, yummiest burgers around in a fun atmosphere, from $4.

Loon Fong Yuen, 393 Spadina. Unpretentious Chinese eatery, meals from $7. Lots of places in Chinatown (around Dundas & Spadina) offer meals at reasonable prices.

The Midtown Café, 552 College St W, 920-4533. Play pool or relax and eat whilst listening to music. Large *tapas* menu at w/ends. Eats for $3-$5. Daily 10 am-2am.

Nefeli, 407 Danforth Ave, 465-4559. One of Danforth's many Greek restaurants. 'It cost around $20 each for two courses and loads of wine. 'Food and atmosphere was lovely-perfect for a special treat.' Take subway to Chester.

Organ Grinder, 58 the Esplanade, 364-6517. 'Noisy but a good laugh.' Pizza, Italian food. 'Entertainment by the only organ of its kind in the world.' Pizzas $7-9. Sun-Thurs 11.30 am-11pm, Fri-Sat 11.30 am-midnight.

Old Spaghetti Factory, Esplanade, east of Yonge, 864-9761. Huge old warehouse. From $7. 'Very delicious. Excellent value and service.'

Sneaky Dees, 431 College St, 603-3090. Serves a bargain bfast for $3.85 from 3 am-11am. Doubles as a night-time hot spot.

Swiss Chalet, a chain with numerous outlets, has 'great' barbecued chicken and ribs at very reasonable prices.

Toby's Goodeats, 925-2171. Locations across the city (including Yonge & Bloor, Bloor & Bay, the Eaton Centre, Yonge & St Clair). Toby's serves up some of the best-value meals in the city. Meals for under $10.

Markets: Westclair Italian Village (little Italy) along St Clair Ave W btwn Dufferin and Lansdown. Sidewalk cafes and restaurants. Don't miss 2 good markets, for fresh produce and a wide variety of food:

Kensington Market, Dundas St West to College St, Spadina Ave to Augusta St.

St-Lawrence Market, 95 Front St East. Over 40 foodstalls in this historic 1844 building, Toronto's first city hall.

OF INTEREST

Art Gallery of Ontario, 317 Dundas St at McCaul, 977-0414. Rembrandt, Picasso, Impressionists, large collection of Henry Moore sculptures, plus Oldenburg's 'Hamburger,' and collections by Canadian artists. Mon-Sun 10 am-5.30 pm; Fri & Weds 'til 10 pm. Wed 5 pm-9 pm, free. Closed Mon in winter. $7.50; $4 w/student ID. 'Don't miss the Art Gallery shop!'

Bata Shoe Museum, 327 Bloor St, 979-7799. The only shoe museum in North America, displaying over 9000 pairs from Elton's platforms to ancient Egyptian sandals. Tues-Sun 11am-6 pm. $4, $1.50 w/student ID.

Black Creek Pioneer Village, 736-1733, on the northern edge of Toronto at Jane St and Steeles Ave. A reconstructed pioneer village of the 18th century. Costumed workers perform daily tasks in the restored buildings. Daily 10 am-5 pm; closed Jan & Feb. $8 or $5.50 w/student ID. If travelling there by subway and streetcar, allow about 1 hr each way from the city centre.

Toronto

1 Old Fort York
2 Black Creek Pioneer Village
3 Art Gallery of Ontario
4 Royal Ontario Museum
5 MacKenzie House

Canadian National Exhibition, 393-6000. Otherwise known as CNE or 'The Ex', held annually next to Ontario Place during the 18 days before Labour Day. Free admission to Ontario Place from the CNE during this time. A sort of glorified state fair, Canadian style, and the largest annual exhibition in the world. Cheap food in the Food Hall, and site of the Hockey Hall of Fame. 'Fabulous.'

Canada's Wonderland, 30 kms north, Rutherford Rd, off Hwy 400, for info (905) 832-2205/832-7000. Ontario's answer to Disney? Includes 5 theme areas, a 150-ft man-made mountain complete with waterfalls, 'splashworld' and all the usual rides and entertainments. $33 for a day pass, $18.50 if don't want to use the rides. May-Sept 10 am-midnight.

Casa Loma, Davenport at Spadina, 9231171. An eccentric chateau-style mansion built by the late Sir Henry Pellatt between 1911 and 1914 at a reported cost of $3m. It was restored in 1967 and the proceeds from the daily tours go to charity. 'Fantastic.' Daily 10 am-4 pm, year round. $8.50. **Spadina House**, next door, is also open to the public. Family mansion. 'Play croquet in the gardens.' Take the subway to Dupont. $6.

Chinatown, along Dundas West and China Court, Spadina, south of Dundas. Usual mixture of tourist and 'real' Chinese. Good place to eat.

City Hall, 100 Queen St at Bay St, 392-7341. $30m creation of Finnish architect Viljo Revell, perhaps most impressive when lit at night. Brochure available for self-guided tour, Mon-Fri 8.30 am-4 pm. The reflecting pool in **Nathan Phillips Sq** becomes a skating rink in winter, and is also home to various special events. Call the **Events Hotline**, 392-0458.

CN Tower, foot of John St, 360-8500. At 1815 ft the tallest free-standing structure in the world. The observation deck is open in summer 9 am-midnight. Elevator to observation deck $13; $16 inclusive to go to the Space Deck. 'Can get in for $6.50 if YHA member—came across discount by accident!' 'The CN Tower has a great view, but don't eat there unless the Air Show is on, when you can have a front row seat and the planes are so close that the pilots wave to you.' 'Expect queues!'

George R Gardiner Museum of Ceramic Art, 11 Queen's Park, 586-8080. The only museum of its kind in North America, with a vast collection of pottery and porcelain. Tue-Sat 10 am-5 pm, Sun from 11am, free last hour every day. Closed Mon. $8, $4 w/student ID. Admission gets you into Royal Ontario Museum and vice-versa.

Harbourfront, 235 Queen's Quay West. 92 acres of restaurants, antique markets, art shows, films, theatre, etc, on Lake Ontario. Free Sun concerts at 1 pm. Great place to spend a sunny summer afternoon.

Mackenzie House, 82 Bond St, 392-6915. Georgian home and print shop of William Lyon Mackenzie, first mayor of Toronto and leader of the Upper Canada rebellion in 1837. Now restored to mid-1800s condition. Tues-Sun noon-5 pm; $4.

Marine Museum of Upper Canada, Exhibition Place, 392-1765. History of shipping and the Great Lakes from fur trading days on. Mon-Sat 10 am-5 pm, Sat/Suns & hols from noon. $3.50.

Metro Toronto Zoo, off junction Hwy 401 and Meadowvale Rd, 392-5901. Year round from 9am; closing time varies with season. $11. Take bus #86A from Kennedy Subway station.

Old Fort York, 392-6907. On Garrison Rd, the Fort was built in 1793 and was the site of the 1812 battle of York when American forces beat British/Canadian and Native defenders. In retaliation British forces later burnt down the White House. The fort now houses restored army quarters and a collection of antique weapons, tools, etc. Guided tours and 'historical activities,' open daily 10 am-4 pm, w/ends noon-5 pm; $6.

Ontario Place on the lakefront, 314-9900. A complex of manmade islands and lagoons, with marina and attractive parkland. Free outdoor rock, folk or symphony concerts given late afternoons and evenings at the Forum; films at Cinesphere on the 'largest screen in the world'; and multimedia presentations of Ontario are shown in several unusual pavilions. There's an amazing children's fun village and fairly cheap food available in several different eating places. Well recommended by previous visitors. $8.50. Take the TTC to Ossington, then bus south using transfer. $3.

Ontario Science Centre, 770 Don Mills Rd and Eglinton Ave E, 429-4100. A do-it-yourself-place which is 'part-museum, part fun fair.' 'Breathtaking.' 'An absolute must.' 'Definitely worth going to.' Daily 10 am-6 pm $8.50; Wed 4 pm-8 pm $2.50. Closed Mon in winter. Take Yonge Subway to Eglinton, then #34 bus to Don Mills Rd.

Provincial Parliament Buildings, Queen's Park ($1/2$ block N of College St, University Ave), 325-7500. Completed in 1892, the Legislative Buildings once provided living accommodation for its elected members. Building open Mon-Fri 8.30 am-6 pm, Sat-Sun 9 am-4 pm; chambers close 4.30 pm. Free guided tours Mon to Fri by request, Sat/Sun every $1/2$ hr 9 am-4 pm, including a $1/2$ hr visit to the Public Gallery. Free gallery passes available at main lobby info desk 1.30 pm.

Q-Zar laser game/Mindwarp, base of the CN Tower. Futuristic live-action laser game and flight-simulator. $8.50 each.

Royal Ontario Museum, 100 Queen's Park. Has the largest Chinese art collection outside China and fine natural history section. Daily 10 am-6 pm; Tue 'til 8 pm. $8, w/student ID $4.50. Free Tues after 4 pm. Next door is the **McLaughlin Planetarium**. Call for showtimes, 586-5736/5750. $8.50, w/student ID $5. Laser and astronomy shows.

The Sky Dome, 341-3663. Located at the foot of Peter St, this impressive structure boasts the largest retractable roof in the world and numerous bars and restaurants. Catch a football or baseball game here starring Toronto's Argonauts or the world champion Blue Jays. Tours available.

Toronto Stock Exchange, The Exchange Tower, 2 First Canadian Place, 947-4670. Visitors Gallery has recorded explanatory guide on tape, Tues-Fri.

University of Toronto, west of Queens Park, 978-5000. The largest educational institution in the British Commonwealth. Free 1 hr tours of the campus available in June/July/Aug, starting from either Hart House or University College; Mon-Fri 10.30 am, 1pm & 2.30 pm

Parks: The best of the city's parks and open spaces are **High Park** (free swimming), **Edwards Gardens, Don Mills, Forest Hill** and **Rosedale**. The ferry ride to **Centre Island** in the harbour costs $4 r/t. Or take a stroll along the boardwalk in the Beaches, south of Queen St E, east from Woodbine.

ENTERTAINMENT

Check the *Globe and Mail, Toronto Star* and *Toronto Sun* for daily entertainments guide, as well as the free weekly guides, *NOW* and *EYE*. Also look for *Key to Toronto*, monthly. There are many bars situated along Queen St W, some of which feature nightly live entertainment: check out especially the **Bamboo** and the **Rivoli**. Also, **Lee's Palace** on Bloor St W, just east of Bathurst and the **El Mocambo** at College and Spadina.

The Big Bop, 651 Queen St W, 504-6699. A multi-storey dance club with different styles of music on each floor and a sofa-lounge upstairs, air-hockey tables/pool tables. Popular with students. Wed, Thurs, Fri, Sat 8 pm-3am. $8, on Wed $2.50 and all drinks $3. Must be 19 or over.

Bourbon St, 180 Queen St. Jazz, often with top-name appearances.

Cineplex Odeon, 1303 Yonge St, 323-6600. One of the largest cineplexes in the world with 17 screens; $5.50 before 6 pm, $8 after 6 pm, $9 Fri/Sat after 6 pm, $4.50 all day Tues. Tkts go fast for the evening performances of new movies so buy early.

Harbourfront, 235 Queen's Quay, 973-3000. Concerts plus movie theatre showing oldies, horror movies, and other classics.

Molson Indy, at the Canadian National Exhibition, 872-4639 for tkts. $75-$110 for 3 days. It varies every year, but usually during the second half of July. 'This race has been on the Indy car circuit since 1986 and has grown more popular each year.'

The Nag's Head, Eaton Centre. Folk music most nights.

O'Keefe Centre, Front & Yonge, 393-7469. Opera, ballet, concerts, jazz, drama. Student rush seats available on night of performance.

St Lawrence Centre for the Arts, Front & Scott, 366-7723. Drama, dance and opera. Season usually ends in May; have some performances during the summer.

Ye Olde Brunswick House, Brunswick & Bloor. 'Good jazz and a lively amateur night.' Bavarian-style long benches and pitchers of beer. Live music upstairs in Albert Hall.

Yuk Yuk's, at Yonge & Eglinton and Bay & Yorkville, offers a night of amateur stand-up comedians. Dinner available. Also **Second City** 110 Lombard at the Old Firehall, , 863-1111. Features excellent nightly shows. 'Canadian humour at its best.'

Festivals: The Festival of Festivals—Toronto Film Festival, first Thurs after Labour Day, tkts available at box office, 92 Bloor St, call 968-FILM; and **Toronto International Dragon Boat Race Festival**, 364-0046, held in June. Celebration includes traditional performances, foods and free outdoor lunchtime concerts.

Swimming: free at **Woodbine Swimming Pool** (subway to Woodbine, bus to

Lakeshore), and **Sunnyside Swimming Pool** (subway to Dundas W, streetcar to Queen), and other pools. Call Recreation Info: 392-7259.

Ticket Info: TO Tix, 208 Yonge St at Eaton's Centre, 596-8211, sell ¹/₂ price tkts for theatre, music, dance and opera on performance day. Tues-Sat noon-7.30 pm, Sun 'til 3 pm but arrive before 11.45 am.

For free tkts to **CBC TV shows** and info on tours, call 205-3311, Mon-Fri 9 am-5 pm.

Five Star Tkts 208 Yonge St, offers half-price tkts on the day of the performance for many of the music, dance and theatre productions in Toronto, Tues-Fri noon-7.30 pm and Sat 11am-3 pm. For info call 596-8211.

SHOPPING
Queen St, west of University Ave, is renowned as the **alternative student shopping area**. 'Vibrant.' Also, check out:

Bee Bee's Flea Market Inc, St Lawrence Market, 92 Front St at Jarvis. Most Sundays all year, 10 am-5 pm. Antiques, crafts. Free coffee or tea.

Eaton Centre Shopping Mall, Yonge and Dundas. An impressive multi-levelled, glass-domed complex of stores, eating places and entertainments. 'Definitely worth a visit.'

Honest Ed, Bloor & Bathurst. 'Just about everything at 40% reduction.' Cheap clothes at **Hercules**, 577 Yonge St. Army surplus store.

Sam the Record Man, Yonge and Dundas. 'Huge selection of cheap records.'

Beneath the **Toronto Dominion Bank** complex, Bay and King Sts, there is a wealth of shops and restaurants, bustling during the day but closed at night. Interconnects into the subway system, the Royal York Hotel and Union Station.

World's Biggest Bookstore, 20 Edward St at Yonge (1 block from Eaton Centre). 17 miles of shelves with over 1 million books. Open daily.

Yorkville, north of Queens Park east of Avenue Rd. 'Lively, open 'til about 1 am on Sat night—street theatre, music, etc.'

INFORMATION
Metropolitan Toronto Convention and Visitors Association (MTCVA), 207 Queen's Quay W, Harbourfront Centre, (800) 363 1990. More convenient office in the Eaton Centre on the lower floor. Watch out for the roving visitor information van as well. Mon-Fri 8.30 am-6 pm, Sun from 9.30 am.

Post Office at Front and Bay Sts. City of Toronto Info: 392-7341.

Travel CUTS student travel office: 187 College St, 979-2406. Smaller office at 74 Gerrard St E, 977-0441. Both open Mon-Fri 9 am-5 pm.

TRAVEL
Airport buses leave the Royal York Hotel and the Sheraton Centre every 20 mins. City buses run to airport (Terminal 2 only) at least every hr from St Lawrence West subway. $3.

Allo Stop driver/rider service: call 531-7668. $26 to Ottawa; $44 to NYC or Québec City. $6 membership.

Bike rentals: Brown's Sport and Cycle Shop, 2447 Bloor St W, 763-4176. $18, $35 w/end, $44 weekly, $200 deposit! Mon-Sat 9.30 am-6 pm, Thur-Fri to 8 pm.

GreyCoach/Greyhound Bus Terminal, 610 Bay St at Dundas, call 367-8747 for info.

The Last Minute Club, at Union Station—ground floor, 441-2582. 'Best place to get really cheap flights.' Mon-Fri 9 am-9 pm; Sat 'til 4 pm. $40 membership.

Toronto Driveaway Service, 5803 Yonge St, Suite #101, 225-7754. Open 9 am-5 pm, Sat 10 am-1pm.

Toronto Transit Commission (TTC) bus and subway, 393-4636: Standard fares operate on this integrated transport system and it is cheaper to buy tokens. Current fare is $2, $3 r/t, 10 tokens $14, monthly pass $69. Free transfers, valid btwn subway and bus lines. Exact fare required for buses and streetcars. Sun and holidays bus pass $5. Bus drivers do not give change.

Route maps available from ticket booths. There is an express bus service from Islington, Yorkdale and York Mills subways to the airport every ¹/₂ hr, $8-12.
VIA Rail Canada: 366-8411. Trains from Union Station to Niagara Falls—about $37 same day return.

HAMILTON Situated on the shores of Lake Ontario roughly midway between Toronto and Niagara Falls, Hamilton is Canada's King of Steel. The city is home to the two principal steel companies in the nation, Stelco and Dofasco, and like its US counterpart, Pittsburgh, is in the throes of an urban cleanup and renewal in the wake of the steel giants. The air and the water are cleaner here these days and many new and interesting buildings have gone up around town. Hamilton is working hard to improve its image.

The city is also blessed with one of the largest landlocked harbours on the Great Lakes, as a result handling the third largest water tonnage in the country. Although primarily a shipping and industrial centre, Hamilton does offer a variety of non-related activities to the visitor. It is also within easy reach of Niagara, Brantford, Stratford and London. *www.city.hamilton.on.ca/*. *The area code is 905.*

ACCOMMODATION
McMaster University, 1280 Main St West, (905) 525-9140, ext 24781.
Shared bath, kitchen facilities, indoor pool. From S/D-$32, S-$189 weekly, approx $390 monthly (call to check prices). Discounts for longer stays. May-Aug.
Pines Motel, 395 Centennial Pkwy, 561-5652. Close to Confederation Park, waterslide and wave pool. From S-$51, D-$60, TV.
YMCA, 79 James St S, 529-7102. S-$29 + $10 key deposit.
YWCA75 MacNab St S, 522-9922. S-$29 + $5 deposit. 'Rsvs a good idea.'

FOOD
Barangas, 380 Van Wagner's Beach Rd, 544-7122. Food with an international flavour, dishes $7-18. Daily 11am-1 am.
Black Forest Inn, 255 King St E, 528-3538. A festive atmosphere for good budget dining. Sample all kinds of schnitzels and sausages, all served with home fries and sauerkraut. Try the Black Forest cake for dessert. Main courses $6-12. Tues-Thurs 11.30 am-10.30 pm, Fri-Sat 'til 11pm, Sun noon-9.30 pm.
Christopher's Cameo Restaurant, 60 James St N, 529-4214. 'Inexpensive.' Sun-Thurs 8 am-7.30 pm, Fri-Sat 'til 9 pm.
Farmers Market, central Hamilton. The largest such market in Canada.
McMaster University Common Building Refectory. 'During the summer, June through Aug, it is possible to eat here. Meals from $4.'
The Winking Judge, 25 Augusta St, 527-1280. Convivial crowd esp at lunchtime and w/ends when the piano player is about. Sample the veal piccata, prime rib and barbecue ribs. Most pub fare items $4-10. Mon-Thurs 11.30 am-midnight, Fri-Sat 'til 2am, Sun noon-11pm.

OF INTEREST
African Lion Safari and Game Farm, W off Hwy 8, S of Cambridge, (800) 461-WILD. 1,500 exotic animals roam this drive-through wild-life park. New animal exhibit showcasing the White Tiger. 'Look deep into the icy blue eyes of these rare large cats!' *www.lionsafari.com*.
The Bruce Trail extends more than 700 km along the Niagara escarpment. Good for hiking, pleasant walks. 'Gorgeous.'
Canadian Football Hall of Fame, 58 Jackson St W, within City Hall Plaza area, 528-

7566. Push button exhibits. Mon-Sat 9.30 am-4.30 pm,Sun from noon. $4, $2 w/student ID.

Canadian Warplane Heritage Museum, 9820 Airport Rd, Hamilton Airport, Mt Hope (1 hr from Niagara Falls/Toronto), (800) 386-5888. Museum houses the world's largest collection of planes remaining from WWII-Jet Age which are kept in flying condition. Watch the 'Flight of the Day,' browse the archive exhibit gallery and memorabilia and experiment with video/audio interactives. Daily year-round 10 am-5 pm, Thurs 'til 8 pm. $7; $6 w/student ID. *www.warplane.com*.

Dundurn Castle, York St at Dundurn, 546-2872. Restored Victorian mansion of Sir Allen Napier MacNab, Prime Minister of United Canada, 1854-1856. *Son et lumière* performances during summer. In August, be sure to hang around for the annual Aug 24th event *An Evening in Scotland—A Celebration of Scottish Heritage* which features music and dance. Mansion open 10 am-4 pm June-Sept, otherwise noon-4 pm. Closed Mon. $6, $4.25 w/student ID.

Hamilton Art Gallery, 123 King St West, 527-6610. Canadian and American art. Wed-Sat 10 am-5 pm, Thur 'til 9 pm, Sun 1pm-5 pm. Donation suggested.

Hamilton Museum of Steam and Technology, 900 Woodward Ave, 546-4797. May-Sept daily 11am-4 pm, otherwise noon-4 pm. Closed Mon; $3.50.

Hamilton Place, 50 Main St W. An impressive $11m showcase for the performing arts and part of the downtown renewal project. Home of 'Hamilton Philharmonic,' one of Canada's finest. Call 546-3100 for schedules.

Hess Village, 4 blocks btwn King & Main Sts. Restored Victorian mansions in a 19th century village. Stroll alongside the trendy shops, antiques, restaurants, etc.

MacMaster University. Has one of Canada's first nuclear reactors and a planetarium. There is also an art gallery on campus in Togo Salmon Hall.

Royal Botanical Gardens, York Blvd. Nature parkland and a wildlife sanctuary called 'Cootes Paradise' where trails wind through some 1,200 acres of marsh and wooded ravines. Free from dawn to dusk daily. A maple syrup festival is held here in March.

TREK Mountain Bike Tours, 546-0627. Discover some of the best mountain bike trails in Hamilton, Dundas, Ancaster, Milton and Cambridge, for beginners as well as experienced/expert riders. Free pick-up/drop-off, use of suspension bike, and helmet, free bottled water and experienced guide with cellular phone. $40. Call for more info/bookings.

INFORMATION/TRAVEL
Hamilton Street Railway (local transit). Basic fare $1.70.
Tourist Information Center, 127 King St E, 546-2666. 'Very helpful.'; and **Greater Hamilton Tourism and Convention Services**, 1 James St South, 3rd Floor, 546-4222.

BRANTFORD Chief Joseph Brant brought the Mohawk Indians to settle here at the end of the American Revolution, the tribe having fought with the defeated Loyalist and British North American armies. Her Majesty's Chapel of the Mohawks was built in 1785 and ranks as the oldest church in Ontario and the only royal chapel outside the United Kingdom. King George III himself was pleased to donate money for the cause.

Chief Brant's tomb adjoins the chapel. The annual **Six Nation Indian Pageant**, depicting early Indian history and culture, takes place at the beginning of August. Visit the Six Nations Reserve to see how Native Indians really live.

The town's other claim to fame is **Tutela Heights**, the house overlooking the Grand River Valley where Alexander Graham Bell lived and to which he made the first long distance telephone call, all the way from Paris, Ontario, some eight miles away. The call was made in August 1876, following Bell's first call in Boston. *http://207.61.5213/brantford/*.

The telephone area code here and the area west of Toronto between the lakes is 519.

OF INTEREST

Bell Homestead Museum, 94 Tutela Heights Rd, 756-6220. Bell's birthplace and museum, furnished in style of 1870s. Tue-Sun 9.30 am-4.30 pm, $4.

Brant County Museum, 57 Charlotte St, 752-2483. Indian and pioneer displays. Tue-Fri 9 am-5 pm, Sat-Sun 1pm-4 pm. Closed Mon & Sun after Labour Day. $4, $2.50 w/student ID.

Brantford Highland Games, held early July. Pipe bands, dancing, caber tossing.

Chiefswood, 8 miles E by Hwy 54, near Middleport, on Indian reservation. 1853 home of 'Mohawk Princess,' well-known poetess Pauline Johnson, daughter of Indian Chief Johnson. Her works include *Flint and Feather* and *Legends of Vancouver*. Newly renovated.

Woodland Indian Cultural Centre and Museum, 184 Mohawk St, 759-2650. Collection of artefacts of Eastern Woodland Indians. Mon-Fri 9 am-4 pm, Sat-Sun 10 am-5 pm. $5.

INFORMATION

Camping Info: Kiwanis Apps Mill Park, RR4 335 Robinson Rd, 753-7442. Retreat centre with dorms and camping sites, situated adjacent to the Grand River Conservation Authority.

Visitors and Conventions Bureau, 100 Willington Sq, 759-4150.

Visitor Information Center , 3 Sherwood Drive, 751-9900.

Daily 9 am-4.30 pm. Organises daily tours of town. Also info centre in the Wayne Gretzy Sports Center just off hwy.

NIAGARA FALLS The Rainbow Bridge (25c) which spans the Niagara River connects the cities of Niagara Falls, NY, with Niagara Falls, Ontario. Whichever side of the river you stay on, the better view of the falls is definitely from the Canadian vantage point. It's an awe-inspiring sight which somehow manages to remain so despite all the commercial junk and all the jostling crowds you have to fight your way past to get there. Try going at dusk or dawn for a less impeded look, and then again later in the evening when everything is floodlit. Snow and ice add a further grandeur to the scene in winter. (*See Niagara Falls, NY, for further details.*) The official website for the Niagara Region of Ontario is *www.community.niagara.com/*.

The area code is 905.

ACCOMMODATION

Tourist homes are the best bet here. Suggest you call first, many tourist homes offer a free pick-up service from the bus depot. Beware of taxi drivers who try and take you to motels or the more expensive tourist homes. 'If arriving on the US side be aware that it's a 45 mins walk with bags and there are no buses.' For accommodation assistance, phone the visitors centre on 356-6061.

Fallsview Tourist Home Backpackers Hostel, 4745 River Rd, 374-8051. Summer accommodation only, $17.

Henri's Motel, 4671 River Rd, 358-6573. Will try to put people who arrive on their own into a dble room to bring down cost. D/T/Q-$45-65. 'Very friendly.' 'Decent rooms.'

Maple Leaf Motel, 6163 Buchanan Ave, 354-0841. 'Near Falls and very comfortable.' S-$42, D-$58+.

Motel Olympia, 5099 Centre St, 356-2614. 'They gave us a student discount.' From S-$32, D-$45, less for longer stays. 'Very friendly.'

Niagara Falls Backpackers Hostel, 4549 Cataract Ave, 357-0770. 2 blocks E of bus and train stations; 30 min walk to Falls and close by Niagara River. Amenities include 2 kitchens, common area, laundry facilities and lockers. Discounts available at the Maid of the Mist, the Whirlpool Jetboat and other locations. Bike rentals are available and Explorer's Pass. Diners, grocery stores and post offices in the vicinty. 'Very cosy and friendly.' $17.

Niagara Park Backpackers Hostel, 4299 #20 Hwy, St Ann's, 386-6720. Rural farm area, 30 min from Niagara Falls. Dorm $20.

Short Hills Outpost Farm Hostel, 2751 Effingham Rd, RR 1, St- Catherines, 864-7518. Close to the luscious Short Hills Provincial Park. Call for varying seasonal prices.

Camping: King Waldorf Tent & Trailer Park, 9015 Stanley Ave near Marineland, 295-8191. 4 miles from Falls. 'Very friendly, Scottish owner, 2 pools, laundry, free showers.' $24 for four. May-Oct.

Riverside Park, 9 miles S on Niagara River Pkwy (on Niagara River banks), 382-2204. Laundry, pool, showers. Sites $23 for four w/hook-up. May-mid-Oct.

OF INTEREST

Fort George, at Niagara-on-the-Lake, 468-4257. Reconstructed 18th century military post. Daily 10 am-5 pm, Sept-May 9.30 am-4.30 pm. $4.50. Whole town of **Niagara-on-the-Lake** is worth a visit. This was the first capital of Ontario and home of the first library, newspaper and law society in Upper Canada. Has a certain 19th century charm. The drive along the Niagara Pkwy from Niagara-on-the-Lake to the Falls is recommended. There is also a bicycle route.

Helicopter rides, 3137 Victoria Ave, 357-5672. Approx $72 for a 9 min tour. 'Expensive, but an amazing experience and impressive views.'

International Winery, 4887 Dorchester Rd, 357-2400. Free tours and samples— Canada's largest winery. Tours run Mon-Sat 10.30 am/2 pm/3.30 pm, Sun 2 pm/3.30 pm.

'Maid of the Mist' boat trip, 358-5781. The boats pass directly underneath the Falls. Oilskins provided. 'Make sure yours is dry or you'll be miserable.' $10.95. Definitely recommended. 'Most memorable thing I did in North America.' Boats run every 15 mins. Daily 9 am-7 pm May-Oct.

Marineland Game Farm, 7657 Portage Rd, 356-8250. Dolphins and sealions. 'Rollercoaster, Dragon's Mouth, incredible.' $22. Daily 9 am-6 pm.

Minolta Tower, 356-1501. 665 ft tall with a restaurant at the top. $6.50.

Shaw Festival, Niagara-on-the-Lake. May-Oct annually is the season of Shaw productions. 20 miles from Niagara Falls. Tkts from $20. Call box office: 468-2172.

Skylon Tower, 356-2651. One of the tallest concrete structures in the world. See-through elevator; revolving restaurant at 500 ft. 'Arrive first around sunset and see the Falls floodlit by night and then by day.' 'Excellent view.' $7.95. Daily 8 am-11pm.

Walk under the Falls through tunnels from Table Rock House, $6. 'Very amusing.' 'A big con.' 'Could only see sheets of water.' Call for info: 356-7944.

Whirlpool and Rapids, 4 miles from Falls by sightseeing tour.

INFORMATION

Visitors and Convention Centre , 356-6061. 'We phoned here as suggested and the helpful staff provided us with various names and numbers of places to enquire regarding cheap accommodation. Very successful!' Daily 9 am-5 pm, w/ends 'til 6 pm.

TRAVEL

To reach **Niagara Falls Airport**, USA, (commuter service to Syracuse and connections) catch city bus. For **Buffalo Airport** take bus from bus station, $14.

VIA Rail runs 2 trains a day (2 hr journey) from Toronto to the Falls. $39 r/t ($22 if bought 1 week in advance). 'A great day trip.' 'Don't catch shuttle bus from station to the Falls. It costs $3.75 and it's only a 10 min walk.'

KITCHENER-WATERLOO A little bit of Germany lives exiled in Kitchener-Waterloo, a community delighting in beer halls and beer fests. The highlight of the year is the Oktoberfest, a week-long festival of German bands, beer, parades, dancing, sporting events and more beer.

Waterloo is often referred to as the 'Hartford of Canada' since the town is headquarters of a number of national insurance companies. The best days to visit K-W (a fairly easy 69-mile excursion from Toronto) are Wednesday and Saturday in time for the farmers' market where black-bonneted and gowned Amish and Mennonite farming ladies and their menfolk sell their crafts and fresh-picked produce. Sixteen miles north at **Elmira**, there's the annual Maple Syrup Festival, held in the spring.

Kitchener: *http://155.194.200.20/* and Waterloo City's *Virtual Tour, www.golden.net/~archeus/wattour.htm.*
The area code is 519.

ACCOMMODATION
Kitchener Motel 1485 Victoria St N, 745-1177. From D-$43.
The Olde Heidelberg Brewery & Restaurant, King St, from S-$45, D-$50
YWCA, 84 Frederick St, Kitchener, 744-0120. $35, bfast included.

OF INTEREST
Kitchener is the site of **Woodside National Historic Park**, 742-5273, boyhood home of **William Lyon Mackenzie King**, Prime Minister from 1921-1930 and 1935-1948. His former home at 528 Wellington St, is open to the public during the summer, 10 am-5 pm daily; free. For info: 571-5684. Admission to park $2.50, $1.50 w/student ID.
Bingeman Park, 1380 Victoria St North, 744-1555. Wave pool, water slides, bumper boats etc. May-Sept. Also, **camping** on one of 600 campsites available for $20-$27.
Doon Heritage Crossroads, south of town on Huron Rd (exit 275 [Doon Blair Rd] off Hwy 401), 748-1914. Re-creation of rural Waterloo County village of 1914. Daily May-Sept 10 am-4.30 pm, after Labour Day only Mon-Fri. $6, $3.50 w/student ID.
Oktoberfest, K-W Oktoberfest Inc, PO Box 1053, Kitchener, (519) 570-4267. Now attracts more than 700,000 people annually for 9 days of celebration, early Oct. Festival halls and tents serving frothy steins of beer and sauerkraut, oompah music, Miss Oktoberfest Pageant, archery tournament, ethinic dance performances, beer barrel races! $5 or up to $30 for an all-you-can-eat-all-night Bavarian smorgasbord. Accommodations in K-W are not always available, but Stratford, Guelph, Cambridge and Hamilton are close by.
Sportsworld, 100 Sportsworld Dr (Hwy 8 N of Hwy 401), (519) 653-4442. 30-acre water theme park, also features go-carts, miniature golf, indoor driving range, batting cages. Daily 10 am-10 pm May-Sept, $12.

INFORMATION
Kitchener Chamber of Commerce , 576-5000. Daily 9 am-5 pm.
Kitchener-Waterloo Area Visitors Bureau, 2848 King St E, (800) 265-6959/748-0800. Stop by for maps and detailed info on the area's attractions. Daily 9 am-5 pm summer, w/days only Sept-May.

GEORGIAN BAY ISLANDS NATIONAL PARK A good way north of Toronto on the way to Sudbury, this is one of Canada's smallest national parks. It consists of 59 islands or parts of islands in Georgian Bay. The largest of the islands, Beausoleil, is just five miles square, while all the rest combined add only two-fifths of a mile. Hiking, swimming, fishing and boating are the name of the game in the park.

The special feature of the park is the remarkable geological formations. The mainly Precambrian rock is more than 600 million years old and there are a few patches of sedimentary rock carved in strange shapes by glaciers.

Midland is the biggest nearby town for services and accommodation but boats to Beausoleil Island go from **Honey Harbour**, a popular summer resort off Rte 103. On Beausoleil, once the home of the Chippewa Indians, there are several campsites. *www.huronet.com/*.

The telephone area code is 705 for Midland, 519 for London and Stratford.

ACCOMMODATION
Chalet Motel, on Little Lake, 748 Yonge St W, 526-6571. From D-$65.
Park Villa Motel, 751 Yonge St W, adjoining Little Lake Pk, Midland, 526-2219. From D-$60, Q-$65. Heated pool.

OF INTEREST
30,000 Island Cruise, at Midland Dock. $2^1/_2$ hr trip among the islands of Georgian Bay at 10.45 am, 1.45pm, 4.30 pm (from June-Sept) and 7.15pm (mid July-Sept). $13. Call for rsvs and info: 526-0161 ext 310/312.
Huronia Museum and Indian Village, off King St, in Little Lake Park, 526-2844. Mon-Sat 9 am-5 pm, Sun from 10 am. $5.
Sainte-Marie Among the Hurons, 3 miles E on Hwy 12, 526-7838. Re-creation of Jesuit mission which stood here 1639-1649 plus Huron longhouses, cookhouse, blacksmith, etc. Orientation centre offers a film about the mission and the excavation work involved in the project. Daily 10 am-5 pm (last admission 4.15pm). $7.50 w/student ID.
Wye Marsh Wildlife Center, Hwy 12, 526-7809. Guided tours, animals, exhibits, floating boardwalk. Daily 10 am-6 pm. $7, $4 w/student ID.

INFORMATION
Georgian Bay Islands National Park: Write to the Superintendent, Georgian Bay Islands National Park, Box 28, Honey Harbour, ON, P0E 1E0, 756-2415.
Midland Chamber of Commerce , 526-7884. Mon-Fri 9 am-6 pm, Sat-Sun 9 am-6 pm.

LONDON   Not to be outdone by the other London back in Mother Britain, this one also has a River Thames flowing through the middle of the city. London, Ontario, also has its own Covent Garden Market. It's a town of comfortable size, and a commercial and industrial centre. Labatt's Brewery is perhaps the town's most famous industry.

London also offers the visitor a thriving cultural life. It is physically a pleasant spot, known as 'Forest City,' and is situated midway between Toronto and Detroit. The University of Western Ontario is here and is said to have the most beautiful campus of any Canadian university. You will find it on the banks of the Thames, in the northern part of the city.

London Pageone is the definitive guide to the city of London, *www.london.page1.org/*.

ACCOMMODATION
For B&B accommodations priced from $35-$65 a night, contact the **London Area B&B Association**, 2 Normandy Gdns, (519) 641-0467.
Spencer Park, 531 Windmere Rd, (519) 432-2646. Camping sites and shelter with bunks. Call for varying seasonal prices.

Univ of Western Ontario, Alumni House, Dept of Housing, 661-3814. Features include laundry, pool, continental bfast. Rsvs required. From S-$28. May-Aug.

FOOD
Fatty Patty's, 207 King St, 438-7281. Burgers, fries and salads in huge portions. Mon 11am-9 pm, Tues-Sat 'til 10 pm, closed Sun.

Joe Kool's, 595 Richmond St, 'right in centre—ask a local.' Tortillas, burgers, etc; 'good music.'

Prince Albert's Diner, Richmond St at Prince Albert. 50s-style diner with great cheap meals.

Say Cheese, 246 Dundas St, 434-0341. Relax and commune over a bottle of wine in the casual, comfortable ambience that prevails here. The traditional menu features all-time favourites as cheese soup, quiches, sandwiches and assorted cheese platters. Ideal for bfast, lunch or dinner and afternoon tea. While you're here, browse in the downstairs cheese shop. Most items $10-13.

Spageddy Eddy, 428 Richmond St, 673-3213. Copious canneloni, seas of spaghetti with lashings of lasagne. Tues-Sun 11am-9 pm.

OF INTEREST
Children's Museum, 21 Wharncliffe Road South, 434-5726. World cultures, communications, music and crafts. Children and adults alike can explore, experiment and engage their imaginations. More up-to-the-minute experiences can be enjoyed in the computer hall, at the photosensitive wall or the zoetrope. 'Excellent.' Tues-Sat 10 am-5 pm, Sun from noon, closed Mon. $3.75, $3.50 w/student ID.

Eldon House, 481 Ridout St. London's oldest house and now a historical museum. Tues-Sun noon-5 pm, $3; and close by **London Regional Art Gallery**, 421 Ridout St N, 672-4580. Open same hours.

Fanshawe Pioneer Village, Fanshawe Pk, off Clarke Rd, 457-1296. Re-creation of 19th century pre-railroad village. Log cabins, etc. Daily 10 am-4.30 pm; $5.w/student ID $4.

Museum of Indian Archaeology and Lawson Prehistoric Indian Village, 1600 Attawandaron Rd, 473-1360. Museum contains artifacts from various periods of Native Canadian history—projectiles, pottery shards, effigies, turtle rattles etc. On-site reconstructed Attawandaron village. Daily 10 am-5 pm, Sept-May closed Mon. $4, $2.75 w/student ID.

Royal Canadian Regiment Museum, Wolseley, on Canadian Forces Base, London, 660-5102. History of Canadian forces from 1883. Tues-Fri 10 am-4 pm, Sat, Sun from noon. Free.

ENTERTAINMENT
Barney's, 671 Richmond St. The local hangout which attracts the young professional crowd. Cheap draught beer in the Ceeps. Arrive early to get a spot on the patio in the summer.

Call the Office, 216 York St, east of Richmond. Live bands.

Grand Theatre, 471 Richmond St, 672-9030. Features drama, comedy and musicals from mid-Oct-May. The theater itself, built in 1901, is worth viewing.

Harness racing, takes place from Oct-June at the Western Fairgrounds track Wed, Fri and Sat. Call 438-7203 for more info.

Jo Kool's, 595 Richmond at Central, 663-5665, is a student hangout.

The Spoke, Somerville House, University of Western Ontario. A popular campus pub.

Western Fair, western Fairgrounds. Agricultural show and fair with midway rides and games. Held annually in mid-September.

INFORMATION
Visitors Center, 360 Wellington Rd S, 681-4047. Daily 8 am-8 pm, Sept-May 10 am-6 pm.

Visitors and Convention Services, 300 Dufferin Ave, City Hall, 661-5000. Daily 8.30 am-4.30 pm.

TRAVEL
Greyhound , 101 York at Talbot, (800) 661-8747.
U-Need-A-Cab, 438-2121.
VIA Rail, on York east of Richmond, 672-5722.

STRATFORD In 1953 this average-sized manufacturing town, on the banks of the River Avon some 50 kilometres north of London, held its first Shakespearian festival. The now world-renowned season has become an annual highlight on the Ontario calendar. The festival lasts for 22 weeks from mid-June, attracting some of the best Shakespearian actors and actresses, as well as full houses every night.

Based on the Festival Theatre, but encompassing several other theatres too, the festival includes opera, original contemporary drama and music, as well as the best of the Bard. In September the town also hosts an international film festival.

There's not much else of interest in Stratford except a walk along the riverside gardens and a look at the swans. Heading west there is Point Pelee National Park before going to Windsor and crossing to the US. For online info to 'The Shakespearean Festival City,' hook-up to *www.sentex.net/~lwr/strat.html*.

ACCOMMODATION
The Festival Theatre provides an accommodation service during the summer. You are advised to contact them first, call 271-4040. Also, the **Festival Accommodations Bureau**, 273-1600, can tell you where to go.
Burnside Guest Home, 139 William St, 271-7076. Turn of the century home, this is the budget traveller's best bet and offers a great view of Lake Victoria. B&B rooms $40-60; student rooms $25; call ahead.
Kent Hotel, 209 Waterloo St S, 271-7805. From S-$27, D-$57, weekly rates available.
Camping: Wildwood Conservation Area, 7 miles W on Hwy 7, 284-2292. Access to beach, pool and marina. Tent sites $17, $21.50 w/hook-up.

ENTERTAINMENT
Festival Theatre, 273-1600. Tkts from $30-60, Festival Theatre, Third Stage and Avon Theatre. The Festival Theatre is at 55 Queen St, Avon Theatre on Downie St, Third Stage on Lakeshore. Order from: Festival Box Office, PO Box 520, Stratford, ON, N5A 6V2. Special student matinees ($11-13) in Sept and Oct often swamped by high school parties. 'Get there early on the day of the performance for returns.'
Jazz on the River, Mon & Fri eves from 6.30-8 pm, mid-June to early Sept.
Lake Victoria, (Avon River) at the middle of town, offers tranquility to take in the outstanding views and have a leisurely stroll.
Stratford Farmers' Market, Coliseum Fairground, Sat mornings.

INFORMATION
Stratford Chamber of Commerce, 88 Wellington St, top floor, 271-5140. Mon-Fri 8.30 am-4 pm.
Stratford Festival, www.ffa.ucalgary.ca/stratford/ is the home of the finest in classical and contemporary theatre and North America's largest repertory theatre company.
Tourism Stratford Information Center, 1 York St, (800) 561-7926. Will send free a visitors guide if you call ahead; willing to help walk-ins. April-Oct; Tues-Fri 9 am-8 pm, Sat-Mon 'til 5 pm.

POINT PELEE NATIONAL PARK   About 35 miles from Windsor, Point Pelee is a V-shaped sandspit which juts out into Lake Erie. On the same latitude as California, the park is the southernmost area of the Canadian mainland.

Only six square miles in area, Point Pelee is a unique remnant of the original deciduous forests of North America. Two thousand acres of the park are a freshwater swamp and the wildlife found here is unlike anything else to be seen in Canada. On the spring and fall bird migration routes, the park is a paradise for ornithologists. There are also several strange fish to be seen and lots of turtles and small water animals ambling around.

Point Pelee is quite developed as a tourist attraction and there are numerous nature trails, including a one-mile boardwalk trail. Canoes and bicycles can be rented during the summer months and the Visitor Centre has maps, exhibits, slide shows and other displays about the park. Entrance to the park is $4.50, w/student ID $2.25. There is no camping in Point Pelee, although there are two sites in the nearby town of Leamington. For info call: 322-2365.

SUDBURY   Sudbury is some 247 miles northwest of Toronto and the centre of one of the richest mining areas in the world. The local Chamber of Commerce will tell you that Sudbury enjoys more hours of sunshine per year than any other city in Ontario (and we have no reason to doubt them), but this is not a pretty area. Part of the empty landscape looks so like a moonscape that American astronauts came here to rehearse lunar rock collection techniques before embarking on the real thing.

However away from the immediate vicinity of the town there are scores of lakes, rivers and untracked forests to refresh the soul after witnessing the ravages of civilisation. The city is often referred to as the 'nickel capital of the world.' Be sure to see the lunar landscape of Sudbury basin, a geological mystery that may have been caused by a gigantic meteor or volcanic eruption.

With more than 30 sparkling lakes and thousands of acres of protected woodlands, Sudbury has plenty to offer outdoor lovers as well. In summer enjoy swimming, canoeing, hiking, and cycling. Alpine and cross-country skiing are big in winter. *www.geocities.com/Thetropics/Shores/6807/* is your cyber guide to the 'Nickel Capital of the World'.
The telephone area code is 705.

ACCOMMODATION
Cheapest in the Ukrainian District, around Kathleen St. There is usually hostel accommodation available here in summer, but as with other cities in Canada locations change year to year. For current hostel info, call Canadian Hostelling Association, (613) 237-7884. To make rsvs at hostels call (800) 237-7884. Your other best bet for lodgings are the chains—**Comfort Inn**, **Ramada Inn**, **Venture Inn** and **Sheraton Caswell Inn.**
Laurentian University, Ramsey Lake Rd, 673-6597. They are helpful and provide accommodation in summer 'til Aug 15th.
Plaza Hotel, 1436 Bellevue St, 566-8080. Approx $65.

OF INTEREST
Big Nickel Mine and Numismatic Park at Hwy 17 West & Big Nickel Mine Dr, 522-3701. Taken underground for a 30 min tour. View a mineral processing station,

measure their weight in gold and enjoy some other video programs. Located 3 miles west of Sudbury. Daily 9 am-5 pm; $8.50, $6 w/student ID.

Copper Cliff Museum, 682-1332 or call Sudbury Parks and Recreation Dept, 674-3141 ext 457. June-Sept, Mon-Fri 10 am-4 pm, closed noon-1pm.

INCO Smelter at Copper Cliff, 4 miles west of town on Hwy 17.
The smelter is the world's largest single smelting operation and is open to visitors. Call 673-5659 for slagpouring info. They'll direct you to the current slagpouring site. Slag is the 2100°F molten waste. 'Hot show.'

Science North, Ramsey Lake Rd and Paris St, 1 miles from Hwy 69 S, 522-3700/3701. Excellent science museum and underground mine tour. Inside you can conduct experiments, such as simulating a hurricane, monitoring earthquakes on a seismograph, or observing the sun through a solar telescope. Also, a water playground, space exploration and weather command centres, and a fossil identification workshop. Daily summer 9 am-5 pm, $8.50, $6 w/student ID.

INFORMATION/TRAVEL
Chamber of Commerce , 100 Elm St W, 673-7133.
Community Information Service and Convention and Visitors Service, 200 Brady St, Civic Sq. Call 674-3141.
Rainbow Country Travel Association, 1984 Regions St South, Cedar Pointe Mall (next to Casey's), 522-0104. Mon-Fri 8 am-5 pm in summer, otherwise from 9am.

SAULT STE MARIE First established in 1669 as a French Jesuit mission, Sault Ste Marie later became an important trading post in the heyday of the fur trade. Today 'The Soo,' as locals call the town, oversees the great locks and canals that bypass St Mary's Rapids. The **Soo Locks**, connecting Lake Superior with St Mary's River and Lake Huron, allow enormous Atlantic ocean freighters to make the journey 1748 miles inland. From special observation towers visitors can watch the ships rising and falling up to 40 ft.

The town is connected to its US namesake across the river in Michigan by an auto toll bridge. If you're going north from here, 'think twice about hitching.' Lifts are hard to come by, the road is long and empty. It's probably best to get as far beyond **Wawa** as possible. Thunder Bay is 438 miles away to the northwest. Two of the most popular local events are the **Bon Soo Winter Carnival**, which runs from January to February, and the **Northern Triathalon** in August. From late September to mid-October, the foliage colours are spectacular and the weather is perfect for hiking. This is also an excellent time to catch the **Agawa Canyon Train.** *www.sault-canada.com/.*

ACCOMMODATION
Whatever you do, make your lodging reservations in advance. For food, try **Ernie's Coffee Shop**, 13 Queen St. 'Big, cheap meals, excellent value.'
Algoma Cabins & Motel, 1713 Queen St E, 256-8681. From D-$42, weekly rates available.
Algonquin Youth Hostel, 864 Queens St E, 253-2311. Cooking facilities. Linen included, on-site parking, canoe rental. Dorms $20-24.
Ambassador Motel, 1275 17 N (Great Northern Road), 759-6199. From D-$56.
Camping: Woody's Campsites, Hwy 17 N, 12 kms N, 777-2638. From $12 for two, w/hook-up.

OF INTEREST
The surrounding area offers great fishing, snowmobiling, cross-country skiing and other sports opportunities.
Lake Superior Provincial Park. A fair ride north of here—some 130 kms—but

nonetheless worth the trip to this rugged wilderness park. Includes nature trails, moose hunting in season, Indian rock paintings and a fine beach. Enjoy 1-7 day kayaking trips with **Lake Superior Kayak Adventures**, 159 Shannon Rd.

Lock Tours, 253-9850. 2 hr r/t cruises through the American (which is one of the world's busiest) lock and the Canadian lock. Departs from the Roberta Bondar Pavilion on the waterfront. Also takes in St Mary's River. Runs daily in summer, $13.50.

MS Norgoma Museum Ship, Norgoma Dock at Foster Dr. The last of the overnight passenger cruise ships built on the Great Lakes, the ship plied the Owen Sound to Sault Ste Marie route from 1950 to 1963. Daily June & Sept 10 am-6 pm; July-Aug 9 am-8 pm. $3.50.

The Old Stone House, 831 Queen St E, 759-5443. Completed 1814 and a rare example of early Canadian architecture. Restored. Daily 10 am-5 pm. $2.50.

For cross-country ski information, call the **Stokely Creek Ski Touring Centre**, at Stokely Creek Lodge, at Karalash Corners, Goulais River.

INFORMATION
Sault Ste Marie Chamber of Commerce , 360 Great Northern Rd, 949-7152. Able to give extensive sports information.
Ministry of Tourism , 120 Huron St. Open daily.

THUNDER BAY On the northern shore of Lake Superior and an amalgam of the towns of Port Arthur and Fort William, Thunder Bay is the western Canadian terminus of the Great Lakes/St Lawrence Seaway system and Canada's third largest port. Port Arthur is known as Thunder Bay North and Fort William is Thunder Bay South. The towns are the main outlet for Prairies grain and have a reputation for attracting swarms of huge, and hungry, black flies during the summer.

The city's new name was selected by plebiscite and is derived from the name of the bay and Thunder Cape, 'The Sleeping Giant,' a shoreline landmark. Lake Superior is renowned for its frequent thunderstorms and since in Indian legend the thunderbird was responsible for thunder, lightning and rain, that was how the bay got its name. The city is 450 miles from Winnipeg to the west, and about the same distance from Sault Ste Marie to the southeast.

For those essential listings and information on special events and recreational activities, go to *www.tourism.thunder-bay.on.ca/*.

The telephone area code is 807.

ACCOMMODATION
Circle Inn Motel, 686 Memorial Ave, 344-5744. 'Reasonably close to the bus terminal.' From S-$48, D-$59.
Confederation College, Sibley Hall Residence, 960 William St. Rooms available until the end of Aug. From S-$30, D-$38. Call 475-6383 for availability.
Lakehead University Residence, Oliver Rd, 343-8612. From S-$25, D-$30 w/student ID. May-Aug only.
Pinebrook B&B, Mitchell Rd (Hwy 527 left on Mitchell Rd on Pine Dr), (807) 683-6114. Dorms from $20, private rooms available.
Thunder Bay Backpackers Hostel, 1594 Lakeshore Dr & McKenzie Stn Rd, 983-2042. Hostel is a central point in the **Backpackers Hostels Canada** network. Run by world travellers and teachers, full of artifacts from around the world. 'World class skiing.' The owner is more than happy to provide information on places to stay all over the country. 'Friendly, warm hostel, baths, TV.' 'The best in Canada.' $17. Tent sites $12, for two $16. *email: longhouse@microage-tb.com/user/jones/hostel.htm* and *www.microage-tb.com/user/jonesl/hostel.htm*.

OF INTEREST

Amethyst Mine. 35 miles on Trans Canada Hwy, then north on E Loon Lake Rd, 622-6908. Daily 10 am-7 pm; $1. Closed Oct-May.

Centennial Park, east of Arundel St, 683-6511. Animal farm, a museum and a reproduction of a typical northern Ontario logging camp of the early 1900s. Daily 8 am-10.30 pm. Free.

Chippewa Park, south off Hwy 61, 623-3912. A wooded park on Lake Superior with a sandy beach, camping, picnic grounds, a fun fair and wildlife exhibit. Daily, late June-Sept.

Hillcrest Park, High St. A lookout point with a panoramic view of Thunder Bay Harbour and the famous **Sleeping Giant,** he of the Indian folk legends from whom the town derives its name. Impressively visible across the bay in Lake Superior.

Old Fort William. On the banks of the Kaministiquia River, 577-8461. Once a major outpost of the North West Trading Company, now a 'living' reconstruction. Craft shops, farm, dairy, naval yard, Indian encampment, breadmaking, musket firing, etc. Daily 10 am-5 pm. $6, $4.25 w/student ID.

Thunder Bay Historical Society Museum, 425 E Donald St, 623-0801. Indian arte-facts and general pioneering exhibits. Tues-Sat 1pm-5 pm (winter), daily June-Aug 11am-5 pm. Free.

INFORMATION

Convention and Visitors Bureau, Patterson Park Info, 520 Leith St, (800) 667-8386.
Pagoda Info Centre, Water St, 345-6812. 8.30 am-8.30 pm daily in summer, other-wise 9 am-5 pm.

TRAVEL

Greyhound/Grey Goose, 815 Fort William Rd, by SKAFF, 345-2194. Open daily. Lockers $1.

Harbour cruises from Port Arthur Marina, Arthur St, 344-2512. Several cruises, daily, mid-May to Oct, from $14. Call for exact times.

ONTARIO'S NORTHLANDS Going north out of Toronto on the Trans Canada Hwy, you can carry on round to Sudbury, Sault Ste Marie and Thunder Bay, or else, at Orillia, you can get on to Rte 11 which will take you up to North Bay, and from there to Ontario's little-explored north country. **North Bay** is 207 miles from Toronto and is a popular vacation spot as well as the accepted jumping off point for the polar regions.

There's not much in North Bay itself, but there is ready access to the **Algonquin Provincial Park,** a vast area of woods and lakes good for hiking, canoeing and camping, and also to **Lake Nipissing.** Pressing north, however, there is **Temagami,** a hunting, fishing, lumbering, mining and out-fitting centre. The Temagami Provincial Forest was the province's pioneer forest, established in 1901 and providing mile upon mile of sparkling lakes and rugged forests. It's quiet country up here; even with modern communi-cation systems, people are few. It's also mining country.

Cobalt is the centre of a silver mining area and **Timmins** is the largest silver and zinc producing district in the world. You can visit mines and mining museums in both towns.

At **Cochrane**, 207 miles north of North Bay, the northbound hwy runs out, and the rest of the way is by rail. The **Polar Bear Express** runs Sat-Thur during the summer (June 27-Sept 7) up to Moosonee on James Bay, covering the 186 miles in 4¹/₂ hrs ($48 r/t). After September, the **Little Bear** runs 3 times weekly ($79 r/t). Rsvs required, call (800) 268-9281 from areas 416,

705, 613, 519 or (416) 314-3750 in Toronto. It's a marvellous ride, the train packed with an odd assortment of people, everyone from tourists to miners, missionaries, geologists and adventurers. Before boarding the train for the trip north there is the **Cochrane Railway Museum** to visit. Housed in an engine and four coaches, the museum traces the history of the James Bay Frontier. **Moosonee** counts as one of the last of the genuine frontier towns and is accessible only by rail or air. Since 1673 when the Hudson Bay Company established a post on nearby Moose Factory Island, this has been an important rendezvous for fur traders and Indians. It's also a good place to see the full beauty of the Aurora Borealis.

This is as far north as most people get, but there's still a lot of Ontario lapped by Arctic seas. Over 250 miles north of Moosonee by air, there's **Polar Bear Provincial Park**. This is a vast area of tundra and sub-arctic wilderness. The summer is short and the climate severe. The rewards of a visit here can be great however. There are polar bears, black bears, arctic foxes, wolves, otters, seals, moose and many other varieties of wildlife to be seen in plenty.

ACCOMMODATION

All the towns mentioned above have small hotels or motels, none of them especially cheap however. If planning to come this far off the beaten track, it is advisable to give yourself plenty of time to find places to stay. Remember that if everything is full in one town your next options may be several hours' driving further down the road. There are many campgrounds in this part of Ontario, but again the distances between them are often considerable.

Orillia area: Horseshoe Valley: Arteclectiks Studio North, 46 Huronwoods Dr, Sugar Bush, Coldwater, (705) 835-5466. Ski chalet, sauna, cross-country skiing, walking trails. Dorms and private rooms available, call for rates.

Thornton: Camp Oba-Sa-Teeka, Scouts Canada, 2665 Yorkland Blvd, 2nd Floor, North York, (416) 490-66364/490-6911 for rsvs. Swimming, cross-country skiing, camping, located east of hwy 400, exit at Thornton or Cookstown. Hostel dorm $16.

Algonquin area: Algonquin Park: Portage HI Hostel, Pembroke, (613) 735-1795. Take Sandlake Gate Park Entrance Rd. Call for rates.

The Portage Store, Box 10009, Algonquin Park, Huntsville, (705) 633-6522/winter phone (705) 789-6955. Not a traditional hostel, but an outfitting company. Tents are provided, canoeing, trekking and mosquitoes! Best park scenery in Ontario, moose and other wildlife.

Temagami area: Temagami HI Hostel, Smoothwater Outfitters, Box 40, Temagami, (705) 569-3539. Canoe rentals, cross-country skiing. Call for rates.
e-mail: temagami@onlink.net.

QUÉBEC

Québec is the largest province in Canada—its area is seven times that of the United Kingdom—and it really has a character all its own. The vast majority of French Canadians live here in La Belle Province, and the French culture is apparent in all walks of life—from the French-only street signs in Montréal and Québec City to the smaller, rural towns where the only language you'll hear is French interspersed with expressions in 'joual'—a dialect used mostly in Northern Québec. Some Québeçois may seem reluctant to speak English to the visitor; in the bigger cities, however, the shopkeepers will understand enough to serve you, and you may find the younger Québeçois eager to practice their English.

The name of the province is derived from the Algonquin Indian word 'Kebec,' meaning 'where the river narrows.' This reference to the St Lawrence River indicates both the important role the river played in the development of the province in the 18th and 19th centuries and its continued importance for Québec's economy today. Four-fifths of the province lies within the area of the barren Canadian Shield to the north. The atmosphere in the smaller, unassuming rural towns contrasts sharply with the cosmopolitan sophistication of Montréal and the Old World charm of Québec City. *www.yahoo.com/Regional/Countries/Canada/Provinces_and_Territories/Quebec.*
National Parks: Forillon, La Mauricie, Auguittuq.

MONTRÉAL Canada's largest city is built around the mountain, Mount Royal, from which it derives its name. Located on the archipelago at the junction of the Outaouais and Saint-Laurent Rivers, Montréal is a natural meeting point for overland and water passages.

Jacques Cartier arrived here in 1535 to find a large Indian settlement, Hochelaga, believed to have been where McGill University now stands. When Champlain arrived, nearly 100 years later, the Indians had gone, and the French subsequently settled there. Their city is now one of the world's greatest inland ports, boasting some 14 miles of berthing space. Since the opening of the St Lawrence Seaway in 1959, the city's port-based industries have greatly expanded and increased, making Montréal one of North America's most important commercial, industrial and economic centres.

More than two-fifths of the total population of Québec live in the Montréal metropolitan area. Two-thirds of Montréalers speak French, and as a result their city is second only to Paris in terms of French-speaking population.

Host city for Expo '67 and the 1976 Summer Olympics, Montréal is forever improving, expanding, renovating. Theatre and the arts flourish. There is always something to do here, and Montréalers consider their city to provide the best of everything in Canada—the best restaurants, shopping, nightclubs, the best bagels, and the best smoked-meat sandwiches (the last of which may in fact be true). This is a cosmopolitan vibrant city whose liveliness is epitomized in Vieux Montréal, on Crescent Street, or on Rue St Denis where you can mingle with the French Canadians and discover a part of the culture and joie de vivre that is neither North American, nor European, but unique unto itself.
The telephone area code is 514.

ACCOMMODATION

For info regarding hostels, hotel and *chambres touristiques* (rooms in private homes or small guest houses), your best resources are the **Québec Tourist Office**, the **B&B Breakfast à Montréal** network, PO Box 575, Snowdon Station, H3X 3T8, 738-9410; and the **Downtown B&B Network**, 3458 Ave Laval, H2X 3C8, (800) 267-5180, which lists homes available downtown. Wander down **Rue St Denis** for least expensive options.

A L'Amèricain, 1042 Rue St Denis, 849-0616. Highly recommended. 'Friendly people, large rooms, and close to Old Montréal.' From S-$42, D-$45-$52.

Alternative Backpackers of Old Montréal, 358 Rue St Pièrre, 282-8069. 'The best hostel I've stayed in, right in the old town. Decor inside very arty. Spacious, clean, very friendly owners. 24 hr access. Definitely recommended.' Dorms $17.

Armor Tourist Rooms, 157 Sherbrooke St, 285-0140. 'Clean and friendly, close to cafés, bus terminal and metro.' From S-$45, D-$50-$60, includes bfast.

Auberge de Montréal HI Hostel, 1030 Mackay, 843-3317. Convenient location, great service and upbeat staff who will gladly assist with nightlife ideas and outings. Kitchen facs, A/C and ride board. 'Clean, safe, friendly.' $16-$21, from D-$20pp.

Collège Français, 5155 Rue de Gaspé, 495-2581. 'Clean and simple.' Take Metro to Laurier. No laundry or kitchen. $12 dorm. Weekly rates available.

Hotel de Paris Backpackers Hostel, 901 Sherbrooke St East, 522-6361. Renovated Victorian hostel $12-$14, linen $2. 'Very cramped and no privacy.' S-$48-58, D-$68-80.

Le Breton, 1609 Rue St Hubert, 524-7273. 'A gem in the city's budget accommodation crown.' Clean, comfortable but rooms fill up quickly. S-$40-45, D-$47-70, TV and A/C.

McGill University, Bishop Mountain hall, 3935 Rue de l'Université, 398-6367. Shared washroom, laundry, kitchenettes, common room with TV and laundry. Garner bldg has best views. Full bfast $5 daily. $37, $28 w/student ID. Weekly rates available. May-Aug only.

Maison André Tourist Rooms, 3511 Rue Université, 849-4092. 'Clean and comfortable.' Non-smokers pref. Satisfied guests have been returning every year. S-$26-35, D-$38-45, XP-$10. Rsvs recommended.

University Residences: Concordia, 7141 Sherbrooke Ouest, 848-4755. S-$26, D-$40, w/student ID $19, D-$38.

Université de Montréal, 2350 Rue Edouard-Montpetit, 343-6531. Easy access by bus. Located on the edge of a beautiful campus; East Tower has best views. 'Highly recommended for value, location, ambience and comfort.' Inexpensive cafeteria on campus. Laundry. Phone/sink in each room. Mid-May-August. $27-$38 (discount w/student ID). Weekly rates available. NB: Both Concordia and McGill are English-speaking universities.

YMCA, 1450 Rue Stanley (downtown), 849-8393. Co-ed. Small rooms with TV and phone. Cafeteria open daily 7 am-8 pm. From S-$35, $2 discount w/student ID. Busy June-Aug. No rsvs June-Sept. S-$30, D-$54.

YWCA, 1355 Rue René Lévesque Blvd Ouest, 866-9941. Clean and safe, located downtown. Kitchen/TV on each floor. From S-$38. Rsvs accepted.

Camping: Call the tourist info centre on 873-2015 for details. Check out **Parc d'OKA**, 479-8337, take Autoroute 20 W to 13 N to 640 W; **Lac des Deux Montagnes**, sites $18-23; and **KOA Montréal-South**, St. Phillipe, 659-8626. 15 miles from city, take Autoroute 15 S over Pont Champlain. Sites for two $18-$23, XP-$3.50. Pool laundry, store, showers and daily shuttle available.

FOOD

For cheap eats, best to stay within the **Rue St-Denis** area. St-Denis, the centre of numerous clubs, bars, cafes, and restaurants, reflects Montréal's French culture and is frequented by a heterogeneous group, including many students from neighbouring universities. A preppier crowd tends to gravitate towards Crescent St. There are many **Greek** restaurants on Prince Arthur E between St Laurent and Carre St Louis. Definitely worth a try. Also, try perusing the free *Restaurant Guide*, published by the Greater Montréal Convention and Tourism Bureau, 844-5400, which gives ideas of where to go depending on what type of cuisine you fancy. Note: Prince Arthur and Duluth Streets both have 'bring your own wine' restaurants (Fr. *apportez vin*) which cool and serve any bottle you bring. Great meals for $10.

Amelio's, 3565 Lorne Ave, 845-8396. Italian-style pizza and pasta, average meal $6-9. McGill 'ghetto,' 'intimate atmosphere.'

Ben's, 990 Maisonneuve. Cheap deli, open 24 hrs. Famous for its Montréal smoked meat. 'Cheerfully tacky deli which is packed at all hours.'

Boeuf à la Mode, 273 St-Paul Est, 866-0963. 'Excellent French food.'

Café Commun/Commune, 201 Milton. Vegetarian food served by volunteers. Close to McGill. 'Artsy.'

Carlos & Pepe's, 1420 Peel, 288-3090. Spicy assortment of Mexican delicacies—burritos, salsas, sangria plus a live band. Average meal $10-$15. Daily 'til 1 am, except Thurs-Sat 'til 3am.

L'Anecdote, 801 Rachel Est, 526-7967. Great burgers and vegetarian tofu hot dogs. Daily 9 am-9.45pm.

La Cabanne, St Laurent, 843-7283. Cheapish shish-kabab-type food in good atmosphere. Upstairs is the Bar St Laurent where you can play pool and drink beer.

La Paryse, 302 Ontario E, 842-2040. 'Best hamburgers in Montréal.'

La Pizzaiolle, 1446A Crescent Est, 845-4158. 'Good, cheap pizza in attractive surroundings. Caesar salad and dessert (L'*indulgent*) are recommended.'

Le Faubourg. Foodhall on Ste Catherine St filled with various cafes and shops selling fresh produce and serving Montréal Bagel Bakery.

Mazurka, 64 Prince Arthur E. 'Good, cheap Polish and continental style food.'

Peel Pub, 1107 Ste Catherine Ouest, 845-9002. Old-fashioned tavern, serves fish and chips, beer by the pitcher. Big student hangout. Strongly recommended by past readers. 'The place to go if on a budget.' Bfast only a meagre $1.69. Daily specials, eg. pizza, for 99¢.

Sun Heung, La Gauchetière E, 866-5912. A little seedy, but has the greatest Chinese food.

Markets: Atwater Market, Marché Maisonneuve, Marché St Jacques and **Marché Jean-Talon** all sell everything from soup to boutiques, handmade articles, fast food and produce for your own preparation. Open daily. Go and haggle. For info on the markets, call 937-7754.

OF INTEREST

Vieux Montréal. Situated on the Lower Terrace, this area includes business and local government sectors. In recent times the buildings lining the old narrow streets have received facelifts, funds being provided from the public, as well as private, purse. The squares and streets are best explored on foot. **Notre-Dame De Bonsecours,** and **St Paul** make for pleasant strolls. Not to be missed, particularly if you don't plan to visit Québec City. During the summer months Montréalers are avid walkers and there is street activity until all hours of the night. As a result, one can enjoy night-life without the burden of urban paranoia. Pick up excellent walking tour leaflets from the city's information bureaux. To get there: metro to Champ-de-Mars, Place d'Armes or Victoria.

The Upper Terrace. Flanking the southern edge of the mountain, the area includes a considerable part of the city stretching east and west for several miles. At its heart was the Indian town of Hochelaga, discovered by Cartier in 1535, standing not far from the present site of **McGill**. The high-rise area through which run **Sherbrooke**, **Maisonneuve**, **Ste Catherine Sts** and **Dorchester Blvd** is the urban centre where metro, bus and rail lines converge. It is also where the major hotels and shops are situated. Beyond Blvd St Laurent, Montréal is entirely French. On the western half of the Upper Terrace is the City of **Westmount**, famous for its stately mansions, fine churches and public buildings.

Bank of Montréal Museum, Place d'Armes, 877-6892. Coins, documents and general banking memorabilia tracing Montréal history as the country's financial centre. Mon-Fri 10 am-4 pm, closed noon-1pm. Free.

Biodôme, 4777 Pierre-De-Coubertin Ave, 868-3000. Offers the chance to explore the 1001 wonders of Naturalia from all remote corners of the planet. Tropical Rainforest,

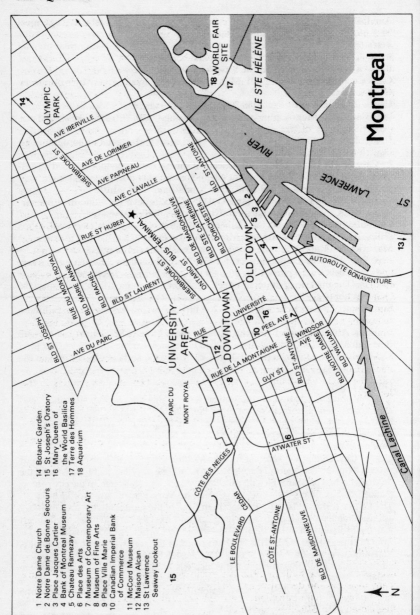

Montreal

1 Notre Dame Church
2 Notre Dame de Bonne Secours
3 Place Jacques Cartier
4 Bank of Montreal Museum
5 Chateau Ramezay
6 Place des Arts
7 Museum of Contemporary Art
8 Museum of Fine Arts
9 Place Ville Marie
10 Canadian Imperial Bank
   of Commerce
11 McCord Museum
12 Maison Alcan
13 St Lawrence
   Seaway Lookout
14 Botanic Garden
15 St Joseph's Oratory
16 Mary Queen of
   the World Basilica
17 Terre des Hommes
18 Aquarium

Desert, Polar and Sea Worlds all under one dome. Located next to the Olympic Stadium and Botanical Gardens. Daily 9 am-6 pm ('til 8 pm in summer). $10, w/student ID $7.

Botanical Garden and Insectarium, Rue Cherbourg, 872-1400. One of the most significant (2nd largest) in the world: 30 specialized gardens spread out over 65 acres, a vast complex of greenhouses, the largest collection of Bonsai and Penjing trees in the western world, a 1700 species orchid collection, a Japanese Garden and a Chinese Garden. Daily 9 am-6 pm ('til 8 pm in summer). $7.

Canadian Centre for Architecture, 1920 Rue Baile, 939-7000. This museum and architecture centre dedicated to the art of architecture is considered to be a world-class institution. Its collection includes 47,000 drawings and master prints, a library with 135,000 books, 45,000 photos as well as important archival finds. Tue-Sun 11am-6 pm, Thurs 'til 8 pm; $6, w/student ID $3.50.

Canadian Railway Museum, 122 St-Pièrre (alias Rte 209) in St Constant, 632-2410. 28 km from Montréal. Largest railway museum in Canada. 120 vehicles dating from 1863. Streetcar demonstrations daily. Bilingual tours geared to non-specialist. Note: public transport to St Constant is a disaster. Call museum to arrange group transportation. Daily 9 am-5 pm May-Sept. $5, w/student ID $2.50. Rsvs: 638-1522.

Chapelle de Notre Dame de Bonsecours, 400 St-Paul Est. Overlooking the harbour and known as the 'sailors' church.' Built in 1771 and the oldest church still standing in the city, it was once an important landmark for helmsmen navigating the river. There is a fine view from the top of the tower. It has been dedicated to sailors since the original chapel was erected in 1657.

Château Ramezay, 280 Rue Notre-Dame Est, 861-3708. Built in 1705 by Claude de Ramezay, a governor of Montréal, the building is a prime example of the architecture of the time and contains a wealth of furniture, engravings, oil paintings, costumes and other items relating to 18th century life. Open 10 am-4.30 pm. Closed Mon Sept-May. $6, $3.50 w/student ID.

Insectarium, 4581 Rue Cherbourg E, 872-8753. Unique in North America, it combines science and entertainment and is home to 350,000 insect specimens from 88 countries. Daily 9 am-8 pm, Sept-May 'til 6 pm. $8. Tkts also give access to the Botanical Garden.

Maison Alcan, 1184 Rue Sherbrooke Ouest, 848-8000. Base of operations for the world's second largest aluminium manufacturer. Art and architecture. Mid-day choral performances in atrium. Eateries.

Mary, Queen of the World Cathedral, Rue de la Cathedrale on Dominion Sq. Small-scale version of St Peter's in Rome. Built 1878. Daily 7 am-7 pm. Nearby: **St Helen's Island** (*Ile Ste-Hélène*). Beautiful park. 'Take picnic for a quiet day away from the city.' Metro from Berri de Montigny.

Museé d'Art Contemporain, 185 Ste Catherine W, 847-6226. The only institution of its type in Canada dedicated exclusively to all forms of contemporary art including paintings, sculpture, multimedia and performance art. Call for info on regular special showings. Daily 11am-6 pm, Wed 6 pm-9 pm free, closed Mon. $8, $5 w/student ID.

Museum of Fine Arts (*Museé des Beaux-arts*), 1379 Sherbrooke St, 285-1600. The oldest established museum in Canada—founded in 1860—housed in a magnificent neoclassical edifice built in 1912. An extensive permanent collection, including many treasures and decorative arts which date from 3,000 BC is found throughout the 34 rooms. Call for info about new displays. Daily 11am-6 pm, Thurs 6 pm-9 pm free, closed Mon. $10, $6 w/student ID.

Notre Dame Basilica, Place d'Armes, 849-1070. The city's oldest parish built in 1829. The wonderful vaulted starry ceiling, extraordinary wood work and beautiful stained-glass windows never fail to impress. Also houses one of the largest Casavant organs ever made. The gilded interior threatens to 'out-Pugin Pugin.'

'Interior decor is breathtaking.' June-Sept 7 am-8 pm; otherwise 'til 6 pm. Tours available. Museum: 842-2925, $2 entry fee.

Place des Arts, Rue Ste Catherine, 842-2112. Montréal cultural complex. Features concert, dance and theatrical performances. Free lunchtime concerts, Sat and Sun.

Place Jacques Cartier. Once Montréal farmers' market. The restored Bonsecours Market building is on the south side of the square. This square also features the first monument to Nelson erected anywhere in the world. You can buy food at the stalls or sit at a street cafe and listen to a jazz band. 'Touristy.'

St Joseph's Oratory, 733-8211. On the north slope of Westmount Mountain which is separated by a narrow cleft from Mount Royal. The Oratory dome is a marked feature of the Montréal skyline. The world's largest pilgrimage centre, includes a remarkable 'way of the cross,' the original chapel and two museums containing memorabilia of founder Brother Andre and religious art. Also famous for its cures said to have been affected through the prayers of the 'Miracle Man of Montréal.' Daily 6 am-10 pm; free. Museum is open 10 am-5 pm. Donations appreciated. St. Joseph is the patron saint of Canada.

St Lawrence Seaway Lookout (*Voie Maritîme du St-Laurent*), Cté Ste Catherine and Beauharnois Locks, 672-4110.

Terre des Hommes (*Man and His World*), St Helen's Isl. Site of Expo '67, now a permanent cultural and entertainment centre. Many of the Expo buildings survive but the whole place shuts up after Labour Day. 'Well worth a day—lots of free exhibitions and music, fascinating buildings.' Also includes **La Ronde**, an amusement part at the eastern end of the island—'sensational waterskiing shows.' Rollercoaster, Le Monstre—'very scary.' For information on both, call 872-6222. Open w/ends in May. Open daily from June 11am-11pm. Day passes to La Ronde, $23.

Parks: Olympic Park, eastern Montréal, 252-4737. Site of the 1976 Olympic Games, now home to Montréal's baseball (the Expos) and soccer teams. Daily tours (bilingual), $6.25. 'Better value: savour a sporting event.' 'Very disappointing—certainly not worth the bother.' 'For lovers of modern architecture only.' 'Go and see a baseball game—much better than the tour.' Tue-Sun 10 am-11pm.

Maisonneuve Park: 4601 Sherbrooke St E, 872-6211. 525-acre park with a botanical garden, golf course, picnic areas and skating rink.

Mount Royal Park: On a fine day the views from the 763 foot slope are spectacular. The view encompasses St Lawrence and Ottawa Rivers, the Adirondacks (New York State), and the Green Mountains (Vermont). It is also an excellent place to admire the nightscape of Montréal. During the summer: open-air concerts, winters: skiing and skating.

Parc Lafontaine, 872-2644. Has picnic areas, outdoor puppet theatre, ice-skating in the winter, tennis courts and a summer international festival of public theatre, June.

ENTERTAINMENT

Read the free *Montréal Mirror* or *Voir* for what's going on. For some real night-time fun, hang out on St-Paul to see street performers, artists and the like. Theatre is big here, so naturally there is a wide variety of theatrical groups, including the **Theatre du Nouveau Monde**, 866-8667; **Theatre du Rideau**, 844-1793; **Centaur Theatre**, 288-3161 for tkt info; **Place des Arts**, 842-2112 for tkts; and **Opéra de Montréal**, 985-2258. Check to see if productions are in English or French.

The Alley, on the McGill campus. Quiet pub and coffee house with live jazz.

Café Campus, student hang-out on Queen Mary Rd near Côte des Neiges. Drinking, dancing, French students. Cheap. Free on Wed nights.

Club Lezards, 4177 Rue St Denis, 289-9819. Eclectic, arty, lively disco situated in the heart of the city. 'Wall and body painting!' From $5 cover. Open nightly 10 pm-3am.

D.J's Pub, 1443 Crescent St, 287-9354. On Thur nights here you can get 6 mixed drinks for under $15. Open 'til 3am daily, happy hour noon-8 pm.

Peel Pub Showbar, 1106 de Maisonneuve W, 845-9002. Live entertainment nightly,

exceptional drink prices, cheap tasty food. Don't miss happy hour Mon-Fri 2 pm-8 pm. Daily 11am-2am. Another location is at 1106 Blvd de Maisonneuve, 845-9002.
Zoo Bar, Rue St Laurent. 'Wild & crazy place.' Be sure to visit a 'bal musette' at the Place d'Armes to hear old Québeçois waltzes played on the traditional accordion and guitar. $5 entrance.
River rafting: Lachine Rapid Tours, 284-9607. 'Excellent fun.'
Tour of Montréal Harbour: Miss Olympia Tours, 842-3871. Summers, starting May through mid-Oct, lasts 2 hrs. $19-40. 'Outstanding.'
Festivals: Montréal is a vibrant theatrical centre with enough performances and styles to suit most tastes.
Montréal International Jazz Festival. Held approx June 26th-July 6th annually, this is a festival of music and fun throughout the city. Over 90 indoor and 240 outdoor shows. With many top-name performers including over 1,500 international perform-ers. 'An ecstatic jazz party that transforms the city into something so beautiful and bizarre, that even the locals sometimes feel like tourists.' For more info call: 871-1881.
Montréal International Music Festival, Place des Arts, Complexe Desjardins, 282-0731. Held annually every Sept, features classes and concerts, conferences and recitals for classical music lovers. See travelling productions of *Cats* or *Les Miserables* at the **Théâtre Saint-Denis**, 1594 St Denis, 849-4211 or for Québeçois works (in French), go to the **Théâtre du Rideau Vert**, 4664 Rue St Denis. Check local papers or call Ticketmaster on 790-2222.
Rock sans Frontières, Aug 28th-Sept 1st annually. International stars share the stage with Québec's promising young musicians, as some 25 bands play for more than 30,000 people over four days. Food, beer and wine are served downtown. In Aug try to catch the **World Film Festival**. The largest celebration of film in North America, ranked with that of Cannes, Berlin and Venice. In 1997 320,000 movie goers viewed 580 screenings of 350 films from 52 countries. Place des Arts, Complexe Desjardins, 848-3883.

INFORMATION

Montréal Tourist Bureaux InfoTouriste, 1001 Rue de Square-Dorchester, 873-2015/outside Montréal (800) 363-7777. Free city guides and maps, and extensive food and housing listings. Daily summer Mon-Fri 7.30 am-8 pm. *www.tourism-mon-treal.org*. For Province-wide info: *www.tourisme.gov.qc.ca*.
Montréal Tourist Info , 873-2015. Info on provincial activities.
Tourisme Jeunesse youth travel office, 3603 Rue St Denis, 252-3117. Free maps, hostel info and advice.

TRAVEL

Allo Stop, 4317 Rue St Denis, 985-3032. Connects travellers with rides. Female drivers may be requested. Membership $6, drivers $7. 'More reliable than hitchhik-ing, cheaper than bus or train.' Average fares $15 to Québec City, $26 to Toronto, $50 to NYC.
Auto Driveaways: 2421 Guenette St at Ville St, 956-1046. $350 security deposit (takes credit cards). Valid licence. Drivers aged 21+, max four riders.
Summer: all destinations, Fall: mostly Florida-bound. Must average 350 driving miles/day.
Central Voyageur bus terminal, 505 Blvd de Maisonneuve and Berri, 842-2281. Also, ride **Greyhound**, 287-1580.
Central Station (Gare Centrale) trains, 895 Rue de la Gauchetière Ouest, under Queen Elizabeth Hotel. Served by VIA Rail, (800) 561-9181, and Amtrak, (800) 872-7245. For info and rsvs: 871-1331. Metro: Bonaventure.
Cycle Tourist bike hire: Metro Île St Hélène, 879-1468. Mountain bikes $20 (9.30 am-7 pm), helmets $2. Passport or credit card, deposit required. Rental also avail-able from the Information Center in Dorchester Square.

Gray Line City Tours, depart from 1001 Metcalfe St, 934-1222. From $18.50 to $37 depending on tour. Call for info on various tour permutations. Metro: Peel.

Mirabel Airport, 55 km from city centre, 476-3010, international flights. **Dorval Airport,** 21 km from city centre, domestic and US flights. Transportation: Gray Line $9.50 to Dorval, $13 to Mirabel from Queen Elizabeth Hotel. For info on reaching Dorval by bus call the airport on 633-3105.

Royal Tours 871-4733, $25 for tour of the city, get on and off where you like.

STCUM Metro and Bus public transport, (built for Expo '67). The metro is fully integrated with the bus system, it whispers along on rubber tyres. Public transit with flair. 'A joy after New York.' Current fare: $1.75, $7.50 for 6 tkts. Ask for transfers (honoured on both buses and metro). Daily 5.30 am-12.30 am. For info call 288-6287. Free maps available at certain stations.

Taxi Pontiac, 761-5522; and **Champlain Taxi Inc,** 273-2435. Both 24 hrs.

LES LAURENTIDES (THE LAURENTIAN MOUNTAINS) This region of mountains, lakes and forests is located just north and west of Montréal via Autoroute 15 and Rte 117. Proximity to Montréal and Québec City ensures that amenities are well developed in this area known for camping, hiking, and skiing, a resort area in both winter and summer.

Ste Agathe, built on the shore of Lac des Sables, is the major town of the Laurentians. Water sports and cruises are major pastimes here. Other towns of interest include: **St Donat,** the highest point in the area (which consequently attracts both climbers and skiers); **St Sauveur des Monts,** an arts and crafts centre; **Mont Laurier,** a farming area; and **Mont Tremblant,** a year-round sports centre which caters to those interested in fishing, watersports and hiking in the summer. In winter, it's probably the most popular ski resort in the area.

In the hills to the northeast of Montréal, north of Trois Rivières, and accessible off Hwy 55, is the unspoiled **La Mauricie National Park.** The park's rolling hills and narrow valleys are dotted with lakes. Canoeing and cross-country skiing are extremely popular here. Moose, black bear, coyote and a great variety of birds are indigenous to the area. The park is open year-round.

Accommodation is plentiful, although somewhat costly. The area is very busy in the summer and from December to March, so it is wise to book ahead. There are a lot of B&B places, inns and lodges to choose from. It is also possible to make day trips out to the Laurentians from Montréal which is a little over an hour away.

QUÉBEC CITY The price and focal point of French Canada is in fact two cities. Below Diamond Rock, Lower Town (*Basse Ville*) spreads over the coastal region of Cape Diamond and up the valley of St Charles. Atop rugged Diamond Rock, 333 ft above the St Lawrence River, is Upper or Old Québec. Originally a fortification located in the heart of New France, it remains the only walled city in North America. It's joined to the charming Quartier Petit Champlain by a 200ft funicular.

In 1759, General Wolfe and his British troops scaled the cliffs in pre-dawn darkness and took Montcalm and his French troops by surprise, thereby securing Canada for the British. The site of this attack, the Plains of Abraham, is now a peaceful public park.

Despite the outcome of that battle, Québec remains quintessentially French. In fact, only five percent of its inhabitants speak English. Walking around narrow, winding streets past the grey-stone walls, sidewalk cafes, and artists on the Rue du Trésor, it's as if one were transported across the Atlantic to the alleyways of Montmartre. The town is best explored on foot and details of a walking tour are available from the Tourist Bureaux. Montréal is situated 150 miles due west. *www.quebec/region.cuq.qc.ca.*
The telephone area code is 418.

ACCOMMODATION

Auberge De La Paix, 31 Rue Couillard, 694-0735. Friendly staff, co-ed rooms with big clean mattresses. Kitchen facilities. Close by great bars/restaurants on Rue St Jean. Free bfast 8-10 am, all you can eat. Curfew 2am. $18. 'Central location, clean.'

Auberge St Louis, 48 Rue St Louis, 692-2424. From S/D-$50, bfast included.

B&B Chez Marie-Claire, 62 Rue Ste Ursule, 692-1556. D-$65 bfast included. 'Central location, bright, clean rooms, friendly hostess.'

Bonjour Québec, 3765 Blvd Monaco, 527-1465. A B&B agency that will set you up with a place to stay, from S-$46, D-$52.

Centre International de Séjour de Québec, 19 Rue Ste Ursule, 694-0755. Laundry, microwave, TV, pool, ping-pong tables, living room, kitchen, cafeteria, limited street parking, linen provided. 'Very nice and well situated.' From $18.

Hôtel Manoir Charest, 448 Rue Dorchester, 647-9320. S-$40, D-$50. 'Clean and friendly.'

Le Manoir Lasalle, 18 Rue Ste Ursule, 692-9953. From S-$32, D-$47-$60, bfast included.

Maison Acadiènne, 43 Rue Ste Ursule, 694-0280. From S/D-$52, bfast included.

Maison du Général, 72 Rue St Louis, 694-1905. 'Very well situated.' No rsvs taken; call or show up after noon (check out time). S-$28, D-$33.

Maison Ste Ursule, 40 Rue Ste Ursule, 694-9794. 3 rooms with kitchen facilities. From S-$38, D-$47.

YWCA, 855 Holland Ave, 683-2155. For women and couples only. S-$32, D-$50.

Camping: Aéroport Camping, 2050 Rue de l'Aéroport (off Rte 138), 871-1574. $14-$23 camping with pool.

Camping Piscine Turmel, 7000 Blvd Ste Anne (off Rte 138), 824-4311. May 15-Sept 15. $18 a night. Showers, laundry, pool, auto mechanics and ice cream parlour. 'Clean and well kept.'

Municipal de Beauport, Beauport (off Rte 40 E), 666-2228. Alternatively drive here by bus #800. Campground on hill, overlooking Montgomery River. Pool, canoes, showers and laundry. $16 w/hook-up, $85-$120 weekly.

FOOD

Stroll alongside the cafés around **Rue St Jean** and **Rue Buade**. Complete 3-course meals (répas complêt), quite economical. Try the traditional *Québeçois* food and the inexpensive *croque-monsieurs*.

Café Buade, 31 Rue Buade, 692-3909. All day bfast, entrees $5-$12. Open 7.30 am-11pm.

Café Ste-Julie, 865 Rue des Zouaves—off St Jean, 647-9368. Big filling bfast $4, burger lunch $4.75. Daily 6 am-8 pm.

Casse Crêpe Breton, 1136 Rue St Jean. Many choices of fillings for your 'make-your-own-crêpe.' Bfast special $3, lunch specials (11am-2 pm). Sun-Thur 8 am-1 am, Fri-Sat 9.30 am-2am. 'Excellent crêpes.'

J A Moisan, 699 Rue St Jean, 522-8268. A cheaper alternative to eating out, buy groceries here for your own food concoctions. Daily 8.30 am-10 pm.

La Fleur de Lotus, 38 Cte de la Fabrique, across from the Hôtel de Ville, 692-4286.

'A local favourite.' Thai dishes $3.50-$10. Mon-Fri 11.30 am-10.30 pm, Sat & Sun from 5 pm.

Le Commensal , 860 St Jean, 647-3733. One of Canada's largest chain of vegetarian restaurants. Self-service hot and cold buffet, pay by weight.

Le Picotin, 4 Petit Champlain, 692-1862. Good filling French meals. For lunch: $6-$12; dinner $15-20. Kitchen closes at 10 pm. Open 11am-midnight.

Marché de Vieux Port open-air market, 160 Rue St André. Daily Mar-Nov.

OF INTEREST

La Citadelle, on Cap-Diamant promontory. Constructed by the British in the 1820s on the site of the 17th century French defences, the Citadel is the official residence of the Governor General and the largest fortification in North America still garrisoned by regular troops. Changing of the Guard ceremony by the 'Van Doos' at 10 am daily. The **Royal 22nd Regiment Museum**, 648-3563, has exhibits of military objects such as firearms, decorations, and uniforms. Museum and Citadelle are open daily from May to Sept 9 am-5 pm, mid-June to Labour Day 'til 6 pm (with reduced hours thereafter). $6 with tour.

The **Fortifications de Québec** are also worth a visit. This is the stone wall that encircles Vieux Québec (the old city). Frontenac erected this wall in the late 17th century in order to fortify the city and guard against British incursion. Tours available. June-Sept daily 10 am-5 pm, with restricted hours the rest of the year. There are great views of the city from the walkways along the wall.

The **Plains of Abraham**. Battlefields Park was the scene of the bloody clash between the French and British armies. A Martello Tower, part of the historic defence system of walled Québec, still stands. There are a number of other historic sites in this 250 acre park including the Wolfe Monument and the Jardin Jeanne d'Arc. Also here is the **Museé du Québec** which houses the original hand copy of the surrender by Montcalm and displays Québec art; visit the jail. Thur-Tue 10 am-5.45pm, Wed 'til 9.45pm (summer), closed Mon Sept-May. $5.50, $3 w/student ID. Call 643-2150 regarding temporary exhibits.

Outside the Walls, at the corner of La Grande Allée and Rue Georges VI, stands **L'Assemblée Nationale**, 643-7239. It was completed in 1886. From the visitors gallery you can view debates in French. Free 30 min tours. Mon-Fri 9 am-5 pm.

Château Frontenac, Rue St Pierre. Named for the 'illustrious governor of New France', this hotel is one of Québec City's most prominent landmarks. There is a spectacular view of the St Lawrence from the Promenade des Gouverneurs.

Ile d'Orléans. This island in the St Lawrence is a slice of 17th century France. Wander around the old houses, mills, churches. Also known for its handicrafts, strawberries and home-made treats.

Museé du Fort, 10 Rue Ste Anne, 692-2175. Diorama sound and light show. Re-live the six sieges of Québec. In summer daily 10 am-6 pm. $5.50, $3 w/student ID.

Notre Dame de Québec, 16 Rue Buade, 692-2533/4. Restored many times, the basilica was first constructed in 1650 when it served a diocese stretching from Canada to Mexico. All the bishops of Québec are buried in the crypt. Daily 9 am-6 pm. Get there early. Tours of the basilica and crypt are available 10.30 am-5 pm, from May to Nov. Free. Sound and light show, 3 times daily. $7, $4 w/student ID. 'An atmospheric introduction to the history of the city.'

Notre Dame Des Victoires, Place Royale, Basse Ville, 692-1650. Built in 1688. Eighty years before its construction, this is where Champlain established the first permanent white settlement in North America north of Florida. The church itself gets its name in honour of two French military victories. Its main altar resembles the city in that it is shaped like a fortress complete with turrets and battlements. Guided tours mid-May to mid-Oct. Free. Mon-Sat 9 am-4.30 pm.

Parliament Buildings, on Grande Allée at Ave Dufferin. The main building built in

1884, is in Second Empire style. The bronze statues in front represent the historical figures of Québec. Open end of June to Labour Day, daily 10 am-5.30 pm. Free. While in the area, notice the architecture of the buildings on Grand Allée and the sidewalk cafes lining the street.

Place Royale has undergone considerable restoration under its current owner, the Government of Québec. In the summer, the roads are blocked off and restricted to pedestrians only, and many plays and variety shows are put on in the parks of the area. This is one of the oldest districts in North America.

The Ramparts, Rue des Ramparts. Studded with old iron cannons, probably the last vestiges of the Siege of Québec in 1759.

INFORMATION

Centre d'information, 60 rue d'Auteuil, 692-2471. Listings of accommodations, brochures, maps and bilingual advice. *Greater Québec Area Guide* can be picked up here free. Daily 8.30 am-8 pm. (Ste-Foy branch), 651-2882. Daily 8.30 am-5 pm, summer 'til 8 pm.

Tourisme Jeunesse, 2700 boul Laurier, (800) 461-8585. Maps, travel guides, hostel membership and insurance sold. Make rsvs here too for hostels.

Tourisme Québec, (800) 361-5405 from anywhere in province or (800) 363-7777 from outside.

TRAVEL

Allo Stop, 467 Rue St Jean, Québec, 522-0056. See 'Montréal' section for description of service.) Daily 9 am-7 pm.

Central bus terminal (Gare Centrale d'Autobus), 525-3000. Daily 5 am-1 am. Also, **Ste Foy bus terminal (west end)**, 651-7015.

CN train station , 3255 Chemin de la Gare, Ste Foy (west end).

Coop Taxis Québec, 525-5191.

Ferry across the St Lawrence, 644-3704. Daily departures from the wharf 6.30 am-3am. Fare: $1.50. Nice views of Québec, especially at sunset.

Québec National Airport, Ste Foy, Blvd Hamel to Blvd de l'Aéroport. 14 miles (23 km) from city centre. For a **shuttle** to the airport call Visites Touristiques Foy d'Erable, 649-9226, $10.

Pelletier Car Rental, 900 Pièrre Bertrand, 681-0678. Mon-Fri 7.30 am-8 pm, Sat-Sun 8 am-4 pm.

VIA Rail, 450 Rue de la Gare du Palais, 524-3590.

Voyageur Bus Terminus, several locations. Québec City: 225 Charest Est, 525-3000; Ste Foy: 2700 Blvd Laurier, 651-7015. Hourly service to Montréal.

LA GASPÉSIE (THE GASPÉ PENINSULA) This is the bit of Québec Province jutting out above New Brunswick into the Gulf of St Lawrence. The word Gaspé is derived from the Micmac Indian word meaning Lands End. You'll appreciate this when standing on the shore at Gaspé for there's nothing but sea between you and Europe. Picturesque fishing villages line the Peninsula; slow, pleasant places in summer, rugged in winter. Inland it's farming country although a large area is taken up by the Gaspésian Provincial Park.

The route from Québec City to Gaspé runs along the mighty St Lawrence where the scenery closely resembles that of the Maritime Provinces. The North Shore is a more interesting drive, but at some point, you have to take a ferry to get to the South Shore. (The narrower the river at the point of crossing, the cheaper the ferry ride.) You can, for instance, take Rte 138 out of Québec City and pass by the **Chute de Montmorency,** the impressive 250 ft waterfall—higher than Niagara. Then, through **Ste Anne de Beaupré,** destination of millions of pilgrimages yearly since 18th century ship-wrecked sailors believed Ste Anne was their saviour. Next, through **Baie St Paul** where there is an interesting museum of old-time French Canadiana, and up to St Simeon where there is a ferry crossing to Riviére du Loup. From here, take Rte 132 as far as **Trois Pistoles.**

Long before Canada was 'officially discovered', Basque whale hunters built ovens at Trois Pistoles to reduce whale blubber to oil. The remains of the ovens can still be seen. Carry on along the south shore of the St Lawrence through the fishing villages, catching all the while the ever changing seascapes. From **Rivière à Claude** access to the top of 4160 ft **Mount Jacques Cartier** is 'easy'. The mountain is in the Gaspésian Provincial Park and is the highest point in the province, guaranteeing a great view and perhaps even some caribou.

Or for the moment carry on round the top of the Peninsula coming first to Gaspé itself where Jacques Cartier came ashore in 1533 and set up a cross to stake France's claim to Canada.

Nearby is **Forillon National Park.** Forillon scenery is typified by jagged cliffs and fir-covered highlands. The park is crisscrossed by many hiking trails and on the way you may see deer, fox, bear or moose. Large colonies of seabirds such as cormorants, gannets, and gulls nest on the cliff headlands and it is possible to see whales and seals basking offshore.

Naturalists offer talks and slide presentations at the Interpretive Centre on Hwy 132 near **Cap des Rosiers.** There are **campsites** at Cap Bon Ami, Le Havre, and **Petit Gaspé.** All three have good recreational facilities.

The views around here are fantastic but none better than at **Percé.** The village takes its name from **Rocher Percé,** the Pierced Rock, which is just off-shore. You can walk there on a sandbar at low tide.

From Percé boat trips go to nearby **Ile Bonaventure,** where there is a bird sanctuary. Be sure to stop off at the **Gaspésian Provincial Park** before heading down to **Chaleur Bay** on your way back to Québec's urban centres. In the park you may catch a glimpse of the caribou herd which spends its summers here. Mornings are the time you are most likely to see them.

ACCOMMODATION
Auberge Le Balconvert Backpackers Hostel, Baie St-Paul, Rte 362, call (408) 435-5587 for seasonal prices and availability.

Auberge de Cap aux Os Hostel, 2095 Blvd Grande-Grève. Gaspé, Forillon National Park, 892-5153. $18. Laundry facs, linen & bike rental. 'Very friendly, bilingual but mostly French.' Voyageur Bus stops at the hostel (June 24-Sept 30). During the off-season take Grey Coach or train from Québec City to Gaspé (25 kms from hostel).

Auberge du Château Hostel, Pointe à la Garde, 788-2048. Castle with a hostel built by the owner, Jean. Laundry, linen rental, free bfast. Dinner served in castle, $8. 'Excellent atmosphere, excellent food, excellent host.' 'Phone before going to get exact location.' Dorms $17.

Collège de la Gaspésie in Gaspé, 368-2749. Year-round. From S-$26, D-$36 (with shared bath). Apt for 6-8, around $84.

Maison Bérubé, 245 Monte Sandy Beach, Gaspé, 368-6402. From S/D-$45.

Motel Fort Ramsay, 254 Blvd Gaspé, 368-5094. May-Sept. S-$39, D-$45. Kitchen facilities.

THE PRAIRIE PROVINCES

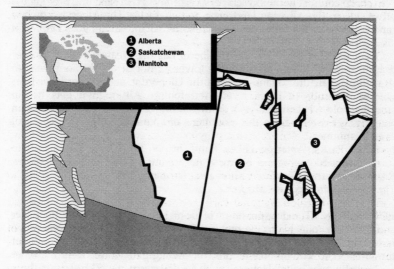

1 Alberta
2 Saskatchewan
3 Manitoba

Although the terrain in Alberta, Manitoba and Saskatchewan is primarily prairie, western Alberta offers the splendour of the Canadian Rockies. Grain was once the foundation of the economy of these provinces, but today mineral wealth and tourism are the industrial leaders.

Although the major cities are fast-growing modern centres of commerce and culture, there remains a touch of the frontier about all three provinces. Vast areas of virgin wilderness are still there for the intrepid to explore and conquer and it is possible to travel for days in some places without ever seeing another human being.

ALBERTA

Once an agricultural backwater with an economy dependent solely on wheat, Alberta is still enjoying the economic boom based on the Province's multi-billion dollar oil and gas industries which took off in the '70s and '80s. The former small-town farming centres of Calgary and Edmonton are now thriving metropolises, their skylines dotted with skyscraping corporate headquarters. With 85 percent of Canada's oil and gas on tap, Albertans are enjoying the lowest taxes, the least unemployment and the highest per capita incomes in the country.

The situation is not without its political implications. The four western provinces and two territories hold less than 30 percent of the seats in the federal Parliament and westerners feel deprived of power by the more populous East. It is not only in Québec that the language of separation is often spoken.

In sharp contrast to the skyscrapers, cattle and grain ranching provide the other side to the Albertan landscape and character. The Albertan cowboy ranches some of the finest beef in the world. As the saying goes here: 'If it ain't Alberta, it ain't beef.'

Of all the Canadian provinces, Alberta has the greatest variety of geographical features, ranging from the towering Rockies in the southwest to the rolling agricultural land north of the US border, and up north the near wilderness lands of lakes, rivers and forests. Although it gets hot in summer, cold weather and even snow can linger into May and come again as early as September. In the mountains of course the nights can be cool even in summer.

National Parks: Waterton Lakes, Banff, Jasper, Elk Island, Wood Buffalo (not developed, no access by road, no accommodation). *www.yahoo.com/ Regional/Countries/Canada/Provinces_and_Territories/Alberta.*
The telephone area code is 403.

EDMONTON   The close proximity of the highly productive Leduc, Redwater and Pembiano oilfields to the provincial capital made Edmonton one of the fastest growing cities in Canada. Coal mining, natural gas, and a couple of throw backs to Edmonton's origins, fur-trading and wheat, were the other factors behind the boom. However, with the downturn in world oil prices those heady days are over and Edmonton is in the process of re-assessment.

During the Klondike gold rush Edmonton was a stopping place for prospectors en route to the goldfields. The town remembers this with joy every July during Klondike Days when the place goes wild for a week. Otherwise it's a sober, hard-working spot, the most northerly major city in North America, boasting as well as skyscrapers a progressive university, the only subway system in western Canada, the world' s largest indoor shopping mall, and, as a result of hosting the Commonwealth Games a few years back, some of the finest sporting facilities anywhere.

Edmonton is centrally situated within Alberta and it's a good starting point for a northbound trip or for going westwards towards the Rockies. Jasper is 228 miles away, but first there's Elk Island National Park just 30 miles east.

The Old Strathcona Pubcrawler lists restaurants, pubs, lounges, nightclubs and live music venues, *www.pub-crawler.com/.*

ACCOMMODATION
Cecil Hotel, 10406 Jasper Ave, 428-7001, downtown. S-$28, D-$33. TV, phone, p/bath.
Commercial Hotel, 10329 82nd Ave, 439-3981. S-$23, S-$28 w/bath, D-$26.50, D-$32 w/bath, key deposit $5. South, in trendy Strathcona.
Edmonton HI Hostel, 10422 91st St, 429-0140. Common room, snack bar, showers, kitchen/laundry. $13-$18. Near West Edmonton Mall. Cycling in river valley, summer festivals. 'Easy walk from downtown. Comfortable.' Bike hire, $13 day.
Grand Hotel, 10266 103 St, 422-6365. S-$25-$37, D-$32-$43, $5 key deposit. Handy location-across from Greyhound bus station.

St Joseph's College, 89 Ave at 114 St near University of Alberta, 492-7681. A better alternative to the more institutionalised and expensive uni accom nearby. S-$21, weekly $130. Full board S-$34. Bfast/lunch/dinner available. Rsvs in summer.

Klondiker Hotel, 153 St and Stony Plain Rd, 489-1906. West End location. From S-$37, D-$43.

University of Alberta Residence, Lister Hall, 87th Ave & 116th St, 492-4281. Open to non-students May-Aug, call for rates.

YMCA, 10030 102A Ave, 421-9622. Dorm rooms $15, S-$33, $38 w/bath, D-$45, $10 key deposit.

YWCA, 10305 100 Ave, 423-9922. Dorm rooms $14.50, S-$32-$37, D-$45.

Camping: Bondiss Skeleton Lake Scout Camp, 14205-109 Ave, (403) 454-8561. 500 acres, 3 km of shoreline, swimming, hiking.

FOOD

Downtown along 104 St is **"Restaurant Row"** with over fifty places within walking distance of each other and an abundance of coffee shops.

Whyte Ave, from 99 St to 109 St, there are lots of eateries along this stretch—close to Uni of Alberta campus. **Strathcona Square**, located at 8150 105 St, is a restored Victorian building containing several restaurants worth looking at.

Amandine, 10130 103rd St, 425-4134. Small French cafe. 'Pleasant place with good food.'

Bones, 10220 103rd St, 421-1167. Specialises in ribs, $7.

Carson's Café, 10331 Whyte 82 Ave, 432-7560. Situated in the middle of the Old Strathcona district. Small selection of daily specials, ranging from chicken dishes to burgers, under $10. Daily 11 am-11 pm.

Chianti's, 10501 Whyte 82 Ave, 439-9829. Italian dishes, ranging from pasta to seafood, and daily speciality wines. Mon-Thurs 11 am-11 pm, Fri/Sat 'til midnight, Sun 4-11 pm.

David's, 8407 Argyll Rd, 454-8527. Come dine here for the true taste of Alberta beef.

Earl's, various locations. Generous servings—one on Uni of Alberta campus.

Hello Deli, 10725 124th St, for sandwiches, bagels, soups, $5-$8.

Smitty's Pancake House, various locations—big bfasts, $5.

OF INTEREST

Edmonton Art Gallery, 2 Sir Winston Churchill Sq, 422-6223. More than 30 exhibitions each year include contemporary and historical art from Canada and around the world. Mon-Wed 10.30 am-5 pm, Thur & Fri 'til 8 pm. Sat/Sun & hols 11 am-5 pm. Thur 4 pm-8 pm, free. $3, w/student ID $1.50.

Edmonton Space Sciences Centre, 11211 142nd St, 452-9100 (info)/451-7722 (recording). Over $2 million worth of exhibits, IMAX film theatre, exhibit gallery and science shop; $6.50 day pass. Sun-Thur 10 am-9.30 pm, Fri & Sat 'til 10.30 pm, closed Mon in Sept.

The John Walter Museum, 10627 93rd Ave, 496-7275, was built of hand-hewn logs in 1874. The house was the district's first telegraph office. Four historic buildings on original site. Sun 1 pm-4 pm, free. Different activities each day.

Legislature Bldg, 97th Ave & 108th St, 427-7362. On the site of the original Fort Edmonton. Built at the beginning of this century. Free tours every 1/2 hr.

Provincial Museum, 12845 102nd Ave, 453-9100. Features displays of Alberta's natural and human history, including native people, pioneers, wildlife, and geology. Sun-Weds 9 am-9 pm, Thur-Sat 'til 8 pm, $3.25.

Muttart Conservatory, 962696 A St, 496-8755. Four glass pyramids nestled in the city centre feature more than 700 species of plants from arid to temperate climates. Sun-Wed 11 am-9 pm, Thurs-Sat 'til 6 pm. $4.25, $3.25 w/student ID.

Ukrainian Canadian Archives and Museum of Alberta, 10611 110 Ave, 424-7580. Traces history of Ukranian pioneers in Alberta. Includes costumes, paintings, folk art. Tues-Fri 10 am-5 pm, Sat from noon. Hours subject to change, phone prior to visit.

Shopping: West Edmonton Mall, 170th St & 87th Ave. World's largest indoor shopping mall with over 800 stores. Employs 15,000 people, and features water-slides, dolphin tank, full size replica of Santa Maria, skating rink, a petting zoo, 10 aviaries, mini golf—you name it! 'Mind boggling.' 'A must see.'

Parks: Fort Edmonton Historical Park, corner of White Mud and Fox Dr, 496-8787. Reconstruction of the original and a replica of a Hudson's Bay Co Trading Post. 'Worth a visit.' Daily Mon-Fri 10 am-4 pm, Sat-Sun 'til 6 pm. $6.50; discounts for HI members.

Polar Park, 22 kms SE on Hwy 14, 922-3401. Preserve for cold-climate and hardy African animals. Cross country trails and sleigh rides in winter. Daily 8 am-dusk, $5.

ENTERTAINMENT
The Red Barn, RR1, about 30 miles out of town, 921-3918. 'Largest indoor BBQ in Canada. Worth a visit.' 'Very popular.' Dance on Saturday. Closed Sun.

Theatre and Concerts, Edmonton Opera and Symphony, plus many live theatres. Call the LIVE LINE at 496-9255 for performance info.

Festivals: Jazz City International Festival, late June. Canadian and overseas jazz musicians. Running simultaneously is **The Works**, a celebration of the visual arts.

Edmonton Folk Music Festival, mid-Aug, Gallagher Park. Features traditional and bluegrass music, country, blues and Celtic music—all under the bright Alberta sun.

Edmonton Street Performers Festival, mid-July. Downtown streets come alive with magicians, jugglers, clowns, mime artists, musicians and comics.

Fringe Theatre Event, (403) 448-9000. For 10 days in mid-Aug, Old Strathcona is transformed into a series of stages for alternative theatre, a rival to Edinburgh's festival. More than 65 troupes attend from around the globe.

Klondike Days. 1890s style provided during the 10 Klondike days, mid-July, full of street festivities and the great Klondike Days Exposition at Northlands Park. 'Excellent entertainment.' The show at MacDonald Hotel, Jasper & 98th St, during this time, is 'not to be missed'. Free entrance to the Golden Slipper Saloon. Immense 'Klondike breakfasts' are served in the open air, massed marching bands compete in the streets, and down the North Saskatchewan River float more than 100 of the weirdest-looking home-built rafts ever seen. 'Where most students drink; good entertainment.'

INFORMATION
Chamber of Commerce, 832 Connaught Dr, 852-3858.

Edmonton Tourism, 9797 Jasper Ave, (800) 463-4667. *www.ede.org*.

Visitors Information Centre, 9797 Jasper Ave (lobby level), 426-4715. Summer: Mon-Sat 9 am-4.30 pm; winter: Mon-Fri from 8.30 am. Another **info centre** at 2404 Calgary Trail Northbound SW, 496-8400. Daily 8 am-9 pm, 8.30 am-4.30 pm after Labor Day.

TRAVEL
Edmonton International Airport, 18 miles S of the city on Hwy 2, about a 45 minute drive.

Airporter shuttle runs Mon-Fri 5.40 am-10.45 pm, Sat & Sun 6 am-10.15 pm and departs every 45 mins from Macdonald Place, various downtown hotels and the Arrivals Terminal. $11 o/w, call 463-7520 for more info.

Greyhound, 421-4211/(800) 661-8747.

Edmonton Transit System Info, 496-1611 for info. Operates the city buses as well as the new, silent, streamlined and comfortable LRT (Light Rail Transit). Basic fare: $1.60.

Red Arrow Express, 425-0820. Coach service btwn Edmonton and Calgary 4 times daily (8 am, 12.15 pm, 4.30 pm, 6 pm) o/w $29, r/t $58.
CN/VIA Rail Station, (800) 561-8630.
Co-op Taxi 425-8310 or 425-2525.
Royal Tours, #600, 1 Thornton Ct, Jasper Ave & 99th St, 488-9040. Daily 3 hr tours of Edmonton from $23, includes admission to Provincial Museum of Alberta. All day tours include admission to the Historical Park and cost $40.

ELK ISLAND NATIONAL PARK   This 75 sq mile park is the largest fenced wild animal preserve in Canada. Apart from the elk, moose, mule deer and numerous smaller animals who live here, there is a herd of some 600 buffalo. Once roaming the North American continent in their millions, the buffalo were hunted almost to extinction by the end of the 19th century. The herd here at Elk Island has been built up from about 40 animals since 1907.

It is possible to observe the buffalo from close proximity, but on the other side of a strong fence. Walking on the buffalo range itself is discouraged! North America's largest buffalo herd, 12,000 strong, is contained in **Wood Buffalo National Park** in the far north of Alberta. This area, however, remains relatively undeveloped.

Elk Island is open throughout the year. The Visitor Centre, just north of Hwy 16, 922-5790, features exhibits and displays. Walks, hikes, campfire talks and theatre programmes are offered by the park rangers. Recreation facilities, including swimming, golf and hiking trails, are available on the east shore of Astotin Lake. There are camping facilities in the park. Admission $5 per vehicle.
www.parks.canada.pch.gc.ca/parks/alberta/elk_island/elk_islande.htm.

OF INTEREST
Ukrainian Cultural Heritage Village, on Hwy 16, 662-3640. Russian immigrants played an important role in taming western Canada and this open-air museum portrays pre-1930s life of the Ukrainian settlers. The authentic buildings have been moved here and then restored. Daily 10 am-6 pm. $5.50, Tues free. After Labor Day 10 am-4 pm, $3.
Vegreville, 25 miles E of the Ukrainian Village, is where to find the world's largest Ukrainian Easter Egg, towering over 30 ft tall! Constructed in 1974 to commemorate the 100th anniversary of the arrival of the Royal Canadian Mounted Police in Alberta, it is possible to camp around the egg. Arrive early July and watch the annual **Ukrainian Festival** with singing, music and leg-throwing folk dances.

JASPER NATIONAL PARK   Jasper National Park is 4200 square miles of lofty, green-forested, snow-capped mountains, canyons, dazzling lakes, glaciers and hot mineral springs. In sharp contrast to one another, within the park are the Miette Hot Springs, one of which gushes forth at a temperature of 129°F, and the huge Columbia Icefields which send their melting waters to three oceans, the Atlantic, the Pacific and the Arctic.

Reached by Rte 16 (The Yellowhead Hwy) from Edmonton, Jasper lies along the eastern slopes of the Canadian Rockies running south until the park meets Banff National Park. This vast mountainous complex of national parkland is an extremely popular resort area throughout the year. Jasper National Park takes its name from one Jasper Hawes who was clerk in the first trading-post at Brul Lake in about 1813.

One of the park's biggest attractions is the 17-mile-long **Maligne Lake**. This is the largest of several beautiful glacial lakes in the area and the tour to the lake from the township of Jasper has been much recommended by previous visitors.

Within the park it is possible to drive through some of the West's most spectacular mountain scenery. **Mt Edith Cavell** (11,033 ft) and **Whistler's Peak** (7350 ft) are two of the more accessible points from Jasper township and the aerial tramway has put Whistler's Peak within reach of even the most nervous would-be mountaineers. In the cablecar at the highest point above the ground you will be 450 ft in the air and once atop the Peak the view is tremendous. In winter this is a favourite skiing spot.

Sixty-five miles from Jasper on the Icefield Hwy between Jasper and Banff (Rte 93) is the **Columbia Icefield**. This is 130 square miles of impressive glacial ice. You can walk across parts of the glacier but it is perhaps best seen by snowmobile. Even on a very hot day take a sweater with you. Also to be seen along this most beautiful of highways are the several glaciers creeping down from the icefields. **Athabasca Glacier** is but a mile from the road and snowmobile trips are available on the glacier.

The resort village of **Jasper** is the Jasper National Park Headquarters and also an important CN railroad junction. Should you arrive by train, take note of the 70-ft Raven Totem Pole at the railway depot. The totem was carved by Simeon Stiltae, a master carver of the Haida Indians of the Queen Charlotte Islands, and gives its name to a famous annual golf tournament held here.

www.worldweb.com/parkscanada-jasper/index.html.

ACCOMMODATION

Recommend contacting the tourist homes/B&Bs for very reasonable rates. The **Chamber of Commerce**, 632 Connaught Dr, 852-3858, has a list of hotels in the area; and **Parks Canada Information Office**, Town Info Centre, 852-6176, provides a list of approved tourist homes.

Youth Hostels general info: contact 10926 88th Ave, Edmonton, T6G 0Z1, (403) 439-3089. Check out website: *www.HostellingIntl.ca/Alberta*. The Pika Shuttle Company runs a shuttle service btwn hostels in Alberta; call (800) 363-0096 for info. Fares vary according to distance. Also check out **Hikers Wheels** and **The Rocky Express** under Banff *Travel* section.

Athabasca Falls HI Hostel, 32 km S from Jasper on Hwy 93; E side of Hwy 93. Propane heating and lighting. Volleyball, basketball, horseshoes, and Athabasca Falls nearby. $9-$15.

Beauty Creek HI Hostel, 87 km S of Jasper; W side of Hwy 93, 439-3089. Cycling destination, and close by Stanley Falls, Columbia Icefield. Partial closure Oct-Apr; in winter pick up key. $9-$14.

Jasper HI Hostel, PO Box 387, Jasper, AB T0E 1E0, 852-5560. 7 km SW of Jasper on Whistler's Mountain Rd, off Hwy 93. Hiking, biking, skiing, barbecue.

Maligne Canyon HI Hostel, 11 km E of Jasper on Maligne Lake Road. Propane heating/lighting. Across the road to Maligne Canyon, access to Skyline Trail. $9-$15.

Mt Edith Cavell HI Hostel, 26 km S of Jasper; 13 km off Hwy 93A (10 1/2 km straight uphill, not accessible by car in winter or spring). Near Angel Glacier, Tonquin Valley & Verdant Pass. 'Superb area for hiking/skiing.' Partial closure Oct-June. $9-$15.

Whistler's HI Hostel, 8 km from Jasper by Skytram. $14-$19.

Camping: Several campgrounds in the area, the nearest ones to Jasper being at **Whistler's** on Icefield Pkwy S (852-3963), and **Wapiti**, also on Icefield Pkwy (852-3992). Approx $12-$16. Gets very cold at night. May-Oct.

OF INTEREST
Columbia Icefield, 762-2241. Snowmobile trips available daily, mid-Apr-mid-Nov, weather permitting, $22.50. Open 9 am-6 pm Mon-Sun (shorter hrs in winter).
Jasper Heritage Folk Festival, held annually Aug 2nd-3rd. This folk festival, set amid the unparalleled grandeur of the Canadian Rockies, includes blues, jazz, bluegrass, country and women's music.
Jasper Raft Tours, for info 852-3613/852-4721 and 852-3332 for rsvs. 2 hr trips on Athabasca River running through May-Sept at 9.30 am, 2.30 pm, 7 pm; $33. Tkts available at the Brewster Bus Depot and Jasper Park Lodge. Also, **Rocky Mountain River Guides White-water Rafting**, offer a 1-day trip, approx $60. 'Excellent! The trips are very well organised and the professional raft guides make you feel safe and at ease. Very safety conscious.' Shop around for the best deal. Don't forget to buy a photo as a souvenir.
Jasper Skytram, 852-3093. 2 miles S via Hwy 93 and Whistler Mountain Rd. Daily mid-May-Oct, 8 am-9.30 pm July through Aug; $10. Bus connections from RR station at 10.15 am, 1.45 pm, 3.15 pm, or walk there.
Maligne Lake Boat Tours. 1¹/₂ hr tour ($27), 852-3370. Views of Maligne Narrows. May-Oct, hourly 10 am-5 pm.

FOOD
The Atha B, 510 Potucia St, 852-3386, is where everyone hangs out in Jasper. Sample local brews and dance to the live bands who play nightly.
The Jasper Pizza Place, on Connaught Dr, 852-3225. Popular with locals, licensed and very reasonable. Under $10 for pizza, burgers, salads and tacos.
Mountain Foods and Café, 606 Connaught Dr, 852-4050. Extensive selection of sandwiches that are perfect for bfast or lunch. Daily 7 am-11 pm.
Scoops and Loops, 504 Patricia St, 852-4333. Sandwiches, pastries, sushi, udon noodles and ice cream all available here to be eaten up! Mon-Sat 10 am-11 pm, Sun 11 am-10 pm.

INFORMATION/TRAVEL
Brewster Transportation and Tours, 852-3332. Provides local transportation and sightseeing. June-Sept, two tours daily. 'Quite pricey.' 'Predictable.' 'A last resort.'
Jasper National Park Interpretive Centre, 500 Connaught Dr, 852-6176. Guided walks, trail maps and information. Daily 8.30 am-7 pm in summer; winter 9 am-5 pm. Or find them on the internet: *www.worldweb.com/parkscanada-jasper.*
Jasper Chamber of Commerce, 632 Connaught Dr, 852-3858. Mon-Fri 9 am-5 pm. Courtesy phone available for accomodation; very helpful and friendly staff. **Travel Alberta** is in the same office. Daily 8 am-8 pm.
Heritage Taxi, 611 Patricia, 852-5558.

BANFF NATIONAL PARK Banff, Canada's oldest national park, was established in 1885 after hot springs were seen gushing from the side of Sulphur Mountain. It takes in an area of 2546 sq miles of the Rockies and the area's dry, equable climate, alpine-style grandeur, hot mineral springs and pools, have brought Banff fame and fortune as a summer health and winter ski resort. **Banff** and **Lake Louise** are the main resort towns. The park gets its name from Banffshire in Scotland, the birthplace of Lord Strathcona, a past president of the Canadian Pacific Railroad.

Operating all year round are the cable cars which take the visitor high into the mountains. Both the **Sulphur Mountain Gondola** and the **Mt Norquay Chair Lift** offer fantastic views, although in winter you can only ride the Mt Norquay lift if you are skiing. During the summer months, hiking is popular on the many trails winding up and around the mountains but it can be tough going and the inexperienced should acquire a guide before venturing forth.

It is possible to walk up **Mt Rundle** or **Cascade Mountain** in a day during summer, but you must first register with a park ranger. If you're on Mt Rundle, make sure that you're on the right trail, since it's easy to mistake the trail and get on to the less scenic one along the river valley. To walk up **Sulphur Mountain Trail** takes around $1^1/_2$ hrs from the **Upper Hot Springs**. The gondola takes around 7 mins and costs $10. If you walk up, the ride down is free!

At the Upper Hot Springs there is a pool fed by sulphur springs at 40 degrees centigrade. Great for relaxing, although it will cost you $5. You can also hire towels for around $1.

If you don't have much time in Banff, there is a beautiful trail walk along the glacial green Bow River to **Bow Falls** near the Banff Springs Hotel. The hotel, the pride of Canadian Pacific, is built in the style of a Scottish baronial mansion. The scenery really is spectacular and the area is not overrun by tourists, especially in winter. Although the Bow Falls are frozen then, they are still breathtaking. You may also see herds of elk on the ice further down the valley. An alternative short walk is the trail up Tunnel Mountain which should take about $1^1/_4$ hrs from bus station to the summit.

Glacial lakes are one of the most attractive features of Banff. **Peyto Lake** (named after Bill Peyto, famous explorer and guide of the 1890s) changes from being a deep blue colour in the early summer to an 'unbelievably beautiful turquoise' later in the year as the glacier melts into it. Tourists have been known to ask the locals whether the lake is drained each year to paint the bottom blue! The glacier which feeds the lake is receding at 70 ft a year.

'The jewel of the Rockies,' **Lake Louise**, lies in a hanging valley formed during the Ice Age and is one of the loveliest spots in the world. It is a placid green lake in a terrific setting—not for swimming though. The water is a chilly 10 degrees centigrade. The town of Lake Louise is 36 miles from Banff on the Jasper highroad. From the town, suggested trips are the 9 miles to the incredibly blue **Moraine Lake**, the **Valley of the Ten Peaks** and back through Larth Valley over Sentinel Peak, or a walk out to the **Plain of the Six Glaciers** via Lake Agnes. You will need lots of time and a pair of stout shoes. In winter these are more likely to be snow shoes, as several feet of snow is the norm in the Rockies!

Be careful of the black and grizzly bears who live in the park. They are out and about in summer, but are occasionally seen in winter. You may also see moose, elk, cougars, coyotes and Rocky Mountain goats and lots of elk— especially in Banff! The lakes and rivers of the park are excellent for trout and Rocky Mountain Whitefish fishing, although you may need a permit to fish in some areas.

www.worldweb.com/parkscanada-banff/index.html

BANFF Situated 81 miles W of Calgary and 179 miles S of Jasper, the village of Banff is always buzzing with activity. With excellent downhill skiing in the winter—a choice of three ski areas within easy reach-and hiking, cycling, golfing, and mountain climbing in the summer, this little town is rarely at a loss for something to do. Banff is also a lively arts centre and is home to the Banff School of Fine Arts, as well as hosting a Festival of the Arts from May 'til late August and the Winter Festival over Christmas and New Year.

Over recent years Banff has become the favourite playground of Japanese tourists, whose multitude is now so great that many of the town's signs are bilingual: Japanese and English. This sudden interest in Banff partly stems from a Japanese soap opera that uses the famous Banff Springs Hotel as its backdrop. As a result, the hotel is constantly full of honeymooners from the Pacific Rim. 'Really touristy but a very attractive town with spectacular surroundings.' For live webcam views from the top of Sulphur Mountain, go to *www.banffgondola.com/*.

ACCOMMODATION

Accommodation options in and around Banff are generally expensive. However, there are many hostels in the area and for the budget traveller they are undoubtedly the best bet. **Central Reservations**, (800) 661-1676. Will find accommodation for a $10 fee. **NB:** Not advisable to arrive in Banff on Sun eve without rsvs.

Banff HI Hostel, Tunnel Mountain Rd, 762-4122. 3 km from downtown, 45 min walk from train or bus station. 'Excellent hostel. Comfortable, friendly and near some great hikes.' Close to Whyte Museum and Banff Hot Springs, plenty of outdoor sports. Pika Shuttle btwn Alberta hostels can be reserved from here. $18-$22.

Castle Mountain HI Hostel, Hwy 1A and 93 S, 762-2367. 1.5 km E of junction of Trans-Canada and 93S. 25 km E of Lake Louise. Access to Norquay, Sunshine, Lake Louise, trails, springs and falls. $12-$15.

Hilda Creek HI Hostel, (403) 762-4122. 8.5km S of Columbia Icefields Visitors Centre, 120km N of Lake Louise on Hwy 93. Close by Mt Athabasca, Saskatchewan Glacier, skiing, telemarking. Hostel has wood burning sauna. 'Basic, but great hiking.' Partial closure Oct-Apr. $10-$14.

Lake Louise HI Hostel (Canadian Alpine Center), Village Rd, 522-2200. Kitchen/laundry, cafe, mountaineering resource library, guided hikes, fireplace, sauna. Book early in high season. 'A palace!' $19-$23, private rooms available $21-$28.

Mosquito Creek HI Hostel, on Hwy 93, 26 km N of Lake Louise next to Mosquito Campground, 762-4122. Hiking, mountaineering, cross-country skiing. $11-$15.

Rampart Creek HI Hostel, 12 km N of Saskatchewan River crossing on the Icefields Pkwy, 762-4122. 'Loads of atmosphere but no common area. Handy for ice climbing and saunas followed by a dip in the creek!!' Hiking, volleyball, mountaineering, ice climbing, wood burning sauna. Partial closure Oct-Apr. $10-$14.

Ribbon Creek HI Hostel, (403) 591-7333, 70km W of Calgary on Hwy 1 (Trans Canada Hwy), then 25 km S on Hwy 40, turn right at Nakiska Skill Hill access, cross the Kananaskis River and left 1.5 km to the Hostel. Hiking, biking, skiing, golfing, rafting, near Kananaski Village. $12-$16.

Tan-Y-Bryn, Mrs Cowan, 118 Otter St, 762-3696. Continental bfast included. 'Super guest house.' S-$30-$50, D-$36-$50.

Whiskey Jack HI Hostel, 27 km W of Lake Louise in Yoho National Park. Hiking to Emerald Lake and President Range. Closed mid-Sept-mid-June. $12-$16.

Y Mountain Lodge, 102 Spray Ave, (800) 813-4138. Laundry, cafeteria, meeting

space. Operated by YWCA team. Winter dorm $18, summer dorm $19. Private rooms available for budget rates (although higher in summer), call to enquire.
YMCA/YWCA, Springs Mountain Hostel, 762-3560. 'Dorms a little cramped but close to the centre of Banff.' $19 (bring sleeping bag), S-$47, D-$53, Q-$58.

FOOD
For unbeatable value, try **Safeway' s** (on corner of Banff Ave & Elk St). For more upmarket possibilities, there's **Keller's** on Bear St, where they offer free coffee while you select your purchases. Pick up a copy of *Dining in Banff* for more options. On **Caribou**, check out **Aardvark Pizza**, 762-5500. 'Cheap, tasty and handy for post pub munchies!'; **The Fine Grind**, (403) 762-2353, great coffee, hot chocolate and snacks; and the **Magpie and Stump**, 762-4067, authentic local cuisine and decor. Reasonable prices.
Athena Pizza, Banff Ave, (403) 762-4022. 'Large deep pan, $15 feeds 4 pp.'
Cascade Plaza Food Court, 317 Banff Ave (lower level). 'Great Chinese/Japanese food. $3.50 for a big plateful.'
Guido's, Banff Ave, 762-4002. 'Generous 3-course meal $8.50-$15. One of the best eating places in Canada.' Daily 4.30 pm-7.30 pm.
Joe's Diner, 221 Banff Ave, 762-5529. 50's style decor & music. 'Good and cheap.'
Melissa's Misteak, 218 Lynx St, 762-5511. Varied menu, large portions, nice atmosphere.
The Scoop, Banff Ave, 762-2928. Not to be missed for delicious ice-cream and frozen yoghurts.
Smitty's, 227 Banff Ave, 762-2533; and **Sam** on Mall, Lake Louise. Great for bfast.
Tommy's Neighbourhood Pub, 762-888. Good food, friendly staff and 2-for-1 specials on five nights a week!

OF INTEREST
Buffalo Paddock. On the Trans-Canada Hwy ¹/₂ mile W of eastern traffic circle. A 300-acre buffalo range. You have to stay in your car. Free.
Icefields Snowmobile trips. See under Jasper.
The Indian Trading Post, 762-2456. A museum-like store which sells everything on display. Indian crafts and furs. Daily 9 am-9 pm, summer.
Lake Louise Gondola, 522-3555, off Trans-Canada Hwy. Daily 8.30 am-6 pm June-Labour Day. $9 r/t ($8 w/student ID). Skiing Nov-May.
Natural History Museum, 112 Banff Ave, 762-4747. Geology, archaeology and plant life of the Rockies plus films. Sept 10 am-8 pm May, 10 am-6 pm rest of year; free.
The Park Museum, 93 Banff Ave, 762-1558. Details flora, fauna and geography of the park. Daily 10 am-6 pm, (winter 'til 5 pm); $2.25.
Peter White Foundation and Archives of Canadian Rockies, 111 Bear St, 762-2291. Library, art gallery, history of Rockies. Daily 10 am-6 pm in summer. $4.50, W/student ID $2.50.
Sulphur Mountain Gondola Lift, Banff, 762-2523. You can see 90 miles around on a good day. Daily May-Oct. $10.
Upper Hot Springs, Banff, 762-15154. Pool temperature is usually around 39 degrees centigrade. Daily 8 am-11 pm in summer, 10 am-10 pm in winter. $5, towel hire $1.

ENTERTAINMENT
Banff Ave is the centre of the local universe, and the shops are generally overpriced and tacky. Try **Canmore** for a more relaxed shopping experience. (22km towards Calgary on the Trans-Canada Hwy). The local rag, *The Crag & Canyon*, has info on local events.' Locals nights' and happy hours should keep you going from Sun-Thurs! On Tues it's only $4 for the **Lux Cinema** on Bear St, 762-8595. Some of the more popular bars and clubs include:
Eddy's Back Alley, off Caribou, 762-8434. Chart and rock music, dead cheap on local nights.

Melissa's Bar, 218 Lynx St (upstairs), 762-5511. Stuff yourself with free popcorn while drinks get cheaper by the hour.

Rose and Crown Pub, 202 Banff Ave, 762-2121. Live music nightly, darts, pool and great food. Home from home!

Wild Bill's, 203 Caribou St. 'Best value in town and live music nightly.' Try a spot of line dancing!

INFORMATION

Banff-Lake Louise Chamber of Commerce, 762-3777.

Banff National Park Interpretive Centre, Banff Ave, 762-3229. *www.worldweb.com/ parkscanada-banff.*

Lake Louise Info Centre, 522-3833.

Parks Info Bureau, 224 Banff Ave, 762-4256. Daily 'til 8 pm.

TRAVEL

The Banff Explorer, is a transit service within Banff. Leaves Banff Springs on the half hour and runs the length of Banff Ave. Every 15 mins a bus leaves for **Tunnel Mountain**, $1.25, summer only.

Big Foot offer camping adventures from Vancouver or Banff. They provide the camping gear, you provide the ability to rough it and keep a sense of humour. 'Highly recommended.' $75 for 3 days. Rsvs through Vancouver HI Hostel, (404) 224-3208 or Banff HI Hostel, (403) 762-4122.

Brewster Transportation, 762-2241. Banff to Jasper, express $44, sightseeing $65; to Yoho Valley and Emerald Lake (recommended, fantastic scenery) from Lake Louise, or from Banff. 'Unless you have a car, forget trying to see both parks.'

Tilden Rent-a-Car has an office in town at Lynx and Caribou Sts, 762-2688.

Canoes/Rowing Boats are on hire at Banff and Lake Louise; and at Lake Minnewanka and Bow River motor boats are available. Motor boats are not allowed on Lake Louise. Hostel and the Y run rafting trips, approx $50. During winter, hiring skis/snowboards is easy and good deals can be found almost anywhere. The buses to the ski areas can prove to be expensive, so if you're staying for the winter season, a pass is the best option.

Hiker's Wheels, 852-2188. Transport services for hikers, bikers and canoeists. Pickups from hotels and campgrounds can be arranged.

Park 'n Pedal Bike Shop bike hire: 226 Bear St, 762-3191. $6 p/hr, $24 p/day; and **Bactrax:**, 339 Banff Ave at the Ptarmigan Inn, 762-8177. Mountain bikes available from $4 p/hr, $16 p/day 8 am-8 pm; and **Peak Experience:** on Bear St, 762-0581. $24 p/day. Daily 9 am-9 pm.

Rocky Express. ' A wilderness adventure you' ll never forget' —and it lives up to it's promise. Departs Sun from Calgary & Banff hostels; fun, flexible tours for small groups covering Banff and Jasper National Parks. Stay in hostels en route; price includes transport only but, at approx $155, is the best way of seeing the maximum in short amount of time. (Total around $280 for six days). Call Banff Int' l Hostel for details, (403) 762-4122.

Saddle horses from **Martins Stables, Banff, Banff Springs Hotel** and **Chateau Lake Louise**. Hired horses cannot be ridden in the park without a guide escort.

Hitching between Banff and Lake Louise could not be easier and it' s very popular. More difficult getting to Jasper, drivers like to view the many wonders of the **Icefield Pkwy** on their own. Not impossible, but be patient.

KANANASKIS COUNTRY Tucked away between Banff and Calgary, Kananaskis Country is a provincial recreation area, containing sections of three provincial parks (Bow Valley, Peter Lougheed and Bragg Creek). This 4,000 sq km backcountry area offers skiing, snowmobiling and windsurfing.

There are excellent hiking trails and plenty of unpaved roads and trails for mountain biking.

Canmore, an old pioneer town, is situated at the north-western tip of Kananaskis Country. Still retaining the haunting presence of the early settlers, this picturesque town has much to offer, including a legacy of the XVth Olympic Winter Games, the Canmore Nordic Centre. The **Canmore Heritage Day Folk Festival** is held annually Aug 3rd-4th. This cosmopolitan event is an annual Heritage Day tradition where each year folkies, families, locals and Calgary music lovers have ventured forth to enjoy the sights and sounds. *www.calexplorer.com/bckana01.html* is a fun online article that lists many of the local activities.

ACCOMMODATION
Ribbon Creek HI Hostel, (403) 591-7333, 70km W of Calgary on Hwy 1 (Trans Canada Hwy), then 25 km S on Hwy 40, turn right at Nakiska Skill Hill access, cross the Kananaskis River and left 1.5 km to the Hostel. Hiking, biking, skiing, golfing, rafting, near Kananaski Village. $12-16.

CALGARY   This fast growing city of 714,000 enjoys a friendly rivalry with Edmonton, 186 miles to the north. Known as the oil capital of Canada, Calgary, like Edmonton, went through a massive boom during the late seventies when growth in the city was astounding. More recently, however, Calgary's growth has stabilized and those gleaming office towers put up during the boom years, are now the Canadian headquarters of the world's largest oil and gas exploration companies.

At one time the city's only claim to fame was the internationally known Calgary Stampede, a ten day revelry devoted to the city's homesteading, steer wrestling, and bull riding heritage. But in 1988 Calgary busted out of its cowboy breeches into a city of international standing as a result of hosting the Winter Olympic Games. The games have left behind various facilities including 70 and 90 metre ski jumps, bobsleigh and luge tracks, and an impressive indoor speedskating oval. (If you are adventurous, you can rent a pair of speedskates and try your luck.)

Geographically, the city is huge. Once annexation plans are complete, Calgary will be the largest city in Canada. Roads are good, however, and the city also has over 100 km of bicycle paths that span the length and width of the city. In addition, Calgary has a fast light-rail transit (train) system.

Despite its northerly location, Calgary gets less snow than New York City and it hardly ever rains here either. Local weather is determined by the chinook, a mass of warm air rushing in from the Pacific which can instantly send the temperature from minus 10°C to plus 15°C.

www.lexicom.ab.ca/calgary/index1.html is a useful source of attractions and events listings.

ACCOMMODATION
Contact the **B&B Association of Calgary**, on 531-0065 for info; for stays especially in July it is never too early to make rsvs.

Calgary HI Hostel, 520 7th Ave SE, 269-8239. $14-19. Located downtown, this modern, pleasant hostel resembles a ski lodge. 'Excellent facilities.'

Circle Inn Motel, 2373 Banff Tr NW, 289-0295. From S/D-$61.

Travelodge, 9206 Macleod Trail S, 253-7070. From S/D-$57.

St Louis Hotel, 430 8th Ave, 262-6341. FromS/D-$25.

YWCA, 320 5th Ave SE, 263-1550. S-$30, D-$40; both $5 extra w/bath, $17 dorm.

University of Calgary, **Kananaskis Hall** and **Rundle Hall**, 220-7243. From S/D-$24. Students only, no rsvs. Monthly rates available. 'Good facilities, gym, cheap meals.'

Camping: KOA Calgary W, 288-0411, 1.6 km W on Hwy 1; and

Langdon Park, about 20 miles E. Sites $18, $20 w/hook-up, XP-$2.

FOOD

Downtown's food offerings are concentrated in the **Stephen Avenue Mall**, 8th Ave S btwn 1st St SE and 3rd St SW.

17th Ave SW, btwn 1st and 14th Sts. Lots of places 'sandwiched' among interesting shops.

Earl's, various locations. 'Great burgers, great prices.'

Electric Avenue, 11 Ave SW btwn 4th & 6th Sts—trendy nightclub area with lots of eateries.

Joey's Only, fish & chips and seafood. All-U-can-eat chips. Inexpensive, good food. For locations call 243-4584.

Kensington's Delicafe, 1414 Kensington Rd NW, 283-0771. Earthy atmosphere, live entertainment, Wed-Sat.

Kensington—Louise Crossing area—Memorial Dr. and 10th Ave NW. Several restaurants to choose from, all reasonably priced.

Nick's Steak House and Pizza, 2430 Crowchild Trail NW, 282-9278. Close to Uni of Calgary, across from McMahon Stadium.

North Hill Diner, 80216 Ave NW, 282-5848.

Smitty's Pancake House, for locations call 229-3838—big bfasts.

OF INTEREST

Calgary Tower, 101 9th Ave at Centre St South, 266-7171. Offers fantastic views of the city and the Rockies. Daily 7.30 am-midnight, $5.95, $3 w/student ID.

Calgary Zoo and Dinosaur Park, Memorial Dr & 12th St E on George's Island, 232-9372. Has a fine aviary and a large display of cement reptiles and prehistoric monsters including one 120-ton dinosaur. Daily 9 am-6 pm, w/ends and rest of year 'til 8.30 pm, $7.50.

Centennial Planetarium and Alberta Science Centre, Mewata Park, 11th St & 7th Ave SW, 221-3700. Phone for show times in planetarium. Museum has vintage aircraft, model rockets and a weather station. $7.50 for any two shows. Daily summer 10 am-8 pm, Fri & Sat 'til 10.30 pm.

Energeum, 640 5th Ave, 297-4293. Hands-on science centre about energy resources, oil and gas, coal, and hydro-electricity. Free. Sun-Fri 10.30 am-4.30 pm.

Fort Calgary Interpretive Centre, 750 9th Ave SE, 290-1875. Calgary's birthplace. Traces early NorthWest Mounted Police life and prairie natural history. Daily May-Oct 9 am-5 pm. $3.

Glenbow Museum, 130 9th Ave SE, 264-8300. Art and artefacts of the west with a large collection of Canadian art and native artefacts. Daily 10 am-6 pm in summer, 'til 5 pm winter. $6, w/student ID $3.50.

Parks: Canada Olympic Park, Hwy 1 W, 247-5404. Bus tour of bobsleigh, luge runs, and olympic ski jumps. In the winter the public can try bobsleigh and luge. Call for prices. Also the **Olympic Hall of Fame** with a heart-stopping audio-visual ski-jump simulator that allows visitors to experience the sensations felt by the athletes. Daily 8 am-9 pm., $4.50, $3 w/student ID, bus tour $5.

Heritage Park, 1900 Heritage Dr, 259-1900. Calgary was once the Northwest Mountie outpost; this and other aspects of the city's past are dealt with in the park. The reconstructed frontier village includes a Hudson's Bay Co. trading post, an Indian village, trapper's cabin, ranch, school, and a blacksmiths, $6. Daily 10 am-6 pm.

Prince's Island Park, on the northern edge of downtown has special events and is just nice for sunbathing, etc.

ENTERTAINMENT
Electric Ave, 11th Ave SW (see under *Food*) is an action packed strip of real estate that comes alive at night, guaranteeing you rockin' times! 'Try **The Warehouse, The King Edward Hotel**, and the **Tasmanian Ballroom**.'

Calgary Centre for Performing Arts, 205 8th Ave. Calgary Symphony Orchestra and live theatre. Call the 24 hr show info line, 294-7444.

Ranchman's, 9615 Macleod Tr S, 253-1100. A Honkytonk, saloon, restaurant, night-club and rodeo cowboy museum. Boot stompin' country music and western dance hall.

Festivals: Afrikadey, held annually every Aug. Featuring the music of the entire African diaspora: Africa, the Caribbean, and the North and South Americas, this festival of African arts and culture is a banquet of sights and sounds.

Calgary Folk Music Festival, held annually July 24th-27th. This 3-day festival, set on the river in a beautiful inner-city park, balances traditional Canadian folk music with the sounds of acoustic and electric folk to Celtic, world beat and country.

Calgary International Jazz Festival, June 20th-July 1st annually. The 10 days of the Calgary International Jazz Festival fit the city like an old glove.

Calgary Stampede. Second week in July. Calgary returns to its wild cowboy past. Rodeo events, chuckwagon races, free pancake breakfasts, bands, parties and tons of Texas two-steppin'. For info & tkts, call 261-0101; for tkts only call (800) 661-1260. '10 days of fun and enjoyment.'

INFORMATION
Calgary Tourist and Convention Bureau, 237 8th Ave SE, 2nd floor, 262-2766/263-8510. Mon-Fri 8 am-5 pm.

Calgary International Airport, 735-1372, at the 'Chuckwagon' on Arrivals level. Daily 7 am-10 pm.

Talking Yellow Pages, 521-5222, provides a wide range of info for only the cost of a local call.

Travel information/accommodation rsvs: (800) 661-1678. *www.visitor.calgary.ab.ca.*

TRAVEL
Calgary International Airport, 735-1372, is located 12 miles N of the city. The Airporter bus leaves every 30 mins from major downtown hotels, $7.50, 6.30 am-11.30 pm. A taxi will cost about $20-$25, call 250-8311. Airport info—292-8477.

Checker Cab, 299-9999 and **Yellow Cab**, 974-1111.

Greyhound Bus Station, 850 16th St SW, (800) 661-8747. Leave terminal by 9th Ave exit and take #79, 103, 10, 102 bus to town, $1.50. 'The only bus south out of Calgary to the USA leaves at 7 am, arriving Butte, Montana, at 7 pm.' $87.

Hitchhiking is illegal within city limits.

DRUMHELLER   In the Drumheller Badlands, northwest of Calgary, the 30 mile **Dinosaur Trail** leads to the mile-wide valley where more than 30 skeletons of prehistoric beasts have been found. Everything from yard-long bipeds to the 40-ft-long Tyrannosaurus Rex.

As well as dinosaur fossils, petrified forests and weird geological formations such as hoodoos, dolomites and buttes are to be seen in the valley. Another survivor of prehistory is the yucca plant found here, also in fossil form. The **Tyrell Museum**, 823-7707 in Midland Provincial Park on Hwy 838 is one of the largest paleontology museums in the world. Daily 9 am-9 pm, $5.50. Also, Drumheller Big Country Tours Association, 823-5885. Drumheller Community homepage, *www.dus.magtech.ab.ca/www/drum.htm*

ACCOMMODATION
Alexandra HI Hostel, 30 Railway Ave N Drumheller, 823-6337. Located inside a refurbished hotel built in the 30's. Close by Royal Tyrell Museum. Games and meeting rooms inside hostel. $14-18.

WATERTON LAKES NATIONAL PARK The other bit of the Waterton/ Glacier International Peace Park (see also under Montana). Mountains rise abruptly from the prairie in the southwestern corner of the province to offer magnificent jagged alpine scenery, several rock-basin lakes, beautiful U-shaped valleys, hanging valleys and countless waterfalls.

There are more than 100 miles of trails within the park which is a great place for walking or riding. It's also a good spot for fishing and canoeing and has four campsites. Several cabins and hotels are provided within the park. Most of Waterton's lakes are too cold for swimming but a heated outdoor pool is open during the summer in Waterton township.

A drive north on Rte 6 will take you close to a herd of plains buffalo. Go south on the same road and you cross the border on the way to Browning, Montana. You can also reach the US by boat. The *International* sails daily between Waterton Park townsite and Goathaunt Landing in Glacier National Park. Park admission $5 or $8 for three day pass. **Waterton Park** townsite, on the west shore of Upper Waterton Lake, is the location of the park headquarters. The park information office is open daily during the summer and park rangers arrange guided walks and tours, and give talks and campfire programmes, etc, about the flora and fauna of the area. **Visitors Centre**, 859-2224, daily 8 am-8 pm.
www.worldweb.com/parkscanada-waterton/.

MEDICINE HAT A town whose best claim to fame is its unusual name. Legend has it that this was the site of a great battle between Cree and Blackfeet Indians. The Cree fought bravely until their medicine man deserted them, losing his headdress in the middle of the nearby river. The Cree warriors believed this to be a bad omen, laid down their weapons and were immediately annihilated by the Blackfeet. The spot became known as 'Saamis,' meaning 'medicine man's hat'. Discover the *Pure Energy* of Medicine Hat, *www.city.medicine-hat.ab.ca/.*

ACCOMMODATION
Assiniboia Inn, 680 3rd St SE, 526-2801. S-$33, D-$38.
El Bronco Motel, 1177 1 St SW, 526-5800. S-$34, D-$38.
Trans-Canada Motel, 780 8th St, 526-5981. S/D-$32-$65, all rooms have kitchens and two beds.

OF INTEREST
Medicine Hat Museum and Art Gallery, 1302 Bomford Cr, 527-6266. Indian arte-facts, pioneer items and national and local art exhibits. Daily in summer Mon-Fri 9 am-5 pm, w/ends 1 pm-5 pm , $3 suggested donations.

INFORMATION
Chamber of Commerce, 513 6th Ave SE, 527-5214; Mon-Fri 8.30 am-4.30 pm.
Information Center, 8 Gehing Rd SE, 527-6422. Daily 8 am-9 pm in summer, 9 am-5 pm after Labour Day.

WRITING-ON-STONE PROVINCIAL PARK   In the south of the province, 40 km from the small town of Milk River on Hwy 501, is this park which is of great biological, geological and cultural interest. The site, overlooking the Milk River, contains one of North America's largest concentrations of pictographs and petroglyphs. Inscribed on massive sandstone outcrops, these examples of plains rock art were carved by nomadic Shoshoni and Blackfoot tribes.

This site is open year round but access is only on the one and a half hour guided tours, daily from May through beginning of Sept. Call for info on special events, 647-2364. Camping $11.

HEAD-SMASHED-IN BUFFALO JUMP   If the name isn't enough to pique your curiosity, then the fact that this historical interpretive centre is a UNESCO World Heritage site may. The Plains Indians who once inhabited this area, hunted buffalo by driving herds of the massive beasts over the huge sandstone cliffs to certain death below. According to legend, a young Indian brave tried to watch one of the hunts from a sheltered ledge below (somewhat like standing underneath a waterfall). So many animals were driven over the cliff, that his people found him after the hunt with his skull crushed by the weight of the buffalo, hence the rather startling name.

The centre is located 18 km NW of Fort Macleod on secondary Hwy 875, 175 km S of Calgary, 553-2731. Daily 9 am-8 pm, 'til 5 pm in winter. $5.50. The home page, *www.head-smashed-in.com/* documents the buffalo hunting culture of aboriginal peoples of the plains.

MANITOBA

Situated in the heart of the North American continent, Manitoba extends 760 miles from the 49th to the 60th parallel; from the Canada-United States border to the Northwest Territories. Surprisingly then the province has a 400-mile-long coastline. This is on Hudson Bay where the important port of Churchill is located.

The first European settlers reached Hudson Bay as early as 1612 although the Hudson's Bay Company was not formed until 1670. You cannot travel far in Canada without becoming aware of the power of the Hudson's Bay Company and its influence in the settlement of the country. At one time its territory included almost half of Canada, its regime only ending in 1869 when its lands became part of Canada. These days the company is relegated back to its origins—you will see the name on a chain of department stores across Canada.

By 1812 both French and British traders were well established along the Red and Assiniboine Rivers and in that year a group of Scottish crofters settled in what is now Winnipeg. The present population of Manitoba includes a large percentage of German and Ukrainian immigrants although the English, Scots and French still predominate. Manitoba became a province in 1870, although only after the unsuccessful rising of the Metis (half Indian/half trapper stock) had been quashed. After the rail link to the east reached here in 1881, settlers flocked here to clear the land and grow wheat. Winnipeg became the metropolis of the Canadian west.

Though classed as a Prairie Province, three-fifths of Manitoba is rocky forest land, but even this area is pretty flat. If you're travelling across the province the landscape can get pretty tedious, prairies in the west and endless forests and lakes in the east. More than 100,000 lakes in all, the largest of which is Lake Winnipeg at 9320 square miles.

National Park: Riding Mountain. *www.yahoo.com/Regional/Countries/Canada/Province_and_Territories/Manitoba/*.

The telephone area code is 204.

WINNIPEG A stop here is almost a necessity if you're travelling across Canada. The provincial capital of Manitoba, Canada's sixth largest city, has plenty to offer, especially if you can time a visit to coincide with one of the festivals happening in and around Winnipeg in the summer months. Among these are the Winnipeg Folk Festival, held annually at Birds Hill Park in July and Folklorama, Winnipeg's cultural celebration, held every year in early August.

Winnipeg (from the Cree word 'Winnipee' meaning 'muddy waters') is very 'culture-conscious', with good theatre, a symphony orchestra, the world-renowned Royal Winnipeg Ballet, and a plethora of museums and art galleries. It's also a major financial and distribution centre for western Canada: hence the chains of vast grain elevators, railway yards, stockyards, flour mills and meat packaging plants.

The Red River divides the city roughly north to south. Across the river from downtown Winnipeg is the French-Canadian suburb, St Boniface. This community retains its own culture while mixing well with the Anglophones in Winnipeg. Many services are, therefore, offered in both languages. Winnipeg is known for its very long and cold winters, but in the summer, the temperatures are comfortably in the high 70s and 80s. Cool in the evenings though.

ACCOMMODATION
Backpackers Guest House Int'l, 168 Maryland St, 772-1272. $13 dorm, S-$25, D-$35. Free pick up (more than 2 people) from stations, bike rentals. 'Highly recommended.'

Ivey House Int'l Hostel, 210 Maryland St (Broadway & Sherbrooke), 772-3022. $13-HI, $17 non-HI. Bike rentals. Check-in 8 am-9.30 am and after 5 pm. Rsvs recommended. 'Very friendly.' Central.

McLaren Hotel, 514 Main St (across from the Centennial Centre), 943-8518. Room for two, w/wash basin $40. En suite, $45. Very central.

University of Manitoba Residence, 26 MacLean Cr, 474-9942. May-Aug, co-ed, $20 pp. Small fee gives access to pool and sports facilities on campus. There are many **B & B** places in Winnipeg. The tourist office has a complete listing, or call 783-9797 for rsvs. Daily 8 am-8 pm.

Winnipeg Hotel, 214 S Main St, 942-7762. S/D $24, w/bath.

FOOD
The multiculturalism of Winnipeg's 650,000 citizens is apparent in the diversity of culinary offerings around the city. Choose from over 1000 restaurants serving everything from Ukrainian and Japanese to regional cuisine.

Alycia's, 559 Cathedral Ave, 582-8789. Ukrainian cuisine, 'try the pirogies, pan fried pasta stuffed with potato and cheese, delicious'. Dishes come separately or in combinations, $4.50-$8.50. Mon-Sat 8 am-8 pm.

Blue Boy Cafe, 911 Main St, 943-1308. Cheap bfast and lunch, $3 up. Open 7 am-10 pm, afternoon closing on the w/end.

Fat Angel, 220 Main St, 944-0396. 'Funky, colourful dining spot'. Entrees, light meals, vegetarian food and pizza, $3-$15. Lunch Mon-Fri 11.30 am-2.30 pm, dinner Mon-Thu 5 pm-midnight, Fri 'til 3 am, Sat 6 pm-3 am.

Hooters, 1624 Ness Ave, 774-9496. Popular US chain famous for its chicken wings and its 'Hooters Girls'; has recently opened its first Winnipeg location. The restaurant features a varied menu including burgers, seafood, salads and sandwiches. Daily 11 am-1 pm, $5-$15.

Grand Garden, 268 King st, 943-2029. Authentic Chinese food including regional specialities, sizzling plates and hot pot selections. Entrees $3-$17. Lunch Mon-Fri 11 am-3 pm, w/end 10 am, dinner

Kelekis, 1100 Main St N, 582-1786. Renowned deli. Good and cheap.

Old Market Cafe, Old Market Square. Numerous speciality kiosks feature a variety of foods. Good in summer. Outdoor patio. Next door is **King's Head**, a British style pub.

Nikos Restaurant, 740 Corydon Ave, 478-1144. Bistro style setting for home-style Greek and Canadian fare. Everything from moussaka to subs. Entrees $6-$9. Daily 11 am-10 pm.

Sweet Place, 1425 Pembina Hwy, S of downtown, 475-7867. Indian specialities including over 35 desserts. Lunch buffet $6, dinner buffet $9. Tue-Sun 11 am-2.30 pm and 5 pm-9.30 pm.

OF INTEREST

Walking tours of historic Winnipeg begin in the renewal zone of the 1960's and wind through the streets and around the buildings of the Exchange District, where the city's commercial and wholesale history began. Tours depart twice daily from Pantages Playhouse Theatre, and last approx 1¹/₂ hrs, $5. Call 957-0493 for schedules.

Assiniboine Park, Corydon Ave W at Shaftsbury, 986-3130. On the Assiniboine River with miniature railway and an English garden. This park is very popular in the summer and there is always some sort of production here, be it Shakespeare, the symphony, or the ballet. In winter there is skating, sleigh rides and tobogganning.

Assiniboine Park Conservatory houses the tropical 'Palm House' and a gallery featuring works by local artists. Daily 9 am-8 pm, free. **Assiniboine Park Zoo**, one of the world's most northerly zoos housing native wildlife. 10 am-9 pm daily, $3.

Legislative Building, Broadway and Osborne, 945-5813. Completed in 1919 and built from native Tyndal stone, this neo-classical style building houses, as well as the legislative chambers, an art gallery, a museum and a tourist office. It is set in a 30-acre landscaped park and the grounds contain statues of Queen Victoria, statesmen and poets. The Golden Boy perched atop the dome of the building, sheathed in 23.5 karat gold, symbolises 'Equality for All and Freedom Forever'. Created in a Paris foundry that was bombed during WWI, the Golden Boy spent 2¹/₂ yrs in the hold of a troop ship before making his way to Winnipeg. 8 am-8 pm daily, guided tours 9 am-6 pm on the hr, free.

Living Prairie Museum and Nature Preservation Park, 2795 Ness Ave, 832-0167. See what the prairie looked like before the settlers came. Daily July-Aug, 10 am-5 pm. Free. Tours available. The prairie is open 24 hrs. 'Take insect repellent!'

Lower Fort Garry, on the banks of the Red River 19 mi N of Winnipeg on Hwy 9, 785-6050. This National Historic Park is the only stone fort of the fur-trading days in North America still intact. It has been used at different times for various purposes. Originally the fortified headquarters of the ubiquitous Hudson's Bay Company, it has also been used as a garrison for troops, a Governor's Residence, a meeting place for traders and Indians, and the first treaty with the Indians was signed here. The park is open daily from May-Sept, 9.30 am-6 pm, tours available, $5. There is also a museum with nice displays of pioneer and Indian goods, maps and clothes. To reach the fort take the Selkirk bus from downtown Winnipeg, $3.75 o/w, Beaver Bus Lines, 989-7007.

Upper Fort Garry Gate, the only bit remaining of the original Fort stands in a small park S of Broadway off Fort St. This stone structure was Manitoba's own 'Gateway to the Golden West'. A plaque outlines the history of several forts which stood in the vicinity. Free.

The Museum of Man and Nature, 190 Rupert Ave, 956-2830, next to the **Centennial Center** concert hall, 956-1360. Features provincial history and natural history of the Manitoba grasslands. Includes dioramas depicting Indian and urban Manitoban history and a replica of the 17th century sailing ship *Nonsuch*, that sailed into Hudson Bay in 1668 and returned to England with a cargo of furs, resulting in the founding of the Hudson's Bay Company. Daily in summer, 10 am-6 pm, Thurs 'til 9 pm. Tues-Sun 10 am-4 pm in winter, $4.

Riel House National Historic Park, 330 River Rd, 257-1783. Built in 1880-81, the Riel home has been restored to reflect its appearance in the spring of 1886. Louis Riel is noted as the founder of the province of Manitoba and lead the Metis revolt of 1870. Although he never actually lived in the house it was here his body was laid in state following his execution in 1885. Daily 10 am-6 pm May-Aug; w/ends only in Sept. Suggested donation $2.

River Interpretive Tours, 986-4928, boat tours exploring the city's waterways. The cruise follows the beginnings of the fur trade, the early forts and shows the importance water transportation played in developing Winnipeg. Tours depart from Forks Historic Docks Site Mon-Fri 9 am, 11 am, 1 pm and 3.30 pm, w/end 10.30 am and 12.30 pm. 1¹/₂ hrs, $5.

Royal Winnipeg Ballet, 380 Graham Ave, 956-2792. Canada's oldest ballet company. Founed in 1939, the RWB has grown to take its place among the world's great companies. Tkts $7.50-$41.

Royal Canadian Mint, 520 Lagimodiere Blvd, 257-3359. One of the largest and most modern mints in the world, strikes all Canadian coins as well as coins for several other countries. Tours every ¹/₂ hr. May-Aug Mon-Fri 9 am-5 pm, last tour 4 pm. Sat Jun-Aug for self guided tours, $2.

The Forks, 983-6757. This development at the confluence of the Red and Assiniboine Rivers celebrates the transformation of the Canadian west. Attractions include **Johnston Terminal**, formerly a 4-storey warehouse, now home to a variety of shops and restaurants.

Forks Market, a vast array of ethnic cuisine, local and national arts and crafts.

The Forks National Historic Site, 9 landscaped acres on the west bank of the Red River offers festivals and heritage entertainment from May 'til Labor day. Also features an open-air amphitheatre, picnic area and dock. For event schedules call 957-7618.

Ukrainian Cultural and Education Centre, 184 Alexander Ave E, 942-0218. Folk art, documents, costumes, and history. Tues-Sat 10 am-4 pm, Sun 2 pm-5 pm, donation appreciated.

Winnipeg Art Gallery, 300 Memorial Blvd, 786-6641. One of the world's largest Inuit art collections. Traditional, contemporary and decorative Canadian, American, and European works. Rooftop jazz concerts regularly throughout summer, $13. Call for schedule. Tue-Sun 11 am-5 pm, Wed 'til 9 pm. $3, $2 w/student ID, free on Wed.

St Boniface. Across the Red River, the city's French Quarter is the largest French-

Canadian community in Canada and is the site of the largest stockyards in the British Commonwealth. A historic and cultural cornerstone of the city, it is the birthplace and final resting place of Louis Riel and original site of the Red River Colony.

St Boniface Museum, 494 Ave Taché, 237-4500. Built in 1846 it was originally a convent for the Gray Nuns who arrived in the area in 1844 and founded the **St Boniface General Hospital**. One of the oldest buildings in Winnipeg and the largest oak construction in N America, it houses displays centred around French-Canadian heritage, the Metis and missionaries who served them, recalling the early days of the Red River Colony. Guided tours by appointment. Mon-Thu 9 am-8 pm, Fri, 'til 5 pm, Sat 10 am-5 pm, Sun 'til 8 pm.

St Boniface Cathedral 190 Ave de la Cathedrale, 233-7304. The oldest basilica in western Canada, originally built in 1818 has been destroyed several times by fire. The latest structure was built in 1972 and still has the facade of the 1908 basilica that survived the fire.

Centre Culturel Franco-Manitobian, 340 Blvd Provencher, 233-8972, and its resident cultural groups, promote French culture through live musical entertainment, art exhibitions, theatre, art courses and a unique gift shop. Taste French-Canadian cuisine in **Le Café Jardin** or on the garden terrace, Mon-Fri 11.30 am-2 pm. The centre is open Mon-Fri 9 am-8 pm, Sat 1 pm-5 pm, free.

Steinbach Mennonite Heritage Village Museum, 40 mi outside Winnipeg, 326-9661. E on Hwy 1, S on Hwy 12. This re-creation of a turn-of-the-century Mennonite village comes complete with mill, store, school, and costumes of the day. Also a good restaurant. May 1-Sept 30, Mon-Sat 9 am-7 pm, Sun noon-7 pm. $3.25. Accessible by Greyhound or Grey Goose Bus Lines.

SHOPPING/EVENTS

Osborne Village, between River and Corydon Junction. Boutiques, craft and speciality shops and eating places. Look out for the Medea, a co-op art gallery found in the Village. The Exchange District and Old Market Square are also interesting places to shop. Portage Ave is the main downtown shopping area. Portage Place has shops, restaurants, and IMAX theatre, 956-4629, with a gigantic 55ft x 70ft screen. S-feature tkts $7, D-feature $10.50 The **Winnipeg Folk Festival** takes place annually at the beginning of July in Birds Hill Provincial Park. This internationally renowned festival features the best in bluegrass, jazz, and gospel music. The park is accessible from Hwy 59 N of Winnipeg or through Winnipeg Transit.

Folklorama, (800) 665-0234, is Winnipeg's multi-cultural celebration held in early August. This two week-long festival highlights the ethnic diversity of Winnipeg with over 40 pavilions featuring the food, dance, and culture of different nations. Day passes available.

Jazz Winnipeg Festival, 989-4656. Features the best in international, national and local jazz performers on free outdoor stages at locations throughout downtown and the Exchange District. Takes place June 14th-21st.

The Fringe Festival, 956-1340, presented by the Manitoba Theatre Centre and held in the Exchange District in mid-Jul. 10 days of theatre performances including, mimes, jugglers, comedy and drama. All shows less than $5.

INFORMATION

Manitoba Visitors Reception Centre, Room 101, Legislative Building, 450 Broadway at Osborne, 945-3777. Maps and literature. Open in summer Mon-Fri 8 am-7 pm, 8.30 am-4.30 pm rest of year. Pick up a copy of *Passport to Winnipeg* for up-to-date information.

TRAVEL

Bike hire: several locations in Assiniboine Park: ask at Visitors Centre.
Greyhound 487 Portage Ave, 783-8840, (800) 661-8747, 301 Burnell St, for **Grey Goose Bus Lines**, 784-4500.

Splash Dash Water Bus, 783-6633. 30 min water taxi tours along the Red and Assiniboine Rivers depart from the Forks Historical Harbour every 10 mins from May-Oct, 11.30 am-sunset. Day pass $6, unlimited usage.

VIA Rail, Broadway and Main St, 949-7400, (800) 561-3949. The train to Churchill takes just over 2 days and must be booked 7 or more days in advance. R/t US $173, C $239.

Winnipeg International Airport, 20 mins W of downtown, is served by the local transit buses, 986-5700. Take 15 (Sargent Airport) from Vaughn and Portage, $1.45. A taxi will cost around $12-$13 o/w, call 925-3131.

RIDING MOUNTAIN NATIONAL PARK   In western Manitoba, the park occupies the vast plateau of Riding Mountain, which rises to 2200 ft, offering great views of the distant prairie lands.

The total area of Riding Mountain Park is about 1200 sq mi and although parts of it are fairly commercialised there are still large tracts of untamed wilderness to be explored by boat or on the hiking and horse trails. Deer, elk, moose and bear are all common and at **Lake Audy** there is a herd of bison. Also good for fishing.

Clear Lake is the part most exploited for and by tourists. The township of **Wasagaming** (an Indian term meaning 'clear water'), on the south shore of the lake has campsites, lodges, motels and cabins as well as many other resort-type facilities, right down to a movie theatre built like a rustic log cabin.

The park is reached from Winnipeg via Rte 4 to Minnedosa, and then on Rte 10. Daily admission $7.50, $16 (4 day pass). 848-7275.
parkscanada.pch.gc.ca/parks/main-e.htm.

CHURCHILL   Known as the 'Polar Bear Capital of the World', Churchill has been a trading port since 1689 and is still the easiest part of the 'frozen north' to see. During the short Jul-Oct shipping season, this sub-arctic seaport handles vast amounts of grain and other goods for export. The west's first settlers came to Manitoba via Churchill.

The partially-restored **Prince of Wales Fort**, the northernmost fort in North America, was built by the British in 1732. It took 11 years to build and has 42-ft-thick walls. Despite this insurance against all-comers, the garrison surrendered to the French without firing a single shot in 1782.

Churchill is a great place to view some of the wonders of nature. From September to April, the beautiful **Aurora Borealis** (northern lights) are visible and good for picture-taking. The summer daylight, however, doesn't provide the best viewing conditions. To make up for it, whale watching is best in the summer months, from July-early September. The beluga whales come in and out with the tides. Polar bears are most frequently seen roaming around the city in September and October and are periodically airlifted to other regions. On the tundra, lichens and miniature shrubs and flowers bloom each spring and autumn and a short distance inland there are patches of *Taiga*, sub-Arctic forest.

Note that Churchill is only accessible by plane or train (no automobiles). Look into the package deals put together by VIA Rail (see Winnipeg).

ACCOMMODATION
Northern Lights Lodge, 101 Kelsey Blvd. S-$58, D-$68, $10 more Aug-Nov. TV, bar.
Polar Inn, 15 Franklin St, 675-8878, D-$84.

OF INTEREST
The **Eskimo Museum**, next to the Catholic Church on LaVerendrye St, 675-2030. Fur trade memorabilia, kayaks and Canadian Inuit art and carvings dating from 1700 BC, that are among the oldest in the world. Tues-Sat 9 am-noon, 1 pm-5 pm, Mon 1 pm-5 pm. Free. 'Worth visiting.'
Fort Prince of Wales National Historic Park, 675-8863, at W bank of mouth of Churchill River, built by the Hudson's Bay Company in the 1700's to protect their interests in the fur trade. After its partial destruction by the French in 1782, it was never again occupied. Now partially restored. Open daily. The fort is only accessible by boat and the Sea North Tour is your only choice. The package includes harbour tour and whale watching and lasts 2 1/2 hrs, $45. Boat departs at a different time each day, tides and weather permitting, Jun-Sep. Call 675-2195 for shedule.

INFORMATION/TRAVEL
Parks Canada, Manitoba North Historic Sites, Bayport Plaza, 675-8863. Daily 1 pm-9 pm.
North Star Bus station, 203 LaVerendrye, 675-2629. Local bus company offering 4-hr tours of the town, $45.

SASKATCHEWAN

Cornflakes country. Known as the 'Wheat Province', Saskatchewan, wedged between Alberta and Manitoba, is the prairie keystone. Although the black ribbon of the Trans Canada Hwy takes the traveller through seemingly endless, flat expanses of wheat fields in southern Saskatchewan, the province does have a more diverse geography. From the scenic hills of the Qu'Appelle Valley to the Cypress Hills in the southwest and the badlands in the southeast, Saskatchewan is anything but wholly flat.

In the south, where visibility can be up to 20 miles, watch the sky—sunsets and rises are beautiful, and cloud formations during a wild prairie storm can be spectacular. As you travel north of the prairies, north of Hwy 16, the yellow landscape gives way to green rolling hills, and, still further north, to rugged parkland—lakes, rivers and evergreen forests.

Saskatchewan derives its name from 'Kisiskatchewan', a Cree word meaning 'the river that flows swiftly', a reference no doubt to the South Saskatchewan River, a gathering place for Northern Plains Indians who came here generation after generation to hunt and fish. The earliest written records of what is now Saskatchewan date to 1690, when Henry Kelsey of the Hudson's Bay Company became the first European to explore the region. Other explorers soon followed, opening the area to the growing fur trade industry. More recently, oil exploration in the south has led to the discovery of helium and potash, in addition to large quantities of 'bubbling crude'. In the summer, the weather is hot and dry while the winters are long, cold and snowy. *www.yahoo.com/Regional/Countries/Canada/Provinces_and_Territories/Saskatchewan/*.
National Park: Prince Albert.
The telephone area code is 306.

REGINA Provincial capital, situated in the heart of the wheatlands, and the accepted stopping place between Winnipeg and Calgary. Regina became capital of the entire Northwest Territories in 1883 just one year after its founding. Situated on the railroad the town served as a government outpost and headquarters for the Northwest Territories Mounted Police until the formation of Saskatchewan as a separate province.

The town was founded and christened Regina after Queen Victoria in 1882 when the first Canadian Pacific Railway train arrived. Its earlier, more picturesque name of Pile O'Bones, referring to the Indian buffalo killing mound at the site, was considered inappropriate for a capital city.

ACCOMMODATION
B & J's B & B , 2066 Ottawa St, 522-4575. S-$25, D-$35, XP-$8. Weekly rates available. Free coffee and pastries in the evening.

Empire Hotel, 1718 McIntyre St, 522-2544. S-$27, D-$38.

Georgia Hotel, 1927 Hamilton St, 569-3226. S-$28, D-$30. AC, TV, shower/bath. Close to downtown and night clubs.

Turgeon Hostel (HI-C), 2310 McIntyre (at College), 791-8165. $12-HI, $17 non-HI. Near downtown, 1½ blks from Wascana Park. Cooking facilities, laundry, common room, library. 'Great place—clean, convenient.' Feb-Dec, check-in 7 am-10 am and 5 pm-midnight.

University of Regina—College West Residence, Wascana Pkwy & Kramer Blvd, 585-4777. $34, bath, TV. May-Aug only. Rsvs essential.

YMCA, 2400 13th Ave, 757-9622. $20 p/night, $5 key deposit. Men only.

YWCA, 1940 McIntyre St, 525-2141. $35 p/night, $2 key deposit. $165 wk, $285 mth plus $125 damage deposit. Rooms have basin, fridge, shared kitchen facs, showers, laundry.

Camping: Fifty Plus Campground, 12 km E on Hwy 1, 781-2810. 'Clean, quiet and quaint', 1km off the hwy. Recreation hall, heated pool, laundry, showers, store. Sites, $12-$18, XP $1. May-Oct.

Kings' Acres Campground, 1km E of Regina on Hwy 1, N service road behind Tourism Regina, 522-1619. Sites 412, $15 w/hook up, XP-$1. Indoor recreation facility, large heated pool, showers, store. March-Nov.

FOOD
Geno's Pizza and Pasta, Albert St N at Ring Rd and Gordon Rd at Rae St, 949-5455. Inexpensive Italian.

The Novia Cafe, 2158 12th Ave, 522-6465. A trendy Regina tradition. 'Don't miss the cream pie.' Open 'til 9 pm.

City Hall Cafeteria, 359-3989, on main floor, McIntyre and Victoria. 'Best lunch bargains in town,' $3-$5.

OF INTEREST
Government House, corner of Dewdney Ave and Pasque St, 787-5726, official residence of the Lieutenant Governors from 1891-1945. Explore rooms that have been restored to Victorian elegance. Tue-Sun 1 pm-4 pm, free.

RCMP Centennial Museum, Dewdney Ave W, 780-5838. The official museum of the RCMP portrays the history of the force in relation to the development of Canada through equipment, weapons, uniforms, archives and memorabilia. Daily Jun-Sep 8 am-6.45 pm, Sep-May 10 am-4.45 pm. Tours in summer only, Mon-Fri 9 am-11 pm and 1.30-3.30 pm. Donations appreciated. The **Sergeant Major's Parade**, is held on the Parade Sq at the Training Academy, 780-5900, Mon-Fri at 1 pm. The **Sunset Retreat Ceremony**, also at the Academy. Colourful ceremony centred around the lowering of the flag and drill display by troops. Every Tue at 6.45 pm Jul-Aug.

Wascana Centre, in the heart of the city, this 2300 acre park built around Wascana Lake, is home to many of the province's top attractions. A place of government, recreation, education and culture. Home to the provincial **Legislative Building**, 787-5357, built in 1908 and designed to reflect the architecture of English Renaissance. Daily May 19th-Sep 2nd, 8 am-9 pm, tours every 30 mins, free. The **MacKenzie Art Gallery**, 3475 Albert St, in the SW corner of Wascana Centre, 522-4242. Historical and contemporary works by Canadian and American and international artists. Daily 11 am-6 pm, Wed and Thu 'til 10 pm, free. The **Royal Saskatchewan Museum**: 787-2815. First Nations Gallery traces 10,000 yrs of Aboriginal culture, the Earth sciences Gallery depicts over 2 billion yrs of geological evolution. Features traditional and contemporary Aboriginal art, books and crafts. Daily May-Sep 9 am-8.30 pm, daily Sep-Apr 'til 4.30 pm. $2 suggested donation. The **Saskatchewan Science Centre**, 791-7900, in the park features over 80 hands-on exhibits, live demonstrations and visiting exhibits. Next door is the **Kramer IMAX Theatre**, 522-4629, watch breathtaking films and special effects on the huge 5 storey screen, 7 shows daily. Mon-Fri 9 am-6 pm, w/end 11 am-6 pm. Museum $5.50, IMAX $6.75, combo tkt $11. Finally, the **Diefenbaker Homestead**, 522-3661, the boyhood home of the former Prime Minister of Canada, is also in the Park. Daily 10 am-7 pm. Free.

Willow Island, at the N end of Wascana Lake, is accessible only by ferry which departs from the dock off Wascana Dr, 522-3611, $2 r/t. The island is a popular picnic and BBQ site, and home to a **Waterfowl Sanctuary**. May-Sep, Mon-Fri noon-4 pm. Part of the **University of Regina** campus is also located in the park. **Guided tours** of Wascana Centre can be arranged through the guide office, 522-3611, wk/days 9 am-4 pm, summer only. Bike rentals are available at park Marina.

Buffalo Days are held in Regina Exhibition Park, Dewdney Ave W, 781-9200, late Jul-early Aug. A celebration of Saskatchewan traditions such as chuckwagon races, logging contest, agricultural fair and exhibition. Also midway rides, grandstand shows, free entertainment stages and casino. The **Buffalo Days Parade** displays over 40 floats in carnival atmosphere. Entrance $7. There is also a three day **Folk Festival** held at the University of Regina in Jun. One of Saskatchewan's biggest attractions is the **Big Valley Jamboree**, 352-2300, in **Craven**, 26 mi N of Regina. From Jul 18th-20th, the population of this small town swells by nearly one hundred times as thousands congregate for free unserviced camping and North America's largest country and western festival, featuring many top names. This is followed by Saskatchewan's largest rodeo, the last weekend in July, 565-0565.

INFORMATION/TRAVEL

Regina Convention and Visitors Bureau, Hwy 1E, 789-5099. Mon-Fri 8 am-7 pm, Sat & Sun 10 am-6 pm. After Labour Day Mon-Fri 8.30 am-4.30 pm.

Saskatchewan Transportation Company, 2041 Hamilton St, 787-3340, (800) 661-8747. Bus to Saskatoon, 3 daily, $26.

Regina Airport is reachable by cab only. Call 586-6555, $8-$10.

SASKATOON Saskatoon started in 1883 as the proposed capital of a temperance colony. An Ontario organisation acquired 100,000 acres of land and settlement began at nearby Moose Jaw. It seems that Saskatchewantonians were unwilling to go without drink. The population of Saskatoon failed to increase, so plans for the temperance colony were essentially scrapped, and the city continued to develop as a trading centre. Some establishments remain dry, however.

The South Saskatchewan River cuts right through the middle of the town and the parklands along its bank make Saskatoon a really pretty place, espe-

CANADIAN WILDLIFE

With so much remote and relatively uninhabited land, Canada is rich in wildlife. Unfortunately however, due to increasing urbanisation many of Canada's native species are known to be extinct or endangered, with most of their decline attributable to habitat destruction. When camping or travelling in wilderness areas, keep a clean and tidy camp, do not intentionally feed wild animals and stick to designated trails. These are some of the more common and/or interesting types the visitor to the backwoods or mountains may come across.

Bears—the dangerous **grizzly**, to be found in BC, Alberta and the Yukon, is very fast but doesn't see well, can't climb trees and runs slowest downhill. Bears are one of the few big game animals in BC for which a spring hunt is still allowed. As a result the grizzly population is fast declining. Smaller **black and brown bears** are found all over and often visit campgrounds and dumps—keep your food locked away and never in the tent! Largest of all is the **polar bear**—that's the white one only in the far north however, where it's common to see them strolling around town! The **beaver** is one of Canada's symbols and is found all across the country. Most likely to be seen chewing its way through a log or having a wash in the very early morning or early evening.

The massive, mean-looking **buffalo** still exists, Wood Buffalo National Park in the Northwest Territories is home to the world's largest free roaming herd. Not to be tampered with. When out in the prairie or bush you may hear the howl of a **wolf** or **coyote** at night. The coyote is a small, timid animal, more of a scavanger than a hunter. The larger, silver grey wolf native to BC and Yukon has been getting better press of late and, is one of the ecosystem's most important predators but seldom a threat to humans. Sadly numbers are dwindling due to government control programs, wolf bounties and elimination of wolf habitat.

The **lynx** is a large grey cat with mainly nocturnal habits. It hunts small animals and is found all over. **Deer** of many kinds can likewise be found everywhere. Canada's **cougar** population once mirrored that of the deer, its chief food supply. This large predator with its distinctive long tail is common only now in the west. Moose too are found across Canada but more commonly in northern woods and around swamps. A large brown, shy animal, the moose is a popular target for hunters. Their distant cousins, **caribou** (or reindeer) live in herds only in the far north. Overhunting and radioactive fallout had severely reduced the numbers of the caribou herds so they are now more carefully monitored. Some Inuit still use caribou for food and for their hides. The more usual smaller animals such as the **squirrel**, **chipmunk**, **raccoon** and **skunk** are common everywhere in Canada and may well be seen around campsites. Although marmots are common all over the country, the **Vancouver Island Marmot**, indigenous to mountainous areas of the Island is one of the worlds rarest mammals, their population now less than 200. Recognised by their chocolate-brown fur with contrasting white faces, buck teeth and high pitched whistle, they've earned the local nickname, 'whistle pig'.

If on either the Pacific or Atlantic, or Hudson's Bay coastline, **whale-watching** may appeal. Canada is a fisherman's paradise, northern **pike**, **bass** and **trout** are the most common **freshwater fish**, while the highly prized **salmon** can be found on the east and west coasts, that of British Columbia being the best.

One of the most mournful and memorable bird calls heard in Canada is that of the **loon**. Once heard over a northern Ontario lake in the late evening, and never again forgotten. More info on Canadian wildlife/wilderness areas via the following sites: *http://www.ca/~eblair/wildside.html*, and *parkscanada.pch.gc.ca/parks/main-e.htm*.

cially in the summer; it's an easy-going town with friendly residents. Saskatoon is 145 mi N of Regina, in the heart of the parklands.

ACCOMMODATION
Patricia Hotel, 345 2nd Ave N, 242-8861. S-$34, D-$40, w/bath, Q-$46. Rsvs recommended. The hotel also runs a year-round **hostel**: $13-HI, $19 non-HI.

The Senator, 3rd Ave S at 21 St E, 244-6141. S-$43, D-$46, Q-$49. TV, bath. Rsvs recommended. Very central.

YWCA, 510 25th St E, 244-0944. $38, $120 weekly, $285 monthly. $10 key deposit. Sports facilities available for use at a minimal charge. Women only. Call to reserve.

FOOD
David's Lounge and Restaurant, 294 Venture Cr off Circle Drive North, 664-1133. Good for big hearty breakfasts.

Louis' Campus Pub, on the University of Saskatchewan campus. Named after the rebellious Louis Riel. A favourite summertime haunt. Lunch on the patio.

Saint Tropez Bistro, 243 3rd Ave S, 652-1250. 'Nice light meals downtown.'

OF INTEREST
Stretching 19km along both sides of the South Saskatchewan River, near Spadina Cres, the **Meewasin Valley Trail**, cuts right through the heart of Saskatoon. Picnic areas, BBQ sites, lookouts and interpretive signs along the way.

Meewasin Valley Centre and Gift Shop, 665-6888. Learn about Saskatoon's history and the river through interactive displays and exhibits. Gift shop sells local arts, crafts and souviners. Mon-Fri 9 am-5 pm, w/end and hols Also in and around the park is the **Mendel Art Gallery**, 950 Spadina Cres, 975-7610. Mendel's permanent art collection and changing exhibitions of international, national and regional artwork. Daily May 19th-Oct 13th, 9 am-9 pm, rest of year noon-4 pm. Free. For a change from the ordinary, try Shakespeare prairie-style at the **Shakespeare on the Saskatchewan Festival**, 653-2300, Jul 2nd-Aug 17th, in the park. Buy tkts in advance. The **University of Saskatchewan**, 996-6607, is home to many attractions including the **Biology Museum**, 996-3499, the **Gordon Snelgrove Art Gallery**, 996-4208, **Museum of Antiques**, 996-7818, and the **Museum of Natural Sciences and Geology**, 996-5683, to name but a few. Call for individual opening times, all attractions are free, donations appreciated.

Musée Ukrainia Museum, 202 Ave M South, 244-4212. Ethnographic collections representing the spiritual, material and folkloric cultural heritage of the Ukraine. Daily June-Aug, Mon-Sat 11 am-5 pm, Sun from 1 pm, $2.

Ukrainian Museum of Canada, 910 Spadina Cres E, 244-3800. Folk art, photographs and exhibits depicting the history of Ukrainian immigrants in Saskatchewan. Summer, Mon-Sat 10 am-5 pm, Sun 1 pm-5 pm, closed Mon rest of year. $1.

The Western Development Museum, 2610 Lorne Ave, 931-1910. Turn of the century 'Pioneer Street'—family life, transportation, industry, agriculture, etc. The museum's collection is 'said to be the best of its kind in North America'. 'Good.' Daily 9 am-5 pm, Sun 1 pm-5 pm. $5, $4 w/student ID.

Saskatchewan Jazz Festival, 652-1421, held in downtown Saskatoon. Emphasis on mainstream jazz and a wide variety of other styles from Dixieland and blues to contemporary fusion and gospel. Over 500 musicians and 200 performers, plus workshops and seminars. Dates change annually, call for details.

Harvest Fest, 931-7149, held in conjunction with the **Saskatchewan Exhibition** Jul 5th-12th. Midway, casino, grandstand, tractor pulls and other contests. The town's biggest event of the year. At Exhibition Grounds S of Lorne Ave.

INFORMATION/TRAVEL
Visitors and Convention Bureau, 6305 Idylwyld Dr N, 242-1206.

The **Delta Lady**, sails from behind the Delat Bessborough Hotel daily. Cruise along the river and take in the local attractions. Boat departs, 10.30 am, 1.30 pm, 4.40 pm and 7.30 pm, $8.

Saskatchewan Transportation, 50 23rd St E, 933-8000, (800) 661-8747. Bus to Regina, 3 daily, $26.

Saskatoon airport is reachable by taxi only. Call 653-3333, $12-$14.

PRINCE ALBERT NATIONAL PARK   This 1496-square mile park typifies the lake and woodland wilderness country lying to the north of the prairies. It's an excellent area for canoeing with many connecting rivers between the lakes. From 1931-8 it was home to Grey Owl, one of the world's most famous park naturalists and imposters. Born Archibald Belaney, old Grey was an Englishman who came to Canada to fulfil a boyhood dream of living in the wilderness. Donning traditional clothing, he presented himself as the son of an Apache woman and carried out valuable research work for the park. Visit the cabin he lived in for 7 yrs. Access by boat or canoe across the lake or on foot in summer. Entrance to the park is $4.

Accommodation in the park includes campsites, hotels and cabins. **Waskesiu** is the main service centre where most hotels and motels can be found at some expense. Saskatoon is 140 mi S. For **Park info: Prince Albert National Park**, 663-5322; or **Prince Albert Convention and Visitors Bureau**, 764-6222. In the park **camping: Beaver Glen**, $13, $16 w/hook-up. **Sandy Lake** and **Namekus**, $10. Campers must register, 663-4522. *parkscanada.pch.gc.ca/parks/main-e.htm.*

THE PACIFIC

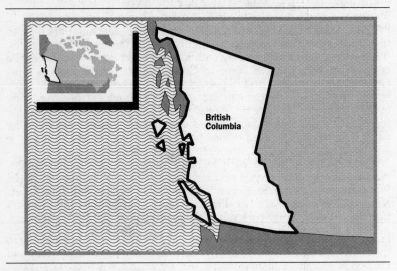

British Columbia

BRITISH COLUMBIA

Sandwiched between the Pacific Ocean and the Rocky Mountains to the west and east and bordered to the south by Washington State and to the north by the Yukon Territory, British Columbia is Canada's most westerly province and arguably the most scenic as well. This is an almost storybook land of towering snow-topped mountains, timbered foothills, fertile valleys, great lakes and mightier rivers, plus a spectacular coastline. The coast has long deep fjords dotted with many islands, and rising out of the coastline are ranges of craggy mountain peaks, in some cases exceeding 13,000 ft.

Inland there is a large plateau that provides British Columbia's ranching country. This is bounded on the east by a series of mountain ranges extending to the Rocky Mountain Trench. From this valley flow the Fraser, Columbia and Peace Rivers. The southwestern corner of British Columbia is considered one of the world's best climatic regions having mild winters and sunny, temperate summers and is consequently popular with Canadian immigrants.

This vast and beautiful province, which is about four times the size of the United Kingdom, was, however, a late developer. As recently as the 1880's there was no real communication and no railroad link with the east. Then as now the Rockies formed a natural barrier between British Columbia and the rest of the Confederation. Although both Sir Francis Drake, while searching for the mythical Northwest Passage, and Captain James Cook came this way, there was no real development and exploration on the Pacific coast until the mid-1800's. Vancouver Island was not designated a colony until 1849 and the mainland not until 1866. British Columbia became a province in 1871.

The whole province still only has a population of three and a half million people, but in recent years has enjoyed one of the highest standards of living in Canada thanks to the rapid development of British Columbia's abundance of natural resources. About 50 percent of provincial monies comes from timber-related products and industries but BC also has an amazing diversity of minerals on tap as well as oil and natural gas. Fishing and tourism are the other major money-makers.

www.yahoo.com/Regional/Countries/Canada/Provinces_and_Territories/British Columbia/

National Parks: Yoho, Glacier, Kootenay, Mount Revelstoke, Pacific Rim. *parkscanada.pch.gc.ca/parks/main-e.htm.*

The telephone area code is 604 in the Vancouver area. Elsewhere it's 250.

VANCOUVER This rapidly-growing West Coast city rivals San Francisco for the sheer physical beauty of its setting. Behind the city sit the snow-capped Blue Mountains of the Coast Range; lapping its shores are the blue waters of Georgia Strait and English Bay; across the bay is Vancouver Island; and to the south is the estuary carved out by its magnificent Fraser River.

Metropolitan Vancouver now covers most of the peninsula between the Fraser River and Burrard Inlet. Towering bridges link the various suburbs to the city and downtown area which occupies a tiny peninsula jutting into Burrard Inlet with the harbour to the east and English Bay to the west. Once downtown you are within easy reach of fine sandy beaches (or ski slopes in winter) and within the city limits there are several attractive parks. Most notable of these are the Queen Elizabeth Park, from which there is a terrific view of the whole area, and the thickly wooded 1000-acre Stanley Park.

Again like San Francisco, Vancouver is a melting-pot. English, Slavs, mid-Europeans, Italians, Americans, and the second largest Chinatown in North America. The politics are very west coast, some people are rabidly right wing, and some are rabidly left wing.

Canada's 'Gateway to the Pacific' has a harbour frontage of 98 miles but the railroads too have an important part to play in Vancouver's communications system; one of the most spectacular rides is that into Fraser Canyon, once the final heartbreak of the men pushing their way north to the gold-fields with only mules and camels to help them. If you're heading back east from here, this is the route to take.

Vancouver's climate is mild, but it does rain a fair amount. January is the coldest month although temperatures then are only about 11° Centigrade cooler than in July. Snow is rare and roses frequently bloom at Christmas. Altogether a great place to visit.

In 1986 Vancouver was host to the world for Expo '86 with the theme of transportation and related communications and technology. You can visit the site and the buildings down at the harbour. Vancouver has now become the city of choice for many American film-makers. This 'Hollywood to the north' (as it has been nicknamed) provides a diverse backdrop for all types of movie sets and at lower costs than for US locations.

ACCOMMODATION

Globetrotters Inn, 170 W Esplanade, 988-2082. Dorm-$15, S-$30, D-$40, $45 w/bath (twin beds). Rsvs recommended.

Hazelwood Hotel, 344 E Hastings St, 688-7467, in Chinatown. Mthly rentals only, $395, $425 w/bath.

Hostelling International Downtown (HI-C), 1114 Burnaby St, 684-4565. Members $18, $21 non. Located in Vancouver's West End, metropolitan neighbourhood, close to shops, attractions, Sunset Beach and nightlife. Open 24 hrs, 'excellent'. Rsvs recommended.

Hostelling International Jericho Beach, 1515 Discovery St, 224-3208. $19, $15 CYH. At foot of Jericho Beach. Take bus #4 UBC from Granville Station to 4th & Northwest Marine Drive, then a 5-min walk downhill to Discovery St. Big hostel with excellent facilities. Book ahead in summer. 'A great place but arrive early' (before 11 pm). Bike rental $20 per day. 'Beautiful area.'

Kingston Hotel, 757 Richards St, 684-9024. S-$40-$60, D-$45-$75. Bfast incl. Very European. Swedish sauna. Cafe outside, TV lounge, laundry. 'Nice place.' 'Good people.'

New Backpackers Hostel, 347 Pender St, 688-0112. Owned by Vincent (see below) but more centrally located than other Backpackers Hostel. $10. S-$25, D-$35. Discounts avaiable

Niagara Hotel, 435 W Pender, 688-7574. S-$45 up. D-$90 up 'Comfortable and close to stores and bus station.'

Patricia Hotel, 403 E Hastings, 255-4301. S-$45 up, D-$60. 'Close to downtown facilities.'

Vincent's Backpackers Hostel, 927 Main St, 682-2441, near to VIA Rail & Greyhound stations. Dorm $10, S-$20, D-$25. $10 key deposit. Mixed reports. Turn right out of the bus station and walk for 10 mins downhill. 'Dodgy area.'

YMCA, 955 Burrard St, 681-0221. S-$41, $43 w/TV, D-$49, $51 w/TV. Co-ed. 'Conveniently situated, friendly staff.'

YWCA, 733 Beatty St, 895-5830, downtown. S-$51-$65, D-$62-$98, T-$90-$108. Co-ed, TV, laundry, walking distance to YWCA pool and fitness centre. Wkly and mthly rates available.

University residence: Simon Fraser University, McTaggart Hall, Burnaby, 291-4503. $20 for 1-2, no linen. S-$33 w/linen. May-end Aug.

UBC Conference Centre, Gage Tower Residence, 5961 Student Union Blvd, 822-2811. S$-22-$60, D-$79-$95, T-$92-$110. Shared kitchen, washroom, recreational facilities, 15 min to downtown and close to Wreck Beach.

Camping: Surrey Timberland Campsite, 3418 King George Hwy, 531-1033. $16, $20 w/hook up. Store and laundry.

FOOD

Granville Public Market, Granville Island underneath the Granville St Bridge. 9 am-6 pm except Mon. Exceptional quality fresh produce, fish and other edibles. An excellent place to stop and have lunch. You can browse the market and be entertained, and then enjoy your meal of Fukomaki (sushi, under $3), Indian Candy (smoked salmon, about $2), fresh fruit, or any of a rainbow of other varied and exotic choices while your eyes feast on a difficult to beat view of sailboats, the city of Vancouver and the mountains rising up to snow-capped heights in the background.

Heavenly Muffins, 601 W Hastings, 681-9104. 'The Italian Crepe is delicious, $4.50.' Open Mon-Fri 6 am-7 pm, Sat 10am-7 pm.

JJ's, 644 Bute St, 682-2068. 'Products of cooking school sold to public. Good main course about $4.50.' Breakfast 7 am-8am, lunch noon-3 pm.

Keg Restaurants, several locations. Inexpensive; salad bar, sea food, burgers. 'Keg-sized drinks.'

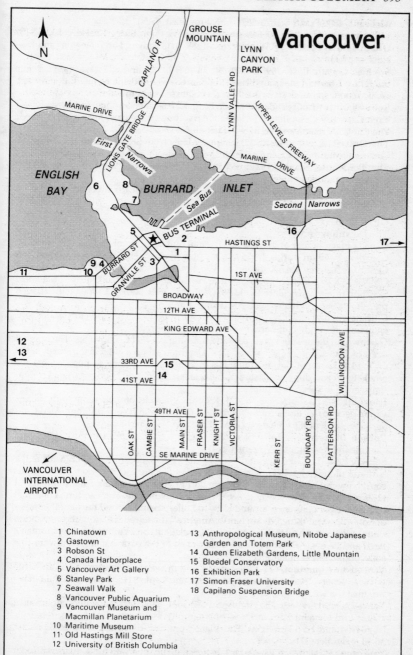

Vancouver

1 Chinatown
2 Gastown
3 Robson St
4 Canada Harborplace
5 Vancouver Art Gallery
6 Stanley Park
7 Seawall Walk
8 Vancouver Public Aquarium
9 Vancouver Museum and
  Macmillan Planetarium
10 Maritime Museum
11 Old Hastings Mill Store
12 University of British Columbia
13 Anthropological Museum, Nitobe Japanese
   Garden and Totem Park
14 Queen Elizabeth Gardens, Little Mountain
15 Bloedel Conservatory
16 Exhibition Park
17 Simon Fraser University
18 Capilano Suspension Bridge

McLeans, 4530 Fraser St, 873-5636. Great for bfast. $5.50.

Milestones All Star Cafe, 2966 W 4th Ave, 734-8616. Pizza, burgers, salad, subs, $5-$15.

Old Spaghetti Factory, 53 Water St, 684-1288, in Gastown. Large portions and reasonable prices.

Sophies Cosmic Café, 2095 W 4th St, 732-6810. 50's and 60's style café serving burgers, pastas and Mexican dishes. Sophies has also become an institution for old fashioned bfasts, and serves the 'best chocolate shake in town'.

Subway, Univ of BC, Students' Union Bldg. Cafeteria style, $3 up for subs.

Taf's Cafe, 829 Granville St, 684-8900. 'Arty atmosphere cafe. Reasonably priced. You can leave messages and luggage here.'

The Only Cafe, 681-6546, 20 E Hastings. Meals from $6. 'Basic but tasty meal. A Gastown institution.' Complete meal $8-$12. 'Queues, popular with locals.'

The Tea House, Stanley Park, 669-3281. Only when you want to splurge. Very expensive, but really lovely.

UBC Campus Pizza, 2136 Western Pkwy, 224-4218. Close to university.

White Spot Restaurants, 731-2434. Good and cheap.

OF INTEREST

The Downtown area

Canada Place, at foot of Burrard St. Unusual building resembling a cruise ship; the Canadian Pavilion during Expo '86, it's now Vancouver's Trade and Convention Centre. A 5-storey IMAX theater is also housed here, 682-4629. For the domed OMNIMAX experience, go to **Science World**, 286-6363, 1455 Quebec St, a short SkyTrain ride away. Science world $9, OMNIMAX $9, both $12. Open daily 10am-6 pm, shows Sun-Fri 10am-5 pm, Sat 10am-9 pm.

Chinatown, on Pender St, between Gore and Abbott Sts. Gift and curio shops, oriental imports, night clubs and many Chinese restaurants.

Gastown, in the area of Water, Alexander, Columbia and Cordova Sts. The original heart of Vancouver. In 1867 'Gassy Jack' Deighton set up a hotel in the shanty town on the banks of the Burrard Inlet. His establishment became so popular that the whole town was dubbed 'Gastown'. Now an area of trendy boutiques, good restaurants, antique shops, and pubs.

Lookout!, 555 Hastings St, 689-0421. Ride the glass elevator 167m up to the observation deck of this tower for a superb view of the city and surroundings. All day tkt $8, $5 w/student ID. Free if you dine at the revolving restaurant!

Robson St, between Howe St and Broughton St. European import stores and Continental restaurants. 'Vibrant. Great at weekends.'

Stanley Park. This, the largest of Vancouver's parks, occupies the peninsula at the harbour mouth and has swimming pools, golf courses, a cricket pitch, tennis courts, several beaches, andn aquarium, an English rose garden, and many forest trails and walks. A nice way to see the park is by bicycle. You can hire a bike just outside the park entrance, around $5 p/h. Rollerblading around the park is another option—'the best thing I did in North America!' If you're walking, a recommended route is the **Sea Wall Walk** past Nine O'Clock Gun, Brockton Point, Lumberman's Arch and Prospect Point. Near the eastern rim of the park is a large and very fine collection of totem poles. Free.

Vancouver Aquarium, 682-1118, located within the park. Features Ocra and blue whales, several performances p/day, 9.30am-8 pm, $11. 'Brilliant. Could have watched the whales for hours.'

Vancouver Art Gallery, 750 Hornby St, 682-5621. Small but innovative collection of classic and contemporary art and photography and lunch time poetry readings. Mon-Wed and Fri 10am-6 pm, Thu 10am-9 pm, Sat 'til 5 pm, Sun noon-5 pm. $9, $5.50 w/student ID.

Vancouver West. Reach Vanier Park by ferry, ($1.75, every 15 mins, 10am-8 pm), or take bus #22 and visit:

Hastings Mill Museum, 1575 Alma Rd, 228-1213. One of the few buildings remaining after the Great Fire of Jun 13th 1886, this is now a museum with Indian artefacts, mementoes of pioneer days and pictures of the city's development. Open daily 11am-4 pm. Sep 16-May 31, Sat and Sun only, 1 pm-4 pm. Donations appreciated.

Macmillan Planetarium, 1100 Chestnut St, 738-7827. Runs numerous stars shows throughout the day and laser shows set to music. Show times vary, call ahead. Rsvs recommended. Star shows $6.50, laser shows $7.50

Maritime Museum, at foot of Cypress St, 257-8309. Exhibits include the RCMP ship *St Roch*, the first ship to navigate the Northwest Passage in both directions and to circumnavigate the continent of North America. Open daily, 10am-5 pm, $6.

Queen Elizabeth Gardens, Little Mountain. When you enter the park keep left for the side with the views overlooking the North Shore mountains and harbour. There is a good view from the Lookout above the sunken gardens. Also, **Bloedel Conservatory**, 872-5513, on top of the mountain has a fine collection of tropical plants and birds. Entrance $3.50. To get to and from Little Mountain, take a #15 Cambie bus from Granville and Pender Sts and get off at 33rd and Cambie. Open Mon-Fri 9 am-8 pm, Sat-Sun 10am-9 pm.

University of British Columbia, at Point Grey, has a population of some 23,000 students. There is a good swimming pool, cafeteria and bookshop. Also an **Anthropological Museum**, 822-3825, $6, the **Nitobe Japanese Garden** and **Totem Park** which has carvings and buildings representing a small segment of a Haida Indian village. To get to the campus take bus #4 or #10 from Granville and Georgia. No charge for museum on Tues after 5 pm.

Vancouver Museum, 1100 Chestnut St, 736-4431. Large circular building fronted by an amazing abstract fountain. Traces the development of the Northwest Coast from the Ice Age through pioneer days to the present. Displays artifacts from native cultures in the Pacific NW. Daily 10am-6 pm, Oct-Apr Tue-Sun 10am-5 pm. $5, $2.50 w/student ID .

Vancouver East, Burnaby

Exhibition Park, bounded by Renfrew, Hastings and Cassiar Sts, is the home of the **Pacific National Exhibition**, 253-2311, **Stadia** and a **Sports Hall of Fame**. The PNE takes place mid Aug-early Sep. $9.50 p/day. 'Fantastic. Includes lumberjack competition, rodeo, demolition derby, exhibitions, fair, etc.'

Simon Fraser University, atop Burnaby Mountain. Constructed in only 18 mths, the giant module design of this ultra-modern seat of learning makes it possible to move around the university totally under cover. The views from up here are superb. To reach the campus catch a #10 bus on Hastings East, change at Kooteney Loop to the 135 SFU.

Vancouver North

Beaches. Near UBC there is Wreck Beach, free and nude; other recommended spots are English Bay, Tower Beach (also naturist), Spanish Banks (watch the tides), Locarno, Jericho and Kitsilano.

Capilano Suspension Bridge, 985-7474. Going north, the bridge is on the left hand side of Capilano Rd. The swinging 137-metre long bridge spans a spectacular 70-m-deep gorge. Entrance to the rather commercialised park costs $9, $6 w/ student ID. 'Not worth it unless you have time to walk the trails.'

Grouse Mountain, 984-0661. The skyride is located at the top of Capilano Rd and you can ride it to the top of the mountain for incredible views, a cup of coffee or a quick hike. Make sure the weather is clear before you go. 'Take food with you and make a day of it'. 'Spectacular. Not to be missed. Best thing I did in North America.' 'We went on a cloudy day and had an amazing time walking in the clouds.' The gondola costs $16, operates daily 9 am-10 pm.

Lynn Canyon Park, 987-5922. Less exploited than Capilano and free. The bridge swings high above Lynn Canyon Creek. Swimming in the creek is nice too and there is an 'excellent' ecology centre by the park entrance. To get there: catch the Seabus at bottom of Granville. At Grouse Mountain take a 228 bus to Peters St and then walk. By car, take the Upper Levels Hwy to Lynn Valley Rd and follow the signs. 'Peaceful and uncrowded.' Open daily 10am-5 pm summer. Winter weekdays.

Whistler Mountain, lies just north of Vancouver and is easily accessible from the city by bus or train. This area of incredible natural beauty is ideal for hiking, biking, rafting or horse-riding and boasts skiing conditions ranking among the best in the world. Even in summer it is possible to ski on the glacier. Trains leave from North Vancouver Rail Station daily at 7am, take 2½ hours and cost $30 o/w. Maverick Coach Lines, 662-8051, run a 2½ hr bus service 6 times a day from Vancouver depot next to VIA rail station $17 o/w.

Whistler Hostel (HI-C), 932-5492, is a timber cabin on picturesque Alta Lake and a good base from which to explore the area. Members $16, $20 non. Great facilities and just 10 mins from the main resort.

ENTERTAINMENT

Jazz Hotline, offers the latest on current and upcoming jazz events. Call 682- 0706.

Jolly Taxpayer Pub, 828 W Hastings St, 681-3574.

Luv-A-Fair, 1275 Seymour St, 685-3288. Downtown Vancouver. Vancouver's hottest club. Hip-hop and alternative music, 'favourite haunt of visiting celebrities in the past.' '80's night on Tue really draws the crowds.' Cover charge $5-$10. Open 9 pm-2am. Sun 'til midnight.

Purple Onion, 15 Water St, 602-9442, Gastown. 'A little bit of everything to please everyone.' 2 rms with live music and DJ's. Open Mon-Thur 8 pm-2am, Fri and Sat 7 pm, Sun 7 pm 'til midnight.

Sea Festival, second wk in July. A week long celebration on the shores of English Bay featuring bathtub races, sandcastle competition, parades, parties, and the city's biggest fireworks display, 'spectacular'.

The Roxy, 932 Granville St, 684-7699. Downtown Vancouver. 'Good atmosphere, extremely popular with locals'. 'Great in-house band.' Cover $3-$6. Sun free. Open 7 pm-2am.

Vancouver Folk Music Festival. Held in mid-July at Jericho Beach Park, 783-6543, features over 50 acts from across Canada and around the world. Tkts $28 p/night, $42 wk day, $75 w/end.

Vancouver International Comedy Festival. From street theatre to cabaret to standup, it's all there early Jul-late Aug at Granville Island, 683-0883. Some performances are free, otherwise tkts $6-$25.

Yuk Yuk's Comedy Club, 750 Pacific Blvd S, 687-5233.

INFORMATION

Chamber of Commerce , Ste #400, 999 Canada Place, 681-2111.

Super, Natural British Columbia Tourism, (800) 663-6000. Info kiosks at airport, Gastown and Eaton's department store. Read *Georgia Straight* and the *Westender*, free from the Tourist Info Centres, for what goes on generally.

Vancouver Travel Information Centre, 683-2000. Waterfront Centre, 200 Burrard St. Open daily 9 am-5.30 pm.

TRAVEL

Hitching is legal and usual in Vancouver but no safer than anywhere else in North America. Exact-fare buses (currently $1.50-$3) operate in the city. The **Skytrain**, a light rapid transit system runs between downtown and New Westminster and connects to the bus system. The ultra-modern **Seabus** also connects to the bus system. A Daypass costs $4.50, available at 7-11, Safeway, Syktrain stops. You can ride anywhere, all day, after 9.30am. Take a ride from the bottom of Granville St to N Van, for stunning views en route. Catch bus #236 to Grouse Mountain.

BC Ferries, (250) 386-3431/ 1-888-223-3779, only in BC. Regular boat service from mainland to surrounding islands. Schedules and prices vary depending on destination, call for details. Victoria $8 o/w.

BC Rail, 1311 W Pemberton St, 651-3500, just over Lion's Gate Bridge, in N Vancouver. Serving surrounding area and points north, Whistler $30.

BC Transit Info, 521-0400. Schedules change every 3 months so call first. There is a free, direct line to BC Transit in the Skytrain stations.

Greyhound Bus Terminal, 1150 Station St, 662-3222/ (800) 661-8747. Calgary $98, Seattle $30.

Gray Line Tours, 879-3363, leave at 9.15am and 1.45 pm daily for 3¹/₂ hour city tours in a double-decker red London bus. They will pick you up from any downtown hotel as long as you call the day before to rsv. $42.

Vancouver International Airport is reached via Hwy 99, Grant McConachie Way. Take city bus #20 from Granville St to 70th Ave. Change to the Airport #100 bus which takes about 45 mins. Perimeter Airport Shuttles run 25 min services every ¹/₂ hr from the Sandman Inn, Skytrain and Seabus stations, Canada Place and other downtown locations. $9 o/w.

VIA Rail located at 1150 Station St, at 200 Granville St, and 1311 West 1st in N Vancouver, (800) 561-8630, in US (800) 561-3949. Train terminals located at 1150 Station St, 200 Granville St, and 1311 W 1st St in N Vancouver. 'Downtown to Downtown' **Vancouver to Victoria** bus service (via ferry) on Pacific Coach Lines, 662-3222, $47 r/t. However, it is much cheaper to go by public transport all the way using the ferry services. Take #601 bus, change at Ladner Exchange to #640 or #404 bus to Tsawwassen ferry terminal. Ferry costs $6.50. From Swartz Bay take #70 PAT bus to Victoria.

VANCOUVER ISLAND The island, and the Gulf Islands which shelter on its leeward side, are invaded annually by thousands of tourists attracted by the temperate climate and the seaside and mountain resorts. Vancouver Island is a 'fisherman's paradise', with mining, fishing, logging and manufacturing the chief breadwinners. There are good ferry and air connections with the mainland. (See under Vancouver and Victoria.)

Victoria, the provincial capital, is situated on the southern tip of the Island. **Nootka**, on the western coast, was the spot where Captain Cook landed in 1778, claiming the area for Britain. In the ensuing years, despite strong Spanish pressure, Nootka became a base for numerous exploratory voyages into the Pacific. The Spaniards were finally dispersed as a result of the Nootka Convention of 1790 but a strong sprinkling of Spanish names on the lower coast bear witness to the past.

Long Beach, 12 mi of white sand W of **Port Alberni** on the Pacific Coast, is recommended for a bit of peace. To get there take Rte 4 from Port Alberni across the mountains towards **Tofino**, the western terminus of the Trans Canada Highway. The beach is part of the now fully developed **Pacific Rim National Park**. Also in the park is the Broken Island Group in Barkley Sound and the 45-mi-long Lifesaving Trail between Bamfield and Port Renfrew. There are campsites in the Long Beach area and on the Ucluelet access road, as well as at Tofino.

The Pacific Ocean is too cold for swimming here, though it's great for surfing or beachcombing. But at **Hot Springs Cove** there are reputed to be the best hot springs in Canada. The least known too, for you can only reach the springs by boat from Tofino and then walk a one-mile trail. The springs bubble up at more than 85° C and flow down a gully into the ocean. The highest pool is so hot that you can only bathe in winter when cooler run- off waters mix with the springs. Sneakers (as protection against possible jagged rocks underfoot) are the only dress worn while bathing.

Back over on the southeastern side of the Island there is a superb drive from Victoria north to **Duncan**, and at Duncan itself the Forest Museum offers a long steam train ride and a large open forestry museum. Going further north you come to **Nanaimo**, the fastest growing town on the island. (By ferry to Vancouver $6.50.) Lumbering and fish-canning are the main occupations in town and it's worth taking a look at Petroglyph Park with its preserved Indian sandstone carvings of thousands of years ago. Nanaimo is also a bungee jumping centre (the only real place to do it in N America) and the starting point for the annual Vancouver Bathtub race across the Georgia Strait in mid-July. There are 'mini hostels' in Duncan and Nanaimo.
The area code for this region is 250.

ACCOMMODATION
Port Hardy: Betty Hamilton's B&B, 9415 Mayors Way—Box 1926, BC VON 2PO, 949-6638. S-$45, D-$55-65.'Really nice after all my hostels and Betty certainly looked after you.'
Nanaimo: Nichol St Mini Hostel, 65 Nichol St, 753-1188. On bus route, communal kitchen, laundry facilities, showers. Registration 4 pm-11 pm. Open May 1st-Sept 1st only. S/D-$15, cottage-$15 pp, up to 5. Camping $8 w/hook-up. Great downtown location, offers discounts to area, BBQ.
Verdun Thomson Mini Hostel, 722-2261, take the #11 bus from the Island Depot and ask the driver to drop you off. Free pick-up between 6 pm-9 pm and ride into town in the morning. Comfortable shared rooms, kitchen, pool table. Hostel $15 p/night, camping $8. No smoking, no curfew.

VICTORIA Former Hudson's Bay Company trading post and fort and now provincial capital, Victoria is noted for its mild climate and beautiful gardens. This small, unassuming little town is located at the southern tip of Vancouver Island on the Juan de Fuca Strait. As a result of its attractive climate, it's a popular retirement spot as well as being popular with British immigrants. Victoria has the largest number of British-born residents anywhere in Canada, and likes to preserve its touch of Olde Englande for the benefit of the year-round tourist industry.

Afternoon tea, fish n' chips, British souvenir shops, tweed and china and double-decker buses all have their place, but if you can get beyond all that, you will find Victoria a pleasant place to be for a time with plenty to explore around the town and out on the rest of the island. There are ferry connections from here to Vancouver and Prince Rupert as well as to Anacortes and Port Angeles, Washington.

ACCOMMODATION
Difficult to find in summer. Book ahead if possible.
Cherry Bank Hotel, 825 Burdett Ave, 385-5380. S-$49-$64 w/bath, D-$58-$73 w/bath. Bfast incl. 'Comfortable, central, recommended by locals.'
Craigmyle Guest Home, 1037 Craigdarrock Rd, 1 km E of Inner Harbour, 595-5411. S-$65, D-$80-95, T-$95. All rms have private bath/shower, full English bfast inc.
Hotel Douglas, 1450 Douglas St, 383-4157. S-$65-$80, D-$80-$95, XP-$10. City centre, close to City Hall.

Selkirk Guest House, 934 Selkirk Ave, 389-1213. Dorm $18. Private rms available. S-$40. XP-$10. D-$60 (w/kitchen and bath). Kitchen/laundry, boat/kayak rental.

Univ of Victoria Residence, 721-8395. May-Aug, students and non-students. S-$37, D-$53 incl full bfast. Half rates for stays over 14 days.

Victoria Backpackers International Hostel, 1418 Fernwood, 386-4471. Shared rooms $12 p/night, $5 key deposit. Private rm w/bath-$35. 4-course Sun dinner $5. 'Very spacious rooms.' 'A great place to stay. Really friendly and run by a complete lunatic!' Open 7.30am-1am.

Victoria International Hostel, 516 Yates St, 385-4511. $19, $15 CYH. Kitchen, laundry, linen rental, lockers, hostel-based programmes. Rsvs essential. Close to bus station and the train station. 'Priority given to members; if you are not one, you'll have to wait until 8 pm to see if there is a bed.'

Victoria Visitors Bureau, 1117 Wharf St, 953-2033 or 387-1642, can help find accommodation for you

YWCA, 880 Courtney St, 389-9280. Dorm-$21, S-$36, D-$55.'New building with coffee shop.'

FOOD
Chinatown. Fishgard St and Government. Inexpensive Chinese eateries.

Fisherman's Wharf, St Lawrence and Erie Sts. Great place to buy seafood.

James Bay Coffee Co and Laundromat, Menzies St. 'Instead of watching clothes go round in the laundromat, hang out in the cafe next door—fabulous idea!'

London Fish & Chips, 5142 Cordova Bay Rd, 658-1921. Has the great British 'chippy' successfully crossed the Atlantic? Decide for yourself—but you'll still have to order 'french fries'. $7.50 for 2 fish and fries.

Scotts, 650 Yates St, 382-1289. Open 24 hr. Meals from $4.50.

Tomoe Japanese Restaurant, 726 Johnson St, 381-0223. 'Delicious, cheap food.'

OF INTEREST
Anne Hathaway's Thatched Cottage, 429 Lampson St, 388-4353. 'Authentic' replicas of things English, plus 16th and 17th century armour and furniture. Tours daily 9 am-7.30 pm in summer, 10am-3.30 pm rest of year, $7.

Art Gallery of Greater Victoria, 1040 Moss St, 384-4101. Includes contemporary and oriental sections. Mon-Sat 10am-5 pm, Thur 'til 9 pm, Sun 1 pm-5 pm. $5, $3 students w/ID. Thurs 5 pm-9 pm free, Mon by donation.

Bastion Square overlooks the harbour. There is a **Maritime Museum** in the square, 385-4222 (open daily 9.30am-4.30 pm, $5, $3 w/student ID) also a number of other renovated 19th-century buildings housing curio shops and boutiques. 'Nice place for just sitting, sometimes there is free entertainment around noon.'

BC Provincial Museum of Natural History and Anthropology, 675 Belleville St, 387-3014. British Columbia flora and fauna, Indian arts and crafts and a reconstructed 1920's BC town. In summer daily 9 am-5 pm. $7, $2.20 w/student ID. 'Great museum.'

Beacon Hill Park, 'Nice for walking and having a peaceful time by the lake.'

Butchart Gardens, 14 mi N of the city off Hwy 17, 652-4422. An English Rose Garden, a Japanese Garden and a formal Italian garden, are the chief features of Victoria's most spectacular park. Floodlit in the evening in summer. Also houses a number of restaurants. Summer hrs, 9 am-11.30 pm, last admission 10.30 pm, otherwise 9 am-4 pm or dusk. $14.50. 'Definitely worthwhile.' 'Don't take the special tour bus.'

Christ Church Cathedral, Quadra and Rockland Sts, 383-2714. One of Canada's largest cathedrals, built in Gothic style. Started 1920's and completed in 1991. The bells are replicas of those at Westminster Abbey in London, England. Stewards are in hand inside the cathedral to show you to places of interest. Open 8.15am-5.15 pm daily. Donation appreciated.

Craigdarroch Castle, 1050 Joan Crescent St, 592-5323. Sandstone castle built in late 1880's by Scottish immigrant Robert Dunsmuir as a gift for his wife, Joan. Now a museum with stained glass windows, Gothic furnishings, original mosaics and paintings. 9 am-7 pm. $7, $5 w/student ID.

Market Square, off Douglas St. Attractive pedestrian mall with shops, fine restaurants and bars.

Parliament Buildings, Government and Belleville Sts. The seat of British Columbia's government is a palatial, turreted Victorian building with a gilded seven-foot figure of Captain George Vancouver, the first British navigator to circle Vancouver Island, on top. Conducted tours available daily throughout summer months. Thunderbird Park, Douglas and Belleville. The park contains 'the world's largest collection of totem poles', a Kwakiutl Tribal Long House, its entrance shaped like a mask, and a flotilla of canoes fashioned from single logs of red cedar. The Undersea Gardens, Inner Harbour, 382-5717. You can look through glass at a large collection of sea plants, octopi, crabs, and other sea life. Also scuba diving shows with Armstrong, the giant octopus. Daily 9 am-9 pm May-Sept; rest of year 10am-5 pm. $7.

INFORMATION
Tourism Victoria Info Centre, 812 Wharf St on the Inner Harbour, 953-2033 Open daily in summer 8.30am-7.30 pm. 9 am-5 pm rest of year.

TRAVEL
BC Clipper, 382-8100, catamaran service to Seattle. $65 o/w, $90 r/t. Takes 2¹/₂ hrs.

BC Ferries, 386-3431/1-888-223-3779 in BC only. Serving Victoria, surrounding islands and the mainland. Vancouver $8 o/w.

BC Transit, 521-0400. New schedule every 3 months so call first. (There is a free, direct line phone to BC Transit in the Skytrain station.) Double decker bus tours of Victoria and Butchart Gardens depart the Empress Hotel. 1¹/₂ hr city tours; buses depart every 30 mins. For rates and info call **Gray Line Tours**, 388-5248.

Island Coach—Pacific Coach, 700 Douglas St, 385-4411/ (800) 661-1725. Buses and connections to and from Victoria and other cities. Vancouver $25 o/w, $47 r/t.

Victoria Regional Transit, local bus, 382-6161.

VIA Rail, (800) 567-8630/(800) 561-3949 in the US, information and rsvs.

From Victoria to Courtenay: the train journey is beautiful—in a small-one car including engine train—spectacular scenery, high bridges. The train stops over Nanaimo's bridge so you can watch the bungee-jumpers.

From Courtenay to Port Hardy, you can only go by bus. $45. Ferry goes from here to Prince Rupert.

KELOWNA   Back on the mainland and going east out of Vancouver, Rte 3 takes you over the Cascade Mountains and down into the Okanagan Valley. One-third of the apples harvested in Canada come from this area. Good therefore for summer jobs, or, if you're taking it slow, for a nice holiday, just lying by the lake in the sun. The **Kelowna Regatta** is held during the second weekend in August, with accompanying traditional festivities.

Beware of the local lake monster. It goes by the name of Ogopogo, and is like the Loch Ness Monster but with a head like a sheep, goat or horse.

Not to be missed are the local wineries. **Mission Hill Winery**, 768-7611, is one of the best, free tours and sampling 10am-6 pm daily. The **Kelowna Centennial Museum** , 763-2417, on Queensway Avenue has nice displays of Indian arts and crafts. Mon-Sat 10am-5 pm. Donation appreciated.

ACCOMMODATION
CYA Hostel, Gospel Mission, 251 Leon Ave, 763-3737. $12 p/night, includes meals. Men only.

Kelowna Backpackers Hostel, 2343 Pandosy St, 763-6024. $10 dorms, private rms $30, $2 linen. Kitchen/laundry, bike rental available.

Same Sun Hostel, 730 Bernard Ave, 763-9800. Rms-$35 pp, up to 4 Dorm-$18. Showers, downtown location, beach views.

Willow Inn, 235 Queensway, 762-2122. S-$66 for 2, D-$95 for 4, incl bfast. Downtown, close to lake and park.

Hiawatha Park Campground, 3787 Lakeshore Rd, 861-4837. Sites $25 for 2, w/hook up. XP-$5. Laundry, store, pool, hotdogs.

INFORMATION/TRAVEL
Kelowna Chamber of Commerce and Tourist Info, 544 Harvey Ave, 861- 1515. Open daily, 8 am-8 pm in summer; 9 am-5 pm winter. www.bcyellowpages.com/ advert/k/kcc/.

Greyhound, 2366 Leckie Rd, 860-3835/ (800) 661- 8747. To Vancouver 6 runs p/day, 5$^{1/2}$ hrs, $49.

Kelowna City Bus Transit, 860-8121. Fare $1-$1.75 depending on zone.

KAMLOOPS The Trans Canada Highway takes the Fraser Canyon/ Kamloops/Revelstoke route through the province. The Highway, incidentally, at 5000 mi long, is the longest paved highway in the world, and Kamloops, situated at the point where Rte 5 crosses it, is a doubly important communications centre, for the railroad also takes this route through the mountains.

Kamloops is useful perhaps as a halfway stopover point between Vancouver and Banff or else a possible jumping-off point for visits to the Revelstoke, Yoho, Glacier, and Kootenay National Parks. The **Kamloops Museum** on Seymour Street deals with the region's agricultural and Indian history. Kamloops is a popular place for skiers and trout fishermen.

ACCOMMODATION/FOOD
Bambi Motel, 1084 Battle St, 3 blks W of Yellowhead Bridge, 372-7626. S- $68-$72 for 2, D-$84 for 4; kitchen available at extra cost.

Kamloops Old Courthouse Hostel, 7 W Seymour St, 828-7991. $15 members, $19.50 non. Downtown location. Kitchen, laundry, TV.

Thrift Inn, 2459 E Trans Canada Hwy, 374-2488. S-$48 for 2, D-$58 for 4, pool, AC, TV.

Mr Mike's Broiler Restaurant, 2121 E Trans Canada Hwy, 376-6843. 'A place for a pig-out. Don't be put off by the exterior.'

INFORMATION/TRAVEL
Greyhound, 725 Notre Dame, 374-1212/ (800) 661-8747. Open 7.30am-9 pm. Vancouver $45 o/w, $79 r/t, if bought 14 days in advance.

Kamloops Visitor Centre, 1290 W Trans Canada Hwy, 374-3377. Open daily 9 am-6 pm.

Kamloops City Bus Transit, 376-1216. Open 8.30am-4.30 pm.

VIA Rail, (800) 561-8630/(800) 561-3949 in the US, information and rsvs.

MOUNT REVELSTOKE NATIONAL PARK   The park, midway between Kamloops and Banff, Alberta, is situated in the Selkirk Range. The Selkirks are more jagged and spikey than the Rockies and are especially famous for the excellent skiing facilities available on their slopes. The summit drive to the top of **Mount Revelstoke** is a 26 km parkway with scenic views. At the summit there is a 9 km trail winding through forests and meadows with fantastic views of distant peaks, glaciers and mountain lakes.

The Trans Canada runs along the southern edge of the park following the scenic **Illecillewaet River** and there are 2 self-guided tours available. One is a tour of the rain forest, with its huge cedar trees, and the other of the rare skunk cabbage plants. You can see it all without ever getting out of the car. Park services are provided in the town of **Revelstoke**, a quiet, pretty place set amidst the mountains. Entrance to the park is $4.

ACCOMMODATION
In **Revelstoke**:
Frontier Motel, at jct of Hwys 1 & 23 N, 837-5119. S-$65 for 2, D-$84 for 4. Price includes 4-course bfast.
Mountain View Motel, 1017 First St W, 837-4900. S-$45 up, D-$48 up, XP-$5; kitchen $8. AC, cable TV. Central location.
R Motel, 1200 1st St W, 837-2164. S-$45, D-$49.
Camping: Canada West Campground, 2¹/₂ mi W of Revelstoke, 837-4420. $15 for 2, $19 w/hook up, XP-$1; laundry, showers, outdoor heated pool, capuccino bar. Free firewood.
Canyon Hot Springs Campground, about 15 mi E of town, 837-2420. $17 for 2, $20.50 w/hook up, XP-$2.

OF INTEREST
Canyon Hot Springs, 837-2420, 15 mi E of town. 39°C mineral waters, or a swim in a pool of 26°C. $5, daypass $7.50.
Revelstoke Dam, 837-6515. Self-guided tours, Mar 18th-Jun 16th, 9 am-5 pm; Jun 17th-Sep 10th, 8 am-8 pm; Sep 11th-Oct 29th, 9 am-5 pm. Free.
Revelstoke Museum and Art Gallery, 837-3067. Mon-Fri 10am-5 pm, Sat 1-5 pm. $2 suggested donation.
Three Valley Gap Ghost Town, 837-2109, about 10 mi W on Trans Canada Hwy 1. Nr site of original mining town of Three Valley with historical buildings moved here from various places in BC. Open daily 8 am-4.30 pm in summer. $6.50. Also has accommodation, D-$84 for 2.

INFORMATION
Tourist Info, 837-3522. Open 9 am-7 pm.
Chamber of Commerce, 837-5345. Open 9 am-5 pm.
Mount Revelstoke National Park, 837-7500. Open 7 am-9 pm.

GLACIER NATIONAL PARK   From Revelstoke carry on eastwards along the Trans Canada and you very quickly come to this park. As its name tells you, Glacier is an area of icefields and glaciers with deep, awesome canyons and caverns, alpine meadows and silent forests. There are many trails within the park and, like Revelstoke, this too is a touring skiers' paradise. The Alpine Club of Canada holds summer and winter camps here.

The annual total snowfall in the park averages 350 inches and sometimes exceeds 600 inches. With the deep snow and the steep terrain, special protection is necessary for the railway and highway running through Glacier. Concrete snowsheds and manmade hillocks at the bottom of avalanche chutes slow the cascading snow, while artillery fire is used to bring down the snow before it accumulates to critical depths. Travellers through Rogers Pass in winter may feel more secure in the knowledge that they are passing through one of the longest controlled avalanche areas in the world.

8 popular hiking trails begin at Illecillewaet campground, 3 km W of Rogers Pass. The **Meeting of the Waters** trail is short and easy and leads to the dramatic confluence of the Illecillewaet and Asulkan Rivers. The longer **Avalanche Crest** trail offers magnificent views of Rogers Pass, the Hermit Range the Illecillewaet River Valley.

Admission to the park is $4 pp daily and climbers and overnight walkers must register with the wardens at **Rogers Pass Info Centre**, 837-6274. Park services and accommodation are available at Rogers Pass. The Info Centre also has displays and exhibits on the history and national resources of Glacier National Park.

ACCOMMODATION
See also under Revelstoke.
Golden Municipal Park, in Golden on Kicking Horse River, 344-5412. $13, $15 w/hook up. Hot showers, outdoor pool. There are **National Park sites** at Illecillewaet River, 3 km W of Rogers pass summit, $13; Loop Brook, 5 km W of Rogers Pass summit, $13. Both campgrounds have firewood, toilets and shelters. Open Jun-Sep. Back country camping at Mountain Creek and Rogers Pass is available with a permit, $6, campers must register at Rogers Pass Info Centre.

INFORMATION
Golden Chamber of Commerce, Caboose, 500 10th Ave N, 344-7125. Open 9 am-7 pm.
Glacier National Park/Rogers Pass Info Centre, 837-6274. Open 7 am-9 pm, winter hrs vary.
Tourist Info, 837-3522. Open 9 am-5 pm.

YOHO NATIONAL PARK   Still going east, Yoho National Park is on the British Columbia side of the Rockies adjoining Banff National Park on the Alberta side. It gets its name from the Indian, meaning 'how wonderful'.

Yoho is a mountaineer's park with some 250 miles of trails leading the walker across the roof of the Rockies. Worth looking at are the beautiful alpine **Emerald** and **O'Hara Lakes**, the curtain of mist at **Laughing Falls**, the strangely shaped pillars of **Hoodoo Valley**, and **Takakkaw Falls**, at 800m one of the highest in North America. The spectacular, rushing **Kicking Horse River** flows across the park from E to W. Entrance to the park is $5 pp.

ACCOMMODATION
There are 5 **campgrounds** and various cabins within the park. The campgrounds are at **Chancellor Peak**, open May-Sep, $15; **Hoodoo Creek**, open Jul-Sep, $14; **Kicking Horse**, open May-Oct, $17; **Takakkaw Falls**, open June-Sep, $12; and Monarch, open Jul-Sep, $12. Yoho operates 6 backcountry campgrounds, 4 in the Yoho Valley and 2 in the Ottertail Valley, $6 pp. Call the **Field Visitor Centre**, 343-6783 Alternatively, Yoho is easily visited from either Lake Louise or Banff. Tours of the park are available from both places.
Whiskey Jack Hostel, 13 km W along the Yoho Valley road (which begins at the Kicking Horse Campground) and 22 km W of Lake Louise on Hwy 1 (Trans-Canada Hwy). $10, $15 non-members. No phone.

INFORMATION
Yoho National Park, 343-6324. Open 8.30am-4.30 pm. *www.worldweb.com/ parkscanada—yoko/*.
Yoho Field Visitor Centre, 343-6783. Open 9 am-7 pm.

KOOTENAY NATIONAL PARK   Lying along the Vermilion-Sinclair section of the Banff-Windermere Parkway (Hwy 93), going S from Castle Junction, Kootenay is rich in canyons, glaciers and ice fields as well as wild life. Bears, moose, elk, deer and Rocky Mountain goats all live here. The striking **Marble Canyon**, just off the highway, is formed of grey limestone and quartzite laced with white and grey dolomite and is one of several canyons in Kootenay.

The western entrance to the park is near the famous **Radium Hot Springs**. There are two pools with water temperatures at almost 60°C. Springs are open daily in summer and entrance is $4. Admission to the park is $5 pp; visitors must obtain a park motor vehicle license at the entrance before driving through. There are campgrounds and motels within the park (beside the Springs and another locations) and accommodation is available in the town of Radium Hot Springs. Camping at **Redstreak Campground**, 2.5 km from Radium Hot Springs, $16, $21 w/hook up. Open May-Sep; **McLeod Meadows**, 27 km N from W Gate entrance, $13. Open May-Sep: and **Marble Canyon**, 86 km N of W Gate entrance, $13. Open Jun-Sep. Park Info: 347-9615.

PRINCE GEORGE   This fairly uninteresting town has become the takeoff point for development schemes in the wilderness Northwest. Travellers en route to Alaska from Jasper use the Yellowhead Hwy (Rte 16). At Prince George change to Rte 97 to Dawson Creek and the Alaska Hwy or Hwy 37 for Alaska or continue on Hwy 16 winding over the Hazelton Mountains to Prince Rupert on the coast. If you are travelling north from Kamloops, Rte 5 picks up the 16 at Tete Jaune Cache.

ACCOMMODATION
Prince George Hotel, 487 George St, 564-7211. S-$48, D-$50, T- $55. XP-$7 English pub, TV.
Municipal Campground, 18th Ave, 563-2313. Sites $13, XP-$3. Hot showers. Free firewood.

BARKERVILLE   The boom town story that triggered off the settlement of British Columbia started here on 21 August 1862 when Billy Barker, a broke, bearded Cornishman and a naval deserter, struck the pay dirt that, within a short time, earned him $800,000, and all from a strip of land only 600 ft long. As a result of his find Barkerville became a boom town.

The shaft that started it all is now a part of the restored gold rush town at **Barkerville Historic Park** located 55 mi E of Quesnel and 130 mi S of Prince George. You will need a car to get there.

In Barkerville you can do some panning, call in at the Gold Commissioner's office, visit Trapper Dan's cabin in Chinatown, have your photograph taken in period clothes and visit the same type of shows the miners once enjoyed at the Theater Royal. A fine museum in the park tells the whole saga of Barkerville with photos, exhibits and artefacts. For info call 994-3332. Open daily 8 am-8 pm.

There is a camp ground near the park or alternatively there is fairly inexpensive motel accommodation in nearby **Wells**. Park admission is $5.50. The park is open year-round with reduced opening hours and no guided tours after Labour Day.

DAWSON CREEK A small, but rapidly growing town NE of Prince George on Hwy 97 which marks the start of the Alaska Highway (see also under Alaska). The Zero Milepost for the Highway is the centre of town.

Dawson Creek was settled as recently as 1912 when the railroad was built to ship wheat from the area. A much older settlement, **Fort St John**, about 50 miles north, was established in 1793 as a fur trading outpost and mission. Today the community thrives on the expanding gas and oil industries in the area.

ACCOMMODATION
Cedar Lodge Motel, 801 110th Ave, 782-8531. S-$45, D-$55.
Windsor Hotel, 1100 102nd Ave, 782-3301. S/D-$40 up. Coffee shop, TV.
Camping: Mile 0 Campsite, 1 mi W of jnct Alaska Hwy next to golf course, 782-2590. $10, $15 w/hook up. Hot showers, laundry.

OF INTEREST
South Peace Pioneer Village, 1 mi SE on Hwy 2, 782-7144. Turn of the century village incl log schoolhouse, trapper's cabin, blacksmith's shop, etc. Daily 9 am-6 pm, Jun-Sep. Donations.
Historical Society Museum, 900 Alaska Ave, 782-9595. In renovated 1931 railway station; local wildlife and history exhibits. Open in summer, daily 8 am-7 pm; Tue-Sat 9 am-5 pm in winter. $1.

INFORMATION
Tourist Info, 900 Alaska Ave, 782-9595. Open in summer, daily 8 am-7 pm.

FORT ST JAMES NATIONAL HISTORICAL PARK Back on Hwy 16 (the Yellowhead Hwy) and heading from Prince George to Prince Rupert, it is perhaps worth a small detour at **Vanderhoof** to the shores of **Stuart Lake** to visit this former Hudson's Bay Company trading post. The 19th century post features restored and reconstructed homes, warehouses and stores. The park is open daily, 9 am-9 pm, May-Oct, and entrance is $4. It must have been an isolated, strange existence for the Hudson's Bay men here in the middle of nowhere 100 years ago. For info call 996-7191.

PRINCE RUPERT Known as the 'Halibut Capital of the World', Prince Rupert is the fishing centre of the Pacific Northwest. The season's peak is reached in early Aug and this is the time to visit the canneries.

This area was a stronghold of the Haida and Tsimpsian Indians and the **Museum of North British Columbia** on First Avenue contains a rare collection of Indian treasures. In front of the building stands a superb totem pole. Inside, there are more totems, masks, carvings and beadwork.

Prince Rupert is marvelously situated among the fjords of Hecate Strait and at the mouth of the beautiful Skeena River. There is also a reversing tidal stream fit to rival the falls at Saint John, New Brunswick. You get a good view of the Butz Rapids from Hwy 16, en route from Prince George.

The town is also a major communications centre being the southernmost port of the Alaska Ferry System, the northern terminus of the British Columbia Ferry Authority and the western terminus of VIA Rail.

ACCOMMODATION

Accommodation hereabouts tends to be expensive. The Visitors Information Bureau may be able to help.

Aleeda Motel, 900 3rd Ave, 627-1367. S-$53 up, D-$65 up, T-$82 up. XP-$6. Courtesy coffee, TV.

Pioneer Rooms, 167 E 3rd Ave, 624-2334. S-$20-$25, D-$35. 'Friendly.' 'Small, clean and cosy.'

Raffles Inn, 1080 3rd Ave W, 624-9161. S-$58.50, D-$70, Q-$84. 'Comfortable and clean.' Nr ferries & bus station.

Park Ave Campground, 1750 Park Ave, 624-5861, $10.50. 1 km from ferry terminal. Covered areas for cooking and eating.

OF INTEREST

Museum of Northern British Columbia, 1st Ave and McBride St, 624-3207. Mon-Sat 9 am-8 pm, Sun 9 am-5 pm, winter hrs vary. $2 suggested donation.

North Pacific Cannery, Port Edward, 658-3238. Old, original cannery buildings, wooden fishing boats, fishing exhibits. Free.

Queen Charlotte Islands, W of Prince George. Miles of sandy beaches. A place for taking it easy and doing some boating. Accessible from Prince Rupert by plane or boat.

Hazelton. A village NW of Prince Rupert off Hwy 16, Hazelton is worth a stop for the interesting **Ksan Indian Village and Museum**, 842-5544. This is an authentic village and consists of a carving house and four communal houses. The houses are decorated with carvings and painted scenes in classic West Coast Indian style, $2. Tours daily May-Oct, $7.

Prince Rupert Grain Elevator, tours of the most modern grain elevators in the world. Rsv through Visitors Info Bureau.

INFORMATION/TRAVEL

Visitors Information Bureau, 100 1st Ave E (cnr of McBride), 624-5637. The nicest way to approach Prince Rupert is undoubtedly by sea. A ferry calls here from Port Hardy on Vancouver Island, making the trip on odd days of the month. $102. One-way it takes about 15 hrs. Leaves 7.30am-arrives 10.30 pm. The scenery is magnificent and if you can afford it, it's a great trip, well worth taking. Ferries also leave here for Haines, Alaska. If you want a shorter trip, take the one to Ketchikan, passing through glaciers and fjords en route. 'Very beautiful.'

THE TERRITORIES

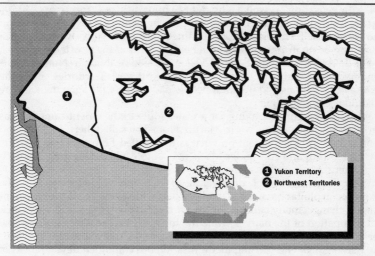

1 Yukon Territory
2 Northwest Territories

Both the Northwest Territories and the Yukon were originally fur-trading areas of the Hudson's Bay Company, only becoming part of Canada in 1870. If planning a trip to either the Yukon or the Northwest Territories, be sure to contact the tourist office in advance. They can send you more detailed information so that you can take advantage of the many package tours available. Or call the North West Territories Tourist Info: (403) 873-7200/(800) 661-0788. *www.yahoo.com/Regional/Countries/Canada/Provinces_and_Territories/ Northwest Territories (or Yukon)/.*
National Parks: Auyuittuq, Nahanni, Wood Buffalo and Kulane in Yukon. *The telephone area code for this section is 403.*

NORTHWEST TERRITORIES

Canada's Arctic is larger than half of the continental USA. It's a vast, mostly unexplored, lonesome area, with a population of 40,000, scattered in 32 communities located on historic trade routes, the Mackenzie, Liard and Peel Rivers, and along the Arctic coast. The territories are not, however, entirely perpetual ice and snow. Although half the mainland and all the islands lie within the Arctic zone, the land varies from flat, forested valleys, to never-melting ice peaks; from blossom-packed meadows to steep, bleak cliffs and from warm, sandy shores to frigid, glacial banks.

In 1993, the Governments of Canada and the Northwest Territories and representatives of the Inuit of the central and eastern Arctic signed a historic land claims settlement. After 20 years of negotiations the Inuit now have control over vast tracts of their original homeland, waters and offshore areas. This is the first adjustment to Canadian boundaries since 1949 and gives the Inuit people outright ownership of 135,000 square miles of the eastern half of the territory, to be named Nunavut. They also received financial 'compensation' as well as the right to hunt, fish and trap across 740,000 square miles of the eastern part of the present territory. The western part of the Northwest Territories will be renamed. The Nunavut Government will come into being in 1999, representing all residents of the new territory.

For their part of the deal, the 17,500 or so Eskimos living in Nunavut surrendered their claim to own the entire Northwest Territories. Both the House of Commons and the Inuit people had to ratify the agreement before it could become binding.

European explorers looking for a water route to the Orient came here as early as the 16th century. Sir Martin Frobisher sailed here in 1576 and founded the first settlement on what is now called Frobisher Bay, in 1578. Henry Hudson and Alexander Mackenzie both explored the area in search of greater trading outlets and profits.

With the more recent discoveries of rich mineral deposits and the promised exploitation of the oil and gas fields, life in the Territories is beginning to change, many believe, for the worse. Fur trapping is still the principal occupation of the natives while the Inuit rely on the white fox and seal for their chief source of income. In many areas the native peoples are fighting hard against encroaching modernisation but continued development of the area's natural resources could threaten their traditional ways of survival.

It's a long, long way north but once you've decided to go there are various alternatives. There are regular scheduled air services from Edmonton, Winnipeg and Montreal into the Territories. Once within the Territories, flights are available to the remoter parts of the Arctic. By road, the Mackenzie Highway starts 250 miles inside the Alberta boundary travelling up to **Hay River** on the Great Slave Lake before striking west to **Fort Simpson**. From Hay River it's a further 600 miles to the capital, **Yellowknife**, on the north shore of the lake. There are daily buses to Hay River and three buses a week as far as Yellowknife from Edmonton, Alberta. When travelling in the Territories, always carry ample supplies of food and fuel since it can be hundreds of miles between towns with few, if any, services enroute.

The Northwest Territories are rich in history and culture. Traditional and modern arts thrive among indigenous communities. Along the Arctic coastline Dene elders are recognised for their skills in producing traditional clothing, snowshoes, baskets and drums. The works of Dene and Metis painters and carvers are collected across North America. Communities along the Mackenzie River produce everything from moccasins and jewelry to canoes and moosehair tuftings. Old time fiddle musicians and young local bands can be found 'shaking their thang' at the dances and festivals held throughout the year in McPherson, Inuvik and Yellowknife. **Raven Mad Daze**, (403) 873-3912, in Yellowknife and **Midnight Madness**, 979-2607, in Inuvik celebrate the summer solstice, 20th Jun, with entertainment in the streets, late night sidewalk sales, traditional drum dances and native cuisine. The **Lake Festival**, (403) 952-2330, takes place in McPherson on the first two days of July. Enjoy musical performances from Canadian artists from the shores of Midway Lake.

The Territories are a place of vast natural beauty, with half a million square miles of unspoilt wilderness, wild rivers, mountain forests and sweeping tundra. The **Canoe Heritage Trail** offers some of the most challenging hiking in North America, a route bushwhacked through the mountains to Yukon during WWII, it's famed for its wildlife and spectacular natural formations in its valleys. Before the snow comes in late August, the northern skies fill with the sinuous dance of Aurora Borealis, the northern lights. A giant electrical storm in the upper atmosphere radiates sheets of coloured light, typically ranging from greens, through yellows and pinks to subtle purples, across the night sky. Visitors come from around the world to witness one of nature's most marvelous spectacles, as familiar here as the summer sun or winter snow. Best seen on clear nights from September to January. The **Mackenzie** is one of the world's greatest rivers, twisting and turning for 1200 miles from the Great Slave Lake, one of the largest and deepest lakes in the world, to the Arctic Ocean, and offering access to more hundreds of navigable miles on the Slave River, the Nahanni, Liard, the Peel and Arctic Red Rivers, and on Great Bear Lake. During the ice-free months (end of May to October) tugs and barges ply up and down the river. The hardiest canoeists and trailer-boaters can join them for one of the loneliest, loveliest trips in the world.

The **Great Slave Lake** is the jumping-off point for the vast developments under way to the north. **Hay River** is a vital freight transportation centre being the transshipment point between rail and river barges.

Yellowknife, the territorial capital until 1999, and less than 300 miles from the Arctic Circle on Great Slave Lake, has 'a wild frontier atmosphere' and two gold mines. Accommodation and food are expensive but new suburbs are springing up and business is booming. B&B's seem to be the best bet for a cheap room, S/D-$50-$75. In June you can take part in a 24 hour golfing marathon made possible since the sun doesn't set here for the whole of the summer. It is also possible to visit the underground gold mines. Tourist information is available from the **Chamber of Commerce**, 4807 49th St, (403) 920-4944, and from **Yellowknife Tourist Info**, 52nd St and 49th Av, (403) 873-7200. One other place to visit is the **Prince of Wales Northern Heritage Centre**, 48th St, (403) 873-7551, which has exhibits and crafts on the history and cultural developments in the Northwest Territories. Open daily 10.30 am-5.30 pm. Free.

Fort Smith, just across from the Albertan frontier, and once the Territorial capital, is a sprawling mixture of shacks, log cabins and more modern government-built establishments. The Hudson Bay Company established a trading post here in 1874, the town later becoming a stopping place for gold-seekers on their way to the Yukon. **Wood Buffalo**, Canada's largest National Park straddling the Alberta/Northwest Territories line, was established to protect the only remaining herd of wood bison. An excellent example of boreal forest with streams, lakes and towering cliffs. The park's unusual geography also yields one of North America's most extensive landscapes of sinkholes, underground rivers, caves and sunken valleys. There are several trails within the park and rangers sponsor guided nature hikes in summer. Camping is permitted: try *Pine Lake*, open May-Sep, $10 p/site, camping is available elsewhere in the park but a back country pass is required, call (403) 872-2349, for details.

For the more adventurous traveller, **Auyuittuq National Park** , (819) 473-8829, is near the Inuit settlement of Pangnirtung on Baffin Island and is notable for its fjords, glacial valleys and mountains. Inaccessible by road, jet connections are available from Yellowknife. Day entrance to the park is $15. **Nahanni National Park**, (403) 695-2310, is north west of Fort Simpson and is a wilderness area of hot springs, waterfalls, canyons and river rapids. Many species of birds, mammals and fish have been observed in the park. This park is also inaccessible by road. Die-hards have been known to hike into the park then canoe down the watershed of the S Nahanni river, but unless you have a death wish, take the plane. Jet connections from various points include Fort Simpson. A large new Visitor Centre in Fort Simpson, features extensive displays on the history, culture and geography of the area, free. Park entrance $10.

The third largest city in the Northwest Territories is **Inuvik**, way up in the northernmost corner. A boom town, ever alert for news of oil strikes, it is an interesting mixture of old timers, traders, delta Eskimos, Indians, oilmen and entrepreneurs. Gold and diamond mining continues to be the staple of the community. There are three hotels, all expensive, but camping is also possible. Even in summer it gets very cold however.

The town of **Frobisher Bay**, way up north on Baffin Island, is the administrative, education and economic centre of the eastern Arctic region of Canada. Frobisher Bay has also, since 1954 and the establishment of the Distant Early Warning Line, become an important defence and strategic site and a refuelling stop for military and commercial planes.

THE YUKON TERRITORY Fur-trading brought the Hudson's Bay Company into the Yukon in the mid-1800's but it was the Klondike Gold Rush of 1898 that really put the area on the map. Thousands of gold-seekers climbed the forbidding Chilkoot and White Passes and pressed on down the Yukon River to Dawson City. In two years **Dawson City**, at the junction of the Klondike and Yukon Rivers, grew from a tiny hamlet to a settlement of nearly 30,000.

There's not much gold around anymore, however. Instead there's silver, copper, zinc, open-pit mining and a big hunt for oil. In fact following the Gold Rush the Yukon practically settled back into its pre-gold hunting and trapping days, once again a remote spot on a map in northwestern Canada until the Japanese occupied the Aleutian Islands in WWII. Then another rush to the Yukon was on, this time of army engineers who constructed the **Alaska Highway** as a troop route in 1942, passing right through the Yukon and up to Alaska.

The 1523 mile Highway begins at Dawson Creek, British Columbia, and winds its way, via **Whitehorse**, the Yukon capital, and a mining and construction centre, to **Fairbanks**, **Alaska**. Services are provided at regular intervals along the route.

Above Whitehorse, many prospectors lost their lives in the dangerous

Whitehorse Rapids. Later, the White Pass and Yukon narrow gauge railway now in restored operation, took the prospectors as far as **Skagway**. For info call: (800) 343-7373 or (907) 983-2217. Round trip excursions from Skagway, $75, and through connections to Whitehorse.

You can also fly into Dawson City or Whitehorse, or else travel by cruise ship as far as Skagway, Alaska, and from there drive on a year round highway to Whitehorse. Hitching is said to be reasonable.

Whitehorse is also the headquarters of the Territory Mounties. A visit here should include a stop at the **WD McBride Museum** on 1st Ave and Wood St, 667-2709, to look at Gold Rush and Indian mementoes including a steam locomotive, a sleigh wagon, guns. shovels, etc. Audio-visual presentations on Yukon history are offered, $3.50, $2.50 w/student ID. Open daily, 10 am-6 pm May 15-Sept 30 (summer); Sunday, 1 pm-4 pm (winter). You can also ride the Yukon River through turbulent **Miles Canyon** on the *MV Schwatka*, named after the explorer, 668-4716. 2 hrs, $17. Be sure to visit the Whitehorse Power Dam to see the salmon leap in Aug. The restored *S. S. Klondike* , 667-4511, on S Access Rd, is a dry-docked 1929 sternwheeler that recalls the days when the Yukon River was the city's sole means of survival. Tkts from the info booth at the parking lot for video and guided tour, $3.25. Open daily June-Sep, 9 am-7.30 pm.

ACCOMMODATION

In Whitehorse: **High Country Inn**, 4051 4th Ave, 667-4471. D-$25 pp, up to 4 people. Cooking and laundry facilities, shared b/room.

98 Hotel, 110 Wood St, 667-2641. S-$30, D-$45 (+$10 key deposit). 16 units (w/out private bath). Open 24 hours, year round.

Robert Service Campground:, 1km from town on S Access Rd, 668-3721. Beside the Yukon River, a convenient stop for campers, sites $10.50.

At **Dawson City** many of the buildings hurriedly thrown up in 1898 still stand. At the height of the Gold Rush more than 30,000 people lived in Dawson, in the settlement at the meeting point of the Yukon and Klondike Rivers. The now declining population capitalises on the tourist trade with things like an old time music hall and gold panning for $5 a pan. Picks, pans, and even bags of unrefined gold are all on view. Food and accommodation prices are high.

ACCOMMODATION

The Bunkhouse, Front and Princess St, 993-6164. Brand new, downtown location. S-$45, D-$50.

Gold Rush Campground, 5th Ave and York St, 993-5247. Showers, laundromat, TV, store. Convenient downtown location. Sites $13, $18.50 w/hook-up. Open 7 am-10 pm, Jun-Aug; 9 am-9 pm, May & Sept.

OF INTEREST

The Dawson City Museum, 5th Ave, 993-5291 or 993-5007. The Yukon's first museum, was established in Dawson City in 1901 in conjunction with the local library. The museum has the largest single collection of recovered artifacts in the Yukon. Its collection of early narrow-gauge locomotives includes a 'Vauclain-type' Baldwin engine, the last one in existence. Historic films and slides are shown nightly during the peak season. Open daily, 10 am-6 pm, June 1 to Sept 3; by appointment only in the winter. $3.50, $2.50 w/student ID.

In the southwestern corner of the Yukon is the mountainous **Kluane**

National Park, 634-7209. The park has extensive icefields and Canada's highest peak, Mt Logan (19,850 ft), as well as a great variety of animals, fishes and birds. The rugged, snowy mountains of Kluane typify the storybook picture one has of the Yukon. In fact the territory is not entirely a land of perpetual ice and snow. Summers here are warm with almost total daylight during June and although winters are cold, they are generally no more so than in many Canadian provinces. The 'Green Belt', along the eastern boundary of the park supports the greatest diversity of plant and animal life in northern Canada. The Alaska Highway, near the park's northeast boundary, provides an easy way to view the eastern edge of the park and glimpse the spectacular peaks beyond. 'This is Big Country to beat Montana.' Camping is available at Kathleen Lake, 27 km south of Haines Junction off Haines Rd, 634-2251. Good hiking and fishing area, free firewood. Open Jun-Oct, sites $10.

The Yukon government provides and maintains more than 50 **campgrounds** throughout the territory, mostly in scenic places along the major highways. Hotel/motel accommodation is available in all the towns mentioned above but it's on the expensive side.

MEXICO

BACKGROUND

This guide is intended primarily for 'on the road' travel in North America and so this chapter concentrates on selected areas of Mexico deemed likely to be of greatest interest for visitors primarily spending time in the USA and Canada. For longer stays, further reading is recommended and necessary, but for a brief visit this chapter gives you valuable general background information and highlights selected areas to visit from the USA.

BEFORE YOU GO

Mexico is anxious to keep formalities to a minimum for the border hopper with dollars to spend. Anyone content with a visit of three days or less to a border town (by land) or seaport (by sea) need only present a passport at the crossing point.

For trips further afield, a **tourist card** is needed. If you try to leave the border area without one, you may be stopped and sent back at customs posts 20 miles inland. Cards are issued by Mexican embassies, consulates and tourist offices, by certain travel agencies and at the border itself: if you are flying in, the airline will handle the formalities. All you need is a valid passport, or for US and Canadian nationals, other proof of citizenship. Travellers under 18 also require an authorisation signed by both parents and witnessed by a Commissioner for Oaths or Notary Public. The card suffices for citizens of the UK, most other European countries, the US and Canada, but nationals of Australia and New Zealand are required to obtain full visas. Those in doubt should refer to their nearest consulate. At the port of entry, both card and passport must be shown, together with a cholera certificate if you have been in an infected area during the preceding five days. No other vaccinations are required.

European visitors receive a card valid for 90 days from the date of entry. US citizens are given 180 days, but in both cases *Migración* officials can vary the duration at whim, often stamping the card with a 30 day limit, as well as charging for the privilege on occasion. The card must be used to enter Mexico within 90 days of the issuing date. So if planning to spend several months in the US first you should obtain the card there at the end of your stay, rather than from the home country. There are Mexican Consulates in most US cities and border towns.

If you are likely to need an extension, request a longer validation when first applying; doing it within Mexico is time-consuming and may involve a trip back to the border to get a new card. In Mexico City you can try your luck at the Visa Renewal office, located at Ave. Chapultepec # 284, Col. Roma , México D.F. Ph. (5) 626-7200. Be prepared for a long wait. The card is issued in duplicate: one part is taken from you on entry, the other as you leave. Once in Mexico you are obliged by law to carry it with you at all times, and you can be fined quite heavily for overstaying the expiry date, particularly if you have a car.

If you are on an Exchange Programme Visa, do not let US officials take your IAP-66, or any other visa documentation, when you cross into Mexico. You need it to get back into the US!. In London, the Mexican Consulate is at 8 Halkin Street, SW1, (0171) 235-6393; and the Mexican Ministry of Tourism is at 6061 Trafalgar Sq, London WC2N 5DS, (0171) 839-3177. In the US the Mexican Embassy is at 1911 Pennsylvania Ave NW, Washington DC 20006, (202) 728-1600.

GETTING THERE

Most travellers (and certainly the overwhelming majority using this guide) will be visiting Mexico via the US. Major American, Mexican or international carriers fly from Los Angeles, Chicago, New York, Miami, San Antonio and other US and Canadian cities to Mexico City and elsewhere in Mexico. It is usually cheaper to fly to the US and shop around there for a flight to Mexico, rather than fly direct from Europe. But because of the continuing devaluation of Mexican currency, the cheapest way to travel is generally to cross into Mexico by land and then travel on domestic flights purchased in pesos.

The most popular (and often fully booked) flight, at present costing about $260 one-way, $520 round trip, is Mexicana's flight from Los Angeles to Mexico City. Mexicana has offices in most US cities: for up to date information in the UK contact Mexicana Tour, 215 Chalk Farm Rd., Camden Town London, NW1 8AF, (0171) 267-3787. Fax (0171) 267-2004.

Tijuana to Mexico City costs about $364 round-trip although it may be possible to find a cheaper fare by shopping around closer to the time of departure. For info, call Mexicana: 1 (800) 531-7921 or Aeromexico: 1 (800) 237-6639. For brief round-trips from the US, it is worth checking with the various airlines as they all offer competitive (and, at press time, largely unpredictable) fares. Major US carriers flying to Mexico include American, Delta and Continental.

Special deals offering discounts on internal flights within Mexico for those with international return tickets are of limited interest, since they typically apply only to trips originating in Europe, not the US, and carry time and other restrictions. Airlines impose a US$12 departure tax on passengers leaving Mexico.

There are 12 major and a number of minor crossing points along the US-Mexico border. The most important are Tijuana (12 miles south of San

Diego), Calexico-Mexicali, Nogales (south of Tucson), Douglas/Agua Prieta, El Paso/Ciudad Juárez, Eagle Pass/Piedras Negras, Laredo/Nuevo Laredo, Hidalgo/Reynosa and Brownsville/Matamoros. If you have a car, the smaller border crossings (such as Tecate, 40 miles east of San Diego) are often less bureaucratic. Car travellers should avoid Tijuana, especially on weekends. There are generally long delays caused by extensive searches for drugs and aliens. El Paso/Ciudad Juárez border is often mentioned by readers as the easiest crossing: 'Mexican officials didn't pay any attention to us'. Matamoros may be the most corrupt: 'We refused to pay a bribe and were kicked out of the country'. Bribees are usually satisfied with US$5; principles notwithstanding, paying a *mordida* is usually cheaper and certainly less time-consuming than travelling to another crossing point. Matamoros is the crossing point closest to Mexico City (622 miles/996 kms); first class bus fare is about US$80.

Even from Ciudad Juárez, a much greater distance, first class bus fare is only about US$120. Amtrak goes to the border at El Paso and Laredo from where you make your own arrangements with Mexican National Railways. Trains also leave daily from Mexicali to Mexico City, but the distance makes it a dreadful trip. It's relatively cheap at around US$50 for a seat in air conditioned first class or half that if you can tolerate second class.

CAR RENTALS

Reservations for car rentals in Mexico can be made in the US with the major companies (Hertz, Avis, Budget, Dollar, Thrifty and National, etc.). The major international car hire companies, plus of course many Mexican companies, have offices throughout the country. In theory all the companies in Mexico charge the same rates for any given car type, as rates are set by the Government, but shopping around, especially among smaller local companies, can often get you significant savings. The official rates are based on time + kilometres at inland towns and daily rates including 200 km/day on the coast. Be sure to check on extra costs for insurance, and to determine whether you are dealing in miles or kilometres. Car hire is not especially inexpensive in Mexico. Expect to pay the cheapest around US$29 per day or $175 per week.

When you drive in Mexico you need to carry a proof of Mexican auto liability insurance which is usually provided by the car rental company. An international driver's license should be used, available from AAA in the US and Canada or in the United Kingdom from RAC or AA.

GEOGRAPHY AND CLIMATE

Running from north to south, the two chains of the Sierra Madre dominate and dictate the country's geography and climate. The vast central plateau lies between the mountain ranges and drops to the Rió Grande valley in the north. Around the area of the capital, just south of the Tropic of Cancer, there is a further jumble of mountains, finally petering out in the narrow and comparatively flat Isthmus of Tehuantepec. From Tijuana in the northwest to Mérida in the Yucatán, Mexico stretches for 2750 miles.

Between the altitudes of 5000 and 8000 feet the climate is mild. The descent to sea level corresponds to an increase in temperature, so that the

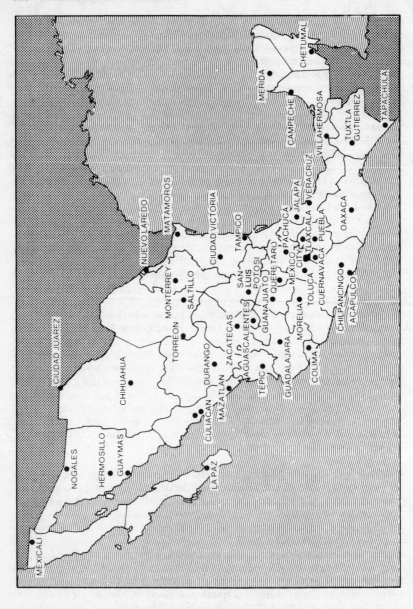

lowlands are very hot in summer as well as being very warm in winter. The Central Plateau, where Mexico City is located (altitude 7350 feet), enjoys a pleasant, springlike climate. It is warm and sunny throughout the year, although regular afternoon showers or storms can be expected from June to October, the Rainy Season.

In the deserts of northern Mexico and throughout Baja California, temperatures of over 100°F are to be expected during the summer months. It is similarly hot on the coast, although the sea breezes are cooling. But in the lush tropical jungle lands to the south of the Tropic of Cancer, humidity is high and the annual rainfall is nearly as great as anywhere else in the world. On the northern side of the Isthmus of Tehuantepec, rainfall reaches a staggering 10 feet a year. The large numbers of rivers and the frequency with which they become rushing, swollen torrents make the land impassable by permanent rail or road systems.

WHAT TO WEAR

Light clothing made of natural fibres (cotton, etc.) is recommended. Bring a jacket or something warmer for Mexico City and the Central Plateau's cool evenings, plus raingear for the rainy season. Shoes, rather than sandals, are a necessity for uneven streets and climbing up pyramids.

Lavenderías automáticas (laundromats) and *tintorerías* (dry cleaners) can be found in larger towns and cities. Many hotels also offer their own laundry service. In smaller places you'll have to rely on two stones and the washing powder you have remembered to pack along with the spare plug for the sink.

TIME ZONES

Virtually all of Mexico, from the Yucatán to the Pacific due west of Mexico City, falls within the zone corresponding to Central Standard Time in the US. The west coast from Tepic up to the border, and including the southern half of Baja California, is an hour earlier, while the northern half of Baja is an hour earlier still and corresponds to Pacific Standard Time in the US. The Mexicans stay on Standard Time throughout the year.

MEXICO AND ITS PEOPLE

Modern Mexico is the product of three distinct historical phases: pre-Columbian (or pre-Cortés) Indian, three centuries of Spanish colonial rule, and since 1821 independent Mexican government. The Revolution of 1910 was followed by ten years of near-anarchy during which one in every eight Mexicans was killed, and although the peasants played a crucial role in overthrowing the corrupt aristocracy, in the end it was (and is) the middle classes who have benefited from the uninterrupted tenure of the Institutional Revolutionary Party (PRI) since 1929. There is at present a higher percentage of landless peasants than when the Revolution began, and the poor live in overcrowded slums where illiteracy is common, malnutrition rampant and basic services often non-existent.

There are however some indications of improvement, albeit very slow improvement. The country is not as desperately poor as it was and the government appears to be making real efforts to root out some of the social ills.

Until now the benefits of industrial and agricultural development have been defeated by the explosive population growth. Although the area of harvestable land has doubled since 1940, the population has risen from 20 million to over 86 million in the same period, and half of these are under fifteen years of age.

Despite relatively successful efforts made to increase earnings from tourism and manufacturing industries, Mexico's economy still relies heavily on oil exports. Mexico is the world's second largest debtor with its external debt at a level of over US$100 billion. It is, however, considered a model debtor by the International Monetary Fund and the international financial community in general, as it has not declared a moratorium on its debt and has implemented a series of economic austerity programmes.

Despite gestures of independence most notably the nationalisation of the oil industry in 1938. Mexico seeks foreign investment and to a great extent is economically dependent on its neighbour to the north. Currently, hopes are pinned on NAFTA—the North American Free Trade Agreement—which will give Mexican business direct access to the US and Canada, and vice versa. The relationship, however, remains epitomised by the ceaseless flow of undocumented immigrants across the US border, and by the steady growth of *maquiladora* (in-bond manufacturing) industries on the Mexican side whereby US companies can take advantage of cheap Mexican labour to produce US products.

POLITICS

At first glance, Mexican politics appears to be an alphabet soup of letters with the parties known as PAN, PRD, PDM, PRT, PARM and of course, PRI. PRI is the Partido Revolucionario Institucional. The party is not very revolutionary but is certainly institutional since it is the most popular and largest party in Mexico, having ruled the country since 1929. The participation and activity of the opposition parties have increased considerably in recent years but as yet they have been unable to topple the PRI's domination. President Ernesto Zedillo Ponce de León won the 1994 election. Mexican presidents cannot be re-elected and hold office for six years. Zedillo got off to a difficult start, being snubbed by the opposition parties, the PRD and PAN, and having to deal with continued unrest in the province of Chiapas.

CULTURE

Mexico is a fascinating and colourful country, physically and culturally, bridging the gap between America North and South. It is a feast of art and history, with more than 11,000 archaeological sites, temples, pyramids and palaces of bygone civilisations, and many museums which are generally regarded as being among the best in the world. (See box) Although Mexico City and resort towns like Acapulco have their share of tall buildings, expensive hotels and general North American glitter, rural Mexico is something else again and the whole pace of life visibly alters the moment you cross the border from the United States.

Three centuries of Spanish rule have left their mark not only on the lifestyle of the country but also on its appearance. The fusion of Spanish baroque with the intricate decorative style of the Indians produced the distinctive and dramatic style called Mexican Colonial. A number of towns rich in Mexican Colonial buildings are preserved as national monuments and new building is forbidden. The most important colonial towns are: Guadalajara, León, Guanajuato, San Miguel de Allende, Morelia, Taxco, Cholula, Puebla and Mérida.

Despite its Spanish architectural and linguistic overtones, Mexico has a distinctly Indian soul: fatalistic, taciturn, reflective and strong on tradition and folklore. You will notice this most sharply in the villages, where it is easy to misinterpret the dignified shyness of the villagers as coldness. Various towns stand out as being Indian in character: Querétaro (where the Mexican constitution was drafted in 1917), Pátzcuaro, Oaxaca, Tehuantepec and San Cristóbal de las Casas. Not to be missed are Indian market days and festivals. Toluca, an hour's drive from Mexico City, has an outstanding Indian market.

MONEY
The exchange rate with the US dollar is (at press time) about N$7.80. Considering the continuous drop in the Mexican peso against the dollar since December 1994, this rate may easily vary in the coming months. The prices given in this section use the above exchange rate.

The Mexican peso is denoted by the symbol N$, meaning *peso nuevo* (new peso). This is to differentiate the new currency from the old peso (still in circulation, although in small amounts). Mexico introduced the new currency in 1993, to simplify calculations. One new peso equals 1000 old pesos. Banknotes in 10, 20, 50, 100, 200, and 500 N$ denominations and coins units of 1, 2, 5, and 10 new pesos are in circulation.

Mexico uses the $ sign for the peso, unfortunately the same as the US dollar sign; where necessary the two are distinguished by the addition of the suffixes MN (*Moneda Nacional*) for pesos and US or 'dls' for dollars. Important note: all peso prices in this section are written as—pesos. US dollar prices are given as US$.

Shop around for the best exchange rates, especially in the large cities and resort areas. Generally the best rates can be obtained at the *casas de cambio* (money exchanges). Try to avoid the hotels for changing money if possible. Many larger stores and some market vendors will accept dollars but check carefully on the rates they are using.

Banks: Banking hours are 9 am-1:30 pm Monday-Friday. (The *casas de cambio* are usually open till around 5 pm.) The larger banks (Bánamex, Bancomer) are the best for changing money if there are no *casas de cambio* around in the provinces. Major credit cards are accepted in most places but the cheaper hotels and restaurants may not take them. Don't take it for granted—always ask first.

Tipping and Tax: 10-15 percent is the standard tip. Service charges are very rarely added to the bill when you receive it so they must be determined by the total before tax. Almost everything you have to buy or pay for, including hotels and restaurant food, has IVA (*Impuesto al valor agregado*)—value added tax—on it which may be included or shown separately.

DISCOVERING MEXICO'S ANCIENT CIVILIZATIONS

Aztecs, Mayas, Mixtecs, Olmecs, Toltecs, Zapotecs—great civilizations have flourished in Mexico for at least 4000 years. To discover their fascinating remains and share their drama, you'll have to journey to the south of the country, where each state's tourism secretariat can provide you with maps, information on tours, brochures and other assistance about the main sites and how to get to them.

Highly recommended, before going to the field, is a first stop in Mexico City at the excellent Museo Nacional de Antropologia, located at Paseo de la Reforma and Calzada Gandí in Bosques de Chapultepec. Mon-Fri 9 am-6 pm, Sat & Sun 10 am-6 pm. For information, call (5) 553-1902. Also look in at the Museo Nacional de Culturas Populares, located at Calle Hídalgo #289, Colonia Coyoacan, also in Mexico City. Mon-Sat 10 am-8 pm, Sun 11 am-5 pm. For information, call (5) 658-1265.

Mexico's pre-Columbian heritage is often divided into three distinct periods: pre-classic (2000 BC to 200 AD); classic (200 AD to 900 AD); and post-classic (900 AD to the Spanish conquest in 1521 AD). This is where to find the main centres.

PRE-CLASSIC—2000 BC to 200 AD
The Olmecs founded one of the earliest great civilizations of Mesoamerica, which is often considered the "mother culture" of the regions. Early advances in agriculture led to the rise of Olmec towns and ceremonial centers in what are now the states of Veracruz and Tabasco. Staple crops of the Olmecs included beans, corn, and squash, though the Olmec diet may have at times included other humans. The Olmecs domesticated dogs and turkeys, had an elaborate religious ceremony and structure, and are famous for their stone carvings, including monumental stone heads between 1.5 and 3 meters tall weighing up to 20 tons.

The primary Olmec cities were Tres Zapotes and La Venta. La Venta, 84 miles west of Villahermosa in Tabasco, is still an interesting site to visit, even though the archaeological finds were transferred in toto to escape destruction from oil drilling in the 1950s. Many colossal Olmec heads of basalt can be seen at the archaeological museum in Mexico City, the Tabasco Museum in Villahermosa, and at Parque Museo La Venta, on Rte. 180 near the airport. Apart from three large stone heads, La Venta has stelae, altars, mosaics and a model of the original city. Self-guided tour map, US$1, daily 9 am-5 pm. For tourist information in Villahermosa, call (93) 16-10-80, 16-50-93, or 16-51-22, Avenida Los Rios #203, in front of the newspaper building Tabasco Hoy. Tourist information can also be found at tourist information booths in the bus stations, railway stations, airport, and around town.

The Zapotecs inhabited what is now Oaxaca in southern Mexico. Their primary city was Monte Albán (the 'White City'), the elaborate ruins of which can still be explored today. The region was later conquered by **the Mixtecs**, who were skilled craftsmen in precious metals, ceramics, and mosaics. For information and maps in Oaxaca, call (951) 6-07-17

CLASSIC —200 AD-900 AD
The dominant influence of the classic period is **the Mayan** civilization. The Maya were the largest homogenous group of Indians north of Perú, and their society stretched from present-day Honduras throughout the Yucatán peninsula. Approximately 6 million Maya inhabit the area today.

The Maya built massive pyramids throughout Central America, including the impressive sites at Uxmal and Chichén Itzá at the tip of the Yucatán and at the ancient partially excavated city of Palenque. For maps and information on reaching these sites call (99) 24-8002 in Mérida, Yucatan.

UXMAL and CHICHEN ITZA   Along with Palenque, Uxmal was one of the chief Mayan cities and the showpiece of that civilization's finest architectural accomplishments. Chichén Itzá, on the other hand, was first a Mayan city and later occupied and built on by the belligerent Toltecs, becoming in the process the most stupendous city in the Yucatán.

Fifty miles of good road lead from Mérida to **Uxmal**, where the clean, open lines of the ancient city create an impression of serenity and brilliant organization on a par with the greatest cities of either Eastern or Western civilization at that time. As white as marble and gilded by the sunshine, the limestone complex of the Nunnery Quadrangle, the Palace of the Governor and the Pyramid of the Soothsayer has a fascinating and almost modern beauty. The friezes of the palaces are decorated with stone mosaics in intricate geometric designs. Daily 9 am-5 pm, US$4.50, free on Sundays.

In the 10th century the peaceful Mayan world was disturbed by the war-like Toltecs, who came down from their northern plateau capital of Tula to conquer the Yucatán cities and make **Chichén Itzá** their southern capital. The monumental constructions you see there are both Mayan (eg. El Caracol, the circular observatory) and Toltec (eg. the Court of a Thousand Columns). The city is dominated by the Great Pyramid, the Temple of Kukulcán, with its stairways of 91 steps on each of four sides, making a total of 364. That figure plus one step round the top totals the days in the year. Other points of interest include the Ball Court and its inscriptions and the Sacred Well into which human sacrifices were hurled.

PALENQUE   About 80 miles inland from Villahermosa are the jungle ruins of the classic Mayan sacred city of Palenque, which flourished AD 300-700. Built on the first spurs of the Usumacinta Mountains, the gleaming white palaces, temples and pyramids rise from the high virgin jungle. Its visually compelling site, compact size (the excavated portion is about three-quarters of a mile by half a mile, out of the 20-square-mile extent of the city) and its dramatic burial chamber make Palenque, to many minds, more outstanding than Chichén Itzá. The 1950 discovery of an ornate crypt containing fantastically jade-bedecked remains of a Mayan priest-king revised archaeologists' theories about Mayan pyramids, which were earlier believed to be mere supports for the temples on top. Although it's a hot, steep and slippery journey, you should climb the Temple of the Inscriptions, descend the 80 feet into its crypt to view the bas-reliefs: chilling and wonderful. Maps and site information are available in Palenque or Chiapas, call (961) 2-45-35 or (961) 3-93-96/99.

The Maya developed advanced mathematics, astronomy, and writing systems. Religious ceremony was central to Maya culture, which at times included human sacrifice. Losers of sporting events might also expect to be beheaded, or tied into a ball and rolled down the steep steps of a pyramid. Although the ancient Maya shared a common culture, like the ancient Greeks they were politically divided into as many as 20 sovereign states, rather than ruled by a unified empire. Such division may ultimately have led to constant warfare and the eventual downfall of their civilization. In addition to the main Mayan sites mentioned here, there are many smaller ruins scattered throughout the Yucatán, such as those at Tulum on the Caribbean coast.

POST-CLASSIC 900 AD-1521 AD.
The Toltecs were mighty warriors who occupied the northern section of the

Valley of Mexico. Their primary city was Tula, approximately 80 km north of Mexico City, where the Temple of Tlahuizcalpantecuhtli was built (yes, Tlahuizcalpantecuhtli). Giant stone warriors, standing nearly 5 meters high, guard the temple.

The Toltecs conquered the city of Teotihuacán, near present-day Mexico City. Teotihuacán is one of the most important ceremonial centers in ancient Mesoamerica, and includes the massive Pyramid of the Sun, 63 meters high, and the Pyramid of the Moon, 42 meters high. The Toltecs spread the cultural influence of the Teotihuacanos, including the cult of Quetzálcoatl (the 'Sovereign Plumed Serpent'), throughout their empire. The rise of the Toltecs, however, transformed much of Mesoamerica from a theocracy to a warrior aristocracy.

The Aztecs, who sometimes referred to themselves as the Mexicas, created the most complex culture in all of Mesoamerica. Their primary city was Tenochtitlán, built in 1325 on small islands in Lake Texcoco where modern-day Mexico City is located. According to legend, the site was chosen when the wandering Aztecs came upon an eagle perched upon a cactus eating a snake, fulfilling a prophecy. Today, the Mexican flag incorporates this scene.

Influenced by the Toltecs, the focus of Aztec life was war and conquest. Only the Incas in Peru had a larger empire in the Americas. However, the Aztecs also built great cities, developed a sophisticated calendar, devised a system of imperial administration and tribute, and made great advances in agriculture.

Among their many gods, the Aztecs continued to worship Quetzálcoatl. When the Spanish arrived in Mexico in 1519, with their light skin and hair, horses, muskets, armour, and great sailing ships, many Aztecs believed their leader, Hernan Cortés, to be Quetzálcoatl. Ultimately, Cortés, aided by Indian tribes who had been mistreated by the Aztecs, was able to conquer Tenochtitlán and overthrow the mighty Aztec empire.

Unfortunately, the Spanairds did a thorough job in eliminating much of the Aztec civilization. Virtually nothing remains of the giant pyramids dedicated to Tlaloc the rain god and Huitzilpochtli the sun god. Some minor remains of the ancient city of Tenochtitlán are located in the suburbs of Mexico City, and some smaller pyramids can be found at Santa Cecilia, Calixtlahuaca, and particularly Malinalco, some 48 km from Toluca, where there are temples dedicated to two Aztec military orders, the Knights of the Jaguar and the Knights of the Eagle. Other Aztec artifacts can be viewed in the Museo Nacional de Antropologia in Mexico City.

WHAT TO SEE NEAR MEXICO CITY
The **Pyramids of Teotihuacan** and **Temple of Quetzálcoatl**. Take Metro to Indios Verdes (last station on north end of line 3), then take bus (50 pesos) marked 'Pyramids'. (NB: no backpackers on Metro.) Frequent buses from Terminal del Norte direct to site, $1^1/_2$ hrs each way. US$1.10. The temples are part of the ruins of the once-great city built even before the Aztecs. The Pyramid of the Sun is 216 ft high (248 steps to the top where the sacrifices were made) and the older Pyramid of the Moon, $^1/_4$ mile away, although less vast, is just as impressive. The Temple of Quetzálcoatl is about $^1/_2$ mile from the pyramids and has some superb Toltec carvings. Daily 8 am-5 pm, US$4 except holidays and Sundays. When climbing pyramids, take care—they're very steep. Traders everywhere—even at the top of the pyramids selling fake artifacts that 'they made at home'. *Son et lumière* six nights per week, in English at 7 pm (not June-Sept).

HEALTH

Medical services are good, and in Mexico City it's easy to find an English-speaking doctor. Fees are reasonable compared to the US, and some hospitals will examine you and give prescriptions free. Nevertheless, where a fee is likely you should ask for a quote beforehand, and insurance is advisable.

'If you travel in the US before Mexico, you'll hear many ghastly tales of internal infections and uncontrollable bacteria, even though the water is so chlorinated that you're more likely to kill off your own bacteria than find any new ones.'

For the long term traveller, acclimatisation is the best policy, but it can take from three days to four weeks. If needed, you can stop *turista* spoiling a brief trip by using Lomotil (which delays the symptoms but will not remove the cause), or Pepto-Bismol, the antibiotic Bactrim, or Kaomycin. Entero-Vioform may still sometimes be on sale, despite being banned everywhere else. It makes you go blind.

If you have decided *not* to 'get used to it', then be cautious. Drink only bottled water. If you are not sure about the water, boil it for 30 minutes or use purification tablets. Be careful when buying food from street vendors: is the fat rancid? Beware of ice cream, salads, unpeeled fruit and vegetables washed in impure water. Eating plenty of garlic, onions and lime juice (which act as natural purifiers and preventatives) may help, but need to be taken in large quantities. *Té de Perro* (dog tea), fresh coconut juice and plain boiled white rice are the native Mexican recommendations.

Anti-malarial drugs are advisable in tropical and southern coastal areas—but as Mexico denies (perhaps rightly) that it has malaria, it's difficult to get any drugs for it there, so bring them with you. It wouldn't hurt to have inoculations against yellow fever, cholera, typhoid and polio, especially if you travel to coastal areas in the south.

'It helps to warn people but hopefully they won't be frightened off.'

It is better to travel with health insurance, available in the United Kingdom from The Assoc. of British Ins., 51 Gresham St., London EC2V 7HQ, tel. (0171) 600-3333.

LANGUAGE

The more alert among you will have guessed by now that it's Spanish, although in some areas Indian languages are still spoken—e.g. Mayan in the Yucatán. The point is, you should learn some Spanish, especially the words for numbers, food and directions. 'Well worth learning some Spanish if you can: don't expect too many Mexicans to know English.' Your efforts in Spanish will normally be encouraged and appreciated by the local people.

COMMUNICATIONS

Mail: Do not have mail sent *Lista de Correos* (Poste Restante) unless you are sure of being able to collect it within 10 days. After that time it is likely to be 'lost'. Letters or postcards to North America are US$0.45; to Europe, US$0.50; to Australia and New Zealand, US$0.65. Important mail should be sent registered mail from a post office, and never put in an ordinary letter box. 'Send mail only from post offices—letter boxes not reliable.'

Chances are that packages sent in or out of the country will not make it to their destination. There are telegraph offices (*Telegrafos Naçionales*) in all cities and towns and many villages too. Domestic cables are cheap and a good way to communicate with other travellers. International cable service is also good and the 'night letter' service, sent after 7 pm, is a good value. Public telex and fax facilities can be found in the larger cities.

Telephones: Public phone booths are found in most cities and larger towns. Elsewhere make use of telephones in stores, tobacco stands, hotels, etc. Public phones with direct dial long distance service (national and international), identified as 'Ladatel' are now being installed in the larger cities. To make a call from one city to another in Mexico, dial 91 + the city code + and the number. Note that the number of digits in phone numbers is not standardized across Mexico. From other public phones dial 02 for the long distance operator for calls within Mexico or 09 for the international operator. In smaller towns look for the '*Larga distancia*' sign outside a store or cafe in the centre of town. Collect calls (reverse charges) are called *llamadas a cobrar*.

Some important phone numbers used throughout Mexico are: emergency assistance—91(5) 250-0123 & 91(5) 5-250-0151; local information 04; country-wide information 01.

For calls to the UK, Ireland or other European countries the code is: 98, then 00 44 for the UK. For the US or Canada the code is: 95, then dial 001 before the number.

PUBLIC HOLIDAYS
Mexico's religious and political calendar supplies many excuses for public holidays. Expect everything to close down on the following dates:

January 1	New Year's Day	November 1**	All Saints' Day
February 5	Constitution Day	November 2	All Souls' Day
March 21	Juárez Birthday		(or Day of the Dead)
March-April*	Holy Thursday	November 20	Revolution Day
March-April*	Good Friday	December 12**	Our Lady of
May 1	Labor Day		Guadalupe Day
May 5	Battle of Puebla Day	December 24**	Christmas Eve
September 15**	Declaration of	December 25	Christmas Day
	Independence	December 31**	New Year's Eve
September 16	Independence Day	*Date varies with year.	
October 12	Día de la Raza	**Usually working half a day.	

On top of these, every town has its own festival and fiesta days, with processions, fireworks, and dancing in the streets. Local tourist authorities will fill you in on the details.

ELECTRICITY
All Mexico is on 110V, 60 cycles AC—in common with the rest of North America. It's a good idea to take a small torch as electricity can be uncertain, especially in small towns.

SHOPPING
The favourable rate of exchange and colourful markets will tempt even those who hate to shop. Mexico is famous for its arts and crafts and the markets guarantee some of the best entertainment anywhere. Look for woven goods, baskets, pottery, jewelry, leather goods, woodcarving, metalwork and lacquerware. A number of towns or states specialize in a particular craft or style. The

government-run FONART shops feature some of the best local works and will give a general idea of price variations. FONART shops are generally a bit higher and will not bargain, but sometimes the quality is superior to what is available in the market. Prices and quality vary. Be sure to look over everything carefully. The vendor may guarantee that the sarape you're holding is *'pura lana'* but you know acrylic when you see and touch it. Bargaining is a fine art and expected.

'The cheapest market by far for sarapes, ponchos and embroidery is Mitla, near Oaxaca. Knock them down to one-third the asking price, and make rapid decisions in order to keep the price down.'

THE METRIC SYSTEM
Mexico is metric. See appendix.

INFORMATION
There are Mexican Government tourist offices in most US cities and border towns. Here are the main addresses:

New York: 450 Park Ave, Suite 1401, New York, NY,10022, (212) 755-7261, FAX (212) 755-2874, *Houston:* 2707 North Loop West 450, Houston, TX 77008, (713) 880-5153, FAX (713) 880-1833; *Los Angeles:* 10100 Santa Monica Blvd, #224, Los Angeles, CA 90067, (310) 203-8191, FAX (310) 203-8316.

Washington, DC: 1911 Pennsylvania Ave NW, Washington, DC 20006, (202) 728-1600, FAX (202) 728-1758. *Toronto:* 2 Bloor St W, Suite 1801, Toronto, Ontario M4W3E2, (416) 925-0704 or (416) 9251876, FAX (416) 925-6061. *Florida:* 2333 Ponce de Leon Blvd. Suite #710, Coral Gables, FL 77008 (305) 443-9160, FAX (305) 443-1186. *Illinois:* 70 East Lake St. Suite 1413, Chicago, IL (312) 565-2778 , FAX (312) 606-9012.

For information 24 hrs a day, call 1-800-482-9832 .

In London, the Mexican Consulate is at 8 Halkin Street, SW1, (0171) 235-6393; and the Mexican Ministry of Tourism is at 60-61 Trafalgar Sq, London WC2N 5DS, (0171) 734-1058 or (0171) 839-3177. FAX: (0171) 930-9202 Delegate Dr. Gerardo Hemken.

On the internet: *www.mexico—travel.com* for information on the main archeological sites; *www.mexnet.com* for Copper Canyon; and *www.indians.org* for info on ancient cultures.

Once in Mexico itself, tourist information is provided at federal, state and local levels and most towns on the tourist track have at least one information office. Bear in mind that the level of service provided is extremely variable, and in particular do not presume that English will be spoken. You might also find maps, directories and brochures available for free at most airports, bus stations, train stations, subway stations and at the border (look for the booth under the name of **Modulos Paisanos.**

NATIONAL PARKS
'Both Mexican and foreign visitors are admitted from 8 am-5 pm throughout the year', according to the official tourism handbook, but most National Parks are without visible regulation and either merge imperceptibly with the surrounding farmland or are undeveloped and inaccessible wilderness. Don't expect the services of Yosemite or Yellowstone. NB: all beaches in Mexico are federally owned and free.

ON THE ROAD

ACCOMMODATION

The range of **hotel accommodation** in Mexico is wide, from ultra-modern marble skyscrapers, and US-style motels along the major highways, to colonial inns and haciendas to modest guesthouses, called *pensiones or casas de huespedes*. There is also a marked difference between north and south Mexico. In the north of the country hotels tend to be older, often none too clean with bad plumbing, and large noisy ceiling fans to hum you to sleep. In southern Mexico hotels 'are a joy'. They are rarely full and often offer a high standard of comfort and cleanliness at low rates. It is fairly common to find hotels which are converted old aristocratic residences built around a central courtyard. Hoteliers will probably offer you their most expensive room first. A useful phrase in the circumstances is: *Quisiera algo más barato, por favor* (I'd like something cheaper, please). Ask to see the room first: *Quiero ver el cuarto, por favor*. Of course a double room always works out cheaper per person than two singles, but also one double bed—*cama matrimonial*—is cheaper than two beds in a room. On the other hand, cheaper hotels often don't mind how many people take a room. 'Travelling in a group of four, considerable savings are possible. Most hotel beds are big enough for two people; therefore a double-bedded room can accommodate four.'

Prices are fixed, and should be prominently displayed by law; though inflation is moving so fast you should not be surprised if your bill bears little relation to the posted rate. In general you should expect to pay about US$10-$14 per person per night in a basic but tolerable hotel a few blocks from the centre of town. An intermediate standard hotel should cost US$20-$35. It should rarely be *necessary* to pay more than this, though if you want to pay US$140 and up for a US-style resort hotel, that's possible too.

Hotel rates may vary between high and low season. High season extends from mid-December to Easter or the beginning of May, the remaining months being low season. Seasonal variations will be more marked at coastal resorts. *As most travellers using this Guide tour North America, including Mexico, in the summer months, low season rates have been quoted.*

'We notice that cockroaches are mentioned by people assessing places to stay. Even the best hotels are full of them—they are part of the scene and should not be regarded as unusual.'

'As it is rare indeed for Mexican wash basins to have plugs, I would recommend travellers to be equipped with this useful item.'

Hostels: There are two youth hostel organisations, the Mexican 'Villas Deportivas' chain and the International YHA-backed SETEJ establishments. The hostels offer cheap dormitory accommodation and we list them here only when a viable option for the tourist.

In general, however, hostels tend to cater more to a Mexican high school clientele, are some distance from town centres, and are rarely worth the small amount saved compared with a cheap hotel room in a better location. For details contact Turismo Juvenil o Causa Joven Cerapío Rendón #76 Col. San Rafael, México D.F., tel: 91-800-716-0092 or (5) 546-7805 ext. 167 & 199. Young travellers can also obtain a discount card for US$4.00, useful for saving up to 50% on hotels, villas, camp sites, airlines and trains. You need to be 12—29 years old, and bring one passport picture to any of the different offices in Mexico City located at Metro Station #1, Patitlán-Aeropuerto, Insurgentes & Chapultepec. Open Mon.-Fri. from 9 am-3 pm. To get the discount card in other parts of Mexico, call Mr. Agustin JR Plata (5) 705-6072.

Camping: Hotels are so cheap it is difficult to justify taking a tent. Where campsites exist, they tend to double as trailer parks and be some distance from areas of interest. Camping independently in the middle of nowhere is definitely pushing your luck, though in some of the beach resorts, nights under the stars are a feasible option. Those who insist on doing things the hard way should get *The People's Guide to Camping in Mexico*, by Carl Franz (John Muir, $14.95.) The Secretaría de Turísmo publishes a detailed state-by-state guide to campsites (in Spanish), available from tourist offices or from Dirección de Turísmo Social, Mariano Escobedo 726, 11590 México DF; Tel: (5) 254-8967

FOOD AND DRINK

Because high altitude slows digestion, it's customary to eat a large, late, lingering lunch and a light supper. (You may be wise to eat less than usual until your stomach adjusts.) Do not eat unpeeled fruit and avoid drinking tap water, unprocessed milk products and ice cubes.

Stick to bottled mineral water, bottled juices, soft drinks or the excellent Mexican beer. Mexican milkshakes or *licuados* are made with various fruits and are delicious; probably best to avoid *licuados con leche* (those made with milk). Go to a *jugos and licuados* shop for *Watershake*, and home-made fruit ice creams.' 'The most important thing is to eat plenty of limes, garlic and onions—all "natural disinfectants"—we didn't have any stomach troubles.'

Mexican cuisine is much more than tacos and beans but the basic menu revolves around ground maize (first discovered by the Mayans), cheese, tomatoes, beans, rice and a handful of flavourings: garlic, onion, cumin and chilies of varying temperatures. The ground maize flour is made into pancake-shaped *tortillas*, which appear in a variety of dishes and also on their own to be eaten like bread. *Tortillas* are also made with wheat flour: restaurants will customarily ask, *'De maíz o de harina?'* (Do you want corn or flour tortillas?) Enchiladas are tortillas rolled and filled with cheese, beef, etc., baked and lightly sauced. *Tacos, tostadas, flautas* and *chalupas* all use fried tortillas, which are either stacked or filled with cheese, beans, meat, chicken, sauce, etc. *Tamales* use softer corn dough, filled with spicy meat and sauce and wrapped in corn husks to steam through. Other dishes to sample: *pollo con mole* (chicken in a sauce containing chocolate, garlic and other spices), fresh shrimp and fish (often served Veracruz style with green peppers, tomatoes, etc). Beans and rice accompany every meal, even breakfast. A good breakfast dish is *huevos rancheros*, eggs in a spicy tomato-based sauce. Mexico is also noted for its pastries, honey and chocolate drinks.

There are over 80 types of chilies in Mexico ranging in taste from sweet to steamroller hot. The different sauces are served from little containers found on tabletops so the diner can determine how mild or hot the dish will be. Best bargain for lunch is *comida corrida* or *menu de hoy*. This can be a filling four-course meal and cost as little as US$4.

breakfast: *desayuno*	beer: *cerveza*
coffee and a roll: *café con panes*	soft drink: *refresco*
lunch: *almuerzo* (lighter) or *comida*	mineral water: *agua mineral*
dinner/supper: *cena*	bread: *pan*
fixed-price meal: *menú corrida*	potatoes: *papas*
eggs: *huevos*	vegetables (greens): *verduras*
fish: *pescado*	bacon: *tocino*
meat: *carne*	ham: *jamón*
salad: *ensalada*	cheese: *queso*
fruit: *fruta*	

I want something not too spicy, please: *Quiero algo no muy picante, por favor*.

The best-known hard liquor is tequila, a potent clear drink made from the maguey plant tasting 'similar to kerosene'. The sharp-spiked maguey is also the source for other highly-intoxicating liquors such as aguamiel, pulque, and mezcal. Look for the fat worm at the bottom of mezcal. It guarantees that you have the real thing. If you don't drink it (and by the time you reach the bottom of the bottle you won't know or care), some people like to fry them for snacks. Margarita cocktails are made with tequila but are primarily popular with turistas. The Mexicans prefer to take their tequila neat with a little salt and lime on the back of the hand. Mexico produces some decent wines but is famous for its beer; don't pass up Dos Equis dark.

TRAVEL

Now for your basic Spanish travel vocabulary: please—*por favor*; thank you—*gracías*; bus—*autobús*; train—*tren* or *ferrocarril*; plane—*avión*; auto—*carro*; ticket—*boleto*; second class—*segunda clase*; first class—*primera clase*; first class reserved seat (on trains)—*primera especial*; sleeping car—*coche dormitorio*; which platform?—*cuál andén?* which departure door/gate?—*cuál puerta?* What time?—*A qué hora?* And inevitably: How many hours late are we?—*Cuántas horas de retraso tenemos?* Street—*calle*; arrival—*llegada*; departure—*salida*; detour—*desviación*; north—*norte*; south—*sur*; east—*este* or *oriente* (and abbreviated *Ote*); west—*oeste* or *poniente* (abbreviated *Pte*). Junction—*empalme*; indicates a route where one must change buses/trains; avoid *empalmes* at all costs. Also, these will be useful : I need your help—*Necesito que me ayude, por favor*; Where is the bathroom, please—*Dónde está el baño, por favor*.

Bus: Bus travel is the most popular means of transportation for Mexicans. Buses cost a bit more than trains, but will cut travelling times by anything from a quarter to a half and in any case are absurdly inexpensive by American or European standards: Tijuana to Mexico City (1871 miles/2995 kms) costs about US$65. All seats are reserved on first class (*primera*) buses, but 'beware of boarding a bus where there are no seats left—you may be standing for several hours for first class fare'. Sometimes it's advisable to book for second class also although in southern Mexico a reader advises: 'Normally there are no standby passengers on first class and you get a reserved seat; on second class buses this is rarely the case'. Standards of comfort, speed, newness of buses, etc., vary more between bus lines than between first and second class, although second class will invariably be slower (sometimes days slower with attendant expenses) and cheaper on longer runs. 'Mexico City to Mazatlán, on a second class bus, took 24 hours. Scenery superb, driving horrifying. Great journey.' Travellers generally recommend deluxe or first class buses: 'By far the best—quite exciting, cheap, fast'. Most towns have separate terminals for first and second class buses. Always take along food, a sweater (for over-air-conditioned vehicle) and toilet paper.

When making reservations you are always allotted a particular seat on a particular bus so if you want a front seat book a couple of days ahead. No refunds are made if you miss the bus; and be careful of buying a ticket for a bus which is just pulling out of the bus station! No single carrier covers the whole country and in some areas as many as 20 companies may be in competition, and while this doesn't mean much variation in fares, it can mean a big difference in service. Greyhound passes are not valid in Mexico, though by waving a student card you can sometimes get a substantial discount—though really this is only for Mexican students during vacations.

Though you shouldn't have too much faith in the precision of its contents, ask for *un horario*—a timetable—showing all bus lines and issued free.
Bus Information from Mexico City.
Transportes del Norte: (5) 587-5511
Transportes Nacionales Terrestres (TNT)
North: (5) 567-9466 **South:** (5) 587-5219
Poniente: (5) 273-0251
Transportes Futurama: (5) 271-0578 or (5) 729-0729
Central del Sur: (5) 522-1111
Transportes de Occidente: (5) 271-0499

Rail: The trains are operated by Mexican National Railways ('N de M' or simply 'Ferrocarriles'). There has been a marked improvement in the quality and speed of the main passenger services—*Servicio Estrella*—in the last few years although in most cases trains are still slower than the buses. The food on board is generally inexpensive and the scenery always magnificent once you are out of the cities. Students can sometimes get a discount. You should avoid travelling on or around any of the main public holidays as the trains get packed. The *Servicio Estrella* trains generally have *Primera Especial*, air-conditioned coaches which are to be recommended whenever available. Overnight trains have sleeping cars with two types of accommodation, *camarín*—berth for 1 and *alcoba* for 2. Reservations should be made in advance for these services at the station of departure (Central reservations in Mexico City, Tel: (5) 682-6213 or (5) 682-7043). Other trains have *Primera Regular* and *Segunda Clase*—much cheaper, no air conditioning and no reserved seats. The toilets are generally dreadful and vendors pass frequently through the coaches selling food, soft drinks and other items. If you travel in *Primera Regular* or *Segunda*, it's best to take your own food and water for drinking and washing. 'If possible choose a carriage far from the station entrance and get a seat in the middle of the carriage, away from the loos and women with screaming babies.' 'Despite discomforts, second-class was great fun—marketplace for parakeets, avocados, tequila, lugubrious serenades by buskers at 2 am for which the Mexicans—incredibly—gave money.' 'Very useful rail timetable for Mexico from Mexican Tourist Office in New Orleans.'

'You dismiss second class rail travel, but huge savings can be made this way for starvation budget travellers who are prepared to rough it. And rough it is the word. You are not guaranteed a seat (they are terribly uncomfortable), toilet facilities are awful, and nighttime finds people bedding down on the floors. My journey from Mexicali to Mexico City took three nights and two days (24 hours longer than by bus) with a five-hour stopover at Guadalajara. But you become totally immersed in Mexican life. The train stops about every 10 miles and this brings all the villagers to the trackside to sell cooked food, fruit and juices. The further you travel southwards the more people board the train to sell their wares.' 'Second class is fine. Lots of room, seats reasonable, loos, as always, revolting. Definitely recommended as a cheap, fun way of travelling.'

Particularly recommended routes are: through the northern desert between Monterrey and San Luis Potosí (10 hours); and from Chihuahua through the spectacular Tarahumara (or Copper) Canyon (four times wider than the Grand Canyon) and down to the west coast at Los Mochis. Enroute the train passes through 87 tunnels, crosses over 36 bridges, crosses the Continental Divide three times, and climbs to 8071 feet at the track's highest point. The Canyon is the home of the semi-nomadic Tarahumara Indians. Stop off at Créel if you want to visit them.

Air: If time is short you may well want to consider city hopping by air. Although obviously more expensive than bus or train, the plane wins hands down for comfort and will give you more time in the places you really want to visit. Mexicana operates the largest number of domestic services (see the 'Getting There' section). Other destinations are served by Aeromexico (which also flies to Paris and Madrid as well as several US cities), AeroCalifornia and Aeromar.

Car: Taking a car to Mexico offers the prospect of unlimited freedom of movement, but also of unlimited hassles if you fall afoul of Mexican bureaucracy. First, you need a car permit, which is issued with your tourist card, and the card itself is specially stamped. (The permit is not strictly necessary for Baja-only trips.) You cannot then leave Mexico without your car; if called away in an emergency, you must pay Mexican customs to look after it until your return, and in theory if the vehicle is written off in an accident it must be hauled back to the border at your expense. Airlines are not allowed to sell international tickets to visitors with the special card, without proof that the vehicle has been lodged with the authorities.

At the border you must produce a valid licence and registration certificate. A UK licence is likely to produce incomprehension in the average Mexican traffic cop: an international one is recommended.

Only Mexican **insurance** is valid in Mexico. You can get it at the border where 24-hour insurance brokers exist for the purpose. It is advisable to increase public liability and property damage coverage beyond the minimum. If you are involved in an accident, the golden rule is to get out of the way as quickly as possible before the police arrive: they tend to keep all parties concerned—whether responsible or not—in jail until claims are settled. A convincing level of insurance may assist your quick release.

Some practical concerns: do not try to drive your Cadillac or BMW from Los Angeles to Oaxaca. Choose a rugged vehicle and take plenty of spares: basic VWs, Dodges and Fords are manufactured in Mexico and are most easily repairable. VW buses are the best for small groups. All main roads are patrolled by the Green Angels fleet, radio coordinated patrol cars with English speaking two man crews (*Angeles Verdes*) in Mexico City (5) 250-8221, Monterrey N.L. (8) 40-21-13, Chihuahua Chih. (14) 29-33-00, Acapulco (74) 83-84-70. They are equipped to handle minor repairs, give first aid and supply information: a raised hood will convey your need of assistance.

Garage repairs are reported as 'often incredibly cheap, particularly if you avoid 'authorised dealers', where you should expect to pay through the nose. Get a quote first!' Although you are not permitted to sell your car in Mexico, in theory you can do so in Guatemala and Belize, though these days purchasers are hard to find.

Pemex, the nationalised gasoline supplier, produces two grades of petrol. 'Don't buy cheap gas. Pemex Nova caused our car to shudder and stall. A mixture of Nova and the (better quality) Extra was a vast improvement.' Extra is however hard to find outside the larger towns, and some travellers detune their vehicles to take low-grade fuel.

It's important to note that all US cars manufactured after 1975 require unleaded gasoline. Outside the big cities unleaded petrol is undependable or not to be found and the use of anything else may damage the catalytic converter and ruin the entire engine. Garage attendants are notorious for swindling tourists: watch the dial carefully. Fuel itself is very cheap, at about US$0.35 per litre. 'Never let the gas level go low, and fill up at every opportunity. Gas stations are few and far between in remoter areas.'

Mexico has good main highways. Petrol stations (Pemex) are infrequent on the road, but most villages will have a 'vendor de gasolina', who will sell you a can-full and syphon it into your tank. Ask: *Dónde se vende gasolina aquí, por favor?* Once off major highways, be on the alert. Branches or rocks strewn across the road are an indication of a hazard ahead. Watch for pot-holes, rocks and narrow bridges (*puente angosto*), and slow down in advance of the sometimes vicious 'speed bumps' (*topes*) near roadside communities. Unless absolutely necessary, *do not drive at night*: many Mexican drivers rarely use headlights, and wandering cattle, donkeys, hens and pedestrians never do.

Car theft is a frequent occurrence: it is worth paying extra for a hotel with a secure car park. And US plates tend to attract the meticulous attention of traffic police. 'You are considered fair game for police along the road, who will stop you and fine you for 'speeding'. Haggle with them—they always come down to five to ten dollars. One man was asleep in his car in Nuevo Laredo when he was arrested for speeding: the car was parked at the time.'

'Drivers should be warned that after entering the country there is a 'free zone' of about 100 miles, with three or four customs stations along the road. You will have to bribe at least one official in order not to have your car ripped apart. But once you leave the 'free zone' you will have no more problems with customs and hardly see any police.'

Mexico's principal highways lead from Nogales, Juárez, Piedras Negras, Nuevo Laredo, Reynosa and Matamoros, all on the border, to Mexico City. The most expensive road in the world is the new toll highway from Mexico City to the Pacific coast resorts, including Acapulco. It costs $82 to drive the full length.

The most scenic road in Mexico is the well-maintained 150D which sweeps through the Puebla Valley past the volcanic peaks of Popocatépetl and Orizaba, climbs into lush rain forests and down through foothills covered with flowers and coffee plantations, to end up in the flat sugarcane country around Veracruz. Note, however, that wherever a car is a definite advantage over the comprehensive bus network, a pretty sturdy vehicle is often needed: this is particularly true in Baja, where a four wheel drive is a major asset.

Some signs: *Alto*—Stop; *No se estacione*—no parking; *bajada frene con motor*— steep hill, use low gear; *vado a 70 metros*—ford 70 metres; *cruce de peatones*— pedestrian crossing; *peligro*—danger; *camino sinuoso*—winding road; (*tramo de*) *curvas peligrosas*—(series of) dangerous curves; *topes a 150 metros*—speed bumps 150 metres; *Ote* (abbr.)—east; *Pte* (abbr.)—west.

Urban Travel: Most cities of any size have a good public transport service on buses, minibuses or converted vans. The flat fare is usually about US$0.60. When choosing a destination note that *Centro* is the centre of town and *Central* is the bus station.

Hitching: Can be hazardous with long waits (not just for a lift but for a car to come along) in high temperatures. However . . . 'found hitching pretty easy in northern Mexico. If you don't speak Spanish at all (like me) show a sign saying *estudiante* and giving your destination. Plan your trip with a map and accept rides only to places you know, unless the driver can make it clear to you in any other language.' 'Water in the desert, I never realised how important it was. Anyone hitching should take a water canteen.' Hitching is *not* recommended for women.

For Women Alone: For better or worse, *machismo* is alive and well in Mexico. The causes and results of *machismo* are frequently discussed and written about but it still doesn't make things any easier for women. Males from 8 to 80 feel compelled to remark on a woman's (and especially a foreigner's) legs, arms, breasts, hair, eyes, etc. In a country of dark-haired people, light or blonde hair has come to symbolize sexiness or higher status. Bare arms and legs, no bra and a casual manner signify that a woman is free and easy. Use common sense—don't hitchhike or enter cantinas. The best way to deal with hassles is to say nothing and continue walking. If possible, travel with a male friend (although *machos* will still try to pick you up) or a couple of women friends.

'I travelled alone and despite many warnings (mostly from US citizens!) I felt very safe. Mexicans seem more curious and friendly than anything else. Not at all like southern Europe.'

FURTHER READING

For anyone planning more than a brief trip to Mexico the following are recommended for additional information.

Let's Go: Mexico. Annually updated, group-researched 560 page guide, full of detailed background and essential practical information. Pan 1993. Price £10.99.

The Rough Guide to Mexico, by John Fisher. More personal guide covering roughly the same ground; slightly less detailed but a smoother read. Harrap-Columbus. Price £9.99.

Mexico: a travel survival kit. A high quality, thorough updating of this excellent guide. Lonely Planet 1997 (6th Edition). Price £14.99.

Insight Guide to Mexico. Interestingly written and illustrated combination of travel guide and historical/sociological portrait. APA Publications 1991. Price £14.99.

Baedeker's Mexico. Thorough, concise, with good maps, colour plates, etc, and a free map of Mexico. Very good for a short stay or tour. AA 1992. Price about £9.95.

Mexico: American Express Pocket Guide. James Tickell. A genuine pocket book, well edited to provide essential facts, colour items, and town & country maps. Mitchell Beazley 1991. Price £7.99.

The People's Guide to Mexico, by Carl Franz. More than a travel guide, this book also tells about the people, the culture, the land and living in a foreign country. Described with wit and wisdom. John Muir Publications. $14.95 in the USA.

NORTHWEST MEXICO

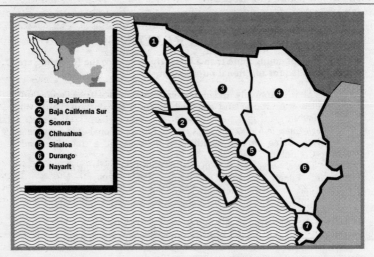

① Baja California
② Baja California Sur
③ Sonora
④ Chihuahua
⑤ Sinaloa
⑥ Durango
⑦ Nayarit

This vast arid region of stark desert, sharp mountains, deep valleys and canyons contains the states of Baja California, Sonora, Chihuahua, Durango, Nayarit and Sinaloa.

The nearness of Mexico to the US is deceptive once you learn that one way or another, you must cross many miles of thinly populated and largely dull terrain in this northern sector in order to get anywhere more interesting.

The coastline offers some relief, especially from Hermosillo southward as it gradually becomes greener, until you reach the lush and humid jungle around Tepic and San Blás.

Baja California has its own peninsula to the west; poorest of Mexican states, beautiful in a bare-bones sort of way, especially on its eastern coast on the warm Sea of Cortéz (also called the Gulf of California).

BAJA CALIFORNIA

TIJUANA Previous editions of this guide have dismissed Tijuana and the other border towns; yet more of its readers visit 'TJ' than anywhere else in Mexico, numbering themselves among the millions of day trippers passing through the city each year. You will do Mexico an injustice if you judge it by the border towns, but you will do yourself an injustice if you fail to take the opportunity provided by a free day in San Diego, El Paso or Laredo to experience an abrupt cultural discontinuity available in few other places on the planet. The most cursory trip across puts into sudden perspective everything the traveller has taken for granted in the course of a trip round the US.

Tourist trap, home of cheap assembly plants, staging post for illegal immigrants en route to El Norte, Tijuana's every aspect depends on its proximity to the border. Possessing few Mexican virtues but pandering to most American vices, the town has long functioned as a commercial and sexual bargain basement for southern California, and although a municipal clean-up campaign has edged the more blatant prostitution and sex shows to the outskirts, hustle is still the name of the game for the storekeepers, street traders and taxi drivers competing for your attention.

There are bargains to be had if you bargain ruthlessly: good deals likely for leather goods, blankets and non-Mexican items such as cameras and name brand clothing. 'You can knock all goods down to a third of the asking price. Take US dollars.' 'Some great buys if you enjoy haggling.' 'If you go in a spirit of sociological enquiry, remember to have fun. Well worth a day visit.' 'I enjoyed every minute of it.'

ACCOMMODATION
Tijuana has over a hundred hotels: those in the southeast section of the city are reputedly the quietest and most salubrious. Expect to pay US$20-$38, and be prepared to haggle. 'Lower prices possible if you don't mind sleaze. There are several small, inexpensive hotels on Ave Madero, to the left as you leave the old Tres Estrellas de Oro bus station.
Hotel Caesar, Revolución & Calle 8, (66) 85-16-06, (66) 85-25-24, S-US$28, D-US$38.
Villa Deportiva Youth Hostel, Via Oriente y Puente Cuauhtemoc, (66) 82-90-67 or (66) 34-30-89, Zona del Río, near the bridge, about US$5 for dormitory bed, make reservation before going down and ask for Mrs. Ivonne Masías.
Hotel Nelson, Revolución 721, (66) 85-43-02 or (66) 85-43-04. 'Clean, decent bathrooms, relatively expensive. S-US$ 25, D-US$ 27. Also has a good restaurant.'

FOOD
Nelson (see Hotel Nelson). Reasonable prices for full-scale Mexican meals, and for breakfasts. 24 hrs during summer, otherwise 7 am-11 pm.
La Especial , Revolución in btwn 3 & 4 , (66) 85-66-54.
La Placita, Revolución in btwn 3 & 4, (66) 88-27-04.
Carnitas Uruapuana, Blvd. Díaz Ordaz 550, (66) 81-61-81 or (66) 81-14-00. Deep-fried pork (carnitas) in various combinations. Popular with locals and tourists. One order US$5.50.
Río Rita Bar, Revolución 744 btwn Calles 3 & 4, (66) 88-37-39. Mon-Sun 9 am-2 am. 'We found the best Margaritas we've ever tasted here. Two drinks for the price of one.' Cheapest food will be purchased from street vendors catering to locals—but same warnings apply as elsewhere in Mexico.

OF INTEREST
Centro Cultural FONART, Paseo de los Heroes & Calle Mina, Zona Río, (66) 84-11-11. New cultural museum of striking modern design with archeological, historical and handicrafts displays. Auditorium with multimedia show in English (afternoons) and Spanish (evenings), also theatre, art shops, and restaurant. Daily 11 am-8 pm. Museum admission US$0.50. Show admission US$3.00—includes free pass to museum.

ENTERTAINMENT
Jai Alai. Fronton Palacio (Revolución and Calle 7, (66) 85-16-12). Fast and furious version of squash using arm baskets to hurl hard rubber ball against court walls. Betting on every game. Mon & Fri. Noon-5.30 pm & 8 pm. Tue, Wed , Thur & Sat 8 pm. Rsvs US$2, free at the door. 'A whole evening's entertainment for $2—a small bet can earn you a few extra dollars.'

Bullfighting. Not every Sunday, so call before you go. The season changes every year, but is from April-Sept approximately. In one of two rings. Tkts US$6 sold in advance at Revolución 921 btwn Calles 5 & 6, (66) 86-15-10 or (66) 86-12-19 at gate. 'Amazing and disgusting.'

Racetrack (*Hipódromo*), Ave Agua Caliente in front of Calimar, (66) 81-78-11. Moorish-influenced building containing enclosed and open-air stands. Races daily 7.45 pm-11.30 pm. Also offers matinee Tues, Sat & Sun 2 pm-5 pm.

INFORMATION
State Tourism Office, (66) 81-94-92/93/94.

TRAVEL
To Tijuana: see section on San Diego, California. From SD Amtrak terminal, the San Diego Trolley will take you to US border suburb of San Ysidro (approx. US$6); then 20 minute walk to centre, or the local bus from the border to Avenue Revolución (Tijuana) costs no more than US$3. Some local buses are: Volante, Diamante & ABC. 'Taxi from border should cost no more than US$7.' If passing straight through, get either the shuttle bus from Amtrak or the Greyhound service from LA and San Diego: these both take you to the new so-called 'central' bus station on the eastern edge of town. The old Tres Estrellas terminal near the border has poor connecting service and a 3 new peso taxi ride is the only other option. Mexicoach offers an excessively expensive centre-to-centre service from San Diego.
Onward: frequent bus services to Ensenada (2 hrs), Mexicali (3 hrs), Santa Ana (11 hrs), Los Mochis (22 hrs), Mazatlán (28 hrs), Guadalajara (40 hrs), Mexico City and points between. Six buses daily to La Paz (22 hrs).

MEXICALI   Inland border town located 136 km east of Tijuana and departure point for bus and rail routes to West Coast destinations. One of the hottest places in Mexico, with few concessions to tourists or to anyone else: accommodation choice is between three hotels priced at US levels or Zona Rosa sleaze. However, for even the short stay border-hopper the trip from Tijuana (the new terminal) is recommended: the three hour ride gives an acceptably brief taste of the starkness of Northern Mexico, and the descent on the eastern side of the mountains towards Mexicali is both hair-raising and dramatic.

ACCOMMODATION
Hotel Plaza, Ave Madero 366, (65) 52-97-57 or (65) 52-97-59. S-US$25, D-US$35. Excellent 24 hr restaurant.
Hotel La Siesta Inn, Blvd Justo Sierra #899, (65) 68-20-01. US$40.
Hotel Del Norte, Ave Madero 205, (65) 52-81-01 or (65) 52-81-02. S-US$22-D-US$26.
Hotel San Juan de Capistrano, Calle Reforma #646 btwn Bravo & Mex. (65) 52-41-04. S-US$39.

FOOD
Cafe Sanborns, Calz Independencia inside Plaza Fiesta, (65) 57-04-11.
Las Campanas Restaurant, Calz Justo Sierra & Calle Haiti Col. Cuahutemoc, (65) 68-12-13.
El Chalet Restaurant, Calz Justo Sierra #899, (65) 68-20-01.

ENTERTAINMENT
Desert Biking. Behind Hotel Riviera, quarter-mile down road on right. US$15 p/hr, US$20 deposit. 'Three wheeler fat tyre motorcycles for desert tracks and sand dunes. Great fun for novices.'
Bodegas de Santo Tomás, Mexico's largest winery, tours and tastings offered Mon-Sat.

State Museum, Avenue Reforma #1998, close to L St, (65) 54-19-77. Gives a comprehensive introduction to Baja California history and culture. Free.

INFORMATION
State Tourist Office Calzada Independencia & Calle Calafia inside Plaza Baja Calif. local #4C. (65) 55-49-50 or (65) 55-49-51.

TRAVEL
Bus and rail stations are near Mateos and Independencia, a mile south of the border: no need to enter the town itself. Buses every 30 mins to Tijuana, hourly to the South. Trains depart at 9 am, tickets available from 6.30 am. 'From Caléxico border to station is 5 minute journey. Not worth waiting for a bus: get a taxi and don't pay more than US$2 pp.'
San Felipe: A 2 hr, 125 mile drive from Mexicali, through desert and beautifully harsh mountains. San Felipe is a likeable, ramshackle fishing village with miles of white sand beaches and superb fishing. After this an unpaved road continues South to join Route 1 from Ensenada.

ENSENADA Slightly hipper version of Tijuana, 70 miles south via a new toll road. A thriving fishing industry fails to impart authenticity to anything but the cheap and tasty seafood. The town is full of Californians, especially at weekends, and is one of the few towns where you will get better value from US dollars than from pesos. But 'the drive to Ensenada along the coast is beautiful—well worth crossing the border just to experience the complete change of environment'.

ACCOMMODATION
'Reservations vital for Saturdays. We didn't have one and spent the night on the streets.' In general expect to pay S-US$20-S30, D-US$35-$45.
Hotel America, Ave López Mateos #309, (61) 76-13-33.
Hotel Bungalows Plaza, Ave López Mateos #1847, (61) 76-14-30.
Hotel Colón, Ave Guadalupe #134, (61) 76-19-10.
Hotel del Valle, Ave Riveroll #367, (61) 78-22-24.

FOOD
El Charro, Ave López Marcos #475, (61) 78-38-81.
La Holandesa, Ave López Mateos #1797, (61) 77-19-65.
Mi Kasa, Ave Riveroll #872, (61) 78-82-11.
Victor's Restaurant, Blvd Lázaro Cárdenas #178, (61) 76-13-13.

OF INTEREST
Shopping: **FONART** store, next to tourist office, Mateos 885, (61) 78-24-11. Daily 9 am-7 pm. High quality textiles, silver, ceramics, etc. No bargaining. Most goods from southern Mexico: a good place to buy if not going further.
El Nuevo Nopal, on northern edge of Ensenada, offers similar range.
BS Beauty Supply (Calle 4 & Ruíz) and **La Joya** (Calle 5 & Ruíz) specialises in tax-free imported goods.
La Bufadora. Spectacular natural geyser, shooting water into the air from underground cavern. 20 miles south of town, and off the main road; own transport needed.
Agua Caliente Hot Springs. 22 miles E on Rte 3. Unpaved but navigable road.
The Tourist Zone. Is located at Ave López Mateos where you will find souvenirs, shops, restaurants and bars.

INFORMATION
State Tourist Office, Blvd Lazaro Cardenas & Ave Las Rocas #1477 (61) 72-30-22 or (61) 72-30-00 ext. 3173, 3138, 3118. A good tourist guide for Ensenada is Mr. Roberto Gonzales (61) 78-41-07.

BAJA BEYOND ENSENADA   After Ensenada the paved but narrow and variable quality Transpeninsular Highway (Mexico 1) leads the bus traveller to the tip of Baja at the resort center of **Cabo San Lucas**, 1,000 dusty miles and 20 hours further on. Known for its sport fishing and beautiful beaches, this is where the Gulf of California and the Pacific Ocean meet. To explore most areas of interest en route you need a car, and often a four-wheel drive vehicle: buses do not prolong their rest stops at the roadside towns, which in most cases is no great loss. Expect visions of desolate beauty and long passages of tedium, especially when the road loses sight of the coast.

OF INTEREST

The mountains, forest and trout streams of **San Pedro Mártir National Park** lies two hours away from **Colonet**, 74 miles from Ensenada. Superb hiking and climbing but check at the turn off that the dirt road is open all the way. Further down the highway, the agricultural town of **San Quintín** offers good markets and restaurants. **Bahia San Quintín**, five miles away by dirt road, has fine beaches, expensive motels and excellent seafood.

The next 250 miles or so consist of bleak inland desert. Those with an interest in salt evaporation plants will enjoy **Guerro Negro**, at the border of Baja California Sur: otherwise its only virtue lies in its proximity to **Scammon's Lagoon**, breeding ground for grey whales and an unmissable spectacle during the breeding period of late December-February. Four wheel drive needed for the 20 mile trek.

San Ignacio, is a delightful oasis village with date palms imported by its Jesuit founders in the eighteenth century, a reconstructed mission, and its own wine. But more and cheaper accommodation will be found 50 miles further on at **Santa Rosalía**, a copper mining town of interest for its friendly inhabitants, ugly galvanised steel church, and thrice-weekly ferry to Guaymas on the mainland, the shortest and cheapest crossing. Boats depart (subject to change): Sun & Wed at 8 am, arrive 3 pm. Transboradores Terminal (115) 2-00-14 or (115) 2-00-13. The 7 hr trip costs US$13.50 salon class, US$27 tourist class, and US$25 for cars. See below for further details.

The desert oasis of **Mulegé** has hotels and restaurants and two hours away by four wheel drive Baja's best cave paintings. Between Mulegé and **Loreto** are a number of beaches accessible by car. Loreto itself was founded in 1697, but most in evidence now is work-in-progress on the Government-sponsored tourist resort.

La Paz follows after another 200 miles of boring inland desert. For years an isolated pearl-fishing centre, the ferry service and completion of Hwy 1 have turned La Paz into a major tourist town, but the centre at least preserves a relaxed charm. Not much to see except the famous sunsets, some good beaches and snorkelling, but many good restaurants and hotels, and the zócalo (main plaza) is spectacularly lit at night. Tourist Information Office, Obregón & 16 de Septiembre, (112) 40-100 or (112) 40-103. Daily 8 am-8 pm.

Ferries: Sematur is located at Guillermo Prieto & 5 de Mayo, (112) 5-38-33. Thurs-Tues services at 3 pm to **Mazatlán**, arrive at 9 am. US$21 salon class, US$41 tourist class. From La Paz to **Topolobampo (Los Mochis)**, US$40 salon class, US$27 tourist class. Wed & Thurs departs at 11 am, arriving at 7 pm. For more information call 91-800-6-96-96.

Cabo San Lucas lies 120 miles further south at the tip of the peninsula, and is a purpose-built tourist town with little time for the budget-conscious, who will have better luck at **San José del Cabo**. The whole southern tip has beautiful and—so far—unspoiled beaches, a couple of which, on Rte 9 out of San Lucas, are accessible to campers. **Sierra de la Laguna National Park**, reached by dirt road from Pescadero, offers pine forests and the occasional puma. The San Lucas-Puerto Vallarta ferry, a gruelling 20 hr trip, is currently suspended. In any case the La Paz-

Mazatlán route, followed by the bus, is the more tolerable alternative.

Ferries: The Baja-Mainland routes make few concessions to tourist convenience or comfort. You must queue for tickets several hours before they go on sale, and be prepared for long waits and customs hassles. Salón class is incredibly cheap, but involves a long and rowdy voyage with two hundred or so others crowded together on bus seats. Tourist class cabins are still a bargain, but frequent air conditioning breakdowns often make them unendurable. Taking a car across demands a willingness to wait several *days* (commercial vehicles always get priority) and pay substantial bribes. As if all this wasn't enough, the food is awful too. The ferry service has recently been privatised and hopefully will improve. Remember that flights duplicate most ferry routes and are definitely a less exhausting, albeit more expensive, option.

OTHER BORDER TOWNS

CIUDAD JUAREZ   Over the bridge from El Paso, and seemingly part of the same urban sprawl, this is the city about which Bob Dylan wrote his most depressing song ever (*Just Like Tom Thumb's Blues*). Souvenirs, gambling, racetracks and brothels, and it's easy to get lost in the rain. But still worth a quick visit (the market is recommended), rather than cowering on the other side of the border: 'it's easy to make the crossing for a much, much cheaper hotel room than you'll find in El Paso.'

ACCOMMODATION
Singles average US$15, doubles US$20.

Hotel Impala, Ave Lerdo N 670, (16) 15-04-31. S/D-US$25, with bath, TV.
Hotel Juárez, Ave Lerdo N 143, (16) 15-02-98, or (16) 15-04-18, S-US$15, D-US$20.
Hotel Kóper, Juárez N 124 & Ave 16 de Septiembre, (16) 15-03-24 or (16) 18-26-86, S-US$10, D-US$15.

INFORMATION
State Tourist Office, Eje Juan Gabriel & Acerradero 2nd floor, Dept Fomento Economico, (16) 29-33-00 Ext.5610.
Tourist Booth, Ave Juárez & Azucena. (16) 14-92-52.

TRAVEL
By bus to Chihuahua, Mexico City or most other destinations. Instead of direct route to Chihuahua it is possible to go via **Nuevo Casas Grandes**, impressive ruins (pyramids, ball courts) of 1000 AD agricultural community. 'Get up early to squeeze this trip into a day.' 'Beware of low flying taxi drivers.'

  NB: Mexican buses to Chihuahua and Mexico City also depart from El Paso Greyhound terminal. By train to Chihuahua and to Mexico City (about US$75 first class). By air, Gonzalez Airport to Mexico City, about US$257 o/w. Call Aeromexico, 1-800-237-6639.

CHIHUAHUA   The first major town on the route down from El Paso, Chihuahua is a prosperous industrial and cattle-shipping centre, once famous for breeding tiny, hairless and bad-tempered dogs of the same name. The city is of interest primarily as the inland terminus for the dramatic **Al Pacífico** train ride from Los Mochis on the coast through the Barranca del Cobre (Copper Canyon). This is one of the world's most spectacular train rides.

ACCOMMODATION

Singles average US$15, doubles US$18.

Hotel Del Carmen, Calle 10 #4 Col. Centro, (14) 15-70-96 or (14) 15-79-05 S-US$12, D-US$18.

Hotel San Juan, Calle Victoria 823, (14) 10-00-35. Off the Plaza Principal. 'Clean and friendly.' 'Lovely patio.' S-US$10, D-US$15.

Hotel del Parque, Calle Ocampo #2400 Col Centro, (14) 15-15-58.'

Hotel Villas del Sol, Ave Tecnologico & Acacias #5701 Col. Granjas, (14) 17-23-90.

OF INTEREST

A crumbling **cathedral** in Colonial style overlooks the Plaza Principal.

The Palacio de Gobierno, where Miguel Hidalgo, the 'Father of Mexico', was executed at 7 am July 30th 1811, is decorated with 'lovely lurid Murals'.

Quinta Luz, The Museum of Pancho Villa is a fortresslike 50 room mansion, Villa's home and hideout, at Calle 10, #301 7 Col. Santa Rosa, (14) 16-29-58. Take bus from Plaza Principal to Parque Lerdo. Calle 10 (unmarked so ask for Calle Diez) is opposite the park, running SE of Paseo Bolívar. Tues-Sat 9 am-1 pm, 3 pm-7 pm, Sun 9 am-5 pm, US$0.65. Now state-run, after being in the hands of Villa's 'official' widow for many years: see Villa memorabilia including weapons and the bullet-scarred car in which he was assassinated in 1923.

INFORMATION

State Tourist Office, Calle Libertad #1300, Col. Centro, (14) 29-33-00. General Information (14) 15-77-56.

TRAVEL

For information about travel to the Copper Canyon, see separate box.

LOS MOCHIS A dull agricultural city of interest only as the southern terminus for the *Al Pacífico* rail journey and its ferry connections with La Paz in nearby Topolobampo. The tourist office is located at Cuahutemoc & Allende, (68) 12-66-40.

ACCOMMODATION

Hotel Beltrán, Hidalgo, 281 Poniente, 2-07-10. Showers, TV, AC. 'Clean.' 'Bus to Los Mochis station leaves from front.' S-US$17, D-US$21.

Hotel Lorena, Ave Obregón, 186 Poniente, (68) 12-45-17. Two blocks from bus station. Shower, AC. 'Clean: what a relief after a long bus trip.' S-US$16, D-US$20. Also has a restaurant.

Hotel Monte Carlo, Flores & Independencia, 2-18-18. Colonial-style, good value, with restaurant and bar, S-US$14, D-US$18.

TRAVEL

Al Pacífico train to Los Mochis: the journey takes at least 18 hrs and often up to 24 hrs. The train is slow, stops frequently, and is hot and crowded. 'Not worth doing unless you have a lot of time and are really bored.'

Trains leave Los Mochis at 6 am. Tickets (see under Chihuahua for prices) on sale from 5:45 am: buy from station, as agents in town can be unreliable. Call (68) 2-93-85 for information. Starting from Los Mochis end reportedly gives best views; sit on the right. Station is 3 miles out of town—allow plenty of time for local bus or take rip-off taxi: 'It took ages to haggle him down from 65¢-25¢.' NB: FCP line from Nogales has different station 30 miles away in San Blás, Sinaloa: it is possible to transfer to Pacífico line here, but at risk of being stranded. Also be aware that Los Mochis station uses Chihuahua time, one hour earlier than local time.

Ferry for La Paz, if operating (see Baja section), leaves from **Topolobampo** for the 8 hour trip, Mon-Sat at 10 pm. Salón class US$13.50. Often sold out 24 hrs ahead.

Nowhere to stay in Topolobampo, but 'a night out under the stars is fun. Fishermen cook freshly caught fish and shrimp over wood fires and invite you to partake. But buying even basics is difficult—don't count on it for food for the ferry.' Going straight from the ferry to the Al Pacifico, or vice versa, is logistically difficult and an exhausting trip: a stopover in Los Mochis is recommended.

MAZATLAN   Big, boisterous and a major gringo tourist town, Mazatlán offers a ten mile strip of international hotels and some superb game fishing: to the south of this, the old section of the town has more affordable hotels, local colour and an element of risk. The El Cid Hotel rents out windsurfers, sailboats, catamarans and snorkel gear. A 10-12 minute parachute/sail along the beach averages US$15. *Piedra Isla*, a tiny island just offshore, has good beaches, diving and camping possibilities: very congenial after the last boat leaves at 4.30 pm.

ACCOMMODATION/INFORMATION
Best value around the bus station and in Old Mazatlán on Aves Juárez, Aquiles Serdán and Azueta.
Hotel Fiesta, Ferruquilla #306, tel. (69) 81-78-88.
Hotel del Río, Benito Juárez #2410, tel. (69) 82-46-54.
Tourism Office, Ave Camaron Sabado & Tiburon Fracc. Sabalo Contry, tel. (69) 16-51-60.

TRAVEL
Local bus, 'Zaragoza', 5 pesos from bus station into town. Ferry leaves 5 pm, daily to La Paz, a 16 hour trip. Be at terminal before 8 am to get ticket. 'The route (Mexico 40) from Mazatlán to Durango is absolutely breath-taking. Although it's just over 300 miles, it took us a long time to cover as the road twists and turns up to 7000 ft where it crosses the Continental Divide. A part of Mexico that should not be missed.' Take Transportes Monterrey-Saltillo bus for the 6 hour trip.

SAN BLÁS   An hour's drive off the highway just north of Tepic takes you through increasingly lush tropical country to San Blás, once a sleepy seaside village, but no longer. 'Signs advertising granola and yogurt, expensive hotels and food, dirty beaches and medium surfing.' 'Very hippified but nice with a good swimming beach.' 'Bring lots of insect repellent—famous for its gnats.' 'We really liked it here. The beach is lovely and the town is small but pretty with nice places to sit and eat.'

ACCOMMODATION
Hotel Bucanero, Juárez 75, near plaza, (328) 5-01-01. 'Clean, popular with young people'.
Hotel Casa María, Batallón 26. 'Mosquito-proofed rooms, showers, clean.'
Hotel Flamingo, Juárez 105. 'Clean, shabby, cell-like rooms, twin beds with shower.'
Hotel Playa Hermosa, dirt road from Batallan. Isolated 'brokendown palace' with big, decrepit rooms and an ocean view. Bar and restaurant. Around US$10 for two.
Posada Portola, Parades 118, off the plaza, (328) 5-03-86. US$14 single, US$20 double. 'Clean mosquito-proofed with shower, stove and fridge. Excellent value.'

FOOD
Try the little cafes along the beach for inexpensive fish, oyster meals. Also check to see if the pool in the bar of the Torino restaurant still has 4 crocodile residents. Restaurant-Bar **La Familia**, Ave H. Batallón 16, (328) 5-02-58. Open 5 pm-10 pm.

INFORMATION/TRAVEL

Tourist Info, opposite plaza, has useful booklet with maps, lodgings, etc. Buses from Tepic to San Blás run fairly regularly. 'Interesting jungle scenery enroute.' The bus station is on Calle Sinaloa, tel (328) 5-00-43. Take a small boat trip into the jungle lagoons and creeks behind the town. Dawn is the best time for you to catch the animals (or vice versa).

THE COPPER CANYON

Copper Canyon (Mochis and Chihuahua) The spectacular Copper Canyon was formed some 20-30 million years ago, when intense volcanic activity raised the Sierra Madre mountain range. Copper Canyon is 300 feet deeper and four times wider than the Grand Canyon. In the high parts of the canyon there is an impressive variety of vegetation and wildlife. During the summer the climate is cool, and during the winter the temperature can drop below freezing. The temperature at the base of the canyon is hot, and the plant and animal life markedly different. The descent to the bottom of the canyon can take two days, and those who make the trek should be in good physical condition. It is recommended to make the descent in winter or spring, to avoid the summer heat of the canyon floor.

The canyon is populated by Tarahumara Indians. Despite the tourism, they live in largely traditional ways and are known for their basketry and long distance running abilities.

How To Get There: The best way to reach and experience the canyon is by train. There is an incredible trip from Chihuahua to Los Mochis, which takes 14 hrs one way. The train passes through 86 tunnels, over 37 bridges and covers more than 400 miles. The train stops at many different points along the way, allowing passengers to see and photograph the spectacular views. Train No. 74 from Chihuahua to Los Mochis costs US$50 and leaves at 7 am daily, Train No. 73 leaves Los Mochis at 6 am daily. For more information, call Ferrocarriles Nacionales de Mexico at (14) 15-77-56, 8 am-7 pm Mon-Fri. Tours of the canyon and accommodations can be arranged in Chihuahua by (1) Turísmo al Mar (14) 16-6-88 or (14) 10-92-32, contact Mr Cobarrubias or Mr Colmenero; (2) Viajes Dorado de Chihuahua (14) 14-64-38 or (14) 14-64-90, contact Mr Juan Rodriguez; or (3) Turísmo Gema (14) 15-65-07 or (14) 15-28-98, contact Mr Jesus Gonzalez. Other tourist information can be obtained from the Mexican Secretary of Tourism at (14) 15-91-24 ext. 4512. For information about Los Mochis you can contact the Mexican Secretary of Tourism at (68) 12-66-40.

Where To Stop Off And Why: **Créel Station**: This is the door to the Sierra Tarahumara. From here you can get to the Tarahumaras Caves, Arareko Lake, rock formations in the Valley of the Mushrooms, the Elephant Stone, and the Valley of the Frogs. Four km from the nearby town of Cusarare are the Cusarare waterfalls. Local tours offer horseback rides and trips to the waterfalls. Tours run between US$8 and US$23. Camping is also possible but bring a tent (summer is rainy season).

Batopilas: One of the more beautiful parts of the Copper Canyon, Batopilas has a descent from 2,200 metres to 460 metres above sea level. From the vantage point of Bufa you can appreciate all of the splendor of this magnificent canyon.

Divisadero Station: An impressive view of the canyon is located at an altitude of 1300 meters, at the Urique River. There is a path to the bottom of the canyon, and an excellent opportunity to experience the variety of vegetation from pine forest to tropical.

Basaseachic National Park: This park has two of the highest waterfalls in Mexico. Basaseachic Falls is 254 metres high and Piedra Volada is 456 metres high. The Candamena Canyon is located here, and excursions to the bottom are offered.

NORTHEAST MEXICO

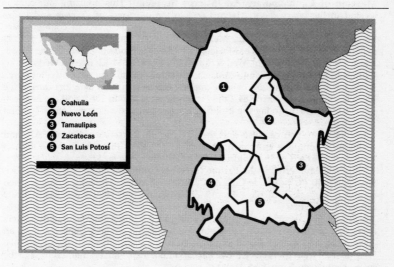

1. Coahuila
2. Nuevo León
3. Tamaulipas
4. Zacatecas
5. San Luis Potosí

The northeast states offer little worth tarrying for. The border towns east of Juárez Nuevo Laredo, Reynosa and Matamoros provide similar experiences to the others, and are worth a quick visit but no more. 'Nuevo Laredo is a corrupt dump and an insult to Mexico'; Matamoros has either exceptionally friendly or unbelievably officious and venal immigration officers people, depending on whom you listen to. All three offer flights to Mexico City (about US$80 one way), and bus and train routes via Monterrey.

From Nuevo Laredo you can catch the *Regiomontano*, leaving daily at 3.15 pm and arriving in Mexico City at 10 am the following day. This is one of the faster and more comfortable Mexican trains.

Another route south is the Pan American highway, Mexico 85, taking you from Nuevo Laredo to Monterrey, Nuevo León.

MONTERREY

NUEVO LEÓN   This state is an important economic center of Mexico. In addition to its modern capital city of Monterey, one of the three largest cities in Mexico, Nuevo León also has interesting deserts, vegetation, water falls, caverns, and museums.

In Monterrey you can find the famous **Macro Plaza** also known as the Gran Plaza, comprising 100 acres in the heart of the city. Completed in 1985, it is one of the world's largest squares. Nearby are shops, restaurants, important goverment buildings, museums, and downtown hotels. In the center of the Macro Plaza is the large Fountain of Life ('La fuente de la vida'), one of several fountains in the plaza.

OF INTEREST

Museum of Contemporary Art (Marcos Museum). This amazing museum is located in the heart of the Macro Plaza in the old town at Zuazua and Padre Raymundo Jordon, (8) 342-4820. The museum, was designed in contemporary Mexican style by the famous Mexican architect Ricardo Legorreta. It has 11 galleries that display the art of Mexico, Latin America, and other parts of the world. Tue & Thur-Sat 11 am-7 pm, Wed & Sun 11 am-9 pm. US$1-$2, free on Weds.

Obispado Museum, (8) 346-0404. The Obispado was built by the Catholic church in 1788. Sitting on a hilltop overlooking the city, it was used as a fort during the Mexican-American War in 1847, the French Intervention in 1862, and the Mexican Revolution in 1915. Today the building is used primarily as a museum. Tue-Sun 10 am-5 pm, US$1.

In Monterrey you can also find the Planetarium Museum of Science, Art, and Technology, complete with an Imax theatre, as well as Plaza Sesamo, an amusement park inspired by the children's TV programme, *Sesame Street*.

Also near Monterrey is the **Parque Nacional Cumbres**, where the famous 75 ft Horsetail Falls ('Cascada de Cola de Caballo') is located. The falls can be reached by foot, horseback, or carriage. From Monterrey, take hwy 85 NW for 145 km. Daily 8 am-7 pm, US$1.50.

South of the city of Monterrey you will find the interesting **Grutas de Garcia** caves that are some 500,000 years old. These caves were once submerged by an ancient sea, and marine fossils can be seen in the walls. To reach the caves, take Hwy 40 west from Monterrey for 40 km to Saltillo, then 9 km on marked road to the caves. Daily 9 am-5 pm, US$ 5.00.

INFORMATION

State Tourism Office, (8) 345-6745 or (8) 645-6805, Zaragoza sur 1300 piso A-1 Building Kalos Suite #137, Monterrey NL.

Saltillo, 50 miles up in the hills to the west, is preferable if you need to break your journey. Further on towards Mexico City, **San Luis Potosí** is a gold and silver mining town of considerable historical interest and with a distinctive regional cuisine.

Zacatecas is the capital city of the state of the same name and is built on the side of a 7000 ft mountain. It's still a silvermining centre and is famous for its baroque cathedral and the Quemada ruins. Yes, those are rattlesnake skins for sale in the market. For 'marvellous views' of the area take a ride on the cablecar (*teleferíco*) north of the plaza. US$2 r/t.

If you cross by car at Reynosa or Matamoros, it is advisable to travel inland to Rte 85 rather than taking the coastal road: while this is the shortest trip to the Yucatan if bypassing Mexico City, the road is in poor repair and the journey offers only unbearable temperatures and polluted beaches.

CENTRAL MEXICO

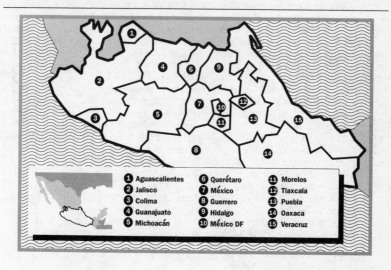

1 Aguascalientes	**6** Querétaro	**11** Morelos
2 Jalisco	**7** México	**12** Tlaxcala
3 Colima	**8** Guerrero	**13** Puebla
4 Guanajuato	**9** Hidalgo	**14** Oaxaca
5 Michoacán	**10** México DF	**15** Veracruz

Mexico seems to save itself scenically, culturally and every other way, in order to burst upon you in central Mexico in a rich outpouring of volcanic mountains, pre-Columbian monuments, luxuriant flowers, exuberant people and picturesque architecture. This is the region where the Mexican love of colour manifests itself and the air is cool and fresh on the high Central Plateau. Be prepared for mugginess on either coast around Acapulco and Veracruz, however.

Mexico City lies in the centre of this region, surrounded by a dozen tiny states from Tlaxcala to Guanajuato. Northwest of Mexico City is the orbit of Guadalajara, second largest city and home to the largest colony of American expatriates. That fact makes its outlying satellite towns of Tlaquepaque, Chapala, Ajijic and so on quite expensive.

MEXICO CITY The Aztec city of Tenochtitlán had a population of 300,000 by 1521, when stout Cortés demolished it to build Mexico City from the remains. Today that figure represents the number of new residents the city acquires *each year*, making it likely that total population will reach 20 million during the lifetime of this guide.

México DF (pronounced 'day effy', for Distrito Féderal) is the nation's cultural, economic and transportation hub, with most of the country's people living on the surrounding plateau. As well as being the largest city in the world, it is probably the most polluted, with a smog level to make LA seem positively bracing and a crime level to make New York City seem like the Garden of Eden on a Sunday afternoon: be alert, especially away from the centre. The altitude—7400 ft—together with the crowds, suicidal traffic and

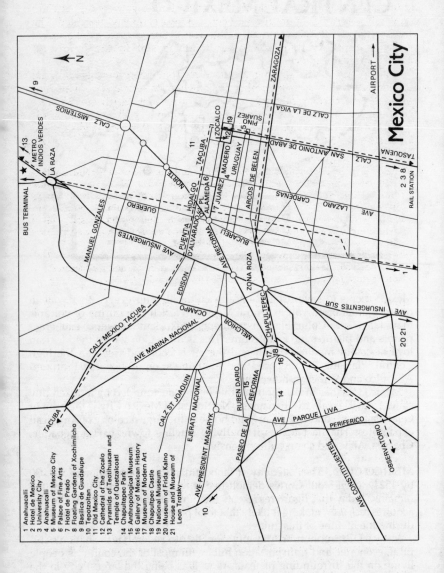

Mexico City

1 Anahuacalli
2 Hotel de Mexico
3 University City
4 Anahuacalli
5 Museum of Mexico City
6 Palace of Fine Arts
7 Hotel de Prado
8 Floating Gardens of Xochimilcho
9 Basilica de Guadalupe
10 Tepotzoltan
11 Old Mexico City
12 Cathedral of the Zocalo
13 Pyramids of Teotihuacan and
   Temple of Quetzalcoatl
14 Chapultepec Park
15 Anthropological Museum
16 Gallery of Mexican History
17 Museum of Modern Art
18 Chapultpec Castle
19 National Museum
20 Museum of Frida Kalno
21 House and Museum of
   Leon Trotsky

incessant din, can quickly exhaust the unacclimatised traveller.

The earthquake of September 1985 overshadowed these problems. In addition to the thousands of deaths, 250 major buildings were toppled and the whole country's communication network was seriously disrupted. The city has now fully recovered from the destruction caused by the earthquakes, except for a few damaged buildings still in the process of demolition and clearance.

Visit the city for its striking architecture from Aztec through Spanish Colonial to modern, from pyramids to enamelled skyscrapers, from modern subways to archeological finds preserved *in situ* at Metro stops. Great wealth and poverty exist side by side but residents at all economic levels tend to be the most hospitable of Mexicans. 'North America is incomplete without a visit to this vast and fascinating city.'

ACCOMMODATION

Singles average US$20, doubles US$15-35. Best area for low price accommodation is around Alameda Park, especially Revillagigedo Street, Plaza San Fernando, Zarazoga, and (further west just before Insurgentes) Bernal Díaz and Bernadino de Sahagun. Also try the area immediately surrounding the Zócalo. Be prepared to add 25% to these prices during summer: during this period pressure on a diminishing reserve of low cost hotels is intense, and a room in Cuernavaca, about an hour away by bus, may be the only viable option.

Asociación Cristiana de Jovenes, Rio Churubusco # 262 Col Carmen, (5) 688-3873 or (5) 688-2066. Mexican version of YWCA. Women only; safe and well-located.

Hotel Bahío, Tonala # 357 Col Roma, (5) 564-0468 or (5) 264-1455.

Hotel Boston, Brazil #137 Centro, (5) 526-1408.

Hotel Cosmos, Lázaro Cárdemas 12, (5) 521-9889. Metro Bellas Artes. Central, D-Q room with or without bath. Ask for a room with a patio.' S-US$15, D-US$20.

Hotel Congreso, Allende # 18, (5) 510-4446. Small rm w/TV and private bathroom. S-US$16, D-US$22.

Hotel Guadalupe, Revillagigedo #36, AC, shower, TV, (5) 537-1779.

Hotel Montecarlo, Uruguay #69,(5) 521-9363. 'Clean and friendly.' Built in 1772 as an Augustine monastery. DH Lawrence briefly lived here. S-US$15, D-US$20.

Villa Deportiva Youth Hostel, Insurgentes Sur, 573-7740. Take bus to Universidad, then another to Olympic Village. Bit of a way from city centre, but safe and comfortable. Breakfast and dinner available. For information call Villas Juveniles Conade Glorieta Insurgentes local # G-11, Col Juárez, (5) 525-2916. Also recommended are **Hotel Paraiso**, Calle I. Mariscal (S-US$12), and **Hotel Metropol**, on Luis Moya (D-US$22), (5) 512-1273.

Outside Mexico City:

Tlamacas Youth Hostel at Popocatépetl, (dorms). 'Near snow line, with magnificent views. Bus from Mexico City (San Lazaro Metro) to Amecameca, then taxi to Tlamacas.' 'Well worth the trip.' US$3 per bed. Rsvs & info. in Mexico City, Tlamaca popopark , Rio Elva #20, 9 floor Col Cuahutemoc, (5) 553-6266.

FOOD

Mexico City is a good place to taste frothy Mexican hot chocolate, a drink once so prized that only the Aztec and Mayan nobility drank it, to the tune of 50 tiny cups a day. A dish invented locally and now popular all over Mexico is *carne asada a la tampiquena* (grilled beef Tampico style). Due to reports of rude waiters and rapacious mariachis, Plaza Garibaldi is no longer recommended as 'best and cheapest'. 'Good cheap eating at small restaurants around Glorieta Insurgentes situated where Insurgentes crosses Avenida Chapultepec. Fewer mariachis than Garibaldi but you can sit in greater comfort to hear them.'

Cafeterias Sanborn are all over Mexico City and they are excellent for breakfast, lunch or dinner. Some of the locations are: Insurgentes Nte. # 70 Col Sta Maria La Riviera, (5) 591-0444. Ave Insurgentes # 1605 Col San José Insurgentes, (5) 662-5077. Insurgentes Sur # 1266 Col Tlacoquemectl del Valle, (5) 575-0550. Parroquia # 179 Col del Valle, (5) 534-7226. Ave Fco I Madero #4, (5) 512-9820. Salamanca # 74 Col Roma, (5) 533-3242.

Restaurant Charleston, Queretaro # 209 Col Roma, (5)574-0261.

Taquería Beatriz, Londres 179, (5) 525-5857. 'All kinds of tacos. Try the tepache.'

'Zona Rosa' is a pleasant place to go strolling and there are some cheap restaurants among the plush sidewalk cafes.

For real Mexican tacos (not to be confused with the Tex-Mex variety found in most parts of the US), try **Beatriz** (several branches downtown and near the Zona Rosa) or **El Caminero** (Río Lerma, just behind the Sheraton Hotel).

OF INTEREST

Anahuacalli (Diego Rivera Museum), Calle 150, near Division del Norte, (5) 617-4310 or (5) 617-3797. Diego Rivera-designed black lava building housing his large collection of Aztec, pre-Columbian artefacts. Open Tue-Sun 10 am-2 pm, 3 pm-6 pm. US$1.27, closed Mon.

Polyforum Cultural Sequeiros, Av Insurgentes Sur in the Hotel de Mexico. A monument designed by and in honor of the artist. 'The March of Humanity mural is indescribably wonderful like being inside an opium dream.' Open 10 am-9 pm. Sound and light show in the evening.

University City, home of UNAM, the Universidad Nacional Autonoma de México. 11 miles south, reached by buses 17 or 19 from downtown or trolley bus from Eje Central Lázaro Cárdenas. Famous for its modern design and colourful murals, mosaics and bas-reliefs by Rivera, Juan O'Gorman, Siqueiros and others.

Torre Latinoamericano, corner of Cárdenas and Madero. A miniature Empire State building that floats, with a magnificent view (smog and weather permitting) from its 44th floor. Open 10 am-midnight. Small admission charge.

Museum of Mexico City, Pino Suárez 30, three blocks south of Zócalo, (5) 542-0487. Built and rebuilt on site of razed Aztec temple (only cornerstone remains), museum provides excellent introduction to city's history with models, murals, photographs. Good background at the start of your visit. Tues-Sat 9.30 am-7 pm, Sun 9.30 am-4 pm. Closed Mon.

Palace of Fine Arts, Sn Juan de Letrán and Juárez. This heavy white opera house contains Mexico's finest art collection. Upstairs are some of the best murals by Orozco, Sequeiros, Rivera and Tamayo. 'Worth every centavo.' Open Tues-Sun, 10 am-7 pm. Small admission fee.

Floating Gardens of Xochimilco (so-chee-meel-coh), 15 miles south. Cheapest to catch 31 or 59 bus from downtown. If you get on, you almost certainly won't get a seat. Very crowded weekends, boats take you around lake, other boats sell food, drink. 'A complete waste of time—muddy canals and gardens.' 'Smelly canals full of refuse.' Boat prices: 'Take one-third off first price quoted.'

Basílica de la Virgin de Guadalupe. Take bus to La Villa, on Reforma, or Metro to Basílica. The holiest of Mexican shrines, it honours the nation's patron saint, The Virgin of Guadalupe. Legend has it that she appeared to an Indian, Juan Diego, in 1531. Devout visitors show their faith by walking on their knees across the vast, cement courtyard. Indians dress in national costume, dance, and parade by on her feast day, December 12. The old cathedral leans in all directions and is slowly sinking into the soft lakebed soil. The new basilica was designed by Pedro Ramírez Vásquez, architect of the National Museum of Anthropology.

Tepotzotlán, 25 miles north by *auto-pista* (expressway). Buses from Terminal del Norte, or Metro to Indios Verdes then local bus. Has a magnificent 18th century **church**, possibly Mexico's finest, with a monastery and an interesting collection of colonial religious art. Open Tue-Sun 10 am-6 pm.

Alameda. A park since 1592, it lies west of the Palace of Fine Arts between Avs. Juárez and Hidalgo. Originally the site of executions for those found guilty by the Spanish Inquisition, it is now the scene of popular Sunday concerts and family outings. On June 13, Mexico's single women line up at the Church of San Juan de Dios and plead with St Anthony to find a for them.

Zócalo, or Plaza de la Constitución, has been the centre of the country from Aztec times. Second only in size to Red Square, vehicular traffic is restricted. The Cathedral, National Palace, Templo Mayor, and much more, are all within 5 minutes of each other.

The Cathedral at the Zócalo is the oldest church edifice on the North American continent (1573-1667) and was built on the ruins of the Aztec temple. Has plumb-line showing how the cathedral has shifted. On the east side of the Zócalo is the **National Palace**, begun in 1692, interesting on its own and for its enormous and impressive murals by Diego Rivera.

Templo Mayor. Just off the corner of the Zócalo, between the Cathedral and the National Palace, is the excavated site of the Aztec Templo Mayor—really twin temples and several associated buildings. Although only the lower and internal parts remain, the ruins are extremely impressive. At the rear of the site is the recently inaugurated Muséo del Templo Mayor which houses many of the artefacts recovered during the excavations, (5) 542-4784 or (5) 542-4786. Open Tues-Sun 9 am-6 pm. Admission US$2.00 except Sun. Guided tours available in English Mon-Fri 2 pm-6 pm. Not to be missed.

Pyramids of Teotihuacán and **Temple of Quetzálcoatl:** for details see 'Ancient Civilisations' box.

Chapultepec Park. Most of the city's important **museums** are in the Park, but it is also an attraction in its own right, especially on Sundays when all the families in the city seem to parade there. 'Should be a compulsory visit—very colourful.' Free **zoo** contains the first captive pandas to be born outside China. Metroline 1 to Chapultepec or line 7 to Auditorium.

Anthropological Museum, (5) 553-1902. The claim that this is the finest museum in the world is well-founded; 'certainly one of the world's top ten'. Contains Mexico past and present. The Museum has recovered some of its most prized treasures which were stolen in December, 1985, but they are not displayed yet. 'Deserves every accolade thrown at it. Worth going here *before* you visit the pyramids at Teotihuacán.' Cameras but no tripods allowed, so bring fast film or flash. 'Worth taking your own photos, since postcards of exhibits are very poor and few (as in all Mexican museums I've visited).' Open Tue-Sat 9 am-7 pm, Sun 10 am-6 pm. Closed Mon. US$4, free Sun. Take Metro to Chapultepec or yellow and brown bus #76 on Reforma Paseo.

Gallery of Mexican History, a cleverly designed building within Chapultepec Castle, with a first-rate presentation of Mexican history since 1500. Open 9 am-6 pm daily.

Museum of Modern Art. Has Mexico's more recent masterpieces. 'Excellent collection, not only of Orozco, Rivera, etc, but some charming primitive paintings.' Be sure to see *La Revolución* by Lozano. Open 10 am-6 pm daily except Mon. Fee US$0.60, At the entrance of Chapultepec park, corner of Reforma and Ghandhi Calle, (5) 553-6233. Metro Line 1: Chapultepec. US$2, Sun free. Open Tues-Sun 10 am-6 pm, closed Mon.

Mural Diego Rivera Plaza Solidaridad, Centro Historico, (5) 512-0754 or (5) 510-2329.

Chapultepec Castle, old castle with original furnishings and objets d'art. Found fame in 1848 when young Mexican cadets fought off invading Americans here. Rather than surrender, the final 6 wrapped themselves in Mexican flags and jumped from the parapets to their death. Unless you want to copy them 'beware stone parapets and banisters, both very unsafe. Castle not impressive but worth visiting for the murals'.

Muséo Rufino Tamayo. Exhibitions of modern art and sculpture, including the personal collection of Mexico's best known living artist, Rufino Tamayo. The building itself is worth a visit. Located opposite the Museum of Modern Art. Open Tue-Sun 10 am to 6 pm, (5) 286-6519. US$1.85.

Two museums in the southern suburb of **Coyoacán**. Take 23A bus south on Burcareli marked Coyoacán or Col del Valle and the journey takes an hour.

House and Museum of León Trotsky, Viena 45, (5) 658-8732. Ring door buzzer to be let in. This is where Trotsky was pickaxed to death in 1940; his tomb is in the garden. His house is preserved as he left it. Open Tue-Sun 10 am-5 pm, closed Mon. US$2. 'Really interesting museum.'

Muséo Frida Kahlo, 5 min from Trotsky house, corner of Allende and Londres 127, (5) 554-5999. Metro Coyoacán (or sometimes called Bancomer), line 3. Open Tues-Sun 10 am-12 pm, 3 pm-6 pm. Closed Mon. US$1.15, Guided tours at 11 am. Frida was Diego Rivera's wife and a prominent artist in her own right. Their colonial style house is filled with their effects and many of Frida's works. The **volcanoes of Popocatépetl and Iztaccihuatl** can be seen on a clear day in the east, although 'for good views take bus to Amecameca from ADO Terminal'. The peaks are some 3000 ft higher than Mts Rainier or Whitney in the USA. 'Mind-blowing view when sitting on the right-hand side of bus from Mexico City to Puebla.'

Mexican Independence Day celebrations, 15 Sept at 11 am. President gives traditional cry of liberty to crowd in the Zócalo amid churchbells ringing, fireworks firing, confetti floating, much rejoicing.

Military parade, 16 Sept down Reforma.

ENTERTAINMENT

Jai Alai, the fastest game in the world, nightly at 6 pm except Mon and Fri at Fronton Mexico, on Plaza de la Republica. Fee. Jacket preferred. Complex betting system; stick to the pre-game parimutual.

Bullfight season runs Nov to March; other times of year, you can see *novilladas* (younger bullfighters, younger bulls) which are cheaper and may please you just as well if you know nothing of bullfighting. Fights Sun at 4 pm; booking in advance recommended. Take 17 bus down Insurgentes Sur to Plaza California, 1 block from the Plaza. Monumental (also known as Plaza México) is at 50,000 seats the biggest in the world; buy '*sol*' seats in *barrera* or *tendido* sections to see anything, (5) 563-3959. Tickets from US$2 to US$12.

Ballet Folklorico at the Palace of Fine Arts, Sun at 9.30 am and 9 pm; Wed at 9 pm. 'A real must—not classical ballet but a series of short dances representing Spanish, Indian and Mexican cultures.' Incredible costumes! Reserve in advance, (5) 512-3636. Tickets from US$10 to US$25.

Casa del Canto, Plaza Insurgentes. Music from all over Latin America, cover charge about US$2.00. 'Terrific.'

Plaza de Garibaldi. Nightly after 9 pm, mariachi music, sometimes free, sometimes not. Can be dangerous—be careful.

Candelero Dinner & Dance, Insurgentes Sur # 1333, (5) 598-0055. Has an eating place inside and plays lots of good music.

SHOPPING

Many good markets including the Saturday market at *Plaza San Jacinto* in the suburb of San Angel; **San Juan market** on Ayuntamiento is a city-run market with many Mexican handicrafts and a good place to practice haggling; the **Handicrafts Museum** is on the Plaza de la Cuidadela at Avenida Balderas and has lots of trash and treasures; the **Thieves Market** (adjoining the Mercado La Lagunilla on Rayón between Allende and Commonfort) is open on Sundays. **La Lagunilla** is also especially interesting on Sundays when vendors come from all over the city to set up booths. Books, guidebooks, American mags: American Bookstore, Madero 25.

INFORMATION

Post Office on **Lázaro Cárdenas** and **Tacuba**, has a *poste-restante* section where letters are held up to 10 days for you. (5) 521-7394. Open weekdays 8 am-10 pm, Sat 8.30 am-8 pm, Sun 8 am-4 pm.

Mexico City News is an all-English paper with good travel section.

Mexican Government Tourist Bureau, Presidente Masaryk 172, (5) 250-8601, north of Chapultepec Park—rather out of the way. Otherwise (5) 250-0123 for English-language tourist information. Open Mon-Fri, 8 am-7 pm. 'Go there in the morning.'

Tourist Police are seen along Reforma and Juárez wearing light blue uniforms with US/Canadian/British flag badges indicating that they speak English. Friendly, well-informed, they provide on-the-spot information.

Radio VIP—CBS Affiliate Station, 88.1 FM.

MEDICAL SERVICES

American-British Cowdray Hospital, Observatorio and Calle Sur 136. Call (5) 230-8000 or in emergencies, (5) 515-8359. Open 24 hours.

EMBASSIES

Britain: Calle Río Lerma #71. (5) 207-2186 or 207-2089. US: Reforma # 305. (5) 211-0042 ext. 3573, 3405 and 3404. Canada: Polanco #529. (5) 724-7900.

TRAVEL

Taxis: 4 types, drivers described as '99.9% cheats—best to find out roughly how much the journey should cost before taking it. Wherever possible, fight to the death!' Regular taxis (yellow) have meters, and you pay 10% more at night. Jitney or 'pesero' taxis (green) cruise the main streets; the driver's finger held aloft indicates that he has space among the other passengers, who fill the taxi like a bus. Sitio taxis (red) operate from ranks on street corners; agree on fare beforehand if possible. Outside hotels, etc, you'll find unmetered taxis; always agree on fare beforehand. 'Taxi meter or not, arrange price beforehand. Hard to bargain, you get overcharged all the time.'

Buses: Municipal buses cost US$0.50, Peseros (white and green mini buses) US$.25. if time is short , Gray Line Tours do a day tour: (5) 208-1163 or 208-1415 contact Mr. Jorge Maldonado. Great city tour cost US$ 38p/p. If staying any length of time it is suggested that you get a street map and a Metro guide. The Mexico City Metro, opened in September 1969, now carries some 4.6 million passengers daily at a ridiculously low price. 'The world's best transport bargain.' 'Use wherever possible, the streets are choked with traffic.' But avoid during rush hours (7-9 am, 7-9 pm) and be prepared to jostle with the rest of them at other times. Work out connections in advance—no overall plans inside stations. Backpacks, suitcases and large packages are *banned* during rush hours (7-10 am, 5-8 pm)—this can be strictly applied. Women and children should take advantage of separate queues and cars provided at worst times, and everyone should beware endemic bag-snatching and slashing. Some stops have artefacts uncovered during excavation: Aztec pyramid foundation at Pino Suarez, more artefacts at Bellas Artes and Zocalo. 'Clean, fast and incredibly simple to use.' When leaving the city, it is best to consult the Tourist Office for info.

Rail: Estacion Buenavista, Insurgentes and Mosqueta, 4 blocks from Guerro Metro. Bus on Insurgentes Norte to downtown. Train information (5) 547-8410 or 547-6593, daily 6 am-9.30 pm.

Air: Benito Juárez International Airport, (5) 784-3600 or 784-4811. Flights to all Mexican destinations. For international flights remember the US$12 departure tax (pesos only). From the airport take the official yellow taxis, buying a fixed price ticket to your destination from desks at the end of the arrivals building. You can also call this service for transport to the airport, but it costs the same or more than a regular taxi. Or Metro to 'Terminal Area line 5'—but transfers involved and remember baggage limitations. For buses getting into or out of Mexico City: 4 terminals, each located near a Metro stop. *North* arrivals/departures at Terminal Central del Norte, (5) 587-1552, change at La Raza and go to Autobuses del Norte, line 5. (Also get there by bus, Insurgeantes Norte then Cien Metros.) *South:* Terminal Sur, at the Taxquena Metro stop, southern end of line 2, (5) 686-4987, *West:* Terminal Poniente, (5) 271-4519 at Observatorio Metro station, west end of line 1. *East:* Terminal Central del Oriente (also known as ADO), (5) 762-5977, at the San Lázaro Metro station, to the east on line 1.

Mexico City travel and tourist info from DF tourist office, Amberes and Londres in the Zona Rosa, (5) 525-9380 or 525-9383. Open daily 9 am-1 pm, 6 pm-9 pm.

OTHER SIGHTS OF INTEREST IN MEXICO

Gray Whales at Baja California   Baja California is the only place in the world where the gray whales immigrate from Alaska to breed and give birth to their young. These fascinating animals usually come down by the end of December and stay until March. When the water starts getting warm, they return north.

The best spots to watch the whales are Ojo de Liebre and San Ignacio Lagoon, both near Guerrero Negro. The third spot is located at La Paz, Baja California at Magdalena's Bay. Tours can be arranged by Eco-Tour Malerrino in Guerrero Negro (115) 7-01-00 with Mr. Luis Enrique Anchón or Turísmo Express in La Paz (112) 5-63-10 with Mrs. Alma or Lorena Barajas.

The cost of the trip ranges from US$40-US$85 pp.

Cliff-diving at La Quebrada in old Acapulco, Guerrero   The famous **high-dive act** takes place off the rocks at the far end of La Quebrada located at 187 Costera Miguel Aleman. The floodlit drops are 25 and 40 metres into 2-metre-deep water, and the *clavadista* hits the water at about 60 mph, timing his dive to meet the incoming surf. Divers wear different types of costumes and often jump with the Mexican flag or torches. You can enjoy the show with dinner at the Mirador Restaurant. Admission is free, but there is a one (expensive) drink minimum. Or you can go down the steps to La Plazeta, located below the restaurant, where admission is US$2. Shows are Sat and Sun only, at noon, 7.30 pm, 8.30 pm, 9.30 pm, 10.30 pm, and 11.30 pm. For more information, call the Secretary of Tourism (SECTUR) at (74) 86-91-67 or (74) 86-91-68.

Los Voladores de Papantla in Veracruz The 'Flying Indian' religious ceremony of the Totonacs, dating back hundreds of years, is still performed in the traditional style. The dance can be seen every Sunday in the main square of Papantla. Four performers climb to the top of a very tall pole that has four extended arms at the top. One performer stands on the ground, dancing and playing traditional pipe music. The other four, dressed to represent the colourful plumage of the macaw, the symbol of the sun, secure themselves by the ankle with ropes and leap into the air. All four fly around the pole exactly 13 times, representing the 52 year cycle of ancient Mesoamerica. For more information, call the Secretary of Tourism (SECTUR) in Jalapa at (28) 12-73-45.

BEYOND MEXICO CITY *All the places mentioned here can be easily reached from Mexico City by bus or car, or, in the case of those towns in the Yucatán Peninsula, also by air.* **Queretaro**, a lovely, lively town, loaded with history, lies about 140 miles to the northwest of the capital. It's a bit off the usual beaten tourist track and is recommended for its freshness, friendly towns-folk and the numerous hidden plazas and cobblestoned by-ways tucked away off the main streets. The Treaty of Guadalupe Hidalgo ending the US-Mexican War was signed here and the present Mexican Constitution was drafted here in 1916.

To the west of Mexico City is the university city of **Morelia** known for its colonial architecture and fine candies! **San Miguel de Allende**, a big draw for American students, writers and artists, is a treasurehouse of art, past and present, put together on the backs of the fortunes made from silver. The town's mountainside setting adds to the charm. To the west, is **Guanajuato**, another Spanish colonial town whose silver mines once supplied one-third of all the world's silver. There's an international arts and music festival here in October and November.

About an hour's drive west of Mexico City, and with some magnificent scenery in between, is **Toluca**. Sitting at 8760 ft, Toluca is the highest city in Mexico and is famous for its main attraction, the **Friday market**. Local Indian stall-keepers come from miles around to sell you local specialties like straw goods, papier mache figures and sweaters. Bargain without mercy but first check out the prices at the government store next to the **Museum of Popular Arts and Crafts**, east of the bus station. You can often do better here than at the market.

Centre of modern Mexico's silver industry is **Taxco**, about 130 miles from Mexico City and sitting high up in the Sierra Madras. The views around here are marvellous and the city is preserved as a national monument thus preventing the construction of modern buildings.

To the east of the capital is **Puebla**. Situated amidst wild and mountainous scenery, Puebla is renowned for its ceramics as well as the snow-capped volcanoes of Popocatépetl (dormant) and Ixtacoihuatl (extinct) and nearby **Cholula**, a pre-Columbian religious centre. Puebla is also the home of *mole*, an unusual sauce made up of the odd combination of chocolate and chilli—usually served over turkey or chicken—and, apparently against all odds, quite delicious.

When the sea beckons, head east to Mexico's chief port since the days of the Spanish invasion, **Vera Cruz**. Cortes landed here in 1519 and with the event of the gold and silver trade to Europe, Vera Cruz became a frequent point of attack by British and French forces. These days, it's a sometimes rough and raucous port city with influences split between old Spain and the Caribbean.

For a more typical resort-type experience, hop on a bus (or drive the very expensive toll road) and head west to **Acapulco** and the other gringo resort towns like **Manzanillo** or **Ixtapa**. Although hit hard by Hurricane Pauline in October 1997, the beach area of Acapulco escaped any lasting damage.

Aiming south from Mexico City, there's **Oaxaca** and the nearby Zapotec centre of **Monte Albán** or the Mixtec site at **Mitla** to explore. (See *Ancient*

Civilisations Sites box.) Moving further southeast into the most beautiful, lush and untouched territory in Mexico, you are in the land of the Maya. The astounding Mayan ruins at **Palenque**, **Chichén Itzá** and **Uxmal** (see Box in *Mexico/Background* chapter) contrast sharply with the bang into the late 20th century Caribbean resort towns of **Cancun** and **Cozumel**.

Prices in Cancun are at New York levels, the hotel strip is as gaudy as anywhere in Florida but the beaches are beautiful and free and the sea is deep blue, warm and inviting. A perfect end to a trip to Mexico? Perhaps, especially if you can combine soaking up the sun on the beach with an excursion to **Tulum** on the coast or Chichén Itzá inland.

Appendix I   TABLE OF WEIGHTS AND MEASURES

Conversion to and from the metric system

Mexico employs the metric system. **Canada** has almost completed the changeover to metric, and the **United States** as yet uses it only sporadically and within its National Parks.

Temperature

```
50°C ─┬─ 120°F
45°C ─┤
      ├─ 110°F
40°C ─┤
      ├─ 100°F
35°C ─┤
      ├─ 90°F
30°C ─┤
      ├─ 80°F
25°C ─┤
      ├─ 70°F
20°C ─┤
15°C ─┤─ 60°F
10°C ─┤─ 50°F
 5°C ─┤
      ├─ 40°F
 0°C ─┤─ 30°F
-5°C ─┤
      ├─ 20°F
-10°C ─┤
      ├─ 10°F
-15°C ─┤
      └─ 0°F
```

Fahrenheit into Centigrade/Celsius: subtract 32 from Fahrenheit temperature, then multiply by 5, then divide by 9. *Centigrade/Celsius into Fahrenheit:* multiply Centigrade/Celsius by 9, then divide by 5 then add 32.

Linear Measure		
	0.3937 inches	1 centimetre
	1 inch	2.54 centimetres
	1 foot (12 in)	0.3048 metres
	1 yard (3 ft)	0.9144 metres
	39.37 inches	1 metre
	0.621 miles	1 kilometre
	1 mile (5280 ft)	1.6093 kilometres
	3 miles	4.8 kilometres
	10 miles	16 kilometres
	60 miles	98.6 kilometres
	100 miles	160.9 kilometres

Weight		
	0.0353 ounces	1 gram
	1 ounce	28.3495 grams
	1 pound (16 oz)	453.59 grams
	2.2046 pounds	1 kilogram
	1 ton (2000 lbs)	907.18 kilograms

Liquid Measure		
	1 US fluid ounce	0.0296 litres
	1 US pint (16 US fl oz)	0.4732 litres
	1 US quart (2 US pints)	0.9464 litres
	1.0567 US quarts	1 litre
	1 US gallon (4 US quarts)	3.7854 litres
	3 US gallons	11.3 litres
	4 US gallons	15.1 litres
	10 US gallons	37.8 litres
	15 US gallons	56.8 litres

The British imperial gallon (used in Canada) has 20 fluid ounces and 4 imperial quarts and is equal to 4.546 litres.

Speed			
	25 km/h	equals (approx.)	15 m.p.h.
	40 km/h	equals (approx.)	25 m.p.h.
	50 km/h	equals (approx.)	30 m.p.h.
	60 km/h	equals (approx.)	37 m.p.h.
	80 km/h	equals (approx.)	50 m.p.h.
	100 km/h	equals (approx.)	60 m.p.h.
	112 km/h	equals (approx.)	70 m.p.h.

Appendix II SOME BUDGET MOTEL CHAINS IN THE US

Budget Host Inns, PO Box 14341, Arlington, Texas 76094, (800) 283-4678.

Chalet Susse International, Chalet Dr, Wilton, NH 03086. (800) 524-2538. *www.sussechalet.com.*

Days Inn, 339 Jefferson Rd, PO Box 278, Parsippany, NJ 07054-0278. (800) 325-2525. *www.daysinn.com.*

E–Z 8 Motels, 2484 Hotel Circle Place, San Diego, CA 92108. (800) 32M-OTEL

Econo-Lodges of America (Choice Hotels), 10750 Columbia Pike, Maryland 20901-4494. (301) 593-5600, (800) 553-2666. *www.hotelchoice.com.*

Exel Inns, 4202 E. Town Blvd, Madison, WI 53704. (800) 856-8013.

First Interstate Inns, PO Box 760, Kimball, NE 69145. (800) 462-4667.

Friendship Inns, Address as Econo-Lodges (above). (800) 553-2666/(301) 593-5600. *www.hotelchoice.com.*

Hampton Inn/Promise Hotels, 755 Crogsover Lane, Memphis, TN 38117. (800) 426- 7866. *www.hampton-inn.com.*

Hospitality International, 1726 Montreal Circle, Tucker, GA 30084. (404) 270-1180, (800) 251-1962.

Knights Inn, HSS 339 Jefferson Road, PO Box 278, Parsippany, NJ. 07054-0278 (201) 428-9700, (800) 722-7220..

Motel 6, PO Box 809103, Dallas, TX 75380. (800) 466-8356.

Quality Inns (Choice Hotels), 10750 Columbia Pike, Silver Spring, MD 20901. (800) 424-6423, (301) 593-5600. *www.hotelchoice.com.*

Red Roof Inns, 4355 Davidson Road, Hilliard, OH 43026. (800) 843-7663. *www.redroof.com.*

Rodeway Inns, Address as Econo-Lodges (above). (800) 228-2000.

Super 8 Motels, PO Box 4090, Aberdeen, SD 57402-4090. (605) 225-2272, or (800) 848-8888.

Travelodge Forte Hotels, See Knights Inn above. (619) 448-1884, (800) 255-3050. *www.travellodge.com.*

Contact any of the above for their directories of motels, containing full information on rates, facilities, locations and often small maps pinpointing each motel.

INDEX

NOTES

NOTES

NOTES

CORRECTIONS AND ADDITIONS

The detail, accuracy and usefulness of future editions of this Guide depend greatly on your help. Share the benefit of your experiences with other travellers by sending us as much information on accommodation, eating places, places of interest, entertainment, events, travel, etc., as you can.

These printed forms are supplied to get you started. Additional information can be sent on separate sheets of paper. *Please do not write on the back of these forms, nor on the back of your own sheets.* When making remarks, bear in mind that a comment on a hotel like 'Quite good' or 'OK' conveys little to anyone—be as descriptive and as quotable as you can, but please also be concise. If suggesting new hotels, eating places etc., please give full information: ie. **correct name, address, phone numbers, price** etc. **This is very important**. Without complete information your special 'hot' tip may not get published.

Please use these slips *only* for this guidebook information and not for any other BUNAC publications. Completed slips and other information should be sent to: General Editor, *The Moneywise Guide to North America*, BUNAC, 16 Bowling Green Lane, London EC1R 0BD, England.
In the USA: BUNAC, PO Box 49, South Britain, CT 06487.

The deadline for information to be included in the 1999 edition of the Guide is 9th October, 1998.

EXAMPLE

Place: LONE PINE, CALIFORNIA	Date: 12 Sept 1998
Subject: ACCOMMODATION	Page no: 247
Correction/Addition	Comments
Redwood Hotel, 123 Spruce Ave. [(209) 976-5432 $28 single, $32 with bath. $35 double, $40 with bath.	Clean, bright, though simply furnished. Vibrating water bed. Friendly and helpful. Turn left out of bus station and walk two blocks.